HANDBOOKS

D1409494

SCOTLAND

LUKE WATERSON

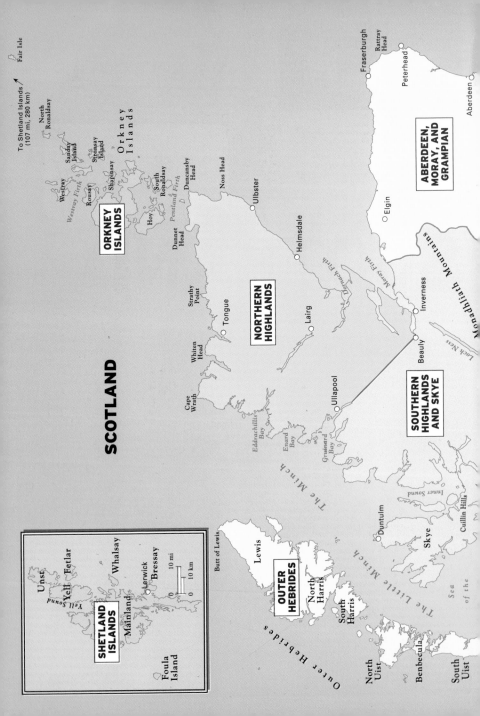

Contents

Discover Scotland

Alone bagpiper wearing a kilt, mist, mountains, lochs, castles, whisky – these are the images coming to mind when you envision Scotland. There are enough bagpipers in castles on mountains for everyone if you know where to look, and when the mist clears, there is nowhere more spectacular.

In its gentle southern half alone, Scotland is a feast for the eye, alternating between flower-carpeted grasslands, ancient pine forests, and wild beaches. A boundary fault ruptures the hilly north into a fretwork of rocky ridges and heather. This is a predominantly rural country; even in Edinburgh, nature is never far away as the Holyrood parklands soar above the city. The Highlands' glorious scenery attracts visitors aplenty but seems to be able to swallow all of them. The remote far north yields miles of bog and vast skies where shaggy cattle are more common sights than other humans. And the islands beyond are so far-flung that airports are in sheep fields and boats are still the main way of getting around.

This mass of moor and mountain provides all the more poignant a setting for the country's history, of which its people are fiercely proud. Everywhere you look, a turbulent past is evident, from battered fortresses to monuments in Highland valleys that saw rival clans fight to their deaths. The past is commemorated in Scotland's many captivating

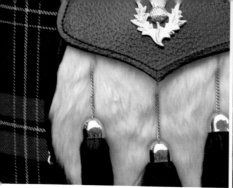

museums and in its intriguing festivals and ceremonies, such as the riding of the burgh boundaries in the Borders and the must-see Highland Games.

Scotland is more than just a feast for the eyes. It's the smell of heather, the breeze brushing your face on a ferry to the isles, and the warmth of a peat fire or a dram of whisky. It's soaking in the sound of an impromptu ceilidh in a pub in the middle of nowhere, when only days ago you were trying to remember directions to a Glasgow nightclub.

This is a place to expect the unexpected, and never is this more evident than in the Scottish people themselves. You'll find that behind that down-to-earth and often tough exterior the Scottish are the friendliest, funniest people you could hope to meet. The old clan tradition of hospitality to passersby is just as strong today as ever, and Scots often go out of their way to make your visit better — showing you their favorite places, giving you a lift when bus connections have failed, or sharing a round of drinks with you. Whatever the encounter may be, it will be the Scots that make your experience of Scotland unique.

Planning Your Trip

▶ WHERE TO GO

Edinburgh and the Lothians

Scotland's capital, Edinburgh is one of the world's most magnificent cities. Spread on the slopes of two extinct volcanoes and dominated by a formidable fortress, it's a photogenic maze of winding alleys, century-old houses, and lush parks. Each August, this is the backdrop to one of Europe's best outdoor festivals, the Edinburgh Festival, a multicultural extravaganza of music and theater. The history-steeped region just beyond the city contains stupendous palaces and scenic seaside resorts.

Borders

Right at the heart of the Southern Uplands, the Borders contain the best of rich lowland forests and high craggy moor. The whole region looks as picture-perfect as a landscaped garden. Peeping out of this sedate scenery are no fewer than four hauntingly beautiful ruined abbeys. Add to that a clutch of Scotland's finest country houses and a whole network of walking trails and you have a place that rivals the Highlands for sheer topographical splendor—without the crowds.

Dumfries and Galloway

Outdoor lovers flock to its interior and solitude-seekers take to its long, winding coasts: Dumfries and Galloway is Scotland at its most gentle and laid-back. Whitewashed coastal villages bypassed by the 21st century peep out of the trees at tracts of sheltered, silvery sand. Scotland's best-loved poet Robert Burns was inspired to pen some of his most renowned verse while living here. Wigtown on the western coast is "Book Town," Scotland's secondhand book capital.

Ayrshire and Arran

Fertile Ayrshire has the legacy of poet Robert Burns stamped all over it, but the

Melrose Abbey, Borders

IF YOU HAVE . . .

Skye Bridge, from Skye

- **THREE DAYS:** Stay in Edinburgh for two days, with a trip up to the Isle of Skye.

- **FIVE DAYS:** Add a couple of days in the Southern Highlands, including a day's walking in Glencoe/Glen Nevis.

- **ONE WEEK:** Add a day and night in Glasgow and a trip down the Clyde to spend some time on the Isle of Arran.

- **TWO WEEKS:** Add at least two or three more days to your time in the Southern Highlands. Consider trips to Knoydart and Ardnamurchan. Spend time in Fort Augustus and on the south side of Loch Ness. From Inverness, you could fit in a day trip to the Orkney Islands. Check out some distilleries in Speyside and spend a couple of days in the East Neuk of Fife.

- **THREE WEEKS:** Add a third day to your time in Edinburgh. Make a trip down south to Kirkcudbright. Do some longer day trips from Edinburgh, such as to the border abbeys. Most of all, spend extra time in the Highlands. On your way up to the Southern Highlands, detour via Oban to the Isle of Mull. Visit Iona. Head up into the Northern Highlands for several days. Explore places with wonderful-sounding names like Ullapool, Assynt, and Cape Wrath. Spend extra time on the Orkney Islands, and do a side trip to one of the outer islands.

main draw lies across the water in forested, mountainous Arran. Known as "Scotland in Miniature," Arran contains all you could ask for in a Scottish island: lonely hills, a ruined castle, a whisky distillery, and plenty of pretty pubs. It's only an hour away from Glasgow, too.

Glasgow and the Greater Clyde

Scotland's biggest city has reinvented itself: If you crave classy restaurants, elegant bars, and opulent nightclubs, there are few better places in Europe to head. The city's culturally booming, too. There is world-class art like the Burrell Collection and a wealth of bright, brilliant buildings designed by celebrated architect Charles Rennie Mackintosh. South of Glasgow is bizarre little Biggar, delighting visitors with its eclectic mix of museums.

Dundee, Angus, and the Kingdom of Fife

The heather-red Angus Glens stretching north of Dundee and the peaceful fishing villages on the East Neuk of Fife have to be two of the most underrated spots to hang out on holiday in the whole country. There are walks in the wilderness, stretches of sandy swimming beaches, and fine seafood restaurants. Then, spanning the region from north to south, are the greatest golf courses in Scotland.

Perthshire

With its three grand forested straths, or valleys, Perthshire is a taste of the Highlands before you've even gotten to the Highlands. Long, lonely lochs perfect for water sports, flanked by high hills, are the order of the day here. Thrown in for good measure are a smattering of castles and distilleries, a Victorian spa town, and Scotland's most stupendous woodland scenery.

Balmoral

Loch Lomond and the Trossachs

Loch Lomond is Scotland's largest loch, a magical, glittering, island-speckled body of water traversed by the West Highland Way, the country's most popular long-distance footpath. Up from its banks rise the Trossachs, a smorgasbord of hills and forests with the wanderings of Scotland's greatest outlaw, Rob Roy, imprinted upon them. Hill-walkers and nature-lovers should head here, taking care not to miss out on the architecturally rich city of Stirling, with a castle to rival Edinburgh's.

Argyll and the Inner Hebrides

Split into thickly forested pieces by snaking lochs and sea inlets, this region has more coastline than all of France put together. Broken castles crown the hills as if to hint at the even richer history lying below them. At Kilmartin you'll find Scotland's most important stretch of archaeological sites. Among the multitude of islands scattered off the coast are dreamy Iona, where Christianity in Scotland began, and Islay, with eight renowned whisky distilleries on its shores.

Aberdeen, Moray, and Grampian

There's no two ways about it: If you are a fan of whisky or fortresses, you want to head here. Over half of Scotland's whisky distilleries are in Speyside in Moray, and Scotland's most glamorous castles, including the Royal holiday home, Balmoral, are dotted throughout the countryside here. Aberdeenshire is big enough to offer you everything: In the northeast are tranquil fishing villages hidden beneath the cliffs, while in the west are some of Scotland's top mountain hikes.

Southern Highlands and Skye

Classic Scotland—in all its grand, gloomy, history-soaked glens, its looming mountains, and its silvery lochs with castles reflected in them—is what awaits you here. The glorious extremes of the country, from its highest peak to its greatest wildernesses to its most romantic island, are all in this region. Whether you're a hill-walker or a history-lover, all the iconic Scottish images you have in your mind are somewhere deep within this rugged landscape.

Northern Highlands

This is the raw, desolate half of the Highlands; the southern half may have the postcard images, but here you'll find little pockets of paradise with not another soul around. It's so wild that the only settlements cling to the

Ardbeg Distillery, Islay

coast, leaving the mountainous interior to solitude-seekers. The best sandy beaches on the mainland, idyllic fishing ports cut off from the real world by miles of hills, and the haunting legacy of the Highland Clearances all wait to be discovered.

Outer Hebrides

This 150-mile-long string of scattered islands off the west coast has the most abundant birdlife and the most glorious beaches in Scotland. It's the most traditional part of the country, too: Gaelic is still spoken as a first language here. Then there's the stone circle of Callanish, one of Britain's most important ancient monuments, standing alone on the stark, empty moor.

Orkney Islands

The first sight for many of this fertile archipelago is a memorable one: the prettiest town of the Scottish islands, Stromness, a vibrant fishing port huddled beneath green hills. The Orkneys entice visitors with the highest concentration of megalithic monuments in northwest Europe. There are enough islands here to give everyone something, from the sandy beaches of Sanday

Shetland ponies

to the unique bird-spotting opportunities of Westray to some of Scotland's most distinctive cuisine.

Shetland Islands

Many of the Shetland Islands lie over 100 miles off the northern coast of Scotland; this is as otherworldly as the country gets, with more in common with the Norse that ruled this archipelago until the 15th century. The bare landscape contains Britain's greatest variety of birdlife and plenty of rich heritage: the stupendous 2,000-year-old tower house of Mousa Broch and Jarlshof, an incredibly preserved 4,000-year-old village.

Callanish stone circle

► WHEN TO GO

The key factors to consider when planning a trip to Scotland are what the weather is going to be like and what events will be taking place. One directly affects the other: Events are cancelled in wet weather and in those rare spells of prolonged glorious weather, impromptu events and festivals are put on to make the most of the sunshine. Visiting in a spell of good weather, at a lively but not overly crowded time of year, is tricky. The height of the tourist season in July and August may be the time when attractions are open the longest and when most events are taking place, but it rarely coincides with the year's best weather.

Edinburgh Festival in August

Weather

Scotland's bad weather is notorious, and whenever you visit, it's the luck of the draw whether you get a string of fine days or a clutch of awful ones. The best of the weather falls between May and October, but the extreme ends of this period generally have weather to surpass that in July and August. Scotland often has long stretches in September and October when the weather is glorious and the light is better than in midsummer—this is an ideal time for photo-snapping. June is a wonderful month, with the longest days of the year. If you're visiting the north of Scotland, then this is the best month because the days barely end. Up in Orkney and Shetland, it will never get dark at this time of year. If winter sports are your thing, then the season is penciled in, weather-dependent, from November to April. With so much of Scotland accessible only by ferry, bad weather also restricts the places you can visit.

Events

July and August are the months with the most hectic events calendars in Scotland. August in Edinburgh, for example, is a solid month of festivities. The summer months see a particular emphasis on outdoors events, making the most of Scotland's gorgeous backdrops. The tourist season runs generally from Easter through the end of September, and during these months there is a more or less continuous program of events across Scotland.

Best Time for Live Music: May to August is the best time to visit Scotland for live music. May sees magical musical events like the Orkney and Shetland folk festivals, while the Edinburgh Festival in August attracts a whole host of performers.

Best Time for Highland Games and Gatherings: The season runs from July to the beginning of September; the Braemar Gathering at the beginning of September is the last Games competition on the calendar.

Best Time for Wildlife Viewing: Scotland may be a year-round wildlife destination, but spring and autumn are the best times for spotting the more unusual animals. Much of the birdlife in Scotland is migratory; September to November are therefore particularly good bird-spotting months.

► BEFORE YOU GO

Accommodations

If you are planning on visiting a town during the time of a major festival, accommodations will be extremely hard to come by, so reserve ahead. Even a city like Edinburgh gets absolutely chockablock during festival season. If you're visiting a small, remote island where there are only a few places to stay, booking in advance is essential if you want to avoid spending the night outdoors.

Getting There

Scotland's major airport is Glasgow International, with direct flights from many parts of America, including daily flights from New York and weekly flights from Las Vegas. Most major cities in Europe and parts of Asia also have direct flights to Glasgow International. Edinburgh International is the other main international airport in Scotland, with Aberdeen and Glasgow Prestwick airports handling flights to and from European countries. Many other cities in North America will have flights to Scotland with a change in a major airport like London Heathrow or Amsterdam. Getting a flight to London Heathrow or London Gatwick airports will give you more flexibility both with flight times and flight prices. If you do arrive at a London airport to start your Scottish holiday, a pleasant alternative to flying is to take the train. High-speed trains can whisk you from London to Edinburgh in a little over four hours, which is, allowing for flight waiting times, as quick as flying.

Getting Around

If you plan on using public transport during your time in Scotland, there are a couple of passes to consider buying (it's not practical to buy them before you arrive in the U.K.). As Scottish public transport, while a whole load of fun, is in many rural areas nonexistent, you may also want to consider renting a car.

Oyster Card: If you have to make transfers from London airports to London stations, purchasing an Oyster Card will give you cheaper subway travel. They can be purchased at all subway stations in the London area.

National Rail Passes: If you are under the age of 26 or a senior citizen, purchasing a rail card is a good idea if you're going to be doing some train travel in England or Scotland. They cost £20–30 but give you big discounts on train fares. As trains are one of the most exciting ways to get around Scotland, it's worth considering. Passes can be purchased at main line railway stations across the United Kingdom.

Car Rental: Renting a car buys you

train crossing Tay Rail Bridge at sunset

Goat Fell, Isle of Arran

more time to visit out-of-the-way places in Scotland. It's better to hire a car in Scotland, as it's cheaper to do so there than in London. If you're arriving at a main city like Glasgow, Edinburgh, Aberdeen, or Inverness, car rental options are plentiful; car hire in smaller, rural areas is much more limited and booking in advance gives you more flexibility.

Cell Phones

If you are planning on doing a lot of remote walking, it's a good idea to take a cell phone in case you get into difficulty (though in many areas there will be no network coverage). Check with your mobile service provider that you will be able to use your phone in Scotland.

Money

It's a good idea to have a supply of British currency before you go. This saves the need to queue up at the airport *bureau de change* for ages. In remoter parts of Scotland, finding a place to change your money or that accepts credit cards can be difficult, so ensure you have a plentiful supply of hard cash. England and Scotland have the same currency: pound sterling.

What to Take

If you're starting a stay in a big city, you'll be able to buy whatever you forget to bring with you. Outside of the big cities, specific items can be hard to find. The most important factor to bear in mind is the weather. Be prepared for all seasons, and never base what you bring with you on a weather forecast. Make sure you pack pullovers, a warm hat, and a warm, waterproof coat. Waterproof trousers and sturdy shoes capable of traversing large expanses of mud are also a good idea. Scotland may not get hot, but sunscreen and sunglasses are useful. Be sure to pack a swimsuit, as Scotland has gorgeous beaches. The other essentials will include a good insect repellent (midges in Scotland are dire) and provision for allergies like hay fever (pollen count is high in Scotland). Finally, there is no better item to have in your luggage than some Scottish literature. Not only will it get you in the mood, but it may come in useful if you get stuck on an island or a long coach journey for several hours.

As for your luggage, you will know what style of backpack or suitcase best matches your needs. Backpacks are the best all-round luggage-carrying device in Scotland. They're easiest to lug into the shelter when a sudden downpour starts. If you're visiting the countryside, bear in mind pavements are sparse and roads are bumpy; dragging a wheeled bag along any distance can be nightmarish.

One thing to go easy on when you're packing is the tartan. Yes, the Scots do wear kilts and the like on special occasions, but if visitors walk tartan-clad down the main street they will most likely be written off as ridiculous tourists. You want to blend in a little bit.

Explore Scotland

Exploring Scotland is a more difficult task than it might first appear from looking at a map. Even the remoter regions are packed full of an array of attractions, which can appear overwhelming. When you take into account that public transportation can be poor (or nonexistent) in just those places that are best to visit, it's often difficult to know exactly what to squeeze in to your holiday. One strategy can be to decide the aspect of Scotland you're most interested in and explore it in more detail.

Don't let Scotland deceive you—it may be small, but the mountains of the Highlands and outlying islands make travel slower, if more spectacular. A combination of rental car, taxi, train, and bus will get you from point A to B on much of the mainland. Having your own transport outside of Edinburgh or Glasgow will make any trip easier, but relying on public transportation is more of an adventure (and less reliable). In remoter places, travel by air and sea is also necessary. In outlying areas, getting there can be the most incredible part of the experience.

Loch Lomond

▶ THE BEST OF SCOTLAND

ruins of Urquhart Castle at Loch Ness

This tour focuses on Scotland's big draws: Edinburgh, Glasgow, and the Highlands, including the must-see Loch Ness and Glen Nevis mountain range. The Highlands also contain the castles and clan history most visitors want to experience. Fourteen days will give a good taste of what Edinburgh and the Highlands can offer. It will also allow for an unforgettable trip to one of Scotland's outlying islands, whisky-sampling, and the chance to relax on golden beaches, with perhaps a game of golf or a fish restaurant thrown in.

ISLAND LOVERS

No trip to Scotland is complete without an excursion and, ideally, a protracted stay on one of Scotland's islands. They are more laid-back and less touristy than the mainland, with a peaceful, addictively charming feel. The best of everything in Scotland seems, in many of these islands, to be condensed into miniature. Whatever it is you are looking for, be it golden sandy beaches, whisky distilleries, or stupendous birdlife, finding it on these far-flung isles is an intensely magical experience. If you want to visit several, consider buying one of the island hopscotch passes from the main ferry operator, Caledonian MacBrayne (Calmac, tel. 0870/565 0000, www.calmac.co.uk).

boat moored at Iona

Islay
Islay has eight single malt whisky distilleries, a clutch of gorgeous golden beaches, and a huge variety of birdlife congregating in its sandy shallows.

Tiree
Tiree offers a different island experience. Over a third of this little island's coast is made up of sandy beaches and that, together with some of the highest winds and longest sunshine hours in Scotland, make it popular with water sports enthusiasts. It's also very good for swimming and has an airport. This means that despite its remoteness it's a busy, well-appointed island.

Iona
Iona is one of the most serene islands in the whole of Scotland, and without a doubt the most spiritual; it was the home of St. Columba, the Celtic missionary who brought Christianity to Scotland. It has a special feel, as well as many good beaches.

Skye
It's cheating a bit now to call Skye an island when it's connected to the mainland by a bridge. However, it does have the most stupendous geology of anywhere in Scotland and the highest mountains of any Scottish island.

Harris, Outer Hebrides
Thanks to the picture-perfect village of Tarbert and white Caribbean-like stretches of sand that make up some of the best beaches in Europe, Harris is far and away the most appealing part of the Outer Hebrides. You're also only a drive away from Lewis, and one of the world's most impressive megalithic stone circles.

Orkney Islands
This archipelago, six miles north of the north coast of Scotland, has a more diverse spread of archaeological sites than anywhere else in Britain. Just seeing all the prehistory on offer could fill up a whole holiday but then you have to factor in one of Scotland's top distilleries and Scotland's prettiest island village, Stromness. There's also a huge array of birdlife here. The other great thing about the Orkneys is the diversity of the smaller islands. Remote, hilly Hoy or gentle Westray, with Britain's best puffin-viewing spot, are the most idyllic.

Day 1

Fly into Edinburgh. Get an airport transfer to the city center, and one of New Town's many evocative hotels, such as Channings. You are now superbly located to spend the afternoon in the Old Town, sightseeing. For an evening meal, allow yourself to be amazed by Scottish cuisine at an atmospheric restaurant like The Witchery, in the Old Town.

Day 2

After breakfast and people-watching at an Old Town café, take a day trip by train to the ruins of the palace of Mary, Queen of Scots at Linlithgow, or to South Queensferry for a leisurely lunch away from the hubbub of the city at The Boat House restaurant, overlooking the Forth Bridges. Return mid-afternoon and spend the rest of the day relaxing in the leafy suburb of Cramond. You could also take a stroll in the Royal Botanic Gardens, or check out the Royal Yacht *Britannia*, in Leith. Leith is a great place to end up for an evening meal at somewhere like Fishers, a beautiful seafood restaurant. Round off your time in the capital by packing into a traditional pub like the Old Chain Pier (Newhaven) or catching some live music at a venue like Hebrides Bar (Old Town).

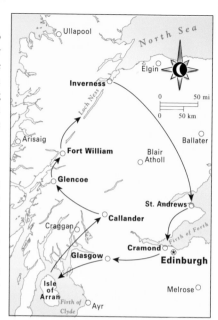

detail of the fountain in the courtyard of Linlithgow Palace

Glasgow

Day 3

Take an early train to Glasgow. Check into Malmaison, a stylish boutique hotel. Take a leisurely late breakfast at a café like Where the Monkey Sleeps (city center). Wander through Merchant City east to Glasgow Cathedral and get a view of the city from the eerie Necropolis. You could then try a spot of lunch at the Willow Tearooms, designed by Charles Rennie Mackintosh. In the afternoon, take a bus out to the Pollock Country Park and the Burrell Collection. Glasgow has more pubs and clubs than any other British city save London—check one or some of these out in the evening. The West End around Ashton Lane is particularly good for experiencing nightlife in this most Scottish of cities.

Day 4

Take the classic Glasgow trip "Doon the Watter" on the world's last oceangoing paddle-steamer to the Isle of Arran. Spend the afternoon exploring Brodick Castle and Gardens, or horseback riding. Stay in the elegant Kilmichael Country House Hotel.

Day 5

Catch a morning ferry to Ardrossan and a bus or train back to Glasgow. Take a bus or drive to Callander. Stay at the relaxed Roman Camp Hotel. Drive out into Rob Roy country in the afternoon to visit his grave at Balquhidder and picnic on Breadalbane ridge. Alternatively, head up to Loch Katrine to do a boat trip. Round the day off with a meal, ale, and maybe a spot of live music at the Lade Inn.

Day 6

Starting early, take a bus or drive to Helensburgh. Visit the architect Charles Rennie Mackintosh's Hill House and landscaped grounds. Take the West Highland Railway or drive to Ardlui at the north of Loch Lomond. Stop off here for lunch at one of the wonderful pubs/hotels like the Drover's Inn, or take your lunch down to the magical Loch Lomond shores. Take a bus or drive to Glencoe in the evening. With your own transport, you should stop for photos on the Pass of Glencoe and an evening meal at the Kingshouse Hotel. Stay at the Clachaig Inn, a classic old pub that does great food.

walking path leading to the mountains, Isle of Arran

CALL OF THE WILD

Puffins are best viewed on Westray in the Orkney Islands.

If you have come to Scotland to see the varied wildlife, these are some of the most unique places to focus your attention. Scottish wildlife will not impress with its size but it will impress with its diversity. These areas are spread out, but feasibly you could have a couple of days in each incorporated into a two-week holiday.

Glen Affric, Southern Highlands
This wild glen runs unchecked for some 20 or 30 miles; you can walk for hours here and see more golden eagles than humans. Also on the agenda are red deer and pine marten and birds like Scottish crossbills, the only exclusively British bird.

Cairngorm Mountains, Southern Highlands
The dramatic combination of ancient Caledonian pine forest, high mountain peaks and marshy lochs makes this a mecca for red deer, red squirrels, wildcats, and badgers. Bird-wise, this is a place where you can feast eyes on Scottish crossbills and osprey.

Loch Maree and Beinn Eighe, Northern Highlands
This area became Britain's first NNR (National Nature Reserve). Incorporating a lonely, island-speckled loch, pine forests, and stupendous mountain scenery, the reserve attracts red deer, pine martens, golden eagles, and other birds such as black-throated divers. It's made all the more magical an experience by the remoteness of its location. There's also a huge array of dragonflies here.

Outer Hebrides
It's not surprising that such numbers of birdlife have chosen the Outer Hebrides to make their home: There are hardly any people around. The loch-bedaubed, sand-dune-backed islands of North Uist, Benbecula, and South Uist are home to the elusive corncrake and greylag geese. West of these islands lies St. Kilda, home to more breeding seabirds of all descriptions than anywhere else in northwest Europe.

Orkney and Shetland Islands
These two archipelagos are world-class bird-watching destinations. Hermaness in Shetland is one of Britain's foremost bird havens, home to gannets, puffins, and skuas that come to nest within its cliffs. Orkney, in addition to plenty of prime seabird-watching places of its own, has in Westray the best puffin-spotting locale in Britain. Just trekking through the bare glens of Shetland and windy green fields of Orkney to find these bird hot spots is an incredible experience.

Loch Leven

Day 7

Today is relaxation or adventure day, depending on your fancy. Try a ramble around the Glencoe and North Lorn Folk Museum to discover the heritage and the clans of this area or a pleasant stroll and picnic along the Loch Leven shoreline. For the adventurous, the walk from the Kingshouse Hotel over the Devil's Staircase is jaw-droppingly beautiful. You could also try hiking into the Lost Valley or picnicking and water sports in Glen Etive. Return to Glencoe in the evening.

Days 8 and 9

Catch an early bus to Fort William. Stay in a glam, town-center guesthouse like The Grange or, better still, stay up in Glen Nevis

King's College, Aberdeen

at Achintee Farm B & B. Spend today and tomorrow relaxing, walking, fishing, and maybe even climbing Scotland's highest peak, Ben Nevis. You could also try a walk along the Caledonian Canal at nearby Corpach. If mountains aren't your thing, consider a train ride on the Jacobite Steam Train to Glenfinnan or Mallaig. There are gorgeous traditional pubs like the rustic Ben Nevis Inn in Glen Nevis or the Grog and Gruel in Fort William for eating.

Day 10

Head up the Great Glen by bus or car to Fort Augustus on the shores of Loch Ness. Take a boat trip to see the monster and spend the rest of the day relaxing and soaking up the view. There are walks to do, good places to eat, and boats on the Caledonian Canal to watch. Stay in the village at a peaceful bed-and-breakfast like the Old Pier House, with its own private stretch of Loch Ness shoreline and activities like boating and horseback riding on offer. Refresh yourself that evening at the traditional-looking Lock Inn.

Day 11

Take a bus or drive to Inverness. From here, either take the train via Keith to Aberdeen

Inverness Castle

or drive cross-country from Keith over the Grampian Mountains to Royal Deeside, the British Royal Family's holiday home. Stop at Keith to see one of Scotland's prettiest distilleries, Strathisla Distillery. From Aberdeen, take a bus or drive along Royal Deeside. Check in to the Inver Hotel, an old coaching inn with welcoming log fires, overlooking the Balmoral Estate. Sightseeing activities here could include looking round the Balmoral Estate, browsing the shops of Ballater with its Queen Victoria memorabilia everywhere or walking and picnicking in the spectacular countryside at the head of the River Dee.

Day 12

Take a bus or drive back to Aberdeen and a train south to Leuchars, in the Kingdom of Fife. Take a taxi to St. Andrews. Check in to the Inn on North Street or Fairmont St. Andrews Hotel and Resort for an afternoon and evening of pampering. Besides just relaxing, activities could include a leisurely round of golf or sightseeing around the historic town center.

Day 13

Continue the pampering by taking a trip to one of the fishing villages on the East Neuk of Fife. Beautiful beaches, a boat trip to the nature reserve on the Isle of May, quaint shops, and country walks: Fife's fishing villages will supply you with whatever you have not had quite enough of on your holiday so far. Round off your holiday with dinner at an award-winning fish restaurant. Head back to St. Andrews in the evening or spend your last night here, in the homey Victorian Spindrift Guesthouse, which rustles up tasty home-cooked meals.

Day 14

After a spot more sightseeing in St. Andrews and an early lunch, take a taxi to the train station and a train back to Edinburgh. There will be time for some souvenir-buying in the afternoon before heading to the airport for your evening flight back.

WHISKY AND PREHISTORY

At first, a few drams and a dose of prehistoric sites might not appear to blend. But they do, they really do: Distilleries and megalithic monuments are things Scotland has a higher concentration of than anywhere else in the world. And remember that whisky is much more than just Scotland's national drink – it's the flavor of Scotland's peaty, stream-laced landscape and the product of Scottish history.

Southern Scotland

Two of Scotland's finest distilleries are well and truly in the lowlands. Near Wigtown in Dumfries and Galloway is the "Spirit of the Lowlands," Bladnoch Distillery; there is also Springbank Distillery in Campbeltown, the oldest family distillery in Scotland and one of the few to carry out the whole whisky-making process from floor malting to bottling on-site. Near Campbeltown, you can see the stone footprints allegedly made by St. Columba, the missionary who brought Christianity to Scotland in the 6th century A.D.

Speyside, Moray

The most obvious place to concentrate your whisky-drinking efforts is in Speyside, in the Aberdeen and Moray region. Within a 20-mile radius of the self-proclaimed whisky capital of the world, Dufftown, lie over half of Scotland's distilleries. Among the most memorable are picture-perfect Strathisla, Glenfiddich, Aberlour, and lofty Glenlivet, high up in one of the region's prettiest glens.

Wick and Vicinity, Northern Highlands

South of Wick at Lybster lie an incredible concentration of ancient stone monuments, including burial cairns, stone circles, and lines of stone menhirs said to represent star constellations or depictions of the night sky. There's

Aberlour, produced by one of Speyside's many distilleries

also one of Scotland's most unique single malts made at Pulteney Distillery in Wick.

Orkney Islands

Highland Park Distillery in Kirkwall is such a good distillery that, even though it's the only whisky-producing place up in this neck of the woods, it's still worth the trek for the single malt connoisseur. It's one of the only distilleries still to have floor maltings. Then, of course, there is the highest concentration of ancient stone monuments anywhere in northern Europe spread among the Orkney Islands.

► HIGHLAND FLING

The Highlands are the main draw for visitors to Scotland. This tour focuses on a seven-day best-of itinerary. Once at the heart of the Highlands, a surprising amount of sights can be seen in a week. You'll be able to spot castles, hike in wild glens, sail on lochs, and absorb plenty of colorful history.

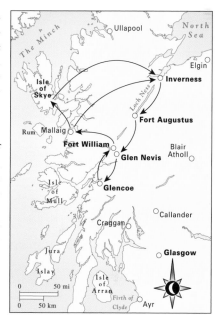

Day 1

Fly into Inverness. Have brunch at one of the cool city cafés/restaurants like the Mustard Seed. Have an afternoon trip by bus to the Clava Cairns or Cawdor Castle just outside Inverness. In late afternoon, make the trip along Loch Ness to Fort Augustus. Check into the Old Pier House bed-and-breakfast and try a spot of refreshment at the Lock Inn.

Day 2

Spend the morning doing a boat trip on Loch Ness, with a look around Urquhart Castle. You could also explore the south side of Loch Ness (you'll need your own wheels). Head southwest to Fort William in the afternoon and base yourself up in Glen Nevis at the Achintee Farm B&B or the Ben Nevis Inn Hostel, ready for some outdoor adventure tomorrow. Dine out on tasty pub fare at the Ben Nevis Inn in the evening.

Day 3

Spend the day hiking at the head of Glen Nevis, climbing Ben Nevis, or trying some different outdoor activities at the Snowgoose Mountain Centre. Try a seafood restaurant like Crannog Restaurant for a well-earned evening meal.

Day 4

Spend the day in Glencoe, south of Fort William. You could do it as a day trip or stay over in an atmospheric inn like the Clachaig Inn, right in the shadow of stupendous mountains in Glencoe village. There are several hikes to do in the glen, or you could check out the history of the Glencoe massacre at the Glencoe

Glencoe from the Clachaig Inn

Trotternish Peninsula, Isle of Skye

and North Lorn Folk Museum. The adventurous should head to Kinlochleven and hike over the Devil's Staircase to the Kings House Hotel before catching a bus back down the glen to Glencoe village.

Days 5 and 6

Get an early bus back to Fort William and hop on the train to Mallaig. You could get a ride on the Jacobite Steam Train, an old steam engine. While on board, it's decision time. At Mallaig you could choose to spend the rest of your holiday in utter wilderness on the Knoydart Peninsula or in classic (but more popular) Scottish scenery on the Isle of Skye. Either way, have lunch at Fishmarket in Mallaig, as gorgeous a fish restaurant as you'll find anywhere.

If you're a wilderness lover, jump on the 2:15 p.m. boat to the Knoydart Peninsula and stay at a bed-and-breakfast like the Gathering. Spend nights 5 and 6 here doing some of the wildest, most wonderful hiking in Scotland.

If you'd rather see Scotland's most popular island, jump on an afternoon boat to the Isle of Skye. Take a bus to Portree, Skye's capital and check in to the Rosedale Hotel. Have an evening meal somewhere atmospheric like the Harbour View seafood restaurant. On Day 6, rent a car or bike to see the Trotternish Peninsula at your leisure. It's where you'll find Scotland's most glorious rock formations and a couple of riveting museums. If you opt for the car, you can fit in a visit to Dunvegan Castle, inhabited by the same family for over eight centuries.

Day 7

From Knoydart, get the morning boat back to Mallaig and in the afternoon head back by train to Fort William, from where you can either get a bus to be back in Inverness or Glasgow for the evening.

From Skye, head back to Inverness over the Skye Bridge and stop off at the picture-perfect Eilean Donan castle en route. Get a later bus to Inverness in time for your flight back.

EDINBURGH AND THE LOTHIANS

Taking in the view from the top of Holyrood Park or Calton Hill, the two spectacular ancient volcanoes that rise up out of the middle of Edinburgh, it's hard not to think Scotland's capital is one of the prettiest in the world. Surrounded by the shimmering Firth of Forth to the north and the heather-clad Lammermuir Hills to the south, Edinburgh not only enjoys a spectacular setting, the city itself boasts picturesque winding lanes within its World Heritage–listed Old Town and a skyline dominated by a castle.

Beauty is not the only thing going for Edinburgh—it also has a cultural appeal that's easy to love, starting with the Edinburgh Festival (Europe's largest), held every August. There are year-round offerings as well, and a stroll down the city's famed Royal Mile in Old Town will give a good sampling of them, starting at Edinburgh Castle and ending at Holyroodhouse Palace and Abbey, with a mix of museums, cafés, and taverns in between.

To the north of Old Town is leafy New Town, itself over two centuries old. Here Georgian houses are set around squares specially designed to offer vistas of the city at its best. New Town lives up to its name as well, offering top-notch shopping facilities and stylish eateries like Valvona and Crolla, a delicatessen-café, by day and a concentration of bars, pubs, and theaters by night.

Beyond the sights and sounds, the city also has an energy, a never-ending buzz that fills the parks and pubs, courtyards and cafés. Every twist and turn of the Old Town tempts you to explore secluded squares and hidden alleyways—this is a wanderer's paradise. Fueled by the mix of people out and about—tourists,

© LUKE WATERSON

HIGHLIGHTS

Edinburgh Castle: The heart of historic Edinburgh, this mammoth fortress has perched on a crag above the city for the best part of a millennium (page 30).

Museum of Scotland: At this dazzling, eclectic museum, you'll find Scotland's most important display of artifacts (page 43).

Calton Hill: Take in the panoramic view from the top of this hill, liberally scattered with outlandish monuments from the ambitious schemes of Victorian developers (page 48).

Dean Village and the Water of Leith: Absorb funky architecture, tranquil scenery, and great galleries in this leafy part of the city (page 49).

Cramond: This plush, lush suburb has swans, sea, and characterful old buildings (page 53).

Rosslyn Glen: Take a trip to Rosslyn with its beautiful, mystery-shrouded chapel in a wooded glen (page 53).

City Ghost Tours: Explore Edinburgh's ghoulish past by night on a tour that treats you to all the gory details (page 55).

South Queensferry: Head to the charming village that inspired Robert Louis Stevenson, full of fabulous pubs and restaurants (page 81).

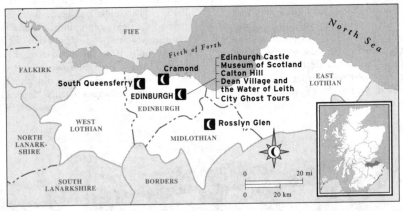

LOOK FOR (TO FIND RECOMMENDED SIGHTS, ACTIVITIES, DINING, AND LODGING.

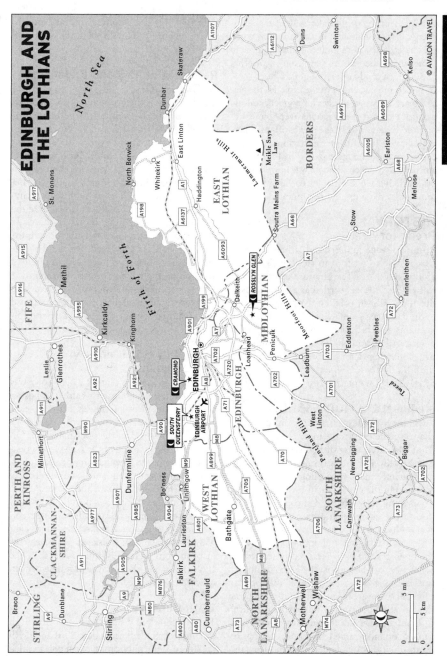

EDINBURGH AND THE LOTHIANS

North Sea

Firth of Forth

FIFE

PERTH AND KINROSS

CLACKMANNAN-SHIRE

STIRLING

FALKIRK

WEST LOTHIAN

NORTH LANARKSHIRE

SOUTH LANARKSHIRE

EDINBURGH

MIDLOTHIAN

EAST LOTHIAN

BORDERS

Lammermuir Hills

Moorfoot Hills

Pentland Hills

Tweed

Meikle Says Law

street performers, picnickers, workers—this energy is most palpable in the summer, when the city is at its most vibrant. You may come to agree with Robert Louis Stevenson's claim that "Edinburgh is what Paris ought to be."

The countryside around the capital is the perfect place to crowd-dodge: it's a green, rolling, wooded expanse of attractions every bit as important as those within the city confines. There is Rosslyn Glen with its mysterious, ornately carved chapel, the huge palace of Linlithgow, where Mary, Queen of Scots was born, and the peaceful village of South Queensferry, home to some classy old pubs and restaurants.

HISTORY
Prehistory
Primitive stone-hunters and fishers were the first people to set foot in the Lothians area, around 5000 B.C. The first use of Edinburgh was at Castle Rock, settled as a key defensive site. It was known as Din Eidyn (Fort of Eidyn) in the dark ages, from where the warriors of the Lothians marched south to defeat at the Battle of Catterick (Catraeth) by the Northumbrians, who, following victory, captured Edinburgh in the 7th century B.C. The city was not regained by the Scots for another 200 years.

Medieval Era (1000-1500)
Edinburgh's oldest surviving building is a chapel in the castle confines, associated with Saint Margaret, sister of the Saxon heir to the English throne, who was entertained by and subsequently married to King Malcolm III of Scotland in the castle late in the 11th century. Their youngest son David I encouraged expansion of the city, which grew throughout the Wars of Independence with England in the early 14th century. Twice Edinburgh was captured by the English and twice it was recaptured by the Scots. Despite the conflict, by 1329 Edinburgh was replacing Berwick on Tweed in Northern England as the area's main outlet for trade, and the Royal Court started to prefer Edinburgh to Dunfermline. Edinburgh consequently became Scotland's capital, and kings gave priority to strengthening its defenses, most notably

following the catastrophic defeat at Flodden, which initiated the building of the Flodden Wall around the city limits after 1513.

Reformation Era and Expansion (1500-1700)
Edinburgh was the epicenter of the Scottish Reformation, an offshoot of the movement started by Martin Luther in 1517 on the continent. It was a stand against the decedent Catholic Church of the time. With a Catholic queen (Mary, Queen of Scots) in power as John Knox emerged into the limelight, the city became a reformation hotbed, with Knox delivering his sermons in St. Giles Cathedral in the Old Town. Increasingly, however, the city's main problem was space. Unable now to expand outward, it expanded upward, becoming a series of medieval tower blocks often 10 or 12 stories high. Trade became threatened as the city quickly descended into an overcrowded slum, taking further blows when both the royal court and parliament moved to England following the Union of the Crowns.

18th- and 19th-Century Improvement
Eventually, in the 18th century, a New Town was built to house Edinburgh's wealthy; imposing Georgian and Victorian houses started spreading to the north and south. The rich moved out of the Old Town, and the poor moved in. On one hand, the building of the New Town kickstarted Edinburgh's reputation as a place of architectural, scientific and intellectual brilliance, due to such people as the architect James Craig, economist Adam Smith, and poet Robert Burns. On the other hand, while grandiose bridges and monuments were erected around them, the plight of the Old Town poor worsened. Improvements in conditions were only implemented in the 1860s following the collapse of a tenement in which 20 people died.

20th Century
The last hundred years have seen Edinburgh expand to include Portobello (1896) and Leith (1920). In 1995, publication of a report entitled

Scotland's Parliament, Scotland's Right led to a resounding vote in favor of a new devolved Scottish parliament two years later. The parliament first met in 1999; its controversial new building in Holyrood contrasts starkly with the graceful Old Town but has brought Scotland into the 21st century in a new wave of independence from England.

PLANNING YOUR TIME

Edinburgh is compact: most notable attractions are located in the Old and New Towns, within easy walking distance of each other. It's possible to see most of the sights on or around the Royal Mile in a day—but that would be nonstop sightseeing. Two days would allow you to experience the city as every visitor should—at a relaxed pace with time to sample some of the many atmospheric bars and cafés. Kick off with a leisurely Old Town breakfast and some people-watching, then head up to the tourist mecca of Edinburgh Castle to begin taking in the Royal Mile sights. There's so much on offer (whisky, tartan, museums, pubs) that it's easy to tailor your time to your tastes. The Royal Mile ends in Holyrood Park, where it's tempting to have a ramble after seeing the palace. Finish the day with a meal in a trendy New Town restaurant (Café Royal Oyster Bar would be hard to beat) and then a theater performance/ghost tour. The next day, climb Calton Hill for the great views and interesting monuments; afterward you could explore New Town architecture and bars, or take a stroll down to the Water of Leith and the nearby modern art galleries. With three days plus, venturing out to Cramond or Rosslyn Glen is recommended. The Lothians region around Edinburgh has plenty of interesting day trips.

SAFETY

For its size (over 448,000 inhabitants), Edinburgh is safe. However, the areas that make it such an agreeable city by day are some of the ones you should be wary of at night: Calton Hill, and the Meadows Area, particularly if you are female and alone. A definite no-no for women by themselves is the red light district in Leith (anywhere around Salamander Street and Leith Links). Other than that, usual common sense applies when in deserted areas after dark.

ORIENTATION

The main sights are located in the Old Town or the New Town, all within 20 minutes' walk of Waverley Train Station. Waverley and Princes Street Gardens separate the Old Town from the New Town. To the south is the Old Town with its main thoroughfare, the Royal Mile, running from Edinburgh Castle down to Holyrood Park. The narrow winding streets do often bring you to dead ends, while flights of steps are not always the shortcuts they appear to be. However, head up from any point around the center and you will inevitably reach the castle. South of the Royal Mile, the most significant street for sights and entertainment is the Grassmarket, right below Castle Rock and running east parallel to the Royal Mile.

The Old Town is bordered on the east by the hilly Holyrood Park and its landmark crags: These should remain east for most of your city explorations. South of the Old Town is the Meadows, another large park. The area south of the Meadows is generally known as Southside, with Bruntsfield and Newington marking its eastern and western periphery. To the immediate west of the Meadows is Toll Cross, while south beyond Bruntsfield are the posh suburbs of Marchmont and Morningside and, much farther out, Rosslyn.

North of Princes Street Gardens is Princes Street, the main thoroughfare of New Town and where the main shopping district is. Where Princes Street's eastern end reaches North Bridge, Leith Street heads northeast, dominated to the east by the city's other significant hill, Calton Hill, which overlooks a clutch of theaters. North of Princes Street and west of Leith Street is where you will find the New Town's architectural merits. At the west end of Princes Street is, in fact, the West End (theater district), and Queensferry Road leads from here to Dean Village. North of the New Town is Edinburgh's other main attraction: the Royal Botanic Gardens, with Leith to the northeast and Cramond along the coast to the northwest.

EDINBURGH

Sights

You can walk easily between all Edinburgh's Old Town sights. The New Town attractions are also close together and wandering between them is an invigorating change to the inside of a museum. The major out-of-the-way attraction is the Royal Yacht *Britannia,* in Leith to Edinburgh's northeast, a short bus ride from Princes Street. Significant sights in the area around the capital include North Berwick's Scottish Seabird Centre and Rosslyn Chapel, but the Lothians area, like the suburbs of Cramond and Stockbridge, are mostly places for a welcome wander in scenic surrounds away from the city bustle.

OLD TOWN

Meandering Old Town, with its cobbled artery of the Royal Mile, stretches east from the ridge of castle rock down to Holyrood Park and south down to Grassmarket where its boundary is the tumbled-down Flodden Wall. Not much to look at now, it was the wall that defined the character of this maze of pirouetting streets, as crowded now with tourists as it must have been with residents in centuries gone. The wall was built to strengthen defenses. This meant the city, hemmed in to the north by the bog that is now Princes Street Gardens, had nowhere to expand. Houses grew upward instead to accommodate the burgeoning population—seven or eight stories, to form what is now an architectural wonderland. Cavernous vaults appeared as forgotten streets were built over. Open land became courtyards, framed by precipitous walls, with windows peeking out from impossible angles. To live here was a nightmare, with a whole social spectrum of people residing under one roof. There was no space for wealthy families to have a whole building; they took the middle floors, not so far up as to strain themselves climbing stairs yet far enough from street level to escape the foul smells. Around them from cellar to attic crammed the tradesmen and the poor. The New Town brought relief, and the Old Town continues as a lively

thriving place. Its fascinating buildings are now renovated into a warren of pubs, restaurants, hostels, shops, and museums, retaining their tradition-rich character.

◖ Edinburgh Castle

Evidence indicates the volcanic Castle Rock was the site of earlier dwellings before building began on the castle as it appears today—unsurprising for such a prominent feature of the landscape. Now Edinburgh Castle (tel. 0131/225 9846, www.edinburghcastle.biz, 9:30 A.M.–6 P.M. daily Apr.–Oct., 9:30 A.M.–5 P.M. daily Nov.–Mar., £12 adults, £9.50 seniors, £6 children), Scotland's finest castle, is a fascinating mix of architectural styles, a result of successive defenses and batterings by English as well as Scottish forces. While Edinburgh residents may wince at the volumes of tourists it attracts (this is Britain's second-most visited attraction after the Tower of London), this city does owe its very existence to this sheer-sided crag. Even the first people in the area recognized the strategic importance of this site, hence why Edinburgh was originally settled.

Visitors approach via **the esplanade,** the large flat area in front of the castle built in 1753 as a parade ground for resident troops. The atmospheric space lends itself well to performances too, including most notably the Military Tattoo, held here every August.

The Gatehouse, the castle's most vulnerable point of attack, was built more for aesthetics in the late 19th century. Standing guard over the entranceway are statues of Scotland's freedom fighters Robert the Bruce and William Wallace, added in 1929. On the left as you approach the shop are the impressive **Half Moon Battery** and **Forewell Battery.** The shattered remains of a former tower are one of many testimonies to the battering the castle has received over the centuries. Rebuilt following the Lang Siege of 1573, the high walls and wide maneuverability for cannons make them key defensive structures.

© LUKE WATERSON

Edinburgh Castle soars up on a crag above historic Old Town.

Passing the castle shop, these days seeming to take up more space than anything, you then reach the **Dog Cemetery,** where officers buried their regimental mascots. Continue to **Mills Mount Battery,** at the far end of which is the **One O'Clock Gun.** Fired at precisely that time every day except Sunday, the tradition dates back to times before accurate timepieces were available—ships in the Firth of Forth could check and reset their chronometers.

The road curves round to the left through **Foogs Gate** to the highest point of the castle, culminating in **St. Margaret's Chapel.** Built around 1110, the chapel commemorates Saint Margaret, wife of Malcolm III and one-time heir to the Saxon throne, who died in the castle in 1093. This is the oldest part of the castle still standing, and one of the most moving. There is a gospel book previously owned by St. Margaret and a stained glass window depicting her along with St. Andrew, St. Columba, and William Wallace. Outside is the famous 15th-century cannon, **Mons Meg,** last fired to celebrate the first of Mary, Queen of Scot's marriages in 1681.

The group of buildings at the top of the castle are arranged around the 15th-century **Crown Square.** On the north side, a former munitions house is now the **Scottish National War Memorial,** opened in 1927 by Prince of Wales (later Edward VIII) as the key monument to commemorate the Scottish dead of the Great War. Opposite, the **Great Hall** was added by James IV before his untimely death at Flodden in 1513. Most noteworthy is its 16th-century hammer-beam roof, supported by intricately carved stone corbels. The **Palace** next door, official residence of the Stewart Kings and Queens, was where Mary, Queen of Scots gave birth to the future King James VI of Scotland and I of England, but most see the highlight of the visit as the **Crown Room.** Here the Regalia of Scotland, otherwise known as the **Scottish Crown Jewels,** are on display along with the **Stone of Destiny** (also known as the Stone of Scone), the traditional coronation seat for Scottish kings and queens. The Scottish Crown Jewels are the oldest in Europe. They include the crown, dating from Robert the Bruce's lifetime, and the scepter, gifted to

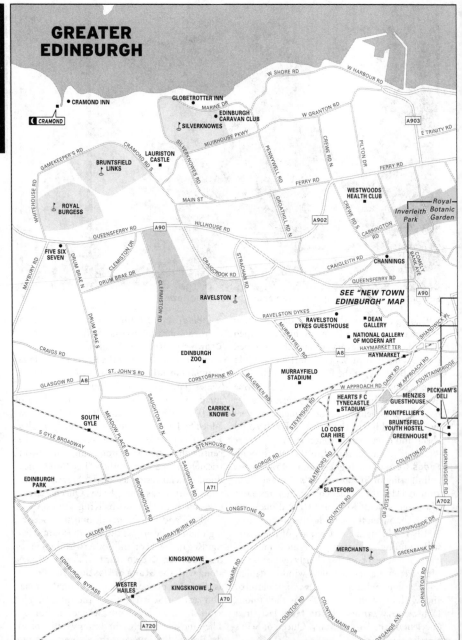

GREATER EDINBURGH

CRAMOND

CRAMOND INN

GLOBETROTTER INN

MARINE DR

EDINBURGH CARAVAN CLUB

SILVERKNOWES

W SHORE RD

W HARBOUR RD

W GRANTON RD

A903

E TRINITY RD

MUIRHOUSE PKWY

LAURISTON CASTLE

BRUNTSFIELD LINKS

CRAMOND RD S

SILVERKNOWES RD

PENNYWELL RD

CREWE RD N

PILTON DR

FERRY RD

WESTWOODS HEALTH CLUB

Royal Botanic Garden

Inverleith Park

WHITEHOUSE RD

GAMEKEEPER'S RD

MAIN ST

GROATHILL RD N

CREWE RD S

CARRINGTON RD

ROYAL BURGESS

QUEENSFERRY RD

A90

HILLHOUSE RD

A902

CRAIGLEITH RD

CHANNINGS

COMELY BANK AVE

MAYBURY RD

FIVE SIX SEVEN

DRUM BRAE N

CLEMISTON DR

DRUM BRAE DR

CLERMISTON RD

CRAIGCROOK RD

STRACHAN RD

QUEENSFERRY RD

A90

SHANDWICK PL

SEE "NEW TOWN EDINBURGH" MAP

RAVELSTON

RAVELSTON DYKES

RAVELSTON DYKES GUESTHOUSE

DEAN GALLERY

NATIONAL GALLERY OF MODERN ART

CRAIGS RD

DRUM BRAE S

EDINBURGH ZOO

MURRAYFIELD RD

A8

HAYMARKET TER

HAYMARKET

GLASGOW RD

A8

ST. JOHN'S RD

CORSTORPHINE RD

BALGREEN RD

MURRAYFIELD STADIUM

W APPROACH RD

DAIRY RD

W APPROACH RD

FOUNTAINBRIDGE

PECKHAM'S DELI

SOUTH GYLE

MEADOW PLACE RD

SAUGHTON RD N

CARRICK KNOWE

STEVENSON RD

HEARTS F C TYNECASTLE STADIUM

MENZIES GUESTHOUSE

MONTPELLIER'S

S GYLE BROADWAY

STENHOUSE DR

LO COST CAR HIRE

BRUNTSFIELD YOUTH HOSTEL

GREENHOUSE

MORNINGSIDE RD

EDINBURGH PARK

BROOMHOUSE RD

SAUGHTON RD

A71

GORGIE RD

SLATEFORD RD

COLINTON RD

COLINTON RD

MYRESIDE RD

SLATEFORD

A702

CALDER RD

MURRAYBURN RD

LONGSTONE RD

MORNINGSIDE DR

MERCHANTS

GREENBANK DR

EDINBURGH BYPASS

KINGSKNOWE

LANARK RD

COLINTON RD

CORNISTON RD

WESTER HAILES

KINGSKNOWE

A70

COLINTON MAINS DR

OXGANGS AVE

A720

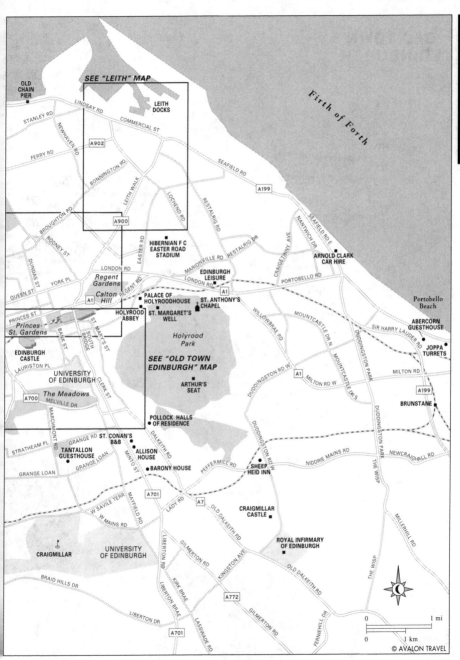

OLD CHAIN PIER

STANLEY RD

LINDSAY RD

LEITH DOCKS

SEE "LEITH" MAP

FERRY RD

NEWHAVEN RD

COMMERCIAL ST

Firth of Forth

A902

BONNINGTON RD

BROUGHTON RD

LEITH WALK

A900

SEAFIELD RD

A199

RODNEY ST

EASTER RD

LOCHEND RD

RESTALRIG RD

MARIONVILLE RD

RESTALRIG DR

SEAFIELD RD E

NANTWICH DR

CRAIGENTINNY AVE

ARNOLD CLARK CAR HIRE

DUNDAS ST

YORK PL

QUEEN ST

LONDON RD

Regent Gardens
Calton Hill

HIBERNIAN F C EASTER ROAD STADIUM

EDINBURGH LEISURE

LONDON RD

A1

PORTOBELLO RD

Portobello Beach

PRINCES ST

Princes St. Gardens

BANK ST

ST. MARY'S ST

REGENT RD

A1

PALACE OF HOLYROODHOUSE

ST. ANTHONY'S CHAPEL

ABERCORN GUESTHOUSE

SIR HARRY LAUDER RD

HOLYROOD ABBEY

ST. MARGARET'S WELL

WILLOWBRAE RD

MOUNTCASTLE DR N

JOPPA TURRETS

EDINBURGH CASTLE

LAURISTON PL

SOUTH BRIDGE

Holyrood Park

DUDDINGSTON RD W

MOUNTCASTLE DR S

DUDDINGSTON PARK

MILTON RD

UNIVERSITY OF EDINBURGH

CLERK ST

SEE "OLD TOWN EDINBURGH" MAP

A1

MILTON RD W

A199

A700

The Meadows

MELVILLE DR

MARCHMONT RD

ARTHUR'S SEAT

BRUNSTANE

STRATHEAM PL

GRANGE RD

ST. CONAN'S B&B

DALKEITH RD

POLLOCK HALLS OF RESIDENCE

DUDDINGSTON RD

NIDDRIE MAINS RD

NEWCRAIGHALL RD

TANTALLON GUESTHOUSE

GRANGE LOAN

MINTO ST

ALLISON HOUSE

PEFFERMILL RD

SHEEP HEID INN

THE WISP

GRANGE LOAN

BARONY HOUSE

A701

W SAVILE TERR

MAYFIELD RD

LADY RD

A7

OLD DALKEITH RD

CRAIGMILLAR CASTLE

W MAINS RD

CRAIGMILLAR

UNIVERSITY OF EDINBURGH

LIBERTON RD

GILMERTON RD

KINGSTON AVE

ROYAL INFIRMARY OF EDINBURGH

OLD DALKEITH RD

MILLERHILL RD

BRAID HILLS DR

KIRK BRAE

LIBERTON BRAE

A772

GILMERTON RD

FERNIEHILL DR

THE WISP

LIBERTON DR

A701

LASSWADE RD

0   1 mi

0   1 km

© AVALON TRAVEL

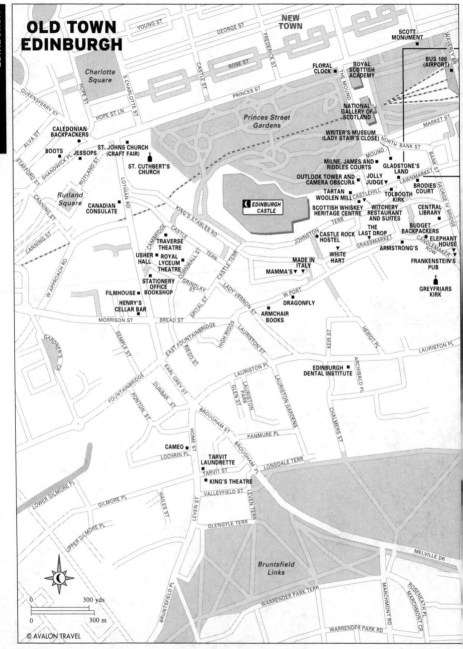

OLD TOWN EDINBURGH

NEW TOWN

YOUNG ST
GEORGE ST
FREDERICK ST
ROSE ST
CASTLE ST
S CHARLOTTE ST
HOPE ST
S ST DAVID ST
PRINCES ST

SCOTT MONUMENT

BUS 100 (AIRPORT)

WAVERLY BR

Charlotte Square

QUEENSFERRY ST
HOPE ST LN

FLORAL CLOCK
ROYAL SCOTTISH ACADEMY

MARKET ST

Princes Street Gardens

NATIONAL GALLERY OF SCOTLAND

THE MOUND

ALVA ST
STAFFORD ST
SHANDWICK PL
CALEDONIAN BACKPACKERS
BOOTS   JESSOPS
ST. JOHNS CHURCH (CRAFT FAIR)
ST. CUTHBERT'S CHURCH
RUTLAND ST
RUTLAND SQ

WRITER'S MUSEUM (LADY STAIR'S CLOSE)

NORTH BANK ST
BANK ST
GEORGE IV BRIDGE

Rutland Square

CANNING ST
LOTHIAN RD
CANADIAN CONSULATE

MILNE, JAMES AND RIDDLES COURTS
OUTLOOK TOWER AND CAMERA OBSCURA
TARTAN WOOLEN MILL
SCOTTISH WHISKEY HERITAGE CENTRE

GLADSTONE'S LAND
JOLLY JUDGE
CASTLEHILL
TOLBOOTH KIRK
WITCHERY RESTAURANT AND SUITES

BRODIES COURT
LAWNMARKET

CENTRAL LIBRARY

W APPROACH RD

KING'S STABLES RD

EDINBURGH CASTLE

JOHNSTON TERR

THE LAST DROP
GRASSMARKET
ARMSTRONG'S

BUDGET BACKPACKERS
CANDLEMAKER ROW
ELEPHANT HOUSE

CAMBRIDGE ST
CASTLE TERR
TRAVERSE THEATRE
USHER HALL
ROYAL LYCEUM THEATRE
CORNWALL ST
CASTLE TERR
CASTLE ROCK HOSTEL
WHITE HART

FRANKENSTEIN'S PUB

CANNING ST
SEMPLE ST
GRINDLAY ST
STATIONERY OFFICE BOOKSHOP
FILMHOUSE
HENRY'S CELLAR BAR
SPITAL ST

MADE IN ITALY
MAMMA'S

W PORT
DRAGONFLY

GREYFRIARS KIRK

MORRISON ST   BREAD ST
EAST FOUNTAINBRIDGE
RIEGO ST
HIGH RIGGS
LAURISTON ST
ARMCHAIR BOOKS

LADY VERNON ST
HERIOT PL
LAURISTON PL

GARDNER'S CR
FOUNTAINBRIDGE
EARL GREY ST
DUNBAR ST
BROUGHAM ST
LAURISTON PL
LAURISTON GLEN PARK
LAURISTON GARDENS

EDINBURGH DENTAL INSTITUTE

ARCHIBALD PL
CHALMERS ST

PONTON ST

LOWER GILMORE PL
GILMORE PL
HOME ST
LOCHRIN PL
CAMEO
TARVIT LAUNDRETTE
TARVIT ST
KING'S THEATRE
BROUGHAM ST
PANMURE PL
LONSDALE TERR
LEVEN TERR

UPPER GILMORE PL
HAILES ST
LEVEN ST
VALLEYFIELD ST
GLENGYLE TERR

MELVILLE DR

Bruntsfield Links

BRUNTSFIELD PL
WARRENDER PARK TERR
MARCHMONT RD
ROSENEATH PL
MARCHMONT CR

0   300 yds
0   300 m

WARRENDER PARK RD

© AVALON TRAVEL

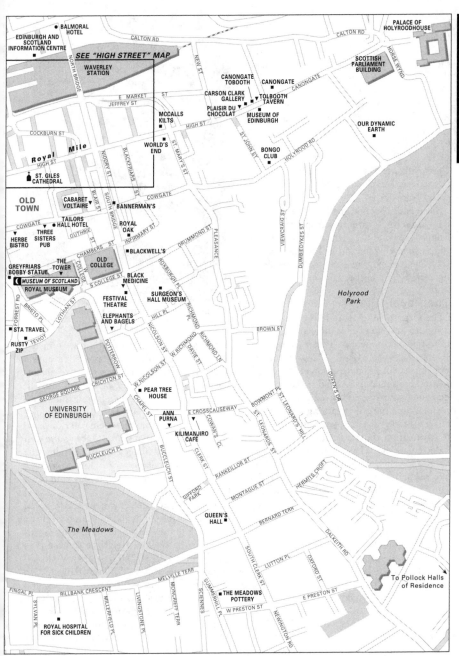

PALACE OF
HOLYROODHOUSE

BALMORAL
HOTEL

EDINBURGH AND
SCOTLAND
INFORMATION CENTRE

CALTON RD

CALTON RD

SCOTTISH
PARLIAMENT
BUILDING

HORSE WYND

SEE "HIGH STREET" MAP

NORTH BRIDGE

NEW ST

WAVERLEY
STATION

CANONGATE
TOLBOOTH

CANONGATE

CANONGATE

E MARKET ST

ST

JEFFREY ST

CARSON CLARK
GALLERY

TOLBOOTH
TAVERN

PLAISIR DU
CHOCOLAT

MCCALLS
KILTS

COCKBURN ST

HIGH ST

MUSEUM OF
EDINBURGH

OUR DYNAMIC
EARTH

Royal Mile

HIGH ST

WORLD'S
END

ST MARY'S ST

ST JOHN ST

BONGO
CLUB

HOLYROOD RD

NIDDRY ST

BLACKFRIARS ST

ST. GILES
CATHEDRAL

COWGATE

**OLD
TOWN**

CABARET
VOLTAIRE

BLAIR ST

SOUTH BRIDGE

BANNERMAN'S

VIEWCRAIG ST

DUMBIEDYKES RD

COWGATE

TAILORS
HALL HOTEL

ROYAL
OAK

INFIRMARY ST

HERBE
BISTRO

THREE
SISTERS
PUB

GUTHRIE ST

DRUMMOND ST

PLEASANCE

*Holyrood
Park*

CHAMBERS ST

BLACKWELL'S

ROXBURGH PL

GREYFRIARS
BOBBY STATUE

THE
TOWER

S COLLEGE ST

OLD
COLLEGE

BLACK
MEDICINE

RICHMOND PL

RICHMOND LN

MUSEUM OF SCOTLAND
ROYAL MUSEUM

SURGEON'S
HALL MUSEUM

HILL PL

FESTIVAL
THEATRE

W RICHMOND ST

DAVIE ST

BROWN ST

QUEEN'S DR

FORREST RD

LOTHIAN ST

ELEPHANTS
AND BAGELS

NICOLSON ST

BRISTO PL

STA TRAVEL

TEVIOT

RUSTY
ZIP

POTTERROW

W NICOLSON ST

PEAR TREE
HOUSE

CHAPEL ST

BOWMONT PL

ST LEONARD'S HILL

ST LEONARD'S ST

CRICHTON ST

GEORGE SQUARE

ANN
PURNA

E CROSSCAUSEWAY

COWAN'S CL

**UNIVERSITY
OF EDINBURGH**

KILIMANJIRO
CAFÉ

HERMITS CROFT

BUCCLEUCH PL

BUCCLEUCH ST

CLERK ST

RANKEILLOR ST

GIFFORD
PARK

MONTAGUE ST

DALKEITH RD

The Meadows

QUEEN'S
HALL

BERNARD TERR

To Pollock Halls
of Residence

MELVILLE TERR

SOUTH CLERK ST

LUTTON PL

OXFORD ST

E PRESTON ST

NEWINGTON RD

FINGAL PL

BILLBANK CRESCENT

MELVILLE TERR

MONCRIEFF TERR

SUMMERHILL PL

LIVINGSTONE PL

SCIENNES

THE MEADOWS
POTTERY

W PRESTON ST

SYLVAN PL

MILLERFIELD PL

ROYAL HOSPITAL
FOR SICK CHILDREN

James IV in 1494 by the Pope. Following the Union in 1707, the old Scots Parliament was dissolved and the Regalia shut away within the castle. As years passed, rumors circulated that they had been stolen by the English. In 1818, authority was obtained to search the castle at the instigation of Sir Walter Scott, who was highly emotional upon the discovery that the Regalia were lying in an oak chest in the Crown Room, "exactly as they had been left in 1707." The **Castle Vaults,** entered from Crown Square, have served a multitude of purposes over the years, including a prison and even a bake-house.

Near Mill's Mount, the **Cart Sheds** nearby housed up to 50 carts to transport provisions from the town to the garrison. Bronze Age artifacts were also found on this site. Now the Cart Sheds host far in excess of 50 people taking refreshment in the tearoom.

The Royal Mile

"The largest, longest and finest street, for Buildings and Number of Inhabitants, not only in Britain but the World" author Daniel Defoe said of the Royal Mile in 1723. Visitors may well agree with this description of Edinburgh's main thoroughfare, today bolstered by a good deal more tourists and souvenir shops than in Defoe's time but still retaining a century-old charm. Made up of the succession of streets that run from the castle down to Holyrood Palace (Castlehill, Lawnmarket, High Street, and Canongate), the Royal Mile is actually one Scottish mile long, in defiance of a law imposing English miles in 1824. It's an easy, enjoyable walk down the architecturally rich Royal Mile, named after the royalty that once used this route between castle and palace, which takes in Edinburgh's main sights.

CASTLEHILL

The **Outlook Tower and Camera Obscura** (tel. 0131/226 3709, 9:30 A.M.–7:30 P.M. daily July–Aug., 9:30 A.M.–6 P.M. daily Apr.–June and Sept.–Oct., 10 A.M.–5 P.M. daily Nov.–Mar., £7.05 adults, £6.50 seniors, £5.50 children) was built in the 19th century. It boasts

© LUKE WATERSON

A bagpiper plays on the Royal Mile.

unsurpassed views of Edinburgh, from the original images of the city projected onto a screen since Victorian times, to three-dimensional views and cameras you control yourself. There are lots of other hands-on exhibits, including the world's largest collection of holograms and a fun exhibit where you can shake hands with your own ghost. Once you've seen enough distorted images you can climb to the top of the Outlook Tower for 360° panoramic views of Edinburgh, popular with (and often full of) children.

The best chance to get your head around the complex history of Scotland's national drink and work out which single malts you are partial to is the **Whisky Heritage Centre** (354 Castlehill, tel. 0131/220 0441, www.whiskyheritage.co.uk, 10 A.M.–5:30 P.M. daily, £9.25). The shop presents 340 types of whisky, and there are free tastings throughout the year. There's a crash-course tour (well worth the admission, but check website for discounts) where you can ride on a barrel through whisky history, including the lowdown on differences

THE DASTARDLY DEACON

Deacon William Brodie was a model 18th-century citizen of Edinburgh, respected cabinet-maker, and leader of the Guild of Wrights and Masons – by day, that is. By night, he was something rather less savory. Things had looked to be going rather well for the deacon when he inherited his father's business and the not-insubstantial sum of £10,000, then enough to set one up for life. But the Deacon had two indulgences: drink and women. Feeding these habits, especially with two mistresses, stretched even his fortunes. Brodie's solution was another kind of income – theft. The means were simple. In his capacity as cabinet-maker he often needed to visit houses to take measurements. When people's backs were turned he made copies of the keys (hung conveniently, as was then the custom, by the back door) and got his partner in crime, a locksmith, to make duplicate keys.

His crimes were thus conducted quietly, and the mystifying robberies plagued Edinburgh's Old Town for some time. No one suspected the respectable deacon; the alcohol flowed and his mistresses were happy. But the ambitions of this successful burglar grew until one night he tried to rob the excise office. He was seen, and despite fleeing from the scene, was caught and sentenced to death by hanging.

For many that would have been the end, but the ever-resourceful deacon even at this black hour had a plan in store. He instructed a surgeon to inset a piece of metal piping inside his throat so that the hangman's noose would not crush his windpipe. However, death proved too much for the deacon to trick: The very gallows he designed were those that executed him. The story of the deacon's two-sided character became the inspiration for Robert Louis Stevenson's *The Strange Case of Dr. Jekyll and Mr. Hyde.*

between malt, grain, and blended Scotch whisky and try a complimentary dram or two. When you've had your fill sampling whisky there's a wonderful restaurant and bar in the basement serving up dishes mostly containing significant amounts of, er, more whisky.

The black, extremely gothic, 74-meter spire of the **Tolbooth Kirk** (tel. 0131/473 2015, information office open 10 A.M.–10 P.M. daily Aug., 11 A.M.–6 P.M. daily Sept.–July) dominates the Royal Mile. Originally housing the General Assembly of the Church of Scotland, this has not been used as a church since 1984 and is now the Hub, a center for information on the Edinburgh Festival. There's an OK—if pricey—café inside (10 A.M.–10 P.M. Mon.–Sat., 10 A.M.–8 P.M. Sun.).

LAWNMARKET

So called because of the famous linen market held here until the mid-18th century, Lawnmarket was a sought-after area to live in, frequented or lived in by some of Scotland's most famous figures including Robert Burns and Sir Walter Scott.

The most fascinating part of the Royal Mile is perhaps just off it. During Edinburgh's housing crisis in the 17th century, space was at a premium. A lot of the land traditionally rented by Edinburgh's craftsmen for their businesses was built over, but these narrow, dark passages, lit by oil lamps, between imposing multistory buildings were designed to give access to the land. The alleyways open up into beautiful secluded courtyards. The best are on Lawnmarket, often leading to an unexpected pub. Among the most impressive are **Brodies Court,** associated with the notorious deacon; **James Court,** where both philosopher and economist David Hume and James Boswell lived; and **Milnes Court,** almost certainly the earliest housing development in the world (1690).

Set deep within the charming courtyard of Lady Stair's Close, the fascinating **Writer's Museum** (tel. 0131/529 4901, 10 A.M.–6 P.M. daily Mon.–Sat., 10 A.M.–5 P.M. daily Oct.–May) explores Edinburgh's and Scotland's rich literary tradition. It exhibits paraphernalia from the lives of Robert Louis Stevenson, Sir Walter

Scott and Robert Burns. The collection includes Burns's writing desk and Scott's chessboard, as well as the printing press on which his Waverley novels were produced. Inscriptions outside commemorate various writers from the 14th century to the present, and admission is free.

The merchant Thomas Gledstanes purchased **Gladstone's Land** (477 Lawnmarket, tel. 0131/226 5856, 10 A.M.–7 P.M. daily July–Aug., 10 A.M.–5 P.M. daily Easter–June and Sept.–Oct., £5 adults, £4 seniors) in 1617. It's an early example of an apartment block, otherwise known as a "land." Gledstanes rented to different groups of people from diverse social groups, and now it's a brilliant insight into what tenement life at this time would have been like. Two floors are authentically preserved in 17th-century style and open to the public. The painted ceilings and reconstructed shop decked out with 17th-century goods are the highlights. Groups should book ahead: Space is at a premium.

HIGH STREET

Although locals refer to the entire Royal Mile as "The High Street," it officially runs from the Royal Mile's intersection with George IV bridge to its intersection with St. Mary's Street.

Worth a quick look, **Parliament Square** is the large complex of buildings set back at the top of the High Street, resonating with plenty of history. Built in 1641, **Parliament House** gave the square its name and until the Union of the Crowns in 1707 was used by the Scottish parliament. The Great Fire of 1824 destroyed many of the buildings in the complex but otherwise the facade of the square is little changed in centuries. Also in Parliament Square are the 18th-century **Law Courts.** The **Heart of Midlothian** in the cobbles here marks the site of a gallows for executing unfortunate inmates of the former Tolbooth (at different times a meeting place for parliament as well as a prison), once located nearby. Spitting on the Heart is something of a tradition (reasons include anything from contempt for prisoners to local football rivalries), so stand well out of range. The **Statue of King Charles II** is the oldest lead-cast statue in Britain.

Right alongside, **St. Giles Cathedral** (9 A.M.–7 P.M. Mon.–Fri., 9 A.M.–5 P.M. Sat., 1–5 P.M. Sun. May–Sept., 9 A.M.–5 P.M. Mon.–Sat., 1–5 P.M. Sun. Oct.–Apr., free, although a £1 donation is suggested) is named after the patron saint of cripples. The cathedral was all but destroyed by Richard II during a siege in 1385 but miraculously rebuilt by the residents of Edinburgh over the following century, culminating in the Crown Spire, added in 1495. During the reformation, the Calvinist John Knox and his followers stripped the church of its Catholic trappings, whitewashing the walls and accounting for much of the plainness of the interior. A statue of Knox, minister of St. Giles for a time, stands at the cathedral entrance. Charles I's visit to Edinburgh in 1633, in which he instructed for St. Giles to be made into a cathedral and reintroduced bishops to the Presbyterian Church, sparked widespread opposition and the signing of the National Covenant, setting in writing the Scottish resistance to the monarch's religious policy. The **Thistle Chapel,** designed in the high gothic architectural style of the 15th century, was added in 1911. The Chapel is approached via an antechamber where all the monarchs from James VII until the time of the Chapel's construction have their names engraved. Most noteworthy here, on the ceiling and in the chapel itself, are a series of simple yet effective carved stone bosses. The Sanctuary marks the heart of the cathedral, where only the four central pillars remain of the oldest part of the building, dating from 1120. In the nave is the Royal Pew designed for Queen Victoria between 1829 and 1833. Several aisles lead off from the center, each with a different theme. The **Moray Aisle,** based on the assassinated half-brother of Mary, Queen of Scots, contains the original 1638 signed copy of the National Covenant.

During extensive redevelopments in the Old Town in the 18th century, many new buildings rose up, some literally built over the top of former streets. **The Real Mary King's Close** (2 Warriston's Close Writers Ct., tel. 0870/241 1414, www.realmarykingsclose.com, 10 A.M.–9 P.M. daily Apr.–Oct., 10 A.M.–4 P.M.

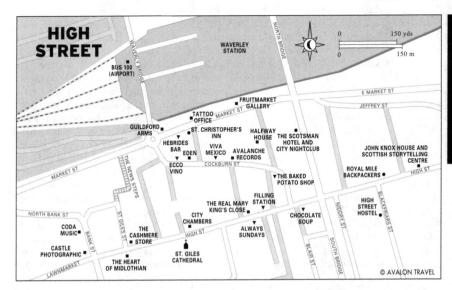

Sun.–Fri., 10 A.M.–9 P.M. Sat. Nov.–Mar.) had supposedly been blocked in by the city council in 1645 with the residents still inside to contain a plague outbreak. When the foundations of the **City Chambers** were built overhead in 1753, the series of streets where people had lived and worked only a century before truly became underground. This dark, eerie warren of streets, including Mary King's Close, is now open to the public with costumed guides to show you around and give a breathtaking insight into life in Edinburgh over four centuries ago. As you can expect with a site where plague victims were buried alive, there are plenty of colorful, morbid stories to experience. Strong footwear is recommended.

Dating from around 1490, **John Knox's House** (10 A.M.–6 P.M. Mon.–Sat., noon–6 P.M. Sun. July–Aug., 10 A.M.–6 P.M. Mon.–Sat. Sept.–June, £3.50 adults, £2.75 seniors) is Edinburgh's oldest tenement, with creaky, overhanging, wooden upper floors. It was home to Protestant reformer John Knox from 1561 until his death in 1572, but the museum also tells the story of the house's other famous residents, including the goldsmith to Mary, Queen of Scots. The house is now part of the Royal

Mile's most recently opened cultural center, the **Scottish Storytelling Centre** (43–45 High St., tel. 0131/556 9579, www.scottishstorytellingcentre.co.uk) with the same operating hours and free entry. The Centre is a great place to experience live storytelling and runs a packed year-round program of literature and theater, supported as ever by a series of flashy multimedia exhibitions.

Off the Royal Mile, following Cockburn Street down onto Market Street will bring you to the bright and airy **Fruitmarket Gallery** (45 Market St., tel. 0131/225 2383, www.fruitmarket.co.uk, 11 A.M.–6 P.M. Mon.–Sat., noon–5 P.M. Sun.), which hosts a variety of innovative exhibitions from contemporary Scottish artists.

CANONGATE

Canongate was traditionally a separate burg to that of Edinburgh, as authorized by David I in 1143. The name refers to the canons of Holyrood Abbey that lived in the street. Canongate was outside the city limits and as a result enjoys spacious house lots and pretty gardens lacking on the rest of the Royal Mile.

If there's one city with a history worth

discovering, it's Edinburgh; the enthralling **Museum of Edinburgh** (142 Canongate, tel. 0131/529 4143, 10 A.M.–5 P.M. Mon.–Sat., also noon–5 P.M. Sun. during festival, free), housed in the gabled 16th-century Huntly House, is the perfect way to do it. It traces the past of the capital from prehistoric times, with highlights including displays of the archaeological finds at Cramond, the National Covenant, and the bowl and collar of Edinburgh's favorite canine, Greyfriars Bobby.

Built in 1591, the **Canongate Tolbooth** was where tolls were collected, as well as being the Council House, Courtroom, and Prison. It now hosts **The People's Story** (163 Canongate, tel. 0131/529 4057, 10 A.M.–6 P.M. Mon.–Sat. June–Sept., 10 A.M.–5 P.M. Mon.–Sat. Oct.–May, also open 2–5 P.M. Sun. during festival, free), recounting tales of the city's colorful residents.

Behind the Tolbooth and unique when built in 1691 in strictly Presbyterian Edinburgh, **Canongate Kirk** (10:30 A.M.–4 P.M. Mon.–Sat. mid-June–mid-Sept., Kirk yard open throughout year) is designed in the shape of a Roman cross. It is believed the builders deliberately designed it so the church could be easily converted for Roman Catholic use should the Reformation of over a century before not succeed. In the nave, a bronze medallion with the name Clarissa by it is the only lasting reference to Robert Burns's mistress. Burns, visiting the Kirk in 1780, found the **Kirk yard** in a poor state and commissioned a fresh headstone for the poet Robert Fergusson, buried there six years earlier. Check Burns's tribute on the back. Also buried in the Kirk yard is renowned Edinburgh economist Adam Smith.

Holyrood Area

At the east (lower) end of the Royal Mile is the verdant area known as Holyrood, predominated by the steep hilly Holyrood Park. This rises to culminate in the distinctive Salisbury Crags.

PALACE OF HOLYROOD HOUSE

The official residence of the royal family in Scotland, this palace (Holyrood Park, tel. 0131/556 5100, www.royal.gov.uk, 9:30 A.M.–6:30 P.M. daily Apr.–Oct., 9:30 A.M.–4:30 P.M. daily Nov.–Mar., £13 adults, £7.50 children) has enjoyed a colorful history. By the 13th century there was already a royal residence nearby Holyrood Abbey. The oldest still-standing part of the palace, to the left of the main entrance, was built between 1528 and 1532 but suffered extensive damage at the hands of Oliver Cromwell's troops. It needed substantial repair work under Charles II, including the addition of the Royal Apartments. The king was forced to flee again before he could make use of the palace. Between 1561 and 1567, Mary, Queen of Scots spent a tumultuous time here but after the 1707 Union, Royals favored other castles; the Palace was often used instead to house poor or distressed noblemen. Bonnie Prince Charlie briefly had his headquarters here during the 1745 Jacobite Rebellion, but it was not until the 19th century that royalty next returned, when Queen Victoria took to staying, furnishing the palace with much of the finery now in place.

In the lavish **Royal Apartments** is an unsurpassed collection of tapestries, many brought by Queen Victoria. The rooms are famed for their ornate plasterwork ceilings and hung with portraits of the real and legendary kings of Scotland by Jacob de Wet. However the palace is more famous for its associations with one Mary, Queen of Scots, and the dramatic episodes that unfolded here during her brief reign. Twice married in the now-ruined abbey nearby, Mary had heated debates with reformer John Knox in her private apartments, approached up a narrow winding staircase in the west tower and including **Queen Mary's Bedchamber,** where Mary witnessed the murder of her secretary David Rizzio by her second husband Lord Darnley. Rizzio made it to the next room, where he bled to death, now marked with a plaque. Among the Stuart relics on display are Mary's needlework and perfume pomander and the **Darnley Jewel**. There's also a café.

Included in the palace admission charge is the impressive ruin of **Holyrood Abbey.** King David I, so the story goes, was out hunting

ILL-FATED MARRIAGES

There are few people in history to whom the phrase "ill-fated" is automatically added whenever their name is mentioned. Mary, Queen of Scots was one of those few. From an early age her life was at the epicenter of the welfare of Scotland. The "rough wooing" by Henry VIII of his son Edward with the infant Mary (an attempt by Henry to securely unite the thrones of Scotland and England), culminating in Scottish defeat by the English at the Battle of Pinkie (1547) led Scotland to seek French assistance. France agreed to help, on the proviso that for safekeeping and education Mary be sent to France.

She returned to Scotland at age 19 already widowed, her husband King Francois II of France having tragically died. She couldn't have picked a worse time to return: Unabashedly practicing her Catholic faith in staunchly protestant Scotland did not win her many favors. She won still fewer by deciding to marry the ambitious but profoundly stupid protestant Lord Darnley. Darnley was always a dislikable character. He had a hankering for the throne of Scotland and England and switched loyalties repeatedly to further his aims, as well as drinking and cavorting with the prostitutes of Edinburgh – male and female alike. He also had a passion for the Queen's much-favored servant David Rizzio, whom he murdered before the Queen's eyes.

The lords whom Darnley had persuaded to play a part in Rizzio's murder were not happy with his behavior during the episode; along with Mary's advisor Lord Bothwell, they planned and executed Darnley's murder. Mary was undoubtedly glad to be rid of her repugnant husband but made the mistake of showing no public grief. Posters began to appear around Edinburgh depicting Bothwell as a murderer and Mary as a mermaid, synonymous with harlotry. Indeed her trusted advisor Bothwell captured Mary as soon as the obligatory 40 days of mourning had elapsed. Now fancying himself as the most suitable candidate for Mary's next husband, he furthered his cause by holding the Queen captive in Dunbar Castle and raping her. Mary consented to marrying the suspected murderer of her former husband, thereby sealing her fate. Within a month Mary was forced to abdicate and her infant son James was declared king. Bothwell fled abroad where he was arrested for piracy, Mary to the only place she could feasibly go – to England and the protection of her cousin, Queen Elizabeth. There, following 19 years of imprisonment, she was executed for her part in a plot to assassinate the Queen. Ever a victim of circumstance, Mary could never have guessed that even the plot she put her name to was a fake, devised by Elizabeth's head of Secret Services to trap her into an act of treason. Treason was punishable by death, and so ended the problems caused by the woman that had been a troublesome thorn in the side of the English from the moment she was born.

when his horse was startled by a stag. Knocked to the ground, the King saw between the very antlers that looked certain to gore him the image of an illuminated crucifix, which he took as a signal to build an abbey. The abbey, named after that Holy Rood, or Holy Cross, was first built in 1128, its design based on Merton Church near London. A grander building replaced it in 1190, and with the exception of a doorway in the southeastern corner from the original church, this is the ruin that remains today. Accessed via a walkway from the Palace, the well-preserved Abbey is the burial place of several Scottish kings. The last major event within its walls was the Scottish coronation of Charles I in 1633. An area extending around the abbey and taking in most of Holyrood Park was also a sanctuary, handy for criminals facing death for offenses as minor as petty theft. Miscreants would take refuge here and extend their period of safety indefinitely. Outside, **Queen Mary's Bathhouse** is where the monarch supposedly used to bathe in sweet white wine. No wonder John Knox thought Catholicism was too decadent. . . .

SCOTTISH PARLIAMENT BUILDING

The design for the new Scottish parliament building (Horse Wynd, tel. 0131/348 5200, www.scottish.parliament.uk, 9 A.M.–7 P.M. daily on business days, 10 A.M.–6 P.M. daily nonbusiness weekdays, 10 A.M.–4 P.M. Sat.–Sun. and bank holidays Apr.–Oct., 10 A.M.–4 P.M. daily Nov.–Mar., free) is based on flower paintings by Charles Rennie Mackintosh and, more obviously if you look at the roof, upturned boats on the seashore. According to architect Enric Miralles, this was a design that would "grow out of the land." It took a while longer to grow than planned, eventually opened by the Queen in 2004, and for the first time since 1707 the Scottish Parliament had an official building to meet in. You can have a look in and see the parliament in action on business days (normally Tues.–Thurs.), but if politics isn't your thing parliament may be best admired from afar.

OUR DYNAMIC EARTH

At Our Dynamic Earth (112–116 Holyrood Rd., tel. 0131/550 7800, www.dynamicearth. co.uk, 10 A.M.–6 P.M. daily July–Aug., 10 A.M.–5 P.M. daily Apr.–June and Sept.–Oct., 10 A.M.–5 P.M. Wed.–Sun. Nov.–Mar., £9.50 adults, £5.95 children) you can somewhat bizarrely experience a real iceberg and a simulated rainforest along with other insights into the earth's history and geology. It's a flashy building with no expense spared on the interactive displays—all good fun, especially if the weather doesn't hold. There is the usual chance to part with substantial amounts of cash in the gift shop. Bear in mind last entry is an hour and 10 minutes before closing time.

HOLYROOD PARK

A far better experience of geology soars right above the palace and surrounding buildings. Holyrood Park lends a taste of wilderness to the city, erupting in the basalt bulk of Salisbury Crags. The crags were carved by the last Ice Age and more recently by quarrying to pave the streets of London. Covering some 650 acres, the park is a mix of marsh, loch, moor, and rocky outcrops.

The high point is **Arthur's Seat,** a dormant volcano and former military lookout. Two key walks take in the premium park attractions and guarantee great views of the city and the Firth of Forth. One cuts from the ruins of **St. Anthony's chapel** to Arthur's Seat and **Dunsapie Loch,** while one runs from the gothic **St. Margaret's Well** to the southern point of the crags. **Duddingston Loch** in the south is a bird sanctuary overlooked by **Duddingston Kirk,** an interesting 17th-century church built on an older Norman site. The Norman door has extraordinary carvings around it. One reclusive reverend named the building "Edinburgh" meaning that persistent visitors could quite honestly be turned away as the owner really was "in Edinburgh." It's a beautiful place to walk, cycle, or picnic.

South of the Royal Mile
GRASSMARKET AREA

Connected to the Royal Mile via the steep Castle Wynd steps, cobbled Grassmarket was for over 500 years a timber and later a cattle market but gained notoriety as a place of execution. A cross at the eastern end marks the site of the old gallows which dispatched among many others the Covenanters that revolted against Charles I. Grisliest of all, it was here that the murderous duo Burke and Hare carried out their morbid trade in a now-vanished close (see *Body Snatchers* sidebar). The area is now home to some of Edinburgh's most tradition-steeped pubs, bars and cafés.

In front of the pulpit of **Greyfriars Kirk** (Candlemaker Row, www.greyfriarskirk.com, 10:30 A.M.–4:30 P.M. Mon.–Fri., 10:30 A.M.–2:30 P.M. Sat. Apr.–Oct., 1:30–3:30 P.M. Thurs. Nov.–Mar.) was where the National Covenant was signed in 1638. A reaction against the religious policies of Charles I, which included turning St. Giles into a cathedral, the Covenant predictably resulted in much bloodshed. In 1679, 1,200 Covenanters were imprisoned in the Kirk yard, awaiting a Grassmarket execution or, for the more fortunate, deportation. The leafy **Kirk yard** still has the Covenanters prison as well as an old section of the Flodden wall. There's a fair share of notable graves, including

BODY SNATCHERS

When William Burke and William Hare arrived in Edinburgh from Ulster in Northern Ireland to work on the Union Canal, no one could have anticipated the gruesome events that would unfold. To get a bit of extra money they indulged in the lucrative trade of grave-robbing: then selling the bodies to Edinburgh medical schools, at the time paving the way in world medicine, for students' dissection lessons. When watchtowers were erected in the recently disturbed graveyards, Burke and Hare decided it would be easier just to murder their victims, luring them back to Hare's lodging house in a now-disappeared close off the Grassmarket. Ensuring the morbid business boomed was one Dr. Robert Knox, who paid good money for the cadavers and asked no questions. Burke and Hare would seize on any chance of a quick kill: Once Burke saved a woman from arrest, claiming he knew her, only for her corpse to turn up on the operating table mere hours afterward.

Suspicions were aroused when one victim, who put up a struggle, was recognized by students in a lecture as Dr. Knox got ready to dissect. Knox is said to have calmed the outcry but then quickly started dissecting – head first. After some 16 murders, the pair of body snatchers was arrested but there was insufficient evidence; Hare, promised immunity from prosecution, was encouraged to testify against Burke, who was subsequently executed. Just like his victims, Burke's body was then passed to the Edinburgh medical schools for dissection. Hare and Knox both escaped, the former to die in poverty in London, the latter to lose popularity and leave his post at Edinburgh University.

New Town architect James Craig, world's worst poet William McGonnegal, and Sir Walter Scott's father. The man who persecuted many of the Covenanters, George "Bluidy" Mackenzie, is also buried here and said to haunt the Kirk yard. A frequent visitor for over 14 years was **Greyfriars Bobby**, a Skye Terrier who came to stand daily guard over his former master's grave until his own death in 1872. Visitors from across the country would come from across the country to await the firing of the One O'Clock Gun, which Bobby took as a signal to break from his vigil to be fed by them.

Just up Candlemaker Row stands the much-photographed **Greyfriars Bobby Statue.** The dog's exploits have recently been made into a film by John Henderson (2005), although this doesn't have a patch on the original made by Walt Disney (1961).

◖ MUSEUM OF SCOTLAND

Directly across from the Greyfriars Bobby statue is Chambers Street, home of Scotland's most important museum (tel. 0131/247 4422, 10 A.M.–5 P.M. daily, free). Purporting to cover "life, the universe and everything in it" the museum brings Scotland's land and culture vividly to life with a world-class lineup of exhibits including Bonnie Prince Charlie's silver set of traveling cutlery and wine beakers and the exquisitely carved Lewis Chessmen, Viking chess pieces with incredibly expressive faces. From the Tower Restaurant upstairs there are great views across the city. A lofty glass-roofed entrance hall leads to the connected **Royal Museum** (same hours, free admission), covering natural history, science, technology, and archaeology exhibits. Undergoing refurbishment until 2011, it contains the remains of Dolly the Sheep, the world's first successfully cloned mammal.

SURGEON'S HALL MUSEUM

Turning right at the end of Chambers Street past the old Edinburgh University brings you to surely the capital's most bizarre museum (Nicholson St., tel. 0131/527 1679, 10 A.M.–4 P.M. Mon–Fri., noon–4 P.M. Sat.–Sun. July–Aug., noon–4 P.M. Mon.–Fri. Sept.–June, £5). The Surgeon's Halls present a fascinatingly morbid display of surgical practices throughout the ages, including gory human remains, exhibits on grave-robbers, and an intriguing

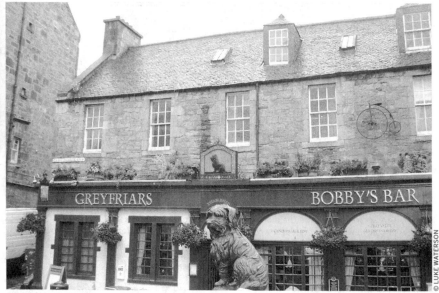

Greyfriars Bobby Statue

display on Sir Arthur Conan Doyle and his relationship to professor Joseph Bell.

NEW TOWN

There were a lot of schemes and proposals in the 18th century to do something about the cramped Old Town, which was rapidly descending into a state of squalor and disrepair. A new town, for the rich to move into with better living standards, was the obvious solution; young architect James Craig won the Town Council's competition to design the New Town layout. Craig's grand plan was based around two large squares (Charlotte Square and St. Andrew's Square) with principal thoroughfares running in between and side streets for shopkeepers and tradespeople. Craig had the foresight to realize the Old Town was not all bad, and his design restricted building to one side only of Princes Street and Queen Street to maximize the aesthetics of the view. Today the New Town, which took 50 years and a series of architects to complete, is Unesco World Heritage–listed, one of the most striking examples of Georgian architecture still surviving.

Princes Street Gardens

One of Europe's most elegant city gardens, Princes Street Gardens (open year-round, free) lies along the valley separating the Old Town from the New Town and its main thoroughfare, Princes Street. This was largely a putrid marsh until the mid-18th century when architect William Playfair, who had overseen the landscaping of Calton Hill, initiated the necessary improvements. East and West Princes Street Gardens are divided by the Mound, a causeway originally made with Old Town rubble in the 18th century.

Below the Balmoral Hotel's distinctive **clock tower,** traditionally three minutes fast so you won't miss your train, the eastern end of the gardens runs by **Register House,** built in 1788 by Robert Adam to house the National Archives. The enormous traffic-blackened gothic tower looming over the eastern side of the gardens is the **Scott Monument** (tel. 0131/529 4068, 9 A.M.–6 P.M. Mon.–Sat., 10 A.M.–6 P.M. Sun. Apr.–Oct., 9 A.M.–3 P.M. Mon.–Sat., 10 A.M.–3 P.M. Sun. Nov.–Mar., £3), housing a statue of Walter Scott and his faithful hound

© LUKE WATERSON

SIR ARTHUR CONAN DOYLE AND THE DEVELOPMENT OF DETECTIVE FICTION

The father of detective fiction may be recognized as Edgar Allan Poe, with his character, the amateur sleuth C. Auguste Dupin, but it was Arthur Conan Doyle who brought this popular genre to the masses some 40 years later. With the publication of *A Study in Scarlet* (1887), Conan Doyle introduced the most famous of fictional private investigators, Sherlock Holmes. The author's brilliant mind invented countless plots involving Holmes and his sidekick, the affable Doctor Watson, yet many of the mysteries solved only by the genius of Holmes' deductions are based on Conan Doyle's experiences in Edinburgh. Between 1876 and 1881, Holmes studied medicine at the University of Edinburgh where, in 1877, he came into contact with the renowned professor Joseph Bell. Bell chose Conan Doyle to become his assistant; he was hired to make patient notes prior to Bell seeing a patient. Bell would then shock both Doyle and the patient by correctly guessing details from the patients' lives he could not possibly have previously known. Bell's seemingly amazing gift was, as with Holmes, based solely on the powers of deduction: He could tell a person's occupation from their hands and the countries they had visited from their tattoos. Bell was also known to wear a deerstalker hat when out walking and had a friend by the name of Dr. Patrick Heron Watson. It is no surprise that Conan Doyle once wrote in a letter to Bell, "It is most certainly to you that I owe Sherlock Holmes."

Maida. A spiral staircase leads steeply up to the spire at the top for good views over the city. Just past the Mound is the **Floral Clock,** the oldest working clock in the world. At the far end of the gardens, **St. Cuthbert's Church** has a watchtower in the churchyard, one of many erected in the days of Burke and Hare to deter grave-robbers.

National Gallery of Scotland

For a relatively small country, Scotland's national collection (The Mound, tel. 0131/624 6200, www.nationalgalleries.org, 10 A.M.–5 P.M. Fri.–Wed., 10 A.M.–7 P.M. Thurs.) is one of the very best in the world, with a superb setting looking out over Princes Street Gardens and Edinburgh Castle. It contains masterpieces by Raphael, Velázquez, Van Gogh, and Cézanne. The main level focuses on the 16th to 19th centuries and includes Titian's *Three Ages of Man* and Rembrandt's *Self-Portrait Aged 51.* An upper level features early Italian paintings such as Botticelli's *The Virgin Adoring the Sleeping Christ Child* (1490) as well as important Impressionist works. On the lower level, dedicated to primarily Scottish art, the highlight is Sir Henry Raeburn's *Reverend Robert Walker Skating on Duddingston Loch* in Room B7. There's a bright restaurant and café (get a window or outside terrace seat for excellent views) with cloakroom and shop as well as study facilities below in what is known as the Western Link.

The link connects the National Gallery with the grand building nearby, the **Royal Scottish Academy** (tel. 0131/225 6671, 10 A.M.–5 P.M. Mon.–Sat., 2–5 P.M. Sun.). Both buildings were designed by William Playfair; the Royal Scottish Academy (RSA) has mighty Doric columns, while the National Gallery is along the more delicate Ionic order. In 1831, an RSA decree stated all academic members must produce one work representative of their art in the discipline of painting, sculpture, or architecture. An interesting collection has been amassed over the years and is displayed in the galleries. The RSA combined with the National Gallery is one of Europe's largest temporary exhibition venues, twice that of Madrid's Prado.

Charlotte Square

Completed in 1820 and easily the more impressive of the New Town squares, Charlotte

EDINBURGH

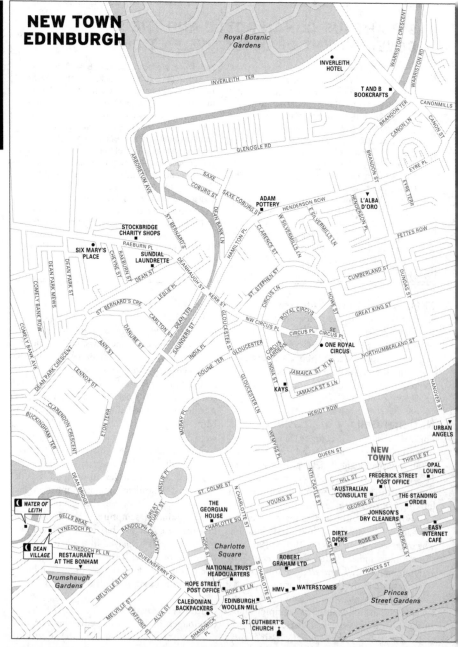

NEW TOWN EDINBURGH

Royal Botanic Gardens

INVERLEITH HOTEL

T AND B BOOKCRAFTS

INVERLEITH TER

WARRISTON CRESCENT

WARRISTON RD

CANONMILLS

BRANDON TER

CANON LN

CANON ST

GLENOGLE RD

BRANDON ST

EYRE PL

EYRE TERR

SAXE COBURG ST

SAXE COBURG ST

ADAM POTTERY

HENDERSON ROW

L'ALBA D'ORO

HENDERSON PL

FETTES ROW

STOCKBRIDGE CHARITY SHOPS

RAEBURN PL

HAMILTON PL

CLARENCE ST

W SILVERMILLS LN

E SILVERMILLS LN

SIX MARY'S PLACE

SUNDIAL LAUNDRETTE

CHEYNE ST

RAEBURN ST

ST. BERNARD'S

DEAN BANK LN

CUMBERLAND ST

DUNDAS ST

DEAN PARK MEWS

DEAN PARK ST

DEAN ST

LESLIE PL

DEANHAUGH ST

ST. STEPHEN ST

CIRCUS LN

HOME ST

GREAT KING ST

COMELY BANK ROW

ST. BERNARD'S CRE

CARLTON ST

DEAN TER

KERR ST

CIRCUS PL

ROYAL CIRCUS

NW CIRCUS PL

SE CIRCUS PL

ONE ROYAL CIRCUS

NORTHUMBERLAND ST

COMELY BANK AVE

DANUBE ST

SAUNDERS ST

INDIA PL

GLOUCESTER ST

CIRCUS GARDENS

INDIA ST

JAMAICA ST N LN

ANN'S ST

DOUNE TER

GLOUCESTER PL

KAYS

JAMAICA ST S LN

LENNOX ST

DEAN PARK CRESCENT

GLOUCESTER LN

HERIOT ROW

HANOVER ST

BUCKINGHAM TER

CLARENDON CRESCENT

ETON TERR

MORAY PL

WEMYSS PL

QUEEN ST

URBAN ANGELS

NEW TOWN

THISTLE ST

OPAL LOUNGE

DEAN BRIDGE

ST. COLME ST

AINSLIE PL

HILL ST

FREDERICK STREET POST OFFICE

GREAT STUART ST

N CHARLOTTE ST

YOUNG ST

NTH CASTLE ST

AUSTRALIAN CONSULATE

THE STANDING ORDER

WATER OF LEITH

THE GEORGIAN HOUSE

GEORGE ST

JOHNSON'S DRY CLEANERS

BELLS BRAE

LYNEDOCH PL

CHARLOTTE SQ

HOPE ST

EASY INTERNET CAFE

DEAN VILLAGE

LYNEDOCH PL LN

RANDOLPH CRESCENT

Charlotte Square

DIRTY DICKS

ROSE ST

FREDERICK ST

RESTAURANT AT THE BONHAM

QUEENSFERRY ST

S CHARLOTTE ST

CASTLE ST

ROBERT GRAHAM LTD

PRINCES ST

Drumsheugh Gardens

MELVILLE ST LN

NATIONAL TRUST HEADQUARTERS

Princes Street Gardens

MELVILLE ST

STAFFORD ST

ALVA ST

HOPE STREET POST OFFICE

HOPE ST LN

HMV

WATERSTONES

CALEDONIAN BACKPACKERS

EDINBURGH WOOLEN MILL

SHANDWICK PL

ST. CUTHBERT'S CHURCH

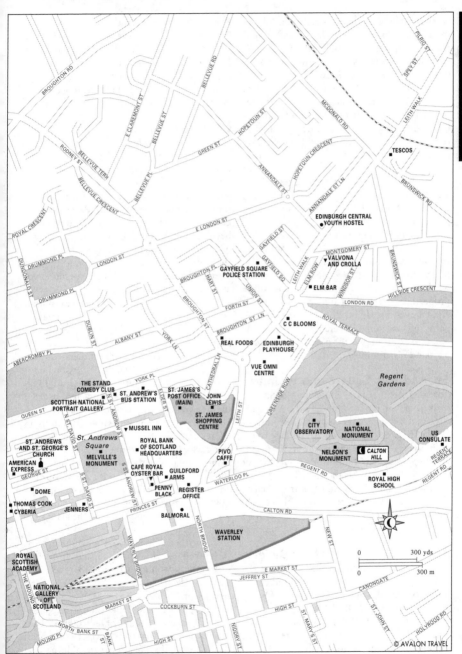

Square was designed by Robert Adam. Adam's specialty was "palace-front" design, and around the grand square are several buildings of note. The **Georgian House** (7 Charlotte Sq., tel. 0131/225 2160, 10 A.M.–7 P.M. daily July–Aug., 10 A.M.–5 P.M. daily Apr.–June and Sept.–Oct., 11 A.M.–3 P.M. daily Mar. and Nov., £5) does for the New Town what Gladstone's Land does for the Old: capturing life as it was for a typical resident in the 18th century with a collection of period furniture, porcelain, and pictures. The rooms are beautifully set out over two floors, the furniture around the edges to leave space in the middle for dancing. The Georgian House is a National Trust for Scotland (NTS) property: if you envisage seeing a lot of NTS-owned sights during your time in Scotland, it may be worth enquiring at the **National Trust for Scotland Headquarters** (28 Charlotte Sq., 9:30 A.M.–5 P.M. Mon.–Sat.) about membership, which gives you free entry to all its properties. You can get into No. 28 for free and enjoy a display of 20th-century Scottish paintings and some Regency furnishings. At No. 6, **Bute House** is the official residence of Scotland's first minister.

St. Andrews Square and Vicinity

Towering over the square is **Melville Monument,** in memory of Henry Dundas, the Viscount Melville, known as the "uncrowned king of Scotland" or just Henry the 9th because of his political power. Just along George Street, the innovatively designed **St. Andrew's Church** (built in an ellipse shape) was the scene in 1843 of a mass walk-out of church ministers, frustrated by the infringements being placed upon the church, from the annual General Assembly. They then formed the Free Church of Scotland.

Scottish National Portrait Gallery

Statues of William Wallace and Robert the Bruce guard the entrance to the red sandstone National Portrait Gallery (1 Queen St., tel. 0131/624 6200, 10 A.M.–5 P.M. Fri.–Wed., extended festival hours 10 A.M.–6 P.M. Fri.–Wed., 10 A.M.–7 P.M. Thurs., free), home to some impressive works such as Sir Henry Raeburn's *Walter Scott,* the portrait of Mary, Queen of Scots, and the striking portrait of Robert Louis Stevenson by Count Girolamo Nerli. From the main hall runs a frieze depicting famous Scots from Thomas Carlyle, who championed the cause of a portrait gallery in Scotland, to St. Ninian.

【 Calton Hill

Calton Hill was Robert Louis Stevenson's favorite viewpoint in the city; from the summit you could see both Edinburgh Castle and Arthur's Seat. Because it rises out of the middle of the New Town east of Princes Street, it offers some of the best views not only over the Old and New Towns but over the Firth of Forth beyond. The Beltane fire festival takes place here each April. As fascinating as the view are the scattering of monuments around the hill, a series of ambitious and not always successful 19th century construction projects.

The **National Monument** (open year-round) is understandably known as the Acropolis, a unique feature of the Edinburgh skyline originally intended to look like a replica of the Athenian Parthenon as a monument to those who had died in the Napoleonic War. Funds dried up soon after building began in 1822, and only one side was ever completed. In a city used to seeing building projects succeed, the construction became known as "Edinburgh's great shame," a bit of a slap in the face for those who had wanted to take away the irony from Edinburgh's then nickname "Athens of the North." However it lends a certain bizarre charm to the hillside, and plans to knock it down or complete it have always been brushed aside—maybe because climbing the giant steps is such fun.

To further enhance your view of the city, for £3 you can climb the 143 steps to the top of **Nelson's Monument** (tel. 0131/556 2716, 1–6 P.M. Mon., 10 A.M.–6 P.M. Tues.–Sat. Apr.–Sept., 10 A.M.–3 P.M. Mon.–Sat. Oct.–Mar.), designed to look like an upturned telescope. The tower has one of only 60 time balls (visual aids for mariners to check the time) left in the world. If sailors in the firth didn't hear

© LUKE WATERSON

Calton Hill viewed from the Old Town

the bang of the One O'Clock gun, they could look up at one and see the ball being lowered. You can still see the ball drop today: look out at noon Greenwich Mean Time, which equates during the summer to 1 P.M.

Timekeeping seemed a principal obsession with the 19th-century Calton Hill developers, and this was the reason the **City Observatory** (tel. 0131/556 4365, call during reasonable hours to arrange a tour) was built in 1818. To the relief of chronologists everywhere, the Observatory was later connected to the time ball on Nelson's monument.

On the south side of Calton Hill, the **Royal High School,** built in 1829, was considered as a venue for the new Scottish Parliament. In the end, 21st-century design won out over the high school's classical Greek style.

◖ Dean Village and the Water of Leith

A haven below the roar of New Town traffic and the imposing bridge built by Thomas Telford, this sedate, gaudily colored village is perfect for a quiet stroll to take in some of the trendy architecture in verdant riverside surroundings. There are no shops (half its appeal), so bring a picnic to eat by the river or try the good but busy café in the Gallery of Modern Art, a short stroll along the Water of Leith walkway. You can follow the path, which runs for 12 miles from Leith to Balerno, in the Pentland Hills, by foot or bike.

Set in parklands to either side of Belford Road are Edinburgh's two galleries dedicated to modern art. The **Gallery of Modern Art** (Belford Rd., tel. 0131/624 6200, 10 A.M.–5 P.M. daily) is housed in a neoclassical former school. Landscaped gardens slope up to its imposing walls, which now contain a variety of important art including early 20th-century French, Russian, Cubist, and post-war art. There are works by Picasso and sculptures by Barbara Hepworth and Henry Moore. Post-war offerings include works by David Hockney, Lucien Freud, Anthony Gormley, Damien Hirst, and Tracy Emin. Scottish art of the 20th century is also well represented. The downstairs space is reserved for exhibitions. The café downstairs is great—pricey and busy—and the garden,

Water of Leith

including an award-winning section based on the chaos theory, is worth checking out.

The second installment of Dean Village's modern art offering, **Dean Gallery** (Belford Rd., tel. 0131/624 6200, 10 A.M.–5 P.M. daily) displays a world-class collection from Dada and the surrealists. There are also important works by Dali and Picasso as well as works by Edinburgh-born sculptor Eduardo Paolozzi. Extensive archives here cover 20th- and 21st-century art, accessible by prior appointment only. A free Gallery Bus runs from the National Gallery on the Mound to both modern art galleries every 45 minutes. Occasionally, both galleries have openings on Thursday evenings.

Stockbridge

Laid-back Stockbridge manages to combine sophisticated restaurants with a wealth of great secondhand shops and cafés and is the perfect antidote to rushing between those Royal Mile sights.

Royal Botanic Gardens

Established in 1670 and moved from its original site in Holyrood due to traffic pollution, the "Botanics" (Inverleith Row, north of city center, tel. 0131/552 7171, info@ rbge.org.uk, 10 A.M.–6 P.M. daily Mar. and Oct., 10 A.M.–7 P.M. daily Apr.–Sept., 10 A.M.–4 P.M. daily Nov.–Feb., free), as it is called locally, has been at its current site in Inverleith, just north of Stockbridge, since 1820 and contain 6 percent of all known plants. The incredibly diverse gardens are an oasis of calm in the city. You can spend hours wandering between the many different sections; be sure to have a look at the Rock Garden and the Chinese Hillside. The **Glasshouses** (£3.50 adults, £3 seniors) contain some wonderful discoveries, best of these are Britain's tallest palm-house; the world's largest collection of rhododendrons, originating from Guinea and Borneo; and a clutch of cycads, plants that were around when dinosaurs roamed the planet.

Edinburgh Zoo

Edinburgh Zoo (134 Corstorphine Rd., 3 miles west of Edinburgh, tel. 0131/334 9171, 9 A.M.–5 P.M. daily Mar. and Oct., 9 A.M.–6 P.M. daily Apr.–Sept., 9 A.M.–4:30 P.M. daily

SCOTTISH PARLIAMENT: A SEAT ON THE MOVE

The Scottish Parliament has never sat anywhere too long. Following its formation in the 14th century, the king and his court traveled around Scotland, meeting in various places including Scone, Stirling Cambuskenneth, and Haddington as well as Edinburgh. Sittings were notoriously jittery affairs, particularly when the infant James VI ascended the throne. In the absence of a king, anyone titled Regent could control parliament. Unsurprisingly, no one regent ever lasted long and, for fear of disturbance, parliament sittings took place tensely behind locked doors. It was Charles I who decided that there should be one meeting place for parliament, and he ordered the Edinburgh authorities to build a suitable building for the purpose beside St. Giles Cathedral. This was first used for a meeting in 1639; however, the rise of the Covenanters and the armed rebellion against the king led to Charles I's execution in 1649.

Scotland recognized Charles II as king, as opposed to the Lord Protector Oliver Cromwell, who then carried out a decisive military campaign against the Scots, making the meeting of any parliament other than that of England illegal. The Scottish Parliament did not meet again in Edinburgh until 1661, following the return to the throne of Charles II. Again, its period of use was short-lived. In 1707 the Treaty of the Union decreed that the English and Scottish parliaments hitherto separate should merge, with Scotland given 45 seats in the 558-seat House of Commons. Devolution during the 1990s ended with the Scottish parliament meeting once more, following elections, in 1999, for the first time in nearly 300 years. Even then, parliament had no settled meeting place. For the first four years of its new life, it would generally meet in the Assembly Halls of the Church of Scotland, although MPs had to use offices rented from Edinburgh Council nearby. Finally the Queen opened the official building at the foot of Holyrood Park, designed by Enric Miralles, in 2004. Following a turbulent 700-year history, finally the Scottish parliament had a place to call home.

Nov.–Feb., £11.50 adults, £10 seniors, £8 children) is one of the leading zoos in the world in protection of endangered species and animal conservation. It's also a fun, fascinating experience with a year-round program designed to educate visitors on zoo species, from keeper talks to the penguin field station. The Indian rhinos, Asiatic lions, and the hilltop safari are some of the highlights.

Craigmillar Castle

In midsummer the crowds at Edinburgh Castle may put you off, but at this fortress (near Royal Infirmary, tel. 0131/661 4445, 9:30 A.M.–5:30 P.M. daily Apr.–Sept., 9:30 A.M.–4:30 P.M. Sat.–Wed. Oct.–Mar., £4.20 adults, £3.20 seniors), southeast of Edinburgh on the road out to Dalkeith, you'll find a formidable ruin remarkably intact without anywhere near so many tourists. The castle, one of the most completely preserved medieval strongholds in Scotland, dates from around 1400. You get great views of Edinburgh and the surrounding countryside from the tower house roof. A 24 or 49 bus from the city center will take you to the Royal Infirmary, from where it's a short walk.

LEITH

A run-down dockland 20 years ago, Leith has experienced a new lease on life with a smattering of top-notch restaurants and bars along the rejuvenated waterfront. Leith is two miles northeast of the city center. Bus 11 goes from the city center (Princes Street) to the Ocean Terminal, from where it's a few minutes' walk to get to the Leith restaurants. Several services including bus 12 run up Leith Walk stopping at Bernard Street, right in the heart of the Leith waterfront area.

Royal Yacht *Britannia*

The rejuvenation of Leith began when the Queen's former yacht (Ocean Terminal Leith,

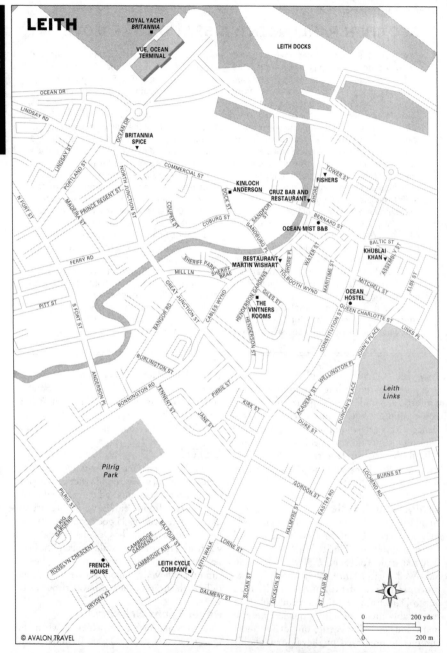

LEITH

ROYAL YACHT
BRITANNIA

VUE, OCEAN
TERMINAL

LEITH DOCKS

OCEAN DR

LINDSAY RD

OCEAN DR

BRITANNIA
SPICE

LINDSAY ST

PORTLAND ST

MADEIRA ST

PRINCE REGENT ST

NORTH JUNCTION ST

COMMERCIAL ST

COUPER ST

N FORT ST

FERRY RD

PITT ST

S FORT ST

COBURG ST

DOCK ST

SANDPORT

SANDBURG PL

SHORE

TOWER ST

FISHERS

KINLOCH
ANDERSON

CRUZ BAR AND
RESTAURANT

BERNARD ST

OCEAN MIST B&B

BALTIC ST

KHUBLAI
KHAN

WATER ST

MARITIME ST

ASSEMBLY

ELBE ST

MITCHELL ST

OCEAN
HOSTEL

QUEEN CHARLOTTE ST

LINKS PL

SHERIFF PARK

SHERIFF
BRAE

MILL LN

GREAT JUNCTION ST

BANGOR RD

CABLES WYND

RESTAURANT
MARTIN WISHART

HENDERSON GARDENS

GILES ST

TOLBOOTH WYND

SHORE PL

THE
VINTNERS
ROOMS

HENDERSON ST

CONSTITUTION ST

JOHN'S PLACE

BURLINGTON ST

ANDERSON PL

BONNINGTON RD

TENNENT ST

PIRRIE ST

JANE ST

KIRK ST

DUKE ST

ACADEMY ST

WELLINGTON PL

DUNCAN'S PLACE

Leith
Links

Pilrig
Park

PILRIG ST

PILRIG
GARDENS

ROSSLYN CRESCENT

FRENCH
HOUSE

CAMBRIDGE
GARDENS

BALFOUR ST

CAMBRIDGE AVE

LEITH CYCLE
COMPANY

LEITH WALK

LORNE ST

SLOAN ST

DICKSON ST

DRYDEN ST

DALMENY ST

GORDON ST

EASTER RD

HALMYRE ST

BURNS ST

LOCHEND RD

ST. CLAIR RD

0   200 yds

0   200 m

tel. 0131/555 5566, www.royalyachtbritannia.co.uk, 9:30 A.M.–4:30 P.M. daily Apr.–Oct., 10 A.M.–3:30 P.M. daily Nov.–Mar., £9.75 adults, £7.75 seniors, £5.75 children) was taken out of service in 1997 after 44 years and finally came to rest in its port. The 125-meter, 5,862-ton vessel had a crew of 220 yachtsmen and 20 officers when at sea, including a 26-man Royal Band. Having traveled the length and breadth of the world and hosted some of the world's most famous people, including Winston Churchill and Nelson Mandela, *Britannia* has some colorful stories attached to it but primarily was where the Royal Family came to escape. The Queen's bedroom has the unique claim of being the only living monarch's bedroom on view to the public, just as it was in 1953 when *Britannia* was launched. The State Dining Room, where the Queen entertained guests, and the sparkling Engine Room with its huge 1950s dials and levers are among the tour highlights. Royal Yacht *Britannia* is moored alongside the Ocean Terminal complex (which obscures most of the yacht for those wanting to sneak a picture without parting with cash) where you can be sure of a shop amply stocked with regal souvenirs. An audio handset available in a range of languages guides you around.

PORTOBELLO

For some faded seaside charm and accompanying kitsch, nowhere beats Portobello, three miles east of the city center. It's easy to see why the miles of golden sands attracted so many Edinburgh holiday-makers here in the 19th and early 20th centuries; it's less easy to understand why Portobello today feels a bit like a ghost town. Expect the locals to be out in force on hot days, mercifully few and far between. The rest of the time, this is a peaceful spot. There are several good places to eat and stay on and around the high street (where it turns into Abercorn Terrace is where the bed-and-breakfasts start). To get to Portobello, take bus 26, 15 or 15A from the city center.

◖ CRAMOND

Two miles northwest of the city center, you would think you are in a different country,

where gorse-dotted fields slope down to the Firth of Forth shoreline, with a series of wood-fringed paths leading along it. Poking out of the trees around a small harbor is the whitewashed village of Cramond. It's home to lots of walks and seabirds, a café, and one of the Lothians best old pubs, the Cramond Inn. Cramond has a detailed history you wouldn't guess from the placid seafront cottages; major archaeological finds in the area such as the Sandstone Lioness (one of Scotland's most noteworthy Roman artifacts) confirm not only that Cramond was an important Roman site but that it was in fact the earliest human site in Scotland, with signs of habitation from 8500 B.C. Much of what was excavated is displayed in the Museum of Scotland or the Museum of Edinburgh.

Cramond Island, linked by a causeway to the mainland, has substantial World War II fortifications. It's worth noting if you come for the peace and quiet that the island is also something of an unofficial venue for punk rock festivals. Check the tide times before crossing or you'll get wet feet. The **River Almond** that empties at Cramond has some of the best fishing in the Lothians. If you're after a stroll in sedate castle grounds, then **Lauriston Castle** (Cramond Road South, near Davidsons Mains, tel. 0131/336 2660, grounds 9 A.M.–dusk daily, castle tours at 11 A.M., noon, 2 P.M., 3 P.M., and 4 P.M. Sat.–Thurs. Apr.–Oct. and noon, 2 P.M., and 3 P.M. Sat. and Sun. Nov.–Mar., £5), a 16th-century tower house, is your bet. It boasts spectacular views over the Firth of Forth and an enchanting Japanese garden. Bus 24 will get you to Cramond from the city center.

◖ ROSSLYN GLEN

Now synonymous with the film *The Da Vinci Code,* Rosslyn (sometimes called Roslin) Chapel has been attracting visitors with its gothic splendor and dramatic setting for over 200 years. Writers Sir Walter Scott and William Wordsworth and painter John Turner were among the many to glean inspiration from the fascinating chapel peeping out of the swaths of woodland tumbling down this rocky hillside. It's not the chapel alone that entices people out

© LUKE WATERSON

Rosslyn Chapel, Rosslyn Glen

here, but also the glorious scenery of the glen itself, which warrants some serious exploration. Its steeply plunging woodland is laced with a series of paths, including walks to the ruined **Rosslyn Castle** (now a private house) and to **Wallace's Cave**—look out for the bats skimming the river below at dusk.

Rosslyn is seven miles south of Edinburgh. To get to Rosslyn, catch a number 15 bus from Princes Street for the 30-minute journey. The bus drops you on Rosslyn high street, from where it's a short walk down to the chapel entrance. Rosslyn village, backed by the Pentland Hills, is a pleasant spot, and there are a couple of good hotels facing each other on the main village street where the bus stops. The lane to the chapel is signposted to the Slatebarns Caravan Site, where you can camp if you want to experience the glen after the tourists go home.

Rosslyn Chapel

The 15th-century chapel (tel. 0131/440 2159, www.rosslynchapel.com, 9:30 A.M.–6 P.M. Mon.–Sat., noon–4:45 P.M. Sun. Apr.–Sept., 9:30 A.M.–5 P.M. Mon.–Sat., noon–4:45 P.M. Sun. Oct.–Mar., £7.50) is shrouded in mystery and remains one of the greatest puzzles in architecture. Rosslyn was one of at least 37 collegiate churches built in Scotland between the reigns of James I and James IV, designed to spread intellectual and spiritual knowledge. Sir William St. Clair, third St. Clair prince of Orkney, founded the chapel in 1446. The mix of architectural styles (Egyptian, Grecian, and Gothic), with 32 different types of arches, leave many questions about the construction unanswered. The famous "Prentice Pillar," for instance, is named for the story of the master mason in charge of the cathedral's carvings. Unable to complete his work, he went to Rome to receive guidance on how to proceed and returned to find his apprentice had completed the work for him. He killed the apprentice in his rage. Work on the roof suggests masons from Strasbourg were needed to assist in the grandiose plans. The carvings on the pillars and ceilings include a multitude of references: the Far East, royalty, biblical figures (from Old Testament sacrifice to the dove associated with peace), devils, and mythical figures. There are also carvings of plants unique to the Americas significantly before 1492, which suggest pre-Columbus travel from Europe to the New World. Among the conclusions to be drawn from these are the chapel's associations with both Freemasonry and the Knights Templar. The Grand Lodge of Scotland (tel. 0131/225 5577) has some interesting materials on these associations. There's a small visitors center charging the entry fee, but you can sit in on one of Scotland's most atmospheric Sunday Services (10:30 A.M., 5 P.M.) and get a glimpse of the interior for free.

SIGHTSEEING TOURS

Edinburgh invites you to explore it yourself: That's the way you'll get your most magical Edinburgh memories. There's not an Old Town turning that won't lead to somewhere intriguing. But some tours can enhance your experience of the city. A word of advice: Don't take a tour because you're short on time and want to see the most important sights (just follow the Royal Mile downhill from the castle for that) but to get a unique and colorful insight into Edinburgh's past.

[City Ghost Tours

Auld Reekie Tours (tel. 0131/557 4700, www.auldreekietours.com, evening tours from £7, nighttime tours from £10) are walking tours focusing on witchcraft and torture, including a visit to an underground pagan temple. Another spooky series of walking tours can be experienced with **Witchery Tours** (tel. 0131/225 6745, www.witcherytours.com, £7.50), where dressed-up characters bring the darkest stories of old Edinburgh to life. There's a Ghost Tour at 7 P.M. and 7:30 P.M. April to October and a year-round Murder Tour at 9 P.M. and 9:30 P.M. The meeting point is Castlehill, outside the Witchery Restaurant.

Other Tours

Based in Rosslyn, **Celtic Trails** (tel. 0131/448 2869, www.celtictrails.co.uk) offers a refreshing alternative to the standard area tours, revealing the Celtic, Druidic, and Knights Templar connections to Edinburgh and the surrounding area. There's an imaginative mix of other tours available on request. Full-day tours of Rosslyn start from £49 per adult.

Cameron Chauffeur Drive (tel. 0131/333 3111, www.cameronchauffeurdrive.co.uk, from £200) tours are good for a spot of fun and splashing out. They offer the chance for

you to be chauffeur-driven around Edinburgh or the Lothians in a luxury E Class Mercedes or Rolls Royce Saloon all day.

Afternoon Tea Tours (tel. 0787/321 1856, info@afternoonteatours.com, £55) does tours of Edinburgh's stately surrounding countryside and historic sights, including that crucial afternoon tea and refreshments at a baronial mansion. This itinerary is geared toward older people.

Edinburgh Bus Tours (tel. 0131/220 0770, www.edinburghtour.com, £13/11 adults/seniors for a 24-hour ticket) is a hop-on/hop-off, open-top bus tour of the city with multi-language facility or live guide. You get Edinburgh's sights explained to you from a bus. However, you'll still have to get off and walk at some point and may just end up feeling pressured.

VISITOR TICKETS

If you are going to be doing substantial sightseeing, consider purchasing the **Edinburgh Pass** (www.edinburgh.org/pass), which costs £24/36/48 for one/two/three-day passes that will save you quite a lot of money. The **Royal Edinburgh Ticket** (www.royaledinburghticket.co.uk) costs £36 and gets you in to the royal attractions of the city (Castle, Holyroodhouse Palace, and the Royal Yacht *Britannia*), as well as two days' unlimited travel on Edinburgh Bus Tours. It's only really worth it if you want the bus tour. Either pass can be purchased from the Edinburgh and Scotland Information Centre.

Entertainment and Events

Scotland's capital is simply awash with great places to drink; characterful century-old buildings contain lots of traditional watering holes, as well as stylish bars and great live music venues. The best source of cultural and entertainment listings is the weekly **List magazine** (£2.20, available in newsagents), which helps you make sense of everything that's going on. If you want tickets to see a theater performance, go to the venue or phone **Ticketmaster** (tel. 0870/606 3424, www.ticketmaster.co.uk) for tickets.

PUBS AND BARS

Nowhere else in Britain has the density of wonderful, bizarre old pubs and bars that Edinburgh does.

Old Town

Five minutes up from Waverley Train Station on secluded (and steep) Fleshmarket Close is one of Edinburgh's most atmospheric pubs, the **Halfway House** (24 Fleshmarket Cl., tel. 0131/225 7101, 11 A.M.–11:30 P.M. Mon.–Thurs., 11 A.M.–1 A.M. Fri.–Sat., 12:30 P.M.–11:30 P.M. Sun.). Being the smallest bar in the city, it can get very crowded but it's a cozy place with plenty of alcoves in which to sit sampling the range of specialty ales. A CAMRA award-winner on several occasions, it also has tasty, cheap food. You won't find haggis, Cullen Skink (haddock and potato soup), or neeps and tatties (turnips and mashed potatoes) at such reasonable prices anywhere else in the Old Town. There have been complaints about the service but there's usually a wild-haired local to keep you entertained, plus lots of railway paraphernalia.

Three floors of Gothic excess, **Frankenstein's Pub** (tel. 0131/622 1818, www.frankenstein-pub.co.uk, 26 George IV Bridge, 10 A.M.–3 A.M. daily) is an ever-popular destination for students and backpackers alike. It's good for big-screen sports but it is the theme nights, including the Full Moon Show and Rocky Horror night, that pull in the liveliest crowds. There is cheap beer

and good cocktails—try the house favorite, the Bride of Frankenstein. Don't be surprised to see someone in fishnet dancing on the table or a Boris Karloff look-alike at the bar.

Taking its name from the fact that, until the 1800s, the Grassmarket was Edinburgh's favored execution spot, with the gallows situated opposite, **The Last Drop** (Grassmarket, tel. 0131/225 4851, 11 A.M.–1 A.M. Mon.–Sat., 12:30 P.M.–1 A.M. Sun.) pulls in just about everyone from 18 to 80. The food is a favorite with backpackers, who get a discount if they are staying at a hostel in the city. Staff can be unfriendly at times but this is a classic watering hole with an elaborate collection of banknotes above the bar and haunted by at least one ghost. Just up from the Grassmarket, funkily decorated **Dragonfly** (52 West Port, tel. 0131/228 4543, noon–1 A.M. daily) is a good place for wondrous cocktails at prices steeper than the steps to the castle.

There are three themed bars in the popular **Three Sisters Pub** (139 Cowgate, tel. 0131/622 6801, 9 A.M.–1 A.M. Mon.–Sat., 12:30 P.M.–1 A.M. Sun.)—Irish, American, and Gothic. The Irish is where most of the serious drinking happens, the American shows big screen sports, and the Gothic, well . . . it's a good place to nurse a hangover, with free Bloody Marys before 11 A.M. The outside courtyard bar is a great size, too, for somewhere so central, but it's best avoided on weekends if large stag and hen parties aren't your thing.

The **World's End** (4 High St., tel. 0131/556 3628, 11 A.M.–1 A.M. Mon.–Fri., 10 A.M.–1 A.M. Sat.–Sun.) lies on an important historical site. When news reached Edinburgh of King James VI's defeat at the battle of Flodden, Edinburgh residents feared the worst and built a wall around the limits of the old city to defend themselves—where the world ended and Edinburgh began. Part of the old wall can still be seen in the basement of this traditional pub, attracting a mix of tourists and locals. Being small, it gets cramped at evenings and weekends. The bar food is good—try the haggis and goat cheese melt.

The **Tolbooth Tavern** (167 Canongate, tel. 0131/556 5348, 11 A.M.–11 P.M. Mon.–Thurs., 11 A.M.–midnight Fri., 11 A.M.–11:45 P.M. Sat., 12:30 P.M.–11 P.M. Sun.) was the location of the former court, jailhouse, and Council Chambers for the borough of Canongate, once outside the city limits. Even in the height of festival season, its location means you are likely to get a table and it's a good place for a quiet drink. The bar is bigger than you'd expect and stocks a good range of ales. Listen for the resident ghost, adept at knocking things over.

Once the novelty of approaching the 17th-century **Jolly Judge** (7 James Ct., tel. 0131/225 2669, www.jollyjudge.co.uk, noon– 11 P.M. Mon.–Thurs., noon–midnight Fri.– Sat., 12:30 P.M.–11 P.M. Sun.) down a narrow passageway and through a pretty courtyard has worn off, the place isn't what it could be. Popular with older tourists and music-free, it's a refreshingly quiet place so close to the Royal Mile but somewhat stuffy inside. Low-beamed ceilings, a good selection of single malt whiskies, and, bizarrely for such a traditional place, free Wi-Fi access are the redeeming features.

Edinburgh's oldest inn, the **Sheep Heid Inn** (43–45 The Causeway, Duddingston, tel. 0131/676 6951, www.sheepheid.co.uk, 11 A.M.– 11 P.M. Mon.–Thurs. and Sun., 11 A.M.– 11:30 P.M. Fri.–Sat.) was known to Mary, Queen of Scots, who would stop off here on her travels between Holyrood and Craigmillar Castle. Incredibly, it traces its history back to the 1360s. On the eastern extreme of Holyrood Park in Duddingston, it's a 20-minute walk around the base of Holyrood Park from the Scottish Parliament Building, ideal for recuperating after those Arthur's Seat excursions. Everything you could expect in a traditional inn is at the Sheep Heid: great ale, great food served every day (noon–8 P.M.—you'd have to be strong-willed not to partake) and the oldest working skittles alley in the world. There's a beer garden with barbecues every weekend from May to September. The list of reasons to come here is longer than the food menu.

New Town

Dating from what was known as the golden age of pub design in Edinburgh, when pub owners wanted to make drinking places more glamorous to compete for people's cash, the **Guildford Arms** (1–5 West Register St., tel. 0131/556 4312, www.guildfordarms.com, 11 A.M.–11 P.M. Mon.–Thurs., 11 A.M.–midnight Fri.–Sat., 12:30 P.M.–11 P.M. Sun.) sports a superb range of real ales in late Victorian surrounds. Think mahogany, chandeliers, and a ceiling so high there's room for a gallery: a restaurant area where you can sit and look down on the drinkers below.

The owner of **Dirty Dick's** (159 Rose St., tel. 0131/225 4610, 11 A.M.–midnight Mon.–Thurs., 11 A.M.–1 A.M. Fri.–Sat., 12:30 P.M.–midnight Sun.) and Bad Ass, the bar/restaurant just down the street, certainly has a sense of humor. Named after a rag and bone man who used to roam the nearby streets, this place has decor (er, 19th-century bric-a-brac) that can only be described as bizarre (check the golf clubs sticking out of the ceiling). That said, it's a good, fun place to spend the evening. It's a magnet for lovers of cask-conditioned ale, which is also the chief ingredient of the famous steak-and-ale pie.

Cozy **Kay's Bar** (39 Jamaica St., tel. 0131/225 1858, until 11 P.M. or midnight daily) is located on a quiet residential street, with a great range of ales and single malts. This bar is at its most appealing in the cold weather, when one of the filling bar sandwiches can be enjoyed beside an open fire surrounded by beer barrels and a welcoming, largely local clientele, often with their dogs in tow.

Originally the site of the Old Physicians Hall, designed by the planner of Edinburgh's New Town James Craig, the opulent-looking **Dome** (14 George St., tel. 0131/624 8624, 10 A.M.–11 P.M. Mon.–Wed., 10 A.M.–1 A.M. Thurs.–Sat., noon–11 P.M. Sun.) is more than just a place to come for a drink. It's also a restaurant, garden café, function room, and conference suite. A separate bar caters to Over-21s only. If leather seats, enormous gilt-framed mirrors, pillars, and palm trees while sipping a specialty cocktail or supping from the Asian-themed menu is your thing, look no further.

In the former headquarters of the Bank of Scotland, the busy, labyrinthine **The Standing Order** (62–66 George St., tel. 0131/225 4460, 9 A.M.–1 A.M. Mon.–Sat., 10 A.M.–1 A.M. Sun.) apparently still houses the 30-ton safe from its days as a bank. It's now part of the Wetherspoons chain and therefore cheap. Don't expect quality service or cask ales; come instead for a pint or three to soak up the character of the place. The books on the shelves can be borrowed for a donation to charity.

Perfect for that pre- (or post-) train journey pint, Czech-themed **Pivo Caffe** (Calton Rd., tel. 0131/557 2925, open until 3 A.M. daily) occupies a slightly dingy location on Calton Street. Inside, however, it's a spacious place with comfy sofas serving beers like Budvar on tap, and in two-pint glasses. Check the "Czeching Out" menu for shooters that will, quite literally, blow your mind. It's something of a pre-club venue at weekends.

For a really traditional local pub in the city, there are a couple of perfect places to try. **Elm Bar** (7–8 Elm Row, tel. 0131/557 4540, 11 A.M.–11 P.M. Mon.–Thurs., 11 A.M.–midnight Fri.–Sat., 12:30 P.M.–11 P.M. Sun.) has fireplaces, fascinating old pictures of Leith on the walls, and surely too many televisions. Then, of course, there's the **Penny Black** (17 West Register St., tel. 0131/556 1106, 6 A.M.–noon Mon.–Fri.) for a comedown pint and breakfast after the night's revelries, alongside postal workers, railwaymen, and tired clubbers.

Leith and Newhaven

Reportedly Edinburgh's only bar on a boat, the deck of the 400-ton ship that is **Cruz Bar and Restaurant** (The Shore, Leith, tel. 0131/553 6699, www.thecruz.co.uk, noon–1 A.M. daily) is a great if slightly pricey place for a few beers on a sunny evening. There's a restaurant serving good seafood and another bar, complete with dance floor inside.

With more the feel of a Masonic Lodge than a bar, the elegant candlelit **The Vintners Rooms** (The Vaults, 87 Giles St., tel. 0131/554 6767, www.thevintnersrooms.com, food served noon–2 P.M. and 7–10 P.M. Tues.–Sat., other

hours by arrangement) is tucked away within the walls of 500-year-old wine vaults. There are over 200 wines on offer and a more formal dining area serving French fare beside an open fire. The Scottish Malt Whisky Society is upstairs in equally elegant surrounds; it's members only (and guests) but it's worth dressing up just in case you can befriend a member, as having a dram at the bar is an unforgettable experience.

Newhaven may not be what it used to be but it's still worth the hike out here for the traditional **Old Chain Pier** (Trinity Cresent, tel. 0131/553 1233, food served noon–9 P.M. Mon.–Sat., 12:30 P.M.–8 P.M. Sun.). This waterfront pub is perched as its name suggests on a weathered seawall. The clientele range from those almost as weathered as the seawall the pub perches upon to the new generation of trendy Leith twenty-somethings. Despite the demise of Newhaven Fish Market, there's still good old-fashioned fresh fish and chips on the menu.

Southside

The city's best beer garden, set in a high-walled courtyard off West Nicholson Street, is the main draw of the traditional **Pear Tree House** (38 West Nicholson St., tel. 0131/667 7533, 11 A.M.–midnight Mon.–Thurs. 11 A.M.–1 A.M. Fri.–Sat. 12:30 P.M.–midnight Sun.). The domed Counting House, upstairs, is a good spot for live music, particularly during the festival. There are two resident bands, and a good pub quiz. South of the Meadows, it's a chic cosmopolitan crowd that frequents **Montpelier's** (159–161 Bruntsfield Pl., tel. 0131/229 3115, food until 10 P.M., bar until 1 A.M.). It's one of the best places on Southside for an evening drink—it has good cocktails and an extensive wine list.

NIGHTCLUBS

Bongo Club (37 Holyrood Rd., tel. 0131/558 7604, www.thebongoclub.co.uk, until 3 A.M. Fri.–Sat., varying hours other nights, cover £3–6) is the undisputed king of the capital's alternative music scene. It's far more than just a club—also a café, rehearsal space, and exhibition center during the day. It focuses on underground music: anything from funk to salsa to reggae to cabaret to burlesque. Headspin on Saturdays from 11 P.M. is a crowd-pleaser. It attracts a varied crowd, including students, backpackers, and those who've danced their socks off in other places and are looking for something a bit different. A cover charge generally applies, but weeknights are often free.

City Nightclub (1a Market St., tel. 0131/226 9560, www.citypeople.info, 11 P.M.–3 A.M. daily, cover £5–6)is growing to be Edinburgh's premium club. With a 1,500-person capacity, it's the place all the beautiful people go to be seen and to dance. Student nights are Monday and Wednesday, and one of Edinburgh's leading DJs, Tokyo Blu, spins on Saturday. Grab a bite to eat at the City Grill—it will help you deal better with the drinks promotions.

CC Blooms (23–24 Greenside Pl., tel. 0131/556 9331, 6 P.M.–3 A.M. Mon.–Sat., 4 P.M.–3 A.M. Sun., no cover) is gay-owned and -operated, taking its name from the iconic performer in the film *Beaches*. This is the gay club with the latest regular opening hours, and it's lively with a mixed clientele (Fridays and Saturdays for the younger crowd).

Opal Lounge (51a George St., tel. 0131/226 2275, 5 P.M.–3 A.M. Sun.–Fri., noon–3 A.M. Sat., no cover before 10 P.M., £4 10–11 P.M., £8 after 11 P.M.) is still the yuppie hangout of Edinburgh. This is a big café/restaurant by day and a bar—then much later a club—by night. Good, innovative Indonesian/Thai food is available, but this venue is more appealing earlier in the day, when there's more space and less of a feeling you've stepped into a waning modeling agency, before the chic gather to party.

Cabaret Voltaire (36–38 Blair St., tel. 0131/220 6176, 10:30 P.M.–late daily, no cover Tues. and Thurs., cover varies other nights) is a dance club surreally located in Edinburgh's subterranean vaults. It hosts some cracking club nights: We Are . . . Electric (electro-punk) on Wednesdays is the thing of the moment. There's also a lot of live music here—up to 30 gigs a month by local, national, and international artists.

SAUNAS

Number 18 (18 Albert Pl., Leith Walk, tel. 0131/553 3222, www.number18sauna.com, noon–10 P.M. Mon.–Thurs., noon–11 P.M. Fri.–Sat., £10) is a popular gay sauna with a steam room and a café.

LIVE MUSIC
Traditional

Hebrides Bar (17 Market St., tel. 0131/220 4213, 11 A.M.–midnight Mon.–Thurs., 11 A.M.–1 A.M. Fri.–Sat., noon–midnight Sun.) is a wee venue attracting a crowd as traditional as the music. There is live music every night of the week. Thursdays and Sunday afternoons/evenings are reportedly best.

The **Royal Oak** (1 Infirmary St., tel. 0131/557 2976, until midnight or 1 A.M. daily) is another intimate bar with live music every night. Downstairs hosts the infamous Wee Folk Club every Sunday (£3); otherwise entry is free. Neil Thomson on a Friday is excellent. Sessions run until 1 A.M. and later Friday and Saturday—get in early if you want to fit through the door.

The Sunday folk music session is the main reason for going to the small 16th-century **White Hart** (Grassmarket, tel. 0131/226 2806, 11 A.M.–midnight Sun.–Thurs., 11 A.M.–1 A.M. Fri.–Sat.) pub. Live folk, rock, or country is on most nights, and as icing on the musical cake, Rabbie Burns apparently stayed here on his last-ever visit to Edinburgh.

Rock and Jazz

Henry's Cellar Bar (8 Morrison St., www.henrysvenue.com, 8 P.M.–midnight or 1 A.M. weekdays, 7:30 P.M.–3 A.M. weekends) is a cozy, friendly place hosting everything from contemporary jazz to blues to funk and hip-hop. There's a cover charge on some nights, well worth paying for the quality of music.

Bannerman's (212 Cowgate, tel. 0131/556 3254, noon–1 A.M. Mon.–Sat., 12:30 P.M.–1 A.M. Sun.) is the most atmospheric venue for live rock music, with resident bands on Tuesdays and Thursdays and live music six nights per week. It's a dark, many-alcoved place with a regular crowd of students and locals.

PERFORMING ARTS

Edinburgh is the best place in Scotland for performing arts, with top quality theaters.

Theater

Drama is the main focus of the lavish **Royal Lyceum Theatre** (30b Grindlay St., tel. 0131/248 4848, www.lyceum.org.uk), built in 1883. It also stages a children's show each Christmas, as well as occasional musicals and ballet.

The **Traverse Theatre** (10 Cambridge St., tel. 0131/228 1404, www.traverse.co.uk) is Scotland's new writing theater, renowned for its quality performances. Originally designed based on the Roxy Theatre in New York, the **Edinburgh Playhouse** (18–22 Greenside Pl., tel. 0131/557 2692, 0870/606 3434 box office) shows musicals, dance performances, and celebrations of classical, pop, and world music. In Bruntsfield, the ornate **Kings Theatre** (2 Leven St., tel. 0131/229 3416, box office tel. 0131/529 6000, www.eft.co.uk) hosts Edinburgh's much-loved annual pantomime and visits from the Royal National Theatre, as well as amateur productions.

Classical Music, Opera, and Ballet

Currently, Edinburgh only has two establishments for operatic and orchestral performances. The **Festival Theatre** (13–29 Nicholson St., tel. 0131/529 6000, www.eft.co.uk) is the former Empire Theatre. With great acoustics, this is a venue for opera, ballet, and contemporary dance. There is also the **Queens Hall** (85–89 Clerk St., tel. 0131/668 3456 or 0131/668 2019, www.thequeenshall.net), home to the Scottish Chamber Orchestra. It additionally hosts a diverse year-round program of music and comedy.

Usher Hall (Lothian Rd., tel. 0131/228 8616, www.usherhall.co.uk) is home to the Royal Scottish National Orchestra. This magnificent venue is closed for refurbishment until spring 2009.

Comedy

The Stand (5 York Pl., tel. 0131/558 7272, www.thestand.co.uk, noon–2 P.M. and 7:30 P.M.– midnight Mon.–Thurs., 7:30 P.M.–1 A.M. Fri.– Sat., 12:30 P.M.–4 P.M. and 7:30 P.M.–midnight Sun.) is Edinburgh's (if not Britain's) leading comedy venue, showing live comedy seven nights a week every week of the year. It also serves cheap, almost gourmet bar food Thursday to Saturday evenings and weekdays and Sunday lunches. Most of the top names in British comedy have performed here.

CINEMAS

Movie buffs are well catered to in Edinburgh, with a choice of art-house film venues as well as multiplex offerings.

Cameo (38 Home St., tel. 0131/228 2806, www.picturehouses.co.uk) is apparently Irvine Welsh's favorite cinema in the world (*Trainspotting* premiered here in 1996). This atmospheric place is one of Scotland's oldest cinemas still in use and shows primarily independent and European films, including the much-loved double matinees on Sunday. Three screens include neoclassical Screen One and a recently refurbished bar for those pre-movie drinks in huge armchairs.

Filmhouse (88 Lothian Rd., tel. 0131/228 2688) is the main venue for the Edinburgh International Film Festival. As you would hope, its mix is eclectic: a range of international, classic, documentary, and art-house films, as well as a monthly film quiz. There's a bar, too.

Vue (tel. 0871/224 0240, www.myvue.com) shows a more diverse range of films than the other big chain cinemas around. Vue has two branches in Edinburgh: one in the Ocean Terminal at Leith and one in the city center (Omni Centre, Greenside Place). The city center branch has three "gold class" screens, with fully licensed bars and luxury seats. Lots of buses head to the Ocean Terminal from the city center, or you can walk to the Omni Centre: it's a short walk down Leith Street from Waverley Train Station.

EVENTS

Edinburgh is a festival hotbed, with multiple events running throughout the spring and summer.

April

The last day of April is one of four ancient Celtic quarter days originally celebrated to welcome in the summer, maximizing the fertility of the land and the chances of a good harvest. That's the reasoning behind **Beltane** (www.beltane.org), a spectacular fire festival held on Calton Hill on April 30. The website contains interesting information on the other three ancient quarter days, which are also celebrated—but this is the big one.

June

The **Scottish Real Ale Festival** (details posted several months in advance on www.camra.org) is Scotland's biggest beer festival. It's the yeast-fest you'd expect with over 50 all-Scottish ales and food and music thrown in. It's usually held the closest weekend to Midsummer (June 24) in the Assembly Rooms.

June also sees the premier event in the Scottish show calendar, the **Royal Highland Show** (Royal Highland Centre Ingliston, tel. 0131/335 6200, www.royalhighlandshow.org). This is an agricultural medley of Scotland's finest cows, sheep, goats, and horses. There's show-jumping, a countryside arena for events like sheepdog trials, and a traditional crafts section including those classic rural pursuits like bagpipe-making and willow-weaving.

July/August

Before Edinburgh goes totally festival mad in August, the **Edinburgh Jazz and Blues Festival** (www.edinburghjazzfestival.co.uk) is held in late July/early August. It's invariably the week preceding the August Festivals and kicks off with a Mardi Gras celebration. There is a wide program of jazz and blues including free outdoor performances. Tickets can be purchased from the Hub.

Held during August and going strong for over 50 years, the **Military Tattoo** (tel. 0870/752 0530, www.edintattoo.co.uk) has always had a special something that separates it from Edinburgh's August festivals. The highlight for most of the 217,000 people that come each year are the Scottish regimental bands, but a host of other military and non-military bands from around the world that have included dancers, elephants, Zulus, and motorcyclists also perform. Whether you are military-minded or not, this is a fascinating spectacle of human achievement held in a spectacular location in front of the castle. There's a performance at 9 P.M. Monday–Friday and two on Saturdays, at 7:30 P.M. and 10 P.M. **The Spirit of the Tattoo Visitor Centre** (555 Castlehill, tel. 0131/225 9661, 9 A.M.–5 P.M. Mon.–Sat., 10 A.M.–5 P.M. Sun., reduced opening hours in winter) is open throughout the year for further information and insight into this historic event.

EDINBURGH FESTIVAL

Europe's largest festival, the Edinburgh Festival is actually a series of different festivals that all overlap each other during August. For any ticketed event, if you want to see something specific book well in advance, particularly with the International and Fringe festivals. The best insight into the festival is offered at the International Festival office at the Hub (Castlehill, tel. 0131/473 2000, www.hubtickets.co.uk, www.thehub-edinburgh.co.uk), in the Tolbooth Kirk on the Royal Mile where there is a ticket office, information center, and café. If you can't afford to go and see a ticketed event, there's a full fest of free shows, too.

The **Edinburgh International Festival** is a rich tapestry of dance, opera, and classical theater held in six major venues as well as numerous smaller ones throughout the city. Its founders recognized the importance in postwar Britain of bringing together and celebrating the culture of Europe, with the aim of the "flowering of the human spirit." To make sense of the extravaganza of performances, there are a series of talks by festival organizers. The festival runs for three weeks in August, ending on the first Saturday of September.

The **Edinburgh Fringe Festival** (office at 180 High St., tel. 0131/226 0026, admin@ed-fringe.com) started out when six Scottish and two English performers didn't make it onto the

© LUKE WATERSON

performer at the Edinburgh Festival

official festival program but turned up anyway and performed on the "fringe" of the main event. Their success gave the green light to artists everywhere, both established and aspiring, to apply to be part of the Fringe; it's now by far the biggest performing arts festival in the world. Theater and comedy account for most of the acts but really the performances are too individual for categorization. The refreshing thing with the Fringe is that you just don't know what to expect. There are plenty of classic established events and over 20 awards for various types of acts but also lots of up-and-coming first-timers. Even if you're a connoisseur of more mainstream performances and big venues like the Assembly Rooms, go to plenty of events you haven't heard of. These might be really good or really dreadful (in 2007 there were 31,000 performances so it's bound to be

a gamble) but the Fringe is the best chance you will get to come away with your unique impression of what the festival, and by extension the capital, is all about. Bear in mind that as a general rule, the lesser known the performer, the harder they are likely to be trying to entertain. These performances are also more likely to be free, and it is the free Fringe events that usually turn out to be the gems of the August festivals. Numerous venues include on the streets, in the pubs, and the not-to-be-missed events on the Meadows.

The **Edinburgh International Film Festival** runs the first two weeks of August and is the longest continually running festival of its kind in the world. It's had its fair share of famous premieres and hosted some renowned directors. The festival was also pioneering in introducing the concept of the retrospective, reassessing the importance of various directors. Main events are held at Edinburgh's Filmhouse (88 Lothian Rd., tel. 0131/228 4051). There is also the **International Book Festival** (5a Charlotte Sq., tel. 0131/718 5666, admin@ edbookfest.co.uk), held in Charlotte Square Gardens, a good chance to hear readings and talks by, as well as meet, a number of different authors. It all happens in a series of tents, including a café and bookshop.

December/January

The Scots take it easy at Christmas and save themselves for the big one: the **Hogmanay Celebrations** (www.edinburghshogmanay.org). Hogmanay is a mega–New Year celebration that starts December 29 and goes on until New Year's Day. Edinburgh sees plenty of events, including ceilidhs, concerts, and fireworks displays. You'll need tickets for some events, including the massive party around Princes Street on December 31. After all that partying, there's the chance to freshen up with the **One O'Clock Run** on New Year's Day.

Shopping

The **Royal Mile** satisfies demands for handicrafts and other Scottish memorabilia, sometimes embarrassingly touristy and often horrendously pricey. **Princes Street** is the main shopping district: here are the department stores and usual high street shops. Princes Street has several malls but none match the **Ocean Terminal** in Leith for size. **George Street** is where all the chic fashion shops are.

FOOD AND DRINK

When you've tried your whisky, haggis, and shortbread and want your own to snack on—or feel a pang of guilt for those back home who haven't tried Scottish fare—head to the **Scottish Whisky Heritage Centre** (354 Castlehill, tel. 0131/220 0441, www.whiskyheritage.co.uk, 10 A.M.–5:30 P.M. daily) for over 300 whiskies and a handy try-before-you-buy policy. There are other good whisky shops as you continue down the Royal Mile, or check old-fashioned **Robert Graham Ltd.** (194a Rose St., tel. 0131/226 1874, www.whisky-cigars.com) for an eclectic range of whisky, cigars, and accessories, often very reasonably priced.

Besides the Royal Mile shops, the fabulous deli/café **Peckham's** (155 Bruntsfield Pl., tel. 0131/229 7054, 8 A.M.–midnight Mon.–Sat., 9 A.M.–11 P.M. Sun.) has several outlets in the city and is the place to go for quality food gifts or picnic items. Vegans will love **Real Foods** (37 Broughton St., tel. 0131/557 1911, 9 A.M.–7 P.M. Mon.–Wed. and Fri., 9 A.M.–8 P.M. Thurs., 9 A.M.–6:30 P.M. Sat., 10 A.M.–6 P.M. Sun.), which even has a selection of organic vegan alcohols. Failing that, there's always the food hall of **Marks and Spencer** (54 Princes St., tel. 0131/225 2301, 9 A.M.–7 P.M. Mon.–Wed. and Fri., 9 A.M.–8 P.M. Thurs., 8:30 A.M.–6 P.M. Sat., 11 A.M.–5 P.M. Sun.) or **Tesco** (7 Broughton Rd., tel. 0131/456 8400, 8 A.M.–9 P.M. Mon.–Fri., 8 A.M.–8 P.M. Sat., 9 A.M.–8 P.M. Sun.) for self-catering or a less-special gift selection.

WOOLENS AND CASHMERE

Sheep-farming is one of Scotland's leading industries and woolen products one of its most classic and sought-after exports. Cashmere, obtained from the soft undercoat of goats and lambs, is as luxury as woolens get. Worth checking out are the **Cashmere Store** (2 St. Giles St., tel. 0131/225 4035) or the **Edinburgh Woolen Mill** (139 Princes St., tel. 0131/226 3840), which was one of the first of the many other similar stores in town. If these don't do it, wander the Royal Mile for more options.

TARTAN

Tartan, a lot of it tack, can be purchased at the top of the Royal Mile. The **Tartan Woolen Mill** (555 Castlehill, tel. 0131/226 1555) has a wide selection (as well as cashmere), crowds, and what you could call a themed museum. If you need to hire a kilt or have one made, there are numerous places all along the Royal Mile. In Leith, **Kinloch Anderson** (corner of Commercial and Dock Sts., tel. 0131/555 1390, 9 A.M.–5:30 P.M. Mon.–Sat.) is another option.

DEPARTMENT STORES

Try Edinburgh's own giant store, **Jenners** (48 Princes St., tel. 0131/225 2442, until 6 P.M. Fri.–Wed., until 8 P.M. Thurs.), around since the 1830s. **Harvey Nichols** (30–34 St. Andrews Sq., tel. 0131/524 8388, 10 A.M.–6 P.M. Mon.–Wed., 10 A.M.–8 P.M. Thurs., 10 A.M.–7 P.M. Fri.–Sat., noon–6 P.M. Sun.) or **John Lewis** (St. James Centre, tel. 0131/556 9121, 9 A.M.–6 P.M. Mon.–Fri., 9 A.M.–6:30 P.M. Sat., 10 A.M.–6 P.M. Sun.) are the other giant stores.

BOOKSTORES

It's a mystery to many how the owner of **Armchair Books** (off Grassmarket on West Port, tel. 0131/229 5927, 10 A.M.–10 P.M. daily) manages to get any rest at all, but this store with its uneven floors, creaking shelves, and old-world charm is an Aladdin's cave of literary treasures.

Best by far of the chain stores is **Waterstones** (128 Princes St., tel. 0131/226 2666) with knowledgeable staff, a wide selection, and a café upstairs with great views of the castle. Also try **Blackwell's** (53–62 South Bridge, tel. 0131/622 8222), another large store.

GIFTS AND HANDICRAFTS

Aside from Royal Mile souvenirs, gift shops in the city offering something a bit different include **Eden** (37 Cockburn St., tel. 0131/220 3372), with wooden ornaments and various gifts. For pottery, a good bet is working shop **Adam Pottery** (76 Henderson Row, tel. 0131/557 3978, www.adampottery.co.uk) or **The Meadows Pottery** (11a Summerhall Pl., tel. 0131/662 4064), although there is much better pottery to be found elsewhere in Scotland. Crystal is a premium Edinburgh specialty. At the **Edinburgh Crystal Visitor Centre** (tel. 01968/672244, www.edinburghcrystal.co.uk, 10 A.M.–5 P.M. Mon.–Sat., 11 A.M.–5 P.M. Sun.) just outside the city at Penicuik you will find the biggest selection; there are also displays in Jenners. Every day during the festival is the decent **Craft Fair in St. John's Church** (Princes St. and Lothian Rd., 11 A.M.–6 P.M.) with ceramics, jewelry, and the like on offer.

For music, the city's flagship **HMV** (129–130 Princes St., tel. 0131/225 7008) should sort you out, or there's trendy **Coda Music** (12 Bank St., tel. 0131/622 7246) for traditional and **Avalanche** (63 Cockburn St., tel. 0131/225 3939) for eclectic.

SECONDHAND SHOPS AND ANTIQUES

Among the best vintage shops are **Armstrongs** (83 Grassmarket tel. 0131/220 5557), which is good for clothes, especially fancy dress. Its sister shop **Rusty Zip** (14 Teviot Pl., tel. 0131/226 4634) is another option. Otherwise, head to the Nicholson Street/Clerk Street area or, better still, Stockbridge, where you'll find several vintage shops. Best of these is **Chic and Unique** (Deanhaugh St., tel. 0131/332 9889, www.vintagecostumejewellery.co.uk) for antique jewelry. On Raeburn Place, the continuation of Deanhaugh Street, you will also find several good charity shops.

MARKETS

Edinburgh Farmers Market (tel. 0131/652 5940, 9 A.M.–2 P.M. Sat.) has some of Scotland's most succulent produce for purchase on Castle Terrace.

Sports and Recreation

Edinburgh lends itself well to outdoor activities, particularly with so much beautiful, lush countryside to be found right on the doorstop.

OUTDOOR ACTIVITIES
Golf
There are lots of golf courses located in and around Edinburgh. Claiming to be the fifth-oldest course in the world (some say it's the oldest), **Bruntsfield Links** (Davidson's Mains, northwest of city center, tel. 0131/336 1479, £60) certainly does have one of the oldest clubhouses, now known as the Golf Tavern.

Cycling
Cycle Scotland (29 Blackfriars St., tel. 0131/556 5560, www.cyclescotland.co.uk, £10–15/day, £50–70/week for cycle hire including helmet, lock, and repair kit). It has branches dotted around the highlands, too. The best feature: if you get started and don't fancy coming back, they offer pick-up service. In Leith, **Leith Cycle Company** (276 Leith Walk, tel. 0131/467 7775, www.leithcycleco.com, from £10/day) does bike hire, including helmet, lock, puncture repair kit, and city map.

The gorgeous countryside of greater Edinburgh is worth taking advantage of, and

© LUKE WATERSON

Cramond makes a great escape from the busy city center.

there are several great rides in and around the city. The **Water of Leith path** out to Leith and the area around Cramond would make good shorter trips, while the **Union Canal path** out to Linlithgow (45 miles round-trip) or the Falkirk Wheel (65 miles round-trip) is accomplishable in a day. Linlithgow and Falkirk have bus/train connections if a one-way cycle is enough. A good source of advice on cycling is www.edinburghbicycle.com, with links to suggested Lothians routes.

Walking
Edinburgh was made to wander around. **Holyrood Park** offers multiple leg-stretches with terrain from crags to lochs to moor. Plush **Marchmont/Morningside** area is good for a residential wander through suburbs staunchly upper-crusty enough to have a film made about them *(The Prime of Miss Jean Brodie)*. The **Water of Leith walkway** (www.waterofleith.edin.org) runs from Balerno High School to Leith docks; pick up a leaflet at the Water of Leith Visitor

Centre (24 Lanark Rd., Edinburgh). Also try the coast path at **Cramond** or the sands at **Portobello.**

Ballooning
To admire Edinburgh's aesthetics gracefully from the air, get in touch with **Alba Ballooning** (tel. 0131/667 4251, info@alba-ballooning.co.uk, £165 per person), where a trip up comes with champagne.

HEALTH CLUBS AND FITNESS CENTERS
After all the hectic sightseeing, checking in to the **Dalhousie Castle and Spa** (Bonyrigg, tel. 0187/582 0153, £220 d) in the southeast of Edinburgh will certainly relax you. Here you'll be able to try out Scotland's first hydro spa and a Roman-style sauna. The room includes breakfast and full use of the spa facilities. Other luxury hotels like the Balmoral or Channings also offer their own lavish fitness/beauty treatments with all the trimmings.

For those within a more earthly budget

wanting a workout, head to **Edinburgh Leisure** (141 London Rd., tel. 0131/652 2178, from £6), with weights, a climbing wall, racket sports, fitness classes, and more.

SPECTATOR SPORTS
Football

The two city teams are Hearts of Midlothian (known as Hearts) and Hibernian F.C. (known as Hibs). Both live in the perpetual shadow of the better-known Glasgow Rangers and Celtic F.C., but they're both still solid Scottish Premier League outfits; a local derby is enjoyable. Hearts play in southwest Edinburgh at **Tynecastle** (Gorgie Rd., tel. 0131/200 7200, www.heartsfc.co.uk, £12–38 for normal home match tickets); in the northeast of the city is Hibs home ground **Easter Road Stadium** (Albion Place, tel. 0131/661 2159, www.hibs.co.uk, around £20 for normal home match tickets).

Horse Racing

Edinburgh is steeped in horse-racing tradition, with races having taken place in the sands on Leith for hundreds of years. In 1816, following complaints the crowd at Leith were too noisy, Lord Roseberry moved the venue to **Musselburgh Race Course** (tel. 0131/665 2859, www.musselburgh-racecourse.co.uk), where you can watch a race for £13.

Rugby

International matches take place out west at **Murrayfield Stadium** (Roseburn St., tel. 0131/346 5000, www.scottishrugby.org).

Accommodations

There is no shortage of accommodations in Edinburgh, to the extent that you will see banners fluttering from residents' windows proclaiming "Homes, not hotels." City center accommodation is plentiful, too. In the Old Town, aside from the usual chains, it is divided between budget accommodations (which can be very classy), catering mainly to backpackers, and upper-end hotels. The New Town has some of the most stunning hotels, and both the New Town and (particularly) the Southside of Edinburgh also have a number of mid-range accommodations, including bed-and-breakfasts and guesthouses. Staying outside the center will give you the chance of finding a parking place, which in the Old Town is almost impossible; Southside guesthouses often have their own parking.

OLD TOWN
Under £50

St. Christopher's Inn (tel. 0131/226 1446, www.st-christopher's.co.uk, 10/8/4-bed dorms from £9.50/17/19.50) is located two minutes' walk from Waverley train station and open 24 hours; even the drunkest party-goers should have no trouble finding their way to this bright, friendly hostel. The staff will ensure your stay is a fun one but be warned: This is a place to meet people, not to get some peace and quiet. One downside is the lack of a kitchen, but food is served with a 10 percent discount for residents and prices include breakfast. The bars are decorated with old movie and music posters, and the plan is to extend the kitsch to the bedrooms. Seven twin/double rooms are available.

The 350-bed, imaginatively furnished ◖ **Castle Rock Hostel** (Johnston Terr., tel. 0131/225 9666, 6- to 16-bed dorms/quads £13/15) boasts some of the finest views of Edinburgh Castle and the Old Town at some of the lowest prices. There's a movie room and reading room complete with piano and board games for when you're rained in. If you're on a budget, it's possible to stay for free and work to earn your keep.

Located in a 400-year-old building, **High Street Hostel** (8 Blackfriars St., tel. 0131/557 3984, highstreethostel@scotlandstophostels.com, dorms from £13, twins £40–50) is run by the same people as Castle Rock and is a friendly atmospheric place conveniently located for Edinburgh's nightlife. Macbackpackers tours of Edinburgh leave from right outside the door (two hours), free if you've stayed at this, Castle Rock, or Royal Mile hostels.

Budget Backpackers (37–39 Cowgate, tel. 0131/226 6351, www.budgetbackpackers.com, 8- and 10-bed dorms from £12.50) is a bright, friendly hostel with more beds in quad and six-bed rooms for £16–22. There are 33 rooms, including mixed and female-only rooms, a well-equipped kitchen and chill-out room, as well as a pool table and Internet access. Ask about discounts for longer stays. Staff members also organize social events like pub crawls.

You could also try **Royal Mile Backpackers** (105 High St., tel. 0131/557 6120, dorms from £12).

Over £100

That **Tailors Hall** (139 Cowgate, tel. 0131/622 6801, www.festival-inns.co.uk, £90 s, £110 d) is one of the more interesting non-chain upper-end hotels in the Old Town does not say much for the choices available. The spacious rooms are comfortable enough, if basic, but sometimes suffer from noise drifting up from the pub next door. The location is very convenient for sightseeing and nightlife.

Once the opulent offices of *The Scotsman* newspaper, the grandiose **Scotsman Hotel** (20 North Bridge, tel. 0131/556 5565, www.thescotsmanhotelgroup.com) retains all the original features. "Basic" rooms begin at £300, including a mini bar and an Edinburgh monopoly game table. Room 303 was the editor's lavish office, and the Penthouse Suite, now with its own library, was where the advertising executives hung out. Only the most important people at the paper were allowed to tread on the hotel's classic marble staircase. The Scotsman has its own gym, sauna, spa, and cinema.

If you're sick of bland hotels, right at the gates of Edinburgh castle are the splendidly theatrical **Witchery Suites** (Castlehill, tel. 0131/225 5613 for reservations, www.thewitchery.com, £295 per suite), lavish even compared to its opulent restaurant. There are seven suites

to chose from, furnished with antiques; they have been frequented by celebrities including Jack Nicholson and Michael Douglas. Named one of the seven wonders of the hotel world by *Cosmopolitan* magazine, this lodging must be booked several months in advance.

NEW TOWN AND VICINITY
Under £50

The modern if slightly stark hostel **Edinburgh Central Youth Hostel** (9 Haddington Pl., tel. 0870/155 3255, dorms £18.50–24.50, twins £37) enjoys great views over Calton Hill. There are dorms, singles from £25, and twin rooms from £37 on offer. There's an on-site café/bistro, well-appointed self-catering kitchen, laundry and drying room, and, usefully, luggage storage from £0.50 per hour. The hostel runs a door-to-door airport shuttle service.

Caledonian Backpackers (Queensferry St., tel. 0131/426 7224, www.caledonianbackpackers.net, 20-bed dorms £8, 12-bed dorms £12, 4-bed dorms £16, twins £36, doubles £38) provides all the quality facilities a tired backpacker could want at prices you can't argue with; amenities include plenty of hot showers, round-the-clock laundry, pool table, and a late-licensed bar. The only thing you may not get is a peaceful night's sleep from all the 24-hour party people also staying.

£50-100

€ **Six Mary's Place** (Raeburn Pl., tel. 0131/332 8965, www.sixmarysplace.co.uk, twins/doubles from £80) is hidden away in a leafy garden in Stockbridge. The Georgian building has eight rooms, seven of which are en suite with very comfortable beds. A conservatory overlooks a beautiful walled garden. The superb vegetarian breakfasts make this place extra special.

With rooms done up in a sleek white, pine beams, and a living room with a brick fireplace to relax in, **The Lodge** (Ravelston Dykes, tel. 0131/332 9300, £50 s, £89 d) is perfectly positioned for the modern art galleries and walks along the Water of Leith. The building was designed by the owners, hence the beautiful use of space.

The **Inverleith Hotel** (Inverleith Terr., tel. 0131/556 2745, www.inverleithhotel.co.uk, £55 s, £89 d) is 15 minutes' walk or a short bus ride from Princes Street. It offers very comfortable rooms overlooking the Royal Botanic Gardens, including one with a four-poster bed. The residents' lounge has a bar well stocked with single malt whiskies. Discounts are available during the off-season.

Over £100

Explorer Sir Ernest Shackleton's former house, **Channings** (12–16 South Learmouth Gardens, tel. 0131/274 7401, www.channings.co.uk, from £85 s, £120 d) is now a boutique hotel with six luxury suites, and rooms decorated with prints relating to the famous explorer. Rooms come with writing desks, jukeboxes, and Molten Brown toiletries. There is a choice of views, over this verdant corner of the New Town or the hotel's private courtyard. You can relax in the wine bar or on the sun deck, where there are barbecues during summer.

The imposing **(Balmoral** (Princes St., tel. 0131/556 2414, www.thebalmoralhotel.com, from £290 s, £345 d) will be one of the first buildings you see arriving in the city by train. It retains all the glamour of a bygone age, starting with the welcome by kilt-attired doormen. The 168 bedrooms and 20 luxury suites offer great views of the castle and Calton Hill. Child-friendly amenities include interactive television, Sony PlayStations, and teddy bear turndown service. The lavish **number one** restaurant downstairs is based on a Hong Kong restaurant, and you can have a drink among the pillars and plants afterward at the Bollinger Bar. Other facilities include conference suites and a spa with swimming pool and steam room.

One of the favorite crash pads of the rich and famous when they drop by Edinburgh is **One Royal Circus** (Royal Circus, tel. 0131/625 6669, mike@royalcircus.com, £140–260 d), a Georgian house built in 1823. It features a drawing room with a book and music library and a classic Brunswick pool table. The gorgeous en suite bedrooms come with Frette linens, and you can get cappuccino or espresso with your breakfast. The experience is a bit like staying in an elaborate museum.

LEITH

If you fancy hitting Leith's chic restaurants and bars without worrying about negotiating night buses back, there are several cheap options. Clean, safe **Ocean Hostel** (55 Constitution St., tel. 0131/556 2700, www.oceanhostel.com, dorm beds £12) could well be the best of them; it has accommodation in 6- to 12-bed dorms and a lounge with table football.

PORTOBELLO

Portobello is a great area to stay in if you want a slightly more relaxed, sedate experience of Edinburgh, and it has the added bonus of being right on the beach.

Abercorn Guesthouse (1 Abercorn Terr., tel. 0131/669 6139, £20–60 pp) is one of the first guesthouses on your right walking away from the main Portobello high street, complete with several gorgeous, light, elaborate-looking rooms. It's a former manse house with a walled garden and a beautiful conservatory.

OUTSIDE CITY CENTER

The main clutches of bed-and-breakfasts and guesthouses are on the main arteries into the city center. Southside (generally speaking, the area south of the Meadows, including Bruntsfield at the western edge and Newington at the eastern edge for the purposes of this book) is a popular area to stay. Even in high season, there are so many accommodations on Minto Street/Mayfield Gardens in Newington that you could probably turn up on the spot and find a room. Booking ahead is, as ever, still strongly advised. Both Pilrig Street and Ferry Road are the main accommodations areas in the North, while west of the city is handy for the airport and transport links.

North and West of City Center
UNDER £50

A step up from your average hostel accommodation, **Globetrotter Inn** (46 Marine Dr., tel. 0131/336 1030, beds £15–18, £46 d) is set in grassy grounds overlooking the Firth of Forth. It has its own kitchen, bar, supermarket, and cinema. It's fun and relaxed, and the beds are solid and comfortable. There is a pick-up service from the city center: The shuttle bus leaves on the hour from 7 A.M. with the last bus at 11 P.M. from Waterloo Place (£2.50 return).

The closest caravan/campsite to the city center is **Edinburgh Caravan Club** (35–37 Marine Dr., tel. 0131/312 6874, pitch £4.60– 7.60 plus £4.40–6 per person). It boasts sweeping views over meadows to the Firth of Forth and the Cramond foreshore, just a short walk away. A site shop is open March to October, and there's even a boule court. Lothian bus 42 stops nearby.

£50-100
Five Six Seven (567 Queensferry Rd., tel. 0131/466 3170, from £30 s, £60 d), which takes its name from its street address, is some ways west of the city center but well connected transport-wise and with private parking. It benefits from huge rooms, with pine floors and white walls (almost) giving the impression of sleeping in an art studio. There's lots of greenery and a beautiful conservatory for alfresco breakfasts. Lothian bus 41 from the city center stops right outside.

With nine bedrooms (seven en suite), sparkling bathrooms, and unusual decor including a variety of strategically placed statues and busts, **Fraoch House** (66 Pilrig St., tel. 0131/554 1353, www.fraochhouse.com, £65– 100 d) is one classy guesthouse. It serves up some of Edinburgh's most creative and tantalizing breakfasts, too.

Southside
UNDER £50
The Southside's main hostel is the large, friendly **Bruntsfield Youth Hostel** (7 Bruntsfield Crescent, tel. 0870/004 1114, dorms from £13.50). Two miles out of the city center, some rooms are crammed full of beds and therefore quite poky (stuffy) despite their size. Some are also a bit of a walk from the wash facilities. Others have great views

looking toward the Old Town; it's a bit of a lottery which you'll get. In the basement is a well-appointed but somewhat gloomy kitchen and dining area; upstairs is a far nicer common room/games room/book exchange. The location, in beautiful parkland and near some chic restaurants, makes up for a lot. Bus 15 will stop nearby.

£50-100
Set back from the road on a leafy Victorian terrace, the reason **Menzies Guesthouse** (33 Leamington Terr., Bruntsfield, tel. 0131/229 4629, £30 s, £30–60 d) remains such a popular place is because of its seven huge value rooms. Some rooms are en suite, but all get a wash basin. There's a large, light breakfast room, and the whole place has been recently refurbished.

On a quiet residential street yet close to the restaurants and bars of Bruntsfield is **Amaryllis Guesthouse** (21 Upper Gilmore Pl., Bruntsfield, tel. 0131/229 3293, www.amaryllisguesthouse.com, £30–40 s, £50–80 d), a townhouse dating from the early 1800s. It has ample rooms, including a family room, and can also arrange local sightseeing tours.

If the idea of heavy Scottish breakfasts makes you queasy, the health-conscious and non-carnivores will welcome the chance to experience **The Greenhouse** (14 Hartington Gardens, Bruntsfield, tel. 0131/622 7634, www.greenhouse-edinburgh.com, £65 s, £70 d). Introducing you to the world of vegetarian and vegan Edinburgh, the Greenhouse offers six comfortable rooms with white-and-yellow decor and colorful furnishings. Down to the homemade soaps and shampoos in the bathrooms, this place is also committed to non-animal-tested, GM-free, organic products. Needless to say, the breakfast—using herbs grown in the Greenhouse garden—is exclusively vegetarian, although meat-eaters are unlikely to complain.

Based in Newington are the **Pollock Halls of Residence** (Holyrood Park Rd., tel. 0131/651 2007, www.edinburghfirst.com, £29–40 s, £59– 84 d). While the students are off (for three weeks during Easter and from approximately the end

© LUKE WATERSON

Newington, on the Southside of Edinburgh, is full of 18th-century houses.

of May to the beginning of September in summer, check website for details), the University of Edinburgh offers surprisingly good accommodation in clean, modern, spartan rooms, many en suite, in a pleasant setting. There may be over 500 rooms available but they fill up very fast—book in advance.

The **Tantallon Guesthouse** (17 Tantallon Pl., tel. 0131/667 1708, £52–74 d) lies just south of the Meadows in Newington. With a wonderful walled garden, this place has two sunny en suite double rooms, well stocked with information on the area.

On a main bus route to the city center, **Allison House** (17 Mayfield Gardens, tel. 0800/328 9003, www.allisonhousehotel.com, £70 s, £120 d) is more a hotel than a guesthouse. Its 11 en suite bedrooms offer complimentary decanters of whisky and sherry. Phenomenal breakfasts can encompass all the classic Scottish fare, from porridge to kippers and everything in between. It's worth checking for last-minute discounts, which at certain times of the year offer beds from £30 pp including a continental breakfast.

Also worth trying on the same stretch are **Barony House** (23 Mayfield Gardens, tel. 0131/667 5806, www.baronyhouse.co.uk, £50–70 d, with occasional discounts available on the website) and **St. Conans** (30 Minto St., tel. 0131/667 8393, £55–65 d), offering doubles in vibrantly decorated rooms.

Food

You are spoiled for choice for eating out in Edinburgh. There's a range of restaurants, often in glamorous old buildings with bags of character adding that special atmosphere to any meal out. Café culture has swept across the city in the last couple of decades, and Scotland's capital can compete with Paris or Rome for its sheer number of stylish breakfast, lunch, and dinner spots. Lunch is generally noon–2 P.M. and dinner 7–10 P.M., but a lot of places in the city are open for food all day. Reliable bets for good food throughout the day are pubs, particularly those in the city center. Each January and February, the **Dine Around Edinburgh** (www.dinearound.5pm.co.uk) scheme sees lots of top restaurants in the city offering two- to three-course meals for £15.

OLD TOWN
Cafés, Tearooms, and Snacks
The ethos behind the light, airy café **Always Sunday** (170 High St., tel. 0131/622 0667, 8 A.M.–6 P.M. Mon.–Fri., 9 A.M.–6 P.M. Sat.–Sun.) is that there is always time for a spot of relaxation and a break from the Royal Mile crowds. It's a popular place, but if you are lucky enough to get a table you can sit with a coffee, people-watching without fear of being rushed. There are great-value lunches—try the sweet potato and spinach salad, washed down with one of the freshly squeezed juices. The menu also includes a range of wheat-free and dairy-free products.

⟨ Elephant House (21 George IV Bridge, tel. 0131/220 5355, 8 A.M.–11 P.M. Mon.–Fri., 9 A.M.–11 P.M. Sat.–Sun.) is where you will find Edinburgh's most eclectic range of coffees. You also get good-value light lunches, big portions of cake, and a view of the castle fringed by enormous potted plants while you partake—what more could you ask for in a café? Not much, and the Elephant House knows this. The atmosphere is a little less relaxed than it used to be, with a somewhat-abrupt staff and long waits for tables at times, but this is a popular

place. There are always the elephants to entertain. Snacks and light meals are £2–8.

The menu in **Chocolate Soup** (2 Hunter Sq., tel. 0131/225 7669, 8 A.M.–7 P.M. daily) includes so many coffees and hot chocolates, it takes up most of one wall. The sweet-toothed can be sure of satisfaction here, with a great selection of cakes on display—the Chocolate Brownie Sandwich is tough to beat. There are also homemade soups with freshly baked bread, ideal for those wet mornings, and hardcore Belgian chocolate soup, ideal for the ultimate binge. Snacks are £1–5.

The **Baked Potato Shop** (56 Cockburn St., tel. 0131/225 7572, 9 A.M.–9 P.M. daily) serves a selection of the city's best baked potatoes with innovative fillings such as vegetarian haggis.

Scottish/International
With 17th-century oak paneling and decorated with tapestries, church candlesticks, and even a bust of Dionysus, the Greek God of wine, **⟨ The Witchery** (Castlehill, tel. 0131/225 5613, noon–4 P.M. and 5:30–11 P.M. daily) offers a magical dining experience. In summer, you can dine on the "Secret Garden" terrace. The menu has a strong seafood theme, with grilled Scottish lobster a particular favorite. Starters are £6–12, mains are £15–35.

Housed above the landmark Museum of Scotland, it's easy to see why Witchery owner James Thomson's **The Tower** (Chambers St., tel. 0131/225 3003, noon–11 P.M.) has gone from strength to strength since it opened in 1998. It's hard to beat dining surrounded with (by general consensus) the best views of any restaurant in the city while you sample a menu ranging from Scottish seafood to game. Starters are £6–10 and mains are £16–30.

You wouldn't think it from the small café upstairs, but descend into the basement of **Herbe Bistro** (44–46 George IV Bridge, tel. 0131/226 3269, 11 A.M.–10 P.M.) and you will not be disappointed. It's an ideal lunch spot serving up Scottish fare with a twist, so think goat cheese and beetroot with the favorite steak burger (£9.50) and haggis, neeps, and tatties in rosemary butter. The mirrors might deceive you, but this is a small place, and booking ahead is advised. Main meals are around £10.

Italian

Stacked with wine bottles and exuding plenty of Mediterranean atmosphere, **Ecco Vino** (19 Cockburn St., tel. 0131/225 1141, noon–1 A.M., food noon–10 P.M. Sun.–Thurs., noon–11 P.M. Fri.–Sat.) is a buzzing place to linger over a meal and a glass of wine. The food is reasonably priced, too, with generous antipasto from £4.

Down in Grassmarket, there is cheap, cheerful **Made In Italy** (42 Grassmarket, tel. 0131/662 7328, 8 A.M.–11 P.M. Mon.–Thurs., 8 A.M.–1 A.M. Fri.–Sat.). It serves a great range of pizzas, pastas, and mean mozzarella, tomato, and basil sandwiches from behind a counter shipped specially from Milan. This is some of Edinburgh's best food for the quantity and quality you get.

American

Eating at the **Filling Station** (235 High St., tel. 0131/226 2488, food served noon–11:30 P.M. Mon.–Sat., 12:30 P.M.–10:30 P.M. Sun.) will do exactly what its name suggests it will. It's huge burgers at huge prices on offer at this hugely crowded pub/restaurant. The bar's on a raised area at the front, with the restaurant at the rear amidst a lot of American-themed kitsch, mostly car license plates. Don't expect the staff to smile as they serve you.

A more convivial venue is **Mamma's** (Grassmarket, tel. 0131/225 6464, noon–11 P.M.). This relaxed place has outside seating on the Grassmarket and juicy American-style pizza for two people at around £6.50.

Mexican

The original Mexican restaurant in Edinburgh, brightly colored █ **Viva Mexico** (41 Cockburn St., tel. 0131/226 5145, www.viva-mexico.co.uk, noon–2 P.M. and 6:30–10:30 P.M. Mon.–Sat., 6:30–10 P.M. Sun.). This establishment enjoys great views over the New Town and has two intimate dining areas. The best is downstairs, with quirky black and white photographs of Mexican life. Recipes are independently re-searched in Mexico, with lunch starting at £3.50 and dinner at £10. Start with the ceviche, followed by tacos, and wrap up with a dessert like the chocolate and chili cheesecake, washed down by an excellent margarita.

NEW TOWN AND VICINITY
Cafés, Tearooms, and Snacks

Set in the basement of a former bakery, the main focus of trendy **Urban Angel** (121 Hanover St., tel. 0131/225 6215, www.urban-angel.co.uk, 10 A.M.–10 P.M. Mon.–Thurs., 10 A.M.–11 P.M. Fri.–Sat., 10 A.M.–5 P.M. Sun.) is its freshly pre-pared, organic, locally sourced food. Largely due to its all-day brunch menu (organic muesli to spinach, feta, and vine tomato omelettes), it caters to all sorts: office workers, locals, stu-dents, and late-risers. No bookings are possible during daytime on weekends.

Scottish/Seafood

If you fancy an offbeat alternative to your aver-age takeaway fish and chips, **L'Alba D'Oro** (7 Henderson Row, tel. 0131/557 2580, 5–11 P.M. Sun.–Wed., 5 P.M.–midnight Thurs.–Sat.) is the place to head. The fish supper of haddock and chips (£5.50) is the classic dish to go for here, but there are surprises like monkfish and chips or prawns in garlic and ginger. The best twist is the great range of wine and champagne you can order to wash it all down. Takeaway dishes are £4 to £6.

Chef Martin Bouyer's award-winning res-taurant, **Restaurant at the Bonham** (35 Drumsheugh Gardens, tel. 0131/274 7444, www.thebonham.com, noon–2:30 P.M. and 6:30–10 P.M. Mon.–Sat., 12:30–3 P.M. and 6:30–10 P.M. Sun.) outdoes even the elegant 19th-century hotel it is contained within. With an interior exuding dark wood, the Bonham does three-course lunches at £16, or mains (din-ner) £15–18. Try the fish pie, a lunchtime special on a Friday, with a glass of wine for £10.50.

Serving a great, reasonably priced range

of seafood in an informal setting, the popular **Mussel Inn** (61–65 Rose St., tel. 0131/225 5979, noon–10 P.M. Mon.–Sat., 1:30–10 P.M. Sun.) restaurant does a superb chowder. It also has sidewalk tables outside. Mains are £6–17, but they do include copious amounts of seafood; starters are £3–6.

With stained-glass windows, walnut wood, and a black-and-white tiled floor, **Café Royal Oyster Bar** (17a West Register St., tel. 0131/556 4124, noon–2 P.M. and 7–10 P.M. for food daily) is Edinburgh's classiest eating institution, going strong for one and a half centuries. The menu strongly focuses on seafood, as you might expect. Fixed lunches kick off at £15.95. Food at the **Circle Bar** (11 A.M.–11 P.M. Mon.–Wed., 11 A.M.–midnight Thurs., 11 A.M.–1 A.M. Fri.–Sat.), approached through a separate entrance beneath, is made in the same kitchens and a little cheaper. The Circle Bar is an elaborate place for a drink, most notable for the tiled pictures of inventors adorning the walls and of course the centerpiece, the 150-year-old bar that lends the place its name.

Italian

Leading the New Town's Italian cuisine by a mile, as it has for 70 odd years, **Valvona and Crolla** (19 Elm Row, Leith Walk, tel. 0131/556 6066, www.valvonacrolla.co.uk, 8 A.M.–6:30 P.M. Mon.–Sat., 11 A.M.–5 P.M. Sun.) is Scotland's oldest deli. The family-owned business has a mouth-watering array of cheeses, salami, home-baked breads, and other treats for picnics. If you can't wait for a picnic, there's an on-site café serving the delicatessen food. Tastings and cooking demonstrations run throughout the year. **Vincaffe** (11 Multrees Walk, tel. 0131/557 0088, 8 A.M.–late Mon.–Sat., 11 A.M.–5:30 P.M. Sun.), an experience in itself with a café and first-floor restaurant/bar serving similar delicacies has now opened near St. Andrew's Square.

SOUTHSIDE

In Southside is the main campus of Edinburgh University, which means the area is not short of good cheap places to go for a drink and a bite to eat. These can rival anywhere on the Royal Mile for quality, at better prices and in a more relaxed, bohemian atmosphere.

Cafés, Tearooms, and Snacks

With friendly staff, unusual Native American-style wooden furniture, and some of the finest coffee in Edinburgh, **Black Medicine** (2 Nicholson St., tel. 0131/557 6269, 8 A.M.–6 P.M. Mon.–Sat., 10 A.M.–6 P.M. Sun.) attracts a crowd of students shirking lectures, shoppers, and other local characters. It has a homey atmosphere and excellent smoothies.

There's plenty of polished wood and a great selection of books to peruse while you people-watch at laid-back **Kilimanjaro** (126 Nicholson St., tel. 0131/662 0135, 8 A.M.–8 P.M. daily). Check out the interesting photographs on the walls, taken in Tanzania by a former employee. The cakes are so good even the most health-conscious will be hard-pressed not to have a try.

About as weird and wonderful as a sandwich bar can get, **Ndebele** (57 Home St., tel. 0131/221 1141, 10 A.M.–10 P.M. daily) has a South African theme. Choose at the deli at the top from a range of exotic fillings that you just won't see anywhere else in the city (the biltong and onion relish pita is delicious). Take your order down, complete with one of the African filter coffees or a Mkul hot chocolate to the café below, filled with coffee sacks and South African masks, not to mention a bit of traditional drum music.

Asian

It's not much to look at, but brightly lit **Ann Purna** (45 St. Patrick's Sq., tel. 0131/662 1807, noon–2 P.M. and 5:30–11 P.M. Mon.–Sat., 5–10 P.M. Sun.) is an Indian vegetarian restaurant that knows all about great-value food. There are three-course lunches from £4.95, while at the top of the price spectrum are amazing thalis (mixtures of many different dishes in separate bowls, including dessert) around £10.

LEITH

Leith has a flank of fine restaurants right alongside the Water of Leith. The area is a

EDINBURGH

© LUKE WATERSON

Leith has reinvented itself as an area of fine dining.

snazzy example of how urban regeneration can be a success: there's a buzz about the dining scene here.

Seafood

A cozy and informal restaurant overlooking the Water of Leith, **Fishers** (The Shore, tel. 0131/554 5666, www.fishersbistros.co.uk., noon–10:30 P.M. daily) dishes up mouthwatering seafood at reasonable prices. Try the smoked fishcakes (£4.85) followed by pan-fried west coast scallops. Testimony to Fishers' popularity is its other branch in the city (not as atmospheric) and plans to open a new restaurant in Fountainbridge, southwest of Edinburgh. Main meals are £15–20.

French

Using Scottish ingredients in a creative French cuisine, **Restaurant Martin Wishart** (The Shore, tel. 0131/553 3557, noon–2 P.M. and 7–10 P.M. Mon.–Sat.) is as excellent as you would expect a Michelin-starred restaurant to be but neither as pricey nor as pretentious. Starters like cured foie gras and mains such as

poached Anjou pigeon in an oyster sauce are served in relaxed surroundings for £20–25.

Asian

Edinburgh's wackiest dining experience is surely Mongolian barbecue–themed **Khublai Khan** (43 Assembly St., tel. 0131/555 0005, www.khublaikhan.co.uk, 6 P.M.–late Mon.–Thurs. and Sat., noon–2:30 P.M. and 6 P.M.–late Fri. and Sun.). Themed around the food favored by the Mongolian marauding hordes of the 13th century, it's hung with tapestries and warriors' weapons, which get you in the mood for the viciously hot food, which includes ostrich, wild boar, and even zebra. The two-course lunch is £5, the three-course evening meal £13.95.

Award-winning **Britannia Spice** (150 Commercial St., tel. 0131/555 2255, www.britanniaspice.co.uk, noon–2:15 P.M. Mon.–Sat., 5–11:45 P.M. daily) mixes copious portions of Indian, Bangladeshi, and Nepalese cuisine with a nautical decor. It's not every day you can tuck into chicken jalfrezi under ships' rigging. Starters are £2–5 and mains on the pricey side at £8–15.

Information and Services

Edinburgh is a well-appointed city, and most of its services are clustered closely together just like its sights are, predominantly in the New Town. Worth bearing in mind is that Edinburgh is the only place in Scotland with foreign consulates.

INFORMATION
Tourist Information Offices
The capital's, and the country's, main TIC is at **Edinburgh and Scotland Information Centre** (3 Princes St., tel. 0845/225 5121, info@visitscotland.com, 9 A.M.–8 P.M. Mon.–Sat., 10 A.M.–8 P.M. Sun. July–Aug., 9 A.M.–7 P.M. Mon.–Sat., 10 A.M.–7 P.M. Sun. May–June and Sept., 9 A.M.–5 P.M. Mon.–Wed., 9 A.M.–6 P.M. Thurs.–Sat., 10 A.M.–5 P.M. Sun. Oct.–Apr.). Located above Waverley train station, this place has multiple advisors, an accommodation-booking service, currency exchange, and a counter selling tickets for Scottish Citylink bus services. There's also Internet access, a substantial free leaflet display, and a gift and book shop.

Handy for those flying in to the capital, the **Tourist and Airport Information Centre at Edinburgh Airport** (tel. 0845/225 5121) is open all year and can help with general enquiries. There's also **Old Craighall Tourist Information Centre** (Old Craighall junction, on the A1 by Musselburgh, tel. 0131/653 6172, daily Apr.–Oct.), which is useful if you are approaching Edinburgh by road.

Maps
The **Stationery Office Bookshop** (71 Lothian Rd., tel. 0131/606 5566, 9 A.M.–5 P.M. Mon.–Fri., 10 A.M.–5 P.M. Sat.) has Edinburgh's best selection of Ordnance Survey (OS) maps. If it's old/antiquarian maps you're after, try the **Carson Clark Gallery** (181–183 Canongate, tel. 0131/556 4710), which also does sea charts.

SERVICES
Currency Exchange
The majority of city center banks now have a bureau de change, including the **Royal**

Bank of Scotland (36 St. Andrew Sq., tel. 0131/566 8555, 9:15 A.M.–4:45 P.M. Mon.–Tues. and Thurs.–Fri., 10 A.M.–4:45 P.M. Wed., 10 A.M.–2 P.M. Sat.). There are convenient currency exchanges at the airport, Waverley Train station, and at the Edinburgh and Scotland Information Centre; unsurprisingly, these will not offer the best rates.

American Express (69 George St., tel. 0131/718 2501, 9 A.M.–5:30 P.M. Mon.–Fri., 9 A.M.–4 P.M. Sat.) offers competitive exchange rates and charges no commission on its own travelers checks. Post offices will often provide the best exchange rates. Convenience-wise, withdrawing cash from an ATM is by far the most hassle-free option—there are commission charges from non-U.K. banks but these are not high enough to be a deterrent.

Communications
The main city **post office** is in St. James's Centre, St. Andrew Square (tel. 0845/722 3344). Other handy offices are at 40 Frederick Street (tel. 0845/722 3344) and 7 Hope Street (tel. 0131/226 6893).

Telephone boxes can be found across the city; sadly, the classic red variety are few and far between. If you are going to be in Scotland for a while, you might want to consider purchasing a pay-as-you-go mobile phone. The best coverage in Scotland is offered by **Vodafone,** with a retail store at 24 Princes St. (tel. 0845/440 0194).

Internet Access
These days, lots of accommodations, from hotels to youth hostels, offer Internet either for free or a price as cheap as you'll find anywhere. Useful Internet cafés include **Connect@edinburgh** (3 Princes St., tel. 0131/473 3800, 50p per 15 minutes) in the Edinburgh and Scotland Information Centre or **easyInternetcafe** (58 Rose St., £1 per hour), within a coffee shop for your online pleasure. Up by Leith Walk, **Coffeehome** (28 Crichton Pl., tel. 0131/477 8336,

www.coffeehome.co.uk, 10 A.M.–10 P.M. Mon.–Sat., noon–10 P.M. Sun., £0.60 for 20 min., then £0.03 per min.) is an efficient joint where you can also photocopy, send faxes, and keep fueled with surprisingly good coffee and muffins.

Libraries

The **Central Library** (George IV Bridge, tel. 0131/242 4800, 10 A.M.–8 P.M. Mon.–Thurs., 10 A.M.–5 P.M. Fri., 9 A.M.–1 P.M. Sat.) is a general lending library with two floors full of Edinburgh and Scottish books.

Consulates

Most consulates are within walking distance of the city center. Farthest out is the **U.S. Consulate** (3 Regent Terrace, tel. 0131/556 8315). Other consulates include **Canada** (50 Lothian Road, tel. 0131/473 6320), **Australia** (69 George Street, tel. 0131/624 3333), and **New Zealand** (5 Rutland Square, tel. 0131/222 8109).

Medical Services and Emergencies

Amazingly, there are no 24-hour pharmacies in Edinburgh. The pharmacy with the longest opening hours is the chemist chain **Boots** (48 Shandwick Pl., tel. 0131/225 6757, 8 A.M.–8 P.M. Mon.–Fri., 8 A.M.–6 P.M. Sat., 10 A.M.–4 P.M. Sun.).

For a dentist, visit the **Edinburgh Dental Institute** (Lauriston Pl., tel. 0131/536 4958, 9 A.M.–3 P.M. and 7–9 P.M. Mon.–Fri., 10 A.M.–noon Sat.–Sun.). Dentists will charge standard NHS rates and should be used in emergencies only. Remember to bring a method of payment with you.

The **Royal Infirmary of Edinburgh** (Old Dalkeith Rd., tel. 0131/536 1000) is Edinburgh's main hospital, with a round-the-clock accident and emergency department. Take bus 33, 49, or (longer) 24. The **Royal Hospital For Sick Children** (9 Sciennes Rd, Marchmont, tel. 0131/536 1000) is for children 13 and under.

The most central **police station** is on Gayfield Square, Leith Walk (tel. 0131/556 9270).

Laundry

Hotels, as well as most hostels, now offer laundry facilities; it's either going to be complimentary or, more likely, the same price per load as anywhere else, around £3–4.

Sundial Launderettes have several branches in the city including one at 7 East London Street (tel. 0131/556 2743, 8 A.M.–7 P.M. Mon.–Fri., 8 A.M.–4 P.M. Sat., 10 A.M.–2 P.M. Sun.). On Southside there is **Tarvit Launderette** (7–9 Tarvit St., tel. 0131/229 6382). If you need a dry cleaner, there is **Johnson's Dry-Cleaners** (Frederick St., New Town, tel. 0131/225 8095, 8 A.M.–5:30 P.M. Mon.–Fri., 8 A.M.–4 P.M. Sat.).

Travel Agencies

The specialists in cheap and budget travel are **STA Travel** (27 Forest Rd., tel. 0131/226 7747, www.statravel.co.uk, 10 A.M.–6 P.M. Mon.–Wed. and Fri., 10 A.M.–7 P.M. Thurs., 10 A.M.–5 P.M. Sat.). Meanwhile, **Thomas Cook** (52 Hanover St., tel. 0131/226 5500, 9 A.M.–5:30 P.M. Mon.–Tues. and Thurs.–Sat., 10 A.M.–5:30 P.M. Wed.) won't get you as good a deal but does have a currency exchange.

Photography

Edinburgh is one of the world's most photogenic cities, with Calton Hill and the Scott monument as well as Salisbury crags and the castle having great views. Get photographic accessories at **Jessops** (150 High St., tel. 0131/557 5575) or **Castle Photographic** (16 Bank St., The Mound, tel. 0131/225 4312).

Getting There

Edinburgh has a smaller airport than Glasgow International but still handles its share of international flights. In terms of train connections, Edinburgh has the best links with London and England of any place in Scotland.

AIR

Edinburgh International Airport is six miles west of the city center. You'll find all the usual services including a selection of shops, cafés, and bars, as well as currency exchange, car rental facilities, and an executive lounge. For additional information on flights outside Scotland see *Getting There* in the *Essentials* chapter.

There are frequent flights to other parts of the United Kingdom, Europe, and more limited services to the Middle East, Asia, and Africa. There are now direct flights from North America from Atlanta, Georgia (Hartsfield-Jackson Atlanta International Airport to Edinburgh with Delta Airlines, daily), and Newark, New Jersey (Newark Airport to Edinburgh with Continental Airlines, daily), but these are in their infancy and therefore pricey. To reach Edinburgh from North America, flying to London and then catching a train could be a better option. Alternatively, fly to Glasgow, from where it is an hour to Edinburgh by train or bus. **British Airways** (tel. 0845/773 3377, www.britishairways.com) serves Inverness, Stornoway, Orkney, and Shetland on a daily basis. Sample flight times from Edinburgh include London Heathrow (1 hour 20 min.), Amsterdam (1 hour 20 min.), Paris (1 hour 55 min.) and Prague (2 hours 25 min.). It takes 7–10 hours to fly to Edinburgh from the U.S. east coast, depending on whether you have to change planes or not.

RAIL

Edinburgh's main station, Waverley, is one of the U.K.'s prettier stations, slap bang in the middle of the city. It has a rail travel center (4:45 A.M.–12:30 A.M. Mon.–Sat., 7 A.M.–12:30 A.M. Sun.) for inquiries and ticket bookings, luggage storage facility (7 A.M.–11 P.M., beside platform one), currency exchange, and a handy Marks and Spencer supermarket, as well as numerous places to eat. Trains to or from the west of Scotland will also generally call at Haymarket (use this station for destinations in west Edinburgh and the airport) and sometimes Edinburgh Park. There's a shuttle service between Edinburgh and Glasgow every 15 minutes (55 min., £10.80) and frequent service to major destinations across Scotland.

National

There are trains at least hourly from Edinburgh to Stirling (50 minutes, £6), Dundee (1.25 hrs., £18), and Aberdeen (2.5 hrs., £36). Trains to Inverness (3.5 hrs., £36) run every one to two hours; there are three to four trains daily to Wick (8.5 hrs., £47). If you book online, you may well get tickets cheaper than the standard fares listed.

International

The east coast line from London Kings Cross to Edinburgh is Britain's fastest. It's less hassle and less costly than flying from London and takes only marginally longer. It will cost around £100 for the journey, which takes as little as four hours and 20 minutes.

BUS

Edinburgh's main bus station is just north of St. Andrew's Square. It's the hub for National Express buses from the south as well as **Scottish Citylink Buses** (tel. 0870/550 5050, www.citylink.co.uk), Scotland's main bus company. Facilities include locker storage of varying sizes (cheaper than Waverley luggage storage) and information desks for the various companies operating (company desks will only answer questions on their own buses). It's quite small but there is a café and a news agent, both of which close early. If you're getting a bus out later in the evening, the St. Andrew's area generally closes down early (around 6 P.M.)—plan ahead to get those journey snacks in.

National

Buses, mostly run by Citylink, run from Edinburgh to most destinations within Scotland including Stranraer (£16, four hours), Dundee (hourly, 1.75 hrs., £10.40), Inverness (several daily, 4 hrs., £19), Aberdeen (several daily, 3.25 hrs., £20), Fort William (several daily, 5 hrs., £23), and Wick (twice daily, 7–8 hrs., £26).

There is also **Megabus** (tel. 0900/160 0900, www.megabus.com) for bargain fare hunters, operating between Edinburgh, Glasgow, Perth, Aberdeen, and Inverness. Megabus does not connect the rural areas, and while it can have fares for £2 or £3, it's worth noting that Scottish Citylink are now matching and often bettering Megabus price-wise for the destinations for which they compete. Book online for Scottish Citylink and Megabus for deals cheaper than the standard fares listed.

International

National Express (tel. 0871/781 8181, www.nationalexpress.com) runs several buses daily from London Victoria coach station to Edinburgh (9–10 hrs., from £22). Other companies plying this route are Megabus and **Silver Choice** (tel. 01355/249499, www.silverchoice.co.uk), which offers round-trip tickets for £24.

CAR

Edinburgh is one hour east of Glasgow by road and between seven and eight hours north of London. Car journey times can be expected to be quicker, although not always that much, than buses. Edinburgh is linked to Scotland's rather minimal motorway system, but this does not seem to help relieve traffic at busy times. When traveling out of Edinburgh, avoid peak commuter hours (7–9 A.M. and 4:30–6:30 P.M.) as roads like the A90 over the Forth Bridge get notoriously congested.

SEA

If you're coming from Europe, one way to beat the hours of driving up through England is with **Superfast Ferries** (www.superfast.com), which run between Rosyth, just across the Forth Road Bridge and Zeebrugge in Belgium (16 hours, £58 weekday standard to £86 weekend in high season).

Getting Around

The best way of getting around Edinburgh's Old Town is on foot. New Town, too, is easily negotiable by walking. If you do get footsore, a taxi is a better bet to get to a destination in New Town from the Old Town. Bus routes and waiting times mean they are more practical for journeys farther out. Edinburgh's public transport system is solely buses.

TRAVEL TO/FROM AIRPORT

An **Airport Shuttle Bus** runs every 15–30 minutes between the airport and pick-up/drop-off destinations within the city (£9 per person, discounts for groups of people traveling to same destination). **Airlink 100** runs every 10 minutes between the airport and Waverley Bridge by the train station from 4:20 A.M. (Waverley Bridge) and 4:45 A.M. (airport) until after midnight. It costs £3 one-way or £5 round-trip. **Bus Service N22** connects the airport with the Ocean Terminal at Leith, running every 30 minutes through the night. **Lothian Bus 35** runs every 15 minutes throughout the day Monday–Saturday and hourly throughout the day on Sundays from the airport to Leith. Bus services cost £1.10 one-way or £0.60 for kids.

A taxi to or from the city center takes 20–25 minutes and should cost around £15. If you're driving to the airport from Edinburgh, follow the A8 west out of town from the city bypass toward Glasgow. If you're coming from the north/west, join the A8 at Newbridge round-about then follow signs.

BUS

Lothian Buses (tel. 0131/565 6363, www.lothianbuses.co.uk) run most routes in greater Edinburgh, while destinations farther out in the Lothians are run by **First Group** (tel. 0870/872 7271, www.firstgroup.com), including to Linlithgow, South Queensferry, and North Berwick.

For exploring areas outside the city center, Edinburgh's bus network is highly reliable once you've mastered it. The problem, especially if you're starting out at Princes Street, is knowing which side of the road the stop is on. The Edinburgh and Scotland Information Centre (3 Princes St.) offers a guide with detailed Lothian bus route maps in the back. If you are unsure about which stop your bus leaves from on Princes Street, the bus stop on Waverley Bridge (Gardens side) tells you the stop you need for certain destinations. Virtually all Greater Edinburgh routes, wherever they go, pass through the city center on or near to Princes Street.

Useful routes include:

- The **15,** which runs from Musselburgh along the coast to Portobello then through the city center south to Bruntsfield (for many of the Southside B&Bs, Morningside, and Rosslyn (for Rosslyn Chapel).

- The **24,** which runs from the Royal Infirmary (for Craigmillar Castle) through the city center northwest to Cramond and then south to Edinburgh Park train station.

- The **11,** which runs from Fairmilehead north through Morningside, Bruntsfield and the city center up to Newhaven, then east to the Ocean Terminal at Leith (for Royal Yacht *Britannia*).

- The **12,** which runs from Portobello through Pilrig to the city center, then west through Haymarket and Murrayfield (for Murray-field Rugby Stadium), past Edinburgh Zoo to the Gyle Centre.

Buses run every 15–30 minutes along most routes. A Lothian Bus one-way fare costs £1.10/0.60 adults/children, but if you're making more than two journeys a day, buy the day pass for £2.50/2 adults/children. If you're staying a while in the city, the **Ridacard** (£13 for one week) might work out cheaper: these can be purchased at a **Lothian Bus Travelshop** (7 Shandwick Pl., 27 Hannover St., or 31 Waverley Pl.). Make sure you have exact change for Lothian Buses, and on all buses, just buy standard tickets on board.

TRAIN

Edinburgh has no metro or separate rail system. Waverley, Haymarket, and Edinburgh Park stations are connected by train, but it's as convenient and cheaper to take a bus. Trains are the quickest, most pleasant way of traveling to destinations within the Lothians.

TAXI

Maybe because of the tricky roads, or maybe because they know they can, Edinburgh taxis charge pretty steep prices by Scottish standards. To avoid a shock, you may want to check when booking what the anticipated journey time is and what the cost will be. There are taxi stands across the city, including at Princes Mall, at the west end of Princes Street, and at Waterloo Place. You can hail taxis, too: available ones should have an illuminated For Hire sign. Taxis are metered; tipping is up to the individual but not necessary. Expect to pay at least £5 for a two-mile journey. Despite their price, bear in mind that longish journeys with a full cab can work out almost as cheap per person as public transport. Cab companies include **Central Taxis** (tel. 0131/229 2468), Edinburgh's largest taxi fleet, as well as **City Cabs** (tel. 0131/228 1211) and **Radio Cabs** (tel. 0131/225 9000).

CAR

Driving is fine for out-of-town destinations like Linlithgow or South Queensferry but in the city is not advised. Streets are narrow, crowded with people, often one-way and just far more pleasant if you're not encumbered by a car. Parking is also difficult; if you're staying outside the center make use of parking facilities there and use public transport. The center of the capital is better negotiated on foot or by bike (see *Sports and Recreation* for bicycle rentals).

Car Rental

All the main car rental companies have offices at the airport and the city center. The big companies will charge about £35 a day for their smallest car to around £135 for a week. It's worth comparing this with a few of the local companies, which will have less variety but better prices. Insurance, a little on top of the standard rental price, is always worth taking. **Arnold Clark** (Seafield Rd. East, Portobello, tel. 0131/312 4444 or 0844/815 0162, www.arnoldclark.com) offers day hire from £17. There is also **Condor** (45 Lochrin Place, Tollcross, tel. 0131/229 6333) and **Lo-Cost** (1a Wardlaw Terr., off Slateford Rd., tel. 0131/313 2220).

West Lothian

West Lothian is mostly pleasantly dull commuter territory, sandwiched between Edinburgh to the east and Glasgow to the west. There are a couple of major exceptions, however: places with bags of their own character and history that make perfect day trips from Edinburgh. These two places, Linlithgow and South Queensferry, sport respectively one of the most impressive ruined palaces and one of the most gorgeous pub-dotted high streets in all Scotland.

LINLITHGOW

Twenty miles west of Edinburgh, Linlithgow retains a lot of its century-old market town charm, unlike a lot of the other commuter towns between Edinburgh and Glasgow. Its prime attraction is the stupendous ruin of Linlithgow Palace, birthplace of Mary, Queen of Scots.

Sights

Set in a park overlooking a loch, vast 15th-century **Linlithgow Palace** (tel. 01506/842896, 9:30 A.M.–5:30 P.M. daily Apr.–Sept., 9:30 A.M.–4:30 P.M. daily Oct.–Mar., £5.20 adults, £4.20 seniors, £2.60 children) is most well known as the birthplace of Mary, Queen of Scots in 1542. Mary did not stay long at the palace. She was taken to Stirling Castle at just seven months; from there, following Scottish defeat at the Battle of Pinkie to Henry VIII, she was sent to France for her own safety. A warren of rooms and passageways are set around a central courtyard in a style similar to that of a French chateau. The cavernous **Great Hall,** with its stone fireplace at one end, is the most striking feature. Bonnie Prince Charlie briefly stopped by the palace in 1745. In the palace courtyard is **The Kings Fountain,** said to be the oldest surviving fountain in Britain, built in 1537. It's decorated with elaborate heads—those of people and mythical creatures. The fountain only spouts water on summer weekends in an effort to conserve the stonework—a far cry from the days when it flowed with wine to welcome the arrival in Linlithgow of Bonnie Prince Charlie. The entrance fee includes access to the grounds. Next to the palace is **St. Michael's Church,** where James IV was visited in 1513 by a spirit telling him not to go to war with England. Had he listened, catastrophic defeat for the Scots at Flodden may have been avoided.

Above the town runs the delightful Linlithgow Canal, accessed up a set of steps up from the police station and then a short walk left. Here prettily painted canal boats are moored beside the **Linlithgow Canal Centre** (www.lucs.org.uk, 2–5 P.M. Sat.–Sun. Apr.–Oct., also 2–5 P.M. Mon.–Fri. July–Aug.), where there is an informative museum on the development of the British canal network (free entry) and a café in a converted stable. The center runs **boat trips** on the canal along the town stretch (half-hourly, 2–4:30 P.M., £3 adults, £1.50 children); out west to spectacular

© LUKE WATERSON

Linlithgow Canal Centre

views from Britain's second-largest aqueduct, the Avon aqueduct (2–4:30 P.M., £8 adults, £6 children); and on various occasions throughout the summer to the Falkirk Wheel (tel. 01506/843194 for details). You can even charter your own boat for £50 per hour. The canal has a towpath making for a good walk or cycle.

Accommodations and Food

There are several bed-and-breakfasts in the town center, but it's worth the seven-minute drive/half-hour walk along the canal to **Belsyde Farm Bed and Breakfast** (tel. 01506/842098, www.belsydehouse.co.uk, £30 s, £60 d), a friendly old farmhouse. Breakfasts are so big there's a menu to list all the courses. Rooms are clean and tastefully furnished; not all are en suite but there are wash basins in the rooms. The beautiful garden has views out to the Ochill Hills. Tucked away in the trees here is also a **caravan site** (berths from £6 per night). Belsyde is just off the A706 out of town.

The best bet for eating or drinking is right by Linlithgow town square. The **Four Marys** (tel. 01506/842171, food served noon–3 P.M.

and 5–9 P.M.) is a welcoming traditional pub serving quality ales and bar food. Linlithgow is also blessed by bakeries and cafés serving freshly baked cakes and bread. Try **Rolls Around** (15 The Cross, tel. 01506/671212, 8:30 A.M.–4 P.M. Mon.–Sat.) or the **Coffee Neuk** (11 The Cross, tel. 01506/847042, 9 A.M.–4:45 P.M. Mon.–Tues. and Thurs.–Sat. and 9 A.M.–3:45 P.M. Wed. and Sun.) clustered around Linlithgow Cross in the town center.

Getting There

On the main Edinburgh–Glasgow line, Linlithgow is well served by trains, with four hourly (20 min., £3.70) to Haymarket and Waverley Stations. The Stirling bus 38/X38 leaves Edinburgh's Waterloo Place four times per hour, reaching Linlithgow after 55 minutes (£2.40).

◖ SOUTH QUEENSFERRY

Often referred to as Queensferry (and not to be confused with North Queensferry, on the other side of the Firth of Forth), this pretty village sits below the massive Forth Bridge and Forth

THE BURRY MAN

Around 9 A.M. on the second Friday in August, South Queensferry's **Ferry Fair** kicks off with a bizarre and rather disturbing sight. A man, covered head to toe in burrs, begins his tentative progress through the town center in one of Britain's last surviving pagan traditions. For two hours before, he will have been dressed in hundreds of the burrs, the sticky spiked fruit of the burdock plant collected during the previous week, leaving only his eyes and mouth free. Then, adorned with a hat of flowers, he will make his way to the first stop of the day, the Provost's House, where he is given a whisky slurped through a straw. He then continues throughout the day, wandering the streets wordlessly (talking being extremely difficult), being plied with more whisky and money wherever he goes.

One cannot help asking, "Why?" The answer is that no one really knows. Many think it dates back to ancient fertility rituals and is a way of ensuring a good crop for the following year; others maintain "burry" is a corruption of "burgh," as South Queensferry was formerly a royal burgh. Whatever the explanation, the Burry Man is believed to bring good luck, spread by showering him with gifts of money or whisky. Bad luck is certainly induced by staring into the Burry Man's deep burr-rimmed eyes.

Road Bridge, consequently looking rather diminutive. Ten miles northwest of Edinburgh, it's established itself as a center of gourmet cuisine with an assortment of pubs and restaurants along the pretty high street to make most places in the capital green with envy. The town is also home to the Burry Man Festival.

Sights

The **Forth Bridges** on either side of the village span a river-crossing with a long history. Queensferry takes its name from the ferry that used to run for the benefit of pilgrims journeying to St. Andrews. In the 11th century, Queen Margaret, wife of Malcolm III, ensured that there was a settlement here to supervise regular ferry crossings to what is now North Queensferry. The popularity of the crossings, which was notoriously uncomfortable and often dangerous, meant that other schemes for crossing the Forth were considered. It was some 800 years before a plan was put into action and the **Forth Bridge**, or Forth Rail Bridge, was opened in 1890. The crossing came at a price: At least 57 men lost their lives and 54,000 tons of steel were used. The ferry kept soldiering through the Forth until 1964, when the **Forth Road Bridge** opened. The two feats of engineering are best viewed from a path leading off the main road to Dalmeny Station, past the bowling green.

For further information on the history of the bridges and the ferry that preceded it, check out the **Queensferry Museum** (53 High St., 10 A.M.–1 P.M. and 2:15–5 P.M. Mon., Thurs., Fri. and Sat., noon–5 P.M. Sun., free) in the district council offices.

In the middle of the Firth of Forth, **Inchcolm Island** has long been an important historical site. Known as the "Iona of the East," with its monastic buildings scattered above a rugged shoreline, it was allegedly visited by Columba in A.D. 567 and named after him in the 12th century. By this stage hermits were already well established on the island, and the remains of a **Hermits Cell,** thought to date from as early as the 9th century, are within the grounds of the well-preserved **Abbey** (tel. 01383/823332, 9:30 A.M.–5:30 P.M. Apr.–Sept., possibly 9:30 A.M.–4:30 P.M. Sat.–Wed. in Oct.) founded in gratitude by King Alexander I after he was sheltered by hermits while marooned on the island in 1123. Throughout the War of Independence the island suffered raids by the English. On one occasion the sailors stole the Abbey's treasures but on running into bad weather thought they were being pursued by the wrath of St. Columba and promptly returned them. Notable rooms within the abbey include the refectory, complete with reading alcove and octagonal chapterhouse. Admission to the abbey is included in the ferry price. There are World War II fortifications, including a tunnel on the island's east side.

Maid of the Forth (tel. 0131/331 5000, info@ maidoftheforth.co.uk) is a ferry company making three trips daily to the island during high season, taking three hours there and back including 1.5 hours on Inchcolm (£14.70 adults, £12.70 seniors including the landing fare).

The work of renowned Scottish architects William Bruce and William Adam, **Hopetoun House** (tel. 0131/331 2451, 10 A.M.–5 P.M. Apr.–Sept., group appointments available by reservation throughout year) is one of the most magnificent examples of Georgian architecture in Britain. Once you've admired the sumptuous ballroom with its Aubusson tapestries and the State Dining Room, where George IV once feasted, check the view from the roof terrace: Hopetoun is set in 150 acres of landscaped parkland, including a deer park, with phenomenal surrounding views. The splendid Stables Tearoom, where racehorses once lived in accommodations as elegant as most nobles of the time, does excellent champagne afternoon teas. Admission to the house and grounds is £8/7 adults/seniors or £3.70/3.20 to the grounds only.

Accommodations and Food

The main reason to come to town may be for the trip out to Inchcolm, but the **Hawes Inn** (under Forth Bridge, tel. 0131/331 3190, food served noon–10 P.M. Mon.–Sat. and until 9:30 P.M. Sun.), right by the Inchcolm Ferry pier, is worth the trip in itself. Dating back 400 years, it was from here that Robert Louis Stevenson was said to have looked out and been inspired to write *Treasure Island*. The bar area itself, with myriad nooks and crannies and an open fire, is big enough to get lost in. You can stay here in one of 14 spacious rooms, named after characters in Stevenson novels. Room number 5 is where Stevenson himself stayed. Try one of the single malt whiskies, said to have revived many a bridge worker at death's door. The wholesome pub food is good value, with mains at £6–10. With 16th-century gables

below a 19th-century railway bridge, the Inn merits a look even if you do not need refreshment. The charming High Street with its elevated pavement is home to **Hawthorne House** (15 West Terr., tel. 0131/319 1447, £25 s, £50 d), where clean rooms done up in cooling colors come with breakfast.

If you try seafood just once during your time in the Lothians, make it at the **Boat House** (19b High St., tel. 0131/331 5429, www.theboathouse.info, noon–2 P.M. Thurs.–Sat., noon–3 P.M. Sun. for lunch, 5:30–10 P.M. Mon.–Sat., 5–8 P.M. Sun. for dinner), with what can only be described as a world-class view from its restaurant over the Firth of Forth. Starters are £3–8, mains £15–19, and there's a terrace overlooking the beach to enjoy that aperitif. It's mainly a place to come and try exquisite seafood; the restaurant is on the lower floor, while there's a quality deli on street level where more fishy things are on offer. The **Ferry Tap** (36 High St., tel. 0131/331 2000), in a charming, whitewashed building on the main street, also does good homemade food, but it's the range of ales that is the real knockout. It's more a local haunt than a tourist bar, so you might get a few inquisitive stares.

Getting There

Regular train services (two per hour from Waverley, four per hour from Haymarket) connect Edinburgh with Dalmeny Station (10–12 min., £3.20), from where it's a 10-minute walk into town or a 5-minute walk to Hawes Inn via a footpath opposite the station exit north along the railway line. First Edinburgh Bus 43 leaves from Edinburgh's Waterloo Place (four per hour, 40–50 min., £2) while Stagecoach Fife 747 runs from Edinburgh Airport to Inverkeithing, with a stop at the Forth Road Bridge Toll for South Queensferry.

Dalmeny House

If you can squeeze in a visit within the scant opening hours, Dalmeny House (off A90 east of South Queensferry, tel. 0131/331 1888, 2–5 P.M. Sun.–Tues. July–Aug., other times by prior arrangement), ensconced within vast grounds stretching along the shoreline from Queensferry to Cramond, is a 19th-century house in an unusual Tudor-Gothic design. The house has the most important Napoleonic collection outside France, including the emperor's shaving stand. Note the bees it is decorated with: These were Napoleon's emblems of luck.

The unspoiled shoreline walk along the Firth of Forth, taking in quirky Bambougle Castle, is open throughout the year; it's 4.5 miles from Queensferry to Cramond. You may or may not be able to coincide your walk with the Cramond Ferry. Dalmeny is two miles east of South Queensferry, off the A90.

East Lothian

East of Edinburgh, golden fields of corn and rich agricultural land rolls away in pastoral swaths to the grassy, sandy coast. It's a great place to go to get a break from the Royal Mile crowds, and there's nowhere better than the seaside resort of North Berwick, right on the northeast coast. In the south of East Lothian, the land rises up into the Pentland and Lammermuir Hills, which separate the capital from the Borders region. Here you'll find great upland walking, all within a short distance of Edinburgh.

NORTH BERWICK

The Victorian seaside town of North Berwick is framed by sandy beaches with a harbor looking out on a string of small rocky islands jutting out of the Firth of Forth. This stretch of coast is known as the "Golf Coast" because of the number of golf courses around town.

Sights

On the rocky promontory between North Berwick's swaths of sands is **The Scottish Seabird Centre** (tel. 01620/890202, 10 A.M.–6 P.M. daily Apr.–Sept., 10 A.M.–5 P.M. Mon.–Fri., 10 A.M.–5:30 P.M. Sat.–Sun. Feb.–Mar. and Oct., 10 A.M.–4 P.M. Mon.–Fri., 10 A.M.–5:30 P.M. Sat.–Sun. Nov.–Jan., £7.95 adults, £4.50 children). It innovatively uses cameras on the Bass Rock seabird colony to send back live panoramas, projected onto giant screens guaranteed to get you closer to a wild seabird nesting colony than you would have thought possible. You can control the cameras yourself, which reveal all from guillemots to

wading birds and even basking seals. Of course there is a wealth of other information on seabirds at the center; children will love the chance to learn about being a wildlife photographer.

Boat trips also run to the former prison and religious retreat of **Bass Rock,** the craggy mound North Berwick looks out over. The rock is caked white from seabird guano: testimony to the amount of birds nesting there (100,000 per summer at the last count). The **Sealife Centre** runs photographic boat trips for groups of up to 11 for £100 per hour (minimum £200). The extra charge allows you to land on the island with an experienced guide. Several other companies run cheaper boat trips to the islands around North Berwick including Bass Rock, some with extras like angling, diving, or trips to the other islands off the coast. Try **Pegasus** (tel. 01620/890022), which does diving. Expect to pay £7.50–20 per person for a Bass Rock excursion lasting around 1.5 hours.

The conical hill of **North Berwick Law** to the east of town is a prominent feature on the landscape for miles around. A steep path leads from the car park off the B1347 to the summit, where there are the remains of a Napoleonic lookout tower and glorious views of the Lothian coastline. Along the coast two miles to the east of town on a rocky headland is **Tantallon Castle** (near North Berwick, tel. 01620/892727, 9:30 A.M.–5:30 P.M. daily Apr.–Sept., 9:30 A.M.–4:30 P.M. daily in Oct., 9:30 A.M.–4:30 P.M. Sat.–Wed. Nov.–Mar., £4.70 adults, £3.70 seniors, £2.35 children) almost an extension of the sheer cliffs it rises from.

This was the stronghold of the Douglas earls of Angus, still standing despite repeated sieges by James IV, James V, and Oliver Cromwell. Even the English Army's chant "Ding Doon Tantallon" (Bring down Tantallon) as they attacked in 1528 did not break the castle. The English invaded and took the castle but could not fell the sturdy curtained walls.

One thing you will certainly see plenty of around North Berwick are **golf courses.** East Lothian has 19 in total: contact the TIC in town for playing details or visit www.golfeast-lothian.com.

Accommodations and Food

Classified as a restaurant with rooms, the accommodation at **No. 12 Quality Street** (tel. 01620/892529, www.no12qualitystreet.co.uk, £60 s, £110 d) is in light and airy rooms with elaborate wrought iron beds and beautiful bathrooms. There's also the happening café/restaurant downstairs, of course. A short distance out of town, **Glebe House** (Law Rd., tel. 01620/892608, www.glebehouse-nb.co.uk, £80 d) is an ivy-clad Georgian manse dating from the 1780s. Rooms are richly but not excessively furnished; one even has a four-poster bed.

The town has many pleasant places to eat. One time-tested option that serves up elegant Scottish cuisine at moderately expensive prices is **The Grange** (35 High St., tel. 01620/893344, lunch and dinner daily) with a two-course set lunch for about £8. Rivaling it for price and often for quality, the **Bass Rock Bistro** (37–39 Quality St., tel. 01620/890875, noon–2 P.M. and 7–9 P.M. Tues.–Sun.) is a tapas bar with fresh seafood as the predominant theme. Mains are £15–17.

Information

The comprehensive **Tourist Information Centre (TIC)** (Quality St., tel. 01620/892197, 9 A.M.–6 P.M. Mon.–Sat., 11 A.M.–6 P.M. Sun. July–Aug., 9 A.M.–6 P.M. Mon.–Sat. Apr.–June and Sept.) has information on golfing and other matters.

Getting There

Trains run from Edinburgh Waverley to North Berwick half-hourly (40 min., £4.20). First Edinburgh bus 124/X5 (1.25 hrs., £3) runs every 20–40 minutes between St. Andrews Square (west side) in Edinburgh and North Berwick.

Dirleton Castle

Two miles west of North Berwick at Dirleton are the rambling ruins of Dirleton Castle (tel. 01620/850330, 9:30 A.M.–5:30 P.M. daily Apr.–Sept., 9:30 A.M.–4:30 P.M. daily Oct.–Mar., £4.50 adults, £3.50 seniors). This bulky ruined fortress rises out of a small rocky crag amid lush gardens that contain, supposedly, the world's longest herb border. You'll find the castle off the A198.

PENTLAND AND LAMMERMUIR HILLS

The range of hills separating the Lothians from the Borders to the South goes under three names: the Pentland Hills (South Lothian) the Moorfoot Hills (Midlothian), and the Lammermuir Hills (East Lothian). This is gently rolling, open-grazing country with few roads, easily accessible in a day trip from Edinburgh and great for walking, cycling, fishing, and even paragliding. For suggestions of walks, visit www.edinburgh.gov.uk/phrp.

BORDERS

Considering the number of visitors approaching Scotland from the south, by rights this region should be crammed with tourists. But most pass on to Edinburgh and the north, and this neglect is the area's main attraction. The ease of access to the Borders' secluded and often deserted countryside cannot be rivaled anywhere else in Scotland. From the yellowy moors in the west to the rocky coves and old fishing ports of the east, it's gentler on the eye than most Scottish landscapes. Around the four graceful border abbeys—far and away the regional trump cards—forests secrete some of Scotland's most masterful stately homes.

The Borders was not always the peaceful place it is today. Back in the 14th century, wars with neighboring England and cattle-thieving were common. Honest folk would patrol their lands on horseback to protect them, and arguments with neighboring communities over boundaries were common. Today, many towns in the Borders have carried on this tradition and hold annual commemorative festivals in which processions of colorfully dressed townspeople follow riders on horseback along the old boundaries. The festival at Duns is one of the most renowned, but rivalry between these towns is traditionally strong—voicing preference for one in the wrong place could make you unpopular! This rivalry comes to a head in the annual Melrose Rugby Sevens championships, the oldest of its kind in the world.

Most visitors head for the attractive towns of Melrose and Kelso, with abbeys, grand houses aplenty, and leafy parks. The River Tweed

© LUKE WATERSON

HIGHLIGHTS

◖ **Melrose:** Catch a game of Rugby Sevens and enjoy the exquisite blend of historical sights and captivating countryside (page 89).

◖ **Dryburgh Abbey:** One of the grandiose border abbeys, peaceful Dryburgh Abbey has an enviable location in river-flanked woodlands (page 93).

◖ **Selkirk:** Bite into a bannock and watch a performance at tucked-away Bowhill Theatre (page 94).

◖ **Kirk Yetholm:** At the foot of the Pennine Hills, this is the base for some top British hill walks (page 97).

◖ **Traquair House and Gardens:** Scotland's oldest inhabited house comes complete with beautiful gardens and its own brewery (page 103).

◖ **Eyemouth Museum:** The museum and its moving tapestry depict the sea disaster that shaped Eyemouth's history (page 105).

◖ **Duns Summer Festival and Common Riding:** Watch this fun summer festival unfold with a Riding of the Bounds, costumed parades, and the town's menfolk competing in a traditional handball match (page 108).

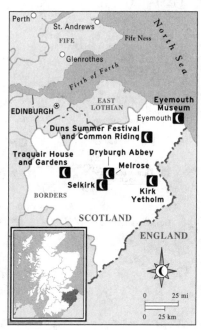

LOOK FOR ◖ TO FIND RECOMMENDED SIGHTS, ACTIVITIES, DINING, AND LODGING.

threads through both towns, and in summer there are great walks on the sheltered banks, making for a calming pastoral feel. Peebles, farther up the Tweed to the west, is an ancient royal burgh from which hills roll away south onto barren Ettrick moor—an outdoor-lover's paradise. Farther east beyond Kelso is the coastal town of Eyemouth, with its haunting tapestry depicting the loss of its townsfolk during a terrible storm in the 19th century.

HISTORY

The Romans came to the Borders but declared the region unconquerable, describing the area as "Britannica Barbarica." In A.D. 122, under the emperor Hadrian, it was decided it would be best to keep the troublesome tribes out

rather than bring them under Roman rule, and to this end a great wall was built. Hadrian's Wall spanned some 70 miles from the mouth of the River Tyne down to the coast of Cumbria (just to the south in modern-day England) but the defensive barrier divided peoples that grew to have a lot in common. The people of the Borders forged close ties with Northumbria in England, mainly through the wool trade which brought prosperity in the 9th to 12th centuries A.D. Abbeys were built at Melrose, Kelso, Dryburgh, and Jedburgh as showpieces of what Scotland had to offer. When Scottish-English tensions flared into the Wars of Independence during the 13th and 14th centuries, the abbeys bore the brunt of the destruction. Prosperity turned to devastation: A whole swath of

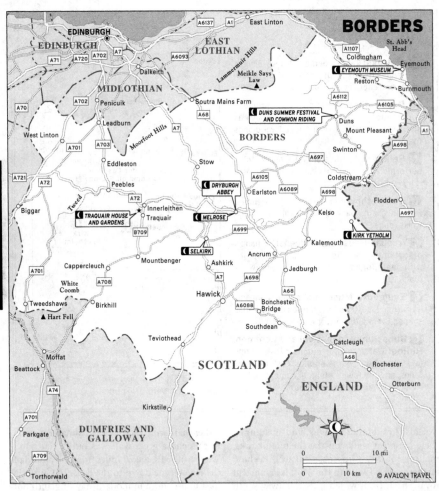

border country became a perilous no-man's-land where families that had formerly traded now carried out vicious raids on each other's territory. Communities were fiercely protective of their territory, and townsfolk would risk their lives to scout boundaries on horseback looking for territorial encroachments by their neighbors. These events became known as "Common Ridings."

Peace had been established again in the region by 1750. In the early 1800s, Sir Walter Scott, drawn to the region by romantic tales of the Border Reivers (raiders), settled here and was inspired to write some of his greatest works. It was a good time to be capturing the Borders in prose; the end of the 18th century saw widespread prosperity return with the boom of the textile trade. Towns like Galashiels and Hawick became major centers of high-quality wool production, and the money flowed for the building of fine town houses and architecturally brilliant country mansions, turning the region into the affluent place it had been centuries before.

PLANNING YOUR TIME

With a couple of days to spare, head for the border abbey town of Melrose, where there's an abbey, pretty shops and restaurants, a historic rugby rivalry to soak up, and umpteen walks in the heart of gorgeous Borders scenery. Melrose is the ideal place for a number of great side-trips, and many other main Borders attractions like Kelso are close by. With four or five days, you could divide up your time between Melrose (two to three days), the west (one day—Traquair House is the highlight) and the east coast (one to two days). There are umpteen country houses to explore and walks to do if you are blessed with more time.

Central Borders

This is the heart of the Borders in every sense: here you'll find the old ruined abbeys and the graceful stately houses exuding wealth and wonderful gardens. This is where the winding wooded riverside valleys and steep, verdant hills combine to form a backdrop every bit as impressive as the buildings it conceals—the ultimate in pastoral aesthetics. Architecture-admirers, walkers, cyclists, horse-riders, and nature-lovers: be prepared to be sidetracked for weeks.

(MELROSE

Stately Melrose cannot really be faulted: an exquisite abbey, bags of attractions, stylish places to stay, and magical ones at which to eat. The River Tweed flows through town; the land around is grassy and flat but rises up in densely wooded hills in the distance, almost like a specially created amphitheater with the town taking center stage. Sir Walter Scott seized inspiration from the surrounding countryside on his wanders; his house at Abbotsford is nearby. Melrose is also home of the sporting scuffle otherwise known as Melrose Rugby Sevens. The best education on this version of rugby is to watch a game at the local stadium.

Sights

Despite being raided four times, **Melrose Abbey** (tel. 01870/822562, 9:30 A.M.–6:30 P.M. daily Apr.–Sept., 9:30 A.M.–4:30 P.M. Mon.–Sat., 2–4:30 P.M. Sun. Oct.–Mar., £5.20 adults, £4.20 seniors), rising out of the grassy fields on the outskirts of the town center, has extensive remains. Ruin-wise, this is possibly the most fun to explore of the border abbeys. After a final wrecking by Henry VIII's forces in 1544, the last monks left the abbey complaining it was too cold to inhabit during winter. The abbey church, almost wholly intact today, continued in use until 1810. The abbey has had some famous patrons over the years. Robert the Bruce helped with refurbishment after Edward II's army attacked Melrose in 1322 and has his heart buried on site; Sir Walter Scott championed the abbey's restoration in the 19th century. The adjoining museum has some interesting artifacts found in the abbey on display.

Sir Walter Scott moved to the impressive residence of **Abbotsford** (tel. 01870/752043, www.scottsabbotsford.co.uk, 9:30 A.M.–5 P.M. daily June–Sept., 9:30 A.M.–5 P.M. Mon.–Sat. and 2–5 P.M. Sun. Mar.–May and Oct., by appointment Nov.–Mar., £6.20) on the banks of the river Tweed in 1799 and lived here until his death in 1832. The move was prompted by his appointment at Selkirk Sheriff Court in 1799. The interior is pretty grand, with suits of armor on display, a collection of artifacts on display, including Rob Roy's Gun, and the magnificent library, which holds the author's collection of over 9,000 books. You can walk the grounds, too; there's a walled garden and a woodland walk to the riverbanks.

Melrose Rugby Heritage Centre (Melrose Rugby Football Club, tel. 01870/822993, 11 A.M.–3 P.M. Mon., Wed., and Fri., free) is located at the rugby club, which now has this exhibition of rugby memorabilia, focusing on

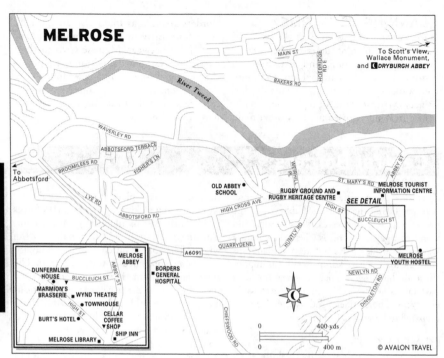

the town's historic links with the origins of "Sevens." With rugby being such a big thing locally, you'll be able to contribute knowledgably to those pub discussions on the subject after a visit here.

Entertainment

The best (and only proper) **pub** in town is the **Ship Inn** (East Port, tel. 01870/822191); it does food (lunches noon–2:30 P.M. Mar.–Dec.) by a warming fire and has a smattering of friendly locals and a beer garden.

The intimate **Wynd Theatre** (off Buccleuch St., tel. 01870/820028) hosts a variety of pantomime, theatrical, dance, and music performances on a sporadic basis, often with a local theme.

Sports and Recreation

Melrose is famous for its **rugby,** mainly "sevens" but also league. The rugby pitch is on Galashiels Road, a couple of minutes' walk from the town center. Contact **Melrose Rugby Club** (tel. 01870/822993) for information on forthcoming matches. In 2008, the 125th anniversary of the birth of "Sevens" rugby, a tournament with guest teams from around the world took place. The Sevens Event occurs each April.

Walking is a justifiably popular local sport. The stretch of the **Borders Abbeys Way** from Melrose to Dryburgh Abbey passes by the distinctive and dramatic **Eildon Hills** and offers easy access to some great scenery. For better views, try following the stretch of the **St. Cuthbert's Way,** which follows a higher route through the Eildon Hills.

A great network of lanes in the surrounding area means **cycling** is popular, too. A 57-mile route forms the **Border Abbeys Cycle Route,** but there are some great afternoon rides to be had: the B6356 via Scott's view linking up with Smailholm Tower and Mellerstain House, for example.

© LUKE WATERSON

Melrose Abbey, one of the magnificent ruined Borders abbeys

Accommodations

In **Melrose Youth Hostel** (Priorwood, tel. 01870/822521, Mar.–Sept., dorms from £13.75) is the proof that Melrose even does budget accommodation with grace. In a park overlooking the abbey, this sedate Georgian mansion frequented by walkers is the essence of border country—a plush building in attractive countryside. The two two-bed rooms are the best deal in town.

The **Old Abbey School** (Waverley Rd., tel. 01870/823432, from £35 s, £54 d) offers three rooms (two double) in a converted schoolhouse, all of which are en suite or with private bath and come furnished with armchairs. There's private parking and bicycle lock-up. One of the most attractive town center bed-and-breakfasts is **Dunfermline House** (3 Buccleuch St., tel. 01870/822411, £30 s, £55 d) with four en suite rooms yielding great views across to the abbey.

Early 18th-century **(Burts Hotel** (Market Square, tel. 01870/822285, www.burtshotel.co.uk, £60 s, £116 d) has been proudly managed by the same family for 35 years: Expect a friendly yet highly professional standard of service. The 20 rooms are attractive, florally finished affairs, and there's a choice of relaxing spots: the private garden, the peaceful first-floor lounge, or the bar with its cask-conditioned ales for the sampling. The formal, starched-linen-tablecloth restaurant is open for lunch (noon–2 P.M.) and dinner (6–9 P.M.) year-round.

The other elegant town center accommodation option is **The Townhouse** (Market Square, tel. 01870/822645, www.thetownhousemelrose.co.uk, £70 s, £100 d), the snazzy, modern counterpart to Burts—it's run by the same people. Three of the bedrooms have hot tubs—think modern with a healthy dose of traditional grandeur thrown in. The restaurant with its ornate, open fireplace and dark wood tables is a stylish place for an evening feast. The four-course evening menu (£28.50) can include anything from char-grilled Aberdeen Angus steak to roast monkfish tails with sesame seeds and chili sauce.

Food

Cellar Coffee Shop (17 Market Sq., tel. 01870/823224, 9:30 A.M.–4:30 P.M. Mon.–Sat.) is a wonderful surprise at the back of Abbey Fine Wines wine shop/deli. Here, a few tables largely commandeered by old gossiping locals have been set out. Order at the counter; the menu is pretty varied and does simple food exquisitely well. You really should try the warmed cheese scones. It gets better: Not only are you now sitting in the middle of one of the Borders' best wine selections, but there's also an on-site glass engraving service. Think about stocking up that larder and buying that present.

(Marmion's Brasserie (Buccleuch St., tel. 01870/822245, www.marmionsbrasserie.co.uk, 9 A.M.–10 P.M. Mon.–Sat.) is special even by Melrose standards: It's been going 20 years and was instrumental in putting the Borders region on the culinary map. Certainly the restaurant seems to go from strength to strength. Boldly innovative mains start at £10.25; try the venison with red wine and chocolate sauce and winter vegetables (£14.25). Melrose theater-goers get 10 percent off their bill. The restaurant is named after "Marmion," the Sir Walter Scott poem.

Information and Services

Melrose TIC (tel. 0870/608 0404, 10 A.M.–5 P.M. Mon.–Sat., 10 A.M.–2 P.M. Sun. Apr.–Sept., extended hours during July–Aug., 10 A.M.–4 P.M. Mon.–Sat., 10 A.M.–2 P.M. Sun. Oct., 10 A.M.–2 P.M. Sat. and Mon. 10 A.M.–4 P.M. Sun. Nov.–Mar.) is at Abbey House, opposite the abbey. It stocks maps and books.

Melrose's post office is on Buccleuch Street, while **Melrose Library** (18 Market Sq., tel. 01870/823052, 10 A.M.–1 P.M. and 2:30–5 P.M. Mon. and Wed., 2:30–5 P.M. and 5:30–7 P.M. Fri.) has free Internet access. If you have a health emergency, **Borders General Hospital** (tel. 01870/826000) is to the west of town off the A6091.

Enterprise Rent-a-Car (David Harrison Ford, tel. 01896/755100) has an office in Galashiels a few miles to the northwest: a free pick-up drop-off service is available. Hire starts at £17.85 daily for a small car.

Getting There and Away

First Bus 8/8A/9/9A makes hourly journeys to **Galashiels** (20 minutes), from where there are frequent buses to **Edinburgh** via **Peebles** (service 62, change sometimes required, two hours). The useful bus 62 also runs from Melrose to Edinburgh five times per day throughout the week. You'll miss the direct buses if you start traveling later in the day.

Services including buses 68 and 71 run to **Jedburgh** about hourly. Bus 72 makes at least eight journeys per day Monday–Saturday to **Selkirk** via the **Borders General Hospital.**

AROUND MELROSE

A trip around the Melrose countryside is a must; few other towns in Scotland have such lovely, undulating country so close. The steeply wooded country around the winding River Tweed also has arguably the finest border abbey, at Dryburgh. You can cover the sights easily by car, but cycling or by horseback is more in keeping with the sedate ambience of this pocket of Scotland.

© LUKE WATERSON

The Wallace Monument gazes down from a hilltop above the lush Melrose valley.

SIR WALTER SCOTT'S PASSION FOR SCOTLAND

You don't have to travel far in southern Scotland to find evidence of Scott's enthusiasm for Scottish heritage: He was at the heart of projects from the rediscovery of the Scottish Crown Jewels in Edinburgh Castle to the restoration of Melrose Cathedral. Few authors have been able to romanticize Scotland like Scott, but his passion was more for preserving or re-creating Scotland's colorful history; writing was just a means for him to do this.

He was an avid historian and collector as well as a writer and was often more enthusiastic about the research he did for his books than he was about the writing of them. When researching his novel *Rob Roy*, for example, he made the long journey to Rob Roy's cave at the north of Loch Lomond and then failed to mention it in the book altogether. Scott was an incredible multi-tasker; while writing the book he was also busy writing articles on chivalry, building his new house at Abbotsford, and showing Washington Irving the best of the surrounding countryside.

It was his childhood passion for the ballads of the Borders region that inspired him to move to the area and write one of his earliest works, "The Minstrelsy of the Scottish Borders" (1802). He spent years making ballad-collecting trips – longer than he devoted to any of his subsequent novels. Again, the end product was a deviation from his painstaking research, with many ballads totally rewritten to his own verses. This anomaly of extensive research and highly fictional write-ups continued throughout his literary career. He would even go to the pains of acquiring artifacts relating to his chosen subjects (such as Rob Roy's gun), but his novels are best known for their romantic flights of fancy. His personal favorites among his novels were the Waverley Trilogy, because they successfully captured an important period in Scottish history, although the novels were not remembered for their historical accuracy.

Scott had a deep effect not only on the Scottish literary scene but also on Scottish mentality, perhaps best evidenced today by the Scottish tourism industry, which glosses over the bad bits of the country's history and hypes up the good bits. Scott always argued with his critics that he was faithful to the "spirit" of Scottish history – perhaps he realized that, whatever the truth may be, we all want a happy ending to the story.

Scott's View and Wallace Monument

Scott's View, Sir Walter's favorite spot to walk to, is a pretty formidable viewpoint: panoramic vistas of Borders countryside framed by the lumpy Eildon Hills, a tract of forest, and the glimmer of the Tweed, brightened with gorse. A little farther along the B6356 road, the Wallace Monument (open year-round) stands dramatically above the bracken overlooking the forest below. The monument was commissioned by David Stuart, 11th earl of Buchan. The earl was passionate about recording Scotland and its heroes but most passionate of all about himself; he once threw a party dressed up as Apollo on Mount Parnassus and invited nine local maidens to play his muses in attendance. Another even more bizarre and fascinating structure commissioned by Stuart stands at the valley bottom near Dryburgh—the Temple of the Muses, a recently refurbished Greek pavilion.

◖ Dryburgh Abbey

Moody, mysterious Dryburgh (tel. 01870/822381, 9:30 A.M.–5:30 P.M. daily Apr.–Sept., 9:30 A.M.–4:30 P.M. daily Oct.–Mar., £4.70 adults, £3.70 seniors) has a totally different atmosphere from the other border abbeys, courtesy of the fact that Dryburgh no longer really exists as a village. Cut off from the nearby village of St. Boswells by the looping River Tweed, which borders it on three sides, the abbey in a glorious patch of flower-carpeted woodland is a secluded spot, and a poignant place to ponder the fate of the monks who once lived here. The exceptionally well-preserved chapter house, along with the remnants of a dormitory above, give a rare insight into what day-to-day life at the abbey would have been like. You can reach the abbey on minor roads from St. Boswells.

Smailholm Tower

One minute you're traveling through sedate farmland, the next you're on an exposed stretch of moor looking out at the wind-buffeted outcrop of rock this tower house (tel. 01573/460365, 9:30 A.M.–5:30 P.M. daily Apr.–Sept., 9:30 A.M.–4:30 P.M. Fri.–Wed. Oct.–Mar., £3.50 adults, £2.50 seniors.) sits upon. It's easy to see what fired Sir Walter Scott's imagination when, as a child, he used to come and stay at this, his grandfather's residence. The Scotts moved from their family home of over a century to a more sheltered location nearby before Walter was born. The superb collections of tapestries on the upper floors reflect Scott's interest in ballads of the region. The tower is four miles northeast of St. Boswells off the B6404.

◖ SELKIRK

The little town of Selkirk tumbles down the steep slopes of the valley of Ettrick Water on the eastern edge of the vast Ettrick Forest. Its attractive center is, unusually, at the top of the town and makes for a good wander. Despite its size, Selkirk has had its fair share of association with the biggest names in Scottish history. It was here that William Wallace was declared guardian of Scotland and that novelist Sir Walter Scott took up the job of local sheriff. The colorful Common Riding is in June.

Sights

Built in 1803, **Sir Walter Scott's Courthouse** (Market Place, tel. 01750/20096, 10 A.M.–4 P.M. Mon.–Fri., 10 A.M.–2 P.M. Sat.–Sun. May–Aug., 10 A.M.–4 P.M. Mon.–Fri., 10 A.M.–2 P.M. Sat. Mar.–Apr. and Sept., 1–4 P.M. Mon.–Sat. Oct., free) is where the novelist Sir Walter Scott dispensed justice to the folk of Selkirkshire. It's

a wealth of information on Scott's life, works, and his time as sheriff.

A drive through thickly wooded grounds brings you to the lavish **Bowhill Theatre, House, and Gardens** (three miles west of Selkirk, off the A708, tel. 01750/222204 (theater), 10 A.M.–5 P.M. daily July–Aug., 10 A.M.–5 P.M. Sat.–Sun. and holidays May–June, 10 A.M.–5 P.M. daily over school Easter holidays in Mar.–Apr., house 1–4:30 P.M. July). It's the home of the Buccleuch family in Scotland and includes a host of world-class paintings. There are works from Raeburn to Gainsburgh and Van Dyck, some original Walter Scott manuscripts, and some of Queen Victoria's gifts to various duchesses. However, one of the main reasons to come here is neither for this nor the extensive woodland walks but for one of Scotland's most memorable theater experiences: an intimate 72-seat venue hosting a range of year-round music and drama, with an attached candlelit courtyard restaurant. House, country park, and courtyard admission is £7 or £3 for just the park.

Events

One of the most history-steeped common ridings of them all is **Selkirk Common Riding** (tel. 01750/20096, www.selkirk.bordernet.co.uk/commonriding), which takes place in June. It's among the longest continuously celebrated Common Ridings and traces its origins to the battle of Flodden in 1513, in which just one Selkirk man returned alive holding the town banner. Selkirk, a former county town, has carried on a tradition of fierce independence ever since. Seeing the townsfolk dressed in the town colors of blue and scarlet on Common Riding day, singing about Flodden and their shoemaking heritage, is an entertaining spectacle.

Accommodations and Food

Not only is the **County Hotel** (3–5 High St., tel. 01750/721333, Selkirk, £39 s, £110 d) the best place to stay in town, it's practically the only one. Unlike a lot of the disappointingly run-down places, this place makes a real effort to offer decent rooms. They come with all the gadgets: Freeview and DVD players as well as extra little touches like bathrobes. Conveniently, this is also the best place to eat in town. The house specialty: Bonnie Prince Charlie Steak (stuffed with haggis and Drambuie sauce).

Don't bother trying to find a prettier place to stay (or to feast, for that matter) than the 17th-century coaching inn that is the ❰ **Cross Keys Inn** (Ettrickbridge, tel. 01750/52224, www.cross-keys-inn.co.uk, £42.50 s, £75 d), some six miles southwest of Selkirk on the B7009. One simply doesn't exist. You're well into the remote Ettrick Forest here and there's a real feeling of isolation. The five crisp en suite rooms, done up in bright pastel colors, will make you think of spring. Tasty pub grub is available (lunches noon–2:30 P.M. Wed.–Sun., evening meals 7–8:30 P.M.), and there are over 40 single malts to sample.

The best place to get a **Selkirk bannock** is **Camerons** (40 High St., tel. 01750/20373). It claims to be the only baker in the world to freshly and authentically bake these local delicacies (you'll get excited about this, too, once you've tried them!).

Information

Head to the pretty, seasonal **TIC** (tel. 01750/20096, 10 A.M.–5 P.M. Mon.–Sat., 10 A.M.–1 P.M. Sun. July–Aug., 10 A.M.–5 P.M. Mon.–Sat., 10 A.M.–noon Sun. Apr.–June and Sept., 10 A.M.–4 P.M. Mon.–Sat., 10 A.M.– noon Sun. Oct.) attached to Halliwell's House Museum (including a re-created ironmongers shop and displays of local art upstairs) for a host of useful local information. A large car park with one of the priciest public toilets around is nearby.

Getting There and Away

First Bus 95/X95 is something of a local lifeline, connecting Selkirk with Edinburgh, Galashiels, Hawick, and Carlisle. It runs every half hour as far as Hawick, every hour all the way to Carlisle. Catch Bus 72 (at least eight per day) to get to Melrose.

THE BANNOCK

The flat, traditionally oatmeal griddle cake otherwise known as the bannock has been adopted in various forms throughout Scotland, but none are quite as famous as the Selkirk Bannock. A thicker, richer, more buttery version of the traditional recipe mixed with fruit, the Selkirk Bannock was first made by Robbie Douglas, who opened his shop in Selkirk in 1859. He could little have anticipated its success, assured forever when Queen Victoria, visiting Sir Walter Scott's granddaughter at nearby Abbotsford, refused all else but the cake to take with her tea.

For such a plain, unassuming snack, its reputation traveled far; bannocks became popular in the eastern provinces of Canada with Scottish emigration there. Somehow the bannock found its way, through Scottish fur traders, to become a Native American favorite, too, from the 18th and 19th centuries onward. The condensed extravaganza of carbohydrate was favored by tribes like the Canadian Metis for the ease with which it could be made while traveling.

KELSO

Kelso has a spacious feel, with a huge cobbled main square (Scotland's largest) and wide streets branching off. It's an attractive, bustling market town—and knows it, too—with the River Tweed arcing like a silver streamer through the center and its abbey just off the main square. The street names give away what a jack-of-all-trades Kelso has been through the ages: Horsemarket, Woodmarket, Coalmarket, Distillery Lane. Up the road from the square is the embedded horseshoe allegedly cast by Bonnie Prince Charlie when he passed by in 1745 on his advance into England. It's a happening town, too; there's something going on most weekends in summer with events you won't see the like of anywhere else in Scotland.

BORDERS

Sights
In front of the Town Hall can be seen the remains of the old **Bull Ring,** where animals were tethered on market days.

Building began on **Kelso Abbey** (Bridge St., 9:30 A.M.–5:30 P.M. daily Apr.–Sept., 9:30 A.M.–4:30 P.M. daily Oct.–Mar., free) to the southeast of the square in 1128; before being reduced to rubble by English soldiers it was one of the finest examples of Romanesque architecture of its day and the wealthiest border abbey. The English found more to loot and therefore the abbey suffered most in the border conflicts. Today the towering remains have less to offer than some of the other abbeys in the area but do have the bonus of being free to explore.

Entertainment and Events
One of the finest old **pubs** in Kelso is the **Red Lion** (Crawford St., tel. 01573/224817) at the back of the town square beyond the Cobbles Inn. It's a proper local's pub where you can toast yourself in front of the best open fire in town as you sip your ale or whisky (a hefty selection of each is available). There's a games room, too.

In June, Kelso hosts Scotland's biggest **Dog Show,** second in the U.K. only to Crufts. Traditionally held on the last Friday and Saturday of July, the **Border Union Show** is the showcase agricultural show of the region, with a setting on Springwood Park, on the banks of the Tweed.

Sports and Recreation
Kelso Racecourse (tel. 01573/224767, www.kelso-races.co.uk) has been voted Britain's friendliest and is also one of Britain's oldest. If horseracing is your thing, or if you fancy seeing what it is all about, the course is one of the most scenic around and has 14 races throughout the season. It's north of town, off the B6461.

Accommodations
Ivy Neuk (62 Horsemarket, tel. 01573/226270, from £25 s, £56 d) is a centrally located amiable Victorian guesthouse. It's a real bargain, too, with three well-appointed rooms and a mean breakfast. Don't book that lunch after all—you really won't need it.

There's a quiet air of magnificence to **Duncan House** (Chalkheugh Terr., tel. 01573/225682, www.tweedbreaks.co.uk/duncanbb.htm, £40 s, £60 d). Get ready for large, antique-furnished rooms with dark wooden beds and sofas, bathrooms with stand-alone baths, and a grand dining room with a table that would not look out of place in a medieval banquet hall. You can admire wonderful views of the meandering Tweed from beside a cozy fire; you'll find it hard to beat them from anywhere else in town.

Old Victorian **Edenbank House** (Edenbank, tel. 01573/226734, www.edenbank.co.uk, £30 s, £60 d) is a country house in sheep fields two miles outside Kelso. It's a great find: the rooms are individually styled and you can look out of your window and practically see where your breakfast has come from before munching away on it in the 1890s dining room, which exudes lots of dark-painted oak. It's little touches like the honey fresh from the house beehives and a pretty seating area for guests in the garden that make this place truly special.

Designed in 1761 by James Nisbet, the architect responsible for the lavish Paxton House, tranquil **Ednam House Hotel** (Bridge St., tel. 01573/224168, www.ednamhouse.com, from £81 s, £106 d) has been in the same ownership since 1928. The establishment is grand enough to boast its own ballroom. Huge, airy rooms have riverside views; go for a double, as the single is a little poky in comparison. After a hard day's fishin' or shootin' (packages can be arranged) you'll feel like relaxing in the riverside restaurant. Try highland venison with fresh tagliatelle or shark fillet. The hotel overlooks a section of the River Tweed called the **Junction Pool,** known to many anglers as the "holy grail" of salmon fishing.

Food
Boo Coffee House (6 Roxburgh St., tel. 01573/223848, www.boocoffeehouse.co.uk,

9:30 A.M.–4:30 P.M. Mon.–Sat.) is a great little place where local folk meet to put the world to rights. You can perch at a table or flop on one of the sofas (both seem equally popular). The coffee, cake, and panini deal has got to be the best lunchtime bargain around—it sets new standards of scrumptiousness in all three areas.

It's hard to find something the 19th-century **(Cobbles Inn** (7 Bowmont St., tel. 01573/223548, food served noon–2 P.M. and 6–9 P.M. daily) doesn't do exceptionally well, be it morning espresso, filling pub lunches, or regionally brewed cask ale. There's a fine malt whisky and wine selection, and the added bonus is that a local folk group meet here on Fridays for a jam—you couldn't ask for a better introduction to Borders hospitality.

If you like fine wines (and don't mind paying the price for them), then **Oscars Wine Bar and Restaurant** (35–37 Horsemarket, tel. 01573/224008, 5 P.M.–late) is surely the place to come. Rest assured: the food here is no afterthought, as the many foodie quotes that fill this place indicate. You could start with the haggis and mozzarella pastry parcels and then move on to a main like the roast rack of border lamb. Mains are around £10.

Information

The **TIC** (Town Square, tel. 0870/608 0404, 9:30 A.M.–5:30 P.M. Mon.–Sat., 10 A.M.–2 P.M. Sun. July–Aug., 9:30 A.M.–5 P.M. Mon.–Sat., 10 A.M.–2 P.M. Sun. June and Sept.–Nov., 10 A.M.–5 P.M. Mon.–Sat., 10 A.M.–2 P.M. Sun. Apr.–May, 10 A.M.–2 P.M. Fri.–Sat. and Mon. Jan.–Mar.) in the town hall building can give pointers on the many things to do in and around town. It also has a good selection of Scottish music.

Getting There and Away

Munros, the main local operator, runs bus 20 nine times daily between Kelso, Jedburgh, and Hawick. Munros also runs bus 52 between Kelso and Edinburgh (about every hour, 1 hr. 50 min.). Bus 67 goes 7–9 times daily via **Coldstream** to **Berwick,** the nearest railway station.

AROUND KELSO

The stately setting of Kelso gives an indication of what to expect in the surrounding countryside: fine country houses and great walking.

Floors Castle

In a wide swath of open green, this castle (tel. 01573/223333, 11 A.M.–5 P.M. daily Easter weekend and May–Oct., £6.50 adults, £5.50 seniors) certainly pulls in the crowds. One cannot help thinking it's because of the restaurant and gift shop as much as what there is to see, but then again, it is the largest occupied house (the word seems a bit out of its depth here!) in Scotland. William Adam designed the somewhat plain-looking mansion, converting it from the tower house it originally was in the 18th century, and William Playfair made some incongruous 19th-century additions. These included the turrets, which look as though they would have crumbled at the first whisper of a cannon.

(Kirk Yetholm

Up in the yellow-green foothills of the Pennine Hills, which soar away south some 250 miles into England, Kirk Yetholm is full of footsore walkers in season gasping upon completion of the arduous **Pennine Way,** one of Britain's toughest long-distance footpaths. The **St. Cuthbert's Way** also passes through en route to Lindisfarne in Northumberland. It's a pretty village centered on a large green and hasn't succumbed too much to tourism like many Scottish hill-walking centers. Other than the gorgeous walking, there isn't a lot happening, although once the village was the home of the Yetholm gypsies, who settled close to the border to avoid persecution from both England and Scotland. The last King of the Gypsies died in the 1880s.

If you want to stay at **Kirk Yetholm Youth Hostel** (by Kirk Yetholm Green, tel. 01573/420639 or 0870/155 3255, Mar.–Sept., dorms £14), book well in advance as hikers are quick to fill up the beds. The **Border Hotel** (Kirk Yetholm Green, tel. 01573/420237, www.theborderhotel.com, £45 s, £90 d) is a good place for a pint of hand-pulled ale and

© LUKE WATERSON

The village of Kirk Yetholm, right on the English border, is a great base for hill walking.

a filling meal beside a blazing fire. There are plenty of sweet stodgy deserts to replenish the carbs. You could always stay if you don't feel like moving, and rooms include Scottish breakfast for a good start.

The village is about eight miles southeast of Kelso, from where Bus 81 makes the hourly journey (20 minutes) to Kirk Yetholm.

Coldstream Museum

Military enthusiasts, prepare to get excited: In the bright little town of Coldstream right on the border is this museum (12 Market Sq., tel. 01890/882630, 10 A.M.–4 P.M. Mon.–Sat., 2–4 P.M. Sun. Easter–Sept., 1–4 P.M. Mon.–Sat. Oct., free), which charters the history of the Coldstream Guards. It's a pretty illustrious history, too: The regiment was formed in Berwick-on-Tweed as part of Oliver Cromwell's New Model Army and is the oldest regiment in continuous service in the British Army today.

Bus 67 from Kelso runs to Coldstream seven to nine times daily en route to Berwick on Tweed in England.

JEDBURGH

Pretty by day and a little creepy by night, Jedburgh is dominated by its abbey. The town relies on this and its association with Mary, Queen of Scots, who stayed here for four weeks while convalescing from a journey and presiding at the local courts, to pull in the tourists. Jedburgh's less appreciated but more meaningful association is with the "father of geology" James Hutton (1726–1797). At Inchbonny Braes, about 300 yards south of the town car park, Hutton discovered rock formations that dated the earth at several million years old, in stark contrast to the few thousand years estimated previously. Unfortunately, the rocks are on private ground.

Sights

The magnificently carved arches of **Jedburgh Abbey** (tel. 01835/863925, 9:30 A.M.–5:30 P.M. daily Apr.–Sept., 9:30 A.M.–4:30 P.M. daily Oct.–Mar., £5.20 adults, £4.20 seniors) can be seen from some distance. Even after being sacked three times it's a formidable first impression of

entrance to Jedburgh Abbey

the town and was originally founded in 1138, largely as a boast. David I wanted to show the English that even as close to their border as this, the Scots could still build just as grandly as their neighbors to the south. The boast held strong for about 150 years, until it became a key target for the English in the Wars of Independence and fell for the first time. The cloister garden is based on a typical abbey garden of around 1500, and there are 8th century carved slabs on display in the visitors center.

Nothing remains of the 12th-century Motte and Bailey fortress destroyed by Scots to deny advancing English forces; the Victorian **Jedburgh Castle Jail and Museum** (Castlegate, tel. 01835/864750, 10 A.M.–4:30 P.M. Mon.–Sat., 1–4 P.M. Sun. Apr.–Oct., £2 adults, £1.50 seniors and children) is now the only building on-site. It's a fascinating insight into prison life and, interestingly, depicts life from both a prisoner's and a guard's point of view. The Jailers House has a duller exhibition on Jedburgh as a royal burgh.

Mary, Queen of Scots was only here for a month in 1566, but nowhere else in Scotland is the complex story of her life told so fully as at the **Mary Queen of Scots House** (Queen St., tel. 01835/863331, 10 A.M.–4:30 P.M. Mon.–Sat., 11 A.M.–4:30 P.M. Sun. Mar.–Nov., £3 adults, £2 seniors) near the abbey in a pretty garden full of pear trees. Mary's stay here was lengthened by an illness that nearly proved fatal; later, when held prisoner by Elizabeth I she is quoted as saying, "Would that I had died at Jedburgh." There are interesting displays of tapestries, armor, and paintings, arranged in chronological order of her stormy life.

Accommodations and Food

Pine is a strong theme at lovely **Meadhon House** (48 Castlegate, tel. 01835/862504, www.meadhon.com, rooms £36 s, £53 d), where the en suite rooms have panoramic views over the abbey. There's also a vividly bright garden to enjoy. As for the town center, well, you're in it!

Distinctly less central (but then, staying in the center of Jedburgh is hardly a highlight of anyone's Scottish holiday) is **The Steadings** (Chesters, tel. 01450/860730, £25 pp). It's one of the first lodgings you'll see trundling into Scotland towards Jedburgh. The Steadings is a converted stables built by the enterprising owner, who is constantly adding to the house. It has warm en suite rooms and does big breakfasts, including the brilliant continental-style breakfast with oodles of cheese, meat, and fruit. It's a well-worth-it seven miles southeast of Jedburgh, a lovely drive down tree-studded lanes (be warned: there are two places called Chesters in these parts).

At 300-year-old **Hundalee House** (tel. 01835/863011, Mar.–Nov., rooms from £30 s, £50 d) you can stay in a four-poster bed, wander a rambling apple orchard, and watch the long-horned cattle moseying through the grounds. Rooms have character but bathrooms are shared. Be sure to try the homemade honey at breakfast, too.

Simply Scottish (6–8 High St., tel. 01835/864696, 9 A.M.–4 P.M. Mon.–Thurs., 9 A.M.–5:30 P.M. and 6–9 P.M. Fri.–Sat.) is a

BORDERS

© LUKE WATERSON

BORDERS

FORTIFYING THE BORDERS

During the Wars of Independence and afterward in medieval Scotland, the Borders, as the gateway to the country, was the most vulnerable area to attack. The threat was not just from the English army but also from marauding parties of border raiders, groups of bandits from the no-man's-land on either side of the hotly disputed border. The Borders' main problem was that it was a predominantly rural region; there were no major towns, and therefore defenses were poor. It was not as if townsfolk had a huge castle like Edinburgh Castle to shelter within in times of attack. Each community traditionally carried out an annual inspection on horseback of its boundaries to check no inroads had been made into them, known as the "Riding of the Bounds." This has been the basis for several key festivals in the Borders region, known as "Common Ridings," in which various towns continue the traditional

district boundary inspection with plenty of extra pomp thrown in. At the time, the "Riding of the Bounds" could be an extremely dangerous pursuit, as riders could encounter those of a neighboring community doing the same thing. Needless to say, disagreements often arose and flared into full-blown fighting.

Ridings were only carried out once a year, however, which was no defense against a sudden attack. Therefore, across the Borders region, fortified keeps or tower houses were built. They were erected primarily as signal towers so others could be alerted of any danger. Wardens of the tower houses had an important task: they had to be ready at any moment to light a signal fire from the top of the tower. To be caught dozing on the job was a serious offense. The tower houses, which became known as Peel Towers, were also designed to be defended with arms if necessary.

stylish place that, with its polished wooden floors and bright tablecloths, has raised the bar a few notches in the Jedburgh dining scene. It's simple but innovative fare and carries on dishing it up throughout the day, from breakfasts through to sizzling steaks at suppertime. Light bites start around £4, mains £9–15.

《 The Nightjar (1 Abbey Cl., tel. 01835/862552, 6–9 P.M. Tues.–Sat.) is an intimate little venue just up from the market square. It's a great bet for an evening meal, blending Scottish cuisine with a Thai slant. It's about as close as Jedburgh restaurants get to being a home away from home. This entails a few tables in a cozy 18th-century building, a cheery informal atmosphere, and a small but spectacular menu featuring the mouth-watering courgette, mushroom, and ewe's cheese strudel. Mains are £10–15.

Information

Jedburgh's year-round **TIC** (Murray's Green, tel. 01835/863170, 9 A.M.–7 P.M. Mon.–Sat., 10 A.M.–6 P.M. Sun. Aug., 9 A.M.–6 P.M. Mon.–Sat., 10 A.M.–5 P.M. Sun. June–July and Sept.,

9:15 A.M.–5 P.M. Mon.–Sat., 10 A.M.–5 P.M. Sun. Apr.–May and Oct., 9:30 A.M.–4:30 P.M. Mon.–Sat. Nov.–Mar.) is a candidate for Scotland's friendliest tourist information office.

Getting There and Away

Munros run most of the local bus services. Bus 20 connects Jedburgh with Kelso and Hawick. Bus 51 runs to Edinburgh hourly (one hour, 50 minutes). Change in Newton St. Boswells for services to Melrose or catch the frequent bus 68, which will stop at Borders General Hospital, too.

HAWICK

The region's main shopping center and town is Hawick (pronounced hoik), which sees a lot of visitors on the hunt for knitwear bargains. There are few reasons to stop in this rather sterile town unless you want to do the same, although it's a good center for information on the surrounding area.

Hawick's **TIC** is contained within **Drumlanrig's Tower** (tel. 01450/377615,

10 A.M.–5 P.M. Mon.–Fri., 10 A.M.–1 P.M. and 2–5 P.M. Sat., noon–3 P.M. Sun. Apr.–Sept., 10 A.M.–5 P.M. Mon.–Fri., 10 A.M.–1 P.M. and 2–5 P.M. Sat. Mar. and Oct., £2.50), a Peel Tower House with an exhibition on the town's history as a hub of border rivalry (far more interesting than its present).

If you're in need of refreshment, the best sit-down option is a branch of the classy coffee-house chain **Beanscene** (tel. 01450/376228, 9 A.M.–11 P.M. daily), something of an arts venue and a surprisingly trendy place in these parts to sip your cappuccino or beer in relaxing environs. Otherwise, there's the huge **Morrisons Supermarket** off Union Street, where the world and his wife seem to hang out.

Being the size it is, you may have to use Hawick for local transport connections. Bus 95 and X95 connect Hawick with Carlisle, Selkirk, Galashiels, and Edinburgh (half-hourly).

Peebles and Ettrick Forest

If it's peace and quiet away from the tourist noise that you want, this is the region to head to. The ancient royal burgh of Peebles has a history of peacefulness, escaping the border conflicts largely due to its status as an ancient royal burgh. The forested valley it sits in isn't typical of the region: The Ettrick Forest, an old royal hunting ground, pushes almost up to its boundaries but is itself mostly open, brown moorland. The area lends itself well to outdoor pursuits, whether fishing on the fat, winding waters of the River Tweed close to town, golfing, or taking off into the hills on foot, horseback, or bike. The major attraction is Traquair House, nestled at the foot of Ettrick Forest near Peebles.

PEEBLES

Peebles is an old prosperous market town hugging the banks of the Tweed in a wide forest-fringed valley that tempts walkers and cyclists with its variety of routes. There are a couple of buildings in town of historical interest, but most people use Peebles as a convenient base for the superb walking, cycling, horseback-riding, fishing, and golf in the area. It's an ideal place to stay for the outdoor enthusiast who likes a few creature comforts come sundown.

Sights

Off Cross Road in town to the west of the High Street are the ruins of **Cross Kirk** (open year-round), founded in 1261. Two miles from Peebles, **Neidpath Castle** (west of Peebles on A72, tel. 01721/720333, 10:30 A.M.–5 P.M. Wed.–Sat., 12:30–5 P.M. Sun. May–Sept.) is a remarkably intact 14th-century tower house castle in a tree-lined gorge by the River Tweed. Off the B7062 two miles southeast of Peebles are **Kailzie Gardens** (tel. 01721/720007, 11 A.M.–5 P.M. daily Mar.–Oct., Wild Garden and Woodland Walks only during daylight hours in winter), featuring a walled garden and Scotland's oldest larch tree, planted in 1725.

Entertainment

For a good pub, head to the **Bridge Inn** (Port Brae, tel. 01721/720589). You can take your ale out to the terrace if you don't fancy sitting with the locals in the cozy interior, but make sure you get views of the river rather than the supermarket. Don't be fooled by the exterior of the **Eastgate Theatre** (tel. 01721/725777): This 19th-century church is ultra-modern on the inside with an auditorium, café-bar, and regular live music/theater performances.

Sports and Recreation

The River Tweed between Peebles and Kelso has great **salmon and trout fishing**—arguably the country's best and certainly the longest salmon season (Feb.–Nov.). Inquire in the TIC about permits and places.

For cycle rentals, the best bet is nearby **Glentress** (bike hire tel. 01721/721736), a candidate for Britain's best biking center with all grades of trails, a bike shop with bike hire, and a café serving good coffee. Glentress is two miles off the A72 east of Peebles (follow 7stanes signs). Bus 62 goes as far as the golfing complex at Cardrona, 1.6 km away (no bikes allowed on the bus).

The big golf course in the area is the **Cardrona** (tel. 01896/833701, www.cardrona-hotel.co.uk, greens fee £45) to the east of town, designed by world-renowned golf course architect Dave Thomas. **Peebles Hydro Hotel** (tel. 01721/721325) offers a variety of family-friendly **horse rides and pony treks** to suit all levels of experience. Rides go off on tracks into the Glentress Forest.

Walk-wise, the **Southern Upland Way** cuts across **Ettrick Forest** south of Peebles, but closer to town is the 13-mile **John Buchan Way** from Peebles to Broughton. There are a number of paths in **Glentress Forest** and **Cardrona Forest.** A good walk goes along the Tweed from the town center along to **Neidpath Castle,** a four- to seven-mile round-trip depending on which trail you follow. Again, the number of trails and paths means a visit to the TIC is a good idea; staff can supply good maps and trail descriptions, and they have walked lots of the paths themselves.

Accommodations

Peebles accommodation is mostly in well-heeled hotels.

In the substantial grounds surrounding the former house of Dr. Thomas Young, who devoted many years to deciphering the hieroglyphics on the Rosetta Stone, is the lush **Rosetta Caravan Park and Campsite** (tel. 01721/720770, www.rosettacaravanpark.co.uk, Apr.–Oct., tent and one adult £5–7.50), with patches of trees providing a sheltered, grassy site—a real find so close to the town center. It's a well-appointed site ticking all the necessary facilities boxes as well as having a shop, television room, and outdoor draughts.

Exuding bygone glamour, the **Tontine Hotel** (High St., tel. 01721/720892, www.tontinehotel.com, from £45 s, £80 d) is a friendly place to stay with a quirky charm absent in some of

the town's more clinical chain hotels. There are 36 en suite rooms with color TV and telephones; the Adam Room restaurant even has a minstrel's gallery. The hotel is involved in local sports and encourages anglers, golfers, and bikers.

The former landlady of the **C Cross Keys Inn** (Northgate, tel. 01721/724222, bunkhouse £22 pp, rooms £35 s, £60 d) was the inspiration for Meg Dodds in Sir Walter Scott's Waverley novels. There's two bunkhouse rooms sleeping four each and simple comfortable rooms at this 17th-century whitewashed coaching house. It's the oldest pub in the area, warmed by a crackling fire with real ales and frequent live music.

Rooms at **Cringletie House Hotel and Restaurant** (Edinburgh Rd., tel. 01721/725750, www.cringletie.com, rooms from £200) range from a traditional four-poster to minimalist modern, all with Molton Brown toiletries and fluffy towels. This place is more a many-turreted baronial mansion than a house and could just be the most interesting accommodation in town. If you're after dinner, you can choose which room you have it in (the Sutherland has an open fire and good views of the surrounding garden). If you want to go out to eat, you can still take afternoon tea in the tearoom (there's a pile of cakes and biscuits to get through). The grounds include a walled garden, dovecote, and croquet lawn.

Food

Eastgate Theatre Cafe (Eastgate, tel. 01721/725777, 10 A.M.–5 P.M. Mon.–Sat. and on show nights) has a modern, open café/bar great for a morning tea or coffee or a pre-show glass of wine. Soups and baguettes start from around £2.50. One of Peebles' most recently opened venues, the **Courthouse Restaurant and Bar** (High St., tel. 01721/723537, 10 A.M.–late daily) is somewhere getting that mix between café and bar just about right. It's furnished with armchairs and has an outside terrace lending itself well to a coffee or beer. Snacks and appetizing lunches are £3–10.

Halcyon Restaurant (39 Eastgate, tel.

© LUKE WATERSON

Traquair House, at over 900 years old, is Scotland's oldest continually occupied house, with its own brewery to boot.

01721/725100, www.halcyonrestaurant.com, noon–2 P.M. and 6–10 P.M. Tues.–Sat.) is the pre-/post-theater restaurant of choice. Credited with bringing flashy fine dining to town, the light, bright Halycon with its walls decorated with artwork serves up some real delicacies: roasted rabbit loin, for instance, with Skye langostines, Puy lentils, and tarragon. Come here to impress your loved one: the three-course set menu is only £17.50.

Information
The business-like **TIC** (23 High St., tel. 0870/608 0404, 9 A.M.–6 P.M. Mon.–Sat., 10 A.M.–4 P.M. Sun. July–Aug., at least 9:30 A.M.–4 P.M. Mon.–Sat. Sept.–June) is a particularly good resource for information on recreational pursuits with a profusion of leaflets on each.

Getting There and Away
First Bus 62 is the most useful public transport, running regularly between Edinburgh, Pencuick, Peebles, and Galashiels with some services going on to Melrose. It's one hour to Edinburgh or Melrose and will call at Cardrona and Innerleithen (for Traquair House).

TRAQUAIR AND ETTRICK FOREST
Above charismatic and history-steeped Traquair House is some of the best walking in Scotland, in the bare hills of the Ettrick Forest (www.ettrickyarrow.bordernet.co.uk). Once a royal hunting ground, today it's more exposed moorland with occasional patches of conifers.

◖ Traquair House and Gardens
In the north, thick woods swoop down to conceal the main attraction in this part of Scotland, Traquair House (tel. 01896/830323, www.traquair.co.uk, noon–5 P.M. daily Mar.–May and Sept., 10:30 A.M.–5 P.M. daily June–Aug., 11 A.M.–3 P.M. Sat.–Sun. Oct.–Nov., £6.50 adults, £3.50 children), the country's oldest continuously inhabited house (well,

WALKING ON THE WILD SIDE

For such a small region, the Scottish Borders has an incredible diversity of walking trails, ranging from paths that commemorate the alleged steps of famous Borderers (local people) to long-distance routes there for no other reason than that they cross cracking good scenery. The longest and best-known path in the region is the **Southern Upland Way** (www.southernuplandway.com), running 212 miles/340 km from Cockburnspath on the east coast across Ettrick Forest on its way to Portpatrick in the west of Dumfries and Galloway. It's Scotland's longest footpath and one of Britain's toughest – it should not be attempted lightly. That said, this walk really does have everything: broadleaf and coniferous woodland, coastal cliffs, heathery moor, and wildlife from red deer to golden eagles. The stretch through the Borders has all of these landscapes: a testimony to the variation of the Borders scenery.

The **John Buchan Way** runs 13 miles/22 km from Peebles through a rich, forested landscape to Broughton, where the John Buchan Centre commemorates the life and works of the novelist. The **Borders Abbeys Way** is a 65-mile/104-km route linking the four Borders abbeys of Melrose, Dryburgh, Jedburgh, and Kelso, as well as the towns of Hawick and Selkirk in five separate stages. Melrose-Kelso via Dryburgh is the prettiest stage; Hawick-Selkirk is the remotest. Regional TICs stock a very good series of accompanying leaflets.

The **St. Cuthbert's Way** (www.stcuthbertsway.fsnet.co.uk) follows the footsteps of the saint from his early monastic life at Melrose Abbey to his later life at Lindisfarne. It also links up with the northern terminus of the **Pennine Way** at Kirk Yetholm. Not enough? Then try the **Sir Walter Scott Way** (www.sirwalterscottway.fsnet.co.uk) or the **Roman Heritage Way,** both of which start at Melrose.

castle), dating back to 1107. This grand former hunting lodge of the kings and queens of Scotland has many fascinating rooms including the library and a secret staircase used by priests. Peacocks strut through the forested grounds, which include a river and one of Britain's oldest breweries. If you're busing it take service 62 from Peebles to Innerleithen, then you'll have to walk 30–40 minutes or take a local taxi (tel. 01896/831333).

Ettrick Forest

Farther south beyond Traquair, grainy yellow hills offer a wealth of paths, most notably a great chunk of the **Southern Upland Way.**

The **Grey Mare's Tail Waterfall** (taking its name from the grey mare in Burns's "Tam o' Shanter"), tumbling down near the lonely A708 in the west of Ettrick Forest, is one of Scotland's highest waterfalls; take care on the path leading up, which is prone to landslides. Brooding **St. Mary's Loch** is noted for fishing. Walking around the loch makes for a pleasant stroll, and good refreshments are on hand

at the **Tibbie Shiels Inn** (at the western end). Inquire at Peebles TIC about walks in the area and make sufficient preparations: this is a barren region and help is a long way if you get into trouble. The south of Ettrick Forest gives way to high farming land and pretty villages like Ettrick.

Accommodations

Well-heated **Gordon Arms Hotel and Bunkhouse** (tel. 01750/82222, www.thegordonarmsyarrow.com, bunkhouse dorm £10 pp) is one of the few budget accommodation options in the entire Borders region, and the only one open year-round. It gets popular particularly with mountain-bikers and walkers. If times get rough, the adjoining hotel does both rooms and meals. Lifts to the Southern Upland Way footpath are available.

There are five en suite rooms with stupendous loch views and camping for small tents at the historic old **Tibbie Shiels Inn** (St. Mary's Loch, tel. 01750/42231, www.tibbieshielsinn.com, £60 d) with a remote location in the west of Ettrick Forest. Being on the Southern Upland Way, it sees a lot of passing trade in season and gets booked up well in advance. Notable visitors have included R. L. Stevenson, Thomas Carlyle, and even British Prime Minister William Gladstone. The conservatory is a good place to loch-gaze, and meals are served 12:30–8:15 P.M. Save room for one of the good stodgy deserts.

East Coast and Lammermuir Foothills

The mix of tumble-down rocky cliffs, rearing grassy headlands, and sandy bays gives the Borders' small but varied stretch of coastline the feel of southwest England. There are only a handful of small former fishing ports here, but each has its own allure: Eyemouth for its tragic, vividly remembered history, Coldingham and St. Abbs for great surfing and important birdlife. Inland, the Lammermuir hills, which separate this region from Edinburgh and the Lothians, rise to the north and west out of gentle agricultural land studded with opulent country houses.

EYEMOUTH

Avert your eyes as you pass the dull housing estate on the outskirts until you get to the corkscrew lanes around the center—now this old fishing port seems quite a charming place with some wonderful old pubs around the harbor. As the museums making up the town's attractions show, fishing has been Eyemouth's nemesis as much as its livelihood. It took the port a century to recover population-wise from the storm that drowned 129 fishermen in 1881. By the time it did, a mixture of overfishing and EU quotas, which imposed annual limitations on how many fish could be caught, had made its waters virtually unfishable. The weeklong Herring Queen Festival in July sees the local fishing fleet escort the elected queen from St. Abbs to Eyemouth.

Getting There and Away

Public transport is extremely limited: Use your own wheels if possible. Infrequent buses do make the scenic run along the A708 between Moffat and Selkirk, some continuing to Galashiels, stopping at points throughout Ettrick Forest. These include, from July to September, **Telford's Coaches** (www.telfordscoaches.com), which does one Tuesday run between Hawick, Selkirk, and Moffat (1 hr., 50 min.).

◖ Eyemouth Museum

Providing insight into fishing life in the 19th century, this museum (Auld Kirk Square, tel. 01890/751701, 10 A.M.–4:30 P.M. Mon.–Sat., 10 A.M.–1 P.M. Sun. Easter–Sept., 10 A.M.–4:30 P.M. Mon.–Sat. Oct., £2.50, ask about discounts for large groups) has as its centerpiece the moving Eyemouth Tapestry, a colorful and masterful depiction of the Eyemouth fishing disaster, produced for the centenary of the tragedy. In case you thought it was only the men who had a hard time of it in Eyemouth, think again. There is also a tribute to the "fisher-lassies" who gutted, salted, and packed thousands of fish into barrels up and down this stretch of coast.

Eyemouth Maritime Centre

A re-creation of an 18th-century frigate inside and out, this building (Harbour Rd., tel. 01890/751020, www.worldofboats.org, £2.50) on the site of the former town fish market is designed to evoke the spirit of the vast collection of maritime heritage in and around it. New in 2007, its opening exhibition was on William Bligh's voyage across the South Seas, although with over 400 boats in its possession, the stories of the sea this place could tell are pretty much infinite. An "upper deck" holds smaller maritime artifacts like figureheads.

Accommodations and Food

Browns (1 Hallydown Cottages, tel. 01890/ 551242, rooms £50) is on the outside of town overlooking St. Abbs Head, with fields sliding to the sea from the door. Expect crisp linens and an atmospheric breakfast experience (the beamed room where you'll be served has a special rustic charm) at this friendly B&B. Berwick/Eyemouth–Edinburgh buses stop at the door.

Not all of the four neat rooms at **Bantry** (20 High St., tel. 01890/751900, from £28.50 pp) have sea views, which is something of a disappointment given its proximity to the waterfront. The big draw here is the rooftop terrace where you can gaze out to sea to your heart's content. Breakfasts can be served on the terrace, and there's a downstairs seafood restaurant.

If there is one place in town that tempts you to linger, it will be (C **Oblo Bar and Bistro** (18–20 Harbour Road, tel. 01890/752527, 10 A.M.–midnight Sun.–Thurs., 10 A.M.–1 A.M. Fri.–Sat.). This is city-style sophistication in a provincial setting—a slick first-floor bar/restaurant with an informal feel, whether it's a beer or coffee or a meal you're after. You can take in any balmy evenings on the outside terrace. The tapas for two is only £11.95 (the standard price for evening meals), or you could try one of the inventive salads.

The locals hit **Giacopazzi's** (Harbour Rd., tel. 01890/750317, 9 A.M.–9 P.M. Sun.–Thurs., 9 A.M.–9:30 P.M. Fri.–Sat.) before moving on to the harborfront pubs of an evening; it's open all day for homemade pizzas and good, cheap fish and chips. However, the specialty is the ice creams (like the delectable Triple Chocolate) and sorbets, made here for over a century.

Information

The **TIC** (Auld Kirk Square, 10 A.M.–5 P.M. daily Apr.–Oct., extended hours in summer) is attached to the Eyemouth museum.

Getting There and Away

Frequent buses run the five miles south to Berwick, the nearest railway station. Buses also run north frequently to Edinburgh. These include the useful **Perryman's** service 235/253, which connects Eyemouth with Berwick, Coldingham, St. Abbs, and Edinburgh. St. Abbs buses are hourly; Edinburgh buses (change in

Coldingham for St. Abbs) are every two hours. It's more difficult getting between Eyemouth and other Borders towns directly; the once-per-day C4 service goes via Duns to Kelso.

COLDINGHAM AND ST. ABBS HEAD

Coldingham with its narrow streets and ivy-swathed closely packed houses has been attracting visitors for over a thousand years, initially to the monastery established here in A.D. 635. A lightning strike in A.D. 679 demolished the abbey—divine retribution, some said, for the allegedly indecent behavior between the monks and nuns at the time. The monastery was rebuilt as a priory, itself now a fascinating ruin. Nowadays the main visitors to Coldingham are water sports enthusiasts and bird-lovers. The village is the gateway to a fascinating stretch of rugged rocky coast pockmarked with sandy beaches and wild waters offering southern Scotland's best diving and surfing. Out of this, St. Abbs Head, an important seabird colony, rears up. From Coldingham a side road twists down to wide, windy Coldingham Bay, popular with surfers. The B6438 then continues the couple of miles to the fishing village of St. Abbs, from where a minor road leads up to St. Abbs Head. St. Abbs, part of the Eyemouth and St. Abbs Voluntary Marine Reserve, has great diving, with seals, whales, porpoises, and sharks for the spotting.

Sights

The sheer, grass-covered cliffs of **St. Abbs Head** are part of an extinct volcano: it's filled with the squabble of breeding seabirds—guillemots (murres), kittiwakes, and fulmars, to name the regulars—in season but is also important for a number of other species. A road leads right up to the reserve and lighthouse at the top, but there's limited parking. You may have to park at the bottom and walk the two miles from Northfield Farm car park in the busy season. This is a blessing in disguise, as this landscape, with its rises, dips, and great views of the ferociously battered cliffs, is spectacular. A Nature Reserve Centre (daily Mar.–Oct.) at

© LUKE WATERSON

beach huts at Coldingham Bay

the car park uses camera technology to allow visitors close-ups of nesting birds.

Diving and Surfing

Although this is one of Britain's and Europe's top cold-water dive sites, there aren't a great deal of dive and surf companies operating, so places get booked up months in advance.

Rockhouse Diving (tel. 01890/771288, www.rockhousediving.com) is based in the whitewashed house by the harbor (doubling as a bed-and-breakfast). It's run by a man with 25 years experience on the waters in these parts as a fishing vessel and dive boat skipper. He provides is a personable diving experience for £20 for two dives. If you're hungry, he and his wife can rustle you up a snack.

Sub Aqua Divers (Scoutscroft Holiday Park, tel. 01890/771669, www.scoutscroft.co.uk), on the way to Coldingham Bay, does various equipment rentals and dive packages. There is a dive shop, and the outfit does suit repair, rents children's wetsuits, and offers all levels of PADI courses and tips on what you can see down in the deeps.

St. Veda's Surf School (tel. 01890/771679, www.stvedas.co.uk) operates out of the brash-looking St Veda's Hotel right by Coldingham Bay. It's an organization with many years' experience; there's an on-site surf shop with board and wetsuit repair, equipment hire, and surfing lessons (£35 a session).

Accommodations and Food

The clean, 36-bed **Coldingham Sands Youth Hostel** (tel. 01890/771298 or 0870/155 3255, Apr.–Sept., dorms £13) in a large house high on the cliffs above Coldingham Bay, has an unbeatable location that compensates for its bland interior. No prizes for guessing who it is most popular with—surfers, of course.

Dunlaverock Guest House (Coldingham Bay, tel. 01890/771450, from £32.50 pp) is a large Edwardian house which sits at the top of Coldingham Bay hamlet. A path leads through its own private gardens to the beach. Rooms are bright, white, and wonderful; to guarantee a sea view you'll have to pay a bit more. Evening meals can be arranged and are a handy option at £18.50 for three courses: otherwise it's the tame fare at St. Vera's Hotel or a mile into Coldingham.

With the wind singing through its white-washed walls, **Castle Rock Guest House** (St. Abbs, tel. 01890/771715, from £30 s, £60 d) is every bit as exposed as its name suggests. Not that you'll mind as you sit in your sea-view room staring out at the wild sea and wondering whether to spend the day bird-watching, walking the cliffs, or trying your hand at diving to see the spectacular marinelife just off the coast. Rooms are all en suite with direct-dial telephones and color satellite TV.

The Lobster Pot (Bridge St., Coldingham, tel. 01890/771315, lunch and dinner daily) is the new, improved version of the New Inn that used to occupy this site; it's now a restaurant under different ownership retaining its old-fashioned charm. The emphasis is on seafood, served in a cozy cellar-style bar; dishes include the green onion, potato, and lobster chowder (£9.25). The owner is into his drinks with a passion—there are three Scottish ales on tap and a burgeoning range of whiskies. These days, the Lobster Pot pulls in a mixed crowd, locals and holiday-makers alike.

Cove Harbour

The tiny hamlet of **Cove,** northwest along the coast from St. Abbs, is perched right on the clifftop, yet somehow a track manages to sneak down to a **harbor,** cut into the foot of the cliff. Few people ever venture down to this place, frozen in time about 150 years ago and full of fishing nets, the odd boat, and the moan of the wind. There's a passage cut through the cliff; if it looks familiar, it's due to Cove's moment of fame in a scene in *Mrs. Brown,* a film about the life of Queen Victoria.

DUNS AND VICINITY

The small sleepy market town of Duns, sitting in pleasant farmland, is a departure from the norm in terms of Borders towns: the surrounding low, fertile hills are more like southern English countryside. It's a handy spot for several off-the-beaten-track attractions. Most activity goes on around the central square.

Don't worry if you get a few stares as you wander around—the locals are just pleased (and surprised) to see you. Information boards on the town square tell you a bit about what there is to do in the area.

Sights

Starting from Castle Street, a key attraction is the climb to **Duns Law** (you'll pass most of the town dog-walking on the way up or down). There are good views over town and toward the **Lammermuir Hills** from the top, where there's an Iron Age settlement. The **Jim Clark Room** (44 Newton St., Duns, tel. 01361/883960, 10:30 A.M.–1 P.M. and 2–4:30 P.M. Mon.–Sat., 2–4 P.M. Sun. Apr.–Sept., 1–4 P.M. Mon.–Sat. Oct.) pays homage to one of the Borders' famous racing drivers.

Just outside Duns on the A6105 is **Manderston House** (tel. 01361/883450, www.manderston.co.uk, garden 11:30 A.M.–dusk, house 1:30–5 P.M. bank holidays, Thurs., and Sun. May–Sept.) one of Scotland's most glam Edwardian houses (Georgian-themed). The highlight is the world's only silver staircase and the octagonal dairy made from marble.

◖ Duns Summer Festival and Common Riding

Each July, the Duns Summer Festival takes place, based on the town's riding of the burgh boundaries. Festivities include a horseback procession up to Duns Law, the crowning of a festival maid (a "wynsome mayde"), a fancy dress parade, and a game of "handba" or handball between the men of the town (the bachelors take on the married men). Going to a Common Riding festival like this one is a great way to get off the beaten path and tap into the turbulent history of the Borders. For more information, call the TIC in Kelso (tel. 0870/608 0404).

Accommodations and Food

Consider staying in the mild farmland surrounding Duns, which has its own special character, rather than the stuffy provincial places in town.

Up in the premiership of places to stay or eat in the area is the pebble-dashed **Allanton Inn** (tel. 01890/818260, www.allantoninn.com, rooms from £55 s, £90 d), with five brilliantly bright and spacious en suite rooms and a menu to send meat-lovers crazy and vegetarians elsewhere. There's a log fire to toast by.

A couple of rivers with good **fishing** are a few minutes walk away, about seven miles east of Duns. If you're hungry in town, pick up some fresh locally grown produce in the fruit and vegetable shop just off the main square or stop at busy **Border Baguettes** (41 Market Sq., tel. 01361/884986), which does exactly what it says on the outside. Choosing can be a challenge.

Getting There and Away

The regular First Bus 60 service between Galashiels, Melrose, and Berwick stops in Duns.

BORDERS

DUMFRIES AND GALLOWAY

Spanning southern Scotland with its gangly peninsulas and deep inlets, Dumfries and Galloway has the country's most varied and fascinating coastline: huge swaths of golden sand, sea-hugging grasslands, rocky shores backed by forests, and brightly painted fishing villages scattered in between. The coast is a key draw, but inland north of Dumfries are the towering Lowther Hills. Inland from Newton Stewart is also the Galloway Heartland, encompassing the United Kingdom's largest forest park. It's favored by outdoor enthusiasts, particularly mountain bikers, who rate its track network as one of the best and most exhilarating in the world.

However you approach the region, it's guaranteed to take your breath away, although not in the conventional Scottish way of castles, lochs, and rearing mountain peaks. It's rather its un-Scottishness that appeals most: a balmier climate, pretty coastal communities that feel as much Cornish as anything, and the refreshing lack of a tacky tourist industry.

Regional capital Dumfries's claim to fame is that Robert Burns, Scotland's national bard, wrote some of his most famous works while living and working in the area. North in the Lowther Hills is remote Wanlockhead, Scotland's highest village, a walker's paradise of huge yellow hills with a fascinating mining legacy to explore. Most visitors, though, want to head west to lose themselves along the miles and miles of unspoiled coastline.

The tracts of sandy beaches, with tranquil fishing villages peeping out from behind trees interspersed with some of Scotland's prettiest

© LUKE WATERSON

HIGHLIGHTS

The Globe Inn: Check out the poetic memorabilia at Rabbie Burns's atmospheric local and, why not, have a drink, too (page 115).

Caerlaverock: Home to the ideal fairy-tale fortress, Caerlaverock has one of Britain's most important bird sanctuaries to boot (page 119).

Kagyu Samye Ling Monastery: You can soak up serenity and splendor at Europe's first Tibetan monastery, near Langholm (page 121).

Wanlockhead: Scotland's highest village has a fascinating mining past (page 123).

Colvend Coast: Kicking back in one of the dreamy villages on this 20-mile stretch of sandy beaches is the region's top way to unwind (page 129).

Galloway Forest Park: This park is an outdoor activity lovers' bliss of hikes and mountain-biking trails through forests and moorland (page 131).

Wigtown: The country's best bookshops, osprey-watching opportunities, and the most charming distillery in the lowlands are among this rejuvenated county town's attractions (page 132).

Portpatrick and Rinns of Galloway: Eat seafood and soak up the silence in pretty Portpatrick and go bird-watching on Scotland's most southerly point (page 136).

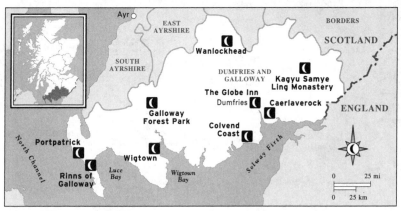

LOOK FOR (TO FIND RECOMMENDED SIGHTS, ACTIVITIES, DINING, AND LODGING.

DUMFRIES AND GALLOWAY

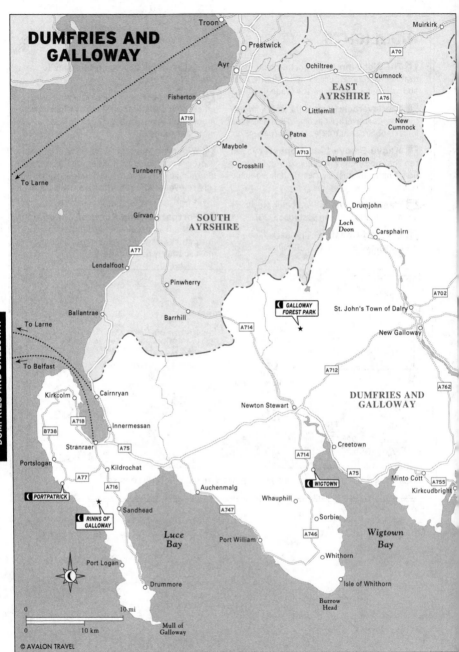

DUMFRIES AND GALLOWAY

Troon

Muirkirk

Prestwick

A70

Ayr

Ochiltree

Cumnock

EAST AYRSHIRE

Fisherton

A76

A719

Littlemill

New Cumnock

Maybole

Patna

A713

Turnberry

Crosshill

Dalmellington

To Larne

Drumjohn

Girvan

SOUTH AYRSHIRE

Loch Doon

Carsphairn

A77

Lendalfoot

A702

Pinwherry

St. John's Town of Dalry

Ballantrae

Barrhill

☾ GALLOWAY FOREST PARK

★

To Larne

A714

New Galloway

To Belfast

A712

DUMFRIES AND GALLOWAY

A762

Kirkcolm

Cairnryan

Newton Stewart

B738

A718

Innermessan

Creetown

Portslogan

Stranraer

A75

A714

A75

Minto Cott

A755

A77

Kildrochat

☾ WIGTOWN

Kirkcudbright

A716

Auchenmalg

★

Whauphill

☾ PORTPATRICK

Sandhead

A747

Sorbie

☾ RINNS OF GALLOWAY

★

A746

Wigtown Bay

Luce Bay

Port William

Port Logan

Whithorn

Drummore

Isle of Whithorn

Burrow Head

0   10 mi

0   10 km

Mull of Galloway

© AVALON TRAVEL

DUMFRIES AND GALLOWAY

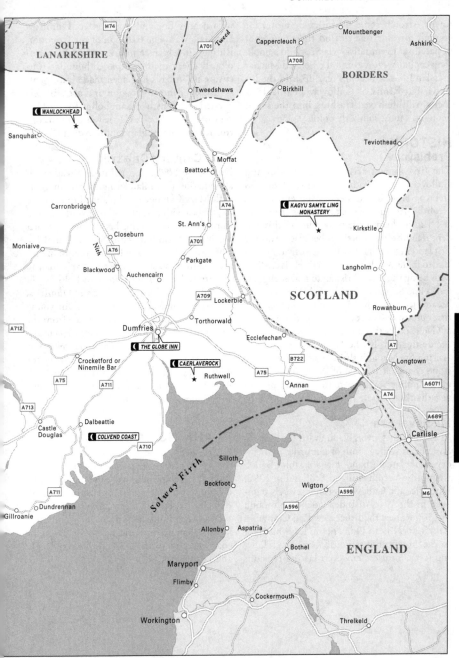

towns, stretch some 60 miles or more, far enough for everyone to find their own spot of paradise. Eventually—via Scotland's bookshop capital Wigtown and the isolated Machar grasslands—the beaches rear up into the little-visited Rinns of Galloway peninsula, a rocky wildlife haven crashing into the sea at Scotland's most southerly point.

HISTORY
Prehistory
The first known arrivals in Dumfries and Galloway were already farming the land and erecting standing stones by the end of the Neolithic Age in 2000 B.C., such as the stones at Drumtroddan. Perhaps because of this evident rich history, or perhaps because it was the first land in Scotland he came across, St. Ninian landed in the Machars in A.D. 397. He is credited with being the first Christian to make religious forays into Scotland. Whithorn, in the Machars, became the site of St. Ninian's first church. This first outpost of Christianity in a barbarous land of Gaels and Picts soon became a major pilgrimage destination. By the 12th century, pilgrims visiting St. Ninian's shrine had built another stone chapel at the Isle of Whithorn, a common landing point where they would pray to give thanks for a safe crossing.

Medieval Era
In 1273, Lady Devorgilla founded the striking Sweetheart Abbey south of Dumfries in memory of her late husband. Her son, John Baliol, went on to become king of Scotland in 1292. Dumfries and Galloway was not severely damaged in the Wars of Independence, although in 1306 Robert the Bruce slew Red Comyn in Greyfriars Kirk in Dumfries to leave his right to the crown unquestioned. Over the following few centuries, however, lasting tensions

with nearby England would affect Dumfries and Galloway. The tradition of the Common Ridings, in which communities would meticulously check their own parish boundaries to ensure no inroads had been made into them, spilled over into the region and are still celebrated in towns like Langholm. In the 17th century, Caerlaverock Castle was built to control access from England into Scotland.

18th Century Onward
During the 1780s, Robert Burns, already with a reputation for philandering, began an affair with Mary Campbell and planned to emigrate to Jamaica with her; plans didn't work out and Burns ended up marrying his long-term partner and instead taking on a farm north of Dumfries. The farm did poorly and Burns, to subsidize his income from poetry, became an exciseman in Dumfries. He died in the town in 1796.

By this time, Gretna, southeast of Dumfries, was becoming a major destination for young couples from England to marry free from the constraints of English law. In the 19th century, the west coast of Dumfries and Galloway saw many Irish immigrants arrive following the devastating potato famine in Ireland in 1845. An Irish influence in the west has pervaded ever since. Dumfries and Galloway has been united as a county since 1975.

PLANNING YOUR TIME
You'll need a good three to four days to do the region justice: the windy roads and out-of-the-way places which make the region such a delight are not designed for rushing around. Although there are a few inland sights like Wanlockhead and the Samye Linig Monastery in Eskdalemuir, focus most of your time on the coast, at places like Colvend, Kirkcudbright and Portpatrick.

Dumfries and Vicinity

This sleepy red sandstone town's nickname, "Queen of the South," will leave you wondering. This is southern Scotland's largest settlement, but only in size does it come out on top (in appeal rather lower down the list). Robert Burns spent some time in Dumfries as an exciseman; visiting the house where he lived (and died) as well as his favorite watering holes are the main reasons to stop by. While parts are run-down, the town's location on the wide, fast-flowing River Nith, together with a great theater and a handful of good places to eat and drink may well entice you to stay. One final thing: Dumfries is pronounced "Dum-freese," not "Dum-frys."

SIGHTS

Burns is the prevalent theme for the few town center attractions, all within easy walking distance of each other.

Robert Burns House

It was while he was living in Dumfries that Burns penned some of his most famous works, some certainly written in this simple sandstone house (Burns St., tel. 01387/255297, www.dumgal.gov.uk, 10 A.M.–5 P.M. Mon.–Sat., 2–5 P.M. Sun. Apr.–Sept., 10 A.M.–1 P.M. and 2–5 P.M. Tues.–Sat. Oct.–Mar., free). You can see the desk and chair where he wrote and a selection of original manuscripts. Enthusiastic staff members provide lots of fascinating extra details. There's a well-stocked, on-site shop.

The Globe Inn

Robert Burns's favorite drinking spot (56 High St., tel. 01387/252335, 10 A.M.–11 P.M. Mon.–Wed., 10 A.M.–midnight Thurs.–Sat., noon–midnight Sun., free) now has lots of Burns paraphernalia in the atmospheric little restaurant, including the chair he once sat on. If the restaurant's closed, the owners may still let you look around. The big bonus of putting this on your sightseeing itinerary is that the Globe is still a fine pub serving great beer and food.

Robert Burns Centre

In Dumfries's 18th-century watermill is this attraction (Mill Rd., tel. 01387/264808, 10 A.M.–8 P.M. Mon.–Sat., 2–5 P.M. Sun. Apr.–Sept., 10 A.M.–1 P.M. and 2–5 P.M. Tues.–Sat. Oct.–Mar., free) dragging it firmly into the 21st century—a well-presented insight into the bard's last years in town. An exhibition includes manuscripts and belongings of the poet, a life-sized Burns model and even a plaster cast of his skull. It's a vivid introduction to the Dumfries Burns package, with a great location on the banks of the Nith and an equally great restaurant. The poignant audiovisual presentation is £1.60 adults, £0.80 seniors and children. There's an arts cinema here showing contemporary films of an evening and, yes, a Burns-related gift shop.

Dumfries Museum and Camera Obscura

This museum (The Observatory, Rotchell Rd., tel. 01387/253374, 10 A.M.–5 P.M. Mon.–Sat., 2–5 P.M. Sun. Apr.–Sept., 10 A.M.–1 P.M. and 2–5 P.M. Tues.–Sat. Oct.–Mar., admission free, camera obscura £2) focuses more on general everyday life in Dumfries and Galloway over the centuries. Highlights include the collection of early Christian stones and, above all, the camera obscura at the top of the windmill, installed in 1836 and giving great panoramic views of surrounding countryside including Mabie Forest.

ENTERTAINMENT

Dumfries has some wonderful traditional pubs to drink in.

Pubs

Go on! Join in that popular local activity of a pub crawl; there's precious little else to do after dark around here, and Dumfries is a great place to do it. You can even use the excuse that you are following in Burns's footsteps and doing it for cultural reasons.

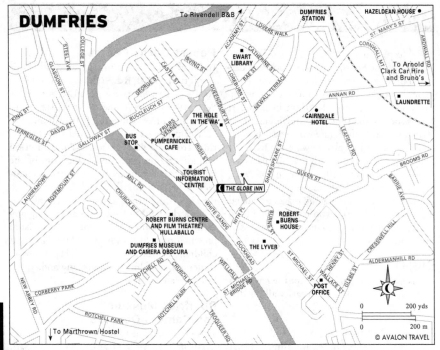

DUMFRIES

To Rivendell B&B
DUMFRIES STATION
HAZELDEAN HOUSE
LOVERS WALK
ST. MARY'S ST
CORNWALL MT
ARROWALL RD
STEEL AVE
COLLEGE ST
ACADEMY ST
CATHERINE ST
To Arnold Clark Car Hire and Bruno's
GLASGOW ST
IRVING ST
EWART LIBRARY
RAE ST
ANNAN RD
LAUNDRETTE
GEORGE ST
CASTLE ST
QUEENSBURY ST
LOREBURN ST
NEWALL TERRACE
KING ST
BUCCLEUCH ST
THE HOLE IN THE WA'
CAIRNDALE HOTEL
LEAFIELD RD
BROOMS RD
TERREGLES ST
DAVID ST
GALLOWAY ST
FRIARS VENNEL
IRISH ST
BARRIE AVE
BUS STOP
PUMPERNICKEL CAFE
SHAKESPEARE ST
QUEEN ST
LAURIEKNOWE
ROSEMOUNT ST
MILL RD
CHURCH ST
TOURIST INFORMATION CENTRE
THE GLOBE INN
BURNS ST
CRESSWELL HILL
WHITE SANDS
NITH PL
ROBERT BURNS HOUSE
ROBERT BURNS CENTRE AND FILM THEATRE/ HULLABALLOO
DUMFRIES MUSEUM AND CAMERA OBSCURA
DOCKHEAD
THE LYVER
ST MICHAEL ST
ALDERMANHILL RD
NEW ABBEY RD
CORBERRY PARK
ROTCHELL RD
CHURCH ST
WELLDALE
ST. MICHAEL'S BRIDGE RD
HENRY ST
WALLACE ST
GLEBE ST
POST OFFICE
ROTCHELL PARK
ROTCHELL PARK
TROQUEER RD
0   200 yds
0   200 m
To Marthrown Hostel
© AVALON TRAVEL

The Lyver (181–183 St. Michael St., tel. 01387/256477, 11 A.M.–1 A.M. Mon.–Thurs., 11 A.M.–2 A.M. Fri. and Sat., 11 A.M.–midnight Sun.) is a traditional, welcoming old pub with some of the longest opening hours in Dumfries and good ales. Way up the High Street, the **The Hole in the Wa'** (156 High St., tel. 01387/252770, 9:30 A.M.–11 A.M. for breakfast Mon.–Sat., until 12:30 P.M. Mon.–Fri., until 1 A.M. Sat., noon–11 P.M. Sun.) has been around since the 1580s. This popular, atmospheric little place where Burns enjoyed many a drink is so-called because in the 17th century women were not allowed inside the pub and had to be served liquor through a hole in the wall. It's a good, fun place to be, with nightly karaoke and a large outside patio. Tucked away down a narrow alleyway, **The Globe** (56 High St., tel. 01387/252335, 10 A.M.–11 P.M. Mon.–Wed., 10 A.M.–midnight Thurs.–Sat., noon–midnight Sun.) is

a cozy wood-paneled pub with a good selection of real ales and single malts. Established in 1610, this was Burns's favorite pub and it has heaps more atmosphere than any other tavern in town.

Cinema
Robert Burns Centre Film Theatre (Mill Rd., tel. 01387/264808) shows an intelligent selection of contemporary/art-house films on a weekly basis.

ACCOMMODATIONS
There are plenty of bed-and-breakfasts around the train station and several more interesting sleeping options in and around Dumfries.

◖ **Marthrown of Mabie Hostel** (tel. 01387/247900, dorm beds £15, duvet rental £3) is a great option in a region where budget accommodation is thin on the ground. The hostel enjoys a Hansel and Gretel–like setting

FISHING THE NITH WAY

Dumfries might be a little old-fashioned, but the way its local fishermen catch fish dates back to Viking times. Being too far upriver to have a fishing fleet as such, the fishing industry on rivers like the Nith involves men wading out with long nets to spread across the river shallows. The ancient custom is a bizarre sight but a very effective method – some say too effective. Anglers farther upriver have complained of vastly reduced numbers of fish. With the tourist industry relying on visitors coming to the region specifically for its great fishing, it looks like this historical fish-catching method could die out for good.

two miles up a forest track (vehicle access possible) just outside of Dumfries. You can stay in a bunkhouse, tepee, or the only traditionally made Celtic roundhouse in the country where a sleepover is possible. The forest has plenty of activities on the doorstep: a sauna, outdoor activity center, and prime location on one of the internationally renowned 7stanes mountain-biking trails. There's a cozy common room where you can cook and huddle by the wood-burning stove and the option of a cooked evening meal and breakfast for a nominal fee. It's easily the most magical place to stay in the area, five miles west of Dumfries in the Mabie forest.

Hazeldean House (4 Moffat Rd., tel. 01387/266178, www.hazeldeanhouse.co.uk, £30–38 s, £50–54 d) is the epitome of a classic Dumfries villa—a gentile red sandstone house in stunning grounds. It has three rooms with four-poster bed and some with a decor that's a little milder on the eye. Rooms are en suite with color TV, and breakfast is served overlooking gardens ablaze with color. From the train station, head left on the Lockerbie road then left up the hill at the next mini roundabout.

Rivendell (105 Edinburgh Rd., tel.

01387/252251, £35 s, £56 d) is a Charles Rennie Mackintosh–themed house with light, minimalist rooms with large digital TVs and Wi-Fi access. The dining room is an interior designer's delight. It is in the north of Dumfries, by the golf club.

With over 90 rooms (big bouncy beds, telephones, and all the trappings), the mammoth **Cairndale Hotel and Leisure Club** (English St., tel. 01387/272410, www.cairndalehotel.co.uk) shouldn't have a problem accommodating you, although it can get booked up with golfers and conference-attendees. It has a heated swimming pool, sauna, steam room, and three café-restaurants.

FOOD

Colorful, cozy **Pumpernickel** (60–62 Friars Vennel, tel. 01387/254475, 8:30 A.M.–5 P.M. Mon.–Sat.) café is a great place to nurse that hangover. It serves excellent teas and coffees and fresh wholesome meals from toasties to bagels, baked potatoes, decent salads, and other traditional mains. Cakes start at £1, fresh sandwiches from £2.25. The owners are catering industry experts, well used to providing for large groups of people.

Drummuir Farm Ice Cream Parlour (Collin, tel. 01387/750599, 10:30 A.M.–5:30 P.M. Apr.–Sept., 10:30 A.M.–5 P.M. Sat. and Sun. Mar. and Oct.–Christmas) is ideal if its hot or if you have children. It's a farm east of Dumfries on the B724 that uses milk from the farm's own cows to make the area's finest ice cream—over 20 flavors of it. Honeycomb is delicious. There are play facilities for kids, outside seating, and other snacks (£1–5) available, from sandwiches and home-baked scones to ice-cream milk shakes.

Bruno's (3 Balmoral Rd., tel. 01387/255757, 5 P.M.–late Mon. and Wed.–Sun.) is a plush, family-run Italian restaurant that has been the haunt of locals in the know for donkey's years. The food is solid, upmarket Italian fare; the fixed three-course dinner is £20. Pasta dishes start around £9.

The **Globe Inn** (56 High St., tel. 01387/252335, 10 A.M.–11:30 A.M. and noon–3 P.M.

daily, dinner by arrangement) has a tiny 17th-century restaurant housed in the original part of the pub where Burns once sat. This is Dumfries dining at its most atmospheric, exuding old wood paneling with a display of Burns items including the chair he allegedly sat upon. The menu is full of traditional pub favorites (around £7.50).

€ **Hullabaloo** (Mill Rd., tel. 01387/259679, www.hullaboorestaurant.co.uk, 11 A.M.–4 P.M. Mon., 11 A.M.–4 P.M. and 6–10 P.M. Tues.–Sat., 11 A.M.–3 P.M. Sun. Easter–Oct., 11 A.M.–4 P.M. Mon., 11 A.M.–4 P.M. and 6–10 P.M. Tues.–Sat. Oct.–Easter) undoubtedly has the town's best dining, overlooking the River Nith in an 18th-century watermill also housing the Robert Burns Centre. For starters, try the tartlet of the day or the hand-dived Wester Ross scallops (£6.25). Then there's an array of exotic sandwiches and superb salads—look for the smoked goose breast salad with plum dressing (£10.50).

INFORMATION AND SERVICES
Tourist Information

The **TIC** (64 Whitesands, tel. 01387/253862, 9:30 A.M.–5 P.M. Mon.–Sat. Apr.–June, 9 A.M.–6 P.M. Mon.–Sat., 10:30 A.M.–4:30 P.M. Sun. July–Aug., 9 A.M.–5:30 P.M. Mon.–Sat., 10:30 A.M.–4:30 P.M. Sun. Sept., 9:30 A.M.–5:30 P.M. Mon.–Sat., 10:30 A.M.–4 P.M. Sun. Oct., 9:30 A.M.–5 P.M. Mon.–Fri. Nov.–Mar.) is a useful place with plenty of local information, as well as a National Express and Eurolines ticket-booking facility.

Services

If you need a hospital, head to **Dumfries and Galloway Royal Infirmary** (Bankend Rd., tel. 01387/246246). The **Ewart Library** (Catherine St., tel. 01387/253820, 9:15 A.M.–7:30 P.M. Mon.–Wed. and Fri., 9:15 A.M.–5 P.M. Thurs. and Sat.) can oblige you with free Internet access. A **post office** (St. Michael St., tel. 01387/253415) and **launderette** (26 Annan Rd., tel. 01387/252295, 9 A.M.–5 P.M. Mon.–Fri., 9 A.M.–4 P.M. Sat.) are in town as well. For car hire, **Arnold Clark** (Annan Rd., tel. 01387/247151) has a branch.

GETTING THERE AND AROUND

Dumfries is 80 miles southwest of Edinburgh on the A76 and 68 miles east of Stranraer on the A75. The A75 is in the stage of being upgraded to accommodate an overtaking (passing) lane—great when it happens but for the moment this means lots of roadworks.

Bus

Buses depart from Whitesands, near the Old Bridge. **Eurolines** runs two buses a day between London and Belfast, stopping at Dumfries and towns along the A75 to Stranraer (Castle Douglas, Gatehouse of Fleet, Newton Stewart). Buses X75/500 run up to 10 times Monday–Saturday and 4 times Sunday between Dumfries and Stranraer via Castle Douglas (35 min., £2.40), Gatehouse of Fleet (one hour, £3.70) and Newton Stewart (one hour 35 min., £5.90) taking 2.5 hours to reach Stranraer (£5.90).

Bus 974 runs four times per day (twice on Sunday) between Glasgow and Dumfries (two hours five min., £6.70) via Moffat. The useful Bus 79 also offers an hourly service between Dumfries and Gretna (one hour).

Train

Dumfries train station is to the north of town, off St. Mary's Street. There are trains every 1.5 hours to Glasgow (1.75 hours, £11.70) and to Carlisle (40 minutes, £7.70) at around the same intervals.

Taxi

A to B Taxis (tel. 01387/710007) will take you where you want to go.

AROUND DUMFRIES

Dumfries and Galloway's main town sits in some great forested countryside.

Mabie Forest

This beautiful old forest south of Dumfries includes one of the renowned 7stanes mountain bike trails. **Marthrown of Mabie Hostel** (tel. 01387/247900) offers plenty of fun outdoor activities in the woods. The popular **Mabie Farm Park** (tel. 01387/259666, www.mabiefarm.co.uk, 10 A.M.–5 P.M. daily Mar.–Oct., 10 A.M.–5 P.M. weekends in Feb. and early Mar.) also offers good country fun with plenty of animal encounters, a dirt buggy track, a boating pond, and a play park as well as a tearoom.

Sweetheart Abbey

A testament to the power of love, Sweetheart Abbey (New Abbey, tel. 01387/850397, 9:30 A.M.–5:30 P.M. daily Apr.–Sept., 9:30 A.M.– 4:30 P.M. Wed.–Sat. Oct.–Mar., £3 adults, £2.50 seniors) is so called because of Lady Devorgilla, who endowed part of her fortune to raise it in memory of her late husband John Balliol, King of Scotland from 1292 to 1296. She loved her husband a great deal, also endowing a sum to Oxford University for a college to be built in his name and carrying his heart around with her in an ivory box. The abbey, relatively unscathed in the wars with England—unlike many of the border abbeys—only fell into ruin after 1600 when the monks left and villagers began using the stone for other buildings. In one of the earliest acts of conservation, villagers agreed to stop this process and preserve what was left in 1779. The arched walls are remarkably intact and make for a great exploration, particularly in summer when the shadows make the abbey extremely photogenic.

█ Caerlaverock

Built to control access to southwest Scotland, picture-postcard **Caerlaverock Castle** (tel. 01387/770244, 9:30 A.M.–5:30 P.M. Apr.–Sept., 9:30 A.M.–4:30 P.M. Oct.–Mar., £5.20 adults, £4.20 seniors), south of Dumfries, fulfills fortress-lovers' wildest dreams. It's one of only a handful with a moat and, more unusually, is triangular in shape (ask the steward for some interesting theories why). Set in a tree-screened park, it's not only outwardly impressive but

© LUKE WATERSON

Caerlaverock Castle, a spectacular fortress that's one of Scotland's last remaining moated castles

also contains the well-preserved 17th-century remains of the Earl of Nithsdale's courtyard residence. Nearby is **Caerlaverock Wildfowl and Wetlands Centre** (tel. 01387/770200, 10 A.M.–5 P.M. daily) where you can learn about and get close to some of the region's most incredible birdlife, including Whooper Swans; this is the best place to view them in the wild in Britain. The center also runs a number of events outside its opening hours, such as Natterjack Toads spawning at night and barn owls bringing back food for their young. If all that watching and waiting makes you hungry, the on-site café does a mean coffee and cake. To get to the castle and wetlands center, follow signs from the A75 southeast of Dumfries. Stagecoach Western bus 371 runs there around nine times daily Mon.–Sat. and twice on Sunday.

DUMFRIES AND GALLOWAY

East Dumfrieshire and Lowther Hills

Much bypassed by visitors pressing north, this region has some delights of which the two main routes through give little inkling. It's mainly wild hill country here, separated by forested valleys. It's a must for walkers and anglers and is a very peaceful place, perhaps why Samye Ling decided to build the first Buddhist monastery in Europe in these lonely rolling uplands.

GRETNA GREEN AND VICINITY

Don't form any impressions of what Scotland may be like from this odd, monstrous village just inside the border. It is the essence of everything tacky about the Scottish tourist industry, and yet there's something bizarrely appealing about it, namely its historical role as Britain's wedding mecca. Year-round, bags of people turn up here to see what all the fuss is about and leave equally mystified.

One of the world's most photographed buildings, the **Old Blacksmith's Shop** (tel. 01461/338441, 9 A.M.–6 P.M. daily Apr.–June and Sept.–Oct., 9 A.M.–7 P.M. daily July–Aug., 9 A.M.–5 P.M. daily Nov.–Mar.) was traditionally the focal point for incoming couples from England wanting to wed. In its **Smithy Museum** is an award-winning multi-lingual audiovisual display on the stories down the centuries of couples seeking marriage and the anvil priests who performed them. There are lots of blacksmiths' tools on display, including the blacksmith's anvil traditionally struck to mark the wedding ceremony. Weddings take place still but the whole experience, both here and at nearby Gretna Gateway village, are as much a monument to Scottish tourist tat as to the history of British marriage.

Gretna's very useful **TIC** (tel. 01461/337834, 10 A.M.–6 P.M. daily Apr.–Oct., 10 A.M.–4:30 P.M. Mon.–Sat., 10 A.M.–4 P.M. Sun. Oct.–Easter) is in Gretna Gateway village.

One thing Gretna is not short on is public transport connections. Stagecoach Bus 79 runs from Carlisle in England to Dumfries several times each hour with a stop at Gretna. It's 50 minutes from Gretna to Dumfries. There are also trains between Dumfries and Gretna running every 1.5 hours (25 min., £6.50).

Around Gretna

Robert the Bruce's Cave (Kirkpatrick Flemming, tel. 01461/800235, open year-round, £1) is allegedly the cave where Robert the Bruce, in hiding during the Wars of Independence, saw the perseverant spider weaving its web that inspired him to victory at Bannockburn. It's in an unlikely location within the **Bruce's Cave Caravan and Campsite** (from £8.50 for tents), a pleasant spot with a site shop and wooded grounds by a river. Pay cave admission to the owner before taking the slippery path down the hillside to the cave itself.

LANGHOLM AND VICINITY

Five centuries ago, isolated, placid Langholm (www.langholm-online.co.uk) was the center of a hotbed of unrest—part of the debatable lands claimed as both Scottish and English territory. Lawlessness was rife; this was the stomping ground of the Border Reivers who carried out nighttime raids of each other's property and livestock and gave the word "bereaved" to the English language. Dumfries and Galloway's only Common Riding Festival celebrates the event. There's a local tourist information point behind the town hall.

Sights and Recreation

On the hillside overlooking Langholm, in the shape of a metallic open book, the **Hugh McDiarmid Memorial** (open year-round) commemorates the famous Scottish poet and founder of the Scottish Nationalist Party. **Thomas Telford** is the area's most famous son; considering he changed the face of Scotland, Telford did not exactly leave his mark on the area. The main exception is **Westerkirk Library** (tel. 013873 70201, phone in advance for hours, open certain

© LUKE WATERSON

vegetables for sale, in Gretna

Sundays during summer) in Telford's home village of Bentpath, to which Telford left a bequest for the purchasing of books. It is Scotland's oldest still-functioning public lending library, annually replenished with new books, in the church where Telford himself was educated.

You don't need to be around at the time of the festival to appreciate the area's varied **walking**—bare hills swooping down to lush, sheltered river valleys and great forest walking around Castle O'er. Visit www.langholmwalks.co.uk for details. **Fishing** is also popular.

Events

The **Langholm and Eskdale Walking Festival** (www.langholmwalks.co.uk/walkingfest) in June is a great time to follow in the Border Reivers' footsteps, with a series of guided walks around the gorgeous countryside of Langholm and Eskdale, inevitably ending up with tasty refreshments.

The last Friday in July is the **Langholm Common Riding Festival.** It's notable for being the only one in Dumfries and Galloway and for the varied emblems used in the procession. The historical inspection of the town boundaries is accompanied by 200 people (see *Borders* chapter for information on Common Ridings).

Accommodations and Food

Wauchope Cottage (Wauchope St., tel. 01387/380479, £25 pp) has one twin room with a self-contained guest lounge and buckets of local information on the area—the owners are instrumental in the town's tourist industry. Look out on a pretty garden (topiary and all) over the big breakfast.

◖ Kagyu Samye Ling Monastery

The West's first Tibetan monastery (by Eskdalemuir, north of Langholm, tel. 01387/373232, www.samyeling.org, temple open 6 A.M.–9 P.M. daily, tearoom and shop 9 A.M.–5 P.M.) is a surreal sight in these quintessentially Scottish forested hills. Take some time to walk around the gardens (walk around clockwise out of respect), visit the splendid red-gold temple (take shoes off before entering), and finish up in the bright

TYING THE KNOT NORTH OF THE BORDER

Years ago, a loophole was discovered in the British legal system. An act passed in 1754 stated that if either party wishing to enter into a marriage was under the age of 21, consent must be sought from the respective parents. This put a lot of young relationships on the rocks, and so generations of young couples trekked north of the English border to Scotland where, provided you were 16, you could get married with or without parental consent. All this led to the first settlement at which they arrived, Gretna, building a rather romantic history for itself. To make matters as official as possible, it fell upon the person amassing the most respect in the village to perform the ceremonies. This was the blacksmith, who would strike his anvil to declare the nuptials finalized. If it was thought the enraged father might be on his way up to prevent proceedings, the anvil priests would urge couples to get into bed promptly.

The English caught on after about a century, passing a law that no wedding in Scotland would be recognized in England unless one of the couple had been living in Scotland for at least three weeks beforehand. This killed off Gretna's romance industry, although anvil priests were still in operation up until the 1940s. When this law was reversed in 1977, couples once again began to flock to Gretna to tie the knot, although with ceremonies having to be performed by real clergy, it was never quite the same.

café/shop. While for the outsider it is more about the peaceful ambience these intricately painted buildings and lovingly tended gardens give off, the monastery organizes retreats and runs courses on peace, well-being, meditation, and Buddhism.

For a unique experience, the monastery offers basic accommodation inclusive of vegetarian meals (dorms £23 pp, rooms £36 s, £56 d). The monastery also has the beautiful **Tibetan Tearoom** (10 A.M.–5 P.M. daily), the coolest place around to eat. It's a bright place with lots of drapes, decorated Tibetan-style and full of all sorts of weird and wonderful people. Simple refreshments are available and there are not many other places where you can be served coffee and cake by a Buddhist monk.

Bus 124 runs at least twice daily between Langholm and Samye Ling; bus 112 from Lockerbie (with a railway station) operates more frequently.

NITHSDALE AND LOWTHER HILLS

This region is a mix of contrasts: a thick, forested valley with good fishing on the gentle River Nith and Wanlockhead, a 300-year-old mining village high up in the barren Lowther Hills.

Drumlanrig Castle, Grounds, and Forest Trails

The ancient woodlands of the Nith valley hide this fine renaissance castle (tel. 01848/331555, www.drumlanrig.com, castle and tearoom open 11 A.M.–5 P.M. daily Good Friday–end Aug., gardens and country park 10 A.M.–5 P.M. daily Good Friday–end Sept., cycle routes and walks throughout year) in a superb setting amidst landscaped gardens surrounded by a web of trails and cycle paths through woodland carpeted with wild flowers. More a palace than a castle, it was built by William Douglas, first duke of Queensberry, to reflect his newfound political power. It features some renowned paintings on the main staircase, including Rembrandt's *Old Woman Reading*. If it's anything like good weather, the grounds are the real temptation. There's a **castle tearoom**, a **snack bar** open in the winter months (11 A.M.–3 P.M. Sat. and Sun. only), **bike rental** (£5/15 per hour/day), and a **visitors center**. A leaflet explains noteworthy trees, including the first Douglas fir planted in Britain. Admission to the house and grounds is £7 adults, £6 children. Bus 246 runs up the main road via Thornhill, some two miles distant.

© LUKE WATERSON

Kagyu Samye Ling Monastery, north of Langholm

◖ Wanlockhead

Scotland's highest village has an otherworldly location on the bare yellow Lowther Hills. It's a little-changed 18th-century former mining community, and the **Museum of Scottish Lead Mining** (tel. 01659/74387, www.leadminingmuseum.co.uk, 10 A.M.–5 P.M. daily July, Aug. and bank holidays, 11 A.M.–4:30 P.M. daily Easter–June and Sept.–Oct., £6.25 adults, £4.50 children) explains that heritage. You can take a guided tour of a real lead mine, visit the 19th-century beam engine that pumped water from these mines, and pan for gold in the mineral-rich burn (gold pans available from reception). Neighboring **Leadhills** (another old mining village) and Wanlockhead have between them the two oldest subscription libraries in Europe. **Wanlockhead Library** is

included in the admission charge for the museum. An enjoyable **Steam Railway** (www.leadhillsrailway.co.uk, 11 A.M.–5 P.M. Sat. and Sun. Easter–Oct.) connects the two villages. The hills around have great walking; the **Southern Upland Way** long-distance footpath passes close by.

Lotus Lodge Hostel (tel. 01659/74544, www.lotuslodge.co.uk, dorm beds £15, twin room £18 pp) is spick, span, and shining as any bed-and-breakfast around and indeed throws in a basic complimentary breakfast. Book ahead as it's popular with Southern Upland Way walkers during season.

Bus 221 runs four times daily between Wanlockhead and Sanquhar in Nithsdale. Wanlockhead is clearly signposted from junctions 13 and 14 of the M74.

Solway Firth Coast

This is quintessential Dumfries and Galloway coastline: sandy bays, tumbling wooded cliffs, and shimmering estuaries dotted with small boats. Kirkcudbright is a vibrant artists' community and the main focal point of the area, but the ample opportunities to lose yourself walking the clifftops and beaches are just as appealing. The low-lying river-laced countryside just inland hides some fantastic ruined castles.

KIRKCUDBRIGHT

The most charming town on this stretch of coast, Kirkcudbright (pronounced Ker-COO-bree) has been a haunt of artists for well over 100 years. The group of artists known as the Glasgow Boys, rebelling against the classical art of the 19th century and famous for painting real scenes of rural life, became associated with Kirkcudbright when their key member, E. A. Hornel, moved to the town. The location of Kirkcudbright on an estuary bobbing with yachts and fishing vessels exudes tranquility. The town has a brilliant light, captured in the pretty houses near the harbor and on the L-shaped main street, smartly painted in pastel blues, greens, yellows, and pinks. It's a peaceful place to putter around and, with galleries, a museum, and a ruined castle, a good base for exploring the region.

Sights

Glasgow Boy E. A. Hornel lived in **Broughton House and Gardens** (12 High St., tel. 01557/330437, house open 10 A.M.–5 P.M. daily July–Aug., noon–5 P.M. daily Good Friday–June and Sept.–Oct., garden open 10 A.M.–5 P.M. daily July–Aug., noon–5 P.M. daily Good Friday–June and Sept.–Oct., 11 A.M.–4 P.M. daily Feb.–Good Friday, £8 adults, £5 seniors) from 1901 until his death in 1933, when he left it for the benefit of local people to enjoy. Hornel amassed an incredible collection of books and manuscripts in his life (some 25,000), which can be seen in the library. The highlight remains the gardens

overlooking the Dee with their strong Japanese theme (dwarf Japanese stone pines and a lily-filled pool), a result of Hornel's visits there.

Maclellan's Castle (tel. 01557/331856, 9:30 A.M.–5:30 P.M. daily Apr.–Sept., 9:30 A.M.–4:30 P.M. daily Oct., £3.50 adults, £2.80 seniors) is a late-16th-century fortress dominating the town center. It is well preserved inside; check the fireplace in the great hall containing a spy-hole for eavesdropping on conversations.

Stewartry Museum (St. Mary St., tel. 01557/331643, www.dumgal.gov.uk/museums, 10 A.M.–5 P.M. Mon.–Sat., 2–5 P.M. Sun. July–Aug., 11 A.M.–5 P.M. Mon.–Sat., 2–5 P.M. Sun. May–June and Sept., 11 A.M.–4 P.M. Mon.–Sat., 2–5 P.M. Sun. Oct., 11 A.M.–4 P.M. Mon.–Sat. Nov.–Apr., free) is a classic Victorian museum with a wealth of exhibits including an important (and in parts, grotesque) natural history collection. The real gems are works by renowned Kirkcudbrightshire artist and friend of E. A. Hornel, Jessie M. King and, bizarrely, Britain's earliest surviving sporting trophy, the Silver Gun. The custodians are just bursting to impart their knowledge of the area.

The best beach in the area is at **Brighouse Bay,** sandwiched between rocky outcrops south of Kirkcudbright off the B727.

Galleries

Ever since Glasgow boy E. A. Hornel lived here at the beginning of the 20th century, Kirkcudbright has been an artists' haunt. The main gallery, the **Tolbooth Art Centre** (High St., tel. 01557/331556, 10 A.M.–5 P.M. Mon.–Sat., 2–5 P.M. Sun. July–Aug., 11 A.M.–5 P.M. Mon.–Sat., 2–5 P.M. Sun. May–June and Sept., 11 A.M.–4 P.M. Mon.–Sat., 2–5 P.M. Sun. Oct., 11 A.M.–4 P.M. Mon.–Sat. Nov.–Apr., free) is in the old Tolbooth where John Paul Jones, founder of the American navy, was once imprisoned. It's a good starting point for an exploration of town, with an audio-visual introduction to the town's artistic history. It's a

© LUKE WATERSON

Kirkcudbright Harbour

wonderful exhibition space—check the tapestry depicting the town on the way up. There's a great little café on the ground floor.

The **Harbour Cottage Gallery** (Castlebank, tel. 01557/330073, 10:30 A.M.–12:30 P.M. and 2–5 P.M. daily Mar.–Dec.) by the harbor has been going strong for 50 years. The town has a lot of artistic clout and shows internationally important exhibitions.

Entertainment and Events

Pick of Kirkcudbright's **pubs** (and it's a hard call) has to be the **Masonic Arms** (19 Castle St., tel. 01557/330517), a dark, cozy, traditional place with real ale on tap plus plenty more bottled beers besides. Kirkcudbright is a happening spot lending itself particularly well to outdoor events—check out www.summerfestivities.com. The buzz is at its height in June for the **Kirkcudbright Jazz Festival.** In July the **Wickerman Festival,** inspired by the 1973 horror film filmed on location in the area, takes place near Dundrennan off the A711 southeast of town. It's a cool, independent arts and music festival going from strength to

strength. Finally, the highlight of the events calendar is the town's very own **Tattoo** at the end of August. It's a night of music and dancing around the castle ruins, culminating with a fireworks display.

Sports and Recreation

Lochhill Equestrian and Trekking Centre (Ringford, tel. 01557/820225, www.lochhill.net) offers a great opportunity to get out into the tangle of pretty lanes and tracks around Kirkcudbright on horseback. For bike rentals, **Trailbrakes** (tel. 01557/870315, www.trailbrakes.co.uk) should be able to sort out any biking queries from hire through to guided rides. It's out of town but is accommodating with pick-up.

Accommodations

Silvercraigs Caravan and Camping Site (tel. 01557/330123 Easter–Oct., tel. 01556/503806 out of season, www.dumgal.gov/silvercraigs, tent £10.50–15) sits on six acres of grassy hillside overlooking town, with electric hookups and laundry facilities. Trees provide some shelter.

An orange Georgian townhouse, **Baytree House** (110 High St., tel. 01557/330824, www.baytreekirkcudbright.co.uk, £60–66 d/ twin) offers three well-furnished en suite rooms with sherry to greet you on your arrival. The conservatory breakfast room looks onto a walled garden; feast on the Creetown haddock and poached eggs as one of the alternatives to a traditional fry-up. A sun deck is available on request.

Reputedly the dower house for McLellan's Castle, the ivy-screened 16th-century ◖ **Marks** (Marks, three miles from Kirkcudbright, tel. 01557/330854, www.marksfarm.co.uk, £30 s, £50 d) is a working dairy and worm farm with three cozy rooms, crackling log fires, and a wealth of wild, tangled grounds and tracks to explore. Marks even has its very own loch. Given that it could be a holiday destination in its own right, the price is a snip.

In a historical building, the rooms at **Gladstone House** (48 High St., tel. 01557/331734, www.kirkcudbrightgladstone.com, £64 d/twin) let in a lot of light, with one overlooking McLellan's Castle. Breakfasts involve homemade bread and jam and vegetables fresh from the garden. Once you sink into one of the comfy chairs in the drawing room, you may not want to get up. If you're in the area retracing your genealogical roots, the owners can give guidance.

Food

A great place for a snack or a meal during the day is the **Solway Tide Tearoom** (16 Cuthbert St., tel. 01557/330775, 10:30 A.M.–4:30 P.M. daily Mar.–Jan.—until 5 P.M. daily during summer). It's an idyllic little tearoom serving Illy coffee and a selection of light bites and cakes, not to mention scrumptious pizzas. In summer, sit in the sun-trapping courtyard at the back.

The **Castle Restaurant** (5 Castle St., tel. 01557/330569, www.thecastlerestaurant.net, from 6:30 P.M. Mon., 11:30 A.M.–2:30 P.M. and from 6:30 P.M. Tues.–Sat. Apr.–Oct., from 6:30 P.M. Mon.–Thurs., 11:30 A.M.–2:30 P.M. and from 6:30 P.M. Fri.–Sun. Oct.–Apr.) is an old-fashioned restaurant that, with crisp linen tablecloths and tartan carpets, serves Kirkcudbright's best food. Under new management since 2006,

it does mains like prosciutto-wrapped monkfish, with an infused roasted red pepper sauce starting at £13. Don't forget to save room for some Cream o' Galloway ice cream and a Bladnoch Distillery single malt.

Information and Services

The brilliant **TIC** (tel. 01557/330494, open at least 11 A.M.–4 P.M. Feb.–Nov.) is at Harbour Square.

The library (tel. 01557/331240, 2–7:30 P.M. Mon., 10 A.M.–7:30 P.M. Tues. and Fri., noon–7:30 P.M. Wed., 10 A.M.–5 P.M. Thurs. and Sat.) is opposite the Tolbooth Arts Centre. You can check the Internet here. The post office is opposite the TIC car park.

Getting There and Away

Buses 501/501A/502A run about hourly between Dumfries and Kirkcudbright. There are no direct buses to Stranraer; take service 501A/502A to Gatehouse of Fleet, then get on the 500 or X75 bus.

Around Kirkcudbright

The A711 winds south around the coast to the generally bypassed tiny village of **Auchencairn,** a clutch of whitewashed houses by a big sandy beach. Two miles beyond it is **Orchardton Tower** (9:30 A.M.–5:30 P.M. daily Apr.–Sept., 9:30 A.M.–4:30 P.M. daily Oct.–Mar., free), Scotland's only circular tower house. Even if this doesn't tickle your fancy, it's worth stopping by Auchencairn to feast on fine food and ale in the ◖ **Old Smugglers Inn** (Main St., tel. 01556/640331, 5–11 P.M. Mon.–Thurs., 5 P.M.–midnight Fri., noon–midnight Sat., 12:30–11 P.M. Sun.) with a good beer garden and a bar made from an old fishing boat. Take bus 505 from Kirkcudbright to get here.

GATEHOUSE OF FLEET

Thanks to entrepreneur James Murray, Gatehouse grew in the 18th century from a mere staging post on the important route to Portpatrick and Ireland to a prosperous cotton mill town boasting so many mills and factories it was dubbed the "Glasgow of the South."

© LUKE WATERSON

Mill on the Fleet, Gatehouse of Fleet

First impression is that it's hard to believe this gentile backwater divided by the water of Fleet ever had such an active industrial life. Now, however, one of the former mill buildings has been restored to vividly preserve the town's history. The legacy of industry that might have put visitors off in the 18th century is today one of the main reasons to stop by.

Sights

Mill on the Fleet (tel. 01557/814099, www .millonthefleet.co.uk, 10:30 A.M.–5 P.M. daily Apr.–Oct.) was built in 1788 as a cotton mill (the large wheel outside powered machinery to spin the cotton). The mill was in use for 150 years; it's now restored as an exhibition venue. It has concentrated on bringing back to life the area's industrial past as well as hosting renowned exhibitions including photographs by Andy Goldsworthy in 2007. It's all about the place itself, though, wandering the carefully restored buildings and getting a feel for what life might have been like for 18th-century industrial workers. The mill hosts talks and arranges guided walks along the wooded fields and riverbanks. The café here has a lovely outside terrace overlooking the river, and there is also a good bookshop on the second floor.

From the battlements of the six-story, 15th-century tower house that is **Cardoness Castle** (tel. 01557/814427, 9:30 A.M.–5:30 P.M. daily Apr.–Sept., 9:30 A.M.–4:30 P.M. Sat.–Wed. Oct., 9:30 A.M.–4:30 P.M. Sat.–Sun. Nov.–Mar., £3.70 adults, £3 seniors), a mile along the A75 from Gatehouse at the head of Fleet Bay, there are exquisite views of the wide stretches of sand lacing Wigtown Bay. You can also have fun exploring the nasty prisons down below.

Accommodations and Food

Appearances can be deceptive: The **Murray Arms Hotel** (tel. 01557/814207, www.murrayarmshotel.co.uk, £79 d) is a big hotel but with extremely friendly service. There are just 12 en suite, spacious-but-cozy rooms. The bar is a relaxed spot with more character than the bland-looking restaurant, with plenty of locals making a show as well as residents. Delightful extras include free tennis, spa breaks, and, for those looking for something out of the ordinary, falconry. You can sit and be inspired in the lounge where Burns penned the first draft of "Scot's Wha Hae."

The marble pillars at the entrance of **Cally Palace** (tel. 01557/814341, www.callypalace.co.uk, from £114 pp including dinner breakfast, and round of golf) set the scene of grandeur—this really is one luxurious place to stay, with lavish antique furnishings in every room and a lounge with fire ablazing. The sumptuous former residence of entrepreneur James Murray, who kick-started Gatehouse's industrial fortunes, even has its own golf course and plenty of wooded nature trails on the grounds. The nature trails are free for anyone to enjoy; the rest you pay substantially for.

Even the basic pub grub at the popular **Masonic Arms** (10 Ann St., tel. 01557/814335, food served noon–2 P.M. and 6–9 P.M.) has a classy air, like the stir-fry fillet of hoisin beef (£10.95). Dine in the conservatory, or prop yourself up by the bar and prepare to sample the range of real ales, which change but regularly feature specials from the Sulwath Brewery in Castle Douglas. The chef used to have his own TV program.

The **Cream o' Galloway** (Rainton, tel. 01557/814040, www.creamogalloway.co.uk, 10 A.M.–6 P.M. daily late Mar.–Aug., 10 A.M.–5 P.M. Sept.–Oct.) is the ice cream pit stop in these parts. It's a farm with 25 wonderful flavors on offer. The tearoom here also does four organic varieties of frozen yogurt along with fair-trade coffee, vegetable soups, jacket potatoes, and salads. There's a play barn, nature trails, and loads more diversions. Take the road signposted to Sandgreen after the main Gatehouse of Fleet turning, from where it's two miles.

Information
The **TIC** (tel. 01556/502611, 10 A.M.–4 P.M. Mon.–Sat., 11 A.M.–4 P.M. Sun. Apr.–June, 10 A.M.–5 P.M. Mon.–Sat., 11 A.M.–4:30 P.M. Sun. June–Sept., 10 A.M.–4 P.M. Mon.–Sat. Sept.–Oct.) is in the car park for Mill on the Fleet.

Getting There
The X75 bus passes Gatehouse of Fleet twice daily (Mon.–Sat.) en route between Carlisle and Stranraer.

CASTLE DOUGLAS AND INLAND
OK, Kirkcudbright as "Artist's Town"—fair enough. Wigtown as "Book Town"—undisputed. But the tourist board's christening of Castle Douglas as "Food Town" may leave you wondering. It's a quiet, unassuming one-street town with pale pastel-colored houses and a loch flanked by a grassy tree-studded park at one end.

Sights
Carlingwark Loch on the western edge of Castle Douglas is an important site for birdlife, including mute swans and the great-crested grebe, which breeds here. Just getting to **Threave Castle** (tel. 0771/122 3101, 9:30 A.M. until last outward sailing 4:30 P.M. daily Apr.–Sept., 9:30 A.M. until last outward sailing 3:30 P.M. Sat.–Wed. Oct., £4.20 adults, £2.10 children), three miles west of Castle Douglas on an island in the river Dee, is half the fun. Park and follow the path through fields for about a mile until you reach the tiny jetty; ring the bell and the custodian will come to ferry you across. The 14th-century tower house is little more than a shell but it is a novel place to explore. McEwans Coach 502 will stop en route from Dumfries to Kirkcudbright at Rhonehouse Road End junction outside Castle Douglas, from where it's a 10-minute walk.

Southwest of town, the A745 leads to **Dalbeattie Forest,** where there is great mountain-biking (a 7stanes course) and good walking.

Entertainment
The **Lochside Theatre** (Lochside Rd., tel. 01556/504506, www.lochsidetheatre.co.uk) is rightly the pride of the town. In a former church, it has the aesthetically pleasing location its name suggests, great acoustics

and a host of innovative performances, run by volunteers.

Accommodations and Food

Castle Douglas is slowly cottoning on to the fact that being proclaimed a "food town" means people expect good restaurants. The brand-new **Bluebell Hotel** (King St., tel. 01556/502882) promises to be a top-notch dining venue.

Lochside Caravan and Camping Park (tel. 01556/502949, Easter–Oct., pitches from £11 for 4 people) is, being on Carlingwark Loch and within a public park, the pick of the places to stay in town location-wise. Pitches are flat and grassy, washing facilities are clean, and if you think it looks pretty during the day, wait for the sunset. It's popular with anglers whose wildest fishing dreams are fulfilled by the loch.

Smithy House (The Buchan, tel. 01556/503841, www.smithyhouse.co.uk, £60–70 s, £70–75 d) is a recently renovated 500-year-old Galloway farm cottage which has some rooms with superb views of Carlingwark Loch. The breakfasts are some of the best around, particularly if you're a fish lover— Kedgeree made with smoked wild salmon or Galloway smoked kippers. It's a short walk to the beautiful Threave Gardens from here.

The big, rambling rooms of the 18th-century **Douglas Arms Hotel** (206 King St., tel. 01556/502231, www.douglasarmshotel.co.uk, from £47.50 s, £75 d) are actually quite modern: all have TVs, telephones, and Internet access. There's a honeymoon suite with four-poster bed available. The child-friendly restaurant of this ancient coaching inn does great dinners beside a roaring fire: char grills with all the trimmings (£13.75) or vegetarian dishes like spicy bean and lentil pancakes (£6.25).

With a conservatory and walled garden, and a leading contemporary art gallery upstairs, **C Designs Gallery and Café** (179 King St., tel. 01556/504552, 9:30 A.M.–5:30 P.M. Mon.–Sat.) is a stylish place to get a bite to eat. The menu is pretty delectable, too—excellent coffee, homemade bread and soups, locally smoked salmon, and beer from Castle Douglas' very own Sulwath Brewery. If you're not up for local foodstuffs, try the spanakopita—a Greek spinach and feta pie (£6.25).

In-House Chocolates and Deli (128 King St., tel. 01556/503037) has not only handmade chocolates but also one of Dumfries and Galloway's best and most eclectic selection of cheeses.

Information

The little **TIC** (tel. 01556/502611, at least 10 A.M.–4 P.M. daily Mar.–Aug., closed Sun. Sept.–Oct.) is by the car park at the top of town.

Getting There

The X75 Bus between Carlisle and Stranraer stops off twice daily (Mon.–Sat.) in Castle Douglas.

C COLVEND COAST

Perhaps the most sublime stretch of Dumfries and Galloway coastline runs in an almost continuous 20-mile swath of sand south from Dalbeattie east around almost as far as Dumfries. Steep wooded cliffs rise from golden bays into dry, stone-walled fields with blazes of gorse. There are not really any specific sights to see but several beautiful spots to lose yourself in for a few days.

Whitewashed **Kippford,** bobbing with yachts, is the best place to stay and to putter around. One of Scotland's most gorgeous coastal walks runs from here to nearby **Rockcliffe** around the silty Urr estuary, with views across to the Lake District and the Isle of Man. Along the road by the estuary just after Kippford, there's a garden with an intriguing series of **carvings** made out of stone and driftwood.

In **Sandyhills,** just east of Colvend, there is a lovely **beach,** although swimming can be dangerous. Golfers will appreciate nearby **Southerness** (tel. 01387/880644, greens fee £45), one of Dumfries and Galloway's best courses.

Transport-wise, bus 372 makes the run between Dumfries and Dalbeattie, stopping at destinations along the A710 (main Colvend Coast road).

Accommodations

The **Anchor Hotel** (Dalbeattie, tel. 01556/ 620205, from £30 s, £50 d) is one of the prettiest buildings in Kippford. It serves up real local ales in the bar and seafood fresh from the pier in the restaurant (11 A.M.–2:30 P.M. and 5:30–11 P.M. daily). Try the moules marinere (mussels in white wine and cream sauce) for £11.95.

Baronial, turreted **Craigbittern House** (Sandyhills, east of Colvend, tel. 01387/780247, £60–65 d/twin) has three ample rooms full of dark wood furniture; it overlooks the shore from its substantial grounds.

Galloway Forest Heartland

The Galloway Forest Park, the largest of its kind in Britain, dominates this region with its gray-green landscape of rocky hillsides climbing out of deciduous and coniferous forest. It's a highland landscape in a lowland setting; you'll have to trek well into northern Scotland before you find another area to rival this for sheer uninterrupted remoteness. The park brushes the edges of the main towns in the region, which are little more than bases from which to explore the park. There is world-class mountain biking on some of Europe's most renowned tracks in the park as well as walks where the only other living creatures in view are wheeling golden eagles. South of New Galloway, the other major attraction is Loch Ken, a snaking 11-mile-long body of water ideal for water sports. To get around the region, it's best to explore by car; public transport in the Forest Park is limited.

NEWTON STEWART AND VICINITY

This unspectacular town by the river Cree knows its place as an accommodation base for exploring the Galloway Forest.

Sights

Five miles south of Newton Stewart in Creetown is the wonderful **Creetown Gem Rock Museum** (Chan Rd., tel. 01671/820554, 9:30 A.M.–5:30 P.M. daily Good Friday–Sept., 10 A.M.–4 P.M. daily Oct.–Nov., 10 A.M.–4 P.M. Sat.–Sun. Dec.–Feb., £3.75 adults, £3.25 children), one of the U.K.'s largest collections of gemstones, minerals, rocks, and fossils.

Exhibits include fossilized dinosaur dung and one of the largest gold nuggets on display in the United Kingdom. A highlight is the cave, where you can see minerals giving off an eerie phosphorescent glow in the darkness.

Accommodations and Food

A former school in a quiet riverside spot, **Minigaff Hostel** (Millcroft Rd., tel. 01671/402211 or 0870/155 3255, dorm £13–14) lies on the back road to Glentrool and Galloway Forest. The hostel has four rooms with at least eight beds in each; it's popular with bikers, as two of the best 7stanes mountain-bike courses (Kirroughtree and Glentrool) are nearby. Bike-wash facilities and cycle storage are available.

The rooms at set-back **Corsbie Villa** (Corsbie Rd., tel. 01671/402124, www.corsbievilla.com, £32.50 s, £59 d) can be poky, but the inviting guest lounge with its private bar and resident tortoise makes up for everything. If you're a walker, you will appreciate the five-day courtesy weather report handed out at breakfast.

For the oldest building in town, **Galloway Arms Hotel** (Victoria St., tel. 01671/402653, £29.50–37.50 s, £59–65 d), a large, revamped, 18th-century coaching inn, offers surprisingly modern facilities. The 17 bright en suite rooms have TVs, and the shiny lounge has leather armchairs and two bars, one decorated bizarrely with vintage airplane parts.

It wouldn't take a supreme effort to be the best place to stay in town; it is therefore to the credit of the **Creebridge House Hotel** (tel. 01671/402121, www.creebridge.co.uk, £60 s, £110 d) that it is head and shoulders above the rest and anything but complacent. Nowhere can match it for how welcoming and cozy it seems, sheltered in its own grounds at the foot of the Kirroughtree Forest. It's also the best place to eat, with a meat and fish-oriented menu (three-course dinner from £14.95).

Information
The seasonal **TIC** (tel. 01671/402431, 9:30 A.M.–4 P.M. Mon.–Sat. Apr.–June and Oct., 9:30 A.M.–4:30 P.M. Mon.–Sat. and 11 A.M.–3 P.M. Sun. July–Aug.) is at Dashwood Square; for Galloway Forest information you'll do better to head to the visitors centers in the forest itself.

Getting There
The handy X75 bus service stops by en route between Carlisle and Stranraer. Newton Stewart is also the jumping-off point for forays into the Machars (Wigtown, Whithorn, and Port William, all of which lie south of the town).

◖ GALLOWAY FOREST PARK
Southern Scotland's wildest landscape is a mixture of close-knit forest slopes divided by patches of open yellow scrubland with bare craggy hills thrusting out of the trees. Be on the lookout for wildlife including wild goats, red deer, roe deer, and, bird-wise, red kites. The highest point in the park and a popular walk is up to the **Merrick** (843 m), best accessed from **Glentrool,** in the west of the park. At Glentrool there is a **visitors center** (tel. 01671/402420, 9:30 A.M.–5 P.M. daily Apr.–Sept., 9:30 A.M.–4:30 P.M. daily Oct.) with information on walks and refreshments.

The most scenic way to get to Glentrool is along the minor road past Minigaff Youth Hostel in Newton Stewart. After the visitors center, follow the road past Loch Trool (plenty of trails branching off) to begin the ascent of the Merrick, southern Scotland's highest peak. You can alternately continue across the moors into Carrick in Ayrshire, a breeding ground for the rare black grouse.

The main road across the park is the zigzagging **Queen's Way** (A712) in the south. Some 12 miles along from Newton Stewart is the large gray

Clatteringshaws Loch with a quaint cottage **visitors center** (tel. 01644/420285, 10:30 A.M.–5:30 P.M. daily May–Sept., 10:30 A.M.–4:30 P.M. daily Mar.–May and Sept.–Oct.).

The **Raider's Road,** a toll road (open summer only) leads from Clatteringshaws alongside the sparkling **Black Water of Dee** and gentle, flower-carpeted **Bennan Wood** to **Loch Ken.** An Art in the Forest initiative has resulted in several interesting sculptures around the park, making good focal points for walks.

ST. JOHN'S TOWN OF DALRY AND NEW GALLOWAY
These two out-of-the-way villages are great access points for the Galloway Forest Park and Loch Ken. They're also the only places to stay in this wild country. St. John's Town of Dalry (understandably shortened to Dalry) is the prettier. Both have an eerie, desolate feel, but fortunately visitors come here to appreciate wildlife, not to admire houses. Bus 503 makes the sporadic journey from Dumfries to New Galloway.

Accommodations and Food
Kendoon Youth Hostel (5 miles north of Dalry, tel. 01644/460268, open May–Sept., dorms £13) is basically a remote log cabin in a field. The friendly hostel, with eight simple four-bed rooms, is on the B7000 halfway to Carsphairn. Outdoor enthusiasts appreciate it particularly. The Castle Douglas–Ayr bus 520 stops on the A713 opposite the hostel, from where it's a 30-minute walk.

The inviting ◖ **Clachan Inn** (10 Main St., Dalry, tel. 01644/430241, £35 pp) with its blazing old stone fireplace, beamed restaurant, and large bar might just tempt you away from that early-morning hike. Rooms are cozy affairs with that Godsend to an outdoors lover— en suite baths. Breakfast is served until 10 A.M. and by then, it's almost lunchtime. It's a popular place to eat, especially since new management has taken over (imagine organic lamb in red wine jus or and a fillet of steak stuffed with haggis soaked in Bladnoch whisky). Views of the mist-flecked Galloway Forest hills are available from almost every window.

Sitting in the courtyard of the scenic **Smithy Tearoom and Craft Shop** (New Galloway, tel. 01644/420269, www.thesmithynewgalloway.com, 10 A.M.–5 P.M. daily), overlooking the gushing burn as you munch on a cheese scone or slurp an Italian coffee, it will take some convincing that there is any better place than New Galloway to kick back of an afternoon. Snacks and unusual soups start from £2; they often end up being a prequel to lunches. The place was actually a functioning smithy until around 1940; it now doubles as a local tourist information point and a decent gift shop.

LOCH KEN

This narrow blue ribbon of water snakes for 11 miles southeast from New Galloway and is a great spot to try out water sports. If this is your thing, look no farther than the **Galloway Sailing Centre** (near Parton, tel. 01644/420626, www.lochken.co.uk) which arranges equipment hire and activities from power-boating to canoeing to sailing and windsurfing. Courses can be anything from 1.5 hours to five days. There are also "dry" activities like mountain biking. The center has a self-catering **lodge** (from £12 pp), **campsite** (£5 pp), and even a bar, if you've the energy left for drinking.

Western Coast and Rinns Peninsula

It doesn't make sense: Even with ringside seats on some of Scotland's most spectacular coastline, still the towns and villages here see comparatively few visitors. Revitalized Wigtown, with Scotland's best book-shopping, is the regional hub—a quiet place where the talk is of secondhand novels and ospreys, reclusive residents spied on the shores nearby. Farther south is the birthplace of Christianity at Whithorn, a good starting point for the wealth of ancient sites scattered across this region. Finding out about St. Ninian, who set up the first outpost of Christianity north of the border and the subsequent pilgrims who braved all to reach the saint's shrine, is a moving experience. The rolling pastures and grasslands of the Machars fold gently down to the coast west of Whithorn, with superb beaches backed by prettily painted villages. Farther west is the Rinns of Galloway peninsula. Its prettiest village, colorful Portpatrick, tumbles down the cliffs and oozes with great places to eat.

⟨ WIGTOWN

I found here, in Galloway, in diverse Rode-Way Innes, goode Cheere, Hospitality and serviceable attendance

– William Lithgow, Travels 1628

These words describe an early traveler's impressions of Wigtown in the 17th century and still stand true today. It's to this friendly, pretty town overlooking the mudflats and sand banks of the Cree estuary, rather than to any of Scotland's fine cities, that book-lovers should flock. Wigtown was looking rather sorry up until about 1998, deprived of its county town status and with the big local employer, Bladnoch Distillery, having closed. It was then decided to make it Scotland's book town, and the results have been incredible. This rejuvenated place now offers by far the biggest and best selection of books both secondhand and new anywhere in Scotland. Most shops (and therefore most sights) are around the spruced-up houses flanking the town square (actually a huge triangle). There is more good news: Bladnoch Distillery has reopened.

Sights

The honey-pink **Wigtown County Buildings** (10 A.M.–5 P.M. Mon., Thurs., and Sat., 10 A.M.–7:30 P.M. Tues.–Wed. and Fri.), formerly the Wigtownshire county administrative buildings, now houses the library, year-round TIC (pick up a copy of the Wigtown bookshops leaflet), and, more intriguingly, the Osprey Exhibition in a room upstairs. After a century's absence, ospreys are back in Dumfries and Galloway. Wigtown has a wonderful local nature reserve stretching along the silty bay and enjoys a unique ecosystem dominated by low-lying salt marsh (merse) often flooded by the sea. This makes the area a bird's (especially osprey) paradise with plenty of goodies left by the outgoing tide and easy fishing in the shallow waters. Guided bird-spotting walks go into the reserve, but a closed-circuit TV link to their nest in the Osprey Exhibition gives the best views (Apr.–Aug.). There are also panoramic views around town and a knowledgeable ranger on hand to quiz on nature-related matters.

Friendly, enthusiastic management has taken over Scotland's most southerly single malt-making center, **Bladnoch Distillery** (tel. 01988/402605, 9 A.M.–5 P.M. Mon.–Fri., 11 A.M.–5 P.M. Sat., noon–5 P.M. Sun. July–Aug., 9 A.M.–5 P.M. Mon.–Fri. Sept.–June, tour £3). It's a bunch of slate-roofed buildings sitting on grassy lawns sliding into the River Bladnoch. The tour here is a very real and vivid experience, not tarted up as at many distilleries. It is a small operation with few staff, making for a very personalized whisky experience. Guided tours including tastings run throughout the year. Distilling began again in 2000, so it's too early to tell if the new brew will be as tasty as before but the signs are promising, and there is plenty of old Bladnoch left to tide over. In case knocking back drams wasn't fun enough, there is riverbank fishing, woodland walks, and regular live music events too.

Bookshops

Of the many bookshops in town, here are a selection of the best.

The Bookshop (17 N. Main St., tel. 01988/402499, www.the-bookshop.com, 9 A.M.–5 P.M. Mon.–Sat.) is Scotland's largest secondhand bookshop—a book-lovers' warren with nine rooms.

The Old Bank Bookshop (7 S. Main St., tel. 01988/402111, 10:30 A.M.–5:30 P.M. Mon.–Sat., noon–5 P.M. Sun. Mar.–Oct., 10:30 A.M.–4:30 P.M. Thurs.–Mon. Nov.–Mar.), with sofas, coffee, creaking boards, and precarious towers

of books everywhere, has any number of specialty areas: military history, travel, a recently bolstered sheet music section, not to mention occasional folk sessions.

ReadingLasses (17 S. Main St., tel. 01988/403266, www.reading-lasses.com, 10 A.M.–5 P.M. Mon.–Sat., noon–5 P.M. Sun.) is a neatly set-out shop with a cheerful, simple café. Its claim to fame: it is the only second-hand bookshop specializing in women's studies and social sciences in the United Kingdom.

Events

Wigtown Book Festival, held in September, goes from strength to strength and pulls in a lot of big names for readings and talks and other, wackier book-related events.

Accommodations and Food

Bladnoch Distillery Campsite (tel. 01988/402605, £6 for tent and two people) is in beautiful grassy distillery grounds by the gently wending river. Fishing costs £5 per day.

A bed-and-breakfast and restaurant, **Glaisnock House** (20 S. Main St., tel. 01988/402249, £27 pp) is centrally located for the best of the bookshops. It offers very comfortable rooms with loud decor and a guest lounge with videos to watch and an open log fireplace.

The flower-festooned **Bladnoch Inn** (one mile down the A746 from Wigtown, tel. 01988/402200, www.bladnoch-inn.com, from £32 s, £54 twin) has five simply furnished, recently revamped rooms. A great bar downstairs has a blazing fire and bare-stone walls; hearty fare is served in the restaurant (mains £9.50–17.50).

The best place for a snack in town is **Café Rendezvous** (2 Agnew Crescent, tel. 01988/402074, breakfast and lunch until 4:30 P.M. Mon.–Sat.). Gloat over your book purchase over coffee, cake, and a good selection of paninis.

Getting There and Away

Bus 415 runs frequently between Newton Stewart and Isle of Whithorn via Wigtown, with 4–5 Sunday services making the full

© LUKE WATERSON

Isle of Whithorn

journey (more Sunday services to Wigtown). Several continue to Port William (only three on Sunday); otherwise change in Wigtown/ Whithorn for more Port William services.

WHITHORN AND THE MACHARS GRASSLANDS

Fascination with building on this windswept grassland south of Wigtown goes back 5,000 years. The area is dotted with ancient monuments, yet it was with the coming of St. Ninian, who established Christianity north of the English border, that the area's most famous landmark was built. Scotland's first church, Whithorn Priory, was constructed in the saint's honor, and the area has been a place of pilgrimage ever since. Whithorn, with its wide main street, is surprisingly untouristy, while the village of Isle of Whithorn three miles south is a pleasant village clustered around a harbor, with the 14th-century St. Ninian's chapel nearby. That is about as much as most visitors see of this remote peninsula, yet the coastline of the Machars (so-called because of the distinctive spiky green grass that grows in profusion along it) hides some real gems—coastal villages with great beaches and even better pubs that barely see tourists and the 5th-century retreat of St. Ninian.

Sights

You can retrace the eventful history of Whithorn and the surrounding area at the **Whithorn Story Visitor Centre** (45–47 George St., Whithorn, tel. 01988/500508, 10:30 A.M.–5 P.M. daily Easter–Oct., £3, with discounts for Historic Scotland members). This is achieved via audiovisual shows and displays of a century of archaeological finds (as bizarre as evidence of Viking cat farming!). There is also access to a dig site and the ruins of the medieval cathedral and crypts (the focal point of the whole experience). In a place of over 15 centuries of Christian activity, the cathedral is historically confusing to say the least; built on the site of St. Ninian's original church (Candida Casa or white house, from which Whithorn takes its name) but itself dating mostly from the 1200s. In the museum beside the cathedral is Scotland's finest collection of early Christian stones. An education in ancient history doesn't

A FAMILY-FRIENDLY DESTINATION

Dumfries and Galloway sells itself, and with some justification, as a child-friendly place. There are really very few other parts of Scotland that have such perfect ingredients for a holiday; you can get a taste of the great outdoors without any strenuous effort and discover museums and attractions that bend over backward to appeal to the younger generation.

Starting in Dumfries, pay a visit to **Caerlaverock Castle** with its moat and ruins. Afterward, you could head to the nearby **Wildlife and Wetlands Centre** to take part in some good animal-spotting fun, looking through Scotland's biggest binoculars at breeding toads or feeding barn owls. **Drummuir Farm** is a good place to stop off for an ice cream, and in Mabie heading toward the Colvend Coast is **Mabie Farm Park** where you can feed animals

and race on the dirt buggy track. The Colvend coast has plenty of beaches and campsites to detain you, but then head inland through Castle Douglas to **Loch Ken** where you can try out a whole range of water sports at the **Galloway Sailing Centre.** Head back down to Newton Stewart to be enthralled at the **Creetown Gem Museum.** Make another ice cream stop, this time at **Cream o' Galloway** (with a play park on-site), then let the children have a look at the **nesting ospreys** in Wigtown while you nip around the bookshops. The **Whithorn Story** is a fun experience for everyone to get a taste of this area's history, then you can continue to the **Rinns of Galloway,** where there are plenty of great campsites right on the beach. The children will be begging to come back another year for more.

come more varied and fascinating than this. The Whithorn Story is also the local tourist information point.

At the **Isle of Whithorn,** follow the harbor around to get to the tussocky path leading to **St. Ninian's Chapel** (open year-round). There's more historical confusion here: The chapel actually takes its name courtesy of the pilgrims who landed at the nearby harbor in the 12th–14th centuries to visit the shrine of the Saint. The ruined building is a poignant reminder of the importance of St. Ninian to Christian pilgrims; it's little wonder that after braving such treacherous sea crossings the pilgrims wanted a place to give thanks for their safe arrival. The **Pilgrims Way** loops through Isle of Whithorn and Whithorn, as well as taking in **St. Ninian's Cave** (where the Saint once lived) on its way through the Machars to Glenluce Abbey. Ask at the visitors center in Whithorn for details. Bus connections are basically the same as for Wigtown.

Accommodations and Food

Just outside of Whithorn past Glasserton on the A747, **Craiglemine Cottage** (tel.

01988/500594, from £23 s, £52 d) is a great place to kick back. It's isolated, sure, but that is compensated for with plenty of books to read, videos to watch, and (on request) evening meals. The two rooms are simply furnished; the double gets great views backed by mountains. The owner is an accomplished baker and has bread and all sorts of goodies for sale.

As close to St. Ninian's Chapel as you can get, one of the delightful buildings clustered around the Isle of Whithorn's harbor is the **Steam Packet Inn** (tel. 01988/500344, www.steampacketinn.com, £30–35 s, £60–70 d), with five of its seven en suite rooms with beautiful sea views. The rooms are large but seem even larger with all the light coming in. The deluxe rooms even have handmade beds. As for meals, the seafood cannot be beaten—you can often watch your meal being freshly landed by the fishing boats on the pier in front of the inn. You could always retire to the bar afterward to toast yourself in front of the fire or take on the locals at a game of dominoes (or pool, but be warned—they're good!).

Picnic-preparers and self-caterers should

© LUKE WATERSON

gourmet seafood served in Portpatrick

check out classy **Ravenstone Deli** (61–63 George St., Whithorn, tel. 01988/500329, 8:30 A.M.–5 P.M. Tues.–Sat.) for specialty Scottish cheeses, homemade bread, fine local meats, massive pizzas, and a good selection of wine. You can sit in and sample the freshly ground coffee.

The Machars Coast

The coast around Whithorn is beautiful but bleak. North of Whithorn is Garlieston with the welcoming blue-and-white **Harbour Inn** (tel. 01988/600685) providing cozy refreshments and the views its name suggests. Farther along the A747, a side road leads to a path down a wooded glen onto the stony beach and **cave** where St. Ninian worshipped in the 5th century. **Gavin Maxwell,** author of that famous book about an otter, *Ring of Bright Water,* grew up in the countryside around here. At Monrieth, the next village west, a **bronze otter statue** lies in the clifftops by the golf course.

Behind **Port William,** a sizeable community in these parts with brightly painted houses, is one of the area's most poignant prehistoric sites, **Drumtroddan Standing Stones.** They're lean, foreboding stone sentinels several millennia old. Cup and ring markings are nearby.

◖ PORTPATRICK AND RINNS OF GALLOWAY

Sprightly, delightful Portpatrick, climbing up a steep hillside from its small and scenic waterfront, was once the area's main harbor. Its history has been much influenced by its proximity to Ireland—smuggling and Irish migration during the time of the Irish rebellion when passengers "of low condition and mean appearance" arrived in the holds of vessels. Portpatrick is the best place to stay on the Rinns, if not in southern Scotland. Aside from some magical walks (the Southern Upland Way begins or ends here), there is no sightseeing in town; this is rather a place to relax, do a round or two of putting, and spoil yourself with the diverse range of places to eat and drink. Portpatrick is the main settlement on the tantalizingly wild Rinns Peninsula, which stretches as far south as Scotland goes and has some fascinating birdlife in store. At the end of August Portpatrick comes alive with the sounds of the **Portpatrick Folk Festival.**

Accommodations and Food

Given its position on the **Southern Upland Way,** Portpatrick has surprisingly little budget accommodation. You're limited to often-tacky (although wonderfully located) campsites around **Luce Bay** seven miles southwest.

◖ **Braefield Guest House** (Braefield Rd., tel. 01776/810255, from £27 s, £54 d) is a big old Victorian guesthouse with a commanding position on the hills above town. This comfortably battered place has stunning views in the morning. You'll need about an hour to get through the breakfasts, tailored to your needs by the chatty owner and involving ample quantities of fresh fruit. A handy flight of steps leads to the center of town (five minutes down, a bit more back up). In a bank-less town, it's worth noting you can pay by credit card for your stay.

The rooms at the **Waterfront Hotel and Bistro** (7 North Crescent, tel. 01776/810800,

© LUKE WATERSON

Mull of Galloway Lighthouse, at the end of the Rinns Peninsula

www.waterfronthotel.co.uk, £45 pp d/twin) are about as stylish as possible, with very comfortable beds and intriguing artwork on the walls. As the hotel is right on the harborfront, many rooms come with wonderful sea views (and go first). There's a restaurant that lacks a little in ambience but makes up for it with a popular outside terrace in summer and scrumptious food. The menu is varied; three-course set dinners are £22.50.

A former customs house, **Harbour House Hotel** (53 Main St., tel. 01776/810456, www.theharbourhousehotel.co.uk, £37.50 pp) dates from 1790. It has light en suite rooms, one with private bath and all with the usual world-class Portpatrick views, above a bar stocked with malt whiskies and real ales. Slide into the cozy fireside booths or the harborside picnic tables outside for a pint or sample the menu (noon–9 P.M.), which includes hefty Aberdeen Angus beef burgers.

◖ Campbell's (1 South Crescent, tel. 01776/810314, noon–2:30 P.M. and 6–9:30 P.M. Tues.–Sat., noon–2:30 P.M. and 6:30–9:30 P.M. Sun.) is the best restaurant in these parts. It's

a stylish, warm place with attentive but unpretentious service. The seafood is the big draw here—it's caught in the restaurant's own boat, which is why it's a special-occasion kind of place (mains from £14.95). Tuck into some scallops with the chunky, locally made cutlery and watch the sea pounding against the harbor only meters away beneath a star-studded sky.

Getting There and Away

Bus 358/367 runs hourly from Portpatrick to Stranraer (20 minutes).

Southern Rinns Peninsula

South from Portpatrick off the B7065 is **Logan Botanical Gardens** (tel. 01776/860231, www.rbge.org.uk, 10 A.M.–6 P.M. daily Apr.–Sept., 10 A.M.–5 P.M. daily Mar. and Oct.), a blaze of color featuring an exotic blend of plants native to South America, New Zealand, and Africa. The gardens have a shop and scrumptious salad bar.

At the very end of the peninsula, fields peter out into Scotland's southernmost point, the **Mull of Galloway.** In a wild location buffeted on all sides by winds is the **Mull of Galloway Nature Reserve** (lighthouse 10 A.M.–3:30 P.M. Sat.–Sun. Apr.–Sept., visitors center 10 A.M.– 4 or 5 P.M. daily Apr.–Sept.). You can climb the 26-meter-high tower for views of England, Wales, Ireland, and even Scotland (about the only place anywhere from which you can see all four countries). The visitors center gives insight into local fauna and flora. Stick to the paths as you explore—cliffs are dangerous and birds nest there. One would assume the chances of finding refreshment out in these parts were pretty much nonexistent, but ☕ **Gallie Craig Coffee House** (tel. 01776/840558, 10 A.M.–6 P.M. daily Apr.–Oct., 11 A.M.–4 P.M. Fri.–Tues. Feb. and Nov., closed Jan. and Dec.) is there to surprise you. This modern, spacious place has a good variety of soups, sandwiches, homebakes, and other light snacks and an enviable clifftop location.

Stranraer and Vicinity

There is no reason to come this shabby ferry port unless you are catching a ferry. If you are marooned, however, do not despair. There are a couple of accommodation options, which, in stark contrast with Stranraer, are attractive.

Castle Kennedy and Gardens (info@ castlekennedygardens.co.uk, 10 A.M.–5 P.M. daily Apr.–Sept.), three miles east of town, is as close to Stranraer as you need to get unless you're ferry-bound. The gardens are some of the most famous in Scotland, poised on a strip of land between two lochs, with a 350-year history and restored to their current vitality in the 19th century. The best times to visit are May and June, to see the dazzling rhododendrons and Chilean fire-bushes ablaze, or September, when the walled garden is at its best. Set aside a few hours to do the 75-acre floral spectacle justice.

Stranraer is full of bland places to stay so it's refreshing to find **North West Castle** (tel. 01776/704413, www.northwestcastle.co.uk, £75 s, £110 d), an old-fashioned place with

the world's oldest indoor hotel curling rink. The Ross Bar was used by former owner and polar explorer John Ross to demonstrate polar navigation to guests. It's a bit too much like the mountain lodge from *The Shining* in places, but thankfully rambling enough to forget about the town you're staying in.

Offering pick-up from the town center with advance notification and therefore another feasible option for ferry-goers is **Corsewall Lighthouse Hotel** (Corsewall Point, tel. 01776/853220, www.lighthousehotel.co.uk, Kirkcolm, from £100 pp) with a variety of classy rooms and suites in an 1815 lighthouse at the north of the hammerhead-shaped Rinns peninsula—one of the most original and luxurious hotels in southern Scotland. Single-night stays are only allowed during the week—this is a place worth devoting more time to, anyway.

Two **ferries** run across to Northern Ireland from the Stranraer area. **Stenna Line** (tel. 0870/570 7070, www.stennaline.com, up to nine crossings daily) operates the service from Stranraer to **Belfast;** the fast ferry makes the journey in 1.75 hours, otherwise it's 3.25 hours.

P&O (tel. 0870/242 4777, www.poirish-sea.com, up to eight crossings daily) operates a service from **Cairnryan** (up the coast from Stranraer) to **Larne.** Journey time is 1–1.75 hours. In either case, prices are extremely variable and depend how far in advance you book.

The main **bus** station is at Port Rodie, near the police station. For **Ayr** take bus 358/360, which runs several times daily (two hours, five minutes, £5.80). The **Dumfries** Bus X75/500 runs up to 10 times daily (2.5 hrs.). To **Glasgow,** Scottish Citylink run a service twice daily (2.5 hrs., £13.80). Buses to **Portpatrick** leave from behind Tesco hourly.

Trains run between Stranraer and Glasgow (8–10 daily, 2.5 hrs., £17.50). Three are direct; otherwise change in Ayr (one hour 20 minutes, £11.70). Bus is a better option if you want to go to Dumfries.

AYRSHIRE AND ARRAN

Scots may get together every January for Burns Night, the world's second-most-celebrated birthday, but it is Ayrshire where the spirit of Scotland's national bard burns strongest. In Ayr, his birth town, lines from his poems are engraved everywhere from hotel rooms to statues, and local football fans still chant the famous lines from Burns's poem "Tam O' Shanter" about a man who stays too long at the pub and then has a dreadful vision: "Auld Ayr, wham ne'er a town surpasses/For honest men and bonnie lasses." Alloway, to the south of town, houses the Burns Heritage Park, including the evocative cottage where the poet was born.

Before you ask what this part of Scotland did before "Rabbie" Burns began attracting visitors, Ayr has answers aplenty. Near the Heritage Park is Rozelle House, an art gallery to rival Scotland's finest, and the town is more widely known as Scotland's leading horseracing venue, hosting the Scottish Grand National. Historic world-class golf courses are just along the coast at Troon, where the long golden sands have long enticed holidaymakers.

The main attraction on the south coast is the fortress of Culzean. Standing on wooded cliffs in Scotland's first country park, the castle has walled flower gardens, forest walks, and rooms devoted to President Dwight Eisenhower, who came to Culzean for his holidays. Farther south is the mysterious Loch Doon and its castle, allegedly a hiding place for Robert the Bruce while he was on the run from the English.

Off Ayrshire's west coast, the Isle of Arran is the highlight for the region. Straddling the

© LUKE WATERSON

HIGHLIGHTS

◖ Alloway: Soak up the life of Scotland's national bard in Burns's home village (page 142).

◖ Isle of Great Cumbrae: This tranquil island is perfect for cycling and offers great water sports (page 149).

◖ North Arran: High hill walking, broken castles, wild beaches, and great places to stay . . . remote North Arran is a taste of the Highlands within easy reach of Glasgow (page 152).

◖ Culzean Castle and Country Park: Former holiday home of Dwight Eisenhower, this elaborate clifftop castle stands surrounded by forested grounds and its own private beaches (page 157).

◖ Loch Doon: Get away from it all as Robert the Bruce once did, discovering mysterious Loch Doon (page 158).

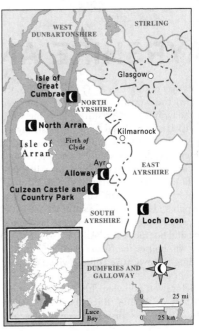

LOOK FOR ◖ TO FIND RECOMMENDED SIGHTS, ACTIVITIES, DINING, AND LODGING.

Highland boundary fault, it's the best place to observe Scotland's stark geographical contrasts, with coastal villages and gentle wooded lowlands alongside austere brown inland hills. The hills offer the region's most outstanding walking but also hide castles, stone circles, a distillery, and a brewery within their folds—little surprise that Arran gets called "Scotland in Miniature."

HISTORY

Early Bronze Age peoples had erected standing stones on the Isle of Arran at locations like Machrie Moor by 1600 to 1800 B.C. Throughout the early medieval period, the Ayr region enjoyed prosperity courtesy of a healthy wool and hide trade. The developing town was important enough in 1315 to host the meeting of the Scottish parliament in St. John's Tower to decide who would succeed Robert the Bruce. Oliver Cromwell passed through Ayr, as he did many towns across Scotland, in 1652. He demolished the old tower to build a fort and used the town as a major garrison base during his Scottish campaign.

Ayr embraced the Industrial Revolution earlier than most parts of Scotland. By the time poet Robert Burns was born near Ayr in 1759, much of Ayrshire was changing irreversibly from a rural to an industrial region. Key industries included hand-loom weaving and gauze production, which made towns

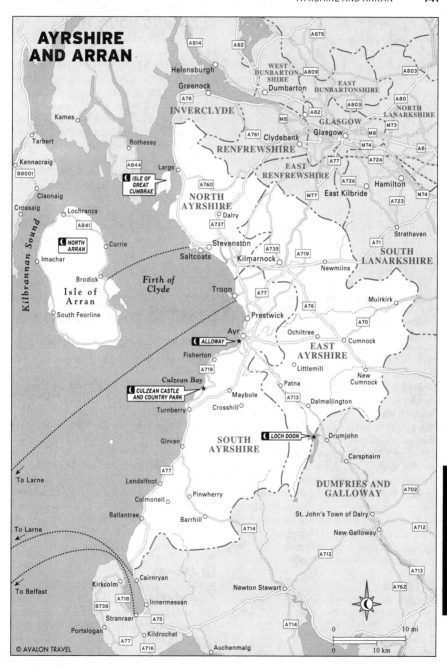

AYRSHIRE AND ARRAN

Helensburgh
Kames
Tarbert
Greenock
WEST DUNBARTON-SHIRE
Dumbarton
EAST DUNBARTONSHIRE
INVERCLYDE
GLASGOW
NORTH LANARKSHIRE
Rothesay
Clydebank
Glasgow
RENFREWSHIRE
Kennacraig
Largs
ISLE OF GREAT CUMBRAE
EAST RENFREWSHIRE
Hamilton
Claonaig
NORTH AYRSHIRE
East Kilbride
Crossaig
Lochranza
Dalry
Strathaven
NORTH ARRAN
Corrie
Stevenston
SOUTH LANARKSHIRE
Imachar
Saltcoats
Kilmarnock
Newmilns
Brodick
Firth of Clyde
Isle of Arran
Troon
Muirkirk
South Feorline
Prestwick
Ayr
ALLOWAY
Ochiltree
Cumnock
EAST AYRSHIRE
Fisherton
Littlemill
New Cumnock
Culzean Bay
Patna
CULZEAN CASTLE AND COUNTRY PARK
Maybole
Dalmellington
Turnberry
Crosshill
SOUTH AYRSHIRE
LOCH DOON
Drumjohn
Girvan
Carsphairn
To Larne
Lendalfoot
DUMFRIES AND GALLOWAY
Colmonell
Pinwherry
To Larne
Ballantrae
Barrhill
St. John's Town of Dalry
New Galloway
To Belfast
Cairnryan
Kirkcolm
Innermessan
Newton Stewart
Stranraer
Portslogan
Kildrochat
Auchenmalg

Kilbrannan Sound

0   10 mi
0   10 km

© AVALON TRAVEL

like Galston in Eastern Ayrshire prosper, and later coal mining. Epitomizing Ayrshire's newfound wealth was Culzean Castle on the coast south of Ayr. The Kennedy family, who owned the property, turned the castle into a set piece of their own power and grandeur. Celebrated architect Robert Adam was employed to transform the fortress into one of the most glamorous in the land.

The trades that ensured affluence in the 19th century declined in the 20th century, and the large parts of the region that had relied on them consequently slumped. Ayr itself enjoyed a rebirth as part of the Clyde Riviera tourist boom in the late 19th and early 20th centuries. The development of Prestwick Airport in the 1950s and 1960s just north of Ayr created an important economical resource for Ayrshire.

PLANNING YOUR TIME

The "Best-of" is doable in a long weekend. Aim to spend at least two nights on Arran (far and away the highlight), with a day climbing Goat Fell and exploring the grounds of Brodick Castle and another day discovering the little-visited north side of the island. On the third day, set aside a few hours for Culzean Castle once you hop back to the mainland before heading to the Burns Heritage Park to find out all about Scotland's number one poet and stroll the pretty parklands. With five days, you could try a round of golf on one of Troon's historic courses, head up to Largs for some traditional seaside fun and a poke around the Vikingar! exhibition, or explore little-visited southern Ayrshire with great walks, particularly on Carrick Moor around Loch Doon.

Ayr

The bustling, red sandstone coastal town of Ayr was always an important center on the Clyde coast. Robert the Bruce held his first parliament in St. John's Kirk, subsequently pulled down by Oliver Cromwell, who decided to locate his Scottish garrison in the town and needed the spare stone to house them in Ayr Citadel, itself long since collapsed. Later Ayr escaped industrialization but did become the region's main holiday resort due to the miles of golden sandy beaches stretching beyond the town. Despite the beaches and the history, and the wealthy benefactors over the years that allowed for the creation of several lush landscaped parks, the town itself is unspectacular and visitors mainly come to explore the heritage of Ayr's most famous son, Robert Burns, in leafy Alloway to the south.

SIGHTS

Ayr's visitor attractions are either in the town center or in Alloway, two miles to the south.

Town Center

Most people come to the town to shop or to catch a horse race, with a couple of notable exceptions, which can be encompassed in a short walk.

The **Auld Brig** (second bridge up the river from the sea) has been immortalized in Burns's poem "The Brigs of Ayr." It's a short walk left up the High Street to the **Tam o' Shanter Pub** where Burns's Tam has a drinking session before his terrible journey home. Continue back down past the Auld Kirk and left up Newmarket Street. Continue up Cathcart Street and Citadel Place to reach **St. John's Tower** (tel. 01292/286385, call ahead to look around), all that remains of St. John's Kirk, where Robert the Bruce held parliament after victory in the Battle of Bannockburn.

◖ Alloway

Ayr's main draw card is in this village just south of Ayr, where Robert Burns was born and spent much of his childhood. The hugely impressive **Burns National Heritage Park** (Murdoch's Lane, tel. 01292/443700, Tam o' Shanter Experience, Burns Cottage, and

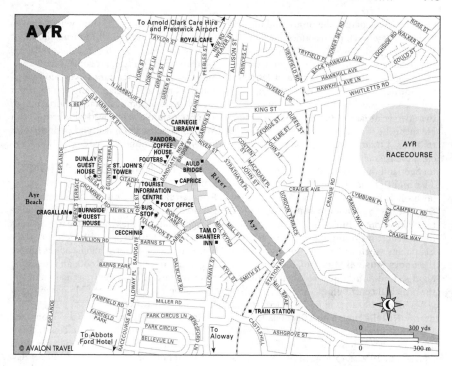

museum open 9:30 A.M.–5:30 P.M. daily Apr.–Oct., 10 A.M.–5 P.M. daily Nov.–Mar., Gardens Monument and Statue House open 9:30 A.M.–5 P.M. daily Apr.–Oct., 10 A.M.–4 P.M. daily Nov.–Mar. weather permitting, Kirk Alloway and Brig o' Doon open year-round, £5 for all attractions) includes the house where the poet was born and spent his early years, as well as a huge range of Burns artifacts. At the time of writing, a substantial renovation program was planned. To the regret of some, to celebrate the 250th anniversary of Burns's birthday, the National Trust for Scotland is taking over in 2009. It plans to relocate the Burns Cottage Museum in an expanded visitors center on the site of the Tam o' Shanter Experience.

There are two main parts to the heritage park. The **Tam O'Shanter Experience** (audiovisual display £1.50) is set in an acre of landscaped gardens and includes a fascinating audiovisual presentation bringing Burns's most famous poem to life. This is where the visitors center is currently located; it includes a large shop, helpful and knowledgeable staff, and a spacious restaurant with superb views into the park. In the **Gardens** (free) nearby is the **Burns Monument** (entry £1), built by Edinburgh architect Thomas Hamilton. It's an impressive structure—a 70-foot-high Grecian-style temple with nine pillars representing the nine Muses of Greek mythology. Climb up to the top for great views of the Doon Valley, including the **Auld Brig o' Doon** (free), a narrow high-arched bridge that Burns used as the setting for Tam's escape in his poem "Tam O'Shanter." In the monument gardens is a **Statue House** containing statues of a more quirky nature—humorous likenesses of Tam o' Shanter, his friend Souter Johnie, and other characters. It's a fitting tribute to the poet, who became good friends with and drew inspiration from people in all walks of life. Also in the park is the ruined and magical **Kirk Alloway** (free); Burns buried his father in the church graveyard.

Farther up the road is the second part of the complex. **Burns Cottage and Museum** (£3 adults, £1.50 children, including museum entry) was built in 1757 by Burns's father; two years later, "Rabbie" was born there. He spent the first seven years of his life in the traditional thatched cottage where he developed the passion for reading, for writing, and for Scotland that would serve him in later life. The highlight is the bed where Burns was born on January 25, 1759. In the adjoining **Burns Cottage Museum** is the most important collection of Burns-related memorabilia in existence, including many manuscripts of his poems (such as "Auld Lang Syne") and the **Scots Musical Museum,** a collection of Scottish traditional music to which Burns was the principal contributor.

Set in over 100 acres of tree-studded grounds nearby, **Rozelle House and Gardens** (Rozelle Park, Monument Rd., tel. 01292/445447, 10 A.M.–5 P.M. Mon.–Sat., 2–4:45 P.M. Sun. Apr.–Oct., 10 A.M.–5 P.M. Mon.–Sat. Nov.–Mar.) is a major display venue with its current highlight being the significant collection of 54 paintings by Alexander Goudie based on the theme of Tam o' Shanter. The artist's fascination with his subject comes across clearly in the bright and often spooky series, and there's no better place to have Burns's poem brought alive for you. Attached to the house is the McLaurin Galleries, a mainly 20th-century collection of paintings, prints, drawings, and sculptures. There is a coffee shop and a good craft shop on-site. Rozelle House doesn't get the volume of tour parties the rest of the Burns Heritage Park gets; the gardens are a tranquil place for a wander and a picnic on a summer day.

ENTERTAINMENT AND EVENTS

Hats off to Ayr: few other places can generate so much business from one poem. The famous **Tam O'Shanter Inn** (230–234 High St., tel. 01292/611684, 11 A.M.–12:30 A.M. summer, 11 A.M.–11 P.M. winter), from where Tam o' Shanter began his eventful journey home, is happily devoid of kitsch (OK, there're Burns quotes over the walls but it comes across as atmospheric). The restaurant serves good meals and does real ales on tap. Not only that, but there's a festival commemorating Burns in Ayr. The **Burns an' a' That** festival takes place in May and is a feast of music and performances loosely based around the bard.

SPORTS AND RECREATION
Golf
Prestwick Golf Course (2 Links Rd., Prestwick, tel. 01292/671020, www.prestwickgc.co.uk) was the venue of the first Scottish Open in 1860. It has a late-19th-century clubhouse adorned with memorabilia on the history of golf in Prestwick since 1860: an interesting place to observe how the sport has changed. Playing on the course costs £115 per round or £170 for a day ticket.

Royal Troon (Craigend Rd., Troon tel. 01292/311555, www.royaltroon.co.uk) offers a deal with morning coffee, lunch, and one round on both of its courses for £220 per day.

Horse Racing
Ayr Racecourse (Whitletts Rd., tel. 0870/850 5666, www.ayrracecourse.co.uk) is the finest place to see a horse race in Scotland. This might seem like a strange field to be making distinctions in, but Ayr and horse racing go way back—as early as the 16th century, in fact. The first official race meeting was in 1777. Today, the town hosts two of the most important events in the Scottish horse racing calendar: the Scottish Grand National in April and the Ayr Gold Cup, one of the most exciting sprint races in the game, in September.

ACCOMMODATIONS
Ayr has the best variety of accommodations in the region, although precious few budget options. If you're traveling in the area on the cheap, Arran has more places to stay. Many accommodation options are a couple of streets back from the esplanade, along Queen's Terrace.

THE PLOUGHBOY POET

When he came to Ayrshire in 1750, William Burness (the family name's original spelling) was a poor but ambitious man and did a variety of jobs to raise money to rent his own plot of land. He built the house soon to be known the world over as Burns Cottage in 1757 and later that year married the young lady he had met at Maybole Fair, Agnes Broun. Robert, their first of seven children, was born in 1759 into poverty and a typical laborer's thatched cottage, in which animals also lived. Unusually for a man in his position, William was determined to provide his sons with an education. Against incredible odds, he not only set aside enough money for a teacher to come to Alloway to teach them, but also the time to write the *Manual of Religious Belief* to instruct his children further.

The fate of children in 18th-century Scotland was to go out and seek work once there was no longer room in the house for them, and William understood that the onus would be on Robert to be the first to go. With that in mind, he found a larger house for the family in 1766. Robert was saved, and, although he helped his father on the farm, he found he had little inclination for manual work and found his mind drifting instead to the fascinating stories recounted by a relation of his mother's, Betty Davidson. Robert recalled that Betty would tell stories of "devils, ghosts, fairies, brownies" and "inchanted towers, dragons and other trumpery"; these kindled the first inclinations to write poetry within him.

As he grew older, another inclination Burns had was for the ladies: Over the course of his short life he would father 12 children. It was infatuation that really got him writing, his first lines inspired by a girl named Nellie Kilpatrick who asked Robert to pick a thorn from her fingers during a day's work. A few years later, moved to anguish by a failed love affair, Robert Burns penned *Poems: Chiefly in the Scottish Dialect* and was catapulted into national celebrity.

A blowy sight welcoming touring vans and tents with an otherwise picturesque view spoiled by proximity to a run-down holiday camp, the **Heads of Ayr Caravan Park** (Dunure Rd., tel. 01292/442269, www.heads-ofayr.com, tent and two people £12) is the closest site to Ayr, five miles south of town on the A719. It's a 15-minute walk from the beach, and at low tide you can walk along the Heads of Ayr into town.

This recently refurbished ivy-swathed **Dunlay Guest House** (1 Ailsa Pl., tel. 01292/610230, £30 pp standard, £35 pp en suite) has been around since the 17th century. The house offers four rooms, two of which are en suite, about as smack-bang in the middle of Ayr as you could hope. Two rooms at the back face an idyllic enclosed courtyard.

Burnside Guest House (14 Queen's Terr., tel. 01292/263192, from £28 pp s/d, from £35 with Burns breakfast) is a traditional guesthouse offering single, double, twin, and family rooms (three en suite). With period furniture and extremely comfortable beds, it's still serving the breakfast that's likely to linger longest in your memory. As you tuck into your full Scottish breakfast, a figure dressed as Robert Burns himself appears on request and recites poetry. Yes, you can even ask for "Address to a Haggis." As you wash it all down with bannocks, cheese, and fruit, the Burns lookalike can inform you about a Burns-related (surprise, surprise) tour of the town (www.walkaboutayr.com). Reduced room rates are available from November to March.

Cragallan (8 Queen's Terr., tel. 01292/264998, www.cragallan.com, from £35 s, from £60 d) is a pale blue terraced guest house containing a wealth of surprises. There are comfortable airy rooms (top floor with sea views), a pretty tartan-carpeted guest lounge, a dining table that converts into a billiard table, and a landlady that will bend over backward to make your stay an enjoyable one.

Coated in ivy, the white, turreted **Abbotsford Hotel** (14 Corsehill Rd., tel.

01292/261506, www.abbotsfordhotel.co.uk, £40 s, £75 d) offers light, reasonably sized en suite rooms, all with TVs. It is a wealth of information on local attractions, most notably golf and horse racing. There's a colorful restaurant with interesting memorabilia on the walls (fish to old-fashioned pots) and a bar with a blazing open fire. To get there, follow Alloway Place south to Racecourse Road and turn left at Racecourse View to reach Corsehill Road.

The ◖ **Brig O' Doon House Hotel** (tel. 01292/442466, www.costley-hotels.co.uk, rooms £85 s, £120 d) is as traditional a hotel as you would expect on the doorstep of the Burns Heritage Park. The large rooms have four-poster beds and antique baths, while downstairs it's all blazing fires and tartan carpets. The bar/restaurant is absolutely huge, with great views of the river and surrounding parkland. The hotel can arrange a host of activities from archery to falconry.

FOOD

Ayr is no stranger to the hospitality trade and has a number of cracking places to eat and drink.

Pandora Coffee House (32 New Bridge St., tel. 01292/289919, 8:30 A.M.–6 P.M. Mon.–Sat., 9:30 A.M.–6 P.M. Sun.) is a plush wood-paneled spot serving coffees, croissants, fresh baguettes, ciabattas, and soup. It's been sating rumbling bellies in Ayr for decades. Sundays are all-day breakfast days—a great place for a browse of the newspapers. The original 1920s lighting is still in place. Snacks and light meals are £3–6.

Still owned by the Mancini family after nearly a century, the **Royal Café** (11–15 New Rd., tel. 01292/263058, 9 A.M.–10:30 P.M. daily) is Ayr's oldest eatery. It's still producing scrumptious fish suppers and—the real draw—a good claim to Scotland's best ice cream. Most of the other mouth-watering Scottish grub that makes a seaside holiday perfect is also served for around £5 or under.

Burns Heritage Centre Restaurant (tel. 01292/443700, 9:30 A.M.–5:30 P.M. daily Apr.–Oct., 10 A.M.–5 P.M. daily Nov.–Mar.) is a place where you are as likely to see a local as a tourist munching on the reasonably priced

food—a sure sign of its pedigree. It's help-yourself, canteen-style service, from coffees, cakes, and light snacks (£2–4) to more substantial, piping hot mains. The fantastic views of the Burns Heritage Park are the main reason to be here—rolling green in front of the wide windows.

Caprice (48 Newmarket St., tel. 01292/ 610916, www.caprice-ayr.co.uk, 9 A.M.– 9:45 P.M. daily, bar open late) is a popular art deco café/bar that doesn't disappoint. You can head here for a morning coffee, a midday glass of wine and light lunch, or a more intimate evening meal in the oak-paneled restaurant downstairs. It's got low lighting, a cozy feel, a good array of continental beers and cocktails, and a menu (mains £9–11) that will have you salivating. The cuisine's mostly Scottish/seafood—try the hand-dived seared king scallops.

Class act ◖ **Cecchini's** (72 Fort St., tel. 01292/263607, noon–2:30 P.M. and 6–10 P.M. Mon.–Sat.) offers some of Ayr's finest dining. It's tasty Italian fare on the menu here with interesting options like homemade crab cakes (£9.95) or the trademark meatballs (£8.95) as well as plentiful pizzas (from £5.50). Main meals are £5.50–12.

Fouters (2A Academy St., tel. 01292/ 261391, www.fouters.co.uk, noon–2:30 P.M. and 6–9 P.M. Tues.–Thurs., noon–2:30 P.M. and 6–10 P.M. Fri.–Sat.) boasts that it is recommended by every guidebook to Scotland; the reason for that is top-notch food and plenty of ambience. Down a flight of steps off a quiet side street, this former bank vault is a magical find. The original bank counter is still in place, and bare stone walls help create that rustic-but-trendy feel. Seafood and venison are popular, and each dish has its own elaborate variation. Try the roast rack of lamb with pine nut, garlic, and herb crust alongside honey-roasted vegetables (£15.95). Most main meals are around £15.

INFORMATION AND SERVICES
Information
The **TIC** (22 Sandgate, tel. 0845/225 5121, 9 A.M.–5 P.M. Mon.–Sat. Apr.–June and

Sept.–Mar., 9 A.M.–6 P.M. Mon.–Sat., 10 A.M.–5 P.M. Sun. July–Aug.) stocks a good selection of local maps.

Services

All town center banks have ATMs and are located on High Street/Sandgate. There is free Internet access at **Carnegie Library** (12 Main St., tel. 01292/286385, 9 A.M.–5 P.M. Mon.–Sat. Apr.–June and Sept.–Mar., 9 A.M.–6 P.M. Mon.–Sat., 10 A.M.–5 P.M. Sun. July–Aug.). You'll find Ayr's primary post office on Sandgate.

Ayr Hospital (Dalmellington Rd., south of town center, tel. 01292/610555) is capable of dealing with most medical emergencies.

Two car rental companies you can try are **Arnold Clark** (Prestwick Rd., tel. 0845/607 4500) and astonishingly cheap **Eurodrive** (Wagon Rd., tel. 01292/619192), where hire starts from £99 per week for a small car—surely the best deal in the country.

GETTING THERE

Ayr's transport connections are about as good as Scotland can offer due to Glasgow's Prestwick Airport being located (confusingly) on its doorstep a few miles north of town.

Glasgow–Ayr trains (two hourly, 7 minutes, £1.70) run to Prestwick.

Glasgow Prestwick Airport (tel. 0871/223 0700, www.gpia.co.uk) handles budget flights from multiple destinations within the U.K. and Europe. Facilities at the airport include a bureau de change, an information desk, cash machines, and left luggage (£4 per day).

Stagecoach Western (tel. 01292/613500) operates buses to Glasgow (no. X77, every 15–30 min., 1 hr., £4.50), Largs (no. 585, hourly, 1.5 hrs., £4.55), Stranraer (no. 358, every 2 hours, 2 hrs. 5 min., £5.80) and Dumfries (no. 246, around 5 per day, 2.5 hrs., £4.80).

P&O (tel. 0870/242 4777, www.poirish-sea.com) runs a ferry between Troon and Larne in Northern Island from March to October (twice per day, 1 hr. 50 min.). Prices fluctuate, generally lower the earlier you book.

GETTING AROUND

To get to Alloway and the Burns National Heritage Centre, take bus 57 from the station or bus 361 from Carrick Street (half-hourly). Bus 14E (half-hourly) is one of the frequent buses that run to Troon (for Royal Troon Golf Course).

For a taxi, try **Ayr Black Taxis** (tel. 01292/284545).

North Ayrshire

North Ayrshire is not going to blow your mind with its beauty, unless you head to the Clyde Muirshiel Regional Park in the far north of the region. Much to this area has fallen victim to heavy industrial blight, but there are a couple of good reasons to visit. For starters, the coast is an almost continual swath of yellow sand from Ayr upward. For the kitschiest British seaside resort experience possible, Largs, in the north, is worth a look. From Largs you can sail to the wonderful little Isle of Great Cumbrae, a bright island a world away from the dull grind of mainland North Ayrshire. The ferry to Arran runs from Ardrossan, south of Largs.

LARGS

Flashing amusements, fish-and-chips shops, and a long windy front signify your arrival in Largs, straggled out for several miles along the North Ayshire shoreline. Once this area was known as the Costa del Clyde because of the holidaymakers it attracted; that stopped in the 1960s with the advent of cheap foreign package holidays but, thankfully for fans of the old-fashioned seaside resort, Largs has been pretty much frozen in time. Each June the **Viking Festival** celebrates the glorious day in 1263 when the Vikings were trounced at the Battle of Largs, thereby ending their dominion in Scotland for good.

CLYDE COAST ICE CREAM

Looking back, it all seemed so logical – poor Italian workers looking for employment in the Glasgow area and the boom in train travel in the late 19th century, which meant a lot of Glaswegians liked to get out of the city on the weekend. The result? Britain's biggest and best ice-cream boom, with ice cream parlors opening up and down the Clyde coast. There were some legendary establishments with legendary queues of city holidaymakers needing refreshment of the ice cream kind. Nardini's in Largs became the largest café in Britain in its day. When "Doon the Watter" ceased to become far enough for Glasgow families to go on a break, the seaside tourist industry declined, but bits of it remain, including the legacy of top-notch ice cream.

The Mancini family are one of those few Italian families on the Ayr coast still in the ice cream business – fourth-generation ice-cream makers with an unbelievable array of flavors available from their Royal Café on New Road in Ayr. Try the Erotic Cocktail sorbet or the blue bubble gum flavor, with that tang of old-fashioned bubble gum. Cast your eye out for ice cream parlors up and down this part of the coast – they could just have a century of experience at creating that favorite of holiday snacks.

Sights

The Battle of Largs and Viking history come to life in **Vikingar!** (Greenock Rd., tel. 01475/689777, 10:30 A.M.–5:30 P.M. daily Apr.–Sept., 10:30 A.M.–3:30 P.M. daily Oct. and Mar., 10:30 A.M.–3:30 P.M. Sat.–Sun. Nov. and Feb., £4.20 adults, £2.50 children), a fun attraction in which a costumed storyteller takes you on a journey through Viking Scotland from the earliest Viking raids to the bitter end in 1263. The insight into their way of life, with the help of multimedia displays, is a vivid experience, particularly for children, who come away far more enthused than from your average stuffy museum.

Covering 108 square miles across the hills behind the Clyde coast, the **Clyde Muirshiel Regional Park** is Scotland's largest regional park. Largs, in its southwest corner, is one of the best access points. The open tracts of moor are barely inhabited; it's amazing to think that Glasgow is less than 20 miles away. It's a true delight for outdoorsy types— nothing spectacular by Highland standards but a refreshing change from Ayrshire's neat farmland. There is some great walking to be had on the fringes: the Greenock Cut in the north and the enticing woods and lochs around Castle Semple in the southeast. You can camp in the park, too. See www.clyde-muirshiel.co.uk for further information on walking and other activities.

Accommodations and Food

Run by a laid-back couple, the working **South Whittlieburn Farm** (Brisbane Glen Rd., tel. 01475/675881, £35 s, £55 d) in the hills above Largs is a great alternative to the typical Largs seaside bed-and-breakfast. The spacious, simply furnished rooms have ample stores of snacks to tide you over until the even more ample breakfasts. The farm is the best-located accommodation option for Clyde Muirshiel Regional Park.

The Viking (32 Gallowgate St., tel. 01475/674949, open until late) is an award-winning exponent of the cheap, no-nonsense Largs fish supper takeaway. Moreover, it's an essential ingredient of any kitschy seafront experience. Admire the huge plastic Viking inside then take your booty (£1–6) down to munch on the seafront.

Information

The Largs **TIC** (tel. 01475/689962, 9 A.M.– 5 P.M. Mon.–Sat. Easter–Oct.) is at the Railway Station.

Getting There

Trains run hourly between Largs and Glasgow

(one hour, £5.85). Bus 585 runs frequently between Ayr and Largs (one hour 25 min., £4.55).

◖ ISLE OF GREAT CUMBRAE

The gentle grassy hills and sandy beaches of tranquil Great Cumbrae are more favored by Scottish holidaymakers than by International tourists but this island is about as relaxed as an island can be. It's not your typical rugged Scottish island; its accessibility from Glasgow and good roads mean outdoor pursuits are even more popular than in other places. The only town, **Millport** (www.millport.org), boasts Britain's smallest cathedral and more bike hire shops per capita than anywhere in the country. The island has some great cycling as well as having one of Scotland's most important water sports centers. If these sound too energetic, strolling the peaceful shoreline is equally rewarding.

Sights, Recreation, and Events

Britain's smallest cathedral, the **Cathedral of the Isles** (College St., Millport, tel. 01475/530353) was built in 1851 by William Butterfield, a key architect of the Gothic revival. Unique features include a pyramidal steeple and the beautifully painted roof depicting wild flowers found on the island. Sunday Service is at 11 A.M. The island is also a birdwatcher's dream, with tawny owls and doves in the cathedral grounds and buzzards on the inland moor. On the west side of the island north of Fintry Bay is **Indian's Face,** a painting using cliff contours to produce the striking profile of an Indian in battle garb.

Scottish National Watersports Centre (Millport, tel. 01475/530757, cumbraecentre@sportscotland.org.uk) offers courses and guidance on everything water sport related, from windsurfing to sea kayaking. There are no set hours so call ahead to make sure the kind of instruction you want is available. **Mapes of Millport** (3–5 Guildford St., tel. 01475/530344) claims to offer not only the cheapest bike rentals on the island, but also in the U.K., at £2 per hour or £4 per day.

The island erupts in waves of quality music with the **Millport Country and Western Weekend** at the end of August.

Accommodations and Food

There aren't many accommodations, so if you want to stay, book ahead. The most unusual place to stay on the island is **The College of the Holy Spirit** (tel. 01475/530353, www.island-retreats.org, £32–37 s, £64–74 d), a character-filled, recently refurbished building next to the cathedral in woodland-dotted fields. The college is also a Christian retreat, and the rooms are simple but very warming. Guests also get use of a well-stocked library. Half or full board (quite worth the splash) is £10/20 extra per person.

Unfortunately, there are no official campsites on Cumbrae, although wild camping is possible.

The **Ritz Café** (24 Stuart St., Millport, tel. 01475/530459) with its 1960s decor is a fun place to grab something to eat. It's Clyde resort–style food at its best: toasties, filled rolls, ice cream, and rock for next to nothing.

Getting There and Away

Calmac Ferries to Cumbrae (£2.85 passenger, £15.70 car) run roughly half hourly from Largs throughout the year. There's little need to bring a car, though, as a bus meets the ferry to take you to Millport, and on an island just 11 kilometers round, walking or cycling anywhere is simple.

KILMARNOCK

This largely ugly industrial town northeast of Ayr has a few remnants of its history left. **Dean Castle** (tel. 01563/522702, www.dean-castle.com, castle open 11 A.M.–5 P.M. Wed.–Sun., country park 11 A.M.–5 P.M. Apr.–Oct., 11 A.M.–4 P.M. Nov.–Mar.) is in fact two fortifications: a keep dating from around 1360 and a palace built about a century later, both surrounded by a curtained wall. The priorities of the Boyd family, who were gifted the castle by Robert the Bruce in gratitude for their support during the Wars of Independence, clearly changed over the centuries. The sturdy, almost windowless keep was built for defense, the palace for comfort without much regard for defense at all. The castle houses the important McKie Collection of Burns-related manuscripts and paintings. It also has an intriguing array of musical instruments. The grassy grounds, in which two rivers meet, are good for a stroll. In the visitors center there is also a **tearoom** (10 A.M.–4 P.M. Sat. and Sun.).

Isle of Arran

It would be hard not to be impressed with the visual excesses of Arran, straddling the highland boundary fault and thus displaying Scotland's contrasts at their most stark: rolling lowlands of forested valleys and coast-hugging whitewashed villages juxtaposed with rearing bare inland hills roamed by red deer. It's a great place to get your Scottish island fix, being easily accessible from Glasgow and yet offering a terrain remote enough to get utterly lost in if you so choose. Arran's topography conceals its greatest treasures, which makes all those things intrinsically Scottish (you'll find castles, stone circles, and great walks as well as atmospheric old pubs, golf courses, and a distillery) all the more magical when you come across them.

BRODICK AND VICINITY

Arran's capital Brodick stretches a long way around its wide sandy bay and, perhaps because of this, lacks the community feel of other places on the island. It is not much to look at either, but visitors' eyes are usually fixed on the village's stunning location. From the shore, steep ranks of conifers shoot upward into looming, black, usually mist-covered hills. It's the island's main ferry port and a good base for exploring Arran, with plenty of visitor facilities.

Sights

Just north of Brodick, **Arran Heritage Museum** (Rosaburn, Main Rd., tel. 01770/302636, www.arranmuseum.co.uk, 10:30 A.M.–4:30 P.M. daily mid-March–Oct., £3 adults, £1.50 children) is a window into bygone Arran life. It has displays on the history of the island, from Clachaig Man, a re-creation of a 5,000-year-old skull found in a cairn on Arran to an early 20th-century smiddy giving horseshoeing demonstrations.

Two miles or a pleasant 30-minute stroll north of Brodick is **Brodick Castle and Gardens** (tel. 01770/302202, 11 A.M.–4 P.M. Apr.–Oct., country park open all year, £10 adults, £7 seniors). It easily wins the prize for Arran's most popular—and overrated—attraction. The castle makes for a great visit, certainly, but the late 16th-century tower is merely a focal point for the outstanding castle grounds. On a steep, conifer-flanked hillside, the rhododendron-splashed gardens are the real draw here. They encompass an icehouse, a hexagonal 19th-century Bavarian summerhouse intricately decorated with fir cones, and umpteen woodland walks, plunged through by a burn (stream). There's an on-site visitors center, shop, and OK restaurant, although there are better eating options just outside the castle grounds.

You can come to the **Isle of Arran Brewery** (tel. 01770/302653, www.arranbrewery.com, Brodick Castle Grounds, 10 A.M.–5 P.M. Mon.–Sat., 12:30 A.M.–5 P.M. Sun. Easter–mid-Sept., 10 A.M.–3:30 P.M. Mon. and Wed.–Sat. mid-Sept.–Easter) for a 45-minute tour and tasting session that costs £2.

Accommodations

Glen Rosa Farm (tel. 01770/302380, camping £3.50 pp) is a traditional, basic site for tents only, with the Rosa burn tumbling through the grounds. To get here, go through Brodick, straight on at the junction to Blackwaterfoot, then turn right on the Glen Rosa track after 100 yards. Book in at the farmhouse first (back on the road, first house on left after the bridge). It's a good two miles from Brodick but is the

© LUKE WATERSON

The Isle of Arran is known for its fine food products – it produces some of the finest cheese in Scotland.

nearest campsite to the ferry and one of the island's prettiest.

Only a 20-minute walk from Brodick's main drag, **Glencloy Farmhouse** (Glen Cloy Rd., tel. 01770/302351, standard from £27.50 pp, en suite from £32.50 pp, from £35 s) feels like 20 miles away. The seven en suite rooms have a homey feel. The chatty owner has bags of advice on local attractions, but you might find yourself praying for bad weather in order to have an excuse to sample the extensive video library or sit at the window gazing out at the distant hills. Barbecues are available during summer.

Whitewashed **Rosaburn Lodge** (tel. 01770/302383, from £30 pp d/twin, suite from £40 pp) is set within its own landscaped grounds and is, geographically, the best place to base yourself for Brodick's attractions, being next to the heritage museum and about as close as it's possible to stay to Brodick Castle. The rooms are comfortable (there's also one luxury suite) but the main pulls are the gardens (plenty of topiary and the river Rosa flowing

right through them) and the breakfasts with eggs fresh from the hens clucking in the yard.

Up a bumpy track above Brodick, **Kilmichael Country House Hotel** (Glen Cloy, tel. 01770/302219, www.kilmichael.com, from £75 pp d/twin) is the epitome of getting away from it all. This hotel is Arran at its most lavish, with elaborate, innovatively furnished rooms, all with unique features: the Forest Room has a four-poster bed and Jacuzzi bath; The Fullarton Suite, decked out in daffodil yellow, has its own sitting room. Common denominators are fresh fruit and a dram of whisky to welcome you on arrival and a mix of Arran Aromatics and Crabtree and Evelyn toiletries, on top, of course, of TVs, CD players, and telephones. This estate was designed to impress outside, too, with emerald-green lawns hemmed by woods.

Food and Entertainment

Conveniently located by the ferry terminal to soothe those lurching stomachs or while away the time until departure, friendly **Copperwheats Restaurant** (tel. 01770/303522, 7:30 A.M.–5 P.M. Mon. and Tues., 7:30 A.M.–5 P.M. and 5:30–7:30 P.M. Wed.–Sat., 10:30 A.M.–5 P.M. Sun.) does a cracking all-day breakfast as well as good coffee and cakes. There's a selection of armchairs to collapse in.

Creelers (noon–2:30 P.M. and 6:30–10 P.M. Tues.–Sun. mid-Mar.–Oct. and Mondays during August and on bank holidays) is probably still the classiest joint in town, or on the island, for that matter. The place specializes in top-notch seafood, but it doesn't have the snobbishness you might fear would be an accompaniment; attached to a smokehouse and shop next door, it's a cheery, laid-back little place. What's written on the blackboard should influence your choice; it will inevitably involve the catch of the day. Staff can advise on which fishy delicacies are in season. Two-course lunches are £7.50, and there is always a vegetarian alternative.

You can watch cheese being made at **Island Cheese Company** (Home Farm, tel. 01770/302788, www.islandcheese.com)

© LUKE WATERSON

Goat Fell, a picture-postcard peak in North Arran

and taste an array of cheese samples before making your purchase (you won't be able to resist). The Isle of Arran Blue is a creamy delight. There's also a presentation on how Arran cheese is made. The shop opens early, and throughout the year. Up the road, **The Wineport** (Brodick Castle Grounds, tel. 01770/302977, morning–early evening Mar.–Oct.) is the color of a chilled glass of Rosé, with a great setting on the grassy approach to Brodick Castle. Popular with puffing walkers recuperating after a day's exertion on Goat Fell, it has a creative menu showcasing local produce; dishes include wholesome homemade soups, a platter of Arran cheese, or a fillet of steak in Lochranza whisky sauce. Fresh paninis cost £3.95; mains are a bargain at £5–8. There is an outdoor patio for those summer diners, weather and midges (biting insects) permitting, of course.

Half-screened by trees, the traditional **Ormidale Hotel** (Brodick, tel. 01770/302293, bar meals served 12:30–2 P.M. and 6–9 P.M.) pulls the best pint of ale on the island. It also offers plenty of single malts, crackling fires,

and good, wholesome bar meals. There's even a disco at weekends.

◖ NORTH ARRAN

The rugged north side of the island is a haven for walkers and wildlife. Expect bare hills and remote, boulder-scattered beaches—and a few cracking places to hole up for the night.

Walks and Sights

The most popular of many walks in Arran's rearing northern hills is that up **Goat Fell** (874 m), starting at Brodick Castle. Taking in a fortress, woods, moors grazed by deer, and a picture-postcard peak, this is one of Scotland's showcase walks. Getting up and back takes about eight hours; if you are lucky there are great panoramic views to the Inner Hebrides on a clear day, but bear in mind rain and mist are frequent uninvited visitors. The only blot on the horizon for some is the number of other people trying to do the same thing; if you're a wilderness-seeker, remember Goat Fell is only the peak of a whole tract of ridge laced with less-trodden paths. **Brodick TIC**

© LUKE WATERSON

Isle of Arran Distillery, North Arran

has information on the network of walks in Arran's hills.

For less grueling walking, **Sannox** on the east coast heading up toward **Lochranza** has the best options: along the wood-fringed coast to **North Sannox Picnic Site** and the **fallen rocks** and, more difficult, on around the **Cock of Arran** to Lochranza itself—a tough 15-kilometer hike. It's a great introduction to the **Arran Coastal Way,** a 100-kilometer path that goes right around the island. It's all beautiful, but the northern section is the wildest.

The **Isle of Arran Distillery** (tel. 01770/ 830264, www.arranwhisky.com, tours daily 10:30 A.M.–4:30 P.M. Mon.–Sat., 11:30 A.M.– 4:30 P.M. Sun. Mar.–Oct., visitors center 10 A.M.–6 P.M. Mon.–Sat., 11 A.M.–6 P.M. Sun. mid-Mar.–Oct., 10 A.M.–4 P.M. Mon., Wed., and Fri.–Sat. Nov.–Mar.) in Lochranza is one of Scotland's newest distilleries and one of the few independently owned. It's certainly a good contender for the most stunningly located, in the shadow of foreboding hills.

The battered remains of photogenic **Lochanza Castle** protrude into the loch at Lochranza. Admission is free, as any of the wheeling seabirds will confirm.

Accommodations and Food
Popular with walkers (who can get ample advice from the staff on island hikes), scenic **Lochranza Youth Hostel** (tel. 01770/830631, dorms £15) sleeps 64 in three- to eight-bed dorms.

☾ **Apple Lodge** (Lochranza, tel. 01770/ 830229, £36–42 pp d/twin) is a former manse, and the north's best accommodation option. There are only three rooms, including one with four-poster bed. Rooms have an Edwardian feel, with lots of old furniture and embroidery. Dinner is £17 for three succulent courses. Bring your own alcohol.

With views either of hills grazed by red deer that rise up behind the house or of Lochranza castle jutting into the loch, it's hard to beat the light rooms at **Kincardine Lodge** (Lochranza, tel. 01770/830267, www.kincardinelodge.co.uk, £27.50 pp twin with shared bathroom, from £30 pp d/twin en suite) location-wise. From some rooms you can even see Loch Fyne, where the kippers you can order for breakfast were caught. There's also a guest lounge, where you can gaze misty-eyed at the view or amuse yourself with a board game.

The charming **Lochranza Hotel** (tel. 01770/830223, www.lochranzahotel.co.uk, from £35 s, £55 d) is one of Arran's oldest hostelries. Much of the insides, including the rooms, are pretty basic (you could say rustically simple), but with this kind of location, you can get away with a lot. Staying here also means being close to the bar, center of the Lochranza social scene. It sports one of Scotland's biggest malt whisky collections and has a strong claim to the best beer garden on the island, if not in the country.

Good news, all you weary whisky-drinkers: at the end of the tour at Lochranza Distillery, the **Distillery Restaurant** (Lochranza, tel. 01770/830328, 10 A.M.–6 P.M. daily Mar.–Oct., also most evenings from 7 P.M. for dinner Mar.–Oct., contact distillery to book) awaits. It surrounds a fountain and has everything from coffee to baguettes to sausage and mash and sizzling steaks. Ask about the specialty Cullen Skink.

If you're feeling faint after the ferry over, **Sandwich Station** (Lochranza Pier, tel. 01770/07917-671913, 10 A.M.–4 P.M. daily) will put the smile back on your face. Never were such an array of succulent sandwiches and cakes crammed into such a small space as this, and not in such an unlikely location either. The substantial snacks start at around £0.80. You can't fill your stomach up on the island for less.

SOUTH ARRAN

Whichever way you go around Arran, the south is a bit of a shock: low-lying with sizeable coastal villages alongside sandy bays, farmland broken up by lush wooded valleys.

Sights

Heading south from Brodick, the first settlement up is **Lamlsh,** where you can take a **ferry** (tel. 01770/600349, around eight crossings daily in summer, reduced sailings spring/autumn, winter by arrangement, £8 pp) across to **Holy Island.** This is where the Celtic Christian saint

St. Molaise lived in the 6th century A.D. His cave is halfway along the western shore, and nearby is a healing well. Those of a rather different faith live on the island now; the island is owned by **Tibetan Buddhist monks** who have set up a center for world peace and health here and lovingly planted the island with trees. You can walk around the shore past the Stevenson lighthouse to the center, coming back over the island's highest point, **Mullach Mor.**

Back on Arran, from **Whiting Bay** a spectacular walk leads up to **Glen Ashadale Falls.** Start from the Coffee Pot Café. The best beaches in the south are around **Kildonan; Lagg,** in a wooded valley, is easily the prettiest village. Farther around the coast are some impressive stone circles (six in all). The most spectacular of these are at **Auchagallon** and on **Machrie Moor.** Some of the Machrie Moor monoliths top 18 feet in height. At 2000–4000 years old, Auchagallon stone circle surrounds a burial cairn, but this is also a bit of Bronze Age boasting: Due to the prominent location, passersby would have seen the monument and

Auchagallon stone circle, South Arran

remarked on its finery, so achieving the builders' wish of their dead living on in people's memories. You'll pass the paths to both sets of stones on the road. Machrie Moor has its own official car park south of the Machrie Golf Club, while Auchagallon lies near a minor road junction north of the golf club.

Accommodations

Seal Shore (tel. 01770/820320, £6 adults, £2 children, £1 for tent) is a relaxed, virtually midge-free campsite. It has an undercover cooking area as well as easy access to the beach, basked upon by seals. The bar of nearby Kildonan Hotel, which does good meals if self-catering gets too much, is also close at hand. The owner, a local fisherman (campers can sample his catch when available) will let you ride his bike if you need to get to town.

For a more unusual sleeping experience, the **Centre for World Peace and Health** (Holy Island, tel. 01770/601100, from £25 dorm, £45 s, £65 twin) has simple pine-furnished dormitories and rooms on Holy Island, off the coast by Lamalsh. There are incredible views (the better the view, the more you pay) and a still more incredible atmosphere, with beautiful ornamental gardens just outside the window. Prices include three vegetarian meals per day. Joining in the meditation schedule after breakfast is optional.

Done up in cool blues and whites, **Lilywhite Guest House** (Lamalsh, tel. 01770/600230, from £25 s, £55 d) has some of the best views out to Holy Island. That being the obvious draw, try to get one of the four sea-facing rooms. Breakfasts are big affairs: fresh grapefruit, organic porridge, oak-smoked kippers, and locally made preserves.

Hotels do not come prettier or more traditional than the **Lagg Hotel** (Lagg, tel. 01770/870255, www.lagghotel.com, £45 s, £80 d), built in the late 18th century and the island's oldest watering hole. The rooms are charming affairs, full of traditional creaky furniture including one room with four-poster bed (£55 pp). Dinner, bed, and breakfast packages start at £75, and there is complimentary

pick-up from the ferry with advance notice. With a river lapping through the gardens outside, it's a peaceful place to spend a few days—a night just isn't enough.

Argentine House (Whiting Bay, tel. 01770/700622, www.argentinearran.co.uk, from £60 s, £76 d) has friendly Swiss owners and offers five modern, colorful rooms. Accommodation is en suite and with TVs. Between the two of them, the owners speak German, French, and Spanish. It's one of those places where mingling is encouraged, courtesy of the large guest lounge stocked with board games. Breakfasts are continental with cold meats and cheeses; cooked breakfasts must be pre-ordered and cost extra. Saturday and Sunday are spaghetti nights during season: it costs £8.50 and there is plenty to go around.

Food

Swathed in plants as it is, you could almost miss the entrance to the tiny **Coffee Pot** (Whiting Bay, tel. 01770/700382, 10 A.M.–5 P.M. Mon.–Sat. Apr.–Oct., 10 A.M.–4:30 P.M. Tues.–Sat. winter), but that would be your loss. This ranks among the island's best places for a snack (£3–6) with an overwhelming display of cakes, as well as soup, sandwiches, and unusually ample servings of salad. Munch away and enjoy great sea views.

Served beside a roaring fire in the oak-beamed lounge or in the restaurant overlooking the garden and river, the food at the whitewashed old **(Lagg Hotel** (Lagg, tel. 01770/870255, open Feb.–Nov.) is anything but traditional. Mains like the crispy duck breast with Asian greens and roasted peach are £8–15. Eat in the bar or, if the weather's fine, in the beer garden with its wonderful river.

With its picnic tables in a grassy garden overlooking the shore, the **Drift Inn** (Shore Rd., Lamalsh, tel. 01770/600270, noon–3 P.M. and 5:30–9 P.M. Mon.–Sat., 12:30–3 P.M. and 5:30–9 P.M. Sun.) is a good bet for a pint and some filling pub grub, like burgers, baked potatoes, or toasted baguettes, all from around £5. There's also pool, darts, and regular live music.

EVENTS AND SHOPPING

If you're around in late May, check out the **Arran Wildlife Festival** to become enlightened on Arran's resident animals. **Brodick Highland Games** is in August.

Arran is a great place for holiday souvenirs. For food and drink (Arran does it tantalizingly well) try **Island Cheese Company** (Home Farm, Brodick, tel. 01770/302788, islandcheese.co.uk) or **Arran Brewery** (Cladach, Brodick, tel. 01770/302353) for fine brewed beers. **Arran Aromatics** (Home Farm, Brodick, tel. 01770/302595, 9:30 A.M.–5 P.M. Mon.–Fri.) has high-quality scented candles and cosmetics.

SPORTS AND RECREATION

The **Arran Golf Pass** (£95, purchase at main hotels on Arran or Brodick TIC) allows for a round of golf on each of the island's seven courses—prepare to be distracted by golden eagles and shore-basking seals.

INFORMATION AND SERVICES

The **TIC** (Brodick Pier, tel. 01770/303774) has a wealth of information and a few good maps. For further books and information you could head to **Books and Card Centre** (Shore Rd., tel. 01770/302991) in Brodick.

Only the banks in Brodick have ATMs: Get sufficient money here before venturing elsewhere.

The island's hospital (tel. 01770/600777) is at Lamalsh. Free Internet access can be had at **Arran Library** (tel. 01770/302835, 10 A.M.–5 P.M. Tues., 10 A.M.–7:30 P.M. Thurs. and Fri., 10 A.M.–1 P.M. Sat.). Brodick has a post office on Shore Road.

For cycle hire, there is **Brodick Boat and Cycle Hire** (Brodick Beach, tel. 01770/302868, 9:30 A.M.–5:30 P.M. Apr.–Oct.) or **Brodick Cycles** (opposite village hall, tel. 01770/302460, Mon.–Sat. summer, Thurs.–Sat. winter), which can help with repairs.

GETTING THERE AND AWAY

Ferry is the only way out of Brodick, as you may find to your cost if you are stuck there in high winds (the ferry cannot get into Ardrossan in high winds). **Calmac** operates 5–6 sailings daily between Brodick and Ardrossan (55 min., £7.25 passenger, £44.50 car). In summer a Calmac ferry runs between Lochranza and Claonaig (eight daily, 30 min., £4.75 passenger, £21.20 car) and in winter once-daily service between Lochranza and Tarbert (1.5 hrs.).

GETTING AROUND

From Brodick ferry terminal, there are two options for exploring Arran: clockwise to the south or counterclockwise to the north. Bus connections are good, with 20 buses per day going to Lamalsh and Whiting Bay and 5–6 continuing to Lagg/Blackwaterfoot. Four to five buses daily make the circuit north to Lochranza and then on to Blackwaterfoot. The chances are you're headed somewhere on the main loop road: ask the driver where to get off. A **rover ticket** allowing transport on any island bus for one day only costs £4.20. Call **Arran Transport** (Ferry Pier, tel. 01770/302121) if you need a taxi.

Cycling and walking are far more rewarding (and windier) ways to get around the island. A popular challenge is the round-the-island-in-a-day cycle ride; a 100-kilometer coastal path also stretches right around Arran.

The best bet for car rental is with **Arran Transport** (tel. 01770/302121, £27 for a full day, less for part-day hire).

South Ayrshire

South and east of Ayr was where the weaving and coal-mining industries boomed in the 18th and 19th centuries and have scarred the region ever since their decline. Today, largely drab farmland gives way to some spectacular patches of coastline and ruptures up in the south into the Galloway Forest Park, one of lowland Scotland's remotest regions.

CULZEAN BAY AND VICINITY
Culzean Castle and Country Park

When Culzean Castle (off A719, tel. 0870/118 1945, www.culzeanexperience.org, 10:30 A.M.–5 P.M. daily Mar.–Oct., visitor center 9:30 A.M.–5:30 P.M. daily Mar.–Oct., 11 A.M.–4 P.M. Thurs.–Sun. Nov.–Mar., grounds open all year until sunset, castle and grounds £12 adults, £8 seniors, grounds only £8 adults, £5 seniors) became the principal seat of the wealthy Kennedy family in 1759, this modest tower house was transformed into one of Scotland's most lavish and intriguing country estates. The 10th earl commissioned renowned architect Robert Adam to design a building that reflected his political status; if the results are anything to go by, the earl was powerful indeed. Perched on the wooded clifftop, the castle, standing in grounds that contain a deer park and five kilometers of beaches, has a dramatic location and Adam created a castle interior to reflect this.

Highlights include the neoclassical **library,** the round **drawing room** with its balcony looking out over the cliffs, and the **Blue Drawing Room,** with elaborate panelled ceilings and friezes—check the gryphon motifs, characteristic of Adam's attention to detail. The centerpiece red-carpeted oval staircase shows Adam's true genius: Although it appears as if the whole design of the castle was based on the staircase, it was actually added at the last minute. High-flying associations with the castle continued into the 20th century, when General Eisenhower was given a flat on the top floor as a gesture of thanks for his part in the allied victory. The apartment is now an **Eisenhower museum** with displays on his life. The castle also has a visitors center explaining the historical contexts of Culzean. There are some brilliant walks through the extensive grounds: a circuit goes through the **deer park** and along the dismantled railway, over a bridge around the **swan pond,** to the peaceful sandy shoreline, which you can follow back to the castle. There are caves to explore and a delightful **boathouse.**

If you are entranced, as many are, by the magic of Culzean, you can stay in the castle: prices kick off from £170 s, £250 d in the **Adam Suite,** while the **Eisenhower Suite** with views over the fountain court goes for £250 s, £375 d. Generous afternoon teas are included in the price, but evening meals are £35 pp extra. There's also a **campsite** in the woods by the entrance (£7.60 pp) for those without such lordly sums of money.

Stagecoach buses 60 and 360 stop at Culzean and Kirkoswald en route between Girvan and Ayr 12–15 times daily.

Electric Brae

On this hill running from the bend overlooking the Croy railway viaduct to Craigencroy Glen south of Dunure, the landscape causes one of its neatest conjuring tricks. As a stone cairn in the middle of the brae explains, although the road has a slight upward grade from the bend at the glen, the land on either side makes it seem to be going downward. A stationary car on the brae with the brakes off therefore seems to be gliding magically uphill. As bizarre as the phenomena itself is the slow-moving line of cars full of children screaming with glee at seemingly nothing. General Dwight Eisenhower entertained many guests with a drive over the Brae during his holidays at nearby Culzean.

Souter Johnnie's Cottage

"Tam lo'ed him like a vera' brother" said Burns of Souter Johnnie, words inscribed

© LUKE WATERSON

Culzean Castle, one of Scotland's finest country houses

on the walls of this recently refurbished thatched cottage (Main Rd., Kirkoswald, tel. 01655/760603, 11:30 A.M.–5 P.M. Fri.–Tues. Good Friday–Sept., £5 adults, £4 seniors) dating from 1786. This was the residence of John Davidson, the Kirkoswald village souter, or shoemaker, the original inspiration for Tam's drinking partner of the same name in Burns's poem "Tam o' Shanter." The cottage is a charming little find in Kirkoswald village and contains a reconstructed souter's workshop, period furniture, and some Burns paraphernalia. There's also a reconstructed ale house and a lovely garden; this is a great place to appreciate what life was like for villagers in the 18th century.

AILSA CRAIG

A notable feature on the horizon almost anywhere along the Ayrshire coast is sheer-sided Ailsa Craig, a volcanic mound home to Britain's third-largest gannet colony. Over 40,000 breed annually on the island, as well as Manx shearwaters, skuas, kittiwakes, and puffins. The ship **MV Glorious** conducts trips to Ailsa Craig from Girvan. It's highly advised to book in advance (for information about sailings and prices, contact Mark McCrindle, 7 Harbour St., Girvan, tel. 01465/723219, mccrindlem@aol.com).

◖ LOCH DOON

South of the large whitewashed village of Dalmellington stretches Loch Doon, a glinting tract of water south of town with some great walking opportunities. Despite its remote location, southern Scotland's largest inland loch has been at the heart of some extraordinary projects over the centuries to tamper with its water levels, including, in the 1930s, a hydroelectric project that threatened to flood the 13th-century **Doon Castle.** As a result, the entire shell of the castle was moved, stone by stone, from an island in the loch to a safe location on its shore. Britain's only relocated castle still stands at the southern end of the loch; the remains of the old Doon Castle where **Robert the Bruce** supposedly hid from the English can still be seen when water levels are low.

Today visitors come for walking and free fishing in and around the loch. The minor road branching right off the A713 one mile south of Dalmellington is a popular starting point for walks; follow the road to where steep-sided **Ness Glen** meets the head of the Loch. There's a car park and visitors center here. Stagecoach Bus 52 heads out to Dalmellington from Ayr (twice hourly Mon.–Sat., 50 min.).

GLASGOW AND THE GREATER CLYDE

Once synonymous with industrial blight, Glasgow has completely reinvented itself. Campaigns such as "There's A Lot Glasgowing On," which once seemed laughable, now seem prophetic. Scotland's largest city, half again as big as Edinburgh with a population 600,000 strong and a million more in its suburbs, is definitely on the up. These days the area is a draw for bar-goers, clubbers, and shoppers not just from Scotland but from across the United Kingdom and beyond.

Stylish bars and clubs frequented by local celebrities like Robert Carlyle and Ewan McGregor challenge London for chic and outdo it with reasonable prices and a friendly, down-to-earth attitude. You'll find the country's best shopping here, as well as several major museums and the Scottish National Opera. Charles Rennie Mackintosh stamped his unique breed of design on many of Glasgow's most famous buildings; these combine with the lavish mansions of the 18th-century tobacco merchants to make the city something of an eclectic architectural feast. Just when the bulk of the metropolis is starting to seem austere rather than fascinating, it finds another way to surprise or delight you. It could be a conversation with a local in one of the traditional old pubs or tapping in to its first-rate live music scene that does it, but a visit to Glasgow is guaranteed to give you an experience you won't get anywhere else in Scotland. It's slick, it's culturally booming, and yet in place of big-city pretentiousness you'll find an almost village-like intimacy suffusing Glasgow. It isn't unusual for complete strangers to laugh, share

© LUKE WATERSON

GLASGOW

HIGHLIGHTS

◖ **Willow Tearooms:** Check out the glorious architecture of Charles Rennie Mackintosh over a drink in these stunning tearooms (page 166).

◖ **Necropolis:** Wandering through the eerie architectural glory of the Necropolis, you can discover the extravagant monuments to Glasgow's famous dead, towering above the city (page 167).

◖ **Glasgow Cathedral:** A mighty church of arches and stained glass, this is one of Scotland's most formidable religious buildings, with the tomb of missionary St. Mungo in a unique sub-church (page 167).

◖ **Pollock Country Park and Burrell Collection:** View one man's vast collection of art and artifacts, housed within a wooded park on the edge of the city (page 173).

◖ **Waverley Excursions:** Voyage down the River Clyde on the *Waverley*, the world's last oceangoing paddle steamer (page 175).

◖ **The Barras:** Take a weekend ramble in Glasgow's bustling Barras market and experience a dose of traditional East End life (page 184).

◖ **Football:** See football passion at its utmost at a Rangers vs. Celtic match (page 185).

◖ **Biggar:** This diminutive town in the hills south of Glasgow offers seven eclectic museums to visit (page 201).

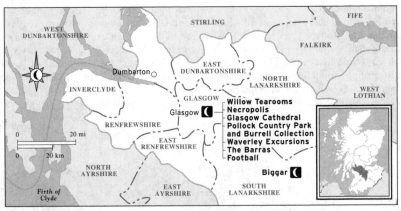

LOOK FOR ◖ TO FIND RECOMMENDED SIGHTS, ACTIVITIES, DINING, AND LODGING.

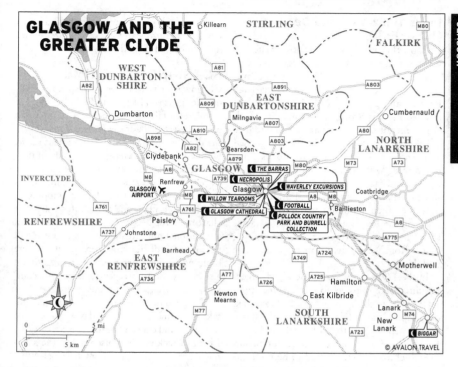

GLASGOW AND THE GREATER CLYDE

© AVALON TRAVEL

jokes, and talk to each other in bars and on the streets. Where other places in Scotland impress with their old-world charm, Glasgow impresses with its modernity, vitality, and innovative urban planning. A trip to Scotland's main metropolis is a must, just to see how a city can turn over a new leaf. Old warehouses have become cafés, galleries, and shopping centers. In once-derelict shipyards sit state-of-the-art museums.

Glasgow's urban tendrils spread out some ways—across most of the central belt of Scotland, in fact. Yet despite its size and sprawl, Glasgow is a gateway to some of the most spectacular countryside in this part of Scotland. Highly recommended is a trip "doon the water" on the world's last oceangoing paddle steamer, the *Waverley,* out to the Isles of Arran or Bute. The West Highland Way, Scotland's toughest long-distance footpath, kicks off in Milngavie, while South Lanarkshire is home

to beautiful parks, stately homes, and some of Scotland's most unusual museums.

HISTORY
Prehistory and Medieval Era

The area around the mouth of the River Clyde was in inhabited in prehistoric times by fishing communities. Late in the 6th century St. Kentigern (later known as St. Mungo) was exiled from Culross Abbey, where his special powers had aroused jealousy, and settled by the River Clyde near to the site of where Glasgow would develop. He baptized Christian converts on the hill where the Necropolis now stands. A number of religious buildings were constructed on the site of Glasgow Cathedral before a stone cathedral was built in the 12th century, by which time Glasgow was a 1,500-strong urban center with the equivalent of city status. By 1471, the city's oldest still-standing building, Provand's Lordship, had been constructed.

Industrialization and Decline (1650-1900)

Glasgow flourished as a city relatively late and was not therefore a major strategic consideration for conflicts in the 15th to 18th centuries. By the late 17th century, with its riverside location and proximity to Edinburgh, it had asserted itself as Scotland's second city. With rich seams of coal nearby and an abundance of fish in the River Clyde, Glasgow burgeoned as a center of commerce. By the 1670s, a tobacco trade with the New World had begun in earnest. Glasgow's tobacco merchants built some of the city's most lavish buildings and developed a reputation for resourcefulness; by the time the American War of Independence killed the tobacco trade they were making money from West Indian rum and locomotive building.

In the 1770s the River Clyde was dredged, meaning large ships could now advance right up the river to the heart of the city. Greenock-born James Watt's developments to the steam engine further paved the path for the Industrial Revolution of the 18th and 19th centuries, during which time there seemed to be no limits to what Glasgow could achieve commercially. Locomotive building, together with the coal and cotton industries, put it at the forefront of world trade and attracted workers in the thousands. Yet the city's urban structure simply could not support the vast numbers of incoming migrant workers. Housing became overcrowded, sanitation was terrible, and cholera and typhoid epidemics rampant. By the beginning of the 20th century, the city's industrial might was waning and Glasgow was a city on the decline.

20th Century

As a result of its importance as a shipbuilding center in the World Wars, the city got badly bombed, and after 1945, ill-planned, soulless housing developments worsened Glasgow's plight. The city became associated with poverty, crime, and violence, and a massive redevelopment plan was implemented. Both the establishment of the Burrell Collection of art in Pollock Country Park in 1983 and the Glasgow's "European City of Culture" award in 1990 helped this effort.

PLANNING YOUR TIME

Glasgow is a city where you can spend as little, or as long, as you like. You can dash around in a day, see a fair amount of what the city can offer in a weekend, or spend a week soaking up the diverse cultural and entertainment scene. Unlike Edinburgh, Glasgow is not about ticking off sights. The ways to really appreciate the city are more time-consuming, like hanging out in the West End charity shopping or people-watching in one of the cafés or bars, or chatting to the locals over a few pints of ale in a traditional pub. Rush Glasgow and you will find it a city of shopping centers and austere buildings. Take your time, and you will find it a city of wonderfully eccentric nooks and crannies, great bars, and gorgeous parks.

With two days, remember that old maxim: take your time. Start off the day with breakfast in a West End café and head up to Kelvingrove Park to check out its museums. In the afternoon, head down to the River Clyde for a cruise up to Clydebuilt Maritime Heritage Centre or look around the Science Centre. Then head to magnificent Glasgow Cathedral and take a stroll around the nearby Necropolis. Spend the evening in a traditional city pub like the Scotia Bar listening to live music or dining out in style at a restaurant like the Corinthian. Day two is southern Glasgow day. Look around the Charles Rennie Mackintosh–designed House for an Art Lover in beautiful Bellahouston Park; in the afternoon visit the spectacular Burrell Collection in Pollock Country Park.

With a couple of extra days, in addition to the above you really have the opportunity to become more immersed in Glasgow culture. A third day could be filled by a more relaxed itinerary of the same kinds of things. Add a couple more traditional pub sessions, fit in a spot of shopping, or catch a football game. If you're visiting over the weekend, be sure to have a browse in Barras market. If you can, take a trip south to Biggar or New Lanark World Heritage Centre.

ORIENTATION

With its sprawl of ring roads and bypasses, Glasgow can be a confusing city to navigate. The main city center road is George Street, with George Square marking an unofficial center. To the immediate north of George Square lie the main shopping centers and Buchanan Bus Station. To the immediate east and south lies Merchant City. Continuing west, George Street reaches Charing Cross after about 10 blocks, becoming West George Street. The River Clyde lies along the southern extent of the city center. To the west, the city center limits are defined by the motorway. Over the motorway to the northwest lies the West End, centered on Kelvingrove Park. South of the River Clyde is Southside, including Pollock Country Park.

SAFETY

Glasgow is a bit rough around the edges and quite often in the center, but, while it is still almost affectionately known as "stab city," visitors are unlikely to feel any more threatened in Glasgow than in most large European cities. Statistics do point to your being three times more likely to be stabbed in Glasgow than in London, however, so exercise more caution here than elsewhere in Scotland. A couple of golden rules: avoid getting involved in a crossfire of Catholic/Protestant rivalry at football matches and avoid large, deserted parts of the city late at night. The red-light district around Anderston Station, the east end of the "Barras" market area, and parts of Glasgow Green are best avoided by women on their own.

Sights

Unlike Edinburgh, which is comparatively compact, Glasgow is a big city covering a wide area. Sights fall into five main areas. The city center has a mix of cultural and architectural delights to discover, and the greener West End is where two of the main museums are located. The area around Glasgow Cathedral in the East End has several major historic attractions. An ever-growing center of interest for visitors is the revamped area around the River Clyde, while the south side of Glasgow contains some important museums and parks. While the city center, Merchant City, and East End attractions can be covered on foot, you will need to take public transport to other city sights. Use the city's subway system to get to the West End and along the River Clyde. For south side attractions, you can use either local buses or the overground railway.

CITY CENTER AND MERCHANT CITY

Much of Glasgow's city center is stark rather than beautiful and generally taken up with that popular Glaswegian pastime—shopping. While shoppers may very well have found paradise, sightseers will have scanter pickings. However, there are several buildings of note worth checking out, and the relaxed area of Merchant City is a great place for a stroll and a people-watching session.

City Chambers

One side of George Square is dominated by this immense, awe-inspiring building (George Sq., tel. 0141/287 4018) with its three high, domed towers. If you want to explore the jaw-droppingly grand interior, latch on to one of the guided tours. The free-of-charge tours of the chambers are on weekdays at 10:30 A.M. and 2:30 P.M. (except public holidays).

Gallery of Modern Art

Behind its grand facade of mighty neoclassical columns, this gallery (Royal Exchange Sq., tel. 0141/229 1996, 10 A.M.–5 P.M. Mon.–Thurs. and Sat., 11 A.M.–5 P.M. Fri. and Sun., free) has a post-war focus on the art it displays. Artists exhibited include Damien Hirst. It's also a venue for arts workshops and contains a good café in the basement.

GLASGOW

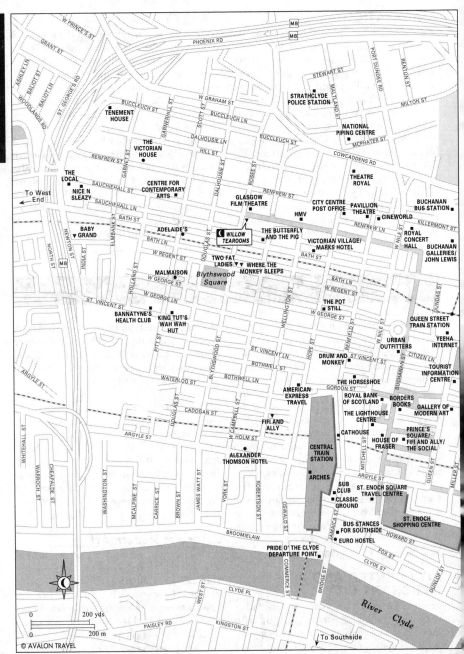

To West End →

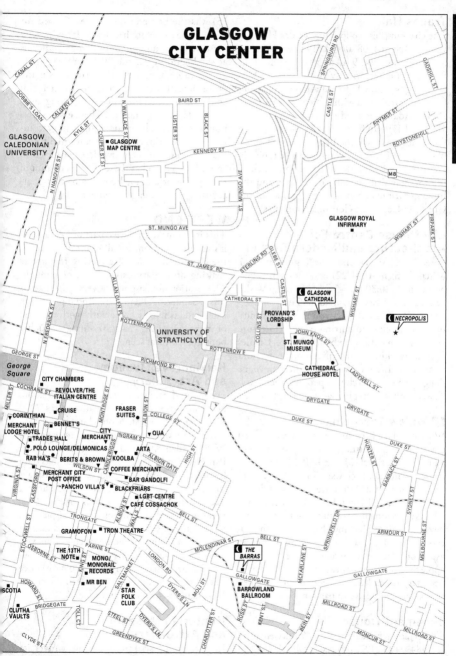

GLASGOW CITY CENTER

GLASGOW

Trades Hall

The city's impressive-looking Trades Hall (85 Glassford St., tel. 0870/403 5194, www.trades-hallglasgow.co.uk, 9 A.M.–5 P.M. Mon.–Fri., 9 A.M.–noon Sat., free) was built to symbolize Glasgow's growing reputation as a trading force to be reckoned with. Celebrated architect Robert Adam designed the building between 1791 and 1795 to incorporate a meeting place for representatives of the 14 incorporated trades of Glasgow. The interior has plenty of typically lavish Adam hallmarks to appreciate, including the magnificent marble fireplace and the immense frieze depicting the 14 trades in the Great Hall, as well as lots of stained glass.

Lighthouse Centre For Architecture and Modern Design

Spread over six floors, The Lighthouse (11 Mitchell Ln., tel. 0141/221 6362, www.thelight-house.co.uk, 10:30 A.M.–5 P.M. Mon. and Wed.–Sat., 11 A.M.–5 P.M. Tues., noon–5 P.M. Sun., £3 adults, £1 children) gives you the opportunity to come up close to cutting-edge architecture and design. It's also an exhibition space, Charles Rennie Mackintosh interpretation center, and a café/shop. Even if you're not a fan of in vogue design, come here to climb up to the Mackintosh Tower, with its sweeping views across the city.

◖ Willow Tearooms

With its silver furniture and colored, leaded glass, these still-functioning tearooms (217 Sauchiehall St., tel. 0141/332 0521, www.wil-lowtearooms.co.uk, 9 A.M.–5 P.M. Mon.–Sat., 11 A.M.–4:15 P.M. Sun.) are among architect Charles Rennie Mackintosh's finest interiors. This is a monument to glam turn-of-the century daytime dining; Mackintosh completed the tearoom in 1904 and had total control over every aspect of its design, even down to the cutlery. To appreciate the finer points, of course, it may be necessary to eat here. It's free to enter the tearooms but you'll have to pay for the food.

Tenement House

This typical tenement house (145 Buccleuch St., tel. 0844/493 2197, 1–5 P.M. daily Mar.–Oct., £5) was the home of one Agnes Toward for some 50 years before her death. It's now been preserved as a monument to living conditions at the beginning of the 20th century, made all the more homey by Mrs. Toward's many possessions. It's so evocative, in fact, that you could almost imagine someone rocking away on the old chair by the Aga. There is an exhibition on tenement living downstairs (it's recommended to see this last) where you will discover that very few tenement dwellers have lived in conditions as good as these. There's no hint of the squalor or cramped conditions that characterized your average tenement.

WEST END

This is the most attractive part of Glasgow—it's an advertisement for all that is great about the city. At first, just wandering the streets soaking up the atmosphere can be enough. The location of Glasgow University here keeps this area buzzing. Here you'll find hip bars and cafés and lush, leafy green parks with the kind of mega-museums that give Glasgow such a booming cultural scene.

Kelvingrove Museum and Art Gallery

Having undergone a massive revamp in 2006, Scotland's most-visited art gallery (0141/276 9599, 10 A.M.–5 P.M. Mon.–Thurs. and Sat., 11 A.M.–5 P.M. Fri. and Sun., free) in the iconic William Adam–designed building in Kelvingrove Park has reopened with even more exhibits than before. It's a broad-ranging series of displays that encompasses a four-meter-high Ceratosaur and Salvador Dali's *Christ of St. John of the Cross* painting. You'll also be able to see displays on talking animals, Chinese symbols, and ancient Eqypt. It really is a phenomenal collection with something to intrigue everyone—set aside a couple of hours to see it. You could also have coffee in the large café and take a stroll in the classic Victorian-designed Kelvingrove Park.

Hunterian Museum and Art Gallery

In part of the striking Glasgow University

complex is this attraction (University of Glasgow, tel. 0141/330 4221, www.hunterian.gla.ac.uk, 9:30 A.M.–5 P.M. Mon.–Sat., free), benefiting from another of Glasgow's generous benefactors, William Hunter. Hunter was a medical teacher and former student at the university and amassed a sizeable collection of items. The collection is contained within two separate sites on the University drive. The museum part contains fossils, minerals, and coral as well as a tribute to the great Glasgow scientist Lord Kelvin. The art gallery comprises two distinct sections joined by the museum shop. A main display space houses prints and paintings and key works by Scottish colorists like John Duncan Fergusson.

A separate section has reconstructed architect Charles Rennie Mackintosh's Glasgow abode with a remarkable degree of authenticity (£3 adults, £2 seniors, with free admission after 2 P.M. Wed.). The original home was dismantled but here Mackintosh lives on; authentic Mackintosh furniture fits like a hand in a glove into this light, white space. There are also displays on the architect, his wife Mary Macdonald, and their relationship.

Botanic Gardens

At the Botanic Gardens (730 Great Western Rd., tel. 0141/276 1614, gardens open dawn–dusk daily, greenhouses open 10 A.M.–4:45 P.M. daily Apr.–Sept., 10 A.M.–4:15 P.M. Oct.–Mar., visitors center open 11 A.M.–4 P.M. daily, free), a peaceful pocket of green away from the west end bustle, is a collection of Victorian greenhouses containing many tropical plants. The 19th-century Kibble Glasshouse is the main draw—a splendid dome containing a forest of ferns, trees, and statues. In the grounds around, flowed through by the River Kelvin, there are plenty of good picnicking spots.

EAST SIDE

East of Merchant City, this serene area of the city is where to head for a wander. You could lose yourself in the colossal Necropolis, marvel at the city cathedral, or check out one of Scotland's most mesmerizing museums in Glasgow Green.

Necropolis

Being able to give the dead a decent burial has long been regarded as a mark of civilization, and the necropolis (open during daylight year-round) that sprawls over a tall hill behind Glasgow Cathedral is a tribute to the extent of Victorian ambition. All graveyards can be creepy places, but the Necropolis with its hodgepodge of weather-beaten tombs has a special spookiness without rival in Britain. Cemeteries with imposing tombs like this are a common thing in Catholic countries but less so in the United Kingdom. Paths zigzag up the hill to the crowning glory—a monument to none other than the Scottish Reformation's number one preacher, John Knox. Plenty of Glasgow greats and not-so-greats are buried in the sea of tombs, however, and the Necropolis has seen about 50,000 burials in its time. Pick up a copy of *Glasgow Necropolis: An Easy to Follow Guide with Full Color Photographs of the Memorable Monuments* by Ruth Johnston, stocked by most Glasgow bookshops.

Glasgow Cathedral

St. Mungo founded a chapel on the site of the cathedral in the 6th century, but the present building dates from the late 12th century. Today the cathedral (Cathedral Sq., tel. 0141/552 6891, www.glasgowcathedral.org.uk, 9:30 A.M.–5:30 P.M. Mon.–Sat., 1–5:30 P.M. Sun. Apr.–Sept., 9:30 A.M.–4:30 P.M. Mon.–Sat., 1–4:30 P.M. Sun. Oct.–Mar., free) is one of the city's most astounding historic buildings. The main thing that hits you as you enter is the profusion of stained glass, creating a somewhat dim, kaleidoscopic light as you move through the immense interior. The oak ceiling high above adds a touch of simplistic grandeur. Breaking the cathedral into two distinct pieces is the ornate choir screen; it's here that you can venture down into a unique sub-church beneath the main one. Here, amidst a dark series of arches, you'll find St. Mungo's tomb. There are explanatory leaflets on sale at the cathedral about the history of the building, as well as a small shop. Photography is permitted.

GLASGOW

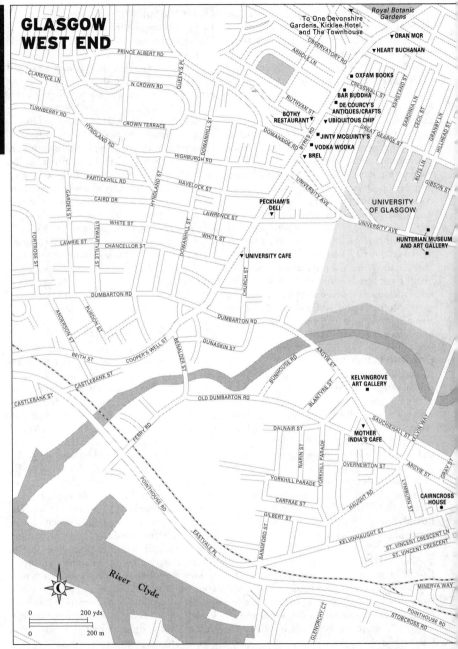

GLASGOW WEST END

To One Devonshire Gardens, Kirklee Hotel, and The Townhouse

Royal Botanic Gardens

▼ ORAN MOR

▼ HEART BUCHANAN

■ OXFAM BOOKS

■ BAR BUDDHA

■ DE COURCY'S ANTIQUES/CRAFTS

▼ UBIQUITOUS CHIP

■ JINTY MCGUINTY'S

■ VODKA WODKA

▼ BREL

BOTHY RESTAURANT ▼

PRINCE ALBERT RD

CLARENCE LN

N CROWN RD

QUEEN'S PL

ARHOLE LN

OBSERVATORY RD

RUTHVAN ST

CRESSWALL ST

KERSLAND ST

SARDINIA LN

CECIL ST

GRANBY LN

HILLHEAD ST

BUTE LN

GIBSON ST

GREAT GEORGE ST

DOWANSIDE RD

BYRES RD

TURNBERRY RD

HYNDLAND RD

CROWN TERRACE

DOWANHILL ST

HIGHBURGH RD

PARTICKHILL RD

HAVELOCK ST

UNIVERSITY AVE

HYNDLAND ST

CAIRD DR

GARDEN ST

PECKHAM'S DELI ▼

UNIVERSITY OF GLASGOW

UNIVERSITY AVE

HUNTERIAN MUSEUM AND ART GALLERY ■

LAWRENCE ST

WHITE ST

STEWARTVILLE ST

DOWANHILL ST

WHITE ST

LAWRIE ST

CHANCELLOR ST

FORTROSE ST

▼ UNIVERSITY CAFE

CHURCH ST

DUMBARTON RD

DUMBARTON RD

PURDON ST

ANDERSON ST

DUNASKIN ST

BEITH ST

COOPER'S WELL ST

BENALDER ST

ARGYLE ST

BUNHOUSE RD

CASTLEBANK ST

OLD DUMBARTON RD

BLANTYRE ST

KELVINGROVE ART GALLERY ■

CASTLEBANK ST

FERRY RD

DALNAIR ST

NARIN ST

YORKHILL PARADE

▼ MOTHER INDIA'S CAFE

SAUCHIEHALL ST

KELVIN WAY

POINTHOUSE RD

YORKHILL PARADE

OVERNEWTON ST

ARGYLE ST

GRAY ST

CARFRAE ST

HAUGHT RD

LYMBURN ST

CAIRNCROSS HOUSE ●

EASTVALE PL

GILBERT ST

SANDFORD ST

KELVINHAUGHT ST

ST. VINCENT CRESCENT LN

ST. VINCENT CRESCENT

GLENORCHY CT

River Clyde

MINERVA WAY

POINTHOUSE RD

STOBCROSS RD

| 0 | 200 yds |
| 0 | 200 m |

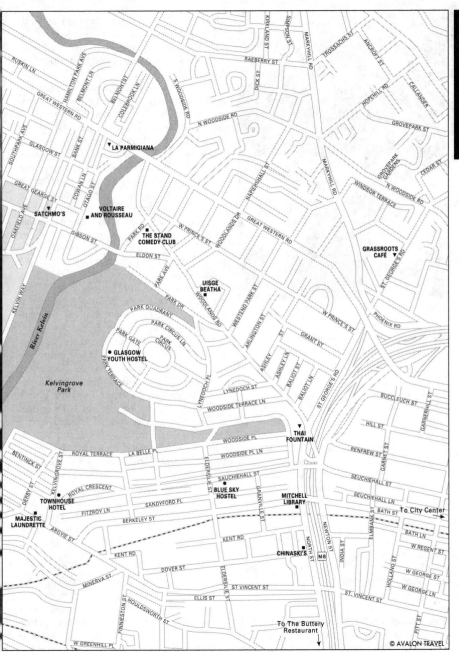

© AVALON TRAVEL

© LUKE WATERSON

Glasgow Cathedral

St. Mungo Museum of Religious Life and Art

A distinctly above-average homage to all types of religious art, this museum (2 Castle St., tel. 0141/553 2557, 10 A.M.–5 P.M. Mon.–Thurs. and Sat., 11 A.M.–5 P.M. Fri. and Sun.) is situated near the cathedral on the site of the former bishop's palace. As befits a multicultural, multifaith city like Glasgow, you'll find exhibits and information on six of the world's predominant faiths. There are three main galleries. The most impressive is the brilliantly colorful gallery of religious art; there is also a gallery dedicated to religious life (including eerie exhibits like the Day of the Dead skeleton from Mexico), a Scottish gallery, and a Zen garden. Across the way is Glasgow's oldest building, Provand's Lordship, dating from 1471.

Glasgow Green

Britain's oldest public space dates back to 1450, when King James II designated the area for common grazing land. It's a refreshing place for a stroll, despite a slightly stark feel, and contains a couple of important attractions.

In the center of the park (to which all paths lead), the **People's Palace and Winter Gardens** (tel. 0141/271 2962, 10 A.M.–5 P.M. Mon.–Thurs. and Sat., 11 A.M.–5 P.M. Fri. and Sun., free) is one of the most fascinating social history museums in Scotland. It traces the story of Glaswegians from 1750 up to the 20th century. Glasgow is a modern city with a lot of important changes relatively recently in its history. Because a lot of the exhibits depict a time within living memory, the museum as a whole has loads more impact and meaning than your average collection of artifacts. There are harrowing displays on cramped living conditions in the famous one-room tenement flats many Glasgow residents remember living in. One of the more bizarre exhibits is the pair of banana boots worn by renowned city comedian "Big Yin" Billy Connolly in the 1970s. A Victorian glasshouse, known as the Winter Gardens, lies next to the Palace. It's chockablock with tropical plants. There's also a café with outside seating for those balmy days.

Glaswegians have guarded their park over the centuries from several land-hungry developers with staunch displays of civic pride. Therefore, when businessmen wanted to locate **Templeton's Carpet Factory** (north of People's Palace) on the northern fringes of the park, the city council rejected several proposals for the building. Then architect Sir William Leiper came up with a design the council accepted, based on the Doge's Palace in Venice. Hence one of the world's most exuberantly decorated factories came into existence; it's blessed with a facade of orange, green, and yellow brickwork along with a mix of churchlike and circular windows. The exterior is the only part worth a look.

RIVER CLYDE

Just as it once was, Glasgow's river is again becoming the living, breathing heart of the city. Once, the River Clyde was a booming center of industry, known for building Europe's best ships. Now it has been carefully and thoughtfully redeveloped, with the maritime industrial

© LUKE WATERSON

Templeton's Carpet Factory

legacy as a key theme. There's certainly a long way still to go, but it's worth a stop here to appreciate the importance of the city's shipbuilding heritage.

Glasgow Science Centre

Looking from the outside like a giant metallic slug, the Glasgow Science Centre (50 Pacific Quay, tel. 0871/540 1000, www.glasgowsciencecentre.org, 10 A.M.–6 P.M. daily Mar.–Oct., 10 A.M.–5 P.M. Tues.–Sun. Oct.–Mar., £7.95 adults, £5.95 children) is a fascinating mix of flash exhibits, interactive shows, and displays. It cements the city's place on the world stage as a center of state-of-the-art attractions. Highlights include a Science Mall, with three floors of fun exhibits and workshops including the chance to make your own lightning.

Your admission ticket will get you into the Science Centre's other attractions for a discounted rate. These include a planetarium (£2 with Science Mall ticket) and the Glasgow Tower (£2 with Science Mall ticket), where you can shoot up to a height of 100 meters to view the new-look Clyde in all its ultra-

modern, glassy, gray glory and the city fanning out behind it. To get here, head to Cessnock Subway station or take an overground train to Exhibition Centre.

Paddle Steamer *Waverley*

Moored right outside the Science Centre is the famous Glasgow ship, the *Waverley* (tel. 0845/130 4647, www.waverleyexcursions.co.uk, daily cruises May–Oct.). It's the world's last remaining seagoing paddle steamer and still takes tourists "Doon the Watter" during season to the Clyde holiday resorts of old, like Dunoon, the Isle of Bute, and the Isle of Arran. Check the website for updated timetable information or contact Glasgow TIC at tel. 0141/204 4400. You could go on the *Waverley* as a day trip from Glasgow or as a novel start to your tour of Scotland.

The Tall Ship

There aren't too many Clyde-built ships left afloat these days; this masterpiece (Stobcross Rd. by SECC, tel. 0141/222 2513, 10 A.M.–5 P.M. daily Mar.–Oct., 10 A.M.–4 P.M. daily Nov.–Feb.) is

CHARLES RENNIE MACKINTOSH: REINVENTING GLASGOW

You can barely read a paragraph of promotional material or walk a block in Glasgow without the name of Mackintosh or a building he had a hand in designing cropping up. The architect's works are, after all, one of the main reasons to visit; these days, there is even a Mackintosh trail to follow, taking in all his architectural achievements.

In the 1890s, when Mackintosh was taking classes at the Glasgow School of Art, the city was still very much in the throes of its Victorian economic buoyancy, which extended to the field of architecture and design. His early projects included an innovative design for the Glasgow Herald building, where he introduced a revolutionary lift and a fireproof floor. His most significant commission was for the Glasgow School of Art in 1897, where his design would incorporate Scottish baronial and Japanese influences. In 1900 he entered a German design competition; his entry, House for an Art Lover, was submitted too late to win the main prize but received a special award for its individuality and boldness. It remained debatable how much of the design was owed to Mackintosh and how much to his wife, however.

The rest of Europe was quick to appreciate the daring modernity of Mackintosh's architecture but in his home country, he felt he was not given the credit he deserved. He relied on a handful of patrons and clients in Glasgow, and these were not always sympathetic to his concept of "total design," a characteristic part of the Mackintosh package. In 1904, in partnership with tearoom interior designer Catherine Cranston, he got the chance to experiment more fully with this style. For the Willow Tearooms, Mackintosh was free to design even the light fittings, chairs, and cutlery. The result was one of his most striking projects: an interior of elaborate leaded glass and high-backed silver chairs. Tearoom customers were happy to pay a penny more for the privilege of sitting there. It was ultimately the narrow-mindedness of potential clients that led to Mackintosh's lack of recognition. Thereafter, he was to fade into obscurity. His life in London during World War I (not a good time for architects) and later in the south of France produced no significant works; he ended his days as a jaded watercolor painter.

one of the few survivors of the River Clyde's once legendary shipbuilding empire. With its distinctive three masts visible from some distance, the vessel, *Glenlee* by name, has various reconstructions on board of what life would have been like in its heyday. These include a cargo hold that would have transported substances like coal and guano (bird droppings) and a galley where you can see the scant substances sailors survived on.

Clydebuilt Maritime Museum

This attraction (Braehead, tel. 0141/886 1013, www.scottishmaritimemuseum.org, 10 A.M.–5:30 P.M. Mon.–Sat., 11 A.M.–5 P.M. Sun.), located downstream at Braehead, is a fun end point to a tour up the city stretch of the Clyde from the city center. It's a must-see for anyone with a love of maritime and

industrial heritage; the story of the beginnings of Glasgow's industry is told in a captivating way. Children will love the opportunity to step into the shoes of a riverboat captain and commandeer a "virtual" vessel. There's also a real vessel you can explore, the ancient MV *Kyles,* constructed in 1863. **Pride o' the Clyde** waterbus (tel. 0771/125 0969, £4 adult, £2 child one-way) runs trips downriver from Central station Bridge to the museum.

SOUTH SIDE

Hidden within the sprawl of southern Glasgow are some of the finest works of Scotland's famous architect Charles Rennie Mackintosh—and pockets of gorgeous parkland. Football fans will want to flock to the area to check out Hampden Park.

Scotland Street School Museum

It says a lot for Charles Rennie Mackintosh that this building (225 Scotland St., tel. 0141/287 0500, 10 A.M.–5 P.M. Mon.–Thurs. and Sat., 11 A.M.–5 P.M. Fri. and Sun.) was far from the most impressive of his architectural masterpieces. Mackintosh designed the building in 1904; its green-and-white tiling and creaking wooden boards set the tone perfectly for a foray into the history of schooling in Scotland since the 19th century. There are reconstructed Victorian classrooms upstairs; some lucky, still-living pupils also get to use them today. Apparently this is the country's only museum of education—one is enough. It's best to take the subway to the museum, as it's not a pleasant walk from the city center. Turn left out of Shields Road subway station; the building is down the road on the right.

House for an Art Lover

Charles Rennie Mackintosh designed this unique building (Bellahouston Pk., tel. 0141/353 4449, www.houseforanartlover.co.uk, 10 A.M.–4 P.M. Mon.–Wed., 10 A.M.–1 P.M. Thurs.–Sun. Apr.–Sept., 10 A.M.–1 P.M. Sat.–Sun. Oct.–Mar., £4.50 adults, £3 children) with his wife as an entry for a competition in 1900. The brief was, simply, to design a house in a thoroughly modern style; this was the first project on which Mackintosh could work unencumbered by specific demands. All the hallmarks of classic Mackintosh design—wide, dazzlingly white rooms; striking contrasts of colored glass; and innovative use of space—are present. Be sure not to miss the fine chairs in the dining room and the music rooms furnished with lanterns and an exquisite-looking piano. Buses 9, 34, 54, and 56 run here from Union Street near Glasgow Central Station.

Scottish Football Museum

A shrine to Scotland's favorite sport, this museum (tel. 0141/616 6139, www.scottishfootballmuseum.org.uk, 10 A.M.–5 P.M. Mon.–Sat., 11 A.M.–5 P.M. Sun., admission only £6 adults, £3 children, admission and tour £9 adults, £4.50 children) is located in Scotland's national football stadium, Hampden Park. It guides you through football history since the beginnings of professional soccer in the 19th century. Among the exhibits are the world's oldest football match ticket and the world's oldest football trophy. For a bit more money you can get a stadium tour of Hampden Park. There are four tours daily November–March and one tour daily April–October. Hampden Park can be reached by train (Mount Florida Station) or buses 5, 31, 37 and 75 (from Stockwell Street in the city center).

◖ Pollock Country Park and Burrell Collection

This large country park (2060 Pollockshaws Rd.) proves just what a city of surprises Glasgow is. In the unlikeliest, blandest area of the South Side is this oasis of greenery—traversed by a river, covered in noble old woodlands, and crowned by a world-class museum. Set aside half a day to do the park justice. The great thing about Pollock is that as soon as you enter the park, you're in a tranquil, wild place a good bit more rural than the average city green space. Buses 45, 47, 48, and 57 regularly head from Jamaica Street by Glasgow Central station to the park. Pollockshaws West is the nearest train station.

On a vast swath of grass in the center of the park is the Burrell Collection (tel. 0141/287 2550, 10 A.M.–5 P.M. Mon.–Thurs. and Sat., 11 A.M.–4 P.M. Fri. and Sun., free), a huge collection of some 8,000 pieces of art collected by shipping magnate William Burrell and donated to the people of Glasgow. You'll see a formidable array of art on display including medieval tapestries, paintings by Rembrandt and Degas, and a substantial collection of Islamic art. Burrell was rich enough to buy more or less whatever he saw and is credited with single-handedly amassing one of the largest collections of art and artifacts ever. The Burrell Collection is unique in yet another way: it's the only museum in Britain to be built according to the needs and specifications of its exhibits. The building is a triumph of light, space, and design, allow a couple of hours for

© LUKE WATERSON

The *Waverley* gives you the chance to take a voyage down the new-look River Clyde on the world's last oceangoing paddle steamer.

a wander around and another hour to sit in the spacious café for a discussion on everything you've seen.

After you've checked out the Burrell Collection, you can head farther down the lane to **Pollock House** (tel. 0141/616 6410, £8 adults, £5 children Apr.–Oct., free Nov.–Mar.), an 18th-century Palladian mansion. Situated within impeccably kept grounds that include a formal rhododendron garden, the house is home to yet more internationally important art. Previous incumbent Sir William Maxwell was something of an authority on Spanish painting in his day, and you can see works by English poet and artist William Blake, Goya, and El Greco.

RENFREWSHIRE AND INVERCLYDE

The area west of Glasgow that stretches along the south bank of the widening Clyde is little more than an extension of the city's urban sprawl. The only reason most people come out here is to catch a ferry west to far more scenic Argyll, just across the Clyde estuary. If you're doing the same, you may well want to hurry on to better things as quickly as possible, but amidst this expanse of grimy industry and dire housing developments are a few sights worth seeing. Working from Glasgow outward, the key places are Paisley, Port Glasgow, Greenock, and Gourock; all have mainline railway stations in close proximity.

Paisley Abbey

This magnificent gray building (Abbey Close, tel. 0141/889 4654, www.paisleyabbey.org.uk, 10 A.M.–3:30 P.M. Mon.–Sat., free, donations welcome) stands in the heart of Paisley. It rivals Glasgow Cathedral for size and splendor. There's some beautiful stained glass, including the swirling tones of the James Shaw Memorial Window, a vast multi-arched nave, some well-preserved cloisters, and the tomb of Scottish King Robert III. You can also visit the abbey for one of several Sunday services, when intoning voices and hymns add to the majesty of this special place.

Newark Castle

This 15th-century castle (near Port Glasgow, tel. 01475/741858, 9:30 A.M.–5:30 P.M. daily Apr.–Sept., £3.50) has a commanding position looking out over the River Clyde. If you've had your fill of modern attractions in Glasgow and crave a good old Scottish fortress, then this place should satisfy you. It's a large, angular stone building extended to its current form in the 16th century by villainous former incumbent Patrick Maxwell, better remembered for murdering two of his neighbors. The castle is on the A8 about a mile east of Port Glasgow. It's better to drive here than to walk, as the A8 is a busy road.

Maclean's Art Gallery

If you want to delve a bit further into the maritime and shipbuilding legacy of this stretch of the Clyde, you will be fascinated by this place (15 Kelly St., Greenock, tel. 01475/715624, 10 A.M.–5 P.M. Mon.–Sat., free), which has plenty of related photographs and artifacts, including models of different ships. There's also a significant art collection and a big tribute to Greenock's most famous resident, James Watt. Watt's developments to the steam engine kick-started the industrial revolution.

Tower Hill

You can do a lot worse while you wait for the ferry than climb up to Gourock's main vantage point. You'll get wonderful views south and east along the Firth of Clyde—bring some snacks and a camera. There's a folly here, too. Tower Hill is a short, steep walk from Gourock town center.

TOURS
City and River Clyde Tours

The **Spirit of Glasgow** (tel. 0141/586 5378, www.spiritofglasgow.co.uk) runs different walking tours through the city with a Victorian, Medieval, or "Gruesome" theme. It's a fun way to discover a side of Glasgow not immediately obvious to the visitor. Tours are at noon Thursday and Saturday, 11 A.M. and 1 P.M. Fridays; horror walks are at 7:30 P.M. on Fridays. A deposit in advance is required for tours; book through the TIC in George Square or your hotel reception.

An easy way of getting around Glasgow is with **City Sightseeing** (tel. 0141/204 0444, www.scotguide.com, £9 adults, £7 seniors, £3 children, tickets valid for two days), aboard a double-decker bus that runs between George Square (City Center), Glasgow Cathedral (East End), the SECC (River Clyde), and Byres Road (West End). Tours run from George Square and call at pick-up points about every half hour. Some buses have live tour guides, and others have multilingual prerecorded guide systems.

The **Pride o' the Clyde** (tel. 0771/125 0969, £4 adults, £2 children one-way) waterbus runs up the River Clyde between the city center and Braehead (for Clydebuilt Maritime Museum) every 45 minutes during the day throughout the week. There are refreshments onboard, and you get to see the Clyde as it should be seen—from the water. The city departure point is from Central station Bridge (just south of Central Station on the north bank of the Clyde).

Out-of-City Tours

Highland Tours (tel. 0141/226 8882, www.timberbushtours.com, from £27) runs selected day tours from Glasgow to different Highland destinations including Loch Ness, Loch Lomond, Glencoe, and Skye.

⟨ Waverley Excursions

You can cruise from Glasgow down the River Clyde on an old paddle steamer with Waverley Excursions (tel. 0845/130 4647, www.waverleyexcursions.co.uk, daily cruises May–Oct.). You'll be able to soak up the city's ultramodern regenerated waterfront and head out to the 19th-century Clyde resorts of Dunoon and Rothesay, in Cowal and Bute. There are a lot of different excursions and trips possible, including Helensburgh and the Isle of Arran. Check the website for updated timetables. From one of its ports of call in Cowal and Bute (part of the Argyll and the Inner Hebrides) or the Isle of Arran (part of the Ayrshire and Arran region), you could jump off and continue your holiday. Round-trip tickets to Rothesay on the Isle of Bute cost £23.95; depending on which day you go you can get up to four hours ashore on Bute as part of a day trip. Cruises depart from the *Waverley's* mooring outside the Science Centre.

Entertainment and Events

Not only is Glasgow the best place in Scotland for pubbing, clubbing, and listening to live music, it's also got a great theater and classic music scene. The Scottish National Opera is located in Glasgow, too. Glasgow has a fair few events throughout the year, including lots of live music and Europe's biggest gay and lesbian festival. There are several information resources in Glasgow for checking out what's going on entertainment-wise. By far the best is *The List* (www.list.co.uk), stocked in newsagents and providing up-to-date events listings from live music to club nights to comedy. You might also want to check out the *Gig Guide* (www.gig-guide.co.uk), which comes out monthly and lists upcoming live music events. Pubs and bars usually have copies lying around. There is also any number of websites with entertainment information, like www.glasgowguide.co.uk.

PUBS AND BARS

Glasgow is not short on places to have a drink or three. There's a full spectrum of watering holes in the city, from traditional century-old boozers to dazzlingly swanky bars like the Corinthian.

City Center

So-called because, shockingly enough, the bar resembles a big horseshoe (it's one of the longest bars in Britain), **Horseshoe Bar** (17 Drury Ln., tel. 0141/229 5711, 11 A.M.–midnight Mon.–Sat., 12:30 P.M.–midnight Sun.) is a popular venue for after-work drinks. In fact, if you find a seat at any time of day you are blessed. It's got a traditional feel with lots of dark wood everywhere and serves a mean pie and a pint of ale. Crowds flock here to watch football on about 20 TVs dotted around.

With nearly 500 whiskies on offer, traditional **The Pot Still** (154 Hope St., tel. 0141/333 0980, www.thepotstill.co.uk, noon–midnight Mon.–Sat., 12:30 P.M.–midnight Sun.), with lots of dark wood, cozy booths and friendly staff, is a lively city-center hangout. It's generally packed because of its diminutive size. The place serves good, cheap food.

Old, dark, low-ceilinged **Scotia** (112–114 Stockwell St., tel. 0141/552 8681, 11 A.M.–midnight daily, food noon–3 or 4 P.M.) has lots of booths and plenty of real ale on tap. It's the city's oldest drinking hole and pulls in an amiable crowd of locals and visitors. Comedian Billy Connolly reportedly started his career here. There's live music several nights a week.

Blackfriars (36 Bell St., tel. 0141/552 5924, 11 A.M.–midnight Mon.–Sat., 12:30 P.M.–midnight Sun.) is a firm hit with real ale drinkers; there are at least five cask ales on the go here at any time and plenty more bottled beer. It's one of those places popular with all sorts, from students to the after work crowd to ninety-something beer guzzlers, and the place serves food, too. There's free blues and jazz on Saturday.

Bar Gandolfi (64 Albion St., tel. 0141/552 4462, www.cafegandolfi.com, 11 A.M.–midnight Mon.–Sat., noon–midnight Sun.) was at the forefront of turning Merchant City into the hip dining and drinking venue it now is. Housed in the old cheese market, it's a great, relaxed venue for a drink—sit at one of the chunky wooden tables and choose from 40 different wines, an array of cocktails, or, to splash out, one of the many types of champagne.

Modeled on a Prague bohemian café with an Eastern European cuisine and drinks range, **Gramofon** (7 King St., tel. 0141/552 7177, 10 A.M.–8 P.M. Mon.–Wed., 10 A.M.–late Thurs.–Sat.) is one cool hangout. It's a relaxed place serving Hungarian goulash, Romanian wine, and good coffee to boot.

A NIGHT OUT ON THE TOWN

Possibly the best thing to do in Scotland's biggest city is experience the absolutely top-class entertainment scene. What makes a night out here so wonderful is the blend of old local boozer bars and sparkling new-style bars. It's only in the last decade or two that Glasgow nightlife has risen to the pinnacle of Europe's nightlife culture. Back in the 1980s, it was perceived by the world as a run-down, rough-and-ready place for a night out. Glasgow has retained the gritty edge to its nightlife but injected a huge dose of glamour. Some extravagant, opulent bars and clubs are now part of the entertainment fix. Many make use of elaborate buildings built to impress by the barons of Victorian industry; a night out therefore also has a cultural aspect. You can gaze up at more Doric columns, statues, and decadent decor as you drink than almost anywhere else in Britain.

A classic night out that combines the best of everything Glasgow can throw at the drinker and clubber involves three key elements: the traditional city pub, the thumping live music scene, and the style bar or club. Most of these places fall into two main areas: the city center and the West End. To pack as much in as possible, start off early in the day at somewhere low-key in the West End. There's no better place to start than **Ashton Lane,** where café tables spill out onto the cobbled sidewalk. Start off at somewhere like **Brel** in early afternoon. It's a Belgian themed bar with a conservatory-type beer garden, loads of good beers, and sidewalk drinking. After a couple of drinks move on to another venue like the lively Irish Bar, **Jinty McGuinty's,** which churns out live music most nights and has an authentic feel. Nearby is also **Vodka Wodka,** the best vodka bar in the city. Just have the one drink here, or you won't last the night. For a great traditional Scottish drinking experience, head east down Great Western Road for a dram at **Uisge Beatha,** Glasgow's most authentic whisky bar.

Now it's time to make your way to the city center. By this time, you'll have worked up an appetite, so what you want now is a bar where you can get some good food. For that, there's nowhere better than opulent Gothic **Arta** in Merchant City. It would be possible to spend the rest of the night in this bar/club, but there are a few more places you should see to round off the city entertainment extravaganza. For a dose of traditional, live music, which by now you will be well in the mood for, try one of the old Clyde-side boozers like **Scotia Bar** or the **Clutha Vaults,** both located by the river. With intimate atmospheres and friendly crowds, these are great places to meet real Glaswegians. If you want a recuperating pint of real ale, then **Blackfriars** in Merchant City will do just as well. Now it's decision time: If you want to go to the most lavish venue the city can throw at you, then head for the **Corinthian.** With a huge glass dome, a late night piano bar, and a club, it will keep you occupied for the rest of the night. For some frantic dancing, head to the small, packed party venue of the **Sub Club.** Dance until the wee hours and make your inebriated way back to your bed, safe in the knowledge you have done Glasgow's entertainment scene justice.

Nice n Sleazy (421 Sauchiehall St., tel. 0141/333 0900, www.nicensleazy.com, 11:30 A.M.–midnight Mon.–Sat., 12:30 P.M.–midnight Sun.) serves good solid grub (try the Nice n Sleazy burger) while providing a cool, grungy place for Glasgow School of Art students (and others) to hang out. The bar's most famous feature is probably the jukebox, but its stage sees its fair share of indie bands performing.

You can say a lot of things about the retro gastro-pub **The Butterfly and the Pig** (153 Bath St., tel. 0141/221 7711, 11 A.M.–3 A.M. daily), but you cannot say it's normal. You sit at plush poufs while you have a glass of wine or eat innovative cuisine with funky art deco cutlery. It's not exactly geared toward your wild night out—more a chit-chat with old friends.

Arches (253 Argyle St., tel. 0141/565 1035, www.thearches.co.uk, 11 A.M.–midnight Mon.–Sat., noon–midnight Sun.) began life as a theater venue but quickly metamorphosed into an elaborate bar and nightclub complex as well. The bar/restaurant is a long, spick-and-span area perfect for a pre-club drink, with high ceilings hung with glittery lights that add a touch of the grand to the experience. The place shows regular theatrical performances.

The bar of the opulent entertainment supercomplex that is the **Corinthian** (191 Ingram St., tel. 0141/552 1101, 11 A.M.–3 A.M. daily) is housed in the ornately decorated, 19th-century former banking hall. Giving you plenty to gawp at as you sip at your drinks (the cocktails are particularly good) is the 30-foot glass domed ceiling. The atmosphere is not what you'd call electrifying, but there's live piano music here in the evenings. It generally attracts a thirty-something-plus crowd.

A surreal, Gothic, operatic romp of blood-red sofas, statues, candelabras, and gilt-framed old paintings, **Arta** (62 Albion St., tel. 0141/552 2101, www.arta.co.uk, 5 P.M.–midnight Wed.–Thurs. and Sun., 5 P.M.–3 A.M. Fri.–Sat.) is not the kind of place you want to try any hallucinogenic substances in. It is, however, a wonderfully wacky place for a drink or three. Food is great here, with lots of pasta and pizza and a few meat and vegetable dishes.

West End

If you want a break from your typical beer-swilling boozer, then come to **Uisge Beatha** (232–426 Woodlands Rd., tel. 0141/564 1596, www.uisgebeathabar.co.uk, noon–midnight Mon.–Sat., 12:30 P.M.–midnight Sun.), one of Glasgow's classic whisky bars. Kilted bar staff will serve you any of the 125 whiskies on display, then you can retire amidst the oh-so-Scottish decor (stag heads, open fires, dark wood, and upturned church pews) with a crowd of students and grizzled locals.

Bar Buddha (142 St. Vincent St., tel. 0141/248 7881, noon–2 A.M. Mon.–Thurs., noon–3 A.M. Fri.–Sat., noon–midnight Sun.) is the original branch of the Far East kitsch bar which now has several outlets in Glasgow. There's a big gold Buddha statue, a touch of lavishness to the decor, and a big selection of fancy cocktails.

Vodka Wodka (31–35 Ashton Ln., tel. 0141/341 0069, www.vodkawodka.co.uk, noon–midnight daily) does for vodka what the Pot Still does for whisky. It's true that most of the vodka "connoisseurs" here are students out to get hammered, but that doesn't detract from Vodka Wodka's great selection of Scandinavian, Baltic, and Russian spirits. It's a crowded hangout but a fun one.

The high-spirited Irish bar of **Jinty McGuinty's** (23–29 Ashton Ln., tel. 0141/339 0747, 11 A.M.–11:30 P.M. Sun.–Thurs., 11 A.M.–midnight Fri.–Sat.) has a great setting; perhaps the best reason for going here is the outside seating on the cobbles—great for a summer beer-slurping session. Unlike a lot of Irish theme bars, genuine Gaels are often seen on the premises.

Of all Glasgow's style bars, chic **Chinaski's** (239 North St., tel. 0141/221 0061, www.chinaskis.com, 11 A.M.–midnight Mon.–Sat., 12:30 P.M.–midnight Sun.) with its potted plants and fish tank wins the prize for most effortlessly attaining the status of "cool." It's themed loosely around the hard-drinking writer protagonist of Charles Bukowski's novels and has pearls of Chinaski wisdom on the toilet walls. As if that wasn't enough incentive, there's also almost always great music playing here.

South Side

There are not many pubs on the south side of Glasgow worth the risk of entering but the **Clockwork Brewery** (1153–1155 Cathcart Rd., tel. 0141/649 0184, http://clockwork-beer.com, 11 A.M.–11 P.M. Mon.–Wed., 11 A.M.–12:30 A.M. Thurs.–Sat., 12:30–11 P.M. Sun.) is one of the few that is. The reason for this place's popularity is that Clockwork has its own microbrewery. In a relaxed, relatively trendy environment, you can drink your way through the range of beers brewed on-site. The fruit beers are favorites but the Red Alt, a soft, fruity, rich red brew fusing Bavarian malt and American hops, also goes down a treat. To get there take a train to Kings Park Station and head west up Kings Park Avenue.

LIVE MUSIC

There's no doubt about it: Glasgow is the capital of live music in Scotland. In fact, after London, it's Britain's main music venue. You're bound to find something that floats your boat: there's jazz, plenty of traditional and folk music, and a great rock/indie music scene. In most cases, for major performances it's best to buy tickets in advance. You can buy tickets at the door at smaller venues, but you risk the performance being sold out. Several pubs also host regular live music. This can be the most fun way of experiencing it as you're hanging out with other Glaswegians; it's a good chance to meet the locals.

The listings below should only serve as a guide: for more information on gigs you should buy a copy of *The List,* Glasgow and Edinburgh's handy entertainment magazine. Music in Glasgow is generally quite organized, unlike elsewhere in Scotland where the best music experiences are more likely to be a spontaneous get-together.

Traditional/Folk/Jazz

Clutha Vaults (167–169 Stockwell St., tel. 0141/552 7520) is a predominantly local venue with live music five nights a week—mostly traditional and folk, but Clutha Vaults hosts all sorts of music, including rock.

Cozy old **Scotia** (112–114 Stockwell St., tel. 0141/552 8681) is where comedian Billy Connolly started out and is a great bet for traditional live entertainment. Wednesday night is Celtic folk night. Glasgow's best-known comedian is still sometimes to be seen having a pint here, they say.

Star Folk Club (1 St. Andrews Sq., by Saltmarket, tel. 0141/563 0454, www.starfolk-club.com) attracts folk, blues, world jazz, and traditional acts. The big night is Thursday—things kick off around 8 P.M.

Irish pub **Jinty McGuinty's** (23–29 Ashton Ln., tel. 0141/339 0747, 11 A.M.–midnight Mon.–Sat., 12:30 P.M.–midnight Sun.) has lively traditional/folk music sessions on most nights of the week, which everybody seems to love, especially after a few pints of Guinness.

The **Drum and Monkey** (93–95 St. Vincent St., tel. 0141/221 6636) has great live jazz sessions around 3–7 P.M. Sunday. **Blackfriars** (36 Bell St., tel. 0141/552 5924) also has regular live jazz.

Rock/Indie

King Tut's Wah Wah Hut (272a St. Vincent St., tel. 0141/221 5279, www.kingtuts.co.uk) is one of the premier promoters of new pop/rock/indie music in Scotland. The likes of Blur, Radiohead, and Travis have all played here; it's also the venue where Oasis were first signed after performing. There's something interesting in the way of live, contemporary music here every night of the week. Tickets range £5–15.

Anyone who is anyone in the world of rock and pop has played at long-established **Barrowland Ballroom** (244 Gallowgate, tel. 0141/552 4601) over the years. It's a medium-sized venue with a 1,900 capacity. Tickets sell out very fast.

Every bit as grungy and well worn as you would expect from a venue beneath a railway line, **Mono** (12 Kings Ct., King St., tel. 0141/553 2400, noon–midnight daily) attract a fair mix of gigs. There are few names you will have heard of, which means that sometimes this venue surprises and delights and at other times appalls.

The famous jukebox in the basement of **Nice n Sleazy** (421 Sauchiehall St., tel. 0141/333 0900) sometimes plays second fiddle to indie acts, which play on the small stage to an appreciative crowd of students and twenty-somethings.

The 13th Note (club 260 Clyde St., bar 50–60 King St., tel. 0141/553 1638) was formerly a jazz venue; this boisterous place now has metal rock and indie bands performing Tuesday–Thursday and a range of alternative music at weekends.

General

The **SECC** (Finnieston Quay, tel. 0141/248 3000, www.secc.co.uk), or Scottish Exhibition and Conference Centre, is, among its many functions, the country's biggest live event and performance space, and live music gigs of all sorts take place here.

GAY AND LESBIAN SAUNAS, BARS, AND CLUBS

Glasgow has far and away the best gay and lesbian scene in Scotland. There's a good mix of lively bars and downright pumping club nights. Many venues are not specifically gay, but cater to a mixed gay and straight crowd. A lot of the city's top clubs like the Arches have gay nights. The heart of the city's gay scene is in laid-back Merchant City. It's a friendly community that mingles well into the vibrant district surrounding it. For further information on gay/lesbian entertainment, check out *The List* magazine or contact the **LGBT Centre** in Merchant City (84 Bell St., tel. 0141/552 4958, open daily), itself with a brand new café/bar here serving decent food.

Relax Central (27 Union St., tel. 0141/221 0415, noon–10 P.M. daily, £8 before 1 P.M., £10 after 1 P.M.) is a complex with two saunas, hot tubs, a private rest lounge, and free broadband Internet access.

Delmonicas (68 Virginia St., tel. 0141/552 4803, noon–midnight daily, no cover) is a loud, brash, lively spot with lots of karaoke

and discos. It attracts a mixed crowd, but there's not much subtlety about this place—most of the clientele here are on the pull, pure and simple.

Polo Lounge (84 Wilson St., tel. 0141/553 1221, 5 P.M.–1 A.M. Mon.–Thurs. 5 P.M.–3 A.M. Fri., noon–3 A.M. Sat.–Sun., cover £5 after 11 P.M. Fri.–Sun.) is decked out like a baronial Scottish mansion, with marble tiles and huge mirrors. It plays all sorts of music, including some live music, from dance to new wave and punk. With three plush levels, this is the city's largest, most lavish gay bar. You'll find plenty of beautiful people here.

A relaxed little venue, **Revolver** (6a John St., tel. 0141/553 2456, 11 A.M.–1 A.M., no cover) has a pool table, a pinball machine, and a free jukebox. It's good for a spot of socializing or as a pre-club venue.

Utter Gutter (Glasgow Art School, Renfrew St., www.uttergutter.com, 11 P.M.–3 A.M., cover £10) club night plays lots of fun, sleazy, cheesy pop on the second Saturday of every month at the Glasgow Art School.

Glasgow's longest-established gay club, **Bennet's** (50–60 Glassford St., tel. 0141/552 5761, www.bennetsnightclub.co.uk, 11:30 P.M.–3 A.M. Tues. and Thurs.–Sun., cover £3–5) plays everything from cheese to dance. It's a sophisticated-looking club with three bars.

NIGHTCLUBS

Arches (253 Argyle St., tel. 0141/565 1035, www.thearches.co.uk, 11 P.M.–3 A.M. Wed.–Sat., cover £7–12) is set in a cavernous set of arches, having a reputation for a huge range of quality club nights. DJs Pete Tongue, David Holmes, and Judge Jules regularly play at the Arches but there's plenty more bizarre nights such as the mad student night, Octopussy on Wednesdays (featuring a Jacuzzi), and Burly, a gay night aimed at over-25's on the first Friday of the month. It's the best club in the city.

Formerly known as the Coco Club, **Classic Grand** (18 Jamaica St., tel. 0141/847 0820, www.classicgrand.com, 11 P.M.–3 A.M. Fri.–Sat., cover £4–6) is the new addition to the city

THE WORLD'S UNLIKELIEST ADVERTISING CAMPAIGNS

Following economic deprivation, mass unemployment, and atrocious, soulless high-rise housing developments, Glasgow's reputation in the mid-1970s was in pretty poor shape. Books such as Alexander McArthur's *No Mean City: A Story of Life in the Glasgow Slums* had helped to shape people's impressions. It was a place famed for knife fights, football violence, run-down industry, and dingy-looking bars. Even its residents were ashamed of it, and certainly no one thought of incorporating it into their Scotland holiday experience.

Clearly, the city was in need of a drastic makeover, and city planners thought the key to halting the spiral of decline was in perception. It wasn't the easiest time to reinvent a city; in the early 1980s, most of Britain was in the grip of an economic depression. Promoting local pride, developers decided, was the key. Campaigns took the form of catchy slogans: There was the "Glasgow Smiles" campaign of the 1970s and the "Glasgow's Miles Better" campaign, launched in 1983. Initially people went from thinking of Scotland's metropolis as a frightening place to a farcical one. The most notorious campaign placard was perhaps that fixed to the side of a rusting gas works, giving motorists a right laugh as they passed on the motorway. The words "Miles Better" might have been visible, but with a background of precious little save industrial blight, they couldn't be taken with any seriousness.

Strangely, however, the campaign did slowly begin to have a noticeable effect: It began to restore civic pride and national interest in Glasgow. Championed by Lord Provost Michael Kelly and advertising man John Struthers, the campaign used Roger Hargreaves' Mr. Men characters (namely Mr. Happy) to get across its point. Even the Queen, pictured smiling under a Mr. Happy umbrella, was involved. Succeeding through doggedness and good PR, the campaign actually got people talking about the city. This was backed up with Glasgow's major cultural ventures of the ensuing years, such as its awards for Garden City of the Year and Cultural Capital of Europe.

Glasgow has kept up the campaigns ever since: 1990 saw the launch of "There's A Lot Glasgowing On" to coincide with its status as European Cultural Capital of the Year. Because of the success of its self-promotion, Glasgow began to change strategies on how it sold itself. The focus was less on proving that it wasn't a bad city and more on showing why it was such a good city: "Scotland with Style" was a more recent catchphrase. While only a blip on the surface of Glasgow's redevelopment program, it was the advertising – once derided – that circulated the buzz that the city had a lot to offer. Glasgow's self-promotion drive remains Europe's best example of a city that has been able to radically alter people's impressions of it through a few slogans.

clubbing scene, aimed at 20- to 30-year-olds and playing an innovative indie, rock, salsa, and hip-hop mix of tunes. Friday night is '80s night.

Making up the opulent Gothic quota of the city's bar/club/restaurant complexes, **Arta** (62 Albion St., tel. 0141/552 2101, www.arta.co.uk, 5 P.M.–3 A.M. Fri.–Sat., no cover before 11 P.M., £5–7 after 11 P.M.) comes alive on Friday and Saturday with a mix of soul, funk, R&B, and pop across its two club spaces.

Moshers, grungers, and thrashers should not look any further than **Cathouse** (15 Union St., tel. 0141/248 6606, 11 P.M.–late Thurs.–Sun.,

no cover on Thurs., £5 on Fri. and Sat.), a heaving two-floor rock venue.

For 20-odd years, the little basement of **Sub Club** (22 Jamaica St., tel. 0141/246 4600, 11 P.M.–3 A.M. Fri.–Sun., cover £6–12) has been treating clubbers to eardrum-busting techno, electronic, and dance. It defies being defined, churning out ever-fresh, ever-innovative music.

PERFORMING ARTS

Part of the reason that Glasgow courses with vitality is its performing arts scene. There's a huge range of theater, the Scottish National Opera, and live comedy venues that have spawned such talent as "Big Yin" Billy Connolly, one of the foremost names in British comedy.

Theater

Housed in an old church, **Tron Theatre** (63 Trongate, tel. 0141/552 4267, www.tron.co.uk, bar open 10 A.M.–late Mon.–Sat., 11 A.M.–6 P.M. Sun.) puts on innovative modern theatrical performances. It's worth coming to the vibrant café/bar for a drink and bite to eat beforehand if you're catching a show here.

The **Pavillion Theatre** (121 Renfield St., tel. 0141/332 1846, www.pavillionthe-atre.co.uk) is one of Britain's few remaining privately run theaters, putting on a mix of pantomimes and plays.

The **Centre for Contemporary Arts** (350 Sauchiehall St., tel. 0141/352 4900, www.cca-glasgow.com) is a real breath of fresh air in Glasgow, putting on all kinds of performances from visual arts to music and film. It's committed to innovative, experimental artistic expression. There's also a good café here.

Ballet and Orchestra

The **Glasgow Royal Concert Hall** (2 Sauchiehall St., tel. 0141/353 8000, www.glas-gowconcerthalls.com) hosts a wide range of classical and world music, as well as folk and country. The home of the Scottish opera is **Theatre Royal** (282 Hope St., tel. 0141/332 3321, www.theatreroyalglasgow.com). The Scottish Ballet also performs here.

Comedy

Edinburgh comedy club **The Stand** (333 Woodlands Rd., tel. 0870/600 6055, www.the-stand.co.uk) has an equally well-regarded venue in Glasgow.

OTHER ENTERTAINMENT
Cinema

The **Glasgow Film Theatre** (12 Rose St., tel. 0141/332 6535, www.gft.org.uk, café/bar open noon–9 P.M. Mon.–Fri., 11 A.M.–9 P.M. Sat., until 8:30 P.M. Sun.) is one of the city's more eclectic movie-going venues, showing hard-to-find art-house films, monthly cult and horror films, and themed screenings from different areas of the world. It also discerningly screens the more alternative end of the mainstream movies. The place has a lively café/bar for before-film drinks.

Cineworld (7 Renfrew St., tel. 0871/200 2000, £6.40 evening) shows mainstream films.

Pool/Snooker

The Local (427 Sauchiehall St., tel. 0141/353 6161, www.the-local.co.uk) is a friendly bar with some American pool tables downstairs; it's a good bet if you fancy a game on the blue baize without trekking anywhere too seedy to do so. The food here is pretty decent, too.

EVENTS

Glasgow cannot match Edinburgh for festivals but, as befits a live music hotbed, there are several good music festivals throughout the year including the wonderful Celtic Connections festival.

Celtic Connections (www.celticconnections.com), held in late January and early February each year, continues to go from strength to strength. It's a celebration of all Celtic music, featuring Celtic rock and dance music as well as more traditional Celtic performances. It's a great time to dispense with prejudices about Celtic music and find out what it's really all about.

Glasgow International Comedy Festival (www.glasgowcomedyfestival.com) is now in its sixth year; the two-week humor fest continues to attract a top lineup. It's held in March.

Opening with a Mardis Gras parade, **West End Festival** (www.westendfestival.co.uk) is an extravaganza of music, theater, film, and dance for two weeks every June.

Glasgow International Jazz Festival (www.jazzfest.co.uk) is held during the time of the West End Festival in June. It features an incredibly diverse lineup of jazz at venues across the city.

Glasgay (www.glasgay.com) is Europe's

largest gay and lesbian multi-arts festival. It's a succession of music, film, art, dance, and club nights across the city in October and early November.

Triptych (www.triptychfestival.com), staged across Aberdeen and Edinburgh as well as Glasgow, is a festival celebrating eclectic music and film in late April.

Shopping

Glasgow has more retail space than anywhere else in Britain, save London. Shopping is understandably one of the top pastimes of Glaswegians; there are more shopping centers than you could shake a bulging carrier bag at. There are designer stores if you want to treat yourself, a good selection of craft and antique shops, and a lot of eclectic music stores.

SHOPPING CENTERS

Below is a selection of Glasgow's best and most useful shopping centers.

Princes Square (Buchanan St., www.princessquare.co.uk, 9:30 A.M.–6 P.M. Mon.–Wed. and Fri., 9:30 A.M.–8 P.M. Thurs., 9 A.M.–6 P.M. Sat., noon–5 P.M. Sun.) is a covered shopping center with mostly fashion and jewelry shops, as well as bars and cafés.

The vast **Buchanan Galleries** (220 Buchanan St., www.buchanangalleries.co.uk, 9 A.M.–6 P.M. Mon.–Wed. and Fri.–Sat., 9 A.M.–8 P.M. Thurs., 10 A.M.–6 P.M. Sun.) complex contains most of the main chain stores including John Lewis.

The Italian Centre (7 John St., tel. 0141/552 6368, 10 A.M.–6 P.M. Mon.–Sat., noon–5 P.M. Sun.) is a cooler, more relaxed place to shop. It's popular with the fashion-conscious, containing Scotland's only Versace location, an Armani store, and lots of lovely Italian cafés and restaurants.

FOOD AND DRINK

The deli/wine/whisky shop of **Peckham's** (Byres Rd., tel. 0141/357 1454, 8 A.M.–midnight Mon.–Sat. 9 A.M.–midnight Sun.) is a mine of Scottish delights, including plenty of brightly packaged foodie gifts.

Tesco Supermarket (St. Rollox Business Pk., tel. 0844/677 9309) is a massive 24-hour supermarket. Tesco has a smaller store by St. Enoch subway station.

Just like a step back in time to a world of gentlemen's clubs and smoking jackets, **Robert Graham Ltd.** (141 West Nile St., tel. 0141/248 7283) has over 50 varieties of Havana cigar and 120 types of malt whisky on offer.

Glickman's (157 London Rd., tel. 0141/552 0880, www.glickmans.co.uk, 10 A.M.–4 P.M. Tues.–Fri., 10 A.M.–5 P.M. Sat.–Sun.) is Glasgow's oldest sweet shop, founded in 1903. It's still every bit as quaint as it would have been 100 years ago. Sweets are still handmade on the premises. Think of all your favorite sweets as a kid: licorice, peanut brittle, and sugared almonds are all here for the taking.

DESIGNER BOUTIQUES AND DEPARTMENT STORES

If you want to look as sharp and well turned out as some of the people you see in the city style bars, there's no shortage of places to find the goods.

Boutique fashion store **Cruise** (180 Ingram St., tel. 0141/572 3232, 9 A.M.–6 P.M. Mon.–Wed. and Fri.–Sat., 10 A.M.–7 P.M. Thurs., noon–5 P.M. Sun.) contains all the big names from Armani to Prada at prices that will make you wince. Nearby is **Cruise Jeans** (223 Ingram St.), where you can get the city's coolest denim.

Fifi and Ally (Princes Sq., tel. 0141/229 0386, 9:30 A.M.–6 P.M. Mon.–Wed. and Fri., 9:30 A.M.–8 P.M. Thurs., 9 A.M.–6 P.M. Sat., noon–5 P.M. Sun.) is a mix of designer products including jewelry and cosmetics, with a good café. There's also a branch at 80 Wellington Street, with a better restaurant.

Glasgow has Scotland's only **Urban**

GLASGOW

Outfitters (157 Buchanan St., tel. 0141/248 9203, 10 A.M.–8 P.M. Mon.–Thurs., 10 A.M.–7 P.M. Fri.–Sat., noon–6 P.M. Sun.), the oh-so-trendy men's and women's clothes store.

An old favorite for department store shopping sprees, **John Lewis** (Buchanan Galleries, tel. 0141/353 6677, 9 A.M.–6 P.M. Mon.–Wed. and Fri.–Sat., 9 A.M.–8 P.M. Thurs., 10 A.M.–6 P.M. Sun.) stocks almost everything worth buying.

BOOKS

Oxfam Books (330 Byres Rd., tel. 0141/338 6185) is a huge, well-organized charity shop bookstore stocking masses of books, many virtually new, at bargain prices.

Voltaire and Rousseau (18 Otago Ln., tel. 0141/339 1811, 11 A.M.–6:30 P.M. Mon.–Sat.) is a book lover's dream: a shop stacked to the rafters with teetering piles of fiction and nonfiction books. What you're looking for will be here . . . somewhere.

A massive store with a good stock of books in all areas, **Borders** (98 Buchanan St., tel. 0141/222 7700, 8 A.M.–10 P.M. Mon.–Sat., 10 A.M.–9 P.M. Sun.) has a section on Glasgow and Scottish interest books.

MUSIC

It's difficult to know what to get most excited about at **Monorail Records** (12 Kings Ct., by Kings Rd., tel. 0141/552 9458, 11 A.M.–7 P.M. Mon.–Sat., noon–5 P.M. Sun.)—the brilliant record shop or the scrummy vegan café.

HMV (154-160 Sauchiehall St., tel. 0844/800 3236, 8 A.M.–9 P.M. Mon.–Wed. and Fri.–Sat., 8 A.M.–10 P.M. Thurs., 9 A.M.–6 P.M. Sun.) is one large music and DVD shop.

SECONDHAND, ANTIQUES, AND HANDICRAFTS

Just like a miniature version of the West End as a whole, **De Courcy's Antique Crafts Arcade** (5–21 Cresswell Ln., tel. 0141/334 6673) has loads of cool secondhand and antique shops, craft shops, and cafés.

Come to **Mr. Ben** (Studio 6, Kings Ct., 101 King St., tel. 0141/553 1936, 10:30 A.M.–5:30 P.M. Mon.–Fri., 10 A.M.–6 P.M. Sat., 2–5 P.M. Sun.) for bargain vintage clothes, some of which are probably quite valuable and all of which are lusted after by browsing students.

MARKETS
ⓒ The Barras

The city's main market (10 A.M.–5 P.M. Sat.–Sun.) is an essential weekend experience—many reckon this to be Glasgow at its most authentic. Situated in the east end of Glasgow along the Gallowgate, it's a squawking hub of activity with local stallholders bawling out their wares, lots of rip-off brands, fruit and vegetables, and good, greasy burger joints. Keep a watchful eye on your wallet.

Craft Markets

Merchant City's craft market takes place on **Merchant Square** (Candleriggs) 11:30 A.M.–6 P.M. every Saturday.

Every year from late November until just before Christmas, streets of Glasgow become lined with the **Festive Market,** rows of stalls selling seasonal goodies from mulled wine to candles, often at cheaper prices than you'd pay in the shops.

Sports and Recreation

The city's favorite sport by some way is football, but there's plenty of interesting walking, especially in the outer areas of Glasgow.

WALKING

Glasgow is on the doorstep of some fabulous countryside, some of it within the city limits.

At **Milngavie** (pronounced Mill-guy) is the start of the **West Highland Way** (www.west-highland-way.co.uk), Scotland's most popular long-distance footpath. The first section, as far as Drymen near the shores of Loch Lomond, is a 12-mile stretch across woods and pasture land, easily accomplishable in a day. Trains run regularly from Glasgow Queen Street to Milngavie.

Pollock Country Park has plenty of good walking, in wilder environs than you generally find in a city. Walks can take in woods and Highland cattle.

HEALTH CLUBS AND FITNESS CENTERS

If you like to work out on your holiday then **Bannatyne's Health Club** (309 St. Vincent St., tel. 0141/248 9788, 6:30 A.M.–10 P.M. Mon.–Fri., 8 A.M.–6 P.M. Sat.–Sun.) is a good place to head.

SPECTATOR SPORTS
Football

To most Glaswegians, "Futba" means only two things: the team they love the most and the team they hate the most. The city's football loyalties are mostly divided into support for one of two rival clubs, Rangers and Celtic. A meeting between these two sides, known as an Old Firm derby, is one of the most fraught, passionate clashes of any domestic football fixtures in the world. The two clubs attract tremendous support and utterly monopolize Scottish football. When either one of these sides is playing in a domestic or European fixture, the whole atmosphere of the city changes noticeably; fans that can't get to see the match live fill the city pubs with their vociferous presence. With passions running so high, it is, of course, best to keep your own preference for the outcome of the game subtle. You just don't know who might be listening! To add to the footballing fun, Scotland's national stadium, Hampden Park, is also located here. Due to Scotland's heartbreaking failure to qualify for international tournaments of recent years, this stadium is a theater of tears as much as it is a theater of dreams.

Celtic Football Club (Parkhead, tel. 0845/671 1888, www.celticfc.co.uk) has its stadium, **Celtic Park**, east of the city center. Buses 61, 62, and 64 run right past the stadium from the city center. Dalmarnock is the nearest train station (10 minutes' walk). Ticket prices are £22–25. **Ibrox Stadium** (Edmiston Dr., tel. 0871/702 1972, www.rangers.co.uk), home of the **Rangers Football Club,** has a subway station with the same name and is in the south of Glasgow. Ticket prices are £20–22.

Scotland has a separate stadium for national team matches, **Hampden Park** (South Side, tel. 0141/620 4000, www.hampdenpark.co.uk). Buses 31 and 37 are among those running to Hampden Park from Stockwell Street.

FOOTBALL RIVALRY

Probably the greatest domestic football rivalry of all time is of that between traditionally Protestant Glasgow Rangers and Catholic Glasgow Celtic. When Celtic was formed in 1888 by predominantly Irish (and therefore Catholic) migrant city workers, a religious divide quickly materialized from the already-established Rangers side. As the two biggest sides in Scottish football, their rivalry has always been at the forefront of the public eye.

More significantly, derby games between the teams have not always been restricted to write-ups in the sports section of the papers. In the past, ever in need of inspiration for ways to taunt the opposition, opposing fans have used political events to incense each other. Rangers-Celtic rivalries came to symbolize the division of the times. During the 1970s troubles in Northern Ireland, Celtic fans vocally supported the IRA, while Rangers fans applauded Loyalist responses. In 2002, Celtic flew Palestinian flags at a local derby match, and Rangers fans flew Israeli flags. It was as late as 1989 before a big-name Catholic player featured in a starting line-up for Rangers.

Both clubs have called for a halt to the actions of the minority of fans stirring up the hatred, but every now and again an incident brings the age-old divisions back to the surface. In 1995 high-profile player Paul Gascoigne infuriated Celtic fans by miming playing a flute, traditionally seen as a sign of empathy with the anti-Irish Loyalist cause. Celtic goalkeeper Alan Boruc infuriated almost everyone in 2006 by crossing himself during a game against Rangers. As a result of the violence between fans, which often spills out into the city after matches, many pubs have wisely chosen to ban football colors on the premises.

History aside, it's only a small proportion of fans causing most of the problems. Generally, the rivalry between the two teams just makes for an electric atmosphere in the stadium and a real desire on behalf of both teams to beat the other. Just be aware of the turbulent history of these two clubs and their supporters; stating a preference for one is making a controversial statement about a lot more than just football!

Accommodations

Glasgow's accommodation options are not as extensive as you might think. The best budget options lie at the Euro Hostel in the city center and in several far nicer West End establishments. It's hard to find a decently priced guesthouse in the city center; most guesthouse accommodations lie in the East End or the West End, with a series of uninspiring places on Great Western Road, west of the city center. There's a range of very good hotels, including lots of boutique hotels, in the city center and the West End. A decent double room in the city costs £50–60 on average. The most pleasant area of town to stay in is the verdant West End.

CITY CENTER AND MERCHANT CITY

If you want to be right in the center of things for your stay in Glasgow, then the accommodation choice is basically between the gigantic Euro Hostel and a range of medium-priced to expensive hotels. Merchant City, despite being very close to the main part of the city center, retains a distinctive bohemian feel and is a desirable area to stay in.

Under £50

Once you've gotten over the dire service, **Euro Hostel** (318 Clyde St., tel. 0141/222 2828, www.euro-hostels.co.uk, beds from £12.95, £29.95 s, £35.90 d) is actually a very pleasant budget option. It's a hostel of truly mammoth proportions with a thumping, friendly bar downstairs. Rooms are quiet, functional, and mostly four-bed or two-bed configurations. You get almost a bed-and-breakfast at bargain rates; it's basic but clean, rooms have en suite bathrooms, and there's even a TV you can pay for the privilege of using. A continental breakfast with good coffee is included in the price. It does feel a bit like you're staying in a rather sterile office block though.

You wouldn't think it, but there are some 60 bedrooms on offer at **The Victorian House** (212 Renfrew St., tel. 0141/332 0129, www.thevictorian.co.uk, £32 s, £46 twin, £60 d). Many rooms sport a likable rustic pine decor. Victorian in name but certainly not in nature, this guesthouse offers some of the cheapest decent city center accommodations. Most rooms are en suite and have color TVs.

£50-100

Adelaide's (209 Bath St., tel. 0141/248 4970, www.adelaides.co.uk, £45 s, £54 d) is a revamped 1870s Baptist church that succeeds where many other Glasgow guesthouses fail— it provides accommodation with a bit of character. All rooms but two are en suite; the two rooms with a shared bathroom have wash basins. The rates do not include breakfast, but it can be ordered.

Set back from the roadside off a quiet street in Merchant City, **(Merchant Lodge Hotel** (52 Virginia St., tel. 0141/552 2424, www.merchantlodgehotel.com, £40 s, £62 d) offers characterful, clean, light rooms at bargain prices. As digs go, they're not exactly huge but all rooms are en suite. The decor is white throughout, except in the pine-beamed basement where breakfast is served. The building dates from the 17th century, although you wouldn't think so to look at it from inside. It does, however, have one of the two turnpike stairways still in use in the city. Try to get a room near the top for good views and good light. It's got a near-perfect location in city center.

The **Fraser Suites** (1–19 Albion St., tel. 0141/553 4288, studio apartments from £108) are a gaudy, boutique-style alternative to a city-center hotel—your very own self-catering apartment. This is not self-catering as you know it, though; Fraser offers 100 or so swanky studio and one- or two-bedroom apartments. You get that extra degree of flexibility as well as additional facilities like a gym and a continental breakfast being available. Rates fluctuate significantly depending on whether they are booked online, how many suites you require, and how long you are staying. Rates drop for more than six nights.

Alexander Thomson Hotel (320 Argyle St., tel. 0141/221 1152, £65 d) is right near Glasgow Central railway station, named and themed after Alexander "The Greek" Thomson, a 19th-century architect. There are lots of dark, elegant old furnishings and hunting scenes on the walls of the public rooms. The bedrooms, however, are a different story; with a cozy pink-beige decor, they exude a generally modern, spacious feel. All rooms are en suite with satellite TV and direct-dial telephones. The only meal you can get here is breakfast, but that's hardly a problem with the amount of eateries close by. It's an ideal place to stay if you're in Glasgow as a quick overnight stop or on business. If you're staying a while in the city, there are places with more soul.

Marks Hotel (121 Bath St., tel. 0141/353 0800, www.markshotels.com, £89 d) is very 21st century; rooms are individually designed with satellite plasma-screen TVs, free Wi-Fi access, fresh fruit, and luxury Arran Aromatics toiletries in the spick-and-span en suite bathrooms. From outside, it resembles a huge, glassy office block. There's a modern bar/restaurant here but it's got very little character—better eateries await outside the doors. It's a handy hotel for Queen Street railway station.

The mini-boutique hotel in Merchant City **Rab Ha's** (81 Hutcheson St., tel. 0141/572 0400, www.rabhas.com, £95 d) has been decorated with a lot of effort and attention to style. It's a proudly individual hotel, affiliated with the bar of the same name, with four vibrant, sparkling rooms on offer. Expect plush

GLASGOW

furnishings, fancy panes of colored glass, flat screen TVs, and en suite bathrooms.

Over £100

The fanciest boutique hotel in Glasgow, **Malmaison** (278 West George St., tel. 0141/572 1000, www.malmaison-glasgow .com, £160 d) is a former Greek Orthodox church boasting over 70 rooms and suites. The decor is in opulent royal reds and purples—truly a pad fit for a monarch. These are modern, cool, spacious rooms, and you won't really want to bother going out and sightseeing if you're staying here. There are all the luxuries that make it such a hit: CD players and CD libraries, trendy toiletries, and round-the-clock nibbles. The love suite is £255 per night, with champagne and chocolate-dipped strawberries.

WEST END

The West End is a quieter, leafier, generally more desirable accommodation alternative to the city center. It's got more attractive budget options and plenty of well-to-do guesthouses and hotels.

Under £50

Blue Sky Hostel (3 Bank St., tel. 0141/221 1710, beds from £13, £38 d) has 2-, 4-, 10-, and 12-bed dorms in a sedate West End residential house. It's a fun hostel with free Internet access, a small self-catering kitchen, and a lively common room area. People have criticized this place for being a bit on the shabby side but it's really not bad.

    Glasgow Youth Hostel (7–8 Park Terr., tel. 0870/155 3255, www.syha.org.uk, beds £14–21) is a big Victorian house right on the edge of Kelvingrove Park. Rooms are large enough, with plenty of light, but the four- to six-bed dorms lack privacy and, truthfully, soul. That said, the building itself is elaborate with high, finely crafted plasterwork ceilings and several massive common areas with plenty of comfy seats. There's even a coffee shop and a pool-room here.

    Among the accommodations available from Glasgow University is modern **Cairncross House** (Kelvinhaugh St., tel. 0141/330 4116, £33.60 d), with a batch of single and twin rooms available. Beds are small and a bit on the hard side, and the rooms aren't much bigger than the beds. For the price, however, these are clean, cozy digs, with use of complimentary laundry facilities and self-catering kitchens.

£50-100

Not to be confused with the Townhouse Hotel, also in this category, **The Town House** (4 Hughenden Terr., tel. 0141/357 0862, www.towhouseglasgow.co.uk, £72 d) is a pleasant guesthouse with good-sized en suite rooms. Rooms are imaginatively wallpapered, and while the patterns may dizzy you if you look at them too long, the decor lends plenty of character to the place. One room gets an en suite bathroom with a stand-alone bath and retro black-and-white tile. The Town House has a reputation for breakfasts every bit as imaginative as the accommodation that include, er, local seafood—one wonders how local that can be in the center of Glasgow, but still. Singles will be hit by almost the full double-occupancy price here.

    Kirklee Hotel (11 Kensington Gate, tel. 0141/334 5555, www.kirkleehotel.co.uk, £59 s, £75 d) is the kind of heartwarming, charming hotel you wish you had the good fortune to wind up at in every town you pass. It's a genteel red sandstone house with nine en suite rooms. Other room facilities include color TVs, radios, and telephones. As for the decor, it's pretty striking stuff: vivid tartan, dark wood, blue and gold. The hotel has a guest lounge, and breakfast is served in your room.

    The **Townhouse Hotel** (21–22 Royal Crescent, tel. 0141/332 9009, www.townhousehotelglasgow.com, £36 s, £60 d) has an enviable location just off Kelvingrove Park. It's a late Victorian white-fronted place set back from the main drag on a quiet road in a fresh, leafy part of town. Rooms have a pale decor and pine furnishings—they're not quite as fancy as you might expect from outside but all are en suite with TVs and telephones.

Over £100

Spread over no fewer than five glam townhouses, **One Devonshire Gardens** (tel. 0141/339 2001, www.hotelduvin.com, standard rooms from £145, suites from £395) has an ever-burgeoning reputation as the celebrity accommodation stop-off of choice. Few places can boast such an exclusive array of rooms and suites. It might be easier to mention what the rooms don't have rather than what they do, but expect as standard soft Egyptian cotton bedding, fluffy bathrobes, mini bars stocked with drinks and snacks, and satellite TV. For all that, the bistro here serves up reasonably priced cuisine for around £10—there's a strong seafood and game theme.

EAST END

The area east of Glasgow Cathedral has some reasonably priced hotels and guesthouses.

Under £50

The high-toned detached villa of **Claremont House** (2 Broompark Circus, tel. 0141/554 7312, www.claremont-guesthouse.co.uk, £25 s, £50 d) is a colorful place inside with several rooms furnished with dark, old wood furniture. En suite rooms are available but marginally more costly. There is off-street parking, and you get a decent breakfast in the morning. The folks who run it are an increasing rarity in the hospitality trade in Scotland—locals.

£50-100

Located in a leafy pocket of Glasgow close to the cathedral, **((Cathedral House Hotel** (28–32 Cathedral Sq., tel. 0141/552 3519, £98 d) is a pleasant accommodation alternative to the city center tumult. There are eight comfortable, spacious rooms here. The spiral staircase you climb to approach them gives you a taste of what to expect—graceful digs with lots of dark old wood; some rooms have four-poster beds and cathedral views. The bar downstairs serves reasonably priced food.

NORTH OF CITY CENTER

People generally stay in the north of Glasgow if they want to be in the vicinity of the start of the West Highland Way at Milngavie. The nearest campsite to the city center is also north of Glasgow.

Under £50

Craigendmuir Campsite (Stepps, tel. 0141/779 4159, www.craigendmuir.co.uk, 2-man tent £14.25) is the nearest campsite to the city center and has space for tents and caravans, as well as chalets. Facilities include an on-site shop and a launderette. The site is northeast of the city center; the best way of getting there is to take a train from Glasgow Queen Street to Stepps station, from where it's an 800-meter walk.

The regal-looking, Edwardian **Laurel Bank** (96 Strathblane Rd., Milngavie, tel. 0141/584 9400, £35 s, £50 d) is a guesthouse with plenty of period furnishings, a mere 10-minute walk from the start of the West Highland Way footpath. It's got two en suite rooms done up in springlike pinks and yellows with hot water bottles and organic toiletries provided. The owners (and their cats) are well used to dealing with walkers; you can expect a good breakfast in the morning.

Food

Glasgow has a vibrant dining scene featuring a worldly mix of cuisine. Lots of the city center eateries are very stylish places. For a more relaxed, informal dining scene head to the West End, which is chock-a-block with wonderful cafés and restaurants. Glasgow has particularly good Italian and Indian restaurants. Lunch is generally noon–2:30 P.M. and dinner 6–10 P.M. To help narrow down the wide choice of restaurants, check out www.5pm.co.uk, which lists Glasgow restaurants offering meal deals on different days. It's a good way of getting to eat inexpensively in pleasant surroundings.

CITY CENTER AND MERCHANT CITY

The city center has lots of glam, glitzy eateries. The main emphasis is on Scottish and seafood restaurants, but you can find every cuisine from Russian to Indian here. The Merchant City area is a more relaxed alternative to the upscale city center dining scene; here there are cafés and bars great for a chat, a spot of people-watching, or some postcard writing.

Cafés, Tearooms, and Snacks

The **Coffee Merchant** (Candleriggs, tel. 0141/552 2600, 8 A.M.–8 P.M. Mon.–Fri., 10 A.M.–6 P.M. Sat.–Sun.) is a low-key place serving wickedly strong coffee, gooey cakes, and sandwiches, in the heart of Merchant City. The great thing about it is that it's totally unpretentious: there's no attempt to make it into a style bar but instead a focus on serving up good, filling fare. There are some sofas to lounge on and the clientele seem content to do just that, for lengthy parts of the day. Snacks are £2–6.

OK, so **Berits and Brown** (6 Wilson St., Unit 2, tel. 0141/552 6980, www.beritsandbrown.com, at least 10 A.M.–9 P.M. Mon.–Sat., reduced hours Sun.) is part of a chain, but it is a very small chain (two stores at the last count) that originated in Scotland and has revolutionized the Scottish café scene.

The Merchant City branch is a fabulous place for coffee and a snack. High walls and shelves are lined with goodies from a wide range of wines to crumbly Scottish and European cheeses, lots of types of olives, and scrumptious pâté. Homemade soups and other snacks are £4–13; £13 will get you a smorgasbord for two and a couple of glasses of wine. Berits and Brown stays open late during the week for wine and nibbles.

One place most distinctly not part of any chain is 【 **Where the Monkey Sleeps** (182 West Regent St., tel. 0141/226 3406, www.monkeysleeps.com, 7 A.M.–5 P.M. Mon.–Fri., 10 A.M.–5 P.M. Sat.). It's tucked away beneath West Regent Street, and a refreshing antidote to the corporate bustle—a dark, relaxed coffee and sandwich bar with stalls to perch on and sofas to lounge in. Frequented by all types, including a high proportion of students finding ways to shirk their essays, the café serves up a range of generous, tasty sandwiches with names as novel as the fillings. You could probably sit in here reading *War and Peace* day in and day out and no one would hassle you to leave. A cool selection of music is always playing, which underlines its growing bohemian reputation. It's the best breakfast stop in the city center by a mile. Snacks/meals are £3–5.

The 【 **Willow Tearooms** (217 Sauchiehall St., tel. 0141/332 0521, www.willowtearooms.co.uk, 9 A.M.–5 P.M. Mon.–Sat., 11 A.M.–4:15 P.M. Sun.) is a place to eat as much as it is a visitor attraction. While you check out the decor of one of architect Charles Rennie Mackintosh's finest interiors, you'll fancy one of the specialty teas or coffees at this idiosyncratic tearoom. Besides, there's nothing like sitting down with a drink and a snack as a means of appreciating fine design. There are all-day breakfast options like scrambled eggs with an Arbroath smokie; delectable light lunches like baked potatoes filled with ratatouille cost £3–6.

Scottish

Few places in the city could claim to look much more modern than **The Social** (27 Royal Exchange Sq., tel. 0141/222 2321, www.socialanimal.co.uk, noon–9 P.M. daily). It's a wide, white, neat space of trim leather chairs, colored glass panels, and bright orange paint—almost like walking in to a design studio. It's a popular people-watching spot with lots of outside tables. The Social is full of varied, reasonably priced cuisine from pizzas and pastas to burgers, steak sandwiches, and succulent salads.

With a silvery, industrial-chic decor, **Fifi and Ally** (80 Wellington Sq., tel. 0141/226 2286, www.fifi-and-ally.com, 8 A.M.–midnight Thurs.–Sat., 8 A.M.–8 P.M. Wed., 8 A.M.–6 P.M. Mon.–Tues.) is about as cutting edge as a razor blade. It's hard to know how to classify its food, which ranges from Scottish steak with Bearnaise sauce to Celtic (Scottish salmon, rustic cheddar cheese) or Italian (red peppers, olives, foccacia) gastronomic smorgasbords. This is the second branch of the restaurant/retail outlet, with its original base at 51–52 Princes Square.

Formerly the Glasgow Ship Bank—and in a later metamorphosis, judiciary courts— **C Corinthian** (191 Ingram St., tel. 0141/552 1101, 5–10:30 P.M. Sun.–Fri., noon–10:30 P.M. Sat.) is a glam, glitzy building with a main dining area of pillars and high ceilings dripping with gold and stained glass. With the lavish atmosphere, the cuisine has a lot to live up to but this place pulls off some fine west coast seafood, game, and Scottish beef (though the service can be markedly less high quality). You could spend hours just choosing your dish from the complex menu. Three-course dinners are £29.95 per person.

Baby Grand (3–7 Elmbank Gdns., tel. 0141/248 4942, noon–3 P.M. and 5–10 P.M. daily), a bright, light venue by Charing Cross, has been pulling in the punters since the 1970s. It's fancy but not pretentious and serves down-to-earth food while live piano music plays in the background. Starters are £3–7, main meals £8–12.

Seafood

City Merchant (97–99 Candleriggs, tel. 0141/553 1577, www.citymerchant.co.uk, noon–10:30 P.M. daily) is an attractive seafood restaurant with a great location in Merchant City. It's a hip-looking, rustically styled eatery. Sandwiches and fishy snacks are £3–8 and a set-price three-course dinner is £27.50.

With an open kitchen so you can see what the chefs are concocting (fabulous pre-dinner entertainment), this second branch of the West End seafood success **Two Fat Ladies** (118a Blythswood St., tel. 0141/847 0088, noon–3 P.M. and 5–10:30 P.M. Mon.–Sat., 1–9 P.M. Sun.) serves the same mouthwatering creations as the first. The cozy, smallish restaurant offers delights like hand-dived scallops, sea bass in red wine sauce, and halibut fillet served up with risotto. You even learn a little about where the fish comes from. Two-course evening meals are £21.

Italian

Gentle music, a big choice of pizzas and pastas and giant Italian-themed murals and sculptures greet you as you enter fun, colorful **Qua** (68 Ingram St., tel. 0141/552 6233, www.quarestaurant.co.uk, 11:45 A.M.–10 P.M. daily). There's a spacious downstairs restaurant and an upstairs bar. As well as the classic dishes, there are treats like deep-fried mozzarella fingers and penne with west coast scallops. Two-course lunches are a mere £6.95 and three-course evening menus are £9.95.

American

Homesick New Yorkers are catered to in Glasgow by the popular American-themed diner, **Ad Lib** (111 Hope St., tel. 0141/248 6645, takeaway sandwiches from 9 A.M., lunch from noon, happy hour 4–7 P.M., dinner until 10 P.M. daily), decorated with a huge mural of Times Square. It's a neat, metallic venue with a glass ceiling. Gourmet burgers are the order of the day here, with a few surprises including the Indian chickpea and potato burger. Meals are £7–10; save room for a chocolate brownie with ice cream if it's possible. The atmosphere lends itself more to a daytime eating binge. There's a second branch of Ad Lib in Merchant City at 33 Ingram Street.

Mexican

Pancho Villas (26 Bell St., tel. 0141/552 7737, 5 P.M.–late Mon.–Sat., noon–late Sun.) is a huge, colorful eatery serving reasonably priced, reasonably authentic Mexican fare. A two-course set lunch is £8.50; evening mains are £9–12. You can't go wrong with the *albondigas* (meatballs) filled with cheese in a hot chili sauce.

Asian

The open, ornate, tapestry-hung restaurant of **Koolba** (109 Candleriggs, tel. 0141/552277, noon–3 P.M. and 5 P.M.–late Mon.–Fri., noon–late Sat., 5 P.M.–late Sun.) combines a striking decor and an eclectic array of Indian dishes to make for a fine eating experience. You can get a range of mixed vegetable and chicken dishes from the spicy to the garlic-infused to the mild and aromatic.

Russian

Done up in bright Communist reds, **Café Cossachok** (38 Albion St., tel. 0141/553 0733, www.cossachok.com, 11:30 A.M.–9 P.M. Tues.–Thurs., 11:30 A.M.–11 P.M. Fri.–Sun.) is Glasgow's only restaurant and art gallery. It's a vivid change from the other dining options in and around Merchant City. The specialties include blintzes, pancakes stuffed with mince and different combinations of vegetables. From Tuesday to Saturday there's a two-course pre-theater menu for £11.95.

WEST END

The West End is Glasgow's culinary heart: Old cobbled streets like Ashton Lane and Ruthven Lane are just plastered in a mix of cool cafés, tasty delis, restaurants, and lively bars. The district has a relaxed, often-bohemian, occasionally continental feel, and lots of the places have outdoor seating.

Cafés, Tearooms, and Snacks

If you're feeling peckish and want a quick fix

of gourmet food, come to **Heart Buchanan** (380 Byres Rd., tel. 0141/334 7626, 8:30 A.M.–9:30 P.M. Mon.–Fri., 9 A.M.–9:30 P.M. Sat., noon–7 P.M. Sun.), a café, deli, and restaurant rolled into one. Come here to pick up delectable takeaway food; if you like, they'll even bake the food you order in your own dish. It's a great stop for getting home-cooked food away from home, like mozzarella with baby tomatoes, pan-fried chicken, or baked aubergine with crème fraiche. The chefs rustle up different fresh goodies every day. You can book the place for an evening party and have your own personal chef attending you.

Catering to young families, hungover students, city workers, and old folk hunched over a cuppa, **University Café** (87 Byres Rd., tel. 0141/339 5217, 9 A.M.–10 P.M. Mon. and Wed.–Thurs., 9 A.M.–10:30 P.M. Fri.–Sat., 10 A.M.–10 P.M. Sun.) is the original and, many say, the best part of the West End café revolution. You can't beat it for sheer time-tested quality; this veteran of the breakfast and lunch business has been churning out great coffee, fat portions of homemade lasagna, and real Italian ice cream since the end of the First World War. Snacks and meals are £1–7.

The food served at **Grassroots Café** (97 St. Georges Rd., tel. 0141/333 0534, 10 A.M.–10 P.M. daily) is every bit as green as the name; expect potent Fair Trade coffee and a healthy organic menu. All day long you can munch on crunchy salads and well-filled sandwiches. The most popular dish is Thai green curry and risotto cakes. A veggie breakfast is served until mid-afternoon on Saturday.

Scottish

The classy **Bothy Restaurant** (11 Ruthven Ln., tel. 0141/334 4040, www.bothyrestaurant.co.uk, noon–10 P.M. daily) is like a Victorian Gentlemen's club mixed with a design studio—leather seats, a fire, and a light, airy feel. Mains like Highland lentil nut loaf or Perthshire lamb are £11–17. The restaurant's slogan is "Food like your granny cooks"—if only we could all have such a granny. A two-course Sunday roast is £13.95.

Scotland's cafés and bars don't come any trendier than those in Glasgow's West End.

There are actually a couple of restaurants and bars housed under the noble spire of this former church that calls itself **Òran Mór** (top of Byres Rd., tel. 0141/357 6200, www.oran-mor.co.uk, brasserie noon–3 P.M. and 5–10 P.M. daily, conservatory restaurant 9 A.M.–9 P.M. Mon.–Thurs. and 9 A.M.–10 P.M. Fri.–Sat.). The dark, more formal brasserie serves a variety of fish and meat-themed Scottish food. Meanwhile, the more relaxed publike conservatory dishes up solid, hearty meals like haggis, neeps and tatties (haggis with turnips and potatoes) and steak pie. Mains are £6–10.

A bit of a Glasgow institution, this: **Ubiquitous Chip** (12 Ashton Ln., tel. 0141/334 5007, www.ubiquitouschip.com, brasserie noon–11 P.M., restaurant noon–2:30 P.M. and 5–11 P.M. daily) has been going since the 1970s. Don't be fooled by the name either, as this is one classy joint. The best bit about the restaurant is that you could go here several nights running and have a totally different culinary experience each time, largely due to the menu but also to the variety of eating spaces. Choose from a cozy main restaurant,

a courtyard with rock features and climbing plants, mezzanine level dining right above, or a roof terrace. There are as many vegetarian options as meat dishes. It's got a menu that will have your stomach rumbling long in advance of the food showing up: Orkney organic salmon, for example, or pastry parcel stuffed with vegetables and Lanarkshire blue cheese. Two-course dinners are £34.85.

A fire gutted the **Buttery** (652 Argyle St., tel. 0141/221 8188, noon–2:30 P.M. and 6–9:30 P.M. Tues.–Fri., 6–9:30 P.M. Sat.), a stylish longstanding West End eatery, in late 2006 but it's now back in business. This is a time-tested restaurant dating back originally to the 1850s; expect lots of grand leather and mahogany, and the rising feeling of stepping back in time about a century into a private Victorian club. One thing you can guarantee here is the quality of the food. Prepare yourself for an Auld Alliance of Scottish and French cooking: meals could be a Perthshire fillet of beef with ream, horseradish, and potato or seafood from the west coast coupled with Provençal vegetables. A three-course lunch is £16: a two-course dinner is around £30.

Belgian

Right at the heart of the West End dining scene is the brightly painted stables of **Brel** (Ashton Ln., tel. 0141/342 4966, www.brelbarrestaurant.co.uk, noon–3 P.M. and 5–10:30 P.M. Mon.–Fri., noon–10:30 P.M. Sat.–Sun.), converted into a lively Belgian-themed bar and restaurant. This is the place to come and sample a plate of moules frites (mussels and chips) washed down with Leffe. Mains like the mussel platters and seafood stew are £9–13; you can also get a good steak here. Of course, a suitably wide range of Belgian beers is available throughout the day.

Italian

Richly painted walls and dark wood paneling combine to give **La Parmigiana** (Great Western Rd., tel. 0141/334 0686, www.laparmigiana.co.uk, noon–2 P.M. and 6–11 P.M. Mon.–Sat.) an opulent, part-Gothic, part-theatrical feel. It serves up food many reckon to be the best Italian dishes in Glasgow and, therefore, the country. There are a lot of wonderful meat dishes on the menu, like venison and veal served with authentic touches like specialty mushrooms and sausages. Pre-theater menus, served until 7:30 P.M., are £13 for two courses. Mains are £15–21.

Spanish

Right by Glasgow University, **Satchmo's** (52 Bank St., tel. 0141/339 7730, noon–3 P.M. and 5–10 P.M. daily) is a tapas bar/restaurant making a handy spot for a good cheap meal. With big comfy seats and a bright, battered decor themed for jazz singer Louis Armstrong, it's perfect for a daytime coffee, sangria and a sandwich, or an intimate evening meal. It's a great people-watching place. You can get three tapas dishes and a drink for £10.

Asian

Smart, chic **Mother India's Café** (1355 Argyle St., tel. 0141/339 9145, www.motherindias.co.uk, noon–10:30 P.M. Mon.–Sat., noon–10 P.M. Sun.) does great Indian-style tapas near Kelvingrove Art Gallery, and at next-to-nothing prices. Fried fish and vegetable pakora, spiced haddock, and spinach with Indian cheese are some of the delicacies on offer. Individual dishes are £3–5; you'll need three to make a meal.

Thai Fountain (Woodside Crescent, tel. 0141/332 2599, noon–2:15 P.M. and 5:30–11 P.M. daily) serves colorful, creative Thai cuisine within a convivial environment; it's the best place to eat Thai food in Glasgow. With the menu being so huge, thankfully there are staff members on hand to advise you on special dishes. For a main course, try one of the creamy Thai curries or the Pad Nua Toi Si, a steak sliced with soybean sauce. Starters are £4–7 and mains are £10–14.

RIVER CLYDE AND SOUTH SIDE

There are a few good eateries to refresh yourself after all that sightseeing in this neck of the woods, although it's not really a part of Glasgow you would go especially to eat.

Cafés

The elegant white **Art Lover's Café** (Bellahouston Pk., tel. 0141/353 4779, 10 A.M.–5 P.M. daily) on the ground floor of Charles Rennie Mackintosh's House for an Art Lover benefits from an outside terrace. You can sit here with one of the specialty crisp salads, couscous, or a risotto (£7–9) and soak up the tranquility of the parkland all around.

Asian

Near the SECC on the slick new-look Clyde waterfront, **Yen Rotunda** (28 Tunnel St., tel. 0141/847 0110, www.yenrotunda.com, noon–2:15 P.M. and 5–11 P.M. Mon.–Fri., 5–11:30 P.M. Sat., 5–10:30 P.M. Sun.) is a two-floor oriental restaurant. One floor does Japanese cuisine, while the floor above offers Cantonese and Thai food. The Japanese floor specializes in Teppanyaki cooking, with a chef making the food right in front of you—it's a hugely entertaining experience. Three-course Japanese meals are £21.95: upstairs you'll be able to eat your fill for £6–10.

Information and Services

Glasgow is the place to do all those fiddly things like sorting out your money and buying maps, before heading into the sticks. It really is a city of enormous resources, offering every service you could possibly require. The handily located central TIC can give you information on where to find Internet cafés, launderettes, hospitals, and the like. Either the TIC or the St. Enoch Travel Centre will be able to tell you how to get around the city, the region, and the country on public transport.

INFORMATION
Tourist Information

Gruff, efficient **Glasgow TIC** (11 George Sq., tel. 0141/204 4400, 9 A.M.–8 P.M. Mon.–Sat., 10 A.M.–6 P.M. Sun. July–Aug., 9 A.M.–7 P.M. Mon.–Sat., 10 A.M.–6 P.M. Sun. June and Sept., 9 A.M.–6 P.M. Mon.–Sat., 10 A.M.–6 P.M. Sun. Easter–May, 9 A.M.–6 P.M. Mon.–Sat. Oct.–Easter) is well used to dealing with all kind of inquiries and has a limited selection of maps.

St. Enoch Square Travel Centre (St. Enoch Sq., 8:30 A.M.–5:30 P.M. Mon.–Sat.) is extremely useful for travel information, including bus and train timetables for the surrounding area. Non-travel inquiries should be directed to the TIC in George Square.

At the airport is **Glasgow International Airport Information Desk** (tel. 0141/848 4440, 7:30 A.M.–5 P.M. daily Easter–Sept., 7:30 A.M.–5 P.M. Mon.–Sat., 8:30 A.M.–3:30 P.M. Sun. Oct.–Easter).

Maps

If the TICs are unable to supply you with maps, try one of the large city center bookstores like **Borders Books** (98 Buchanan St., tel. 0141/222 7700, 8 A.M.–10 P.M. Mon.–Sat., 10 A.M.–9 P.M. Sun.). **The Glasgow Map Centre** (50 Couper St., tel. 0141/552 7722, 9 A.M.–6 P.M. Mon.–Tues. and Fri., 9:30 A.M.–6 P.M. Wed., 9 A.M.–7 P.M. Thurs., 9 A.M.–2 P.M. Sat.) has a huge array of local and national maps available. The shop is part of Tiso Outdoor Centre.

SERVICES

You'll find a plethora of banks spread across the city, as well as several post offices and places to check your emails.

Money and Exchange

There are banks with ATMs across the city and *bureaus de change* or moneychangers at both of Glasgow's airports and Buchanan Street bus station. Most banks also offer a currency exchange service.

American Express Travel (115 Hope St., tel. 0870/600 1060, 8:30 A.M.–5:30 P.M. Mon.–Tues. and Thurs.–Fri., 9:30 A.M.–5:30 P.M. Wed., 9 A.M.–noon Sat.) will even hold mail for American Express cardholders.

The main branch of the **Royal Bank of Scotland** (tel. 0141/567 0065) is at 10 Gordon Street.

Communications

A couple of good post offices are **City Centre** Post Office (228 Hope St., tel. 0845/722 3344, 9 A.M.–5:30 P.M. Tues.–Fri., 8:30 A.M.–5:30 P.M. Mon., 9 A.M.–1 P.M. Sat.) and **Merchant City Post Office** (59 Glassford St., tel. 0141/552 7557).

Internet Access

At the **Gallery of Modern Art** (Royal Exchange Sq., tel. 0141/229 1996, 10 A.M.–8 P.M. Mon., Tues., and Thurs., 10 A.M.–5 P.M. Wed. and Sat., 11 A.M.–5 P.M. Fri. and Sun.) there is free Internet access in the library basement. The **Mitchell Library** (North St., tel. 0141/287 2999, 9 A.M.–8 P.M. Mon.–Thurs., 9 A.M.–5 P.M. Fri.–Sat.) also offers free access.

Yeeha Internet (48 West George St., tel. 0141/332 6543, 8:30 A.M.–late daily) offers services that include faxing, printing, and CD burning. It's near Queen Street rail station.

Medical Services and Emergencies

Glasgow Royal Infirmary (84 Castle St., tel. 0141/211 4000) has an outpatient department;

head here if you need a doctor. It's in the east of the city near the cathedral. For dental matters, get in touch with **Glasgow Dental Hospital** (378 Sauchiehall St., tel. 0141/211 9600, 9 A.M.–3 P.M. Mon.–Fri.).

Strathclyde Police (50 Stewart St., Cowcaddens, tel. 0141/532 3000) is the main city center police station.

Laundry
Majestic Laundrette (1110 Argyle St., tel. 0141/334 3433, 8 A.M.–6 P.M. Mon.–Fri., 9 A.M.–4 P.M. Sat., 10 A.M.–4 P.M. Sun.) in the West End offers dry cleaning and washing.

Travel Agencies
STA Travel (122 George St., tel. 0871/468 0622, 10 A.M.–6 P.M. Mon.–Sat.) are good at arranging budget holiday itineraries and flights—and the agency doesn't just serve students.

Getting There

Glasgow is one well-connected city, one hour's drive from Edinburgh and seven hours' drive from London. Its connections have, over the years, probably been its greatest asset. Some 40 miles west of Scotland's capital, Edinburgh, Glasgow is at the hub of the Scottish motorway network. It has direct bus and train connections to most national destinations and some international destinations. Visitors also have two airports and even sea connections to points in western Scotland at their disposal.

AIR
Glasgow is the best-connected city in Scotland for international flights. It has two airports. Glasgow International Airport serves points throughout Europe, North America, and Mexico. Glasgow Prestwick serves U.K. destinations and other points mainly in Western Europe.

Glasgow International Airport
Glasgow International Airport (tel. 0141/887 1111, www.glasgowairport.com) is 10 miles west of the city center, near Paisley. There are flights to many destinations in Europe and also several direct flights to North America including New York (daily), Toronto (several weekly), and weekly flights to Vancouver and Las Vegas. It's worth noting that even though this is Scotland's major airport, you will almost certainly have more options by flying to London and then

changing. At the airport you'll find a tourist information center, a *bureau de change,* left luggage, and all the other facilities you would expect of a big airport. The airport is served by regular buses from the city center; they'll arrive/depart from stance one outside the terminal.

Glasgow Prestwick Airport
Glasgow Prestwick Airport (tel. 0871/223 0700, www.gpia.co.uk), 30 miles southwest of the city, handles budget flights from multiple destinations within the U.K. and Europe. Facilities at the airport include a *bureau de change,* an information desk, cash machines, and left luggage (£4 per day).

BOAT
The Glasgow suburbs in Inverclyde have a couple of key ferry connections to outlying parts of Western Scotland. Gourock and Wemyss Bay, the ports in question, are both served by regular train connections from Glasgow.

The Clyde estuary twists and turns in such a way that heading across the water from **Gourock to Dunoon** is by far the quickest way to reach Dunoon on the Cowal Peninsula in the Argyll and Inner Hebrides region. **Calmac** (www.calmac.co.uk, 25 mins, £3.35 passenger, £8.15 car one-way) runs hourly ferries throughout the week.

Calmac also plys the route from **Wemyss Bay to Rothesay** on the Isle of Bute (35 mins,

£3.90 passenger, £15.55 car one-way) every 45 minutes throughout the week, slightly less frequently on Sundays in winter.

TRAIN

There are two main train stations in Glasgow, Glasgow Central (trains to the south) to the south of the city center and Glasgow Queen Street (trains to the north and east of Scotland), a 10-minute walk to the northeast.

National

Glasgow Queen Street is where to catch trains to Edinburgh and northbound destinations. There are trains to Edinburgh (four hourly, 50–55 min., £10.80), Stirling (at least three hourly Mon.–Sat., two hourly Sun., 25–45 min., £6.80), Inverness (every 1.5 hrs., 3.5 hrs., £38.20) Aberdeen (hourly, 2 hrs. 35 min., £38.20) and Fort William (three to four daily, 3.75 hrs., £22.20).

International

The city's main rail station is Glasgow Central, terminus for trains from the south, including trains to London Euston (one to two hourly, 4.5–6 hrs., £102).

BUS

Glasgow has a very effective system of national and international buses operating out of **Buchanan Street bus station** (Killermont St. by Buchanan Galleries, tel. 0141/333 3708, 6:30 A.M.–10:30 P.M. Mon.–Sat., 7 A.M.–10:30 P.M. Sun.). At the station you'll find a cash point, a *bureau de change,* a travel booking center, a few shops, and a café.

National

Scottish Citylink (tel. 0870/550 5050, www.citylink.co.uk) is the key national bus operator, with regular buses to Edinburgh (four hourly, one hr., 20 min., £5.10). There are also buses to Stirling (hourly, 45 min., £5.40), Aberdeen (Citylink and Megabus, hourly, 3.25 hrs., £21.70) and Inverness (Citylink and Parks of Hamilton, 4 hrs., £21.20). There are several daily buses to Highland destinations like Oban and Fort William.

International

National Express buses (tel. 0870/580 8080, www.nationalexpress.com) leave London Victoria coach station several times daily for Buchanan Street bus station in Glasgow. Journey times range 8–10 hours. The no-frills journey can be as low as £16 if you book it online (remember to print out the ticket and present it to the driver).

Silver Choice (tel. 01355/230403, www.silverchoicetravel.co.uk) has a nightly bus service to London Victoria coach station. A one-way fare is £25; if you book a round-trip it will cost less.

Getting Around

Glasgow has a better public transport system than any other city in the U.K., save London. With a useful subway system and trains that serve most outlying destinations in the suburbs—not to mention a top notch bus network—it's very easy to get about. You can walk between most places in the city center.

TO/FROM GLASGOW INTERNATIONAL AIRPORT

The nearest train station to the airport is Paisley Gilmour Street, one mile from the terminal building. Several buses connect the railway station and the terminal. It's less hassle just to take bus 500 from Buchanan Street bus station, however; it runs directly to the airport several times hourly. It's £3.95 one-way, £5.95 round-trip. A metered taxi to the airport will cost £18–22.

TO/FROM GLASGOW PRESTWICK AIRPORT

Prestwick Airport is somewhat unique in being served by its very own train station. Trains run from Glasgow Central Station half-hourly throughout the week (50 min., £5.95) and make by far the most practical means of getting to the airport.

Stagecoach bus X77 also runs regularly throughout the day from Buchanan Street bus station to the airport (one hour 10 min.). Public transport runs between 6 A.M. and midnight. Outside of these hours, there is the X99 bus, which has a couple of services from Buchanan Street bus station through the night (£8 one-way).

IN THE CITY CENTER

Although Glasgow has a better infrastructure than most places, it's best to keep car use in the city to a minimum as roads still get very congested. With a good public transport system in place, there's little need to use a car. Parking for free is very difficult, and Glasgow's traffic wardens have a reputation for being overzealous; use a multistory car park if you have to.

Subway

One of the oldest underground systems in the world, Glasgow's subway is known as the "Clockwork Orange" because of the loop it forms. It's of use when traveling to the River Clyde or the West End. A **discovery ticket** allowing unlimited travel for one day is £1.90 provided you use it after 9:30 A.M. Subway tickets can only be purchased with cash.

The stops include **Hillhead** (for West End), **Kelvinhall** (for Kelvingrove Park), **Ibrox** (for Ibrox Stadium), **Cessnock** (for the Glasgow Science Centre), **St. Enoch** (for the main city center shops), and **Buchanan** (for transfers to national rail).

Train

In addition to the subway, Glasgow has an extensive overground train network, particularly useful if you are traveling into the south side or into Renfrewshire and Inverclyde. Generally speaking, trains run to northern destinations from Glasgow Queen Street and southern destinations from Glasgow Central

station. Families should consider purchasing the **Daytripper Ticket,** allowing a day's travel of overground trains, subway trains, and most buses in the Glasgow and Strathclyde area (£15 for two adults and up to four children).

On the South Side, the main stations visitors need to know about are **Mount Florida** (for Hampden Park and the Scottish Football Museum) and **Pollockshaws East** (for Pollock Country Park and the Burrell Collection). There will be around four trains hourly.

For Renfrewshire and Inverclyde, at least four trains per hour run from Glasgow Central Station to **Paisley** for Paisley Abbey (20 min., £2.50). Three hourly trains run directly to **Port Glasgow** for Newark Castle (40 min.), **Greenock** for the Mclean Art Gallery (45 min., £4.70), and **Gourock** for ferries to Dunoon (55 min., £4.95). There are also hourly trains to **Wemyss Bay** for ferries to Bute.

Bus

Glasgow has a good system of buses; you will rarely have to wait longer than 10 minutes during the day for a bus to your destination. Buses around the city cost around £1–1.50. You need to have exact change when you board all buses. Bus shelters around the city will have maps of the numbered routes each bus from that stop takes.

The useful **St. Enoch Travel Centre** (8:30 A.M.–5:30 P.M. Mon.–Sat.), just by the St. Enoch subway station, can help with most bus travel inquiries. **Buchanan Street bus station** (tel. 0141/333 3708) can also help with bus inquiries. The main city operator, **First Group** (www.firstgroup.com) publishes the highly useful *MapMate,* listing all public bus routes in the city. It costs £1 and is available from TICs and Travel Centres. You can also download a copy for free from First Group's website.

Taxi

There are lots of taxis cruising the city center that can be hailed if their For Hire sign on the roof is on. Taxis are generally limited to five passengers.

Glasgow Taxis (tel. 0141/429 7070), will,

in addition to normal service, even do tours of the main sights of the city with a commentary from the cabbie as you go. To hire a taxi for this purpose will cost you £30 per taxi. **Glasgow Airport Millennium Taxis** (tel. 0141/558 2285) is another reputable cab company.

IN THE REGION
The city's excellent transport connections spread out across the Clyde Valley area.

Train
There are a couple of trains hourly during the week to **Lanark,** usually requiring a change. Journey time is about 50 minutes. There are also regular trains to Hamilton.

Bus
Buses depart from Buchanan Street bus station in Glasgow to destinations across the Clyde Valley. The main operator is **First Group** (tel. 0871/200 2233 for timetable inquiries, www.firstgroup.com).

Car Rental
Roads in the region are very good, generally consisting of motorways, dual carriageways, or main trunk roads. Because of all the competition, hiring a car is cheaper in Glasgow than anywhere else in the country. Petrol/gas is also about as cheap as it comes in Scotland. Don't spend too much time driving in the Glasgow urban area, though. One-way streets and slip roads that will end you up on a motorway headed in the wrong direction make driving unpleasant and frustrating.

   Arnold Clark (40 Hamilton Rd., Mount Vernon, tel. 0141/778 2979) does car hire from £17 per day. **Enterprise Rent-A-Car** (tel. 0141/842 1000) is one of the big rental companies with a branch at Glasgow International Airport.

Clydesdale Valley

The farther you head southeast from Glasgow, the more you realize that Scotland's metropolis is actually located in some magnificent countryside. The main feature is the curling, kinking upper reaches of the River Clyde—a part of the river unrecognizable to its clamoring industrial section through the city. It's a landscape best appreciated by getting off the motorway running south to England. You can follow the Clyde up through some steep-sided forested valleys and below increasingly stark hills, which provide the backdrop to some of Scotland's best museums. Here you'll find New Lanark and its strikingly preserved 18th-century milling village and Biggar, a tiny town with terrific museums on every corner. There are still more unusual architectural attractions, including one of the biggest mausoleums in the northern hemisphere.

LANARK AND NEW LANARK
Lanark, the smart capital of Lanarkshire, combines the very best of what the Clyde valley has to offer: pockets of great countryside and a fascinating industrial heritage. It's the first town worth stopping in south of Glasgow. There are a few good pubs and restaurants, but most people come here to check out New Lanark World Heritage Village, a time capsule of 18th-century industrial life just south of town. Here is your best chance to see Scotland's industrial roots, sitting in a stunning river gorge setting.

Sights
Lanark itself has little to do: the main attractions are in New Lanark. Eighteenth-century **St. Nicholas Church** (Lanark, tel. 01555/662600, open for Sunday service at 11 A.M. or by arrangement), however, is home to the world's oldest bell.

   There are few more dramatic approaches to a visitor attraction than the way most people arrive at **New Lanark World Heritage Village** (tel. 01555/661345, www.newlanark.org, visitors center 10:30 A.M.–5 P.M. June–Aug.,

GLASGOW

© LUKE WATERSON

New Lanark World Heritage Village, a spectacularly preserved 18th-century milling village

11 A.M.–5 P.M. Sept.–May, £6.95 adults, £5.95 children). As you descend from the car park, the forest opens out before you into a gorge charged through by the brown-white waters of the River Clyde. Hugging the banks, in a formidable collection of pale stone buildings, is a preserved 18th-century cotton-milling village, rightly given the status of World Heritage site because of its absolute uniqueness. Visionary mill manager Robert Owen transformed the village during his spell in charge, doing away with the terrible working conditions synonymous with milling life at the time. He created a village where workers could enjoy a decent standard of living in close proximity to the mills. Among the innovations that came a good century ahead of their time were free health care and decent schools.

A tour should start off at the mill **visitors center,** where you can buy a passport to all sites on the complex. Getting top marks for innovation is the journey into the history of New Lanark and the visionary ideas of Robert Owen. Your virtual guide is Harmony, a 23rd-century girl who explains the lasting importance of the site, even in future centuries. There is also **Robert Owen's House,** where you can see how milling folk would have lived in the 1820s and 1930s (when the mill experienced a new lease on industrial life after its earlier closure). The latest attraction is the **Roof Garden,** where you get great panoramic views of the whole complex. The mills also hide a large cafeteria/restaurant that would impress even Owen's privileged workers.

It's a wonderful hour's walk from New Lanark to the **Falls of Clyde** (visitors center tel. 01555/665262, 11 A.M.–5 P.M. daily Mar.–Dec., noon–4 P.M. daily Jan.–Feb., £2 adults, £1 children), where the river drops through the wood-flanked river cliffs in a series of four foaming white waterfalls. The highest fall, the 90-foot Corra Linn, had its beauty captured in a poem by William Wordsworth on a visit to the gorge in 1802. The obvious starting point for a walk to the falls is at the Falls of Clyde visitor center, where you can get a CCTV-aided glimpse of a peregrine falcon nest or find out about life as a badger. To get to the visitor center and the Falls of Clyde, just follow the river upstream. The path to the falls is well marked.

Accommodations and Food

Also featuring in the conversion village is **New Lanark Youth Hostel** (tel. 01555/661345, www.syha.org.uk, beds £15), sitting atmospherically in a former mill workers' cottage. Slightly above the majority of the village, it gets great views of the Clyde and has mostly four-bed dorms. You can use the nearby hotel's pool and leisure facilities for £5.50.

A converted cattle byre, **Kirkfield Mains** (Kirkfieldbank, tel. 01555/660094, www.kirkfieldmains.co.uk, £45 s, £70 d) pulls off almost boutique-style rooms with chocolate brown and multicolored furnishings and special en suite massage showers. It's a plush, peaceful little place ideally located for visiting New Lanark. Rooms also have TVs and DVD players.

One of the huge former cotton mills at New Lanark is now the imposing **New Lanark Mill Hotel** (tel. 01555/667222, www.newlanarkhotel.co.uk, £74.50 s, £109 d). Its attractiveness slowly grows on you. Among its sumptuous 38 en suite rooms are some that have been adapted for wheelchair users. With views of the Clyde tumbling past from many of the rooms and the large restaurant, this place really is one-of-a-kind. If you want to stay at least three nights, there are more attractive self-catering water-houses, with a slightly more idyllic, rustic feel to them.

For top-notch pub grub, the cozy, lively old watering hole that is the **Crown Tavern** (17 Hope St., tel. 01555/664639, dinner served 5–9:30 P.M. daily) is the place to head. Char-grilled steaks are the thing to go for here, with a great selection for £13–16.

Information

Lanark TIC (Horsemarket, Ladyacre Rd., tel. 01555/661661, 10 A.M.–5 P.M. daily Easter–Oct., 10 A.M.–5 P.M. Mon.–Sat. Nov.–Mar.) is by the big car park near Lanark Station.

Getting There and Around

Trains run to Lanark from Glasgow twice hourly (50 mins., £4.95); you'll need to change at Holytown. There are hourly **buses** from Lanark Train Station to New Lanark, which also makes for a great one-hour walk. Approaching on foot from above is certainly the most spectacular way. You can stop off at the TIC for a free map of the area. You reach New Lanark from Lanark via Braxfield Road.

◖ BIGGAR

Sitting just where South Lanarkshire begins to rise up into the bare yellow hills that make up the Southern Uplands, little Biggar earns its title as "Museum Town" with no fewer than seven museums in and around it. This means the town has more museums per head of population than any other place its size in Britain and, quite probably, the world. Biggar has a hilly location astride a ridge between Scotland's two major lowland rivers, the Clyde and the Tweed. Early settlers, Romans, and Normans all favored the land around town, and a flourishing settlement of farmers, millers, and even gas producers developed over the 17th, 18th and 19th centuries. Biggar's museums reflect this patchwork of heritage but also delve into a few subjects even the most diligent history buff could not have guessed, like puppets. It's safe to say this is one of the most bizarre towns you will come across in Scotland, all surrounded by spectacular, undulating hills.

Sights

Moat Park Heritage Centre (Kirkstyle, tel. 01899/221050, 11 A.M.–4:30 P.M. Mon.–Sat., 2–4:30 P.M. Sun. May–Oct., £2 adults, £1 children) is a good place to kick-start your travels around the town's museums. In this old church, now converted into a center dealing with 500 million years of history in this part of Scotland, you can see fossils, find out about the Norman Motte and Bailey fort built right next door, and view some interesting natural history displays.

In a delightful streamside setting backed by woodsy fields, **Greenhill Covenanters House** (Burnbrae, tel. 01899/221050, 2–4:30 P.M. Sat.–Sun. Apr.–Oct., £2 adults, £1 children) is a revamped 17th-century farmhouse done up with rooms that reflect Biggar's history at the time. It's a beautifully simple museum that sets the turbulent contexts of the times (the period leading up to the Union of the Crowns) and then juxtaposes how ordinary people lived their lives with all this going on around them. Exhibits and costumed figures, including a local diarist who recorded what life was like in the Biggar area during this period, make this a colorful insight into the local history.

Biggar's High Street shops may be more individual and traditional than those in most towns but even they can't match the enclosed street of preserved 19th-century shops that constitutes **Gladstone Court** (tel. 01899/221050, North Back Rd., 11 A.M.–4:30 P.M. Mon.–Sat., 2–4:30 P.M. Sun., £2 adults, £1 children) for good old-fashioned charm. Highlights include a host of colorful old shop signs and a photographic shop containing Victorian camera equipment.

Despite the slightly unfortunate name, **Purves Puppet Theatre** (Broughton Rd., tel. 01899/220631, www.purvespuppets.com) is a great place to bring the kids. It's a magical little puppet theater, putting on shows like Nessie the Loch Ness Monster, Sinbad the Sailor, and Snow White throughout the year. There are shows most Fridays and Saturdays, and often during the week. Tickets for performances are £7.

Shopping

It's worth a stroll down Biggar's High Street just to see the refreshing lack of chain stores. Instead, you'll find a fascinating mix of locally run places. **Atkinson-Pryce Books** (27 High St., tel. 01899/221225, 9:30 A.M.–5 P.M. Mon.–Sat.) is a goldmine of Scottish and local interest books; try here if there's any aspect of Biggar history you want more information on.

Accommodations and Food

School Green Cottage (Kirkstyle, tel. 01899/220388, £28 s, £50 d) is the only obvious choice for town center bed-and-breakfast accommodation, and it's a pretty decent one. This small stone-built cottage sits bang in the middle of Biggar, with two simple rooms decked out in white. One room is a twin with a private bathrooms and one is a double with en suite facilities.

Surrounded by a landscape of open green sheep fields merging into the hills is the picturesque **Skirling House** (near Biggar, tel. 01899/860274, www.skirlinghouse.com, £60 s, £100 d). The five amply sized rooms have great views of the surrounding scenery and are done up in soothing whites and primrose yellows. All rooms have en suite bathrooms with baths; one has a Victorian roll-top bath. Over the years the owners have built up a substantial collection of wines to complement the evening meals they provide. Skirling House is just down the A72 a few miles north of town toward Peebles.

A charming, wonderfully old-fashioned coaching inn dates back over 400 years, **Elphinstone Hotel** (145 High St., tel. 01899/220044, food served noon–2:30 P.M. and 5–9 P.M. Sun.–Fri., noon–2:30 P.M. and 5–10 P.M. Sat.) provides the most atmospheric environment for a meal in Biggar. You'll find plenty of fresh local fare like Cullen Skink and fishermen's pie, and be able to enjoy it in front of an open fire under an oak-beamed ceiling.

Getting There and Away

Bus 100, running between Dumfries and Edinburgh, stops off in Biggar hourly from Monday to Saturday. Buses run hourly throughout the week from Biggar to Lanark (30 min.), from where there are two hourly trains to Glasgow.

HAMILTON

Hamilton is a dull satellite town of Glasgow, but with one of southern Scotland's most eccentric buildings in the vicinity, not to mention a wild country park centered on a lush river gorge, it's worth a stop off here. Visit it as a day trip, though—there's no need to spend the night.

Chatelherault Country Park (Carlisle Rd., near Hamilton, tel. 01698/426213, house 11 A.M.–4:30 P.M. Sun.–Thurs. Apr.–Sept.,

© LUKE WATERSON

Chatelherault, the Duke of Hamilton's hunting lodge

visitor center and grounds 10 A.M.–6 P.M. daily Apr.–Sept., 10 A.M.–5 P.M. Mon.–Sat., noon–5 P.M. Sun. Oct.–Mar.) is far more than just a rare bit of green for city folk to walk in on weekends. This 500-acre park includes a wonderful network of trails through lush open grassland and thickly forested river gorge; it feels 100 miles away from Glasgow rather than just 10. The centerpiece of the park is the Duke of Hamilton's former hunting lodge—possibly the most elaborate joke in Scotland. Celebrated architect William Adam built the hunting lodge between 1732 and 1744 for the fifth Duke of Hamilton. The Duke only wanted it done to create a grand view from his palace and to satisfy the great pretensions of the time by commissioning a construction that would be a suitably lavish demonstration of his wealth. The hunting lodge certainly does dominate the landscape and fools even the clued-up visitor today into thinking it is far more lavish than it is. Most of the length of the building is merely a decorative wall, joining up two equally ornate buildings a mere one room thick. Behind the house is a courtyard, formal garden, and visitors center, where you can pick up leaflets on paths through the grounds. The best walk leads to the ruins of Cadzow Castle and some magnificent, gnarled 500-year-old oaks (2 km). You'll find the park just south of Hamilton on the A72 toward Lanark.

Getting There and Away

Trains run from Glasgow Central to Hamilton Central every 20 minutes (25 min., £3); from there you can get a bus from the bus station to Chatelherault. **Buses** to Larkhill, including Whitelaws 254 service, stop near the gates and run regularly Monday–Saturday.

DUNDEE, ANGUS, AND THE KINGDOM OF FIFE

Home to marmalade, the world's worst poet William McGonagall, and the explorer Robert Scott's HMS *Discovery,* Dundee wouldn't really blend in to any region of Scotland. Indeed, with a gentle sandy coast dotted with ancient fishing ports and golf courses to the south of the city and the equally timeless rolling red Angus Glens to the north, it really does seem as if Scotland's fourth-largest metropolis has just touched down in its location from another planet.

It's a starkly modern city, the inhabitants of which (Dundonians) are some of Scotland's friendliest people, once their distinctive regional accent has been mastered. The views from Dundee, especially up at Dundee Law and Mills Observatory, are some of the best the east coast has to offer.

Toward the north you'll find the distinctive culinary delicacies of the region, including the Arbroath Smokie and Forfar Bridies. From Kirriemuir, where the author of *Peter Pan* J. M. Barrie was born, the lonely Angus Glens cut gently up wooded valleys toward the Cairngorm Mountains behind, hosting fabulous walking opportunities. In summer the sun barely sets and the red of the bracken on the hills contrasts with the yellow-green of the woods below. And the kind of adventurous single-track roads that make driving Scotland such fun seem to lead enticingly on and up forever.

Across the Firth of Tay to the south, Fife is characterized by emerald-green golf courses and quaint whitewashed fishing villages with picture-postcard harbors. Best known as the capital of golf, St. Andrews has all the dignity and lavish

© LUKE WATERSON

HIGHLIGHTS

◖ HMS *Discovery* and Discovery Centre: Exploring the fascinating HMS *Discovery* at Dundee gives you a taste of what polar exploration was like on board North Pole adventurer Robert Falcon Scott's original ship (page 208).

◖ Mills Observatory: At Britain's only full-time public observatory, you can train your eyes on the heavens through a 19th-century telescope from the top of a pretty park above Dundee (page 211).

◖ Smokie Shops: Hunt out a smokie shop and taste an Arbroath Smokie fresh from the pier in Arbroath (page 217).

◖ Edzell and Glen Esk: Start off with a wander around a magical castle and then head up into an even more magical valley, dotted with great walks in the wild Angus Glens (page 222).

◖ Angus Sculptured Stones: Around Glamis are many of the world's best examples of Pictish carved stones, mesmerizing depictions of battles and ancient kings over 1,000 years old (page 223).

◖ Falkland: A village with a palace, great hill-walking, and delicious places to eat, Falkland is a former royal hunting ground that hosted notable Scottish monarchs including Mary, Queen of Scots (page 228).

◖ Crail: One of the tranquil East Neuk fishing villages, known for their good seafood and beautiful beaches, photogenic Crail is an artists' haven with steeply twisting streets full of craft shops and galleries (page 231).

LOOK FOR ◖ TO FIND RECOMMENDED SIGHTS, ACTIVITIES, DINING, AND LODGING.

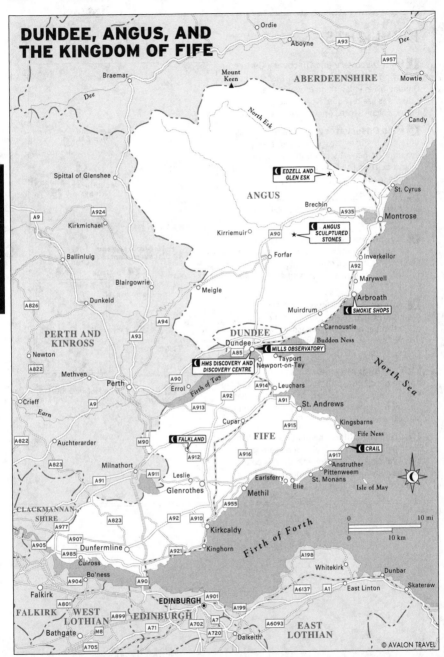

DUNDEE, ANGUS, AND THE KINGDOM OF FIFE

Ordie
Aboyne
A93
Dee
A957

Mount Keen ▲
Braemar
ABERDEENSHIRE
Mowtie

Dee
North Esk
Candy

Spittal of Glenshee
EDZELL AND GLEN ESK ★

ANGUS
St. Cyrus

A924
Brechin   A935
Montrose

A9
Kirkmichael
Kirriemuir   A90   ★ ANGUS SCULPTURED STONES

Ballinluig
Forfar
Inverkeilor
A92
Marywell

Blairgowrie
Meigle
Arbroath
SMOKIE SHOPS

A826
Dunkeld
Muirdrum
Carnoustie

A94
DUNDEE
Buddon Ness

PERTH AND KINROSS
Dundee   MILLS OBSERVATORY

Newton
HMS DISCOVERY AND DISCOVERY CENTRE   Tayport
North Sea

A822
Methven
Newport-on-Tay

A90   A914   Leuchars

Perth
Errol   Firth of Tay   A92
A91

Crieff
A9   A913   St. Andrews
Kingsbarns

Earn
Cupar   A915   Fife Ness

Auchterarder
FALKLAND   FIFE   CRAIL

A822
A90   A912   A916   A917   Anstruther
Pittenweem

A823
Milnathort   A911   Leslie   Earlsferry   St. Monans
Isle of May

CLACKMANNAN-SHIRE
Glenrothes   Methil   Elie

A977
A955

A905   A907   A92   A910

A985   Dunfermline   Kirkcaldy

Cuiross   A921   Kinghorn   Firth of Forth

A904   Bo'ness   A19B
Whitekirk   Dunbar

Falkirk
A90   A6137   A1   East Linton   Skateraw

A801
EDINBURGH   A901

FALKIRK   WEST LOTHIAN   A899   EDINBURGH   A199   EAST LOTHIAN

Bathgate   M8   A71   A702   A7   A6093
A720   Dalkeith

A705

0   10 mi
0   10 km

© AVALON TRAVEL

resorts you would expect to go with it. Here is the chance to pamper yourself and empty your wallet at a fancy hotel, wander the historic town center, or try your hand at a round of Scotland's best-loved game. Continuing south, East Neuk of Fife fishing villages such as Anstruther are wonderful places to relax with succulent seafood on offer. Great, golden beaches beckon farther down along the coast. Inland, in the mauve foothills of Fife Regional Park, is Falkland, a village with a palace. Keep heading south within Fife, and you will reach Dunfermline, the ancient burial place of the kings of Scotland.

HISTORY
Prehistory and Medieval Era

Angus was the main stomping ground in Scotland of the Picts, the indigenous peoples who lived and worked in the area until the 9th century A.D. They left behind them an important legacy of sculptured stones and very little else. Kenneth MacAlpin set off from Dundee in A.D. 834 to conquer the region's Picts and became king of Scotland as a result of his success. By the 12th century, St. Andrews was becoming Scotland's Episcopal center, and Scotland's first university was established here around 1410. Dunfermline was patronized by Royals from the 11th century onward. It was at Arbroath Abbey that Scottish nobles declared independence from England and loyalty to Robert the Bruce in 1320.

18th Century Onward

The region has a long history of being an entrepreneurial center for commerce. East Neuk fishing villages were instrumental in Scotland's trade with the continent as early as the 15th century. The region was quick to capitalize on being the world's key golfing center and by the early 18th century St. Andrews was manufacturing golfing merchandise and selling it to America for high prices. One of Scotland's key fishing industries was and still is on the east coast of Angus and Fife. In the 19th century the countryside population drained to seek work in Dundee, the world's jute-manufacturing capital. Smuggling gave East Neuk villages as much income as anything else and Angus had one of Britain's highest witch-executing rates in the 17th century: Forfar in the north and Culross in the south saw a lot of action. The region also inspired some of the country's most famous writers, notably JM Barrie had his childhood in the Angus Glens and William McGonagall, officially recognized as the worst poet ever.

PLANNING YOUR TIME

Both the number of attractions and their out-of-the-way nature will detain you in Angus and Fife; it may be a small area geographically but size should not be underestimated. You'll need four or five days at least. Key areas to spend your time are the Angus Glens (the small town of Kirriemuir is a good base) and the East Neuk of Fife fishing villages, throwing in a visit to St. Andrews. With more time, plan on adding Falkland to your itinerary. Bus connections are quite good in Fife but almost nonexistent in the Angus Glens.

Dundee

Revisit most Scottish places and year-in, year-out, little will have altered. Ever-changing, starkly modern Dundee is the exception. It reinvented itself out of necessity. In the premiership of Scottish cities with a 150,000-strong population, it lacks the charming buildings of Edinburgh or Stirling, the vibrant nightlife of Glasgow, and the scenic location of Inverness; it is often dismissed as boring. But the "City of Discovery," as it is now dubbed, has pushed itself to the forefront of the Scottish culture, arts, and science scene. Dundee's history has been long tied with industry, particularly the production of jute, a cheap Hessian-like fiber used to make fabric. The city rose to riches with the jute boom in the 19th century and declined with its collapse in the 20th. Jute is bouncing back, though—it's the force behind Dundee becoming the first U.K. city to go totally plastic-free.

In the 21st century Dundee's industrial past is just the reason you should visit: a history brought vividly alive by some of the country's most unusual museums. The city also has Scotland's only full-time public observatory and one of Britain's most atmospheric wining and dining scenes. A new fashionable hotel or bar always seems to be opening—Dundee is even becoming a weekend getaway destination. Chances are Dundee will grow on you; it ain't pretty or nearly as cosmopolitan as it thinks it is but compensates with bundles of friendliness. If you're in the area and fancy a day or two of urban dynamism, this is your city.

ORIENTATION

Dundee is best approached the way most people approach it: from the south across the wide, silvery River Tay. Unfortunately you're met with an often-confusing tangle of road intersections before you can appreciate the best of the city (enough to put many off). Three main areas are of interest. The waterfront is immediately to your left and right with its two historic ships, the HMS *Discovery* and Frigate

Unicorn. In from the waterfront to the west (follow A991) is the cultural quarter; city center lies straight ahead. Dundee Law is the large hill to the north, and the hill to the west is Balgay Park where the Mills Observatory is located. The A92 leads east to the suburb of Broughty Ferry.

SIGHTS

Dundee is blessed with several one-of-a-kind attractions, divided between two principal areas. The waterfront area contains Dundee's important ships, while most other sights are in the city center/cultural quarter area.

Waterfront
◖ HMS *DISCOVERY* AND DISCOVERY CENTRE

You can hardly miss the ship (Discovery Quay, tel. 01382/201245, www.rrsdiscovery.com, 10 A.M.–6 P.M. Mon.–Sat., 11 A.M.–6 P.M. Sun. Apr.–Oct., 10 A.M.–5 P.M. Mon.–Sat., 11 A.M.–5 P.M. Sun. Nov.–Mar., £7.50 adults, £5.75 children) that polar explorer Sir Robert Falcon Scott used on his North Pole voyages, moored on the waterfront as the set piece of Dundee's burgeoning cultural scene. The tour begins in the Discovery Centre (gift shop and tourist information point), and it doesn't take long to become enraptured with the theme: one of the most grueling and heroic ventures ever made by human beings. You can see how the explorers lived and follow their journey, made all the more poignant by the fact that Dundee was where Scott lived and had his ship built. The highlight is stepping onboard the ship itself; you can see where Scott's men lived and worked through two Arctic winters and visit Scott's restored cabin.

HMS FRIGATE *UNICORN*

The *Unicorn* (tel. 01382/200900, www.frigate-unicorn.org, 10 A.M.–5 P.M. daily Apr.–Oct., noon–4 P.M. Wed.–Fri., 10 A.M.–4 P.M. Sat.–Sun. Nov.–Mar., £4 adults, £3 seniors) is the

oldest British-built ship afloat and the world's last intact warship from the great days of sail. You can return to the glory days of Britain ruling the waves and explore what it would have been like to be a sailor onboard. Men endured incredibly bleak conditions for King and Country with precious little reward. There are moving displays, but it's mainly all about soaking in the atmosphere of this magnificent, creaking warhorse.

City Center and Cultural Quarter

CITY SQUARE AND ALBERT SQUARE

On the wide, plain City Square look out for the **Desperate Dan statue,** remembering Dundee's contribution to the comic-book industry (*The Dandy* is printed here). Head down Reform Street to get to Albert Square, home to the largest Albert memorial outside London. Here is the **McManus Galleries and Museum** (Albert Sq., tel. 01382/432084, www.mc-manus.co.uk), undergoing refurbishment at the time of writing to return the building to how the original architect envisaged it. It will

© LUKE WATERSON
HMS *Discovery*

still house its important collection of 19th- and 20th-century Scottish art and whaling collection, depicting Dundee's stint as one of Britain's chief whaling ports. The scheduled reopening is late 2009.

VERDANT WORKS

The jute industry tripled Dundee's population during the 19th century and at its height employed 50,000 people in over 100 mills, producing a phenomenal 1 million bales of jute annually. This lovingly restored late 19th-century jute mill (complete with brook) and works (West Henderson's Wynd, tel. 01382/225282, www.verdantworks.com, 10 A.M.–6 P.M. Mon.–Sat., 11 A.M.–6 P.M. Sun. Apr.–Oct., 10:30 A.M.–4:30 P.M. Wed.–Sat., 10:30 A.M.– 4:30 P.M. Sun. Nov.–Mar., £6.25 adults, £3.85 children) brings the city's main story to life, particularly vivid because it focuses on what it was like for both poor workers and prosperous jute barons. The highlight is the machinery, still making jute in the traditional methods.

DUNDEE LAW

Climb up here for great views over the city and River Tay. You can walk or drive up to the car park, which is where the view starts opening up (head through woods to the war memorial at the top). It's a particularly good vantage point to appreciate the **Tay Rail Bridge**—get out the cameras. The original Tay Bridge collapsed in 1879, taking with it the train that was crossing and more than 75 lives, immortalized in truly terrible verse by resident poet William McGonagall. The current bridge was built in 1887, at that time the longest bridge in the world at over two miles.

DUNDEE CONTEMPORARY ARTS CENTRE

At the heart of the cultural quarter and the city's art scene is this vibrant exhibition space, cinema, and café/bar (152 Nethergate, tel. 01382/909900, www.dca.org.uk, 10:30 A.M.–5:30 P.M. Tues.– Wed. and Fri.–Sat., 10:30 A.M.–8 P.M. Thurs., noon–5:30 P.M. Sun.). It's an ultra-modern meeting point for the trendy and artistically

THE WORLD'S WORST POET

"All of a sudden my body got enflamed, and instantly I was seized with a strong desire to write poetry, so strong in fact that in imagination I thought I heard a voice crying in my ears – Write, Write!" recalls William Topaz McGonagall in his autobiography. The fact that he did write – and so prolifically, and on such tedious topics – confirmed his place in history as the worst poet ever to make his words public. His most remembered lines commemorate the Tay Bridge railway disaster of 1879:

> Beautiful Railway Bridge
> of the Silv'ry Tay!
> Alas I am very sorry to say
> That ninety lives have been taken away
> On the last Sabbath day of 1879,
> Which will be remember'd for a very
> long time.

Although the lines are by no means the worst in McGonagall's career of over 200 literary works, they do epitomize the lack of sensitivity for subject or audience. Even when he was pelted with fruit during performances of his poems, the poet was apparently oblivious to the fact that his work was being mocked. Perhaps McGonagall had the last laugh, though. He was thick-skinned to the point where it was possible that, knowing full well his work was universally derided, he played up to the crowds with particularly pompous and awful lines to gain further notoriety. Sadly, neither the tomes of his autobiography or poems shed any light on this. Certainly, critics have been a little unfair to McGonagall; he was, after all, a hand-weaver with no education. Over a century after his death, he is still a renowned poetic figure with his own appreciation society, albeit for the wrong reasons – just the literary recognition he felt he deserved.

minded, with five floors of galleries and a year-round program of events and talks.

◆ MILLS OBSERVATORY
In leafy Balgay Park to the west of the city center, Mills Observatory (Glamis Rd., tel. 01382/435967, 11 A.M.–5:30 P.M. Mon.–Fri., 12:30–4 P.M. Sat.–Sun. Apr.–Sept., 11 A.M.–10 P.M. Mon.–Fri., 12:30–4 P.M. Sat.–Sun. Oct.–Mar.) is the only British observatory open full-time to the British public, a great asset in Dundee's open-house scientific discovery program. There's a planetarium, displays on historical sky-gazing equipment, and a 19th-century telescope trained on the stars. The dome is open on clear nights October–March.

Broughty Ferry
The bright seaside suburb of Broughty Ferry is a bustling spot of bright pubs and restaurants, a breath of fresh air after the somewhat dour city center. Wander along the silvery banks of the Tay to **Broughty Castle Museum** (10 A.M.–4:30 P.M. Mon.–Sat. 12:30–4 P.M.

Sun., closed Mon. Oct.–Mar.), sticking out on a promontory into the Tay estuary with some good displays on local history and whaling within a 15th-century castle. There's a first-floor coffee shop.

ENTERTAINMENT AND EVENTS
Thanks to a large student population, the area around Dundee University known as the **Cultural Quarter** is pretty hip, with plenty of lively bars and restaurants. Head here, or east to attractive **Broughty Ferry** by the shore, for quality eating and drinking options. Once pubs close, that's pretty much it for the night—there are few worthwhile nightclubs. A couple of the country's leading performing arts venues are in the city.

Pubs, Bars, and Live Music
The area known as the Cultural Quarter along Nethergate/Perth Road has lots of different bars: It's just a matter of finding one to your tastes. They're mostly at the trendy, modern

GOLF TOUR OF DUNDEE AND FIFE

Start things off at one of the area's finest parkland courses at rolling **Downfield** (Turnberry Ave., tel. 01382/825595, www.downfieldgolf.co.uk, £50-55 high season) in Dundee. Head north up the coast for a round at **Carnoustie** (Links Parade, tel. 01241/853789, £115), which Tiger Woods believes to be one of the best courses in the world. Continue up to **Montrose** (Traill Dr., tel. 01674/672932, www.montroselinks.co.uk, £52 weekends) for some of the area's best links golf. One of the most picturesque inland courses of Angus is at **Edzell** (High St., tel. 01356/648462, www.edzellgolfclub.net, £42 weekends).

Back in Fife, if you fancy your skills you should try the difficult but classic **Old Course** (£125) and the almost as challenging **New Course** (£65) at **St. Andrews Links** (www.standrews.org.uk). A new addition to the St. Andrews courses will be two miles from town along the Craill Road at **Fairmont St. Andrews** (tel. 01334/837000, £95), with two courses; the Devlin course is open, and the Torrance should be up and running in 2009 and promises to be an exceptional course. Continue south to the impressive links at **Kingsbarns** (7 miles southeast of St. Andrews, tel. 01334/460860, www.kingsbarns.com, £130-160) on the East Neuk, and finish off with a round farther south at **Aberdour** (Seaside Pl., tel. 01383/860080, www.aberdourgolfclub.co.uk, £22), another beautiful links course.

All golf clubs are signposted from their respective towns, but it's almost essential to pre-book as this is the golfing hot spot of the country that calls itself the capital of golf. Contacting the clubs beforehand also means you can get a whiff of any special offers floating about.

---

age of the spectrum of Dundee drinking spots, or at least think they are.

One of the best places for a drink in the city is the **Trades House Bar** (40 Nethergate, tel. 01382/229494, 11 A.M.–11 P.M. daily). With tiled floors, stained glass windows, booths, and big screen sports, this is a popular old pub frequented by all sorts.

The **Reading Rooms** (57 Blackscroft, tel. 01382/450432, www.thereadingrooms.co.uk, 7:30 P.M.–2:30 A.M. Wed.–Sat.) is the leading live music venue in Dundee. Long-standing **Fat Sams** (31 South Ward Rd., tel. 01382/228181, www.fatsams.co.uk, until 2:30 A.M. daily) is about the best of Dundee's scant selection of nightclubs, attracting regular live music and the city's top DJs. The cover is usually £5–8 on weekends.

Performing Arts

Caird Hall (City Sq., tel. 01382/434451, www.cairdhall.co.uk), with immense Doric columns, is the city's leading concert and performance venue. **Dundee Rep Theatre** (Tay Sq., tel. 01382/227684, www.dundeereptheatre.co.uk)

hosts an exciting year-round program of drama, dance, and comedy. Not to be underestimated, it has Scotland's only resident ensemble of actors and, many say, Scotland's best dance company.

Events

The **Dundee Blues Bonanza** (www.dundeebluesbonanza.co.uk) is a live blues and rock festival at the end of June and beginning of July.

SHOPPING AND RECREATION
Shopping

Dundonians like shopping. If you do, too, try three-level Wellgate in the city center, reputedly haunted. For a bookshop, **Borders** (42 East Dock St., tel. 01382/454845, 8:30 A.M.–9 P.M. Mon.–Fri., 9 A.M.–8 P.M. Sat., 10 A.M.–8 P.M. Sun.) is a good bet.

Sports and Recreation

Angling is good along the waterfront in Broughty Ferry. **Golf** is the chief sporting delight in the region—Dundee sees a lot of passing trade up towards Carnoustie and down to St. Andrews.

ACCOMMODATIONS

Dundee city itself doesn't exactly have a great range of accommodations—plenty of quantity, less so for quality. The suburb of Broughty Ferry offers some pleasant alternatives to the city center options.

City Center and Vicinity
UNDER £50

Dundee is awakening to the need for budget accommodation: The newly restored **Dundee Backpackers Hostel** (71 High St., tel. 01382/224640, 4-bed and 6-bed dorms £15) opened in 2008 after a few teething problems. It offers 90 beds with en suite rooms, self-catering facilities, and a games room.

Smack bang in the middle of the cultural quarter, the **Aauld Steeple Guesthouse** (94 Nethergate, enquiries@aauldsteepleguesthouse.co.uk, £23–25 s, £40–44 d) is one of the best accommodation deals in the city. It's a solid old-fashioned place with 13 clean rooms, crisp linens, and filling breakfasts. Rooms have basins but bathrooms are shared.

Out toward the hospital, the **Scottish Art Studio** (Menzieshill Rd., tel. 01382/665879, www.scottishartstudio.com, from £25 s, £46 d) is a quiet West End house that mixes bed-and-breakfast with artist's studio. The two come to a head at breakfast, as you look out over the Tay from large windows in a room full of paintings. Some rooms are en suite, while some have a shared bathroom.

£50-100

The **Shaftesbury Hotel** (1 Hyndford St., tel. 01382/669216, www.shaftesbury-hotel.co.uk, £55 s, £69 d) is a former jute baron's mansion that now offers large, light rooms in Dundee's West End. The hotel boasts two restaurants, including one overlooking the garden. There's also a DVD room with a huge selection of DVDs.

Great for stylish breaks and business trips, **Number 25** (25 South Tay St., tel. 01382/200399, www.g1group.co.uk, £60 d) is the only boutique hotel in the city. This townhouse in the city's cultural quarter has only four shiny, modern-looking rooms available;

pick from claret, yellow, blue, or brown. All rooms are en suite.

Five miles northeast of Dundee, **Duntrune House** (Duntrune, tel. 01382/350239, www.duntrunehouse.co.uk, £45 s, £100 d) dates back to 1826. It offers fresh fruit in each of its en suite rooms and free laundry if you're staying two nights or more. The price goes down by £10 pp if you stay two nights or more, too—why don't you just stay two nights?

Broughty Ferry
UNDER £50

Riverview Caravan Park (Monifieth, tel. 01382/535471, pitches from £13) is spread out along a sandy stretch of beach by Monifieth. This is the nearest campground to the city (five miles east of Dundee center) with heated toilet/shower block, games room, gym, and sauna. It's a pleasant, grassy site.

£50-100

Better known for the charismatic old pub below, the **(Fisherman's Tavern** (10–16 Fort St., tel. 01382/477466, www.fishermanstavern.co.uk, £39 s, £64 d) has rooms that are pale-colored, spartan, modern, clean, and all en suite. Most have direct-dial phones and color TVs. The best bit, of course, is that you are staying in a converted 17th-century fisherman's cottage above the best pub in Broughty.

Ten large rooms overlook both the Tay and the verdant, sloping gardens at the **Taychreggan Hotel** (4 Ellieslea Rd., tel. 01382/778626, www.taychreggan-hotel.co.uk, £45 s, £70 d). There are writing desks for postcard-writing and TVs with Freeview channels. Breakfast choices include a selection of Sri Lankan teas, porridge with cream, or Stornoway black pudding. High Tea can be taken on the patio.

FOOD

Particularly in its charming Cultural Quarter, Dundee is getting a good reputation as a place to eat out. It does cafés particularly well. The attractive suburb of Broughty Ferry is, and has been historically, a great place to eat out, right on the waters of the wide Tay Estuary.

City Center and Vicinity
CAFÉS, TEAROOMS, AND SNACKS

If any place could take the traditional out of tartan, the **Tartan Coffeehouse** (58 Perth Rd., tel. 01382/332338, www.tartan-coffeehouse.com, 8 A.M.–4 P.M. Mon.–Fri., 8 A.M.–5 P.M. Sat., 10 A.M.–3 P.M. Sun.) would be it. Proudly organic and Fair Trade, this recent addition to the Cultural Quarter café scene is an informal place decorated with artwork including, yes, tartans (funky ones, by the manager of Dundee's McManus Galleries). It's understandably popular with students and arty types; the food is wholesome and cheap and the coffee is top-notch. Healthy mains are £4–6: the homemade soup is a perk-up in the cold weather.

The ◖ **Jute Café/Bar** (152 Nethergate, tel. 01382/909246, food 10 A.M.–4:30 P.M. and 5–9:30 P.M. Mon.–Sat., noon–8:30 P.M. Sun.) is part of the Dundee Contemporary Arts Centre. It occupies a vast, airy space but still fills up fast with arty, well-heeled types. Bar and restaurant areas are divided. There are great breakfast paninis and mains (pasta, fish, steak, and salads) from £7.50.

You can trust the **Fisher and Donaldson Bakery/Café** (12 Whitehall St., tel. 01382/223488, until 5:15 P.M. Mon.–Sat.) to provide you with a memorable sugary snack—it's been going strong for decades. It stocks the stickiest, tastiest cakes and pastries for takeaway or sampling in its little café, and a wide range of teas and coffees and soups to go with them in elegant surrounds.

SCOTTISH/INTERNATIONAL/SEAFOOD

The Tasting Rooms (5 South Ward Rd., tel. 01382/224188, www.thetastingrooms.co.uk, open for breakfast until late) is yet another proof that Dundee is spot-on when it comes to offering innovative, modern cuisine. It's essentially a wine-appreciation venue, where you can go and sample the best selection of wine in the city (buy a bottle between 3 and 6 P.M. to receive a free tasting platter) and enjoy it in the light, spacious café/bar until you get a little peckish. There's lots of food to complement the wine: a great selection of wraps like chorizo with raclette cheese (£4.95), scrumptious salads, and the tasting room platters (including cheese, olives, carni/meat, and seafood) from £5.50. You could always order some more wine to go with that.

The **Social** (10 South Tay St., tel. 01382/202070, food served noon–5 P.M. Thurs.–Tues., all day and night Wed.) is a cheap, chic place to eat, drink, and party: a flagship for what the new trendy Dundee is about these days. The food encompasses nachos, bruschetta, whole-baked camembert and good mezze plates. Haggis fritters are also a favorite. Good meals are £3–10. It can get noisy with parties but never intimidatingly so; all walks of life stop by, from students to tourists. The bar has a drink range as internationally diverse as the food it offers.

The traditional fish and chips at **Deep Sea** (81 Nethergate, tel. 01382/224449, 11:30 A.M.–6:30 P.M. Mon.–Sat.) has been providing locals with hearty fish suppers for nigh on 60 years. You can get takeaway, but sitting in is good fun, too; this is what Scottish eateries were like before anyone knew about the word "pretentious."

ASIAN

The pearl-white, purpose-built **Dil Se** (99 Perth Rd., tel. 01382/221501, 5 P.M.–1 A.M. Sun.–Thurs., noon–1 A.M. Fri.–Sat.) is the sister restaurant of the better-known Balaka Restaurant in St. Andrews. It does superb Bangladeshi/North Indian cuisine in huge portions and has given multicultural dining in Dundee a real boost. Mains are £8–15.

MIDDLE EASTERN

Let's face it: with the handy location **Twin City Café** (4 City Sq., tel. 01382/223662, 7:30 A.M.–5:30 P.M. Mon.–Sat., 10:30 A.M.–4:30 P.M. Sun.) has on the main city square, it could be appalling and still the footsore shoppers of Dundee would stop to flop (there's few other options). That they can do that here in style is credit to the staff and management, a friendly bunch despite being rushed off their

DUNDEE AND MARMALADE

Dundee has long been associated with this bitter, orange-based preserve, dating back to the 1700s when a Spanish ship with a cargo of Seville oranges moored in Dundee to shelter from storms. Local grocer James Keiller, so the story goes, acquired a vast amount of the oranges at a knock-down price but then discovered how bitter they were; none of his customers would buy them. However, when his wife took charge and crushed them down instead of the normal quinces when making preserves, the result was universally popular. It makes for a good breakfast anecdote, but the truth is that world trade had probably meant citrus fruit was common enough in Brit-ain in the 17th century for aspiring marmalade-makers to begin experimenting.

As for Keiller and Dundee, both still get a substantial share of marmalade fame. In 1797 he really did open a marmalade factory in Dundee along with his mother, producing a citrus preserve with the revelation of thick chunks of fruit and peel rather than the previously used smoother paste. Rather than having any great foresight of how popular this would prove in the preserve industry, Keiller and his firm were probably just looking to cut down on fruit waste. The new chunky marmalade hit it off more because of how the peel helped with digestion than because of its superior taste.

feet. You have to scratch a little beneath the surface to discover the Middle Eastern theme, but falafel, hummus, and Turkish sweets are available in addition to the good coffee and croissants. It's a great people-watching spot.

Broughty Ferry

When it's hot in Broughty, there will be a gradual but guaranteed procession down to **Visocchi's** (40 Gray St., tel. 01382/779297, 9:30 A.M.–7:30 P.M. Mon.–Thurs., 9:30 A.M.–9:30 P.M. Fri.–Sat., 9:30 A.M.–5:30 P.M. Sun.), a die-hard Italian ice cream parlor. Apart from dishing up Dundee's best ice cream, there are also delicious cakes like Italian gateaux.

Going strong as a pub since the early 19th century, the 🅒 **Fisherman's Tavern** (10–16 Fort St., tel. 01382/775941, www.fishermanstavern.co.uk, food served noon–7:30 P.M. daily, open until late) has allegedly featured in every good ale guide to Britain ever written—the only pub in Britain to do so. The dark nook-and-cranny eating area is by the bar, and fish is the focus of the menu. A beer festival is held annually in the enclosed garden at the rear.

Art deco and glass-fronted, **Glass Pavilion** (The Esplanade, tel. 01382/732738, www.theglasspavilion.co.uk, 10 A.M.–10 P.M. daily) is a bistro that was originally constructed as a bathing shelter—hard to believe these days as it serves up wonderful high teas while you scan the lapping estuary waters outside for dolphins. Mains like seafood linguine or Shetland salmon are from £10.

INFORMATION AND SERVICES
Tourist Information

At the helpful **Dundee TIC** (21 Castle St., tel. 01382/527527, 9 A.M.–6 P.M. Mon.–Sat., noon–4 P.M. Sun. June–Sept., 9 A.M.–4 or 5 P.M. Mon.–Sat. Oct.–May), you can buy maps and book bus or Calmac Ferry tickets.

Services

There are multiple banks on Reform Street. Most have exchange facilities and all have ATMs.

You can check **Internet** at the TIC or **Dundee Central Library** (Wellgate, tel. 01382/431500, 9:30 A.M.–6 P.M. Mon.–Tues. and Fri., 10 A.M.–6 P.M. Wed., 9:30 A.M.–8 P.M. Thurs., 9:30 A.M.–5 P.M. Sat.). One of the main city branches of the post office is at 4 Meadowside.

For medical services, **Ninewell's Hospital** (tel. 01382/660111, open 24 hours) is the region's main hospital, to the west of the city center at Menzieshill. Take bus 96 (also from St. Andrews), 72, or 42.

Albertay Launderette and Dry Cleaning (78 Albert St., tel. 01382/451070) will attend to your laundry needs.

GETTING THERE AND AWAY

The city is the regional transport hub, with some flights and good bus/train connections.

Airport

Dundee City Airport (Riverside, tel. 01382/662200) is one of the more photogenic places to land in Scotland, right by the banks of the Tay a few minutes' drive west of city center. **Air France** operates a daily service from London City Airport to Dundee.

Train

There are trains to Glasgow (about hourly, 1 hour 10 min., £21.40), Edinburgh (one to two hourly, 1 hour 10 min., £17.60) and Aberdeen (two hourly, 1 hour 15 min., £22.60).

Bus

Scottish Citylink runs buses about half-hourly between Dundee and Edinburgh (2 hours, £10.40, stopping at Dunfermline) and between Dundee and Glasgow (2 hours, £10.90). There are also frequent buses to Perth (35 min., £4.90) and Aberdeen (1 hour 20 min., £10.90). Change at Perth for Inverness service with Scottish Citylink and **Megabus;** journey time is 3.25 hours. **National Express buses** will also stop at Dundee en route between London and Aberdeen (11 hours, from £16 to Dundee).

Car Rental

Reliable **Arnold Clark** (East Dock St., tel. 01382/225382) has a branch in the city.

GETTING AROUND

If navigating is too much, call **Tele Taxis** (tel. 01382/669333) or **Tay Taxis** (tel. 01382/450450).

The Angus Coast

The stretch of coast north of Dundee is a mix of sand and spectacular rocky clifftops, with great dunes around Montrose. The diversity of coastal habitats makes it a popular stopover for many unusual migrating birds, as well as year-round home to many other wonderous winged species. Arbroath, the main port of call, is the adopted home of the Arbroath Smokie, a fishy delicacy.

ARBROATH

This old red sandstone town is distinctly mediocre for the most part, thanks to a number of bland shopping precincts. However the splendid abbey and clattering harbor, with its fish shops on every corner, retain a whiff of the charm of Arbroath's glory days and make the town well worth a visit. Be sure to taste the local delicacy, the Arbroath Smokie, a salted, smoked fish. The original recipe was invented by accident when a fish-drying room caught fire. Arbroath assured its place in the history books by hosting the "Declaration of

Arbroath," in which Scottish nobles swore their independence from England in 1320.

Sights

The most interesting area of Arbroath is around the harbor, known as **"Fit o' The Town,"** a colorful old fishing community.

The ruddy red ruins of **Arbroath Abbey** (tel. 01241/878756, 9:30 A.M.–5:30 P.M. daily Apr.–Sept., 9:30 A.M.–4:30 P.M. daily Oct.–Mar.) are pretty impressive, dating back to 1178. It was here that the Declaration of Arbroath was signed. There is a visitors center with insights into the abbey's history.

Arbroath has seen some important maritime developments (the Stevenson's Bell Rock Lighthouse, the oldest sea-washed tower still in existence, was built just off the coast here, for example). The **Signal Tower Museum** (Ladyloan, tel. 01241/875598, 10 A.M.–5 P.M. Mon.–Sat., 2–5 P.M. Sun. July–Aug., 10 A.M.–5 P.M. Mon.–Sat. Sept.–June, free) charters all of them. You

© LUKE WATERSON

Arbroath Abbey

can discover all about the Arbroath Smokie and learn about a clutch of other events and personalities that have shaped Arbroath over the centuries. The museum is housed in the shore station for the lighthouse.

(Smokie Shops

One of the best places to try the much-hyped Arbroath Smokie, a succulent wood-smoked haddock with a unique taste, is at **Stuart's Fresh Fish** (46 Ladybridge St., tel. 01241/874772), serving simply heavenly seafood. It's not just a great option for one of the traditional "Smokies" but also for something different, like dressed crab or Smokie pâté.

Accommodations

Don't come to **Harbour Nights Guest House** (4 Shore, tel. 01241/434343, www.harbour-nights.co.uk, from £50 d) expecting a typical sea-side B&B. Harbour Nights not only has a prime location by the harbor but also offers prime facilities. Ample, comfortable rooms look out over bobbing boats and smokie shops—just what the town is all about. The superior double is worth

the extra splash; it has an armchair for window-gazing and even a globe. Look out for the ornamental elephants. As with most places, you'll pay more for sea views; singles don't get a good deal here, paying almost the double-occupancy rate.

On the edge of Arbroath is **Rosely Country House Hotel** (Forfar Rd., tel. 01241/876828, www.theroselyhotel.co.uk, rooms £40–50 s, £55–65 d), about as traditional and countri-fied a place as Scotland can offer (tartan, dark wood, and many, many stags heads). In a historically significant Victorian house within four acres of its own grounds, it's a laid-back place offering en suite rooms with TVs.

The characterful red sandstone **(Ethie Castle** (Ethie Mains, off A92 north of Auchmithie, tel. 01241/830434, www.ethiecastle.com, from £70 s, £94 d) is the second-oldest inhabited castle in Scotland and was inspiration for Sir Walter Scott's novel *The Antiquary*. Rooms, including one with four-poster bed, overlook the courtyard or the extensive garden and all have private/en suite bathrooms. You can feast on breakfast in the Tudor Kitchen in front of a huge crackling inglenook fireplace.

DUNDEE, ANGUS, AND FIFE

© LUKE WATERSON

Arbroath Harbour is bright, brash, and full of places to try Arbroath Smokies.

Food
The Old Boatyard (Fishmarket Quay, tel. 01241/879995, from 10:30 A.M. daily) is a large café/restaurant right on the harbor, decorated with signs from old shipyards and with sofas and an outside patio. There's a good selection of coffee and cakes. A two-course set lunch is £10.95; Lobster Thermidor is the most expensive of the main meals at £17.95.

The **But n Ben** (1 Auchmithie, tel. 01241/ 877223, noon–2:30 P.M. and 7–10 P.M. Wed.– Sat., noon–2:30 P.M. Sun., 7–10 P.M. Mon.) is located in Auchmithie, where the Arbroath smokie originated. In keeping with this little village's fishy legacy, the delightful little cottage perched above the harbor here serves up a great seafood-dominated menu. The service can be a bit curt but it's worth it for the experience. For a sample of the mouthwatering fare, try the high tea. Mains start from £8.

Getting There and Away
Buses 39/73/73A take about an hour to travel between Arbroath and Dundee (four per hour).

Bus 39 also continues to Montrose (hourly, 25 min.). Trains run from Dundee to Arbroath (two hourly, 20 min., £4.10) and continue from Arbroath to Aberdeen (1 hr., £17.40).

MONTROSE BASIN AND INLAND
The wide wildlife-rich lake that is the Montrose Basin stretches west from the dunes that flank this part of the coast; it drains at low tide to form a vast mud puddle patronized by a huge variety of birdlife. Nearby is the House of Duns, while farther inland, linked by a steam railway with the basin, is the tiny city of Brechin with a wonderful cathedral and an intriguing museum exploring the area's Pictish history. Some of the last remaining evidence of Picts in Angus stands in the form of a collection of sculptured stones in the nearby village of Aberlemno.

Sights
The Montrose Basin attracts a great variety of birds with its freshwater, seawater, and salt marsh habitats and the **Montrose Basin Wildlife Centre** (near Montrose on A92, tel.

01674/676336, 10:30 A.M.–5:30 P.M. daily Mar.–Nov., 10:30 A.M.–4 P.M. Fri.–Sun. Nov.– Mar., £3 adults, £2 children) gives visitors the chance to tap into this rich pageant of bird-life. The visitors center complete with basic café tells you more about which birds you can expect to see at which time of year. These in-clude kingfishers, shelducks, waders, and pink-footed geese. Telescopes and CCTV cameras give up-close views of the birds. You can follow a limited number of paths around the basin it-self. Make sure you respect the diverse birdlife by sticking to the paths. In autumn be sure to sign up for the truly magical pink-footed goose breakfasts, when you can witness thou-sands of these migratory birds flying in to the basin and round things off with breakfast at the visitors center.

Railway enthusiasts reopened the **Caledonian Railway** (tel. 01356/622992, www.caledonian-railway.co.uk), a branch line from Brechin to Bridge of Dun Station, in 1993. If you're in the area and fancy a visit to the Montrose Basin or to William Adam–designed **House of Dun** (tel. 01674/810264, 11:30 A.M.–5:30 P.M. daily July–Aug., 12:30–5:30 P.M. Wed.–Sun. Apr.–June and Sept.), which is a 15-minute walk from the station, traveling on this steam train from Brechin is a fun way to do it. Trains run Sunday May–September and Saturday July–August.

The little city of Brechin has a splendid 13th-century **Cathedral** (9 A.M.–5 P.M.) but the most interesting attraction comes in the form of **Pictavia** (Brechin Castle Centre, tel. 01356/626241, 9:30 A.M.–5:30 P.M. Mon.–Sat., 10:30 A.M.–5:30 P.M. Sun. Apr.–Oct., 9 A.M.–5 P.M. Mon.–Sat., 10 A.M.–5 P.M. Sun. Oct.–Mar., £3.25 adults, £2.25 seniors). The Picts left their mark on Angus 2,000 years ago, and this place tells their story. You can also pick up information on the Angus Pictish Trail here. If you're headed out to Aberlemno and want to learn something about the sculp-tured stones there beforehand, this is a useful frame of reference, too. There's tourist informa-tion available, too.

Out on the B9134 towards Forfar are the huge, riveting **Aberlemno Sculptured Stones,** set in the roadside and at the village kirk (church). Etched with disc symbols, snakes, and centaurs, these exquisitely carved slabs set you thinking about the quality of the work-manship necessary more than a millennium ago to survive so clearly today. The stone at the kirkyard is best preserved; the back depicts a battle scene from A.D. 685. Stones are boxed for protection from weather October–May.

Accommodations and Food

Head out of dull Montrose to the pretty city of Brechin for a place to stay. Here, 19th-century **Liscara** (3a Castle St., Brechin, tel. 01356/625584, www.liscara.co.uk, £28–32 s, £50 d) has rooms on two stories, all endowed with private or en suite bathrooms.

On the B9134 toward Aberlemno, con-cealed by rolling fields, this idyllic **Blibberhill Farm** (near Aberlemno, tel. 01307/830323, www.blibberhill.co.uk, £24–26 s, £48–52 d) is a working farm with three homey en suite rooms and a guest's conservatory overlooking the garden. Only a long, broken track links it to the real world. Blibberhill is a popular stop-off for Greylag Geese in season; the farm takes its name from the sound a goose makes while searching for food in the water—blibbering. The ruined **Melgund Castle** is nearby.

The 18th-century timber-beamed **Old Bakehouse** (26 High St., Brechin, tel. 01356/625254, 9:30 A.M.–4:30 P.M. Mon.–Sat.) is a lively local café hangout, dealing out tasty, ri-diculously cheap paninis and homebakes. A combination of the two is around £4.50.

Getting There and Away

Stagecoach Strathtay Bus 30 runs hourly be-tween Brechin and Montrose (20 min.) via the House of Dun. The same company oper-ates Service 21, running hourly to Aberlemno and on to Forfar. Some Service 21 buses con-tinue to Dundee direct; otherwise change in Forfar for regular Dundee buses. You can ac-cess the Montrose Basin Wildlife Centre from Montrose, which has two hourly trains (Mon.–Sat.) and two trains every two hours (Sun.) to Dundee (35 min., £8).

Angus Glens

These rolling red glens (www.angusglens.co.uk) spread out in splayed fingers from Kirriemuir: Glen Isla, Glen Prosen, Glen Clova, Glen Doll, and farther east, Glen Esk. They are far and away the highlight of any trip to Angus: a taste of what the highlands have to offer with the bonus of great accessibility. With public roads cutting up through the majority of each, the outdoor enthusiast can really make the most of these long, remote valleys in a way not always possible farther north and get far closer to the wildlife within them. The combination of steep-sided woods, rivers, and moor makes for great, varied walks and excellent picnicking.

KIRRIEMUIR

Cobbled streets, attractive red sandstone and whitewashed houses, some great museums, and one of the best settings of any town in Scotland, it seems "Kirrie" has everything. The author of Peter Pan, J. M. Barrie, was born in town and inspired to write by the fairy-tale surrounding landscape. The town's also confirmed its place in the hill-walking history books; Hugh Munro, mountain-classifier and climber, was born here, too.

Sights
J. M. Barrie's Birthplace and Camera Obscura (9 Brechin Rd., tel. 01575/572646, 11 A.M.–5 P.M. Mon.–Sat., 1–5 P.M. Sun. July–Aug., noon–5 P.M. Sat. and Mon.–Wed. 1–5 P.M. Sun. Apr.–May and Sept., £5) is a restored weaver's cottage, made to reflect what it was like when the creator of Never-Never-Land was born and grew up under its roof. Through a wealth of family memorabilia and drawings, the inspirations for Barrie's later writings become apparent; the ninth of 10 children, Barrie was deeply affected by the death of his brother at only 13, supposedly influencing him to write about the "boy who never grew up." Barrie wrote and performed his first play at the ripe old age of seven in the wash house. An adjacent cottage contains the "Peter Pan Experience." There are

costumes from an early production of Peter Pan on display. Barrie donated the Camera Obscura and the cricket pavilion in which it stands, to the town in 1930. It sits on Kirrie Hill overlooking the town, the most scenically located of Scotland's three Camera Obscuras.

Run by a World War II RAF veteran, the **Aviation Museum** (tel. 01575/573233, 10 A.M.–5 P.M. Mon.–Thurs., 11 A.M.–5 P.M. Fri.–Sun. Apr.–Sept., other times by arrangement, free) is one of Scotland's most incredible museums. It focuses mainly on Scottish RAF history (medals to uniforms to aircraft models to navigational instruments) but the owner is a mine of information on all aspects of flying and of the glens themselves. Head down the road from the TIC past the car park to get there: The museum is on the right.

Accommodations and Food
You'll leave **Crepto** (Kinnordy Pl., tel. 01575/572758, £23–26 pp) feeling full; the rooms in this modern house come with surely the biggest supply of biscuits of any bed-and-breakfast in Scotland. Then you have to get through the breakfasts themselves (the home-made preserves are also for sale). The rooms are simple but perfectly decent affairs. Bathrooms are shared, and parking is ample.

The **Airlie Arms Hotel** (St. Malcolm's Wynd, tel. 01575/572847, £40 s, £65 d) is the best hotel in town: cozy, central, and white-washed, with lots of hanging baskets of flowers. The comfortable en suite rooms are quirkily done up in blue, red, and white deckchair-like stripes. The upstairs Wynd Restaurant is pretty good (evening meals from 5 P.M.) but they stop serving, like most places in Kirrie, ridiculously early: You'll have to power walk those hills to make it down in time for dinner. Avoid the soulless downstairs bar.

Intentional or not, there's an air of the Wild West about the **Old Fire Station** (St. Malcolm's Wynd, tel. 01575/574624, food served until 9 P.M. daily)—the decked seating and choice of background music might have a lot to do with it. It's the most reliable dining option in town and as a result charges through the nose (mains £10–16). The American-themed food is tasty, however—even the salads.

Information

In the Gateway to the Glens Museum is the friendly **TIC** (The Townhouse, tel. 01575/575479, 10 A.M.–5 P.M. Mon.–Sat. Apr.–Sept., 10 A.M.–5 P.M. Mon.–Wed. and Fri.–Sat., 1–5 P.M. Thurs. Oct.–Mar.) with bags of information and maps on walks, wildlife, and geography. Outside is a statue of Peter Pan.

Getting There and Away

Stagecoach Strathtay runs buses two or three times hourly to Forfar/Dundee. Dundee's a one-hour ride. **Country Cabs** (tel. 01575/575050) will give you a ride up to the glens (about £25 up to the Glen Clova Hotel).

GLENS CLOVA AND DOLL

With its bubbling, grassy-banked river, tussocky fields, and tracts of conifer woods all backed by increasingly craggy hills etched with corries (hillside hollows), Glen Clova is the most conventionally pretty of the glens, mainly because of its variety of terrain. Great picnicking spots jump out at you from the roadside, and there's the added enticement of a very good hotel at the head of the glen. If hill-walking is your thing, head here. From the head of Glen Clova, Glen Doll extends further into the hills and almost begs you to don your hiking boots and set off on an adventure. There are a couple of **Munros** for the bagging, and the **Angus Glens Ranger Service** is also located in Glen Doll (Braedownie, tel. 01575/550233).

In the shadow of **Ben Tirran** to the northeast of the head of Glen Clova are two glacial lochs. They are lonely, eerie spots, connected to civilization by a path from the **Glen Clova Hotel** (tel. 01575/550350, www.clova.com, from £60 s, £90 d, bunkhouse £11, food noon–8:30 P.M. Sun.–Thurs., noon–9 P.M. Fri.–Sat.). Even if you don't like the idea of walking, you can sit in this wonderful whitewashed drover's

inn and feast on good home cooking while soaking up the atmosphere of this peaceful place. Bunkhouse self-caterers: be aware there's no shop to stock up on food, but you can get breakfast at the hotel.

A **post bus** leaves Kirriemuir for the Glen at 8:30 A.M. Monday–Saturday, going as far as Braedownie; there's also a Monday–Friday service at 3:10 P.M.

GLEN PROSEN

Quiet Glen Prosen has an intimate feel. It's one of the smallest, gentlest, and least-visited glens, with some great **walks** up on to the moor on either side through its thick woods, including the **Minister's Path,** a popular walk over to Glen Clova. A **cairn** at the roadside before Glenprosen village marks the favorite view of polar explorer **Robert Falcon Scott.**

Up a track from the telephone box in the village is the 18-bed **Prosen Hostel** (tel. 01575/540238, £18 pp). At any time of year, it's best to phone in advance if you want to guarantee a bed, as there are no other sleeping facilities nearby. Amenities include a wood-burning stove and Internet access. You can make a foray into the glen a circuit by coming up through Courtachy and returning via Pearsie. The **Glen Clova Postbus** stops at Courtachy.

GLEN ISLA

This is the only glen where a through-road extends right along it and is consequently the most fertile and populated of the glens (we're talking in Scottish terms here—that still only means a few hamlets and grassy fields in front of the heather). Its big asset, aside from its beauty, is its accessibility: If you're pushed for time you can work Glen Isla into part of your onward journey north or south.

At the foot of the glen is **Peel Farm** (tel. 01575/560205, www.peelfarm.com, 10 A.M.–5 P.M. daily) by the southwest corner of the Loch of Lintrathen, a great rustic coffee shop with an adjoining courtyard exhibiting the work of around 30 local craftspeople. You can park here and walk the sign-posted half mile to the cascading falls of **Reekie Linn** (year-round). This white torrent of a water-fall tearing through the trees looks impressive at any time of year, but particularly in winter and spring after heavy rainfall. A **post bus** leaving Blairgowrie at 7 A.M. makes the slow journey per day to various points in Glen Isla.

◖ EDZELL AND GLEN ESK

Quiet, handsome Edzell, with the rambling ruins of its castle a mile to the west, is quite literally a gateway to Glen Esk: From the south you have to pass through the hallmark Dalhousie arch to enter the wide main street of the village and the glen behind it. There's talk of opening a TIC by the wide central green, but that hasn't happened yet. The bare red-brown hills of Glen Esk, some 15 miles long, are mainly used by huntin', shootin', and fishin' types. The industry is the main-stay of the economy in the glen, and the land is managed accordingly with less forest and more moor than in other glens. It's the most interesting glen to explore; a road does make the long cut-through over Mudlee Bracks to Aboyne in Aberdeenshire, but isn't driveable after Invermark Castle.

Sights

Up a track backed by woodland in grassy, steeply rolling countryside, the 16th-century ruin of **Edzell Castle** (tel. 01356/648631, 9:30 A.M.–5:30 P.M. daily Apr.–Sept., 9:30 A.M.–4:30 P.M. Sat.–Wed. Oct.–Mar., £4.70 adults, £3.70 seniors) is the definition of peacefulness. The main feature is the gardens, designed by Sir David Lindsay in 1604 to entertain guests including Mary, Queen of Scots. Lindsay was so passionate about them he neglected to finish building the castle. Within walls set with stone carvings of the cardinal virtues and special bird-nesting holes are hedges cut into the shapes of the fleur de lis and the Scottish thistle, as well as a two-story summer house.

The **Brown and White Caterthuns** (open year-round) are two dramatic Iron Age hill forts that stand on an exposed bulk of moorland five miles from Edzell. The heather has all but reclaimed the older Brown Caterthun, but the White Caterthun still has the remains of its thick white-painted walls almost 2,000 years after it was last inhabited. The forts are sign-posted off the B966 Brechin-Edzell road, but it's easy to get lost on the network of tiny twisting lanes. It's a climb of under 1 kilometer to either fort—both good picnicking spots. The views are gorgeous around here, with steep, grassy, heathery hills and hardly any visitors.

Pretty **Glenesk Folk Museum** (The Retreat, tel. 01356/648070, noon–6 P.M. Sat.–Sun. Easter–June, noon–6 P.M. daily July–Oct., £2 adults) has a lot of farming, costume, and dairy artifacts and important local history archives for tracing ancestry. There is information on the glen and a tearoom—by the time you've made it this far up the glen you'll be glad of it.

In **Glen Mark** a monument commemorates the spot where Queen Victoria once stopped to drink at a spring. To get here, head left on the rough route towards Loch Lee.

Accommodations

Places to stay are thin on the ground in the glen itself, but **Glenesk Caravan Park** (1.5 miles north of Edzell, tel. 01356/648565, tent pitches, electric hookup, and awning from £12) at the beginning of Glen Esk proper is a handy option set in woodland.

Dominating Edzell High Street is the large green-and-white **Panmure Arms Hotel** (52 High St., tel. 01356/648950, www.panmurearmshotel.co.uk, from £50 s, £75 d) with its garishly striped but otherwise comfortable rooms. The steaks are recommended off the hearty restaurant menu; there are a wide variety of accompanying sauces.

Getting There and Away

You can get to Edzell from Forfar on **Stagecoach Strathtay** Bus 21 (about hourly, 40 min.) or from Montrose on **Bus 30** (about every two hours, 50 min.). From Edzell it's about a mile walk to the start of the glen.

GLAMIS AND DEAN WATER

On the map, this 10-mile stream looks as if someone has tried to draw a line between Forfar Loch and Meigle in a very shaky hand with a leaking blue pen (lots of squiggles and splodges). Forfar sits surrounded by small lochs good for fishing and is renowned for its Bridies, meaty snacks encased in pastry. Glamis is a charming 300-year-old village; the jewel in its crown is the magnificent Glamis Castle, a home and haunt of members of the Royal Family for over 600 years. Less visited but every bit as interesting are the series of sculptured stones just beyond Glamis—a fascinating insight into the region's Pictish past.

Sights

Childhood home of the Queen Mother and birthplace of HRH Princess Margaret, **Glamis Castle** (tel. 01307/840393, www.glamis-castle.co.uk, Glamis, 10 A.M.–6 P.M. daily Mar.–Dec., £8 adults, £7 seniors, £5 children) is a forest of grand turreted towers at the end of a long drive through tree-studded parkland. It creates a suitably grand first impression for a place that has reared and been visited by so many high-pedigree royals. The grand rooms include the **Victorian dining room** with its lavish plasterwork ceiling. The nearby **crypt,** where castle minions would eat and sleep, gives an indication of the differences in lifestyle between the servers and the served. The **chapel** is decorated with panels depicting the Twelve Apostles; there can be few more finely finished religious buildings in the country. When you have finished gaping at the finery inside the house, the **grounds** have their own herd of Highland Cattle and an Italian and walled garden. Throughout spring and summer there is the pink of rhododendrons, the yellow of daffodils, and the frequent flash of a red squirrel. Set a whole day aside with a break for lunch in the **Victorian kitchen restaurant.** Glamis Castle even has its own brand of beer.

The **Angus Folk Museum** (Glamis village, tel. 01307/840288, 11 A.M.–5 P.M. Mon.–Sat., 1–5 P.M. Sun. July–Aug., noon–5 P.M.

Sat.–Sun. Mar.–June and Sept.–Oct., £5 adults, £4 seniors) sits behind the Strathmore Arms. Converted 18th-century cottages contain a collection of agricultural exhibits re-creating the rural history of the area. Check out the horse-drawn hearse.

You'll be hard-pushed squeezing Glamis into a day trip, and besides, a visit is best crowned with a few pints of local ale in the evening. Helping you out in this capacity is the **Strathmore Arms Hotel** (The Square, tel. 01307/840248, £65 d), a snug old tavern in the village center.

◖ Angus Sculptured Stones

At **Meigle Museum** (Perthshire, tel. 01828/640612, 9:30 A.M.–12:30 P.M. and 1:30–4:30 P.M. daily Apr.–Sept., £3 adults, £2 seniors), just over the border, is one of the world's most important collections of Medieval sculpture: no fewer than 26 intricately carved Pictish stones dating mainly from the 8th to the 10th centuries A.D. Another elaborately carved slab is at **Eassie** to the east of Meigle. The stone is in the old churchyard. As at Aberlemno Sculptured Stones, a protective cover is put on during the winter season.

Forfar

Forfar had a reputation for burning witches in the 17th century; now it is best known for its Bridies, the Scottish version of the Cornish pasty. Two main places in town do them, and opinion is strongly divided on whether **Saddlers** (35 East High St., tel. 01307/463282) or **McLarens** (8 The Cross, tel. 01307/462762) does them best. With your snack in hand, beat a hasty retreat; Forfar is a shabby place with nothing to detain the visitor.

Getting There and Away

Being so near Forfar, Glamis is quite well connected. **Bus** Service 20/22/22A connects Glamis with Dundee and Kirriemuir four times per day. Bus service 57 runs hourly Monday–Friday from Dundee to Meigle and on to Perth.

St. Andrews and Northern Fife

Golf has been going strong in St. Andrews for six centuries and attracting well-to-do visitors ever since. There's also a good university here (Scotland's first), traditionally frequented by the wealthy English (recently including Prince William), which accounts for the eclectic selection of Britain's rich wandering around. As the Birthplace of Golf, a lot of town is devoted to courses and lavish hotels, but St. Andrews is large enough absorb all this and offer every visitor something. There are well-preserved historical buildings and plenty of chic places to eat and drink. This is a polished, touristy town though: Don't expect to get chatting to locals, and do expect to pay through the nose for everything.

SIGHTS

It's hard to separate St. Andrews and golf, especially with the world's oldest **golf course** lying by the seafront in town. Golf has been played on the links here since around A.D. 1400, and watching golfers (many of them professionals) perform under crowd pressure is an amusing pastime.

British Golf Museum

An almost essential accompaniment to the history-steeped Old Course, this museum (Bruce Embankment, tel. 01334/460046, 9:30 A.M.– 5:30 P.M. Mon.–Sat., 10 A.M.–5 P.M. Sun. Apr.–Oct., 10 A.M.–4 P.M. daily Nov.–Mar., £5.50 adults, £4.50 seniors) tells you all you ever wanted to know about golf, from history's celebrated players to how a golf ball is made. The galleries of golfing through the ages show how the game has changed and, in some senses, stayed exactly the same over the centuries.

St. Andrews Castle and Visitor Centre

Follow the windy path from the Golf Museum along to The Scores, lined with attractive old houses and leading to St. Andrews Castle (tel. 01334/477196, 9:30 A.M.–5:30 P.M. daily Apr.– Oct., 9:30 A.M.–4:30 P.M. daily Nov.–Mar., £5

adults, £2.50 children), the former home of the bishops of St. Andrews and one-time headquarters of the Church of Scotland. The original 13th-century building is all but demolished thanks to the Wars of Independence; the spread-out ruins are now mostly from the 16th century. Be sure not to miss the Bottle Dungeon carved out of solid rock or the long tunnel dug underneath the castle during a siege in an attempt to destabilize the walls. If you're planning on doing the rounds of the historical buildings, buy the joint castle-cathedral ticket (£7 adult, £3.50 child), which will also allow entrance to the Cathedral.

St. Andrew's Cathedral

The magnificent ruins of St. Andrew's Cathedral (tel. 01334/472563, 9:30 A.M.–5:30 P.M. daily Apr.–Oct., 9:30 A.M.–4:30 P.M. daily Nov.– Mar., £4 adults, £2 children) once represented the largest cathedral in Scotland. One of the best views of the town is from its St. Rule's Tower.

Tours

Meet outside the Greyfriars Hotel for St. Andrews' very own **Witches Tour** (tel. 01334/655057, 7:30 P.M. Thurs.–Fri. year-round, £7).

ENTERTAINMENT, EVENTS, AND RECREATION

Most of the snazzy places in town are as much restaurants as bars; specific drinking places can be hard to find. St. Andrews has the hectic program of events you would expect of a vibrant, historic town, but most visitors are in town for Scotland's best golfing. Playing here is a true test of skill and a trip through history to the very roots of the sport.

Pubs and Theaters

The **Old Castle Tavern** (22 South Castle St., tel. 01334/474977) is an atmospheric but tiny place for a drink. Otherwise, the **Inn on North Street** (North St., tel. 01334/473387) is the

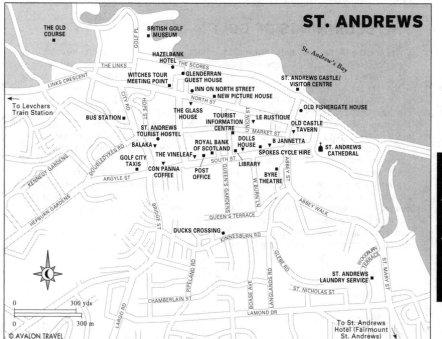

ST. ANDREWS

best bet—old, dark, and traditional and including the lively **Lizard Lounge.**

For film, check out the **New Picture House** (North St., tel. 01334/473509); for theater head to **The Byre Theatre** (Abbey St., tel. 01334/475000, www.byretheatre.com). Both are stylish, welcome diversions from all the golfers and tourists everywhere (they're less conspicuous in subtle light during performances).

Events

As befits an ancient town, St. Andrews has plenty going on. Standing out is, of course, July's **Open Golf Championship** (www.open-golf.com) held in many towns throughout Scotland but guaranteed to be on the historic courses in town about every six years.

Named first and foremost after the saint, not the town, **St. Andrews Festival** takes place for a week over St. Andrews Day (November 30). If you're intrigued by Scotland's patron saint and want to discover what it means to the Scots (an excuse for a party, basically) then you might want to be part of this extravaganza of dance and drama, arts and craft exhibitions, and food and drink. The Byre Theatre sells tickets for events.

Golf

The **Old Course at St. Andrews Links** (greens fee £125) is one of Scotland's toughest; it's right in the town center, and there are lots of intrigued tourists watching you if you mess up your shot. The **New Course** (£65) was laid out in 1895; expect hidden greens and sudden winds. Winds can also prevail at challenging **Eden Course** (£35), while **Balgove Course** (£12) is ideal for beginners.

Cycling

Spokes (37 South St., tel. 01334/477835) has a branch in town, renting bikes by the hour, half day, or full day.

THE BEGINNINGS OF GOLF

China and the Netherlands both lay claim to the origins of golf; much of Europe was playing variants of the sport by the Middle Ages. In the 15th century the Dutch knew the game as "Kolf" and the English as "Goff." Why Scotland is credited with being the birthplace of the game owes much to the sandy, rolling grassy ground that characterizes Scotland's east coast. In those days, "Gowf" was hitting a pebble around with a stick in the sand dunes — the rolling ground helped matters. Some of the most controversial moments in early golfing also took place in Scotland: King James IV complained as early as 1452 that it was side-tracking his men from archery practice and banned the game several times. In 1567 Mary, Queen of Scots was widely criticized for playing a round only two days after the murder of her husband. However, James VI of Scotland (later I of England) and his own passion for the sport played a key role in the permanent establishing of golf as a Scottish institution — no longer was it the sport of miscreants. Lovers of the game began to get together for tournaments, and at Leith in Edinburgh the first recorded international golf match took place. By the beginning of the 18th century, St. Andrews was established as a "metropolis of golf" with an enterprising local family, the Robertsons, credited as being the first professional golfing manufacturers. Soon golfing equipment was being shipped to America, and the news of Scotland as a golfing mecca spread across the globe.

a game of golf on the Old Course at St. Andrews

© LUKE WATERSON

ACCOMMODATIONS

The golfing sect ensure there's a wide choice of accommodation; they also ensure most of it is extremely expensive. Places can get booked up at any time of year, so phone ahead if you want to stay.

Under £50

Thank goodness for the **St. Andrew's Tourist Hostel** (Inchape House, St. Mary's Pl., tel. 01334/479911, www.standrewshostel.com, dorms £14); there's a big jump in lodging prices if you can't get a bed here (and that can be tough). The hostel is colorfully done up with a lounge, TV and video room, and free tea and coffee. It has a good central location.

£50-100

Dating from around 1650, **Old Fishergate House** (35 North Castle St., tel. 01334/470874, £40 pp) is one of the oldest houses in town, a stone's throw from the castle. Done up with a rosy pink, the two en suite rooms (surely the biggest this money can buy) have their own sitting rooms and make for a cozy stay. You can order a continental breakfast of cold meats and cheeses if you can't manage the traditional Scottish option.

The three unusually furnished rooms in Victorian **Ducks Crossing** (Dempster Terr., tel. 01334/477010, Mar.–Oct., £35–50 pp) include pictures of rabbits and ducks—just what you need as you wake up in the morning. The tangle of garden is a cluster of flowers with its own burn (brook).

There's a refreshingly individual feel to **Glenderran Guest House** (9 Murray Pk., tel. 01334/477951, www.glenderran.com, £35–60 pp), so close to the blander chain hotels jostling for position around the Old Course. The five en suite rooms, decorated in royal reds and whites, are spread out over three floors; downstairs is a guest lounge for evening mingling. Try the Inverawe kippers for breakfast. Winter golf packages are available.

Over £100

It was from a bath in **Hazelbank Hotel** (28 The Scores, tel. 01334/472466, www.hazelbank.com, from £86 s, £127 d) that golfer Bobby Locke was called to be presented with the 1957 Open Championship trophy after fearing he would be disqualified. This former tea planter's house has seen plenty of notable guests over the years, enough of a testament to the quality of its accommodation. Try to get one of the four bay-windowed rooms with views over the bay. Rates are significantly less November–April.

Rooms at **The Inn on North Street** (North St., tel. 01334/473387, from £50 pp) are special—proof that you don't have to be a bland hotel to offer creature comforts. Whether your end-of-the-day dream is lying between crisp linen sheets watching DVDs or relaxing in a hot tub, this place can make it come true. It's every inch the ultimate traditional hostelry—dark wood, open fires—but with facilities as modern as they come.

FOOD

There are a wealth of eating establishments in town—over 40 at the last count.

Cafés, Tearooms, and Snacks

For a good cup of Fair Trade coffee, tea, or orange juice and a cake, head to popular **Con Panna Coffee Shop** (203 South St., tel. 01334/479289, mornings and afternoons). It's a good people-watching spot, and they sell the coffee they serve in packages if you get hooked. The premier ice cream venue in town, with over 50 flavors and over 100 years of experience, is **B Jannetta** (31 South St., tel. 01334/473285, www.jannettas.co.uk). There's also a café of the same name next door.

Scottish/International

With high wooden beams, polished wooden tables, and evocative landscape and seascape paintings on the walls, **The Vineleaf** (131 South St., tel. 01334/477497, 7–9:30 P.M. Tues.–Sat.) gets the balance right between trendy Scottish and traditional Scottish. Two courses are £21.95; the gourmet menu focuses on seafood and game with some vegetarian options.

With an open kitchen/bar, bare stone walls,

DUNDEE, ANGUS, AND FIFE

and an outside patio on the upper floor, **Glass House** (80 North St., tel. 01334/473673, www.houserestaurants.com, lunch noon–4 P.M., early evening menu 4–6:30 P.M.) is a sleek addition to the local dining scene and surprisingly inexpensive—you can have a two-course lunch for £5.95. Stone-baked pizzas are done exquisitely here, as are the evening pasta dishes, all £6–10.

Some of the best food in St. Andrews (like oak-smoked duck) is to be had just out of it at this charming but pricey **Grange Inn** (Grange Rd., tel. 01334/472670, Tues.–Sat. and Sun. afternoons). It's a 17th-century inn overlooking St. Andrew's Bay. Mains are around £15.

French
On a cobbled side street, cozy **Le Rustique** (5 College St., tel. 01334/475380, 11 A.M.–late) serves the best French cuisine in town. Meals are £4.95–14.95, with a range as equally suited to a lunchtime bite at an outside table as to an evening meal.

Asian
Elegant, award-winning **Balaka** (3 Alexander Pl., tel. 01334/474825, www.balaka.com, noon–3 P.M. Mon.–Sat., 5 P.M.–1 A.M. daily) is an Indian and Bangladeshi restaurant serving filling curries from £8.50. In case you wanted proof of the freshness of the ingredients, there's over an acre of herb garden at the back fueling the dishes; the owner is a keen gardener and happy to supply people with fresh herbs.

INFORMATION AND SERVICES
Tourist Information
The **TIC** (70 Market Square, tel. 01334/472021, 9:30 A.M.–5 P.M. Mon.–Sat.) is open year-round; if you haven't booked your accommodation you can head here for some help. During summer it's open on Sunday as well and until 7 P.M. other days.

Communications
Free Internet access is available at the library (Church Sq., tel. 01334/659378, 9:30 A.M.–5 P.M. Mon., Fri., and Sat., 9:30 A.M.–7 P.M. Tues.–Thurs.).

Money
There are numerous banks in town along South Street and High Street, like Royal Bank of Scotland (113 South St., tel. 01334/472181).

Laundry
For a launderette, head to **St. Andrews Laundry Service** (14b Woodburn Terr., tel. 01334/475150). Most hotels and guesthouses here will do laundry.

GETTING THERE AND AWAY
Bus 99 runs four times per hour to Dundee (35 min.). St. Andrews has no train station but **Leuchars station,** five miles northwest has hourly connections to both Edinburgh (1 hr., £10.60) and to Dundee (one to three per hour, 10 min., £3.90). From Leuchars, bus 99 as well as 94 and 96 will take you into St. Andrews for under £2, although for Dundee you might as well stay on the bus.

For connections between St. Andrews and the East Neuk of Fife fishing villages, **Stagecoach Fife 95** (one to two hourly, 50 min. to Elie) makes the rounds to Crail, Anstruther, Pittenweim, and Elie.

GETTING AROUND
For a taxi, call **Golf City Taxis** (tel. 01334/477788); it's about £10 from the town center to Leuchars station. For car hire, you're better off heading to Dundee.

◖ FALKLAND
On the edge of the little-visited Fife Regional Park, the Royal burgh of Falkland sits below heathery hills and has a gloriously isolated feel. King James II first used Falkland Palace as a hunting lodge, and the impressive palace buildings still dominate its one main street. The remnants of the once-booming linen weaving industry are also scattered across the village around a series of steep, narrow streets.

Sights
It's hard to miss the soaring walls of **Falkland Palace** (High St., tel. 01337/857397, 10 A.M.–5 P.M. Mon.–Sat., 1–5 P.M. Sun. Mar.–Oct., gift

© LUKE WATERSON

DUNDEE, ANGUS, AND FIFE

the main square in Falkland

shop open throughout year, £10 adults, £7 seniors), transformed by King James V into this example of classic renaissance architecture in the early 16th century. Mary, Queen of Scots would often come here to wander the wooded grounds and relax from her hectic life in Edinburgh. By the 19th century it had fallen into disrepair, when the Crichton-Stuarts purchased keepership of the palace and repaired rooms to an acceptable standard. Sir Walter Scott passed by in 1800 and was distinctly unimpressed, but had he seen the subsequent refurbishment the palace would have met even his high standards. The **chapel** and adjoining **tapestry corridor** are the undoubted highlights. Today the palace is part plush and part ruin. The **royal tennis courts** in the grounds, also built by James V, are supposedly the world's oldest.

A short, steep walk leads up from the village to East Lomond Hill, with great views from the grassy summit.

Accommodations and Food

Burgh Lodge (Back Wynd, tel. 01337/857710, dorms £12) is one of the best budget accommodation options in all Scotland. It's a big, informal house offering nine rooms of varying sizes far more reminiscent of a rambling manor house than a hostel (only one is a dorm in the traditional backpacker sense). There is a self-catering kitchen, a common room stocked with games and DVDs with a blazing fire, and an enclosed garden. It's closed during winter.

The cozy en suite rooms at the **Covenanters Hotel** (High St., tel. 01337/857163, £20–35 pp) look out on the delightful main village street and have sparkling clean bathrooms. The real reason to come here is the food. The restaurant serves up authentic Italian pizza from a wood-fired oven—something you don't get to taste every day in Fife. There's a cozy bar area and plans to include a deli; the owner's wife is Italian so this promises to be a real treat, too.

The **C Pillars of Hercules** (by Falkland off A912, tel. 01337/857749, www.pillars.co.uk, 9 A.M.–6 P.M. daily), a café in the woods on a farm just north of Falkland, serves the best organic food for miles around.

There are few things more appealing than sitting with a cappuccino and a brownie watching squirrels cavorting in the treetops. There's a very good organic shop, too. On a bright day in autumn you won't find a more magical place for refreshments anywhere else in Fife.

Getting There and Away

Like much of the rest of the world, public transport seems to pass Falkland by. Bus 36 runs about every hour between Glenrothes in Fife and Perth via Falkland and Auchtermuchty. To Glenrothes is 20 minutes, Perth is one hour and five minutes.

East Neuk of Fife

The undoubted jewels in the crown of Fife are the whitewashed East Neuk fishing villages, with their 300-year-old cottages tumbling down steep hillsides to harbors that time seems to have passed by. Visitors come here to soak up the peace and quiet, wandering the tranquil twisting streets or the gorgeous beaches, but the top priority should be sampling the freshly landed seafood. Watching the fishing boats coming in of a morning is a spectacle in itself—then nip along to one of the classy restaurants to have the catch served to you.

ANSTRUTHER AND VICINITY

The largest and most-visited of the East Neuk fishing villages, Anstruther spreads out some way. It has a long, attractive waterfront and the best old pubs for miles around concealed within a sharply twisting warren of streets. The main attraction is the Scottish Fisheries Museum, which encapsulates the history of the area's fishermen.

Sights

Housed in a collection of the town's oldest buildings, the **Scottish Fisheries Museum** (Harbourhead, tel. 01333/310628, www.scotfishmuseum.org, 10 A.M.–5:30 P.M. Mon.–Sat., 11 A.M.–5 P.M. Sun. Apr.–Sept., 10 A.M.–4:30 P.M. Mon.–Sat., noon–4:30 P.M. Sun. Oct.–Mar. £5 adults, £4 seniors) has been growing in size since its founding in 1969. Take your time exploring the complex; it's divided into different periods of fishing history, brought to life with photographs and artifacts. There are some truly incredible sights:

the haunting chapel commemorating fishermen lost at sea and a 78-foot Zulu fishing boat. Moored nearby is the highlight: *The Reaper,* a Fifie sailing herring drifter, one of those that ruled these waters over the last 200 years. Tourist information is available.

Just off Anstruther's coast lies the rocky **Isle of May** with the remains of a 12th-century monastery and of three lighthouses (including Scotland's oldest). A host of wildlife including gray seals and puffins can also be seen. There's one sailing per day to the island (Apr.–Sept.) with the *Isle of May Princess* (tel. 01333/310103); tickets can be purchased from the kiosk at Anstruther harbor.

Accommodations and Food

Accommodation of any kind is hard to come by in Anstruther, budget accommodation even more so.

The Grange (45 Pitanweem Rd., tel. 01333/310448, Mar.–Nov., £30–35 s, £60–70 d) is an Edwardian villa set back from the main road. It has four comfortable rooms (three en suite) and the big bonuses of a wonderful sun lounge for guests to relax in and a shrub-screened back garden complete with sundeck.

The detached Victorian (**Spindrift Guesthouse** (Pitanweem Rd., tel. 01333/310573, www.thespindrift.co.uk, £55–76 d) offers eight en suite rooms, including one done up by the original owner of the house—a tea clipper captain—as the replica of a ship's master cabin. There's a comfortable guest lounge with an honesty bar as well as a small library, lots of board games, and an award-winning breakfast made extra special by having the morning papers to peruse.

In a former bakery right on the harborfront, **The Waterfront** (18–20 Shore St., tel. 01333/312200, www.anstruther-waterfront.co.uk, £20–38 s, £40–76 d) has one of the best locations in town. It doubles as a guesthouse with self-catering facilities. Light spacious rooms have the feel of artists' studios, and downstairs, the equally modern glass/timber restaurant offers all the traditional favorites (Cullen Skink, Fisherman's Pie) in pretty classy surroundings.

If you eat fish and chips only once during your time in Scotland, let it be at the **Anstruther Fish Bar** (42–44 Shore St., tel. 01333/310518, www.anstrutherfishbar.co.uk, 11:30 A.M.–10 P.M.). The first good sign is that it's nearly always packed—with locals. The second is that you can watch a video of the fish you'll be eating being caught, meaning the wait is easily the most enjoyable of any takeaway around. Third: when the food comes, you can taste the freshness. If there's no room in the lively restaurant, just take your spoils down to the harbor outside. There's fantastic ice cream, too.

The wonderful 16th-century **Dreel Tavern** (16 High St. West, tel. 01333/310727, lunch and dinner daily) is the most atmospheric place around to dine, with stone walls, a cozy open fire, and dark wood beamed ceilings (as well as a bright conservatory). Pub favorites like prawns in garlic butter or a classic cheese ploughman's lunch start at £5.95. There is an excellent range of single malts and cask-conditioned ales.

Getting There and Away

Stagecoach Fife Bus X95 connects Anstruther and all of the East Neuk villages with St. Andrews.

⬛ CRAIL

It doesn't take long to realize why Crail is something of an artist's haunt—17th- and 18th-century houses lined with flower-bedecked gardens, sloping steeply down to cluster around a picturesque harbor. It's a colorful village enhanced by a number of galleries and craft shops that capture the magical light of the place. The **Crail Arts Festival** runs for two weeks at the end of July, including pottery classes, puppet-making, dance, and story-telling.

Sights

Four miles west of Crail at the village of Troywood, the labyrinthine **Scotland's Secret Bunker** (tel. 01333/310301, www.secretbunker.co.uk, 10 A.M.–5 P.M. Mar.–Oct.) within the grounds of a farm house is built 100 feet underground and encased with 15 feet of reinforced concrete. Had nuclear war broken out, this is where key government members and military personnel would have taken refuge. It's a great place to explore and relive those incredibly devious times of the Cold War.

Galleries and Crafts

Crail is a haven for craftspeople and artists, and the fruits of their labors are displayed in premises across the village. **Crail Potteries** (75 Nethergate, tel. 01333/451212, www.crailpottery.com, 9 A.M.–5 P.M. Mon.–Fri., 10 A.M.–5 P.M. Sat.–Sun.) has a flower-filled yard full of colorful pots and fruit trees, while on the road to the harbor in a refurbished 17th-century fisherman's cottage is **Crail Harbour Gallery** (tel. 01333/451896, www.crailharbourgallery.co.uk, from 11 A.M. Mon.–Sat. Mar.–Oct.). Not only is there a gallery in the cellar here; there's also a delightful tearoom from where you can survey the artwork.

Accommodations

Sauchope Links Holiday Park (the Links, tel. 01333/450460, www.caravan-leisure-park.co.uk, Apr.–Oct., 2-man tent £14–18) is an attractive park right on the rambling rocky shore north of Crail. It's big enough to find your own peaceful pitching spot and has a heated swimming pool and on-site shop.

Barnsmuir Farmhouse (Barnsmuir, tel. 01333/450342, £20–30 s, £40–60 d) is primarily a horse-riding school—a cheery old

DUNDEE, ANGUS, AND FIFE

rambling farm with creaking uneven floors, large rooms, and a deep bath to soak in. The very jolly owner will do anything to make your stay an enjoyable one and doesn't adhere to any of the petty rules many bed-and-breakfasts seem to. The farmhouse is between Anstruther and Crail on the A917 just after the gatehouse of an old lodge on the left (from Crail, it's just before the lodge, on the right).

C The Marine Hotel (tel. 01333/450207, from £25 s, £35 d) is a whitewashed, flower-festooned hotel. Ten rooms with private bathroom get great views down across a private garden to the wild beach.

Information

The seasonal **TIC** (tel. 01333/450869, 10 A.M.–1 P.M. and 2–5 P.M. Mon.–Sat., 2–5 P.M. Sun. June–Sept., weekends Apr.–May) is in Crail Museum and Heritage Centre.

PITTENWEEM AND ST. MONANS

St. Filan came to Pittenweem in the 7th century to convert local Picts to Christianity. He set himself up in a cave in the village; legend has it that he had a luminous left arm so he could work in the dark. Most of the action today goes on in the harbor below; it's the main center of the East Neuk fishing industry, and catch is landed most mornings to be sold at the Fish Market. Pittenweem and St. Monans have an air of authenticity to them as a result. There's less of the tourist gloss of neighboring Anstruther and Crail here but every bit as much charm.

Sights

St. Filan's Cave (Cove Wynd) contains the well and altar allegedly used by the saint. Get the key from the **Gingerbread Horse Coffee Shop and Gallery** (9 High St., tel. 01333/311495, 10 A.M.–5 P.M. Mon.–Sat., noon–5 P.M. Sun.), where you may also want to stop off for a snack.

Accommodations and Food

You're better off heading to Anstruther or Crail for a place to stay: most options here

are self-catering (check www.pittenweem-accommodation.com). You could also try one of the three rooms at **St. Abb's House** (4 St. Abbs Cres., tel. 01333/311964, www.stabbshouse.co.uk, £25 pp).

Heron Gallery and Bistro (15a High St., tel. 01333/311014, lunch noon–2:30 P.M.) is the best spot for gooey cakes and does great toasted sandwiches and jacket potatoes (£3–5.50) as well as more filling lunches. The walls are festooned with colorful, mostly harbor-inspired paintings. Being a seaside village, there are also good fish dishes, like smoked mackerel pâté and toast (£3.95).

C The Seafood Restaurant (16 West End, tel. 01333/730327, www.theseafoodrestaurant.com, noon–2:30 P.M. and 6–9 P.M. Mon.–Sat., 12:30–3 P.M. and 6–9 P.M. Sun., closed Mon.–Tues. in winter) is a special place offering gourmet cuisine along a quiet, picture-postcard seaside village street. The smoked salmon comes from the smokehouses down the road; the lobsters are caught off the Isle of May visible from the restaurant windows. The outside terrace is opened in decent weather. A two-course lunch menu is £21; the three-course evening menu is £35.

ELIE AND EARLSFERRY

The twin burghs of Elie and Earlsferry sit on either side of one of the best beaches in the area. Once some of the richest communities in Scotland due to their trade in salted fish, they are now popular places for water sports due to their sheltered waters and sandy bay. **Elie Watersports** (Elie Harbour, tel. 01333/330962, www.eliewatersports.com) offers reasonable rates for instruction in water-skiing, canoeing, and windsurfing; it also has pedal boat hire.

You can walk along the cliffs east of the village up to **Lady's Tower** (open year-round) built for Lady Janet Anstruther as a bathing house in the 18th century. Lady Janet liked to swim naked in the sea below the tower; she sent a bell-ringer around Elie to warn the townsfolk to keep away, although this often had the opposite effect. Also on the road to the

© LUKE WATERSON

sunset over the beach at Elie

harbor at Elie is the blue-and-white **Ship Inn** (tel. 01333/330246, www.ship-elie.com, rooms £40 pp) offering five rooms with stunning sea or lighthouse views, warming bar meals and one of the only British pub cricket teams to play on the beach.

Southern Fife

The ancient kings of Scotland were once crowned and buried at Dunfermline, the region's main town; despite having been industrialized and agriculturalized, Southern Fife's nationally important heritage remains to be explored. Many pass by on their way to more acclaimed places farther north, but there are architectural delights in store for those who linger: Dunfermline Abbey and Culross Palace. On the gentle, emerald-green coast every field seems like a golf links, and safe, sandy swimming beaches lie concealed beneath fringes of trees.

DUNFERMLINE AND VICINITY

The "Auld Grey Toon" of Dunfermline gets some bad press but it's really not such a nasty place. The fascinating historical buildings and museums have not been wiped out by the plague of ugly industrial developments, and the town boasts one of the most gorgeous urban parks in Scotland. On the coast east of Dunfermline are some gorgeous swaths of golden sand and cliffs flanked by woods that make for great walking.

Sights

The **Andrew Carnegie Birthplace Museum** (Moodie St., tel. 01383/724302, www.carnegiebirthplace.com, 11 A.M.–5 P.M. Mon.–Sat., 2–5 P.M. Sun. Apr.–Oct., free) follows the story of the onetime richest man in the world, and the cottage where the Carnegie family lived before emigrating to the United States. A working

Jacquard handloom is displayed on the ground floor; it's a fitting tribute to the rise of the bobbin boy and telegraph operator who went on to become a multimillionaire and the Steel King of America. Carnegie did a lot of good with his considerable wealth: his funds had paid for half the libraries in the United States built before 1919, as well as 660 throughout the U.K. and Ireland.

Dunfermline Abbey and Palace (tel. 01383/739026, 9:30 A.M.–5:30 P.M. daily Easter–Sept., 9:30 A.M.–4:30 P.M. daily Oct., 9:30 A.M.–4:30 P.M. Sat.–Thurs. Nov.–Easter, £3.70 adults, £3 seniors) has been a religious site since the 11th century, when King Malcolm II married Queen Margaret in a ceremony on the site. That nemesis of Scottish historical buildings, Edward I, destroyed the abbey in 1302 during the Wars of Independence. Robert the Bruce helped with funds for its rebuilding: he's buried in the abbey. Today the abbey is in quite a ruinous state, as is the palace. They're well worth an exploration, though, particularly under the palace kitchens. In total, six former kings of Scotland are buried here.

Known locally as the glen, **Pittencrieff Park** (year-round) is a wild spot, encompassing sweeping gardens, nature trails, and a statue of Carnegie, who donated the park to the Dunfermline people.

Aberdour easily wins the competition of the prettiest town on the stretch of coast near Dunfermline (although the competition is feeble). **Aberdour Castle** (tel. 01383/860519, 9:30 A.M.–5:30 P.M. daily Apr.–Sept., 9:30 A.M.–4:30 P.M. Sat.–Wed. Oct.–Mar., £4 adults, £3 children) is a fortified house worthy of exploration. The walled gardens are a blaze of color in summer. Aberdour also has a very pretty and popular **beach,** good for an ice cream and a game of **putting** on a sunny day.

Accommodations and Food
Davaar House Hotel and Restaurant (126 Grieve St., tel. 01383/721886, www.davaar-house-hotel.com, £40 s, £70 d) is a traditional detached Victorian villa with 10 rooms, all en suite, with antique furnishings.

You'll definitely want to relax of an evening in the lounge with its comfy red chairs hugging the fire; there's also a bar well stocked with single malts.

At Hawkcraig Point near Aberdour, the **Forth View Hotel** (tel. 01383/860402, www.forthview-hotel.co.uk, from £35 s, £55 d) is tucked at the foot of the cliff below the car park down a steep track. It's just you, the surf, and the seabirds here; you really feel cut off from the mainland. Rooms get sea views but not all bathrooms are en suite. You may want to sample the restaurant with its fresh fish–oriented menu.

At the art deco Carnegie Hall Theatre, **Tiffany's** (Dunfermline, tel. 01383/602302, 10 A.M.–11 P.M. Thurs.–Sat., 10 A.M.–3:30 P.M. Mon.–Wed., always open 2 hours before any theater performance) is a very modern place with great views down to the River Forth. For seating areas, choose from the conservatory, beer garden, or terrace. Bread-based snacks are available, like the bacon and brie ciabatta (£4.95), as are mains like pan-fried salmon or venison sausages (£6.50).

Information
The regional **TIC** (1 High St., tel. 01383/720999, 9:30 A.M.–4 P.M. Mon.–Fri.) is a good source of local information. It's open year-round but opening hours are subject to change.

Getting There and Away
Dunfermline is very well connected and a likely transfer point if you want to explore Southern Fife. A new bus station in Queen Anne Street was up and running in 2008.

Hourly **Scottish Citylink buses** go to Edinburgh (35 min., £5) and Dundee (1 hr. 35 min., £7.90). Likewise, there are three trains hourly to Edinburgh and two hourly to Dundee (change at Inverkeithing, about 1 hr. 20 min.). Note that Dunfermline has two train stations, Dunfermline Town and Dunfermline Queen Margaret; either is good for Edinburgh.

Stagecoach Fife Service 7 will get you from Dunfermline east to Aberdour (half-hourly, 35 min.) en route to Leven. Aberdour also has regular, direct trains to Edinburgh.

CULROSS

It's a pity the people that built the charming, colorful houses of Culross aren't still around; they could do lots for modern architecture. On the banks of the industrialized Forth valley and hidden from the main road beneath steeply wooded hills, Culross is Scotland's most stunning collection of 16th- and 17th-century buildings.

Sights

The **National Trust for Scotland** (tel. 0844/493 2189) has preserved (and owns) the village's old buildings, including the mustard-

© LUKE WATERSON

a side street in Culross, a colorful 300-year-old village

colored **Culross Palace** (noon–5 P.M. daily June–Aug., noon–5 P.M. Thurs.–Mon. Apr.–May and Sept., noon–4 P.M. Thurs.–Mon. Oct.). The palace fruit and herb garden offers great views over the Culross rooftops to the Forth. Even the BP refinery at Grangemouth looks good from here. A steep £8 admission also includes entry to the nearby **Townhouse** (guided tour only). A wander of the steep cobbled streets lined by pastel-colored, curved-walled cottages hemmed by well-tended gardens should include the ruined 13th-century **Culross Abbey** sitting half a kilometer above the town.

Food

The charming **Red Lion** (tel. 01383/880225, food served noon–9 P.M.) is the village pub, with a bar pulling a fine pint of ale and a wood-paneled restaurant distinguishing itself with fine salads and a ploughman's/herdsman's lunch for £5.50. Also handy in the sustenance department is **Biscuit Café** (tel. 01383/882176, www.culrosspottery.com, 10 A.M.–5 P.M. daily), claiming to be open every day of the year. How does sitting munching organic cakes in a conservatory overlooking one of the prettiest gardens in Culross sound?

Information

The pottery shop in the village center by the Mercat Cross doubles as a friendly **TIC,** also open year-round.

Getting There

Dunfermline–Stirling buses sometimes call at Culross (Palace). Service 78 will take you there every two hours from either Dunfermline or Stirling.

DUNDEE, ANGUS, AND FIFE

PERTHSHIRE

From the undulating red sandstone of the Ochill Hills near the Gleneagles Hotel to the vividly purple and red gardens of Perth and the high green moorland forests by Pitlochry in the north, Perthshire is a place of colorful extremes. Framing the picture-perfect panoramas at every turn are the region's trees, for which it is deservedly renowned. It was here in the 18th century that modern-day forestry began. Ancient arboreal giants lace the landscape—huge ranks of sequoia more reminiscent of the Canadian Rockies than of Scotland and gnarled yews around in the days of Pontius Pilate.

It's Perthshire's tracts of trees that make its main attractions extra special. You'll find them fringing Scone Palace, the fortress at the heart of Scottish history, where ancient kings of Scotland were crowned. Literature buffs won't want to miss the wood at Birnam, the very one that rose up to defeat Shakespeare's Macbeth, the last Gaelic king of Scotland. Pale green in spring and brilliant amber in autumn, forests add a lush coating to the hills, carpet the valleys, and make this one of Scotland's bonniest regions. This, after all, is where the lowlands meet the Highlands: The region straddles the Highland boundary fault and provides the kind of views Scotland shows off to the world on shortbread tins. Mountains mingle with gentle pastures, hiding some of Scotland's most classic castles and many of its finest distilleries.

The north of Perthshire, rising steeply to meet the Highlands, is the main draw of the area. The main settlement, Pitlochry, promotes itself as the gateway to the Highlands. Rising to back its claim is the grand castle at Blair

© LUKE WATERSON

HIGHLIGHTS

◖ Scone Palace: Stroll round Scone Palace, where ancient kings of Scotland were crowned, and round the day off watching a polo match (page 240).

◖ Perth's Café Quarter: Soak up the summer sun in the sophisticated café quarter of this handsome county town (page 244).

◖ White-Water Rafting: The stretch of water from Loch Tay down to Grandtully will get the pulses of the most hardy canoeist racing with its mix of magnificent scenery and thrilling rapids (page 254).

◖ Birnam Wood and the Hermitage: Tour Britain's most majestic trees and a gorgeous 18th-century planned nature trail at

Birnam, culminating in the Hermitage, a 200-year-old folly (page 257).

◖ Edradour Distillery: Perched picturesquely above Pitlochry, Scotland's smallest distillery still makes the country's most eclectic single malt whisky with a team of just three workers (page 261).

◖ Blair Castle: A grand abode with Europe's only remaining private army, this fortress contains finery that contrasts sharply with the wild grounds on which it stands (page 263).

◖ Rannoch Moor: Hike in the glorious mountain plateau wilderness of Rannoch Moor, one of Europe's remotest spots (page 265).

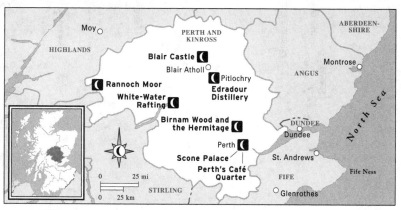

LOOK FOR ◖ TO FIND RECOMMENDED SIGHTS, ACTIVITIES, DINING, AND LODGING.

Atholl and Scotland's smallest, most charming distillery at Edradour. Pitlochry is the place to get your cultural fix, with a superb festival theater boasting panoramic views across the forested valley. Its fish ladder is a great place to watch salmon returning after swimming 6,000 miles to their spawning grounds high above in the tributaries of Loch Tummel. Soon enough, you'll want to follow them, and let the thrills of Highland isolation descend. If you like walking, mountain climbing, or cycling,

you can follow the roads to where they peter out into Rannoch Moor, one of Scotland's last great wildernesses.

HISTORY
Prehistory

Hunter-gatherers had already settled in the area around 8,000 years ago, but civilization in Perthshire really began when the Picts adopted the region as the center of their empire. Many believe the seat of power to have been in the

PERTHSHIRE

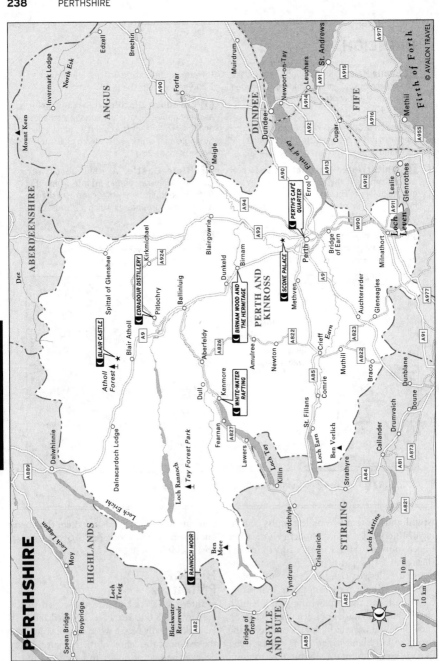

PERTHSHIRE

© AVALON TRAVEL

Strathearn valley west of Perth. The first king of Scotland, Kenneth MacAlpin, was crowned at Scone in A.D. 843; Scottish kings would be crowned at Scone for the next 800 years.

1100-1745

Perth was already a well-established center of culture and trade by the time Alexander I founded an abbey at Scone in the 11th century. Between 1200 and 1300 Perth would rival Berwick and Aberdeen as one of the great trading centers of Britain. As all historically significant places are, however, Perth was vulnerable to attacks; King Edward I of England, the "Hammer of the Scots" invaded in 1296. Despite its prosperity, Perth was never able to establish itself as the true capital of Scotland. King James I and his court spent much of their time in the town but the monarch was murdered in 1437 and replaced on the throne by his six-year-old son James II, whose mother deemed Edinburgh a safer place for the young Royal to have as his power base.

Perth was supportive of the Jacobite uprisings, and the valley of Strathearn to the east became almost a dividing line for where loyalties lay. Northward was where Bonnie Prince Charlie and the Jacobite cause was favored; to the south support lay with the Hannoverian king's government troops. Crieff in Strathearn became notorious as a hanging place for Highland rebels.

18th Century Onward

Improvements made by General Wade to the road network in 1730 enabled other curious individuals to explore the area. Robert Burns was a notable visitor; he urged the Duke of Atholl by means of a poem to plant his lands with beautiful trees. As a result the Duke became widely acknowledged as the father of modern-day forestry. Across the board, there was a buoyancy about Perthshire, and by the late 18th century it was one of the first places in Britain to develop a tourism industry. Queen Victoria toured Perthshire on two notable occasions, which further promoted the tourist trend. Crieff—its hanging days behind it—developed as a luxury Victorian health resort. A hotbed of industry and agriculture kept the region from too much devastation by the Clearances and made it boom with the coming of the railway. Even the World Wars affected Perth far less than other places.

PLANNING YOUR TIME

With four days in Perthshire, your starting point should be Perth, making sure to include a wander around Scone Palace. Most of Perthshire's sights are spread along three valleys where the going can be slow and where the attractions are thick on the ground, so don't try to cram in too much. Another good base is Pitlochry, well poised for trips to some of the regional highlights like Rannoch Moor and Blair Castle. If you have to pick a valley to explore, make it that of the Tay Forest Park. There is a good week's worth of wild moor and woodland walks here, and the farther you go from civilization, the better it gets. Roads in Perthshire are of a high standard, with the exception of roads in the Tay Forest Park. Perth is the cheapest place in the area to stock up on petrol. Public transport is pretty good in Perthshire; you can get to some of the main sights (Perth, Gleneagles, Birnam, Pitlochry, and Blair Atholl) by train. Public transport is poor in the Tay Forest Park.

Perth and Vicinity

Being on the doorstep of Scotland's ancient seat of power at Scone, Perth was for a time in the late 14th and early 15th centuries the capital of the country. It's a quieter place today but wears its history with dignity; there's a buzz to those ancient streets with classy restaurant tables spilling on to the sidewalks and a lively theater scene. It's one of Scotland's most vibrant large towns and is the perfect introduction to any holiday you have in this region. The county town of Perthshire epitomizes everything that is great about the region. It's a handsome, affluent place in a stunning forested valley, brightened by lush flower gardens and studded with castles.

SIGHTS

Most of the main sights are scattered within a five-mile radius of Perth.

Branklyn Garden

It is places like this that make you wish you lived in Perth just so you could go wandering through it every morning. This little garden (116 Dundee Rd., tel. 01738/625535, www.branklyngarden.org.uk, 10 A.M.–5 P.M. daily Mar.–Oct., £5 adults, £4 seniors) has a full spectrum of color of greet the eye: the blue of Himalayan poppies through to the pink of rhododendrons and the red of Acers. You can buy most of the plants you see in the potting shed on-site.

Kinnoull Hill

For the best views of one of Scotland's most attractive towns and the silvery lace of the River Tay flowing through it, head out on the minor road by Branklyn Garden toward Kinfauns. From the car park, woodland trails lead up to the Kinnoull Tower, a folly poised right on the edge of a leafy cliff looking down over the river. Red squirrels play among the pine trees. It's a lovely place to bring a picnic.

◖ Scone Palace

The history of Scone is, in many ways, the history of the country. Scone was the capital

of the ancient Pictish kingdom and later the crowning place of the Kings of Scotland. The palace (Scone, tel. 01738/552300, www.sconepalace.net, 9:30 A.M.–5:30 P.M. Apr.–Oct., grounds close at 6 P.M., £7.50 adults, £4.50 children) is a grand, sprawling red sandstone building set in equally grand grounds. It was built based on a 16th-century design during the early 1800s. The palace rooms are full of worldly finery; highlights include the collection of ivory in the state dining room and the old oak fireplaces of the inner hall. The porcelain in the library is said to be the best collection of its kind of any private house in Britain.

It's all well and good but it's the grounds that make Scone a really special place. Most significantly, close to the Palace is Moot Hill, a sacred site for the best part of two millennia. This is an artificial mound supposedly created with earth brought in the boots of lords swearing allegiance to the king. The tiny chapel on top of the hill is where the crowning of the kings of Scotland took place. Scottish kings from the first king of Scotland Kenneth MacAlpin to Charles II were crowned at Scone, from the 9th century to the 17th century. The grounds form dazzling parkland with 340 kinds of pine tree, a maze, a field of Highland cattle, and lots of strutting peacocks and prospects that make the views back to the palace all the grander.

Located in the grounds of Scone Palace is **Perth Racecourse** (tel. 0783/136 5194, www.scottishpolo.com). There are two grandstands, a clubhouse, and even a wooden horse for practicing. Watching a polo game here is great fun—matches are at 7 P.M. Wednesday, 11 A.M. Saturday, and 2:30 P.M. Sunday. The race course and polo ground are just north of Scone Palace off the A93 north of town.

Elcho Castle

This castle (River Tay near Rhynd, tel. 01738/639998, 9:30 A.M.–5:30 P.M. daily Apr.–Sept., £3 adults, £1.50 children) is one of Scotland's best-kept secrets with its high,

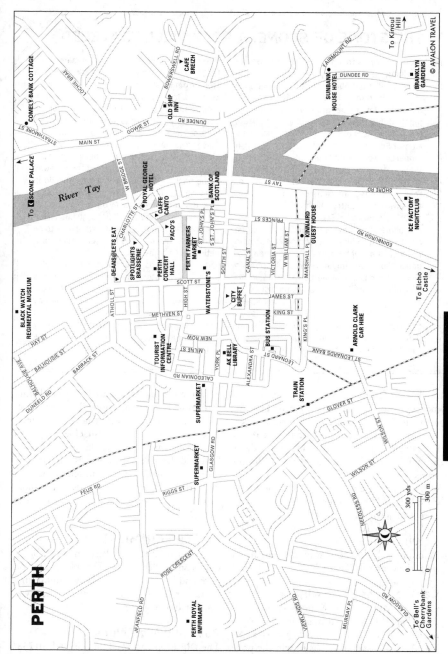

PERTH

PERTHSHIRE

To Kinoul Hill

BRANKLYN GARDENS

© AVALON TRAVEL

SUNBANK HOUSE HOTEL

FAIRMOUNT RD

DUNDEE RD

CAFE BREIZH

BOWERSWELL RD

OLD SHIP INN

DUNDEE RD

ICE FACTORY NIGHTCLUB

SHORE RD

EDINBURGH RD

To Elcho Castle

TAY ST

STRATHMORE ST

COMELY BANK COTTAGE

LOCHIE BRAE

GOWIE ST

MAIN ST

To SCONE PALACE

River Tay

W BRIDGE ST

CHARLOTTE ST

ROYAL GEORGE HOTEL

CAFFE CANTO

PACO'S

DEANS@LET'S EAT

SPOTLIGHTS BRASSERIE

PERTH CONCERT HALL

PERTH FARMERS MARKET

ST JOHN'S PL

ST JOHN ST

SOUTH ST

CANAL ST

PRINCES ST

VICTORIA ST

W WILLIAM ST

MARSHALL PL

PRINCES ST

KINNAIRD GUEST HOUSE

BANK OF SCOTLAND

ATHOLL ST

SCOTT ST

HIGH ST

METHVEN ST

WATERSTONE'S

CITY BUFFET

JAMES ST

KING ST

BUS STATION

KING ST

ST LEONARDS BANK

ARNOLD CLARK CAR HIRE

BLACK WATCH REGIMENTAL MUSEUM

HAY ST

BALHOUSIE ST

BARRACK ST

DUNKELD RD

BALHOUSIE AVE

NEW ROW

MILNE ST

YORK PL

CALEDONIAN RD

AK BELL LIBRARY

ALEXANDRA ST

LEONARD ST

TOURIST INFORMATION CENTRE

SUPERMARKET

TRAIN STATION

GLOVER ST

KING'S PL

FEUS RD

RIGGS ST

GLASGOW RD

SUPERMARKET

WILSON ST

WILSON ST

NEEDLESS RD

To Bell's Cherrybank Gardens

GLASGOW RD

MURRAY PL

VIEWLANDS RD

ROSE CRESCENT

JEANFIELD RD

PERTH ROYAL INFIRMARY

300 yds

300 m

0

0

THE STONE OF SCONE: A ROCK WELL TRAVELED

Stories vary as to what the Stone of Scone originally was: Some say it was the traveling altar of St. Columba during his missionary work in Scotland; some even say it was the biblical pillow of Jacob. Both theories are highly dubious. What is certain is that, from the time of Kenneth MacAlpin, the first true king of Scotland in the 9th century, Scottish monarchs were seated upon the stone during their coronation ceremony. Over the centuries it has come to be the most important piece of rock in Scotland due to its dramatic associations with the country's history.

In 1296 Edward I of England, alias the "Hammer of the Scots," allegedly captured the stone and took it with him to Westminster Abbey in London as a trophy of the Wars of Independence. Some say this never really happened and that monks, hearing Edward was on his way, hid the rock in the river. As part of peace talks with Scotland 32 years later, it was agreed the stone, real or fake, should be returned to Scotland, but this was not done, and when James VI of Scotland and I of England came to the throne and had his court in Westminster,

the stone stayed put. So things remained until 1950 when four Scottish students captured the stone from Westminster Abbey to return it to Scotland. In the process the stone was broken in two and smuggled back in an old car over the border, despite the roadblocks that had been put up. The stone then fell into the care of a Glasgow stonemason who repaired it before it ended up placed in Arbroath Abbey. British police discovered this and escorted the runaway stone back to Westminster. It was agreed in 1996, seven centuries after its wrongful capture, that the stone actually did belong in Scotland. Its new home was in Edinburgh Castle, but even now the stone is unable to rest, due to be transported back to Westminster for any coronation ceremonies.

It is little surprise that the rocky relic is also known as the stone of destiny; its journeys between Scotland and England over the centuries have more or less been paralleled by the ups and downs in Scottish history. The last time the stone was in Scotland, the country was in its heyday – perhaps history is now free to repeat itself.

thick walls, corridors, walkways, and turrets making it a great ruin to explore. The immense main tower house is completely intact, and from outside, you'd be hard pushed to tell it wasn't still lived in. Considering it dates from around 1570, it's remarkably well preserved—there is still plaster on some of the walls. Make sure you look at the doo'cot or dove cote in the grounds; doves would have been a major food source for castle residents of this period. To reach Elcho, turn left from the A912 heading out of Perth just before the junction with the motorway. It's four miles from the center of town.

Cairn o Mohr Fruit Winery

Cairn o Mohr Fruit Winery (Errol, tel. 01821/642781, www.cairnomohr.co.uk, shop open 9 A.M.–6 P.M. Mon.–Fri., 10 A.M.–5 P.M. Sat., 12:30–5 P.M. Sun.) has to win the prize

for the most bizarre attraction in Perthshire and would be only too happy if it got that accolade. It's a winery as you've never seen wineries before: a wonderful ramshackle setup with wine made from anything that grows well in Scotland, from leaves to berries and flowers. See the winemaking process in action and taste the surprisingly delicious results in the shop. Errol is off the A90 heading east to Dundee from Perth.

ENTERTAINMENT

Quiet during the week Perth may be, but it erupts on weekends. There are plenty of good pubs and bars and a lively theater and dining scene. Perth also has a race course where you can watch polo games.

Pubs and Nightclubs

The **Old Ship Inn** (31 High St., tel. 01738/

624929) is an old boozer, traditionally the haunt of actors, musicians, and farmers. It's a great place for a drink with a dark, cozy atmosphere and lots of real ales on tap.

If you feel like dancing, plenty of it is going on at the **Ice Factory** (6 Shore Rd., tel. 01738/630011, www.icefactory.co.uk, 10:30 P.M.–2:30 A.M. Thurs.–Sun.). This is a funky, colorfully decked-out dance club that regularly hosts top DJs. It's more a complex than anything, as there are six bars here. The same people also own the **Loft** on South Street; the entrance fee covers both clubs on some nights. Entrance can be £8–15 depending on who is playing.

Performing Arts and Events
Perth Concert Hall (Mill St., tel. 01738/ 472700, www.horsecross.co.uk) hosts a good variety of music and has a good café/bar (10 A.M.–6 P.M. Mon.–Sat.).

On the first Saturday of each month 9 A.M.–2 P.M. you can sample the fruits (and vegetables) of Perthshire's fertile soils at **Perth Farmer's Market.**

SHOPPING
Perth's town center precincts are pleasant places for a spot of shopping, largely cobbled and pedestrianized.

Antiques
If you like the antique furnishings of the hotel you're staying in and want your own little souvenir to take home, there are few better places to get one than the longest-established family antiques firm in Scotland, **Michael Young Antiques** (Glencarse, tel. 01738/860001, www.michaelyoungantiques.com, 10:30 A.M.–5:30 P.M. Mon.–Sat.). You'll be able to dig out those relics, Scottish and otherwise, to your heart's content. Glencarse is on the A90 to Dundee.

Food
There are several supermarkets at the town center end of Glasgow Road including **Aldi** (21 Glasgow Rd.).

SPORTS AND RECREATION
Polo
Perth Racecourse (Scone Palace, tel. 0783/ 136 5194, www.scottishpolo.com) is Scotland's main polo club. The season runs April–September, with the main cup competitions held in August. There are two grandstands, a clubhouse, and even a wooden horse for practicing. Watching a polo game is a great experience; matches are played on Wednesday evenings (7 P.M.), Saturday mornings (11 A.M.), and Sunday afternoons (2:30 P.M.). The racecourse and polo ground are just north of Scone Palace (on palace grounds) off the A93 north of town.

ACCOMMODATIONS
Perth is a smart town with some smart places to stay. There are any number of decent options in elegant old Georgian houses, particularly along **Dundee Road.** The accommodations listed here offer a little something special.

The rich woodland of the Scone Palace grounds forms the backdrop of the large but nicely divided up **Scone Palace Camping and Caravan Site** (Scone Palace grounds, tel. 01738/552308, tent pitch and one adult £9.85). It can get quite noisy at times but has spotlessly clean facilities.

Comely Bank Cottage (19 Pitcullen Cres., tel. 01738/631118, www.comelybankcottage.co.uk, from £26 s, £52 d) is an elegant, traditional bed-and-breakfast with rooms that would put far more expensive places to shame; they're big, clean, warm, white, and well-furnished with old, dark-wood furniture. Rooms are en suite with TVs. The porridge at breakfast time is a treat.

Bein Inn (Glenfarg, tel. 01577/830216, www.beininn.com, from £50 d) is a country inn with a difference. The owner's passion is live music; the bar, restaurant, and some of the rooms here are decked out in rock memorabilia (they look like clean versions of a grungy teenager's bedroom). The pub is on a busy road, but you'll sleep like a baby in the quiet, average-sized rooms, which get en suite facilities, color TVs, telephones, and views of the woods. The restaurant here serves up good home-cooked food. The inn is south of Perth on the A912 (come off the motorway at junction 9).

The Georgian terraced **Kinnaird Guest House** (Marshall Pl., tel. 01738/628021, www.kinnaird-guesthouse.co.uk, from £40 s, £55 d) is right on the doorstep of South Inch Park. The seven rooms here are lovely, mellow places in gentle whites and blues; this is a country retreat right at the heart of town. Bathrooms are all en suite, and there's an antique-furnished guest lounge. You'll get porridge and a huge cooked breakfast in the morning. The place is nothing exceptional, but it ticks all the boxes for good town center digs.

Staying at the handsome ◖ **Sunbank House Hotel** (50 Dundee Rd., tel. 01738/624882, www.sunbankhouse.com, £79 s, £90 d) with a quiet location above the river Tay, you could easily imagine yourself as a character in a Jane Austen novel. The rooms have an old-fashioned elegance, as does the residents' lounge with its period furniture and long windows. The twist is that the accommodation is full of 21st-century touches like Wi-Fi access and luxury toiletries. The restaurant, run by the joint owner, is full of foodie delights like homemade pasta and oak-smoked salmon. The hotel has private parking and a large grassy garden that secludes it from the hubbub of daily life. Just up the road is **Branklyn Garden,** and the splendid walk up to **Kinnoull Hill.**

The **Royal George Hotel** (Tay St., tel. 01738/624455, www.royalgeorgehotel.co.uk, £75 s, £90 d, £120 suite) is a pocket of tranquility on Perth's handsome riverfront. Rooms mostly look over flower-studded grounds to the river. All are en suite with radio, telephone, TV, and a charismatic elegance to them. All are large and light-filled, but the undoubted highlight is the Chinese Suite, with oriental furniture and its own cinema. As you take your afternoon tea in the sun-filled conservatory, you'll be as taken with this noble old hotel as Queen Victoria was when she visited the establishment in 1848.

FOOD

The best food you eat in Perthshire will be here.

◖ The Café Quarter

Café culture is booming in Perth and on a sunny day the sidewalk tables of the elegant town center cafés entice you with their charm and sophistication. You'll hardly be able to walk a block without seeing a couple of good places to stop off for a coffee and a bite to eat—head for the area around St. John's Kirk for some of the best ones.

Caffe Canto (62–64 George St., tel. 01738/451938, 10 A.M.–5 P.M. Sun.–Wed., 10 A.M.–8 P.M. Thurs.–Sat.) is an airy venue just perfect for a coffee and a snack during the day. It's full of all types chatting and perusing the papers. It does evening meals, too—excellent homemade pasta dishes and risottos—but lacks that cozy restaurant feel so important for a dinner out. Light bites are £2–6, or you could go for the evening deal of a starter, main, and glass of wine for £11–12.

Café Breizh (28–30 High St., tel. 01738/444427, www.cafebreizh.co.uk, 9 A.M.–9 P.M. Sun.–Thurs., 9 A.M.–9:30 P.M. Fri.–Sat.) uses bare stone walls and dark-wood furniture to create the cozy, rustic-but-stylish feel to perfection. This French restaurant is a great place for a light lunch or evening meal. It's popular but laid-back enough to allow a relaxed eating environment. Even solitary diners won't feel conspicuous here. The coffee is delicious, and you can get scrumptious mains like venison with poached pear and blackcurrant sauce. Three-course meals are £13.90.

Other Cuisine

The daily eat-as-much-as-you-like Chinese buffet at **City Buffet** (171 South St., tel. 01738/440055, lunch and dinner daily) is nothing short of excellent—filling, tasty and cheap. Feast for as little as £5.99.

The ◖ **Spotlights Brasserie** (8 North Port, tel. 01738/563032, www.spotlightsbrasserieperth.com, 11 A.M.–2:30 P.M. and 5–9 P.M. Tues.–Thurs. and Sun., 11 A.M.–2:30 P.M. and 5–9:30 P.M. Fri., 11 A.M.–9:30 P.M. Sat.) is a tiny, intimate venue in an 18th-century former dairy: with its wood paneling, wrought iron chairs, cushion-covered old seats, and old

parade to commemorate the end of the First World War, in Perth's Café Quarter

stage memorabilia on the walls it is the kind of restaurant that a city like Edinburgh or London would kill for. The decor gives it away: This is a prime pre-theater dining venue, but Spotlights lets you discover its quiet charms for yourself rather than boast about them. The Scottish/contemporary menu is not too varied but you're not going to mind with this type of ambience. Start off with the oven-baked beef with tomato and mozzarella and progress to the red onion and gruyere cheese tart. Main meals are £12–14. Consider rounding things off with one of the liqueur coffees.

Paco's (3 Mill St., tel. 01738/622290, 9:30 A.M.–11 P.M. Mon.–Sat., 4:30–11 P.M. Sun.) is a fun restaurant with memorabilia-lined walls and fountain courtyard. The Italian-American slanted menu centers on pizzas, pasta, steaks, burgers, and fish; it's solid, filling fare with a fancy touch. Each dish takes several lines to describe: A seemingly straightforward pasta dish like fettucini comes with blackened salmon, pine kernels, spinach leaves, and cream. Mains are £9–14.

Deans @ Let's Eat (77–79 Kinnoull St., tel. 01738/643377, www.letseatperth.co.uk, noon–2 P.M. and 6:30–9:30 P.M. Tues.–Sat.) really kicked off Perth's reputation as a good place to eat, and it's still at the top of its game. The service here is, to a large extent, why this bistro-restaurant is such a big hit. There are cozy sofas to lounge on with a drink while your table is being prepared and always a member of staff to greet you with a sunny smile. With linen tablecloths and an open fire, the restaurant is smart without being overly formal. Mains like the Blairgowrie beef and winter vegetables are fantastic at £15–22.

INFORMATION AND SERVICES

Perth has all the urban facilities you would expect of a county town.

Tourist Information

Perth TIC (tel. 01738/450600, 9:30 A.M.–6 P.M. Mon.–Sat., 11 A.M.–4 P.M. Sun. July–Aug., 9:30 A.M.–4:30 P.M. Mon.–Sat., 10 A.M.–2 P.M. Sun. Apr.–June and Sept.–mid-Oct., 10 A.M.–4 P.M. Tues.–Sat. Oct.–Apr.) is in the handsome Lower City Mills.

© LUKE WATERSON

PERTHSHIRE

PERTHSHIRE'S FAMOUS TREES

Tourist boards have the habit of giving the districts they cover fancy and often rather optimistic titles to attract visitors, but Perthshire County Council's decision to dub the region "Big Tree Country", has to be one of the most appropriate. Trees in all shapes and sizes cover the county, and the nature lover will be hard-pressed to know which arboreal areas are most worthy of a visit.

At **Meikleour** near Dunkeld is the tallest hedge in the world, a 30-meter-high row of beeches. Over at Fortingall in Glen Lyon is what villagers claim is Europe's oldest living thing: the black, gnarled trunk and branches of the **Fortingall Yew**. The tree is said to be somewhere between 2,000 and 9,000 years old. The **hermitage** at Birnam has to be on any tree lover's list; one of the Douglas firs is a candidate for the tallest tree in Britain. There are any number of magnificent trees in the woods at **Birnam,** including the last survivors of the great ancient woodland which in Shakespeare's *Macbeth* was said to move and thereby fulfill the prophesy of the Scottish king's fate. Another tree-rich area is **Diana's Grove** on the Blair Castle estate; the inky green Japanese larches are the ones to gawp at here, checking in at over 150 feet high. Then there is the ancient **Tay Forest Park,** one of the few surviving tracts of the ancient Caledonian pine forest that once covered Scotland. You can stand amidst these timeless trees and imagine life as it must have been in the Highland over 1,000 years ago.

Maps

Waterstone's Bookshop (St. John's Centre, tel. 01738/630013, 9:30 A.M.–5:30 P.M. Mon.–Wed. and Fri.–Sat., 9:30 A.M.–6 P.M. Thurs., 11 A.M.–5 P.M. Sun.) stocks local maps, as well as fiction and local interest books.

Services

The **Bank of Scotland** (50 St. John St., tel. 01738/412600) has an ATM. The High Street also has lots of banks on it.

AK Bell Library (York Pl., tel. 01738/444949, 9:30 A.M.–5 P.M. Mon., Wed., and Fri., 9:30 A.M.–8 P.M. Tues. and Thurs., 9:30 A.M.–4 P.M. Sat.) has a family history section.

If you're in need of medical attention, **Perth Royal Infirmary** (Taymount Terr., tel. 01738/623311) is to the west of town.

GETTING THERE

Perth is well connected by train and bus. It's also where the M90 terminates, so it has good southbound road connections.

Train

Perth is served well by trains to Glasgow (1 hour 10 min., £12.20), Edinburgh (1.5 hrs., £11.70), Inverness (2 hours 5 min., £20.40), Dundee (25 min., £5.90) and also Stirling. One daily direct Inverness service will call at Perth en route from London Kings Cross (London–Perth 6 hours, £105).

Bus

Frequent buses run to Edinburgh and Glasgow (1.5 hrs., £7.70) from Perth. Operators are generally **Scottish Citylink** (tel. 0870/550 5050, www.citylink.co.uk) and also **Megabus** (www.megabus.com) or **Parks of Hamilton** (tel. 01698/281222). Half-hourly buses run to Dundee (40 min., £4.90) which has the nearest airport.

GETTING AROUND
Train

The railway station in Perth is at Kings Place, to the northwest of South Inch Park. You can get to Gleneagles, Dunkeld and Birnam, Pitlochry, and Blair Atholl by train from Perth.

Bus

Buses depart from Leonard Street. Main operators within the Perthshire region are **Stagecoach Strathtay** (tel. 01382/227201, www.stagecoach.com/strathtay) and **Scottish Citylink.**

Taxi

Call **Perth Radio Taxis** (tel. 01738/580058) if you need a cab.

Car Rental

Arnold Clark (St. Leonard's Bank, tel. 01738/442202) does car and van hire from £17 per day for a small car.

South Perthshire

Hilly South Perthshire has two main points of interest for the visitor. Brightening the dull motorway corridor from Dunfermline is Loch Leven, Scotland's largest lowland loch, crowned by a fortress on one of its islands. The Ochill Hills that form the backbone of the region have had their part to play in history. They provided a defense for the Kingdom of Fife and handed Stirling its importance—the city became the main through-route to the Highlands as a result of the hills making other access difficult. Today the hills are a playground for the outdoor enthusiast and shelter one of the most lavish resorts in the country, the Gleneagles Estate.

LOCH LEVEN AREA

With a diameter of about 16 kilometers, Scotland's largest lowland loch seems to sparkle like a piece of tin foil whatever the time of year. A fine castle where Mary, Queen of Scots was imprisoned and a priory decorate the loch's islands. There are some easy, gentle walks around its shores. It's a pity that the ugly housing estates of Kinross threaten to tarnish the western shore.

Sights and Activities

Loch Leven is among Scotland's most renowned trout-fishing lochs. Permits at **Loch Leven Fisheries** (the Pier, Kinross, tel. 01577/863407, www.lochlevenfisheries.co.uk) start from £5 per hour.

The fairytale ruin of **Loch Leven Castle** (tel. 0777/804 0483, 9:30 A.M.–5:30 P.M. daily Apr.–Sept., 9:30 A.M.–4:30 P.M. Sat.–Wed. Oct., last island-bound ferry one hour before closing time) stands on a small wooded island a short way toward the middle of the loch. It's

a 13th-century building with a 14th-century tower fortified by Robert the Bruce, one of the oldest still-standing towers of this sort in Scotland. It was the prison of Mary, Queen of Scots in 1567; she only escaped by agreeing to abdicate (and miscarried to boot). The admission charge including the ferry trip to the island is £4.50 adult, £2.25 child. The ferry departure is from the west bank of Loch Leven, signposted from Kinross.

You can do the short walk along the west shoreline from the car parks to Kinross House, the first Palladian-styled mansion in Scotland. It's not open to the public, but **Kinross House Gardens** (Loch Leven shore, www.kinross-house.com, 10 A.M.–7 P.M. daily Apr.–Sept., £3) are; they make for a scenic Sunday stroll.

Accommodations and Food

Great for a day trip, Loch Leven is. Great to stay over, it is not, as this will mean basing yourself in depressing Kinross. If you're hungry, you are best off taking a picnic down to the loch side.

Thankfully, **Burnbank** (79 Muirs, tel. 01577/861931, www.burnbank-kinross.co.uk, £33 s, £60 d) is on the outskirts of Kinross, so there's really no need to go into the center at all! You can stay in this popular guesthouse in bright blue-and-white en suite rooms, from where you can gaze wistfully at the Lomond Hills. All rooms get TVs and VCRs. Burnbank was a former mill shop and has a somewhat intriguing, open layout as a result. Homemade bread is a breakfast specialty. To get there, turn off the M90 at junction 6 and turn left on the A9222, headed north. The house is at the end on the right.

It says little for Kinross that its most

GLENEAGLES: HOSTING HIGH SOCIETY AND THE WORLD'S MOST POWERFUL LEADERS

Almost since it opened as a hotel, Gleneagles Hotel has been firmly on the agenda of the rich and famous. It was well established as part of the high-society season by the 1950s: The wealthy would do yachting at Cowes, polo in Deauville, and grouse-shooting at Gleneagles. Renowned golfer Jack Nicklaus created a new PGA golf course on the estate in 1993 to complement the existing courses and underline Gleneagles' reputation as a prime golfing venue. It wasn't just its hotel or golf courses that were getting a reputation, though; it was also becoming a lavish conference venue.

In July 2005 Gleneagles hosted its most important event yet: the annual G8 summit. The occasion had been billed as that when global policy on climate change had to be addressed once and for all. The buildup to the summit was one of the most fraught of recent years. As with all G8 summits, this one was the focus for a variety of different campaigns; the Make Poverty History march in Edinburgh four days before the Summit began was the biggest in Scottish history, with over 200,000 people turning up. On the opening day of the Summit the "Live 8" concert in Edinburgh aimed to bring home to the masses the plight of those in developing countries, to try to force the leaders at the conference into acting to increase aid to impoverished countries. Meanwhile, in the grounds of Gleneagles, U.S. President George W. Bush collided with a policeman while riding his bicycle. He had been waving at the security staff

to thank them for turning up when he lost control of the bicycle and hit the policeman, who needed three months off duty to recover.

Despite vehicles transporting staff and attendees for the Summit being held up by the roadblocks of protesters, and despite the perimeter fence being breached by 200 activists, the Summit went ahead. For all the hype, the meeting of the world's most powerful leaders at Gleneagles was an anticlimax, largely overshadowed by the terrorist attacks in London on July 7. An anti-terrorism stance ultimately dominated the agenda, although world leaders did agree that action needed to be taken to address the debt of developing countries. Plans were drawn up to cancel debt from the poorest nations in the world and to inject a further US$25 billion annually in aid to such countries. However, despite British Prime Minister Tony Blair addressing those present at Gleneagles by saying that climate change was "long-term, the single most important issue we face as a global community," targets to reduce greenhouse gas emissions could not be reached. The best that can be said about the G8 Summit at Gleneagles was that there was finally wide-scale recognition of the problems climate change was causing. Countries like Brazil, Mexico, and China, for example, agreed to make future commitments to improving their environmental policies. The question now is whether all this proposed change will be too little, too late.

pleasant place for a snack is at a motorway service station. However, it would be wrong to tar **Le Jardin at Dobbie's Garden Centre** (Turfhills Tourist Centre, tel. 01577/863327, 9 A.M.–6 P.M. Mon. and Wed.–Sat., 9 A.M.–6:30 P.M. Tues., 10 A.M.–6 P.M. Sun.) with scathing preconceptions. It's a decent pit stop just off the M90 motorway and has a spacious restaurant serving up all manner of goodies. People sit with purchases from rakes to radish seeds on the tables and seem generally content with the home baking, all-day breakfasts, and

baguettes on offer. There's a bunch of local tourist information at the garden center, too.

Getting There and Away
Stagecoach Fife bus 56 runs from Perth to Kinross hourly en route to Cowdenbeath. **Scottish Citylink buses** between Edinburgh and Perth will stop off in Kinross.

OCHILL HILLS
The Ochills may not be the highest range of hills in Scotland, but they are some of the

© LUKE WATERSON

Gleneagles estate

most distinctive. Evidence of Perthshire's position astride the Highland boundary fault, they are cut from old red sandstone and glow russet from the rock or yellow from the bracken-coated slopes. The hills cradle the lavish resort of Gleneagles, a world-class hotel and conference center with several championship golf courses.

Gleneagles

Once described as the "eighth wonder of the world," Gleneagles (Auchterarder, tel. 0800/389 3737 U.K. only, 866/881-9525 U.S. only, www.gleneagles.com, from £295 d) is a sumptuous gray hotel that's not only a place to stay but a place to have a holiday. In its gently rolling, tree-dotted grounds are three of Scotland's leading golf courses, one of its leading restaurants, one of the world's major conference centers, a health spa, and the opportunity to fish and shoot, walk and horseback ride, or participate in falconry. The grounds were designed by one of the most famous landscape gardeners of all time, Capability Brown, in the 18th century. Bedrooms here (232 of them) include every degree of luxury you could hope for and use of all hotel facilities. It's £65 for a three-course meal in the celebrated Andrew Fairlie restaurant (reservations recommended). When you've slept and eaten, you can see if your wallet will allow any of the other indulgences on offer. Gleneagles is a great family destination, with loads of things to keep children amused.

Getting There and Around

Gleneagles has its own railway station, on the Perth to Stirling line. Perth **trains** come around twice hourly (10 min.). There are five **buses** daily (Mon.–Sat.) between Gleneagles, Auchterarder, and Perth.

Strathearn Valley

Starting with the genteel Victorian holiday resort of Crieff, lovely Strathearn is in many ways the ideal Scottish valley. It sports a distillery, some imposing castles, and a loch—and for all that, gets relatively few visitors. Historically, it was always a prosperous place: during the 19th-century Clearances it was one of the prime destinations for impoverished Highland families to resettle. The valley runs along the Highland boundary fault and benefits from a gorgeous mix of grassy, rolling lowland hills and sharper, more severe mountains. In the sunshine the entire area glows gold-green at the bottom and russet-red in the heathery uplands. What with all the fine hotels in the vicinity, you might find yourself wanting to stay and pamper yourself awhile, whether with picnics in the countryside or beauty treatments in the refined resorts.

CRIEFF AND VICINITY

The Victorians made Crieff into a fashionable holiday resort and to a large extent, this smart old-fashioned town has changed little. Tumbling down from wooded Knock Hill to the Strathearn River, it remains a town of proud 19th-century houses where people come to try the latest health, beauty, and relaxation treatments. The surrounding scenic countryside is good for walking and picnicking and contains some of Perthshire's most bizarre and fascinating attractions.

Sights

Famous Grouse is Scotland's leading blended whisky; find out why at **Glenturret Distillery** (The Hosh, near Crieff, tel. 01764/656565, 10 A.M.–4:30 P.M. daily Jan.–Feb., 9 A.M.–6 P.M. daily Mar.–Dec., £7.50), better known as the Famous Grouse Experience. You'll get a unique tour, seeing not only how Glenturret single malt is produced but also how blended whiskies are made. It's an ego-tickling insight into how Famous Grouse is at the top of the liquor game, but you will get plenty of chances to taste the product. There are whisky "nosings" in the depths of the distillery for significantly additional fees. You'll find the experience at a scenic location just outside Crieff on the Comrie Road.

In a charming white building in lonely wooded Innerpeffray village is **Innerpeffray Library** (tel. 01764/652819, http://innerpeffraylibrary.co.uk, 10 A.M.–12:45 P.M. and 2–4:45 P.M. Wed.–Sat. and 2–4 P.M. Sun. Mar.–Oct., at other times by prior appointment, £5 adults, children free), one of the most remarkable collections of books in Scotland. This library was founded in 1680 as Scotland's first free public lending library, flourishing for three centuries until its closure in 1968. It contains extremely rare 16th- and 17th-century books. Today you can appreciate this special spot and browse the books once again. In the trees nearby are the ruins of a chapel, also worth exploring.

Northeast of Crieff, mesmerizing **Glen Almond** has all the key ingredients to a great day out in the Scottish countryside: glinting rivers, undulating fields grazed by sheep, and towering grassy hills breaking out of forested valleys. The whole of the glen makes for a good drive, with plenty of grassy places to pull over for a picnic.

Accommodations and Food

The large Georgian **Galvelmore House** (Galvelmore St., tel. 01764/655721, www.galvelmore.co.uk, from £52 d) has a good reputation for offering comfort at a decent price. The rooms here are enormous with feisty, original furnishings ranging from crimson to peach; they're all en suite, with extra touches like ornaments and writing desks that make this place a real home away from home. For some quality "you" time, hang out in the wood-paneled resident lounge by the open fire.

There are seven pale pink-and-white rooms at the characterful **Tower Hotel** (81 East High St., tel. 01764/652678, www.towerhotelcrieff.co.uk,

© LUKE WATERSON

Glen Almond, the perfect place for a picnic

£30 s, £60 d). It's a distinctive whitewashed building at the top of town, originally designed to house medical students. Only five are en suite but if you can grab one of the back rooms facing out on Crieff tumbling away down the hillside, you won't be complaining. With all the formality of most places in Crieff, this is a refreshingly down-to-earth, family-run accommodation option. On a summer's day, take your beer out into the garden, the best drinking spot in town. There will often be a boule match on.

Whether it's a traditional room you want (red and gold drapes and cornicing) or a more contemporary feel to your accommodation (white and minimalist), the **Crieff Hydro** (tel. 01764/651670, www.crieffhydro.com, £45 s, £100 d) can sort you out. It's developed a reputation over 140 years as a place to come and relax, and there are a range of activities on the 900-acre estate, ringed by the slopes of Ben Vorlich. A set three-course evening meal in the formal Victorian restaurant is £24.50.

So how does being pampered in a castle sound? Everything about **Roundelwood Health and Lifestyle Spa** (Drummond Terr.,

tel. 01764/650088, www.roundelwoodhealth-spa.co.uk, £90 d) spells "relax." The rooms are wide, white, soothing spots with Molten Brown toiletries in the en suite bathrooms. There's a restaurant with lots of healthy alternatives to the greasy, traditional Scottish fare and every kind of treatment and therapy under the sun. The spa does packages of treatments and/or accommodation from £99.

Delivino (King St., tel. 01764/655665, 9 A.M.–6 P.M. daily) is a snazzy deli/bistro that's a great spot for breakfast, with a number of healthy options like bagels, bruschettas, and huge bowls of fruit and yogurt, all lovingly presented and served alongside Crieff's best cup of coffee. There are some tasty looking morsels in the deli section if you're hunting for picnic things.

Information

Crieff TIC (Town Hall, tel. 01764/652578, 9:30 A.M.–6:30 P.M. Mon.–Sat., 10 A.M.–4 P.M. Sun. July–Aug., 9:30 A.M.–5 P.M. Mon.–Sat., 10 A.M.–2 P.M. Sun. Apr.–June and Sept.–Oct.) also contains a fun exhibition named Stones,

Stocks and Stories—evidence Crieff was not always the tranquil place it is today.

The **Bank of Scotland** (1 Galvelmore St., tel. 01764/654056) has an ATM.

Getting There and Away
Bus 15 runs between Crieff and Perth hourly Monday–Saturday. There are seven services on Sunday.

COMRIE AND LOCH EARN
The enchanting village of Comrie spreads itself out along one main street, proudly sitting on the Highland Boundary fault. There's been more seismic activity here over the last 200 years than anywhere else in Scotland. As you head up the valley, the lush greens and springy turf of the rolling, livestock-grazed fields change to darker, starker mountain scenery. On one side is Breadalbane Ridge and on the other the sheer slopes of Ben Vorlich, both with wonderful walking. Down on Loch Earn is the opportunity to try your hand at water sports.

Sights
Accessed via a steep hump-backed bridge on the western edge of Comrie in the middle of a peaceful grassy field stands the **Earthquake House** (year-round), monument to Scotland's past geological turmoil. Comrie, as it dubs itself, is the earthquake capital of the country. For visitors from California, Japan, or indeed almost any other part of the world, the seismic activity seen by Comrie could be described as very slight, but that is all part of the charm of this place. A quake occurred near here in 1597 that was felt as far away as Atholl and Breadalbane (neither point is more than 40 miles away). Built originally in the 19th century, the Earthquake House was restored in 1988 as the center of earthquake monitoring in Britain. Visitors can look at old and new seismological equipment and find out about the history of earthquakes in the vicinity.

The walk up wooded **Glen Lednock** to the **Deil's Cauldron** (year-round), a spectacular waterfall, is a great advert for what Strathearn can offer the outdoor enthusiast. At the top is the granite **Melville's monument,** an obelisk commemorating Henry Viscount, the first Earl of Melville. The best time to go is in early autumn, when the whole route is a blaze of reds, gold, and greens. It's about 8 kilometers there and back. You can start from the village car park in the west of Comrie (after the A85 kinks sharply to the right).

Sports and Recreation
Just on the junction of the A84/A85 is **Lochearnhead Watersports Centre** (Lochearnhead, tel. 01567/830330, www.lochearnhead-water-sports.co.uk, center open 9 A.M.–8 P.M. daily mid-May–Sept., 10 A.M.–6 P.M. Sat.–Sun. Apr.–May and Sept.–Oct.), one of the country's best places to try your hand at water sports. It's a friendly, relaxed, well-equipped center where you can have a go at windsurfing, canoeing, and sailing. Water-skiing is also popular here, with lessons starting at £20 for 15 minutes. For £5 you can bring your own craft and launch it here; remember that if you want to bring a boat with a powerful engine you should seek permission first. You can refresh yourself at the wonderful Lochside Café on-site.

Comrie Croft (Braincroft, tel. 01764/670140, www.comriecroftbikes.co.uk) is a great place to hire a bike; you can ride straight off into the hills on off-road trails from here. Day hire starts from £16.

Accommodations and Food
When you stay at the spacious converted former croft house of ◖ **Comrie Croft** (Braincroft, tel. 01764/670140, www.comriecroft.com, dorm beds £15, £35 d) in the hills above Comrie, you won't mind what the weather does. Sunshine? You can hire a bike and take to the hills. Rain? You'll relish the opportunity to snuggle up in the huge lounge watching TV or playing board games. The kitchen is first rate, too: large, solid, and well appointed. Then there are the rooms, all clean and en suite with a choice between dormitories and private rooms. You're paying next to nothing for near-perfect views and facilities that surpass a lot of hotels. There

© LUKE WATERSON

Earthquake House, Comrie

is even a small tourist information center and shop on-site. The staff are very competent and know lots about outdoors activities. It's two miles to Comrie from here along the A85.

The exquisite, ivy-coated **Royal Hotel** (Melville Sq., Comrie, tel. 01764/679200, www.royalhotel.co.uk, £80 s, £130 d) is the best rural getaway in a valley full of rural getaways. There are 11 rooms here done up in bright whites and beiges with Molton Brown toiletries; three rooms have four-poster beds. You'll be contented just lying on the beds all day, with perhaps a sojourn to the restaurant here and there. It's a cozy, countrified place to eat, with elegance and light. The rack of roast lamb is good. A three-course dinner is £26.50.

Isolated on the shores of steely Loch Earn, the **Four Seasons Hotel** (St. Filans, tel. 01764/685333, www.thefourseasonshotel.co.uk,

£110 d) is the one glimmer of white in a sea of green forested hills. It's refreshingly modern inside, with large light rooms decorated with findings from the owner's travels to the Far East. There are also some chalets perched up in the trees behind the hotel; you can stay here and still make use of hotel facilities.

Getting There and Away

Hourly buses run to Comrie from Perth (1 hour 15 min.) via Crieff. It's service 15 you're looking out for; some buses will continue to St. Filans on Loch Earn, otherwise change in Crieff or Comrie. The useful Dundee to Oban service operated by **Scottish Citylink** (www.citylink.co.uk) runs mid-May–early October twice daily via points in Strathearn (3 hours 30 min.). It's a scenic journey and saves changing buses in Glasgow.

Strath Tay Valley

The inky green, wooded sides of this valley channel the waters of the River Tay, at first gently and then violently down its course: producing some of the best white-water rafting rapids in Britain. Strath Tay is as popular with water sports enthusiasts as it is with walkers—and adventure seekers don't have to stop there. The highest mountain in Central Scotland beckons, as does the longest glen. For those who fancy something more sedate, farther downstream are the twin villages of Dunkeld and Birnam. There is a magnificent cathedral here and some of the most awe-inspiring ancient woodland in Perthshire.

ABERFELDY AND LOCH TAY

For all the many attractions in and around Aberfeldy, the main town on this stretch of the Tay is a somewhat shoddy, gray place. It's good as a base to explore the surrounding area, and for precious little else. However, as the proclaimed capital of adventure water sports in the United Kingdom and with gorgeous walking and heaps of archaeology on its doorstep to boot, it's not a place where architectural aesthetics really matter.

Sights

One of several woodsy areas in Perthshire popularized by Robert Burns, the **Birks of Aberfeldy** is a walk culturally as well as aesthetically pleasing. Burns penned "The Birks of Aberfeldie" up here in 1787. He conjures up the image of this dark wooded gorge well: "The foaming stream deep-roarin' fa' us." Burns's Birks flank the thundering waters by the **Moness Falls.** You can start in the center of town; a path goes into the woods from by the Courtyard Restaurant. It's 1.5 miles to the falls.

The **Watermill** (Mill St., Aberfeldy, tel. 01887/822896, www.aberfeldywatermill.com, 10 A.M.–5 P.M. Mon.–Sat., noon–5 P.M. Sun., free) is many things to many people: the Highlands' biggest bookshop, a wonderful upstairs gallery set off by the restored mill workings, and a downstairs reading/café area. It's one of those cultural extravaganzas in the back of beyond in Scotland that never cease to amaze—some top-notch exhibitions go on here. Importantly for Aberfeldy, it's also the saving grace of the gloomy town center.

Of all the ways to come to terms with Scotland's often hard-to-grasp archaeology, the **Scottish Crannog Centre** (near Kenmore, tel. 01887/830583, www.crannog.co.uk, 10 A.M.–5:30 P.M. daily Mar.–Oct., 10 A.M.–4 P.M. Sat.–Sun. Nov., £5.75 adults, £4 children) is one of the best. Crannogs are ancient lochside dwellings dating back as much as 5,000 years ago; evidence of many similar structures has been found all along Loch Tay. At this center you'll find out all about the people who lived in them before actually going into a re-created crannog, jutting out on a wooden platform into the water. This isn't just a pretty face—it's built on the site of an actual crannog and built as much as possible with the materials and in the methods Iron Age people would have used. This is not just one more prehistoric site but an engaging attempt to acquaint the visitor with Scotland's past.

◖ White-Water Rafting

The upper waters of the River Tay, from Loch Tay down as far as Grandtully, have developed a reputation for having some of the finest white-water rafting rapids in the country. Several companies offer rafting trips on the 12-mile stretch of the river from Kenmore on the edge of Loch Tay during season. The trip is gentle for the most part and passes some great scenery before the hair-raising rapids at Grandtully. One of the main companies is **Activity Scotland** (Dunalistair Hotel, Kinloch Rannoch, tel. 01882/632323, www.activityscotland.com), with rafting trips for £40 per person. You can also hire kayaks for use on Loch Tay.

Accommodations and Food

The accommodation at **Dunolly Adventure Outdoors** (Taybridge Dr., Aberfeldy, tel. 01887/820298, www.dunollyadventures.co.uk, beds from £11) is on two sites in leafy Taybridge Drive; best is the 48-bed Victorian house, but there is also a separate 15-bed cottage. Dorms are cozy and carpeted with sturdy pine beds. It's a quiet place understandably popular with water sports enthusiasts: Dunolly Adventures runs rafting and kayaking courses along with a host of other adventure pursuits. It's a good thing those beds are comfy.

Set on the lip of gorgeous Glen Lyon above fields tumbling down into the valley, the one-story farmhouse of **Tomvale** (Tom of Cluny, near Aberfeldy, tel. 01887/820171, www.tom-vale.co.uk, from £24) has oodles of space in its three rooms. Bathrooms have under-floor heating, and the cozy guest lounge is full of snug sofas with a TV and, of course, those gorgeous valley views.

The imposing **Weem Hotel** (Weem, tel. 01887/820381, www.weemhotel.com, £60 s, £90 d) is a gleaming white building dating back to the 16th century; when General Wade was building his famous bridge nearby, this was most likely where he stayed. It's had a bit of a renovation since then. The bar actually seems so cavernous and modern it's almost unwelcoming. Fortunately the en suite rooms are crisp and spick and span without losing their snug feel. The view is of the hills or the pretty courtyard garden. Hearty bar meals are £8–15, and you'll get the best selection of real ales around. There is a fire to warm you up, too.

The █ **Kenmore Hotel** (Kenmore, tel. 01887/830205, www.kenmorehotel.co.uk, £109 d) is supposedly Scotland's oldest pub, dating from 1572. It certainly looks the part: From the moment you catch sight of the black-painted tree trunks that form the entrance way you know you're in for a bit of rural heaven. There are 40 bedrooms, which although well-furnished and done up in warming pinks and whites, disappointingly lack the traditional character of other parts of the inn. For some this could be just the reason to stay—you'll be in a characterful old-world pub with every convenience of the 21st century. Some rooms even have whirlpool baths. Many rooms are also in the lodge across the way. You won't want to pass over the opportunity of downing a pint and even eating in the country's oldest hostelry anyway, regardless of whether you are staying or not. The poet's bar is one of the oldest parts of the place; it was here that guest Robert Burns rushed back to pencil on the chimneybreast a poem he had just been inspired to write while looking out over the Tay. The poem is still there today, as is every inch of the traditional coziness you'd hope for from a Highland tavern.

Choose from a fine leaf tea, cappuccino, or scrumptious slab of cake and sit in the spacious downstairs café of the █ **The Watermill** (Mill St. Aberfeldy, tel. 01887/822896, www.aberfeldywatermill.com, 10 A.M.–5 P.M. Mon.–Sat., noon–5 P.M. Sun.). You're encouraged to take books down with you to read; you can perch at a table or lounge on one of the red sofas. Light bites and snacks are £2–5.

Information

Aberfeldy TIC (The Square, tel. 01887/820276, 9:30 A.M.–6:30 P.M. Mon.–Sat., 10 A.M.–4 P.M. Sun. July–Aug., 9:30 A.M.–5 P.M. Mon.–Sat., 10 A.M.–2 P.M. Sun. Apr.–June and Sept.–Oct.) has lots of useful information.

Getting There and Around

Hourly buses run between Perth and Aberfeldy Monday–Saturday. It's Service 23 you want (one hour 20 min.). On Sunday you can take Service 83, which connects Perth with Aberfeldy and Pitlochry.

Five buses run daily between Aberfeldy and Dunkeld (30 min.), and there are two daily buses running to Blairgowrie (Mon.–Fri.) from Aberfeldy. There are buses on Tuesday (two services) and Saturday (four services) along Strathtay to Kenmore and Killin from Aberfeldy, run by **Caber Coaches** (tel. 01887/820090).

Call **David McDougall** (tel. 01887/820370) for a **taxi** if you don't fancy chancing public transport.

PERTHSHIRE

GLEN LYON

Scotland's longest enclosed glen stretches some 30 miles from Castle Menzies at its eastern end through Fortingall to where the road fades out at Loch Lyon. It's windswept agricultural land in the east and thick woodland in the west, separated by a row of three mountains from Bridge of Orchy on the A82 to the west. The mountains that hem it in are possibly its greatest asset. Few people take the time to explore the far reaches of this dead-end glen; those who do will find themselves alone in a lush valley with only the thundering waters of the River Lyon for company.

Sights

In the churchyard at Fortingall is what local residents insist is Europe's oldest living thing: **Fortingall Ancient Yew** (open year-round). The thing in question is not a village elder but a tree, dated at between 2,000 and 9,000 years old (the lower end of the spectrum is more realistic). Its gnarled old trunk is split into many different smaller branches, a result of Victorians chopping bits of wood off as souvenirs. Pontius Pilate is said to have been born in Fortingall; if that's true, then you are gazing at the same tree that he must have looked at in his early years.

Ben Lawers (north of Loch Tay by Lochan na Larigee) is the highest mountain in the Loch Tay area with a **visitors center** at the foot explaining the geological history of Ben Lawers. Geology thrust it up to 3,980 feet but for local residents this was simply not good enough: in the 1850s a group of men built a cairn on top to guarantee the mountain a height of 4,000 feet above sea level. The cairn has since crumbled but the incredible views from the summit remain. To get to the car park and visitors center from where the walk starts, follow the minor road north from the A827 on Loch Tay or south from the Bridge of Balgie in Glen Lyon. The walk starts at 1,400 feet up; allow seven hours to get up to the top and back.

Accommodations and Food

Smack bang in the middle of the ancient Caledonian pine forest in Glen Lyon is idyllic **Milton Lodge** (Bridge of Balgie, tel. 01887/866318 or 01887/866337, www.miltone-onan.com, £30 s, £60 d) on the site of a Pictish water mill. There are three traditionally furnished rooms here done up in pale colors, which makes them seem even bigger than they are. Two have their own bathrooms with baths or showers. Complimentary tea and cakes are served in the lounge by the open fire. You might have need of the excellent evening meals in these isolated parts; they're £15, and there is always a veggie alternative. In the grounds is Milton's very own waterfall and lots of resident animals.

In summer months, you can get refreshments at the charming **Bridge of Balgie Post Office/ Tearoom** (Bridge of Balgie, tel. 01887/886221, 10 A.M.–5 P.M. daily Apr.–Oct.).

Getting There and Away

Caber Coaches (tel. 01887/820090) run two buses on a Saturday between Aberfeldy and Fortingall. For other destinations in Glen Lyon, charter a bus from Caber Coaches or call a taxi.

DUNKELD AND BIRNAM

These two pretty villages facing each other across the River Tay have long been pulling in the tourists for precious little reason. Dunkeld has a great cathedral and a well-preserved 18th-century center, while Birnam makes its tourism bucks from being mentioned as the site of the moving wood in Shakespeare's *Macbeth*. The ancient woods above the villages, however, particularly the Hermitage northwest of Dunkeld, are awe-inspiring places: Beatrix Potter was one of those inspired and wrote *The Tale of Peter Rabbit* while on holiday in the area. The Birnam Institute in Birnam features displays on her life and works. Dunkeld is the more pleasant of the two places to spend the night. It has a bank with an ATM, a couple of shops, and even a seasonal TIC in its vast car park.

Dunkeld Cathedral

The main event in Dunkeld is the cathedral (by River Tay west of Cathedral St., www.dun-keldcathedral.org.uk, 9:30 A.M.–6:30 P.M. daily

© LUKE WATERSON

Dunkeld town center

Apr.–Sept., 9:30 A.M.–4 P.M. daily Oct.–Mar., free), one of the most splendid cathedrals in Scotland. Its location on a tree-studded riverbank helps; you're screened from the rest of Dunkeld here and transported back centuries even before you've stepped inside. The cathedral's history as a religious site goes back to A.D. 848, when Kenneth MacAlpin, King of the Scots, rebuilt the previous wattle-constructed monastery in stone. Check the fragments of these 1,000-year-old cathedral building blocks in the choir. The building is a mix of Norman and Gothic in style and has some fine stained glass, such as the Great East window. In the Chapter House Museum (same hours as above) you can get to know the famous people connected with the Dunkeld and Birnam area: the legendary fiddler Neil Gow, the Duke of Atholl, and Beatrix Potter. There is an 11 A.M. Sunday service.

◖ Birnam Wood and the Hermitage

If you want to see Birnam's ancient trees, you can do a wonderful **walk** touring the best of them. Start at Birnam railway station and head under the A9 road to Birnam village (an alternative start point and a better parking point). Continue straight ahead by the side of the Tap Inn car park to follow signs to **Birnam Oak,** last remainder of the ancient woodlands that allegedly rose against the last Gaelic king of Scotland, Macbeth. It's propped up by lots of wooden crutches so you won't miss it. For good measure, the Douglas fir standing nearby is the tallest tree in Britain. The path continues along the riverside to the **Hermitage.** An 18th-century planned walk through woodland leads to the folly built to entertain visitors by the Duke of Atholl. By the fast-tumbling River Braan, this is a magical spot indeed. Return by heading up to cross Rumbling Bridge in Strathbraan before descending again through woods. Allow 3.5 hours for the round-trip walk. The Hermitage can also be accessed by car off the A9 one mile northwest of Dunkeld; there is a large car park and wildlife information boards.

Meikleour

This little village east of Dunkeld gets into the record books for having the highest hedge

Dunkeld Cathedral

in the world. It's a 100-foot-high (30-meter) beech hedge, flanking the main A894 road. Meikleour has a good hotel for a drink once you've done your hedge-spotting.

Accommodations and Food

You could fall on the beds at **Waterbury Guesthouse** (Birnam, tel. 01350/727324, www.waterbury-guesthouse.co.uk, £42 s, £62 d) and they're so soft there would barely be a sound. The carpeted rooms of this distinctive turreted guesthouse are done in pinks and yellows. You'll find color TVs and Arran Aromatics toiletries in the en suite bathrooms. Breakfasts in the large rustic dining room could involve smoked salmon from the Dunkeld Smokehouse.

The rooms at the **Royal Dunkeld** (Atholl St., Dunkeld, tel. 01350/727322, www.royaldunkeld.co.uk, £90 d), a former coaching inn, are not nearly as impressive as the outside and downstairs of the hotel would have you believe. Even so, all the signs of an enjoyable stay are there: plenty of space, comfortable

beds, en suite bathrooms, color TVs, and direct-dial telephones. All of this is presented in neutral tones that may not win medals for innovative design—but might pick up a few prizes for coziness. Two-course evening meals are £15; the best place to eat is in the snug 1809 bar.

If only all live music in Scotland was as good as that featuring on a regular basis at the **Taybank** (Tay Terr., Dunkeld, tel. 01350/727340, www.thetaybank.com, food noon–9 P.M., bar until late). This hotel on the banks of the Tay is a great place to come for a drink. If you do, you'll almost certainly witness a spontaneous jamming session between local or not-so-local musicians, who are enticed from miles around to play here to their hearts' content. Now under new management, the place seems to be continuing in much the same vein. You can get good pub grub here, too. Expect all manner of performers to sound all manner of instruments until the wee hours.

Birnam Wood

Darjeeling (3–5 Atholl St., Dunkeld, tel. 01350/727427, www.darjeeling-dunkeld.com, noon–11 P.M. daily Apr.–Sept., noon–2 P.M. and 5–11 P.M. daily Oct.–Mar.) is a pine-decked, contemporary-style Indian restaurant: it's the best place to eat out in Dunkeld or Birnam. There's a wide range of Indian food available, including a mean chicken jalfrezi. A two-course lunch is £5 and evening mains kick off at £9–12.

Getting There and Away

Trains run from Dunkeld and Birnam station (in Birnam) to Perth (every 1–2 hours, 20 min.) and on up north to Inverness. There are seven trains daily Monday–Saturday to Glasgow, with a few Sunday services.

Stagecoach Strathtay runs two buses (Service 62, 30 min.) on Tuesday, Wednesday, Friday, and Saturday between Dunkeld and Blairgowrie.

Highland Perthshire

Many people rate Perthshire as the loveliest part of all Scotland, and when you come here you'll understand why. The Victorians championed this area as the epitome of Highland charm; it was relatively easy to access, and the rewards were unsurpassable views. Dense tracts of the ancient Caledonian pine forests that once covered all of Scotland carpet the valleys of Perthshire's own little bit of the Highlands. They frame sparkling lochs, which in turn wrap themselves around mountains. As you get farther away from Pitlochry, the bustling village that acts as capital of the area, the remoteness kicks in more strongly. Distances between villages grow and soon you'll find yourself in the uninhabited expanses of Rannoch Moor, one of the most barren-looking places on the planet. Wherever you go, you'll develop a tendency to keep one hand on your camera; vistas have a habit of opening up every few minutes, and just by ideal picnicking spots, too. This is a wild part of the world, but not always a desolate one. You'll find distilleries, castles, and one of the most interesting theaters in Scotland.

PITLOCHRY

In a verdant part of the Tummel Valley sitting on either side of a wide river, Pitlochry has benefited from an idyllic location and from being connected early in its history to one of General Wade's main military roads. Mountains rise enticingly behind the village: first Ben Vrackie and beyond that the peaks of the Cairngorm National

Park. If you headed north from Pitlochry you would encounter one of the largest areas of Britain untouched by roads. The village itself gets almost city status in this remote neck of the woods, with plenty of shops, restaurants, and far more swarms of tourists than many cities generally see. It's not many places, after all, where you can go to the theater and overlook mountains, or watch salmon trying to jump upstream.

Scottish Hydro-Electric Visitor Centre and Fish Ladder

Right at the southern end of Loch Faskally is a large hydroelectric dam (tel. 01796/473152, 10 A.M.–5 P.M. daily July–Aug., 10 A.M.–5 P.M. Mon.–Fri. Apr.–June and Sept.–Oct., £3 adults, £2 seniors, children free). The dam is an eyesore, but far more entertainingly, you can watch the salmon jumping up the river. The dam might make Pitlochry residents complain, but it presented far more of an obstacle to the 54,000 salmon that make the annual pilgrimage up the River Tummel to their spawning grounds in Loch Tummel. They now scale the rapids by a series of salmon pools, complete with resting places where they are not fighting against the current. Because you can get so close to the hardworking fish, watching them is a very special spectacle.

Pass of Killiecrankie

This deep, dramatic wooded gorge (off the B8079 north of Pitlochry, tel. 01796/473233,

PERTHSHIRE

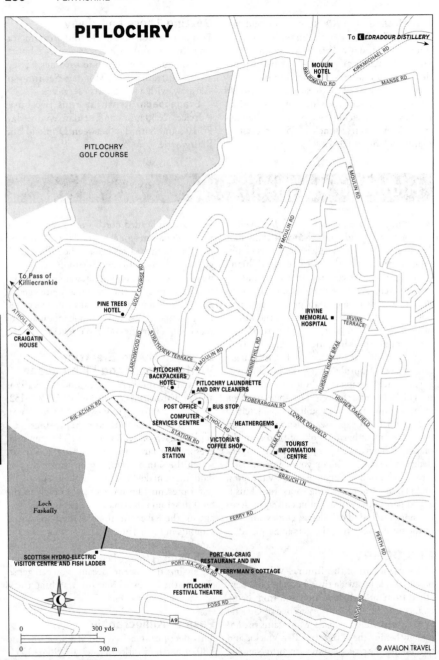

PITLOCHRY

To **EDRADOUR DISTILLERY**

MOULIN HOTEL

KIRKMICHAEL RD
BALEDMUND RD
MANSE RD

PITLOCHRY GOLF COURSE

E MOULIN RD

W MOULIN RD

To Pass of Killiecrankie

PINE TREES HOTEL

GOLF COURSE RD

IRVINE MEMORIAL HOSPITAL

IRVINE TERRACE

ATHOLL RD

CRAIGATIN HOUSE

LARCHWOOD RD

STRATHVIEW TERRACE

W MOULIN RD

BONNETHILL RD

NURSING HOME BRAE

HIGHER OAKFIELD

PITLOCHRY BACKPACKERS HOTEL

PITLOCHRY LAUNDRETTE AND DRY CLEANERS

TOBERARGAN RD

LOWER OAKFIELD

BIE-ACHAN RD

POST OFFICE   BUS STOP

COMPUTER SERVICES CENTRE

ATHOLL RD

HEATHERGEMS

ELM CT

STATION RD

TRAIN STATION

VICTORIA'S COFFEE SHOP

TOURIST INFORMATION CENTRE

BRAUCH LN

Loch Faskally

FERRY RD

PERTH RD

SCOTTISH HYDRO-ELECTRIC VISITOR CENTRE AND FISH LADDER

PORT-NA-CRAIG RESTAURANT AND INN

PORT-NA-CRAIG RD

FERRYMAN'S COTTAGE

PITLOCHRY FESTIVAL THEATRE

BRIDGE RD

FOSS RD

A9

0   300 yds
0   300 m

© AVALON TRAVEL

www.perthshirebigtreecountry.co.uk, visitors center 10 A.M.–5:30 P.M. daily Mar.–Nov., site open year-round) has lots of lovely woodland trails, on the site of the Battle of Killiecrankie, the most important conflict in the first of the Jacobite uprisings in 1689. You can walk down the gorge to see Soldier's Leap, where Duncan Macbean, a soldier pursued by the Jacobites, supposedly leapt 5.5 meters (18 feet) across the River Garry to reach safety. At the visitors center you'll find information on the battle and on wildlife in the gorge—look up for red squirrels and down for otters.

Edradour Distillery

Edradour Distillery (tel. 01796/472095, www.edradour.co.uk, 9:30 A.M.–6 P.M. Mon.–Sat., 11:30 A.M.–5 P.M. Sun. Mar.–Oct., 9:30 A.M.–4 P.M. Mon.–Sat., 11:30 A.M.–4 P.M. Sun. Nov.–Dec., 10 A.M.–4 P.M. Mon.–Sat., noon–4 P.M. Sun. Jan.–Feb., free) is Scotland's smallest single malt whisky distillery. It's a rarity in this age of mass production, which even traditional Scottish whisky distilleries are affected by—an outfit relying on the whisky-making abilities of just three men. Edradour produces so little whisky that it's barely able to sell its bottles commercially. Certainly, if you leave Perthshire without having sampled some, you may never see a bottle again. It's a rare malt whisky and a highly sought-after one, and the distillery in itself is a unique place. The brightly painted window frames of the white-washed, cottage-like buildings look out on a grass-banked stream; the tour here is pleasing on the eye as well as the tongue.

Entertainment and Events

Pitlochry Festival Theatre (Portnacraig Rd., tel. 01796/484600, tel. 01796/484626 box office, www.pitlochry.org.uk, café/restaurant 10 A.M.–9 P.M. daily summer, 10 A.M.–5 P.M. daily winter) promised to be such a great concept: a theater with cutting edge city sophistication in the heart of the Highlands. Opinion is rather divided on whether the festival theater has been a success. It's not the most beautiful of buildings, and some would say it looks

downright ugly in the lush green fields by the River Tummel. But inside it's an undeniably impressive venue with a huge glassy café/bar/restaurant good for a bite to eat even if you're not seeing a show. The year-round program isn't the least bit provincial; theater and opera companies from around Europe regularly play here.

For a unique Highland gift, the factory of **Heathergems** (22 Atholl Rd., tel. 01796/474391, www.heathergems.com) behind the TIC in Pitlochry makes gems out of heather. Yes, really. The heather stems are dried and compressed into hard, colorful orbs. There is a great selection of designs; you can bring your piece of heather home without fear of it ever wilting. A shop is on-site.

Pitlochry has a year-round program of events, but **Enchanted Forest** (www.enchantedforest.org) is the most magical—a light and sound show in the woods near the village. In 2007, the theme was creation with lights and sounds to illustrate magma and volcanoes. The lights illuminate woodland as you have never seen it before, and the streets of Pitlochry are full of music and partying. It takes place in mid-October to early November. Check the website for details from July onward.

Sports and Recreation

You can hire bikes at **Escape Route Bike Hire** (3 Atholl Rd., tel. 01796/473859, £18 per day).

Accommodations

You would have to be desperately unlucky not to find a room in accommodation-rich Pitlochry.

Pitlochry Backpackers Hotel (tel. 01796/470044, www.pitlochrybackpackershotel.com, dorm beds £13, £28–32 d) is a great, creaking old former hotel that has been taken over as a hostel. You get pretty much the same standards of faded luxury as before, only now at a fraction of the price. It's some of the best value budget accommodation in all Scotland, as most of the rooms are doubles rather than dorms. There are hot showers, towel rental from £0.20, and hearty breakfasts served until late for a pittance. It's right in the center of Pitlochry, too, with a lively games room/common room invariably full of people who appear to live there. If you're touring the Highlands on the bare minimum, don't expect every hostel to be this good.

The snug stone **Ferryman's Cottage** (Portnacraig Rd., tel. 01796/473681, www.ferrymanscottage.co.uk, £30 pp) has been around 300 years; it was originally built to help with the cattle that would have been swum across the river here. It's a bright, well-cared-for place with homey triple and twin rooms available. Rooms are en suite with color TVs, with light color schemes. There is a guest lounge with an open fire, but what you are really getting for your money here is the best riverside view in Pitlochry and a quiet location on the theater side of the river. In the summer there's even a mini ice cream parlor outside.

Tucked away in an early Victorian house in secluded grounds to the north of Pitlochry is the closest you'll get to a boutique hotel in this neck of the rather dense woods: **Craigatin House and Courtyard** (165 Atholl Rd., tel. 01796/472478, www.craigatinhouse.co.uk, £70 d). The rooms look like showrooms: you can hardly believe they're for sleeping in with their Gothic blood-reds, zebra stripes, and loft conversions. Suffice it to say that this is ultra-modern layered upon the ultra-old. Try the apple pancakes with grilled bacon and maple syrup served up at breakfast.

The **Moulin Hotel** (11–12 Kirkmichael Rd., Moulin, tel. 01796/472196, www.moulinhotel.co.uk, from £70 d) has been a coaching inn for over 300 years. Rooms here are lavish, with many having clan tartan themed furnishings. All are en suite or with private bathrooms. As befits such a traditional hotel, you can stay in a four-poster bed here, but whichever room you stay in there is a feeling you're on top of the world. The towels are soft and the views are incredible; the Moulin sits high on the hills above town in a conservation village. The resident lounge looks out over the babbling Moulin burn. The other big bonus is that you're right next to one of Scotland's best pubs.

Set in 10 acres of grounds on the edge of the village, the Victorian mansion that is

the **Pine Trees Hotel** (Strathview Terr., tel. 01796/472121, www.pinetreeshotel.co.uk, £120 d) has 20 amply furnished rooms. They're all plush affairs, full of dark wood with some four-poster bed rooms available. The Garden Restaurant here has a good reputation; it serves up delicacies like sea bass, venison, and guinea fowl.

Food

Pitlochry is hardly short of tearooms or restaurants but few stand out.

Victoria's Coffee Shop (45 Atholl Rd., tel. 01796/472670, www.victorias-pitlochry.co.uk, 10 A.M.–late daily) is a dark little joint that's just about perfect for a coffee, cake, or a panini. Breakfast things like croissants are served from 10 A.M. but the evening bistro menu is pretty varied and reasonably priced for Pitlochry. There are salads, steaks, pasta dishes, and even a seafood platter. Light lunches are £3–6 and evening meals are £10–14.

The tranquil riverside setting already makes **Port na Craig Restaurant and Inn** (Portnacraig Rd., tel. 01796/472777, www.portnacraig.com, noon–9 P.M. daily Nov.–Mar., 10 A.M.–9 P.M. daily Apr.–Sept.) a winner; it's handily located near the theater for that pre-show feast. The rustic restaurant itself has inside and outside seating, lending itself equally well toward lingering on a long winter evening or on a sunny afternoon. There are some innovative pasta and fish dishes for around £8 like the tagliatelle with roast garlic, spinach, basil, and white wine. More expensive meat dishes are £13–17.

Despite the numerous competition in Pitlochry, there is no beating the whitewashed coaching inn of the ◖ **Moulin Hotel and Micro Brewery** (tel. 01796/472196, www.moulinhotel.co.uk, food served noon–9:30 P.M. daily) for an evening meal. It's full of locals and weary hikers, most of them downing ales from the hotel's very own microbrewery. The bar and the restaurant are equally cozy and pleasant; you can tuck yourself into one of the booths at the back. The main courses (£9–14) are hearty affairs designed to satisfy the famished outdoorsy type; you can't go wrong with a venison steak with blue cheese and chips. When you've eaten at the Moulin, it's safe to say you've eaten at a proper Scottish pub. You get dark wooden beams, a good choice of beer and whisky, a relaxed atmosphere, and lots of chatter centered on which hills have been climbed or which rivers have been fished.

Information and Services

The staff at **Pitlochry TIC** (22 Atholl Rd., tel. 01796/472215, open at least 9:30 A.M.–5 P.M. Mon.–Sat. 9:30 A.M.–4:30 P.M. Sun. mid-Apr.–Oct., Mon.–Sat. Nov.–Mar., extended hours in summer) are friendly despite being rushed off their feet. There's maps and local walking information—you'll be charged for a lot of it as this is a touristy place.

You can check your email at the **Computer Services Centre** (67 Atholl Rd., tel. 01796/473711, 9:30 A.M.–5:30 P.M. Mon.–Fri., 12:30–5:30 P.M. Sat.). You'll find a post office and banks with ATMs on Atholl Road.

Irvine Memorial Hospital (Irvine Terr., tel. 01796/472052) is a small hospital in the center of Pitlochry. Do your laundry at **Pitlochry Laundrette and Dry Cleaners** (3 West Moulin Rd., tel. 01796/474044).

Getting There and Away

Trains from Edinburgh or Glasgow to Inverness stop off in Pitlochry, going via Perth. Trains to/from Glasgow/Edinburgh (about every 1.5 hours, one hour 45 min.) and to/from Inverness (about every 1.5 hours, one hour 45 min.) both run through gorgeous scenery.

There are at least five **buses** daily between Pitlochry and Inverness (two hours, £10.90) operated by Scottish Citylink. The same company runs buses south from Pitlochry via Perth to Edinburgh (two hours 20 min., £10.90) and Glasgow (2.5 hrs., £10.90) about every two hours daily.

ATHOLL FOREST

This vast expanse of forest north of Pitlochry has as its only settlement the little village of Blair Atholl. Dominating the village is the magnificent white Blair Castle: home to the only private army in Europe. The vast Atholl estates cover the entire region but these lands were not always so verdant. The poet Robert Burns visited Bruar Falls on the estate in 1787 and found the riverbanks bare and rocky. He set about writing a poem, entitled "The Humble Petition of Bruar Water" in which he urged the Duke at the time to plant the banks with trees for future generations to enjoy. After Burns's death the Duke acquiesced and the rich woodland here is the result.

Blair Castle

This grand castle (Blair Atholl, tel. 01796/481207, www.blair-castle.co.uk, 9:30 A.M.–4:30 P.M. daily Easter–mid-Oct., £7.90 adults, £4.90 children) has a history going back some 750 years, during all of which time it has been the home of the Duke and Duchess of Atholl. It is home to Europe's last private army, the Atholl Highlanders and boasts some of the wildest estates of any private stately home in the country. It's full of old-fashioned pomp and ceremony: During opening hours a piper will even stand and play as you approach up the castle drive.

Thirty rooms are open to the public, including displays on the Atholl Highlanders. Other highlights are the staircase lined with Georgian pictures of the Atholl family and the magnificently opulent tapestry room. Hanging here are the Mortlake Tapestries once belonging to King Charles I before his execution. In the ballroom hangs Sir Henry Raeburn's portrait of Scotland's most famous fiddler, Neil Gow, who often played for the second and third Dukes of Atholl. The downside of the castle is that as this is the most-visited private home in Scotland, you'll be hard-pushed to dodge the tour parties. They don't venture very far into the grounds though, so there is a refuge of sorts.

The grounds are a refreshing antidote to the sometimes stifling finery inside, with gardens full of swaggering peacocks and statues. Beyond the formal gardens stretch the Atholl Forest with a network of trails for walkers and game hunters. You can walk to **Diana's Grove** and see some of the tallest trees in the country as well as to the dark thundering torrent of **Bruar Falls** in the west of the estate. You can also access Bruar Falls from the car park of the ugly House of Bruar shopping complex on the B8079. If you are sightseeing in the area, ask about the Treasure Ticket (£15), which gives entry to other attractions like Scone Palace as well as Blair. The number 87 Pitlochry bus will run from the castle along to the House of Bruar for Bruar Falls.

Atholl Country Life Museum

Before museums became all flashy and glassy and modern, they were like this museum (tel. 01796/481232, 10 A.M.–5 P.M. Mon.–Fri., 1:30–5 P.M. Sat.–Sun. July–Aug., 1:30 A.M.–5 P.M. daily Easter–June and Sept., £3): Musty old treasure troves of bizarre artifacts and lovingly arranged displays. You can see a post office as it would have looked in the 1930s and a horse-drawn sleigh used by rural doctors as well as the highlight, the world's largest rifle shooting trophy! You'll be struggling to relate all of what you see to Blair Atholl or even Scotland but that won't matter—enjoy the oddities and re-created rural scenes.

Events

Blair International Horse Trials (www.blair-horsetrials.co.uk), held in August, is full of good horsy fun. There's pony shows, a show-jumping competition, and lots of side shows. It's held in Blair Castle grounds.

Accommodations

Sumptuous, Gothic-looking **Atholl Arms Hotel** (Blair Atholl, tel. 01796/481205, www.athollarmshotel.co.uk, £75 s, £90 d) takes up most of the tiny village of Blair Atholl. The rooms are dark, traditional, and tartan-themed here; this is Highland hospitality to the hilt. There is a spacious Baronial-style restaurant and a snug bar.

Getting There and Away

Blair Atholl Station is on the Inverness-Edinburgh railway line. About five **trains** daily go to Perth; it may then be necessary to change

to get to Edinburgh or Glasgow. There are 5–8 **buses** Monday–Saturday (three Sunday) between Blair Atholl and Pitlochry, from where you can get on connecting services to other parts of Perthshire.

TAY FOREST PARK

The remarkable aesthetics of Loch Tummel and Loch Rannoch, which stretch throughout the dark, dense trees of Tay Forest, have been admired since the days of Queen Victoria. She took tea before the fine views of Loch Tummel in 1866. This is a wild, sparsely inhabited part of Perthshire, but the way the scenery is set out, from shiny loch to coatings of coniferous trees to angular hills, gives it the feel of a landscaped garden at times. The farther west you head through the forest park, the wilder it gets: Kinloch Rannoch is the last outpost of civilization before the road heads a further 16 miles up onto Rannoch Moor. Don't expect a lot of tourist facilities, and do expect most of them to be closed for most of the year. The area's metropolis, Kinloch Rannoch, has pricey petrol, a shop, a hotel, and little else. Come here to savor the remoteness, to tackle the wide variety of walks, to breathe the sharp pine-scented air, and to enjoy one of the most postcard-perfect wildernesses in Scotland.

Loch Tummel

Right at the beginning of the B8019 road through the Tay Forest Park is this two-mile walk to the **Linn of Tummel** (open year-round), a series of enchanting rapids at the point where the rivers of Garry and Tummel meet. You can link this up with paths through to the Pass of Killiecrankie on the A9. The **Queen's View** (B8019, viewpoint year-round, café and visitors center in summer only) yields the best views of Loch Tummel. You'll find a café and ample parking and picnicking space here.

Loch Rannoch

At the eastern edge of Loch Rannoch (www.visitrannoch.com) is **Kinloch Rannoch,** a small, pretty village with a wonderful waterfall and basic tourist facilities (fuel, a shop, and a couple

Queen's View, Loch Tummel: looking towards Rannoch Moor, one of Scotland's last great wildernesses

of places to stay). After here, you're really on your own. The boulder-strewn shores of Loch Rannoch reach 10 miles long from end to end, but in a landscape of seemingly never-ending hills and forests it seems a lot more. You can drive right around the loch; the road along the southern shore is the more scenic. If you want to climb the pointy ridge of Schiehallion (an easy ascent as Munro Mountains go, with excellent views), the best access is by heading along the minor road east from Kinloch Rannoch to the Braes of Foss car park some six miles farther on.

◖ Rannoch Moor

West of Loch Rannoch, the road comes to an end at Rannoch Station, a collection of houses and a railway track dwarfed by a sweeping vista of heather. Here begins Rannoch Moor, the kind of wilderness you don't really believe can exist in Britain. It is right in the edge of Perthshire, with much of it spilling over into the Southern Highlands. In area it covers only 50 square miles, but beyond it are other

similarly wild regions just given different names, giving it a vast, desolate feel. Rannoch is a windswept plateau, spattered with lochans and mountains rising to over 3,000 feet. It can be the most beautiful place and it can be the bleakest, depending on weather that can change in the blink of an eye.

It's one of those places walkers whisper excitedly about—a walk into this wilderness is one of the most rewarding things to do in Perthshire. It could also potentially be one of the most dangerous. Out here, there's no friendly hostel with lots of information on treks: You really are on your own. Never attempt a trek into the wilderness without very good maps, sturdy footwear, plenty of provision for atrocious weather, and a good idea where you are going. It's no joke being stuck 20 miles from civilization without any shelter or mobile phone reception.

The main **walk** in the area is from Rannoch Moor railway station across to the Kingshouse Hotel at the top of Glencoe. It's 10 miles; if you're coming with your own transport then you'll need to turn right around and head back the same way. There is a relatively good track along the route, but be warned: Workers on the railway across the moor would often do this trek across to the Kingshouse regardless of the time of year and perish from exposure on the return leg after a few drinks too many.

If you're planning a trek, one of the few buildings to provide shelter for walkers is **Ben Alder Cottage,** a bothy on the west coast of Loch Ericht near its southern end.

Accommodations and Food

There are seven rooms at **Loch Tummel Inn** (Strathtummel, tel. 01882/634272, www.loch-tummelinn.co.uk, £50 s, £90 d) with grand Loch Tummel views. They're full of creaking old furniture, and one of the bathrooms even has its own fireplace. The whole point of staying here is that this place hasn't changed much in centuries, so don't come here expecting 21st-century conveniences. Try the old-fashioned pursuits of board games and books instead— these the inn has in abundance. You can get evening meals at the inn. If you can brave the midges, the picnic tables across the road are a great spot to sit.

Staying at the fancy old hunting lodge of **Bunrannoch House** (near Kinloch Rannoch, tel. 01882/632407, www.bunrannoch.co.uk, £30 s, £52 d) is a real pleasure. You get the sense of weathered charm while enjoying light, airy rooms—the best are right at the top of the house. One has its own bath, and both have lots of unexpected corners and recesses. There are also two rooms with four-poster beds. As eating options in these parts are pretty thin, you'll be glad to know that three-course evening meals are provided. They are the stuff of Scottish legend—roast rack of venison and duck.

When you get to the end of the road at Rannoch Station and can't face the drive back, the **Moor of Rannoch Hotel** (Rannoch Station, tel. 01882/633238, www.moorofrannoch.co.uk, £52 s, £88 d) comes in handy. Five white, en suite, freshly painted rooms have windows that let in that sharp, special Rannoch Moor light. There is only one single

room, and prices go down for longer stays. You can get quite a good choice of evening meals here, too; it's typical Scottish fare like venison and lamb for the most part. Expect solid home-made food, blazing fires, and a bar buzzing with the wild tales of hikers. Ask at the hotel about walking on the moor—they'll have a few handy tips.

Post Taste (Kinloch Rannock, tel. 01882/632333, 10 A.M.–5 P.M. Tues.–Sun.) is absolutely ingenious: a post office meets internet café and restaurant. In the day Post Taste will do cheap snacks and light bites, but on certain evenings it becomes a full-fledged restaurant. It's essential to book in advance to guarantee a table; if you manage it you can sample the gorgeous chicken and leek pie. Meals are £3–8. The place also acts as an invaluable source of tourist information and a souvenir shop.

Getting There and Away

One of the wildest regions in Scotland is best explored with your own wheels, but sporadic public transportation services do exist. The most fun way to get around is on the **post bus,** which makes one run Monday–Saturday between Pitlochry and Rannoch Station, calling at all points in the Tay Forest Park. **Broon's Buses** runs an additional five daily services (Mon.–Fri.) between Kinloch Rannoch and Pitlochry. In summer it operates Loch Rannoch circular buses, useful for walkers.

GLENSHEE

The landscape changes drastically on the A93 from Blairgowrie to Braemar: You're catapulted from gentle, lush fruit plantations into a landscape of daunting, jagged peaks. This is the beginning of the Cairngorm Mountains, and you'll see precious little but rock until you get to the Spittal of Glenshee, Scotland's main skiing area right on the border with Aberdeenshire.

Skiing

Like a lot of ski areas, **Glenshee Skiing Centre** (tel. 01339/741320, www.ski-glenshee.co.uk) can seem ugly out of season when there are just a few chair lifts hanging above the rock and scarring the view. In season, how-ever (Dec.–Apr.), there are 36 runs catering to most skiing abilities. Lift passes are £24 adults, £18 children. You can buy or rent equipment from the Cairnwell Mountain Sports Store, and there are a couple of restaurants. Most of the runs are red and blue (intermediate), but there are a couple of challenging black runs, too. Runs extend over three valleys all together, with plenty of variety of terrain. It's also a good place to try snowboarding.

Accommodations

Attached to the hotel of the same name, the **Spittal of Glenshee Bunkhouse** (Glenshee, tel. 01250/885215, www.spittalofglen-shee.co.uk, beds £19.50, reduced rates for larger groups) is a clean, sturdy, comfortable bunkhouse sleeping up to 17 in one- to four-bed dorms. Note that you cannot cook here, but the Spittal of Glenshee Hotel offers meals throughout the day. You'll see it signposted off the A93 from Blairgowrie to Ballater.

Dalmunzie Hotel (near Spittal of Glenshee, tel. 01250/885224, www.dalmunzie.com, from £65 s, £100 d) is a Highland laird's mansion set on its own 6,500-acre estate. It comes with its own golf course, tennis courts, and bags of walking trails. All the rooms here exude an-tique furnishings and grandeur; they try to re-create what it would have been like to stay in a hunting lodge when the house was first built. You can stay in the shooting lodge or the laird's former suites of rooms in creaking old four-poster beds. There is also a restaurant, a fireside lounge, and a library. The hotel is 1.5 miles down the dead-end lane through Spittal of Glenshee.

Getting There and Away

From June until August, the **Heather Hopper bus service** connects Pitlochry with Glen Shee and Deeside, stopping in Braemar and Ballater. At other times of the year, you'll be reliant on your own wheels or the **post bus** from Blairgowrie to Glen Shee. It leaves from Railway Road, Blairgowrie, at 7:30 A.M. for the 3.5-hour journey.

PERTHSHIRE

LOCH LOMOND AND THE TROSSACHS

It is the hilly, forested countryside of this region where the gentle glens of central Scotland rupture into the stark, dark peaks of the Highlands. The signs start appearing the farther north you venture: Lochs begin dividing the country into inaccessible clumps, and craggy Munro mountains thrust their way out of the formerly grass-topped hills. The centerpiece of the region is Loch Lomond, Scotland's largest freshwater loch. It's a snaking, forest-flanked expanse of water that seems to sparkle with a magic all its own, even on the dullest day. There are tree-swathed harbors to stroll along and historic islands to sail to, as well as restaurants along the shore for admiring the view. It was a treasured enough spot to be designated Scotland's very first National Park, in recognition of the versatile walking in the vicinity.

To the east, the lonely Trossachs Hills were the stomping ground of Scotland's favorite outlaw Rob Roy; he used the area as a hiding place from his enemy, the Duke of Montrose. You can follow in his footsteps, across the peat bogs and lochs, to the Braes of Balquhidder that shelter his grave. From here the windswept ridge of Breadalbane sweeps up to tempt the outdoor enthusiast further. This has traditionally been the gateway to the Highlands, where underdogs could take refuge from the law and where brigands could defeat brutal aristocracy. The region is steeped in a legacy of bloody history and the heroes and villains who engineered it. It was said that whoever controlled the lofty castle at architecturally rich Stirling, the main town in the area, effectively controlled Scotland. The must-see castle has a vantage

© LUKE WATERSON

HIGHLIGHTS

◖ Hill House: Check out the quirky design of renowned architect Charles Rennie Mackintosh's greatest work at Hill House in Helensburgh (page 272).

◖ Eastern Shoreline of Loch Lomond: The loch's scenic eastern shore, on the route of Scotland's most popular long-distance footpath, has plenty of peaceful places to stay and picnic (page 276).

◖ Loch Katrine: Take a steamboat trip down the middle of this glittering lake or walk the shores in the footsteps of Scotland's most prestigious author, Sir Walter Scott, in the heart of the Trossachs (page 282).

◖ Rob Roy's Grave: Visit the legendary outlaw's resting place beneath the Braes of Balquhidder (page 283).

◖ Stirling Castle: This immense, lavish castle, bursting out of the wooded slopes above Stirling, is arguably the most important building in Scottish history, with events from the Battle of Bannockburn to the crowning of Mary, Queen of Scots unfolding close to or within its walls (page 287).

◖ Falkirk Wheel: Marvel at the world's only revolving boat lift, and board a boat to be lifted by this triumph of 21st-century engineering almost eighty feet through the air (page 293).

◖ Dollar Glen: The steep wooded valley above the tranquil town of Dollar is crowned by photogenic Castle Campbell and laced with walking trails (page 294).

LOOK FOR ◖ TO FIND RECOMMENDED SIGHTS, ACTIVITIES, DINING, AND LODGING.

point over undulating southern Scotland and the wild, mountainous north. Rival armies and power-mongering monarchs have played out some of the most important events in Scottish history in or under its walls.

The wild country west of Stirling is counterbalanced by the heavily industrialized Forth Valley to the east. The legacy of industry to explore spans three centuries, with the crowning glory being Scotland's greatest work of construction since the Victorians bridged the River Forth. This is the Falkirk Wheel, the world's only revolving boat lift, re-establishing an east–west coast canal boat route for the first time in 70 years.

HISTORY
Prehistory to Medieval Era

The volcanic plug of rock that juts out of the earth at Stirling holds the key to this region's history: It made the ideal vantage point between the lowlands and the Highlands. There's

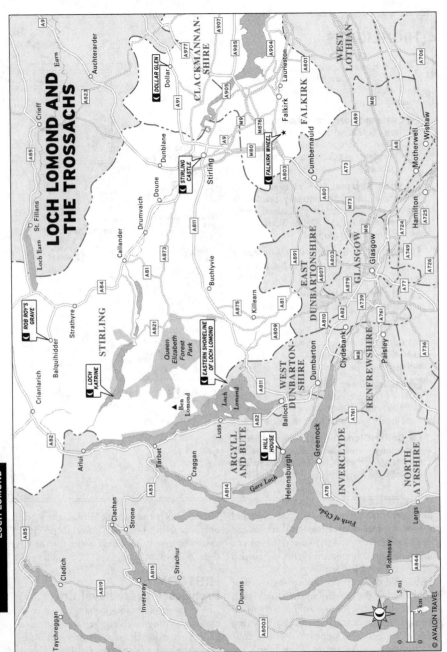

LOCH LOMOND AND THE TROSSACHS

© AVALON TRAVEL

evidence to show that this rock, on which Stirling Castle now stands, has been inhabited since prehistoric times. The Romans made the region the northernmost extent of their empire through necessity rather than choice. They lacked resources to tackle the barbarous tribes of the north and built the Antonine Wall to mark their territory in the 2nd century A.D. By the 12th century Stirling had established itself as one of the most important settlements in Scotland; Scottish kings resided and died there, and in 1228 it was awarded burgh status. As it was growing in importance, so was the desire of King Edward I of England to bring Scotland under his control as he had Wales. Stirling became the main setting for his attempts to bring the country under English rule, and occupancy of Stirling Castle became synonymous with control of the country. After decades of warring, Robert the Bruce was handed Stirling Castle in 1314, a decisive step in Scottish independence from England being restored.

1400-1746

Stirling came to be the home of the Stewart monarchs from 1437. At the age of four Mary, Queen of Scots hid at Inchmahome Priory near Aberfoyle from King Henry VIII of England, who was trying to attain the Scottish throne by marrying Mary to his son. The infant Mary had been crowned at the Chapel Royal at Stirling Castle in 1543, but after her son King James VI of Scotland became king of England as well, he moved his court to London. As a result Stirling dwindled in importance. Hostilities between the north of Scotland and the south, with Stirling again at the center of things, flared up again with the advent of Jacobinism, a movement dedicated to restoring the ousted Stuart monarchs to the British throne. The area north of Stirling was a Jacobite hotbed; in 1715 the Duke of Argyll established himself in Stirling Castle to ensure the movement spread no farther south. He was largely successful in his attempts, and in 1746 Bonnie Prince Charlie failed to successfully lay siege to the castle. By the time

of Bonnie Prince Charlie's demise, the region around Stirling had descended into a place of lawlessness. Cattle-thieving was the main way of survival in the Trossachs hills, orchestrated by groups of brigands known as Catalans, of which the most famous was Rob Roy. By contrast, the valley of the River Forth was becoming a place of industry as early as 1700.

Victorian Era to Present Day

By the beginning of the 19th century, figures like William Wallace and Rob Roy roaming these far northern hills had become the embodiment of romantic nostalgia for a colorful bygone age. After Sir Walter Scott published the poem "The Lady of the Lake" in 1810, tourism in the area mushroomed overnight; Victorian tourist villages like Tarbet on Loch Lomond and Aberfoyle in the Trossachs were the result. The railway brought a lot of wealth to the region from the 1850s onward: Wealthy people moved to towns like Stirling to live and commute to Glasgow for work. Improvements continued throughout the 20th century, and today the area is thriving. Since the millennium, east–west coast canal access has been re-established for the first time in 70 years, courtesy of the Falkirk wheel. Stirling was declared a city in 2002.

PLANNING YOUR TIME

The main delights of the area are of an outdoor variety, but really appreciating the countryside of the region takes time. This is not a region to tick off sights from the car window. Its touristy areas are very touristy, and if you want to avoid the people and appreciate the majesty of the hills and lochs, allow 4–6 days. Loch Lomond and the Stirling area can be easily explored by public transport, but buses are few and far between in the Trossachs and Breadalbane. Aim to spend 1–2 days in the Loch Lomond area and about the same amount of time in each the Trossachs and Stirling. You could use Stirling as an exploration base for the Forth Valley and Strathallan and the Campsie Fells.

Loch Lomond and Vicinity

If any expanse of water besides Loch Ness was to make it into Scotland's hall of fame, it would be this vast, glittering island-peppered expanse of water. At 24 miles long, 5 miles wide, and up to 600 feet deep, this is Scotland's largest freshwater loch, in surface area. Brushing the side of the main route north from Glasgow, Loch Lomond almost demands a visit, and there are innumerable reasons to do just that. A lot of visitors will want to know whether the loch lives up to the hype—the much sung-about "Bonnie banks of Loch Lomond" are every bit as beautiful in reality. Catch the waters on a summer day and they will reflect in sparkling detail the surrounding hills, including Scotland's most southerly Munro mountain, Ben Lomond. Catch the same scene in winter and you'll find it equally intriguing—still and mysterious with the dim outlines of bobbing boats and islands. It was officially recognized as a place of outstanding natural beauty in 2002, when Loch Lomond and the surrounding mountainous area became Scotland's first national park. This is some of Scotland's most magnificent and popular walking country, with 20 Munro peaks within its confines. The western shore is the busier, more touristy part of the loch with several large developments; the eastern shore remains a tranquil, densely wooded place.

BALLOCH AND VICINITY

Balloch is the largest, dullest, and noisiest of the communities on Loch Lomond's shores. This owes much to the village being the terminus of the railway from Glasgow and having good road connections to major urban centers. The business and tackiness was at least doubled by the completion of the Loch Lomond Shores development in 2001, a large visitors complex on the outskirts. This is a tourist-swamped place with lots of pleasure boats and a couple of worthwhile attractions. Southwest of Balloch at Helensburgh is Hill House, generally thought to be the crowning glory of

celebrated Glasgow architect Charles Rennie Mackintosh. For a stroll in Balloch, head to Balloch Castle Country Park.

Sweeney's Cruises

This company (tel. 01389/752376, www .sweeney.uk.com, hourly cruises Apr.–Sept., by arrangement Oct.–Apr.) runs one- and two-hour cruises around the islands of Loch Lomond. Commentary in different languages is available, and prices start from £5.50 per adult. The one-hour cruise alone takes in several stately homes and goes over to the island of Inchmurrin, home to lots of wildlife and Scotland's very first nudist club.

◖ Hill House

Renowned Glasgow architect Charles Rennie Mackintosh designed this house (Upper Colquhoun St., Helensburgh, tel. 0844/493 2208, www.nts.org.uk, 1:30–5:30 p.m. daily Easter–Oct., £8) in 1902 for Glasgow publisher Walter Blackie. The building is said to be the architect's finest creation, sitting resplendently above the northern bank of the River Clyde and offering great views south to Glasgow. It's a visual feast inside and out, with an asymmetrical layout designed to maximize the use of natural light by use of colored glass and pale decor. Contrasts are always apparent though—compare the dark entrance way with the brilliance of the drawing room. A few of the rooms still have Mackintosh-designed furniture. You can wander the gardens, too, which frame the house perfectly between hillside, sea, and sky. To get to Helensburgh from Balloch, head north on the A82 and turn left on the B831, then left again on the B832.

Sports and Recreation

The south of Loch Lomond is a sheltered, safe place for water sports; **Can You Experience** (Loch Lomond Shores, tel. 01389/602576, www.canyouexperience.com, Apr.–Oct.) hires out a variety of vessels, including canoes and

© LUKE WATERSON

sunset on the River Clyde from Charles Rennie Mackintosh's Hill House

pedal boats. They also have mountain bikes for rent from £17 daily.

Food

If you get peckish in Balloch and really can't wait for the far nicer places to eat fanning out on both sides of the loch, then head to the **Loch Lomond Shores** complex, where eateries at least get lochside views (yet almost zero atmosphere).

Information

The **National Park Gateway Centre** (Loch Lomond Shores by Balloch, tel. 0870/720 0631, www.lomondshores.com, 10 A.M.–7 P.M. daily Apr.–June and Sept., 10 A.M.–8 P.M. daily July–Aug., 10:30 A.M.–4:30 P.M. daily Oct.–Mar.) is a large building by the lochside with books, maps, and interactive displays on Loch Lomond sights and activities. It also has a children's corner.

Getting There and Away

Trains run from Glasgow Queen Street to Balloch (half-hourly, 45 min., £3.90) and to Helensburgh (half-hourly, 45 min., £4.60).

Getting Around

McColl's (tel. 01389/754321) bus service 309 operates between Alexandria, Balloch, Drymen, and Balmaha at least 10 times Monday–Saturday and 8 times on Sundays.

To get to Helensburgh from Balloch, take the train to Alexandria and hop on service 306, also run by McColl's. If you're going to be taking a lot of buses in the area, buy a rural rover ticket from the driver when you get on the first bus. It costs £5 and is valid on most buses in the Loch Lomond/Trossachs area for that day.

WESTERN SHORELINE

The main road to the north of Scotland, the A82, trundles along the western shore of Loch Lomond and makes this the more touristy side of the loch. It's not the tacky tourism that overrides Balloch, however, and there is the pretty village of Luss, the shambling Victorian holiday resort of Tarbet, and the delightful hamlet of Ardlui for stopping points along the way.

Luss

This tiny 19th-century village, built up mainly

LOCH LOMOND

to house workers toiling in the nearby slate quarries, is by some ways the prettiest place on the loch. The deluge of visitors increased after it became the setting for the Scottish soap opera *Take the High Road.* Even so, its picturesque conservation village cottages with their colorful gardens cannot fail to impress at any time of year. It's hard to believe that Luss was once known as Clachan Dhu (the dark village). An Irish missionary, St. Kessog, brought Christianity to Loch Lomond's shores and was martyred nearby. Devotees embalmed his body with sweet herbs, which spread from his grave across the area. With the plants, a new village name sprang up, from the Gaelic *lus* (herb).

Luss is a village for wandering around. Besides strolling past the pretty village center cottages, a clutch of easygoing **woodland and shoreline walks** branch off from Luss. There are information boards in the large car park on the walks, or you can inquire in the visitors center also by the car park.

Ardlui

At the northern end of the loch, Ardlui has a railway station, a few houses, and a good hotel. It's the starting point for a demanding ascent of **Ben Vorlich** (the route starts beside the station). There's also a **marina** here; if you have your own boat you can sail up from Balloch and stay overnight. A ferry will, on request, also take you to the eastern shore, where there are some good pike fishing places.

Accommodations and Food

Loch Lomond Youth Hostel (tel. 01309/ 850226 or 0870/155 3255, www.syha.org.uk, Mar.–Oct., beds £15.75–17.75) is a secluded 19th-century country house that remains glamorous despite being a hostel. It is two miles north of Balloch, on a minor road opposite Duck Bay Marina. Well hidden by woodland, this large hostel still has great loch views, a ballroom, and amply sized three- to eight-bed dorms. The hostel has a shop and Internet access as well.

At the very head of the loch (it's only a stream at this point) is ultra-traditional **Drover's Inn**

(Inverarnan, tel. 01301/704234, www.droversinn.co.uk, £35 s, £68 d). Expect tartan carpets, stags heads, and four-poster beds at this old wayside hostelry, mixed with modern touches like hot tubs. Not all rooms are en suite, but this is the liveliest place to stay in the Loch Lomond shores, oozing with 300 years of character. There's a lodge with plusher rooms, too. The bright, warming colors of the rooms are every bit as welcoming as the convivial downstairs bar/restaurant. In a dark bar full of smoke from the open fire you can sit at candlelit wooden tables, sip real ale, and feast on stalwart Scottish food including the famous haggis, neeps and tatties (haggis, turnips, and mashed potatoes).

The whitewashed **Inverbeg Inn** (Inverbeg, tel. 01436/860678, www.inverbeghotel.co.uk, £90 d) is set back from the main road two miles north of Luss and has been welcoming travelers since the early 19th century. There are 20 rooms here, well sized and well cared for with armchairs and even decanters of sherry to greet you. Rooms are en suite (some get baths), as well as being blessed with color TVs and telephones. Under the main road from the inn is the Lochside Lodge, under the same management, where rooms open up onto a quiet stretch of shoreline. The inn was refurbished in spring 2008.

The Coach House Coffee Shop (Luss, tel. 01436/860341, 10 A.M.–5 P.M. daily) is a large, convivial place, and one of the most expensive cafés you'll eat at in Scotland. Then again, it is in Luss, one of its most charming and popular villages. You can get a range of teas, coffees, and soft drinks as well as some interesting meals (£9–11) like quiche with haggis clapshot.

In an old church, the dark, opulent, good-humored **Ben Lomond Restaurant** (A83, Tarbet, tel. 01301/702393, www.thebenlomond.com, 10 A.M.–late, early evening menu 5–7 P.M., evening menu from 7 P.M. daily) serves up fresh, simple fare like baguettes, fish and chips, pizza, and salads (£4–7). You can eat your meal in a pew if you like. The fancier restaurant part is separate from the café; watch

THE HIGH ROAD OR THE LOW ROAD?

The "Bonnie Banks O' Loch Lomond" is going to be one of the first, if only songs you'll either learn or have engrained onto your memory during your stay in this part of Scotland. Undoubtedly the most famous verse is the second one:

Oh! You'll take the high road and
I'll take the low road,
And I'll be in Scotland afore ye;
But me and my true love
Will never meet again
On the bonnie bonnie banks of Loch Lomond.

However, the ballad is far more than just a scenic description of a loch and the surrounding topography. It's actually an astute political commentary on one of the most crucial periods of Scottish history. The song is thought to date to the times of Bonnie Prince Charlie and allegedly refers to two soldiers left behind the prince's retreating troops after the failed uprising of 1745. Government forces caught up with the pair in Carlisle, just south of the Scottish border; one was set free and one sentenced to death. The singer of the ballad, of course, is the still-living soldier as he trudges over the mountainous "high road" back to the Highlands. The high road would have been used by fugitives from the law, as the main through route to the north of Scotland would have been on the easier-going "low road," well guarded by government troops. There is a double irony here. The first is that the "high road" would have historically been the easy route between two points, as in "High Street" where high means principal or primary. That the high road in the song is the wilder, more arduous route is indicative of the turmoil in Scotland at the time. The second irony is that the "low road" to which the balladeer is referring, despite being the quicker route from England to the Scottish Highlands in 1745, would not be so for his doomed companion. Instead the soldier would be traveling back slowly as a corpse in a coffin, some time after his freed companion had taken flight over the hills back to his homeland.

Another interpretation of the song has only one soldier in it. He is caught by government troops and sentenced to death (this would have been more in keeping with the brutality of troops at the time that would have been unlikely to show leniency by letting one soldier go free). His Highland sweetheart is the singer of the ballad who, hearing of her lover's capture, journeys to Carlisle in the hope of arranging his pardon. This is not granted and so her journey back to Scotland is alone, through the high hills. As for the meeting at Loch Lomond, this would have been a central point of the lands of the Lennox clan, to which the lover and the soldier in the ballad are thought to have belonged.

out for the ghost that is said to haunt both this and the adjoining craft shop.

Information
Luss National Park Centre (tel. 0870/720 0631, daily Easter–Oct., Sat.–Sun. Nov.–Dec.) is in the village car park.

Tarbet TIC (tel. 0870/720 0623, 9:30 A.M.–6 P.M. Mon.–Sat., 10 A.M.–5 P.M. Sun. July–Aug., 10 A.M.–5 P.M. Mon.–Sat., 11 A.M.–5 P.M. Sun. Apr.–June, 10 A.M.–5 P.M. Mon.–Sat., noon–5 P.M. Sun. Sept.–Oct.) is a friendly little place in a car park right by the A82/A83 junction.

Getting There and Away
The infrequent **trains** on the West Highland Railway from Glasgow to Oban provide the most enjoyable way of getting to and along the west shore. Three to four services daily will call at **Arrochar and Tarbet** and **Ardlui** stations (1.25–1.5 hrs., £9–12).

Buses heading north on the A82 (and therefore along most of the western shore) are pretty regular and will drop you off at the bus stop nearest to your destination. The worst-case scenario is that you get dropped off in either Balloch or Tarbet and take another bus to your destination.

© LUKE WATERSON

Loch Lomond is the perfect place for a boat trip.

Scottish Citylink (tel. 0870/550 5050, www
.citylink.co.uk) is the most regular operator, with
Oban- and Fort William–bound buses passing
Balloch (often stopping a 10-minute walk from
the village just north of the roundabout on the
A82), the layby by Loch Lomond Youth Hostel,
Luss, and Tarbet (1 hr. 5 min., £6.90).

Getting Around

There are several west–east ferry crossings
on the loch, making the west coast a viable
accommodation option for West Highland
Way walkers.

The Inverbeg to Rowardennan service (tel.
01360/870273) runs according to demand,
as do the Inveruglas to Inversnaid crossings
(tel. 01877/386233), run by the Inversnaid
Hotel. There is also a crossing from Ardleish
to Ardlui (tel. 01307/704243, 9 A.M.–8 P.M.
daily May–Aug., 9 A.M.–7 P.M. daily Apr.
and Sept.–Oct.). These are run by Ardlui
Hotel, which will also operate out of season
by arrangement.

🄲 EASTERN SHORELINE

The eastern coast of the loch is far more
secluded than the west. Roads only reach

halfway along; after Rowardennan the only
route through is the West Highland Way
footpath, Scotland's most popular long-
distance walk. There are wild stony beaches
ideal for lochside picnics, lush forest walks,
and rugged mountain walks including the
ascent of Scotland's most southerly Munro,
Ben Lomond. Drymen and Balmaha are
the main (indeed, the only) settlements; at
Balmaha is a National Park Centre. Despite
the often-deserted feel, this side of the loch
has the better accommodation options.

Walks

The West Highland Way runs along the shore
seven miles to **Inversnaid** and a further eight
miles to rejoin the road at **Inverarnan.** The
79-mile **Rob Roy Way** (www.robroyway.com)
also starts at Drymen, running across the
Trossachs to **Pitlochry** via **Callander** and
Loch Tay.

Sports and Recreation

Lomond Activities (Drymen, tel. 01360/
660066) offers bike rentals. You can hire a
rowing boat or a motorboat at **Macfarlane &
Son** (Balmaha Boatyard, tel. 01360/870214).

WALKING THE WEST HIGHLAND WAY

This is Scotland's most popular long-distance footpath, stretching 95 miles/152 kilometers from Milngavie just north of Glasgow to Fort William in the heart of the Highlands. It's not difficult to see why so many people choose to get their hiking boots on for this one. For a start, you can walk it in a week, which fits in to most people's holiday plans. The route passes through some of Scotland's most glorious terrain, there's plenty of visual variety, and the accommodation en route is better than on any other Scottish footpath. It's a deeply satisfying walk: You start on the edge of Glasgow, walk through arable lowlands and along the shore of Scotland's largest mainland loch, and climb into its wildest mountain scenery. There's also a tradition on the walk of climbing Scotland's highest point, Ben Nevis, the day after tramping into nearby Fort William.

The walk is broken into 13 stages for a reason: These are the points where the accommodations are. Wild camping is possible, provided you don't do it irresponsibly. For all its popularity, this is not a walk to be undertaken lightly: it does, after all, cross Rannoch Moor, one of the most desolate spots in Western Europe. Often the only accommodation available on the path is in basic hostels or on campsites. If these are the places you plan to stay, you'll need your own sleeping bag and rucksack. There are bed-and-breakfast inns and hotels, but these often involve a trek off the path to reach them. Lots of places to stay run a pick-up service from the path and back again next morning. There is also the option of not carrying your luggage at all on the walk but paying a luggage drop-off service to bring your bags to wherever you are staying. No matter how you travel, be prepared for unpredictable, rapidly changing weather at all times.

You don't have to walk the whole path, of course. One of the most rewarding parts of the walk (Rowardennan to Inverarnan) is along the bonnie banks of Loch Lomond. The West Highland Way is one of those walks you never forget. It takes in distilleries, castles, craggy peaks, lonely glens, and isolated pubs with crackling log fires – in short, everything that makes Scotland so good to visit. You can find out more about the path by checking out www.west-highland-way.co.uk.

Accommodations and Food

There's a very special feeling about spending the night on Loch Lomond's east shore: You're right on the edge of one of Scotland's most visited lochs, and yet tourists prefer the west coast haunts, leaving the east relatively unspoiled.

Cashel Caravan and Camping Site (Rowardennan, tel. 0845/130 8224, www.forestholidays.co.uk, Mar.–Oct., tent and 2 people £15.20) is one of the most photogenic campsites in the whole of Scotland. There are over 100 tent pitches on the tree-dotted banks of the loch here, and you'll be able to find your own special place to camp even in the busiest season.

◖ Rowardennan Lodge Youth Hostel (Rowardennan, tel. 01360/870259 or 0870/155 3255, www.syha.org.uk, beds £15) is as far as the road around the eastern shore of the loch goes—it's already deteriorated to a rough track through gorgeous woodland by the time it reaches this wonderfully isolated hostel. Accommodation at this 19th-century lodge is mostly in four- to eight-bed dorms. Being a popular West Highland Way stop-off, it gets booked up fast throughout the tourist season. Meals are available.

The road around Loch Lomond may have petered out, but first-class hospitality is only just beginning at the **Rowardennan Hotel** (Rowardennan, tel. 01360/870273, www.rowardennanhotel.co.uk, £95). This white-and-black hotel stands sandwiched between the forest and the loch shore, originally dating from the late 17th century. Comfy, pale-colored rooms with tall windows range over three floors, and the bar has an open fire perfect for drying sodden walkers. The food here is nothing fancy but it is filling, the haggis, as they say, is "freshly caught."

The C **Oak Tree Inn** (Balmaha, tel. 01360/870357, www.oak-tree-inn.co.uk, bunkroom beds £25, rooms £75, food served noon–9 P.M. daily) has a timeless quality to it. The snug bar of this tavern with its blazing open fire can feel like something out of the 18th century, although in reality the building, constructed out of locally quarried slate and ancient pieces of wood, has only been around a decade. There are eight light, en suite rooms: all solid, white-painted, and pine finished. The two bunkrooms here are kitted out in a similar style. In a spacious rustic restaurant, you can feast on wholesome pub-style main meals like red wine and venison casserole, or check out the sausage of the day. Fill yourself up for £12–14. You can also get takeaway handmade pizza until 10 P.M. if you want to eat elsewhere (tel. 01360/870440).

Information and Services
Balmaha National Park Centre (tel. 01389/722100, 10 A.M.–5 P.M. daily Easter–Oct.) is in the large car park in Balmaha by the Oak Tree Inn. There is an ATM opposite the Buchanan Arms Hotel in Drymen.

Getting There and Away
McColl's Coaches run regular buses (service 309) from Balloch to Balmaha via Drymen. There are at least 8–10 services operating throughout the week.

The Trossachs and Breadalbane

The busy villages of this area can more than double in population in hill-walking season and make a fine trade from their proximity to Munro mountains and gorgeous green valleys. The scenery here is dominated by glens with bubbling rivers and tree-covered passes and as a result is often more photogenic than the mountains farther north. It will take your breath away initially with its beauty—and all over again as you toil through its thick lush forests and up its steep peaks. The main settlements can be thronged with tourists in summer, but the hills, glowing golden green in the sunshine, have plenty of spots to find peace and quiet. Wherever you go, you'll be tramping the trails local legend Rob Roy did 300 years previously. His daredevil defiance of the villainous Duke of Montrose gave him celebrity status and lends these hills an extra romantic charm. Novelist Sir Walter Scott was one of the first to be captivated by the tale of the heroic brigand, visiting the Trossachs several times during his career. After touring Loch Katrine he was inspired to write the poem "The Lady of the Lake." A Victorian visitor boom began almost overnight, and the Trossachs have never looked back.

CALLANDER AND VICINITY
This small, upbeat town is the appealing place from which to launch an exploration of the Trossachs. You'll find the best, most reasonably priced accommodations for the region here as well as being able to get your share of pampering in before sampling the outdoor thrills of the surrounding landscape. Whether it's fell walking, forest walking, water sports, boat trips, or bird-watching that tickle your fancy, Callander is your ideal base. It's also has all the luxuries like post offices, half-decent supermarkets, banks with ATMs, and petrol pumps.

Sights
Just south from Leny Road (opposite the Old Rectory Guest House), a car park offers access to this lush riverside area of **Callander Meadows** (open year-round), ideal for afternoon strolls. You can then follow a dismantled railway line track to the west, all the way to the foot of Ben Ledi. The route passes a Roman

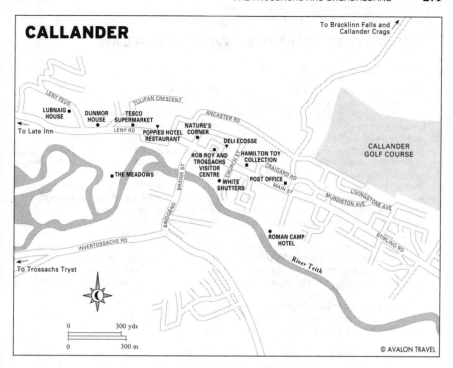

fort, woods, and a waterfall. In the east of Callander, Bracklinn Road leads up by the side of the church for half a mile to the car park for **Bracklinn Falls** (year-round). It's a half-hour walk from the car park to the spectacular waterfall itself, where white water crashes through a wooded ravine. You can walk on from here to **Callander Crags,** from where there are great views over the town and out to Loch Lomond and Ben Lomond.

Shopping

Callander is the major shopping center in these parts. **Tesco Supermarket** (west end of Main St., 6 A.M.–11 P.M. daily) is good for getting those convenience products at irregular hours in the wilds. **Nature's Corner** (2a Cross St., tel. 01877/330200, http://natures-corner.com, 9:30 A.M.–5:30 P.M. Mon.–Sat., noon–5 P.M. Sun.) is the best place to stock up on tasty organic fruit, vegetables, and meat.

Sports and Recreation

You can do a limited selection of **water sports** on **Loch Venacher** southwest of town. The loch can be accessed from the minor road near Trossachs Tryst Backpackers or the main A821 road. Get in touch with **Trossachs Leisure** (tel. 01877/330011, www.venachar-lochside.co.uk) who do boat hire and can arrange fishing trips. The complex is three miles along the A821 from Callander.

Callander has a number of great **cycling** routes fanning off from the center of town: along the remote side of Loch Lubnaig, for example. You can hire a bike at Trossachs Tryst Backpackers (tel. 01877/331200, www.trossachstryst.com).

Accommodations

Trossachs Tryst (Invertrossachs Rd., tel. 01877/331200, www.trossachstryst.com, beds £15) is a secluded hostel doubling as the best

LOCH LOMOND

ROB ROY: SCOTLAND'S FAVORITE OUTLAW

Robert Roy MacGregor, or Rob Roy, had better cause than most to be angry with the powers that be. Rob Roy and his father had, as many Highland clans did, joined forces with Viscount "Bonnie" Dundee in the first Jacobite rising of 1689. After Dundee was killed, Donald MacGregor was arrested on dubious charges and imprisoned for a long time. He was eventually released, but only after his wife had died. The young Rob Roy during this time became a renowned cattle thief. The trade essentially involved stealing someone's cattle and then blackmailing them for its return. He also set about increasing his own herd of cows and borrowed a large sum of money from the Duke of Montrose to finance a deal that would further this aim. The chief herder ran off with the cash he had been entrusted with, and the Duke of Montrose suspected Rob Roy of being involved in the ruse. Despite attempts to clear his name and offers to immediately pay back as much of the money as possible, the cattleman was declared bankrupt and a thief to boot. Rather than face imprisonment like his father before him, he took refuge in the hills.

So began a battle that lasted several years. The Duke of Montrose seized Rob Roy's lands, and Rob Roy retaliated by carrying out raids on the Duke's property. The outlaw caused further anger by helping those who had fallen victim to the Duke's notorious brutality. He was eventually tricked into capture by the Duke of Atholl but bribed his prison guards and escaped. By this point, even Montrose and Atholl were getting weary of chasing Rob Roy, and the anti-hero's life quieted down somewhat. He lived a relatively peaceful later life and died in his 60s. It was the visits of two of the most famous authors of their day to the Highlands that ensured Rob Roy a lasting reputation. Daniel Defoe wrote a greatly elaborated account of his life in 1723 entitled *Highland Rogue*, and Sir Walter Scott further glamorized the cattleman's reputation with the publication of the novel *Rob Roy* in 1817.

budget accommodation in the Trossachs and a bike rental store. Accommodation is in single rooms (with one bunk bed) or eight-bed dorms. Family rooms are also available. Dorms get several en suite bathrooms. Breakfast (cereal, toast, coffee, and juice) is included in the price. There is a large, well-appointed kitchen and two common rooms, one with buckets of area information and one with views of the Trossachs hills. Turn on to the A81 from the A84 in the center of Callander and take the minor road on the bend, which will lead you to the hostel. It's about one mile from town.

White Shutters (6 South Church St., tel. 01877/330442, £18 s, £36 d) has to be one of the best deals for a night's stay anywhere in Scotland. This charming, cozy-looking terraced house has three, large, rambling rooms with TVs, wash basins, and a shared bathroom. The traditional Scottish breakfasts are not huge but they are filling. When you think that there are youth hostels you'll pay more for, this is very good value for its friendliness and bang-in-the-center location.

A Glasgow merchant's former holiday home, **Lubnaig House** (Leny Feus, tel. 01877/330376, www.lubnaighouse.co.uk, from £72 d) has been done up with eight open, attractive rooms, including two in a peaceful annex. Rooms are decked out in white with color TVs and en suite bathrooms. The long tree-rimmed garden is great for a wander; you can look at it as you have breakfast in the conservatory-style dining room.

Dunmor House (Leny Rd., tel. 01877/330756, www.dunmorhouse.com, £70 d) is a large leaf-fringed detached house with four impressively sized rooms, all pearly white with flash red furnishings. You'll get facilities above and beyond the call of your typical guesthouse here: color TVs with video/DVD players and hospitality trays of chocolates and mineral water. Rooms are all en suite, with views of Callander Meadows. One room has a king-size bed and a bay window. Breakfast here is like two meals rolled into one: you start with a continental-type affair (cheese and fruit) and can finish with a full Scottish fry-up.

The **Roman Camp Hotel** (off Main St., Callander, tel. 01877/330003, www.roman-camphotel.co.uk, £85 s, £135 d) was the favorite of J. M. Barrie (author of *Peter Pan*) when he was in town. If you want to stay at a country retreat right in the town center, then do it here. The large, lovely Roman Camp is set in 20 acres of its own grounds, wound through by a river. The rooms here are the epitome of old-fashioned luxury; surely no occupant of the house since it was built in the early 17th century had it quite as fine as the hotel guests of the last few decades. There are 14 rooms here; larger rooms come with fires and antique furnishings, and even some of the standard rooms have four-poster beds. Dinner in the restaurant is £25 for three courses, but a walk in the grounds is free for guests. At a pink house on the right on the A84 through town to Stirling is a sign indicating the drive to the hotel.

Food

The homey **Deli Ecosse** (10 North Ancaster Sq., tel. 01877/331220, 8:30 A.M.–5 P.M. Mon.–Tues. and Thurs.–Fri., 8:30 A.M.–5:30 P.M. Sat.–Sun.) is not only the walk-in larder of your dreams, it is also a café where you can sate your suddenly rumbling stomach. The deli has preserves, freshly baked bread, meats, cheeses, wines, and ales. It's the wonderful coffee and fine homebakes that are most popular in the café.

Many dismiss **Poppies Hotel Restaurant** (Leny Rd., tel. 01877/330329, www.poppieshotel.com, noon–2 P.M. and 6–9 P.M. daily) as a staid, older person's eatery, but it's charming and cozy inside and a good relaxed spot for some quite-classy cuisine. The menu goes for quality rather than quantity; a highlight is the Trossachs trout with prawns and roasted tomatoes. Most options are meat- and fish-oriented. Mains are £11–15. The wine cellar here is extensive, and staff are on hand for advice. Eat in the lounge bar or restaurant depending on your fancy.

Renowned for its live music on Friday and Saturday and great ale, the **Lade Inn** (near Callander, tel. 01877/330152, www.theladeinn.com, noon–9 P.M. Mon.–Sat., 12:30–9 P.M. Sun.) is also a great place to have a meal. You can get a huge portion of haggis, neeps and tatties (turnip and potato mash) and homemade beef burgers. Mains are £7.50–14.50. The **Scottish Real Ale Shop** is attached to the premises; needless to say, many selections of these are available at the bar. Try one of the Lade Inn specialty beers, like the amber, velvety Ladeback. The inn is on the A821 by the junction with the A84, northwest of town.

Information

The **Rob Roy and Trossachs Visitor Centre** (tel. 01877/330342, www.visitscottishheartlands.com, 10 A.M.–5 P.M. Mar.–May and Oct., 10 A.M.–6 P.M. June–Sept., 10 A.M.–4 P.M. Nov.–Feb., winter hours can change subject to demand) is an exceedingly helpful place. There's an audiovisual presentation where you can make your own mind up whether Rob Roy was a hero or a villain.

Getting There and Away

First Group runs an hourly service (no. 59) between Callander and Stirling Monday–Saturday. From May to October, **Scottish Citylink** (tel. 0870/550 5050, www.citylink.co.uk) buses run a once-daily service between Edinburgh and Fort William, via Callander. It's 1.75 hours from Edinburgh to Callander and a further 2.25 hours from Callander to Fort William. Buses also run from Callander to local destinations like Killin and Aberfoyle.

Getting Around

MacPhail Taxis (tel. 01877/331240) will get you to outlying destinations like Killin or Balquhidder; Callander to Balquhidder costs around £20.

QUEEN ELIZABETH FOREST PARK

An immense forest of steeply pitching swaths of conifers, renowned for its daredevil twisting roads and glittering, mystery-steeped lochs, stretches west from Calendar as far as Loch Lomond. The north of the region is marked by popular Loch Katrine, which you can tour on a steamship. Other than that, it's mostly out-doorsy types attracted to the region—there's precious little civilization to distract them. The center of this wild treescape is tourist-inundated Aberfoyle. The village provides a welcome base for flagging adventurers and one other important service: It keeps the tourist hordes within its commercialized confines and leaves the rest of this region almost empty.

Achray Forest

The A821 twists steeply up beyond Aberfoyle into the Achray Forest (www.forestry.gov.uk), an area of the wider Queen Elizabeth Forest Park high in the Menteith Hills. It's a wild-looking part of the country where trees give way to patches of heathery moor. The area was made accessible with the completion of the steep Duke's Pass road in the 19th century, which connected Aberfoyle with Callander.

If you fancy exploring the area, then start off at the **David Marshall Lodge Visitor Centre** (Achray Forest, tel. 01877/382258, 10 A.M.–4 P.M. Mar.–Dec., free) with informa-tion on the myriad of forest trails and informa-tion on local birdlife. A lot of birds live in the area immediately around the lodge; through live video link-ups you can see blue tits and ospreys beavering away obliviously from the Wildlife Room. Energetic visitors may like to try the high-level ropes course here. There's a good café here.

((Loch Katrine

Novelist Sir Walter Scott visited this loch (www.lochkatrine.com) and was inspired as a result to write the famous poem "Lady of the Lake." Visitors have been visiting this forest-rimmed loch northwest of the Achray Forest ever since. In the southeast part of the loch you will find the road ending at a long, at-tractive wooden jetty, a decent restaurant (10 A.M.–5 P.M. daily), and a bike hire store (Katrinewheelz, tel. 01877/376316, adult cycle hire £10 half day, £14 full day).

You can take a **cruise** (tel. 01877/332000, 1–2 cruises daily Easter–Oct., 1.75 hrs., £8 round-trip) aboard the on the Loch Katrine Steamship *Sir Walter Scott,* up the loch as far as the pier at Stronachlachar in the northwest corner. A small island in the loch near here is known as "Factor's Island," where rebellious Rob Roy once impris-oned the Duke of Montrose's Factor (estate manager). Shorter 45-minute cruises on *Ellen's Isle* run around the islands. Loch Katrine's wa-ters are disproportionately busy with boats, but cruises come here for a reason: Few lochs of its size can boast such a diversity of terrain around their shores (thick forests to bare hills swooping right to the shore). Hikers and mountain bikers often take the boat up to Stronachlochar and make their own way back along the delightful track around the shore.

Inchmahome Priory

Three miles east of Aberfoyle is the Lake of Menteith, one of the very few lakes (as op-posed to lochs) in Scotland. It's thought to be a corruption of the Gaelic word *laich,* which merely means "low ground." It's surrounded by farmland and the red-brown Menteith Hills. On an island in the middle of the lake is tree-rimmed Inchmahome Priory (information tel. 01877/385294, 9:30 A.M.–4:15 P.M. (last out-ward sailing) daily Apr.–Sept.), which has been visited by Robert the Bruce and used as a ref-uge by Mary, Queen of Scots. Boats run from the shore near Port of Menteith. Admission, including a return boat trip, is £4.70 adults, £2.35 children.

Accommodations and Food

The haughty Victorian villa of **Stoneypark B and B** (Lochard Rd., Aberfoyle, tel. 01877/382208, www.stoneyparkb-b.co.uk, from £50 d) has three white, rustic-styled en suite rooms right below the craggy hill of Crag Mhor on the outskirts of Aberfoyle. The decor is traditional, in keeping with the age of the bed-and-breakfast. Guests get use of a lounge with an open coal fire and two acres of grounds to wander in.

Having a drink in the flower-covered **Forth**

Inn (Main St., Aberfoyle, tel. 01877/382372, www.forthinn.com, £45 s, £70 d, food served noon–9 P.M. daily) is an integral part of a visit to Aberfoyle—it's certainly the best way of passing the time. It has a large, relaxed bar/restaurant area with an open fire, frequented by locals and tourists alike. Main meals include good vegetarian options and mix up a variety of local produce in inventive ways. If you're lucky, the menu will feature locally caught brown trout. You'll pay £9–15 for dishes. You can also stay here in one of six large, bright, en suite rooms.

Information
As befits a tourist trap, Aberfoyle has a TIC (Main St., tel. 0845/225 5121, 9:30 A.M.–6 P.M. daily July–Aug., 10 A.M.–5 P.M. daily Apr.–June and Sept.–Oct., 10 A.M.–4 P.M. Sat.–Sun. Nov.–Mar.) in the Trossachs Discovery Centre.

For forest-related information, head to the **David Marshall Lodge Visitor Centre** (Achray Forest, tel. 01877/382258).

Getting There and Away
First Group bus service 11 runs four times daily Mon.–Sat. (45 min.) between Aberfoyle and Stirling via Port of Menteith; on Sundays the same service connects Aberfoyle with Glasgow only. Getting to rural destinations around Forest Park can be more difficult.

There are two **post buses** Monday–Friday and one on Saturday between Callander and Loch Katrine; on weekday afternoons the service continues to Aberfoyle. The other option for getting around the forest during summer months is the **Trossachs Trundler** circular service, heading on the A821 from Callander to Aberfoyle via Loch Katrine and Achray Forest, returning via Port of Menteith. The trips are timed to coordinate with steamship sailing times on Loch Katrine. Inquire at the Rob Roy Visitor Centre in Callander for timetable information.

BREADALBANE RIDGE
The wide rugged expanse of moor that erupts into the Breadalbane Ridge is known as the

Rob Roy's grave, Balquhidder

© LUKE WATERSON

LOCH LOMOND

"High Country" because of the 20 Munro mountains contained within it. Solitude-seekers will love this lonely, hilly region; there are only a few small settlements cowering in the valleys. As soon as you step into the shadow of one of the craggy peaks it will not be difficult to conjure images of Scotland's favorite outlaw, Rob Roy, running through the heather, as he would have done here 300 years ago in a landscape not so very different from today. The main settlements in the area are the unexceptional hill-walking centers of Crianlarich and Tyndrum.

◖ Rob Roy's Grave
Right in the shadow of the Balquhidder Braes in scattered Balquhidder village is the final resting place of the celebrated outlaw Rob Roy MacGregor. You'll find the grave in the church, along with an explanatory board detailing the other graves of note in this tiny churchyard. The gravestone itself was a 20th-century innovation, in case you're marveling at how remarkably shiny it looks. On the grave is etched the

most famous epitaph in Scotland: MacGregor Despite Them. It's an appropriately wild spot, with none of the tourist kitsch too often prevalent at Scottish attractions.

Hill Walking

The **West Highland Way** passes through the area at Tyndrum. Within walking distance of Crianlarich alone there are 11 Munro peaks—a book could be filled with hikes from here. One of the most impressive climbs in the area is to the summit of **Ben Lui,** a dual-peaked mountain with hair-raising drops into jawlike corries (hollows). There are two main approaches: from Cononish Farm in the northeast (easier) and from Dalrigh near Tyndrum on the A85 (longer but with more rewarding views). The summit sits at 3,700 feet. The TIC in Tyndrum can give you printouts of any walk you fancy doing and offer advice on the most spectacular.

Accommodations and Food

If you have your own sleeping bag then **Strathfillan Wigwams** (tel. 01838/400251, www.wigwamholidays.com/strathfillan, £11 pp, tents £5) is about the most intriguing accommodation option in these parts. You can stay in your very own centrally heated wigwam, each of which can sleep up to five. There is a self-catering block nearby, and linens can be rented. It's great fun for the children, especially since the farm shop stocks lots of barbecue supplies, including wild boar, ostrich, and venison. You can also do the normal camping thing here.

The **Crianlarich Youth Hostel** (tel. 0870/ 004 1112, www.crianlarichyouthhostel.org.uk, daily Mar.–Oct., Fri.–Sat. Nov.–Feb., beds £13) is an SYHA-affiliated place with a handy location by Crianlarich station; it offers accommodation in six-bed, single-sex dorms. There are a few separate rooms for families or couples, two of which are en suite. There's also a large common room and well-appointed kitchen.

Located between Crianlarich and Tyndrum, the former church manse of **Strathfillan House** (tel. 01838/400228, www.tyndrum.com, £50 d) has three wide white rooms with sturdy wooden beds. There are en suite

and shared bathroom facilities. Each room has wireless Internet access. The owners will give you a free lift to and from Tyndrum to get back on the West Highland Way path and do pick-ups from Inverarnan to Kingshouse if you want to walk several stages and stay in one place. Coming from Crianlarich, the track to Strathfillan House is on the right of the A82.

Kingshouse Hotel (near Balquhidder, tel. 01877/384646, www.kingshouse-scotland.co.uk, £60 d) has been a spot of fine Highland hospitality since 1599, when the kings of Scotland had a hunting lodge on the site. Two centuries later the current whitewashed inn was built, run by red-coat soldiers to make the drovers that passed through feel more at ease! You'll find big, white, en suite rooms here, with views of Balquhidder and Breadalbane. Now bypassed by the main road, this place has become a tranquil spot to pass a night or three. You can get a good meal in the bar/restaurant by an open fire and amongst the excited chatter of walkers. You'll find the hotel by the junction of the A84 with the Balquhidder road.

Information

Tyndrum Tourist Information (Main St., tel. 01838/400246, 10:30 A.M.–5 P.M. daily Apr.–June and Sept.–Oct., 10:30 A.M.–6 P.M. daily July–Aug.) is one of Scotland's best information centers with information not just on the local area but on destinations throughout Loch Lomond and the Trossachs.

Glencoe Mountain Rescue (tel. 01855/ 811986) should be contacted if you are worried about someone out on the hills.

Getting There and Away

Three to four **trains** daily run from Glasgow to Crianlarich (1 hr. 50 min.) and Tyndrum (2 hrs.). Fares range £14.20–15.30.

Scottish Citylink buses (tel. 0870/550 5050, www.citylink.co.uk) call at Crianlarich and Tyndrum en route to Fort William or Oban from Glasgow. It will take one hour 40 minutes to Tyndrum from Glasgow (a little less to Crianlarich); standard one-way fare is

© LUKE WATERSON

Falls of Dochart, Killin

£12.70. There are **post buses** (two Mon.–Fri., one Sat., 35 min.) between Crianlarich and **Killin** stopping at points on the A85. To get to **Balquhidder,** take a Killin-bound bus from Callander (three weekly).

Getting Around
Call **Crianlarich Cars** (tel. 01838/300307) for a taxi. Book the journey as much in advance as possible; such services are much in demand.

KILLIN
It's difficult to fault this scenic, whitewashed village poised at the confluence of the bubbling Dochart and Lochay Rivers. Behind it the dramatic hill-walking country of the Breadalbane ridge slopes up and in front of it is long, shimmering Loch Tay. It has a cracking good pub, an interesting visitors center, and enough walks to keep you returning, as many do, year after year. What makes Killin a particularly good hiking base is the variety of trails that lead off from here. Some head along the lesser-traveled south shore of Loch Tay, some go up to the rugged Ben Lawers ridge, and some along delightful

Glen Lochay. Lots of the trails are accessed by drivable roads, which heightens the sense of adventure you feel in this special place. The one drawback is that this is a special place appealing to more and more visitors; fortunately there are still enough hikes to lose them all.

Sights
Breadalbane Folklore Centre (tel. 01567/ 820254, www.breadalbanefolklorecentre.com, 10 A.M.–5 P.M. Apr.–June and Sept.–Oct., 10 A.M.–5:30 P.M. July–Aug. £2.75 adult, £1.80 child) is housed in an old water mill overlooking the Falls of Dochart. It also houses the healing stones of St. Filan, a Celtic missionary. Inside it's a visitors center/tourist information point where you can find out more about St. Filan and local clans and plan your own tour through the surrounding hills on a touchscreen computer.

If ever there was a castle reminiscent of Scotland's bloodthirsty past, **Finlarig Castle** (year-round) would be it. In the dark ivy-clad ruins of this 16th-century fortress by Killin village you'll find not only a hanging tree but

LOCH LOMOND

also a beheading pit (legend says that the commoners were hanged and the nobles beheaded, as it was a quicker death). Head east through Killin and turn right over a bridge after the Killin Hotel and before a campsite to reach the castle.

Accommodations and Food

As befits all good hill-walking villages, Killin has a budget accommodation option. **Killin Youth Hostel** (Main St., tel. 0870/004 1131, www.syha.org.uk, beds £14) is pretty good as they go, set in a sedate, old, large-windowed Victorian house amidst greenery on the northeast edge of the village. It sleeps 40 people in spick-and-span 4- to 12-bed dorms. Views of Loch Tay stretch away enticingly. There is a self-catering kitchen.

If you could imagine the ideal place to unwind after a day out in the country, the (**Falls of Dochart Inn** (Falls of Dochart, tel. 01567/820270, www.falls-of-dochart -inn.co.uk, £55 s, £70 d) would undoubtedly be it. There's been no effort made to adapt to the 21st century at this old whitewashed pub; rooms are simple, white, and rustic-looking, with great views of the Falls of Dochart, which tumble under the bridge opposite. It's a listed (historically significant) building, and the wood used in the refurbishment is in keeping with how it was originally built. You needn't

look any further than the cozy bar with its open fire for an evening meal or, on a fine day, sit at the front in the beer garden overlooking the Falls. The menu is dominated by fish and game, with traditional mains like guinea fowl with Drambuie sauce.

Capercaillie Restaurant with Rooms (Main St., tel. 01567/820355, 10 A.M.–9 P.M. daily) is a light, sunny restaurant, set on stilts with prime views over lush gardens and the River Dochart. It puts on some great home baking and a variety of solid main meals (£4–8). The fine views make the dining seem even finer. Bed-and-breakfast rooms are also available.

Getting There and Away

Because it's so far from anywhere, public transport to Killin is minimal. **Post buses** connect it twice per day with Crianlarich and Tyndrum and the **C60 bus service** (tel. 01877/384768) connects it on Tuesday, Thursday, and Saturday evenings with Callander. The C60 will call at Balquhidder if booked in advance by the previous day.

There is also a post bus to Aberfeldy in Perthshire on weekdays. In summer, the highly useful **Scottish Citylink** (tel. 0870/550 5050, www.citylink.co.uk) Dundee to Oban bus service has been calling at Killin (two services daily May–Oct.). Hopefully this will continue to run in the future.

Stirling and the Forth Valley

Huddling on steep slopes below a magnificent castle, Stirling owes a lot to its location. With the first sight of Stirling and its castle atop a crag, you're seeing a city as perfectly situated as can be, with commanding views across the forested central belt of the country. Magnificent it may appear, but sitting on the cusp between lowland and Highland Scotland, Stirling is a strategic settlement. It was said in centuries gone by that he who controlled Stirling Castle controlled Scotland. For all its vivid past, including a stint as the home of

the Scottish monarchy, Stirling only achieved city status in 2002. This increased the flow of comments likening Stirling to a miniature Edinburgh, which the city was all too keen to lap up, but such comments are barely justified. Granted, Stirling Castle rivals Edinburgh's for immensity and historical intrigue, but the rest of Stirling is no more than a jumped-up town with precious few other noteworthy buildings, an art gallery, and some half-decent pubs and restaurants. Still, as urban areas of Scotland go it's an attractive place and a good base for a

© LUKE WATERSON

Stirling Old Town

clutch of attractions in the surrounding area. Beyond Stirling, the Forth Valley has its heavily industrialized heritage to discover. To the northeast and southwest press two steep ranges of hills, the Ochill Hills and the Campsie Fells, both teeming with great walks.

SIGHTS

As befits a place so integral to Scottish history, Stirling has its fair share of historic sights. The old town that spreads out below the castle is good for a wander. For all the fighting the area has seen, most sights are remarkably intact.

Stirling Castle

Standing on a volcanic crag soaring out of the trees, this castle (tel. 01786/450000, 9:30 A.M.–6 P.M. daily Apr.–Sept. 9:30 A.M.–5 P.M. daily Oct.–Mar., £8.50 adults, £6.50 seniors, £4.25 children) is the dominant feature of Stirling and possibly of all central Scotland. There have almost certainly been buildings on the castle site for the best part of a millennium, but the castle standing today dates from as early as 1496. The castle's

position above the lowest crossing point on the River Forth and the main lowland–Highland route meant that historically, there were few worthwhile movements that escaped the eye of its incumbents. It's a testimony to its incredible defenses that the fortress has been able to survive 16 assaults during its colorful history.

The castle has overseen many of the turning points in Scottish history. William Wallace and Robert the Bruce recaptured the castle from the English in 1297 and 1314 at the Battle of Bannockburn. The Stewart monarchs made the castle their home between 1400 and 1600: Mary, Queen of Scots was crowned in the Chapel Royal next to the Great Hall in 1543. Today the castle makes for not only a lengthy exploration (set at least half a day aside) but also a great photo-snapping spot. You're high above Stirling here and have great panoramic views to William Wallace towering across the valley. The castle's café offers homebakes and even roast dinners. There's a car park at the top to save you the walk up.

The thick **Outer Defences,** the most apparent part of the castle, are its most recent

LOCH LOMOND

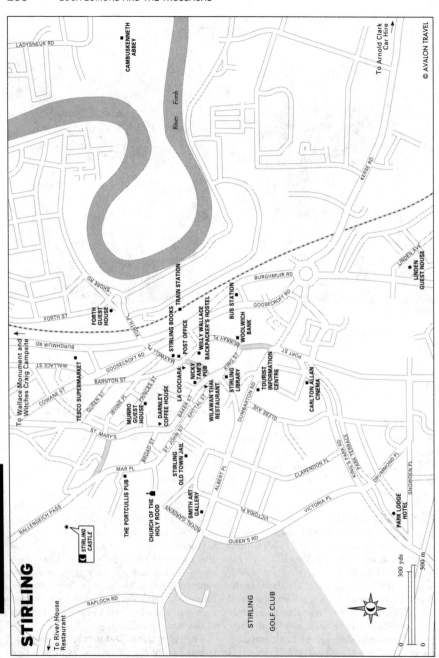

addition; Mary of Guise, wife of James V and mother of Mary, Queen of Scots, ordered construction of the first of these outer walls in 1559. These were strengthened again in 1711 in response to the Jacobite threat of the time. The major development in the Outer Defences was that of the French spur, a jutting artillery tower from which soldiers could fire to the south and east, as well as to the front; this enabled the castle to defend itself against Bonnie Prince Charlie, who laid siege to it in 1746.

As you approach the Outer Close through the forework, the palace is on your left and the great hall is straight ahead. To the right are the **kitchens.** A good sense of the incumbent's priorities in the late 17th century can be grasped here, as these were covered by the **Great Battery,** an added line of defenses to protect the castle on this, its weakest side.

The **palace** at Stirling Castle was designed to rival the best designs in France, and to increase accommodation at the fortress. James V began work on the palace and his wife continued the building after his death. It's a grand and extensive building, with a set of three rooms apiece for king and queen but appears unfinished in places. Perhaps after the death of James V such large apartments were considered unnecessary. Historic Scotland intends to restore the king's and queen's lodgings back to their state during the glory days of the 16th century.

The resplendently white **Great Hall** is the most impressive part of the castle. It's hosted some appropriately lavish events in its time, including the christening of Prince Henry in 1594; seafood was served to guests from a ship that fired cannons in celebration of the event. Like much of the castle, the Great Hall was historically prey to military priorities rather than architectural ones. In the 18th century extra floors were added for storage space and the previously elaborate hammer-beam roof was altered. In 1999, Queen Elizabeth II opened a refurbished Great Hall that had taken 30 years to restore to its fine early 16th-century state. Make sure to pay a visit to the exquisite tapestries hanging in the **Chapel Royal:** They depict scenes from *The Hunt of the Unicorn,* a series of late 15th-century tapestries depicting a group of nobles pursuing the mythical beast.

Stirling Old Town Jail

This thought-provoking attraction (St. John St., tel. 01786/450050, www.oldtownjail.com, 9:30 A.M.–5:30 P.M. daily June–Sept., 10 A.M.–5 P.M. daily Apr.–May, 10 A.M.–5 P.M. daily Oct., 10 A.M.–4 P.M. daily Nov.–Mar., last entrance one hour before closing, £5.95 adult, £4.50 senior or student, £3.80 children, £15.70 family) uses a host of sinister characters and grisly displays on a number of prison inmates to re-create life in this jail in the 19th century. You'll get insight into life as an inmate, a hangman, and a prison reformer, before completing your education with a comparative look at today's prisoners in Scotland. It's all good fun and a highlight for children on the trail of Stirling's daunting number of historical attractions.

Smith Art Gallery

This museum (Dumbarton Rd., tel. 01786/ 471917, www.smithartgallery.demon.co.uk, 10:30 A.M.–5 P.M. Tues.–Sat., 2–5 P.M. Sun., free) is a fitting testimony to the grandeur of Stirling. The huge art collection of Thomas Stuart Smith (1815–1869), the gallery's founder, contains one of the most important series of British and world exhibits in Scotland outside Edinburgh. Highlights include one of the best portraits of Bonnie Prince Charlie and the oldest curling stone in existence.

Wallace Monument

You'll see monuments to Scottish freedom-fighter William Wallace across the country, but none as big as this one (off Hillfoots Rd., Causewayhead, Stirling, tel. 01786/472140, www.nationalwallacemonument.com, 9 A.M.–6 P.M. daily July–Aug., 10 A.M.–6 P.M. daily June, 9:30 A.M.–5:30 P.M. Sept., 10 A.M.–5 P.M. daily Mar.–May and Oct., 10:30 A.M.–4 P.M. daily Jan.–Feb. and Nov.–Dec., £6.50 adults, £4 children). Built with a typical Victorian propensity to grandeur, it sticks out of a forested hill across the valley

LOCH LOMOND

from Stirling Castle and looks very nearly as impressive. You can climb up through an over-the-top trumpeting of Scottish history (one floor is devoted to a hall of heroes and one to the story of how the monument was built) before you emerge at the top of 246 steps for some of Scotland's best views. Up here, with the River Forth nothing but a thread below, you're looking out on the ground where some of the most important battles in Scottish history were fought.

Cambuskenneth Abbey
Cambuskenneth Abbey (Cambuskenneth, 9:30 A.M.–6:30 P.M. daily Apr.–Sept., free) was at its height in the late 13th century and reduced to rubble soon after by successive armies during the Wars of Independence; it's incredible that any of this lonely ruin by the wending River Forth survives at all. The only building now standing is the Bell Tower but in the remains of the church is the tomb of James III. It's indicative of his unpopularity that this monarch should be buried in these scant ruins. The flat grassy ground on which the abbey stands has good views to the greater structures of Stirling Castle and the Wallace Monument. The abbey lies to the east of Stirling, on the other side of the looping River Forth.

Tours
City Sightseeing (tel. 01786/446611, www.citysightseeingstirling.net, £7.50 adult, £5 students and seniors, £3 children, under 5 free) runs 1.5-hour tours to all the main attractions in Stirling starting from the rail station, every 45 minutes daily Easter–October and weekends October–Easter.

ENTERTAINMENT AND EVENTS
Stirling is the nightlife capital of the region. There are no amazing clubs but plenty of style bars and a few lively pubs. There's a freshness to the air in this history-rich town, which makes it a charming spot to linger over a meal or a few drinks.

Pubs and Bars
Nicky Tams (29 Baker St., tel. 01786/472194, 11 A.M.–midnight Sun.–Thurs., 11 A.M.–1 A.M. Fri.–Sat.) is allegedly haunted: a great lively old pub popular with students, locals, and tourists alike. It's on the main Stirling pub crawl route, but it's an individual place with a good Sunday night quiz.

The **Portcullis** (near Stirling Castle, tel. 01786/472290, www.portcullishotel.com, 11 A.M.–midnight daily), a dark old bar right by the castle with a stone-walled outside beer garden, is great for a drink and a meal. The bar is all shiny wood, and you can cozy up by the fireside in the cold weather. The building is an 18th-century schoolhouse, and it's hard to tell which century you're in at this place.

Cinema
The **Carlton Allan Cinema** (28 Allan Pk., tel. 01786/475242) shows mainstream films for £6.

Shopping
This basement shop of **Stirling Books** (18 Maxwell Pl., tel. 01786/461816, www.stirling-books.co.uk) is stacked with secondhand books and has Internet access (£1 for 30 min.). You'll also get Stirling's finest takeout coffee here. **Tesco** (Wallace St., tel. 0845/677 9658) is one of the large supermarkets just to the north of the city center.

ACCOMMODATIONS
Stirling doesn't exactly jump out at you as a place brimming with great places to stay but you'll find plenty of pleasant accommodation, mainly in the form of guest houses which make up for the lack of really good hotels.

Witches Craig Caravan Site (Blairlogie, tel. 01786/474947, www.witchescraig.com, Apr.–Oct., tents £6.50) is the nearest place to pitch a tent to Stirling. With the Ochill Hills towering over the site, it's an unusually scenic spot to camp so close to the city center. There's a mix of grass and trees for shelter and spick-and-span toilet blocks. The site is at the beginning of the A91 road to Alva and Tillicoultry.

Willy Wallace Backpacker's Hostel (77 Murray Pl., tel. 01786/446773, www.willy-wallacehostel.com, beds £14, £35 d) is a loud, friendly hostel offering good clean accommodation mostly in gaudily painted dorm rooms. Too many beds are crammed into some rooms, but partitions add a sense of privacy. There's a light guest lounge, a well-furnished kitchen, and a reception area full of information on local attractions.

At the comfortable, terraced **Munro Guest House** (14 Princes St., tel. 01786/472685, www.munroguesthouse.co.uk, from £28 s, £46 d) you'll find five cozy, clean rooms, all with en suite or private bathrooms. There is a guest lounge with a fire. The carpets and tartan furnishings combine to make this a very convivial place to stay. You can't argue with the location, either—10 minutes' walk to the castle and five minutes to the bus/train station.

The **Forth Guest House** (23 Forth Pl., tel. 01786/471020, www.forthguesthouse.co.uk, £50 d) bills itself as Stirling's most conveniently situated guesthouse (it's close to the city's main bus and train connections). This pretty terraced house dates from the 1820s. The six rooms here have a loud floral theme but they are spacious and en suite, with TVs. You'll get a good traditional Scottish breakfast in the morning, as well as the option of porridge, in the elegant dining room. You can walk to the center of Stirling in five minutes.

Linden Guest House (22 Linden Ave., tel. 01786/448850, www.lindenguesthouse.co.uk, £45 s, £100 d) offers four bright, modern en suite rooms that positively gleam after their recent refurbishment. The family room is absolutely massive. Rooms come with color TVs and the breakfasts are big (fruit, cereal, and a fry-up if you want).

This antique-furnished 19th-century **Ⓒ Park Lodge Hotel** (32 Park Terr., tel. 01786/474862, www.parklodge.net, £75 s, £105 d) overlooks the King's Park and Golf Course. It's the most elegant hotel in the city with a walled garden and a French restaurant. The nine rooms have en suite facilities, color TVs, and telephones.

FOOD

The good restaurants in Stirling are fairly evenly spread between the city center and the wealthy suburb of Bridge of Allan, north of center near the University.

City Center

Darnley Coffee House (18 Bow St., tel. 01786/474468, 10:30 A.M.–4 P.M. Mon.–Sat.) is supposedly where Lord Darnley stayed while his wife Mary, Queen of Scots lived the high life up at Stirling Castle. It's got bags of charm and ambience; enjoy the 16th-century atmosphere as you sit with your baguette and specialty coffee in the heart of the old town. Snacks and meals are £2–6.

The owners of **Wilawan** (9 Baker St., tel. 01786/464837, www.wilawanthairestaurant.moonfruit.com, 12:30–3 P.M. and 5:30–11 P.M. daily) ensure diners get some authentic Thai cooking here in an ornate restaurant decked out with statues. The pad Thai is a tasty option. Booking is advisable as there are not too many tables. Dinner will cost £10–20 depending on the number of dishes ordered.

If there was one place in Stirling to while away the day over a bottle of wine or two, it would be **Ⓒ La Ciociara** (41 Friars St., tel. 01786/451552, noon–10 P.M. daily). This is a café with an Italian restaurant upstairs. You can enjoy an espresso and people watch at the window seats downstairs and retire upstairs for a good pizza or pasta meal in the evening. Meals are around £10–12. You can get takeaway pizza, too.

River House (Castle Business Pk., tel. 01786/465577, www.riverhouserestaurant.co.uk, noon–10 P.M. daily) may be based on the design of a traditional Scottish crannog (ancient lake dwelling) but it offers modern, contemporary cuisine from the unlikely location of a retail park on the outskirts of Stirling. Mains, like vegetarian chili, salmon fillet with Parma ham, and pan-seared scallops, are £12–16, in a spacious restaurant overlooking the water.

Bridge of Allan

This laid-back, scenic northern suburb of Stirling is a great place to eat.

Allan Water Café (15 Henderson St., tel. 01786/833060, www.allanwatercafe.co.uk, 8 A.M.–10 P.M. Tues.–Sat., 8 A.M.–9 P.M. Sun.–Mon.) has to be one of the most idyllic places to eat fish and chips in Scotland. You can sit upstairs and gaze out over Henderson Street through the wall-to-ceiling windows or munch your takeaway down by the river (head right out of the building—you can't miss it). They've been hand-making ice cream on-site for about a century, as well. Meals are £2–6.

If you're planning a riverside picnic, don't even think about going anywhere other than **Clive Ramsay Deli** (Henderson St., tel. 01786/833903, www.cliveramsay.com, 7 A.M.–7 P.M. daily). This place has received the Cheese of the Year award in Scotland several times. You'll also find olives, chorizo, specialty beers, and homemade bread. Takeaway sandwiches and other snacks start from £1.

The **Old Bridge Inn** (2 Inverallan Rd., tel. 01786/833335, www.oldbridgeinn.co.uk/bofa, food noon–2 P.M. and 6–9 P.M. daily, bar open until 11 P.M. Sun.–Thurs., until midnight Fri.–Sat.) serves pub food worth traveling to find. The bar/restaurant is an inviting spot: an open-plan setting with a cozy fire to create that feeling of rustic intimacy as you dine on pub classics like venison and ale pie or just a good steak. Mains are £6–13.

Seafood is the specialty at **Campbells@ Chambo** (Mine Rd., tel. 01786/833617, 12:30–2:30 P.M. and 5:30–9:30 P.M. daily). It's delightful enough just soaking in the atmosphere here at this converted old Victorian spa house with its circular restaurant, let alone trying the cuisine. The food is anything but the pretentious fare you might expect in this affluent neighborhood: scallops, steak sandwiches, and even tapas. Two-course lunches are £10.95 and three-course early evening meals are £15.95.

INFORMATION AND SERVICES

Stirling is the main service center for the region, with the biggest area hospital.

Tourist Information

Stirling TIC (41 Dumbarton Rd., tel. 0870/720 0620, 9 A.M.–5 P.M. Mon.–Sat. Apr.–May and mid-Sept.–mid-Oct., 9 A.M.–6 P.M. Mon.–Sat. and 10 A.M.–4 P.M. June and early–mid-Sept., 9 A.M.–7 P.M. Mon.–Sat. and 9:30 A.M.–4 P.M. Sun. July–Aug., 10 A.M.–5 P.M. Mon.–Fri. and 10 A.M.–4 P.M. Sat. mid-Oct.–Mar.) has lots of brochures, information, and local maps, but the service here borders on rude at times.

Services

You'll find most banks in the area around Murray Place, including **Woolwich** (16 Murray Pl., tel. 0845/071 8099) which has a *bureau de change*.

The characterful **Stirling Books** (18 Maxwell Pl., tel. 01786/461816) has Internet access (£1 for 30 minutes). Free Internet access is at **Stirling Library** (Corn Exchange Rd., 9:30 A.M.–5 P.M. Mon., Wed., and Fri., 9:30 A.M.–7 P.M. Tues. and Thurs., 9:30 A.M.–5 P.M. Sat.). **Stirling Post Office** is on Barnton Street near the junction with Maxwell Place.

Stirling Royal Infirmary (Livilands, tel. 01786/434000) is just south of the city center and is the main hospital for the city and for Loch Lomond and the Trossachs.

Superwash Laundrette (9 Barnsdale Rd., tel. 01786/473540) will do self-service and full-service cleans. You'll find it south of the city center in the St. Ninians district.

GETTING THERE

Stirling is near the head of the M9 Motorway with good transport connections southwest to Glasgow and southeast to Edinburgh.

Train

There are thrice-hourly trains to Glasgow (35 min., £6.70) and Edinburgh (1 hr., £6.50). Trains also run hourly to Perth (30 min.) and every 1.5 hours to Inverness (3 hrs.).

Bus

Scottish Citylink (tel. 0870/550 5050, www.citylink.co.uk) runs buses to Edinburgh (hourly, 1 hr. five min., £4.90) and Glasgow (hourly, 50 min., £4.90). You can also take the regular service to Perth and change there to get to Inverness.

© LUKE WATERSON

the Falkirk Wheel, the world's first rotating boat lift, in action

GETTING AROUND
Train
From Stirling, you can get to **Falkirk** in the Forth Valley and **Dunblane** by train. Train travel is also possible in the west of the region, from Glasgow to **Balloch** and from Glasgow to **Helensburgh** and points along **Loch Lomond** up to **Crianlarich and Tyndrum** (the West Highland Line).

Bus
Stirling bus station (tel. 01786/446474) is on Goosecroft Road. Stirling is the major hub for bus travel in the area and is almost the only way of getting to the Trossachs and destinations in the Forth Valley.

Taxi
Albion Taxi's (tel. 01786/811111) are licensed by Stirling Council and will do journeys in four- to eight-seater cabs.

Car Rental
Arnold Clark (Kerse Rd., tel. 01786/478586) has an office here; hire is from £17 daily.

THE FORTH VALLEY AND CLACKMANNANSHIRE
Heavy industry is both this area's curse and its blessing; it's the reason a lot of visitors are put off the region and also what makes the attractions here unique. The undoubted highlights are the masterful Falkirk Wheel, the world's only revolving boat lift, which has rejuvenated the main canals in the area, and the dramatic Dollar Glen in Clackmannanshire's Ochill Hills. Near Falkirk you can also follow the remains of the Antonine Wall, built by the Romans to signify the northern extent of their empire almost 2,000 years ago. North of the Forth Valley is the "wee county" of Scotland, Clackmannanshire. It's a loveable little place characterized by its distinctive towers and dramatic-looking hills. The Ochill range of hills shoots up from a series of villages known as the Hillfoots (villages at the foot of the hill) in steep, scenic glens that provide commanding views of the surrounding countryside.

◖ Falkirk Wheel
For a long time the Union Canal from

LOCH LOMOND

Edinburgh and the Forth and Clyde Canal from Glasgow were connected by a series of 11 lochs, but these had fallen into disrepair by the 1930s. At Falkirk the two ran close but were separated by a distance of 78 feet. It was decided by British Waterways to link the two canals once more as part of a millennium project; this ingenious design got the go-ahead. The Falkirk Wheel (tel. 0870/050 0208, www.falkirkwheel.co.uk, 9:30 A.M.–6 P.M. Mon.–Fri., 9:30 A.M.–7 P.M. Sat.–Sun. Aug., 9:30 A.M.–6 P.M. daily Easter–July and Sept.–Oct., 10 A.M.–4:30 P.M. Mon.–Fri., 10 A.M.–6 P.M. Sat.–Sun. Nov.–Easter), the world's first and only rotating boat lift, lifts boats the equivalent height of an eight-story building between the two waterways. It's helped by the weight of a boat coming down from the canal at the top. For the first time in 70 years the Falkirk Wheel connected Central Scotland's east and west coasts. You can find out about how the Falkirk Wheel was built and how it operates at the visitors center, where there is a very good café. The whole thing is a great celebration of modern design and architecture—a very different kind of attraction from most of Scotland's history-themed sights. Boat trips up on the wheel are possible; they run about three times per hour roughly 10 A.M.–4:30 P.M. April–October, and about five times per day the rest of the year. Boat trips cost £8 adult, £4.25 child. Admission to the visitors center is free.

You can walk the half mile from the wheel to paths to **Rough Castle Fort** (year-round), the best-preserved section of the Antonine Wall, built in A.D. 142. Regular buses run from Falkirk High train station and from the town center to the wheel.

Clackmannanshire Towers

Fifteenth-century **Alloa Tower** (Alloa, tel. 01259/211701, 1–5 P.M. daily Mar.–Oct.) is one of the most magnificent buildings of its type in Scotland, refurbished by the 6th Earl of Mar, John Erskine, who lived in the tower in the late 17th and early 18th centuries and instigated the industrialization of

Clackmannanshire. The tower has a fine portrait collection and a dungeon. **Clackmannan Tower** (Clackmannan, tel. 01259/216913, www.clacksweb.org.uk) was where, in 1787, Robert Burns was knighted with a sword supposedly belonging to Robert the Bruce. The tower is not currently open to visitors but still makes for a good, muddy walk.

Dollar Glen

The steep-sided Ochill Hills cut down sharply into a series of glens clung to by what are known as the Hillfoot villages. The most impressive of these is Dollar, an intriguing village of handsome gray houses. Dollar was made affluent by the establishment there in 1818 of one of Britain's largest private schools, which has since attracted the area's wealthy families. Above Dollar a road climbs into woodland and tails off at a car park, from where a path twists around **Castle Campbell** (near Dollar, tel. 01259/742408, 9:30 A.M.–5:30 P.M. daily Apr.–Sept., 9:30 A.M.–4:30 P.M. daily Oct., 9:30 A.M.–4:30 P.M. Sat.–Wed. Nov.–Mar., £4.50 adults, £2.25 children). The fortress was the lowland stronghold of the Campbell family, who built it as a demonstration of power and wealth. The castle, which seems to teeter on the edge of a wooded precipice, dates from the 1400s. Dollar Glen is a great access point onto the hills; from here you can walk up to Ben Cleuch, the highest point on the Ochill Hills.

Accommodations

Westbourne House (Dollar Rd., Tillicoultry, tel. 01259/750314, www.westbournehouse.co.uk, £40 s, £54 d) is a Victorian mill-owner's house set in an acre of tree-studded grounds beneath the Ochill Hills, a real haven from the busy Stirling–Dollar road. The elegant rooms are decked out in soothing whites and come with color TVs and en suite/private bathrooms. There is a sitting room with wood-burning stove and a croquet lawn in the garden.

Getting There and Away

Trains run half-hourly to Falkirk from Stirling (20 min., £3.60) and five times per hour to Edinburgh (35 min., £5). **Bus** service 62 connects Stirling, the Hillfoot Villages, and Alloa every 20 minutes Monday–Saturday, with reduced Sunday service. To get to Clackmannan, there are half-hourly buses from Stirling via Alloa.

STRATHALLAN AND THE CAMPSIE FELLS

Allan Water rises in the Ochill Hills and wends its way down to join the River Forth just outside Stirling. The river was ideally located for the milling industry, and the handsome towns of Dunblane and Doune here owe their development to textile mills. The gentle, lush countryside quickly rears up to the southwest in the shape of the Campsie Fells, an extensive range of hills that separate the Stirling area from Glasgow to the south. In the hills nestle some great walks and several beautiful, isolated villages perfect for kicking back awhile.

Dunblane

Dunblane is a quiet town laced by Allan Water and scarred by the tragedy of March 13, 1996, when a gunman killed 16 primary school pupils and a teacher before turning the weapon on himself. The tragedy is remembered by the Dunblane commemoration stone in the splendid cathedral, which forms the centerpiece of the town.

Walking along the banks of the River Allan is very pleasant but the main attraction in town is the immense **cathedral** (tel. 01786/823388, 9:30 A.M.–5:30 P.M. Mon.–Sat., 2–5:30 P.M. Sun. Apr.–Sept., 9:30 A.M.–4:30 P.M. Mon.–Sat., 2–4:30 P.M. Sun. Oct.–Mar.), a charming gray-pink building set on the wide grassy square in the center. The building commemorates St. Blane, who founded a monastery on this site in the 7th century A.D. The nave contains the Dunblane commemoration stone; there is also some wonderful stained glass. Donations are welcome, and there is a Sunday service at 10:30 A.M. year-round.

Kippen and Fintry

These two villages make great bases for walking in the Campsie Fells. With a snug location in the Fells foothills, Kippen is a collection of charming 17th-century black-and-white houses. Kippen Cross has an information board detailing various local walks and activities. In the heat of the Fells six miles south of Kippen, the one-street village of Fintry stretches along Endrick Water in the heart of the steep, green Campsie Fells. It may only be 15 miles from the northern sprawl of Glasgow, but Fintry is an isolated spot. The village has a couple of places to stay, good pubs, and an impressive 90-foot series of cascades, the **Loup of Fintry** (near Cairnoch Hill, open year-round), which lies east of the village on the B818.

Accommodations and Food

In the Dunblane area, a good place to stay is **The Water Tower B and B** (Ashfield, tel. 01786/820217, www.thewatertower.co.uk, £25 s, £50 d), 1.5 miles north of town at Ashfield, in the heart of Strathallan. It's a recently renovated house right on the river. The rooms have a mix of en suite or private bathrooms. They are quite minimalist, and the breakfasts are organic.

There are pubs aplenty in Dunblane but the best place to feast is just outside at the **Sheriffmuir Inn** (tel. 01786/823285, www.sheriffmuirinn.co.uk, noon–2 P.M. and 5:30–9 P.M. Wed.–Sat., noon–2 P.M. and 5:30–8:30 P.M. Mon., noon–2:30 P.M. and 5:30–8:30 P.M. Sun.), a traditional, countrified gastro-pub with a touch of the modern about it. It's in a really isolated spot, despite being only five minutes' drive from Dunblane. You'll eat very well here (from haggis to braised squid—take your pick) and with such a setting, meals are worth the price tag of £10–15. You'll find it on the road across Sheriff Muir from Bridge of Allan, past Cauldhame.

In Kippen, the beautiful **Cross Keys Hotel** (Main St., tel. 01786/870293, from £60 d, food served noon–2 P.M. and 5:30–9:30 P.M. Mon.–Sat., 12:30–2 P.M. and 5:30–9:30 P.M. Sun.) has three boutique-style rooms, all en suite and two with great views of the fells. Food here in the 17th-century coaching inn is a great deal: Wholesome meals like traditional fish and chips start at around £6. There's also the classy **Berits and Brown Deli** (Main St., tel. 01786/870077, kippen@beritsandbrown.co.uk, 10 A.M.–5 P.M. Mon.–Sat., 11 A.M.–5 P.M. Sun.) just up the road, serving the finest coffee in the Campsie Fells and a host of other goodies.

The best place to stay in Fintry is at **Culcreuch Castle** (north Fintry on B822, tel. 01360/860228, www.culcreuch.com, £136 d), a fortress set within its own forested estate. The 10 suites here look like something out of a period drama, with four-poster beds and antique furniture, with one room even having hand-painted Chinese wallpaper. Wide-screen TVs are in every room. You can also rent a four-person woodland lodge from £239 per week. The best place to dine here is in the dungeon bar/restaurant, with bare stone walls, an intimate feel, and lots of real ales on tap. A candlelit meal here will set you back £30 per person. If you fancy a meal lighter on the stomach/bank account, head a few miles farther along the B822 toward Kippen to **The Courtyard Café** (Knockraich Farm, near Fintry, tel. 01360/860466, 10 A.M.–4:30 P.M. daily Apr.–Sept., 10 A.M.–4 P.M. Oct.–Mar.) with meals from £5, including fine homemade soups, all in a gorgeous rustic setting on a farm.

Getting There and Away

You can get to Dunblane by **train** from Stirling (four hourly, £2.50). **Callander bus** service 59 calls at Doune en route to/from Stirling. They run hourly Monday–Saturday; there is no Sunday service.

For Kippen, there are two daily buses (Mon.–Fri.) from Stirling, terminating in **Balfron,** southeast of Kippen. You can also get to Balfron via a regular bus service running daily. There is a bus on the first Saturday of every month from Balfron to Fintry. Alternatively, Fintry is a pleasant five-mile hike along Endrick Water from Balfron.

ARGYLL AND THE INNER HEBRIDES

Argyll and its nearby Hebridean islands are a land of shores: sea shores and loch shores. Taking in each isle and inlet, this part of Scotland alone has more coastline than France. It's a land dominated by water; even in innermost Argyll huge blue-gray lochs almost cut this part of the mainland off from the rest, and the mountains finish the job. The region has traditionally looked outward to the sea for its income, and the importance of towns here is still denoted by their fishing industries and whether they are ferry ports or not. When on dry land in Argyll, you will often get the impression that civilization, where it exists at all, sits crouched as close to the water as it can get, peering out at the waves for signs of activity.

Wilderness rules: vast hills and thick sweeps of forest make a mockery of human attempts to settle here. Yet the buildings of Argyll are often as stunning as the scenery. Great Gothic mansions dominate hillsides, crumbling castles command the shorelines, pearl-white villages huddle around bays, and wild woods open up in to tropical gardens warmed by the Gulf Stream. For millennia, people have wanted to live here despite the isolation and danger posed by warring tribes. Historically, the motivation was that a house or castle built here had the natural defenses of water and mountains. You would see your enemy approaching from a great distance. More recently, the reason to linger here has been just to soak up the scenery and the serenity. Since the days of celebrity writers Boswell and Johnson and their famous tour of the isles in the late 18th century, visitors to the area have bolstered its economy. As

© LUKE WATERSON

ARGYLL AND INNER HEBRIDES

HIGHLIGHTS

Kerrera: This hilly island makes the perfect day out from Oban, with wild walks, perfect picnicking spots, and a bunkhouse and tea garden for those who can't bear to leave (page 304).

West Highland Railway: Riding the West Highland Railway to Oban is the ideal introduction to Argyll, with sleepy stations sheltering beneath stupendous loch-laced moorland scenery, and all from the comfort of your carriage (page 307).

Kilmartin Glen: An exploration of the mega-archaeology of Kilmartin Glen can include standing stones, burial chambers, forts, and castles spanning 5,000 years (page 314).

Crinan Canal and Knapdale Forest: Watch the yachts sail down Britain's most photogenic man-made waterway, surrounded by wild mountain forest (page 317).

Tobermory: With a brightly colored, bustling harborfront, this lively island capital is packed with gourmet restaurants and charismatic places to stay (page 324).

Isle of Iona: Spiritual Iona is the fount of Christianity in Scotland, with one of the world's most beautiful cloistered abbeys as well as plenty of swimming beaches (page 333).

Windsurfing: There's no better surfing spot in Britain than **Tiree,** a windy island with a coastline made up almost entirely of superb sandy beaches (page 337).

Port Charlotte and Rinns of Islay: All that is best about the Isle of Islay in one

LOOK FOR ([TO FIND RECOMMENDED SIGHTS, ACTIVITIES, DINING, AND LODGING.

wonderful peninsula of distilleries, picturesque villages, wildlife reserves, and exquisite bays (page 343).

Walking on Jura: Hiking opportunities in this island wilderness include the trek to the Corrywreckan, one of the world's largest whirlpools (page 347).

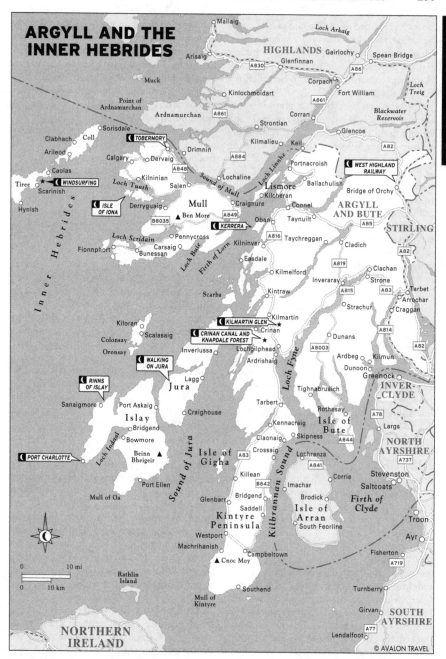

ARGYLL AND THE INNER HEBRIDES

Mallaig
Loch Arkaig
HIGHLANDS Gairlochy Spean Bridge
Arisaig Glenfinnan A86
A830 Corpach Loch Treig
Muck Kinlochmoidart Fort William
Point of Ardnamurchan Corran Blackwater Reservoir
Ardnamurchan A861 Strontian Glencoe
A861 Kilmalieu Keil Glencoe A82
Sorisdale Portnacroish
Clabhach Coll (**TOBERMORY** Drimnin (**WEST HIGHLAND RAILWAY**
Arileod Calgary Dervaig A884 Lochaline Ballachulish
Caolas Kilninian A848 Salen Lismore Kilcheran Bridge of Orchy
Tiree (**WINDSURFING** Loch Tuath **Mull** Craignure **ARGYLL AND BUTE**
Scarinish Derryguaig (**ISLE OF IONA** ▲ Ben More A849 Oban Connel A85 **STIRLING**
Hynish B8035 Pennycross (**KERRERA** Taynuilt A82
Loch Scridain Carsaig A816 Taychreggan Cladich
Fionnphort Bunessan Kilninver Easdale A819 Clachan Tarbet
Firth of Lorn Kilmelford Inveraray Strone A83 Arrochar
Scarba Kintraw A815 Strachur Craggan
Kilmartin A814
(**KILMARTIN GLEN** Crinan A8003 Dunans A82
Kiloran (**CRINAN CANAL AND KNAPDALE FOREST** Lochgilphead Ardbeg Kilmun
Colonsay Scalasaig Inverlussa Ardrishaig Dunoon Greenock
Oronsay (**WALKING ON JURA** Loch Fyne Tighnabruaich **INVER-CLYDE**
(**RINNS OF ISLAY** Lagg **Jura** Tarbert Rothesay A78
Sanaigmore Port Askaig Craighouse Kennacraig **Isle of Bute** Largs
Islay Bridgend Claonaig Skipness A844 **NORTH AYRSHIRE**
Bowmore Crossaig Lochranza A737
(**PORT CHARLOTTE** Beinn Bheigeir ▲ Isle of Gigha A83 Killean A841 Corrie Stevenston
Loch Indaal Bridgend B842 Imachar Saltcoats
Port Ellen Glenbarr Saddell Brodick **Firth of Clyde** Troon
Mull of Oa Westport Kintyre Peninsula South Feorline **Isle of Arran** Ayr
Machrihanish ▲ Cnoc Moy Campbeltown Fisherton A719
0 10 mi Rathlin Island Turnberry **SOUTH AYRSHIRE**
0 10 km Mull of Kintyre Southend Girvan
NORTHERN IRELAND Lendalfoot A77
© AVALON TRAVEL

Inner Hebrides
Sound of Jura
Kilbrannan Sound
Loch Linnhe
Sound of Mull
Loch Bute

Boswell explained in the account of his travels, he was attracted to visit this region "to find simplicity and wildness, and all the circumstances of remote time or place." Over 200 years later, tourists are enticed by much the same reasons.

Scattered down a hillside plunging into the sea, Oban is the delightful regional capital and main transport hub, and yet it is decidedly remote. The journey here is grueling and dramatic, passing nothing but sprinklings of houses in the moors of Lorn. From Oban, most of the ferries go to the islands of the Inner Hebrides, which lie to the west. Once the islands were a powerful dynasty in their own right, governed by the ancient Lords of the Isles who wielded might with fleets of war ships. These islands still have a self-important swagger. They are thriving little places: There is Mull with its picture-postcard capital of Tobermory and remote walks, Iona with its 1,500 years of religious heritage, Tiree with its exotic white-sand beaches, and Islay with its whisky distilleries.

Topography means that the roads in Argyll and on the islands are few, long, winding, and wonderful. Public transport is limited—you're better off getting around on your own wheels. However, it may be quicker and certainly more rewarding to sling a backpack over your shoulder and set off cross-country on foot to reach your destination.

HISTORY

From the beginnings of time, Argyll and the Hebrides have had their own separate and unique histories; it's only been considered part of the same land as Scotland for the past six centuries.

Prehistory

As early as 3000 B.C. the first of the great stone monuments were being erected in Kilmartin Glen, when huge stone burial cairns were built as memorials to the chieftains of warring tribes. Migrants from Ireland known as the Scoti began to settle here around A.D. 500. They recognized the importance of an area

littered with standing stones and burial chambers and built another monument, the hill fort of Dunadd, which became the capital of their kingdom. Their empire grew in importance over the following 300 years. It was a king of Dalriada, Kenneth I, who conquered the Picts and went on to become the first lord of a unified land, in A.D. 843.

In A.D. 563 St. Columba founded a monastery on the Isle of Iona and is credited with introducing Christianity to Scotland. By A.D. 800 the kingdom of migrants was invaded by more migrants: the Vikings, who asserted their authority and thrust their language on the area.

1100-1746

In 1156, the political and military leader Somerled capitalized on the deaths of two kings in Scotland to seize the Inner Hebrides, the Isle of Skye, and the Outer Hebrides, along with the Isle of Man off the English coast for himself. This new empire heralded the beginnings of the dynasty of the Lords of the Isles. At the Battle of Largs in 1263, the empire sided with the Norse against the Scottish, lost heavily, and was forced to recognize the overriding authority of the Scottish crown. By the 15th century, the dynasty of the Lords of the Isles had all but collapsed. The power game in the region was no longer about showing reckless military might but about politically supporting the right sides in the bigger picture of Scottish politics. Therefore the MacDonalds and the Campbell clan supported Robert the Bruce and made huge political gains at the expense of the MacDougalls, who opposed Bruce and were consequently decimated. The 13th–15th centuries were uncertain times. Castles were built in haste as protection; no family knew who would stab who in the back next to make territorial gains. Ultimately, it was the Campbells who proved the more tactically shrewd and asserted their power in the region.

18th Century Onward

By the demise of the Jacobite Rebellion in 1746, the Campbells, now under the title of the government-allied Dukes of Argyll, embarked upon strengthening and improving the lands they had inherited. The 3rd Duke of Argyll began with the construction of the first planned village in Scotland, Inveraray, in the 1740s. This region developed a more sophisticated reputation; early 19th-century travelers had Argyll and the Hebrides at the top of their itineraries. Wealthy families moved to the area, built grand houses, and left their marks of gentility. The railway arrived at Oban in the late 19th century, providing an important industry link. Meanwhile, those who had made their money in Glasgow began to explore the Cowal peninsula and the Isle of Bute by steamboat. By the time the days of steam were over in the early 20th century, road connections had given Argyll another link to the outside world.

PLANNING YOUR TIME

The Hebridean islands are the best thing about the Argyll region—and the most time-consuming thing. Depending on how many islands you want to visit, you'll need anything from one week to two weeks to do this region any justice at all. Whatever you do, don't try to see everything. Distances are long and roads are generally poor, making long detours around lochs to get to places only a couple of

miles across the water. So long are the roads, in fact, that it is often quicker to walk or cycle between destinations than to drive them. On the islands, nearly all roads are single track, even the ones marked as main roads. Relying on public transport limits your options further, as you'll only be able to go to the best-known places and will miss out on better, more isolated ones. The other time-consuming factor is the ferries. You'll need to take them to get to a lot of the best places, and scheduled crossings are sporadic and subject to weather conditions that can change in the blink of an eye. It's quite common to be stuck in one place for longer than you might want. To speed things up, there are three airports in the region: at Campbeltown at the south of the Kintyre peninsula and on the islands of Islay and Tiree. With four days or less, you should concentrate on one specific area of this region. The best idea would be to head to Oban, from where you are in touching distance of many of the highlights of Argyll. You can get ferries to many of the best islands from here, like the Isle of Mull. Given one week, fair weather, and your own transport, you can see one or two of the Inner Hebridean islands as well as Mid-Argyll and the Kintyre peninsula.

Oban and North Argyll

Tumbling down the hillside into a forest-fringed bay, the port of Oban is the colorful capital of Argyll and the main gateway to the Hebridean islands beyond. It's a slightly bizarre clutch of rambling, turreted Victorian townhouses mixed up with a red-and-black distillery, glassy state-of-the-art restaurants, and, crowning it all, a part-finished Coliseum. Like most of Argyll, Oban traditionally made its trade from the sea but the added bonus of being connected to the railway line helped it mushroom into Argyll's main town. These days it's a bustling place, full of tourists preparing to voyage from its ferry port to one of the many islands off the coast. Oban boasts a lot of good

viewpoints and picnicking places, including the nearby wild island of Kerrera.

SIGHTS

Oban is a spectacular place just to look at. If you're after those sweeping views of town, forests, and islands scattered in the distance, head to either McCaig's Tower or Pulpit Hill farther south.

McCaig's Tower

You'll see this elaborate Roman coliseum-style building (east of town up Laurel Rd., year-round) dominating the Oban skyline, sitting above the town atop a forested hill. It

© LUKE WATERSON

Oban, the gateway to the Inner Hebrides

was the brainchild of one John Stuart McCaig who wanted primarily to build a lasting monument to the McCaig family and secondly to keep local stonemasons employed during winter. Building began in 1895 but by McCaig's death only the outer walls had been completed. Original plans for the tower involved an enclosed art gallery, but the family had other ideas on how to spend the money in his will and the tower remains part-finished to this day. It's still a very impressive building, with wonderful views of Oban through the windows.

Oban Distillery

The iconic red chimney of Oban distillery (Stafford St., tel. 01631/572004, www.discovering-distilleries.com, 9:30 A.M.–7:30 P.M. Mon.–Fri., 9:30 A.M.–5 P.M. Sat., noon–5 P.M. Sun. July–Sept., 9:30 A.M.–5 P.M. Mon.–Sat. Easter–June and Oct., 10 A.M.–5 P.M. Mon.–Fri. Mar.–Easter and Nov., 12:30–4 P.M. Mon.–Fri. Feb. and Dec., £5) is almost as much a landmark in the town as McCaig's Tower which it sits beneath. It's the historic heart of the town: Oban grew up around the

distillery after its founding in 1794 by the town's notorious entrepreneurs, the Stevenson brothers. The adult admission price can be applied to the purchase of a bottle of single malt. This is one of Scotland's oldest distilleries and the 14-year-old medium, peaty whisky has a pretty special taste with a hint of sea salt.

Dunollie Castle

The MacDougall Clan, descendents of the Lord of the Isles and lords of Lorne, inhabited this castle (north of town along coast road to Ganavan, open year-round) on and off from the 13th century until after 1746. They were a rather luckless clan and made the mistake of warring against Robert the Bruce and, subsequently, the Duke of Argyll. On both occasions their castle and land were taken from them (and on both occasions eventually returned). The ruins today are 15th century, wrapped tightly by creepers. It's one of the most magical castle ruins on the west coast, sticking out of a small forested clump above the sea, and makes for a good out-and-back walk from Oban (around a mile each way). Alternately, you can access the

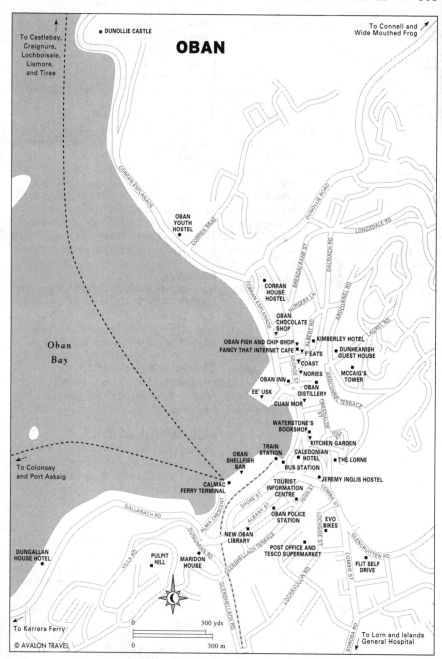

To Castlebay,
Craignure,
Lochboisale,
Lismore,
and Tiree

To Connell and
Wide Mouthed Frog

■ DUNOLLIE CASTLE

OBAN

*Oban
Bay*

OBAN
YOUTH
HOSTEL

CORRAN ESPLANADE

CORRAN BRAE

CORRAN ESPLANADE

DUNOLLIE ROAD

LONGSDALE RD

LAUREL RD

BREADALBANE ST

DALRIACH RD

ARDCONNEL RD

NURSERY LN

ALBERT RD

■ CORRAN
HOUSE
HOSTEL

OBAN
CHOCOLATE
SHOP

OBAN FISH AND CHIP SHOP
FANCY THAT INTERNET CAFE

● KIMBERLEY HOTEL

▼ F'EATS

● DUNHEANISH
GUEST HOUSE

▼ COAST

▼ NORIES

MCCAIG'S
TOWER

GEORGE ST

OBAN INN ▼

ARDCONNEL TERRACE

TWEEDDALE

EE' USK ▼

OBAN
DISTILLERY

CUAN MOR ▼

WATERSTONE'S
BOOKSHOP ■

KITCHEN GARDEN

HILL ST

TRAIN
STATION

OBAN
SHELLFISH
BAR

CALEDONIAN
HOTEL

■ THE LORNE

BUS STATION

To Colonsay
and Port Askaig

CALMAC
FERRY TERMINAL

TOURIST
INFORMATION
CENTRE

● JEREMY INGLIS HOSTEL

SHORE ST

ALMA CRESCENT

GALLANACH RD

DUNAPHAN RD

ALBANY ST

OBAN
POLICE
STATION

HIGH ST

COMBIE ST

LOCHSIDE ST

EVO
BIKES

GLENCRUITTEN RD

NEW OBAN
LIBRARY

DUNGALLAN
HOUSE HOTEL ●

VILLA RD

PULPIT
HILL

● MARIDON
HOUSE

GLENSHELLACH TERRACE

POST OFFICE AND
TESCO SUPERMARKET

LOCHAVULIN RD

COMBIE ST

● FLIT SELF
DRIVE

GLENSHELLACH RD

SOROBA RD

To Kerrera Ferry

0   300 yds

0   300 m

© AVALON TRAVEL

To Lorn and Islands
General Hospital

castle from beside a small lay-by on the A85 just north of Oban.

Kerrera

The rugged, barely populated isle of Kerrera is a great antidote to the tourist buzz of Oban: a hilly, woodsy place great for rambling. A six-hour walk leads from the ferry docks south along the coast to Gylen Castle, around to Ardmore in the west, and back along an old drove road (a road traditionally used for cattle herding) to the ferry pier. You'll get some great views of the Argyll coastline. The only ferry to the island runs from two miles south of Oban on the Gallanach Road. It takes five minutes and costs £3.50 round-trip. Ferries run half-hourly in summer and about every two hours in winter. Bus number 431 heads south from Oban to connect with a couple of Kerrera sailings during summer. If you miss the bus, it's not a bad walk back to town. Be sure to check the last return ferry times (it will be around 6 P.M.).

Tours

Most tourists coming to Oban want tours of the islands, not of little-visited Lorn. The Firth of Lorn that Oban looks out on is teeming with marinelife from minke whales to seals; ask at the TIC for details of tours to see it.

Bowman's Tours (Railway Pier, tel. 01631/ 563221, www.bowmanstours.co.uk, Apr.–Oct.) offers "three isles" day tours across to Mull and down to Fionnphort for the ferry to Iona. It also takes in a visit to Staffa and Fingal's Cave. The advantage (or disadvantage!) is the early start, thereby avoiding lots of the crowds. The cost is £44/22 adults/children inclusive of return ferry from Oban to Mull, return bus from Craignure to Fionnphort, and return ferries to Iona and Staffa. It's good if you want to see the best of the islands in a rush, but it spoils the magic of these places to flash past them so quickly. You could also do exactly the same trip under your own steam.

ENTERTAINMENT

Oban has its own official pub crawl (www.oban-pubcrawl.com); you get a T-shirt at the end of the endurance test.

Pubs

Dating from the 1790s, the whitewashed **Oban Inn** (Stafford St., tel. 01631/562484, 11 A.M.–1 A.M. Mon.–Sat., 12:30 P.M.–1 A.M. Sun.) is the town's most charismatic pub, with a rotating selection of ales. There's a jukebox and food on offer, too; you can't go wrong with the Moules Marinere (£6.95).

If you wondered where all the locals had gone in tourist-dominated Oban, chances are you will find them at **The Lorne** (Stevenson St., tel. 01631/570020, www.maclay.com, 11 A.M.–1 A.M. Sun.–Thurs., 11 A.M.–2 A.M. Fri.–Sat.). This place keeps buzzing into the wee hours longer than most, has a great selection of cask ales, and live music at weekends. There's also a covered beer garden with heaters for smokers and drinkers to congregate in.

Shopping

Waterstones Book Shop (12 George St., tel. 01631/571445, 9:30 A.M.–5:30 P.M. Mon.–Tues. and Thurs.–Sat., 9:30 A.M.–5:30 P.M. Wed., 11 A.M.–5 P.M. Sun.) stocks a reasonable range of new books and maps.

Sports and Recreation

Evo Bikes (29 Lochside St., tel. 01631/556996), opposite Tesco Supermarket, offers mountain bike rentals.

ACCOMMODATIONS

Nowhere in Scotland outside the capital can rival Oban for its array of quirky budget places to stay. The quantity of opulent Victorian houses around town means that upper-end accommodation is not in short supply either.

Under £25

If you fancy getting away from the hubbub of Oban for a night or two, you can stay on barely inhabited Kerrera island at the cute little converted stables of **Kerrera Bunkhouse and Tea Garden** (Lower Gylen, Kerrera, by Oban, tel. 01631/570223, www.kerrerabunkhouse.co.uk, beds £12–14). The place will sleep just seven people, but those seven will have the time of their lives—this epitomizes everything most appealing about Scottish hostels. You get an isolated location, a small lounge with a music system, and a self-catering kitchen. The hostel is stocked with basic provisions. There's also a cozy rustic byre (barn) to rent out for evening entertainment and a tea garden serving Fair Trade coffee and spring water from its own spring—not bad for the wilderness!

Staying in one of the unique, peaceful rooms at **Jeremy Inglis Hostel** (21 Airds Cres., tel. 01631/565065, shared rooms £11 pp, rooms £18–20) is more akin to a holiday with an eccentric uncle than an average hostelling experience. It's a combination of charismatic staff, the homemade jam and scones for breakfast, and the homey old rooms festooned with local artwork that make this the most original and friendly budget accommodation around.

With an enviable location on the waterfront, **Oban Youth Hostel** (Esplanade, tel. 0870/004 1144, www.syha.org.uk, hostel beds from £15, lodge beds from £18 pp) is a good budget option. This grand Victorian house has big windows just full of sparkling sea views; there's also a purpose-built lodge just behind the main building. Accommodation options also include dorms and one- to three-bed en suite rooms. The lodge is fancier but the main hostel gets the best views. There is Internet access, large and light common rooms with comfy chairs, and a self-catering kitchen.

Over £25

Maridon House (Dunuaran Rd., tel. 01631/562670, maridonhse@aol.com, £28 s, £50 d) is the pretty blue building up from the ferry terminal at the foot of Pulpit Hill at the south end of town. It offers quiet, cool, pastel-colored rooms, all en suite and most with baths. Some even have DVD players. You're away from the tumult of the town center here, and the owner, a mine of local information, runs this place with a courteous, no-nonsense attitude. This is Scottish hospitality at its height.

Kimberley Hotel (Dalriach Rd., tel. 01631/571115, www.kimberleyhotel.co.uk, £45–65 d)

is a small hotel or a large guesthouse, depending on your viewpoint. High above town, this tranquil place was once a maternity hospital, and a stay in the big, creaking old rooms here is certainly going to revitalize you. There are 12 rooms available, mostly with sea views. Right at the top of the house is the turret room; the sleeping area is inside the turret itself. You get homemade tablet fudge in your selection of room goodies. With a light conservatory bar/restaurant and a dark lounge full of shiny leather and an open fireplace, there are plenty of spots here to relax during the day too.

At the top of town off the road to McCaig's Tower, the whole of Oban falls away spectacularly from the garden of superbly located ❿ **Dunheanish Guesthouse** (Ardconnel Rd., tel. 01631/566556, www.dunheanish.com, £80 d), yielding great views of the harbor, Kerrera, and out to the Inner Hebrides. When you peel your eyes away from the windows, this guesthouse's rooms are equally impressive: huge and traditionally furnished, some with four-poster beds and open fireplaces. Breakfasts can be traditional, continental, or smoked salmon affairs. The big dining room windows let vistas of Oban Bay spill in.

On a peaceful road overlooking the Island of Kerrera, **Dungallan House Hotel** (Gallanach Rd., tel. 01631/563799, www.dungallanhotel-oban.com, from £65 s, £130 d) is the huge, turreted former summer house of the Duke of Argyll. The rooms here are tastefully and subtly done up in white-and-brown decor that is gentle on the eye. All rooms are en suite with TV, and most have sea views. There are several acres of wooded grounds to walk in and a cocktail lounge with a grating decor that appears modeled on a Picasso painting.

Now under new management, the large, grand, old **Caledonian Hotel** (Station Sq., tel. 01631/562998, www.obancaledonian.com, from £65 d) was built as a fitting accompaniment to the arrival of the railway in Oban at the end of the 19th century. It emerged from a makeover in 2002 with a huge range of well-appointed rooms and a pleasant outside seating area.

FOOD

With its proximity to the sea and a steady influx of fresh fish straight from the fishing boats, Oban really is a place to embrace Scottish seafood.

Cafés, Tearooms, and Snacks

Not only can you watch through a window as a tantalizing array of chocolates are produced before your eyes at ❿ **Oban Chocolate Factory and Shop** (tel. 01631/566099, www.obanchocolate.com, 10 A.M.–5 P.M. Mon.–Sat., noon–4 P.M. Sun. July and Aug., 10 A.M.–5 P.M. Mon.–Sat. Apr.–June and Sept., 10 A.M.–5 P.M. Tues.–Sat. Oct.–Dec. and Feb.–Mar.) but you can then sit and sample a selection of them with a drink in the modern, spacious café. Chocolate prices start from £1.

F'Eats (John St., tel. 01631/571000, 9 A.M.–5 P.M. Mon.–Sat., 10 A.M.–4 P.M. Sun.) manages that happy medium of being reasonably priced yet sophisticated, drawing in a chatty, mostly local crowd. Perch on a stall to get your caffeine fix or relax at a table with the newspaper awaiting one of the house specialties—sumptuous paninis, ranging £2.50–4.

Kitchen Garden (14 George St., tel. 01631/566332, www.kitchengardenoban.co.uk, 8:45 A.M.–5:30 P.M. Mon.–Wed., 8:45 A.M.–9 P.M. Thurs.–Sat. Easter–Oct., 8:45 A.M.–5:30 P.M. Mon.–Sat. Oct.–Easter) is the best place in town to stock up on picnic treats. It's an extensive deli full of phenomenal cheese, biscuits, and malt whiskies and brimming with shelves of neatly labeled preserves and mustards. The upstairs part of the café gets fine views over the bay. This inexpensive place offers bagels, croissants, toasted sandwiches, and original salads like blue cheese and walnut.

Seafood/Scottish

You should head to **Oban Shellfish Bar** (Railway Pier, 9 A.M.–6 P.M. daily), no more than a green shack on the quayside behind the Waterfront Restaurant, for the best-value seafood in town. You'll pay no more than £5 for takeaway portions of scallops, smoked crab, smatterings of oysters (about £0.50 each), and wonderful salmon sandwiches.

The harborfront chippy of **Nories** (88 George St., tel. 01631/563736, noon–2 P.M. and 4–11:30 P.M. daily June–Sept., noon–2 P.M. and 4–11:30 P.M. Mon.–Sat. Oct.–May) is, however, the local's favorite—and they know a thing or two about the subject. You'll also find other fast-food favorites like pizza, pasta, and haggis on offer. Fish and chips and other fried goodies are £1–6.

Cuan Mor (60 George St., tel. 01631/565078, noon–4 P.M. and 6–10 P.M. daily) is Oban's slick new gastro-pub, sporting a spacious, bare stone–walled, rustic look. It does good, inexpensive seafood dishes as well as a few surprises such as Isle of Skye chicken, crammed with pistachios and Stornoway Black Pudding. Main meals are £8–12.

Every so often, a new eatery hits the headlines in Oban as somewhere that stands out against the masses of others. **Coast** (102–104 George St., tel. 01631/569900, www.coastoban.com, noon–2 P.M. and 5:30–9 P.M. daily) is doing just that. This place is next to a contemporary art gallery; with its white walls, wood finishing, and chic layout it looks like an exhibition space itself, and the menu is as contemporary as the decor. For £12–19 you can get lovingly prepared seafood or game, like char-grilled Loch Linnhe langoustines and roast partridge, and you can tell that presentation really matters here. Coast does get very busy, though.

In a vast, glassy, classy setting at **Ee'usk** (North Pier, tel. 01631/565666, www.eeusk.com, noon–3 P.M. and 6–10 P.M. summer, noon–2:30 P.M. and 6–9:30 P.M. winter) you can pay through the nose to enjoy some of Oban's most exquisite seafood with great, bustling harbor views (the means justifies the end). Main meals are £12–20. They range from homey fare like salmon and potato cakes to the lavish seafood platter with piles of oysters, mussels, and langoustines.

INFORMATION AND SERVICES

Oban is one of the few places in Argyll you can be guaranteed to find all types of services year-round.

Tourist Information

Oban TIC (off Argyll Sq., tel. 01631/563122, 9 A.M.–7 P.M. daily July–Aug., 9 A.M.–5:30 P.M. Mon.–Sat., 10 A.M.–5 P.M. Sun. Apr.–June, 10 A.M.–5 P.M. daily Sept.–Oct., 10 A.M.–5 P.M. Mon.–Sat., noon–5 P.M. Sun. Nov.–Mar.) is a large, helpful place that can help with ferry and accommodation bookings.

Money

Oban has lots of banks: ATMs can be found along George Street and at Tesco.

Communications

Oban Library (Albany St., 10 A.M.–1 P.M. and 2–7 P.M. Mon. and Wed., 10 A.M.–1 P.M. and 2–6 P.M. Thurs., 10 A.M.–1 P.M. and 2–5 P.M. Fri., 10 A.M.–1 P.M. Sat.) has a new location (it's not at Corran Halls anymore) with improved disabled access and free Internet. **Fancy That** (108 George St., tel. 01631/562996) also has a number of computer terminals for getting online.

One of the town's post offices (tel. 01631/510450, 8 A.M.–6 P.M. Mon.–Sat.) is at Tesco, on Lochside Street.

Medical Services and Emergencies

For medical attention, you have the options of **Lorn Medical Centre** (Soroba Rd., tel. 01631/563175) or **Lorn and Islands District and General Hospital** (Glengallan Rd., tel. 01631/567500), which has accident and emergency facilities.

Contact **Oban Police Station** (Albany St., tel. 01631/562213) regarding crimes or (more likely out here) mountain rescue inquiries.

GETTING THERE AND AWAY

Oban has plenty of connections with the outside world, all of which take a long time. To give you an idea of how roundabout even the best roads are, Oban is 50 miles from Glasgow as the crow flies but nearly twice that (97 miles) by road.

Train

◖ WEST HIGHLAND RAILWAY
The glorious West Highland Line trains run 3–4 times daily from Glasgow to Oban (3 hours 10 min., £18.30). En route you'll pass the glittering Clyde estuary, Loch Lomond, Munro peaks, and remote, rolling moorland with more deer on it than houses. It's one of those railway journeys you'll remember forever, and you have to admire the sheer audacity of the Victorians who constructed it, essentially across nothingness. If you're coming from Fort William to Oban, catch the morning train to Crianlarich, where you can change and get a train that arrives in Oban just before midday. Either way, these will be several of the most fun hours of train travel you'll have in Britain.

Bus

Scottish Citylink has three or four buses Monday–Saturday and two buses on Sunday from Glasgow to Oban (2 hours 50 min., £15).

GETTING AROUND
Boat

From Oban you can get a boat to the islands of Mull, Colonsay, Coll, Lismore, and also the Outer Hebrides.

Train

You can get from Oban to **Connel** (for Connel Rapids), **Taynuilt** (for Bonawe Iron Furnace), **Falls of Cruachan** (for Cruachan Power Station), and **Loch Awe** by train. All stations are on the West Highland Railway line, with three or four trains daily to these destinations. If you're not in a rush, it's a very pleasant way of getting about.

Bus

The main bus stances are on the road along the harborfront by the train station and close to the ferry terminal. From Oban you can get buses north to Benderloch, east to Loch Awe, and south to Lochgilphead, where you may have to change for southbound services to Campbeltown. **Scottish Citylink** (tel. 0870/550 5050, www.citylink.co.uk) and **West Coast Motors** (tel. 01586/552319, www.westcoastmotors.co.uk) are the main operators.

Car

Roads in mainland Argyll are generally poor and slow-going. Petrol prices are higher than in most other parts of the country.

TAXI

For a cab, call **Lorn Taxis** (tel. 01631/564744).

CAR RENTAL

Flit Self Drive (Glencruiten Rd., tel. 01631/566553) offers the best rates for car rental (around £25 per day for a small car) and is by far the most professional car hire company.

LOCH ETIVE COAST

This spectacular sparkling blue loch would be one of the most visited in Scotland if only it had roads along its shores. Its mouth is at bustling Connel, where it rushes in white torrents into the sea at the Falls of Lora. Then it cuts inland, past Taynuilt with its impressive legacy of iron mining, into increasingly steep-sided looming hills. There are isolated walks past the white specks of croft houses along its banks. You can also appreciate its silent magnificence from the water: You won't find many more remote lochs you can take a boat trip on.

Sights

At **Connel Rapids** (Connel), Loch Etive is kicked up into a frenzy of white rapids at ebb tide as it pours over a submerged rock shelf down to the lower Loch Linnhe. It's an impressive spectacle, so check out the tide times before you go. Connel has a couple of pubs to have a drink in while you wait.

After its founding in 1753, the group of dramatic buildings making up **Bonawe Iron Furnace** (Bonawe, by Taynuilt, tel. 01866/822432, 9:30 A.M.–5:30 P.M. daily Apr.–Sept., £4 adults, £3 seniors) above the shores of Loch Etive formed the most successful Highland iron furnace during the late 18th and 19th centuries. This is a different kind of tourist attraction to most—a remarkably well-preserved industrial legacy in this remote region. The buildings, set up a grassy slope, include the furnace itself and the charcoal stores higher up. With a good supply of trees around for fuel and a fast-flowing stream to drive power, it's possible to see why this site was a success for so long. One of the buildings houses a series of museum displays. What is most interesting about Bonawe as a tourist destination is that, rather than contemplating the wealthy, obscure family that inhabited some castle, you're instead thinking about how common people tried to eke out a living in these parts in centuries gone by.

Loch Etive Boat Trips (tel. 01866/822430, at noon and 2 P.M. daily Easter–mid-Oct., from £6 adult, £4 child) offers trips out on the waters of Loch Etive, giving you the chance to see mountains, mussel farming, and—because most of the shoreline is unreachable by road—a host of wildlife including otters and a seal colony. There are 90-minute and three-hour cruises available.

Accommodations and Food

The **Wide Mouthed Frog Restaurant with Rooms** (Dunstaffnage Marina, tel. 01631/567005, www.widemouthedfrog.co.uk, £60 s, £90 d) has a serene location and pulls in a well-heeled crowd of mostly yachting types. Rooms are spacious, neat, well kept, and very welcoming. You can eat well here, too; there's a gorgeous patio for those sultry summer days. Whether you're eating or sleeping, you are almost guaranteed a view of the Oban bay.

The **Taynuilt Hotel** (Taynuilt, tel. 01866/822437, www.taynuilthotel.com, from £30 s, £80 d) is a coaching inn with plush white and cream-colored rooms sporting big beds and en suite bathrooms. Most get a color TV, and there's a four-poster bed room for splurging out. The traditional old bar/restaurant does wholesome, generously portioned meals for £9–12. If you're passing by on a Sunday, the roast dinner is very good.

If only more villages had places like **Robin's Nest Tearoom** (Main St., Taynuilt, tel. 01866/822429, 10 A.M.–5 P.M. daily spring–end Oct.) to snack in, the world

© LUKE WATERSON

Barcaldine Castle, Benderloch

would be that bit more bearable. This cheery café decked out in green, white, and pine greatly enhances Taynuilt's appeal. Its menu focuses on good home baking and simple light lunches (£2–6). The cinnamon scones here are easily Argyll's best.

Getting There and Away

Connel and Taynuilt both have stations on the West Highland Railway between Glasgow and Oban. Three to four **trains** daily stop by. **Buses** to Connel and Taynuilt, including the 403, 415, and 975 services, stop by more than hourly to/from Oban, with a marginally reduced Sunday service.

BENDERLOCH AND LISMORE

Benderloch is the name given to the hammerhead-shaped peninsula nudged from either side by Loch Linnhe and Loch Creran but is used to refer to the whole of this forested region immediately west of Loch Etive. Villages, where they exist at all, seem as if they have been pushed to the very edge of the water by the inland mountains. The isolated feel persists:

the main reasons to visit the area today are to stay in some of Argyll's most lavish accommodations and to appreciate the panorama of incredible mountain scenery from the little Isle of Lismore.

Sights

The **Scottish Sealife Sanctuary** (Barcaldine, tel. 01631/720386, www.sealsanctuary.co.uk/oban1.html, 10 A.M.–5 P.M. daily Mar.–Oct., £10.50 adult, £33 family of two adults and two children) is a step up from your average sealife sanctuary. It has plenty of marine fauna from octopus to sharks to starfish (which you can hold!). The center is also committed to rehabilitating seals and has a revolutionary seal rescue center where injured animals from Loch Creran and around are nursed back to a condition where they can be returned to the wild. It's great fun for children, and good for those all-too-frequent wet days. There are regular seal-feeding demonstrations—the crowds just flock.

For one of the finest views of a fortress in Scotland, head to Castle Stalker View for a panorama of **Castle Stalker** (near Portnacroish, tel. 01631/740315, www.castlestalker.com, open during May, Aug., and Sept. on various dates). This stout tower house dating from 1320 is one of Scotland's most photographed castles, standing on an island in the middle of an inlet of Loch Linnhe.

From a distance, it's very hard to tell the **Isle of Lismore** (www.isleoflismore.com, ferries run twice daily from Oban and regularly from Port Appin) is an island at all. It sits so surrounded by high hills and mountains in the giant fissure of Loch Linnhe that it's not easy to see water between it and the mainland. It's a fertile island of flower-filled fields, great for a walk or picnic and for contemplating the rugged majesty of the mountain scenery soaring away in all directions. The focal point of the community is **Lismore Stores** (tel. 01631/760272, 9:30 A.M.–5:30 P.M. Mon.–Tues. and Thurs.–Fri., 9:30 A.M.–1 P.M. Wed. and Sat.) with groceries and Internet access. Lismore is a long narrow island with two ferry terminals; they are at the northern tip, where the passenger-only Port Appin ferry docks, and at the main community, Achnacroish, where a ferry from Oban docks.

Accommodations and Food

Barcaldine Castle (northwest of Benderloch village, tel. 01631/720598, enquiries@barcaldinecastle.co.uk, rooms £125) is the 16th-century fortress of the Campbells of Barcaldine. It has two rooms that get booked up months in advance. This is hardly surprising: The unique rooms are full of 16th-, 17th-, and 18th-century furniture and paintings, with open fireplaces, big beds, and Molten Brown toiletries. One room has an original Victorian roll-top bath. A wonderful sitting room with an open fire and big breakfasts await. Turn off the A828 at the school in Benderloch; the castle is two miles down the lane.

The first of many novel features of the **Isle of Eriska Hotel** (Isle of Eriska, Ledaig, tel. 01631/720802, www.eriska-hotel.co.uk, £290–400 d) is that you'll be staying on your own private island. It's a luxury country hotel, with

a separate swimming pool and spa complex and wonderful wooded grounds. The rooms are vast—the en suite bathrooms (with baths) alone are bigger than suites at other hotels. The color scheme tends toward the light and modern. You get separate seating areas overlooking the grounds and the quiet seaweed-fringed coast. Areas for guests to relax in consist of a light and airy lounge, a piano room, and a library. The restaurant has an extensive menu: You could start with rabbit and move onto a main like monkfish or Aberdeen Angus steak. Dinner is £39.50 per person. For in-between refreshments, try the bar with its range of single malt whiskies.

You'll pay more for your dog to stay at the ◖ **Pierhouse Hotel and Seafood Restaurant** (Port Appin, tel. 01631/730302, www.pierhousehotel.co.uk, £90 d) than you will for yourself elsewhere, but this is worth forking out for. The culinary feast on offer in the restaurant warrants a stopover just so you can savor the magical atmosphere without rushing. First, the rooms: just the kind of refreshingly decorated, relaxing places you would want to flop in after stuffing yourself with seafood. They have a neutral white decor, color TVs, en suite facilities, and even use of a Finish sauna. Luxuriously prepared fish is the supreme theme of the restaurant here. The pierhouse has its own creel (lobster pot) for catching the lobsters it serves, and the oysters are locally caught in Loch Linnhe. Start with a clam chowder and then progress to a main meal (£15–25) like the Pierhouse Platter, full of goodies from the local lochs. If you have one meal out in this part of Argyll, make it here.

Getting There and Away

The attempts to put a railway through Benderloch ended in failure; these days it's just served by surprisingly regular **buses.** These run from Oban up the A828 to Benderloch, the Scottish Sea Life Sanctuary, Barcaldine, and Appin hourly Monday–Saturday, with about five services continuing to Fort William. It's a pleasant two-mile walk from where buses stop on the main road in Appin to the Port Appin ferry terminal.

The Isle of Lismore is served by **ferry** from Oban (two to four Mon.–Sat., £2.10 adult, £22.20 car one-way) and Port Appin (Calmac, half-hourly to hourly, £1.50).

Mid-Argyll

Even the most central region gets its fair share of coastline courtesy of the spread-eagled Loch Awe, with watery tendrils splaying out some 20 miles. The main village here is touristy Inveraray, with a setting you cannot help but fall in love with. Farther west is Kilmartin Glen, which some describe as an area with archaeology as important as the pyramids in Egypt. North of Kilmartin are the Slate Islands, known for centuries as "the islands that roofed the world" because of the amount of slate mined there. The islands are fascinating, haunting places to explore.

INVERARAY AND VICINITY

This grand village was the brainchild of the third Duke of Argyll; he razed the previous settlement to the ground to make way for an extension to his castle and set about rebuilding Inveraray in the attractive black-and-white design that survives today. Don't be fooled by the grandeur and the number of visitors—this is still a relatively small place. Its architectural delights are set against an irresistible backdrop of forested hills. Within the trees are a couple of vividly bright formal gardens brimming with subtropical plants.

Sights

Britain's most celebrated architects had a hand in the design of grand, gray, 18th-century **Inveraray Castle** (tel. 01499/302202, www.inveraraycastle.co.uk, 10 A.M.–5:45 P.M. Mon.–Sat., noon–5:45 P.M. Sun. Apr.–Oct., £6.80 adults, £4.60 children). Sir John Vamburgh, architect of the former home of British Prime Minister Sir Winston Churchill, as well as William and Robert Adam were involved in the plans. Since completion in 1789, this has been the home of the Dukes of Argyll,

intertwined since 1745 with the development of Inveraray. The exterior, with its four cylindrical towers, is impressive but gives no hint of the extravagance within. The opulent state dining room was the grandest room in Britain when it was designed, but the undoubted highlight is the armory. This room has one of the highest ceilings in the country (21 meters high) and contains weaponry illustrating the history of the Campbell Clan and of the castle and town. Once you've taken your fill of the two floors of finery, you can take a walk in the 16 acres of grounds—a mix of woods and park. There is a shop and one of Inveraray's nicer tearooms on site.

The fun attraction of **Inveraray Jail** (tel. 01499/302381, www.inverarayjail.co.uk, 9:30 A.M.–6 P.M. daily Apr.–Oct., 10 A.M.–5 P.M. daily Nov.–Mar. £7.25 adults, £5.50 concessions, £4.25 children over 5) isn't exactly novel, but it's delivered with typical Inveraray hype and gloss. These buildings were the former courthouse and prison for Argyllshire, and you can take a trip back in time to a reconstructed courtroom and experience life as an inmate here. A few celebrated prisoners tell their sorry tales, and there's a fascinating exhibition of prison memorabilia from across Scotland. Then there are the just plain bizarre parts, like where you can meet the prison cow and learn about paranormal activity in the jail.

The forested hills swooping up from Loch Fyne above Inveraray certainly give the village a magnificent setting, but it's the **folly** (fake castle) at the pinnacle of the **Dun Na Cruaiche woodlands** that gives the area a downright fairytale feel. The path can be accessed from Inveraray Castle grounds; the summit is one of the best viewpoints in Argyll.

The jewel in the thickly wooded Loch Fyne

© LUKE WATERSON

a war memorial in Inveraray

coast south of Inveraray is **Crarae Woodland Gardens** (tel. 0844/493 2210, www.nts.org.uk, visitors center 10 A.M.–5 P.M. daily Easter–Sept., site year-round, £5), centered on the Crarae Burn that tumbles through a gorge here. A series of bridges and paths link the burn with the surrounding 100 acres of woods; you'll find an incredible collection of rhododendrons and a lush array of conifers and beeches hugging the steep banks.

Events
Held in late August and early September in the grounds of Inveraray Castle, the lively **Connect Music Festival** (www.connect-musicfestival.com) debuted in 2007. It gets a good lineup—the likes of the Beastie Boys and Idlewild alongside court jesters.

Accommodations and Food
The amply sized **Killean Farmhouse** (four miles south of Inveraray, tel. 01499/302474, www.killean-farmhouse.co.uk, rooms £54 d, cottages £25 pp) is a good place to base yourself

for Loch Fyne's attractions. You can choose from five large en suite bedrooms done in blues, whites, and oranges. For bigger groups, there are also some attractive rustic cottages you can rent by the day. Prices include breakfast, served in the conservatory of the main house.

It will come as little surprise to learn that Inveraray's master planner the Duke of Aryll was behind the construction of the lively and elegant whitewashed ⟨ **George Hotel** (Main St., tel. 01499/302111, www.georgehotel.co.uk, £35 s, £70 d, food served noon–9 P.M. daily) in the 18th century. Originally it was built as two churches for the English- and Gaelic-speaking communities of Inveraray. Rooms have a glorious antique elegance; expect four-poster beds, tartan carpets, couches, and creaking old furniture, not to mention whirlpool baths in the en suite bathrooms. All rooms have gone through recent refurbishment. The hotel also manages self-service accommodation just down the road at the **Paymasters House,** another 18th-century building. The bar/restaurant area is just as authentic, with flagstone floors and an open peat fire—a cozy joint for a whisky or a seafood meal.

Claonairigh House (Bridge of Douglas, tel. 01499/302160, www.argyll-scotland.com, £40 s, £50 d) is a former laird's residence in the oldest dwelling in Inveraray. It has its own salmon river within gorgeous woodsy grounds, and there are even midge-magnets, which make sitting outside on those warm, sunny evenings more pleasurable. The well-appointed rooms are warm and en suite, with DVD players and Wi-Fi Internet access. Some rooms have open stone fireplaces; one has a four-poster bed.

You can't really go wrong with the rooms at the magnificent, turreted **Fernpoint Hotel** (by Inveraray Pier, tel. 01499/302170, www.fern-pointhotel.co.uk, rooms from £77 d, suites £130), built just after the 1745 rebellion. All are done up in soothing, cozy whites, most with en suite baths. Views are of either Loch Fyne or the hotel's Japanese garden. The suites on the first floor are designed to pamper with whirlpool baths and coal fires. You can get a meal in the restaurant for £10–14.

Inveraray is simply awash with tearooms, but at least **Inveraray Castle Tearoom** (tel. 01499/302112, www.inveraray-castle.com, open during castle hours 10 A.M.–5:45 P.M. Mon.–Sat., noon–5:45 P.M. Sun. Apr.–Oct.) is in an atmospheric 18th-century castle to help it stand out. Down in the basement of the fortress, with bright paint splashed on its old stone walls, it's a cheery place for a light meal, fresh salads, or refreshments. The tearoom is self-service: light snacks and meals are £3–8.

Information and Services

Inveraray TIC (Front St., tel. 01499/302063, 9 A.M.–5 P.M. daily May–June, 9 A.M.–6 P.M. daily July–Aug., 10 A.M.–5 P.M. Mon.–Sat., noon–5 P.M. Sun. Apr. and Sept.–Oct., limited winter hours) is a small but useful source of tourist information.

Getting There and Away

Scottish Citylink buses from Glasgow stop at Inveraray six times daily Monday–Saturday (1.75 hrs., £9.20) and five times daily Sunday. There are several daily services from Inveraray to Oban (1 hr. 5 min.) and to Campbeltown (2 hrs. 20 min.).

LOCH AWE COAST

Splitting mainland Argyll almost in two, Loch Awe is a massive 73 square miles and takes up the same amount of space as Greater London. Apart from its northern tip, it's a very remote stretch of water best known for its excellent fishing (the biggest brown trout caught in the British history books was from the deeps here). The loch's most-photographed feature is Kilchurn Castle, perching photogenically on an island at its northern end, but the shores are also home to a power station where you can actually venture into a manmade cavern in a mountain. There are good walks around the forested shores, too: check www.loch-awe.com. Mainly, though, the shores around this silvery body of water are places for relaxing.

Sights and Recreation

Don't let the name put you off: **Cruachan**

Power Station (Cruachan, tel. 01866/822618, www.visitcruachan.co.uk, 9:30 A.M.–5 P.M. daily Apr.–Oct., £5.50 adults, £2 children) is one of the region's unique visitor attractions. Known as the "Heart of the Hollow Mountain," the power station here is built a kilometer into the rock of Ben Cruachan. It was the first pump storage hydro system in the world. On the tour it will take you a while to get to grips with how exactly power is generated. That's mainly because you'll be sidetracked by the neatest part of the experience—actually being inside a man-made cavern in a mountain, tall enough to swallow the Tower of London. It's like being in the villain's lair in a James Bond movie.

Mid-15th-century **Kilchurn Castle** (accessible during Apr.–Sept. by boat) has a great setting on a tiny island in Loch Awe. On a bright day, there are few more photogenic fortresses in Scotland, with the mirror-like waters of the loch reflecting the castle and the mountains behind it. You can access the castle by steamboat near Loch Awe Railway Station during the summer (tel. 01838/200440).

At **Loch Awe Boats** (The Boathouse, Ardbrecknish, tel. 01866/833256, 8 A.M.–6 P.M. daily) you can rent fishing equipment, boats, or canoes and explore Scotland's longest inland loch; boat hire is from £30 per day.

Accommodations

Loch Awe, despite its vast area of coastline, is decidedly remote and offers little in the way of decent accommodations.

The exquisite **Ardanaiseig Hotel** (Taychreggan, tel. 01866/833333, www.ardanaiseig.com, from £124 d) is so far from anywhere, you'll be expecting some rural, back-of-beyond establishment with basic facilities and intermittent electricity by the time you arrive. You're in for a surprise, though: Ardanaiseig is as luxurious as Argyll accommodation comes. The mid-19th-century hotel is full of fancy antique furnishings and crackling log fires but has 16 very modern-looking rooms done up in bright, fruity colors that give them almost a boutique feel. The highlight room is, without a doubt, the converted boat shed down by the lochside; it's like an airy art gallery on water. When you see the restaurant, overlooking the loch, you'll understand why dinner here is £45 per head. Taychreggan is at the end of the B845 south of Taynuilt.

Getting There and Away

It's easiest to get to the northern part of Loch Awe, with two railway stations on the West Highland Railway line including Loch Awe (2–4 trains daily to Oban, 40 min.) and a major Scottish Citylink bus route running by (several daily, 2.25 hrs. to Loch Awe from Glasgow).

You're better off exploring the south of the loch with your own wheels. The southern tip of Loch Awe can be reached by a 2.5-mile hike from the B840 road junction north of **Kilmartin village,** which has bus connections to Oban.

C KILMARTIN GLEN

This lush green valley north of Lochgilphead is the most archaeologically diverse area of mainland Scotland. A long time before the great pyramids were built, hunter gatherers were already in the Kilmartin area, building the first of their great monuments. Within a six-mile radius of the little village of Kilmartin, you'll find burial chambers, standing stones, cup and ring markings, and castles. The center of the scattering of some 350 ancient sites, tranquil Kilmartin contains a heritage center that goes a long way to explaining the 5,000 years of history on its doorstep.

Sights

With the exception of the museum, all the sites in Kilmartin Glen can be accessed free and are open year-round. There are specially surfaced pathways to most sites.

Kilmartin House Museum (Kilmartin village, tel. 01546/510278, www.kilmartin.org, 10 A.M.–5:30 P.M. daily Mar.–Oct., £4.60 adult, £1.70 child) is the obvious starting point for any serious exploration of the Kilmartin area. It serves as a TIC for other local information as well as giving the lowdown on the area's archaeology. The museum explains

pretty much everything you could want to know about this archaeologically rich area; it provides the cultural background and shows you how the builders of these monuments likely lived. Most importantly, it does all this in chronological order, to give you a sense of how this huge complex of cairns and standing stones developed. It's well worth buying the guide to all the monuments in Kilmartin to make sense of them all. At the very least, be sure to take one of the explanatory leaflets available in the museum reception area with you as you tour the sites.

If all this history has made you hungry, you'll be grateful for the presence of the very pleasant Glebe Cairn Café (10 A.M.–5 P.M. daily Mar.–Oct., evening meals Thurs.–Sat.) on-site, which rustles up some mouthwatering fare.

Kilmartin Church (access to grave slabs year-round) opposite the Kilmartin House Museum has an extensive collection of carved medieval stones. The well-preserved late 16th-century **Carnasserie Castle** at the north of the glen was the home of John Carswell, the translator of the first Gaelic book to be printed. Around the grassy mound on which it stands are several cairns.

The **linear cemetery** is the name given to the series of five clearly aligned cairns stretching south from outside the windows of Kilmartin House. The northernmost is Glebe Cairn, followed by Nether Largie North, Nether Largie Mid, Nether Largie South, and Ri Cruin Cairns. The only chambered cairn is Nether Largie South, and it is probably most impressive: Fragments of drinking vessels dating back to 2500 B.C. were found in the burial chamber, along with human and bovine remains. A pathway connects the four most northerly cairns.

Temple Wood Stone Circle is the most photogenic of the area's monuments in many ways, surrounded by bluebell woods planted by Victorians to enhance the beauty of Kilmartin. There are two stone circles, built to mark and reflect the winter solstice. These are some of the oldest Kilmartin monuments, built before 3000 B.C.

Nether Largie Stones stands to the south of this bunch of prehistoric monuments. Nether Largie is two pairs of standing stone sentinels, one of which reaches nearly three meters high. They're just to the south of the Temple Wood Circle. Evidence suggests the alignment could have been used to predict solar and lunar eclipses. There are another group of stones at Ballymeanoch to the south.

Rising out of the flat plain of the River Add, **Dunadd Fort** was at the height of its power in the 6th to 8th centuries A.D. You can follow a steep, rocky, slippery path up the mound to its summit, where you'll have one of the most commanding viewpoints in the area. The fort was the capital of the empire of the Dalriadic kings; you can see the supposed footprint of one of them in the rock at the top, along with a Pictish symbol of a bull. The fine detail is still incredibly preserved after as much as 1,500 years. You can see north up the glen and south to the Crinan Canal and Loch Fyne. It really is an imposing feature on the landscape, with good picnicking spots in the grassy tussocks at the top.

No one is any the wiser today as to what the strange symbols carved into the rocks at the **Achnabraek Cup and Ring Marks** may actually mean. What is certain is that this is the most extensive series of rock carvings in Britain. Markings take the form of cup-like hollows surrounded by concentric circles, rather like the depiction of planets in the universe. You can access this site from a forestry track off the A816 opposite the turn-off to Cairnbaan. The track leads to a car park with information panels about the markings.

Accommodations and Food

Whitewashed **Kilmartin Hotel** (Kilmartin, tel. 01546/510250, www.kilmartin-hotel.com, £65 d) is the center of village life and right opposite the carved stones in Kilmartin Church. Accommodation here is simple but comfortable in six rooms, four of which are en suite. There's a convivial bar selling lots of malt whiskies and real ale, and a popular restaurant selling warming bar meals for £7–11, like haggis

with mashed potatoes and turnips. It's a perfect end to a day's hectic monument spotting.

Getting There and Away

It's possible to get to Oban or Lochgilphead from Kilmartin by **bus** service 423. Buses run four times daily Monday–Friday and twice on Saturday. At Oban (1 hour 20 min.) or Lochgilphead (20 min.) you can link up with Scottish Citylink buses to Glasgow.

SLATE ISLANDS

A slate boom began in these islands in the late 17th century and has influenced the course of events here ever since. Until 1881, when sea flooded one of the principal slate quarries, these were known as the "islands that roofed the world" because of the amount of roofing slate gouged out of their hills. The most interesting of the islands are Seil and Easdale, both of which are bustling little communities with fascinating displays on their industrial heritage. Seil is also the jumping off point for excursions to the other uninhabited slate islands and trips to the tidal whirlpool of the Corrywreckan.

Seil

You reach Seil via the grandiosely named **"Bridge Over the Atlantic,"** so-called because it crosses a narrow inlet of Seil Sound, just about dividing Seil from the mainland. The island is a charming, grassy place until you reach the more somber western shore and the main village of **Ellenabeich** (also known as Easdale, and not to be confused with the Isle of Easdale, a stone's throw away across the water.) Around this conservation village (the houses are preserved as quaint whitewashed miner's cottages), the shiny black hills are reflected in the still waters of the loch.

A trip out around the surrounding islands with **Sea.Fari Adventures** (Ellenabeich, tel. 01852/300003, www.seafari.co.uk, booking office 9 A.M.–5:30 P.M. daily, cruises throughout year) will quench your thirst for adventure for a while. It runs trips in a rigid inflatable boat out to see the Garvellach Isles visited by

© LUKE WATERSON

slate-cutting, Ellenabeich

St. Columba, as well as tours of the world's third-largest whirlpool off the coast of Jura. Besides island-spotting, you can see whales and lots of birdlife. You also get the chance to land on the most remote of the Slate Islands. Whirlpool tours are £30.

Isle of Easdale

The main reason to come to this flat, slatey island is to check out the **Easdale Island Folk Museum** (tel. 01852/300370, 10:30 A.M.–5:30 P.M. daily Apr.–Oct.), something of a time capsule of 19th-century life in the slate mines here, now filled with water. It's a more evocative museum than its counterpart across the water, and if you've had enough of slate you can retire to the island's convivial **Puffer Bar** (tel. 01852/300500). At the time of writing the Puffer was closed for refurbishment but was heroically managing to open on Fridays and Saturdays 9 P.M.–1 A.M. For the epic five-minute crossing, there's a horn by the pier—this will summon the boat across to Ellenabeich pier at most decent hours throughout the week.

Accommodations and Food

Tigh an Truish (Clachan Seil, tel. 01852/300242, www.tigh-an-truish.co.uk, rooms £50, food served noon–2 P.M. and 6–8:30 P.M. daily Apr.–Oct., extended height of season hours and reduced low season hours) is a gem in West Argyll's clutch of lively old pubs. The bar is teeming with activity at most times of the year and is popular with passing yachties. You can get a range of local ales and sit in the dark, wonderfully wood-paneled bar and restaurant with a good solid main meal (£6–9) like all pubs should do, like prawns with brown bread and garlic mayonnaise. There are two self-contained apartment-style rooms with their own kitchens (where self-service breakfast can be made) if you fancy staying—many do.

Head south from the Slate Islands down the A816 to sample another real Scottish country pub, the ivy-clad **Cuilfail Hotel** (Kilmelford, tel. 01852/200274, www.cuilfail.co.uk, £60 s, £80 d). It's a family-run venture in the equally charming backwater of Kilmelford (bus stop and organic village shop nearby) and makes a great base for either

Kilmartin to the south or the Slate Islands to the north. Accommodation comes in the form of 12 snug rooms carved into individual shapes and lots of nooks and crannies by the old roof and walls. They are bright, rustic affairs with en suite bath or shower, and there's a resident lounge containing a lot of antique furnishings. The hotel also sports a beer garden and a traditional old bar with flagstone floors, an open fire, and a bundle of single malt whiskies. Bus services are the same as for Kilmartin.

Getting There and Away

West Coast Motors bus service 418 runs from Oban to Ellenabeich five times daily Monday–Saturday and four times daily Sunday. Journey time from Oban is 45 minutes.

Kintyre Peninsula

This wild peninsula may be just about joined to the mainland but it is island in all but name; it's a 70-mile romp from the Crinan Canal, which marks its northern extremity, to where it crashes into the sea at the Mull of Kintyre. Paul McCartney introduced this little-visited expanse of moor and lonely, thickly forested coast to the world with his 1977 song "Mull of Kintyre," but it hardly brought the tourists pouring in. Kintyre has historically been separate from the rest of mainland Scotland. Conniving Norse warlord Magnus Barelegs seemed to reach an arrangement with King Malcolm of Scotland that he could re-take for his country sovereignty of all the western islands of Scotland in the 11th century. King Magnus sat in his boat while his minions pushed it over the narrow isthmus that joined Kintyre to the rest of Scotland at Tarbert. As he had therefore "sailed" across the isthmus, Magnus claimed all Kintyre belonged to him. As befits an isolated place, the main pleasures of Kintyre are in walking and experiencing its diverse wildlife.

◖ CRINAN CANAL AND KNAPDALE FOREST

The ingenious Crinan Canal is easily the most picturesque waterway in Britain. In a country full of canal networks, this is no mean feat. The canal was begun in the 18th century to provide easy access from the River Clyde to Scotland's western isles without the time-consuming and often dangerous voyage around the Kintyre peninsula. It cuts through simply gorgeous scenery en route from Ardrishaig on tranquil Loch Fyne to Crinan, overlooking the island-speckled waters of the Sound of Jura. When you see the white sails of the yachts gliding by the charming whitewashed canal front houses, it is like an image from sedate middle England overlaid upon the wild upland forest scenery of Knapdale. The forest, which swoops up from the canal banks, is split up by lochs into a barely inhabited wilderness with its own unique archaeological heritage. For services and shops in this area, head to Lochgilphead, just off the canal north of Ardrishaig.

Crinan Village

The narrow B805 road is this village's only connection with the outside world unless you come through the canal. It winds up into the fringes of Knapdale Forest before tumbling down again to this collection of whitewashed houses by the canal side. Crinan is little more than a scenically located hotel, a harbor-master's office, and a series of lochs at the end of the Crinan Canal, but it can absorb you for hours. It's a flurry of year-round activity, with yachties pulling up and conducting repairs on their vessels and refueling at the pub, and battered old boats being enthusiastically restored. You can take a walk along the canal towpath here and boat-watch or even help open the lock gates for passing yachts. When you're done with boats, you can have a drink at one of the most picturesquely positioned bars in Scotland at the Crinan Hotel. The beauty of everything you see is doubled by its reflection in the still canal waters.

Gemini Cruises (tel. 0777/608 2256, departing twice daily) runs two- to three-hour excursions from the gentle waters of the Crinan Canal into the treacherous waters of the Corrywreckan, the world's third-largest whirlpool. For the slightly hair-raising experience of voyaging into the middle of what feels like a giant, gurgling plughole, it costs £20. Cruises depart from outside the coffee shop.

Knapdale Forest

Thought to be one of the earliest surviving castles in Scotland, the splendid fortress of **Castle Sween** (year-round) south of Knapdale Forest juts out on a rocky headland over Loch Sween. To get there, take the minor road off the B8025 about a mile after it leaves the Crinan Canal. If you follow the minor road beyond Castle Sween you'll reach tiny, isolated **Kilmory Chapel** (open year-round) at Kilmory. Inside this humble stone building is one of Scotland's most extensive assortments of early Christian carved crosses, some dating from the 14th century.

Accommodations and Food

It's mostly yacht owners that stay in this neck of the woods, which means pricey (and jaw-droppingly incredible) accommodation.

Bellanoch House (Bellanoch Bay, Crinan Canal, tel. 01546/830149, www.bellanochhouse.co.uk, £55 s, £90 d) is an old Gothic house standing on a quiet grassy bay stacked with lobster pots and ancient upturned fishing boats. Yachts bobbing in the background make up the views from the brightly colored rooms, which are en suite and hung with old artwork and tapestries. Scottish baronial splendor meets here with attractive country cottage simplicity. You can sit in front of an open fire with a book from the library or watch the boats sailing past outside. A choice of evening meals is available in the elaborate dining hall.

If you want to linger for a few days in this relaxed part of the world, then the self-catering accommodation at **Seafield Farm Cottages**

(Seafield, Knapdale, tel. 01546/850274, www.scotland2000.com/seafield, £55 per day), in the heart of the Knapdale Forest, is ideal. There's a choice of converted stone steadings (farm building outhouses) or a timber-built lodge smack bang on the shore of Loch Sween. Both places are fully appointed (washing machine, oven, TV/VCR/DVD); Kirkland, the timber lodge, even comes with a stack of firewood. There's a three-day minimum stay but this could just be the excuse you need to kick back in this secluded spot. The cottages are on the minor road toward Castle Sween.

The huge, light, luxury rooms at the **Crinan Hotel** (Crinan, tel. 01546/830261, www.crinan-hotel.com, £115 s, £210 d) gaze out at either the Sound of Jura or the canal side—any closer to the water's edge and this large hotel would tumble right in. Many of the 20 en suite rooms get their own balconies so you can be that little bit nearer to the waterside activity. The hotel is ideally poised to have seafood as its specialty, served in the large ground floor restaurant. This could be jumbo prawns or freshly landed halibut, depending what the fishermen catch. The **Crinan Coffee Shop** (Crinan, 10 A.M.–5 P.M. daily) could just be the best place for a shot of caffeine or a light lunch in Scotland. It's a chic, rustic-styled place that dishes out a variety of wonderful homebakes and good fresh coffee right by the canal side and is intriguingly decked out in canal-themed paraphernalia. It's run by the Crinan Hotel.

Information

There is a seasonal **TIC** (Lochnell St., tel. 0845/225121, 10 A.M.–5 P.M. Mon.–Sat., noon–5 P.M. Sun. Apr.–Oct.) at Lochgilphead.

Getting There and Away

Dull Lochgilphead is the regional transport hub. It's served by buses from Glasgow (three daily, 2 hrs. 40 min.) and local bus service 423 (four times Mon.–Fri., two times Sat., 1 hr. 45 min.) from Oban. Buses also go on south to Ardrishaig. The Ardrishaig end of the Crinan Canal is easily accessible: buses from Lochgilphead to Campbeltown or half-hourly local buses will drop you nearby.

© LUKE WATERSON

Tarbert, the gateway to the Kintyre peninsula

Anderson Coaches (tel. 01546/870354) operates a bus on Tuesday and Thursday mornings from Lochgilphead to Crinan and a daily afternoon service during school holidays. The nine-mile canal has a towpath; the seven miles from Lochgilphead to Crinan are a very enjoyable walk.

TARBERT

The A83 seems to twist above the silent stony shores of Loch Fyne forever before dropping through forest to the blue, pink, yellow, and white houses of Tarbert, perched around an inlet guarded by a castle on a narrow isthmus just about holding Kintyre peninsula to the mainland. It's the gateway proper to the Kintyre peninsula and one of the most idyllic villages in Scotland. This is still very much a lively fishing port, having carved out a reputation for itself as the seafood capital of western Scotland, and the terminus for ferries to the Isle of Arran and Cowal.

Walking

Tarbert is the starting point of the **Kintyre Way** (www.kintyreway.com), which follows the coast down the east of the Kintyre peninsula. The path runs for 87 miles (at least five days of hiking), encompassing the peninsula's most idyllic scenery, down to Southend on the southern tip of Kintyre.

Events

Held at the end of May each year, the **Scottish Series** (www.yacht-race.com) is second in the British yachting calendar only to Cowes. Yachts race first from Glasgow to Tarbert and then compete in events over three additional days on Loch Fyne.

Tarbert Seafood Festival (www.seafood-festival.co.uk) is an extravaganza of seafood that takes place on the first weekend in July; you'll see cooking demonstrations (celebrity chef Nick Nairn is a regular performer) and hear lots of live music.

Accommodations and Food

Colorfully decorated in maritime blues and whites, **Struan House** (Harbour St., tel. 01880/820190, www.struan-house-lochfyne.co.uk,

£25 s, £50 d) is a pretty Victorian abode near the ferry terminal. The three rooms are named after Scottish islands, with red, beige, and white color schemes. One room is en suite and all come with their own wash basin, TV, and radio. You can have breakfast in the bright breakfast room or, if you are leaving early, take it with you.

If you're staying in Tarbert in order to catch a ferry across to Islay or as a journey-breaker down south along the Kintyre peninsula, the attractively rustic **Rhu House** (West Loch Tarbert, tel. 01880/820231, www.rhu-house.co.uk, from £52 d) four miles south of the village is perfect. The three blue, white, and pink wallpapered rooms are en suite (some have twin beds) and get great views of the tangle of garden. You can stroll through the thickly wooded grounds down to the lonely loch shore of West Loch Tarbert.

You couldn't hope for a brighter, friendlier, more cheerful place to stay than the **Victoria Hotel** (Barmore Rd., tel. 01880/820236, rooms from £45 d, bar meals noon–2 P.M. and 6:30–9:30 P.M.), Tarbert's only yellow harborfront building. It has recently refurbished, simple rooms, some of which are en suite. You can dine on local seafood in the sunny conservatory restaurant or sit in the darker bar with a whisky or real ale.

Displaying paintings and jewelry and serving coffee and cake, **Lucken Booth Gallery and Coffee Bar** (Harbour St., tel. 01880/821234, www.luckenbooth.net, until 5 P.M. Mon.–Sat.) makes for a perfect daytime refreshment stop.

Since French chef Pascal opened up his cozy little **Corner House Bistro** (Harbour St., tel. 01880/820263, lunch and 6–9 P.M. daily), Tarbert has established itself firmly on the gourmet map of Scotland. Log fires and candlelit tables set the scene for sampling the exquisite seafood on offer at this restaurant. Main meals are £12–20 but it's worth splashing out here on dishes like the halibut with langoustine sauce (£18.95). All the fish is caught in the owner's boat. Wash it all down with one of many whiskies on offer.

Getting There and Away
Buses in Tarbert stop at the Turning Circle,

on the road to Campbeltown. Tarbert is on the bus route from Glasgow to Campbeltown. At least three Scottish Citylink buses daily connect it with Glasgow (3 hrs. 15 min., £12.90) and Campbeltown (1 hr. 5 min., £6).

During winter (late Oct.–Mar.) a daily **ferry** links Tarbert with **Lochranza** on the Isle of Arran. It's £3.85 adult, £19.80 car one-way.

EAST KINTYRE
Being bypassed by the main road south down the peninsula to Campbeltown has allowed the lovely east coast of Kintyre to remain one of Scotland's unspoiled secrets. You'll find great places to munch seafood, rocky seaweed-laced bays frolicked in by otters, sandy coves, a ruined abbey, and vast, lovely expanses of tree-fringed wilderness in between.

Skipness
This is where the loneliness of the Kintyre peninsula really kicks in: Skipness is a tiny hamlet strung out around a shingle shore overlooking the Kilbrannan Sound. You'll find a small shop stocked with tasty treats, a dramatic fortress, and one of the best places to munch seafood in Kintyre.

Sticking out of the forest on the shores of Skipness is the black, largely intact ruin of **Skipness Castle** (open year-round), built in the 13th century. You can climb quite high up the ruins and explore a small chapel dedicated to St. Brendan nearby.

Saddell Abbey
The primarily 12th-century abbey at Saddell (open year-round) was founded by Somerled, the legendary Lord of the Isles, and building was continued by Somerled's son after his death in 1168. Somerled is buried on the site. You can see several good examples of medieval carved grave slabs, on display in the visitors center. Admission is free. The abbey sits above the golden sandy curve of Saddell Bay.

Accommodations and Food
The small, neat, art deco **Dunvalanree Hotel** (Port Righ, Carradale, tel. 01583/431226,

PAUL McCARTNEY AND THE MULL OF KINTYRE

By 1977, former Beatles frontman Paul McCartney had gotten together with a new band, Wings. McCartney had a recording studio and farmhouse in the Mull of Kintyre and wanted to write a song to express the magic of the place. He came up with "Mull of Kintyre," with lyrics about how he loved the peninsula and wanted to be back there whenever he went away. Featuring the Campbeltown Pipe Band in the background, the record catapulted the peninsula to nationwide fame after its release. It went on to become the best-selling single in the U.K. at the time and had nine weeks at the top of the charts. It was less of a success in the United States; as a result McCartney has never played "Mull of Kintyre" during his tours there. Paul McCartney and his late wife Linda owned several farmhouses on the Mull of Kintyre and spent a lot of time bringing up their family there. Even before the success of the "Mull of Kintyre" single, the area had inspired McCartney to write famous lyrics: The Beatles' hit "The Long and Winding Road" was also written with the peninsula in mind.

www.dunvalanree.com, rooms £60–100 d) has undergone a complete refurbishment over the last few years. It's got an idyllic location right by the bay in Carradale and offers two kinds of rooms. The larger en suite rooms get color TV, bath robes, and generally sea views, while smaller rooms look out toward the steeply rising forest at the back of the house and have shared bathrooms. The range of rooms here makes it popular with a lot of holidaymakers. Breakfast is served in an art deco room full of mirrors and painted glass.

The **Skipness Seafood Cabin** (grounds of Skipness Castle Estate, tel. 01880/760207, 11 A.M.–6 P.M. daily late May–Sept.) is a wonderful surprise; it's been dishing out cheap, good-quality seafood in this tranquil location for 20 years. There are fresh crab rolls served with salads mostly from leafy plants grown in the garden, pots of mussels, and smoked fish. It's licensed as well. Sit out at one of the picnic tables on the grassy lawn and enjoy the views of the castle. Meals are £2–8.

Getting There and Away

Skipness in the north of Kintyre is best accessed from Tarbert; Carradale and Saddell are accessed from Campbeltown.

For Skipness, there are three daily buses linking it with the **Claonaig ferry terminal** and **Tarbert.** Carradale and Saddell are served by five daily buses Monday–Saturday from **Campbeltown.**

You can get a **ferry** from Claonaig near Skipness to Lochranza on the Isle of Arran. There are eight to nine services daily from March to October (£4.75 adult, £21.90 car one-way).

MULL OF KINTYRE AND WEST COAST

The Mull of Kintyre is the name given to the fist-shaped southern tip on the long limb of the Kintyre peninsula. It's not as beautiful as the east coast but still justifies Paul McCartney's lyrical reminiscences about it in the singer's 1977 hit of the same name. The best places to stay are concentrated around Southend, in the south.

Campbeltown and Vicinity

Campbeltown has a lovely location on lush green hills sloping into Campbeltown loch; it's just a pity about all the ugly gray council houses, which give the town a seedy and even menacing feel. Still, the chances are if you've made your way down here that you won't have the time or inclination to head straight back up again, and Campbeltown has a couple of worthwhile attractions. Catching a film at the **Art Deco cinema** is an entertaining way of passing the time. There's no reason to stay or eat here, though.

On the south side of **Davaar Island** in the Kilbrennan Sound is a series of caves above the boulder-studded shore that have become something of a pilgrimage site. The reason is the cave painting of Christ on the cross, done in 1887 by a local schoolteacher. The island can be reached via a causeway at low tide; inquire about tide times in the Campbeltown TIC. The cave is identifiable by a small plaque and lots of nearby cairns built by pilgrims.

Springbank Distillery (85 Longrow, Campbeltown, tel. 01586/552085, www.springbankdistillers.com, tours Mon.–Thurs. Apr.–Sept. by prior appointment only, £3) is about the only distillery in Scotland to do every part of the distilling process on-site, from floor maltings through to bottling. This makes the tour one of the most interesting and comprehensive of any distillery. Three different single malt whiskies are distilled here (Springbank, Hazelburn, and Longrow), each using a different production process, which makes the tastings at the end of the tour a lot of fun.

The long, lovely, blowy stretch of golden sand at **Machrihanish Bay** is popular for walking, kiteboarding, and surfing.

Mull of Kintyre Headland

The long Kintyre peninsula culminates in steep grassy cliffs at the end of a higgledy-piggledy 18-mile road from Campbeltown. The lighthouse here was built by Robert Louis Stevenson's father. To the east lies the peaceful village of Southend, with sandy Dunaverty beach nearby. At **St. Columba's Chapel** (one mile west of Southend, open year-round, free) is a rock known as St. Columba's footprints, allegedly where the missionary saint first set foot upon Scottish soil on his quest to introduce Christianity to the Picts.

Isle of Gigha

The main draw on the west coast of Kintyre is Gigha, a low-lying, verdant place renowned for its friendliness and the spectacular **Achamore Gardens** (tel. 01583/505388, morning–dusk daily, £3.50), with an abundance of subtropical plants. Tours can be arranged in advance with the head gardener. With good restaurants and regular ferry connections, the island is perfect for a day trip from Kintyre.

Entertainment

Campbeltown Picture House (26 Hall St., tel. 01586/553899, www.weepictures.co.uk, film showings at 8 P.M. Sat.–Thurs.) is a gem amidst the direness of Campbeltown, an art deco–style cinema, supposedly the oldest still operating in Scotland. It shows mainly mainstream films.

Accommodations and Food

An open, grassy site, at **Machrihanish Caravan and Camping Park** (Machrihanish Bay, tel. 01586/810336, www.campkintyre.com.uk, Feb.–Oct. and Dec., tent pitches for 2 adults £11, wigwams from £24) you can choose whether to pitch a tent or stay in a spacious wigwam. Facilities for campers include a small room with a kitchen. The wigwams get basic kitchen facilities and pretty good heating. A pub is nearby and, of course, you get those sweeping views of gorgeous golden beach.

There are just two bed-and-breakfast rooms on offer at the small holiday park of **Pennyseorach Farm** (near Southend, tel. 01586/830217, www.pennyseorach.co.uk, £50 d), You can choose from a family room and a twin room, both en suite and with color TV and DVD players. Both are large, wonderfully light places to kick back. The holiday park (a few caravans in a field, nothing more) is two miles east of Southend, near Macharioch.

It's easy to see why the cozy **Isle of Gigha Hotel** (Gigha, tel. 01583/505254, £70 d) is popular with visiting yachties (apart from it being Gigha's only hotel, that is). There are 12 neat, en suite rooms here with a pale, soothing decor; some get views out to Ardminish Bay. The bar, decked out with lots of dark wood, serves food based on what local fishermen have caught.

Balinakill Country House (Clachan, tel. 01880/740206, www.balinakill.com, £75 s, £90 d), lying toward the north of the peninsula by the mouth of West Loch Tarbert, has bags of good old-fashioned charm. It's a Victorian mansion with great views out to the Sound of Jura. You can stay in a room with an open fire or one with an en suite bath: there's antique furniture in all 10 rooms, lending a

BOSWELL AND JOHNSON: THE ORIGINAL SCOTTISH TOURISTS

James Boswell, a Scottish lawyer and diarist, and Dr. Samuel Johnson, one of the most renowned essayists and lexicographers of his day, agreed to team up together on a tour of the Western Highlands and islands of Scotland in 1773. In the idea they were some ways from being original; the unfortunately named author Martin Martin had published an account of his journeys in the Hebrides as early as 1707. Martin was a relative unknown when he wrote his work though, and both Boswell and Johnson were renowned figures in their respective fields. Both were also particularly wordy men and described their travels at some length and not without a great deal of self-aggrandizement. According to Boswell, a page of his writing was "like a cake of portable soup. A little may be diffused into a large portion."

The two set out on their tour in the August of 1773. They began in Edinburgh and spent two months traversing the Highlands, Skye, Coll, Mull, Iona, and Argyll before returning to Glasgow in late October. Boswell used his account of the trip, "The Journal of a Tour to the Hebrides (1785)" as a precursor to his greater work: a biography of Samuel Johnson. Boswell's account of the grand tour is a lively affair. It was the number of renowned Scottish places they passed in a relatively short space of time, together with the way that Boswell wrote, that so captured the public imagination. Boswell was a gifted writer eager to carve a reputation for himself as a man of hedonistic exploits. His passions were drink, women, and a desire for adventure and he wanted these three things to come across clearly in his prose. His Highland and Hebridean tour came across very colorfully; what he did was to sketch lands previously thought of as barbarous in a sympathetic and engaging way. Like a lot of later tourists, Boswell and Johnson were far from role-model visitors. At times they showed ingratitude to their hosts, at times they cursed the land they were traveling through, and quite often they would assume the moral high ground over the people they met. Yet largely as a result of their escapades a whole generation of Romantic writers and artists decided to adventure to the west of Scotland and the area's tourism industry hasn't looked back since.

certain haughty elegance. The set-price dinners (£28.95) could include fresh local scallops, quail, or venison, followed by sticky toffee pudding (one hopes the latter is always on offer!).

Maybe, in a dim and distant past before the age of pretentious yuppie bars and style cafés, all tearooms were sophisticated affairs like **Muneroy Tearoom** (Southend, tel. 01586/830221, www.muneroy.co.uk, open until 5:30 P.M. daily). You can sit in this art deco place and choose from a range of cheap meals (£6–8) like breaded lobster or cheese and broccoli bake. The tearoom is attached to Muneroy stores in Southend village.

Information

Sunny **Campbeltown TIC** (tel. 01586/552056, 10 A.M.–5 P.M. Mon.–Sat. Apr.–Oct., 10 A.M.–4 P.M. Mon.–Fri. Nov.–Mar., open extended hours including Sun. June–Aug.) on the ferry pier in Campbeltown will give you bundles of ideas of things to do in the surrounding area you wouldn't even have dreamed possible.

Getting There and Away

From **Machrihanish Airport,** three miles west of Campbeltown, there are two daily flights to Glasgow with British Airways, even on Sunday.

There are three **buses** daily from Glasgow to Campbeltown (4 hrs. 25 min., £15.90) via Lochgilphead and Tarbert. There are five to seven buses daily Monday–Saturday between Campbeltown and Southend.

Long-distance buses will drop you at points down Kintyre's west coast, including Tayinloan (for the Gigha Ferry). You can also hop on the hourly bus service 200 to get to Machrihanish.

Getting Around

Kintyre Express (tel. 01294/270160, www .kintyreexpress.com) offers a solution to transport difficulties in Campbeltown: a high-speed power boat carrying up to 12 passengers, which can be chartered to take groups and individuals from Campbeltown to destinations as far flung as Northern Ireland.

Mull, Iona, and Vicinity

After Skye, these two islands are the most popular to visit of the Inner Hebrides. But within minutes of arriving on remote, forested Mull you will see the island pull off its greatest party trick: the people just seem to vanish. The reason is simple. Tourists head in hordes to the prettily colored capital of Tobermory or down to Fionnphort in the southwest for the boat trip to Iona and its famous abbey and leave the rest of the islands almost deserted. Mull, the second largest of the Inner Hebrides, often has its size underestimated. It's a landscape of mountains, moor, and forest-fringed lochs that all but cleave the island into pieces. Nearly all of the roads are single-track—it's a superb island for walking. Iona has had a spiritual aura to it since St. Columba introduced Christianity to Scotland after founding a monastery on the island in A.D. 563. Beyond these islands are the wild peaceful lands of Coll and Tiree, islands best known for their wildlife and sandy beaches.

ORIENTATION

Mull is shaped like a squashed version of Britain. Most ferries arrive at Craignure in the east. Then visitors will head in one of two directions: northwest to the main population center, Tobermory, or southwest to Fionnphort, where the ferry for Iona departs. Coll lies west of the northern section of Mull, and Tiree lies just southwest of Coll.

GETTING TO MULL

Mull is accessible by three ferries, the least used of which runs from Tobermory. Other ferry crossings are to points on the east coast of Mull, south of Tobermory. All ferries are run by Calmac (www.calmac.co.uk).

Journey time on the **Tobermory-Kilchoan** crossing (every two hours daily May–Aug., every two hours Mon.–Sat. Mar.–Apr. and Oct., three daily Mon.–Sat. Nov.–Mar., £4.05 adult, £21.15 car one-way) is 35 minutes. The crossing is commonly used by holidaymakers who want to see both Mull and Ardnamurchan and make the experience into a round-trip in conjunction with the Fishnish–Lochaline ferry. The **Craignure-Oban crossing** (three to five daily, 45 min., £3.35 adult, £24.85 car one-way) is the most common approach to Mull, from Oban on the mainland in Argyll to Craignure. This is a big car ferry, with a bar. The **Fishnish-Lochaline crossing** (about every 45 min., duration 15 min., £2.55 adult, £11.15 car one-way) is the shortest crossing to Mull, from Lochaline on the Morvern peninsula to Fishnish north of Craignure. The only disadvantage is that it's a very long way from Lochaline to anywhere else.

Buses (about hourly) run between Craignure and Tobermory via Fishnish to connect with ferry departure times. Journey time is 45 minutes.

◖ TOBERMORY

With its bright blue, yellow, and pink houses fanning around a quiet bay, Tobermory's harbor has to be the most photographed harbor in Scotland. The bustling capital of Mull may these days be most associated with the children's TV series, *Balamory*. The program was filmed in and around Tobermory and gets more than its fair share of young families wandering around trying to spot the sets. Even so, this is a place that still epitomizes everything that is most charming about a Scottish island coastal village, with great restaurants, cafés, pubs, and places to stay. Its steep streets soar into woodland and

© LUKE WATERSON

Tobermory, the capital of Mull

give great views of the westernmost point of the British mainland, Ardnamurchan.

Sights

Perhaps the best thing to do in the village is simply to stroll along its colorful harborfront with its eccentric clock tower, experiencing the friendly pace of island life. You'll see fishing boats, pretty shops, and good restaurants.

An Tobar (Argyll Terr., tel. 01688/302211, www.antobar.co.uk) is the island's main art center, putting on a range of exhibitions throughout the tourist season.

Tours

If wildlife is your passion, then **Discover Mull** (tel. 01688/400415, www.discovermull.co.uk, tours depart 10 A.M. from south harbor car park, £34) is a great way to see it: A 4x4 vehicle takes up to eight people looking for golden eagles, porpoises, seals, red deer, and mountain hares in the remote north of Mull. Lovely packed lunches are included. Tours are specially timed to catch the first ferry of the day from Oban to Tobermory.

Half-day trips to see the wealth of marine-life just off the coast of Tobermory with **Sea Life Surveys** (tel. 01688/302916, www.sealifesurveys.com) start from £45. Some trips are not suitable for children. You can see minke whales, porpoises, dolphins, and seals.

Entertainment

Pick up a copy of the *Oban Times* to find the nearest ceilidh (get-together involving music and dance).

Macgochans (south of waterfront, tel. 01688/320250, www.macgochans.co.uk, 11 A.M.–2 A.M. daily during summer, slightly earlier closing in winter), the daffodil-yellow building by the distillery, is one of the brightest places both inside and out to spend a while drinking. There's live music here at weekends, cask ales to try, and an outside beer garden overlooking Scotland's prettiest harbor view. You can get good pub grub here for £8–14.

Shopping and Recreation

Tobermory's Main Street has a supermarket and the more tempting **Island Bakery Shop**

Tour of Mull car rally

© LUKE WATERSON

(23 Main St., tel. 01688/302225) to sort out self-catering needs.

Archibald Brown and Son (21 Main St., tel. 01688/302020) is an Aladdin's cave of a place doing bike rentals, as well as issuing fishing permits and selling nuts, bolts, and Tobermory whisky.

Events

Mull provides an atmospheric backdrop for a number of live musical events. **Mishnish Music Festival** (www.mishnish.co.uk/music-festival.htm) is a three-day extravaganza of traditional Gaelic folk music.

As if Mull's roads aren't bad enough, a riveting bit of mayhem in October sees the round-island **Tour of Mull car rally** (www.2300club.org) take off. Mull is jammed for the duration; buses stop running and even the roads that stay open have battered rally cars along them.

Accommodations

Tobermory Campsite (Dervaig Rd., tel. 01688/302624, www.tobermory-campsite.co.uk, £5 pp) is the nearest campsite to Mull's capital,

an easy 20-minute walk from town. You're high above the town here on a moist grassy site fringed by trees. It all feels very pastoral, while having a lively town close at hand. There are a couple of midge magnets to keep Scotland's most pesky insect away.

There are actually not many places on Tobermory's famously colorful harbor-hugging Main Street to stay; **Tobermory Youth Hostel** (Main St., tel. 01688/302481, www.syha.org.uk, beds £14–15) is one of the few, and it's a great hostelling experience. It's very spacious, with five- to six-bed dorms, a good kitchen, laundry facilities, a garden, and great sea views from most rooms. Unusually for a hostel, you're also bang in the center of things.

Don't come to **Cuidhe Leathain** (Breadalbane St., tel. 01688/302504, www.cuidhe-leathain.co.uk, £65 d) expecting your typical minimalist hotel room; the three rooms at this bright, whitewashed guesthouse are intriguingly and thoughtfully furnished and more resemble a Victorian hideaway. They're done up in bold festive reds and greens with drapes and dark-wood furniture. There's a guest lounge with an open fire and big sofas and a similarly cozy dining room.

You can't fault the modern, white **Ptarmigan** (tel. 01688/302863, www.bed-and-breakfast-tobermory.com, rooms from £95 d) and its sparkling, airy rooms. Not only do they deliver all the creature comforts you would expect from a well-appointed guesthouse, but they also come with a swimming pool. The owner has considerable experience in the hospitality trade in different parts of the globe and provides friendly, quality service. The house sits above Tobermory Bay.

Gothic-looking **(◖ Glengorm Castle** (Mishnish, tel. 01688/302321, www.glengorm-castle.co.uk, rooms from £140 d) is a clutch of towers and pinnacles in an isolated location in the far north of the island. Rooms are vast, yet not without a sense of coziness. As befits any castle, there's a room with four-poster bed, complete with an antique en suite bath. All the rooms have beds big enough to get lost in, grand views over the grounds, and a library of books to enjoy. You can make your way down to the old library for a complimentary evening dram or three. The dining room is nothing short of a banqueting hall. There are a whole holiday's worth of activities in the grounds of this estate alone. You could wander with the sheep through fields to the wave-blasted shore, or sit in nearby Glengorm Coffee Shop, enjoying potent coffee and tempting homebakes. Glengorm even has its own art exhibition space. The castle lies four miles northwest from Tobermory, off the Dervaig road.

Food

Right at the top of town on Argyll Terrace is **An Tobar** (Argyll Terr., tel. 01688/302211, www.antobar.co.uk, 10 A.M.–4 P.M. daily Mar.–Dec.), the relaxed, airy café of the Mull arts and cultural center. It's set in an old Victorian school with huge windows. There's no better place to enjoy a tea, coffee, or homebake while you gaze over the sound of Mull. You can get there via the steep, pedestrian-only Post Office Brae, running uphill from the post office.

If you like chocolate, you will have found heaven in the light, modern **Tobermory**

Chocolate Shop Cafe (Main St., tel. 01688/302526, www.tobchoc.co.uk, 10 A.M.–4 P.M. Mon.–Sat., extended summer hours). The place offers a simple menu but does, of course, include plenty of samples of the wonderful chocolate produced here for the tasting, as well as generous, strong coffees and pastries.

For great takeaway fish and chips, **Tobermory Chip Van** (Fisherman's Pier, off Main St., tel. 01688/302390, noon–9 P.M. Mon.–Sat.) is the place to come, right by the clock tower on the harborfront. It has even won awards, which is not bad for a humble chip van. Fish, including delicious scallops, is piled fresh straight into the van and cooked superbly. Snacks/meals are £2–6.

The pretty navy blue and white-decked **(◖ Anchorage** (28 Main St., tel. 01688/302313, 10 A.M.–3:30 P.M. and 6–9 P.M. daily) is a café by day and a gourmet seafood restaurant by night. Whatever kind of catch you fancy, from langoustines to crab, you'll find it on offer here. The fisherman's platter is £8.95. You can also get non-fishy favorites like highland venison.

The **Highland Cottage** (Breadalbane St., tel. 01688/302030, www.highlandcottage.co.uk, 7–9 P.M. Mar.–Nov.) is the hotel where you will have one of the most intimate, exclusive dining experiences possible in the Hebrides. The menu is varied: you could start with crab cakes and a celeriac and carrot salad and move on to a main like roast lamb with Dauphinoise potato and black olive sauce. A set dinner is £42.50. Wash it all down with a dram of Tobermory 10-year-old single malt.

Information and Services

Tobermory TIC (The Pier, tel. 01688/302182, 9 A.M.–5 P.M. Mon.–Fri., noon–5 P.M. Sat.–Sun. Apr.–Oct.) is a small but helpful information center.

Clydesdale Bank (Main St.) has an ATM, generally with huge queues outside. You'll find Tobermory Post Office (Main St., tel. 01688/302058) by Post Office Brae. **Dunaros Hospital** (tel. 01680/300392) is 10 miles south of Tobermory at Salen.

Getting There and Around

Tobermory is a lovely place to stroll around. Buses from Tobermory run with reasonable frequency south to Craignure and on down to Fionnphort (for the Iona ferry). Buses run less often west to Calgary. Roads on Mull are almost all single track; it takes almost two hours to drive from Tobermory to Fionnphort.

MacKay's Garage (Tobermory, tel. 01688/302304) by Tobermory Distillery does car hire. **Mull Taxi's** (tel. 0776/042 6351, www.mulltaxis.co.uk) has seven-seater cabs available.

NORTH MULL

The remote northern chunk of Mull is best identified on the map as the hunched, bulbous head of the fetal shape of the island. It extends west from Tobermory and south to the narrow isthmus of land where the sizeable village of Salen sits. The treacherously zigzagging B8073 skirts the edge of the region. At the time of writing, the main attraction, Britain's smallest (and cutest) theater at Dervaig was closed, but there's still lots to see in the area including some stunning walks, one of Mull's loveliest sandy beaches, and its best heritage center.

Sights

Far northwestern Mull is home to one of the island's best beaches, the sweep of white sand that is **Calgary Beach** (B8073, by Calgary).

Mull is the best place in Scotland to see sea eagles; visits are possible to a **sea eagle hide** (tel. 01688/302038 for inquiries) in North Mull. The meeting point is on the B8073 road between Tobermory and Dervaig: you have to go as part of a guided tour and book in advance. Tours last, on average, two hours; there is limited optical equipment at the hide.

With no paved roads and a permanent population of some 16 crofters, the **Isle of Ulva** (www.ulva.mull.com, ferries run 9 A.M.–5 P.M. Mon.–Fri.) is a good bet for remote walks. You can head out along a reasonable track on the north side of the island to **Gometra** (crossed via a tidal stretch of sand) at the far end. It's

around 14 miles to Gometra's lonely pier and back. There are some haunting ruins on the south coast. Watch out for red deer and lolling seals. Ferries to Ulva sail regularly on Sundays, too, from June to August and at other times by prior arrangement. No ferries run on Saturdays. To summon the boat, uncover the red panel on the wall of the ferry house. The Ulva Ferry is signposted off the B8076, south of Lagganulva.

Shopping

Delightful **Coffee and Books** (Dervaig, tel. 01688/400234, 10 A.M.–5:45 P.M. Mon.–Sat., 1–3:15 P.M. Sun.) is part specialty convenience store, part coffee shop, and part bookshop. If you want any local interest book, head here first. There are two rooms stacked with fiction and nonfiction, and the owner knows lots about all the titles he stocks.

Accommodations and Food

The ◖ **Calgary Hotel** (Calgary, tel. 01688/400256, www.calgary.co.uk, from £49 s, £72 d) is a unique place to stay on Mull. The hotel and restaurant here should consider proclaiming themselves a separate village; there is little more to Calgary than what you'll find here. There are nine light, pine-influenced rooms here, set around an attractive central courtyard, with four on the ground floor. One room has its own spa, and one has a separate bunkhouse section, perfect if you're traveling with kids. All rooms are en suite. There's the feel of a peaceful commune rather than a hotel. As you investigate the public rooms, you'll notice the unique sculptures, handmade by the owner. If you like what you see, you can follow a sculpture trail out of the hotel grounds into the woods just beyond, where the trees hide more unusual carvings. The charming Dovecote Restaurant forms the other side of the courtyard: it is open nightly during season and during the day for wickedly strong coffee and cakes. The Isle of Mull cheese-makers also showcase their wares here. Evening meals, like the fresh fillet of salmon, are £11–15.

As you drive around the B8073 from Calgary, you'll come to a scattering of houses by a minor road junction; the red telephone box marks the entrance to hidden-away **The Old Mill** (Torloisk, tel. 01688/500259, www.old-millmull.com, £30 s, £55 d). It's a converted mill with a burn flowing through the tree-studded grounds and monstrously sized bedrooms that look right out over them. The Old Mill isn't a place you'll want to leave in a hurry. There are some great walks up into the moors from here and lots of hidden beaches to discover.

Supposedly the oldest inn on the island, dating back to the turn of the 17th century, the **Bellachroy Inn** (Dervaig, tel. 01688/400314, www.thebellachroy.co.uk, £60 s, £85 d, food served noon–2:30 P.M. and 5:30–9 P.M.) is an old Drover's Inn. This pub is renowned for its food, but you can stay here, too, in six warm beige rooms that—in stark contrast to the bar downstairs—seem very modern. Rooms are en suite with TV/DVD players. Now onto the real business: food and drink. This is a dark, homey bar with a restaurant where you can get your teeth into some of Mull's finest pub grub, like venison sausages with braised cabbage. Main meals are £7–9. Make sure you wash it all down with one of the real ales available, and make the most of this place—such inns on the island are few and far between.

The whitewashed ◖ **Boathouse Café** (Ulva, 9:30 A.M.–4:30 P.M. Mon.–Fri. Easter–May and early to mid-Sept., 9:30 A.M.–4:30 P.M. Mon.–Fri. and Sun. June–Aug.) by the pier on Ulva isn't just a place to wait for the ferry; it's a reason to come across to this tiny island in the first place. You can sit in the café or on the outside picnic tables and munch on Ulva seafood, like oysters with Guiness. There are also homemade soups and rolls. Meals are £3 to £10.

Getting There and Around

Buses run from Tobermory via Dervaig to Calgary. Salen is the nearest point reached by public transport to Ulva. You'll then need to get a taxi if you don't have your own wheels. Buses

(tel. 01688/302220) run four or five times daily from Tobermory to Dervaig and Calgary.

CENTRAL MULL

This remote, hilly, central part of Mull has little in the way of civilization, save for Craignure, the island's main ferry terminal, in the east. The village itself is little more than a couple of hotels, a shop, and a petrol station. Still, the contrast between the Craignure Area and the rest of Central Mull could hardly be more marked. There are enough tourists flocking around Craignure, Mull's main ferry terminal, to justify Scotland's only island railway line, which runs to the first of Mull's two great castles, Torosay Castle. Duart Castle is just to the south. After that, you'll barely see another house during your exploration of Central Mull. This is a land of deep rocky lochs and patches of forest from which soars the island's highest mountain, offering Mull's remotest walking.

Craignure and Vicinity

The ferry docks at Craignure and most tourists quite rightly hop on one of the first buses heading either northeast to Tobermory or southwest to Fionnphort.

Torosay Castle and Gardens (off A849 by Craignure, tel. 01680/812421, www.torosay.com, castle 10:30 A.M.–5:30 P.M. daily Easter–Oct., gardens 9 A.M.–dusk daily, £5.50 adults, £3 children) was a mid-19th-century Scottish baronial construction, more mansion than castle. There are some fine rooms to look around inside the castle: you'll learn about the colorful lives of the incumbents and see a portrait of William Wallace. Save plenty of time for a stroll through the gardens and grounds; you'll find the refreshingly bright reds and blues of plants like Himalayan poppies and azaleas and a statue walk featuring a collection of limestone figures from an Italian villa.

You can reach the castle via the only passenger rail service in the Scottish islands, **Mull Rail** (tel. 01680/812494, www.mullrail.co.uk, train runs four or five departures Easter–mid-June and Sept.–Oct. and half-hourly departures mid-June–Aug.). Mull Rail runs from Craignure; to get to Craignure station, turn left from the Pier and left again in a few hundred meters. The journey takes 20 minutes and costs £3.50 adult, £2 child one-way.

Duart Castle (Duart Bay, tel. 01688/812309, www.duartcastle.com, 10:30 A.M.–5:30 P.M. daily May–early Oct., 11 A.M.–4 P.M. Sun.–Thurs. Apr.) is the proper fairy tale fortress on Mull, accessed via a side road from the main A849 curving around Duart Bay. It was built in 1350 and became the stronghold of the MacLean clan. The castle has dungeons and great views of Mull and the mainland coast from the top of the keep.

Burgh and Ben More Estate

The wild area to the west of Central Mull is a haven for wildlife and walkers. It's a wild 12-mile (round-trip) walk along the coast of the rocky Burg peninsula to reach the 12-meter-high **Burgh Fossil Tree** (accessed from NTS car park by Tioran off B8035). Its tree trunk still stands against the cliffs since being preserved as the result of a lava flow between 50 and 60 million years ago. The path there ends at a sheer cliff, scaled by a somewhat rickety iron ladder, from where it's a tough one-mile hike along a boulder-strewn beach to the tree. You have to return the same way.

Ben More (accessed from car park on B8035) is Mull's highest mountain at 966 meters above sea level and the only Munro peak in Scotland's islands outside of Skye. The best access point is from the car park on the B8035 at Abhain Dhisieg, southwest of Salen after the road climbs up from the shores of Loch na Keal. The car park is near where a bridge crosses the Abhain na h-Uamha. You should allow at least five hours for the boggy, often pathless trek to the summit.

Accommodations and Food

Shieling Holidays (Craignure, tel. 01680/812496, www.shielingholidays.co.uk, tent and two people £15.50, carpeted tents £28) is a campsite with a difference: you don't even have to bring your own tent! That's an option, of course, but the best accommodation here is in innovative carpeted tents or Shielings, complete with their own common room and stove heater. Some of the Shielings are en suite. It's a delightful grassy site sheltered by trees from the most biting of breezes. The complex is only 800 meters from the Craignure ferry terminal; turn left on the Fionnphort road.

Barn Cottage (Gruline, tel. 01680/300451, www.barncottagemull.co.uk, £46 d) is a small farm cottage poking out between trees by Gruline, a great bargain in these remote parts. There are just two simple rooms on offer at the farm, with views of the moist, wild, central belt of Mull. Both are clean, countrified rooms; one is en suite and the guest lounge is shared (lots of CDs, DVDs and board games). To get there, follow the B8035 south from Salen past the B8073; it's the track on the left signposted to Macquaries Mausoleum.

Lying on a bed in one of the seven rooms at **Tiroran House** (tel. 01681/705232, www.tiroran.com, £138 d) is like floating on a cloud. Think of the crispest, coolest linen and the softest king-size beds, then visualize views over lush, verdant grounds to a lonely rocky loch shore with distant hills beyond; at Tiroran, you don't have to imagine—you can experience it all first-hand. Meals can feature grapes from Tiroran's very own conservatory vine in season. It's cordon bleu cuisine here, but if you can afford to stay then the main meals are a snip at £36.50 per head.

Getting There and Away

Craignure is the main hub for buses to the south and to Tobermory but there are no public transport connections to any of the sites in Central Mull. The exceptions are Torosay Castle, served by bus and train, and Duart Castle (Fionnphort buses stop 1.5 miles away).

SOUTH MULL AND THE ROSS

The south coast of Mull is easily its loveliest and most varied. It's got the full spectrum of coastal features, from lonely bays where castles

© LUKE WATERSON

fishing catch being landed, Fionnphort

stand as sentinels to formidable rock arches and stacks to fine sandy beaches.

Loch Buie

The road to Loch Buie twists past the slate-colored Loch Spelve and eventually twists down to the wide, quiet shingle bay at Loch Buie village. Here you'll find the ruins of sheer-sided **Moy Castle** overlooking the shoreline and Mull's most impressive **stone circle.** The stones are accessed by a path from a road bridge on the approach to Loch Buie village.

Carsaig

Carsaig, little more than a house and a phone box, is the starting point for **walks** in both directions along a splendid stretch of wild South Mull coast. You can walk northeast along the coast to Lochbuie (allow three to four hours for the four-mile hike). The walk southwest along the coast to **Carsaig Arches** from Carsaig is one of the most rewarding walks on Mull. It's a two-hour hike to the arches themselves, via **Nun's Pass,** with a

cave that has crosses carved into its walls dating from A.D. 800. Then you reach the arches—dramatic basalt rock formations that were originally sea caves. There are two arches to see, one of which has a precariously positioned rock stack on top. Expect to see wild goats, seals, and otters. Giving yourself time to photo snap, you'll need at least five hours for this walk.

Fionnphort

The small village of Fionnphort (pronounce it "Finn-a-fort") clusters at the very tip of the Ross of Mull peninsula. It's the hopping-off point for ferries to Iona and has a heritage center exploring the life of St. Columba, a supermarket, a couple of pubs, and Mull's best beaches just down the road. Drive down the minor road south from Fionnphort to Knockvologan to get to the area's best sandy **beaches.** The sands link Mull with the tidal island of **Erraid,** where Robert Louis Stevenson, who spent much of his youth in the area with members of his family on lighthouse-building duty, was inspired to write *Kidnapped.*

ST. COLUMBA: LIGHTING UP THE SCOTTISH DARK AGES

St. Columba was an Irish missionary saint exiled from his homeland after a dispute with a fellow priest. The dispute had ended with a battle with a great loss of life: St. Columba's mission was to sail to Scotland to convert at least as many people to Christianity as had died in battle. The saint set sail and landed in Kintyre in 563. He is said to have wished to found a monastery there but to have climbed to the top of the nearest hill, realized he could still see his homeland, and so headed north. Scotland is peppered with places that claim an association with the saint's route upon his arrival; if all of them are accurate then the route must have been a rather circuitous one.

Later in A.D. 563 he landed on Iona and founded a monastery after being granted lands there. St. Columba became a respected figure with the resident Pict population. The facilities he set up could hardly be argued with: as well as a religious center, Iona was also the only center of literacy in a vast area. The island became host to a school of missionaries and book transcribers through the saint's efforts; he so impressed the Pictish king that he was allowed a say in the politics of the kingdom. With Iona as his base, St. Columba went on a series of missionary trips through the glens of Highland Scotland. His travels took him as far east as Aberdeenshire; the High Steward of Buchan gave the saint the town in reverence, according to the *Book of Deer* that St. Columba later wrote.

The saint's travels even brought him through the Great Glen. Here he is said to have come across a group of Picts burying a man who had been killed by a monster. St. Columba turned to the beast, made the sign of the cross, and told it "You will not go further," at which point the monster fled in terror. This is the first recorded mention of the Loch Ness monster. St. Columba had even amassed a following in Ireland, the country that had exiled him, by his mid-70s. One morning in early June 597, he climbed the hill overlooking the monastery he had built and blessed the land around him one last time. At the midnight mass that evening, he went early to the church and fell dead before the altar.

Columba was still writing the Scottish history books 700 years after his death; the Scots were said to have the saint's relics with them, inspiring them to victory at Bannockburn, despite the heavy odds stacked against them. A heroic figure St. Columba certainly seems; however, much of his missionary life is only known about through an account written by the ninth abbot of Iona, who was quite possibly trying to give either himself or his abbey a boost in prestige during the dark times following St. Columba's death.

Accommodations and Food

Unless you camp in the wild, you will not get more beautiful views or more basic facilities than at **Fidden Farm Campsite** (Fidden, by Fionnphort, tel. 01681/700427, camping £4 pp), 1.5 miles down the dead-end road toward Knockvologan. The site sits on its own beach. The camping area is huge, with intermittently hot showers and water for washing dishes.

On the road to Lochbuie, the whitewashed barn conversion at **Barrachandroman** (Kinlochspelve, by Lochbuie, tel. 01680/814220, www.barrachandroman.com, £64 d) has just two rooms, each with its own entrance and looking as if it could have come out of another century. Both rooms are en suite and one has a bath; expect dark antique furniture, bare stone walls, and oak beamed ceilings. It's where the Lochbuie road meets the road around Loch Spelve.

The **Pennyghael Hotel** (Pennyghael, tel. 01681/704288, www.pennyghaelholidays.co.uk, £65 s, £80 d) is a long, low, white hotel, sitting in a very useful location to catch all the tourists who underestimated the length of time it takes to drive Mull's grueling roads. For a long way to the east, west, and north it is the only notable place to stay. From outside, it looks a little like an American Midwest motel, but it's a charming place inside with clean, compact rooms that come with TV/DVD player and en suite bathrooms. A set five-course menu is £28 and includes lots of seafood goodies like Loch Etive salmon. If you want cheaper food, head up the road to the Kinloch Hotel.

Staffa House (Fionnphort, tel. 01681/700677, www.staffahouse.co.uk, £64 d) sits handsomely overlooking the Iona Sound. It has four light rooms with pale decor and period furnishings; each has en suite facilities and some rooms get a bath. There's a wonderful conservatory to sit in and ponder the views over to Iona. One of the owners is a chef who rustles up not only tempting evening meals (£15) but also packed lunches, made up according to the size of your adventure (you have to be really hungry to manage the larger one).

With its bare stone work and cozy open fire, the **Keel Row** (Fionnphort, tel. 01681/700458, food served noon–3 P.M. and 6–8:30 P.M.) is a pub that looks better from the inside than outside. It serves an informal menu (bar meals £8–12) and a good array of ales and whisky.

Red Bay Cottage (near Kintra, Fionnphort, tel. 01681/700396, evenings Mon.–Sat. during summer) is one of the best culinary finds in the Inner Hebrides. The main problem you'll have with this place is finding it at all: It's up the dead-end road to Kintra, accessed from the A849 east of Fionnphort. Then you have to branch off onto a rough farm track and open and close a couple of gates to get to a small farm cottage restaurant perched on the cliffs overlooking Iona and the Treshnish Isles. Yes, dogs are barking and no one seems to be at home but that is half the charm. You get wonderful views from the restaurant itself. The menu is not extensive, but it's very tasty, particularly the salmon. Mains are £10–15.

Getting There and Away

Bus service 496 runs five times daily Monday–Friday and twice daily Saturday between Craignure and Fionnphort via Pennyghael. Places like Lochbuie and Carsaig have no bus services.

◖ ISLE OF IONA

As soon as you step onto Iona's green, treeless, spiritual shores a magical sensation arises within you: You are arriving somewhere pretty special. Celtic missionary St. Columba was credited with founding the first outpost of Christianity in Scotland on the island in A.D. 563, but even before this it had been a place of fascination for druids. Since the 6th century, Iona has grown into one of the world's most important religious pilgrimage sites. Iona Abbey, with its magnificent cloistered courtyard, is the focal point for visitors, and the tourist attractions spread out from there. As a result there is an 800-year-old nunnery, a rather more recent heritage center, a religious retreat, and a clutch of places to stay and eat. Iona remains a resolutely tranquil place despite the tourist hordes; once you get off the main abbey drag, you'll find you have much of it to yourself. For an island just three miles long and less than one mile wide it contains an improbable number of sandy beaches where you can soak up the peace and quiet of the eastern shore. North of Iona is uninhabited Staffa, with some of

cloisters, Iona Abbey

© LUKE WATERSON

Scotland's most impressive rock formations and the famous Fingal's Cave, which inspired Felix Mendelssohn to compose an overture.

Sights

Nothing remains on the site of **Iona Abbey** (north of ferry pier, tel. 01681/700512, 9:30 A.M.–5:30 P.M. daily Apr.–Sept., 9:30 A.M.–4:30 P.M. daily Oct.–Mar., opening hours dependent on ferries running from Fionnphort, £4.50 adults, £3.70 seniors, £2.35 children) of the original wattle and daub monastery founded by St. Columba in the 6th century A.D. By 1200 the building had been transformed into a masterful stone Benedictine abbey. Like many religious sites, the abbey suffered at the hands of invaders: Both the Vikings and the Reformation in 1560 played their part in reducing it to a ruin. It was only in the 1930s with the founding of the Iona Community that restoring the abbey to its former glory really got underway.

The first building up on the approach to the abbey is the oldest, St. Oran's Chapel. Somerled, the first Scottish Lord of the Isles, built the chapel in the mid-12th century, but the chapel's name comes from one of St. Columba's followers, St. Oran, who volunteered to be buried alive as a sacrifice to prevent the original church from collapsing. Here in the graveyard known as Relig Odhrain is where the ancient Kings of the empire of Dalriada and later Scotland were buried. In the abbey itself, centered on a glass plot flanked on four sides by Britain's most magnificent cloisters: a series of arches moving mainly for the simplicity of their design. On the far sides of the cloisters is the abbey church with its statue to the 8th Duke of Argyll. It was the Duke's idea to begin restoration of the abbey in 1899. You'll also find an abbey shop and information boards on the history of the island.

Several individuals have had schemes of revamping Iona into a major Christian pilgrimage site; one of the first was Reginald MacDonald of Islay, one of the sons of Somerled. At the same time his men rebuilt Iona Abbey in stone, he also founded **Iona Nunnery** (north of ferry pier, open year-round). Today the nunnery is an extremely well-preserved ruin. You can pass through the peaceful grounds en route from the ferry to the abbey.

The best **beach** on the island is at **Ardriona** in the north; it's a belt of white machair-backed sand. Head north past the abbey to Ardriona Farm and then northeast to get to the beach.

If you have ever looked at a map and seen an intriguing point on the coast but lost hope of ever going there because the place is not on any ferry route, listen up. **Alternative Boat Trips** (tel. 01681/700537, year-round), operated by Mike Jardine, runs everywhere the ferries don't, to all those places you dream of. Whether it's a picnic trip to a little-known beach on the Iona coast or a simple sailing lesson you want, this one-man outfit can oblige. Trips are on a sailing boat, with the option of a motor if passengers prefer. It's £42 for chartering the boat for the first hour and £10 per subsequent hour, but the cost can be split between up to eight people.

The Vikings named rocky **Staffa** (boat trips with MB *Iolaire* of Iona, Tigh na Traigh, Iona, tel. 01681/700358, www.staffatrips.co.uk, leaving Iona Pier daily at 9:45 A.M. and 1:45 P.M., Fionnphort at 10 A.M. and 2 P.M.) after their term for "pillar." The island's immense basalt rock formations reminded them of their houses. Six miles north of Iona, Staffa's striking black basalt columns and series of immense sea caves have enthralled travelers for over two centuries. Author Sir Walter Scott, poet William Wordsworth, and composer Felix Mendelssohn all visited. Mendelssohn was inspired by the sound of waves crashing in **Fingal's Cave** to write his Hebridean Overture: making the cave one of the most famous rocky recesses in the world. Wordsworth already thought in the 1800s that the number of visitors took the edge off the wild beauty of Staffa; the same is true today but it's hard not to be mesmerized by this rocky place bashed by the full ferocity of the Atlantic. You'll get an hour ashore on the excursion. A landing isn't guaranteed if the weather is too rough.

Shopping

Several shops catch the eye on Iona; maybe this is because there are not that many other buildings.

© LUKE WATERSON

Iona fishing boats

The chances are that as you pass eclectic little **Iona Bookshop** (tel. 01681/700699, sporadic opening hours dependent on ferry crossings) it will be open: hours for the time of year are usually posted on the window. It's not just religious and spiritual books here but a whole host of wonderful antiquarian and secondhand volumes.

Iona Gallery and Pottery (tel. 01681/700439, www.iona-gallery.co.uk, 11 A.M.–4 P.M. Mon.–Sat.) is one of a select group of craft shops on the island that is worth a look for a souvenir of Iona. The pottery here is particularly evocative of the colors and shapes of the island; the on-site workshop is in the small converted croft house.

You'll find a bizarre assemblage of products at the **Spar Shop** (up from ferry pier, tel. 01681/700321, 9 A.M.–5:30 P.M. Mon.–Sat., noon–5 P.M. Sun.) for a picnic to take to the beach, like homemade bread and groceries.

Sports and Recreation
Finlay Ross (tel. 01681/700357) is the place to head on Iona for bike hire. You'll find the shop by heading left after the ferry pier at the eyesore of the Martyr's Bay Restaurant.

Accommodations and Food
Situated on a 60-acre working croft with grounds extending to one of Iona's best beaches, **Iona Hostel** (Langandorain, by Camus Cuil, An T'Saimh beach, tel. 01681/700781, www.ionahostel.co.uk, beds £17.50) is a great place to stay, with six dormitory rooms sleeping 2–6 people on bunks and single beds. There are lots of solid pine furnishings, a well-equipped kitchen, and a lounge with a stove to toast yourself by.

You can stay in two simple, light rooftop rooms at **Tigh na Tobrach** (south of ferry pier, tel. 01681/700700, www.bandb-iona.co.uk, £55 d); you'll get a bird's-eye view of the sandy beaches of southwest Mull, as this guesthouse is quite high up. This place is in a quiet location and offers good value. To get to the modern, white house, turn left after the pier and you'll see it near the golf course and the machair after about a mile.

Bishop's House (tel. 01681/700800, www.argyll.anglican.org/bhi.htm, rooms £50 pp full board) is an Anglican retreat center welcoming all pilgrimage groups or individuals. It's one of three spiritual retreats on the island, in a long stone building overlooking the Sound of Iona. Thirteen comfortable rooms are available (none en suite), and there is a house chapel with daily services. Prior booking is essential. Head along past the Argyll Hotel to get to the retreat.

The ◖ **Argyll Hotel** (harborfront, tel. 01681/700334, www.argyllhoteliona.co.uk, £52 s, £72 d, lunch noon–2:30 P.M., dinner 7–8:30 P.M.) isn't the most outwardly attractive building, but inside this is every inch the charming island hotel. There are 16 rooms here—cozy, intimate places with all but one of them en suite, and with Isle of Coll–produced toiletries. The restaurant is even more of a pull: it's not just quality seafood here but also tasty meals like lamb casserole with chorizo and pumpkin tagine. It's all served in a countrified restaurant with prim white tablecloths and an open fire.

Information and Services
There is no bank on Iona. You will, however, find a basic grocery store and post office (by ferry pier, tel. 01681/700515, 9 A.M.–1 P.M. and 2–5 P.M. Mon.–Tues. and Thurs.–Fri., 9 A.M.–1 P.M. Wed., 9 A.M.–12:30 P.M. Sat.).

Getting There and Around
The only ferry to Iona is from Fionnphort on the Ross of Mull. Ferries run about hourly throughout the year, with reduced sailings on Sundays during winter (there's still about five sailings on such days). It's £3.95 adult, £2.30 bicycle round-trip. Unless you have mobility problems, Iona really isn't a place for a car: There are barely any roads and you need a special permit to take a car across on the ferry. You are better off walking or hiring a bike on the island itself. You can only visit Staffa with your own vessel or via a boat tour from Iona/Fionnphort.

ISLE OF COLL
Coll changes kaleidoscopically the closer you get to it. On the approach by ferry from Oban it seems to be a daunting place of craggy coasts. Closer still and it seems to be a flat, lochan-spotted moor, but this too gives way on its east coast to a paradisiacal series of empty shell sand

beaches. Arinagour, near the ferry docks, is the lively main settlement (OK, the only one) and has a petrol pump, village stores, and a café. The main reason visitors come, however, is to escape from the modern world and appreciate the diverse wildlife, consisting of many varieties of flowers and birds.

Beaches
Coll has numerous pockets of golden sandy beaches all along its north coast. The best are at **Hogh Bay,** with its expanse of sand dunes, and **Feall Bay,** a huge, flat, empty golden beach where you can sight whales offshore in summer.

Accommodations and Food
Tigh Na Mara Guesthouse (Arinagour, tel. 01879/230354, www.tighnamara.info, £32.50 s, £60 d) is a smart, modern bungalow with five smallish, simple rooms on offer, two of which are en suite. The view out of the breakfast room, of rocks shelving into a twinkling sea scattered with the distant outlines of the mysterious Treshnish Isles, will make you glad you stayed here. It's handy for the ferry, being the first house after you leave the pier before Arinagour village.

The **Coll Hotel** (Arinagour, tel. 01879/230334, www.collhotel.com, £40 s, £80 d) is a contender for most stunning hotel garden in Scotland; the whitewashed hostelry sits on delightful sloping grassy grounds above the sea, decorated with shrubs and plants. Inside, the rooms get white paint and eye-boggling swirly furnishings, and the bar gets wood paneling. You can eat good seafood in the restaurant for £12–15 or splash out and try the delicious seafood casserole concoction for £25. The hotel does ferry terminal pick-up.

The **Island Café** (by ferry pier, tel. 01879/230262, www.firstportofcoll.com, 10 A.M.–7:30 P.M. Fri., 11 A.M.–7:30 P.M. Sat., 11 A.M.–4 P.M. Sun., 10 A.M.–5:30 P.M. Mon., also Tues. Easter–Oct.) is a bit of a gossiping point for locals, but it's a cheerful happening place to go for a coffee, a filled roll, a hot meal like game pie, or, yep, an organic beer. You'll pay £5–10 for the filling fare on offer.

Getting There and Away

There is a daily **Calmac ferry** from Oban to Coll (3 hrs., £13.40 adult, £79 car one-way) March–October. The reduced winter service runs four days per week. The same ferry will also run from Coll to Tiree (1 hr.) and can be used to get between the two islands.

ISLE OF TIREE

The flat, bright island of Tiree looks like no more than a brushstroke on the horizon from a distance. It gets the most sunshine of any place in the country according to meteorological stats, and almost as much wind. As a result, it's one of the best destinations in Britain for water sports enthusiasts, and also highly popular with bird-life taking a rest from battling the gales. Remote Tiree may be, but lifeless it is not—there are several bustling villages and plenty of places to eat and drink. Then, of course, there are the beaches: 35 percent of this little island's coast is made up of stretches of sand.

Sights

The pretty scattering of buildings at **Hynish** includes the derelict buildings used by Robert Louis Stevenson's uncle Alan Stevenson during construction of the daunting Skerryvore Lighthouse, located offshore. The Hebridean Trust has been revamping these buildings and the signal tower here has been converted into the Hynish Centre (open 9 A.M.–5 P.M. daily, free) which includes information on the mammoth engineering feat that constructing the lighthouse became.

If you saw Tiree from the air, your eyes would be fixated on its wide rim of gold and white sand **beaches.** The biggest and best are on the south coast at **Gott Bay,** to the east of the where the ferry comes in, and **Hynish Bay,** an even wider expanse of sand to the west (particularly at Sorobaidh Bay). It can get windy on these beaches but swimming is still good fun. The beaches here are also great for walking or trying out a sport like kiteboarding or windsurfing.

◖ Windsurfing

The island is growing in popularity with the surfing sect; for the adventure-seeking surfer, things don't get better than Tiree's flat, empty, sandy beaches, a rip-roaring wind, and plenty of crashing waves. In **Wild Diamond Water Sports** (Burnside Cottage, Cornaig, tel. 01879/220339, www.surfschoolscotland.co.uk) Tiree has a very good surf school. Five-hour windsurfing courses inclusive of all equipment start at £60. There are not many places where you can ride the surf and feel higher than the surrounding land. You can also go kiteboarding or kayaking.

Accommodations and Food

Tiree now has a campsite in the west of the island near Balemartine at Balinoe. It has a decent spread of accommodation options for an island of its size.

◖ **Millhouse Hostel** (by Loch Bhasapol, tel. 01879/220435, www.tireemillhouse.co.uk, beds £13, twin rooms £31) is a converted mill near Cornaig and still has a functioning water mill. There are two dorms filled with comfy single beds and two twin rooms. It's a light, brightly painted place and a godsend for budget travelers on the island. The lounge area has lots of board games and books, and there's a self-catering kitchen. It's in the northwest corner of the island. Loch Bhasapol is Tiree's second-largest loch.

It's strangely appropriate for an island many people consider paradise to offer accommodations in a converted church. **Kirkapol House** (by Gott Bay, tel. 01879/220729, www.kirkapoltiree.co.uk, £32 s, £60 d) is the prettiest, classiest guesthouse on the island with six dainty en suite bedrooms. There is a library with lots of books and music. Views from most of the rooms are of stunning Gott Bay, one of the island's best beaches.

Scarinish Hotel (Scarinish, tel. 01879/220308, www.tireescarinishhotel.com, £40 s, £70 d) is the island's bright hotel. It has nine rooms, all of which are immaculate with a pale, neutral decor occasionally brightened by a picture of a vivid blue Hebridean sea or sky. Don't come here expecting anything too fancy—it's a friendly, low-key kind of place. Six of the rooms are en suite; the rest get shared or private bathrooms. **The Old Harbour Restaurant** is still one of the best places on the island to eat and almost certainly the most varied. Main meals are £8–18, with a strong fishy theme including whole crabs and lobsters.

Co-op Supermarket (Scarinish, tel. 01879/ 220326, 8 A.M.–8 P.M. Mon.–Fri., 8 A.M.–6 P.M. Sat., noon–6 P.M. Sun.) is the place to stock up for self-caterers; you can also pay with a debit card here and get cash back.

Information and Services

There are **tourist information touch screens** at the airport and Calmac ferry terminal, as well as several other locations on the island. You can access the Internet at the **An Iodhlann Centre** (Scarinish, tel. 01879/220793, 9 A.M.–5 P.M. Mon.–Fri. July–Sept., 10:30 A.M.–3:30 P.M. Mon.–Fri. Oct.–June), which acts as something of a local history archive for the island.

Getting There and Around

The **ferry sailings** and prices are the same as for Coll. Ferries take four hours to reach Tiree from Oban, via Coll. Tiree also has an airport with one **flight** per day Monday–Saturday (www.britishairways.com) to Glasgow.

Tiree Motor Company (tel. 01879/220469) is the place to hire a car.

Islay and Vicinity

Balmy Islay, home to eight working distilleries and some of the best beaches in the Inner Hebrides, is a gently rolling, luscious island. It's a world away from the mountainous bleakness of larger Hebridean islands like Mull or Skye with swaths of inky green forest and farmland that merges into flower-flanked machair (grass-covered dunes) and long tracts of golden sand. The island is also a mecca for bird-watchers, who are attracted by the many wild geese that become Islay residents every autumn. Colonsay, to the north of Islay, is a lush place with a subtropical garden and a priory patronized by St. Columba. Wild Jura, the other main island in this group, is a paradise for hill-walkers.

ORIENTATION

Ferries come into Islay at the southern end at Port Ellen or in the northeast at Port Askaig. The capital of Islay, Bowmore, lies about 10 miles north of Port Ellen and 10 miles southwest of Port Askaig.

GETTING TO ISLAY

Calmac ferries to Islay run from Kennacraig on the Kintyre peninsula south of Tarbert (£8.45 adult, £45 car one-way). They run to either Port Ellen (northeast Islay, 2 hrs. 20 min.) or to Port Askaig (south Islay, 2 hrs. 5 min.) four times daily.

British Airways has **flights** from Glasgow to Islay Airport twice daily Monday–Friday and once daily Saturday. Flight time is around 40 minutes. The airport is in the south of Islay by Laggan Bay.

SOUTHERN ISLAY

The south of the island is pretty hilly by Islay standards: heathery moor with thick patches of conifer forest in the east. The high moor channels fast-flowing burns down to the rocky southern coast, helping to flavor the whisky produced in the three renowned distilleries at the bottom. In the west is the huge golden strip of sand known as Laggan Bay, backed by grassy, flower-filled dunes known as machair. The main settlement in these parts is Port Ellen, the island's chief ferry port, with Islay's very own airport nearby.

Port Ellen and the Oa

Port Ellen, Islay's main ferry and airport link to the outside world, is a shabby place and has little to offer the visitor beyond a means to enter or exit the island. It does, however, have some of Islay's finest leisure facilities: a top-notch cybercafé, tennis courts, and a putting green. To

© LUKE WATERSON

Ardbeg Distillery, by Port Ellen

the west of Port Ellen is the squat peninsula known as the **Oa,** a low-lying, lochan-daubed moor renowned for its birdlife. At its southwestern end stands the lighthouse-shaped **American Monument,** erected to commemorate the loss of two American troop ships in 1918; more than 2,000 lives were lost in the disaster.

Northward from Kintra near Port Ellen stretches a seven-mile sweep of uninterrupted golden sand, known as Laggan Bay or the "Big Strand." You can see lots of wildlife in the flower-carpeted dunes behind the beach.

South Coast Distilleries

The coast east of Port Ellen is where three of the island's finest, most peaty whiskies are distilled. Tour costs of each can be largely redeemed against a purchase in the distillery shop.

Abutting the gentle waters of the south coast is this long, low distillery, **Laphroaig** (by Port Ellen, tel. 01496/302418, www.laphroaig.com, tours 10 A.M. and 2 P.M. Mon.–Fri. Sept.–June, £2). Originally a farm, it's one of the most picturesque Islay distilleries. You get a generous dram at the end of the tour. Inquire about

becoming a "Friend of Laphroaig," which will get you your very own plot of land! The distillery cuts its own peat. Make prior arrangements for tours.

The next distillery along this coast is **Lagavulin** (by Port Ellen, tel. 01496/302730, www.discovering-distilleries.com/lagavulin, tours Mon.–Fri. by prior appointment only, £4). Once, as many as 12 (often illicit) distilleries stood around the site where Lagavulin now stands. The liquor produced here is known as the "aristocrat" of Islay whiskies and epitomizes everything that is finest about them: it's got a heavy, strongly peat-influenced taste. Lagavulin whisky is probably the most famous of all the Islay malts.

The whiskies just seem to get peatier the farther east you head along the south coast, and the climax comes at **Ardbeg** (by Port Ellen, tel. 01496/302244, www.ardbeg.com, 10 A.M.–5 P.M. daily June–Aug., 10 A.M.–4 P.M. Mon.–Fri. Sept.–May, £2.50). No single malt whisky in the world comes peatier than this. Ardbeg is the most visitor-friendly distillery of these three; there is a

© LUKE WATERSON

driftwood collecting near Kildalton

section in the shop where you can taste away to your heart's content before making a purchase, and a pleasant café/restaurant.

Kildalton and Vicinity

In the grounds of the lonely ruined chapel at Kildalton stands the most complete **Celtic High Cross** in Scotland. It was intricately carved during the 9th century A.D. by a craftsman from Iona. The road continues beyond Kildalton to **Ardtalla,** where there are some fine deserted sandy beaches.

Entertainment and Events

Check the island newspaper, the *Ileach,* for details of what's going on. Most shops stock copies. Most events, including the principal festivities of the Islay Malt and Music Festival and the Islay Show, take place at Islay House near the island's capital, Bowmore.

Each Monday evening throughout the tourist season, Islay runs a series of **welcome evenings** for visitors in different locations across the island. They offer a good introduction to what there is to see and do, and there's

a guest appearance from one of the island distilleries, offering sample drams. Check in the Bowmore TIC for the location of upcoming welcome evenings.

Accommodations and Food

Homey **Kintra Farmhouse and Camp Site** (Kintra, tel. 01496/302051, www.kintra-farm.co.uk, from £56 d, tent pitches £10), at the end of the great golden curve of Laggan Bay, has three rooms available, sharing two bathrooms. There are also two resident lounges where you can sit, gaze at the views, and peruse the selection of local history books, all in front of an open fire. The campsite, amongst the dunes, is a delightful spot to pitch a tent. Farm buildings have been converted into basic wash facilities. Shelter from the wind is limited, so bang those pegs in well.

Glenmachrie (Glenmachrie, tel. 01496/302560, www.glenmachrie.com, £90 d), an old whitewashed farmhouse, seems to bridge the gap between traditional and modern. The result is elegant rooms with antique furnishings and fresh, soothing decor with orthopedic beds

© LUKE WATERSON

sand castle near Ardtalla

and en suite bathrooms. Glenmachrie champions home-grown, organic produce, and you can see from the breakfast room how most of the food got on your plate. From the conservatory or sunhouse you can soak in the stupendous views of a golf course overlooking sand dunes and a nature reserve. Deer and otters are regularly seen on the 450-acre working farm. Next to Glenmachrie is a second house offering more rooms; this is where breakfast is served. The friendly, gushing hosts have a long list of ideas for days out.

The **Old Kiln Café** (tel. 01496/302244, www.ardbeg.com, noon–5 P.M. daily June–Aug., noon–4 P.M. Mon.–Fri. Sept.–May) in Ardbeg Distillery is a great spot for a light lunch. Tables are set out in the former peat kiln, where peat for the distillery would have been burnt. There are some great homebakes on offer, and there isn't a better place for coffee and scones on the south coast. Snacks and light meals are £1–6.

Information

Who says the cybercafé is dead? It lives on in style at **Mactaggart Community Cyber Café and Corner Kitchen** (30 Mansefield Pl., tel. 01496/302693, www.islaycybercafe.co.uk, food served 11 A.M.–3 P.M. and 5–8 P.M. Mon.–Sat., 11 A.M.–5 P.M. Sun., cybercafé open until 10 P.M. Mon.–Sat.). There is Internet access (£1 for 20 minutes), lots of pool tables, and a café serving cheap snacks.

Getting There and Around

Port Ellen is the southern terminus for the Islay **bus** network. Buses run north to Bowmore, where you'll probably need to change, although a few services run right the way through to Portnahaven daily. Four buses daily run along the south coast as far as Ardbeg.

If you don't want to take public transport, get in touch with **Fiona's Taxis** (tel. 01496/302622 or 0780/830 3200). **Islay Car Hire** (tel. 01496/810544, www.islaycarhire.com) rents cars from £32.50 per day, £175 per week.

BOWMORE AND VICINITY

The one main street of Islay's self-proclaimed capital soars up from the harbor to the distinctive round church at the top. It's a pretty little place with a fine distillery, lots of arty-crafty shops, and a couple of good places to eat. If your palate is burning from all that whisky, Islay House to the north of Bowmore is home to the Islay Brewery, which makes several good beers.

Sights

The white **Round Church** (top of Main St., Bowmore, www.theroundchurch.org.uk, 9 A.M.–6 P.M. daily) at the top of the steep high street gives Bowmore a somewhat individual appearance: it was supposedly built like this so that there were no corners for the devil to hide in.

The oldest distillery on Islay, **Bowmore Distillery** (Bowmore, tel. 01496/810441, www.bowmore.co.uk, 9 A.M.–5 P.M. daily July–mid-Sept., 9 A.M.–5 P.M. Mon.–Sat. Easter–June, 9 A.M.–5 P.M. Mon.–Fri., 9 A.M.–noon Sat. mid-Sept.–Easter, £4) is a charming whitewashed building with its name painted in black letters on the front. A distillery has stood here on the edge of Loch Indaal since the 1770s. Bowmore does one of Islay's best distillery tours. One of the factors in the uniqueness of the tour here is that the distillery still has its own floor maltings, one of few distilleries in Scotland to do so. The flavor of the sea comes across in the taste of the finished whisky: Barrels are stored in damp vaults below sea level. Tours include a tasting of the "angel's share" in the warehouse at the end. There are four tours daily except on Saturday during low season, when there is just one.

Shopping and Recreation

The closest Islay gets to a shopping center is the tasteful development at **Islay House Square** (north of Bridgend off A846). The stables of the main house have been converted into a series of arts and craft shops, the **Islay Brewery** (tel. 01496/810014, www.islayales.com), and a **coffee shop.**

You can hire **bikes** from the post office at the top of Main Street (tel. 01496/810366).

Events

The **Islay Festival of Malt and Music** (www.islayfestival.org), or "Feis Ile" as it is known in Gaelic, is a festival that celebrates Islay culture in the form of a little music and a lot of whisky-based events. It's held in the last week of May.

The island's big event is the **Islay Show,** a fun agricultural event showing off the best of local livestock and showcasing Islay's produce (including whisky-tasting stalls). It's one of the most important agricultural events on the west coast of Scotland, culminating in the sheaf toss, in which burly local men fling a sack of wheat on a pitchfork over an increasingly high barrier—absolutely brilliant. The show is held on a Thursday in early August each year.

Accommodations and Food

The seven stylish studio-like rooms at the **Harbour Inn and Restaurant** (Harbour, Bowmore, tel. 01496/810330, www.harbour-inn.com, £115 d) have the pick of the views across Loch Indaal Bay. They're soothing places to relax for a few days, with pale-colored decor and en suite baths. Once you settle down in one of the easy chairs in the guest lounge, you could spend hours gazing at the view. The snug restaurant is without doubt the best around; the menu has lots of locally caught seafood, including oysters. Lunch for two is £32.50.

The **Bowmore Hotel** (Jamieson St., Bowmore, tel. 01496/810416, www.bowmore-hotel.co.uk, £79 d) has somewhat old-fashioned rooms in an endearing, graceful old black-and-white building. Accommodations have a mixture of en suite and shared bathroom facilities, and all rooms get Sky TV. Rooms are simple, average-sized affairs; the restaurant here puts on a hearty spread of food. You can try anything from venison and fine Islay lamb to the specialty shellfish cream with brandy sauce (a concoction of all the freshest local seafood). Mains are £10–16.

Under new management and new inflated prices, the **Bridgend Hotel** (Bridgend, tel. 01496/810212, www.bridgend-hotel.co.uk, £70 s, £125 d) has come on leaps and bounds. Pearly white rooms are en suite, with Sky Digital TV and DVD players. They're good, but possibly not good enough to stop you wincing at the price. The pleasant restaurant does

© LUKE WATERSON

some bagpipers taking a rest, Islay

filling main meals (£5–9.50) like venison casserole and deep-fried scampi. There is a decent bar with a lovely beer garden. Fishermen, listen up: the hotel has boats on two local trout-fishing lochs.

Information and Services

As the island capital, Bowmore has a decent spread of tourist facilities.

Bowmore TIC (The Square, tel. 01496/810254, 9:30 A.M.–5:30 P.M. Mon.–Sat., 2–5 P.M. Sun. Apr.–Aug., 10 A.M.–5 P.M. Mon.–Sat. Sept.–Oct.) has the area info you need.

Bowmore has a couple of banks with ATMs. If you have financial matters to resolve on Islay, do it here. Bowmore post office (tel. 01496/810366) is at the top of Main Street. **Islay Hospital** (Gortonvoggie Rd., Bowmore, tel. 01496/301000) has an outpatient department.

Getting There and Away

Bowmore is as near as Islay gets to having a center. It's the convergence point for Port Ellen, Port Askaig, and Rinns Peninsula buses. About 10 buses daily (30 min.) run from Port Ellen to Bowmore. Five buses run between Port Askaig and Bowmore daily, coinciding with ferry departure times.

◖ PORT CHARLOTTE AND RINNS OF ISLAY

Whitewashed houses standing in a long line above a grassy, rocky bay, the best restaurants on the island, and an intriguing museum: appealing Port Charlotte is the epitome of Islay charm. It's the main village on a peninsula full of similarly scenic villages, wild sandy beaches, and geese. Scotland's most westerly distillery has also just opened here.

Sights

Housed in a former church, the **Museum of Island Life** (Port Charlotte, tel. 01496/850358, 10 A.M.–5 P.M. Mon.–Sat., 2–5 P.M. Sun. Apr.–Oct., £3) takes a detailed look at life on Islay from Mesolithic times through to the 20th century. It's a cluttered hodgepodge of items grouped into themes like dairy implements and blacksmith tools. You can see an illicit still and

© LUKE WATERSON

Bruichladdich Distillery, Rinns Peninsula

an interesting archaeological collection including the skull of an elk preserved in peat bog from 10,000 years ago.

Since the originally Victorian **Bruichladdich Distillery** (Bruichladdich, tel. 01496/850190, www.bruichladdich.com, tours Mon.–Sat. year-round, £5) has been reopened by a group of whisky enthusiasts and private investors in 2000, it's gone from strength to strength. The whisky is still made using Victorian machinery to keep its original taste all those decades ago unchanged. A tour here includes a dram and will involve a visit to the bottling hall; it's the only distillery to have one on Islay. There's a shop here, as well as the Single Malt Academy, which promotes weeklong whisky production courses. Tours are three times daily during the week and twice daily on Saturdays.

The southern end of shallow, sandy **Loch Gruinart** (visitors center tel. 01496/850505, 10 A.M.–5 P.M. daily, free, donations gratefully accepted) is renowned for its birdlife, full of mating wading birds come spring, and even the odd elusive Corncrake. The highlight of the ornithological calendar is in autumn, when

thousands of barnacle and white-fronted geese arrive. There is a center telling you about the wealth of birdlife that visits and a bird hide with telescopes to zoom in on unsuspecting birds. A minor road leads up the west shore of Loch Gruinart to Ardnave, where you can do a walk along the glorious dunes to Ardnave Point.

Kilchoman Distillery (Rockside Farm, by Machir Bay, tel. 01496/850011, www.kilchomandistillery.com, 10 A.M.–5:30 P.M. daily July–Aug., 10 A.M.–5:30 P.M. Mon.–Sat. May–June and Sept., £3.50) is Islay's newest; even if you've seen all seven others, coming here will be no run-of-the-mill experience. Every part of the distilling process, from barley growing to bottling, is done on-site at the farm of Kilchoman, and it's been set out in a very attractive, rustic way. The visitors center is top notch, giving a run-through of the history of farm distilling on Islay. Then there's a good **craft shop** and **organic food shop,** as well as an excellent **café** serving coffee, cakes, and salads. You can, of course, tour the endearing little distillery itself, which is fast approaching its first bottling in 2010. The dram on offer at present consists of a part-distilled liquor that, while interesting in taste, is not going to be winning any awards just yet! The admission charge is redeemable against products in the shop.

The two more-or-less joined settlements of **Portnahaven and Port Wemyss** are as idyllic as island villages come: whitewashed cottages gathered around the edge of a steep, grassy drop to a picturesque harbor. There is little to do besides buying an ice cream from the post office and having a wander, with possibly a gaze across at the lighthouse built by Robert Louis Stevenson's grandfather on the Isle of Orsay. You can stare back at the seals as they bask on the seaweed-covered rocks. There's plenty of good picnicking spots, too.

There are several splendid sandy **beaches** on the western edge of the Rinns Peninsula: the best are at Machir Bay (off the B8018 on the northern end), where swimming can be dangerous, and Lossit Bay (accessed via a minor road north from Portnahaven). Getting to Lossit Bay involves a one-mile walk through fields often full of bulls.

Accommodations and Food

The **Islay Youth Hostel** (Main St., Port Charlotte, tel. 01496/850385, www.syha.org.uk, beds £13–15) is a former whisky warehouse with an adjoining wildlife center, with 30 beds available in mostly three- to seven-bed dorms. It's remarkably warm for a youth hostel and has self-catering facilities and a drying room.

Staying at whitewashed **Port Charlotte Hotel** (Port Charlotte, tel. 01496/850360, www.portcharlottehotel.com, £70 s, £120 d) is a real treat: rooms are done up in white with en suite bathrooms with baths, direct-dial telephones, and color TVs. Make sure you get a room with a sea view to justify the price tag. Pretty Port Charlotte is well located for access to lamb, game, and seafood—just what's on offer on the menu in the rurally decked out bar/restaurant. You can try a dram of Islay's finest whisky at the bar.

The popular, light-filled café restaurant **Croft Kitchen** (Port Charlotte, tel. 01496/850230, 10 A.M.–5 P.M. and 6:30–

8:30 P.M. daily) overlooks the rocky beach in Port Charlotte. During the day it serves up coffee, tea, gooey cakes, and scones. By night it does atmospheric meals like steak with peppercorns. Daytime light meals are from £4. There is also a craft shop and bookshop here.

An Tigh Seinnse (11 Queen St., Portnahaven, tel. 01496/860224, food midday–8 P.M. daily) is pretty new on the scene, a cozy little bar/restaurant with a great location on the headland at Portnahaven (follow the road down to the harbor, around to the very end). There are lots of Islay ales to try and limited but very good grub. This place is all about location and has oodles of rustic maritime charm.

Getting There and Away

Five to six services daily make the 55-minute journey from Portnahaven to Bowmore and back, all calling at Port Charlotte.

NORTHEAST ISLAY

The northeast of the island is mostly rough moor, with a pocket of lush forest around the main villages of **Ballygrant** and **Port Askaig,** Islay's chief ferry terminal (for ferries to Jura and Kennacraig on the mainland). On a loch in this wild region is an island containing the ruins of the capital of the former empire of the Lord of the Isles. There's some good walking to be had, including a gentle woodland hike from Ballygrant via **Loch Ballygrant** to Port Askaig.

Sights

The ancient Scottish kings known as the Lords of the Isles made the area around **Loch Finlaggan** (enquiries@finlaggan.com, www.finlaggan.com, Visitor Centre open 2:30–5 P.M. Sun.–Fri. May–Sept., 2:30–5 P.M. Tues., Thurs., and Sun. Apr. and Oct.) their home from as early as the 13th century. It's worth starting out at the visitors center at the entrance, which provides interpretive displays on the numerous ruins you can see on-site. Numerous ancient monuments litter the loch's largest island, Eilean Mor, accessed by a walkway from the center. These include the crumbling walls of the Lords of the Isles

THE DYNASTY OF THE LORDS OF THE ISLES

The history of Scotland's western islands and outlying peninsulas during the first millennium A.D. was one of various Gaelic and Norse warlords vying for control. Ineptitude by the kings of Scotland and Norway, who disputed overall control of the region until the Battle of Largs in 1263, left a power void in the far western islands and Highlands. The area was far from the main seat of power in the country, and various men were able to amass armies and declare themselves lords of the region without any real fear of reprisal. The incentive to rule was great: Here was an empire stretching from the Isle of Man in England to the tips of the Outer Hebrides.

In a land of islands, war ships were the currency of might and power, and one man had more of these than anyone: Somerled. Somerled first emerged on the scene in A.D. 1140, marrying the daughter of Olaf, then king of Mann and the Isles. On Olaf's death in 1153, Somerled acted while other leaders floundered and he seized control, giving himself the title of King of Mann and of the Hebrides. Divides between Gaels and Norse were healed, as Somerled had equal amounts of both in his veins. With fewer internal power struggles, the empire formed was one that would in time grow stronger and richer than all other authorities in Britain, save the English and Scottish kings themselves.

The new ruling elite in the islands were called Gall-Gaidheal, or foreign Gaels. Somerled's own rule would only last six years, until 1164. Somerled's son Ragnald became the new king, with his power base on Loch Finlaggan on Islay. Until 1263, Gall-Gaidheal leaders kept the title of king, but in 1263 they sided with Norway against mainland Scotland in the Battle of Largs. The Norse were resoundingly beaten and future leaders of the Isles had to make do with the title of "Lord," recognizing the kings of mainland Scotland as their superiors. In the late 13th century, the dynasty of the Lords of the Isles reached its zenith. The three most powerful figures of the dynasty, the respective heads of the family branches of the promiscuous Somerled, were respected and feared by Scottish monarchs. Although by the 14th century the relative importance of this empire was dwindling, lords were appeased by various Scottish kings because of their might. Robert the Bruce was keen to keep leader Angus Og on his side during the Scottish Wars of Independence and both English and Scottish leaders were eager to win the favor of Angus Og's son John. John was even granted further lands to add to his empire, and by his death in 1380 the Lordship of the Isles included lands in Ardnamurchan and Kintyre.

Hopes that this might begin another golden age were short lived. John's heirs were politically incompetent. His grandson, Alexander of the Isles, fell victim to King James I's steps to rein in his powerful rivals. Lord Alexander was arrested by the king when he believed he was attending a conference; he was later released but the empire was by then in disarray. Alexander's son John made the fall of the dynasty complete by agreeing to become a vassal of the English king. In so doing he gave the crown of England carte blanche to grant or deny the Lords of the Isles a title at all. Given this choice, and the intimidating history of the might of the island empire, King James V of Scotland decided to no longer grant the title. The once mighty dynasty fizzled to an embarrassing end.

former stronghold and a 14th-century chapel with some medieval carved grave slabs. At the south of the island are the remains of the most important building, the Great Hall, where Lords of the Isles would have feasted and held council. Only foundations and rubble remain now, so you'll need a strong sense of imagination to re-create the glory days of this empire in your mind. The Finlaggan complex is on the A846 by Ballygrant.

Accommodations and Food
The **Port Askaig Hotel** (Port Askaig, tel. 01496/840295, www.portaskaig.co.uk, £39 s, £90 d) wins lots of prizes for location; it's a delightful, whitewashed hotel stretched out along the harborfront. The bar/restaurant, serving meat dishes throughout the day, has the best beer garden on the island—and quite possibly in the country. It's a grassy area superb for people- and boat-watching; you might like it so much you don't want to leave. In that case, you'll find pale-colored, smallish rooms, most of which are en suite and have color TV and all of which have great views of the woods or the Sound of Jura. The two single rooms are cheaper because they are not en suite, but they still get private bathrooms.

Getting There and Away
Buses run five times daily between Port Askaig, Ballygrant (for Finlaggan), Bridgend, and Bowmore.

ISLE OF JURA
George Orwell, who holed up on Jura to write his novel *1984,* described this rugged island as "an un-get-atable place." Things haven't changed much since. Few islands this large in Scotland can claim to be so inaccessible or remote. The life that does exist on the island does so on a strip of fertile land on the south coast. The name Jura in Gaelic means "deer island," and you're more likely to see a red deer than a human being here. If an absolute break from the outside world (the bank comes once a week, and mobile phone reception and Internet access are virtually zero) is not enough of a motive to

make the trek out here, then there are other reasons to come. You can tour a distillery, see some exquisitely beautiful walled gardens, go deer spotting, and trek to see the world's third-biggest whirlpool, the Corrywreckan.

Sights
The key to **Jura Distillery** (Craighouse, tel. 01496/820240, www.isleofjura.com, open year-round, tours 11 A.M. and 2 P.M. Mon.–Fri. Easter–Oct. and at other times by appointment, free) is the nearby burn that crashes down from the hills. If you want a tour, book in advance.

That the verdant spread of plants and flowers at **Jura House Gardens** (Ardfin, tel. 01496/820315, www.jurahouseandgardens.co.uk, 9 A.M.–5 P.M. year-round, £2.50) can even flourish in the exposed peaty wilderness of Jura seems unbelievable. This charming walled garden has an array of exotic plants, trellised pathways, ferns, and a wildflower meadow. Admission includes a booklet detailing walks through the grounds. From June to August a tea tent sells tasty homebakes. Beware of midges here.

🄲 Walking
With huge, wild, heathery mountains pushing civilization right to the edge, Jura is a great place to take off into the countryside.

The distinctive **Paps of Jura** are high hills visible from a great distance around. These three conical hills form Jura's backbone; they're not that high (the tallest is 2,785 feet or 785 meters), but they are big in reputation and are the only features of Jura's vast, desolate peaty north. A good access point for ascending the Paps is from the minor road to Glenbatrick on the western coast. The route to the top will be a scramble over scree, so bring good footwear and a good map. Set six hours aside for the hike to the top.

The public road heading northeast up Jura's coast dies out at **Inverlussa,** where there is little more than a vehicle barricade and a rubble track leading across the moor. From Inverlussa it's an adventurous seven-mile hike to the northern tip of Jura, from where you can see the **Corrywreckan Whirlpool.** After four miles is **Barnhill,** the ruin where George Orwell wrote the novel *1984.* The track dies out completely at **Kinuachdrachd,** from where it's two tough miles farther to the tip of the island.

Here is the best land point from which to see the Corrywreckan, the world's third-largest maelstrom. The bed of rock below the treacherous waters of the Strait of Corrywreckan is pockmarked with reefs and great pinnacles of rock that jut sharply up from the deeps. As a result the tides here go crazy, resulting in a dramatic series of eddies, up-thrusts, and tidal flows. To see the effects maximized you want a good westerly wind. If you still don't feel you are close enough to the thrilling vortex, it's possible to swim it. However, this should only be tried at certain tide times and under the strict supervision of professional swimming guides who are familiar with the waters.

Accommodations and Food

Facilities on Jura, in stark contrast to Islay, are very limited.

The **Jura Hotel** (Craighouse, tel. 01496/ 820243, www.jurahotel.co.uk, £70 d) advertises its status in big black letters on its white walls and well may it boast: it's the only pub on the island, and easily the best-appointed place to stay. The rooms are comfy and old-fashioned, with a mix of en suite and shared facilities. There is a resident lounge and a bar where you can pick up a decent evening meal.

If you're planning a stay on Jura and you haven't booked a room in the Jura Hotel, it is highly recommended you do not stay at all, although camping in the lush gardens of the Jura Hotel is possible.

Getting There and Around

A **ferry** (tel. 01496/840681) runs regularly across the Islay Sound from Feolin in southwestern Jura to Port Askaig on Islay. Ferries are dependent on school term times but are generally every half hour 8 A.M.–6:30 P.M., with later sailings on Wednesdays. The Jura **bus** service (tel. 01496/820221) will meet ferries and

run up through Craighouse to Inverlussa; it's always best to phone in advance if you need the service.

COLONSAY AND ORONSAY

These two islands, joined by a sandy causeway, are among the remotest of the Inner Hebrides and also among the brightest. Colonsay basks in the relative warmth of the Gulf Stream and as a result has not only a splendid formal garden but carpets of rich wild flowers across its grassy, rocky hills. You'll be wanting excuses to sit down and have picnics every few minutes. The shelves of shoreline rock make good resting places for seals as well as humans. Celtic missionaries St. Columa and St. Oran are said to have stopped by the islands en route to Iona, and the latter gave his name to the ancient priory which still stands on Oronsay. For those not grabbed by flora, fauna, or archaeology, almost everywhere you look are wonderful white sandy bays.

Sights

On such a windswept shore it is heart-lifting to see the astounding color of the 20-acre **Colonsay House Woodland Garden** (near Kiloran Bay, tel. 01951/200211, www.colonsay.org.uk, daylight hours daily year-round) surrounding Colonsay House. It has one of Scotland's best collections of rhododendrons and trees like eucalyptus, myrtle, and magnolia.

Remains at **Oronsay Priory** (Oronsay, open year-round) date back to the time that St. Columba first set foot in Scotland in the 6th century, but the ruins of the priory left today date back to the mid-14th century, when Lord of the Isles "Good" John MacDonald had it rebuilt. He did a good job, as most of the priory remains intact, with an intricately carved Celtic cross nearby. Come for the adventure and the atmosphere, though; the trek here is across a sandy causeway pockmarked by puddles of retreating sea with this gray stone building standing beyond against the grass and white sand.

Accommodations and Food

◀ **Colonsay Keeper's Lodge** (Kiloran, for bookings tel. 01951/200312, dorm beds £12–14, twin rooms £32) is a Victorian gamekeeper's house. The house and the two rustic bothies nearby really are in the middle of nowhere. There are twin rooms and a dorm room in the house; dorm beds are available in the sleeping bothy, complete with bare stone walls inside. There is a lounge with open fire and self-catering kitchen, too. You can hire bikes on-site; otherwise it's a two-kilometer walk/drive to the pub.

There are three clean, simple rooms at **The Hannah's** (4 Uragaig, tel. 01951/200150, thehannahsbandb@aol.com, £34 s, £54 d), a modern bed-and-breakfast with rooms with en suite/private bathrooms and color TVs. View-gazing in the guest lounge is a popular activity; you're right next to gorgeous Kiloran Bay in the north of the island here. Ferry pick-up is available.

The Colonsay (tel. 01951/200316, www. thecolonsay.com, £60 s, £90 d, lunch noon–2:30 P.M., dinner 6–9:30 P.M.) is the island's

hotel with chic new rooms, two of which now boast Egyptian linens on the beds and flat-screen TV/DVDs. All the rooms are light, some with sea views and one with a four-poster bed. It's an unerringly modern place in this isolated setting. The evening menu focuses on locally caught seafood; the hotel also offers unique "pre-ferry" suppers on Friday and Sunday while you wait for the late-night ferry back to the real world. If you're taking off around the island, you can get a packed lunch here.

Getting There and Around

The ferry between Oban and Colonsay (once daily Mon., Wed.–Fri. and Sun., 2 hrs. 20 min., £11.90 adult, £59 car one-way) runs throughout the year. On Wednesday April–September there is a connection between Colonsay, Port Askaig on Islay, and Kennacraig on the Kintyre peninsula. It can be done as a day trip, in which case you get six hours on Colonsay.

Cowal Peninsula and Bute

Most of the sparsely inhabited Cowal peninsula is easier to reach by boat than by land: it's a thickly forested place, almost cut into an island by the long arms of Loch Fyne and Loch Long. The main town of Cowal, Dunoon, was a Gaelic-speaking village that made a living from cattle-droving and illicit whisky distilling until the steam ships from Glasgow began to bring over Victorian tourists. The tourist industry made Dunoon boom, then steamships declined and most of the region became a backwater once more. The visitors that pass Cowal by miss out on a tranquility that's increasingly hard to find in this region of Scotland. The lush vegetation includes some of the most magnificent gardens on the west coast and a panorama of thickly forested, almost Amazonian loch shores twisting into a series of jaw-droppingly beautiful viewpoints. Add to that a clutch of the most idyllic watering holes in Scotland, and there are plenty of reasons to linger in Cowal. A stone's throw away from Cowal, the island of Bute saw its

heyday come and go with the age of steam, too. Rothesay, the island capital, has kept its glorious Victorian kitsch theme and is a fascinating place to soak up faded resort-style glamour. The south of Bute is home to one of the country's most lavish 19th-century houses, Mount Stuart.

EAST COWAL

For somewhere only a few kilometers across the water from Glasgow's suburban sprawl, the east coast of the Cowal peninsula is a surprisingly quiet place. Outside Dunoon, you could blink and miss the houses poking out of the trees on the isolated shores of Holy Loch, Loch Long, and Loch Goil. The places that do exist thrived in the days they could be reached by steamship, but now that they are not, most communities have the air of passed-by backwaters. Highlights include charming rural pubs like the Coylett Inn and, if you're there at the right time of year, the largest Highland Games in Scotland, the Cowal Gathering.

Dunoon

It was in 1779 that the first Glaswegian "tourist" set sail in a small boat for Dunoon, a green-looking blur across the water from industry-driven Glasgow and its suburbs. He found a tiny, unruly village making a trade from cattle-droving and the distilling and smuggling of illicit liquor. The trickle of tourists soon became a deluge, and Dunoon turned its hand to the more respectable trade of catering for them. Elegant Victorian houses sprung up and Dunoon prospered. Then the glory days of steam were replaced by the glory days of the motor car, and people didn't arrive in Dunoon so often anymore. Today it's a somewhat shabby place, but pockets of plush houses remain in the suburb of Hunter's Quay. On a small hill above the ferry terminal is a statue to Highland Mary, sweetheart of Robert Burns. Mary Campbell spoke English with a singsong Highland lilt (hence the nickname) and inspired several verses in the renowned Scottish bard. Seen the statue? Time to leave Dunoon.

Kilmun

On the opposite side of Holy Loch to Dunoon, this strung-out village has the intriguing 15th-century **St. Munn's Church,** on the shoreline of Holy Loch, the traditional burial place of the Dukes of Argyll. Back on the main A815 road north toward Loch Eck, an avenue of giant, 50-meter-high redwood trees marks the entry to 120-acre **Benmore Botanic Garden** (by Kilmun, tel. 01369/706261, www.rbge.org.uk, 10 A.M.–6 P.M. daily Apr.–Sept., 10 A.M.–5 P.M. daily Mar. and Oct., £4 adults, £3.50 seniors). Inside, you'll see one of the world's most vivid and diverse collections of rhododendrons. Because of the mild climate, cross-sections of the world's plants can be found here, including a section devoted to the Chilean rainforest and one dedicated to plants and flowers from Bhutan. There are guided tours of the gardens at 2 P.M. four afternoons per week during season.

Arrochar

Clustered around the head of Loch Long, this pretty, touristy village of white-and-black houses is the gateway to the Cowal peninsula and a popular hill-walking base, courtesy of its proximity to the **Arrochar Alps.** The A83, running up Glen Croe from Arrochar to the junction with the B828 to Lochgoilhead at the Rest and Be Thankful, is a good access route to these peaks. From tiny Succoth you can do the popular climb up **Ben Arthur** (The Cobbler) near Glen Croe. It's one of the most impressively ridged mountains in Scotland, the outline of which is said to represent a cobbler hunched over his shoemaking tools. The path starts out well enough, but reaching the top involves a scramble over scree. To reach the highest summit of the three, you have to crawl through a hole on to a ledge one meter wide with sheer drops on either side—not for those with vertigo.

Events

The **Cowal Gathering** (www.cowalgathering.co.uk), held at the end of August over three days, is the largest, most spectacular Highland Games in Scotland. Lots of Highland Games say they're the best—this one actually is. Expect lots of grunting kilt-wearing bulky men running, jumping, and throwing things. Ask for details from Dunoon TIC.

Accommodations and Food

If you think the outside of the **Hunter's Quay Hotel** (Marine Parade, Dunoon, tel. 01369/707070, www.huntersquayhotel.co.uk, £69 s, £88 d) looks like your ideal, charming, whitewashed retreat then wait until you see the rooms. These monstrously sized bedrooms are more like light, white apartments; all have flat-screen Freeview TV and are en suite. A four-poster bed is on offer, too. You're right on the Holy Loch waterfront here, and most rooms get a view of it. The resident lounge has a cavernous open fireplace; someone is usually on hand to recommend a single malt whisky from the bar.

It's hard to imagine why any stray travelers passing through this area would want to stop anywhere but **€ St. Munn's Old Manse** (Kilmun, tel. 01369/840311, www.stmunnsoldmanse.com, £28 s, £50 d). You won't get better value for your money anywhere in the west of Scotland. Set in the spacious old Victorian manse (minister's house) for St. Munn's Church, rooms have huge windows soaking up the views of shimmering Holy Loch, as well as antique furniture, brass beds, and lots of endearing little touches like CD players, dressing gowns, and old-fashioned beauty cases. Rooms are not en suite, but you won't be worrying about that as you sink into the antique Victorian bath. There are sumptuous breakfasts the following morning.

It's hard to say what the highlight of the mid-17th century **Coylet Inn** (Loch Eck, tel. 01369/840426, www.coylet-locheck.co.uk, £54.50 s, £79 d, food served noon–8:30 P.M. daily) is. The old coaching inn has cozy rooms with loch views, an old dark-wood bar stocked full of whiskies and ales, and the superb, rustic-style restaurant, also with loch views. The rooms are warm, modern, and en suite despite the age of the building; from one, you can lie in the bath and gaze at the mountains across the loch. The inn is a wonderful place to eat or drink—well worth the drive into the wilderness to do so. Mains like the venison burger or mushroom and red wine risotto are £7–10. There's also a more expensive seafood platter of goodies caught in local lochs.

You couldn't ask for a better location for the gracious, whitewashed **Shore House Inn** (Lochgoilhead, tel. 01301/703340, www.shorehouse.net, £70 d, lunch Fri.–Mon., dinner Wed.–Mon.). This hostelry has four smart white-and-beige rooms on offer. There are oodles of space and antique furniture in the rooms but these are modern and airy as an art studio, with big-windowed views out over the loch or the golf course. Some rooms have open fires and writing desks. It's a sizeable complex, this place, with a more traditional rustic bar and restaurant and a new pine-built separate eating area. The menu includes seafood, sizzling steaks, and wood-fired pizzas. The views of Loch Goil from here are splendid.

Superbly located **Ardgartan Caravan and Camping Site** (by Arrochar, tel. 0845/130 8224, www.forestholidays.co.uk, Mar.–Oct., tent and 2 people £12.50) hugs the shore of Loch Long: it's one of those sites where you can find the terrain that suits you, with open grassy plots, lochside plots, and tree-sheltered plots. There are 200 pitches for tents and caravans, and a small shop. It's possible to use this as a base for climbing the Arrochar Alps.

If you're stuck in Dunoon for any reason, check out tantalizing **Black of Dunoon** (144–148 Argyll St., tel. 01369/702311, 8 A.M.–5 P.M. Mon.–Sat.), a baker where you can buy home-baked treats like shortbread and even sit in with them in the small attached café.

Information

Dunoon TIC (7 Alexandra Parade, tel. 0870/720 0629, 9 A.M.–5:30 P.M. Mon.–Fri., 10 A.M.–5 P.M. Sat.–Sun. Apr.–Sept., 9 A.M.–5 P.M. Mon.–Thurs., 10 A.M.–5 P.M. Fri., 10 A.M.–4 P.M. Sat.–Sun. Oct.–Mar.) have heaps of information on the Cowal peninsula.

Ardgartan Ranger Centre (Glen Croe, Arrochar, tel. 01301/702432, Apr.–Oct.) is handily located along the climb up to the Rest and Be Thankful on the A83 just after the road leaves Loch Long. It's set within woods and has several good hill-walking trails. There are year-round information boards on walking in the area.

Getting There and Away

The nearest Cowal comes to having a railway station is Tarbet and Arrochar station, a couple of miles outside Arrochar and on the West Highland Railway line.

Ferry is an important means of getting around in Cowal. The highly useful **Calmac ferry** between Gourock, a suburb of Glasgow in Inverclyde, to Dunoon is the best way of accessing Cowal. Ferries run half-hourly and cost £3.35 adult, £8.15 car one-way. From Gourock, you can connect with a train to Glasgow.

West Coast Motors runs bus service 486 five times daily to Inveraray via the Loch Fyne Oyster Bar.

Getting Around

Six **buses** daily Monday–Saturday run between Dunoon and Lochgoilhead. To access the Arrochar Alps, get a bus to the Loch Fyne Oyster Bar or on to Inveraray and then wait for a Glasgow-bound bus, which will drop you off at the Rest and Be Thankful on the A83.

For a cab, call **Tucker's Taxis** (tel. 01369/701710).

WEST COWAL

The west side of the peninsula is a quiet place that sees few tourists. The calm inlet of Loch Riddon, splitting into the Kyles of Bute, is one of the most magical places in the country to improve your sailing skills, with a sailing school at tiny Tighnabruaich. Western Cowal is also known for its fine viewpoints across loch-ravined tracts of forest. At the northern end there is the little matter of Scotland's best rural seafood restaurant, at the head of Loch Fyne.

Tighnabruaich

This picturesque village slopes steeply down a forest-swathed hillside and along the shoreline of the Kyles of Bute. The village has a shop, a hotel, and a good café. **Tighnabruaich Sailing School** (tel. 01700/811717, www.tssargyll.co.uk) runs courses for youths and adults in sailing, powerboating, and dinghying. Courses start from £212 for five days.

As the A8003 climbs up the west shore of Loch Riddon, at the summit before the plunge into Tighnabruaich you are treated to one of the finest panoramas in Cowal, looking right down the Kyles of Bute to Cumbrae and beyond. It's a vista of glittering channels of water edged by ranks of dark green conifers.

Accommodations and Food

The commanding whitewashed property of **Tregortha** (Tighnabruaich, tel. 01700/811132, www.tregortha.co.uk, £30 s, £70 d) stands at the top of the village of Tighnabruaich. It has a blossoming garden and three large plush rooms. Beds and furnishings are as neat and white as wedding cakes. All three have en suite facilities, color TV, and elegant iron beds.

It's not every day you get to eat in the place where a national chain of restaurants originated. To begin with, the (Loch Fyne Oyster Bar

(Clachan, by Cairndow, tel. 01499/600236, www.lochfyne.com, 9 A.M.–7 P.M. daily, occasional later hours on weekend evenings) was nothing but a shed selling fresh seafood; now it's a stylish restaurant with a large, modern conservatory dining area tacked on to the side of a whitewashed building. Oysters on ice are £1.40 each; sampling the seafood on offer will cost you £4–30. The restaurant is on the shore of Loch Fyne on the A83 to Inveraray.

Getting There and Away

Buses run from Dunoon to Colintraive (three to four daily on school days) for the ferry to Rothesay. There are five buses daily from Dunoon to Tighnabruaich on school days (seven Sat.), with a few continuing to Portvadie for the ferry to Tarbert.

Calmac run hourly **ferries** (25 min., £3.30 adult, £14.95 car one-way) from Portvadie in the west of Cowal to Tarbert on the Kintyre peninsula from late March to October. It makes for a useful island-hopping connection from Arran or Bute.

ISLE OF BUTE

Split in two by the Highland boundary fault, the traditional Glaswegian holiday destination of Bute is an island of two distinct parts. The north is more in keeping with the rugged, forested moor land of the Cowal peninsula; the fertile, low-lying south with its patches of sandy coast bears more resemblance to the southwest of Scotland. Sandwiched in between is the main town, Rothesay, exuding the quiet, worn feel of a small southern England seaside resort. Bute is an island that doesn't feel like an island. Set in a wide inlet of the River Clyde estuary, it's surrounded by the Cowal peninsula to the north, the Kintyre peninsula to the west, the Isle of Arran to the southwest, and Ayrshire to the east. The open sea lies only to the south. Visiting Bute is a very different experience to visiting most Scottish islands, offering gentle waters, relatively calm weather, and a busy tourist infrastructure that's been in place for the best part of two centuries. There is also the splendid mansion of Mountstuart,

© LUKE WATERSON

Rothesay Castle

the most magnificent piece of Gothic revivalist architecture in Britain; it's a 300-year-old symphony in opulence.

Rothesay

The **Isle of Bute Discovery Centre** (Esplanade, tel. 01700/505156, 9 A.M.–5:30 P.M. Mon.–Sat.) in the restored winter gardens has an exhibition on the island and acts as the island's TIC.

Completely surrounded by houses and one of the few castle moats in Scotland, the high, thick-walled, 13th-century **Rothesay Castle** (off High St., tel. 01700/502691, 9:30 A.M.–5:30 P.M. daily Apr.–Sept., 9:30 A.M.–4:30 P.M. Sat.–Wed. Oct.–Mar., £4.20 adults, £2.20 children) is a great focal point to the town. As Bute was one of the more easily accessible islands in the empire of the Lords of the Isles, the fortress saw several attacks despite its strong defenses.

It's well worth the entrance charge of £0.20 to set foot in the **Victorian Toilets** (Rothesay Pier, open year-round), Scotland's finest public convenience. Decked out with green, cream, and black glazed ceramics and even mosaics, these toilet blocks, dating originally from 1899,

have been revamped to their full Victorian glory. There are even display boards inside (it's the done thing to wait until the urinals aren't in use before you look too closely in the gents).

Northern Bute

Even in the tourist heyday, this part of the island remained a little-visited, refreshingly wild place. Today the moor land has been planted with extensive conifer woods, making for a mix of scenic woodland and coastal walks. The **West Island Way** skirts the coast; the rough section from **Rhubodach** (where the Cowal ferry comes in) around to Ettrick Bay is 10 miles. You'll pass the **Maids of Bute,** two rocks resembling old women with a bit of paintwork to enhance the impression, and the ruined **Kilmichael Chapel.** Wildlife-wise, you could see roe deer and buzzards.

Southern Bute

The south of the island is low-lying agricultural land: the glamorous Victorian palace-mansion of Mount Stuart rather steals the show but there's also some pleasant coastal scenery.

Mount Stuart (south of Kerrycroy, tel. 01700/503877, www.mountstuart.com, 11 A.M.–5 P.M. Sun.–Fri., 10 A.M.–2:30 P.M. Sat. May–Sept., gardens 10 A.M.–6 P.M. daily May–Sept., out of season by appointment, house and grounds £8 adults, £4 children) is Bute's main tourist attraction, and a lavish one at that. It's a house fusing different architectural styles in a seemingly ongoing cycle of opulence (the completion of the grand 19th-century design plan for the house continues). The Stuarts of Bute built the original Mount Stuart mansion in the first decade of the 18th century. Fire destroyed it in 1877, and ambitious plans for its rebirth as the gem of the Gothic revivalist movement commenced. The interior—solid marble, vaulted ceilings, and red silk—has the finery of a dozen churches. There is a hall that soars up in arches made from Italian marble to a roof some 80 feet above ground level and a drawing room, with stained glass windows of Greek muses and paintings by Titian and Veronese. Lady Bute's boudoir is covered in red silk, as Lord Bute believed this best presented his wife's complexion. The gardens are no less grand in their scale; the temperate climate allowed for tropical plants to add that colorful touch of class. One part of the grounds has been laid out to represent the Via Dolorossa, the route Christ took to his crucifixion.

The ruined 12th-century Norman **St. Blane's Chapel** (south of island near Garrochty) and the surrounding buildings are a good excuse to venture to the south end of Bute. It's accessed from down the minor road to Garrochty, from where a path leads to the site.

Events

The island erupts into life for the **Isle of Bute Jazz Festival** (www.butejazz.com) in early May, with U.K. and international artists on the festival's five-day music agenda.

Accommodations

Palmyra Guest House (12 Ardbeg Rd., Rothesay, tel. 01700/502929, from £56 d) is a whitewashed waterfront house surrounded by a clutch of exotic greenery. The rooms here are large and warm; you'll get an en suite shower or bath and color TV. Breakfast is taken in a gorgeous, light-filled conservatory.

The most architecturally distinctive building on the drag of glam-looking Rothesay guesthouses, **◖ Glendale Guest House** (20 Battery Pl., Rothesay, tel. 01700/502329, www.glendale-guest-house.com, £35 s, £60 d) looks a bit like a lighthouse tacked on to a sophisticated Victorian villa. The 10 letting rooms work around the wide glass windows and curving walls: each is individual, most get sea views, and all are en suite. Some have a slightly gloomy feel; maybe it's all the shiny leather and antique wood furniture. One room with four-poster bed is available. The lounge in the "lighthouse" part has a circular window seat at which you could spend hours, just watching the to-ing and fro-ing of boats. Innovative breakfast options include creamy homemade yogurts and brioche filled with scrambled egg.

An elegant Georgian townhouse, **Cannon House** (Battery Pl., tel. 01700/502819, www .cannonhousehotel.com.uk, from £45 s, £70 d) has several richly furnished rooms in soothing pale pastel blues and pinks. Lying on one of the beds, you'll think you've been whisked away on a cloud—they're that soft. Rooms are en suite with color TV. The lavish, candlelit dining experience here is magical; the four courses last so long you'll think you've been trapped in time about two centuries ago.

Glecknabae (North Bute, tel. 01700/505655, £37 s, £75 d) is the pick of places to stay in wild North Bute: a peaceful 19th-century house with three charming en suite rooms full of light and sea views. Glecknabae also has a gorgeous garden with a burn flowing through it. You're right by the shore here, too—look out for sun-bathing otters! Evening meals can be arranged. To find the house, head north on the B875 past Ettrick Bay: it's on the right-hand side after a couple of miles.

An elegant 19th-century hotel with high arched windows, **St. Blane's Hotel** (Kilchattan Bay, tel. 01700/831224, www.stblanesho tel.com, rooms from £60 d, four-poster suites

£80 d) is right in the south of the island, looking out over a tranquil bay. Lots of the rooms here have hand-carved wooden beds, including two four-poster bed rooms. The color scheme is elegant whites; it feels like the fabric furnishings must have been cut from Liberty wedding dresses. The bar serves plenty of draught ales and whiskies, and you can eat a good home cooked meal here in the evenings. A spectacularly set beer garden overlooks the shore, and you can moor your boat for free right outside the hotel.

Food

Part of the refurbished Victorian pier complex in the winter gardens, **The Galley Restaurant** (Rothesay Pier, tel. 01700/505500, 10 A.M.–4:30 P.M. and 5:30–9 P.M. Tues. and Wed., 10 A.M.–4:30 P.M. Thurs., 10 A.M.–4:30 P.M. and 5–10 P.M. Fri.–Sat., noon–5 P.M. Sun.) is easily Rothesay's most atmospheric eatery, serving an innovative bistro/restaurant menu at reasonable prices. The coffee is superb, the cakes are tasty, and the filled paninis/baguettes are meals in themselves. Snacks and light lunches are £4–8. In addition to the decor, this place is great for the friendly service.

Whitewashed **Kingarth Hotel** (Kingarth, tel. 01700/831662, www.kingarthhotel.com, noon–8 P.M. Sun.–Thurs., noon–9 P.M. Fri.–Sat.) is an atmospheric country pub with two relaxed, open-plan bars. Bar meals start at £6, with the steaks at the top end of the spectrum being £13. The steak baguette with chips and coleslaw is one of the many heartening meals on offer. On a sunny day you can sit at an outside deck area with your drink and play bowls on the nearby green for a nominal fee.

Getting There and Away

The Isle of Bute has two **ferry** terminals: Rhubodach in the north, just a sliver of sea away from southern Cowal and Rothesay, which has a ferry connection with Wemyss Bay in Inverclyde. Rhubodach-to-Colintraive ferries run half-hourly (5 min., £1.25 adult, £7.85 car one-way). Wemyss Bay-to-Rothesay ferries run every 45 minutes (35 min., £3 adult, £12.20 car one-way).

There are four **buses** per day with West Coast Motors from Rothesay to Colintraive (via boat), where you continue to Dunoon or change for services to Portvadie for the Tarbert ferry. It takes one hour 40 minutes to get to Dunoon from Rothesay via bus and boat.

Getting Around

Buses bound for Dunoon and Portvadie call at points in Northern Bute en route from Rothesay. As for the rest of Bute, bus 93 heads south from Rothesay to Mount Stuart hourly Monday–Saturday. You're better off exploring the area on your own four wheels or by bike, however.

ABERDEEN, MORAY, AND GRAMPIAN

Scotland's third city in size, culture, and cuisine, gray Aberdeen sits on the northeast coast facing the North Sea, the source of its wealth contained within—oil. It spreads its granite bulk across the mouths of two rivers and along one of the longest continuous stretches of sandy beach in the country. The only way the city falters is in its appeal for visitors. The surrounding fertile farmland, together with the fishing and oil industries, might have made Aberdeen the wealthy capital of the wealthiest region of Scotland since medieval times, but it's hard to find reasons to linger in the city with such a fascinating corner of Scotland on the doorstep. Oil revenue has given Aberdeen a self-confident swagger, in the form of fancy restaurants, interesting museums, and plenty of glassy, glitzy buildings. Much of the development, though,

has been far from tasteful and is not worthwhile to explore.

Aberdeenshire is renowned for its castles, which start springing up everywhere inland from the capital. Fortresses range from fairytale ruins to extravagant baronial-style buildings sporting floors of ornate rooms; you'll be hard-pressed not to find one to your fancy. Moray in the northeast of the region is a mecca for malt whisky fans. It's best known for an area known as Speyside, dotted with more whisky distilleries than the rest of Scotland combined. The streams used in the process flow over heathery moor down into fertile barley-growing country and produce a distinctive regional flavor to these single malts, including the world-famous Glenfiddich.

The region is not all about drinking;

HIGHLIGHTS

(Aberdeen Art Gallery: Northern Scotland's most absorbing art gallery contains important works by Scottish artists including William Dyce and Sir Henry Raeburn (page 362).

(Footdee: Stroll around Footdee, a former fishermen's community by Aberdeen Beach that has weird and wonderful houses (page 364).

(Stonehaven: This historic town sitting below majestic Dunnotar Castle boasts the region's most atmospheric fine dining (page 372).

(Huntly Castle: Get off the beaten track discovering the ancient strongholds of Central Aberdeenshire like Huntly Castle (page 375).

(Strathisla Distillery: Touring a Speyside distillery like Strathisla, with its iconic twin pagodas in the heart of Scotland's whisky-producing country, should be a top priority for single malt lovers (page 377).

(Elgin Cathedral and Biblical Garden: The spectacular ruins of Elgin Cathedral and the landscaped bible-themed gardens nearby form one of Scotland's most striking religious sites (page 383).

(Findhorn Foundation: Wander around this wacky spiritual eco-village situated in woods alongside shifting sand dunes (page 386).

(Portsoy: Relax in a northeast fishing port like Portsoy, with one of the region's best pubs and a colorful annual traditional boat festival (page 390).

(Walks in the Grampian Mountains: Take to the peaks on the wild long-distance walks around the Linn of Dee (page 400).

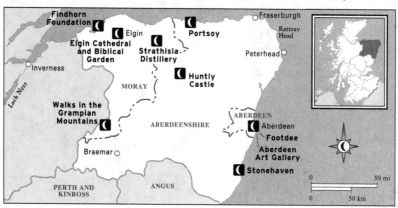

LOOK FOR **(** TO FIND RECOMMENDED SIGHTS, ACTIVITIES, DINING, AND LODGING.

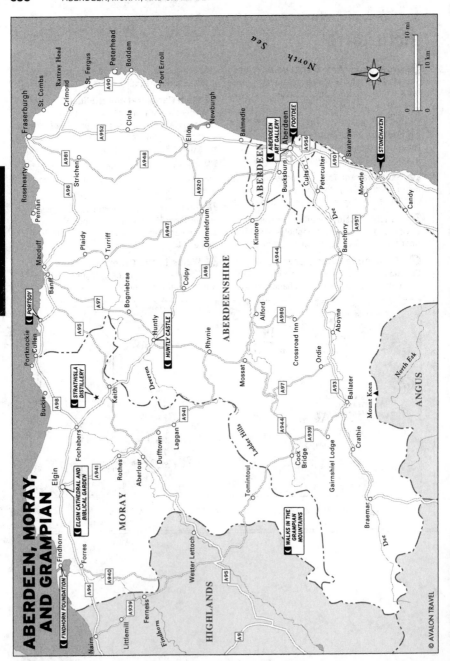

ABERDEEN

ABERDEEN, MORAY,
AND GRAMPIAN

© AVALON TRAVEL

eating, too, is a popular activity. Aberdeen has a fine dining scene, and regional delicacies feature Cullen Skink, a fish-and-potato soup originating on the north coast, and Walker's Shortbread, made in Aberlour. The Aberdeenshire and Moray coast also has some of the finest fish-and-chip shops and ice-cream joints in Scotland. The coast here is an enticing tract of long, tropical-seeming white sand beaches and idyllic fishing villages perched at the foot of immense cliffs, but the main attraction for visitors lies inland. The tree-lined valley of the River Dee houses Balmoral, the holiday destination of the Royal Family since the days of Queen Victoria. Royal Deeside is a hot spot for tourists wanting to soak up some monarchical heritage and is sure to fulfill all your wildest romantic images of Scotland. Rich forests and fortresses backed by the foothills of the Grampian Mountains run all along the length of the ride before fading into a walker's paradise of moor, rocky ridges, and tumbling streams.

HISTORY
Prehistory
Perhaps because of the profusion of enduring granite in the area, there is plenty of evidence of prehistoric activity in the region. By the end of the third millennium B.C., Garioch, near modern-day Inverurie, was an important center of habitation. Early settlers, including many from Scandinavia, were attracted by the rich coastal farmland. Aberdeenshire was the heartland of the Pictish empire during the first millennium A.D.

Medieval Era to 19th Century
As early as 1127, Elgin was making a name for itself as the center of the country's leading medieval bishoprics. During the 10th, 11th, and 12th centuries, Aberdeen also grew from a small fishing port into a large town, held by the English during the Wars of Independence. Local residents helped Robert the Bruce oust the English from the town, and Bruce made Aberdeen a Royal burgh in gratitude. Aberdeen consequently thrived to become the major center of learning in northern Scotland and the country's second-largest city by 1600.

In the 18th century, the high remote glens of Moray and the Grampian Mountains were places of lawlessness, roamed by powerful bands of brigands who were organized enough to take control of castles in the region. Illicit whisky distilling was another popular way of making ends meet: Glen Livet in Moray had as many as 200 stills at this time. Aberdeen, however, was an increasingly prosperous place, with major historical happenings in the field of commerce. Farming, fishing, and, by the early 1800s, whaling, were the main sources of income. By the 1820s, Peterhead was one of Britain's two major whaling ports, and speedy clipper ships built in the reputable boatbuilding center of Aberdeen harbor were trading commodities as exotic as tea from India.

Victorian Era and 20th Century
In 1848, following a tour of the Highlands, Queen Victoria and Prince Albert acquired the Balmoral estate on the River Dee and built a castle as a holiday home there. This began an unprecedented flood of royal tourism, helped by the building of the railway along Deeside. The tradition of the Royal Family vacationing on Deeside has lasted ever since. Industry, now in the additional forms of tourism and whisky distillation, advanced on all fronts. The economic face of the city was altered forever by the discovery of oil in the North Sea in the 1970s. This has shaped the city in every sense, providing revenue to spend on public buildings and facilities. The oil boom has not always been a success story, however; on July 6, 1988, the Piper Alpha oil production platform some 120 miles northeast of Aberdeen exploded, taking with it 171 lives.

PLANNING YOUR TIME
Aberdeenshire is one of those perfect holiday destinations where you can just pick the terrain that suits you. If you're a beach-lover, you can head to the northeast coast; if you're a whisky-lover, head to Speyside; and if you're a fan of hiking or of the Royal Family, head to Royal Deeside—these

ABERDEEN

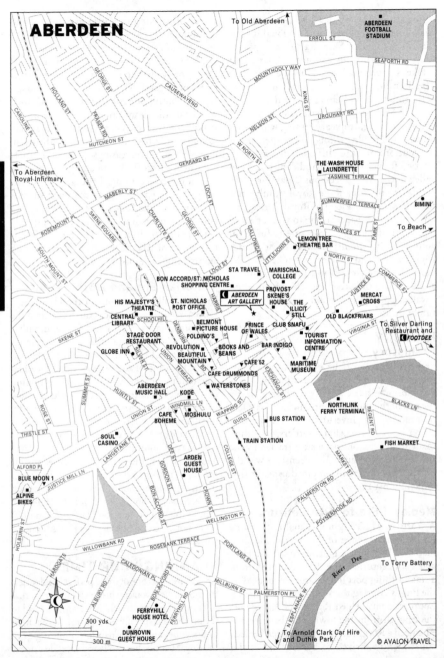

ABERDEEN

To Old Aberdeen

ABERDEEN FOOTBALL STADIUM

ERROLL ST

SEAFORTH RD

HOLLAND ST
CAROLINE PL
GEORGE ST
FRASER RD

MOUNTHOOLY WAY

KING ST
URQUHART RD

CAUSEWAYEND
HUTCHEON ST

NELSON ST
W NORTH ST

GERRARD ST

THE WASH HOUSE LAUNDRETTE
JASMINE TERRACE

To Aberdeen Royal Infirmary

MABERLY ST

ROSEMOUNT PL
SKENE SQUARE
CHARLOTTE ST
GEORGE ST
LOCH ST

SUMMERFIELD TERRACE

KING ST
PRINCES ST
PARK ST

BIMINI

To Beach

SOUTH MOUNT ST

GALLOWGATE
LITTLE JOHN ST

LEMON TREE THEATRE BAR

E NORTH ST

STA TRAVEL
MARISCHAL COLLEGE

COMMERCE ST
JUSTICE ST

BON ACCORD/ST. NICHOLAS SHOPPING CENTRE

LOCH ST
HARRIET

ABERDEEN ART GALLERY

PROVOST SKENE'S HOUSE

MERCAT CROSS

HIS MAJESTY'S THEATRE
ST. NICHOLAS POST OFFICE

THE ILLICIT STILL

CENTRAL LIBRARY
SCHOOLHILL

BELMONT PICTURE HOUSE

PRINCE OF WALES

CLUB SNAFU

OLD BLACKFRIARS

To Silver Darling Restaurant and FOOTDEE

SKENE ST

DENBURN RD

POLDINO'S

TOURIST INFORMATION CENTRE

VIRGINIA ST

STAGE DOOR RESTAURANT

REVOLUTION

BOOKS AND BEANS

BAR INDIGO

GLOBE INN
SILVER ST

BEAUTIFUL MOUNTAIN

UNION TERRACE

CAFE 52

MARITIME MUSEUM

EXCHANGE ST

CAFE DRUMMONDS

SUMMER ST

ABERDEEN MUSIC HALL

WATERSTONES

HUNTLY ST
UNION ST

KODE

WINDMILL LN

NORTHLINK FERRY TERMINAL

BLACKS LN

ROSE ST

CAFE BOHEME

MOSHULU

WAPPING ST

GUILD ST

BUS STATION

REGENT RD

THISTLE ST

SOUL CASINO

LANGSTANE PL

DEE ST

TRAIN STATION

FISH MARKET

MARKET ST

ALFORD PL

BLUE MOON 1

JUSTICE MILL LN

GORDON ST

ARDEN GUEST HOUSE

COLLEGE ST

CROWN ST

PALMERSTON RD

ALPINE BIKES

HOLBURN ST

BON-ACCORD ST

WELLINGTON PL

POYNERNOOK RD

WILLOWBANK RD

ROSEBANK TERRACE

PORTLAND ST

HARGATE

ALBURY RD

CALEDONIAN PL

BON-ACCORD ST

FERRYHILL RD

MILLBURN ST

PALMERSTON PL

River Dee

To Torry Battery

FERRYHILL HOUSE HOTEL

DUNROVIN GUEST HOUSE

N ESPLANADE W

To Arnold Clark Car Hire and Duthie Park

0   300 yds
0   300 m

© AVALON TRAVEL

three are the prime areas to factor into a visit. Because of the region's size, it's best to concentrate your time on one or two of these areas; each is some distance apart, so you'll spend all your time driving if you try to fit too much into too few days. Four days, for example, is barely enough time to do justice to the Royal Deeside area alone. Five to seven days will give you time to get a taste of all areas of the region.

The roads in Aberdeenshire are of a high standard; however, be warned that this is the region of Scotland with the most fatalities from car accidents. The roads in the mountainous west of the region, while double track, are notoriously dangerous due to their poor weather conditions.

It can be difficult to access some of the northeast fishing ports by car due to the narrow streets.

ORIENTATION

The central artery of Aberdeen is Union Street, which runs two blocks north of, and parallel to, the train and bus stations. At the east end of Union Street is Castlegate, and east of this again is the beach. At the south end of Aberdeen's beach is Footdee and Aberdeen Harbour. Aberdeen Harbour is an extensive network of docks stretching inland as far as Market Street, one block east of the train and bus stations. Old Aberdeen lies one mile north of Union Street and the city center.

Sights

Being built almost entirely of granite has earned Aberdeen the nickname of "The Granite City." Some people go a bit too far and refer to it as "The Silver City" because of the way the granite sparkles on a summer day. All this means there are some very distinctive buildings to check out in Aberdeen, although after a while these will start to come across as stark rather than splendid. Sights are concentrated in three areas: the Union Street area, Old Aberdeen, and the harbor and beach. It's possible to walk between Union Street and the harbor and beach. For Old Aberdeen attractions, get a bus from Union Street or undertake the dull half-hour walk.

UNION STREET AND CITY CENTER

The smart granite buildings lining the city's main thoroughfare, Union Street, seem to stretch on forever. This is one of the longest main city streets in Britain and has its fair share of historical sights. The area around Union Street is known as the city center.

Castlegate and Mercat Cross

At the east end of Union Street is Castlegate, the oldest area of the city, where it's worth checking out the Mercat Cross, a decorated, arched building where public hangings were conducted in days gone by.

Marischal College and Museum

Founded in 1593 to create a Protestant alternative to King's College in Old Aberdeen, the immense college building has been recognizable in its current form since 1906. It checks into the record books as the world's second-largest granite building, the first being Monasterio del Escorial in Spain. It took 71 years to complete the ornate frontage of the building facing Broad Street: It's a dizzying angular Gothic display of high walls soaring into pinnacles, spires, and an 85-meter (279-foot) tower. The granite facade encloses a courtyard containing intriguing Marischal Museum (Broad St., tel. 01224/274301, www.abdn.ac.uk/historic/museum), closed for refurbishment until summer 2010. The museum's fascinating collection includes an Egyptian coffin and figurines, North American tribal masks, and Pictish stones from Aberdeenshire. At press time, a temporary exhibition was due to open in Old Aberdeen. Contact the museum, which remains open for phone and online inquiries, for further updates. Behind the museum is the

ABERDEEN

Mitchell Hall, with its huge window depicting the history of Aberdeen.

Provost Skene's House

This 16th-century house (Guestrow, tel. 01224/632133, 10 A.M.–5 P.M. Mon.–Sat., 1–4 P.M. Sun.) looks like a cross between a fortified house and a Victorian woolen mill. It's a colorful museum named after previous incumbent provost George Skene. The imposing building has rooms furnished in 17th- and 18th-century styles, as well as an Edwardian-themed nursery. The costume gallery puts on monthly exhibitions exploring fashion through the ages. At the top of the house are temporary displays on the social history of Aberdeen.

◖ Aberdeen Art Gallery

The city's art gallery (Schoolhill, tel. 01224/523700, 10 A.M.–5 P.M. Mon.–Sat., 2–5 P.M. Sun., free) is a vast, undeniably impressive, marble-lined space behind an elegant columned facade. It has a great program of temporary exhibitions, but the permanent collection is the highlight. Here you'll find works by Aberdonian artists William Dyce and John Phillip, along with paintings by John William Waterhouse, Claude Monet, and Dante Gabriel Rosetti. The highlight is Francis Bacon's painting of Pope Innocent X, considered the artist's masterpiece. There's also a good selection of works by 18th-century artists like Sir Henry Raeburn through to more modern art. At the back, the large white circular space capped by a dome is a moving memorial to those who lost their lives in the World Wars and in the Piper Alpha Oil Rig disaster.

Duthie Park

This late Victorian park (www.aberdeen-city.gov.uk, winter gardens open 9:30 A.M.–dusk daily) is the city's premier public space. Within it you'll find a mound covered with 120,000 roses, a boating pond, and the winter gardens, which contain several greenhouses of exotic plants. It all makes for a pleasant weekend afternoon wander. You'll find Duthie Park in the south of the city, by Polmuir Road. Bus 16 (orange line) runs there from Holburn junction (west end of Union St.) every few minutes.

OLD ABERDEEN

The area of the city around the University of Aberdeen campus, a mile north of the city center, was a separate burgh until 1891 and retains a fiercely independent air. It's not as old as the buildings on Union Street but with its cobbled streets and verdant surrounds, it certainly has more of an old-world feel. Take bus number 1, 2 or 15 from Union Street or bus 20 from Littlejohn Street to get to Old Aberdeen.

St. Machar's Cathedral

This thick-walled cathedral (The Chanonry, tel. 01224/485988, www.stmachar.com, 9 A.M.–5 P.M. daily, free) is more like a castle than a place of worship—check the twin towers at the western end with spiral staircases leading to battlements! St. Machar, a devotee of St. Columba, founded the first church on this site around A.D. 580, but the current building

Marischal College, one of the world's largest granite buildings

© LUKE WATERSON

FROM MITSUBISHI TO MADAME BUTTERFLY

Many might lament that the Scotsman heralded in Japan as the most famous foreigner to grace their shores did not choose to make a career for himself in his native county of Aberdeenshire. Had he done so, Thomas Blake Glover may well have ignited Scotland's industrial drive to the extent that he did Japan's.

Glover, however, was much inspired by a visit to Japan with his brother in 1857, and he moved to Nagasaki two years later. By 1863, he had done well enough for himself as a tea merchant and opium trader to build Glover House on a hillside above Nagasaki Harbor. It's the oldest Western-style building in Japan today and the top visitor attraction in the area. Soon enough Glover was running a key local coal mine and making improvements to Japan's harbors. He oversaw construction of Japan's first Western-style harbor, ordered three British warships for the country, and kick-started the railway industry there by introducing trains. He also organized the education of many Japanese abroad and helped found the Kirin Beer company. In fact, there were few facets of Japanese industry Glover did not get involved in at the time, but in 1870 his entrepreneurial enthusiasm had overstretched him: He was declared bankrupt. The shipbuilding legacy he had created was taken over by the firm that would become Mitsubishi, a leading Japanese company ever since.

Glover's fame does not even end there. In 1867 he married the daughter of a local Samurai chief, Tsura, who wore butterfly motifs on her clothes. The couple inspired a story by John Luther Long on which the composer Puccini later based the opera *Madame Butterfly*.

dates from almost a millennium later, built around 1520. The most spectacular feature of St. Machar's today is the heraldic ceiling, containing 48 shields relating to various Scottish and religious notables. Services are at 11 A.M. and 6 P.M. every Sunday.

Glover House

This angular gray house (79 Balgownie Rd., tel. 01224/709301, 11 A.M.–4 P.M. Thurs.–Mon., £3 adults, £2 children) was the home of Aberdeen entrepreneur Thomas Blake Glover, who devoted a lot of his talents to modernizing and improving industry in Japan. This is a Victorian home with a difference: In many rooms are the bright additions of Far East memorabilia. The highlight is the reproduction suit of Samurai armor. To get there, take red route bus number 1 toward Danestone; this service will drop you virtually at the gates.

HARBOR AND BEACH

Covering six kilometers of quays, Aberdeen harbor eats into the eastern portion of the city in a honking hive of activity. Among the 25,000 vessels operating out of here annually are ferries to Orkney, Shetland, and Bergen in Norway. For all the industrial bustle, there's a lot of interest to see around the harbor. Starting with the colorful village of Footdee on the northern side of the harbor mouth, the coast opens up into one of the longest golden tracts of sand in the country, backed by cafés and restaurants.

Aberdeen Maritime Museum

Standing above the harbor, the Aberdeen Maritime Museum (Shiprow, tel. 01224/337700, www.aagm.co.uk, 10 A.M.–5 P.M. Mon.–Sat., noon–3 P.M. Sun., free) is a testimony to how the city has made its wealth from the sea, both by fishing and from the oil industry. There are models of ships built and used here over the centuries; the city's last shipbuilding yard closed in 1992, and there's information here relating to the vessels that came off the production line. You can also see a lighthouse lens and some whalers' harpoons. The museum encompasses the oldest dwelling in the city, Provost Ross's House, built in 1593. You'll find a café on the ground floor.

ABERDEEN

Footdee

This old fishing village is a clutch of brightly painted, bizarre-looking houses, cottages, and sheds to the north of the harbor. You could pass an hour or so here just strolling the quiet streets: no two houses are the same. Lots of fishing nets and maritime memorabilia decorate the dwellings.

Entertainment and Recreation

ENTERTAINMENT AND EVENTS

Aberdeen folk like to party, and there's plenty of scope for doing it in the city. Whether you want a traditional old pub, a style bar, or a club to dance the night away, Aberdeen can oblige.

Pubs and Bars

Aberdeen is chockablock with watering holes of all kinds. In fact, most of Aberdeen's social activities involve drinking (lots) at one bar or another.

The Illicit Still (Guest Row, Broad St., tel. 01224/623123, www.illicit-still.co.uk, 10 A.M.–midnight Mon.–Wed., 10 A.M.–1 A.M. Thurs.–Sun.) is a mine of dark nooks, crannies, sofas, and bizarre decor. It serves decent food and pitchers of lethal cocktails and attracts a crowd of students on drinking binges and those just after a gossip with friends. Football is shown on big screens, too.

Come to **Old Blackfriars** (52 Castle St., tel. 01224/581922, 11 A.M.–midnight Mon.–Thurs., 11 A.M.–1 A.M. Fri.–Sat., 12:30–11 P.M. Sun.) for a break from the style bars, a good range of cask ales, hearty pub grub, and discerning locals who appreciate all these qualities. The dark place has bare stone walls and some stained glass good enough to grace a cathedral. If you want to fit in, just refer to the place as "Blackfriars" like the locals do.

Aberdeen's **Revolution** (25 Belmont St., tel. 01224/645475, noon–late daily) is one of Scotland's only branches of the vodka bar chain, with its own special uniqueness. It's a simply massive place on two levels: a ground floor with lots of sofas and a downstairs bar and conservatory restaurant offering good views out over the city. There are fun vodka-tasting sessions and a relaxed, relatively sophisticated clientele.

The **Prince of Wales** (7 St. Nicholas Ln., tel. 01224/640597, 11 A.M.–11 P.M. or midnight daily) will inevitably feature on pub crawls of the city; it does, after all, have the longest bar of any watering hole in the country. This is a reasonably traditional pub that serves no food except for scrumptious cheese-and-ham toasties. The clientele ranges from the weird to the wonderful and the reasonably young to the ancient.

The Globe (13–15 North Silver St., tel. 01224/624258, www.the-globe-inn.co.uk, 11 A.M.–midnight Mon.–Thurs., 11 A.M.–1 A.M. Fri.–Sat., 12:30 P.M.–midnight Sun.) is an old pub with dark, turn-of-the-20th-century wood paneling and a great selection of beers and ales. The Globe is a spacious boozer with a low-key but lively buzz. There's live music at weekends, usually around 9 P.M.

Nightclubs

Aberdeen has a decent clubbing scene.

If rock music is your thing, then head to **Moshulu** (Windmill Brae, tel. 01224/594785, from 10:30 P.M. Wed. and Fri.–Sat., cover £5–6). Friday is alternative rock night, while Adventures in Stereo on Saturday sees a mix of indie, rock, and dance. Across the road, **Kode** (40–42 Windmill Brae, tel. 01224/210174, 10:30 P.M.–3 A.M. Fri.–Sat.) is a hardcore rave, trance, and techno club formerly known as Drum; many clubbers swear it still has the best atmosphere of any club in Aberdeen.

The music and comedy venue **Club Snafu** (Union St., tel. 01224/596111, www.club-snafu.com, 10 P.M.–2 A.M. Mon.–Thurs., 10 P.M.–3 A.M. Fri.–Sat., cover £3–6 Fri.–Sat., cover varies other nights) plays mostly electric, house, and experimental music. It's a cozy, boutique venue with a 1960s slant to the decor.

Bar Indigo (20 Adelphi, tel. 01224/586949, 5 P.M.–2 A.M. Sun.–Thurs., 5 P.M.–3 A.M. Fri.–Sat., no cover Sun.–Thurs., £2–3 Fri.–Sat.) was formerly Oh Henry's; it is one of the premier gay venues in Aberdeen. It's a lively spot at weekends and quieter the rest of the week.

Live Music and Performing Arts
Café Drummonds (1 Belmont St., tel. 01224/619931, www.cafedrummond.co.uk) is a great live music venue, as well as being famed for its comedy and open mic nights. Among the budding bands that have played here are Supergrass and the Cosmic Rough Riders. Entry is often free, but sometimes tickets go up to £4 for certain performances.

His Majesty's Theatre (Rosemount Viaduct, tel. 0845/270 8200, www.boxofficeaberdeen .com) dates originally from 1906; this grand venue now hosts a program of drama, musicals, and dance. A modern, glassy reception and bar/café have been built onto the side to turn this into a top venue.

Aberdeen Music Hall (Union St., tel. 01224/632080, www.boxofficeaberdeen.com) is where the city's classical music concerts take place.

Cinema and Other Entertainment
Aberdeen has several cinemas, including an eccentric old cinema that shows a range of eclectic movies and several chain cinemas.

The first film shown at **Belmont Picturehouse** (49 Belmont St., tel. 0871/704 2051, www.picturehouses.co.uk) in 1898 featured footage of Queen Victoria at Balmoral; these days this atmospheric venue shows a mix of art-house and discerningly selected mainstream films. There is a basement café/bar.

It's hard to know how much more "wrong" things can get than a glamorous casino in a former house of God, but there you go: Aberdeen is full of watering holes in opulent old buildings like **Soul Casino** (333 Union St., tel. 01224/587711, www.pbdevco.com, food served

7 P.M.–4:15 A.M. nightly). You don't have to come here to gamble, of course, although it's about the most beautiful building in the country to do it. Sit in this church surrounded by stained glass and choose from an extensive drinks list and a pretty decent menu (mains £7–11).

Events
For a city its size, Aberdeen doesn't have that much going on: far smaller towns in Aberdeenshire have a far better range of events. Still, music-wise, the city can oblige with the **Aberdeen Jazz Festival** (www.jazzaberdeen.com), which has proved a success since it kicked off five years ago. It's reinventing itself as of 2009 as the Aberdeen International Jazz Festival. The event will be held biannually in September and seems set to pull in an even more diverse array of jazz and blues performances.

SHOPPING
Aberdonians love shopping. Unfortunately, while oil revenues have meant there are plenty of flashy shopping malls and every chain store you could think of, there are few interesting stores in the city. It's all bland, functional shopping, which will prove useful if you need to get something in a hurry and just dull otherwise.

Shopping Centers
The **Bon Accord/St. Nicholas Shopping Centre** is the largest shopping center in Aberdeen, with retail stores like John Lewis and Marks and Spencer. Along the length of **Union Street** you will find all the main chain stores.

Markets
Aberdeen Fish Market, a fresh fish market/sale, takes place every weekday morning from 4 A.M. between Commercial Quay and Albert Basin.

Bookstores
Books and Beans (22 Belmont St., tel. 01224/646438, www.booksandbeans.co.uk, 8 A.M.–4:30 P.M. daily), a friendly, cluttered establishment, has a formidable range of reasonably priced books.

Waterstone's (3–7 Union St., tel. 01224/

592440, 9 A.M.–6 P.M. Mon., Wed., Fri., and Sat., 10 A.M.–6 P.M. Tues., 9 A.M.–8 P.M. Thurs., 11 A.M.–5 P.M. Sun.) is a big bookshop that stocks most titles.

SPORTS AND RECREATION

As in much of Scotland, the most popular recreational sports activities include a round of golf or watching the city's football team enjoy a rather up-and-down rate of success.

Aberdeen's grassy, sandy coastal strip lends itself well to both golf and walking. There's also good coastal walking from Torry Battery south of Aberdeen Harbour.

Golf

In late 2006 and early 2007, American billionaire Donald Trump caused controversy with his plan to set up a new multimillion-dollar golf course north of Aberdeen and develop the area into an open championship venue. This is still in the cards but hasn't happened yet.

Royal Aberdeen Balgownie Links (Links Rd., tel. 01224/826591, www.royalaberdeen golf.com, greens fee £80), on the gorgeous coastline just north of Aberdeen before Bridge of Don, is an excellent place for a round of golf. It's the sixth-oldest course in the world.

Cycling

A disused railway line converted into a cycle track runs from the city (at Duthie Park) to Banchory in Royal Deeside.

Alpine Bikes (64–70 Holburn St., tel. 01224/211455, www.alpinebikes.com) is a conveniently located bike rental and repair center.

Football

Aberdeen Football Club (Pittodrie Stadium, tel. 01224/650400, www.afc.premiumtv.co.uk, tickets £15–25) is only a shadow of its former glory, but it has enjoyed a smattering of success in Europe of late. Matches are played generally on Saturday afternoons. Buses 1, 2, 4, and 11 go north to Pittodrie Stadium (on Pittodrie Street) from Union Street.

Accommodations

Seeing a constant flux of passing oil workers, rooms in the city are at a premium. Budget accommodation is limited, as rooms are more geared toward workers than travelers. Even the cheapest guesthouses will set you back over £50 on average for a room. Guesthouses and bed-and-breakfasts are often impersonal and bland and will serve breakfast at working hours (8:30 A.M. is the absolute latest in most places), not holiday hours. Your best option is to opt for a small hotel, which will cost little more than a guesthouse and offer better service.

UNDER £50

Tucked away in the leafy west end of Aberdeen in a large, rambling Victorian building, **Aberdeen Youth Hostel** (8 Queen's Rd., tel. 01224/646988 or 0870/155 3255, www.syha.org.uk, beds £15–16) is the best budget option if you're staying in Aberdeen overnight. It's a bit soulless—it doesn't seem to be the done thing to actually talk to anyone else staying here. The facilities, though, are very good. There are large, clean bathrooms and a well-stocked kitchen. Rooms are generally four-bed dorms, and a decent night's kip is possible. To get here, follow Union Street west until Holburn junction, then head along Albyn Place. Queen's Road is on the other side of the roundabout. It's one mile from the train station.

Dunrovin Guest House (168 Bon Accord St., tel. 01224/586081, www.dunrovinguest-house.co.uk, from £25 s, £40 d) is a smart-looking guesthouse that stands out against the plethora of bland places to stay in this area of the city. It has high-end rooms with a white decor and a mix of en suite and shared facilities. Rooms are small but have color satellite TVs. The place has friendly owners, decent breakfasts, and even a pretty garden.

Stone-built **Arden Guest House** (61 Dee St.,

tel. 01224/580700, www.ardenguesthouse.co.uk, from £40 s, £50 d), central to the thick of the action in Aberdeen, pretty much fulfils your dreams of the ideal city center guesthouse. It's got a mix of decent-sized rooms with en suite and shared bathrooms, done up in summery, flowery decor. The breakfasts are big and varied, and the service is courteous and personal. Union Street is a five-minute walk and Aberdeen's waterfront is 20 minutes' walk away.

£50-100

The **Globe Inn** (13–15 North Silver St., tel. 01224/624258, www.the-globe-inn.co.uk, £57.50 s, £62.50 d) is one of the best sleeping options in the city center. There are seven stylishly refurbished rooms here above the lively old pub of the same name. The rooms are immensely cozy, well-appointed places, done up in bright colors and with en suite facilities and color TVs. The continental breakfast is a bit of a downer—you might want to take advantage of the reasonably priced bar meals the night before to keep the wolf from the door.

On the south side of town, **Ferryhill House Hotel** (169 Bon Accord St., tel. 01224/590867, www.ferryhillhousehotel.co.uk, £50 s, £65 d) is a refreshing change from all the similar guesthouses. It's a pretty, traditional hotel set in its own large gardens and screened by foliage from the busy road. There are nine cool, pale-toned en suite rooms. Rooms are on the large side and get color TV and direct dial telephones. There is an air of faded grandeur about this hotel, but it's not too faded just yet. You can enjoy breakfast or lunch in the ornate conservatory restaurant.

Sadly, the modern **King's Hall** (College Bounds, Old Aberdeen, tel. 01224/273444, www.abdn.ac.uk/kingshall, June–Sept., £49.50 s, £74.50 d), smack bang in the middle of old Aberdeen, is only offering accommodation during student holidays as of 2008. It's the best accommodation option in this part of the city, complete with wide flat-screen TVs

and local tourist information. The Hall, part of the Aberdeen University complex, offers smart, light, pine-furnished rooms. It's possible to make use of university sports facilities for an additional charge.

OVER £100

Simpson's (59–63 Queens Rd., tel. 01224/327777, www.simpsonshotel.co.uk, £140 d) is a great example of the old saying, "You get what you pay for." This place might be almost twice the price of most lower-end hotels, but it is at least five times as good, because it has character—something sorely lacking in a lot of Aberdeen accommodations. You can't help being impressed with this elegant hotel/bistro's high arches, lofty ceilings, terracotta floors, palm trees, and general class. The rooms are a mixture of executive pads and suites. Expect warming pastel colors, elaborate iron framed beds, and Molten Brown toiletries in the en suite bathrooms. Four-poster bed rooms are available. Meals in the delightful brasserie are £16–18.

The serene, whitewashed **Marcliffe Hotel** (North Deeside Rd., Pitfodels, tel. 01224/861000, www.marcliffe.com, £195 s, £215 d) has a countryside location just three miles from the city center. It's easily the finest place to stay in Aberdeen and strikes a good balance between antique charm and contemporary spaciousness. There are 42 rooms on offer here, seven of which are suites. All rooms come with refrigerated mini bars, en suite bathrooms hung with bathrobes, a bowl of fresh fruit, and maid service at night. Even amidst all this luxury, the restaurant is a delightful surprise: an intimate, neat conservatory restaurant serving interesting seafood. A plate of Russian red king crab (according to the proprietor, as good as seafood gets) will set you back £35. There's outside dining to be had, too, where you can overlook the acres of charming wooded grounds.

Food

Leaving aside Edinburgh and Glasgow, Aberdeen has the best dining scene in the country, from funky cafés to atmospheric restaurants serving up different world cuisine.

CAFÉS, TEAROOMS, AND SNACKS

Books and Beans (22 Belmont St., tel. 01224/646438, www.booksandbeans.co.uk, 8 A.M.–4:30 P.M. daily) was the first Fair Trade coffee shop in Aberdeen, and it's still one of the most bizarre. It combines that time-tested winning formula of books and coffee, excelling on all fronts. It's a creaking, three-floored place with two floors of teetering bookshelves laden with titles; tables and comfy armchairs are squeezed in wherever possible. Books are artfully displayed so that while you're browsing you are likely to be so tantalizingly close to someone sitting with his coffee, cake, or snack that your stomach will beg you to stay. Coffees, sandwiches, and salads are £1–4.

Think of your breakfast and lunchtime fantasies and indulge them at the superb café that is (**Beautiful Mountain** (11–13 Belmont St., tel. 01224/645353, www.beautifulmountain.com, 8 A.M.–4:30 P.M. Mon.–Fri., 8 A.M.–5 P.M. Sat., 10:30 A.M.–4 P.M. Sun.). Imagine a breakfast of pancakes drizzled with honey and covered in fruit; imagine crisp baguettes with hummus and red peppers; imagine bagels with peanut butter and cream cheese. This is the kind of fare you can expect at this place, which prides itself on its made-to-specification sandwiches. There is a takeaway section downstairs and a dark café stretching around two sides of a room upstairs, furnished with church pews. Sandwiches are £3.50–5. When you're done with savories, sample the cake menu, which includes fudge brownies festooned with walnuts.

At seafront-hugging **Sand Dollar Café** (2 Beach Esplanade, tel. 01224/572288, www.sanddollarcafe.co.uk, 9 A.M.–5 P.M. Sun.–Wed., 9 A.M.–5 P.M. and 6–9 P.M. Thurs.–Sat.), a hefty dose of maritime-themed imagination has clearly gone into the decor. Think a Caribbean blue-and-yellow color scheme, driftwood, and, um, sand. The place has plenty of what most of the other places by Aberdeen's beach lack: individuality. All-day breakfasts are £5.50, lunches are £6–10, and evening meals like smoked salmon and steaks are £10–16.

SCOTTISH/INTERNATIONAL

Up by Aberdeen university campus at Bridge of Don in a converted mill is the **Olive Grove** (Grandholm Village, Bridge of Don, tel. 01224/821700, 9:30 A.M.–10 P.M. Mon.–Sat., 10 A.M.–10 P.M. Sun.), part of the Olive Tree chain that has set Aberdeen's dining scene alight over the last decade. The difference with this branch is that it's somewhere everybody can afford to eat (helped no doubt by its proximity to a large population of broke, hungry students). It serves up coffees, teas, generous breakfasts, and a mix of pizzas, pastas, and burgers with a classy, individual flair. Main meals are £8–14.

It's not often outside of Edinburgh and Glasgow that you walk into a place to eat in Scotland and feel underdressed. Be prepared, then, for **Café 52** (52 The Green, tel. 01224/590094, www.cafe52.net, lunch noon–3 P.M., tapas 3–6 P.M., dinner 6:30–9:30 P.M.), the coolest industrial-themed joint in town. Slick, sharply dressed staff serve contemporary cuisine looking as if it had been prepared for a cookbook photograph. A medley of different food is on offer, from kedgeree to steak to a risotto with rhubarb and dill. The café is great at any time of day, with great coffee, pricey but gooey puddings, and a good selection of white wines. Enjoying a glass of wine on one of the outside tables in the sunshine is probably the best thing to do in the city.

The vast, glam **Stage Door Restaurant** (26 North Silver St., tel. 01224/642111, 5:30 P.M.–late Mon.–Sat.) somehow manages to keep itself out of the spotlight despite having some of the best pre- and post-theater dining around.

In what used to be Aberdeen's Union Hall and Theatre, it's colorfully decorated with crowd scenes around the walls and plants screening the tables. You could go for Highland venison or fish pie and finish up with a cranchan, a Scottish delicacy of whipped cream, berries, honey, and, of course, whisky. Three courses or "acts" and coffee cost £24.

Silver Darling (Pocra Quay, North Pier, tel. 01224/576229, www.silverdarlingrestaurant.co.uk) is a glassy restaurant sitting on top of a castellated building on the quayside with wonderful views over the Aberdeen coastline. The views aren't quite wonderful enough to justify the prices, but the seafood served here is very good—try roast monkfish served with a cumin puree. The wines on offer are excellent; this is a great seaside dining experience. Starters are £11–15, mains are £19–22.

FRENCH AND ITALIAN
A sophisticated little piece of traditional Paris in Aberdeen, **Café Boheme** (23 Windmill Brae, tel. 01224/210677, www.cafebohemerestaurant.co.uk, noon–2 P.M. and 6–10 P.M. or later Tues.–Sat.) is a cozy French eatery. Candlelit and with old French jazz music in the background, Café Boheme serves up some great cuisine. You have to be prepared to splash out to really enjoy the food on offer. Start off with the snails with chorizo and move on to a main like the pan-fried steak. Starters are £4–7 and main courses £14–21.

A spacious modern restaurant lined with huge vases and busts, **Poldino's** (7 Little Belmont St., tel. 01224/647777, www.poldinos.co.uk, noon–2:30 P.M. and 6–10:45 P.M. Mon.–Sat.) has a colorful dining area set between high arches. It's the most atmospheric joint for Italian food in the city. Main courses range £8–18: At the lower end are pizzas and at the higher end are interesting beef and veal dishes.

ASIAN
Blue Moon 1 (11 Holburn St., tel. 01224/589977, www.bluemoon-aberdeen.co.uk, noon–2 P.M. and 5 P.M.–1 A.M. Mon.–Fri., noon–1 A.M. Sat.–Sun.) is one of the more interesting Indian restaurants in town. It's a bright, light eatery with walls decorated with contemporary art. It pulls in the business crowds during the day and all types in the evenings. It's got a good range of vegetarian dishes and fish specialties like the spicy salmon jalfrezi.

Information and Services

Aberdeen is a well-appointed city with every service visitors could need, including a helpful TIC and a hospital.

INFORMATION
Considering it's in such a big city, **Aberdeen TIC** (23 Union St., tel. 01224/288828, 9 A.M.–6:30 P.M. Mon.–Sat., 10 A.M.–4 P.M. Sun. July–Aug., 9:30 A.M.–5 P.M. Mon.–Sat. Sept.–June) offers a far friendlier, more personable service than you might expect, although it charges through the roof for information you'd get free elsewhere. You can get local and regional maps here; if you don't have any luck try one of the big bookshops on Union Street. You'll find the TIC on the corner of Union Street and Shiprow.

SERVICES
Money and Exchange
You'll find banks with ATMs up and down Union Street. Most banks will change travelers checks and U.S. dollars, as will many post offices. The airport has a *bureau de change*.

Communications and Internet Access
St. Nicholas Post Office (489 Union St., tel. 0845/722 3344, 9 A.M.–5:30 P.M. Mon.–Sat.) is one of the most central post offices in Aberdeen. The **Central Library** (Rosemount Viaduct, tel. 01224/652000, 9 A.M.–8 P.M. Mon.–Thurs., 9 A.M.–5 P.M. Fri.–Sat.) has free Internet access. You can also check your email at **Books and**

Beans (22 Belmont St., tel. 01224/646438, www.booksandbeans.co.uk, 8 A.M.–4:30 P.M. daily); the top floor of this bookstore has several computers available for Internet use.

Medical Services

Aberdeen Royal Infirmary (Foresterhill, tel. 01224/681818) is the major hospital in the region, with an outpatient department. Stagecoach Bus 10 and First Bus 12 pass nearby.

Laundry

Head to **The Wash House** (250 King St., tel. 01224/638999) for laundry needs.

Travel Agencies

STA Travel (30 Upperkirkgate, tel. 0871/468 0601, 10 A.M.–6 P.M. Mon.–Wed. and Fri.–Sat., 10 A.M.–7 P.M. Thurs.) specializes in arranging vacations for students and others on a budget.

Getting There

Aberdeen has a high standard of road and rail links to other U.K. cities, as well as national and some international air links. Even so, it's probably better to fly into a larger airport like Glasgow or Edinburgh, which will give you more choices in price and flight times. Aberdeen is not on the U.K. motorway system but does have good duel carriageways connecting it to the motorway at Perth.

AIR

Aberdeen Airport is six miles northwest of the city, at Dyce. You'll find limited restaurant facilities at the terminal as well as a *bureau de change*. It's a well-connected international airport with flights to U.K. destinations including Orkney, Shetland, and London and limited international flights to Scandinavia and other destinations in Western Europe. Many international flights change in Amsterdam. The airport is linked to the city center by regular local buses.

BOAT

Aberdeen's lively harbor has several ferries operating out of it. You'll find the harbor to the east of the city (turn right on Guild street out of the train station and right again on Market Street; the harbor is on the left).

Northlink Ferries (tel. 0845/600 0449, www.northlinkferries.co.uk) runs ferries from Aberdeen to Kirkwall on Orkney and Lerwick

in Shetland, departing Aberdeen at 5 P.M. (7 P.M. Mon. and Wed.). A one-way ticket to Lerwick costs £32.70 adult, £116.60 car.

At the time of writing, it was no longer possible to take a ferry from Aberdeen to Bergen, although plans to reintroduce a Scotland-Scandinavia connection from Rosyth, near Edinburgh, have been discussed.

TRAIN

Aberdeen's railway station is on Guild Street. You'll find ATMs and couple of restaurants here, as well as a left-luggage service (7:30 A.M.–5:30 P.M. Mon.–Sat., 9 A.M.–5 P.M. Sun.).

National

Trains run south to Dundee and Edinburgh and northwest to Speyside and the Moray coast. Trains run south to Dundee (three times per hour, 1 hr. 10 min., £22.60), Edinburgh (half-hourly, 2.5 hrs., £38.20) and Glasgow (hourly, 2 hrs. 40 min., £38.20). Trains also run regularly to Inverness (every two hours, 2 hrs. 20 min., £22.30).

International

Direct trains run from London King's Cross to Aberdeen once daily (seven hours, £116). Otherwise, change in Edinburgh. After Edinburgh on the way up, it's a gorgeous journey (sit on the right).

ABERDEEN

BUS
National

Scottish Citylink Buses and **Megabus** run services between Aberdeen and Edinburgh (about hourly, 3 hrs. 5 min., £21.80) with a change at Perth. Direct buses run between Aberdeen and Glasgow (3.25 hrs., £21.70). Glasgow buses are more frequent. To get to Inverness, take Stagecoach Bus 10, which runs hourly Monday–Saturday and also has Sunday service; the journey takes just under four hours.

International

The grueling journey by bus from London Victoria coach station takes 12 hours. **National Express** (www.nationalexpress.com) run a daytime and a nighttime service for as little as £18.

Getting Around

Aberdeen is a well-connected city and has many trains and lots of buses running to local, national, and some international destinations.

TO/FROM THE AIRPORT

Bus services 10 and 307 run regularly from the bus station to the airport (allow 40 minutes). Buses also run there from Union Street. A one-way fare is £1.30.

You can also get a taxi to the airport (£15–20).

TRAIN

Aberdeen train station is off Grant Street. You can get trains to Stonehaven, Huntly, Keith, Elgin, and Forres from Aberdeen. In Keith you can change to get on a branch line to Dufftown.

BUS

Aberdeen bus station is a run-down affair off Grant Street, east of the train station, with buses to most destinations in the region. The main local operator is **Stagecoach** (tel. 01224/597590). You might want to take a bus if you are heading to a bed-and-breakfast in the south of Aberdeen or to Old Aberdeen (services 1, 2, or 15).

TAXI

Rainbow Airport Taxis (tel. 01224/725500) are a reputable airport taxi firm. You could also call **Central Taxis** (tel. 01224/898989).

CAR

Arnold Clark (Girdleness Rd., tel. 01224/249159) has the cheapest car hire in town; it's by the Citroen garage south of the River Dee.

South Aberdeenshire

South of Aberdeen, the coast rises up into some dramatic cliffs hosting Britain's second-largest nesting seabird population. It's a fertile, sun-kissed region of rippling cornfields and pockets of woodland, petering out inland into bare hills. The main town is the appealing resort of Stonehaven. Being caught between the major tourist destinations of the Angus Glens to the south and Royal Deeside to the northwest means few visitors stop by. If you fancy seeing a bit of gentle rural Aberdeenshire without the crowds of visitors, this is the perfect place.

【 STONEHAVEN

Home to a sandy beach and a great ruined castle, historic Stonehaven has lots of lively pubs and restaurants clustering around its 17th-century harbor.

Sights
The prettiest area of Stonehaven is around the **old harbor.** From here, boardwalks connect along the coast to the open air swimming pool and paths head south up to the cliffs at **Dunnottar Castle** (tel. 01569/762173, www.dunnottarcastle.co.uk, 9 A.M.–6 P.M. daily late June–Sept., 9 A.M.–6 P.M. Mon.–Sat., 2–5 P.M. Sun. Easter–June and Sept.–Oct., 10:30 A.M.–sunset Fri.–Mon. Oct.–Easter, £5). The thick walls of this fortress are so close to the cliff edge they seem like a continuation of the rock face that plummets to the crashing waves below. The dramatic site has been of importance since Pictish times, when St. Ninian set up a church here. The castle ruins are mainly 14th century. This was the home of the powerful Earls Marischal, one of the three most important titles under the Scottish crown at the time. The castle, surrounded by sea on three sides, is one of the best-defended sites around—defendants were even able to hold out against the forces of Oliver Cromwell for eight months in the 17th century.

If you fancy a swim with a difference, **Stonehaven Open Air Pool** (tel. 01569/762134, www.stonehavenopenairpool.co.uk, 11 A.M.–7:30 P.M. Mon.–Fri. 11 A.M.–6 P.M. Sat.–Sun. July–mid-Aug., 1–7:30 P.M. Mon.–Fri., 10 A.M.–6 P.M. Sat.–Sun. May–June, 1–7 P.M. Mon.–Fri., 10 A.M.–6 P.M. Sat.–Sun. mid-Aug.–Sept., £3.90 adults, £2.20 children), a heated art deco swimming pool, has been a huge attraction with visitors to Stonehaven since 1934.

Events
New Year's Eve sees Stonehaven take center stage in the northeast's festivities as masses descend upon Stonehaven to see the fireball-swingers at **Hogmanay Fireballs Ceremony.** These consist of some 60 locals who take to the streets on the stroke of midnight, waving fireballs above their heads before chucking them into the harbor.

Accommodations and Food
Set above the main part of Stonehaven in a tree-screened cul-de-sac, the old, ivy-clad sandstone house of **Pitgaveny B&B** (Baird St., tel. 01569/764719, www.pitgavenybedandbreakfast.co.uk, £27.50 s, £55 d) has four rooms on offer, including one with four-poster bed. They're cozy affairs, all done up in a pale decor with plenty of old wood furniture and lots of space. There's private parking, and the town center is less than 10 minutes' walk away.

Nowhere beats the characterful old 【 **Ship Inn** (5 Shorehead, tel. 01569/762617, www.shipinnstonehaven.co.uk, £50 s, £75 d, food served noon–2:30 P.M. and 5:15–9 P.M. Mon.–Thurs., noon–2:30 P.M. and 5:15–9:45 P.M. Fri., noon–9:45 P.M. Sat.–Sun.) at Stonehaven Harbour as a place to stay or drink watching the boats bobbing outside the window. The six rooms are decently sized with a white decor and en suite facilities. Two of the rooms have four-poster beds and five get great harbor views. The traditional old bar has over 100 malt whiskies to try. If you want to enjoy the nice weather, you can take a pew on the outside picnic tables and have your food there. You could go for a regular main dish (£7.50–12) or try the ostrich steak with stilton sauce.

The **Carron Fish Bar** (1 Alladrice St., tel. 01569/765377, 4:30–10:30 P.M. Mon., noon–2 P.M. and 4:30–10:30 P.M. Tues.–Sat., 4–10 P.M. Sun.) is a great little fish-and-chip shop, where you can take your deep-fried fare down to the river that runs right by the takeaway. This place also claims to be the home of that gorgeous, greasy piece of gastronomy known as the deep-fried Mars bar.

Elegant art deco **C Carron Restaurant** (Cameron St., tel. 01569/760460, www.carron-restaurant.co.uk, noon–2 P.M. and 6–9:30 P.M. Tues.–Sat.) could occupy you a long while with its appearance alone. Set behind a grassy courtyard, its magnificent centerpiece is a nine-foot glass mirror, etched with a naked woman and edged with mosaic tiles. The artwork is thought to be Picasso's work but this has yet to be proved. The food here is nothing too complicated but it's made with lots of TLC. Dishes are mainly fish, like the herb-crusted sea bass, or meat, like the haunch of venison. Main courses are £10–17.

Right down by the harborside in Stonehaven, the **Tolbooth Restaurant** (Stonehaven Harbour, tel. 01569/762287, www.tolbooth-restaurant.co.uk, noon–2 P.M. and 6–9:30 P.M. Tues.–Sat.) is an irresistibly charming building with white-painted stone walls and wooden floors that give the dining experience a rustic character. It's a place that has seen a colorful history over the centuries—as the town's oldest building it's acted as a tollbooth and prison. Seafood is the specialty here; main meals range £15–18.

Getting There and Away

Two **trains** hourly run from Stonehaven to Aberdeen (25 min., £3.90). You can also get trains south to Dundee and Edinburgh direct from Stonehaven. Stonehaven is also served by regular **buses** from Aberdeen, including the half-hourly 107 and 117 services (50 min.). There are even a couple of night buses back from Aberdeen on Friday and Saturday if you want to go partying in the big city.

FOWLSHEUGH BIRD RESERVE

The towering 200-foot old red sandstone cliffs south of Stonehaven at Fowlsheugh Bird Reserve (near Crawton, tel. 01346/532017, year-round) are home to Britain's second-largest population of breeding seabirds. Skylarks and meadow pipits are attracted to the crop fields at the cliff edge while puffins, kittiwakes, guillemots, and shags are among the species chattering in crevices in the sheer cliffs. With around 130,000 birds breeding here at the height of the season, this place will mesmerize ornithologists.

The cliffs are accessed from the minor road at Crawton, four miles south of Stonehaven.

Coastrider buses heading south from Stonehaven to Montrose will drop you off at the turn for Fowlsheugh. Buses run hourly from Monday to Saturday and several times daily on a Sunday.

ABERDEEN

Central Aberdeenshire

This vast farming region is often dismissed as an area of dormitory commuter settlements too near to Aberdeen to have much vitality of their own. The centerpiece is the River Don, channeling off the Grampian Mountains and gushing into a steep, still valley lined with woods. Unlike the tourist-infested Deeside to the south, the area around the River Don is a place where you can still find tranquil walking and fishing spots and little-visited castles. Fortress-spotting is probably the main attraction in Central Aberdeenshire. There are dozens to be found, from the whitewashed tower of Corgarff Castle to the grand history-steeped ruin of Huntly Castle and opulent Fyvie Castle with its collection of fine paintings. These magnificent medieval buildings provide the main diversion in the area and the greatest insight into its eventful past.

DONSIDE

With the exception of a few adventurous walkers, knowledgeable anglers, and tourists that have gotten lost between Speyside to the north and Royal Deeside to the south, the valley traversed by the River Don remains relatively unknown. It rises in the Grampian Mountains and flows east through forests and via castles before turning south to reach the sea at Aberdeen. It's a peaceful place that offers a mix of terrains for visitors. These range from the high hills at Corgarff near its source to the castles and the sedate backwater of Alford along its middle course. The main activities, besides castle-bagging, are walking and fishing—the Don is one of the best places in the country to catch brown trout and salmon.

Sights

Corgarff Castle (tel. 01975/651460, 9:30 A.M.–5:30 P.M. daily Apr.–Sept., 9:30 A.M.–4:30 P.M. Sat.–Sun. Oct.–Mar., £4.70 adults, £3.70 seniors, £2.35 children) stands in an isolated location where the River Don channels its way off the Grampian Mountains, a brilliantly white fortress standing out starkly against the fertile green foothills. The wild location of this 16th-century castle has led it to be taken over by bandits and used as a Jacobite garrison base over the years. Inside is a reconstructed barracks room and an illicit whisky still. There's also a small visitors center and a shop on-site. The castle is a couple of miles west of the junction of the A939 and the A944, at the bottom of the road to the Lecht Ski Centre.

Kildrummy Castle (near Kildrummy, tel. 01975/571331, 9:30 A.M.–5:30 P.M. daily Apr.–Sept., £3.50 adults, £2.50 seniors) is the best-preserved 13th-century castle in Scotland: It may not look like much until you consider just how well its walls have done to survive the best part of 800 years. It would have originally been one of the most impressive fortresses of its day but being besieged by Edward I of England and the Scottish king David II did very little to preserve its glory. Today it's a great ruin to explore.

In a land dominated by castles and distilleries, **Grampian Transport Museum** (Alford, tel. 01975/562292, www.gtm.org.uk, 10 A.M.–5 P.M. daily Easter–Oct., £5.50 adults, £2.80 children) is quite a refreshing change. It's a collection of all kinds of vehicles from the glory days of steam, road, and rail travel, including a pre–World War I steam wagon. While not perhaps a reason to venture into this neck of the woods, it's all good fun for children, who can take rides and clamber on some of the old vehicles. There's a varied assortment of vehicle miniatures. The museum has refreshments and a shop.

The partly recumbent **Easter Aquorthies Stone Circle** stands in fertile rolling farmland just north of the River Don and west of Inverurie. It's the most impressive stone circle in the region, dating from the tail end of the Neolithic era around 2000 B.C. To find the circle, head north up the A96 to Inveruri; you'll see it signposted from the roundabout directly west of Inverurie, from where it's three kilometers.

Accommodations

Cozy little **Jenny's Bothy** (near Corgarff, tel. 01975/651449, www.jennysbothy.co.uk, beds £9) is up a long, lonely forestry track near Corgarff and makes even the castle (its nearest neighbor) seem positively well connected to the outside world. The magical little stone-built croft can sleep up to 10 people in accommodations that include a family room, with a woodburning stove for warmth. To find the hostel, head west on the A939 for a couple of miles after the junction with the A944: you'll see it signposted along the old military road. After almost a mile, the bothy is the second dwelling along.

There is no better place to stay in this area than **Kildrummy Castle Hotel** (tel. 01975/571288, www.kildrummycastlehotel.co.uk, £95 s, £169 d), right, as its name suggests, by Kildrummy Castle. Located west of Alford and east of Corgarff, it's an elegant place of wide corridors lined with heavy tapestries, ornate hand-hewn staircases, beamed ceilings, and blazing fireplaces. There are 16 considerably sized bedrooms, several with fourposters. All have en suite facilities. Local game features heavily on the menu.

Getting There and Away

Public transport is good to the eastern end of Donside and nonexistent to the western end. Inverurie has a **train station** (Aberdeen trains about hourly, £4), handy if you are visiting Easter Aquorthies stone circle.

Bus 220 runs hourly Monday–Saturday and a few times Sunday to Alford from Aberdeen. Three daily buses go from Alford to Kildrummy, but none goes beyond Strathdon, which is eight miles from Corgarff. Getting to Corgarff will require either your own wheels, a taxi, or a long walk.

Getting Around

Alford Taxis (tel. 01975/562244) are a taxi company based in Alford.

HUNTLY

The old market town of Huntly is where the tame farmland that characterizes much of

Central Aberdeenshire begins to rise into lofty wooded hills and valleys. It's got a history dating back to the 12th century but is essentially a planned 18th-century town centered on a handsome main square. The great, rambling ruin of the castle north of town makes this an essential stop en route from Aberdeen to Speyside and the Moray Coast.

◖ Huntly Castle

Perhaps because of its location in a tree-studded park or perhaps because of its action-packed history, Huntly Castle (tel. 01466/793191, 9:30 A.M.–5:30 P.M. daily Apr.–Sept., 9:30 A.M.–4:30 P.M. Sat.–Wed. Oct.–Mar., £4.70 adults, £2.35 children) is one of the most worthwhile ruined fortresses to visit in Aberdeenshire. Of all the castles in Scotland, Huntly Castle's incumbents deserved being attacked the most. The fourth Earl of Huntly had religious quarrels with Mary, Queen of Scots, which incited her to attack the castle. The sixth earl of Huntly joined a plot to assassinate King James VI in 1594; again the monarchical response was to attack the castle, making it a pitiably damaged fortress. Around 1600, the sixth Earl made repairs to the castle and wrote his name in large letters across the outside, together with the date repairs were completed. The impressive frontispiece above the door dates from this period. Examining the ornate carvings and exploring the largely complete series of corridors and rooms inside is a time-absorbing activity—set aside a couple of hours plus time to stroll the woodsy grounds afterward. It's a very peaceful place, separated by a long drive from the main part of town.

Shopping

Just like a traditional old Scottish market town should, Huntly has several tasty food shops. **Deans of Huntly** (Depot Rd., tel. 01466/792086, www.deans.co.uk, 9 A.M.–5 P.M. Mon.–Sat., 10 A.M.–4 P.M. Sun.) is renowned for its shortbread and has a shop, café, and shortbread factory viewing gallery.

Accommodations and Food

As you'd hope from a town so architecturally

impressive, Huntly has a selection of grand places to stay. Food-wise, it's worth noting that the town is renowned for the **buttery,** an infamous Aberdeenshire snack similar to a heavy, extra-buttery croissant. Pop into **Strathbogie Bakery** (Gordon St.) to try a buttery.

The **Huntly Hotel** (18 The Square, tel. 01466/792703, www.thehuntlyhotel.co.uk, from £35 s, £50 d) is one of the two grand gray hotels making up most of Huntly's charming town square, offering 11 well-turned-out rooms with en suite or private bathrooms. Seeing as most hotel rooms get a view of the square, it's one of the best accommodation options. You can eat inexpensively at the hotel—the steak is very popular.

The most stylish place to stay for miles around is the (**Castle Hotel** (tel. 01466/ 792696, www.castlehotel.uk.com, £73 s, £103 d), farther along the lane leading to Huntly Castle. It's large enough to make even the castle seem like a gatehouse. The sumptuous rooms come with huge ornate beds, writing desks, en suite bathrooms, and views sliding away over the surrounding parklands, and that's just the standard ones. There are four-poster bed rooms and suites available, too. In the bright, big-windowed restaurant, expect crisp tablecloths and classy cuisine as you sit down to a three-course meal starting at £24.50.

The traditional old **Coffee House** (6 The Square, tel. 01466/799466, 9 A.M.–4 P.M. Mon.–Sat.) has spacious upstairs seating overlooking the square and does a great line in homebakes, snacks, and light meals (£1–5).

Information
Head to **Huntly TIC** (The Square, tel. 01466/792255, 10 A.M.–1 P.M. and 2–5 P.M. Mon.–Sat. Apr.–Oct.) for local information. Posted in the office window are details of castle and whisky tours you can do from Huntly.

Getting There and Away
Trains run every 1.5 hours between Aberdeen and Huntly (50 min., £9.50). **Stagecoach bus** 10 between Aberdeen and Inverness also stops off in Huntly.

CASTLE TRAIL NORTH OF ABERDEEN
There's a vast tract of Aberdeenshire north of the capital with nothing much to see except the pleasant, dull farmland that has kept the region one of the richest in the country for centuries. Nothing much, that is, except castles. If fortresses are your thing, and you want to find a few off the beaten track, then this is where you should head. The castle-bagging area lies north of Oldmeldrum, approximately following the course of the main road to Banff.

Fyvie Castle
Fyvie Castle (Fyvie, tel. 0844/493 2182, www.nts.org.uk, castle open 11 A.M.–5 P.M. daily July–Aug., noon–5 P.M. Sat.–Wed. Mar.–June and Sept.–Oct., grounds open dawn–dusk daily, £8 adults, £20 family) has been around for eight centuries and seen the coming and going of five families. It's a vast stone castle of thick circular towers and soaring parapets and has entertained guests including Robert the Bruce. The castle is in great shape for its age and contains lots of lavish Edwardian furnishings. Art lovers will want to investigate the great portrait collection, which includes works by Thomas Gainsborough and a significant number of works by Sir Henry Raeburn. Once you've checked out the inside, you can head onto the grounds, which include an American garden, an icehouse, and an old bowling alley, all against a lochside backdrop. The castle is said to be haunted by at least two ghosts.

Tolquhon Castle
Tolquhon Castle (by Pitmedden, tel. 01651/ 851286, 9:30 A.M.–5:30 P.M. daily Apr.–Sept., 9:30 A.M.–4:30 P.M. Sat.–Sun. Oct.–Mar., £3.70 adults, £1.85 children) is one of the region's most magnificent ruined fortresses. Its most impressive feature is its twin-towered, highly decorated gatehouses. Beyond, craggy walls sheer up in broken fingers to the sky. There's an on-site shop and toilet facilities. To reach the castle, head east on the A920 from Oldmeldrum, from where it is signposted.

Delgatie Castle

This high, pale gray castle (by Turriff, tel. 01888/563479, www.delgatiecastle.com, 10 A.M.–5 P.M. daily, £5) stands amidst cow fields east of Turriff. You can see the bed chamber where Mary, Queen of Scots stayed for several days and, most impressively, the fine 16th-century painted ceilings. Somewhat puzzlingly, these feature animals with human heads representing the castle's past inhabitants.

Getting There and Away

Stagecoach bus service 305/325 runs at least hourly throughout the week from Aberdeen to Oldmeldrum, Fyvie, and Turriff (for Delgatie Castle) en route to Macduff. Change in Oldmeldrum for regular services to Pitmedden, where you can jump off for Tolquhon Castle. Frequent Ellon buses from Aberdeen also stop at Pitmedden.

Speyside

The granite Grampian Mountains swoop down here through a series of emerald-green glens to the north-facing coast. Tumbling with the glens are a series of rivers, flowing at first furiously through the hills and then more gently through sun-kissed, barley-growing country to the sea. The defining feature is the wide, winding River Spey, and the landscape around it lends itself perfectly to the production of single malt whisky. Over half of Scotland's whisky distilleries are in this region, which, in concentrated areas of production like Dufftown, is thick with the smell of malt. So strong is the allure of distilleries offering tours with complimentary drams of their finest products at the end that it's easy to overlook this region's simply stunning scenery. There are superb low-level river walks and hilltop hikes over desolate moor to be had. One of the great long-distance footpaths of Scotland, the Speyside Way, offers a chance to see the best of this lush landscape.

PLANNING YOUR TIME

If you are in Speyside for the whisky and want to see as many distilleries as possible, bear in mind that distillery tours only operate a few times per day, so seeing two distilleries in a day is realistic. A good reason for not cramming in more is that, if you want to sample the fruits of the distillation process, you'll be over the limit by the time you hit the third or fourth distillery.

KEITH

Mellow Keith has over the centuries committed itself almost absolutely to whisky-making. There are four distilleries in and around town; the most interesting to visit is Strathisla Distillery. There are some pleasant walks along the wooded banks of the River Isla, but if you're not a whisky fan there's little reason to stop here, other than to hop on the picturesque branch line railway to Dufftown.

Keith and Dufftown Railway

This scenic, 11-mile mini-railway (Dufftown Station, tel. 01340/821181, www.keith-dufftown-railway.co.uk, trains run several times daily Easter–Oct.) links Keith, on the main rail network, with the world's malt whisky capital, Dufftown. Keith Station is on Station Road in Keith.

◖ Strathisla Distillery

This is probably Speyside's most picturesque distillery (Seafield Ave., tel. 01542/783044, 10 A.M.–4 P.M. Mon.–Sat., 12:30–4 P.M. Sun. Easter–Oct., £5), standing in peaceful woodland at the edge of little-visited Keith. It's set off by its striking twin pagodas. It's Speyside's oldest working distillery and produces a golden, fruity malt with a strong hint of wood. Tours are pretty comprehensive. On the opposite side of the road are some enjoyable woodsy walks.

Accommodations

If you want to stay anywhere in Keith, you'll want it to be **Craighurst Guest House** (Seafield Ave., tel. 01542/880345, www.craighurst-guest-house.co.uk, £70 d), conveniently located next to the Strathisla Distillery. There are four special themed rooms here: the castle, the coastal, the whisky, and the royal. Each room has en suite bathrooms and easy chairs to relax in. There's also a large lounge with a welcoming open fire.

Getting There and Away

Trains run from Aberdeen to Keith (at least eight Mon.–Sat., several Sun., 1 hr. 5 min., £12.40 en route to Inverness, via Elgin. There are also hourly **buses** between Keith and Elgin Monday–Saturday.

DUFFTOWN

The sweet scent of malt hits you as you arrive in gray Dufftown, dubbed the malt whisky capital of the world because of the seven working distilleries in and around it. A love of liquor is the reason to come here; among the distilleries opening their doors to visitors is the most famous single malt maker of them all: Glenfiddich.

Glenfiddich Distillery

You'd better believe it: Tours of Glenfiddich Distillery (tel. 01340/820373, www.glenfiddich.com, 9:30 A.M.–4 P.M. Mon.–Fri.), the distillery that produces the world's favorite single malt whisky, are free. Full credit to the folk at Glenfiddich for this, as you'd think they could charge £10 and still get the hordes turning up for tours. It's a serene distillery, with photogenic buildings reflected in a large pond in the grounds. One of the unique aspects to a tour here is that Glenfiddich has its own cooperage (barrel-making plant). It's also the only Highland distillery to distill and bottle its own whisky on-site. The Malt Barn Café on-site offers a range of refreshments in appropriately rustic surroundings.

Balvenie Distillery

Small, intimate Balvenie (tel. 01340/820373, www.balvenie.com, tours 10 A.M. and 2 P.M.

Glenfiddich Distillery

© LUKE WATERSON

Mon.–Thurs. and 10 A.M. Fri., £25) is one of the last family-owned distilleries in Scotland. Balvenie Farm, next door to the distillery, grows the barley that goes into the malt. The wonderful tour includes a visit to one of the last on-site floor maltings in Scotland. In the warehouse, you also get to bottle your own Balvenie single malt. At the end of the experience, you retire for nosings and tastings. Tours of Balvenie start at Glenfiddich, its sister distillery.

Dufftown Whisky Museum

Mostly staffed by retired distillery workers, Dufftown Whisky Museum (Fife St., tel. 01340/820507, www.dufftown.co.uk, daily Apr.–Oct. or by arrangement) is a treasure trove of historic whisky distilling exhibits, including an illicit still (no longer in use). It's a good old-fashioned museum, and you can be chatting to the staff for hours. If the museum is closed, inquire at either the whisky shop up the road or the TIC; someone will usually open up. As of March 2009, the museum will be changing premises; at press time, a new location had not been finalized.

A BRIEF HISTORY OF WHISKY

The word whisky derives from the Gaelic "Uisge Beatha," translating as "water of life." That, for many centuries, was exactly the function Scotland's most popular drink performed. The Celtic missionary monks are credited with first introducing whisky to Scotland in the sixth century A.D. – it could even have gone hand in hand with introducing Christianity to the country. A potent, fiery drink, whisky caught on in a cold, wet climate, and many crofters produced a similar liquor simply as a means of keeping warm during winter in leaking croft houses.

In these dark times, whisky was the drink of the very poor, while the rich in Scotland favored claret. This was hardly surprising. The "Auld Alliance," an agreement between France and Scotland born out of a shared need to curtail English expansion, ensured a steady influx of the finest French wine into Scotland at vastly reduced prices. Whisky couldn't compete, and the pleasure the Scottish elite took from French wine was increased significantly by the fact that it meant the English were left with an inferior product.

After the Union of the Crowns in 1707, Scottish wine privileges were lost and the price of their prized drink went up. It was only now that more people began to look to other liquor to drink. While the wealthy had been sipping claret, whisky had been steadily advancing as a palatable product. For a long time it was an unbearable, foul-tasting liquid that was often dangerous to drink. The poor taste was due to a lack of refinement in the production technology available.

In the 1530s, the dissolution of the monasteries under Henry VIII ousted many monks from their century-old homes and forced them into the one other trade they knew: distillation. Purpose-built distilleries, manned by monks and generally within monasteries, had begun to appear as early as 1300. Distillation, originally used for medicine and winemaking, was a process that the then-educated classes (mostly monks) would have had almost exclusive knowledge of. Others soon learned the technique, though. In countries without ready supplies of grapes, it was whisky distillation rather than wine distillation that boomed, with cereal crops like barley used as the base ingredient of the liquor.

As whisky grew in popularity, the Scottish parliament jumped on the financial bandwagon and began imposing heavy taxes on those who produced it. This simply drove the whisky-making process underground. Although the government had excise men to police the production of whisky, many of the stills making whisky were high up in the glens and guarded by teams of locals. By 1820, things had got rather bad for the government: More than half the whisky in Scotland was produced without contributing any money in duty. As a result, it was proposed in government to provide financial incentives to produce whisky legally. New, sophisticated distilleries with government backing were established, often right in the thick of illicit distilling country. The illegal distillers opposed this government venture but could do nothing to stop their trade from dying out. When a plague of beetles destroyed vineyards across France in the 1880s, the Scottish whisky industry filled the void in the drink market and surpassed brandy to become the world's favorite spirit.

ABERDEEN

Entertainment, Shopping, and Events

The **Royal Oak** (30 Fife St., tel. 01340/542118) is a great spot for a drink, with roaring fires and stupendous numbers of whiskies to try.

The Whisky Shop (1 Fife St., tel. 01340/821097, www.whiskyshopdufftown.co.uk, daily Apr.–Oct., Mon.–Tues. and Thurs.–Sat. Oct.–Apr.) has to be lined with more eclectic bottles of single malt than almost anywhere else in the country. It also acts as a whisky information point; it's happy to recommend distilleries in the local area to tour and sample its products.

In May each year is the **Spirit of Speyside Whisky Festival** (www.spiritofspeyside.com), a four-day fest of whisky-themed action. If you miss the occasion, don't worry: It's on again at the end of September.

The **Dufftown Highland Games** (www.dufftownhighlandgames.org) is one of the country's most visitor-friendly Highland Games, with loads of fun track and field events to watch and one for visitors to participate in. The games are held at the end of July.

Picnicking in an upturned whisky still is an option in Dufftown.

© LUKE WATERSON

Accommodations and Food

Just outside of Dufftown in the grounds of the Drummuir Castle estate is the idyllic campsite and water sports center of **Loch Park** (Drummuir, tel. 01542/810334, www.loch-park.co.uk, tent and two people £12). It's a lush, grassy site at the head of a tree-flanked loch with basic camping facilities. The adventure center here runs activities like canoeing, kayaking, and archery—a fun, refreshing break from all that whisky-swilling. There were plans afoot at the time of writing to change the bunkhouse (£15 per person) in Drummuir village into self-catering cottages. The Keith and Dufftown Railway makes a stop at Loch Park.

Tannochbrae (22 Fife St., tel. 01340/820541, www.tannochbrae.co.uk, £64 d) is a guesthouse with six cozy, wallpapered rooms, all of which have en suite facilities and safes for valuables. The accommodation is done up in soothing, welcoming white tones. The traditionally styled guest lounge is full of shiny leather furniture with a blazing fire and a selection of over 100 whiskies to sample.

The vividly colorful, family-friendly, whole-food café that is **Noah's Ark Bistro and Fournet House** (18 Balvenie St., tel. 01340/821428, www.noahsarkbistro.com, £45 d, food served noon–8:30 P.M. daily) concentrates its menu on fresh, organic food. With colorful pictures, many by children, on its walls and an open fire, it's a great spot for some healthy cuisine. There are loads of vegetarian dishes, including veggie sausages and veggie moussaka. Main meals are £6.50–12.50. Noah's Ark/Fournet House also has one room upstairs (bed-and-breakfast from £22.50 per person)—a twin room with a lavish bathroom—and a guest lounge with a log fire.

Information

Dufftown TIC (tel. 01340/820501, Easter–Oct.) is in the clock tower in the center of town.

Getting There and Away

Bus 336 runs hourly Monday–Saturday and four times daily Sunday to Elgin and Forres.

In summer, you can also hop on the Keith and Dufftown railway to Keith, on the Aberdeen-Inverness rail line.

ABERLOUR AND VICINITY

Otherwise known by its other more tongue-twisting name of Charlestown of Aberlour, this relaxed village on the banks of the Spey is the most picturesque of the Speyside whisky centers. It's here, certainly, that you'll have your most magical single malt experiences, whether at one of the distilleries or in one of the excellent whisky bars. Aberlour's culinary claims to fame don't stop with the liquor: This is also the home of Walker's Shortbread, and great restaurants abound.

Aberlour Distillery

Aberlour Distillery (tel. 01340/881249, www.aberlour.com, 9 A.M.–5 P.M. daily Apr.–Oct., 9 A.M.–5 P.M. Mon.–Fri. Nov.–Mar., tours at 10:30 A.M. and 2 P.M., £10) makes a soft, sherry-like whisky not generally ranked among the single malt greats. This is compensated for by the fact that this is a simply wonderful distillery to tour. It's an intimate experience that involves nosings and tastings with expert guidance and the chance to bottle your own exclusive bottle of single malt (you hand pour it from a cask). Arrangements to tour should be made ahead of time.

Walks

There is some lush walking alongside the River Spey: start from the car park down behind the Mash Tun pub. The 80-mile **Speyside Way** passes through en route from Aviemore in the southern Highlands to Buckie on the Moray coast.

Accommodations and Food

Aberlour is a great place to stay, if for no other reason than that once you have partaken of the fest of food and drink that give the town its distinctiveness, you'll be in no state to leave.

C **The Mash Tun** (8 Broomfield Sq., tel. 01340/881771, www.mashtun-aberlour.com,

rooms from £80) has adopted the name for a reason: It's a glorious homage to single malts. These days, you can stay at the Mash Tun in one of four bright red-and-white rooms or in the even more luxurious suite. Expect iron-framed beds, en suite bathrooms (one with a roll-top bath), and oodles of space. Each is named after a whisky. The best bit of this building is its whisky bar, decked out in wood from distillery wash backs and serving lots of single malts and real ales. It serves food, too, like venison sausage and mash.

There's no denying what a special place the **C** **Craigellachie Hotel** (Craigellachie, tel. 01340/881204, www.craigellachie.com, Spey-facing rooms from £155 d) is, rising out of the trees from the River Spey in all its white-washed glory. The 26 huge rooms, done up in cozy white and pastel colors, have sofas, armchairs, and en suite showers/baths. Many rooms face the River Spey. Guests can relax in the drawing room, in front of a blazing fire. The Quaich Bar at the hotel is famous for having one of the largest collections of whiskies anywhere in the world; currently around 700 bottles line the walls. There's a very good restaurant here, too.

Whether it's oatcakes, shortbread, fruitcake, meats, or cheeses that you're after, you're sure to find it at the friendly, long-established **Spey Larder** (96–98 High St., tel. 01340/871243, 9:30 A.M.–5:30 P.M. Mon.–Sat.). There's something both delightfully old-fashioned and very contemporary about this huge deli. If you're hunting for picnic ingredients or wanting to get a good takeout coffee and filled sandwich/panini, this is the place.

You can come to the factory shop of the famous shortbread manufacturing base at **Walkers Shortbread Factory** (tel. 01340/871555, shop open 8:30 A.M.–5 P.M. daily) and buy Walkers shortbread in all its tartan-clad forms, at knock-down prices.

Getting There and Away

Dufftown to Forres **buses** (hourly Mon.–Sat., several Sunday buses) stop at Aberlour High School and Craigellachie Hotel en route.

TOMINTOUL AND THE GLENLIVET ESTATE

South of the snaking waters of the River Spey, two high ridges of hills cut up to the wilder Grampian Mountains beyond; the roughly 2,000 acres in between is known as the Glenlivet Estate. On the edge of the Cairngorm Mountains—1,160 feet up—is the neat, chilly village of Tomintoul, a village set out by the Duke of Gordon in the 18th century. The Duke's aim was to provide housing and employment for those on his estates so they were content enough not to rise up against him in a repeat of the 1745 rebellion. It's a prime outdoor activities base, with walking, cycling, and skiing being popular activities. The Glenlivet Estate also contains one of Scotland's highest single malt whisky distilleries.

Glenlivet Distillery

Remarkably, Glenlivet Distillery (Ballindalloch, tel. 01340/821720, www.theglenlivet.com, tours at 10:30 A.M. and 2 P.M. Mon.–Sat. and 12:30–4 P.M. Sun., free), up in a remote glen between Speyside and Tomintoul, owes much of its development to illicit distilling. Historically it was too cut off and dangerous for excisemen to visit, which allowed the area to become a whisky-producing hotbed. The wild setting helps to create the flavor of Glenlivet. At a higher altitude and in a colder climate than other distilleries, the liquor at Glenlivet comes to the boil at a different temperature and enhances the distillation process. The finished product is a soft, flowery malt well worth doing the tour to sample.

Sports and Recreation

Way up above Tomintoul in the stark peaks of the Grampians, the **Lecht Ski Centre** (tel. 01975/651440, www.lecht.co.uk, 8:30 A.M.–5 P.M.) is one of the country's main ski centers: A chairlift takes you up to 2,500 feet. There are 20 runs, six of which are either ⌐d or black runs. You can also try your hand ⌐wboarding, and novices can get lessons. ⌐ent rental is £15.75 per day, while a lift ⌐ cost £22.50 adults, £14.70 children.

In summer, you can still go quad-biking at the Lecht. To get there, follow the A939 south from Tomintoul.

Walking-wise, a branch of the long-distance footpath, the Speyside Way (www.moray.gov.uk/area/speyway) runs 15 miles from Ballindalloch to Tomintoul, taking in Glenlivet Distillery and one of the finest viewpoints in Moray, Carn Daimh. You'll see Glen Livet dropping away below you in a patchwork of pale greens and browns. It's the hardest part of the Speyside Way footpath. Near Glenlivet Distillery there are three **smugglers' trails** that follow in the footsteps of the glen's illicit distilling past through hills and woods.

Accommodations and Food

Tomintoul Youth Hostel (Main St., tel. 01807/580364, www.syha.org.uk, Easter–Sept., £13–14) is an intimate hostel in a Victorian schoolhouse with 20 beds in four rooms available here. There is a good, clean self-catering kitchen and plenty of tourist information available. It's tucked up on the dead-end road, to the left of the main junction in the village.

The stone cottage of **Argyle House** (7 Main St., tel. 01807/580766, from £23 s, £46 d) on Tomintoul's long Main Street is a great bargain, offering five white twin, family, and double rooms at some of the lowest prices around. The en suite rooms here are slightly more expensive. Beds are comfortable and breakfasts are generous.

In this part of the world, it makes sense to have hotels located near popular distilleries for those merry whisky buffs who have had one dram too many after their tours. This is the kind of market ◖ **Minmore House Hotel** (by Glenlivet Distillery, tel. 01807/590378, £83 s, £136 d) caters toward—those who have vast amounts of money to spend. With nine huge rooms, all of which are en suite (thank goodness, at this price), this is a luxurious place with grand views over wild Glen Livet. The dinner menu here might include gravadlax made with Scottish salmon or succulent roast guinea fowl. This is by far the best hotel in the region.

There's something oddly Canadian about the rustic **Old Fire Station Tearoom** (37 Main St., tel. 01807/580485, 9 A.M.–5 P.M. daily). Most likely, this could be put down to the contrast between the frozen outside of Tomintoul and the warm, welcoming interior, where pancakes dowsed in maple syrup with bacon is the favorite on the menu. It will serve hot, hearty food amidst a decor of fireman's hoses and uniforms. There's even underfloor heating in winter.

Information

Tomintoul has two tourist information offices, the main one being **Tomintoul TIC** (The Square, tel. 01807/580285, 9 A.M.–5:30 P.M. Mon.–Fri., 9 A.M.–1 P.M. and 2–5:30 P.M. Sat., 1–5 P.M. Sun. July–Aug., 9:30 A.M.–1 P.M. and 2–5 P.M. Mon.–Sat. Apr.–June and Sept.–Oct.).

Glenlivet Estate Office (Main St., Tomintoul, tel. 01807/870070) is handy for further information on outdoor activities on the huge Glenlivet Estate. It's at the south end of Main Street.

Getting There and Away

From May to September, the **Heather Hopper** Bus 208 runs daily from Grantown on Spey in the Southern Highlands over the mountains via Tomintoul to Ballater. At other times of year, public transport is extremely limited. There is one service daily Monday–Wednesday and Saturday between Dufftown, Glenlivet Bus Shelter, and Tomintoul.

ABERDEEN

Moray Coast

The green and gold farming lands in the north of Moray are rimmed by long tracts of sand and dunes attracting thousands of wading birds. You would expect the combination to attract hundreds of holidaymakers, but in truth these are lonely shores, where you can lie on the sand and feel like you are stranded on your own desert island. With the beaches and the gentle forests that stretch south from the coast, this is a paradise for cyclists and walkers.

The mesmerizing archaeology of the area, taking the forms of abbeys, palaces, and monasteries still inhabited by monks, sets a distinctly spiritual tone to this softly undulating landscape. A more recent addition to this coast is the ecologically and spiritually motivated community that is the Findhorn Foundation. Since setting up on these shores they have proved to the world that environment-sustaining living is achievable; a visit to the community is one of the most bizarre and enlightening experiences you will have in Scotland.

ELGIN AND VICINITY

The smart market town of Elgin, capital of the Moray region, has a lot going for it: most notably Scotland's most splendid ruined cathedral. Scattered in the area around the town are some other hugely impressive architectural sights, but this area is not all about old buildings. Lossiemouth, north of Elgin, has recently hit the headlines as part of entrepreneur Richard Branson's plans to launch space tourism in the United Kingdom. Commercial flights into space could be running from spaceport Lossiemouth by 2010 if all goes to plan. To the west of Elgin is Gordonstoun, Scotland's most famous school, where most of the country's aristocracy, including three generations of British royalty, have gone for their education.

C Elgin Cathedral and Biblical Garden

Dating from the 12th century, the ruins of this cathedral (tel. 01343/547171, 9:30 A.M.–5:30 P.M. daily Apr.–Sept., 9:30 A.M.–4:30 P.M. Sat.–Wed. Oct.–Mar., £4.70 adults, £2.35 children or £6.20 adults, £3.10 children with combined admission to Spynie Palace) lie on a flat plot of grass just north of the town center. Once this grand building was known as the "Lantern of the North" and was Scotland's second-largest

ABERDEEN

© LUKE WATERSON

Elgin Cathedral

cathedral, surpassed in stature only by St. Andrews. It was devastated in the Reformation but the mighty columns of stone and towering walls have retained their magnificence even in the state of ruin. You can still see the outlines of the high circular window in the presbytery and the elaborate ceiling of the chapter house. It really is a stupendous place to explore or even just to stare at, with some medieval carved grave slabs standing in the grounds.

Around the corner from the cathedral is the Biblical Garden (10 A.M.–7 P.M. daily Apr.–Sept.), Scotland's first and foremost bible-themed formal grounds. You'll find all 110 plants mentioned in the bible and sculptures depicting the scriptures.

Spynie Palace

There's little left of the traditional residence of the Bishops of Moray (tel. 01343/546358, 9:30 A.M.–5:30 P.M. daily Apr.–Sept., 9:30 A.M.–4:30 P.M. Sat.–Sun. Oct.–Mar., £3.70 adults, £1.85 children or £6.20 adults, £3.10 children with combined admission to Elgin Cathedral) save for the squat, square bulk of David's Tower.

Although large, it wasn't quite big enough for the Bishops' needs, hence the other ruins scattered around. You can climb up to a walkway midway up the building for good views of the surrounding woods plunging away to the north. The palace is two miles north of Elgin off the A941.

Lossiemouth

With its wide streets of old gray houses and thick sweeps of golden sandy beaches on either side, Lossiemouth (www.lossiemouth.org) is, rather than a major tourist attraction, better known as the RAF base from which Richard Branson's Virgin Galactic company plans to launch space tourism. Crowds flock to its sands in season but the main thing to see here is the **Lossiemouth Fisheries Museum** (Pitgaveny Quay, information at tel. 01343/543221, 10 A.M.–4:45 P.M. Mon.–Sat. Apr.–Sept.) tracing the story of the Scottish fishing industry in these parts. It also features a display on James Ramsay MacDonald, Lossiemouth's most famous son who went on to become Britain's first Labour Prime Minister in 1924. Lossiemouth is north of Elgin, on the A941.

Pluscarden Abbey

Pluscarden (fax 01343/890258, www.plus-cardenabbey.org, 4:30 A.M.–8:30 P.M. daily, free, donations gratefully accepted) is a unique place: It's Scotland's only medieval monastery still inhabited by monks. This gives visiting the beautiful building in the wooded, rolling countryside southwest of Elgin a significantly enhanced appeal. The abbey was founded in 1230 by Alexander II of Scotland, and a look around should include the church with its multicolored stained glass. A visit is most rewarding because you are able to see monks living out their day-to-day lives much as they would have done over 500 years ago. The monks are difficult to contact by telephone but you can just turn up to look around.

Accommodations and Food

The large tree-screened Victorian house of **Auchmillan** (12 Reidhaven St., Elgin, tel. 01343/549077, £50 d) has nine double rooms available. They're simply furnished en suite rooms done up in cooling whites and have 24-hour room service. Rooms differ in size and quality and are priced accordingly. A surcharge for single occupancy of a double room applies.

One of Elgin's more intriguing town houses, with its distinguished-looking turret, **The Lodge Guest House** (20 Duff Ave., Elgin, tel. 01343/549981, www.thelodge-elgin.com, from £32 s, £50 d) is a former tea planter's house set in its own gardens. There are eight en suite rooms here, including four singles. The rooms are smart, immaculate places with a white decor. You'll find a comfy lounge with the kind of armchairs you could sink to a deep sleep in. For breakfast, the specialty is salmon served on English muffins with scrambled eggs.

Kings of Scotland once supped and slept at **Thunderton House** (Thunderton Sq., tel. 01343/554921, www.thundertonhouse.co.uk, 11 A.M.–12:30 A.M. Sat.–Wed., 11 A.M.–1:30 A.M. Thurs.–Sun.), and you can refresh yourself at this history-rich building, too. The modern pine-furnished restaurant serving basic baguettes and other pub grub for £6–10, as well as several ales.

The Ashvale (11–13 Moss St., tel. 01343/552441, noon–9 P.M. daily) is the place in Elgin to eat fish and chips in style—it's part of the mini-chain that began in Aberdeen. Fish ranges £7–10.

Information and Services

Elgin TIC (17 High St., tel. 01343/542666, 10 A.M.–6 P.M. Mon.–Sat., 11 A.M.–4 P.M. Sun. July–Aug., 10 A.M.–5 P.M. Mon.–Sat., 11 A.M.–3 P.M. Sun. Apr.–June and early Sept., 10 A.M.–5 P.M. Mon.–Sat. Mar.–Apr. and mid-Sept.–Oct., 10 A.M.–4 P.M. Mon.–Sat. Jan.–mid-Mar. and Nov.–Dec.) is a compact but extremely helpful information center.

Doctor Gray's Hospital (tel. 01343/543131 or 0845/456 6000) is on the corner of Pluscarden Road and High Street.

Getting There and Away

There are **trains** every 1.5 hours from Aberdeen to Elgin (1.5 hrs., £14.20). Trains continue onward to Inverness. You can also catch a number 10 **bus** to Aberdeen (2.5 hrs.) or Inverness (1.5 hrs.). Elgin has direct bus services to most points in Speyside and on the Moray coast.

FINDHORN AND BURGHEAD BAY

Lying within shifting dunes, and historically at the mercy of violent storms that destroyed the two previous sites of the village, Findhorn is a quiet scattering of houses right on the beach, with a heritage center, a couple of great pubs, and lots of wildfowl and wading birds in its grassy dunes. More famous than the village, however, is the community of spiritually driven people who formed the Findhorn Foundation, just down the road, in the 1960s. These days the eco-friendly spiritual center is a thriving community of businesses, shops, and environmentally designed houses in the woods. You may hear a few stories about how these woods miraculously rose out of the barren sandy soil because of spiritual faith. As long as you can take this kind of mumbo-jumbo with a pinch of salt, a visit to the thought-provoking Foundation is highly enjoyable.

ABERDEEN

Findhorn Foundation

The founders of Findhorn (tel. 01309/690311, www.findhorn.org, visitor center open 10 A.M.–5 P.M. Mon.–Fri., 1–4 P.M. Sat.–Sun. May–Sept., 10 A.M.–5 P.M. Mon.–Fri., 1–4 P.M. Sat. Mar.–Apr. and Oct.–Nov., 10 A.M.–5 P.M. Mon.–Fri. Dec.–Feb.) began the eco-village and spiritual retreat center from a caravan near Findhorn Bay in the 1960s. The fundamental principle of the community has always been cooperation with nature; over the years it has attracted a lot of souls dedicated to the cause, who move here and keep the eco-ball rolling. Against the odds (and the skepticism), it's a remarkable economic success story and an example to the world of how environmentally friendly living can be achieved. Every year the park runs an "experience" week, when visitors can spend time getting to know the ins and outs of the foundation. In fact, tourism is an essential part of Findhorn these days: There's a café, caravan park, and plenty of accommodation offered by residents in their houses in the park. You can wander around the complex yourself; it's like a countrified version of a university campus. You can see intriguingly designed eco-friendly houses and wind turbines, but this place is also about atmosphere—there's an unmistakably spiritual feel. The guided tours (£3) certainly give you a much better insight into how the community operates. These take place on Mondays, Wednesdays, Fridays and Saturdays throughout the year.

Events

The **Burning of the Clavie** (Burghead, east of Findhorn) is a pagan ceremony that involves carrying a cask of burning tar through the village of Burghead and up to a headland. It's held to mark the start of the New Year according to the Julian calendar. If you're in the area on January 11 (January 10 if the 11th falls on a Sunday), don't miss it—it's one of the more bizarre spectacles you'll see. The most entertaining bit is when procession-followers tussle over bits of smoldering wood to burn on their own fires for good luck.

Accommodations and Food

Yellow Sands (Findhorn, tel. 01309/691351, www.yellowsands.com, £27.50 s, £55 d) is a great little hideaway in the woods on the edge of Findhorn. The rooms here are plainly decorated and spacious, but it's the magical feeling of being in a Hansel and Gretel–type cottage you're staying here for. Rooms are en suite, and some bathrooms have baths.

The **Crown and Anchor** (Findhorn, tel. 01309/690243, www.crownandanchorinn.co.uk, £38 s, £64 d) beefs up the center of Findhorn considerably. It's an attractive hostelry sporting seven cozy, en suite rooms with TVs and one of the best bar/restaurants in the area. It's decked out in dark shiny wood and serves wholesome pub grub for around £10, alongside a range of over 100 malt whiskies.

Located in the leafy grounds of the Findhorn Foundation, sunny **Blue Angel Café** (www.blueangelcafe.co.uk, 10 A.M.–5 P.M. daily) serves up a variety of refreshments and light lunches for £2–5. There's no better place around for a mean organic espresso. Signs inside the Findhorn complex will lead you there.

Getting There and Away

From Findhorn, there are hourly connections Monday–Saturday to Forres, Elgin, and Dufftown courtesy of the 336 **bus** service, which has just four services on Sunday.

FORRES

Ablaze with bright formal flower gardens, Forres has been a Royal Burgh for almost 900 years. It's a sedate little town in the extreme northwest of Moray, surrounded by attractive forests brimming with trails for walking and cycling.

Sights

Checking in at over six meters high, **Sueno's Stone** (East Forres, by old Findhorn Rd.) is easily the tallest-standing Pictish carved stone in Scotland. It's in a protected glass case, making it harder to examine the fascinating carvings on the sides. These include a large cross

THE WOLF OF BADENOCH

Even by the barbarous standards of the 14th century, the figure known as the Wolf of Badenoch stood out as an irrationally evil and ruthless man. The Wolf, a.k.a. Alexander Stewart, was the son of King Robert II and ruled over vast portions of lands in the Buchan, Badenoch, and Strathspey area in the north of Aberdeenshire. He was known for his fiery temper, destroying the lands of and imprisoning those who displeased him. He ruled, with help of his army of lawless Highland caterans (brigands), with a violence that alienated him from other landowners, including the Bishop of Moray. After he left his wife, the Countess of Ross, she appealed to the Bishop of Moray, who made the mistake of siding with her, and against the Wolf. The Wolf's retaliation was swift and dramatic. He set out on a spree of destruction, burning the town of Forres and the ecclesiastical base of the Bishopric of Moray, Elgin Cathedral. Townsfolk, including women and children, were driven away from their homes and into the countryside. King Robert, whose own Royal reputation was suffering as a result of his wayward son, ordered his son to do penance for his crimes against the church. The Wolf obliged, was allowed back into the church, and continued to profit through the misfortune of others.

For all his territorial gains, the Wolf was to lose his position of power just as quickly. His lack of inclination or inability to control his Highland brigands was seen as a sign of ineffectiveness, and when Robert III ascended the throne, he took steps to take lands and influence from the Wolf. For such a violent figure, it is perhaps surprising that the Wolf ended his days in relative obscurity. This allowed tales to circulate as to the eventual nature of his demise. The best hypothesis was that he was visited at his home of Ruthven Castle in 1405 by a tall, thin man dressed in black, who challenged the Wolf to a game of chess. The stranger won, at which point a turbulent storm blew up. When the storm subsided, the Wolf and all his men were found hanging dead from various places along the outside walls of the castle. The Wolf was not buried locally, but at Dunkeld Cathedral in Perthshire instead.

on one side and depictions of death in many gruesome forms on the other. It's signposted from the main road into Forres from the east (the B9011).

Dallas Dhu Distillery (south of Forres, tel. 01309/676548, 9:30 A.M.–5:30 P.M. daily Apr.–Sept., 9:30 A.M.–4:30 P.M. Sat.–Wed. Oct.–Mar.) is a distillery with a difference: It no longer produces whisky but has been preserved as a monument to the time-honored whisky-making process. This means visitors can get that much closer to understanding how whisky was made here. The tour has no intensely malty smell, no toiling workmen, and no noise, but you can see the old malting floor and peer into the cavernous wash backs. Dallas Dhu ceased production in 1983, but the tour still includes a dram (it's a blend, however). The distillery is a couple of miles of south of Forres, off the A940. It's signposted from the roundabout at the end of Bridge Street.

Part of the verdant Logie Estate, **Logie Steading** (tel. 01309/611378, www.logie.co.uk, 10 A.M.–5 P.M. daily Mar.–Dec.) is a visitors center forming the focal point of the forest that flanks the valley of the Findhorn River. It's a countrified development with a café, saddlemaker, secondhand bookshop, and guided walks. You can use the Steading as a base for the warren of paths, tracks, trails, and lanes that wind through the forest and alongside the Findhorn River. One path leads to **Randolph's Leap,** a delightful rocky river gorge. Logie is six miles southwest of Forres on the A940.

Accommodations

There's nothing quite like staying in a converted old church, and **◀ The Old Kirk** (Dyke, tel. 01309/641414, www.oldkirk.co.uk, £39 s,

ABERDEEN

© LUKE WATERSON

Cullen, home of Cullen Skink

£58 d) comes complete with some of the original stained-glass windows. The church was built in the 1850s, and the conversion retained lots of the old features, including bare stone walls in the upstairs rooms. All three rooms are en suite, with a lot more light and warmth than in your average 19th-century church. The little village of Dyke is just west of Forres, signposted off the A96.

Getting There and Away

To get to Forres from Aberdeen take a **train** (every 1.5 hours, 1 hr. 50 min.) or **bus** number 10 (hourly, 2 hrs. 50 min.), both of which stop at Elgin first and continue to Inverness afterward.

CULLEN AND VICINITY

The pleasant, low-key resort of Cullen, sloping steeply down a hill into the sea, has its name on almost every restaurant menu in Scotland, courtesy of the creamy fish, potato, and onion broth known as Cullen Skink, which has its origins here. Cullen is bisected by an impressive railway viaduct, which photogenically frames the lower part of town known as Seatown. Seatown is a collection of prettily painted 19th-century fishermen's cottages fanning around a broad sandy beach. Cullen has a couple of culinary claims to fame: In addition to a few places where you can sample Cullen Skink, it also has one of Scotland's best ice-cream parlors. Geologists love Cullen, too; near the town the coast erupts into some interesting rock formations.

Sights

Wandering through **Seatown** is a rewarding experience: it's the most complete collection of purpose-built fishermen's cottages in Scotland.

The remains of Robert the Bruce's second wife, Elizabeth de Burgh, are buried at **Cullen Auld Kirk** (open year-round), one of the few examples of a pre-reformation church in Scotland. The building is next to Cullen House approximately half a mile southwest of town.

Cullen's best **walk** is along the coast west from Cullen to Portknockie to some impressive rock formations. Start at the golf club car park by the beach and follow the shore-hugging path

ABERDEEN

© LUKE WATERSON

© PHOTO CREDIT

Cullen's Seatown, a historic fishing harbor

along to the **Whale's Mouth** rock arch and, more famously, the **Bow and Fiddle Rock,** another rock arch at angles to the sea. Allow two hours there and back from Cullen.

Accommodations and Food

Cullen has some good places for ice cream (try the shop by the viaduct on Seafield Street).

The traditional old **Seafield Arms Hotel** (17–19 Seafield St., tel. 01540/840791, www.theseafieldarms.co.uk, £55 s, £85 d) on the approach to the coast is a great journey-breaker. Rooms are a medley of traditional tartan furnishings and lighter, more modern color schemes. All are en suite. Some of the bathrooms really are a monument to a bygone age of glam sanitation, with dark green tiles and huge baths. Even if you don't fancy staying here, it's worth popping into the old-fashioned restaurant to try that local delicacy, Cullen Skink.

Getting There and Away

Hourly **buses** connect Cullen with Elgin (1 hr.) and Macduff (35 min.). These buses also continue to Aberdeen (2.5 hrs.).

Northeast Fishing Ports

In the past, fishermen along this stretch of coast must have been desperate for a place to harbor; they risked the likelihood of landslides and devastating storms when they built their villages along Aberdeenshire's northeast shores. As a result, communities have grown up tumbling down steep hillsides and perched precariously at the base of cliffs, so close to the sea as to be almost falling in. The landslides and storms came, sure enough, and all but devastated villages like Portsoy and Pennan, and yet somehow these age-old ports have stubbornly survived and remain idyllic spots to kick back in. In a flurry of wide sandy bays, whitewashed cottages, grassy cliffs, and the odd stately home, this coast wends its way east to the huge modern harbor of Peterhead. Here, fishing is more than a matter of photogenic bobbing boats. These ports land much of Scotland's commercial fish catch and keep the kitchens of Scotland's finest fish restaurants well stocked.

PORTSOY

This 17th-century harbor village has been associated with its fair share of great names in the history books: it was granted burgh status by Mary, Queen of Scots, and the marble quarried nearby was used to build Louis XIV's palace at Versailles. It's a dreamy, irresistible little place, full of narrow, twisting streets and traditional pubs. There's also a safe, sandy swimming beach.

Shopping and Events

Portsoy Marble Shop (10 A.M.–5 P.M. Mon.–Sat.) is a charming shop on the harbor selling the famous red-green Portsoy marble in all its rough, polished, and hybrid forms.

Held in June each year, **Portsoy Traditional Boat Festival** (www.sbf.bizland.com) is an extravaganza of parading traditional boats and vessels that compete in a number of shows and races. The people of Portsoy also put on displays of music, a food fair, and a road race.

Accommodations and Food

The **Portsoy Caravan Park** (The Links, tel. 01261/842695, www.aberdeenshire.gov.uk, two-person tent £7.10) occupies a grassy site fanning around a sandy bay right by Portsoy. There are 19 pitches for tents and limited facilities including hot showers free of charge.

Harbour View House (Schoolhendry St., tel. 01261/843556, www.harbourviewhouse.co.uk, from £65 d) has three richly decorated rooms to let, all done up in bold festive colors. The 1880s stone building looks down on Portsoy harbor, and all rooms have sea views. Rooms are en suite, with color TVs. There's a lounge for guests.

Full of dark polished wood and nautical artifacts, the blue-and-white decked out **Shore Inn** (Old Harbour, tel. 01261/842831, food served noon–2 P.M. and 6–9 P.M.) is one of the most charming pubs in Scotland both inside and out. It's a snug former wine merchant's house, serving real ales along with good surf and turf (seafood and game) for £7–10.

Getting There and Away

Bus 305 runs hourly from Aberdeen to Portsoy via Macduff; many services continue to Inverness.

BANFF AND VICINITY

Banff and Macduff, twin towns separated by the Deveron River, are the main settlements on the northeast coast. With a long stretch of golden sand and a history spanning almost a millennium, Banff is by far the better of the two towns to visit. Even so, there's an austere feel about the place; fortunately, this can be eased by a wander around the finest mansion in these parts, Duff House. East of Macduff are the cliff-foot villages of Gardenstown and Crovie, full of narrow streets, old fishing cottages, and bags of 18th century maritime charm.

Sights

The square, imposing-looking mansion that is **Duff House and Gallery** (Banff, tel. 01261/818181, www.duffhouse.com, 11 A.M.–5 P.M. daily Apr.–Sept., 11 A.M.–4 P.M. daily Oct.–Mar., £6.20 adults, £16.70 family) was designed in the early 18th century by William Adam. It's a treasure trove of important paintings and furnishings, including works by English artist Thomas Gainsborough and Scottish artist Sir Henry Raeburn, as well as Chippendale furniture. You'll need a couple of hours to take in all the grandeur, especially since Duff House encompasses an exhibition of contemporary art by various rotating artists and a tearoom. The entrance to Duff House is by the large car park on the main road into Banff from Macduff.

Gardenstown and **Crovie** are two villages of charismatic old-world fishermen's cottages, eking out a remarkable existence on the narrow strip of land between the foot of the steep grassy north coast cliffs and the sea. Space is so limited in Crovie that it is one of the few villages in the Western world not to have a driveable road running through it (just a footpath). Both villages are great places for a wander and picnic.

Accommodations and Food

The glorious swath of sandy beach on which **Banff Links Caravan Site** (Banff Links, tel. 01261/812228, www.aberdeenshire.gov.uk/caravanparks, two-person tent £7.10) sits is the jewel in the crown of Banff and has quite a separate feel from the rest of the town. You'll find ample space to pitch a tent, a shop, and lots of hot water for showers.

Decorated in a mix of rich reds, blues, and whites, the rooms at **Fife Lodge Hotel** (Sandyhill Rd., Banff, tel. 01261/812436, www.fifelodgehotel.com, £75 s, £85 d) are vast—many could accommodate whole families. Rooms all have top-notch hotel facilities, including en suite bathrooms, and gaze out over the private grounds toward distant undulating fields. The menu here includes good, solid Scottish food as well as fancier options; main meals are £7–17.

The elegant French restaurant of the early-19th-century **County Hotel** (32 High St., Banff, tel. 01261/815353, www.thecountyhotel.com,

5:30–9 P.M. daily) offers convivial dining with plenty of polished wood and chandeliers. The a la carte menu is £8–16, or you can opt for the three-course "menu gourmand" for £25, with specialties like duck confit or pork with prunes. There are armchairs to round off the meal with a malt whisky. Reservations are essential.

PENNAN

The pearl-white village of Pennan, huddled in a long line of cottages beneath steep, grassy cliffs, was relatively untouched by tourism until 1983, when it became the film set for *Local Hero,* starring Burt Lancaster. Pennan's red telephone box was catapulted into everlasting stardom as a result of the movie, devotees of which still flock to have their picture taken here. Sadly, the Pennan Inn that featured in the film is closed. It's a village for soaking up the atmosphere rather than sightseeing, although east around Pennan Head is a decent sandy beach, Aberdour Bay.

Accommodations

These days, (**Driftwood Bed and Breakfast** (tel. 01346/561287, www.driftwoodpennan.com, £50 d) is the only place to stay in the village, which makes the experience even more magical; there's just one room available with a four-poster bed and en suite spa bath. What with all the creaking wood and picture-perfect coastal views here, you'd be forgiven for thinking you had actually set out to sea when you wake up next morning. When the self-catering cottage isn't in use, there is additional room for bed-and-breakfast guests.

Getting There and Away

Bus 473 makes one call daily en route between Gardenstown and Fraserburgh at the (defunct) Pennan Hotel. Bus 273 stops off twice on Saturday between Fraserburgh and Macduff.

FRASERBURGH AND PETERHEAD

For over a century, these two towns were among Europe's leading fishing ports, seeing booms in whaling and herring during

ABERDEEN

the 19th century. By the 1980s it was white-fish: More than 120,000 tons were landed at Peterhead annually, serving a thriving fish market some 400 meters long. EU quotas have since instigated a decline in the fishing industry, and these two dour places have suffered as a result. There's precious little reason to stop in either port unless you're visiting the excellent Museum of Scottish Lighthouses in Fraserburgh. However, the two towns are linked by a long, lovely stretch of golden sand, and the coast in this far northeastern corner of Aberdeenshire contains a couple of interesting sights.

Sights

Fraserburgh was the site of the first lighthouse built by the Northern Lighthouse Board on the Scottish mainland in 1787. It's with this in mind that the fascinating **Museum of Scottish Lighthouses** (Kinnaird Head, tel. 01346/511022, www.lighthousemuseum.org.uk, 10 A.M.–4 P.M. Mon.–Sat., noon–5 P.M. Sun. July–Aug., 11 A.M.–5 P.M. Mon.–Sat., noon–5 P.M. Sun. Apr.–June and Sept.–Oct., 11 A.M.–4 P.M. Mon.–Sat., noon–4 P.M. Sun. Jan.–Mar. and Nov.–Dec., £5 adults, £2 children) was set up here. It's a wealth of lighthouse-related artifacts, many donated by the Lighthouse Board. You can climb inside the original lighthouse for spectacular views both south and west along the Aberdeenshire coast. In the revamped former lighthouse keeper's cottages, there are displays on the colorful characters who used to operate the lights prior to lighthouses becoming automated. You can also learn about the family of author Robert Louis Stevenson and the part they played in establishing Scotland's lighthouses. In the garden outside is a collection of lighthouse bouys and lights. There's a café and a shop at the museum, which also acts as a regional TIC.

South of Fraserburgh, the small seaside village of **St. Combs** is little more than an access point to some of the longest sand dunes and sandy stretches of beach in Scotland, extending over 10 miles south to Peterhead.

The gaunt, lonely ruins of **Slains Castle** (open year-round) that stand above the cliffs east of Cruden Bay were the inspiration for Bram Stoker's *Dracula*. With the wind whistling through the crumbling walls and the seagulls wheeling overhead, images of the Gothic are easily evoked here. There are no signposts marking the way to the castle; to get there, follow the bay around on foot or access from a small car park at a kink in the A975 north of Cruden Bay.

Shopping

Located at Peterhead's harbor entrance opposite Albert Quay, **Peterhead Fish Market** (from 7 A.M. Mon.–Sat.) is one of Britain's premier fish markets.

Getting There and Away

Stagecoach Bluebird bus services 260 and 263 run to Peterhead from Aberdeen (half-hourly Mon.–Sat., hourly Sun., 1 hr. 20 min.) with a call at Cruden Bay (for Slains Castle). Service 267 runs to Fraserburgh from Aberdeen (half-hourly Mon.–Fri., hourly Sat.–Sun., 1 hr. 25 min.).

To get from Fraserburgh to Peterhead, take a number 269 bus (hourly Mon.–Sat., several times daily Sun., 35 min.), which will stop at St. Combs and close to many other points from which you can access that nice long sandy beach.

Royal Deeside and the Grampians

Ever since Queen Victoria and Prince Albert purchased the Balmoral estate in the 1840s and began the trend of the Royal Family taking their annual holidays there, Deeside has been at the top of travel itineraries. Visitors swarm up this forested valley in summer to see Balmoral, the castle and grounds where monarchs retreat for their own piece of paradise. As a result, this is one of the most popular tourist destinations in Scotland, and rightly so. The wide, gently flowing River Dee with noble, steeply shelving pine forests soaring up on either side into the mountains is a majestic setting fit for queens (and kings). It's one of those valleys that gets more gorgeous the higher up you go. The handsome main settlements of Ballater and Braemar are well used to coping with visitors and abound in quality restaurants and hotels. Off the main tourist trail, the tranquil south side of the Dee and the Grampian Mountains that stretch beyond Ballater have Aberdeenshire's best walking. There are routes to suit all abilities, from riverside rambles to tough multi-day hill hikes.

BANCHORY AND VICINITY

This small town of smart gray houses full of flourishing turrets and gables is the self-proclaimed gateway to Royal Deeside. It suffers from the same problem that other "gateways" to beautiful parts of Scotland do, namely that there is no reason to stop in a gateway. Being this far down Deeside with a wide main road cutting right through it gives Banchory a slightly sterile feel but there's one very good reason to come here: the glorious Crathes Castle, situated on the outside of town.

Sights

Robert the Bruce was generous to the Burnett family: Not only did he grant them the estate at **Crathes Castle** (tel. 0844/943 2166, 10:30 A.M.–5:30 P.M. daily Easter–Sept., 10:30 A.M.–4:30 P.M. daily Oct., 10:30 A.M.–3:45 P.M. Wed.–Sun. Nov.–Mar., £10 adults, £25 family) in 1323, but he even presented them with an ancient horn as a token of appreciation for their support during the Wars of Independence. When Crathes was built on the estate in the 16th century, the symbol of the horn appeared on everything. It's even carved into the Laird's bed. Crathes is a fascinating castle of soaring turrets and parapets. Despite managing to avoid conflicts throughout the centuries, the Burnetts clearly feared attack; check the trick step on the staircase designed to hinder attackers. As impressive as the castle is the series of eight walled gardens, featuring immense yew tree hedges. New for 2008 will be Skytrek: an adventure course through the canopy of trees in the grounds. The castle is just to the east of Banchory, off the A93.

Drum Castle (Mains of Drum, tel. 0844/493 2161, castle open 11 A.M.–5 P.M. daily July–Aug., 12:30–5 P.M. Mon., Wed.–Thurs., and Sat.–Sun. Apr.–June and Sept.–Oct., garden open noon–6 P.M. daily Apr.–Oct., £8 adults, £5 seniors) is one of Aberdeenshire's more sumptuous castles, occupied by the Irvine family for over 600 years until 1975. The castle is of the early 14th century, but the medieval tower house has been extended into a veritable complex by the later additions of a Jacobean mansion house and several improvements during Victorian times. There's also a tranquil garden full of roses from as far afield as Japan. The castle is off the A93 east of Banchory.

Food

A mile south of Banchory, the stone-built cottage of **Falls of Feugh Restaurant and Tearoom** (Bridge of Feugh, tel. 01330/822123, www.thefallsoffeugh.com, 10 A.M.–5 P.M. daily) sits right on the riverbank. You couldn't ask for a more peaceful place to have breakfast, lunch, or afternoon tea. The menu is innovative, with plenty of twists on common dishes. You could go for a plate of oatcakes with cheese, celery, and apple or salmon with a crusty peppercorn topping. You can take afternoon tea on the tables overlooking the river.

© LUKE WATERSON

Craigievar Castle, by Aboyne

ABOYNE AND VICINITY

As you work your way upriver through Deeside, the communities get prettier and the conifer-clad hills close in around you. Aboyne is a large, sedate village with a couple of great historic sights in the area, including one of Aberdeenshire's finest castles. It's a refreshing alternative base to touristy Ballater.

Sights

Tomnavurie Stone Circle (Tarland, open year-round) is a scattering of gray, mostly recumbent stones on an exposed green hillside above Aboyne. It's a poignant spot to contemplate the surrounding views. The circle was probably constructed around 1800 B.C. The site is a 200-meter walk off the B9044, south of the village of Tarland and north of Aboyne.

Castles in Scotland don't come more picture-perfect than the fortress-lovers' fantasy of 17th-century **Craigievar Castle** (tel. 0844/493 2174, www.nts.org.uk, noon–5:30 P.M. Fri.–Tues., castle closed until 2009, grounds open year-round, £10). With its rounded pink-brown walls swooping up into turrets and parapets above grounds peppered by monkey-puzzle trees and rhododendrons, it's a real architectural feast. Unfortunately, the castle was closed during 2008 for essential conservation work but is due to reopen in summer 2009. With the exception of a couple of portraits by Sir Henry Raeburn, though, visitors will not really be missing out. Delightful as the inside is with its twisting rooms and stairways, it's enough to just be in the vicinity of the castle. Its quirkiness is best appreciated from the grounds outside, which remain open throughout the year.

Accommodations

Struan Hall (Ballater Rd., Aboyne, tel. 01339/887241, www.struanhall.co.uk, £39.50 s, £69 d) is set in two tranquil acres of woods and grounds just outside of Aboyne. There are four sparkling white rooms, all with en suite or private bathrooms and color TVs. Breakfast is a departure from the norm here, with goodies like banana sandwiches and cinnamon-flavored French toast as well as the

A ROYAL HIGHLAND PARADISE

Queen Victoria and Prince Albert first visited the Scottish Highlands in 1842, just two years after their marriage. The Queen, who kept a scrupulous journal of her forays into Scotland, described the place as "lovely, grand and romantic" and spoke of how the "great peace and wildness pervades all, which is sublime." Being so taken with the region, Victoria and Albert returned two years later and spent a lot of their time sheltering from the persistent rain in a shooting hut. Here they learned of the lands at Balmoral, and over the drab days the idea of having a permanent base in the place they both loved became increasingly attractive to the Royal couple. They leased Balmoral for the first time in 1848, at which point they had not even seen the estate. This was some undertaking, for they were committing, in effect, to developing and patronizing the grounds for the rest of their lives. In 1852 they concluded the purchase of the estate.

Prince Albert was instrumental in planning how the new castle would look, and building was completed in 1856, by which point Queen Victoria was in love with the estate. She especially liked how Prince Albert's influence was apparent everywhere in the laying out of the estates. The Queen continued to visit Balmoral after Albert's death in 1861 and erected a monument to her husband. A tradition was established with the Queen of associating with the locals and patronizing the nearby Highland Games, the Braemar Gathering. There was one particular local she took a shine to: locally born John Brown, who served the Queen loyally but made disparaging remarks about other members of the Royal Family. The relationship between monarch and servant is explored in the film *Mrs. Brown*.

By the late 1860s, the railway had reached Ballater and Deeside was officially a Royal tourism destination. Train connections not only made it easier for the Queen to reach her castle but also for the general public to visit. There were plans drawn up to have the railway line extended, but Queen Victoria refused; she did not want the line passing Balmoral, which would have been a noisy inconvenience.

By the time of her death in 1901, a Royal legacy of spending leisure time at Balmoral had been established. Queen Victoria's grandson, King George V, said "I am never so happy as when I am fishing at the pools of the Dee, with a long day before me." An affection for the Deeside area was inherited by later members of the Royal family. Queen Elizabeth II and Prince Phillip, the Duke of Edinburgh, are as in love with the place as any previous Royal couple. This has been evidenced by the Duke taking on several ambitious gardening projects to enhance the overall appearance of Balmoral.

more conventional options. The minimum stay is two nights.

BALLATER AND BALMORAL

The old railway through Royal Deeside ended at Ballater; the legacy of the village being the jumping off point for visiting Balmoral, the Royal family's summer residence, has lasted ever since. The railway became redundant in the 1960s but by then Ballater was, and is, firmly engrained in people's minds as a hot spot of Royal tourism. Ballater cunningly plays up to its large influx of visitors, providing plenty of accommodation and well-to-do restaurants. This manages to mask the fact that

there's actually precious little to do in the village itself. There are, however, great walks in the forested hills around. Royal Family enthusiasts are well catered for: You can see the station where Queen Victoria once alighted and then head to Balmoral, the castle she and subsequent monarchs have holidayed in over the last century.

Sights

The main attraction in Ballater itself is the slightly kitschy **Old Royal Station Visitor Centre** (Station Sq., tel. 01339/755306, 9 a.m.–6 p.m. daily July–Aug., 9 a.m.–5 p.m. daily Sept.–June, free), now a bustling, converted café/shop/museum complex. However commercialized the station might now seem, Ballater owes its development to the railway from Aberdeen constructed here during the 1860s. It provided an important link for royalty en route to Balmoral Castle and for commoners wanting to get a taste of the lands the Royals holidayed in. You can see a number of costumed Victorian models on the platform and even the lavatory on which Queen Victoria once placed her royal posterior. There's barely room to move for all the tourists, but, importantly, the station does contain the TIC for Ballater and has a good restaurant open throughout the day.

Located just outside of Ballater off the Tomintoul road, the **McEwan Gallery** (tel. 01339/755429, 11 A.M.–5 P.M. Tues.–Sat., 2–5 P.M. Sun.) holds a fascinating collection of 18th-, 19th-, and 20th-century paintings, mostly watercolors by British artists. Most works are for sale.

At Crathie, by the entrance to Balmoral, is **Crathie Kirk** (9:30 A.M.–5 P.M. Easter–Oct.),

Crathie Kirk, near Balmoral, the Royal Family's place of worship when on holiday

the church used by the Royal Family to worship. Queen Victoria laid the foundation stone in 1893. Royals have their own special entrance at the south transept. Sunday service is at 11:30 A.M.

After all the gradually built-up hype as you approach **Balmoral** (Crathie, tel. 01339/742534, www.balmoralcastle.com, 10 A.M.–5 P.M. Mar.–July, £7 adults, £6 seniors, £3 children) through Deeside, many people find the Queen's summer residence itself a bit of a disappointment, due to the little you can actually see and to the fact that you have to share the most interesting parts of the grounds with several hundred others. Massive tour parties cram into the grounds during their limited annual opening hours and make even the most tranquil part of the formal gardens about as soothing as the subway at rush hour. There's also only a small portion of the castle open to the public. This includes the ballroom and the carriage hall, in which you'll find a series of carts engaged on a variety of Royal errands and outings. You'll see a few paintings of various Royals and a tartan designed by Prince Albert (modeled by a bagpiper). The rest of the castle is the Queen's private living quarters. The grounds do have several interesting monuments marking various points in the history of the Royal Family at Balmoral. Most moving, perhaps, is the granite obelisk raised in memory of Prince Albert by Queen Victoria. If you go to Balmoral, as thousands do despite the crowd warnings, about the best impression you can take away is that it would be beautiful if it weren't for all the people. It's no wonder the Queen wants to get rid of them all and closes the grounds for her own holiday in August. What a lucky lady she is.

Sports and Recreation
Cycle Highlands (The Pavillion, Victoria Rd., tel. 01339/755864, www.cyclehighlands.com) have plenty of bikes for hire from £15 adults, £7 children.

Shopping
The **Chocolate Gallery** (8 Bridge St., tel. 01339/755388, www.chocolategallery.co.uk,

10 A.M.–5 P.M. Mon.–Sat.) is an award-winning combination: a shop that enticingly shows off a huge range of chocolate products and a coffee bar where lots of the chocolates you've been trying to avoid appear on the menu.

Accommodations and Food

Netherley Guest House (2 Netherley Pl., tel. 01339/755792, from £35 s, £50 d) is a gorgeous white-and-blue cottage right in the center of Ballater. The rooms are neat, boldly decorated affairs in greens, whites, and yellows. All are furnished with sparkling, tiled, en suite bathrooms. It's a good place to stay for outdoor enthusiasts, with a drying room and free mountain bike use for guests (on a first-come, first-served basis).

Characterful **◖ School House** (Anderson Rd., tel. 01339/756333, www.school-house.eu, from £24 dorm bed, £47 s, £75 d) is a Victorian property with a great mix of accommodations in airy, light rooms with wood furnishings. There are rooms for one to six people available, with each room getting an en suite bathroom. Most rooms get great views of the surrounding hills. There's a lounge with large comfy sofas and an open fire to relax by in the evenings. The owner is a professional storyteller, and he's happy to oblige guests with a performance for a small fee. The School House also offers evening meals for £7.50–12.50.

A former church, **Auld Kirk** (Braemar Rd., tel. 01339/755762, www.auldkirk.com, £57.50 s, £85 d) with its elegant spire has six well-appointed, decent-sized rooms done up in a mix of contemporary styles. Some rooms have the old church windows as lookout points. You'll find the equivalent facilities of a small, smart hotel here, including en suite bathrooms, color TV, and telephones in all rooms. Downstairs is a popular, well-to-do restaurant hung with chandeliers. Evening meals cost £30 for three courses. You can try rabbit soaked in Scottish ale, finished off with a whisky at the bar (complete with its own baptism font).

The attractive gray stone **Green Inn Restaurant with Rooms** (9 Victoria Rd., tel. 01339/755701, www.green-inn.com, £70

d, food served 7–9 P.M.) with its pretty green decking is an eye-catcher in the trim streets of Ballater. The light, white rooms here are all en suite; some come with king-size beds. This is one of the more exclusive eateries in Ballater: a favorite dish is the partridge from a local estate, served with foie gras, wild mushroom sausage, and caramelized apple. It costs £31.50 for a starter and two courses.

Inver Hotel (Crathie, tel. 01339/742345, www.inverhotel.com, from £80 d), an 18th-century coaching inn, has been around longer than the castle most of its guests stay here to see. It sits on the doorstep not only of Balmoral but also of a great salmon fishing river. Rooms are uncomplicated, white affairs with plenty of dark antique furniture, TVs, and en suite facilities. The bar is furnished with tartan, burnished leather sofas, open fires, and lots of varieties of whisky. Coming from Ballater, it's a couple of miles past Crathie on the main road.

You can't help but be charmed by **◖ La Mangiatoia** (Bridge Sq., tel. 01339/755999, 5–10 P.M. Mon.–Fri., noon–10:30 P.M. Sat.–Sun.), an Italian restaurant housed in converted stables and serving pizza out of a wood-fired oven. Other delights on the menu include sizzling steaks and grilled chicken. Main courses are £6–12.

Information

Ballater TIC (tel. 01339/755306, 9 A.M.–6 P.M. daily July–Aug., 9 A.M.–5 P.M. daily Sept.–June) is part of the Old Royal station complex.

Getting There and Away

Buses 201, 202, and 203 run about hourly Monday–Saturday to Ballater from Aberdeen, with a few Sunday services. They'll also stop off at Crathie (for Balmoral) en route to Braemar. In summer, you can also jump aboard one of two **Heather Hopper services.** One runs along the A93 to Braemar and on to Perth (daily July–mid-Aug.) and one runs north up the A939 to Tomintoul and on to Grantown on Spey in the Southern Highlands daily May–September.

BRAEMAR

By the time you get as far upriver as the remote parish of Braemar, the noble forests that flank the River Dee lower down are dropping away and the Grampian massif is rearing its bare, craggy bulk. The A93, on which Braemar sits, is not a dead-end road—you can continue south from here into Perthshire—but in winter it might as well be. Bad weather and accidents make this one of the first roads to close in Scotland at this time. Braemar itself is a small, attractive, tourist-packed village best known for its Highland Gathering, patronized by the Royal Family. The numbers of people passing through make it easy forget that Braemar has only limited facilities: a petrol station, chemist, bank with ATM, and combined supermarket/post office.

Sights and Tours

The main pleasures of Braemar are most certainly scenic. Pick up a booklet entitled *Short Walks and Cycles Around Braemar* for an idea of the best short to medium-length hikes around. The best viewpoint in the vicinity is from **Morrone Hill**, a three-hour hike from the village. Follow the road via the duck pond to the south of the village, from where a path up forks off.

The average visitor to Braemar may have a great time at the Gathering or enjoy gazing at the views from a café or hotel window. Many, however, will get that wistful look in their eyes as they imagine what it will be like to be actually in amongst the hills rather than seeing them from below. That's where **Braemar Highland Safaris** (tel. 01339/741420, www.braemarhighlandsafaris.co.uk) comes in—operators will take you up in a 4x4 vehicle on some high mountain tracks to get a taste of the more rugged scenery, without you even breaking a sweat. A two-hour drive costs £20 per person; longer drives can be arranged.

Events

Held on the first Saturday in September, **Braemar Gathering** (www.braemargathering.org, tickets £14) is the king among Highland gatherings. The main reason is that it is patronized by the Royal Family and has been since the days of Queen Victoria. Any number of Royals can be found in attendance, so the urge for burly Highland men to strive to play the pipes harder, throw heavy objects farther, and run up hills the faster is all the more intense. The mountains provide a glorious backdrop. The only downer is the crowds; accommodations get booked up here months in advance. For anyone who is not a hardcore Highland Games addict, the Gathering is a cue *not* to be in Braemar during the events.

Sports and Recreation

Glenshee Ski Centre (tel. 01339/741320, www.ski-glenshee.co.uk), one of Scotland's key ski destinations, sits a 10-minute drive south of Braemar on the Perthshire border (see *Skiing* under *Glenshee* in the *Highland Perthshire* section of the *Perthshire* chapter for details).

Accommodations

The **Invercauld Caravan and Camping Site** (Glenshee Rd., tel. 01339/741373, Dec.–Oct., tents £5.50 pp) sits on the edge of Braemar village. It's got toilets, showers, laundry, and bags of room. It's also one of the few campsites in Scotland to be open in the middle of winter.

The **Braemar Youth Hostel** (21 Glenshee Rd., tel. 01339/741659, www.syha.org.uk, beds £14–16) is a spacious former Victorian shooting lodge, an attractive property set back from the road in its own grounds. It offers accommodation in mostly four- and five-bed dorm rooms and has a kitchen and large lounge with a pool table.

A Victorian manse with period furniture set in its own pocket of lush, secluded grounds, looking out over the distant mountains . . . there couldn't be a better introduction to Royal Deeside than **Clunie Lodge Guest House** (Cluniebank Rd., tel. 01339/741330, www.clunielodge.com, £52 d). The rooms are spacious, sunny affairs with en suite showers/bathrooms. There's a lounge full of board games and one of the most convivially rustic breakfast rooms around. You can soak up the tranquility with a wander around the grounds.

Callater Lodge (9 Glenshee Rd., tel. 01339/741275, www.callaterlodge.co.uk, £35 s, £66 d) is a granite, mid-19th-century mansion with six bedrooms done up in soothing colors like pink, mauve, and purple. It's a serene place to spend a night or two: Rooms are warm and decently sized. Some rooms benefit from views of the mountains and en suite baths. Variations on the breakfast theme are potato scones, cold meats, cheeses, and croissants. If you're peckish after you check in, the lodge offers an array of wholesome snacks to tide you over until dinnertime.

A large gray-stone former shooting lodge, **Braemar Lodge** (Glenshee Rd., tel. 01339/741627, www.braemarlodge.co.uk, bunkhouse beds £11, lodge rooms £60 s, £120 d) offers rooms in three forms. In the lodge itself are neat, simple rooms exuding rustic coziness and a smattering of dark wood; all have TVs and en suite bathrooms. Then there is the bunkhouse with 12 sturdy beds, decent storage facilities, and a kitchen in pine-paneled surrounds. Lastly, there are the log cabins, well-appointed self-catering options. The lodge has a lounge with a roaring fire and rather too many stag heads leaning off the walls.

Food

The bright, modern café at **Taste . . .** (Airlie House, tel. 01339/741425, www.taste-braemar.co.uk, 10 A.M.–5 P.M. Sun.–Thurs., 10 A.M.–5 P.M. and 6:30–8:30 P.M. Fri.–Sat., reduced winter hours) is a welcome addition to the local dining scene, especially if you like wonderful homemade soups, sandwiches, and wickedly strong coffee. It's spacious inside and more geared toward daytime munching than evening dining, but this versatile eatery offers both options anyway. The evening menu is limited. Lunchtime snacks are £2.50–7 and dinner is £9–10.

The Gathering Place Bistro (Invercauld Rd., tel. 01339/741234, www.gathering-place.co.uk, 12:30–2:30 P.M. and 6–9 P.M. Wed.–Sat., 6–9 P.M. Tues. and Sun. summer,

6:30–8:30 P.M. Thurs.–Sun. winter) is an intimate little restaurant set back from the main road on the approach to Braemar. It has an equally small and enticing menu: Gourmet main dishes (£12–17) are largely meat- or fish-based.

Information and Services

Braemar TIC (The Mews, tel. 01339/741600, 9 A.M.–6 P.M. daily Aug., 9 A.M.–5 P.M. daily June–July and Sept.–Oct., 10:30 A.M.–1 P.M. and 2–5 P.M. Mon.–Sat., 1–4 P.M. Sun. Jan.–May and Nov.–Dec.) has plenty of information on walks in the area. Next door is a heritage center and shop with approximately the same year-round opening hours showing a film about the Braemar area. It's all set around a pretty courtyard.

Braemar Police and Mountain Rescue (Balnellan Rd., tel. 0845/600 5700) will deal with all urgent mountain rescue inquiries.

A useful convenience store is **Alldays Store/Post Office** (Mar Rd., tel. 01339/741201).

Getting There and Away

There are two ways to get to and from Braemar by public transport, of which only one is a year-round option. About eight **buses** daily Monday–Saturday and three buses Sunday leave Aberdeen going right through Deeside to Braemar (2.25 hrs.). In summer it's also possible to traverse the wild A93 south to Perth. The **Heather Hopper service** runs via the Spittal of Glenshee once daily from July to mid-August.

THE GRAMPIAN MOUNTAINS

This long, wild range of mountains runs southwest to northeast between the Great Glen and the Highland Boundary Fault, effectively separating the Highlands of Scotland from the rest of the country. The range includes Scotland's highest peak, Ben Nevis, at the western end. Confusingly, it's large enough to be referred to by different names in different parts, including the Cairngorm Mountains. It's the eastern part of the range that's contained within Aberdeenshire. From Tomintoul, at the

ABERDEEN

northeastern end of the Grampians, you could walk southwest into the peaks and not pass another human being, road, or house for several days. Even to the seasoned mountaineer, this series of soaring granite peaks on which snow rarely melts is a wilderness as formidable as it is photogenic. Braemar in the south and Tomintoul on the northeastern edge, where the land slides away into the whisky-producing region of Speyside, are the main access points. If you need advice or guidance on mountain-walking, the two main information centers are in Braemar in Royal Deeside and Tomintoul in Speyside.

Walks

There are hundreds of trails through the Grampians, of which only a fraction can be detailed here. It's recommended you pick up a walking guide in one of Aberdeenshire's TICs, as well as a detailed map of the area. Good maps include Pathfinder series *Cairngorm Walks,* published by Jarrold Publishing, which covers most of the Aberdeenshire Grampians and the Cairngorm Mountains to the north.

You don't have to be a professional mountaineer to enjoy the spectacular scenery of the Grampians. From Braemar you can head seven miles west along the upper reaches of the River Dee via a lane to the **Linn of Dee.** It's all rich conifer woodland around here, ideal for photo-snapping. The lane to Allanaquoich crosses the Dee at the Linn. You can see the river raging in a white torrent through a slimy rock gorge. There's lots of trails signposted through the pine woods; most are out-and-back routes. There's a large car park and toilets at the Linn of Dee.

Adventurous types, listen up: this is the jumping off point for one of Scotland's best high-level mountain hikes. The route will take you up **Glen Lui** to the very source of the River Dee at the **Pools of Dee.** You can then follow the old cattle droving route over the pass of the **Lairig Ghru** through to the Glenmore Forest and Aviemore. You'll be heading up to the shoulder of Scotland's second-highest peak, **Ben Macdui.** It's 35 kilometers from the Linn of Dee to Aviemore.

Queen Victoria favored following the lane around from Linn of Dee to where it ends at **Allanaquoich;** a woodsy path leads up from here to one of her favorite picnic spots. It's about one kilometer there and back, with further trails leading off through the trees. Many people agree with the Queen and find this a more leisurely option.

Skiing

There is a ski center at **Lecht** (tel. 01975/651440, www.lecht.co.uk), southeast of Tomintoul. See *Sports and Recreation* under *Tomintoul and the Glenlivet Estate* in the *Speyside* section of this chapter for further details.

Getting There and Away

There is no reliable public transport to the Linn of Dee; Braemar is the nearest transport link.

SOUTHERN HIGHLANDS AND SKYE

This region is the set piece of Scotland's tragic, wonderfully preserved history. Lonely hills almost cry out with stories waiting to be told, of cruelly betrayed clans and bloody skirmishes in the heather. The legendary story of Bonnie Prince Charlie—triumphs against the odds, eventual defeat, and flight from government forces—is imprinted everywhere on this remote landscape. Waging a valiant campaign to defeat English forces and restore a Scottish king to the throne, Charlie rallied his forces on barren Ardgour in the west of the region, was defeated at Culloden outside Inverness in the east, and then evaded capture on the Isle of Skye.

The Southern Highlands, hotbed of two rebellions against the crown, was historically perceived as a land of barbarians. Most people south of the region were positively terrified of it. The hills were "black and frightful," according to one visitor; 18th-century travelers Boswell and Johnson were branded reckless adventurers for even wanting to set foot here. The air of wild history and mystery remains, although now it's a draw rather than a deterrent.

To most visitors, this region is the most iconic part of Scotland. The country's deepest loch; its most ancient forest; its highest, darkest mountains; and its most history-steeped glens can be found here. Starting at vibrant Inverness, the main gateway to all of this, great fjord-like lochs cleave southwest, splitting Scotland almost in two. Among them is Loch Ness, Scotland's most famous loch and one of its deepest. Once you're done with monster-hunting, there are fascinating side trips up into

© LUKE WATERSON

HIGHLIGHTS

◖ Leakey's Bookshop/Café: Browse Leakey's, Scotland's biggest secondhand bookshop, housed in a church, and enjoy a coffee in the former choir stalls above (page 411).

◖ Fort Augustus: Watch boats come through the Caledonian Canal while you have a local beer in a traditional pub alongside in this pretty village on the banks of Loch Ness (page 419).

◖ Shinty: Seeing Newtonmore take on Kingussie at shinty, a rough-and-ready form of hockey, is one of Scotland's most entertaining sporting experiences (page 429).

◖ Glen Nevis: Head up gorgeous Glen Nevis and climb Ben Nevis, Scotland's highest mountain (page 436).

◖ Walks Around Glencoe and Kinlochleven: Hiking in the hills around Glencoe village and Kinlochleven gets you up close and personal with some of Scotland's most dramatic mountain scenery: rocky ridges, raging rivers, and moody valleys (page 439).

◖ Knoydart Peninsula: Accessible only by boat or on foot and home to mainland Britain's most isolated pub, this rugged peninsula has some of Scotland's best hiking and mountain climbing (page 444).

◖ Ardnamurchan Point: Make the journey out to far-flung Ardnamurchan Point, the very western extreme of Britain, with a lighthouse to climb (page 448).

◖ Trotternish Rock Formations: Get lost among the bizarre rock formations of Skye's rocky northern peninsula, like the Old Man of Storr, a volcanic rock tower looming out of a lunar-like ridge of hills (page 459).

◖ Plockton: This charming coastal village has a climate placid enough to be palm tree fringed, along with a picture-perfect array of pubs and restaurants (page 463).

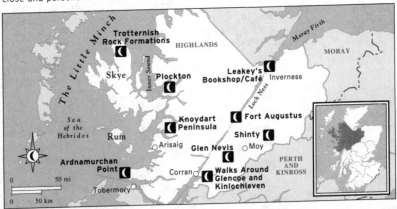

LOOK FOR ◖ TO FIND RECOMMENDED SIGHTS, ACTIVITIES, DINING, AND LODGING.

SOUTHERN HIGHLANDS

the thick conifer forests and mountain slopes on either side. Southwest of Loch Ness, glorious Glen Nevis rises to reach Britain's highest mountain, Ben Nevis. Beyond, land falls away in greens and purples to crystal-clear sea coasts; to Knoydart, Britain's wildest expanse; and to the stupendous geology of the Isle of Skye.

Even on a gray day the light makes Skye, alive with the spirit of the Bonnie Prince, magical. To the north, the land has been wrenched into strange rock formations like the Old Man of Storr, while the sheer, craggy Cuillin Mountains boast Britain's best mountaineering. Yet the peaks overshadow another Skye: a fertile plain with some of Scotland's finest castles and where Gaelic swords are forged.

HISTORY
Prehistory to Medieval Era
The country's earliest evidence of habitation, however, is traced to the Island of Rum off the coast of Locaber, in 7500 B.C. Iron Age peoples left their mark too, in defensive stone towers called brochs at Glenelg, in Lochalsh. The Southern Highlands was at the center of the old Pictish kingdom, which had its capital at Inverness. In the 6th century, the Pictish king Brude was visited here by Irish Celtic missionary St. Columba. Celtic Christianity was slowly accepted in the area. It was in 1040 at Inverness Castle that the real Macbeth supposedly murdered Duncan. Inverness remained an important settlement and was made a royal burgh by King David I in the 12th century. By the mid-14th century the Lordship of the Isles, ruled by the mighty MacDonald clan, wielded a lot of power in the west of the Highlands. Inverness, as a key strategic site, was a target for attack by both the abbot of Arbroath and the Lord of the Isles Alexander MacDonald in medieval times.

17th and 18th Centuries
Oliver Cromwell's forces built a citadel in Inverness in 1652 and sailed up Loch Linnhe to build a still more significant fort at Inverlochy. Following the Glorious Revolution of 1688, unrest amid the Highland clans grew into evident opposition. Clans bitterly resented a foreign, Protestant influence on the throne, and in the first of many moves to bring the rebellious Highlanders under rein, the British government organized the Glencoe Massacre. The old tradition of clan hospitality was bloodily betrayed. In these uncertain times no one knew who to trust. The wary government commissioned General Wade to fortify the region following uprisings formed almost completely by Highland men in 1689 under Bonnie Dundee and again in 1715. Garrison settlements like Fort Augustus grew up around this time. The last great stand of the old Highland clan system came in 1745. The son of the "Old Pretender," "Bonnie Prince Charlie" arrived in the Outer Hebrides in August. He sailed to the mainland, rallied a sizeable force of Highlanders, and raised his standard at Glenfinnan. Despite early success, Bonnie Prince Charlie's troops were decimated at Culloden near Inverness in just one hour by the Duke of Cumberland's forces in spring 1746. Charlie escaped to France, never returning to Scotland; Lochaber was laid to waste by Cumberland's troops.

19th Century
Centuries of conflict had torn the Southern Highlands apart by the late 18th century. Salvation for the region was to come in the form of the Caledonian Canal, which improved transport links in the area after 1822, and in the form of tourism. The region slowly became a fashionable visitor destination, helped by Queen Victoria, who favored the spa resort of Grantown on Spey in the 1860s. By the mid-19th century, however, another menace befell the Southern Highlands in the form of the potato famine in 1849. The only crop that could be grown in such a bleak climate was blighted. Highland clearances now kicked off in earnest. As croft ruins began to litter the landscape, a further dispute came with the rise of the Free Church in the 1840s, which traditionalist landlords in the Southern Highlands resented. Ministers were banned from performing ceremonies in churches. Services took place in graveyards and in Strontian, a "floating

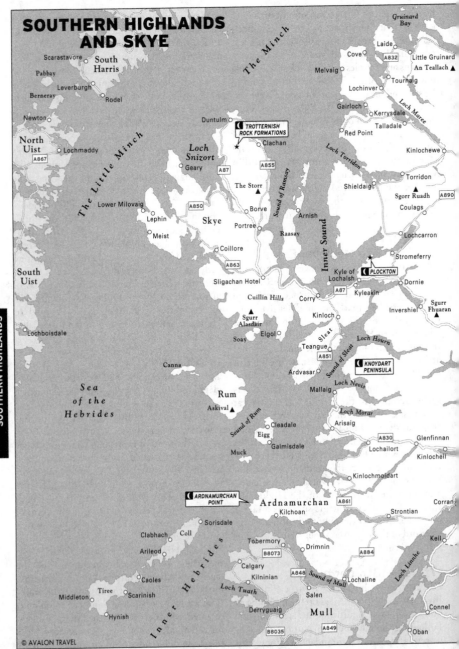

SOUTHERN HIGHLANDS AND SKYE

SOUTHERN HIGHLANDS

The Minch

Gruinard Bay

Scarastavore
South Harris
Pabbay
Berneray
Leverburgh
Rodel
Newton
Lochmaddy
North Uist
A867

Laide
Cove
A832
Little Gruinard
An Teallach ▲
Melvaig
Lochinver
Gairloch
Kerrysdale
Talladale
Red Point
Loch Maree

The Little Minch

Duntulm
TROTTERNISH ROCK FORMATIONS
Clachan
Loch Snizort
Geary
A87
A855
The Storr ▲
Lower Milovaig
A850
Skye
Borve
Lephin
Meist
Portree
Coillore
A863
Sligachan Hotel
Cuillin Hills
Sgurr Alasdair ▲
Soay
Elgol
Arnish
Raasay
Sound of Ramsay
Inner Sound

Loch Torridon
Kinlochewe
Torridon
Shieldaig
Sgorr Ruadh ▲
Coulags
A890
Lochcarron
Stromeferry
PLOCKTON
Kyle of Lochalsh
A87
Kyleakin
Dornie
Invershiel
Sgurr Fhuaran ▲

South Uist
Lochboisdale

Sea of the Hebrides

Corry
Kinloch
Sleat
Teangue
A851
Ardvasar
Mallaig
Sound of Sleat
Loch Hourn
KNOYDART PENINSULA
Loch Nevis

Canna
Rum
Askival ▲
Sound of Rum
Cleadale
Eigg
Galmisdale
Muck

Loch Morar
Arisaig
A830
Lochailort
Glenfinnan
Kinlocheil
Kinlochmoidart

ARDNAMURCHAN POINT
Ardnamurchan
Kilchoan
A861
Corran
Strontian
Keil

Sorisdale
Clabhach
Coll
Arileod
Caoles
Tobermory
Drimnin
B8073
Calgary
Kilninian
A848
Sound of Mull
Lochaline
A884
Loch Linnhe

Inner Hebrides
Middleton
Tiree
Scarinish
Hynish
Loch Tuath
Derryguaig
Salen
Mull
Connel
A849
B8035
Oban

© AVALON TRAVEL

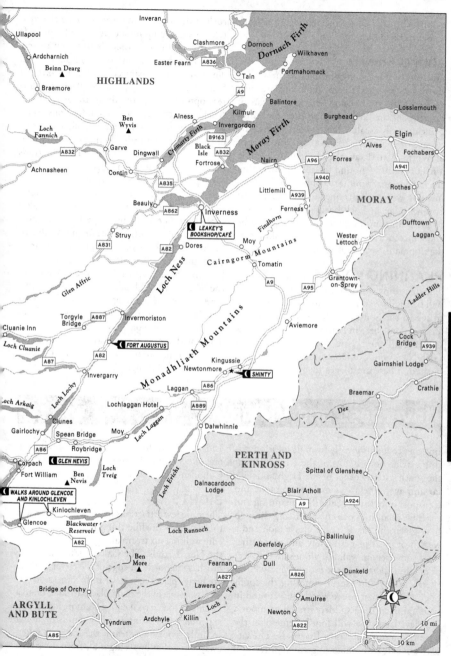

minister" preached to his congregation from a boat in Loch Sunart.

20th Century

Tourism to the region continued to grow once the railway reached the region in the late 19th century and got a boost in 1933 with a spate of sightings of the Loch Ness monster. Sightings coincidentally escalated only months after the release of the movie *King Kong*. The advent of World War II saw the Highlands become a major training ground for troops, including the revolutionary military concept of the commandos, which were trained in the area around Spean Bridge, by Loch Lochy. In the latter half of the 20th century, tourism continued to be a key income, prompting the rise of ski resort developments such as Aviemore.

PLANNING YOUR TIME

The first thing worth bearing in mind is that it will be nigh on impossible to see all you want to see in the Southern Highlands and Skye. Visitors come here in hordes for a reason: This is where all the classic Scottish sights from Loch Ness to Eilean Donan Castle to Skye are located. These are places to be enjoyed, not

rushed through. Many people make the mistake of signing up for a tour of the Highlands specifically because there is so much to see, cramming the main sights in to a short time. The result is that many come away thinking of Scotland as a kitschy postcard place with few real opportunities for adventure or relaxing. Any one of the region's six subdivisions could absorb you for days; it's best to pick one or two of these areas and really do them justice if you are pushed for time. Good road connections between Inverness, Loch Ness, Aviemore in the Cairngorm Mountains, and Skye means that you can dash between these areas with relative ease. The remote region of Lochaber takes more time to explore but is perhaps the most thrilling and untouristy area of any. With two to three days, focus your energies on the Great Glen and Skye. With five to seven days, you have the scope to see the best of several areas of the Southern Highlands. This could include, for example, the many sights around Inverness like the Clava Cairns, or out-of-the-way places like Newtonmore or the villages of Lochaber. Those with more time should consider the glorious walking country of Knoydart for some unforgettable hiking.

Inverness and Vicinity

Inverness benefits greatly from its location: sitting astride both banks of the River Ness at the southeastern corner of the Highlands, it's far and away the area's main settlement and transport hub. Intelligent urban planning and the huge quantities of tourists passing through have given the city a smart, classy look and a wealth of great places to stay and eat. Other than some serene walking alongside the river or dolphin-spotting in the nearby Moray Firth, there's little to do except sampling the spoils of city life. When you're wandering around in your raingear on a sodden stretch of moor a few days later, you will fondly remember the cosmopolitan comforts of Inverness. The city is the base for a number of great architectural

and historical attractions nearby, including one of Scotland's finest stately castles and the Culloden Battle Site.

SIGHTS

There are few attractions in the city center itself; the most worthwhile thing to do is undoubtedly walking upstream along the River Ness to the Ness Islands. The Caledonian Canal also brushes the northern edge of the city, but there are better places to look at it. Inverness, nevertheless, is one of the main places to latch on to a Highland tour. You'll have a far more interesting experience of visiting the Highlands by doing so under your own steam; the magic is taken away somewhat by seeing it all from the sterile confines of a minibus. However, those without their own transport or with limited time can make use of a huge variety of tours. With so many to choose from, tour quality can vary drastically. It's worth shopping around before you sign on to any particular tour: Ask exactly what will be included and how long you will have at different places. The Inverness TIC and word-of-mouth recommendations from other travelers are good sources of information. You could also try asking the staff at your hotel. Be aware that even a company with an established reputation can become complacent and offer a shoddy service.

River Ness

Walking down Bridge Street brings you to the wide, shallow banks of the River Ness. Inverness cannot be said to have the most glamorously developed waterfront, but upstream it's a different story: The banks are greener and there's a more scenic feel. A good way to approach the walk here is to cross Ness Bridge and begin on the west side of the river; you'll pass the red sandstone Inverness Cathedral and the revamped Eden Court Theatre. Then you can cross over on a footbridge and continue on the east bank another 15 minutes to the **Ness Islands** (open year-round), where a number of tributaries and dividing eddies of water form a shady, wooded series of islands on the river linked by pathways, cycle-ways, and bridges.

Tours

A plethora of tours are available, both in and out of Inverness. Tours depart from the TIC, where you can ask about tour departure times.

There is no m ore appropriate-looking character to guide you around the colorful historic sights of Inverness than **Greg Dawson Allen** (tel. 01463/233729 or 0784/069 2766, walks nightly or by arrangement, £7 adults, £5 children). Clad in Highland garb, he runs guided walking tours around the city to bring its past evocatively to life. Greg Dawson Allen can also be hired as a guide to longer tours of the surrounding area by car/minibus.

The Moray Firth by Inverness is one of

the best places to see dolphins in Britain, and **Inverness Dolphin Cruises** (tel. 01463/717900, www.inverness-dolphin-cruises.co.uk, several times daily Mar.–Oct., £12.50 adults, £9 children) runs cruises to see them. They depart from Shore Street Quay east of the city center; you can walk or take a free bus there.

Jacobite Cruises (tel. 01463/233999, www.jacobite.co.uk, several cruises daily year-round) has been running cruises along Loch Ness for a very long time. The tours include a bus journey to the start of Loch Ness proper from Inverness and then loch cruises of up to six hours, depending on how much you want to see. The two-hour freedom tours, which include some time at Urquhart Castle, start from £14. The longer you go, the more off-the-beaten-track attractions you can see. The six-hour cruises, for example, take in monster museums and cairns as well as the castle.

The best company offering out-of-Inverness tours is **Puffin Express** (tel. 01463/717181, www.puffinexpress.co.uk, daily Mar.–Oct. or by arrangement). They operate small, intimate tours and inject passion into the tours on offer. Operators can be chartered to take you wherever you want to go in the Highlands and Islands, including the Isle of Skye.

Canny Tours (tel. 01349/854411, www.cannytours.com) still offers original, private tours to off-the-beaten-path places like Black Isle and Glen Affric.

ENTERTAINMENT

Inverness is a lively wee city. There is a selection of nightclubs but these are best avoided by anyone with a degree of discernment. The best nightlife is rather to be found in the city's pubs and bars, which offer a spirited array of drinking options and plenty of live music between them. Inverness also has very good theater.

Pubs, Bars, and Live Music

The Market Bar (32 Church St., tel. 01463/233292, 12:30–11 P.M. Sun.–Tues., 12:30 P.M.–1 A.M. Wed.–Sat.) is a teeming, traditional local watering hole up a winding flight of steps from the Victorian market. It's not surprising

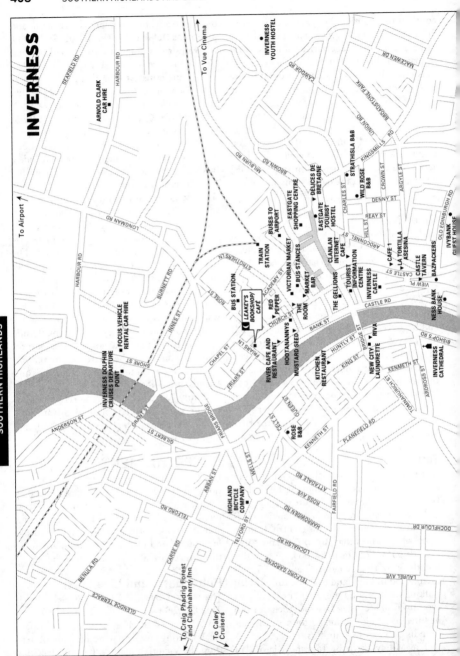

INVERNESS

To Vue Cinema

To Airport

INVERNESS YOUTH HOSTEL

ARNOLD CLARK CAR HIRE

STRATHISLA B&B
WILD ROSE B&B

DELICES DE BRETAGNE
EASTGATE SHOPPING CENTRE
EASTGATE TOURIST HOSTEL

BUSES TO AIRPORT

CLANLAN INTERNET
TOURIST INFORMATION CENTRE
INVERNESS CASTLE

CAFE 1
LA TORTILLA ASESINA
CASTLE TAVERN
BAZPACKERS
IVYBANK GUEST HOUSE

TRAIN STATION

BUS STATION

VICTORIAN MARKET
BUS STANCES
MARKET BAR
THE GELLIONS

LEAKEY'S BOOKSHOP/ CAFÉ

RED PEPPER
THE ROOM

FOCUS VEHICLE RENTAL CAR HIRE

INVERNESS DOLPHIN CRUISES DEPARTURE POINT

RIVER CAFE AND RESTAURANT
HOOTANANNYS
MUSTARD SEED

KITCHEN RESTAURANT

NESS BANK HOUSE

NEW CITY LAUNDRETTE
RIVA

INVERNESS CATHEDRAL

ROSE B&B

HIGHLAND BICYCLE COMPANY

To Craig Phadrig Forest and Clachnaharry Inn

To Caley Cruisers

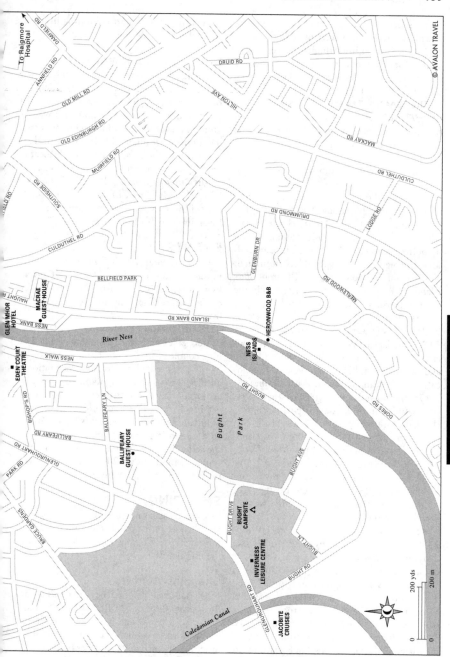

SOUTHERN HIGHLANDS

To Raigmore Hospital

DANEFIELD RD
ANNFIELD RD
OLD MILL RD
OLD EDINBURGH RD
DRUID RD
HILTON AVE
MURFIELD RD
SOUTHSIDE RD
FIELD RD
CULDUTHEL RD
MACKAY RD
CULDUTHEL RD
DRUMMOND RD
LODGE RD
GLENBURN DR
MELROSE RD
BELLFIELD PARK
HAUGH RD
MACRAE GUEST HOUSE
GLEN MHOR HOTEL
NESS BANK
ISLAND BANK RD
HERONWOOD B&B
River Ness
NESS WALK
NESS ISLANDS
EDEN COURT THEATRE
BISHOP'S RD
BALLIFEARY LN
BUGHT RD
BALLIFEARY RD
Bught Park
DORES RD
GLENURQUHART RD
PARK RD
BALLIFEARY GUEST HOUSE
BRUCE GARDENS
BUGHT DRIVE
BUGHT AVE
BUGHT CAMPSITE
BUGHT LN
INVERNESS LEISURE CENTRE
BUGHT RD
GLENURQUHART RD
Caledonian Canal
JACOBITE CRUISES

0   200 yds
0   200 m

© AVALON TRAVEL

that it's teeming, being as tiny as it is. There's live music pretty much every night of the week. It's a sometimes intimidatingly local venue (because of its size), but they're really a friendly bunch. You won't find a cozier old spot to hole up with a pint of beer.

The Castle Tavern (1 View Pl., tel. 01463/718178, until 11 P.M. Sun.–Thurs., until midnight Fri.–Sat.), with its flowery outside garden and mean Sunday roasts (£6.95), is a great spot for a drink, particularly if you get an outside table in the sunshine. These days, it pours a good pint of ale.

Locals stand their ground against the influx of tourists in the traditional **The Gellions** (11–17 Bridge St., tel. 01463/233648, 11 A.M.–1 A.M. Mon.–Sat., 12:30 P.M.–midnight Sun.), where a lot of Inverness characters drink. There are ceilidhs, live big screen sports, and lots of different ales. You'll find two bars here—the front one's friendlier. It's supposedly the oldest pub in the city and boasts an outside courtyard.

The Room (73 Queensgate, tel. 01463/ 233077, www.theroomandno27.com, 10:30 A.M.–late daily) is a relaxed, spacious modern bar serving food with live music on Friday and Saturday. It pulls in a mixed crowd from locals to tourists and is popular with families.

On the western outskirts of Inverness, the wonderful old coaching inn that is the **Clachnaharry Inn** (17–19 High St., Clachnaharry, tel. 01463/239806, www.clachnaharryinn.co.uk, 11 A.M.–11 P.M. Mon.–Wed., 11 A.M.–midnight Thurs.–Sat., 12:30– 11:45 P.M. Sun.) has some fine ales to try and a great atmosphere to try them in. It's right on the Caledonian Canal, one mile west of Inverness on the A862.

Hootananny (67 Church St., tel. 01463/ 233651, www.hootananny.co.uk, until late daily) might have been going a long time now, but it's still the best and most important bar in Inverness. Inside, it's spread over three floors. The colorfully decked out first floor is dedicated to nightly live folk music, while rock and indie bands perform live to a younger crowd upstairs. The place is open until late, sometimes just closing whenever the music stops, but 8 P.M. onward

is when the crowds start cramming in for the cheap drinks promotions.

Other Entertainment

Reopened in November 2007 after a refurbishment, **Eden Court Theatre** (Eden Ct., Bishops Rd., tel. 01463/234234, www.edencourt.co.uk) is the place to come in Inverness for all kinds of theater and for cinema screenings of mainstream, foreign language, and arthouse films. The complex has a lovely location on the green east bank of the River Ness.

Vue Cinema (Inverness Retail Park, Eastfield Way, tel. 0871/224 0240) is a multiplex on the edge of Inverness showing mainstream movies. Bus number 6 heads out here.

EVENTS

Held in late August/early September each year in venues across the Highlands, **Blas Festival** (www.blas-festival.com) is a huge weeklong celebration of Gaelic culture, mostly through live music.

The **Highland Feast** (www.highlandfeast .co.uk) takes place every September and lasts for a couple of weeks. The Highland Feast is a handy event to look out for; as a celebration of all that is glorious in Highland cuisine, there are lots of free food-tasting events. Local chefs get involved in this good old promotion of Highland produce. The feast is held in different locations across the Highlands but a lot of the action happens in and around the culinary capital of Inverness. In 2007, events took place in Cawdor Castle, near Inverness.

SHOPPING

Inverness is as far north as the chain stores go, and there is an incredible concentration of all the High Street names you could hope for in the Highlands.

Shopping Centers

Most retail chain stores can be found at **Eastgate Shopping Centre** (Millburn Rd., 9 A.M.– 5:30 P.M. Mon.–Wed., 9 A.M.–7 P.M. Thurs., 9 A.M.–6 P.M. Fri.–Sat., 11 A.M.–5 P.M. Sun.), including a branch of Waterstones Bookshop. It's directly south of the train station. The covered, elaborate **Victorian Market** (Academy St.) complex has lots of more offbeat shops.

⟨ Leakey's Bookshop/Café

Scotland's biggest secondhand bookshop (Greyfriar's Hall, Church St., tel. 01463/239947, 10 A.M.–5:30 P.M. Mon.–Sat.) is set in an 18th-century former church stacked with books as high as its stained-glass windows, with a log fire in winter. You're guaranteed to find something that will interest you here; there's a very good Scottish interest section and huge towering bookcases of fiction. If you feel daunted by the array of titles, the charismatic owner will be able to point you towards the right book. A spiral staircase leads to an upper-level café, where you can peruse your chosen purchase over a coffee and homemade cake. This cavernous place has the added advantage of being near the bus and train stations, ideal for spending time in between transport connections.

SPORTS AND RECREATION
Walking

The best places for a walk in Inverness are along by the banks of the River Ness or in Craig Phadrig Forest, northwest of the city. If you like the idea of long-distance walking and want an easy(ish) introduction to it, the 73 mile **Great Glen Way** (www.greatglenway.com) path between Inverness and Fort William follows mainly the towpath of the Caledonian Canal and gentle forest tracks. You're experiencing majestic mountain scenery without having to do very much climbing. Further information can be gleaned from Inverness TIC.

Cycling

Highland Bicycle Company (16a Telford St., tel. 01463/234789, www.highlandbikes.com) rents out bikes for £12 daily. The rate goes down for longer-term hires.

Boat Rental

You can hire a boat with **Caley Cruisers** (tel. 01463/236328, www.caleycruisers.com, daily Apr.–Oct.) and sail right down the length of the Great Glen on the Caledonian Canal. It takes three days to do the 60-mile jaunt down to Fort William. Instruction is given and boats come fully equipped.

Fitness Centers

If it's exercise you are craving, head to **Inverness Leisure Centre** (Bught Pk., tel. 01463/667500). The center here has a gym and swimming pool.

ACCOMMODATIONS

Inverness accommodations have some of the most wildly fluctuating prices of any place in the country. Rooms can be reasonable or pricey depending on season and demand. Many also advertise single rooms but charge surcharges for single occupancy at peak times of the year. In order to bump up custom, many places will offer you their best and priciest room when they have cheaper ones available. For this reason the full price ranges for rooms are given here where appropriate. Most of the decent accommodation is either in hostels or guest-houses, with relatively few good hotels.

Under £25

⟨ **Bazpackers** (4 Culduthel Rd., tel. 01463/717663, dorm beds from £13) is the best hostel in the city—a small 30-bed place that fills up mighty quickly. It's got a mix of six-bed, four-bed, and two-bed rooms and feels every bit the 19th-century cottage. Expect small, twisting rooms and corridors, a cozy lounge with an open fire, a Victorian walled garden and the welcome 21st-century addition of pounding hot showers. Laundry can be done here for £5 a load.

Huge, modern, comfortable, and devoid of any atmosphere, **Inverness Youth Hostel** (Victoria Dr., tel. 01463/231771 or 0870/155 3255, beds £15–17) is just west of central Inverness. Dorms are single-sex with four to six beds. When other places in the city are full, it's a good place to turn to, set in a pleasant green part of town. Bathroom and kitchen facilities are top-notch. The hostel is a 10-minute walk west of the city center, off Millburn Road.

A mile from the city center (and a very pleasant mile, too) is the nearest campsite to Inverness, **Bught Caravan Site** (Bught Ln., tel. 01463/236920, www.invernesscaravan-park.com, Apr.–Oct., two-man tent £12). It's a well-appointed grassy site with bags of room for backpackers. It can still get very full in season.

£25-50

A friendly, eccentric host and spacious rooms make **Strathisla** (42 Charles St., tel. 01463/235657, £25 s, £40 d) a great place to stay. Rooms are not all en suite but include wash basins and flat-screen TVs. There's an impressive collection of whisky bottles in the dining room. The owner will be happy to point you in the direction of local attractions.

Wild Rose B&B (10 Hill St., tel. 0771/722 0869 or 0771/722 1453, www.the-rose-bb.com, from £36 d) is a charming whitewashed cottage with three rooms available in a quiet location at the top of town. The rooms are simple but clean and have a shared bathroom with a bath. The owners also run the similarly styled three-room Rose B and B at 64 King Street, sharing the same telephone numbers.

Farther upstream from the city center, the River Ness gets increasingly idyllic until, just after the Ness Islands, you come across little **Heronwood B&B** (16a Island Bank Rd., tel. 01463/243275, from £48 d), right by the wooded river banks. The 19th-century house has three light, white rooms, including one with a king-size bed. Bathrooms, including one with a bath, are all private. The number 11 bus to the airport passes by the door from the city center.

£50-100

The █ **Macrae Guest House** (24 Ness Bank, tel. 01463/243658, £35 s, £64 d) has a grand location on the banks of the River Ness. It's a flower-flanked building with a Far East flavor to the decor; a lot of care and attention has gone into making guests' stays enjoyable. The three large rooms have private bathrooms and cozy armchairs to lounge in. The breakfast is

continental-style, but with heaps of cold meats, cheese, and croissants to choose from you won't be going away hungry.

Rising splendidly behind a colorful garden is well-kept **Ness Bank House** (7 Ness Bank, tel. 01463/232939, www.nessbankguest-house.co.uk, £24–35 s, £48–70 d), a Georgian guest house offering a mix of single, double, and family rooms. The rooms are of a decent size, with peaceful white decor and color TVs. There are both en suite and shared facilities, and the price varies accordingly.

You won't get a more stylish guesthouse than **Ivybank Guest House** (28 Old Edinburgh Rd., tel. 01463/232796, www.ivybankguest-house.com, £25 s, £56 d) anywhere in the city for this price tag. It's a listed building with a red-trimmed sandstone Georgian tower as the main part of it. With oak beamed ceilings, glossy dark wood furnishings, and a couple of open fires, the whole house has an ambience of traditional elegance. Not all rooms are en suite, but there is an en suite four-poster bed room that will have you wandering which century you have woken up in. The guest lounge even has a baby grand piano.

Ballifeary Guest House (Ballifeary Rd., tel. 01463/235572, www.ballifearyhouseho-tel.co.uk, £76 d) is a sedate Victorian house with six large en suite rooms boasting color TVs and Internet access. With dark wood period furniture and room-high bay-view windows, this place has bags of old elegance. You'll find the property in a laid-back residential area of Inverness to the west of the river.

Over £100

Crisp white sheets set against dark wood furnishings and windows looking out onto the river—that's what the amicable **Glen Mhor Hotel** (Ness Bank, tel. 01463/234308, www.glen-mhor.com, £95 s, £105 d) offers. In a stretch of undeniably appealing riverfront properties, the hotel has Freeview TV and Wi-Fi Internet access in all its rooms. Some rooms look out over the hills to the rear of the hotel. Glen Mhor also has restaurants and a cozy bar filled with sofas. It puts on regular live music.

FOOD

Inverness has a very good reputation for food these days. There are a number of top-quality restaurants; places like Café 1 and the Mustard Seed really revolutionized dining in these parts. There is also a small but significant range of world cuisine to sample, including Spanish and Italian.

Cafés, Tearooms, and Snacks

Your obvious choice for a tasty morning or lunchtime sandwich is **The Red Pepper** (Bow Ct., 74 Church St., tel. 01463/237111, 7:30 A.M.–4:30 P.M. Mon.–Fri., 9 A.M.–4:30 P.M. Sat.). It's a popular local haunt and can get very busy. There's a pleasant seating area in the café itself, or you can get takeaway (£1–4).

For a good strong coffee and a light bite to eat, there's nowhere more unusual than **Leakey's** (Greyfriar's Hall, Church St., tel. 01463/239947, 10 A.M.–4:30 P.M. Mon.–Sat.), an upper-level area of tables inside an old church stacked with secondhand books. You can get quiches and tasty soup here. Snacks are £2–6.

The **River Café and Restaurant** (10 Bank St., tel. 01463/714884, www.rivercafeand-restaurant.co.uk) is perfect for breaking up those riverside rambles. This often-crowded place dishes up generous helpings of stuffed jacket potatoes, soups, sandwiches, and salads. Nothing can live up to the High Teas, though: a selection of hearty meals like lasagna and steak accompanied by tea or coffee and piles of bread, preserves, and homebakes (£9). Most main meals are £7–10.

Scottish/International

Is it a bar, or is it a restaurant? **The Room** (73 Queensgate, tel. 01463/233077, www.the-roomandno27.com, food served 10:30 A.M.–9:30 P.M. daily) really can't seem to make up its mind. Supposedly American-themed but hardly shouting the fact at you, it's a vast, friendly place with decked seating areas and regular live music on weekends. The "American" menu features a lot of good, cheap dishes, and the food comes in hearty portions. Fish and chips in their varying, innovative forms bulk up the menu (£7–9). At many times of the day, it can be the best bet in the city for a decent, casual, filling meal.

A strong contender for the coolest eating venue in Inverness, **⟨ Café 1** (75 Castle St., tel. 01463/226200, www.cafe1.net, noon–2 P.M. and 5:30 P.M.–late daily) is an elegant space of wooden tables and huge artworks; it's like a cross between a medieval banqueting hall and a factory. During the day the front area is a hip café serving some of the finest coffee in the city. In the evening, Café 1 concentrates on turning out original, inexpensive, quality Scottish food, like collops of monkfish with Stornoway black pudding. You get slick, professional service here, too. Lunches are £8–12, evening meals £9–18.

The **⟨ Mustard Seed** (16 Fraser St., tel. 01463/220220, www.mustardseedrstaurant.co.uk, noon–3 P.M. and 5:30–10 P.M. daily) wins the prize for the classiest eatery in Inverness. Housed in a former church with wine bottles stacked up the walls and done up in primrose yellow, it has two huge dining levels. Just to appreciate the building fully, the balcony is the best part, although there's also a gorgeous rooftop terrace with views of the river. The eclectic menu has mainly Scottish dishes, but with lots of worldly variations on traditional Scottish cuisine. Roast chicken, for example, comes with basmati rice and a curry-infused tomato sauce, while the sea bass comes with a pineapple and passion fruit salsa. You can enjoy a two-course early evening meal for £11.95, while main meals are £9–14.

The modern, open plan, two-story **Kitchen Restaurant** (15 Huntly St., tel. 01463/259119, www.kitchenrestaurant.co.uk, noon–3 P.M.) serves up innovative lunches and dinners from inside a space more resembling a design studio than a place to eat. There are great views over the river as you tuck into creative Scottish cuisine dishes like corn-fed chicken with asparagus. Two-course lunches are £5.95. Evening main meals are £9–15.

Other Cuisine

With its bright blue, white, and yellow tile, **La Tortilla Asesina** (99 Castle St., tel. 01463/

709809, www.latortillaasesina.co.uk, noon–10 P.M. Sun.–Wed., noon–midnight Thurs.–Sat.), this tapas restaurant creates a soothing Mediterranean vibe. It's a refreshing new dimension to the Inverness dining scene with two parts to it: the main restaurant and the cozy sherry bar upstairs. Tapas dishes like *calamares* (battered squid) or the gorgeous *albondigas* (chicken and chorizo meatballs) are £2–5. A set menu is three pieces of tapas per person (£9). The place has been dubbed the most authentic Spanish tapas bar in Scotland, an accolade it wholly deserves.

A cozy French brasserie/patisserie, **Delices de Bretagne** (4–6 Stephens Brae, tel. 01463/712422, 9 A.M.–5 P.M. Mon.–Sat., 10 A.M.–5 P.M. Sun.) does a cracking range of European coffees and hot chocolates as well as crepes and croissants. Inside, it really does feel like a little piece of Paris in the Highlands.

Riva (4–6 Ness Walk, tel. 01463/237377, www.rivarestaurant.co.uk, noon–2:30 P.M. and 5–9:30 P.M. daily) is a friendly, intimate Italian restaurant serving up good quality pasta, fish, and meat dishes (£9–15) like linguine tossed with an array of shellfish. The mouth-watering deserts include a selection of Italian cheeses with Hebridean oatcakes. It's a reasonably formal establishment with a good wine selection.

INFORMATION AND SERVICES

Inverness TIC (tel. 01463/234353, 9 A.M.–5 P.M. Mon.–Sat. Apr.–mid-May, 9 A.M.–6 P.M. Mon.–Sat., 9:30 A.M.–4 P.M. Sun. mid-May–June and early–mid-Sept., 9 A.M.–7 P.M. Mon.–Sat., 9:30 A.M.–5 P.M. Sun. July–Aug., 9 A.M.–5 P.M. Mon.–Sat., 10 A.M.–4 P.M. Sun. mid-Sept.–Oct., limited hours Nov.–Mar.) is a hugely helpful TIC. It has bags of free information, lots of free guidebooks to different areas of Scotland, local maps for sale, and a *bureau de change.*

Besides the TIC, plenty of banks will exchange money—and Inverness is littered with banks.

If you need to go online, head to the TIC or **Clanlan Internet Cafe** (29 Castle St., tel. 01463/240880).

Raigmore Hospital (Old Perth Rd., tel. 01463/704000) is a main hospital not just for Inverness but for much of the Highlands. It's just east of the city center.

New City Launderette (17 Young St., tel. 01463/242507) even has Internet access (£1 per 20 mins) while you wait for your clothes to wash.

GETTING THERE

Inverness is the farthest place north to experience anything like a normal, decent bus and rail service. Both buses and trains connect Inverness regularly to Edinburgh, Glasgow, and Aberdeen. Inverness also has an airport with both national and international services. The city is the main transport hub not only for the Southern Highlands but also for the Northern Highlands.

Air

If you want to save time on the long journey up here, Inverness Airport comes in mighty handy. You'll find the airport 10 miles east of the city center, on the A96. There are five daily departures to various London airports, as well as several to Edinburgh, Stornoway in the Outer Hebrides, Kirkwall on Orkney, and Sumburgh on Shetland. You can get to all these destinations on weekends as well on a reduced service. The main operator is British Airways (tel. 0870/850 9850, www.britishairways.com) and its affiliated airlines.

Train

Trains run to many Scottish towns and cities from Inverness including Edinburgh (every two hours daily, 3 hrs. 40 min., £38.20) and Glasgow (every two hours, 3 hrs. 25 min., £38.20), as well as regular trains to Aberdeen.

There's one direct train per day from Inverness to London (8 hrs., £117). Otherwise, change at Edinburgh or Glasgow, which have regular services. If you don't mind a change, there are about five trains daily between Inverness and London. There's also the Caledonian Sleeper, which runs nightly (except Saturdays) from London Euston to Inverness (11 hrs.).

Bus

Inverness Bus Station is located off Academy Street, north of the train station. It's a modern place with a quite pleasant café and a frequent bus service to various destinations within the Southern Highlands and beyond, to Edinburgh, Glasgow, and London.

The main operators are **Scottish Citylink** (tel. 0870/550 5050, www.citylink.co.uk) or **Megabus** (tel. 0900/160 0900, www.megabus.com). Buses run to Edinburgh (hourly, 4–5 hrs., £21.20) and Glasgow (hourly, 4 hrs., £21.20). To get to Aberdeen, take Stagecoach Bus 10, which runs hourly Monday–Saturday and has Sunday service; the journey takes three hours 50 minutes. One direct bus runs between Inverness and London Victoria coach station; the 12- to 13-hour journey can cost as little as £20.

GETTING AROUND

Inverness is a relatively compact city; you can walk between most of the sights, accommodations, and restaurants. Several attractions are scattered some distance outside the city limits, though, connected by a decent bus network. The bus and train stations are located near each other, off Academy Street.

Train

Trains run about every 1.5–2 hours from Inverness to Aviemore and Nairn. Trains also run to Plockton and Kyle of Lochalsh from Inverness. Other train stations (connected to Glasgow) are at Fort William, Spean Bridge, Glenfinnan, Arisaig, and Mallaig.

Bus

Generally speaking, public transport in the Southern Highlands means buses. Buses to destinations within the Southern Highlands will depart from the main bus station. Local buses will use bus stances on Union Street, opposite the train station. Rapsons/Highland County offers one day Rover Passes for £9 adults, £6 children, valid on any of its buses for one day.

Stagecoach Bus service 1 links the Aquadrome (for Bught campsite) with the city center and Culloden half-hourly Monday–Saturday. Stagecoach 5A/6/6A links Union Street in the city center with the Vue Cinema four times hourly Monday–Saturday and hourly on Sunday.

Rapsons (tel. 01463/710555, www.rapsons.co.uk) service 11 runs regularly to the airport throughout the week (hourly on Sundays) with buses often continuing to Fort George.

Car Rental

Focus Vehicle Rental (Inverness Car Hire, 36 Shore St., tel. 01463/709517) has an office at Inverness Airport and offers the best rates in town, with prices starting at £115 per week.

Arnold Clark (Citreon Garage, Harbour Rd., tel. 01463/236200) has daily hire from £17.

AROUND INVERNESS

The fertile, wooded ground around Inverness contains a wealth of historic attractions that illustrate the importance of this area since prehistoric times. Most visitors will venture out into this area to see the Culloden Battle Site, where the last hope of a Scottish king, Bonnie Prince Charlie, was defeated once and for all at the hands of government forces in 1746. More impressive, however, are the monuments to different eras nearby: Neolithic cairns and a majestic 14th-century castle associated with Shakespeare's *Macbeth*. The sights can be seen as part of a day trip from Inverness.

Culloden Visitor Centre and Battle Site

The blackest day in Scottish history was April 16, 1746, when Bonnie Prince Charlie's Jacobite rebel forces were decimated by government troops on the poorly chosen battleground known as Culloden Moor. The Bonnie Prince fled the scene, but 1,250 of his men died in the space of an hour; many more were executed afterwards. The lonely, boggy moor hasn't changed much since it saw the last hope for a Scottish king crushed forever. This age-old battle site got an all-new look for 2008, presumably in an attempt to draw in

THE REAL MACBETH

Macbethad mac Findlaich, known in English as Macbeth, was born around A.D. 1005. His family held one of the most important stewardships in the Celtic kingdom at the time. He killed the reigning king, Duncan I, in battle and through a series of favorable events including marriage to former king Kenneth III's granddaughter, rose to become king. Despite having gained the throne through dubious means, Macbeth proved to be a good ruler. He was a just and brave monarch, according to the historical resources available, endeavoring to bring a degree of order to a barbaric kingdom. Late on in a reign that spanned between 14 and 17 years, Macbeth is known to have visited Rome on a pilgrimage and flung gold at the crowds there. He also worked hard to keep the Northumbrian interest in the Scottish throne at bay. Ultimately, however, he was defeated in battle by Malcom Canmore in 1054, who had Northumbrian backing and became king in Macbeth's place. His rule seems to have been a comparatively fair and uneventful one by the standards of the times – far from the treacherous and corrupted monarch he is remembered as.

After his death, however, historians came to look upon Macbeth in an increasingly romantic light. Many considered him to be the last Gaelic king of Scotland. His later fictionalization came courtesy of the renowned historian Andrew of Wyntoun, a monk of St. Andrews, in Fife. The monk was one of the principal chroniclers of the 11th century in which Macbeth ruled. Unfortunately, the monk was also known to have an obsession with old myths and incorporated many of these into his written histories, published around 1406. The elements of the supernatural as embodied in the Shakespeare play by the sinister witches who predict Macbeth's destiny became tied in with the story of Macbeth around this point. By the time Shakespeare was searching for material for his play, he did not have to make many further embellishments and elaborations of the truth to make his account of Macbeth's life almost purely fictional. Further, Shakespeare was writing the play to perform in front of James I of England (VI of Scotland). He knew the monarch loved stories of mystery, magic, and prophesy and so threw in plenty of each to ensure his play entertained the king. In so doing, he also cemented poor Macbeth's reputation as a self-deluded monarch who stops at nothing, least of all murder, to seize the crown. Fortunately, time discrepancies of several centuries save the real Macbeth's reputation. Cawdor Castle, of which he was supposedly Thane, was not built until over three centuries after his death.

even more tourists and make the atmosphere even less reminiscent of that day back in 1746. Archaeologists discovered the previous site of the complex was not on the site of the actual battle at all (unlucky for previous visitors), and so a new visitors center (Culloden Moor, tel. 0844/493 2159, 9 A.M.–6 P.M. daily Apr.–Oct., 10 A.M.–4 P.M. daily Nov.–Mar., site accessible year-round, £10 adults, £7.50 children) has now been built on the more precise location of the Jacobite demise. There will be a whole new series of interactive exhibits to help visitors better understand the conflict. The poignant memorial cairn and the graves of the clans along the road through the battle site are interesting, but ultimately this is an underwhelming visitor experience. A piece of bare moor can only have so much appeal. Culloden is six miles west of Inverness; bus 1 and Rapsons bus 12 head here from the city center.

Clava Cairns

In a clearing in a wood near Culloden lies a far more impressive historic attraction, which hardly anybody ever visits. Screened from the road by a covering of gnarled old trees are three huge 4,000-year-old burial cairns. There are three main cairns at the site (open year-round). The northeast and southwest cairns are the better preserved; they're stone burial chambers accessed by passage-ways. The northeasterly one was aligned with the winter solstice, with the chamber built so the sun set against the far wall on the shortest day of the year. Clava Cairns are down a warren of little lanes about a mile southwest of Culloden, signposted off the B9006 east of Culloden. There are lots of great places to have picnics in the area. Public transport doesn't reach the cairns but you could take the bus to Culloden and walk.

Cawdor Castle

Handed an everlasting dose of fame through its associations with Shakespeare's play *Macbeth,* Cawdor Castle (tel. 01667/404401, www.cawdorcastle.com, 10 A.M.–5:30 P.M. May–2nd Sunday in October, £7.90 adults, £6.90 seniors, £4.90 children) is a wonderfully romantic fortress that makes for an engrossing and time-absorbing visit. Shakespeare's protagonist was based very loosely on the real Scottish king of the same name, but giving Macbeth the title of Thane of Cawdor in his play was pure artistic license on the part of the bard. In reality, Cawdor Castle was built several centuries after the actual Macbeth died, but that doesn't detract at all from the appeal of the fortress. It's a simply colossal 14th-century castle with several rooms worth checking out inside. A humorous self-guided tour takes you through the dining room, hung with portraits of famous Campbells, then up to the ornate tapestry room and down to an evocative period kitchen. Everywhere you go is the famous Cawdor tartan. The experience is made by the room notes, which offer insight into the quirks and eccentricities that make a family history so interesting. The castle also has a good bookshop and restaurant, and the grounds are every bit as splendid as the castle. They include a formal walled garden, a putting green and golf course, and several nature trails. Cawdor Castle is off the B9090 five miles southwest of Nairn. Rapsons bus 12 heads to Cawdor from Inverness.

Fort George

Jacobite forces may have been crushed after the Battle of Culloden but just possibly they had the last laugh. The uneasy government commissioned the hugely expensive construction (£1 billion in today's money) of Fort George (by Ardersier, tel. 01667/460232, 9:30 A.M.–5:30 P.M. daily Apr.–Sept., 9:30 A.M.–4:30 P.M. daily Oct.–Mar., £6.50 adults, £3.25 children) to ensure any repeat Jacobite uprising could be easily quelled. The fort, reckoned by military historians to have most perfect defense of any fortress in the world, never saw combat. On a windy headland by the Moray Firth, it's a monstrous military fortification. It's easily the biggest of its kind in Britain and quite possibly in Europe. There's one mile of walls surrounded by heavy ditches, and barracks space for 1,600 troops. Its appeal, as it remains almost completely intact, is in the insight into 18th-century military activities it offers. Fort George is still occupied by government troops today and contains the Regimental Museum of the Queen's Own Highlanders (open daily Apr.–Sept. and Mon.–Fri. Oct.–Mar.). Fort George is 11 miles northeast of Inverness; take the A966 east to Nairn, from which it's signposted. Bus 11, the airport service, runs to Ardersier or Fort George very two hours.

Nairn

Tucked away in the easternmost corner of the Southern Highlands, the pleasant town of Nairn is a fair-sized seaside resort with some spectacular walks along its sandy coast. The Victorians heralded Nairn as the "Brighton of Scotland" in the 1880s, but the claim doesn't really stand up today. Brighton is a heaving southern English town, and Nairn is a passed-by backwater.

The most interesting part of the town is **Fishertown,** a cluster of colorful 19th-century fishermen's cottages near the shore. Nairn's coast is a glorious swath of golden sand, perfect for a walk. It's also clearly a bit of coast the local council is keen to promote; lots of information boards tell you tidbits of local history as you wander along. Farther east from Nairn is the **Culbin Forest,** with many wonderful paths to explore. Trains run from Inverness to Nairn every two hours or so. Stagecoach buses also stop by in Nairn between Inverness and Aberdeen hourly Monday–Saturday.

Loch Ness and Vicinity

Scotland's most renowned loch probably deserves all the hype: Even discounting Nessie, the monster that may or may not lurk within the deeps, it's a spectacular body of forest-flanked black water that all but cuts the Highlands off from the rest of Scotland. The loch is part of the Great Glen, the deep, forested valley that runs southwest from Inverness, on the country's east coast, to Fort William, on the west coast. At 23 miles long and up to 754 feet deep in parts, Scotland's largest body of freshwater would be as good a location as any for a large creature to hide. Monster appeal has burgeoned a tacky tourist industry that spoils the intense beauty of the loch, and with a main road cutting along the north shore, it's not the easiest loch in Scotland to appreciate.

Loch Ness, however, is worth giving some time. There is the picture-perfect Urquhart Castle lying on its shores and the engineering masterwork of the Caledonian Canal to appreciate at its southern end. The canal, constructed by Thomas Telford in the 1820s, used the vast lochs in the Great Glen to give the Highlands an invaluable coast-to-coast route. Contrary to popular belief, it's possible to escape the tourists on Loch Ness. Traveling along the south shore, you will encounter a lonely stretch of inky forest, secreting one of the most magical waterfalls in the Highlands. North of the Great Glen are other wild spots like Glen Affric.

NORTH SHORE

Traversed by the traffic-snarled and often treacherous A82, the north shore of Loch Ness gets the worst of both worlds: lots of tourists and few places to pause and actually look at the loch. The places there are to stop get consequently very busy. There is Urquhart Castle, a magnificent fortress mirrored in the dark waters of the loch and the village of Drumnadrochit with no fewer than two Loch Ness monster museums.

Sights

It was St. Columba who made the first recorded sighting of the Loch Ness monster. He was engaged in missionary work when he came upon a group of men burying a comrade who had been bitten by a giant fishlike creature. As the burial continued, the monster reared its ugly head to strike again but St. Columba commanded it back into the deeps by holding up a crucifix. The spirit of the monster is alive as ever 1,500 years later, nowhere as much as at **Drumnadrochit.** "Drummy," as locals call this village, is where you'll find unashamedly touristy **The Original Loch Ness Monster Centre** (Loch Ness Lodge Hotel, tel. 01456/450342, www.lochness-centre.com, 9 A.M.–5 P.M. daily, £5 adults, £3.50 children), which takes a fun look at the sightings of the monster through the ages.

On a grassy promontory jutting into Loch Ness is **Urquhart Castle** (tel. 01456/450551, 9:30 A.M.–5:30 P.M. daily Apr.–Sept., 9:30 A.M.–5 P.M. Oct.–Mar., £6.50 adult, £3.25 children), one of Scotland's most romantic and most visited ruined castles. There have been buildings on the strategically important site the castle stands upon for almost 1,500 years, at least since the time when St. Columba baptized a Pictish noble on the foreshore here in the late 6th century. The castle itself dates from the 13th century; it saw action during the Jacobite rebellion, when a small garrison of men loyal to the government defended the castle against vastly superior numbers of the Jacobite army. It's all about location at Urquhart, though. The only significant part of the ruin, the tower house, has its broken battlements reflected in the deeps of Scotland's most famous loch. There is, of course, one big reason besides the ruins that visitors come here—to catch a glance of Nessie, the Loch Ness Monster, from the shoreline. By the entrance you'll pass through a riveting visitors center.

Walks

The best walk in the vicinity is to the summit

of **Craigmonie Hill:** it gives a rare bird's-eye view of the loch from the north shore. Turn right out of the Drumnadrochit TIC car park and you'll see the footpath sign 100 meters down the road. Keep bearing uphill through woods to Craigmonie Crag; a path continues past a viewpoint with amazing views of the loch to a waterfall, the **Falls of Divach.** The TIC and Loch Ness Backpackers Lodge have information on this walk.

Accommodations and Food

You can't help falling in love with the friendly little **Loch Ness Backpackers Lodge** (Coiltie Farmhouse, East Lewiston, tel. 01456/450807, beds from £12.50); it puts many other hostels around to shame with its character and coziness. It sports a snug lounge and an equally snug set of mixed dorms. There's not much space but you are guaranteed to meet plenty of interesting like-minded backpackers. Breakfast of coffee and toast is included in the price. Follow the A82 south for almost a mile after Drumnadrochit; the road to the hostel is on the left, signposted for the Loch Ness Inn.

The best bed-and-breakfast on the northern shore is in the converted church of **Glenkirk** (Drumnadrochit, tel. 01456/450802, www.lochnessbandb.com, from £55 d). It's a peaceful place with three large, light rooms and lots of original church features (pews and big windows). The large guest lounge has board games and is a particularly good spot to contemplate the view across the garden, particularly with some of the owner's complimentary homemade shortbread.

There's no denying it: the **Loch Ness Lodge Hotel** (Drumnadrochit, tel. 01456/450342, www.lochness-hotel.com, from £80 d) is about as traditionally furnished a hotel as you could get—tartan, bare stone work, and dark wood paneling. Once the home of a colonial tea planter, the hotel now shelters mainly tour groups and monster-followers (one of the Loch Ness monster museums is next door).

Up a secluded tree-lined drive about half a mile from the center of Drumnadrochit, **Benleva Hotel** (tel. 01456/450080, www

.benleva.co.uk, 3–11 P.M. Mon.–Thurs., 3 P.M.–1 A.M. Fri., noon–midnight Sat., 12:30 P.M.–midnight Sun.) is the best place around to get a good hearty meal and a pint of real ale. Plenty of traditional Scottish fare like haggis, neeps, and tatties (haggis with turnip and potato mash) features on the menu for £7–12. The dining area is an intimate little place—watch out for the soppy dog that likes to join everyone for dinner.

Getting There and Away

The **Rapsons Inverness to Fort William** service 19 stops off along the north shore of Loch Ness at Drumnadrochit, Urquhart Castle, and the Loch Ness Youth Hostel. There are two buses every two hours.

C FORT AUGUSTUS

The drive along the A82 southwest along Loch Ness can be almost bland in places, with an endless wall of conifers between you and the lochside. By far the brightest place you'll come across, Fort Augustus is clustered around the head of the loch. The location of this bustling little village means it pulls in the crowds; it spans a magnificent stretch of the Caledonian Canal, completed by Thomas Telford in 1822. With some great places to stay and something irresistibly charming about it despite the tourist hordes, Fort Augustus makes a great journey-breaker. It's an alternative spot to base yourself for a boat cruise on the loch or canal and has shops, good restaurants, a petrol station, two ATM machines, and canal boat facilities.

Sights and Activities

The main things to do in Fort Augustus are watching the boats go up and down the Caledonian Canal's five-flight series of locks, laid out in a dramatic staircase above Loch Ness. The Great Glen Way also passes through Fort Augustus.

Run by British Waterways, the **Caledonian Canal Visitor Centre** (Canalside, tel. 01320/366493, 10 A.M.–5 P.M. daily Apr.–Oct., free) tells you about the history of the canal. It sets out the vision for, and the realization of, one of Britain's greatest 19th-century construction feats. The visitors center is just up from where the main road crosses the canal.

Comfortably seating 120 passengers on two decks, the boat run by **Cruise Loch Ness** (tel. 01320/366277, www.cruiselochness.com, cruises at 2 P.M. daily Mar.–Oct., weekend cruises only Nov.–Dec., £9.50 adults, £5.50 children) is fitted with sonar equipment and cruises Loch Ness for one hour to see if any signs of the Loch Ness Monster can be found. There's nothing quite like sitting with a beer on the top deck in the summer, scouring the surface of a loch for monsters.

You can hire a bike at **Clansman Centre Bicycle Hire** (Canalside, tel. 01320/366444).

Accommodations and Food

In the woods above Fort Augustus is cheerfully done-up **Morag's Lodge** (Bunoich Brae, tel. 01320/366289, www.moragslodge.com, beds £16, £42 d), a whitewashed house in quiet grounds. There are clean four- and six-bed dorms, as well as twin and double rooms. If you don't feel like self-catering, you can get decent food here in the mornings and evenings. There's a bar, too. The hostel is up the road by the petrol station in Fort Augustus.

Banks often occupy stunning buildings, but they are not usually surrounded by Highland scenery and still less often have a guesthouse right next door. **Bank House** (Station Rd., tel. 01320/366755, £60 d) has three large rooms available. Rooms are light, airy, and en suite, with color TVs. There is a resident lounge and even a small library full of Scottish interest books.

There are not too many bed-and-breakfasts like the ⟨ **Old Pier House** (by Fort Augustus, tel. 01320/366418, from £40 d) in the Loch Ness area. Few others can boast a huge tract of the coast of Loch Ness amongst their grounds and still fewer can offer a relaxed, unpretentious, and unspoiled environment for their guests. Yet the Old Pier House has happily avoided the trappings of crass tourism and instead focused on providing genuine top-notch farm hospitality. The 100-year-old farmhouse has three pine-furnished bed-and-breakfast rooms and several

delightful self-catering cabins—purportedly prime monster-spotting pads. There is a lounge with an open fire, and activities like horseback riding and boating are available. The Old Pier House is up a track to the left as you reach the edge of Fort Augustus from the northeast.

The Scots Kitchen (A82 by car park, tel. 01320/366361, 10 A.M.–5 P.M. daily) is a great little café for a light bite to eat during the day. Best of all are breakfasts, where the coffee is strong and the French toast with maple syrup and bacon is heavenly and crisp. In summer, the kitchen is also open for evening meals. You'll find it opposite the garage, just before the canal bridge as you approach from Inverness. Snacks are £2–6.

The sunny **Bothy** (Canalside, tel. 01320/366710, www.lochnessrestaurant.co.uk, lunches noon–4 P.M., dinners 5–9 P.M.) with its conservatory-style seating and a great location makes an atmospheric spot for a meal. In the daytime, try a fine homemade soup. For dinner, tuck into some Loch Linnhe salmon or feast on duck with wild berry sauce. Main meals are £8–14, with seafood platters setting you back £24.

The **Lock Inn** (Canalside, tel. 01320/366302, lunches served noon–5 P.M. daily) is a nearby traditional pub.

Information

Fort Augustus TIC (tel. 0845/225 5121, 10 A.M.–4 P.M. daily Easter–Oct.) is a small but friendly and useful TIC in the main car park in Fort Augustus.

The village post office (Canalside, tel. 01320/366373) also contains a *bureau de change*.

Getting There and Away

Bus service 19 stops off in Fort Augustus twice every two hours en route between Inverness and Fort William; it's one hour from Inverness to Fort Augustus.

SOUTH SHORE

Hemmed by the lunar-like Monadhliath Mountains, the south shore of Loch Ness rises and falls from high yellow moor to inky green forest. Remarkably few people follow the road that runs right along it from Fort Augustus to Inverness. Here you'll find the loch's best viewpoints, the majestic Falls of Foyers, and some peaceful forest walks. There are a couple of routes to take along the loch, including one that follows the course of one of General Wade's 18th-century military roads. Jacobite rebels were particularly grateful for the road along Loch Ness and used it to their advantage far more than government troops did.

Sights

The main pleasures of the South Shore are scenic ones. One of the best viewpoints in the Great Glen is along the B862 as it climbs up to Stratherrick on the south side of the loch.

The best attraction on the south shore is a spectacular waterfall. The **Falls of Foyers** (by Foyers, open year-round, free) was a key attraction on Loch Ness in the 19th century, but now it is often overlooked in favor of the more gimmicky north shore tourist draws. By the post office and stores in Foyers, a series of paths lead down to a viewpoint above a primeval gorge. Here, against sheer, water-slimed cliffs, one of Britain's most magnificent waterfalls plunges 140 feet down toward Loch Ness in a Jurassic-like setting; it feels like a dinosaur could emerge from the foliage at any moment.

The trees here are also favored by an abundance of increasingly rare red squirrels; this is one of the best places in Scotland to catch them at their antics. There are live CCTV links observing the squirrels, linked to a monitor in the **Red Squirrel Café** (by Foyers post office, Easter–Sept. on CCTV, year-round live) where you can sit with a cappuccino and get hours of squirrel entertainment.

One of the best places to appreciate the thick, lush forest on the south shore of Loch Ness is at **Farigaig** (by Inverfarigaig, year-round), farther northeast along the B852 from Foyers. A number of forestry commission tracks lead up into the trees.

Accommodations and Food

You may very well fancy staying along the tranquil south shore; **Foyers House** (by Foyers,

tel. 01456/486405, www.foyershouse-loch-ness.com, from £50 d) is the best of these few places on offer. Tucked away in the woods up a track just down from Foyers post office, rose-pink Foyers House has eight rooms to let. There are a mix of shared and en suite facilities in the light, white rooms, all of which have comfortable twin or double beds and TVs. If you're an early riser, heading up to the splendid roof terrace to watch dawn breaking over Loch Ness is an experience you will never forget. The other big reason to stay here is to make use of the cozy restaurant (Easter–Sept.) serving dishes like venison, duck, and salmon. Accommodation does not include breakfast, offered at £7.50 per person.

Getting There and Away

D & E Coaches (tel. 01463/713181) runs a once-daily service (302) down the south shore of Loch Ness to Foyers from Inverness.

SPEAN BRIDGE AND VICINITY

Marking the end of the Great Glen is the village of Spean Bridge in a remote, thickly forested spot by Loch Lochy. It's a spread-out place dominated by the tourist-infested Spean Bridge Woolen Centre, where you can watch commercialized weaving demonstrations. Despite being the meeting point of two main roads, Spean Bridge feels like one of the loneliest, most foreboding places in the Southern Highlands. This stark moorland setting lends itself particularly well to a couple of noteworthy attractions: the memorial to the World War II commandos that used this area for training and one of Scotland's top ski centers.

Sights and Activities

The **Commando Memorial** (northwest of Spean Bridge off A82, open year-round) stands in a lonely location above the head of Loch Lochy, remembering the commando units of World War II that trained in the area. The commandos were a novel fighting force in the 1940s: elite, handpicked, highly trained, almost guerrilla-style troops that spearheaded operations like the D-Day landings. Sixty years

© LUKE WATERSON

Commando Memorial, by Spean Bridge, commemorating the world's first military commandos, who trained in the lonely countryside nearby

on, it is standard practice for armies to have commando units, but the men remembered by this memorial were among the pioneers.

Skiing at the **Nevis Range Ski Centre** (by Spean Bridge, tel. 01397/705825, www.nevisrange.co.uk) in sight of Scotland's highest mountain, Ben Nevis, is a memorable experience. This is the newest of the country's five ski centers and offers 35 runs in mountain scenery topping 4,000 feet. The key mountain here is Aonach Mor with both exposed and sheltered runs; snow buildup is probably greater here than at any other ski center in Scotland. There's equipment hire and the Snowgoose Restaurant for a refreshment stop. The resort is divided into two zones; day passes to either cost £24 for adults. The center is southwest of Spean Bridge, off the A82.

Getting There and Away
Rapsons Bus service 19 runs twice every two hours between Inverness and Fort William with a stop at Spean Bridge bus shelter. These buses will stop at the entrance of the road to the Nevis Range Ski Centre, but it is better accessed by a Rapsons service 42 from Fort William (about five times daily Mon.–Sat., three times daily Sun.).

GLEN AFFRIC
Ten miles north of Loch Ness in distance—and light years away in atmosphere—Glen Affric is a remote valley of rich green folds of conifers beneath hills that blaze red with heather. It stretches for some 30 miles west of the area's main settlement, Cannich, but most of it is only accessible by foot. The area referred to as Glen Affric is actually a series of three glens linked by the wooded River Glass. Glen Affric is the most southerly of the three, traversed by two lanes and renowned for the twinkling cascade of water known as Plodda Falls. Glen Cannich and the long and lovely Glen Strathfarrar lie to the north. All three glens are notoriously glorious hiking, fishing, and wildlife-spotting country. This wild, unspoiled landscape leaps up into the peaks of Lochalsh but seldom becomes bare or rocky: it's a gentle

feast for the eye in stark contrast to the daunting rocky crags that make up many glens. One of Scotland's top hill walks leads from Glen Affric to Glen Shiel, in Lochalsh.

Sights

The deeper you get into the glens, the more wildlife you are likely to see. Watch out for badgers, foxes, golden eagles, and red deer. Glen Affric sees so few humans that animals sometimes seem fearless; it's possible to get quite close to some.

Three miles west of Tomich, the minor road to Cougie skirts the path to the spectacular **Plodda Falls** (northeast of Cougie, open year-round). The combination of slumbering ancient conifer forest, the white torrent of water, and the black plunge pool at the bottom make this a special place. It's a one-mile walk to the viewing platform from the car park.

Walks

At first glance, Glen Affric appears to have pretty good facilities, but away from the hamlet of Cannich, these facilities go from sparse to virtually nonexistent. If you are contemplating a long-distance hike through the glen, bear in mind that once you leave the Tomich Hotel there is nothing save the Glen Affric Youth Hostel until you reach the Cluanie Inn in Glen Shiel. That said, you could not ask for a better experience of the Scottish countryside than walking up into the loch-daubed moor in the high reaches of the wide valley of Glen Affric. There are paths of various lengths, including some wooded trails around Plodda Falls.

The most mammoth hike is from Cannich up Glen Affric to the forestry commission car park on the north shore of Loch Affric and on to the croft of **Altbeithe** and **Glen Affric Youth Hostel** (20 miles). From here it's another 7.5 boggy miles to the road lay-by on the A87, a mile east of the Cluanie Inn in Glen Shiel. The walk is hard going, and best split into a two-day hike, with a break at Glen Affric Youth Hostel.

Accommodations

The remote croft of Altbeithe is where you'll find **Glen Affric Youth Hostel** (tel. 0870/155 3255, www.syha.org.uk, beds £14); in the upper reaches of Glen Affric, it's probably the most inaccessible hostel in the country. It's 18-bed basic accommodation in little more than a glorified shed. The nearest road access is 7.5 difficult miles south at Glen Cluanie, at the head of Glen Shiel in Lochalsh.

Glamorous, whitewashed **Kerrow House** (by Cannich, tel. 01456/415243, www.kerrow-house.co.uk, £60 d) is a former hunting lodge high in the forested hills southwest of Cannich. This place retains every inch of its Victorian glory; there are four-poster beds and lots of ornate dark wood furniture offset by a cool white decor. The delectable breakfast occasionally includes smoked salmon. As if you needed more perks, there's also complimentary fishing on the River Glass in the woodsy grounds. It's right in the heart of Glen Affric, and a perfect base for exploring the area. The house is one mile south of Cannich on the minor road to Tomich along the south bank of the river.

An old Victorian hunting hotel, the **Tomich Hotel** (by Cannich, tel. 01456/415399, www.tomichhotel.co.uk, £67.50 s, £105 d) has a selection of well-appointed, innovatively decorated rooms. All are en suite with TVs; many have extra features like whirlpool baths, king-size beds, and CD/DVD players. The downstairs restaurant is one of the best places around for a bite to eat. It's a comfortable relaxed place with an open fire and candlelit dining, and it serves food all day.

Getting There and Away

Public transport in Glen Affric is poor but not as bad as you might think. The highly useful **bus** service 17, run by Rapsons, heads to Drumnadrochit and then up to Cannich and Tomich four or five times daily Monday–Saturday. In summer, you can go by bus from Cannich right up to Loch Affric, but you could probably walk in the time you'll be waiting for the bus to show.

Cairngorm Mountains

Carved out by glaciers 10,000 years ago, the Cairngorm Mountains are known as the "roof of the world" due to their uninterrupted extent of high altitude plateau. This is as close as you'll come to the Rockies or the Alps in Britain—a largely subarctic terrain of dark, stark peaks etched with snow-filled corries and occasional verdant valleys. Part of the wider Grampian mountain range, which runs from Fort William northwest as far as Aberdeenshire, the Cairngorm Mountains are a magnet for skiers, mountaineers, and hill-walkers. The main center for all this outdoor activity is Aviemore, from where you can head up through the majestic ancient pine trees of the Rothiemurchus Forest to the Cairngorm Ski Centre. From here a bare series of mountains spreads southwest with barely a road or a house to break the view until Fort William, some 50 miles away. Southwest of Aviemore are the remote settlements of Newtonmore and Kingussie. Between them they share a world-class folk museum and an age-old shinty rivalry. Watching the two towns come head to head in a game of shinty, a rougher version of hockey with fewer rules, is one of the more bizarre experiences the Highlands can throw at you.

AVIEMORE AND ROTHIEMURCHUS FOREST

Year upon year, people traipse to ugly Aviemore, the winter sports capital of Britain, to try their hand at skiing or snowboarding at the nearby Cairngorm Ski Centre. It's best to avoid the crass tourist development of Aviemore at all costs, but east of town the road up to the ski center passes through the ancient, hauntingly beautiful Rothiemurchus Forest. Centered on the brooding silvery mirror of Loch Morlich, the forest has great picnicking spots and walks.

Rothiemurchus Forest

Inky green Rothiemurchus Forest (www .Rothiemurchus.net) climbs from the gentle River Spey right up the Cairngorm Mountain plateau. It's a rich, luscious spread of trees, a large number of which form the largest remaining bastion of the ancient Caledonian pine forest that once covered Scotland. The best access point is from along the road up to Cairngorm Ski Centre, but the forest stretches southwest of Aviemore almost as far as Kingussie. It's a vast and easily accessible area for a range of outdoor activities from walking to canoeing to pony trekking.

The best frame of reference comes from the **Rothiemurchus Centre** (Coylumbridge by Aviemore, tel. 01479/812345, 9:30 A.M.– 5:30 P.M. daily Feb.–Oct.), a visitors center located one mile south of Aviemore on the road to the Cairngorm Ski Centre. It has bags of information on what there is to do in the forest.

Britain's only herd of reindeer can be found in the grounds of Glenmore Lodge, in upper Rothiemurchus, at the **Cairngorm Reindeer Centre** (tel. 01479/861228, www.reindeer-company.demon.co.uk, reindeer visits at 11 A.M. daily, also at 2:30 P.M. daily in summer, winter visits dependent on whether the free-ranging herd can be found, £2.50 adults, £1.50 children). It's a fun experience, and the reindeer are quite docile. The center is by Glenmore Forest Caravan and Camping Park.

If you like the idea of a world-class mountain view but aren't so keen on hiking to attain it, then the **Cairngorm Mountain Railway and Ski Centre** (tel. 01479/861261, www.cairn-gormmountain.org.uk, railway trips every 10–20 min. 10 A.M.–4 P.M. year-round, ski center accessibility dependent on snow conditions) is the trip for you. From the Cairngorm Ski Centre Base Station at the very end of the road up through Rothiemurchus, this mountain railway takes you up to Ptarmigan Top Station, just below the jagged summit of Cairn Gorm (4085 feet or 1245 meters). The trip costs £9.25 adults, £5.85 children. The base station is also where you should buy ski and snowboarding passes. Half-day ski passes cost £21.50 adults, £15 children. This may be Scotland's biggest ski area, with over 20 miles of piste, but don't expect anything too dramatic; drizzle is the order of the day more often than snow. The snow conditions, which are as erratic as any other weather condition in Scotland, are best checked at the Aviemore TIC before you build your hopes up.

Shopping

For groceries and provisions, there is **Tesco** (Grampian Rd., 8 A.M.–10 P.M. Mon.–Sat., 9 A.M.–6 P.M. Sun.) For outdoor gear, head to the sizeable branch of **Nevisport** (89 Grampian Rd., tel. 01479/810239, 9 A.M.–5:30 P.M. Mon.–Fri., 9 A.M.–6 P.M. Sat.–Sun.).

Walking

Aside from the hikes in Rothiemurchus and the Cairngorm Mountains themselves, the 84-mile **Speyside Way** (www.speysideway.org) footpath now extends to Aviemore. One of the best hikes to get a taste of the dramatic Cairngorm Mountain scenery is the 20-mile hike through the mountains to **Linn of Dee** in Royal Deeside, Aberdeenshire. It's a wonderful yet grueling route that follows the old drovers route via the Lairig Ghru Pass and takes in great views of Britain's second-highest mountain, Ben Macdui. If you're a keen hiker you should pick up one of the many walking books that cover the Cairngorm Mountains, like *Walking in the Cairngorms* by Ronald Turnbull, published by Cicerone Press.

Accommodations

It's worth swapping a ceiling over your head for canvas to stay right up in the heart of Rothiemurchus Forest at **Glenmore Caravan and Camping Park** (tel. 01479/861271 or 0845/130 8224, www.forestholidays.co.uk, from £18 for two people and a tent). This site is in the trees by the shores of Loch Morlich—a wonderfully peaceful place with a café/shop nearby and plenty of space.

Purpose-built **Aviemore Bunkhouse** (Dalfaber Rd., tel. 01479/811181, www.aviemore-bunkhouse.com, beds £15, £40 d) sits right next to the Old Bridge Inn. It has basic 6- to 12-bed dorms with floor heating, a drying room, storage lockers, and free Wi-Fi Internet access. Private rooms can be made available for couples.

Ravenscraig Guest House (141 Grampian Rd., tel. 01479/810278, £28–35 s, £56–70 d) is a pleasant Victorian property set back from the road. It packs in 12 rooms—six in the main part of the house and six in an adjoining annex. The annex rooms are big enough for four people, and one is suitable for disabled guests. Breakfasts at Ravenscraig have a good reputation, including the locally produced marmalade.

Ardlogie Guest House (Dalfaber Rd., tel. 01479/810747, www.ardlogie.co.uk, £38 s, £56 d) is a bright, white, modern house with five en suite rooms furnished in pine and a crisp combination of pinks, whites, and blues. If you're a solo traveler, you'll be given a double room. It's a friendly place with a terrace overlooking a tranquil enclosed garden, where you can play boule. Smoked salmon and croissants with whisky marmalade are on the breakfast menu. Another bonus of staying here: you get free access to gym/sauna facilities at a nearby country club. The house is located farther down the road from the Old Bridge Inn.

Great, gray, turreted, and maybe a bit past its prime, **Cairngorm Hotel** (Grampian Rd., tel. 01479/810223, www.cairngorm.com, £50 s, £80 d) has a wealth of rooms to meet visitors' needs. There are around 30 well-kept, neutrally decorated rooms with all the standard hotel amenities (en suite bathrooms, TVs, and telephones). None will make you gasp with amazement but most will give you a good, comfy night's sleep. On weekends the music from the bar downstairs can throb a little around some rooms.

In the Victorian era, when **C Corrour House Hotel** (Rothiemurchus, by Aviemore, tel. 01479/810220, www.corrourhousehotel.co.uk, £70–110 d) was built, the exquisite emerald green grounds were laid out in such a way that the house looks straight down a fairway-like lawn with forest on either side framing the cloud-flecked Cairngorm Mountains perfectly behind. The rooms have a relaxed elegance about them; there are eight in total, all en suite with TVs, telephones, and a healthy dose of dark wood furniture. There's a cozy lounge with an open fire and a bar at which to try a few single malts. Red squirrels, pine martens, and deer are all regular visitors to the grounds. Breakfast in the charming dining room is included; ask about evening meals.

Food

Wood-paneled **Mountain Café** (111 Grampian Rd., tel. 01479/812473, www.mountaincafe-aviemore.co.uk, 8:30 A.M.–5:30 P.M. daily) does a superb coffee and a range of healthy snacks (like chowder) throughout the day. If the weather is bad, huddling here over a hot snack is just the therapy you need. Snacks and light meals £1–7.

Cool **Café Mambo** (Units 12–13 Grampian Rd., tel. 01479/811670, noon–8:30 P.M. Mon.–Thurs., noon–7:30 P.M. Fri.–Sat., 12:30–8:30 P.M. Sun.) is easily the most interesting of Aviemore town center's tame culinary offerings. It's a great place to relax with a coffee or hot chocolate in the daytime, when you can also get a good range of burgers and baguettes. Come evenings, Café Mambo caters to the cocktail-drinking brigade—the selection is huge and the names are intriguing.

La Taverna (High Range Holiday Complex, Grampian Rd., tel. 01479/810683, noon–9 P.M. daily) is a cozy restaurant with tables set around a stone wood-fired oven. It served monstrously sized pizzas and a wide range of Italian wines and international beers. With checked tablecloths and low wooden beams, it pulls off an extremely authentic Italian experience despite the unlikely exterior. Meals are £7–15. You'll find the restaurant south of Aviemore town center and just north of the junction with the B970.

After a few minutes in the crass, tourist-infested center of Aviemore, you'll be only too pleased to take refuge in the atmospheric **Old Bridge Inn** (Dalfaber Rd., by Aviemore, tel. 01479/811137, www.old-bridgeinn.co.uk, noon–2 P.M. and 6–9 P.M. Mon.–Thurs., noon–2 P.M. and 6–9:30 P.M. Fri.–Sat., 12:30–2 P.M. and 6–9 P.M. Sun.). With the beamed ceilings, fires, and dark,

shiny traditional-look wood, this is a proper Scottish pub serving solid Scottish food like venison or roast lamb. OK, it's Aviemore, so it isn't cheap, but at £10–16 for main meals and much less for one of the real ales on offer, it's the nicest place around for a drink.

Information and Services

Proficient **Aviemore TIC** (tel. 01479/810363, 9 A.M.–5 P.M. Mon.–Sat., 10 A.M.–4 P.M. Sun.) is open throughout the year to deal with your queries.

For a launderette, try **Aviemore Laundrette** (Unit 1–2 Myrtlefield Shopping Centre, tel. 01479/810462) or the Rothiemurchus Caravan and Camp Site at the **Rothiemurchus Centre** (by Aviemore, tel. 01479/812345, www.rothie-murchus.net, 9:30 A.M.–5:30 P.M. daily Feb.–Oct.).

Getting There and Away

Trains connect Aviemore with Inverness every 1.5–2 hours (40 min.). Aviemore trains also continue south to Perth and Edinburgh: the town's on the main Inverness line. Buses also run to Aviemore from Inverness about hourly, including **Rapsons** service 15, which goes via Rainmore Hospital and Grantown on Spey several times daily, sometimes with a change in Grantown on Spey required.

Getting Around

Buses run from Aviemore up to Coylumbridge and on to the Cairngorm Ski Centre about hourly (20 min.).

For a taxi, call **Aviemore Taxis** (tel. 01479/810118).

STRATHSPEY

In between the stark mountain surrounds, the verdant Strathspey Valley offers a few more refined accommodation options than Aviemore, all of which are also suitable outdoor activities bases. The prettiest of these is Boat of Garten, linked to Aviemore by the scenic Strathspey railway. The village has dubbed itself, with some justification, "Osprey Village," as a result of the ospreys on the nearby RSPB Centre.

Sights

Run by train enthusiasts for train enthusiasts, **Strathspey Steam Railway** (tel. 01479/810725, www.strathspeyrailway.co.uk, 2–4 services daily Easter–Oct., sporadic service Dec.–Feb.) links Aviemore and Boat of Garten. The branch line traverses some gorgeous countryside, and you can dine on the train, too (although it's only 15 minutes between the two stations). A round-trip journey costs £10.50 adults, £5.25 children.

Ospreys have been nesting at Loch Garten in the Abernethy Forest since the 1950s. Superb CCTV links with a fish eagle nest site at the **Loch Garten Royal Society for the Protection of Birds (RSPB) Centre** (Abernethy Forest, tel. 01479/831476, 10 A.M.–6 P.M. daily Apr.–Aug., £3 adults, £2 children) reserve give you one of the best opportunities in Scotland to see these amazing birds up close and personal. The RSPB Centre also runs "Caper Watch" starting at 5:30 A.M. from April to May for the viewing of Capercailles, birds of the grouse family with elaborate mating rituals. It's the enthusiastic, knowledgeable staff here as much as anything that makes this such an invaluable experience.

Accommodations and Food

The **Old Ferryman's House** (Boat of Garten, tel. 01479/831370, £51 d) is a charming stone-built former ferryman's cottage is right next to the River Spey. The peaceful, homey rooms, all with shared bathrooms, look out on a garden backed by forests and hills. With no TV and a lounge where the main entertainments are reading and toasting yourself by the wood-burning stove, this is somewhere to forget about the hurried pace of modern life. Excellent meals are available in the evenings, and you'll get snacks on arrival. To find the house, follow the main road through the village from the A9 and cross the River Spey; the house is immediately on the right.

The snug, traditional **Boat Hotel** (Boat of Garten, tel. 01479/831258, www.boathotel.co.uk, food served noon–3 P.M. and 6–9 P.M. daily, £85 s, £110 d) has high-quality rooms and an equally top-standard restaurant. Bedrooms here have a touch of class—even standard rooms are large and light, with dark wood furnishings and smart, old-fashioned fabrics. There are even four-poster bed rooms and suites with stand-alone baths. All rooms have en suite facilities. Once you're settled in, you can chow down on some great home cooking in the convivial Osprey Bar/Bistro. Main meals like braised lamb shank with garlic roast potatoes cost £8–13.

The former sporting lodge of **Dalrachney Lodge** (Carrbridge, tel. 01479/841252, www.dalrachney.co.uk, from £80 d) offers sumptuous accommodation on the leafy edge of Carrbridge off the A938 to Grantown on Spey. There are great views of the conifer-flanked estate and the Spey valley from the large windows of the rooms. Rooms have en suite or private facilities, TVs, and armchairs. It's all very formal, with crisp white tablecloths in the dining room and the kind of lounge where it is easier to imagine Victorian gentlemen smoking after dinner than 21st-century guests relaxing. The lodge has its own river fishing, too.

Getting There and Away

Rapsons Bus service 15 runs from Inverness to Carrbridge, Grantown on Spey, and Boat of Garten en route to Aviemore several times daily. In the summer the best and most fun way of getting from Boat of Garten to Aviemore is via the **Strathspey Railway** (regular departures).

NEWTONMORE AND KINGUSSIE

Farther up the river Spey from Aviemore, high up in the hills are the quiet twin settlements known better for the sport they play than anything else. Newtonmore and Kingussie are the two great exponents of the version of Highland hockey known as shinty. Under the watchful eye of the Cairngorm Mountains to the south and the Monadhliath Mountains to the north, the two village sides slog it out on Newtonmore's pitch several times between March and October.

© LUKE WATERSON

Ruthven Barracks, above Kingussie, one of the defenses put up by government forces to quell the Jacobite uprisings

Other than the obvious draw of the mountains, there's another very good reason to come here: the superb Highland Folk Museum, which offers an imaginative insight into Highland life in times gone by. Kingussie is the brighter of the two communities to spend time in and has better restaurants.

Sights

Newtonmore and Kingussie are only separated by one mile of road, with a footpath running the entire length.

Located on two sites in Newtonmore and Kingussie, the **Highland Folk Museum** (tel. 01540/673551, http://highlandfolk.museum, Newtonmore site open 10:30 A.M.–5:30 P.M. daily Easter–Aug., 11:30 A.M.–4:30 P.M. daily Sept.–Oct., Kingussie Site by prior arrangement only, free, donations appreciated) is a moving immersion experience in traditional Highland culture. You're not simply viewing a museum here—you're actually part of it. There is a re-creation of an 18th-century township, reconstructed using traditional materials, as

well as a farm and several early 20th-century shops. You can take part in a typical 1930s school class and view intriguing demonstrations of typical Highland crafts. An old-fashioned bus trundles around the mile-long site. The best thing about this open-air complex is that it doesn't fall into the trap many Highland museums do (i.e., a few pieces of rusting farm machinery in a barn) but really makes an effort to engage visitors with the history on display. The Kingussie site is open only to pre-booked groups. The Newtonmore site is well signposted from the center of Newtonmore village.

The extensive ruins of **Ruthven Barracks** (B970 south of Kingussie, year-round, free) stand on a hill above Kingussie with a commanding view over the Spey valley. The government built the barracks to quell Jacobite uprisings in the early 18th century, but they crumbled following a Jacobite siege. There are several buildings to explore and great views of the surrounding hills.

If ever a settlement in Scotland looked like it had been picked up and transported stone by

© LUKE WATERSON

Newtonmore's shinty pitch

stone from the Canadian Rockies, **Dalwhinnie,** 14 miles southwest of Newtonmore, off the A9, would be it. It's a remote, chilly, spread-out place with the highest distillery in Scotland at 1,073 feet above sea level, **Dalwhinnie Distillery** (tel. 01540/672219, 9:30 A.M.–5 P.M. Mon.–Sat., 12:30–4:30 P.M. Sun. July–Aug., 9:30 A.M.–5 P.M. Mon.–Sat. June and Sept., 11 A.M.–4 P.M. Mon.–Sat. Oct., 9:30 A.M.–5 P.M. Mon.–Fri. Easter–May, 11 A.M.–2 P.M. Mon.–Fri. Nov.–Easter (£5). This collection of white-washed buildings in the wide, desolate valley of Glen Truim is a lonely, beautiful sight, although more beautiful is a taste of the spirit distilled here, flavored with snow-fed waters. There are two to three tours daily.

Shinty

A few other Highland teams partake in the rough form of hockey known as shinty but pale in comparison to the game's giants: Newtonmore and Kingussie. Newtonmore has the best shinty pitch, the Eilan, at the west end of the village, with matches taking place generally on Saturdays between March and October.

Invariably these matches take place with neighboring Kingussie, as the two sides are some of the only big shinty teams around.

The rules of the game have been made stricter of recent years. It used to be that matches could take place on any size of pitch with any number of participants (whole villages used to compete); these days, it's 12 a side. From a distance, a match resembles a hockey game; closer up, it's more or less an anything-goes battle where sticks called cannas are wielded with gay abandon. Shoving, trampling of the opponents, or, in fact, almost any means are used to get the ball into the opponents' goal. It's a hugely entertaining and passionate affair with local family pride often at stake. Newtonmore's club website (www.newtonmoreshinty.com) has information on fixtures and gives a run-down of the history of the sport.

Walking

With a range of mountains on either side, this area is a hotbed of exciting walks. The free car park in Kingussie has an information board detailing local walks; you can also inquire at

Newtonmore Gallery TIC (tel. 01540/673912). The best walk in the area is the four-mile trek over **Creag Bheag** through forest to a dramatic viewpoint (signposted from the free car park in Kingussie). The **Monadhliath Mountains** are a great place to get away from it all, as few walkers head here, but this also means help is not necessarily on hand if you get into difficulty. A good starting point is **Glen Banchor,** a gorgeous picnic spot north of Newtonmore.

Accommodations and Food

Strathspey Mountain Hostel (Main St., Newtonmore, tel. 01540/673694, beds £12) has to be some of the best-value budget accommodation in Scotland—a testament to how many walkers pass through the area in season. It's a convivial Victorian house with 18 beds in four rooms, a fire and plenty of wood to stoke it, and a free washing machine.

Located right by Ruthven Barracks with views over the wide River Spey valley, ◖ **Ruthven Farmhouse** (by Kingussie, tel. 01540/662328, www.bedandbreakfastcairngorms.co.uk, from £60 d) is one of those delightful off-the-beaten-path discoveries. The two rooms are in converted steadings (outbuildings) and are consequently vast. The "Tractor Shed" with its handmade furniture and exposed wooden beams is the pick of the two. The other room is also en suite and has a handmade bed. As an alternative to the huge Scottish breakfast on offer next morning, you could try pancakes stuffed with apple and sultanas. There are discounts for longer stays.

The **Columba House Hotel** (Manse Rd., Kingussie, tel. 01540/661402, www.columbahousehotel.com, £110 d) has 10 huge en suite bedrooms, most with either four-poster or king-size beds in them. The accommodation is a wonderful blend of traditional and modern, and most of the bathrooms get double-sized baths. All rooms are furnished with top-notch refreshments including proper Scottish shortbread and freshly ground coffee. There is a candlelit restaurant with great views of the grounds; dining in the attractive walled garden is possible in good weather.

The best place for a wickedly strong coffee and a panini in Kingussie is at **Gilly's Kitchen** (57 High St., tel. 01540/662273, 10 A.M.–5 P.M. Tues.–Sat.), a bright, flower-bedecked coffee shop with seafood, good curries, homemade bread, and crusty brownies (£1–6).

The cozy ◖ **Tipsy Laird** (68 High St., Kingussie, tel. 01540/661334, www.tipsy-laird.co.uk, food served noon–9 P.M. daily) is the best tavern around for a pint of real ale.

Information and Services

Newtonmore Craft Centre (Main St., Newtonmore, tel. 01540/673026, 8 A.M.–10 P.M. daily summer, 8 A.M.–6 P.M. daily winter) has gifts, Internet access, and a tourist information point.

Getting There and Around

Newtonmore and Kingussie are both linked to the Perth-Inverness **train** line but trains do not always stop here. There are four to five trains daily from Aviemore to both Newtonmore and Kingussie and onward to Perth and Inverness. **Scottish Citylink buses** also run from Inverness to Newtonmore (six daily, 1.25 hrs., £9.70).

Glen Nevis and Glen Coe

It's hard not to be overwhelmed by the sheer, craggy stupendousness of these two glens. With high, mighty black peaks, heather-brown foothills and emerald-green valleys tumbled through by rivers, they offer some of Britain's best-loved mountain walking. Lovely Glen Nevis has Britain's highest mountain, Ben Nevis, as its crowning glory, while Glen Coe is flanked on both sides by a series of daunting jagged peaks. Glen Coe was the scene of the most notorious massacre in Scottish clan history and has an added melancholy as a result. On a blowy day when the wind shears through the rocky passes, it's almost as if you can still hear the cries of the MacDonald clan members as they were murdered by men they believed to be their allies. The main service center in this area is Fort William, which offers an array of distractions for when the weather closes in. There is enough high-level hiking here to fill up several holidays: In sunshine there is no more beautiful part of Scotland, and when the rain sets in, nowhere gloomier.

FORT WILLIAM AND VICINITY

Dual carriageways, a lot of shoddy development, and a pocket of particularly abysmal weather: it's hard to think of ways that gray Fort William could be any more of a blot on an otherwise spectacular landscape. The town huddles around the northern end of Loch Linnhe beneath the heathery bulk of Ben Nevis. It's the gateway to some of the most stunning hill walks in Scotland. The Great Glen and Loch Ness lie just to the northeast, while the magical Road to the Isles lies to the northwest. It's also the meeting point for some major road and rail connections and, as a result, pulls in huge numbers of visitors. If you spend much time in the Highlands you'll be hard pushed to avoid Fort William. Those who do stay find plenty of top tourist facilities: a good range of accommodation, some cracking pubs, and even a couple of worthwhile attractions. Stay long enough to stock up on all those holiday essentials and

get out to the Highlands proper. Nearby Glen Nevis makes a far more desirable base.

Sights

Fort William has a few innovative attractions unique to the Southern Highlands.

What a wonderful surprise: on Fort William's bland High street is the **West Highland Museum** (Cameron Sq., tel. 01397/702169, www.westhighlandmuseum.org.uk, 10 A.M.–5 P.M. Mon.–Sat., 2–5 P.M. Sun. July–Aug., 10 A.M.–5 P.M. Mon.–Sat. June and Sept., 10 A.M.–4 P.M. Mon.–Sat. Oct.–May, £3 adults, £2 children), a huge, eclectic collection of artifacts that bring to life the history of the Highlands. It's easily one of the top museums in Northern Scotland. What makes it harrowing is that it tells the story of ordinary people (and extraordinary animals). From Neolithic hunter-gatherers to Jacobite rebels to government regiments and World War II commandos, these people's lives are brought vividly forward into the present day through a series of exhibits and artifacts. As fascinating as any of that, though, are the displays on the geology and natural history of the area. There are also exhibitions on torture weapons and ancient charms and remedies. It's about the most informative introduction to the Highlands you could hope for.

There are trains from Fort William to Mallaig year-round, following the route of the "Road to the Isles," but going on **Jacobite Steam Train** (bookings tel. 01524/737751, www.steamtrain.info, one run daily July–Aug., one run Mon.–Fri. May–June and Sept.–Oct.) adds an extra touch of magic to the route. You'll pass over surely the most iconic British railway image of the Glenfinnan Viaduct. A round-trip fare for the two-hour journey to Mallaig costs £43 first class, £29 standard. Trains depart from Fort William main station; you'll get just over an hour in Mallaig on a day trip.

The talents of the great 19th-century Scottish engineer Thomas Telford gave rise to many feats

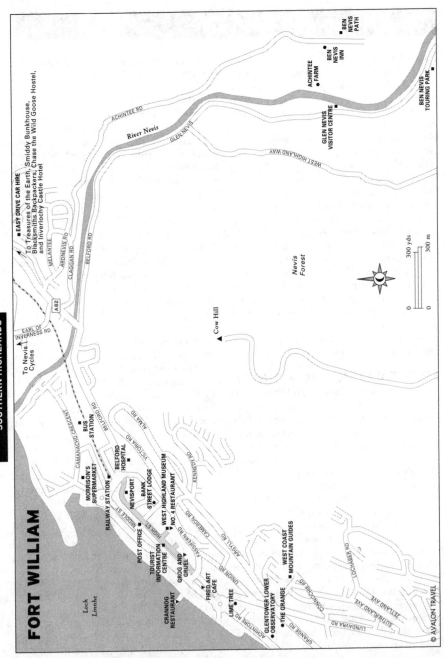

FORT WILLIAM

Loch Linnhe

Nevis Forest

Cow Hill

River Nevis

ACHINTEE RD

GLEN NEVIS

WEST HIGHLAND WAY

BEN NEVIS PATH

BEN NEVIS INN

ACHINTEE FARM

GLEN NEVIS VISITOR CENTRE

BEN NEVIS TOURING PARK

■ EASY DRIVE CAR HIRE

To Treasures of the Earth, Smiddy Bunkhouse, Blacksmiths Backpackers, Chase the Wild Goose Hostel, and Inverlochy Castle Hotel

To Nevis Cycles

A82

EARL OF INVERNESS RD

MELANTEE

ARDNEVIS RD

CLAGGAN RD

BELFORD RD

CAMANACHD CRESCENT

BUS STATION

BELFORD RD

MORRISON'S SUPERMARKET

BELFORD HOSPITAL

ALMA RD

VICTORIA RD

RAILWAY STATION

MIDDLE ST

NEVISPORT

BANK STREET LODGE

HIGH ST

WEST HIGHLAND MUSEUM

NO. 4 RESTAURANT

KENNEDY RD

POST OFFICE

FASSIFERN RD

CAMERON RD

TOURIST INFORMATION CENTRE

GROG AND GRUEL

ARGYLL RD

CRANNOG RESTAURANT

FIRED ART CAFE

UNION RD

LIME TREE

ACHINTORE RD

GLENTOWER LOWER OBSERVATORY

THE GRANGE

WEST COAST MOUNTAIN GUIDES

GRANGE RD

CROMACHIE RD

LOCHABER RD

LUNDAVRA RD

SOUTHLAND RD

ZETLAND AVE

© AVALON TRAVEL

300 yds

300 m

0

0

of construction across Scotland from harbors to bridges, including his most visually impressive work, **Neptune's Staircase** (for information contact Fort William TIC tel. 01397/703781, open year-round) which lies a couple of miles northwest of Fort William at Banavie. The Great Glen runs down all the way from Inverness, effectively cutting Scotland in two, and through it runs the Telford-built Caledonian Canal, providing a coast-to-coast waterway. At Banavie the canal drops in a spectacular series of eight locks over the hilly ground to the sea, and watching a boat working its way through the locks is an enjoyable activity.

The **Treasures of the Earth** (A830 Mallaig Rd., Corpach, tel. 01397/772283, 9:30 A.M.–7 P.M. daily July–Sept., 10 A.M.–5 P.M. daily Feb.–June and Oct.–Dec., £3.95 adults, £2.50 children) is one of the best collections of minerals, gemstones, and fossils in the country. You'll see mammoth-sized crystal caves, trilobites, a saber-toothed tiger skull, and a rather ridiculous-looking re-created dinosaur.

Tours and Activities Courses

Fingal Cruising (the Slipway, Corpach, tel. 01397/772167, www.fingal-cruising.co.uk, weekly cruises Apr.–Oct.) run a number of tours along the Caledonian Canal and the Great Glen. You have several options: walking it, cycling it, or sailing it. It's possible to cruise the whole length of the canal, starting at Banavie and finishing at Inverness. The four-day mini-cruises and seven-day cruises give you the opportunity to uniquely experience some of Britain's finest mountain scenery from a canal barge. Cruises include accommodation and meals and start at £595 per person (mini-cruises £295 pp).

Whatever your outdoor activity preference is, **Snowgoose Mountain Centre** (Corpach, tel. 01397/772467, www.highland-mountain-guides.co.uk) is the company most likely to make it a reality. Snowgoose is experienced in canoeing, kayaking, rock-climbing, mountaineering, and hill-walking trips in and around the Fort William/Glen Nevis area. Two day hill-walking/rock-climbing courses start from £90 per person. Check the website or phone for a full list of courses offered. The company will do its best to meet individual budgets and time scales. Snowgoose also offers equipment hire, often not included in the course cost.

Shopping

Fort William is the last outpost of chain stores on the west coast.

Nevisport (Airds Crossing, tel. 01397/704921, 9 A.M.–5:30 P.M. Mon.–Sat., 9:30 A.M.–5 P.M. Sun.) is the original branch of this successful outdoor shop chain. The branch has Internet access, a restaurant, and, more importantly, a whole range of great books and maps on mountaineering and hill walking. It also sells outdoor equipment.

Morrisons Supermarket (An Aird, 8:30 A.M.–8 P.M. Mon.–Wed., 8:30 A.M.–9 P.M. Thurs.–Fri., 8 A.M.–8 P.M. Sat., 9 A.M.–6 P.M. Sun.) is a truly huge supermarket, with a petrol station close by, on the other side of the Fort William roundabout/dual carriageway complex.

Sports and Recreation

You can hire a bike at **Nevis Cycles** (4 Lochy Cr., tel. 01397/705555, www.neviscycles.com). Prices start from £15 per day and include waterproof clothing and route maps.

Accommodations

Fort William has several decent hostels and a plethora of guesthouses, many with their own unique charm. If you're in Fort William to do some walking, Glen Nevis makes a far better accommodation base. In addition, the nearby villages of Corpach and Banavie have some of the best hostels around, as well as a couple of the key attractions.

UNDER £25

The **Smiddy Bunkhouse and Blacksmiths Backpackers** (Corpach, by Fort William, tel. 01397/772467, www.highland-mountain-guides.co.uk, beds £8–14) is pine-furnished, alpine lodge–style accommodation in two bunkhouses a two-minute walk from Corpach railway station at the Snowgoose Highland Mountain Centre. There are 26 beds available in two separate two-dorm buildings. Blacksmiths Backpackers has more space and a better living/kitchen area. The added bonus for outdoor enthusiasts is that there's a wealth of information on mountain walks and loads of outdoor activities on hand. The hostels are both open all year. Corpach is four miles northwest of Fort William on the A830.

Pretty new on the hostelling scene is this cozy, brightly decorated **Chase the Wild Goose Hostel** (tel. 01397/772531, www.greatglen-hostel.com, beds from £9.95), sitting bang on the Great Glen Way and the Caledonian Canal. Accommodation is in well-spaced four-, six- and eight-bed bunkrooms. It's a well-appointed place and friendly to boot, running a range of activities for guests. Whether you're here to watch boats sail past on the canal nearby or get on the walking boots for some serious hikes, this hostel is the ideal base. Trains stop at Banavie station, from where it's a short walk up the B8004 road to the hostel.

The **Bank Street Lodge** (Bank St., tel. 01397/700070, www.bankstreetlodge.co.uk, beds £13, £30 s, £45 d) is one of the best budget options in Fort William due to the variety of rooms it offers (dorms, singles, doubles, en suite, and family rooms). It's a place that bridges the gap between hostel and bed-and-breakfast accommodations with relative success. The dorms are on the ground floor and the light en suite singles and doubles on the upper floors. There's a drying room, a TV lounge, and, perhaps not surprisingly, the feeling that some guests may have moved in here permanently. It's not as sociable a place as some of the other hostels around but it is central; the High Street is 100 meters' walk away. Breakfast is not included.

£50-100

Located in the former Ben Nevis observatory, the **Glentower Lower Observatory** (Achintore Rd., tel. 01397/704007, www.glentower.com, rooms £58 d) is a rose pink building offering seven grand, light-filled rooms in color schemes of pale maritime blues, greens, and whites. All rooms have en suite power showers and color TVs. Breakfasts include a healthy vegetarian option.

The high-quality room, art gallery, and restaurant experience at the **Lime Tree** (The Old Manse, Achintore Rd., tel. 01397/701806, www.limetreefortwilliam.com, £80 d) is a phenomenon in the local accommodations scene. The nine airy, white, en suite rooms with their exposed oak beams and paintings on the walls are not part of the art gallery itself but all look as though they could be. The gallery at Lime Tree displays art produced in the on-site studio (vibrant, moody land and seascapes) as well as hosting a range of other exhibitions; art produced here also graces the rooms. There's a modern-looking restaurant here, too.

OVER £100

Quite possibly the grandest and most eccentric place to stay in Fort William is **The Grange** (Grange Rd., tel. 01397/705516, www.thegrange-scotland.co.uk, £110 d). It's a delightful, whitewashed, turreted building that sums up all the eccentricities of Scottish architecture under one roof. The four rooms live up to the outside appearance; they're lavish yet uncomplicated affairs with antique wood and complimentary sherry. The Rob Roy room with the King Louis XV antique bed and the opulent marble bathroom was actress Jessica Lange's favorite when she was on location filming *Rob Roy* here. The Grange is set in acres of secluded grounds.

With bags of baronial magnificence, the Victorian **Inverlochy Castle Hotel** (Torlundy by Fort William, tel. 01397/702177, www.inverlochycastlehotel.com, £410 d) is the place to stay if money is no object. This fortress is one of the grandest hotels in the country with 17 enormous, palatial rooms. Even Queen Victoria, who once stayed for a week, considered it the loveliest place she had ever seen. There are phantasmagorical suites, four-poster bed rooms that look like opera sets, sumptuous lounges, and little touches like personal laptop computers with Internet access provided as standard. You could have a varied holiday without ever leaving the vast grounds—try your hand at activities from tennis to clay pigeon shooting. The hotel is off the A82 a couple of miles northeast of Fort William.

Food

Standing head and shoulders above a huge number of bland cafés is **Fired Art Café** (47 High St., tel. 01397/705005, www.fired-art.co.uk, 10 A.M.–5 P.M. Mon.–Sat.) at the far end of the High Street. It's got the best coffee in town, mean fruit smoothies, and a good range of sandwiches, bagels, waffles, and other snacks. It's a unique venue that lives up to its name by offering the chance to select and paint your own piece of pottery—great fun for children on a wet day. Snacks and light meals are £1–6.

The **Grog and Gruel** (66 High St., tel. 01397/705078, www.grogandgruel.co.uk, food served noon–9 P.M. daily) is just what you need after a damp day on the hills. It's an alehouse downstairs, serving cask-conditioned beers, including some from the local Atlas Brewery and the Isle of Skye Brewery. Upstairs, it's a restaurant serving hearty meals like steak and ale pie or wild boar burgers for £7–13. You can eat on both floors; the alehouse is the more atmospheric of the two.

To get your dose of maritime magic while you're staying in town, head to **Crannog Restaurant** (Town Pier, tel. 01397/705589, www.oceanandoak.co.uk, noon–2:30 P.M. and 6–9:30 P.M.). It's as close to Loch Linnhe as you can get without falling in and serves probably the best seafood in the Southern Highlands. It's a venture that combines catching seafood, smoking seafood, serving seafood, and selling seafood. On the spacious restaurant's menu, the highlights are the bouillabaisse (mixed seafood soup) and, surprisingly, non-seafood dishes like prime Angus steak. Mains are £9–20.

With its mix of wood paneling, bare stonework, and attractive conservatory-style dining, it's no surprise that **No.4 Restaurant** (Cameron Sq., High St., tel. 01397/704222, www.no4fortwilliam.com, 11 A.M.–5 P.M. and 6:30–9:30 P.M.) has risen to the very top of the Fort William dining scene. The menu features a selection of meat and seafood dishes like venison or a fillet of Scottish salmon; follow that with white chocolate cheesecake.

Information and Services

Fort William TIC (Cameron Sq., tel. 01397/703781, 9 A.M.–7 P.M. Mon.–Fri., 9 A.M.–6 P.M. Sat., 9:30 A.M.–5 P.M. Sun. July–Aug., 9 A.M.–6 P.M. Mon.–Sat., 10 A.M.–4 P.M. Sun. June and Sept., at least 9 A.M.–5 P.M. Mon.–Fri. Oct.–May) should only be approached if absolutely necessary. It's the most unhelpful, unfriendly information office in Scotland, and constantly packed.

Fort William has several banks with ATMs, a post office (Caol Shopping Centre, 9 A.M.–1 P.M. and 2–5 P.M. Mon.–Fri., 9 A.M.–1 P.M. Sat.), and the handy **Belford Hospital** (tel. 01397/702481, Belford Rd.) near the train station.

Finally, it's worth noting that the stark, foreboding north face of Ben Nevis attracts a lot of mountaineers, not all of whom are experienced; get advice and guidance on various ascents at **West Coast Mountain Guides** (Calluna, Heathercroft, tel. 01397/700451, www.west-coast-mountainguides.co.uk).

Getting There and Away

The bus station and the train station are located next to each other at the north end of town. Fort William is at the end of a branch of the West Highland Railway line and has three to four **trains** daily Monday–Saturday and two to three daily Sunday to Glasgow. The journey takes three hours 40 minutes and costs £22.20. Fort William also has trains to Mallaig (four or five daily, £9.20). In summer, there are also old-fashioned steam trains running this route.

There are four **buses** per day from Glasgow to Fort William (3 hrs., £17.80), which stop in Glencoe on the way. Rapsons Buses run from Fort William to Inverness every two hours.

Getting Around

Take regular Bus 45 to get to Corpach (for Neptune's Staircase); it runs every 20 minutes.

Call **Caberfeidh Taxis** (tel. 01397/703335) if you need a cab.

Easy Drive Car Hire (North Rd., tel. 01397/701616) hires out cars here from £32 daily.

◖ GLEN NEVIS

Glen Nevis seems more than able to handle the huge numbers of tourists it sees each year arriving to climb Britain's highest mountain, Ben Nevis. It starts off as a wide, gentle-looking valley with the main mountains set back but the heathery hills close in as you follow the water of Nevis up into an increasingly narrow, sharp-sided gorge. There are several great accommodation options here, which should be considered as an alternative base to Fort William if you're going to be in the area walking. Movie buffs may recognize the scenery here as the backdrop for films like *Braveheart*.

Ben Nevis

If you're an outdoor enthusiast, purchasing OS Landranger Map 41 is a good idea: it covers both Glen Nevis and Glencoe and will give you a few different ideas for hikes.

Glen Nevis Visitor Centre (bottom of Glen Nevis, tel. 01397/705922, 9 A.M.–5 P.M. daily Easter–mid-Oct.) is a great reference point for the glen as a whole. It's worth a visit if you're planning a climb up Ben Nevis. It has a lot of free information on walks and wildlife in the glen. The center is situated in a pleasant car park with lots of picnic tables. You can begin an ascent of Ben Nevis from here.

Britain's highest mountain, Ben Nevis is 4,406 feet, or 1,344 meters. It's the most popular mountain to scale, which means it's climbed by a great deal of people not generally used to climbing. Whereas on other peaks you'll pass mostly lean muscle machines of walkers who look as though a topple down a hundred-foot ravine wouldn't shake them too badly, Ben Nevis is traipsed up by a sometimes-alarming mix of the very young, the terribly unfit, and the incredibly frail as well. A large number of these get into difficulties on the way up or down; there are more deaths on Ben Nevis

than any other British mountain. In the height of the season there are almost queues to start on the ascent—don't expect a serene hill walk here. The path to the summit is clear all the way; it will take you about five hours up and about three hours down. Views from the summit are something of a lottery. Regardless of the weather when you set out, you're likely to encounter wind, sleet, snow, and mist on any day of the year.

It's folks who are not prepared for all eventualities that generally get into trouble. A standard kit should include a comfortable rucksack, sturdy hiking boots, a waterproof jacket, cold weather clothes like an extra pullover and hat, plenty of water (at least one 1.5-liter bottle per person), a good detailed map, a compass, a whistle, sunscreen, midge repellent, a camera, and plenty of snacks. The summit is surrounded by very sheer cliffs; when the mist has come down, many have died from exposure just trying to find the safe path back down. Finally, it's also a good idea to let someone know you are going up. A trip up should be achievable by most fit, able-bodied people and will be a memorable experience—hiking as high up as Britain goes.

The best starting point is from the Ben Nevis Inn. The route starts off green enough; take photographs in the early stages while the weather is still clear. The latter stages are over scree, with merely cairns (piles of stones) to mark the path, and in the mist one path looks much like another. Rather worryingly, you'll also pass crosses marking where the bodies of climbers have been found. The summit itself is an eerie, flat lunar land with a somewhat surreal ruined observatory. Note that the main tourist path up Ben Nevis is the only one that should be taken by walkers unless they are experienced mountaineers.

Upper Glen Nevis

Beyond the Glen Nevis Visitor Centre and the turn-off for Ben Nevis, the rest of Glen Nevis is relatively peaceful. The road gets narrower and higher and eventually dies out at a car park from where you can walk to one of Scotland's highest waterfalls, **Steall Falls.** It's a steep and slippery path through woodland; allow 1.5 hours for the two-mile route.

Accommodations and Food

Glen Nevis Touring Park (tel. 01397/702191, www.glen-nevis.co.uk, small tent and two people £11) is a gorgeous, grassy site with great facilities, including immaculate washrooms and a bar/restaurant. It's three miles along the glen from Fort William.

Achintee Farm (Achintee, Glen Nevis, tel. 01397/702240, www.achintee.co.uk, beds £13), beside the river at the start of the trek up Ben Nevis, offers both bed-and-breakfast and hostel accommodations. The main farmhouse has large, plain rooms with sparkling en suite facilities, while the hostel alongside has a mix of smaller twin and bunk rooms with shared facilities. It's a traditionally furnished place (old wooden furniture and tartan) but the light color schemes give it a modern look. The views from the rooms, of the purple-green glen closing in on both sides, are just breathtaking.

In these parts, everybody wants to cater to the hiking set, so the lively **Ben Nevis Inn** (Achintee, Glen Nevis, tel. 01397/701227, www.ben-nevis-inn.co.uk, food served noon–9 P.M. daily Apr.–Oct., noon–9 P.M. Thurs.–Sun. Oct.–Apr., beds £14) offers a sturdy bunkhouse in addition to a great pub. The bunkhouse comprises 24 beds, divided into separate sections to give a feeling of intimacy. It's not the warmest hostel you'll come across but there are immaculate showers and washrooms, a small kitchen, and a stone-walled garden perfect for an evening drink (until the midges get you). You can spend most of your night in the pub, in any case. With bare stone walls, huge wooden tables, and plenty of good *craic* (conversation), this is a great place for real ales and a wholesome meal like Thai green curry for £8–14. To get to the inn, leave Fort William and head straight over the roundabout after the Ben Nevis Inn. Take the first right on Claggan Road and continue to bear right at the Claggan Spar shop. The inn is at the end of the road.

Getting There and Away

In summer several buses daily run from Fort William bus station to Glen Nevis Youth Hostel.

GLEN COE AND KINLOCHLEVEN

The 10-mile romp from the Kings House Hotel on barren Rannoch Moor down to Glencoe village on the banks of Loch Leven is a slideshow of increasingly sharp, dramatic ridges. First up at the head of the glen is Buachaille Etive Mor, closely followed by Buachaille Etive Beag, two colossal, pyramidal peaks that rise like sentinels out of the brown-white subarctic tundra. As the glen, traversed by the main A82 road, sinks slowly toward Loch Leven, the mountains on either side rise still higher. To the north is Scotland's hardest hill-walking challenge, the Aonach Eagach ridge, tapering to a rough, rocky knife edge. South of the glen are the toothlike peaks of the Three Sisters of Kintail, hiding the monster mountain of the lot, Bidean nam Bian. These peaks may not be of Himalayan proportions, but what makes Glen Coe such a powerful place is how close you can get to this majestic mountain scenery without even breaking a sweat. These peaks cast a shadow over the emerald green valley threading between them. It's a place resonating with a tragic history: The MacDonald clan, which once ruled the glen, was slaughtered by their guests, the Campbells, one midwinter day in 1692. Finally, the road tumbles down to Glencoe village, one charming street of houses and an excellent museum.

Glen Coe

In a typical 300-year-old thatched croft house on the main street of Glencoe village is the fascinating little **Glencoe and North Lorn Folk Museum** (Glencoe village, tel. 01855/811664, 10 A.M.–5:30 P.M. Mon.–Sat. Apr.–Oct., £2 adults, £1.50 seniors), which has displays on Glencoe's history, an unusually violent and turbulent sequence of events even by Scottish standards. The Glencoe Massacre is a central topic,

© LUKE WATERSON

Glencoe, from the Clachaig Inn

and there's an interesting display of weapons found concealed in the thatch of local houses up to two centuries after Culloden. The museum also features artifacts from local farming and blacksmith trades.

Glencoe Visitor Centre (A82 in Glen Coe, tel. 01855/811307, 9:30 A.M.–5:30 P.M. daily Apr.–Aug., 10 A.M.–5 P.M. daily Sept.–Oct., 10 A.M.–4 P.M. daily mid-Feb.–Mar., 10 A.M.–4 P.M. Thurs.–Sun. Nov.–mid-Feb., £5 adults, £4 children) is the area's new-look visitors center, acting as both a TIC and a museum. It's as near as possible on the site of the Glencoe Massacre. It's a hive of information on local history and an invaluable resource on walks and wildlife in the glen. The museum exhibition has lots of hands-on displays that tell you about the geology of the region. There's also a spacious self-service café serving good coffee and cakes. The visitors center is on the A82 south of Glencoe village, situated a mile up into the glen.

The dreamy dead-end valley of **Glen Etive** (south of Glen Coe) is a quiet place to appreciate the contrasts of Highland scenery. At the head of the road down from the Kings House Hotel on the A82 road to/from Glen Coe stands the fierce-looking bulk of Buachaille Etive Mor, one of Scotland's most iconic mountains. Initially the glen is all open moor and stark mountain views, but as it wends towards Loch Etive it changes from icy rock-faces to gentle woodsy lochside, all in the space of a few miles. The head of the loch is a great canoeing spot.

Kinlochleven

Kinlochleven is an out-of-the-way village at the head of glittering Loch Leven, offering easy access into the hills. As well as being at one end of the notorious hill-walking scramble of the Devil's Staircase, it also offers a great back route to the Nevis range of hills, up a long track ending at Mamore Lodge Hotel. One of the best breweries in the Highlands is the **Atlas Brewery** (Kinlochleven, tel. 01855/831111, tours Mon.–Sat. Easter–Sept.), with free guided tours at 5:30 P.M. in season. Best of the brews is the dark, fruity Three Sisters ale.

THE GLENCOE MASSACRE

Following the Glorious Revolution of 1688, which resulted in William III and Mary I replacing the exiled James II on the British throne, unrest was high. James II had been a Catholic, Stuart king with Scottish blood. William and Mary were both Protestants, with Mary descended from Charles I of England. A strong Anglo-Scottish rivalry developed, and the clans of the Highlands particularly resented the sovereignty of William and Mary. Plots to mount an insurrection were devised. By 1690, Jacobite rebelliousness was causing the government considerable distress, and everyone was suspected of having Jacobite sympathies.

Lord Breadalbane was a cunning man who appeared to bridge the rift between the pro-Jacobite and pro-government camps and was given sums of money to bribe Highland leaders into showing government allegiance. Rather than quell the rift, Breadalbane antagonized matters further and caused one leader, MacDonald of Glencoe, to storm out of a meeting. Breadalbane was of the Campbell clan, already much hated by the MacDonalds; the Campbells had made numerous territorial gains over the previous centuries at the MacDonalds' expense. The government issued a proclamation to all Highland clan chiefs in 1691, giving leaders four months to swear loyalty to the government. Already, encouraged by Breadalbane, the government had devised a scheme to speed this process along by making an example of one clan to illustrate the price of disloyalty. MacDonald of Glencoe was that clan. Already an enemy of Breadalbane, MacDonald was also slow to agree to the proclamation, and although he did sign (albeit late), by that stage Sir John Dalrymple had already declared the government's intention to dispense with the MacDonald clan. The Campbells were chosen as the agents.

In early February 1692, a battalion of Campbells passing through Glencoe requested that the MacDonalds provide them with shelter, as was Highland custom. The MacDonalds acquiesced, and Campbell men were housed in MacDonald homes throughout the village. After 12 days of enjoying the hospitality of their hosts, the Campbells received the government order to dispatch every MacDonald man under the age of 70. The Campbell captain, who had the night before played cards with his hosts, commenced the butchery around 5 A.M. on February 13. Maclain, the MacDonald chief, and 37 others were murdered. The overzealous Campbells killed children and raped the MacDonald women, in addition to carrying out their government orders. The women and children that survived were thrown out of their houses, which were set alight. They would now suffer a slower, more excruciating fate than their menfolk, perishing in the cold as they tried to find shelter. The public outcry at the brutality of the massacre did little to help the now virtually decimated MacDonald tribe. The victims of the massacre are remembered by a monument in Glencoe village.

◖ Walks

There are infinite walks in the Glencoe/Kinlochleven area, ranging from hilly hikes to serious mountaineering routes that should only be tackled with the proper equipment; make sure you know what a walk entails before you set out.

The Devil's Staircase is a nine-mile (one-way) walk, part of the West Highland Way. It kicks off at the Kings House Hotel and follows the old military road for three miles before leaving the glen to climb the staircase. There are great views across to the Mamores from the top, before the long descent to Kinlochleven.

The Lost Valley is about as rewarding a two-mile walk as you're likely to find in Scotland, through the lands the ill-fated MacDonalds used to hide cattle they had stolen from the Campbells. It starts from the upper of two car parks on the A82 just before the Meeting of the Three Waters Waterfall. The walk is a great opportunity to strike into the mountain scenery without having to dangle off any precipices to do so, and the top end of the valley is completely hidden from the lower part.

Sports and Recreation

Vertical Descents (Inchree Falls, Onich, north of Glencoe, tel. 01855/821593, www.verticaldescents.com, year-round) offers every outdoor activity under the sun, from kayaking to white-water rafting to mountain biking. Operators try hard to cater to individual needs and are happy to listen to location preferences. Daylong kayaking courses are £50 (6–8 hrs.).

You can rent bikes from **Glencoe Mountain Bike Centre** (Clachaig Inn, by Glencoe village, tel. 01855/811252, from £12 daily). Be warned: it's a tough cycle up Glen Coe.

Accommodations and Food

The **Red Squirrel Campsite** (by Glencoe village, tel. 01855/811256, www.redsquirrelcampsite.com, £7 pp) is a wonderful, woodsy campsite by the river on the old minor road to Glencoe village. The **Glencoe Hostel and Bunkhouse** (by Glencoe village, tel. 01855/811906, www.glencoehostel.co.uk, beds £9.50–18) is the pick of the budget accommodation in Glencoe. It's down a rough track off the old minor road to Glencoe, just over a mile up from the village. You can choose between the three-room hostel and a more basic alpine-style bunkhouse; between them they sleep 46. There's an atmospheric log cabin that sleeps two or three people.

Scorrybreac Guest House (Glencoe village, tel. 01855/811354, www.scorrybreac.co.uk, from £46 d) is a peaceful, white-washed bungalow tucked up the lane to the hospital amidst the trees with six rooms of varying hues and sizes. There's good heating, en suite/private bathrooms with power showers, and a drying room. Rooms also have color TVs and CD/DVD players. It's solid, homey accommodation.

The 300-year-old **◖ Clachaig Inn** (by Glencoe village, tel. 01855/811252, www.clachaig.com, £42 s, £84 d, food served daily throughout the day) is a legendary outdoor enthusiasts' hot spot. There are 23 rooms here either in the oldest part of the pub or in the more recent addition of the lodge. The rooms are snug affairs with a light color scheme and en suite bathrooms. If you want an en suite bathtub, get a room in the characterful Ossian wing. More famous than the rooms here are the bars: Expect a dark, lively atmosphere full of the smell of smoke and the blaze of an open fire where hikers discuss their exploits. Then there's the small matter of the best meals in the glen to sample; main dishes like mixed bean chili or boar sausages are £7–15. The Clachaig is on the old minor road to Glencoe village.

In a wild, isolated spot on the edge of Rannoch Moor high up above Glen Coe, the **Kings House Hotel** (tel. 01855/851259, www.kingy.com, £27.50 s, £55 d) is an 18th-century former barracks for government troops. It's a very traditionally Scottish labyrinthine place (tartan and blazing fires) with two massive, dark, old bar/restaurants. There are 23 rooms at the hotel, geared more toward tired walkers than anything. About half of the rooms are en suite. Even if you just come here to contemplate the incredible mountain views from the lounge window over a pint of real ale and a meal of local game, it's worth it.

Information and Services

You should head to the **Glencoe Visitor Centre** (A82, Glen Coe, tel. 01855/811307) for tourist information. **Glencoe Police** (tel. 01855/811222) double as the mountain rescue contact.

Getting There and Away

Rapsons Bus 44 heads from Fort William to call at the Glencoe village road junction en route to Kinlochleven hourly through the week. **Scottish Citylink** buses from Glasgow to Fort William (four daily) will also stop at Glencoe village.

Lochaber and the Small Isles

Lochaber is the broad term given to the vast loch-riven wilderness west of Fort William. It is by some distance the most remote region of Britain; the impenetrability of the mountains and lochs here means even parts of the mainland can only be accessed by boat or via a tough spot of hill-walking. The only visitors Lochaber sees are those en route to one of the main islands lying off its shores or real adventure seekers. The place names alone—Moidart, Ardnamurchan, and Morar—conjure up otherworldly, almost frighteningly bleak images. The main road and indeed the only road into the region is steeped in history; it was along here that Bonnie Prince Charlie rallied his allies and raised his standard against the ruling Hanoverian monarchy in 1745. South of the road lies a series of brown, hilly tracts of moor segmented by lochs and culminating in the Ardnamurchan Peninsula, the most westerly point on the British mainland. North is a still more delightfully remote stretch of land, where the hiker's mecca of the Knoydart Peninsula beckons. Munro mountains and empty, elemental glens hide Inverie, the most isolated community in the country. At the very end of the road lies the main town of the area, Mallaig, a bustling fishing village hemmed in by hills with ferries linking it to the tiny islands scattered off its coast. This archipelago, known as "The Small Isles," may be small in stature but for many visitors, a trip here represents the crowning glory of Lochaber. These humps in the Atlantic Ocean contain an opulent castle, shimmering golden beaches, and an abundance of unusual wildlife.

THE ROAD TO THE ISLES

It was not surprising that the communities linked by the Road to the Isles, which runs west from Fort William to Mallaig, gave their support to Bonnie Prince Charlie in 1745. Dire poverty and a general feeling of being sidelined by the powers that be pervaded, and few people around thought highly of the reigning King George II and his government. The road first passes Glenfinnan, where the Bonnie Prince raised his standard, and Arisaig, renowned for its hypnotically beautiful beaches, before terminating at Mallaig. The land stops here but the sea connections start—this is the departure point for ferries to the Small Isles and to Skye. If you don't have your own transport, you can travel in glamour on the Jacobite Steam Train along the Road to the Isles.

Glenfinnan

Glenfinnan is perhaps best known to the world as being the location of the viaduct the Hogwarts Express train passes over in the Harry Potter films. It lies in a lonely forest-backed location at the head of Loch Shiel. Glenfinnan was where the Jacobite rebellion really began; here Bonnie Prince Charlie officially declared his intention to regain the crown in the name of his grandfather, James II of England. A **monument** (Glenfinnan, open year-round) remembers the Jacobites who gave their lives during the 1745 rebellion. The visitors center nearby has limited tourist information.

If you visit one railway station in Scotland to taste the glory of the bygone age of rail travel, let it be Glenfinnan, housing the **Glenfinnan Station Museum** (tel. 01397/722295, www.glenfinnanstationmuseum.co.uk, 9 A.M.–5 P.M. daily June–mid-Oct., £1). Glenfinnan is a still-operational station in a glorious Highland setting with an old train in one of its sidings that you can stay and eat in. As if that were not enough for you to recall the heady days of classic train journeys, part of the station has been converted into a museum of old railway memorabilia. Photographs, old station signs, billboards, and brightly painted engine parts trace the history of the West Highland railway line over the 19th and 20th centuries.

Arisaig and Vicinity

This peaceful little coastal village sits on the shores of the peninsula of the same name and is known for its glorious beaches and beautiful accommodation.

The **Land, Sea and Islands Visitor Centre** (Arisaig village, tel. 01687/450263, 10 A.M.–4 P.M. Mon.–Fri., 1–4 P.M. Sun. Apr.–Oct., £2 adults, £1 children) has enthusiastic staff and loads of interesting local history tidbits that larger museums would skirt over. Arisaig's past, affected by early Christian missionaries, Bonnie Prince Charlie, and specialist World War II operations, is all covered here. Glorious **Camusdarach Beach,** where *Local Hero* was filmed, lies about five miles north of Arisaig village by Loch Morar.

Accommodations and Food

In Glenfinnan, you can spend the night in ☾ **Glenfinnan Sleeping Car and Dining Car** (tel. 01397/722295, www.glenfinnanstationmuseum.co.uk, beds available June–mid-Oct. or by arrangement, £12, food served 9 A.M.–5 P.M. daily June–mid-Oct., other times by arrangement), a charismatic sleeping compartment of an old 1950s train in a siding at Glenfinnan Station. Four compartments here have been lovingly converted to offer a total of 10 beds, including one family compartment. The dining car is next door, still with the original elegant dark wood dining berths from the days when this train ran; it serves excellent coffee, ice cream, pizza, and other light meals for £1–5. You can phone to see about arranging an evening meal (usually until 8:30 P.M. Fri.–Sun.).

Charming, mid-18th-century, and whitewashed, **Glenfinnan House Hotel** (Glenfinnan, tel. 01397/722235, www.glenfinnanhouse.com, Mar.–mid-Nov., food served noon–9 P.M. daily, from £115 d) has a clutch of grand rooms full of dark mahogany furniture. With views of Loch Shiel or the hotel garden, all rooms get sparkling, tiled, en suite bathrooms. A four-poster bed suite is available, as are three-course dinners (£30).

The best place to stay in Arisaig is at the **Old Library Lodge** (Arisaig village, tel. 01687/450651, www.oldlibrary.co.uk, rooms £90 d, food served noon–2:30 P.M. and 6:30–9:30 P.M. daily), a 200-year-old whitewashed restaurant with rooms. It's large, light, peaceful accommodation here; all rooms are en suite and most have stunning sea views. Three-course meals in the rustic restaurant are £18–25. You could start with venison pâté and move on to a main like the salmon doused in whisky sauce. If you want to stay and eat at a modern, forward-thinking, innovative place that combines a historical building with a prime coastal location, the Old Library Lodge is the spot to try.

Camusdarach Camp Site (by Morar on B8008, tel. 01687/450221, tent and two adults £14) is one of the most idyllic spots to pitch a tent in the country, a short walk away from the vast white sand beach where the film *Local Hero* was shot. There are good washing facilities and a shop that visits twice a week. Morar is four miles north of Arisaig; the B8008 is the old coast road heading west from Morar and the main A830 road.

Getting There and Away

Four to five **trains** daily stop off at Glenfinnan and Arisaig stations en route to Mallaig. Mallaig-bound **buses** from Fort William will also drop you off at either Glenfinnan or Arisaig; there's one bus per day Monday–Saturday with Shiel Buses (tel. 01967/431272). Shiel also operates bus service 47, which runs south from Mallaig to Morar and Arisaig several times daily Monday–Friday.

MALLAIG

Bustling Mallaig is the jumping-off point for ferries to Skye; the Small Isles of Rum, Eigg, Muck, and Canna; and to barren Knoydart. It's a lively fishing port that sees a lot of passing tourist trade. The community has turned to the sea to make ends meet; it's connected to the rest of the world only by a long stretch of lonely moor and has few other places to look for its trade but the water surrounding it. Not too many people stop off in the village itself, which is their loss—it's a fascinating place. Just watching a working West Highland port in all its bustling action is an interesting experience; thank goodness for places like this, happily devoid of tourist gloss.

THE HIGHLANDS AND ISLANDS ON THE BIG SCREEN

As you make your way through the Highlands, you may notice that certain parts of the landscape look oddly familiar, particularly if you know your movies. With misty mountains, broken old castles, bags of romance and history, and a special lurid light, it's no surprise that the Highlands have been the setting for some epic TV series and lots of Hollywood blockbusters. The poignant scenery and tragic past provided the ideal backdrop to pull at the heartstrings: Filming on location in Scotland was almost half the way to making a successful movie. Filmmakers were using Scotland as a setting as early as the 1930s, but it was the most melancholy, magical glen of them all, Glencoe, that got the ball rolling as far as Highland film backdrops were concerned. The Alfred Hitchcock film *The 39 Steps* was filmed in the glen in 1935.

By 1945, *I Know Where I'm Going*, filmed on the Island of Mull, had made Highland film backdrops a trend. The film, about a girl who goes to live on a remote Scottish island to marry a rich elderly landowner but falls in love with a naval officer instead, got critics raving about its evocative imagery. "I've never seen a picture which smelled of the wind and the rain in quite this way," Raymond Chandler would say. The joke about the film was that starring actor Robert Livesey had committed to a West End show in London during filming and so the scenes featuring him had to be shot

in a studio. Still, total immersion in Scottish Highland scenery became a big theme for movie-shooters.

In 1948, Glencoe and Glenfinnan were used as the backdrop for *Bonnie Prince Charlie*, starring David Niven. The 1960 big-screen adaptation of Robert Louis Stevenson's book *Kidnapped* was shot on location in Ardgour and Glen Nevis. In 1975, Glencoe and Castle Stalker, along the coast to the south, became the setting for *Monty Python and the Holy Grail*, while Bill Forsyth's *Local Hero* (1983) used the beaches near Morar, south of Mallaig, as a main location. The Highlander series of movies used a clutch of famous Scottish locations: *Highlander I* was shot around Glencoe and Rannoch Moor, and *Highlander III* used Castle Tioram by Ardnamurchan as a central setting.

The biggest year of Highland movies was 1995. *Rob Roy*, starring Liam Neeson as the famous Scottish rebel, and *Braveheart*, starring Mel Gibson as freedom-fighter William Wallace, were both filmed then. Glen Nevis and Glencoe were again key locations, as well as parts of Ardnamurchan. TV series from *Dr. Finlay's Casebook* (1960s) to *Monarch of the Glen* (1990s) have also been filmed in the Highlands. The biggest film of recent years to be graced with a Highland setting was *Harry Potter and the Chamber of Secrets*. The Glenfinnan viaduct starred in the movie as part of the route taken by the Hogwarts Express train.

Sights

Aside from watching the boats in the harbor or catching one of them to the outlying islands or Knoydart, there isn't a lot to do in Mallaig.

The silent waters of **Loch Morar,** Scotland's deepest loch at over 1,000 feet deep, lie southeast of Mallaig, supposedly inhabited by a monster named Morag. You can do a wonderful walk from **Bracorina,** where the road ends on the northwestern side of the loch, to **Tarbet,** seven miles farther east along the north shore. Allow three hours for this isolated

trek. You can pre-book the Bruce Watt cruise ferry to pick you up at Tarbet (it only turns up on demand). Ferry times (see *Getting There and Away* in this section) are subject to change. Hop on bus 47 to get to Morar from Mallaig.

The invaluable **Bruce Watt Sea Cruises** (tel. 01687/462320, www.knoydart-ferry.co.uk, morning and afternoon calls to Inverie Mon.–Fri., afternoon calls to Tarbet Mon.–Fri. May–mid-Sept., morning and afternoon calls to Inverie Mon., Wed., and Fri., afternoon calls to Tarbet Mon. and Fri. mid-Sept.–May) runs cruises from Mallaig to Inverie, the only settlement on Knoydart. After Inverie, the cruise continues to Tarbet, near Loch Morar, and then heads farther up Loch Nevis to tiny Seal Island. The cruise calls at Inverie at 11 A.M. and 3 P.M. and Tarbet at 3:30 P.M. The cruise costs £12; if you want to use it as a ferry service the one-way Mallaig–Inverie fare is £9 and Tarbet–Mallaig is £13. You cannot get directly from Tarbet to Inverie.

Shopping
You can mail order fresh fish from **Andy Race Fish Merchants** (by Mallaig Pier, tel. 01687/462626), as well as pop in to see what seafood treats are in store.

Sports and Recreation
Cycles 2U (Burnside Cottage, tel. 01687/461021, 9 A.M.–5 P.M. daily) hire out bikes and tandems for £16/32 per day.

Accommodations and Food
Brilliantly bright with swaths of flowers and plants surrounding it, **Sheena's Backpackers Lodge and Tea Garden** (Harbour View, tel. 01687/462764, beds £13.50) is a pleasant little hostel with basic dorm accommodation, sparkling clean shared bathrooms, a comfy guest lounge, and a well-stocked kitchen. Downstairs is the plant-covered patio and tea garden where you can sit with a decent coffee or a plate of haddock and chips and watch the world go by. In the summer this little place diversifies even more and offers evening seafood meals.

There are a number of amicable whitewashed guesthouses fanning around the wide arc of East Bay but **Western Isles Guest House** (East Bay, tel. 01687/462320, from £56 d) is the most appealing, run by Bruce Watt of Bruce Watt Cruises fame. There are four amply sized rooms here in this long, low, modern bay-facing house. The rooms are all en suite and have color TV. Locally smoked kippers are on the breakfast menu.

You don't necessarily expect Mallaig to have a classy restaurant, so spacious 【 **Fishmarket** (Station Rd., tel. 01687/462299, 11:45 A.M.–2:45 P.M. and 6–9 P.M. daily) with its tiled floor and clumpy iron chairs comes as a surprise. Conservatory-style windows look out over the harbor where some of the largest seafood catches in the west of Scotland (indeed, in the west of Europe) are landed. It's appropriate, then, that seafood should be the specialty here, £7–14. Delectable fishy specialties on offer include seafood chowder.

Information
Mallaig TIC (East Bay, tel. 01687/462170, 10 A.M.–4 P.M. Mon.–Fri., 10:15 A.M.–3:45 P.M. Sat., 1:45–3:45 P.M. Sun.) is an independent information center with lots of details on activities, attractions, and accommodations in the "Road to the Isles" area, which includes Knoydart and the Small Isles.

Getting There and Away
The main **ferry** link from Mallaig is the **Calmac ferry** (tel. 0870/565 0000, www.calmac.co.uk, to Armadale on Skye). Ferries to Skye from here are regular (30 min., £3.50 adult, £18.75 car one-way). There are also ferries to the **Small Isles** with Calmac and to the **Knoydart Peninsula** with Bruce Watt Charters.

There are four to five **trains** between Fort William and Mallaig daily. The journey takes one hour 25 minutes and costs £9.20 (more for the Jacobite Steam Train).

Shiel Buses operates one service per day to Mallaig via Glenfinnan (Mon.–Fri., 1.5 hrs., £5.40) from Fort William (change in Fort William for services to Glasgow).

【 KNOYDART PENINSULA
Wilderness lovers should skip the rest of Scotland and come straight to this enormous peninsula of brown hills and silent lochs for a hefty dose of pure, unadulterated isolation. The unique thing about Knoydart is that it has a road and a thriving village not connected by any other road. After a 20-odd mile trek across the mountains, it's heartening to see the white string of houses of Inverie lying along the shore of Loch Nevis. There are plenty of places

to stay in the wilderness here, not to mention Britain's remotest and quite possibly best pub. Munro mountains combined with real ale and crackling open fires make this place the stuff hikers' dreams are made of.

Walks

The real reason to come to Knoydart is to do some walking. You can get the ferry across and sit in the same pub that your gasping fellow drinkers have spent a day or more hiking to, but this feels like cheating somehow. Munro baggers come to Knoydart to climb the peaks of **Ladhar Bheinn, Luinne Bheinn, Meall Buidhe,** and **Garbh Chioch Mhor.** Some of these peaks are best accessed from **Upper Glendessary,** at the end of the road via Loch Arkaig. Quite possibly the best walk, in any case, is the walk in to **Inverie.** Whatever you do, don't undertake a foray into Knoydart without a map. Most of the folks in Inverie can help recommend some great day hikes once you arrive.

Accommodations and Food

Knoydart is not short on places to stay and in the Old Forge is blessed with one of the best pubs in the country. Wild camping is possible on the beach 10 minutes southeast from the ferry pier. Running water is provided; there's no charge but donations are appreciated.

Knoydart Foundation Bunkhouse (half mile southeast of Inverie, tel. 01687/462242, www.knoydart-foundation.com, beds £14) is the cheapest hostel around Inverie and has 25 beds available in four large rooms (a two-bed room and six- to 10-bed rooms). There's even Internet access here.

A whitewashed bungalow set within a stone-walled field, **The Old Byre** (near Inverie, tel. 01687/460146, www.theoldbyreknoydart.com, beds £25) is a step up in class from your average hostel and several flights of steps up from the cow shed that it started its days as. Its three four-bed dorm rooms and two twin rooms all have underfloor heating, and it's far neater and better-appointed than many guesthouses you'll see. Not only is there a rustic stone-walled sitting room but also a hot tub for post-hike

relaxation. The hostel is 15 minutes' walk from the ferry pier.

The spick-and-span accommodations at the **The Gathering** (Inverie, tel. 01687/460051, www.thegatheringknoydart.com.uk, £45 s, £70 d) is ideal for large groups; many of the en suite rooms can sleep up to four people in a mix of bunks and beds. TVs are provided but there's no reception, so you'll have to help yourself to the extensive video collection or feast your eyes on the view instead. Vegetarians and those with dietary requirements are catered for, but with shops so far away a little advance warning is necessary.

The fatigued walker's paradise that is the **The Old Forge Pub** (Inverie, tel. 01687/462267, www.theoldforge.co.uk, food served noon–2 P.M. and 6:30–8:30 P.M. Fri.–Mon. and Wed., 6:30–8:30 P.M. Tues. and Thurs., additional hours on demand from Apr.–Oct.) is officially Britain's remotest pub, which seems to make everything its specialty: real ales, beers from as far afield as Poland, freshly caught seafood, and even Italian espresso. You can munch down a steak doused in Tallisker whisky sauce or, perhaps best of all, the home-made fish pie. Main meals are £8–15. Expect to be coerced into participation in the more-or-less spontaneous sing-alongs and ceilidhs.

Getting There and Away

There are two ways to reach Inverie on Knoydart: by **ferry** from Mallaig and **on foot** from Kinloch Hourn. Although it would be technically possible to traipse across the mountains to Knoydart from any number of places, only the Kinloch Hourn route is recommended—at least it follows the vague semblance of a path.

Ferries are operated by **Bruce Watt Cruises** (tel. 01687/462320); see *Sights* in the *Mallaig* section of this chapter for route, time, and price details.

Hiking from Kinloch Hourn

You can walk to Knoydart from Kinloch Hourn, which lies a long, spectacular 27 miles from Invergarry in the Great Glen southwest of Loch Ness. At the time of research there was no public transport to Kinloch Hourn. At Kinloch Hourn farmhouse bed-and-breakfast accommodations and a tearoom are available. From here it is a tough 17-mile hike to Inverie, Knoydart's only village, but it's one of the best hikes in Scotland. The walk is doable in one day but many people prefer to allow two, with a break at Barisdale (a seven-mile hike, on a bay on the south of Loch Hourn). You'll find rudimentary accommodations at **Barisdale Bothy** (tel. 01599/522302, www.barisdale.com, tent pitches £1, bothy beds £3). The path now heads over the pass of Mam Barisdale southwest to Inverie. You'll need a good map of the area and will have to carry all your own provisions. Even when you reach Inverie, there's no shop.

THE SMALL ISLES

Against the odds of sheer remoteness and mass Highland clearances in the 19th century, the Small Isles of Rum, Eigg, Muck, and Canna have a vibrancy to match anywhere on mainland Lochaber. Rum is a hilly nature reserve with one of Scotland's most opulent castles tacked rather surreally on the side. Eigg is the liveliest of the four islands, with some glorious beaches, while the outposts of Muck and Canna have some classic walks and the added blessing that hardly anyone ever visits them. You may not bring a car to any of these islands; in any case, the isles are virtually roadless and small enough to be explored on foot, which adds to their charm.

Isle of Rum

Mountainous Rum (www.isleofrum.com) is the largest of the Small Isles. Its 40 square miles of wild, brown moor were mostly cleared of people in the 1820s during the Highland clearances. The majority of the population went to Newfoundland and left a landscape that was largely uninhabitable in any case. By 1957, Rum had become a designated nature reserve, having far more wildlife than human inhabitants.

Due to its status as a nature reserve, access on Rum is limited. Wildlife spotting is a key pastime; watch out for Manx shearwaters, red deer, golden eagles, and eider ducks. The focus for activity on Rum is at Kinloch, where you'll find the extravagant red sandstone **Kinloch Castle** (tel. 01687/462037, guided tours when ferries run, £6 adults, £3 children), completed in 1900 for young millionaire industrialist and then owner of the island George Bullough. (Bullough caused cartographical confusion for the best part of a century after his stint at Kinloch by having the island's name changed from Rum to Rhum, to avoid his name and title being associated with any reference to alcohol; happily, the island name has now been changed back to the original Rum.) The castle's construction involved importing sandstone from Dumfries and Galloway and took three years to build, but Bullough enjoyed it as a luxury pad only until 1914, when World War I broke out. In contrast to simple, stark Rum, the castle is a wealth of bronze statues, stained glass, elaborate four-poster beds, and silk wall coverings. It was one of the first residences in Scotland to have electricity. Distinguishing itself even among all this opulence is the presence of one of the world's most unusual musical instruments, the orchestrion. A network of paths lead through the grounds around the castle.

You can stay at the back of the castle in the **Castle Hostel** (tel. 01687/462037, beds £14, £55 d). The hostel dorm beds are in the old servants' quarters, but you can also stay in one of the Oak Rooms which, while nothing elaborate by the castle's standards, offer suitably Gothic accommodation in four-poster beds. The castle serves three-course evening meals in the bistro (£13.50).

Isle of Eigg

Eigg (www.isleofeigg.org) is a lively little island with some golden sandy beaches and interesting walks. Seals and otters cavort in the gentle bays, and corncrakes cower in the flower-dotted meadows. The ferry will come in at Galmisdale, where you'll find the island shop and post office (stocked with lots of different goodies). The main population center is at Cleadale.

On the northwest side of the island at Camas Sgiotaig lies Eigg's best beach, the **Singing**

Sands, a beautiful sandy beach with great views across to Rum. The best walk on Eigg goes to the sharp, dramatic ridge of **An Sgurr,** known as the Sgurr of Eigg. It's a five-hour walk to the summit (1,289 feet or 393 meters) and back, do-able at a push on a day trip to the island. You can hire out bikes to explore Eigg at **An Laimhrig** (tel. 01687/482406), close to the pier.

Eigg has several self-catering bothies and hostels, the best of which is the excellent **Glebe Barn** (tel. 01687/482417, bunkrooms £14 pp, twin room £16 pp) sleeping guests in a spacious, modern series of two- to eight-bed rooms. The barn is a mile up from the ferry pier; your hosts will meet you at the pier. Another good bothy-style hostel is white-washed **Sandavore Bothy** (west of ferry pier at foot of An Sgurr, tel. 01687/482480, £30 for the whole hostel). New for 2008 is electricity; the bothy will sleep four people, and firewood is provided. For a guesthouse, try **Kildonan House** (tel. 01687/482446). There are plenty more self-catering options. With all accommodations, it's highly recommended to book before departing on the ferry. Eigg also has an excellent tearoom by the ferry pier.

Isle of Muck

Once deriving an income from selling seaweed, this tiny fertile island is now essentially one farm, with the sea acting as the only fence. Gleaming white croft cottages sit on the rich green, low-lying shores. While Muck may not be the island to blow your mind, it is home to some intriguing wildlife, including the only type of coral found in Britain, **Cup Coral.** Walking is good on Muck, and at low tide you can walk to **Horse Island,** a seabird colony where puffins can be spotted. Ask at the **Craft Shop and Tearoom** (tel. 01687/462362, 11 A.M.–5 P.M. daily July–Aug., evening meals by arrangement, other hours hit and miss) about the island boat, available for charter.

Isle of Canna

Lying to the northwest of Rum is the thin, green island of Canna, owned by the National Trust for Scotland and home to a thriving population of 16. Canna is a haven for **seabirds** including razorbills and puffins. Contact the **Trust** (tel. 0844/493 2242, www.nts.org.uk) for further information of visiting and staying on Canna.

Getting There and Away

Ferries to the Small Isles run from Mallaig. Eigg, being the nearest, is generally the first call, followed by Muck, Rum, and Canna. There is a different circuit of the Small Isles every day of the week, just to add the spice of variety to proceedings. In season, there are one or two daily services to **Eigg** (Mon.–Tues. and Thurs.–Sat., £5.75 one-way), to **Muck** (Tues. and Thurs.–Sat., £8.70 one-way), to **Rum** (Mon., Wed., and Fri.–Sat., £8.50 one-way) and one service to **Canna** (Mon., Wed., and Fri.–Sat., £10.75 one-way). Bringing bicycles costs £2.50 between any two points. A reduced service runs in the winter.

ARDNAMURCHAN PENINSULA

The wild lands south of the Road to the Isles are fissured by lochs which all but transfigure the purple-brown, forest-carpeted hills into separate islands: Ardgour, Morvern with its fine beaches, and lusciously forested Sunart and Moidart. All these tracts of land taper out eventually into the long Ardnamurchan Peninsula, which after a straggling 25-mile single track road crashes into the sea at Britain's most westerly mainland point. While it contains little but the sound of the wind, this terrain is not as bare as it seems from the map, and the solitude seekers who venture here find themselves very well catered for. The area has some of the best accommodation and dining options on the west coast of Scotland. The main settlement is Strontian in Sunart, with a petrol pump and tourist information center. Most attractions and facilities are concentrated here and to the west, on the road to Ardnamurchan Point. Ardnamurchan's main settlement is pretty little Kilchoan, which also has a tourist information center. The appeal of the Ardnamurchan area is almost exclusively in its scenery: silver sand beaches where

© LUKE WATERSON

SOUTHERN HIGHLANDS

Ardnamurchan Lighthouse, the most westerly point in mainland Britain

no one goes and some of Scotland's grandest forests (www.sunartoakwoods.org.uk). There is good seal-spotting in Ardgour along the road south of Corran.

Ardnamurchan Natural History Centre

This absorbing center (Ardnamurchan Peninsula, tel. 01972/500209, www.anhc.co.uk, 10:30 A.M.–5:30 P.M. Mon.–Sat., 12:30–5:30 P.M. Sun. Apr.–Oct.) is a showcase for Ardnamurchan's wildlife. It includes the fabulous turf-roofed "Living Building;" many of the birds and animals indigenous to the area live in this natural habitat environment where visitors can see them close up. There is useful information and exhibits on wildlife in the center as well as a shop and a wonderful café serving tasty cakes. Admission is free although a charge applies for access to the Living Building (£5 adults, £2.50 children). To find the center, turn along the B8007 to Ardnamurchan Point; it's nine miles down the road from Salen.

◖ Ardnamurchan Point

Slowly, the forests of the Ardnamurchan Peninsula drop away as you near the most westerly point on the British mainland and are replaced by bumpy, grassy hills. The single-track road threads delightfully up and down to reach, in the middle of nowhere, a traffic light. Here you have to wait in a lay-by, without even a house in sight, for the light to turn green—the first of the many charms of the outpost of Ardnamurchan point.

Farther along the road you reach the **Stables Café** (tel. 01972/510210, 10 A.M.–5 P.M. daily Apr.–Oct.) a stone-built converted stables for the lighthouse-keepers in the nearby lighthouse. Straight ahead rises the grassy headland that marks the farthest west point in mainland Britain, crowned with the 36-meter tower of **Ardnamurchan Lighthouse** (tel. 01972/510210, tours hourly 11 A.M.–4 P.M.). The lighthouse was built by the family of Robert Louis Stevenson in granite shipped from the Isle of Mull, which you can see to the south. To the west lies the Isle of Coll, while to the north are the Isles of Eigg and Muck. Good views of all can be had from the top of the lighthouse (you get to check out the light and the balcony if weather allows). Below, in the former head lighthouse keeper's cottage, is the intriguing **Kingdom of the Lights Visitor Centre** (10 A.M.–5 P.M. daily Apr.–Oct., £2.50 adults, £1.50 children, with lighthouse tour £5 adults, £2.50 children). Here you can see the brightly painted red-and-green engine room and gain an insight into how lighthouse keepers lived. There's even a display on how to build a lighthouse. Watching the sun set here is a magical finishing touch to the experience.

Accommodations and Food

Backed by woods and fronted by one of the bays of snaking Loch Sunart, grassy **Resipole Farm Campsite** (tel. 01967/431235, www.resipole.co.uk, two-man tent and two people £13) is situated on a working farm eight miles west of Strontian. Wash facilities, a pay phone, and basic provisions are available.

With a serene location in the lush woods

north of Strontian, the ◖ **Ariundle Centre** (tel. 01967/402279, www.ariundle.co.uk, beds £12, food served 8 A.M.–9:30 P.M. daily May–Oct., 9 A.M.–8 P.M. daily Mar.–Apr., 9 A.M.–7 P.M. daily Nov.–Feb.) is a craft shop and restaurant complex with a basic, well-kept bunkhouse. The chalet-style bunkhouse has 26 beds in mostly eight-bed rooms, but it's the café/restaurant here that's the real draw. It's a spacious, light-filled place with a high wood-beamed roof. Service isn't exactly speedy, but then, it's not the kind of experience you'd want to rush. Great coffee and a range of light snacks and meals are served throughout the day. The evening menu is Scottish, with a variety of dishes that would put many city center restaurants to shame; the blue cheese and leek soup is heavenly. Main meals are £8–12.

On a remote shoreline backed by thick woods in Moidart, north of Ardnamurchan, **Glenuig Inn** (Glenuig, by Lochailort, tel. 01687/470219, www.glenuig.co.uk, bunkhouse beds £13, £88 d) offers pricey but picture-perfect accommodation in large, pine-furnished, en suite rooms. Some can accommodate up to four people in a mix of king-size beds and bunk beds. Simple food is available in the bar.

The finest place to stay in the whole vast Ardnamurchan area is undoubtedly **Kilcamb Lodge** (by Strontian, tel. 01967/402257, www.kilcamblodge.co.uk, £140 d), on a wooded bay overlooking Loch Sunart. The hotel was originally an 18th-century military barracks, used by government troops trying to track down sympathizers of Bonnie Prince Charlie. The luxurious en suite bedrooms dazzle with their king-size beds, snug yellow-and-white tones, and grand loch views. There's a welcoming lounge with an open fire, lots of whisky to sample at the bar, and an award-winning restaurant to dine in. The hotel is just west of Strontian, on the A861.

Information

There are two information centers in the Ardnamurchan area. **Strontian TIC** (Strontian village, tel. 0845/225 5121, 10 A.M.–5 P.M. Mon.–Sat., 10 A.M.–4 P.M. Sun. June–late Sept., 10 A.M.–5 P.M. Mon.–Sat. Apr.–May and late Sept.–Oct.) is an official tourist board information center, while **Kilchoan TIC** (Community Centre, Pier Rd., tel. 0845/225 5121, 10 A.M.–4:30 P.M. Mon.–Fri., 10 A.M.–3:30 P.M. Sat.) offers year-round tourist information.

Getting There and Away

Road access to Ardnamurchan is via the Road to the Isles; both entry points are from the A861, which does a loop from east of Glenfinnan to join the main road again at Lochailort.

Bus connections in Ardnamurchan are poor. **Shiel Buses** (tel. 01967/431272) is the only operator, with one service departing Kilchoan each morning Monday–Saturday for the 2.5 hour journey to Fort William via Strontian and Corran in Ardgour. The return service leaves Fort William in the afternoon. There is also a service from Lochaline pier via Strontian to Fort William. Two services from Acharacle via Glenuig to Fort William Monday–Saturday.

There are also three **ferries** in operation in the Ardnamurchan area. The **Onich-Corran Ferry** (tel. 01855/841243, every 20–30 min. daily, cars £5.20) is a five-minute crossing to Corran on Ardgour from Onich, south of Fort William. You save a long drive around via Glenfinnan by taking this boat. The **Lochaline-Fishnish Ferry** (Calmac, www.calmac.co.uk, every 45 min. daily, £2.60 adult, £11.40 car one-way) crossing connects Lochaline, in southern Morvern, with the east coast of the Isle of Mull. It's popular with locals as it's the cheapest, easiest way of getting a car across to Mull. Journey time is 15 minutes. The **Kilchoan-Tobermory Ferry** (Calmac, www.calmac.co.uk, every 2 hrs. daily May–Aug., every 2 hrs. Mon.–Sat. Mar.–Apr. and Oct., three daily Mon.–Sat. Nov.–Mar., £4.05 adult, £21.15 car one-way) runs from Kilchoan, right at the end of Ardnamurchan to Tobermory on the Isle of Mull. It's most commonly used to make a round-trip of a visit to the Ardnamurchan area and Mull combined, rather than an out-and-back journey. Journey time is 35 minutes.

Skye and Lochalsh

There is something unarguably romantic and ethereal about the Isle of Skye. Going some way toward building this impression are its historical connections with Bonnie Prince Charlie. Against the odds, the prince evaded capture by government forces on the island in 1746 with the help of local lass Flora MacDonald. As a result he was able to escape safely back to France. This would have been more than enough material for the legend-makers to make a meal of, but then an un-known hand penned the "Skye Boat Song" and wrote the island into the history books as a place of romance and adventure. The largest and most popular of Scotland's islands could probably have cemented a reputation for itself as a place of romance and adventure without Bonnie Prince Charlie's help. In the razor-sharp rocky ridges of the Cuillin Hills and the Trotternish Peninsula it has Scotland's most phenomenal geology. The dominance of these black mountains seems to makes the glens greener, the sea bluer, and the island's clutch of top-notch castles all the more ap-pealing. Skye is a walkers' and mountaineers' paradise. These days, however, this 50-mile sweep of stupendous scenery can be merely a backdrop to a totally different Skye of gour-met restaurants and captivating museums. Whatever you do and whenever you go, the icing on the cake is the incredible, lurid light that bathes all of this. The contrasts of bare uplands and lowland pastures mean that mist, shafts of sunlight, and vivid rainbows con-gregate over Skye in a dazzling array of col-ors. Lochalsh, the path of mainland to the east of Skye, often gets overlooked but offers similarly gorgeous views with only a fraction of the tourists. Places like palm tree–fringed Plockton are ideal places to relax for a few days and forget that the real world exists.

GETTING TO SKYE

Trains run to Kyle of Lochalsh from Inverness, from where it's a quick bus ride or even a walk over the bridge on to Skye. Now that it has a bridge, Skye's **bus** connections are not bad. **Scottish Citylink buses** run from Portree to Glasgow with stops en route at Broadford and Kyleakin. There are two to three buses daily (four in summer). The journey takes around 6.5 hours and costs £31.40. There are also buses to Inverness from Portree, stopping at Broadford and Kyleakin en route.

Two **ferries** still run to Skye in spite of the bridge. The main ferry terminal now is **Armadale,** where the Mallaig ferry comes in (Calmac, www.calmac.co.uk, regular cross-ings daily, 30 min., £3.50 adult, £18.75 car one-way). A smaller ferry runs from **Kylerhea,** south of Kyleakin, to Glenelg in Lochalsh (Skye Ferries, tel. 01599/522273, www.skye-ferry.co.uk, five min., car and four passen-gers £8.50).

SOUTHERN SKYE

For most people, this is the main access point to Skye. The peaceful villages of Kyleakin (the road gateway) and Armadale (the main ferry gateway) are not the most flattering ap-proaches to an island of Skye's mountainous magnificence, but this will be about as green and leafy as Skye gets. The Sleat Peninsula, which forms the bulk of Southern Skye is nicknamed the "Garden of Skye" because of its lush greenery. The main village, Broadford, is a service center for Skye with a petrol sta-tion, supermarket, hospital, and some of Skye's best shops.

Kyleakin

It was the village of Kyleakin that was hardest hit by the building of the Skye Bridge. Not only was Skye's island status technically gone but there was suddenly no reason to stop at this former main ferry port at all. This back-water with its wide village green still makes a pleasant stop, and on the green clump of hill to the immediate east of Kyleakin stands **Castle Moil** (open year-round), a broken

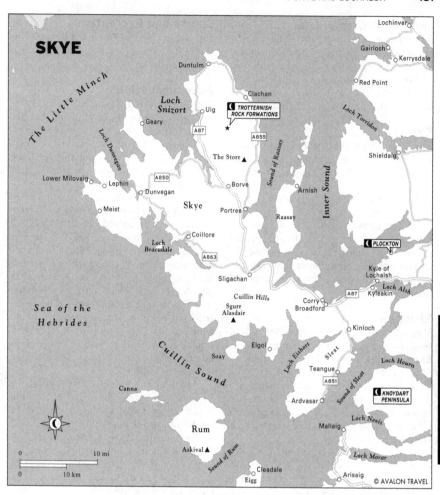

SKYE

14th-century ruin making a good stroll from the village.

Shadowed by the Black Cuillin immediately to the north, **Elgol** is a beautiful little spot with a scattering of houses shelving steeply down toward its pier. There isn't a great deal to do here besides having a snack in the café by the car park or going down to the pier to imagine Bonnie Prince Charlie departing Scotland for good from this same spot in 1746. Getting here along the single-track B8083 from Broadford is half the fun, however.

The Sleat Peninsula

Known as the Garden of Skye, this peninsula is mainly visited for the Clan Donald Centre, a splendid country house and garden that goes a long way to earning the area its verdant reputation.

The **Clan Donald Centre** (by Armadale, tel. 01471/844305, www.clandonald.com, 9:30 A.M.–5:30 P.M. daily Easter–Oct., £5.60 adults, £4 children) comprises **Armadale Castle,** where former Lords of the Isles the MacDonalds of Sleat once ruled the roost;

some 40 acres of **formal gardens** and flower-flanked meadows; a **museum** filling you in on the long, bloody past of the MacDonald clan; and an extensive **library** full of Scottish interest books and archives. It's a wonderful spot, whether you fancy a woodland wander or insight into clan history.

Events

The **Skye Music Festival** (www.skyemusicfestival.co.uk) is wonderful musical event takes place on Broadford airstrip and has in the past had a great lineup including Primal Scream and Echo and the Bunnymen. It's held in late May each year.

Feis an Eilean (www.feisaneilean.com) is a festival mainly using Armadale Castle, part of the Clan Donald complex, as the magical backdrop. It's a celebration of theater, books, and all kinds of music and takes place for two weeks each July.

Shopping

Skye has long had a reputation for fine silverware; you can watch it being made at **Skye Jewellery** (Main St., Broadford, tel. 01471/820027, www.skye-jewellery.co.uk, 9 A.M.–5 P.M. Mon.–Fri.). Mainly, though, this is a shop where you either select from a number of fascinating designs encapsulating the varied geology of Skye. You'll find it opposite the Dunollie Hotel.

It's easy to see why Broadford has a bustle to it: The source of the activity is invariably the **Co-Op Supermarket** (Main St., Broadford, 8 A.M.–10 P.M. Mon.–Fri., 10 A.M.–4 P.M. Sat.–Sun.), which boasts a round-the-clock ATM and a petrol station, as well as a supermarket.

Mor Books (Old Pier, Broadford, tel. 01471/822669, 11 A.M.–6 P.M. Mon.–Sat.) is a great secondhand bookstore.

Based out in the sticks on the road to Elgol, **Castle Keep** (the Steading, Strathaird, tel. 01471/866376) is where you should go if you want your own hand-forged Celtic sword. Swords cost between £200 and £700.

Sports and Recreation

You can rent bikes at **Fairwinds Bicycle Hire** (Elgol Rd., Broadford, tel. 01471/822270), which also does repairs.

Accommodations

Dun Caan Hostel (Kyleakin, tel. 01599/534087, www.skyerover.co.uk, beds £13) is the best hostel in the south of Skye in a whitewashed terraced cottage at the quiet east end of the village, It has four- and six-bed dorms, hot showers, and an attractive wood-paneled kitchen. You also get free tea and coffee.

Built in the 1800s to house workers on the nearby lime quarry, **Limestone Cottage** (4 Lime Pk., Broadford, tel. 01471/822142, www.limestonecottage.co.uk, £70 d) has been lovingly restored to provide Broadford's best accommodation. It epitomizes the pastoral ideal to which all country cottages must aspire. It's set back behind a garden abounding with flowers and shrubs, with ivy climbing the walls and bedroom windows peeping through a pitched roof. There's one downstairs room suitable for disabled guests and two gorgeous upstairs rooms with sloping ceilings and exposed stone walls.

Down in the tranquil little village of Isleornsay, so near to the Sound of Sleat that it's all but splattered by the sea spray, **Hotel Eilean-Iarmain** (Isleornsay, tel. 01471/833332, www.eileaniarmain.co.uk, rooms/suites £90–120) is a Victorian hotel with 16 rooms and suites oozing with traditional Scottish ambience. No two are the same: some get pine paneling, some get plush mahogany beds, some are covered in chintz, and one has a fireplace. The common denominators in all rooms are absolute comfort and old-fashioned class. The suites, with huge bedrooms and pretty big lounges, are in the converted 19th-century stables. The hotel restaurant serves game from the immense estate and langoustines landed at the pier outside the door. Also outside the door is the hotel's very own distillery.

The **Torvaig House Hotel** (Knock Bay, Sleat, tel. 01471/833231, www.skyehotel.co.uk, £69.50 s, £120 d) has a commanding location overlooking Knoydart Peninsula in the verdant south of Skye. It's had an overhaul of recent years. The nine bedrooms are now flashy, well-appointed places with lots of little incentives to make the Torvaig your holiday destination of choice: flat-screen TVs, complimentary whisky and fruit, and en suite showers or baths. The decor ranges from pastel to lavish gold. There is a sumptuous lounge with stunning sea views, where you can relax by an open fire.

Food
Pasta Shed (tel. 01471/844264, daily year-round during ferry operating hours) is a little booth right by the Armadale ferry terminal that serves seafood and chips in generous portions for £5–10. **Creelers** (by the Old Mill, Broadford, tel. 01471/822281, www.skye-sea-food-restaurant.co.uk, noon–9:30 P.M. Tues.–Sat.) is one of Skye's finest and least pretentious restaurants. It serves up succulent fresh seafood from a small white cottage. In an intimate, modern-looking space decorated with lots of bright artwork, you can sample a huge array of seafood (from swordfish steaks to a seafood pizza), but the prize dish is a spicy seafood gumbo, a stew that contains all kinds of fishy things. Starters are £5 and mains are £9–15. To get there, follow signs for the Serpentarium on the eastern edge of Broadford; the restaurant is just up the hill to the left.

Information and Services
Broadford TIC (the car park, tel. 01471/ 822361, 10 A.M.–5 P.M. Mon.–Fri., 11 A.M.– 4 P.M. Sat. Apr.–Oct.) might be tiny but it's packed with information and staffed by knowledgeable people.

Broadford Hospital (High Rd., tel. 01471/ 822491) deals with minor injuries only.

Getting There and Around
The main operator on Skye is **Rapsons** (tel. 01463/710555, www.rapsons.co.uk). Bus 50/55 runs between Kyleakin, Broadford, and Portree hourly Monday–Friday and hourly between Kyleakin and Broadford only on Saturday. For Elgol, bus 49 heads there from Broadford three times daily Monday–Friday and twice on Saturday. There are three or four buses daily from Broadford to Armadale and Ardvasar, in the south of the Sleat Peninsula.

CUILLIN HILLS
These dark, toothlike rocky ridges form, quite simply, the finest mountain scenery in Scotland. Formed out of jagged basalt and carved by sheer corries and clefts that shoot almost straight out of the sea, the Cuillin absolutely dominate the Skye landscape. The highest point is Sgurr Alisdair at 3,325 feet (993 meters) in the Black Cuillin, but mountaineers come for what is generally considered the most difficult rock-climbing in the country. This is illustrated vividly by climbs like the Inaccessible Pinnacle, a sheer spur of rock towering above Glenbrittle that proves too much to ascend even for many Munro-baggers. On the other side of Glen Sligachan are the less daunting and less climbed Red Cuillin. There are plenty of opportunities to appreciate this rockscape without getting out your crampons and climbing gear; even being in the shadow of these mighty mountains is an awe-inspiring experience.

Walks
There are as many walks in the Cuillin Hills as there are ways to ascend the many peaks, and several more besides. The best sources of information on walking are at the Sligachan Hotel and at Broadford TIC. The best way to appreciate the mountains all around you is to climb up to **Coire Lagan** from **Glenbrittle**, on the west side of the Cuillin. The 5.5-mile walk starts at Glenbrittle campsite.

Accommodations and Food
The group of buildings at **Croft Bunkhouse, Bothies, and Wigwam** (Portnalong, tel. 01478/640254, www.skyehostels.com, beds £10–14) offers accommodation at five different sites. The main bunkhouse has one twin room and a large dorm, but the most bizarre of the options is two double-glazed wigwams sleeping four each. You'll find the hostels 500 meters along from the pub in Portnalong.

SOUTHERN HIGHLANDS

© LUKE WATERSON

Cuillin Hills

In a lonely location overshadowed by needle-like mountain peaks sits the 36-bed, four-room **Glenbrittle Youth Hostel and Campsite** (tel. 01478/640278, www.syha.org.uk, beds £12.50), so popular with mountaineers that they're almost fighting to get through the doors come summer. It's a smart Norwegian-style building, but most guests are just thankful for the hot showers and central heating.

Well located for the Tallisker Distillery, a clutch of Cuillin Hills, and just generally relaxing by the lochside, the (**Old Inn** (Carbost, tel. 01478/640205, www.carbostf9.co.uk, beds £13, £40 s, £70 d, food served 6:30–10 P.M. daily) sits dreamily on the shores of Loch Harport. The separate guest lodge has refreshing white-painted rooms, with TVs and en suite facilities. All rooms have loch views. The Waterfront Bunkhouse, also separate from the main pub, has the best budget accommodations in these parts: a bright studio-like space with pine furnishings and a balcony overlooking the loch. There are dorm rooms available, en suite and not, sleeping four each. The pub itself is a rustic little gem; there's not too much

space and plenty of locals drinking and talking as exuberantly as the tourists. On a sunny day you can take your beer down to drink beside the glittering lochside.

For many hill-walkers and mountaineers, the vast **Sligachan Hotel** (Sligachan, tel. 01478/650204, www.sligachan.co.uk, beds from £10, rooms £90 d) has been synonymous with hiking and climbing on Skye for years. It's big enough and cozy enough that you can forget about the wet, windy wilderness on the doorstep when you've had enough of it. Likewise, when you need to get rid of that hangover after a few at the convivial bar(s) the night before, there those mountains are, just enticing you back into them from outside your bedroom window. You can stay in the hotel with its smart, refurbished en suite rooms, the bunkhouse with 20 beds, or even the campsite. Whichever you opt for, you're likely to make use of the Seumas Bar, with over 200 malt whiskies on offer. Even the children will be happy: there's a ball pool, video games machines, and a pool table. When you factor in the on-site brewery and museum, showing

BONNIE PRINCE CHARLIE IN SCOTLAND

Charles Edward Stuart, known to his supporters as Bonnie Prince Charlie, spent less than a year on British soil trying to regain the crown that had been taken away from his grandfather James II. He landed on a stormy day on the Isle of Eriskay in the Outer Hebrides in early August 1745, 57 years after James II had been exiled and replaced as monarch. The Bonnie Prince had been convinced by his advisors that he would find sufficient support to raise an army against then-king George II. It must have seemed a daunting prospect on the remote shores of Eriskay but the young king was resolute nonetheless. Alexander Macdonald of nearby Boisdale met him hastily and urged him that his campaign was a foolish one and that he should return home to France. In perhaps his most oft-quoted words, Charles replied, "I am come home Sir."

The Outer Hebrides were not hard for the Bonnie Prince to win over, and heartened by this show of support, Charles set sail for the mainland. Amidst a further show of men loyal to his cause, he raised the Jacobite standard at Glenfinnan on August 19. He officially proclaimed his intentions to restore the Stuart monarchy to the British throne. Time was now of the essence: It was important for the rebel forces to put their grand words into action. By September the Bonnie Prince and his forces had marched to Perth and Edinburgh and taken both places. Encouraged, the rebel army decided to march into England on November 1.

News of the "young pretender," as the British government called Bonnie Prince Charlie, was spreading fast, so it was important that Charles advance to London as quickly as possible, to press home his advantage while a government army was insufficiently prepared. "I must either conquer or perish in a little while," Charles wrote. Miraculously, the rebel army met with no resistance as it surged south; the troops got as far as Derby before, against the wishes of Charles, his advisors persuaded him that retreat to Scotland was the best course of action. To Bonnie Prince Charlie, this seemed like quitting when victory was within the Jacobite grasp. With

increasingly fatigued men and low resources, however, the Jacobite forces did retreat to Scotland, where they defeated government troops again on January 7, 1746 at Falkirk.

Fighting in the depths of winter on meager resources was not easy, however. Bonnie Prince Charlie became convinced that the only way toward victory was to engage in open combat with whatever force the British government could throw at them. The spot they picked at Culloden, east of Inverness, was poorly chosen. Culloden was an open stretch of moor, marshy and uneven. The classic guerrilla-style surprise charge that had worked for underdog forces in the past was not an option on open ground where walking was hard enough and where the rebel troops were exposed to the vastly superior artillery of the Duke of Cumberland. The battle, on April 16, 1746, proved disastrous for the Bonnie Prince; when he saw his forces were losing, he fled the scene. He made his way west again, heading for the coast to get a boat back to France, a £30,000 reward on his head convincing him even some of his supporters may be tempted to betray him. He tried to arrange a passage to France on the west coast but could not, in the end sailing to the Outer Hebrides. It was a bitter contrast between his time here now and his original arrival in Scotland on the same land some nine months before.

During May and June of 1746, he evaded capture, but it became increasingly apparent that government forces would begin scouring the islands for him. Helped by local lass Flora MacDonald, Bonnie Prince Charlie sailed for Skye dressed as a maid on June 27. The voyage was immortalized forever by the words of "The Skye Boat Song," written perhaps appropriately by an unknown hand. Charles spent a week hiding out on Raasay, at Sligachan, and at Elgol, where finally a boat was arranged to take him away from Skye. On July 20, a French vessel picked him up and returned him to France. The chance of Scotland having a Scottish king was gone. Jacobite unrest would continue in the Highlands for some time, yet Charles Edward Stuart would never return to Scotland, dying an old man in Rome.

a scale model of all the Cuillin, you really do have a lot to be getting on with while you recuperate from the day's hiking. The only problem is that the place is a bit too popular: there doesn't seem to be enough staff to cope.

Getting There and Away
Bus 53 heads from Portree to Sligachan, Carbost, and Portnalong three times daily Monday–Saturday. There are a few more buses along this route from Sligachan only.

PORTREE AND RAASAY
Portree is a collection of blue, pink, and white houses that look from a distance as if someone has spilled some particularly good pieces of candy around a forest-backed harbor. Skye's capital is a thriving little place with lots of great restaurants—it's perfectly positioned for exploring the Trotternish and Waternish Peninsulas. Facing it across the

water is wild Raasay, a barely inhabited hill-walkers' paradise.

Sights
Portree is a pretty village to wander around, particularly by the harbor.

An Turieann translates from Gaelic as "The Spark," and the impressive new arts venue in the island's capital that is **An Tuireann Arts Centre** (tel. 01478/613306, www.antuireann.co.uk, 10 A.M.–5 P.M. Mon.–Sat.) really has ignited the Skye art scene. The year-round exhibition program has featured a range of artists using mixed media including ceramic, glass, and textiles. The center provides the space and international exchange of ideas to make rural art flourish, and various artists exhibit their thought-provoking pieces here.

With **The Lady-B Cruises** (tel. 01478/612093, www.skyeboats.com, £12 adults, £6 children), you can take two-hour wildlife

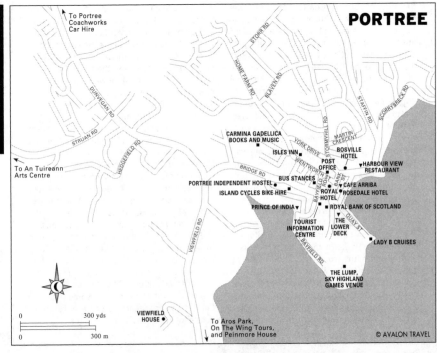

cruises from Portree Harbour down the coast of Skye and Raasay. You get to appreciate Skye's mountainous bulk from the water (from where it looks more impressive) and the chance to see Britain's largest bird of prey, the white-tailed sea eagle. You can also do some seal-feeding.

On The Wing (Aros, tel. 01478/613649, www.aros.co.uk, £12 pp) run tours of Northern Skye which wham together castles, sea eagles, geology, and even a little culture into a thoroughly enjoyable three-hour frenzy. Tours leave from the Aros Centre, one mile west of Portree on the road to Broadford.

Rambling **Raasay,** spreading along the coast east of Portree and much of mainland Skye, is a grassy, wooded island mainly of interest to walkers. Naturalists should also watch out for the unique Raasay Vole that makes its home here. At 14 miles long with its ferry port at the southern end, Raasay requires a car or bike for exploring. The best walk on the island is up to the highest point of **Dun Caan,** a curious flat-topped hill where 18th-century gentleman traveler Dr. Samuel Johnson danced a jig in 1773. At the north of the island you'll find the ruins of **Brochel Castle** with its crumbled walls almost indistinguishable from the abrupt cliff it stands on. Raasay has no TIC and no petrol station—stock up on information and fuel before you come here.

Entertainment and Events
The huge complex of the **Royal Hotel** (Portree, tel. 01478/612525, www.royal-hotel-skye.com) contains a couple of bars: the vast, mellow Macnab's Inn and the lively Lounge Bar, often with live music on. Between the two of them they show big screen sports, attract drinkers both young and old, and have a great range of malt whisky and beer to try. The lively **Isles Inn** (6 Somerled Sq., tel. 01478/612129) has a roaring open fire and attracts a good mix of locals and tourists. It's done up Jacobean-style and serves decent food, too.

The **Skye Highland Games** (www.skye-highland-games.co.uk) is good caber-tossing fun held in August each year. The location—on

a grassy hillock above the harbor in Portree—is impressive enough alone. Add to that a few hefty men sweating it out in track, field, and piping events and you've got a great day out. Tickets for all attractions are £6.

Shopping and Recreation
Carmina Gadellica (Wentworth St., tel. 01478/612585, 9 A.M.–5:30 P.M. Mon.–Sat.) is a great bookshop; you can also buy enough Celtic music here to last you a lifetime, with lots of local folk bands represented.

Hire bikes at **Island Cycles** (The Green, tel. 01478/613121).

Accommodations
The pretty, yellow-painted former post office in the middle of Portree is now the 60-bed **Portree Independent Hostel** (The Green, Portree, tel. 01478/613737, www.hostelskye.co.uk, beds £13), sleeping guests in large 6- to 12- bed dorms. There is one twin room. The kitchen is about as big as it's possible for kitchens to be, and there's a pleasant common room.

Located two miles south of Portree of the B883, **Peinmore House** (tel. 01478/612574, www.peinmorehouse.co.uk, from £80 d) may be a 19th-century former manse (minister's house) but it boasts accommodation that is very 21st century. The five large, light rooms are done up with a neutral decor and all are en suite; some even have sofas. The enormous oak-floored resident lounge with its open fire and supply of books is a great place to relax in the evening. The house is surrounded by rambling gardens and is an extremely peaceful place to kick back for a few days.

The **Bosville Hotel** (Bosville Terr., tel. 01478/612846, www.bosvillehotel.co.uk, £59 s, £86 d) has 19 immaculate, airy, en suite rooms above its renowned Chandlery restaurant. Expect crisp sheets and a touch of class to the decor. The Bosville is good for a romantic night in—you can arrange for your room to be furnished with handmade chocolates and champagne.

In 20 acres of wooded grounds on the edge of Portree is vast, early-19th-century **Viewfield**

House (tel. 01478/612217, www.viewfield-house.com, from £90 d). To call it a house, however, is hardly doing it justice; it looks more like a church. It's a peaceful place with 11 very Victorian-looking bedrooms. The color scheme is often a little on the fussy side but you can't argue with all the dark antique furniture and the crackling log fire. As you approach Portree from Kyleakin, the house is off to the left by the petrol station.

Right down by the harborfront, the stylish **Rosedale Hotel** (Beaumont Cres., tel. 01478/613131, www.rosedalehotelskye.co.uk, £30–55 s, £60–130 d) is a row of whitewashed former fishermen's houses knocked through to offer 19 delightfully old-fashioned rooms. There are a mix of views and room types, from singles to family rooms (sea views cost more). All accommodation is furnished with color TVs and telephones. A four-poster bed room is available. From the restaurant you can watch today's fishermen bringing the catch to the kitchen ready to make up the menu.

The **Isle of Raasay Hotel** (Isle of Raasay, tel. 01478/660222, www.isleofraasayhotel.co.uk, £80 d), Raasay's only hotel, provides 12 decent en suite rooms. The rooms come in two types: standard rooms with color TVs and mostly views across the Sound of Raasay and superior rooms, with handmade chocolates and special toiletries.

Food

The open, modern **An Tuireann Arts Centre Cafe** (tel. 01478/613306, www.antuireann.co.uk, 10 A.M.–4:30 P.M. Tues.–Sat.) serves some of the best coffee on the island. It's a suave place to come for a drink and a bite to eat, whether it's cake or something healthier like the couscous and Mediterranean vegetables. There's also Wi-Fi access.

Café Arriba (Gladstone Buildings, Quay Brae, tel. 01478/611830, www.cafearriba.co.uk, 7 A.M.–10 P.M. daily summer, 8 A.M.–5:30 P.M. daily winter) is a bright new addition to the breakfast and lunch scene in Skye's capital, up above the steep street leading to the harbor. You'll get a good cup of coffee here as well as a creative, healthy menu featuring excellent freshly squeezed juices, crisp salads, all-day veggie breakfasts, and a good wine menu. If your taste buds have had as much fish as they can handle on Skye, this is a great alternative for a bite to eat.

Serving up gorgeous seafood in a cozy, cottage-like restaurant, the whitewashed **Harbour View Restaurant** (Bosville Terr., tel. 01478/612069, www.harbourviewskye.co.uk, noon–10 P.M. daily) is one of Skye's finest eateries. Feast upon moules marinere, langoustines, or seafood chowder while looking out on the colorful curve of Portree's harborfront houses. Lunches are £4–9 and evening main meals are £11–16.

Right down by the harbor and done up with a suitably nautical theme, **The Lower Deck** (The Pier, tel. 01478/613611, noon–2:30 P.M. and 6–9 P.M. daily) is another great bet for enjoying quality seafood in snug surrounds. The best thing to go for is the catch of the day. Main meals are £12–15.

Information and Services

Portree TIC (Bayfield Rd., tel. 01478/612137, 9 A.M.–6 P.M. Mon.–Sat., 10 A.M.–4 P.M. Sun. July–Aug., 9 A.M.–5 P.M. Mon.–Sat., 10 A.M.–4 P.M. Sun. Apr.–June and Sept.–Oct.) has Internet access and lots of friendly help and advice.

One of a few banks in Portree with ATMs is **Royal Bank of Scotland** (Bank St., 9:15 A.M.–4:45 P.M. Mon.–Tues. and Thurs.–Fri., 10 A.M.–4:45 P.M. Wed.). At Portree post office (Wentworth St., tel. 01478/612533, 9 A.M.–5:30 P.M. Mon.–Sat.) you can exchange currency.

Getting There and Around

Portree is where buses from Glasgow to Skye terminate. There are two to three buses daily (four in summer). The journey takes around 6.5 hours and costs £31.40. There are also three to four daily buses from Inverness to Portree (3–4 hrs., £18.60). All these buses will also stop off at the **Sconser ferry terminal** south of Portree, from where you can get a ferry to

© LUKE WATERSON

the striking rock formations of the Trotternish Peninsula

Raasay (15 min., nine daily Mon.–Sat., two daily Sun. Mar.–Oct., reduced winter service, £2.80 adult, £10.95 car one-way). Portree has its own set of bus stances in Somerled Square—it's all very organized.

Portree Coachworks (Portree Industrial Estate, tel. 01478/612688) is where you can hire a car on Skye; rates kick off from £38 per day. It will be cheaper to rent a vehicle in Inverness or Fort William, though.

TROTTERNISH AND NORTHWEST SKYE

North and west of Portree, Skye stretches away in all its classic beauty, tailoring off into three rugged peninsulas. Perhaps the most enticing of these is bare, rocky Trotternish, to the north of Skye's capital. The peninsula is home to some of Scotland's weirdest, most wonderful rock formations. The farther you head up Trotternish's east coast, the more the landscape twists itself into bizarre ridges and pinnacles. To the east are the peninsulas of Waternish and Duirnish, containing the magnificent Dunvegan Castle and Skye's

most atmospheric restaurants. The main settlements in this region are Uig on Trotternish and Dunvegan on Waternish. Uig is a pretty ferry port from where you can sail to Tarbert in the Outer Hebrides.

Trotternish Rock Formations

The east coast of Trotternish is festooned with some truly fantastic rock formations. These bizarre humps, lumps, columns, and cliffs of basalt are the highlight of any trip to Skye. First on the route north from Portree is the **Old Man of Storr.** This basalt pinnacle stands in front of the sharp Storr ridge and can be accessed from a car park to the west of the A855, near Beareraig Bay. It's a spectacular walk up through woodland onto the grassy hillside where the Old Man stands; allow a good two or three hours for meandering up, around, and back again. From **Mealt Falls,** where the A855 passes Loch Mealt, are the best views north along the coast to **Kilt Rock,** 200-foot cliffs characterized by vertical basalt lava folds that resemble the creases of a kilt. Farther north, as you round Staffin Bay is arguably the most impressive rock formation of the lot, **The Quairang,** which contains no fewer than three stupendous rocky sights. Thrust up by the earth's crust 150 million years ago, the Quairang comprises the frenzied fretwork of the needle, the prison, and the table, a grass-covered spot once popular with locals for shinty matches.

Skye Museum of Island Life

You won't see a much more photogenic group of croft cottages during your time on Skye than those standing by this museum (tel. 01470/552206, 9:30 A.M.–5 P.M. Mon.–Sat. Easter–Oct., £2.50 adults), with their low stone walls, honey-colored thatch and brightly painted cart wheels. Inside, there are evocative reminders of what life was like on Scotland's islands until well into the 20th century: box beds, hand spinning wheels, and the like. Even so, you can't help thinking previous inhabitants would have used fewer cleaning products. You'll find the museum by Kilmuir, north of Uig on the A855.

Macurdie's Exhibition (near Kilmuir, open sporadically year-round) is the ultimate antidote to museums, so much so that the only way of planning a visit here is simply to turn up. You'll find it down a minor road by Kilmuir, from where it's signposted (it's the white shack with the green paintwork that you want). Normally, a man just comes and opens up when he sees people arriving. It's a wonderful collection of whimsical objects, put together with a whole lot of imagination, charm, and above all a sense of humor.

Dunvegan Castle

This fortress (by Dunvegan, tel. 01470/521206, www.dunvegancastle.com, 10 A.M.–5:30 P.M. daily mid-Mar.–Oct., 11 A.M.–4 P.M. daily Nov.–mid-Mar., £7.50 adults, £4 children) represents one of Skye's most popular tourist attractions. It's understandable: Dunvegan is, say the incumbents, the only castle in Scotland to have stayed intact and retained its family for eight centuries. The fortress has been the Macleod family seat since the 14th century, but only the castle keep dates from this time. The secret to the Macleods' success, while other fortresses were falling into ruin across Scotland, is said to lie in the Fairy Flag, a sacred banner said to bring victory for those who wield it. The Macleods display the flag still in the castle, along with the other notable clan treasure: a 14th-century bull horn. The horn belonged to a demented bull slain by the third Macleod chief. Male heirs to this day still have to prove their manhood by drinking a horn full of claret. The magnificent grounds of Dunvegan include rhododendron gardens and lush woodland walks. There is also the opportunity to take a boat from Dunvegan Castle to see a local seal colony; trips leave regularly during opening hours.

Accommodations and Food

The north of Skye has some great accommodations and dining on offer, but it comes at a price. For those on a budget, there is a decent campsite, a hostel, and bed-and-breakfasts at the ferry port of Uig and an excellent hostel at Flodigarry.

Just north of the Flodigarry Country House Hotel in the far north of Trotternish is the vibrantly decked out **Dun Flodigarry Hostel** (Flodigarry, by Staffin, tel. 01470/552212, beds from £12.50, £28 d). It has a striking pink, yellow, and turquoise color scheme and a mix of clean dorm and private rooms. With a remote location, large self-catering kitchen, and Internet access, it's the best hostel in the north of Skye. You can camp here, too.

The nearest place to get a meal and a pint of ale inside you is 100 meters away at the █ **Flodigarry Country House Hotel** (Flodigarry, by Staffin, Trotternish, tel. 01470/552203, www.flodigarry.co.uk, £100 d), the rambling grounds of which Scottish heroine and savior of Bonnie Prince Charlie, Flora MacDonald, had as her former home. It's traditional Scottish hospitality here; think four-poster beds, tartan furnishings, and open fireplaces. Not all rooms have an old-world charm, however; some look quite modern and are done up in light colors. Rooms come with

TVs and Scottish nibbles like shortbread. There are 11 rooms in the main hotel and several in Flora MacDonald's wonderful little cottage. There are a number of dining options; most magical is the conservatory restaurant, overlooking the sea. The hotel is on the A855 just south of the Dun Flodigarry Hostel.

Rosebank (by Struan, tel. 01470/572780, www.rosebank-skye.co.uk, £35 s, £60 d) is a spacious modern house in a dreamy location overlooking snaking Loch Harport and the distant Cuillin Hills. The two comfortable rooms with accordingly gorgeous views and private bathrooms make for a great place to stay, but it's the breakfasts that really sell this place. It's a full Scottish and continental breakfast rolled into one with croissants, fruit, and cheese even before you embark on the huge fry-up. Rosebank is just west of the bridge over the inlet of Loch Harport on the A863 north to Dunvegan. Rosebank also offers handicraft-making retreats.

Once, in another life, the **Three Chimneys** (Colbost, Duirnish, tel. 01470/511258, www.threechimneys.co.uk, 12:30–1:45 P.M. Mon.–Sat. mid-Mar.–Oct., 6:30–9:30 P.M. daily year-round, £255 d) was a humble croft cottage, although it's hard to believe these days. If you've got the money and the time to enjoy it, then the Three Chimneys is as good as accommodation on Skye gets. It's another example of the "restaurant with rooms" concept, but in this case, it's very difficult to tell which excels more. The lavish rooms and suites all have designer fittings, en suite bathrooms with baths, and individual access to the pretty garden. For the princely price you get fresh fruit, handmade chocolates, mini-bars, and flat-screen satellite TV/DVD sets. Tack on another £100 per night for two people to eat a three-course evening meal in the low-beamed, candlelit restaurant. Lunches cost as little as £22.50 for two courses, and dishes could include combinations like west coast skate, scallops, winkles, and claret.

Dating from the late 18th century, the ◖ **Stein Inn** (Stein, Waternish, tel. 01470/592362, www.steininn.co.uk, from £60 d, food served noon–4 P.M. and 6–9:30 P.M. Mon.–Sat., 12:30–4 P.M. and 6:30–9 P.M. Sun.

Easter–Oct., noon–2:30 P.M. and 5:30–8 P.M. Mon.–Thurs., 5:30–8 P.M. Fri., noon–2:30 P.M. and 5:30–8:30 P.M. Sat., 12:30–3 P.M. and 5:30–8 P.M. Sun. Nov.–Easter) is the oldest tavern on Skye and quite possibly the most idyllically situated. It's a vast whitewashed building hugging the west coast of the rocky Waternish peninsula, with a grassy beer garden sloping to the sea. The five characterful rooms available are decorated in fresh spring-like colors with sloping ceilings, nooks, and crannies. All rooms are en suite and exude a peaceful, traditional, countrified feel. The bar and restaurant are probably more famous than the bedrooms, however. Whether you want to dine on top-quality seafood in the wood-paneled restaurant or down a couple of whiskies at the bar, this tavern is rich in atmosphere and views. Nearby is the isolated little **Loch Bay Seafood Restaurant** (Stein, Waternish, tel. 01470/592235, www.lochbay-seafood-restaurant.com.uk, 11 A.M.–2 P.M. and 6:30–9 P.M. Tues.–Sat. Mar.–Oct.), with just a few tables in an intimate little dining area decorated with artwork. Seafood is the specialty, with a highlight being the shellfish platter for two: a four-course fest of fish. If you want to eat here, it's advisable to book in advance.

Services

Columba 1400 Community Centre (Staffin, Trotternish, tel. 01478/611400) is a good Internet access point.

Getting There and Away

Rapsons runs bus 57, which does a circuit of the Trotternish Peninsula, calling at Staffin, Flodigarry, and Uig several times daily. Just ask the driver where to get off. There are also buses every two hours Monday–Friday and three times on Saturday to Dunvegan.

LOCHALSH AND GLEN SHIEL

This region was remote before the Skye Bridge was built—more remote, in fact, than Skye itself. But now the A87 through Glen Shiel and Lochalsh continues in a giant leap over the small stretch of water to Skye, there's precious little need to pause in this land of giant bare hills and idyllic, forested coast. No need, perhaps, but plenty of incentive: This untouched corner of the country is free of the commercialism that plagues much of the Southern Highlands and Skye. The warren of lanes north of Kyle of Lochalsh and west of Glen Shiel around Loch Duich lead to one of Britain's highest waterfalls and to Scotland's most iconic castle. The fortress of Eilean Donan Castle on the shores of Loch Duich has featured on more cookie boxes, calendars, and postcards of Scotland than any other building. Mirrored moodily in the waters of Loch Duich, it has lost none of its magnificence despite its popularity.

Sights

There has been a fortress on the site of **Eilean Donan Castle** (Dornie, tel. 01599/555202, castle open 9 A.M.–6 P.M. daily July–Aug., 10 A.M.–6 P.M. daily Mar.–June and Sept.–mid-Nov., visitors center open 10 A.M.–5 P.M. daily Mar.–mid-Nov., £4.95 adults, £3.95 children) since the 6th century, and no wonder—you could scarcely conceive of a more picture-perfect location. The current castle is a 13th-century ruin blitzed by the Jacobite forces and rebuilt to its former splendor only in the 20th century. Visitors here, though, will hardly have time to think about the history; most come just to gaze at Scotland's most renowned castle image. It looks just as splendid in the flesh as on the postcards, jutting out on a promontory into the shimmering Loch Duich with the Lochaber hills rearing behind. Most of what you'll see inside is 20th-century re-creation rather than medieval splendor. The castle has been used for numerous film settings from *Bonnie Prince Charlie* (1948) starring David Niven to the James Bond movie *The World Is Not Enough* (1999). There's also a visitors center and café here. It gets absolutely crammed with tour groups in season, so get an early start if you want to take the perfect holiday snap.

One mile south of the backwater of Glenelg are the well-preserved **Glenelg Brochs** (open year-round), Dun Telve, and Dun Troddan, in a wooded setting. These brochs were mighty stone tower houses, built around 2,000 years ago by Stone Age farmers. The broch walls are some of the most complete on the British mainland.

Hill Walking

Lochalsh has some formidable hill walks, including no less than 23 Munro peaks. The best of these branch off from the vicinity of the Cluanie Inn, high up in Glen Shiel. The other main access point for the high hills is farther down the A87 toward Kyle of Lochalsh, on the minor road to Carnach. Detailed information on walks can be obtained from the Cluanie Inn. You could try the boggy slog up to the Glen Affric Youth Hostel at **Altbeithe** (7.5 miles) with a through route down into **Glen Affric,** or do the popular traverse of the five distinct ridges known as the **Five Sisters of Kintail.** For this walk, start from a forest plantation in Glen Shiel, one mile up toward the Cluanie Inn from the Glenshiel Battle site.

Accommodations and Food

On the quiet far shore of Loch Duich on the Glenelg road is **Ratagan Youth Hostel** (Loch Duich, tel. 01599/511243, beds £13–14), with mostly eight-bed dorms, good self-catering facilities, and views of otters playing on the rocky coast if you're lucky. It's one of the most idyllically located hostels in Scotland.

The massive **Cluanie Inn** (Glen Shiel, tel. 01320/340238, www.cluanieinn.com, £49.50 s, £99 d) lies high on the mountain pass through to the Isle of Skye; Bonnie Prince Charlie took refuge in a cave near here in flight from government forces after Culloden. He was looked after in the area by the "seven men" of Glenmoriston who got deported for their trouble, but hospitality standards at this whitewashed hostelry have remained pretty consistent ever since. It is comfortable en suite accommodation on offer here: the light rooms vary in size from singles to four-bed rooms with both bunks and beds. There's even a suite with a whirlpool bath, which some weary walkers feel they deserve. The Cluanie village offers an information point for walking in the area and a large bar/restaurant on two levels—a dark, worn, wooden place with an abundance of single malt whiskies. With no other building for miles around, it remains just as welcome a resting place today as it was in previous centuries. For a fee, staff at the inn will give you a run to points along Glen Shiel to cut out the road walking part of your hike.

The folks who run the **Old School House** (Dornie, tel. 01599/555482, £55 d) have big plans. They want to make Dornie, the village by Eilean Donan Castle, a place people visit in its own right. That's just what Dornie will become if this place keeps doing what it has been: providing comfortable, light accommodation at affordable prices. All rooms are sizeable and en suite, and there's some interesting artwork displayed around the house. This rambling 19th-century stone building sits by the water's edge on an inlet of Loch Duich. Guests have use of the well-appointed kitchen.

When restaurants with rooms like **Grants at Craigellachie** (Ratagan, tel. 01599/551331, www.housebytheloch.co.uk, food served 7 P.M.– late Wed.–Sat. Apr.–Oct., 7 P.M.–late Thurs.– Sat. mid-Feb.–Apr., £59.50 s, £99 d) start to grace the isolated far shores of Loch Duich, it's time to get excited. There aren't too many places you can both stay and eat in such jaw-droppingly spectacular mountain scenery, except, it seems, on this remote road to Glenelg. There are two en suite rooms available, pressed by views of the woods and loch. One is a ground-floor twin room; the class act, the upstairs double, is a gorgeous more traditionally furnished room. It's a versatile menu here, too, with dishes including rabbit with cognac and apricots, as well as a range of seafood and game.

If you want a really isolated location to stay in, on the silent, wooded shores overlooking the Isle of Skye, then there's nowhere to match the **Glenelg Inn** (Glenelg, tel. 01599/522273, www.glenelg-inn.com, £70 d). The pale-colored rooms seem to soak up a lot of the glittering, magical light that Glenelg has hanging around. They're attractive rooms with bundles of space and comfy creaking chairs to sit in. Guests get a morning lounge to sit in with an outside balcony (midge magnets close at hand). There's a

bar stacked up with firewood downstairs where you can chow down on some local seafood.

Getting There and Away

The main transport hub for the region is Kyle of Lochalsh. Kyle has two to three **trains** daily to Inverness (2.5 hrs., £17.30). There are also **bus** connections from Kyle to Portree, on Skye, Fort William (2–4 daily, 1 hr. 50 min., £17) and Glasgow (three daily, around 5 hrs., £27.90). Buses all head through Glen Shiel and stop off at the Cluanie Inn, Shiel Bridge (for Ratagan Youth Hostel), and Eilean Donan Castle. There is no scheduled public transport service to Glenelg.

A regular **ferry** (tel. 01599/522273, www .skyeferry.co.uk) runs from April to September between Glenelg and Kylerhea on Skye. It takes five minutes for the crossing: a car and four passengers costs £8.50.

◀ PLOCKTON

You'll soon see when you arrive in magical Plockton why it's not really a village for "doing" things. With its welcoming band of whitewashed houses hugging the gently lapping waters of Loch Carron and Loch Kishorn, this is a place where you come to get away from it all. Plockton's fame as the set of the 1990s British drama *Hamish Macbeth*, starring Robert Carlyle, has died down somewhat. These days most people come to eat fine seafood in one of the picture-perfect pubs or just to wander the palm tree–fringed waterfront, wondering whether they are dreaming or not.

Sights and Shopping

A tour to see the seals in the bay is the best thing to do in Plockton. The village is also something of an artists' community these days—not all of the art is good but you'll find some wonderful souvenirs if you look around.

You can cruise Loch Carron to see seals and get unique views of the wild Lochalsh landscape with **Calum's Seal Trips** (tel. 01599/544306, www.calums-sealtrips.com, £7 adults, £4.50 children for one-hour trips). Excursions depart from either the pontoons by Bank Street or the Main

© LUKE WATERSON

Plockton, a place where you come to get away from it all

Pier at the end of Cooper Street; village notice boards have information on daily departures.

Accommodations and Food

In the whitewashed former station building is the attractive, spick-and-span little **Plockton Station Bunkhouse** (Nessun Dorma, Burnside, tel. 01599/544235, beds £12) with 20 beds available in four- and six-person dorms. It's got sturdy pine furnishings, a self-catering kitchen, and a comfy lounge with TV. The rooms share three sets of shower rooms/toilets and have use of a washing machine for a nominal extra charge.

Tigh nan Saor (Harbour St., tel. 01599/544241, www.tigh-nan-saor.co.uk, Mar.–Oct., rooms £56 d) is a charming bed-and-breakfast offering three light rooms decorated with homey old furniture. All rooms are en suite, and one has a king-size bed. It's far better to appreciate the delights of this place as a couple—you'll pay the same price as singles will.

Right on Plockton's serene waterfront is **(Plockton Hotel** (tel. 01599/544274, www.plocktonhotel.co.uk, £80 s, £110 d), with spacious white en suite rooms and a cozy, traditional bar/restaurant. When you wake up in the morning here and gaze out over palm trees by the bay, you won't regret splurging on the accommodations here. All rooms have seats to sit in and survey the view, and one room is a characterful daffodil yellow with a four-poster bed. Not surprisingly for a scenic fishing port pub, the menu in the restaurant features lots of locally caught fish. There are salmon and fresh prawns along with fine, thick steaks for £7–12. You can savor all this with a pint of local ale. The hotel is the dark gray building on the waterfront.

Getting There and Away

Plockton has **trains** to Inverness (2–3 daily, 2 hrs. 20 min., £16.80) and to Kyle of Lochalsh (2–3 daily, 15 min., £2) from the station about half a mile up from the waterfront. **Bus** services are sporadic: Rapsons Bus 62 makes a daily journey between Plockton, Kyle of Lochalsh, and Ratagan Youth Hostel. In Kyle there are connecting services to Portree on Skye and Fort William.

NORTHERN HIGHLANDS

This is Scotland at its most beautiful, bleak and unspoiled. The most chiseled hills, the most resplendent lochs, the wildest moors, the most shattered castles, and the most idyllic coastal villages come together in the Northern Highlands in a landscape that is at times postcard perfect and at times so hostile it appears like the surface of another planet. In places, this is a land untouched by time: Kinlochbervie's fishing community and Loch Shin's crofting communities have carried on in much the same way as they have since centuries ago. In other places, time has left its ugly scars. This was the part of Scotland hardest hit by the Highland Clearances, where landowners replaced their tenant farmers with sheep. Many people were forced to abandon traditional ways of life and immigrate to North America. If they did not leave willingly, they were evicted brutally, and today the ruins of their villages are a moving sight.

Roads are mostly single track and not always paved, with many closing in winter and most blocked with sheep intermittently throughout the year. This is a sparsely populated part of the world—one of the least inhabited places in Western Europe. The main settlement and draw on the west coast is Ullapool, a pretty fishing village with some unforgettable walks and drives nearby. Then there is the trek to Britain's highest waterfall and the journey over Applecross Pass. There are islands that rarely see human life and villages without roads to get to them. Where overland transport fails, boats take over and can be chartered to many destinations.

Lochs do the visitor a favor: They lace the

© LUKE WATERSON

HIGHLIGHTS

◖ **Live Music in Ullapool:** Experience Ullapool's amazing live music scene at an event like Loopallu (page 470).

◖ **Sandwood Bay:** Walk to north Scotland's remotest and most spectacular beach via some poignant ruins from the Highland Clearances (page 479).

◖ **Applecross Peninsula:** Jump on board for one of Britain's most exhilarating drives, heading over the Bealach na Ba pass to a serene coastal village with a cracking pub (page 483).

◖ **Cape Wrath:** Stand on mainland Britain's tallest cliffs, only accessible by boat or a grueling day's hike (page 487).

◖ **Tongue:** Poised on a spectacular causeway between two lochs, this laid-back village is about as remote as villages get – it's just you, a couple of pubs, and walks to isolated beaches and ancient castles on the doorstep (page 489).

◖ **Taking the Train Through Flow Country:** Take one of Europe's wildest railway journeys through the desolate Flow Country and alight at one of the remotest stations ever built to experience life, quite literally, in the middle of nowhere (page 494).

◖ **Helmsdale:** Charming, vibrant Helmsdale, site of Scotland's mini Gold Rush, offers one of Northern Scotland's best museums, fine dining, and the chance to go gold-panning (page 496).

LOOK FOR ◖ TO FIND RECOMMENDED SIGHTS, ACTIVITIES, DINING, AND LODGING.

◖ **Strathpeffer:** Relive Victorian Scotland's answer to healthy living in this bizarre old spa village (page 503).

region and make the going slow. Most people find this the most incredible thing about the whole Northern Highland experience—just being surrounded by the haunting, hostile beauty of the landscape. In the extreme northwest, Cape Wrath is a must-see, with mainland Britain's highest cliffs soaring 800 feet straight up out of the sea. This is mainland Britain's last hurrah: Cloud-swept moorland tinted pink by heather gives way to forested valleys, boulder-strewn beaches, and sandy coves with bountiful hiking opportunities. The east has gentler

scenery, with brightly painted villages like Helmsdale. Here you can go gold-panning in the footsteps of those who experienced the short-lived Gold Rush in northeastern Scotland.

Inland, there are even fewer people and even more ruins of human attempts to forge a living from this land over the last few millennia. Standing stones and cairns and old croft houses wait to be discovered in the heather. This is also Flow Country, a 21,000-acre tract of low-lying peat bog, crossed by almost nothing except, bizarrely, the railway. If you get off at lonely Altnabraec station and walk out of sight of the platform, you can easily believe you are at the end of the world.

HISTORY
Prehistory to 19th Century

Roman occupation of Britain pushed the Pictish peoples northward. They left their mark on the area in the shape of their distinctive brochs, or defensive towers. The Norse arrived in the 10th century and left their mark, too—a coastline littered with Nordic place names and a language that survives in the regional dialects of the Northern Highlands still. The Northern Highlands was not so affected by the coming of Bonnie Prince Charlie in 1745 as areas farther south, but the fate of Scotland's last hope of a king was allegedly decided on the bleak land south of Tongue on the north coast. The Prince had deployed some 1,500 of his troops to retrieve a shipment of gold dumped in a loch by government troops. The 1,500 were apprehended en route, but had they been available at Culloden, where the Prince's forces were defeated by the English, the outcome for Scotland might have been very different.

During the 18th and 19th centuries, the fishing industry brought previously unheard-of prosperity to some coastal areas. Inland, however, the potato famine of 1847 to 1856, in which tenants were left with neither a food source nor an income to give to their landlords, spurred estate owners to clear their lands. This made way for more economically efficient wide-scale sheep farming. The Sutherland family owned some 1.5 million acres of land in the far north, the biggest single estate in Britain. The effects of the Clearances on the tenants of this estate were some of the most notoriously brutal in the Highlands. The glens were said to resound with the wails of women and children. From a church in Croik near Black Isle, the plight of the Highland people was famously brought home to the public in England by a correspondent for the *Times* newspaper, which incensed the public but did little to stem the tide of mass eviction across the Scottish Highlands. Most people were left with little choice but to immigrate.

20th Century

Even the introduction of new industries like aluminum smelting did not stop people from leaving the Northern Highlands to make their fortunes elsewhere. It has only been since the late 1950s, with the advent of tourism, that people are slowly returning. Industries and development, as ever, continue to bring their controversies, such as the nuclear power station at Douneray and more recently, wind farms.

PLANNING YOUR TIME

The beauty of the Northern Highlands is that you can take as little or as long as you like to explore, although bear in mind that no road, however short it may appear, should be undertaken lightly. Nearly all roads in the Northern Highlands are single track. Be prepared for blockages by sheep and landslides. Above all, don't get frustrated—just be prepared to drive slowly. You'll need five days to get a feel for the region—any less and you'll be in the car almost constantly just trying to get to places. With public transport, you are extremely limited as to what you can see: most places only see one bus per day (if that), which means one visitor attraction per day. Many of the best attractions, like the walk to Britain's most remote beach or a visit to Cape Wrath are time-consuming activities; you'll need the best part of a day for each. Set aside at least two days if you want to explore Wester Ross. Don't try to fit too much into a short time: Most of the places worth going to are also worth spending several days in. Villages, although not far apart by North American standards, do have distances of up to 40 miles between them and will feel at least twice that because of the roads.

NORTHERN HIGHLANDS

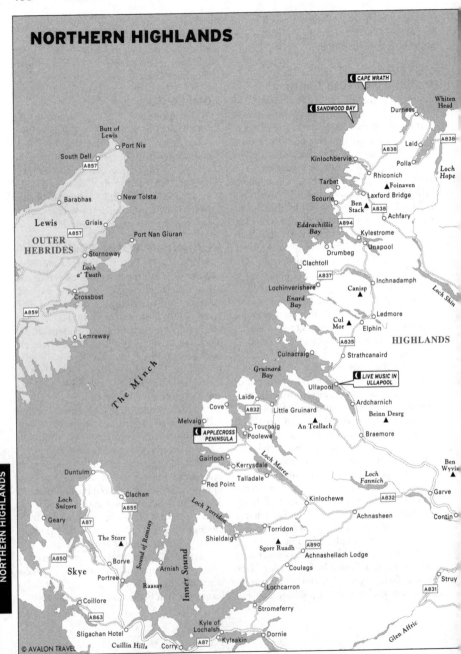

NORTHERN HIGHLANDS

© AVALON TRAVEL

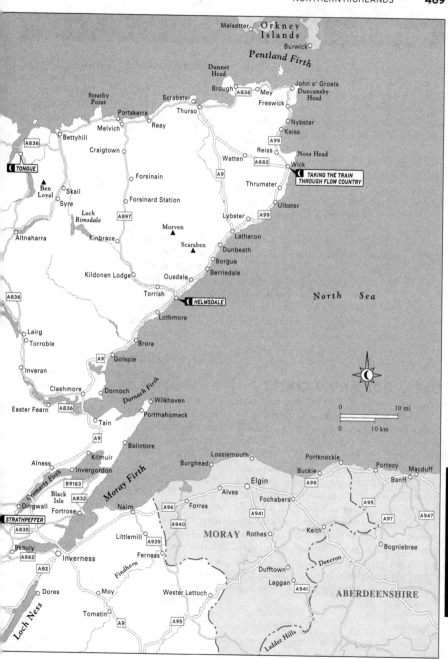

Northwest Highlands

Mountains and moors fissured by deep lochs, ruined castles on rocky outcrops, pearl-white fishing villages hugging shimmering harbors, and stretches of golden sand with not a soul on them: here is the Scotland you see on postcards minus the tourist trappings. Don't come to this region if you like creature comforts. The only creatures comforting you here will be the golden eagles and red deer that thrive on the remote mountain passes and wild, lush valleys where humans have failed to make an impact. The Northwest Highlands is the remotest part of mainland Britain and feels it every step of the way. People come here to tread on golden sands few have trodden on and walk in hills where few have walked. The rocky region also has some of the most fascinating geological rock formations in the world, and most of it makes up one of the 37 UNESCO World Geoparks. For all this, the area also has delightful surprises in store; restaurants and bookshops have a habit of jumping out from the wilderness just when you would think it least likely.

ULLAPOOL AND VICINITY

The drive up the A835 from Inverness takes only an hour but seems longer, traversing the barren flanks of Wester Ross with precious little but heather and peat bog until you descend into the trees that shelter this picturesque little town from the rugged terrain around. A clutch of whitewashed cottages jutting out into Loch Broom, Ullapool is the major urban center of a vast area of mountainous moorland. Being the main port for ferries to Stornoway on Lewis gives it a year-round bustle, but it's a destination in its own right with enough shops, cafés, and nightlife to keep you amused. Ullapool is a great place to relax awhile—if you can resist the urge to explore the gorgeous scenery hemming it in on all sides.

Sights

Ullapool is more about atmosphere than sightseeing.

Ullapool Museum (7–8 West Argyle St., tel. 01854/612987, www.ullapoolmuseum.co.uk, 10 A.M.–5 P.M. Mon.–Sat. Easter–Oct., £3 adults, £0.50 children) is contained within a restored Thomas Telford–built Presbyterian church. This place is worth a look if you're stopping for a while in Ullapool. It tells the grueling story of the early settlers in the Loch Broom area, as well as the first emigrants. Perhaps more fascinating than all of this are the tapestries and quilts handmade by local people in 1988 to celebrate Ullapool's bicentenary. You can hear the stories of locals set in panels in the wall.

Originally used for cattle-grazing, thickly wooded **Ullapool Hill** is great for a short walk from town. There are a number of trails taking 30 minutes to 1.5 hours to hike. Access the woodland trails from about halfway along North Road, heading from Shore Street toward Ullapool River.

◖ Live Music

Ullapool has a phenomenal live music scene. When you couple this with the village having one of the best backdrops of any place in the British Isles, what you have is an intimate, but world-class, music venue. Entertainment enough is getting a slice of Highland life from the *Ullapool News,* printed weekly; it also has listings of what's on.

There's usually something interesting going on at the bar of **The Ceilidh Place** (14 West Argyle St., tel. 01854/612103, http://ceilidh-place.com) every weekend. Remember the nature of a ceilidh is that it's a spontaneous getting together—these are not things planned weeks in advance!

The Arch Inn (West Shore St., tel. 01854/612454) is a pleasant waterfront boozer. It's making a name for itself in quality cuisine—no easy task in this town. Try a starter like the seafood chowder followed by stuffed pork belly with buttered leeks (mains £6–8) followed by the biggest draw of all: regular live music. The

© LUKE WATERSON

lobster pots by the pier

inn has had bands from across the world play in its homely atmosphere; again, check the *Ullapool News* for up-and-coming events.

The reason for the Arch Inn's musical success can certainly be put down to its owner, who also organizes Ullapool's renowned music festival, **Loopallu** (www.loopallu.co.uk), held in September each year. It's a largely contemporary music event on the edge of Loch Broom. In the three years it's been running it has already pulled in its fair share of big names: The Stranglers, Franz Ferdinand, The Undertones . . . and the Ullapool Pipe Band. It's one of the best music events in Scotland, helped by a stunning backdrop and friendly people. There are also sideshows and performances all over Ullapool. Get tickets well in advance.

Shopping
One of the most ingenious craft places in town, **Gaia Designs** (West Shore St., tel. 01854/612429) uses pieces of driftwood found on local beaches to create beautiful clocks, mirrors, and other items.

Ullapool Bookshop (Quay St., tel. 01854/

612918, 9 A.M.–9 P.M. Mon.–Sat., 11 A.M.–5 P.M. Sun.) is a mine of different titles, mostly new and local interest with some secondhand books. Outside is a useful 24-hour touchscreen information point.

Somerfield Supermarket (north of Seaforth Rd.) is the place for self-caterers to stock up.

Events
With its eclectic selection of bookshops, both in town and in the surrounding area, it makes sense for Ullapool to hold the **Ullapool Book Festival** (www.ullapoolbookfestival.co.uk), one of Scotland's best book festivals, in May each year. There are lots of English/Gaelic talks from some of Scotland's most renowned writers. The music festival **Loopallu** (www.loopallu.co.uk) takes place in September.

Accommodations
Right on the tip of where the village juts out into Loch Broom, **Broomfield Holiday Park** (tel. 01854/612020 or 01854/612664, www.broomfieldhp.com, £5–11 per pitch) is a simply heavenly place to camp. You'll be

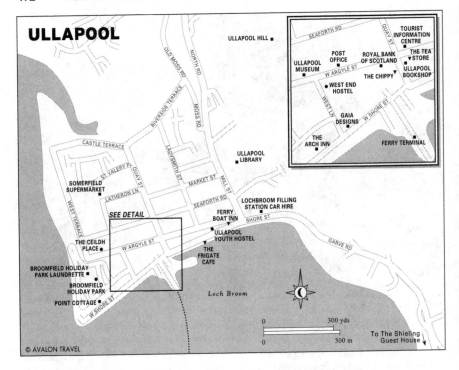

surrounded on two sides by twinkling water, and there are plenty of grassy plots available. There are coin-op showers, laundry facilities, and, handily, midge magnets.

Prettier outside than in, the white-washed **Ullapool Youth Hostel** (Shore St., tel. 01854/612254, www.syha.org.uk, beds £12.50–15.50) is still one of the best budget places in the Northern Highlands for knowledgeable local service and spectacular sea views. The rooms are warm, if a little on the drab side, but the lovely kitchen is a pleasant contrast. There is bike storage, laundry, and free hill-walking/sightseeing information sheets. To make the stay worthwhile you'll want to get a street-fronting dorm with sea views.

There is a great vibe to the **Scotpackers Hostel** (West House, West Argyle St., tel. 01854/613126, www.scotpackers-hostels.co.uk, dorms £12); it's a funkier alternative to the SYHA youth hostel on Shore Street. The place

is cozy, it's clean, it's sociable, and you get all the hostel facilities you'd expect nowadays (free hot showers, Internet, laundry, and a lounge with TV/DVD player). Rooms have four or six beds, with doubles also available. Some rooms have their own TV. This really is like a guesthouse at a budget price.

The two white bedrooms at **Point Cottage** (West Shore St., tel. 01854/612494, www.point-cottage.co.uk, rooms £44–60 d) are none too large but they are en suite and have views to die for; the mountains of Wester Ross seem perfectly framed across the garden and loch. Almost as wide as the panoramic view from the windows is the choice at breakfast: piles of fresh fruit, tattie (potato) scones, a fry-up full of local produce or smoked fish.

The Sheiling (Garve Rd., tel. 01854/612947, www.thesheilingullapool.co.uk, from £60) is a great place to stay with six large, warming rooms in a whitewashed house within an acre of its own grounds by the shores of Loch Broom. Bedrooms are all en suite (some with bath, some with shower) but you'll want an upstairs room for the best views. You'll find a resident lounge with an open fire, and there's even exclusive residents' fishing on the Sheiling's own stretch of glorious loch. A lodge within the grounds has its own sauna. The house is on the road heading out of town on the way to Garve.

◖ **The Ceilidh Place** (14 West Argyle St., tel. 01854/612103, http://ceilidhplace.com, £96–136 d, clubhouse rooms £15–20 pp) should consider setting itself up as a separate village. If it did, it would have more facilities than most places in this part of the world. It's a huge place on two separate sites—whatever type of accommodation you are looking for and whatever your mood, this hostel/hotel can oblige. The hotel rooms are themed around books; each room is named after a contemporary Scottish literary figure who has selected books for that particular room. The idea is to pick the room with the books you most want to read and that will be the accommodation for you. Rooms are large and light, with a touch of the ethnic about them, and have en suite bathrooms. In the colorful resident lounge is an honesty bar. There's also a cozy parlor to relax in with an open fire downstairs. Despite the charm, it is fearfully overpriced, with notices instructing you on how to clean up after yourself (part of the hotel's environmentally friendly campaign). You are paying for a unique experience, though. In a separate building is the colder but charmingly rustic Clubhouse (bunkhouse), with several small dorms full of solid wooden furniture looking out onto Loch Broom. There are no self-catering facilities but the café/restaurant back in the main building opens for breakfast.

Food

You can tell by the queues: **The Chippy** (Quay St., tel. 01854/613756, 9 A.M.–10 P.M. daily Apr.–Sept., 9 A.M.–9 P.M. daily Oct.–Mar.) does good fish and chips. But this award-winning takeaway can also rustle up battered squid or scallops for customers (portions £1–5), and all without too much grease. You can read about how prestigious The Chippy is while you wait.

The **Tea Store** (tel. 01854/612995, www .teastore.co.uk, 8 A.M.–8 P.M. Mon.–Sat., 10 A.M.–4 P.M. Sun.) does what a greasy spoon should do: It serves reasonably priced all-day breakfasts with friendly service and newspapers on hand for a browse. Snacks start at £2.

With a prime waterfront location, ◖ **The Frigate** (Shore St., tel. 01854/612969, www .ullapoolcatering.co.uk, 9 A.M.–5 P.M. Mon.–Sat., 10 A.M.–5 P.M. Sun.) is a hip colorful local hangout doing fancy coffees. You can be sure that what you eat is prepared by the best—the Ullapool Catering Company is based here. You can pick up a filled bagel for £3.50 or opt for a wholesome salad with salmon or Parma ham. The picnic goodies in the deli are as tempting as what's on the menu. Mains are £6.50–8.50. Evening meals are available during summer months.

Cozy wooden tables by an open fire are what you'll find at the **Ferry Boat Inn** (Shore St., tel. 01854/612366, www.ferryboat-inn.co.uk, 11 A.M.–11 P.M. Mon.–Sat., from 12:30 P.M. Sun., food served until 9 P.M., bar food only during winter months), known locally as the FBI. It's a lively, local hangout, with good fresh seafood and lots of ever-changing ales to try. Tuck into a main course for £7–12.

The Ceilidh Place (14 West Argyle St., tel. 01854/612103, http://ceilidhplace.com, 8:30 A.M.–late daily) is a coffee shop, restaurant, all-day bar, live entertainment spot and bookshop all rolled into one. With comfy seats, open fires to toast yourself by, and everything from French toast in the morning to venison and Cullen Skink (traditional fish and potato soup) in the evening, the Ceilidh Place can provide any kind of culinary experience you feel like. Meals are £7–17. The *craic* (conversation) is good, the coffee better, and the beer better still.

Information and Services

The very good **Ullapool TIC** (Argyle St., tel.

01854/612486, 9 A.M.–5 P.M. Mon.–Sat. 9 A.M.–4 P.M. Sun. June–Aug., 9 A.M.–5 P.M. Mon.–Sat. Apr.–May and Oct., reduced hours approx. 9 A.M.–3 P.M. Mon.–Fri. Nov.–Mar.) can provide information on walks in the area as well as maps.

The **Royal Bank of Scotland** (West Argyle St.) has an ATM—just about the only one in the Northwest Highlands. **Ullapool Library** (Mill St., tel. 01854/612543, 9 A.M.–5 P.M. Mon., Wed., and Fri., 9 A.M.–5 P.M. and 6–8 P.M. Tues. and Thurs.) has free Internet access. The post office is on West Argyle Street.

Broomfield Holiday Park (tel. 01854/ 612020) has long been established as Ullapool's laundry of choice.

Getting There
Scottish Citylink Buses (tel. 0870/550 5050, www.citylink.co.uk) runs two of the five daily services Monday–Saturday between Inverness and Ullapool. Journey time is about 1.25 hours (£8.90). In summer there are a few more services, almost (but not quite) hourly. From Glasgow, you'll have to change in Inverness to get to Ullapool by bus; total journey time will be five to six hours.

Calmac Ferries (www.calmac.co.uk) make the often-rough crossing from Ullapool to/from Stornoway on the Isle of Lewis two times per day (three daily Wed. and Fri. June–Aug., £15.30 adult, £75 car one-way). Journey time is 2.75 hours.

Getting Around
Public transport in the Northwest Highlands is poor, often nonexistent.

A key local **bus** operator is **Tim Dearman Coaches** (tel. 01349/883585, www.timdearmancoaches.co.uk), which runs seasonal services up the Northwest Highlands coast. The other bus operator in the region is **Rapsons** (www.rapsons.co.uk).

Ewen's of Ullapool (tel. 01854/612619) is a **taxi** company that also does minibus hire. For **car rentals**, contact **Lochbroom Filling Station** (tel. 01854/612298, www.lochbroom.com, from £35 per day).

ULLAPOOL TO GARVE
There is precious little to define the eastern fringe of Wester Ross apart from the main road that forges its way south from Ullapool to Inverness. The main feature you'll notice is the isolated Glascarnoch Dam. It's all inky patches of forest, wide lochs, and steep, open, bumpy hills, but it's a magnificent and wild area for walking. A popular ascent is up to grassy-topped Munro mountain Ben Wyvis. The Aultguish Inn is an invaluable source of information on walking in the area. The major sight is the spectacular Corrieshalloch Gorge, and Garve is notable for having a railway station, as near as you can get to Ullapool by train.

Corrieshalloch Gorge
The name of this deep gouge in the landscape made by the Abhain Droma river does not do the place justice. "Ugly Hollow" is what Corrieshalloch translates as from Gaelic, but the place is quite the opposite. The Falls of Measach plummet around 40 meters here down a wet, wooded gorge and then rumble along in a white torrent along its narrow, rocky bottom. The sense of drama is heightened by a wobbly wooden bridge built by John Fowler, who also constructed the Forth Rail Bridge north of Edinburgh. You can cross the bridge and walk through the woods to another viewing point further down. There's a car park but no toilets at the top of the gorge (open year-round, free).

Accommodations and Food
Mossford (Lochluichart, near Garve, tel. 01997/414334, from £20 pp) could just be the best accommodation deal in the Highlands—a lovely bungalow sitting above Loch Luichart with the friendliest owner imaginable. Rooms are cozy little affairs with sparkling en suite bathrooms and the trees almost pushing to get in through the windows. You get use of a lounge, which has wonderful views over the loch and mountains; you'll hardly be able to keep your eyes on your breakfast, which comes on a huge platter for you to help yourself. To

get here, take the A832 road for about four miles west of Garve.

The **Aultguish Inn** (tel. 01997/455254, www.aultguish.co.uk, bunkhouse beds £17.50, £59 d) may not be too pretty to look at but this place is a godsend for walkers in the area. It's a veritable mine of information on hiking in the region with good accommodations and a lively bar to boot. It's wood-paneled more or less throughout. The double rooms look like just the kind of places you would want to collapse in after a day on the moor and are cozy, clean places to stay. The bunkhouse also offers four-bed dorms. Breakfast is included in the price of all rooms. The latest edition to the Aultguish is a coffee shop, to add to the main bar. You can get hearty meals here 11 A.M.–9 P.M. daily. In this wild neck of the woods, make sure you use the system in operation (for your own safety) of letting staff know where you'll be walking and when you'll be returning.

Getting There and Away

Inverness to Ullapool buses stop at the Aultguish Inn. It's the only building you can see near the big Loch Glascarnoch reservoir. Let the driver know where you want to get off, just in case; it might be some time before the next bus passes through.

LOCHINVER AND ASSYNT

Set around two sides of the loch of the same name, Lochinver is pretty even by the high standards of Northern Highlands villages. The loch cuts inland some way from the open sea and in calm weather the white houses are mirrored perfectly in the water with the distinctive peaks of Suilven Mountain framed behind it. Assynt, comprising some of the wildest upland scenery in Britain, lies on the doorstep of the village. It spreads north and east in picture postcard yellow-green hills that break into ridges, split into deep silent lochs and swoop to remote stony bays. You'll find strong candidates for the most photogenic mountains and castles in Scotland and Britain's highest waterfall within a short distance of Lochinver. Look

hard at the rocks around here—you're seeing craggy Lewisian Gneiss, the oldest rocks on the planet.

Sights

The highly useful **Assynt Visitor Centre** (Main St., Lochinver, tel. 01571/844340, 10 A.M.–5:30 P.M. Mon.–Sat., 10 A.M.–4 P.M. Sun. May–Oct., free) doubles as a tourist information center and exhibition on Assynt's incredible geography and geology. There are hands-on exhibits and a clutch of information on outdoorsy activities. There is information on the area's walks, including the trek up Suilven (allow all day). Another good leaflet to pick up is the *Rock Route,* telling you about geological phenomena in the area.

Eas a Chual Aluinn Waterfall (Loch Glencoul off A894, year-round) is Britain's highest waterfall, gushing 200 meters down a steep hill south of Loch Glencoul. The best access route on foot is from the A894 south of Loch na Gainmhich. It's a torturous 2.5 miles over rocky Glas Bheinn and then very boggy ground to see the waterfall, and even then you can only get to within about a mile. You can take a boat trip on board **The Statesman** (tel. 01971/502345) to see the waterfall from Kylesku old ferry pier. By the pier is also **Kylesku Hotel** (tel. 01971/502231, www.kyleskuhotel.co.uk), good for a meal afterward. The falls are better appreciated from the loch. Trips leave Kylesku Sunday to Thursday at 11 A.M. and 3 P.M. and on Fridays at 11 A.M. and 2 P.M. Kylesku is by the lochside on the A894 north of Loch Assynt, after the junction with the B869.

The shattered shell of **Ardvreck Castle** (Loch Assynt, year-round), built during the 1490s, remains one of the most gloriously set castles in Scotland. Jutting out into the steel-gray waters of Loch Assynt, its beach is grazed on by sheep and highland cattle, and the still waters reflect its gaunt outline and the hills behind. If you want a picture of a Scottish castle to hang in your house, this is about as photogenic as they get. Access is on the A837 just south of the junction with the A894.

© LUKE WATERSON

Ardvreck Castle, on Loch Assynt

Knockan Crag (Knockan, by Loch Urigill, www.knockan-crag.co.uk, year-round) is one of the most important geological sites in Europe. It's integral to understanding how the landscape of northern Britain was originally formed. The essence of it is that at Knockan, older rocks lie over the top of newer rocks, thanks to something called the Moine Thrust. It is the first place in the world such a phenomenon has been discovered. There is a car park and an always-accessible visitors center full of information on rocks. Pick up a copy of the *Rock Route* leaflet in Lochinver TIC, which takes you on a trail of the other geological wonders of Assynt. Knockan is on the A835 south of the junction with the A837.

Accommodations and Food

The 36-bed croft that is **Achamelvich Beach Youth Hostel** (near Achamelvich off B869 northwest of Lochinver, tel. 01571/844480, www.syha.org, beds £10) has a simply stunning location for a youth hostel, right by one of the best white sand beaches in the highlands. It was traditionally a very basic hostel but now sports such modern facilities as a shower.

The towering **Ardglas Guest House** (Lochinver, tel. 01571/844257, www.ardglas.co.uk, £28 pp) has a great position in Lochinver with the village spread out around the shore below. The rooms here are small and a little on the dull side, with shared bathrooms and just about the best views around. You'll be guaranteed a huge breakfast and stunning bay views in a two-level lounge. Head north through the village, then turn off the main road at a narrow stone bridge to get to the guesthouse. Ardglas is up the hill on the left.

You get what you pay for at idyllic **Albanach Hotel** (Baddiderach, by Lochinver, tel. 01571/844407, www.thealbanach.co.uk, £250 d). There are six huge rooms done up in light browns and whites with wonderful en suite bathrooms and views across the stone-walled garden to the sea. The room price includes dinner and breakfast. Seafood in the classy restaurant is locally caught (or dived). The hotel is

© LUKE WATERSON

Lochinver, set around the loch of the same name

down a dead-end road in the back of beyond; you'll find it a very peaceful stay.

Achins Bookshop and Coffee Shop (Inverkirkaig, by Lochinver, tel. 01571/844262, www.scotbooks.freeuk.com, 10 A.M.–5 P.M. daily Apr.–Sept., 10 A.M.–5 P.M. Mon.–Sat. Oct.–Mar., bookshop open 9:30 A.M.–6 P.M. daily Apr.–Sept., 9:30 A.M.–5 P.M. daily Oct.–Mar.) is off a tiny road in a wooded gorge south of Lochinver. The bookshop is the main thing here, having a 35-year reputation and a great selection of titles, particularly in Scottish interest and natural history. You can peruse books in the friendly coffee shop, decorated with artwork and serving cakes, homemade soup, and light lunches (£2–5). While you're here, you can do a great walk up to **Kirkaig Falls.**

Lochinver Larder (Main St., Lochinver, tel. 01571/844356, 10 A.M.–8 P.M. Mon.–Sat.) is a charming rustic bistro with bare stone walls. It's full of urban classiness with the addition of jaw-dropping Assynt scenery looming from the window. Try the Larder's famed Lochinver Pies for £5–7—they really do have

a national following. The wild boar, pear, and prune pie at £5.65 is simply delectable. Other bistro-style lunches are available.

The whitewashed **Shorehouse** (Tarbert, by Scourie, tel. 01971/502251, www.seafood-restaurant-tarbert.co.uk, noon–8 P.M. daily July–Aug., noon–8 P.M. Mon.–Sat. June, noon–7 P.M. Mon.–Sat. Apr.–May and Sept.), in a cottage overlooking Handa Island, is hardly what you are expecting in this remote part of Assynt: a delicious seafood restaurant serving up haddock, prawns, and lobster straight from Loch Laxford. It sits just above a charming bay and makes for a great evening meal out. Expect to pay around £15 for main dishes. It's just north of Scourie, off the A894.

Getting There and Away

Tim Dearman Coaches runs a daily service from Inverness via Ullapool and Lochinver to Durness (late Apr.–late Sept. only). The journey from Inverness takes just under three hours. Ullapool to Lochinver costs £6.50. If you're traveling around the area, you can by the **rover ticket,** allowing travel on six consecutive days, for £28. Bicycles cost £3 to be transported.

There's also a **post bus** that runs between Drumbeg, Lochinver, and Lairg daily Monday–Saturday. It departs Drumbeg at 7:45 A.M. and returns from Lairg in the afternoon.

INVERPOLLY FOREST NATURE RESERVE

This is the region of yellowy-brown hills you can see south of Lochinver and north of Ullapool. The region has a stark beauty and some distinctive hills, the peaks of **Suilven** and **Stac Pollaidh** being two of the most popular for rambling. In the treeless wilderness of Inverpolly there is no shelter from the severe climate. A dramatic example of how people have had to adapt their lifestyles in order to survive is at the Hydroponicum Centre, which hosts a marvelous collection of flowers and plants, all grown without soil. A couple of minor roads snake through the region, including the great back route to Lochinver from Drumrunie.

© LUKE WATERSON

Tatties for sale in Kinlochbervie – houses in the Scottish countryside often have produce for sale outside their doors.

Sights

The Hydroponicum Eco Centre (Achiltibuie, tel. 01854/622022, www.thehydroponicum.com, 11 A.M.–4 P.M. daily Apr.–Sept., 11 A.M.–4 P.M. Mon.–Fri. Oct., £4.50 adults, £2.50 children) is devoted to hydroponics, the study of growing plants without soil. It's the leading center of its kind in the country. You can see some incredible plants here, an array of tropical fruits and flowers within greenhouses that face out onto often freezing shores. Perhaps the best bit: you can sample some of the tasty plants grown here in the Lilypond Café. This has to be one of the healthiest cafés anywhere in the Highlands.

At the **Achiltibuie Smokehouse** (Achiltibuie, tel. 01854/622353, www.summerislesfoods.com, 9:30 A.M.–5 P.M. daily Apr.–Sept., at other times telephone first to inquire), you can witness the smoking process, which is a popular way of preparing fish in coastal Scotland. There is also a shop where you can buy the finished products, which include smoked cheeses and smoked meats.

Summer Isles Cruises (tel. 01854/622200, www.summer-isles-cruises.co.uk) runs trips twice a day Monday–Saturday (May to Sept., £20) from Badentarbert pier in Achiltibuie to the laid-back **Summer Isles.** The islands have the claim to fame of having the only offshore post office in Britain to issue stamps. You can hire kayaks on the island and go paddling around the various bays and inlets. You'll get one hour ashore on the cruise and will see lots of birdlife. It's possible to take the morning ferry and be picked up by the later one (giving you six hours ashore) but the price wouldn't change and you'd miss out on the guided wildlife-watching.

Accommodations and Food

Few places to stay jump out at you as you make your way along the bleak exposed roads to Achiltibuie: that's because there are precious few houses. Then you reach the village itself and there you are: The **Summer Isles Hotel** (Achiltibuie, Inverpolly, tel. 01854/622282,

© LUKE WATERSON

Sandwood Bay, Scotland's remotest beach

www.summerisleshotel.co.uk, from £132 d) is everything you've ever dreamed of accommodation-wise in one classy, pricey establishment. This whitewashed house, screened by bright flowers in summer, offers a mix of rooms and suites. The suites, like the Norwegian suite made out of pine and with a wood-burning stove, actually work out to be better value at £240 for four people. The financial blow that staying here will entail is best halved—only the astronomically rich could afford the single rooms. The hotel does lunches and dinners from £15. Seafood is the specialty.

Getting There and Away

Believe it or not, sporadic public transport reaches Achiltibuie. **Spa Coaches** (tel. 01997/421311) run two buses Monday–Friday (one on Saturday) to Ullapool. The journey takes one hour.

KINLOCHBERVIE AREA

Remote Kinlochbervie is the settlement at the heart of this area of steeply rolling green hills. Nearby are the most isolated white sand beaches anywhere in the Highlands.

◖ Sandwood Bay

This is the best beach on the Scottish mainland. It is also the remotest beach in Scotland and therefore the vast tract of Caribbean-quality sand gets hardly any visitors. You follow the Oldshoremore road north of Kinlochbervie around to Blairmore, where there is a large car park, information board, and drinking fountain. Then you set off on foot on a fairly good, often swampy path all the way to Sandwood Bay. You'll pass poignant croft ruins and lochs chattering with birdlife before arriving at a series of steep dunes that you negotiate to get to the shore. Allow 4.5 hours for the walk there and back and plenty of time for just being on the beach soaking up the atmosphere.

If you don't fancy the hike but are longing for a beach then head to **Oldshoremore** (two miles north of Kinlochbervie), another stunning sandy bay. The swath of sand is backed by sheer rocky cliffs at one end that provide plenty of shelter. There is a car park with toilets at Oldshoremore.

Accommodations and Food

The **C Old School Restaurant and Rooms** (Inshegra, by Kinlochbervie, tel. 01971/521383, www.oldschoolklb.co.uk, £45 s, £55 d), an attractive Victorian stone-built school, stands high in the fields overlooking Loch Inchard. Rooms come with simple white decor, plump white beds, TVs with DVD players, and telephones. Then, of course, there is the restaurant (in the old classroom); expect starched white tablecloths, cozy lighting, and great steaks. Main courses run £9–18. There's outside dining too, weather permitting. The Old school is a couple of miles east of Kinlochbervie on the B801.

Getting There and Away

There is only one **bus** daily to Lairg (Mon.–Sat.). Otherwise, you can only get to the village seasonally (late Apr.–late Sept.) by public transport, when one Tim Dearman bus per day will call by. You can get up to Durness on this bus and also down to Ullapool and Lairg. A **dial-a-bus** (tel. 01971/511343) can take you on Wednesday throughout the year up to Durness. Book the service in advance.

Wester Ross

Mention the two words above to the seasoned British hiker and chances are their eyes will get that dreamy look. This vast area stretching south and west from Ullapool is an outdoor enthusiast's dream: high mountains, vast moors beautified with pockets of forest and gushing rivers, and, above all, lochs. Roads didn't reach Wester Ross until the 19th century, and the sea lochs that cut into its hilly interior were the only way in and out. Scatterings of houses, where they exist at all, huddle by the coasts. Fishing was, and still is, big business here, and the best of it is served up in the region's restaurants. You can fill your days exploring the area's glorious wildness and fill your evenings discussing adventures over seafood with ringside views of the loch-chiseled hills.

GAIRLOCH AND POOLEWE

These two pretty villages are the thriving heart of Wester Ross, largely due to the historic importance of their harbors. The sheltered location of Poolewe meant it was one of the most important harbors on the west coast in times gone by, but today it's a collection of serene white houses better known for nearby Inverewe Gardens. Gairloch is a collection of three villages (Gairloch, Auchtercairn, and Charlestown) strung out around the loch of the same name. They're service centers for a number of outlying areas and offer excellent tourist facilities.

Sights

At the Drumchork Hotel in Aultbea you'll find **Loch Ewe Distillery** (tel. 01445/731242, www.lochewedistillery.com, open year-round). The owner has long been known for his passion for whisky; his hotel has been officially recognized as having the second biggest collection of malt whiskies in the world. Yet there's a more special reason to come to this corner of Lochewe: For a different distillery experience, this hotel makes its own whisky with an illicit sized still. The Drumchork Hotel runs whisky tasting and distilling courses. You're taught to distill in the way it was done in Scotland 200 years ago and get loads of the liquor you produce to take home with you (or drink there and then!). Contact the hotel to arrange a package that suits or to take a look at the still. You'll find it on the northern corner of Loch Ewe on the A832.

Inverewe Gardens (Loch Ewe northeast of Poolewe, tel. 0844/493 2225, www.nts.org .uk, garden open 9:30 A.M.–8 P.M./sunset if earlier daily Mar.–Oct., 10 A.M.–3 P.M. daily Nov.–Mar., visitors center and shop open 9:30 A.M.–6 P.M. daily May–Aug., 9:30 A.M.–5 P.M. daily Mar.–May and Sept., 10 A.M.–4 P.M. daily Oct., £8) is a vibrant, exotic splash of reds, blues, yellows, and greens on this exposed landscape and contains everything from rhododendrons to eucalyptus. It's the fruits of the labors of Osgood Mackenzie of Gairloch, who began experimenting with growing different plants here in the 19th century. By 1870 a walled garden had already been established, and today the 54 acres of gardens on the Inverewe estate are the finest in Scotland. Not a bad feat for somewhere on the same latitude as St. Petersburg, Russia. Find out more about the garden in the adjoining visitors center.

If you want to see your dinner being caught and get a taste of life on a fishing boat, then see about **Dry Island Boat Trips** (tel. 01445/741263, www.dryisland.co.uk, trips depart at 9 A.M. during summer or on request, £15 adults, £10 children). Dry Island will take out a maximum of five passengers for 1.5-hour trips from its pier in Badachro. **Loch Maree Boat Trips** (tel. 0787/117 4600, on request, weather permitting) will take you out on a boat on the prime bird-spotting waters of island-speckled Loch Maree on the A832 southeast of Gairloch. You could see sea eagles, sand pipers, and black-throated divers. Trips can go to whichever of the islands you wish and are £12 per adult, with a maximum of five people.

Entertainment and Events

To find out where the latest ceilidh is, you should check the *Gairloch and District Times*. It costs £0.20 (available in Gairloch village stores).

Between March and October, Poolewe has a bustling **market** in its village hall on 10:30 A.M.–2:30 P.M. Tuesdays. You can buy local products (wrought iron to homebakes to preserves to pottery to antiques) and meet local people. Places like this are great windows into the community way of life in this remote area, and vitally important for its survival.

Accommodations and Food

Isolated Wester Ross may be, but tucked out of the way here are some distinctive and memorable places to stay and eat. Most unusual of the bunch is the **Rua Reidh Lighthouse** (north of Melvaig, tel. 01445/771263, www.ruareidh.co.uk, hostel beds £10, rooms £32 d), jutting out on a headland into the ocean up a bumpy single-track road 12 miles from Gairloch. Weather can change in an instant in such an exposed location, and the sky forms a whole kaleidoscope of colors and shapes. You can watch all this from the windows of the rooms at the lighthouse, choosing from en suite rooms, standard rooms, or hostel beds. There are open fires and a host of books around the place, including the wonderful conservatory dining room. Meals are not included in the price but you can order breakfast (£5.50) and dinner (£15.50).

Kerrysdale House (Gairloch, tel. 01445/712292, www.kerrysdalehouse.co.uk, from £52 d) is a charming listed farmhouse built in 1793. It sits surrounded by redwood trees fronted by stone-walled farmland. Three rooms are available here, all with private bathrooms complete with baths. The decor is all pale pastels, with walls covered in abstract artwork that gives this old building a modern twist. Kerrysdale is south of Gairloch on the A832 and just north of the junction with the B8056.

The **Poolewe Hotel** (Poolewe, tel. 01445/781241, www.poolewehotel.com, from £47 s, £94 d) is a large coaching inn that pulls in the crowds to its lively bar and spacious restaurant. If you can catch it when the tour groups aren't there, you'll hardly hear a sound here save the roar of the wind and the bleating of nearby sheep. Rooms are recently refurbished, with a white decor and a bold mix of furnishings.

The Old Inn (Charlestown, Gairloch, tel. 01445/712006, www.theoldinn.net, £89 d) keeps picking up awards for both its ale and food, and it's so easy to see why. From the moment you approach this whitewashed pub via a small stone bridge over a stream, you know you are in for something special. Rooms here are lavish affairs with distinctive, comfortable furnishings and en suite bathrooms or showers. You can stay in a four-poster bed room, too. Backed by woods, you are totally cut off from it all at the Old Inn and transported into a world of dark wood, smoking fires, strong whisky, and ever-changing real ales (try the Blind Piper of Gairloch). If the idea of all this rustic bliss is making you hungry, then you have the comforting knowledge that you can chomp down on some just-landed seafood in the evenings.

The **Badachro Inn** (tel. 01445/741225, www.badachroinn.com, open for lunch and dinner daily) is a candidate for the most gorgeously located pub in the country. With a scenic woodsy spot in Badachro facing Gairloch across the loch, this pub is a tempting place to linger for days—it's a pity you can't stay over. Decked seating overlooks the tree-studded harbor, the perfect place to enjoy one of the 50 single malt whiskies available, or one of the extensive range of beers. Food at the Badachro is appropriate to the setting: wholesome, rustic, and with a strong seafood theme (mains £8–15). You might even see local fishermen making their deliveries to the kitchen. There is also a traditional bar with a cozy fire.

Along the remote northern edge of Wester Ross is **Maggie's Tearoom** (Camusnagaul, tel. 01854/633326, 10 A.M.–4:30 P.M. Mon.–Sat. Apr.–Sept.), a great refreshment pit stop. It's a tearoom and craft room gazing out over Loch Broom with mountains soaring up right behind it. A lot of effort has gone into making this a very sophisticated (if tiny) place: outside seating in the garden, tasty food like Orkney sweet pickled herring or quiche with salad (£5.25), and quality pottery and other crafts in the shop. They'll do evening meals by arrangement, which is a real blessing in this neck of the woods.

Information

There's a **TIC** (daily May–Sept.) in the car park by the museum in Gairloch. Auchtercairn has a **health center** (tel. 01455/712229) for those wilderness emergencies. You'll even find a rather large bank with an ATM between Auchtercairn and Charlestown.

Getting There and Away

Westerbus (tel. 01455/712255) runs on Monday, Wednesday, and Thursday between Ullapool and Gairloch, stopping at Poolewe and Dundonnell. It's always best to call the evening to notify the company that you will be taking the bus.

GLEN TORRIDON

Wide, verdant Torridon valley is primarily a hill-walking center for the peaks that tower loftily around it. The hiking is superb, but the cyclist and driver will also find a number of adventurous, often dead-end routes to explore. Being in the stony gray hills looking down over purple-green moor to the lush valley below is a thrilling experience, but this is also a place for relaxation and tasting some good local seafood.

Hiking and Hill-Walking

Walking is the reason people generally come to Torridon. Rugged Glen Torridon northeast of Torridon village boasts the most rocky and dramatic of the mountain scenery. A good, well-marked walk climbs to the western slopes of **Beinn Eighe;** there is a car park on the A896 below Sgurr Dubh. Allow seven to nine hours for the 11.5-mile route. The views are so loch-dominated they resemble the aftermath of the Great Flood. For a gentler stroll, try the coast around the gorgeous whitewashed village of **Shieldaig.** You can get further information on walks from Torridon Youth Hostel.

Accommodations and Food

Purpose-built **Torridon Youth Hostel** (Torridon, tel. 01445/791284, www.syha .org.uk, beds £13–14) may not be the loveliest building to look upon but inside, it's actually a very nice place. There are warm dorms, a lounge with TV that's cozy enough, a very large and well-appointed kitchen and eating area, and competent staff. If you're here for hill-walking, be sure to tell someone where you are going for your own safety. It's just up the minor road along the north shore of Upper Loch Torridon, on the right.

The magical **Tigh An Eilean Hotel** (Shieldaig, tel. 01550/755251, www.steve-carter.com/hotel, rooms £70 s, 150 d, food

© LUKE WATERSON

Bealach na Ba, Applecross Peninsula

11 A.M.–9 P.M. daily) is a rustic, whitewashed place that serves up fresh seafood accompanied by homemade bread; try the gorgeous seafood stew or other wholesome mains for £7–15. You can eat in the bar, at picnic tables looking over Loch Shieldaig, or in the restaurant. Just to make things perfect, you can stay here, too. The warm, wallpapered, intimate rooms do not have TVs (just world-class sea views) but they are all en suite, with real coffee provided.

Getting There and Away

A useful **post bus** runs from Strathcarron railway station on the Inverness–Kyle of Lochalsh line via Lochcarron to Shieldaig once daily Monday–Saturday. At the last check, it left Shieldaig at 9:05 A.M. and Strathcarron station at 9:55 A.M. for the 45-minute journey. Another postie runs daily Monday–Saturday from Torridon via Shieldaig and via the coast of the Applecross Peninsula to Applecross.

The **Skyeways bus** from Applecross calls at Shieldaig on the big journey to Inverness, via Lochcarron (Mon., Wed. and Sat., book by evening before tel. 01520/722205).

APPLECROSS PENINSULA

The road up to the summit of the Bealach na Ba is the most exciting to travel in Britain—a narrow, steeply twisting road that seems to rise into the clouds forever. It's an appropriate introduction to this wild, barely inhabited peninsula, which is absolutely cut off by the mountains forming its frontier with the outside world. The one and only real settlement, Applecross, sits beneath these steep slopes in a lush swath of woodland, facing out over the sea to the Isle of Skye. The limited accommodation and food options are, despite being of an excellent quality, few and far between. Walkers, wildlife-lovers, and wilderness-seekers shouldn't hesitate to explore this area; for many this is the highlight of Wester Ross. A loop road goes right around the peninsula, from Loch Kishorn at the southern entry point around to Loch Torridon and Shieldaig village on the northern side.

Sights

The peninsula has some of the most unspoiled villages in Scotland, particularly south of Applecross village.

NORTHERN HIGHLANDS

The **Bealach na Ba** is an amazing road, twisting up from sea level by Kishorn up through the foreboding rocky slopes of the Bealach na Ba to reach the summit at over 2,000 feet above sea level. The road goes as high as roads in Britain go but the journey up is as much fun as the getting there. First the road skirts Loch Kishorn, then continues up the grassy foothills of Bheinn Bhan in a series of sharp, steep bends. If you are view-gawking, take care to do it in designated parking places, not passing places. From the car park at the top you can continue by foot to the summit (marked with aerial masts) or just stare at the different world you have ascended into: a lochan-spattered moonscape of broken boulders. You get great views, looking back the way you have come, at all the Torridon range of mountains.

Accommodations and Food

Applecross Campsite and Flower Tunnel (tel. 01520/744268 or 01520/744284, camping huts £12, food from 9 A.M. daily Mar.–late Oct.) is the perfect antidote to the stark scenery of Applecross Pass—a gently sloping grassy campsite screened by trees where you can pitch a tent or stay in a tepee-like camping hut. Among the facilities is the flashy Flower Tunnel café, a wide arcing glassy roof that covers a patio full of tropical flowers and tables where you can be served pizza from wood-fired ovens and top-notch beers and coffee. It's not one of those sites where you have to worry about getting soaked. Meals start at £5. The complex is just above Applecross village on the Bealach na Ba road.

The **Applecross Inn** (Applecross, tel. 01520/744262, food served daily noon–9 P.M., rooms £30 pp) forms the bulk of the settlement of Applecross and is its living beating heart. It's a cozy hostelry with fine Scottish ales, seafood straight from the loch, and seven rooms (three en suite) to stay in.

Getting There and Away

Skyeways (tel. 01520/722205) runs three weekly buses direct to Inverness from Applecross (3 hrs. 25 min.), going there and back on Monday, Wednesday, and Saturday. Request a place by telephoning the evening before or it might not come.

You can get the **post bus** from Applecross south to Toscaig and also around the peninsula to Shieldaig. There is one service in the morning Monday–Saturday.

LOCHCARRON AND VICINITY

A row of pearl-white cottages strung out along the loch shore, this peaceful village makes a great base for exploring the south part of Wester Ross. This is prime Munro-bagging territory, but the low-lying land beneath the dramatic mountains is surprisingly gentle on the eye, with winding grass-banked rivers and the vividly bright landscaped garden of Attadale. Don't pass Lochcarron village off for a backwater—it has a touch of cosmopolitan chic about it and you can go sailing, play golf, or sit with a good coffee in a bistro here.

Sights

You'll begin to notice a pattern once you've been in this region awhile: Some of the most barren countryside in Britain secretes some of its prettiest landscaped gardens. This is certainly true of **Attadale Gardens** (south of Strathcarron on A890, tel. 01520/722603, www.attadale.com, 10 A.M.–5:30 P.M. Mon.–Sat. Apr.–Oct., £4.50), part of the 30,000-acre Attadale estate. The estate is part Huntin' Shootin' and Fishin' country and part ingeniously designed garden. Transformed after storms in 1980, the gardens are now a blaze of red, gold, and green sheltering beneath the heather-coated hills. You'd think you were walking into a painting, especially when you see the Monet-like bridges carefully framed by lily ponds, rhododendrons, and ferns. You'll see unusual plant species here, too, like the Korean fir, but this place is all about setting and how such a fairytale array of plants could blossom amid these stark mountains. There is a tearoom, but Attadale House is not open to the public.

When Strome ferry stopped running across the Loch in the 1970s following construction of a road from Loch Carron to the Kyle

© LUKE WATERSON

Strome Castle, by Loch Carron

of Lochalsh, places like **Strome Castle** (by Stromemore, southwest of Lochcarron, open year-round) got passed by. This has to be one of the most spectacularly located castles in the Highlands. It won't take long to explore the ruins of this broken fortress jutting out into Loch Carron, but it can take hours to fully appreciate the exquisite views of a silver-blue loch occasionally chugging with small fishing boats, a wild beach, and distant rearing hills.

The village of **Strathcarron** has a railway station, a charming hotel, and a year-round **TIC** in the post office (tel. 01520/722218) where you can also buy wellies and takeaway cappuccinos.

Sports and Recreation

Lochcarron has a beautiful **golf course** (Lochcarron, tel. 01599/577219, www.lochcarrongolf.co.uk, greens fees from £14 daily) and **Lochcarron Sailing Club** (east of village center, www.lochcarronsailing.com), which organizes all kinds of fun water-based events.

Accommodations and Food

There is something delightfully rustic about **The Old Manse** (Church St., tel. 01520/722208, www.theoldmanselochcarron.co.uk, from £50 d); it almost feels as if you are waking up in a Jane Austen adaptation, with long windows that let in the enticing Loch Carron light and heavy curtains. The rooms are big here, and well-kept, one with a four-poster bed. It's about five minutes' walk to the village center.

The **Lochcarron Hotel** (Main St., Lochcarron, tel. 01520/722226, www.lochcarronhotel.com, £55 s, £70 d), an extensive, whitewashed hostelry in the center of Lochcarron, is a former drovers' inn. It's been doing business since the 1880s. There are 10 charming, warming rooms on offer—go for one of the six that get the loch views. All are en suite with private bathrooms, and the creamy decor and neatly placed furniture add to their appeal. All rooms have color TVs, but there is a sea view supplement. There's a light restaurant strung out along the road to maximize the loch-viewing potential and a dark bar with an open fire.

If people knew somewhere like the **Waterside Café** (Main St., Lochcarron, tel.

01520/722203, 9:30 A.M.–7:30 P.M. Mon.–Sat., 10 A.M.–6 P.M. Sun. Apr.–Oct., 9:30 A.M.–6:30 P.M. Thurs.–Sat. Nov.–Mar.) awaited them at the end of a day in the wilds, then the whole of the country would be taking off to remote spots. OK, the setting helps: sidewalk tables looking out at the silvery shallows of Loch Carron. But it's just as good inside, with cozy seating and a varied menu including locally caught prawns and haddock. There's even a takeaway section if you want to hurry on up to the Applecross Peninsula with your latte. The plum crumble makes a good snack.

In a wooden hut at the **Kishorn Seafood Bar** (tel. 01520/733240, www.kishornseafoodbar.co.uk, 10 A.M.–9 P.M. Mon.–Sat., noon–5 P.M. Sun. Apr.–Sept., 10 A.M.–5 P.M. Mon.–Thurs. and Sat., 10 A.M.–9 P.M. Fri., noon–5 P.M. Sun. Oct., 10 A.M.–5 P.M. Thurs. and Sat., 10 A.M.–9 P.M. Fri. Nov.–Mar.), get ready for one of the best seafood experiences you will have in Scotland. It's all top-quality fresh fish served here, from crabs to oyster to lobster, reasonably priced at £2.50–8 for main meals. You can get an array of fishy things in the seafood platter for £17.95. All around are wild Wester Ross hills, with barely another house in sight. The bar is on the A896 west of Lochcarron, just before the road meets the shores of Loch Kishorn.

Getting There and Away
Strathcarron railway station is three miles east of Lochcarron village. The station is on the Inverness–Kyle of Lochalsh line and sees three trains per day Monday–Saturday and one train per day on Sunday. A **minibus** meets trains (Mon.–Sat.) to connect with Lochcarron village.

All this means that you can (theoretically) leave London on the Caledonian Sleeper at 9:15 P.M. and be in Strathcarron around 10:30 A.M. the next morning (changing in Inverness). Minibuses are well used to the trains being late and will wait. The bus from Applecross to Inverness (Mon., Wed., and Sat.) passes through Lochcarron.

The North Coast

Scotland's north coast stretches from Britain's tallest mainland cliffs through golden sandy coves and deep, silent sea lochs and wild bracken-covered hills to windswept expanses of peat bog. The extreme edge of the country captures each of these different terrains and juggles them to form a landscape that has looks more like another planet than the rest of Britain. The recognizable features are all there, but with a difference. The castles on the hilltops seem a bit more broken and moody, the bare hills a bit more lunar, and the single-track roads even more blocked with stray sheep. Beautiful to look at the region may be, but beautiful to live in it was historically not. This part of the country was one of the worst hit by the Clearances of the 19th century; tumbled-down piles of stone in the heather are the continual reminder of how tough times were.

DURNESS AND CAPE WRATH
Durness (www.durness.org), Britain's most northwesterly village, is a clifftop oasis in the barren yellow hills of the far north. You'll want to stop off here for days—not so much for sightseeing as to soak up the balmy atmosphere. It's a place that has inspired the very best: John Lennon wrote the song "In My Life" from the *Rubber Soul* album about his holidays here as a teenager. Here you will find oodles of golden sandy beaches and dramatic cliff scenery. Perched above the largest accessible cave in the country, this spread-out little village entices you with great walking, some truly gorgeous places to eat, and one of Britain's last great frontiers, the rearing cliffs of Cape Wrath.

Balnakeil Craft Village
A former World War II military encampment half a mile from Durness has been turned

into a gaudily painted hippie village of crafts shops, artist galleries, and cafés. It's a bizarre sight on the bare hills and a great place to wander around. Facilities are generally open 10 A.M.–6 P.M. daily year-round.

Smoo Cave

Not too many caves have their own website, but if one is going to, Smoo Cave (www.smoocave.org, year-round when tide permits, free) is a deserving candidate. Set into the limestone cliffs, it's about 200 feet long and 130 feet wide—Britain's largest cave so readily accessible from land (it's down a series of steps from the car park at the east end of Durness village). Bring a torch to have an adventure into the recesses. Wildlife is as fascinated with the cave as humans are: some of the troglodytes to be found here are rock doves, rockpipits, and even the odd sleeping seal.

◖ Cape Wrath

One of the wildest parts of Britain, Cape Wrath has gales on an average of 38 days per year. It was once on the busy Viking sea route from the west coast to Norway; Cape Wrath actually derives from the Norse for "turning point," where Vikings would turn their boats for home. One of the few roads in Britain not connected to any other road leads into this towering rocky wilderness. At the cape you'll find a **Stevenson lighthouse** built in 1825 and, above the bay of Kervaig to the east of the lighthouse, the highest **cliffs** (a stupendous and slightly dizzying 1,000 feet) in mainland Britain. Why would you want to come here? Well, mainly because you can, and because it's an adventure. There's an exhilarating feeling about standing on this headland, the most fittingly dramatic extremity of Britain, with the wind blowing in your face.

In good weather between May and September, a boat makes the 10-minute crossing of the Kyle of Durness from where a minibus service connects to Cape Wrath. From Cape Wrath there is a tough, remote, 12-mile **walk** to Sandwood Bay and on to Kinlochbervie. Allow six to eight hours one-way.

Sports and Recreation

Framed by beaches and bumpy green hills, **Durness Golf Club** (tel. 01971/511364, www.durnessgolfclub.org, greens fee £15 per day) is the best place for a game of golf in the Northern Highlands. It might have just nine holes but the ninth is a real beauty: You have to play across the Atlantic Ocean when the tide is in. The course is on the western edge of Durness.

Accommodations and Food

You can't argue with the location of **Sango Sands Campsite** (Durness, tel. 01971/ 511262, one person with tent £5)—it's right on the grassy cliffs where the north coast of Scotland crashes into the sea. The pub is smack bang on your doorstep, and the facilities are open all year-round (the hot water ends in October, though).

The Lazy Crofter Bunkhouse (Durness, tel. 01971/511202, www.durnesshostel.com, beds £14) is a modern, purpose-built hostel and benefits from brand new, spick-and-span facilities. Accommodation is in a mix of bunk bed–filled dorms and private rooms. It has a drying room, good hot showers, and a well-appointed kitchen.

Port na Con (Port na Con, Loch Eriboll shore, tel. 01971/511367, Mar.–Oct., from £40 d) has to be one of the remotest bed-and-breakfasts in the country. Everything about it exudes tranquility. It's set on the shores of deep, dark Loch Eriboll, on one of the few British roads where you are as likely to see red deer as passing traffic. There are three rooms with private bathrooms, no TV reception, and a library full of books and other amusements. One of the best ways of passing the time is to just sit in the conservatory seeing if you can spot minke whales from the window. The house is around six miles southeast of Durness (practically next door in these parts).

Some serious renovation has gone into the 19th-century **Mackays Rooms and Restaurant** (Durness, tel. 01971/511202, www. visitmackays.com, £80 d), making it a stylish place to stay in these far northern climes. The

BROCHS

These giant stone towers, the remains of which you'll see littering the Northern Highlands and islands, were the original Scottish castles. When they were built between 400 B.C. and A.D. 100, they represented a drastic change in living style; stone had been generally reserved for ritual or burial purposes, and if it was used for living quarters it was in dwellings far lower to the ground. Most of the brochs in the far north sprung up, were lived in, and were abandoned in a relatively short space of time, perhaps 200 years from boom to bust. They would have been impressive features in the landscape in their heyday, with walls up to three meters thick and fifteen meters tall.

Many historians believe that the purpose of their construction was not only defensive but also aggressive. Iron Age farming families built them to protect their families and livestock from attack in the turbulent times of prehistoric Scotland, but they were also built as a boast and a warning to others. You'll find brochs in prominent locations: on exposed hills and at the edge of a loch or stretch of coast. They were built there so they would be visible from miles around. In Orkney and Shetland, they were often built facing each other across the water by rivaling tribes: a clear statement from the builders that their people were powerful and to be treated with respect. What is remarkable about these brochs is the way many have survived in better condition than many castles built well over 1,000 years later. This is partly due to their generally isolated locations but also a testament to their solid construction. Even after they were abandoned by their Iron Age residents, some were inhabited by later peoples, up to almost 1,500 years later, still choosing to live in brochs rather than construct their own separate houses.

en suite rooms have been done up in heartwarming cozy colors and get modern conveniences like iPods and DVD players. There's Sutherland lamb and locally caught crab available in the restaurant. There is one single room here—not as nice as the doubles and almost as expensive.

Come to the unassuming, brightly done-up little **Seafood Platter** (eastern edge of Durness, tel. 01971/511215, 6–9 P.M. daily) to try the best seafood in Durness, not to mention good, sizzling steaks. The shellfish platter is £18, with other mains £10–15. **Cocoa Mountain** (Balnakeil Craft Village, tel. 01971/511233, www.cocoamountain.co.uk, 9 A.M.–6 P.M. daily Easter–Oct. 10 A.M.–5 P.M. Oct.–Easter) bills itself as the most geographically remote chocolatier in Europe. In a brightly painted former RAF base building, you can sample the cocoa-themed goodies and get a good shot of caffeine to go with it. It's a wonderful experience but not a cheap one; small handmade truffles cost £2–3 each. There is an often-midge-infested courtyard outside.

Information and Services

Durness Tourist Information and Visitor Centre (tel. 01971/511368, 10 A.M.–5 P.M. Mon.–Sat., 10 A.M.–4 P.M. Sun. June–Aug., 10 A.M.–5 P.M. Mon.–Sat. Apr.–May and Sept.–Oct.) stands right by the big car park on the grassy cliffs overlooking Durness beach. It's a very good information center with an exhibition (free) on the area's history and lots of written material on local points of interest. There's an accommodation booking service available.

Mace Supermarket (tel. 01971/511209) in the village center has petrol pumps, a post office, and an ATM.

Getting There and Away

There is a daily bus from Durness to Lairg (2.5 hrs.) via Kinlochbervie. You can change in Lairg for a train to Inverness. You can also get the **Tim Dearman bus** from Inverness to Durness via Ullapool late April–September. A one-way fare is £16.85 and journey time is about five hours. It's an adventure!

KYLE OF TONGUE AND INLAND

The deep, glimmering sandy inlet of the Kyle of Tongue and the area of rolling, peaty country around it is easily defined. Its eastern edge is Strathnaver with its haunting crofting ruins and its western edge is the desolate road via Dun Dornaigil broch. It's a sparsely inhabited place; you're more likely to see sheep than humans. Yet where the peaty hills rush north down to the sea there are great golden expanses of sandy beach and irresistibly charming hamlets like Tongue and Bettyhill. South of Bettyhill, you can see the most evocative remnants of the 19th-century clearances anywhere in Scotland, along desolate Strathnaver.

(Tongue

Above tiny Tongue sits the ruins of **Castle Varrich** (open year-round), a 14th-century stronghold that sits on the site of an older Norse fort. This is the oldest stone building in the north of Scotland; it has a dramatic location and makes a great two-mile walk from Tongue. **Dun Dornaigil Broch** (Alltnaccaillich, open year-round) is one of the best-preserved brochs on the Scottish mainland, isolated in the shadows of Ben Hope. You'll find it on the minor Loch Hope road to Altnaharra.

Bettyhill

In the white parish church of St. Columba in Bettyhill is the superb **Strathnaver Museum** (tel. 01641/521418, www.strathnavermuseum.org, 10 A.M.–1 P.M. and 2–5 P.M. Mon.–Sat. Apr.–Oct., £1.90 adults, £1.20 seniors, £0.50 children) which traces the area's history from prehistoric times through to the Clearances. Displays on the Clearances are the most moving but there are also good archives here, particularly on the Mackay Clan. Pick up some information on the **Strathnaver Trail** here, which guides you around all the historical sites in the area. It's an eerie trip along the B871 that cuts down wooded **Strathnaver,** site of about the most brutal Clearances in all the Highlands back in 1814. At **Achanlochy** and at **Syre** are the two main village sites. To get to Achanlochy you'll need to go down the minor road than runs parallel with the B871 on the other side of the River Naver, accessed from the A836 south of Bettyhill.

Accommodations

(**Tongue Youth Hostel** (Kyle of Tongue, tel. 01847/611789 or 0870/155 3255, www.syha.org.uk, Mar.–Oct., £14) has to be one of the most dramatically situated hostels in Scotland, right by the causeway over the wide sandy inlet of the Kyle of Tongue. There's a choice of twin, double, and dorm rooms and a light common room with great views of the Kyle. It's a friendly place with its own shop. The **Spar Supermarket** (8 A.M.–5:30 P.M. Mon.–Fri., reduced weekend hours) is just under a mile away.

Built into a converted 19th-century church, **Cloisters** (Talmine, tel. 01847/601286, www.cloistertal.demon.co.uk, £27.50 s, £45 d) is an isolated spot to spend a few days. There are just three twin-bed rooms here, furnished in loud colors that grate a little with the peaceful stone-and-whitewashed exterior. Views of sandy Talmine Bay greet you just outside the windows.

Tongue Hotel (Tongue, tel. 01847/611206, www.tonguehotel.co.uk, from £90 d) was the Duke of Sutherland's former hunting lodge and was never a stranger to luxury. The rooms here are just stunning and retain a lot of former elegance. They're vast and colorful with features like period furniture, cast iron fireplaces, marble sinks, and an imaginative mix of colors. The welcoming bar is a good place for a drink, and you can get a mean Aberdeen Angus burger in the restaurant.

(**Elizabeth's Café and Crafts** (Bettyhill, tel. 01641/521244, 10:30 A.M.–5 P.M. Mon.–Thurs., 10:30 A.M.–8 P.M. Fri.–Sat., noon–5 P.M. Sun. June–Aug., 10:30 A.M.–5 P.M. Mon.–Sat., noon–5 P.M. Sun. Apr.–May and Sept.–Oct.) is the place to come for that much-needed cuppa on the long road along the north coast. It's also the only place, but that doesn't detract from its charm. There are two levels; upstairs, mingled with the crafts, is the nicer in which to sit. The place does fine tea and scones, crisp salads, filled rolls, and hearty basic meals on weekend evenings during summer like pizzas and burgers. You'll find Elizabeth's next to the Strathnaver Museum off the main A836 road in Bettyhill. Look out for the car park and the tourist information center. For the kids, there is Orkney ice cream inside and a good beach outside.

Getting There and Away
Daily **post buses** Monday–Saturday connect Tongue with Thurso and also with Lairg via Altnaharra, but seeing as the inland area is barely inhabited, you'll need your own wheels. The post bus leaves Lairg at 9:30 A.M. and Thurso at 9:40 A.M. From Bettyhill, there are four to five daily buses to Thurso.

THURSO AND SCRABSTER
No visitor is going to be particularly enamored with cheerless Thurso, but if you're heading north to Orkney or west around the north coast it's quite possible you'll be unlucky enough to have to spend the night here. The town boomed with the construction of Douneray Power Station nearby and became the North Highlands' chief population center. With the decline of nuclear power, Thurso's future is now uncertain and tourism could become a primary source of income. For once, the bleak North Sea waves are helping with this—they're big enough to make Thurso a prime surfing spot. The town's still far from tourist-friendly, but there are some decent places to eat and spend the night. Scrabster is the busy harbor village from where boats depart for Orkney. Although tiny, it's generally a more heartening place to spend your time.

Sights and Activities
The graceful 15th-century ruin of **Old St. Peter's Church** (Wilson Ln.) is worth an exploration, if only to take your mind off the gray council houses that set the architectural trend here. Thurso East (the area on the east of Thurso River) is, however unlikely it may sound, Scotland's premier **surfing** destination, with swells on its reef of 2–15 feet. You

should head to the mouth of the River Thurso by the castle for the wave action. **Tempest Surf** (tel. 01847/892500, www.tempest-surf.co.uk, 10:30 A.M.–6 P.M. daily, board hire from £10 daily) at Thurso Harbour rents and sells equipment.

Shopping
There is a huge **Lidl supermarket** (8 A.M.–8 P.M. Mon.–Sat., 10 A.M.–6 P.M. Sun.) on the road to Scrabster.

Accommodations and Food
With your own transport, there's no need to stay in town; head to the far more scenic Dunnet Bay to the northeast.

Sandra's Backpackers Hostel (24–26 Prince's St., tel. 01847/894575, www.sandras-backpackers.co.uk, beds from £9 per night) is Thurso's clean but basic budget option; all eight dorms are en suite.

There are seven simply furnished spick-and-span rooms on offer at the recently refurbished **Holborn Hotel** (16 Princes St., tel. 01847/892271, from £40 s, £60 d). They've been done up with a modern touch, all en suite and with TV. The added bonus is that you're above a bar/restaurant that has none of the grunginess of many other places in town. It's a spacious, appealing place for a drink or a meal (mains £8–15) with lots of armchairs, light, and even a garden. On the menu, the fillet of Mey pork with grapes and crème fraiche looks best.

The best thing about **Forss House Hotel** (near Thurso, tel. 01847/861201, www.forss-househotel.co.uk, £75 s, £110 d) is all the trees screening it from the bare, bleak hills just beyond. In this 20-acre estate, you're in a pocket of tranquility with a river for fishing and woodland walks. The rooms really are the definition of rural ecstasy—you could get lost in them, they are so big. Refurbishment in 2008 resulted in even better rooms with broadband Internet access, TVs with DVD players, and spanking new bathrooms with stand-alone baths. The bar here has 300 malt whiskies to try. Forss House is four miles west of Thurso on the A836.

Whether it's a light lunch or an intimate evening meal that you're after, **Le Bistro** (Trail St., tel. 01847/893737, lunch and dinner until 9 P.M. Tues.–Sat.) is the spot to try. It actually manages to feel rustically French and Scottish simultaneously inside, with green-and-white checked tablecloths, low lighting, and bumpy white walls hung with fishing nets. It's the best place in town to while away the rainy hours with a wickedly strong coffee. Try a scrumptious light meal like Orkney herring with oatcakes (£4.80) for lunch. Main meals are around £10–14. It's a good idea to book a table; everyone in search of a quality dining experience in Thurso comes here.

Inside this stone vaulted restaurant known as the **Captain's Galley** (Scrabster, tel. 01847/894999, www.captainsgalley.co.uk, dinner 7–9 P.M. Tues.–Sat.), some of the tastiest seafood in the north of Scotland is prepared and served. Maybe the secret lies in this place's proximity to the harbor—it's so close to where the fish are landed that the fishermen could virtually throw their catch on to the tables themselves. Three- to four-course dinners are £30–36.

Information and Services

Thurso's **TIC** (tel. 0845/225 5121, core hours 10 A.M.–5 P.M. Mon.–Sat. Apr.–Oct., open Sundays June–Aug.) is on Riverside Road. It's good for getting local transport information.

Getting There and Away

Thurso is just about as well connected as places this far north can be and boasts Britain's most northerly railway station. Four **trains** Monday–Saturday and one on Sunday (3 hrs. 40 min., £15.30) run from Thurso to Inverness; it's one of Britain's wildest train journeys. You can also get the train to Wick a few times daily.

Buses leave from George Street, north of the river. **Scottish Citylink/Rapsons** runs five buses between Inverness and Thurso (3 hrs. 35 min., £16.50 one-way) with one direct to Scrabster to coincide with Northlink Ferry departure times.

You can get a **boat** with **Northlink Ferries** (tel. 0845/600 0449, www.northlinkferries.co.uk) from Scrabster to Stromness on Orkney. There are three daily departures.

Getting Around

For a taxi, call **Thurso Taxis** (tel. 01854/893031).

The main **bus** operator in the area is **Rapsons** (tel. 01847/893213, www.rapsons.com), which runs hourly buses to meet with John o' Groats ferries to Orkney or Wick. Courtesy buses will pick you up from the train station to meet with ferries from Scrabster. The buses will also connect from Thurso town center to Scrabster.

WICK AND FLOW COUNTRY

Hardly the jolliest place, Wick still seems positively shimmering after Thurso and is by a whisker the better of the big northeast towns to spend the night. It's also got one of the best heritage centers in Scotland and a clutch of gaunt ruined castles on its cliffs. Once, this was the busiest herring port in Europe. Today, the best that can be said about the town is that it does as well as it can in one of the bleakest locations in Scotland, with flat, brown, bare peat bog stretching away in all directions.

Sights

Wick Heritage Centre (18–27 Bank Row, tel. 01955/605393, www.wickheritage.org, 10 A.M.–3:45 P.M. Mon.–Sat. Easter–Oct., £3) is a step above your average heritage center—several flights of steps, in fact. It takes a colorful look at Wick's history, from traditional domestic life (you get to see the distinctive Caithness chair and the uncomfortable-looking box beds) to the herring industry (there's even a real herring boat to look at). It could take hours to look all around, but if you only have a short while head for the Johnston Collection of photographs. This represents the work of three generations of family photographers who portrayed Wick life from the 1860s to the 1970s, focusing on the common people involved in Wick's industries and on footage of herring boats. Few towns are blessed with such a vivid portrayal of their history. You can climb to the terraced gardens at

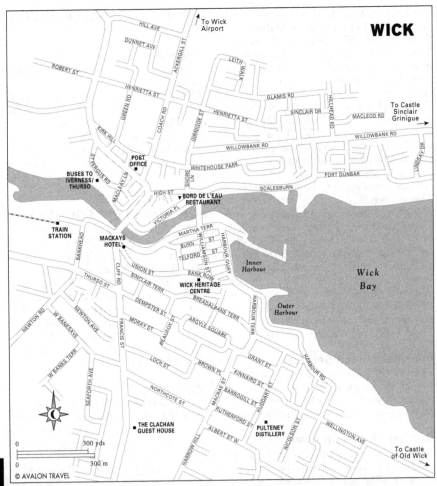

the back of the museum to get a good view of Wick. Knowledgeable guides are on hand.

Wick has two ruined **castles** sitting on its coast. Just south of town is the solitary **Castle of Old Wick** (year-round), an early 14th-century tower poised above a ravine in the cliffs. You can walk one mile along the coast from Wick to reach the castle. **Castle Sinclair Girnigoe** (www.castlesinclairgirnigoe.org, not currently open) is the most spectacular fortress in the north of Scotland, so near the cliff edge it's almost falling in. Turn up Henrietta

Street and follow signs for Staxigoe and Noss. The road ends at a car park by the lighthouse. Nearby is spectacular Sinclair Bay.

Pulteney Distillery (visitors center on Huddart St., tel. 01955/602371, www.old-pulteney.com, tours 10 A.M.–4 P.M. Mon.–Fri.) is the most northerly distillery on the Scottish mainland and produces a cracking single malt, full of the flavor of the sea breeze. Back in the days of the herring boom, most of the distillery workers were also fishermen and used their boats to ship whisky across to Norway. It's also

THE HERRING HEYDAY

Herring fishing on the east coast of Scotland is nothing new: from Viking times onward, this small oily fish has been recognized as one of the most important commodities around. But for a very long time it was thought that the fishermen weren't making the most of the fish-full seas. The government was unhappy with the catch coming in and in 1718 introduced barrel bounties: bonuses on each barrel of gutted and cured fish produced. The effect was almost instantaneous: annual fish catches, caught mainly by fleets of small boats that could be launched quickly, began to rise. This still wasn't enough for the government.

One of the main problems was the harbors where the fish catch were landed: They were simply insufficient for the number of boats. In 1768 Sir John Sinclair of Ulbster decided to promote Wick as a center for Herring fishing. He built a quay, which renowned engineer Thomas Telford later developed into a harbor. Like many towns along the east coast, Wick was on the up. Despite an outbreak of cholera that forced many fishermen to seek work elsewhere, by 1860 Wick was Europe's leading herring port, with over 1,000 boats operating out of its harbor. It was a big industry: not only did it employ some 6,000 fishermen but also the women who followed wherever the catch was landed to gut, salt, and pack the herring. Then there were the 300 coopers employed to make barrels for all the herring to be packed

in. Even Wick's distillery got involved, supplying barrels for the cause.

The inhabitants of Wick were lucky; at least they had the industry on their doorstep. Others risked everything for the herring. Women from as far away as Lewis and Shetland would make the grueling journey on foot to pack fish in the east coast ports, spending months away from home. In Shetland, women would follow their menfolk down the coast as the fishing season progressed. When one area was fished clean, fishermen would move on to the next, from Wick south to Aberdeen, Eyemouth, then Lowestoft in England. In many places the trade eventually dwindled through pricing disputes and competition from other countries. In Wick, it was just overfishing; no precautions had been taken to conserve stocks.

By 1900, things were on the decline. To cheer up the dispirited fishermen, authorities decided to inject a bit of frivolity into the industry. They appointed a girl who had to have at least one parent connected with the herring trade to be the annual "Herring Queen." The queen was taken out to sea on a brightly decorated drifter with members of the fishing fleet. The last Herring Queen was elected in 1953, by which time there were barely any herring to be queen of. The legacy of the salty fish that shaped the course of the 19th century in the Wick area can be explored at the Wick Heritage Centre.

noteworthy for being the only distillery in the north of Scotland to bottle at the source. A tour costs £3.50, redeemable against a purchase. The distillery is south of the town center.

Accommodations and Food

On the southern outskirts of town, **The Clachan** (14 Randolph Pl., tel. 01955/605384, www.theclachan.co.uk, £35 s, £46 d) offers good value for money with just three warm, florally decorated rooms. Porridge and homemade marmalade are on the breakfast agenda.

Grand old 19th-century **Mackays Hotel** (Union St. off Cliff Rd., tel. 01955/602323,

www.mackayshotel.co.uk, £70 s, £95 d) stands on Britain's smallest street, a whopping three meters from end to end. As for the hotel, it's relatively larger. Inside, this is easily the most luxurious accommodation option in town. The big, elegant old rooms have every modern convenience: wide screen TVs and DVD players and en suite bathrooms. You will even get a guide to local attractions put together by staff and a newspaper delivered to your room in the morning. You can get meals, including good lamb and venison, throughout the day in the bistro.

Bord de L'eau (2 Market St., tel. 01955/604400, 6 P.M.–late Tues.–Sat., 2:30–6:30 P.M.

Sun.) is far and away the best place to eat in the area. This swanky French restaurant right by the river serves up innovative dishes like wild pheasant and mushroom terrine followed by pork medallions with roquefort cheese. It also does three-course seafood meals. Mains are £10–15.

Getting There and Away
You can fly from Wick Airport to Aberdeen three times daily with **Eastern Airways** (tel. 01652/680600, www.easternairways.com). Fares depend on how much in advance they are booked. You can also fly once daily from Wick to Edinburgh.

Scottish Citylink and **Rapsons** provide five services daily between them to Wick (3 hrs., £16.50) from Inverness.

◖ TAKING THE TRAIN THROUGH FLOW COUNTRY
There are four trains daily between Wick and Inverness (4 hrs. 10 min., £15.30). This is the most otherworldly railway journey in Europe—you go through a land of flat, brown, peaty nothingness. It's incredible that the railway even crosses this landscape, and still more so that in the middle of it, there's a station (Altnabraec Station). We're talking a station and nothing else here, except for, of course, peat. Get off, experience life at what seems like the edge of the earth, and make sure there's a train you can take back to civilization again.

THE FAR NORTHEAST
It's a bleak, peaty approach to the most northeasterly part of Scotland. Many visitors head for overcommercialized John o' Groats to pose beside Most Northeasterly Point in Britain signs, but the coast here holds far more worthwhile reasons to visit. The late Queen Mother took her summer holidays in the Castle of Mey for nearly 50 years and had the renovations done on this fascinating stately home. The coast forms extremes in this windswept place; as well as being the mainland's most northeasterly and northerly points, it also alternates from curving sandy beaches to towering rock stacks.

John o' Groats and Vicinity
First of all, who really cares about visiting the most northeasterly point of a country? It's not even as impressive as either the most northerly or the most easterly. Secondly, John o' Groats isn't even the most northeasterly point of Britain (that's at nearby Duncansby Head), only the most northeasterly village. Thirdly, because of the hype, you have to endure fearfully expensive public toilets, crowds of people, and kitschy tourist shops, all in the name of a compass point. Bear this in mind as you force your way out of the car against the driving wind to stand on this godforsaken part of Scotland. That said, it will continue, despite the best advice of those who have gone before, to lure people fascinated by this extremity of British atlases. At least there are places to get something to eat to take the edge off your disappointment. You can get a passenger ferry to Orkney from here. Two miles northeast of John o'Groats, **Duncansby Head and Stacks** (year-round) marks the proper most northeasterly point of Britain, and is refreshingly devoid of the tackiness of John O' Groats. It's actually devoid of pretty much everything.

Castle of Mey
The most northerly castle on the Scottish mainland, the Castle of Mey (Canisbay, tel. 01847/851473, www.castleofmey.org.uk, 10:30 A.M.–4 P.M. daily May–Sept. with a short break late July–early Aug., £8 adults, £3 children) was where the Queen Mother stayed every summer from the early 1950s until her death in 2002. She herself oversaw the renovation. This is an impressive stately home made unique by the fact that there are touches of the Queen Mother everywhere. You can see some of her vast repertoire of hats, the bowls from which she fed her corgis, the library where she would write letters and play after-dinner games, and, best of all, the fruit and flower gardens she helped tend herself. Check the Queen Mother's very own favorite rose, which she managed to establish by the high garden wall. The castle lacks the visual excesses of other stately houses but compensates with a homey elegance. It's

a charming shrine to the Queen Mother's life here and gives a very real insight into how she liked to fill her days.

Dunnet Head and Dunnet Bay

Dunnet Head is the most northerly point on the British mainland, and if you're doing the rounds of all the compass point extremities, this is a particularly rewarding one—just a small car park by the high grassy cliffs overlooking the Pentland Firth. Dunnet village has a lovely sandy **beach:** it's on the A836 around seven miles east of Thurso. Dunnet Head is directly north of Dunnet.

Accommodations

You can pitch your tent at **Dunnet Bay Caravan Club** (Dunnet, tel. 01854/821319, Mar.–Oct., tents from £7.10) above the most gorgeous beach on the northeast coast. It's an impeccably spotless site but it can get windy. The views of grassy dunes and golden sand compensate, and the pub is not too far away.

The **Castle Arms Hotel** (Mey, tel. 01854/851244, www.castlearms.co.uk, £57 s, £90 d) is a 19th-century former coaching inn sporting eight decently sized en suite rooms with color TV.

Getting There and Away

Hourly **buses** run Monday–Friday, with fewer Saturday services, between Thurso and John o' Groats, stopping off at points on the way. **Passenger ferries** from John o' Groats go to Burwick on South Ronaldsay, Orkney, two to four times daily May–September.

East Highlands Coast

The stretch of coast from Wick down to Inverness is mild by the rather rugged standards of the Highlands. You still get the huge hills, but they're appeased with sheltered, forested valleys, beaches and picturesque villages. This is an archaeologically and culturally rich area of prehistoric sites and brilliant heritage centers that delve into their history. Dotted down the coast are some of the country's most appealing villages, such as brightly colored Helmsdale, the Victorian spa town of Strathpeffer, and the graceful sandstone-built Cromarty. Inland by Loch Shin, the Highlands' often-desolate feel returns, but it's here that you'll find some of Scotland's unique places to stay.

LYBSTER AND VICINITY

On the yellow-green sloping moor south of Wick, Lybster is another former herring boom port. Once Scotland's third-largest fishing fleet operated out of the harbor, but today the area is a showcase for a rather more distant period of history. In the moor around the village is scattered one of the most diverse spreads of archaeological sites anywhere in Britain. The bleak location adds an especially poignant feel to each; historians will be champing at the bit to explore them all.

Sights

You get a great insight into Lybster's fishing-oriented past at the vibrant stone-built visitors center of **Waterlines** (tel. 01593/721520, 11 A.M.–5 P.M. daily May–Sept., £2.50), right by Lybster harbor. You can find out how kippers are made and see live CCTV images of nesting birds. It's also a good idea to come here to get a sense of the archaeology to explore in the Lybster area.

The villages of Whaligoe and Ulbster are situated on cliffs high above the sea. Not to be outdone by other ports during the days of the herring boom, locals cut a steep series of steps known as the **Whaligoe Steps** (Ulbster, year-round) into the cliff. That way herring boats could still land by the pier at the bottom and catch could be carried up to the village. It's a magical experience coming down the steps to the quiet shore. Imagine scaling these steps with a load of just-landed herring on your shoulders, and then walking with it six miles into Wick; the local women had to do this on a regular basis. To get to the steps from Lybster, head past Whaligoe village and take the sharp turn right by the phone box, opposite a sign to the Cairn of Get. There's a big car park from where you can follow a track down beside houses to the steps. An old man often materializes from one of the cottages by the car park and begins telling you the history of the steps.

South from the Cairn of Get turn-off you'll pass Whaligoe and Bruan and, one mile after Bruan, see a signpost to **Hill o' Many Stanes** (year-round), slightly inland to the east. It's an incredible series of 22 rows of eight stones in a fan formation on the hillside. These tiny stones or "stanes" are thought to have been built around 1800 B.C. for astrological observance, probably set out to depict stars in the cosmos.

Two miles south of the turning to the Hill o' Many Stanes at Occumster, a minor road leads to the **Grey Cairns of Camster** (by Camster, open year-round). This is as good as Neolithic burial chambers get on the British mainland. You'll find two stunning examples here, both around 4,500 years old.

Achavanich Standing Stones (Achavanich, year-round) are about 30 still-standing stones of an estimated original 60, standing in a horseshoe shape above the loch of Stemster. It's a powerful, lonely sight: It's just you, these gray Bronze Age monuments, and the brown moor here. To get there, take the minor road to Achavanich, which heads northwest from Lybster village. The stones are just south of the junction with the main A9 road.

Accommodations and Food

The Croft House (Swiney, Lybster, tel. 01593/721342, £30 s, £46 d), just south of Lybster, has two ample, comfortable, en suite rooms and bags of local information. There's a conservatory to sit in on rainy days and watch the world go by. The showers are candidates for some of the best in Scotland: hot, fast, and furious! In the morning, guests sit down at one central table and find it extremely difficult to

leave again, the breakfasts are so big. You'll be offered such treats as thick, creamy porridge, homemade preserves, and kippers.

The **Bayview Hotel** (Russell St., Lybster, tel. 01593/721346, food served until 8:30 P.M.) is a cozy spot for a meal, down in Lybster village. You get big portions of Scottish food, including mammoth plates of vegetables. It's a meat-dominated menu, but there are veggie options too. There are plenty of booths to tuck into and a lively bar separate from the restaurant.

Getting There and Away

Scottish Citylink and **Rapsons buses,** between Inverness and Thurso, stop up to five times daily in Lybster.

◖ HELMSDALE AND VICINITY

You can see why Dame Barbara Cartland made the little town of Helmsdale her holiday destination of choice. It lies at a pretty major crossroads for these parts: not only do two roads meet here but the railway and the River Helmsdale also pass through. Perhaps that's why this brightly painted cluster of houses seems to bustle with life so. It's the highlight of a visit to the East Highlands coast with a wonderful heritage center, some characterful pubs, and great places to eat. You can even try gold-panning on the site of Scotland's very own Gold Rush near Helmsdale.

Sights

You can't help but enjoy the **Timespan Heritage Museum** (Dunrobin St., tel. 01431/821327, www.timespan.org.uk, 10 A.M.–5 P.M. Mon.–Sat., noon–5 P.M. Sun. Easter–Oct., £4)—if only history was always this much fun. It fixes on the most captivating parts of Helmsdale's history (the Vikings and the Gold Rush) to create a colorful display. There's even a lovingly created smithy and croft. Upstairs is a wonderful exhibition space overlooking the river. Overlooking the bridge and Helmsdale's own Victorian ice-house is the heritage center's spacious café, with wonderful views and even better coffee.

The peaceful harbor of **Dunbeath** about

15 miles northeast of Helmsdale was the birthplace and childhood inspiration of Neil Gunn, the author of *Ring of Bright Water*. In quiet, thought-provoking **Dunbeath Heritage Centre** (tel. 01593/731233, www.dunbeath-heritage.org, 10 A.M.–5 P.M. daily Easter–Oct., £2 adult, £1 children) you can find out about Gunn and also the rich archaeology of the area. It's very well presented; the highlight is probably the runic Ballachly Stone, found by one of the museum's founders in her back garden! From the north, take the side road off to the right, which loops under the main road and to the center.

Activities

You can go **gold-panning** free of charge at **Kildonan Burn** on the Suisgill Estate just south of **Kildonan Lodge.** You do have to follow strict laws if you want to take advantage: It must take place upstream of the stone bridge at Baile an Or, and you cannot gold-pan for commercial purposes or financial gain. You can buy gold-panning kits at the Strath Ullie Crafts and Tourist Information Centre in Helmsdale. Follow the A897 eight miles northwest from Helmsdale to get to the burn.

Accommodations and Food

Helmsdale Hostel (tel. 01431/821636, www.helmsdalehostel.co.uk, beds £15, family rooms sleeping up to four £60) is a charismatic and very popular wood-paneled hostel just up from the town center on the main road north. There are two eight-bed dorms, two great value family rooms, and a well-appointed kitchen. Each room gets its own showers.

The 19th-century, family-run **Belgrave Arms Hotel** (Dunrobin St., tel. 01431/821242, www.belgravearmshotel.co.uk, from £56 d) has nine good-value rooms. Only a few are en suite (they are a little dearer); the rest have shared bathrooms. It's light, cheery accommodation with a pale decor, although some rooms can get quite cold. As hotels go, it's nothing fancy but this is an immensely characterful place with a lively, friendly bar/restaurant done up with lots of dark wood and made cozy by a coal fire. There is plenty of single malt whisky behind the bar.

The pretty white-and-green decked **Bridge Hotel** (Dunrobin St., tel. 01431/821100, www.bridgehotel.net, £65 s, £95 d) dates from 1816 and, after a recent revamp, has the best of both modern and traditional facilities. It's a massive place with 19 spacious rooms, full of antique Spanish furniture. A complimentary glass of champagne is included in the bed-and-breakfast price. The residents' lounge has an open fire, and there's even an aquarium full of lobster. The downside is a rather off-putting number of stag's heads—you just can't escape them. Be prepared for a huge dining room and a more laid-back bistro; the culinary highlight is the whole Helmsdale lobster (£27.50).

The tasty ⓒ **La Mirage** (7–9 Dunrobin St., tel. 01431/821615, www.lamirage.org, serving all meals) restaurant pays homage to Barbara Cartland, who used to be a regular visitor in town. The former owner Nancy modeled herself on Barbara down to the hair and pink nails. It's under different management now, but Nancy still pops in: if you don't see her in the flesh you'll see her on the wall posing with a number of the celebrities who have also been attracted to this fun, colorful place. It's delightfully kitsch, dripping pink decor and fluffy lamps. You'll get anything from langoustines to monkfish to T-bone steaks to jacket potatoes here, with sweets like meringue to wrap things up. Light snacks start around £3, while main meals are £5–15.

Information

At **Strath Ullie Crafts** (The Harbour, tel. 01431/821402, 9 A.M.–5:30 P.M. Mon.–Sat. Apr.–Oct., 10 A.M.–4:30 P.M. Nov.–Mar.) there is an informal tourist information center, where you can rent gold-panning equipment.

Getting There and Away

Four **trains** (2.5 hrs.) run between Helmsdale and Inverness daily Monday–Saturday, with one Sunday service. Five buses daily run by either **Scottish Citylink** or **Rapsons** pass through Helmsdale en route between Thurso/Inverness.

BRORA AND GOLSPIE

These two pleasant but dull large villages sit five miles apart on the best sandy beaches on the east coast. They're well-appointed places to spend the night if you're headed north and are practically resorts by East Highlands standards, with a smattering of shops and places to eat. Brora is the more attractive of the two places and has one of the most photogenic distilleries in Scotland, backed by heather-brown hills. Down in its center, the famous Capaldi's ice cream, said by some to be Scotland's best scoop, can be sampled at Gow's bakery. Just north of Golspie is the resplendent Dunrobin Castle.

Sights

The **Clynelish Distillery** (Clynelish, by Brora, tel. 01408/623000, 9:30 A.M.–4:30 P.M. Mon.–Fri. Mar.–Oct., 9:30 A.M.–4 P.M. Tues.–Thurs. Nov.–Feb., £4) is often described as the liquid part of the gold rush. It really is a very good single malt, and tours (cost redeemable against the purchase price of a bottle) run several times daily in season. The distillery is signposted on a minor road northeast of the center of Brora.

Soaring above the treetops one mile north of Golspie, **Dunrobin Castle** (off A9 northeast of Golspie, tel. 01408/634081, 10:30 A.M.–5:30 P.M. daily June–Aug., 10:30 A.M.–4:30 P.M. Mon.–Sat., noon–4:30 P.M. Sun. Apr.–May and Sept.–Oct., £7) is the biggest house in the Highlands. This white, turreted expanse of opulence has no fewer than 189 rooms. There are some imposing family portraits and plenty of lavish touches. For all their hugeness, there is a touch of the snug about the rooms, too, with oak and larch furnishings rather than the sickly plasterwork that characterizes other stately homes. You could imagine this as a lived-in house—and indeed it has been, right since the 13th century, making it one of the country's oldest continuously inhabited houses. The landscaped grounds, complete with regular falconry demonstrations, add to the grandeur, but give the museum (full of hunting trophies) a by-pass. The restaurant is themed around a Victorian horse-drawn fire engine.

The 100-foot-high statue commemorating the first Duke of Sutherland (by Golspie, year-round) stands on top of the Beinn a Bhragaidh hill behind Golspie. One of the most bitterly ironic statue inscriptions of all time graces the plinth: to "a judicious, kind and liberal landlord" from "a mourning and grateful tenantry." This is the same tenantry who were being burned out of their homes and forced to emigrate by the Clearances in the 1830s, which in Sutherland were particularly vicious. You can climb the 1,300 feet to the statue from Golspie.

Accommodations

Glenaveron Guest House (Golf Rd., Brora, tel. 01408/621601, www.glenaveron.co.uk, £62–68 d) is a large detached house perfect for relaxing. There are three pastel-hued, plump-bedded rooms here, all en suite and some sporting antique furnishings. It's on a tranquil side road skirting high above Brora Harbour. Any fan of landscaped gardens should check out the back garden here, ideal for a summer day with grass, flowers, and trellises. There is a residents' lounge, and guests can use the swimming pool at the **Royal Marine Hotel** (Golf Rd., Brora, tel. 01408/621252, www.highlandescapehotels.com, £85 s, £130 d) nearby, another grand place to stay with tartan- and antique-furnished rooms with en suite bathrooms, writing desks, TV, and telephones. The hotel comes with its own extensive leisure facilities and has boats on Loch Brora that you can rent.

The large, distinguished old **Sutherland Arms Hotel** (Old Bank Rd., Golspie, tel. 01408/633234, www.sutherlandarmshotel.com, £45 s, £80 d) is a coaching inn with 14 formal-looking rooms, some with delightfully sloping ceilings to lend a cozier feel. If you want fancy extras like fruit and flowers, you can order them in advance. You'll get a filling breakfast included in the price and can have a packed lunch or afternoon tea to keep you going until supper. This place really does blend the old with the new; despite all the tartan and old oak furnishings, you can get free wireless Internet access.

Done up in warm Mediterranean colors and serving equally warming Mediterranean food, **Il Padrino** (Station Square, Brora, tel. 01408/622011, noon–10 P.M. Tues.–Sun.) is the newest and most exciting eatery in town. There is a good range of pizza and pasta available. Mains are £12–18.

Getting There and Away

There are four **trains** (2.25 hrs., £14.20 adult one-way) daily Monday–Saturday between Brora and Inverness, as well as several buses.

DORNOCH

Small in stature but large in personality, Dornoch is a genteel cathedral town with impressive architecture, good pubs, and great sand dunes to wander in nearby. The cathedral is the beating heart of the community, and most of the action here is in close proximity. There's a seasonal TIC on the main square.

Sights

The gray, angular bulk of **Dornoch Cathedral** (www.dornoch-cathedral.com, open year-round during daylight hours) dates originally from the 13th century but was not properly repaired from a fire in 1570 until the 19th century. The stained-glass windows on the north side of the chancel remember Andrew Carnegie, who took holidays at nearby Skelbo. It was only in 2001 that the cathedral really hit the headlines, as the place where Madonna had her son christened; someone hid in the organ pipes to film the ceremony.

Accommodations and Food

You can **camp** on Dornoch's sandy, grassy, links at **Dornoch Caravan and Camping Park** (tel. 01862/810423, www.dornochcaravans.co.uk, two-person tent £11).

The 15th-century fortress of **Dornoch Castle Hotel** (Dornoch, tel. 01862/810216, www.dornochcastlehotel.com, £70 s, £113 d) outdoes even the cathedral opposite it for aesthetics. After glimpsing the castellated outside, it's almost to be expected that the 24 rooms are huge, lavish, and full of antique furnishings. Most rooms look onto the walled garden at the back of the hotel. For eating, you can choose

between the garden restaurant and the cozier chairs and tables clustering around the enormous old open fireplace. You just want to reach out and touch those cool, thick, 500-year-old walls. Note that there is only one single room, otherwise singles will be paying the full double room price in high season.

Getting There and Away

Scottish Citylink and **Rapsons buses** en route from Inverness to Wick and Thurso (five daily Mon.–Sat.) will stop off at Dornoch.

LOCH SHIN AND INLAND

Long, snaking Loch Shin forms the center of this scattered area, which suffered badly in the Clearances and has as many ruins as it does inhabited houses. The main town is the former sheep-droving center of Lairg, a dismal place with a railway station and a top-notch visitors center. The lochs that lace the surrounding countryside are great places for fishing, and the exposed russet-red hills abound with walking possibilities, yet for an area some 50 by 50 miles there are few specific attractions around. You should rather look upon this vast region as the starting point for an incredible adventure, with a clutch of Britain's (and Northern Europe's) most isolated roads branching off from Lairg. Out in the wilderness you will also find some of Scotland's most unusual accommodation options.

Sights

If for any reason you find yourself in Lairg, head for the wonderful **Ferrycroft Centre** (tel. 01549/402160, 10 A.M.–5 P.M. daily June–Aug., 10 A.M.–4 P.M. daily Apr.–May and Sept.–Oct., free), a great source of information on the region and the history of the landscape. Doubling as a ranger base, it organizes lots of forays into the surrounding wilderness to look at the wildlife. You'll find a great café here. A number of forest nature trails branch off from the center.

The **Falls of Shin** (B864 south of Lairg, tel. 01549/402231, www.fallsofshin.co.uk, 9:30 A.M.–5:30 P.M. daily Apr.–Sept., 10 A.M.–5 P.M. daily Oct.–Mar., free) is the closest you get to a tourist attraction in this neck of the woods. A slightly overhyped visitors center is perched above a waterfall, where you can watch Atlantic salmon leaping up en route to their spawning grounds. Salmon do their leaping between June and September. The waterfall is a gorgeous spot and there's a special platform for salmon-viewing, but the big coach parties with the luminous waterproofs hogging the pathways are a bit of an eyesore. You can find some solitude in the woodland trails however. The **restaurant** has good views of the falls and some tasty food (mains £5–7). You'll even find a **miniature golf course** here.

From the quiet village of Bonar Bridge 11 miles south of Lairg, you can head up 10 miles into thickly forested Strathcarron to delightful **Croik Church** (www.croikchurch.com, open daily), screened by trees. It was here in 1842 that one of the most poignant images of the Clearances (people thrown of their lands and living in a shelter in the church) was brought home to the British public. You can attend a service in the church at 3 P.M. on the second Sunday of each month April–September.

Accommodations

◖ Sleeperzzz (Rogart Station, tel. 01408/641343, www.sleeperzzz.com, Mar.–Nov., compartment £12) is the only place in the country where you can stay on a first-class train in your own compartment. There is a 10 percent discount for rail users and cyclists. There are three carriages with compartments for the washing facilities, the common room, and the kitchen, then the sleeping compartments. Sleeperzzz is berthed by a pretty garden that divides it from the real train station on the Inverness-Wick line. The pub in the village is, conveniently, one of the best bets for food around.

Until the Scottish Youth Hostel Association totally goes down the pan, they will be able to say, with justifiable pride, that at least they have **Carbisdale Castle Hostel** (tel. 01549/421232, www.syha.org.uk, Mar.–Oct., £17–18). Even those averse to the idea of hostelling will be content to stay in this grand Highland castle built for the dowager Duchess of Sutherland. This isolated place soars out of the trees of Carbisdale woods, every inch the fairy-tale fortress. There are marble statues in the corridors and stained glass in some of the windows. There are one- to eight-bed rooms available, as well as Internet access. Reportedly good breakfasts and evening meals are on offer. It's even got its own railway station (Culrain Station, three to four trains from Inverness daily) 500 meters down the hill. You can walk to the Falls of Shin in around one hour.

An early 19th-century travelers' and drovers' hostelry, the **◖ Crask Inn** (by Lairg, tel. 01549/411241, £25 pp) is remote, situated some 12 miles up on the moor from Lairg on a working sheep farm. It's popular with anglers and walkers and anyone who happens to be stuck out in the middle of nowhere. There are three bedrooms and a 12-bed basic bunkhouse, a light breakfast room, and a dark bar where you can hear the wind creaking in the rafters. This might just be the most Scottish place you ever stay, with lots of books, fishing charts, and even a piano for evening entertainment (in addition to the bar brimming with whiskies). You'll get a good evening meal for around £10.

The **Overscaig Hotel** (tel. 01549/431203, www.overscaig.com, £44 s, £88 d, food noon–2:30 P.M. and 5:30–8:30 P.M.) enjoys a tranquil location along Loch Shin, popular with fishermen who've come to reap the benefits of the nearby trout and salmon waters. There are eight pale-toned en suite rooms, most with loch views and all with TV. You can get lunches and dinners based on the two local food supplies—fish and lamb.

Getting There and Away

Lairg has good train connections, with three trains per day to Inverness (1 hr. 40 min.). **Macleods Coaches** (www.macleodscoaches.co.uk) also runs six services daily to Tain Monday–Saturday (50 min.).

Black Isle and Easter Ross

North of Inverness is a relatively gentle, undulating landscape made up of low, heather-dark hills and agricultural land. This is the outer fringe of the Highlands proper and there's none of the topographical drama you'll find farther north. Yet in the hillier areas are some of the east coast's most captivating woodland walks. Then there is Scotland's oldest royal burgh, its most famous spa town, and a clutch of laid-back coastal communities filled with good pubs and restaurants and fronted by sandy beaches. In the pretty sandstone cottages of Cromarty on Black Isle and the creaking Victorian splendor of Strathpeffer, the region has its share of architectural eccentricity, too.

BLACK ISLE AND BEAULY

Black Isle is neither black nor an island. It's rather a flat, diamond-shaped peninsula almost completely surrounded by water. The Vikings knew the large harbor inlet of Cromarty Firth to the north of Black Isle as a sandy safe haven for their ships. As they looked inward to the snow-covered hills in winter, Black Isle was the only place where the snow did not settle due to its mild maritime climate. Black Isle is equally untouched by either the railway or by major roads, making it a very relaxed part of the country. It's mostly fertile farmland with a few patches of magical forest. The main settlements of Fortrose and Cromarty have some interesting buildings: grand red-sandstone Fortrose Cathedral and the 18th-century cottages of Cromarty. There are also some good dolphin-spotting places.

North Kessock and Vicinity

Most people overlook North Kessock as they zoom over the Moray Firth from Inverness on the A9. Those people miss out. Just after you cross into Black Isle, there's a year-round **tourist information center** for Black Isle on the left with a car park. The best way to approach the village itself is down steps from here. You can also drive to the next exit and get to this cut-off village from there. It's a line of tranquil white-washed houses hugging the shoreline.

On the other side of the main A9 road from North Kessock, one mile west of the village of **Munlochy** lies the intriguing **Clootie Well** (open year-round, free) in a patch of woodland near the side of the A832 road. It's an eerie patchwork of colored rags and cloths tied around trees, a throwback to times when pilgrims would visit certain sites and leave offerings in the hope of becoming cured.

Tucked away on North Kessock's main street is one of Europe's only **Targemakers** (tel. 01463/731577, www.targemaker.co.uk). A targe is essentially a shield, in this case embossed with the designs of different clans who fought with Bonnie Prince Charlie at Culloden. You can get your own made up for around £200.

Fortrose and Rosemarkie

No more than a few sandy fields divide these two handsome settlements on the south coast of Black Isle, which boast a couple of great pubs.

Taking the grassy center stage in Fortrose are the somewhat diminished but nonetheless grand red sandstone remains of lovely **Fortrose Cathedral** (open year-round). There are some interesting tombs including that of cathedral benefactor Euphemia, Countess of Ross. Much of the building was destroyed by Oliver Cromwell.

Just as the Cromarty road twists out of neighboring Rosemarkie it passes the entrance to **Fairy Glen** (open year-round). You can park here to do one of the most enchanting woodland walks in Scotland, alongside a tumbling stream. It's just over a mile to the folklore-steeped glen.

Cromarty

This small, quiet coastal town of gorgeous yellow sandstone houses with colorful gardens is well worth a wander.

The only thatched house left in Cromarty

Clootie Well, Black Isle

is **Hugh Miller's Birthplace Cottage and Museum** (Church St., tel. 0844/493 2158, 1–5 P.M. daily Mar.–Sept., 1–5 P.M. Wed.–Sun. Oct., £5), where the famous writer/geologist was born. Next door is the three-story **museum** with incredible displays of fossils from the High Miller Collection. His life's work during the 19th century revolutionized the way geologists thought at the time.

Beauly

Beauly, to the southwest of Black Isle at the mouth of the Beauly Firth, has an interesting ruined priory and little else to detain you.

Mary, Queen of Scots is said to have commented as she passed through this town in 1564, "Que beau lieu" (What a beautiful place). Today the largely ruinous **Beauly Priory** (tel. 01667/460232, 9:30 A.M.–6:30 P.M. Apr.–Sept., access possible year-round, free) is about the only beautiful thing in Beauly. It was founded around 1230 and was already falling into disrepair before the reformation. The high walls are still an imposing sight, though, and the chancel

and transepts are still magnificent. If you find the site closed inquire in the tourist information center next door.

The **House of Beauly** (Station Rd., tel. 01463/782821, www.houseofbeauly.com, open daily) is a quality shopping center with plenty of tartan gloss, full of the pungent smell of Highland soap. The idea is that you can get a selection of the best products available in Scotland here, only at twice the price. If you're passing through, it offers a good array of gifts of the food and fabric variety and has a decent, spacious restaurant. There are occasional food demonstrations.

Accommodations and Food

The Black Isle area has precious few places to stay but several good spots to get a meal.

Fortrose and Rosemarkie have between them a couple of top-notch accommodation/eatery options. **The Anderson** (Fortrose, tel. 01381/620236, www.theanderson.co.uk, £45 s, £75 d, £85 four-poster bed) is a phenomenal place to stay and eat. There are nine elegant en suite rooms here but the pub (full of dark wood with an open fire and over 200 single malt whiskies to try) is the real draw. There is a wide choice of cuisine from Scottish game right through to Caribbean. The pub also does a healthy line in Belgian beers. Over in Rosemarkie is another great pub, **The Plough** (48 High St., tel. 01381/620164, food noon–2:30 P.M. and 6–9 P.M. Mon.–Sat., noon–4 P.M. Sun.). It is an old timber-framed place serving Black Isle Brewery beers in two beer gardens.

If you're hungry in Cromarty, gravitate to **Sutor Creek** (21 Bank St., Cromarty, tel. 01381/600855, www.sutorcreek.co.uk, 11 A.M.–9 P.M. Wed.–Sun.), claiming to be the only wood-fired pizza place in the Highlands. The food is certainly first-rate; real pride and effort goes into making the pizzas and a variety of other dishes—try the slow-roasted Black Isles venison. Mains are £7–12. Sutor Creek is best appreciated for an evening meal but it's open all day for good coffee, paninis, and the like.

Getting There and Away

Bus 26 runs at least hourly Monday–Saturday (40 min.) from Inverness to Cromarty via North Kessock, Munlochty (for the Clootie Well), and Fortrose/Rosemarkie. Two Sunday services run as far as Rosemarkie only. For Beauly, regular **trains** run from Inverness (15 min., £2.50).

STRATHPEFFER AND VICINITY

This town was big business in Victorian times; the discovery of sulfurous springs here the century before led to Strathpeffer being declared the healthiest spa town in Britain. It's full of elegant 19th-century houses spread down a wooded hillside, looking more like a German mountain resort than a typical Highland community. The days of the fashionable spa trains arriving direct from London may now be over but this place still retains a lot of its former magnetism and has some fascinating architecture to check out. The town regularly rakes in large busloads of tourists.

Sights

With an atmospheric setting in the restored Victorian train station at the bottom of town (trains no longer run), the **Highland Museum of Childhood** (Old Station, tel. 01997/421031, www.highlandmuseumofchildhood.org.uk, 10 A.M.–7 P.M. Mon.–Fri., 10 A.M.–5 P.M. Sat., 2–5 P.M. Sun. July–Aug., 10 A.M.–5 P.M. Mon.–Sat., 2–5 P.M. Sun. Apr.–June and Sept.–Oct., £2 adults, £1.50 children) is a wonderful collection of old-fashioned toys and photographs. OK, so there's the obligatory collection of sinister-looking dolls but also some wonderfully intricate dollhouses and lots of Victorian parlor games and old board games. There's a good café here, too.

At the **Pump Room** (The Square, tel. 01997/421415, 10 A.M.–6 P.M. Mon.–Sat., 2–5 P.M. Sun. May–Sept., £2.50) you can step back in time to find out about those funny-looking Victorians "taking the waters" of this Highland village. There are some hilarious old photographs and displays and you can taste the sought-after spa water.

The best village walk is to gushing **Rogie Falls,** approached through pine forests and starting at the old Strathpeffer Youth Hostel at the top of town. You follow the edge of Loch Kinellan through fields, then it's in trees for the rest of the way. You can then continue along Loch Garve to **Garve,** from where you can return by bus to Stathpeffer. Get walk information from the Square Wheels Bike Shop in the Square.

Accommodations and Food

You can stay at **The White Lodge** (The Square, tel. 01997/421730, www.the-white-lodge.co.uk, £54 d) in one of Strathpeffer's oldest buildings, a late-18th-century house with a small garden and two en suite old-fashioned rooms. They may boggle your mind with their swirly decor but they're comfortable places to spend the night. You can also sample the attached **Wee Swally Tearoom** (around 11 A.M.–4 P.M. Tues.–Sat.), a Victorian tearoom with delightful home baking.

The three rooms at **Craigvar** (The

Square, tel. 01997/421662, www.craig-var.com, £37 s, (£66 d) will make you think you've stepped back in time a century or so. Accommodation consists of the blue room, pink room, and beige room; one room has its own four-poster bed and Victorian bath. This place is reminiscent of the spa hotel glory days, full of thoughtful touches like fresh fruit and decanters of sherry for guests. Craigvar is set back from the road behind a hedged garden. Don't worry: you still get all the 21st-century trappings (TV, en suite facilities, hairdryers). The rear garden is a secluded place to relax.

Grand **Richmond Hotel** (Church Brae, tel. 01997/421300, www.richmondhighlandhotel.co.uk, from £30 pp) looks pretty imposing from the outside, sitting on the hillside above the Square and setting the haughty architectural tone for the town. Inside, it's less grand but still pretty impressive. You can expect lots of wood paneling, an open fire in the bar, and great views over the surrounding wooded hills and pretty, well-kept gardens. There are nine rooms in total, all en suite and comfortably furnished with the best of the Strathpeffer vistas from the windows. One room has a four-poster bed.

Based in the Old Pavilion, the **Red Poppy** (tel. 01997/423332, www.redpoppycatering .co.uk, 11 A.M.–8 P.M. Tues.–Thurs., 11 A.M.–9 P.M. Fri.–Sat., noon–4 P.M. Sun.) has a growing reputation for fine food. It's very spacious inside this white-and-green decked building. You can get main courses ranging from steak to game to fish for £9–15. It's simple, no-nonsense Scottish cooking in fairly elegant surrounds. You'll be in good hands; the chef/proprietor has even cooked aboard the *Orient Express*.

Information and Services

There's a lot crammed into the tiny **Square Wheels Bike Shop** (The Square, tel. 01997/421000, www.squarewheels.biz, open Wed.–Mon.). Bike rental is possible from £15 per day, but this place is also a key self-service information point with maps and advice on the surrounding countryside.

Just down from the Square, **Digit Works**

(10 A.M.–9 P.M. summer, 10 A.M.–6 P.M. winter) has Internet access and, next door, coffee and cakes.

Getting There and Away

Inverness to Ullapool **buses** (2–5 daily Mon.–Sat.) stop at Strathpeffer.

TAIN AND VICINITY

The past is far more colorful than the present of this rather drab town on the Dornoch Firth. Tain doesn't let you forget its former grandeur, and you can trace over 900 years of its history as Scotland's oldest royal burgh and as a medieval place of pilgrimage in its excellent museum. Glenmorangie whisky is also distilled in town. The peninsula jutting out east from Tain is also worth exploring, mainly for the picture-perfect fishing village of Portmahomack.

Sights

Thanks to St. Duthac, an 11th-century saint born in Tain, the town became a place of medieval pilgrimage. The story is told in the captivating **Tain Through Time** (Tower St., tel. 01862/894089, www.tainmuseum.org, 10 A.M.–5 P.M. Mon.–Sat. Apr.–Oct., £3.50) museum. It includes displays on James IV, who came to Tain to do penance. Also included in admission is a tour of the church built in the late 14th century to house the remains of St. Duthac. It was to become one of Scotland's key pilgrimage destinations over the following centuries and was restored in the 19th century. The museum also acts as an independent tourist information center and is a very good place to get advice on the area.

As you might know from television advertisements, Glenmorangie means "The Glen of Tranquility." As far as the visitor is concerned, **Glenmorangie Distillery** (A9 on north side of Tain, tel. 01862/892477, www.glenmorangie.com, 9 A.M.–5 P.M. Mon.–Fri., 10 A.M.–4 P.M. Sat., noon–4 P.M. Sun. June–Aug., 9 A.M.–5 P.M. Mon.–Fri., 10 A.M.–4 P.M. Sat. Apr.–May and Sept., 9 A.M.–5 P.M. Mon.–Fri. Oct.–Mar.) is undoubtedly one of Scotland's best experiences of whisky distillation. You'll see a lot of spiel about the "sixteen men of Tain" on the distillery tour—that's how many people are given the hefty responsibility of producing this fine single malt. Be sure to check out the stills themselves here; they're smaller than the distillery norm but have unusually high columns, meaning only the lightest vapors can rise to be condensed into the spirit. The distillery is off the main A9 road heading north from Tain.

Accommodations and Food

Tain's exciting attractions warrant a stopover. You could base yourself in nearby Portmahomack, which is prettier and has sandy beaches and good places to try seafood.

Mansfield Castle Hotel (tel. 01862/892052, Scotsburn Rd., Tain, www.mansfield-castle.co.uk, rooms from £140 d) is set in acres of its own landscaped grounds. It's a grandly wood-paneled place that towers both physically and in sheer class above any other accommodations in the area. Celebrated architect Andrew Maitland did the refurbishment on the castle in the early 20th century, and the interior today bears the fruits of his labors. The rooms have a lavish, warming, floral decor; the en suite bathrooms are almost as magnificent. You even get a decanter of sherry, but only some of the rooms have whirlpool baths. The castle is also haunted. Meals (mains £13–21) are served in the restaurant, in front of an open fire.

The **Caledonian Hotel** (tel. 01862/871345, www.caleyhotel.co.uk, Portmahomack, £88 d) is a good hotel made great by its location, overlooking as it does the swaths of sand in Portmahomack village. Pale blue, white, and red rooms get TVs and en suite bathrooms with a bath or shower, but only a couple have that sought-after sea view. The rate includes dinner and breakfast, based on a two-night minimum stay.

Getting There and Away

Inverness to Thurso **buses** run by **Scottish Citylink** and **Rapsons** stop off in Tain (seven Mon.–Sat., four on Sun., Inverness 1 hr. 20 min.). There are also **trains** from Tain to Inverness every two to three hours.

Stagecoach Inverness service 35 runs from Tain to Portmahomack five times daily Monday–Friday.

OUTER HEBRIDES

In 1598, King James VI, along with a group of gentleman adventurers from Fife resolved to "set up civilization in the hitherto most barbarous isle of Lewis." Attracted by the archipelago's fishing possibilities, he eventually had his way against the then-ruling MacLeod clan. As a result, Stornoway, the main town on the Isles, became a royal burgh. For the people of these outer islands, however, this did little to change their way of life.

This is truly a corner of Britain that time passed by. On this string of islands over 150 miles long, the Gaelic culture long forgotten in much of Scotland is still the main driving force. Visitors from Bonnie Prince Charlie to today's tourists have done little to change the way of life. Living off the barren land and sea here always was, and still is, hard; weaving Harris Tweed from the wool of island sheep, peat-cutting, and fishing are the time-tested ways of making ends meet.

Lewis and Harris are largely peat bog and rocky hills, hemmed by some of Europe's best beaches and dotted with enough Neolithic monuments to make history buffs positively giddy with excitement. A short ferry trip south, the isles of North and South Uist are the places to visit for an internationally important spectrum of birdlife. More beaches run almost uninterrupted down both, with white sands and turquoise waters. The added delight of the coast here is the colorful machair (flower-covered grasslands that back the dunes). Right at the bottom is Eriskay, an idyllic island where Bonnie Prince Charlie first set foot on Scottish soil. Just south is Barra; flying to the island and landing

© LUKE WATERSON

HIGHLIGHTS

◖ Lews Castle and Grounds: This woodsy park centered around a castle on the edge of Stornoway is a network of peaceful paths with a craft shop, heritage center, and tearoom, making it ideal for an afternoon stroll (page 510).

◖ Callanish: Not one but three of Britain's most glorious stone circles, a stupendous series of Neolithic temples as much as 4,500 years old (page 516).

◖ South Harris Beaches: The tracts of unspoiled sand and turquoise water on South Harris rival anything in the Caribbean (page 521).

◖ St. Kilda: Britain's remotest island outpost, a fretwork of jagged cliffs frequented by some of the world's most diverse seabird life, is the end point of one of Europe's most adventurous sea voyages (page 522).

◖ Smokehouse Shops: Tasting smoked fish on North Uist is a truly unique experience – no other smokehouse in the world smokes fish with Scottish peat (page 524).

◖ South Uist: Deviate from the beaten track and discover remote side-roads to wild hills, traditional crofting settlements, and ancient ruined churches (page 526).

◖ Eriskay: This balmy beach-rimmed island has a history including Bonnie Prince Charlie and a shipwrecked stash of whisky (page 528).

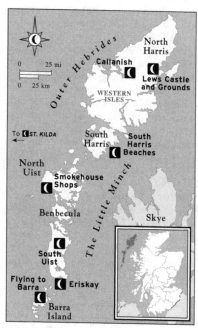

LOOK FOR ◖ TO FIND RECOMMENDED SIGHTS, ACTIVITIES, DINING, AND LODGING.

◖ Flying to Barra: Landing on Barra Airstrip, the world's only beach runway, is a memorable introduction to a placid island home to tranquil sandy coast, Neolithic heritage and the most photogenic castle on Scotland's islands (page 530).

on one of the world's few beach runways is one of the best travel experiences in Europe.

Most island folk consider visitors prepared to trek in the drizzle to see a few prehistoric stones a "wee bit strange." The islands still haven't really grasped tourism and for the visitor, this just might be the main incentive to come. The Outer Hebrides (also known as the Western Isles) offer a chance to gain insight into Scottish life that's almost impossible to apprehend elsewhere. The traditional Gaelic culture that's still in full swing means that for the visitor, a trip here can mean seeing croft farming as it was done centuries ago, hearing Gaelic spoken in the pubs, and dancing at ceilidhs until dawn.

HISTORY
Prehistory to Medieval Era
Prehistoric times seemed to be the boom period for the Outer Hebrides. The Greek historian Diodorus Siculus makes the first known reference to the islands in the 1st century B.C., describing "Hyperborea" (the island of the north) with its round temple devoted to lunar appreciation. This is a reference to Callanish, a complex of stone circles dating to the 4th millennium B.C. By the 8th century A.D. the islands were coming under Norse control, a development that escalated centuries of almost continual conflict. After 1156 Somerled became King of the Hebrides (Inner and Outer) along with the Isle of Man. This empire became known as the dynasty of the Lords of the Isles and flourished until the 15th century. The Outer Hebrides were one of the first places where rule collapsed; several feuding clans rose to quarrel for control of the islands. Different branches of the Macleods took control in Lewis and Harris, the MacDonalds and Clanranalds in North and South Uist and the proudly defiant MacNeils on Barra. A story goes that at the time of Noah's flood the MacNeil chief was invited aboard the ark but haughtily claimed, "MacNeil has a boat of his own!"

The 19th-Century Clearances
With such carryings on local tenants became progressively disillusioned with their so-called leaders. Landlords increasingly spent long periods of time away from the island. Many made their money in Scotland's brief 18th-century kelp boom and lost it when Spain began to undercut Scotland on kelp prices. As ever, it was the tenants who would feel the consequences. Landlords instigated large-scale land clearance to make way for more commercially viable sheep farming. The Outer Hebrides were one of the worst hit areas during these clearances. Notoriously cruel landlords like Colonel Gordon of Cluny systematically cleared their land of tenants, right to the rocky shores. There was no choice left for many but to emigrate to America or Australia. Colonel Gordon also spent years trying to persuade the government to make Barra a penal colony. A more enlightened landlord, Sir James Mattheson, was responsible from 1844 onward for the development of Stornoway. He built schools and developed Stornoway's harbor with money he had made in the opium trade.

20th Century
The biggest tragedy of World War I for the islands was undoubtedly just after it had ended. In early morning on New Year's Day 1919, 205 servicemen were returning home to their families when their ship ran aground on rocks at the mouth of Stornoway harbor. Unable to see the shore in the darkness, the vast majority of the men drowned. There was not one family in the Outer Hebrides unaffected. Emigration steadily continued after the war and life on the islands grew progressively bleaker. It is only since the advent of a bilingual council, the Comhairle nan Eilean, to control the islands in the 1970s that the tide has turned. With Gaelic TV and Gaelic education, the culture that many were losing hope of has suddenly bounced back. The 21st century still sees the traditional ways of making ends meet very much at the forefront of daily life, although these days much is done in the name of tourism, and it spins a tidy bit more income than it used to.

PLANNING YOUR TIME
If you want to see all of the Outer Hebrides, you'll need a minimum of five days due to how

spread out the islands are. Because of the length of the isles, it's a good idea to come in at either the north end (Stornoway) or south (Tarbert or Castlebay on Barra) and leave from the other to avoid doubling back. Given five days, base yourself in Stornoway if you like urban comforts or, if you would prefer a smaller, prettier village, Tarbert in Harris. With less time, base yourself in Harris, which is the prettiest part and also well located for trips down to the Uists and up to Callanish. To save waiting for ferries, carry a copy of Calmac's ferry timetables for the Outer Hebrides with you. In the southern Outer Hebrides, Eriskay and Barra are most deserving of your time, and are linked conveniently by regular ferries. Allow four hours (driving and sailing) for travel between Eriskay and Stornoway.

GETTING THERE AND AROUND
Getting There
Calmac (tel. 0870/565 0000, www.calmac.co.uk) runs the **ferry** from Ullapool in the Northern Highlands to Stornoway (at least two daily Mon.–Sat., 2 hrs. 45 min., £15.30 adult, £75 car one-way). The crossing traverses the notoriously rough stretch of water known as The Minch; even in summer be prepared for ferry cancellations. Calmac also runs ferries from Uig on Skye to Tarbert in Harris (two daily Mon.–Sat., 1 hr. 45 min., £10 adult, £48 car one-way); Uig to Lochmaddy in North Uist (two each day, 2 hrs. 45 min., £10 adult, £48 car one-way); Oban in Argyllshire to Lochboisdale on South Uist (four weekly, 4 hrs. 45 min., £21.95 adult, £81 car one-way) and Oban to Barra (one ferry daily, 4 hrs. 45 min., £21.95 adult, £81 car one-way).

You can **fly** to Stornoway from a number of airports including Glasgow, Edinburgh, and Inverness. Service operators are either **Loganair**

(tel. 0870/850 9850, www.britishairways.com) or **Highland Airways** (tel. 0845/450 2245). You can also fly from Aberdeen with **Eastern Airways** (tel. 0870/366 9100, www.easternairways.com). Flight times are all around one hour.

Getting Around
There are three **airports** on the Outer Hebrides: Stornoway, Benbecula, and Barra. There are two daily flights on weekdays from Stornoway to Benbecula. Prices vary drastically; book in advance to get lower fares.

Harris and North Lewis are connected by a chain of **ferries** via the Uists to Eriskay and Barra. Ferries run from Leverburgh in South Harris to Berneray at the top of the Uists three to four times every day of the week (1 hr., £5.75 adult, £26 car one-way). All other main islands are connected by road bridge or causeway, except Barra, which is accessed by ferry from Eriskay (10 daily ferries, 40 min., £6.15 adult, £18.05 car one-way).

The **bus** station is right by the ferry terminal in Stornoway. Buses run Monday–Saturday, not Sundays. Buy a rover ticket from the bus station/bus driver if you are going to be making a few bus journeys in the day. **Galson Motors** (tel. 01851/840269) runs most of the local services.

If you are going to be getting around by **car,** bear in mind that roads are generally single track, although the main road south through the islands (A859/A867/A865) is mostly a good double-track road. Occasional long, straight stretches of double-track road are essentially treated as racecourses by the island's drivers. Even the main north–south road in the isles has a lot of narrow, twisty bits. There are petrol stations on Lewis, Harris, North Uist, Benbecula, South Uist, and Barra.

Stornoway and Lewis

You'll most likely arrive onto the Outer Hebrides in Lewis, and you might not be able to believe your eyes. Out of the lumpy, brown, peaty hills appears a town that looks like it has just landed from another planet. Stornoway, this metropolis of the Outer Hebrides, may be far from pretty but it's as cosmopolitan as these islands get with a few great places to eat and an increasingly vibrant cultural scene. Take your fill of the cosmopolitanism—once you leave town, that's it. The rest of Lewis is a wind-ravaged peat bog of open skies, which you'll need to venture into to discover some of Britain's most important ancient monuments.

STORNOWAY (STEORNABHAGH)

The capital of these outer isles, Stornoway is a higgledy-piggledy town you'll most likely end up having to pass through at some point during your time here. Stornoway folk make a point of emphasizing how different from the rest of the islands their town is, and it's true; nowhere else in the Outer Hebrides comes close to being as dreary or disappointing. It's still a real hub of island life, though, with a wonderful arts center, an important museum, and the gorgeous wooded grounds of Lews Castle to wander in.

Museum Nan Eilean

Housed in an imposing, gray, Victorian former school, this museum (Francis St., tel. 01851/709266, www.cne-siar.gov.uk/museum/index.htm, 10 A.M.–5:30 P.M. Mon.–Sat. Apr.–Sept., 10 A.M.–5 P.M. Tues.–Fri., 10 A.M.–1 P.M. Sat. Oct.–Mar., free) is an essential starting point for anyone wishing to get a better understanding of island culture and life over the centuries. There is a wealth of riveting information in here: old photographs of Stornoway, the history of peat-cutting, and on the herring trade that took many Stornoway women over the seas as far as the east coast of Scotland and England. The museum guides you through over 6,000 years of history on the islands.

An Lanntair Arts Centre

This vibrant arts center (Kenneth St., tel. 01851/703307, www.anlanntair.com, 10 A.M.–late Mon.–Sat.) is housed in a modern, state-of-the-art building in Stornoway and has added a previously absent vibrancy to the town. It's fit to grace any city in the country, a huge, airy venue that runs a number of cultural events and exhibitions. There's often live music and also a cinema here showing several special interest and mainstream films weekly. Pop your head in—there's always something absorbing going on, and invariably a free something.

◖ Lews Castle and Grounds

Sir James Matheson built square-looking, bulky Lews Castle (year-round, free) with the fortune he'd accumulated in the opium trade and had thousands of tons of soil shipped over from the mainland for the construction of the castle grounds. In a swath of dark woodland, this is a spectacular place. There is a network of woodland paths and trails, some of which hug the coast. The center of things is the recently built Woodlands Centre guarded by replicas of the Uig chessmen. This place acts as an information point, shop, and spacious, atmospheric café (tel. 01851/706916, 10 A.M.–5 P.M. Mon.–Sat.). It's a shame no one has yet restored the castle itself (currently unsafe to enter), as this would be the crowning glory of Stornoway's finest attraction. A golf course is also within the grounds. It's enough of a distance away from the town center to make for a good afternoon picnic.

Tours

Out and About Tours (Great Bernera, tel. 01851/612288, www.hebridean-holidays.co.uk, £120–140 per group per day, inclusive of transport) offers knowledgeable tours for individuals and groups. It's especially good for doing off-the-beaten-track walks. Operators are very adaptable to individual needs and would certainly suit the older or less mobile traveler.

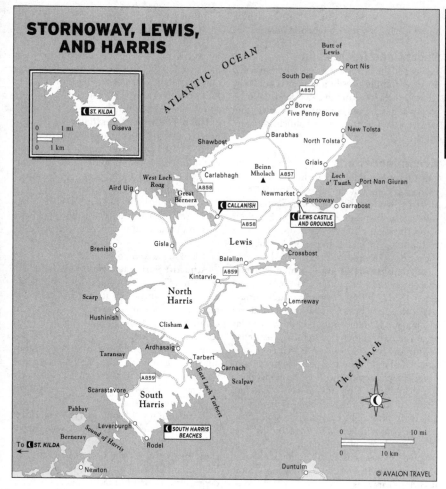

STORNOWAY, LEWIS, AND HARRIS

ST. KILDA

ATLANTIC OCEAN

Butt of Lewis
Port Nis
South Dell
A857
Borve
Five Penny Borve
Shawbost
Barabhas
North Tolsta
New Tolsta
Griais
Oiseva
Beinn Mholach
A857
Loch a' Tuath
Port Nan Giuran
Carlabhagh
Newmarket
Stornoway
Garrabost
West Loch Roag
A858
Aird Uig
Great Bernera
CALLANISH
LEWS CASTLE AND GROUNDS
A858
Lewis
Brenish
Gisla
Balallan
Crossbost
Kintarvie
A859
Scarp
North Harris
Lemreway
Hushinish
Clisham
Ardhasaig
Tarbert
Taransay
Carnach
Scalpay
Scarastavore
A859
South Harris
East Loch Tarbert
The Minch
Pabbay
Leverburgh
SOUTH HARRIS BEACHES
Berneray
Sound of Harris
Rodel
To ST. KILDA
Newton
Duntulm
© AVALON TRAVEL

Entertainment and Events

If you really want to hit the town in Stornoway, the best pub is **McNeils** (11 Cromwell St., tel. 01851/703330), a small, snug place where a lot of seasoned drinkers go. It has regular live music. The best that can be said about it is that it is neither sleazy or bland, categories every other drinking place in town would fall under.

The **Hebridean Celtic Festival** (www.heb-celtfest.com) in July is one of the highlights of the events calendar. It's a mesmerizing festival of Celtic music (down to the words), with events taking place in Lews Castle grounds and other venues throughout town.

Shopping

You can get a modern selection of books and maps at **Baltic Bookshop** (8–10 Cromwell St., tel. 01851/702802, 9 A.M.–5:30 P.M. Mon.–Sat.).

Award-winning Stornoway black pudding awaits at **Charles MacLeod** (Ropework Park, tel. 01851/702455, www.charlesmacleod.co.uk,

8 A.M.–5:30 P.M. Mon.–Sat.)—don't even think about leaving town without coming here.

Sports and Recreation

Lewis and Harris are particularly renowned for their **fishing** possibilities. Lewis holds the record for a U.K. salmon catch, and there are plenty of good spots both near Stornoway and farther afield. Check www.fishhebrides.com for details.

Accommodations

The Outer Hebrides unique brand of accommodation comes in the form of **Gatliff Trust Hostels** (www.gatliff.org.uk), budget accommodations in remote, wonderful locations across the islands. They're cheap (under £10 per bed) but it's impossible to pre-book them; just show up and people are rarely turned away.

Laxdale Holiday Park (1.5 miles north of Stornoway town center on A857 Barvas road, tel. 01851/706966, www.laxdaleholiday-park.com, dorm beds £12, backpacker and tent £6) is a handy budget option in the Stornoway area; the park enjoys a peaceful tree-screened setting and has a bunkhouse as well as a campsite. The bunkhouse is a pine-floored, modern, clean place to stay with accommodation in four-bed dorms. Curtains divide these in half again, so you get a fair amount of privacy for a bargain price. The campsite has quite basic facilities but with a mix of grass and fir trees it makes a lovely place to pitch a tent so close to town. Showers cost £0.50 in the bunkhouse and the campsite. You can also stay in the more luxurious caravans.

Heb Hostel (25 Kenneth St., tel. 01851/709889, www.hebhostel.co.uk, beds £15) is an early Victorian house that's been given a makeover: newly refurbished and opened in 2007 as a 26-bed hostel. The best of the Victorian trappings have stayed, giving the place a genteel grace, but everything else is modern and comfy. The pine bunk beds are handcrafted and the guest lounge is full of big comfortable chairs. Bed sheets and a continental breakfast are included in the price, and Internet access is available.

Thorlee (1–3 Cromwell St., tel. 01851/705466, www.thorlee.com, £35 s, £55 twin) is a good find right in the town center: simple single and twin rooms, done up in cooling whites. Rooms are not en suite but there are hand washbasins and TVs in the rooms. It's a family-friendly place on the harborfront next to the Stag Bakery (where you can also inquire about available rooms).

Hal o' the Wynd Guesthouse (2 Newton St., tel. 01851/706073, www.halothewynd.com, £50 d) is one of Stornoway's most interesting and beautiful places to stay: a 300-year-old whitewashed harborfront house. Cool white rooms, tartan bed sheets, and color TVs are the order of the day. Not all rooms are en suite. The service is usually as cold as a Stornoway summer but then maybe that's because the owners know they offer some of the best-looking accommodation in town.

Attractive **Park Guest House** (30 James St., tel. 01851/702485, £44 s, £76 d) is a stone-built Victorian house: it may not have the most serene location in town but it's got eight comfortable, clean rooms and a well-regarded restaurant. Breakfasts are superb—just ask for your morning food fantasy and they'll probably be able to rustle it up. Try to get a room that isn't street-facing; these can get quite noisy with morning traffic. All rooms are en suite or with private bathroom.

The charming 19th-century ◖ **Royal Hotel** (Cromwell St., tel. 01851/702109, www.royal-stornoway.co.uk, from £49 s, £78 d) is always eager to please. It's the best place to stay in Stornoway by several miles, and rooms have undergone recent refurbishment. Some rooms are at the back with quiet outlooks over the town. A room facing the marina and Lews Castle wooded grounds is a little bit pricier, but worth it for the view. You can sit in your window seat and begin to soak up the Stornoway bustle. All rooms have nice en suite bathrooms; some have fancy wood paneling for that touch of grandeur. The hotel's restaurants are the best places to eat in town.

Food

The Coffee Pot (5 Kenneth St., tel. 01851/703270, 7:30 A.M.–7 P.M. daily) is a good place

THE RELIGIOUS DIVIDE ON THE ISLANDS

You won't have to be on the Outer Hebrides long on a Sunday to realize that the islands are devoutly religious places, more so than any other area of Great Britain. The Sabbath is still very much the day of rest here: Everything closes down, from bus services to shops to many pubs and restaurants. There is a very strong (but peaceful) north-south divide in religions, though: The northern Hebrides are Protestant and the Southern Hebrides (from South Uist downward) are Catholic. As you drive down to South Uist you will see shrines appearing at the side of the road and a statue of the Madonna on the hillside.

The specific reasons for the split are thought to be that people of South Uist and Barra proved more resistant to conversion. Even when threatened with fines and beatings by various landlords for their faith, the people of the Southern Hebrides held firm. In practical terms, for the visitor this means that on South Uist and Barra places do still open on Sundays. Do not expect this in the North; there are plenty of examples of how strict Protestantism can be here. Sunday is for prayer and bible-reading, and even the playground in Stornoway is locked. In the 1970s a priest famously cursed a cinema for showing the film *Jesus Christ, Superstar;* the cinema was struck to the ground by lightning only days later. In 2005, the local council refused to conduct formal same sex marriage ceremonies for couples wishing to register under the Civil Partnerships Act of 2004. Services, despite their associations with what many consider to border on religious fanaticism, are very moving ceremonies. Formal dress has to be worn, with women wearing hats and dresses. They take place in simple minimalist buildings, generally in Gaelic. The sound of psalms being sung can be an enchanting sound as it echoes out of the building and through the almost totally deserted streets.

to be while you're waiting for the ferry—there's nowhere else open at this time in the morning. A lot of Formica tables stretch back into the darkness. The fry-ups are cheap and filling and you can also get other basic meals (£3–6). It's the number one favorite with the locals.

There's something immensely pleasurable about watching a boat pull in and out of port, even if it's at Stornoway's ungainly harbor. (**An Lanntair Arts Centre Café/ Restaurant** (Kenneth St., tel. 01851/703307, www.anlanntair.com, 10 A.M.–late Mon.–Sat.), the stylish modern café contained within the arts center of the same name, is the best place in Stornoway to do it. It's in a building that easily stands out on the shabby harborfront. It really is a very good place to eat—nuzzle into the huge comfortable sofas or perch at a window-side table. You'll get a good shot of caffeine here and some tasty main courses, like pan-fried pigeon breast and beef and Guinness pie. Mains with occasional Italian and Thai themes are £8.50–15.

HS-1 (Cromwell St., tel. 01851/702109, www.royalstornoway.co.uk, lunch noon–4 P.M., dinner 5–9 P.M. daily) is the coolest hangout in town: an open, lively place with bare brick walls, abstract artwork, and a choice of booths or sofas to plonk yourself in. The coffee and the cakes are to die for; the warm, tasty tomato soup is a lifesaver on a cold day; and the roast dinners (£10.99) are about the best thing to happen in Stornoway on Sundays. Main meals are £6–12.

Corner Tapas (26 Francis St., tel. 01851/ 700101, 5–9 P.M. Tues.–Sat.) is Stornoway's own little piece of the Mediterranean. It comes in the form of local seafood-themed tapas, a tasty alternative to the Scottish cuisine options elsewhere in town. It's one of the few tapas joints in the world where you can get Stornoway black pudding and chorizo as a dish. A good choice of wines is available.

Evening is the time to come to the candlelit, sophisticated restaurant **Digby Chick** (5 Bank St., tel. 01851/700026, until 10 P.M. Mon.–Sat.)

to try modern Scottish cuisine. The seafood is the obvious choice here; there's a "catch of the day" specials board with delights like langoustines or a fillet of local herring. You can also try game like roast Lewis venison in red onion marmalade. Evening meals are around £15, including the three-course set dinner available in early evening only.

Information and Services

Stornoway Tourist Information (26 Cromwell St., tel. 01851/703088, 9 A.M.–6 P.M. Mon.–Sat. Easter–mid-Oct., 9 A.M.–5 P.M. Mon.–Fri. mid-Oct.–Easter) has a good selection of local maps and books. It's also open one hour after every ferry arrives, which means it will reopen late on most evenings.

The **Royal Bank of Scotland** (17 North Beach St., tel. 01851/705252) is one of the banks in Stornoway with an ATM.

For health ailments, head to the chemist chain **Boots** (4–6 Cromwell St., tel. 01851/701769, 9:45 A.M.–5:30 P.M. Mon.–Sat.) or to the **Western Isles Hospital** (MacAulay Rd., tel. 01851/704704), which is the main hospital on the isles with a casualty department.

Stornoway Public Library (19 Cromwell St., tel. 01851/708631, 10 A.M.–6 P.M. Thurs. and Fri., 10 A.M.–5 P.M. Mon.–Wed. and Sat.) has Internet access with a limit of one hour.

Stornoway's post office is at 16 Francis Street.

Getting There and Around

Stornoway has an **airport** with two daily flights on weekdays from Stornoway to Benbecula.

Calmac (tel. 0870/565 0000, www.calmac .co.uk) runs a **ferry** from Ullapool in the Northern Highlands to Stornoway (at least two daily Mon.–Sat., 2 hrs. 45 min., £15.30 adult, £75 car one-way). The crossing traverses the notoriously rough stretch of water known as The Minch; be prepared for ferry cancellations at any time of year.

The **bus station** (South Beach St., tel. 01851/704327) is right by the ferry terminal in Stornoway.

Mackinnon Self Drive (18 Inaclete Rd., tel. 01851/702984, www.mackinnonself-drive.co.uk) is the best company to rent a car with; prices for day hire of a small car start from £24.50.

Try **Central Cabs** (20 MacMillan Rd., tel. 01851/706900) if you need a cab.

LEWIS (LEODHAIS)

As you head northwest from Stornoway, the landscape quickly becomes one of the bleakest Britain can offer: seemingly endless, bumpy, brown peat bog spattered in hundreds of mirror-like lochans (small lochs). It's an apt introduction to Lewis; with the exception of pockets of coast on either side, most of the island's like this. Once you've gotten used to the feeling of vast and sometimes unnerving emptiness, you'll find some of Britain's best prehistoric sites to explore. The most magical and extensive complex of stone circles in Britain is at Callanish, while Clach an Truiseil is the country's tallest standing stone.

Tolsta (Tolastadh) and Vicinity

Tolsta has a couple of gorgeous golden **beaches** and is the start of a path up across the moor along the coast to Ness (Nis). Allow six hours for the 10-mile (16-km) trek.

Butt of Lewis (Rubha Robhanais)

At the very northern tip of Lewis stands a characteristic redbrick **lighthouse,** the Butt of Lewis (yes, the potential for jokes is limitless). This makes the Guinness Book of Records as the windiest location in the United Kingdom. You'll see signs to it from the village of Ness (Nis). Note the interesting (and very diplomatic) way in which the farming land is divided up around here: long thin fenced strips with different sections for different crofters.

Clach an Truiseil

This monstrous standing stone towers near six meters high: the tallest in Scotland. It makes the house below it seem like a toy—a good one for the photographs. Heading north on the A857, it's down a little side road to the left by the village of Baile an Truiseil.

© LUKE WATERSON

Tolsta Beach, north of Stornoway

Gearrannan

At Gearrannan (Carloway, tel. 01851/643416, www.gearrannan.com, 9:30 A.M.–5:30 P.M. daily, £2) is the chance to see a crofting village as it might have looked 300 years ago. The experience is made all the more moving when you realize these basic stone houses were occupied in much the same way until as recently as the 1970s. For the visitor, it's an undeniably charming place—a cluster of traditional blackhouses on a slope above a sandy bay. Its original residents would have appreciated its charms less: Gearrannan is an isolated spot even by Hebridean standards. Its women would have traveled all down Scotland's east coast gutting and salting herring, its men across the globe on whaling missions, all just to make ends meet. As pretty as Gearrannan seems with the squat-walled houses and thatch roofs, living here was tough. It's little wonder that given the option of moving into more modern accommodation nearby, most inhabitants jumped at the chance. By the mid-1970s Gearrannan was deserted but has now been restored with every effort made

to preserve the original village. Of course, there are a few modern additions: a shop, a good café, and an even better restaurant, as well as a Gatliff Trust hostel and several rustically stylish self-catering cottages.

Dun Carloway Broch (Dun Charlabhaigh)

The scenery as you near Carloway village gets a little more interesting: Pockmarked, grass-covered rocky hills rise up out of the heather. The builders of Dun Carloway chose one of the most dramatic of these hills for this fortress, built sometime around 100 B.C. It's the best preserved example of a broch outside of Shetland, with one wall towering high above the ground. Stairs lead up inside the walls to give a good vantage point; you can get better views of the broch and the snaking Carloway Loch below by climbing farther up the hill behind. At the bottom is a **visitors center** (tel. 01851/643338, 10 A.M.–5 P.M. Mon.–Sat. Apr.–Sept., free). Although quite basic, it is a helpful and friendly place that will give you a good idea

© LUKE WATERSON

the stones at Callanish

of the broch's history, including its stint as a refuge for local cattle thieves. You can still get to the broch if the visitor center is closed.

▐ Callanish (Calanais)

Standing on a green hump of exposed moor beneath a blue-gray sky, the ancient gray standing stone monoliths that make up the Callanish complex of stone circles are a lurid contrast of colors and shapes. There are no fewer than three stone circles in the surrounding area. **Callanish I** is by far the most impressive (hence the visitors center and exhibition). The **visitors center/café/shop** (tel. 01851/641422, www.calanaisvisitorcentre.co.uk, visitors center 10 A.M.–6 P.M. Mon.–Sat. Apr.–Sept., 10 A.M.–4 P.M. Wed.–Sat. Oct.–Mar.) is a good point of reference for the history of the stones, but in all honesty, it's mostly theoretical and the mystery is half the appeal. The site (accessible at all times) consists of two double rings of standing stones and an avenue of stones leading downhill from it. Note the vastly contrasting shapes of the stones: The wider stones and the tall thin stones are more

or less placed alternately, probably representing the female and male components of fertility. Theories abound, though; there are also strong arguments put forth for the whole site being solely a lunar observation station. There are more than 50 stones in Callanish I, for the most part standing as tall today as they were when erected about 3,500 years ago. You can go up and touch all of the stones and picnic nearby, constructing your own theories as to why they were built—far more moving than any visitors center display. **Callanish III,** back by the main road to the southeast, is a poignant double ring of stones, too. You're also more likely to have the place to yourself and get a shot of the stones without a bright-coated tourist in the frame. **Callanish II** is just to the west. A path does link all three complexes but it's poorly maintained and quite boggy.

Great Bernera

July 22, 1953, was a great day for the residents of Great Bernera: A bridge spanning the 150 meters between it and the mainland was constructed and depopulation was halted.

BLACK HOUSES AND WHITE HOUSES

What are referred to today as blackhouses were for a long time the typical residences of Hebridean islanders. The basic design of each was similar: a long low-lying stone building with inner and outer walls of mortar filled with turf for warmth. A roof of turf and thatch would then be laid on top of a wooden frame, weighted down by fishing nets secured with lots of rocks. Despite how insecure this sounds, especially given that many such dwellings were perched on the edge of wind-blasted cliffs, such dwellings were sturdy enough to last for many centuries. Humans and animals would share the same living space, at the center of which would be a peat fire. There was no chimney – houses would have been constantly full of smoke.

This might have seemed a backward way to live, but builders of these houses only had at their disposal materials they could find locally: often old bits of boats and, of course, boulders.

The chimney-less design was almost certainly intentional, too; the sooty deposits that accumulated on the ceiling and walls would have been scraped off and used for fertilizer. The assumption is often made that blackhouses are so called because they are stained black with soot, but blackhouses only developed their name in the 19th century. At this time, alternative accommodation began to be built on the Outer Hebrides. As more of the islanders began to live in these newer houses the term "white house" was developed, probably more in reference to their internal (cleaner!) appearance than their external ones. To differentiate between new dwellings and old, the old crofting houses were termed "black houses." Traditional they may be, but the blackhouses you see either restored or in ruins as you travel around the Outer Hebrides aren't necessarily as old as you might think: Some were inhabited up until about thirty years ago.

It's now a thriving little island, home to the very good **Bernera Museum** (Breacleit, tel. 01851/612331, 11 A.M.–5 P.M. May–Sept., by arrangement Oct.–Mar., £2 adults, £0.50 children includes admission to the Iron Age Village), where a collection of old photographs and an audiovisual presentation trace the island's heritage. One room is devoted to the Iron Age village in the north of the island. The hours seem to change quite often; it's best to phone if you're set on having a look. You'll find a good café here, too. By Bostadh, in the north of the island, a remarkable **Iron Age village** (year-round access) has been discovered. Five houses have been excavated and one restored as authentically as possible to its condition over a millennium ago. It's right on the edge of one of Great Bernera's exquisite sandy coves.

Uig

Uig (www.uigandbernera.com) is a pocket of the Caribbean tucked away in remote western Lewis, centering on a wide winding tract of golden sand sheltered by rocks and forming one of the best beaches in the Outer Hebrides. After all those peat bogs, this is a bit of a change—lots of bouncy machair with the distant Harris hills making the photogenic backdrop complete. A belt of remote lochs and moor all but cut it off from the rest of Lewis. As if the scenery weren't enough, it was on this beach in 1831 that one of the most important Viking valuables ever was found: 78 12th-century ivory chess pieces. A cow, the sea, and a local fisherman are all given credit for finding them by various sources. None of the Uig Chessmen are in Uig; you can see some in the British Museum and some in the National Museum of Scotland in Edinburgh.

For a real adventure, **Seatrek** (tel. 01851/672464, www.seatrek.co.uk) runs daily trips during summer to the mystery-steeped Flannan Isles, seven outcrops of rock sticking out of the Atlantic 25 miles northwest of Lewis. Several lighthouse keepers disappeared here during the 19th century. Running time is about one hour (wildlife-dependent). Excursions cost £90 and depart from Miavaig pier.

peat-cutting on Lewis

Accommodations and Food

Lewis is a big place with very spread-around facilities.

In the **Butt of Lewis** area, the best place to stay is **Galson Farm and Bunkhouse** (Galson, tel. 01851/850492, www.galsonfarm.co.uk, from £36 pp, hostel beds £12), an enterprising 18th-century farm where accommodation comes in two forms. The bed-and-breakfast option is three en suite rooms done up in whites and rich wine reds. There are no fewer than two residents' lounges, complete with open fires. Then there is the six- to eight-bed pine-furnished hostel next door. It's a cozy little place with a self-catering kitchen. Renting the whole bunkhouse will only cost you £44. You don't have to stay here to benefit from the huge four-course dinners in the large farmhouse kitchen. It's hearty Aga-cooked food, and there are lots of choices of wine and single malts. The farm is off the A847 in the north of Lewis.

For light refreshments in this neck of the woods, there is **Europie Tearoom** (tel. 01851/810729, www.eoropaidh.co.uk), the U.K.'s (and allegedly Europe's) most northwesterly tearoom. The brightly painted croft house in Europie village just south of the Butt of Lewis has picnic tables outside in the grassy garden and a less blowy interior. You can choose from teas, coffees, sandwiches, or very good ploughman's salads.

In the **Callanish and Carloway area** you should head to ◖ **Gearrannan** (Gearrannan, tel. 01851/643416, www.gearannan.com, www .gatliff.org.uk, cottages 2 nights from £125, hostel beds £8) for the area's most atmospheric accommodation. Here you'll find amidst this reconstructed blackhouse village a few houses that you can actually stay in. The self-catering cottages have bare stone walls but are a good sight plusher in every other sense to traditional blackhouses, with stoves and underfloor heating. The hostel was the first blackhouse to be restored. There are 14 beds, lots of heating, and basic but clean showers and kitchen. It's one of the Gatliff Trust hostels.

You can get solid refreshments at **Callanish Visitor Centre Café** (Callanish, tel. 01851/621422, 10 A.M.–6 P.M. Mon.–Sat. Apr.–Sept., 10 A.M.–3:30 P.M. Wed.–Sat. Oct.–Mar.) and

© LUKE WATERSON

you get to look out on Britain's most spectacular stone circle. This café/restaurant, decked out in wood, has huge light windows that make a meal here a real pleasure. The cuisine is nothing gourmet but it does very good coffee, soups, toasted sandwiches, and cakes, all £1–5.

In **Uig** it's possible to camp at the basic but stunningly beautiful **campsite** (tel. 01851/672248) on the southern side of the bay or to wild camp in a secluded position at the back of the beach. **Bonaventure** (Aird Uig, tel. 01851/672474, www.bonaventurelewis.co.uk, 6:30–9 P.M. daily, reservations advised) is an unexpectedly classy French restaurant doing three-course set meals for £30.50 in a former radar station building on Gallan Head. It's big and comfortably modern inside with mains like Minch langoustines in garlic butter and profiteroles with Moroccan ice cream. The cuisine is about as adventurous as the trip out here.

Getting There and Away

Three main **bus** services cover the main visitor attractions.

The Stornoway–Point of Ness service has 9–11 buses daily on a route via Barvas and then up the A857 to Europie and the Butt of Lewis. It's 55 minutes to Europie.

The West Side circular service goes from Stornoway via Barvas, Carloway, and Callanish, with five full circuits daily. You may have to change in Barvas or Carloway for services to Gearrannan or Callanish. It will be about one hour five minutes to Callanish.

On the Stornoway–Uig service, five buses daily will run as far as Timsgarry, just east of Uig. Journey time is one hour 35 minutes.

Harris

It can at first be hard to differentiate where exactly Lewis becomes **Harris (Na Hearadh).** At first it's just a continuation of the same hilly gray-green landscape, yet where Lewis is bleak, Harris quickly proves itself to be beautiful. Its chirpy, whitewashed main village, Tarbert, is the prettiest community in all the Outer Hebrides. Mountainous North Harris has some incredible walking opportunities; in South Harris, the most picturesque sandy beaches in all Scotland beckon.

The story goes that once, long ago, two feuding branches of the ruling Macleod clan split: one to control the larger northern end of the biggest island in the Outer Hebrides, one to control the rocky southern tip. The MacLeods, who got the southern bit (Harris) may have felt hard done by as there was less farming land, but from a modern perspective, they got the better deal.

TARBERT (AN TAIRBEART)

Tarbert is a gorgeous village of gray and white houses sitting on an isthmus between two lochs.
It's hemmed in by the rocky lunar-like hills that characterize much of Harris, which accentuates its charms. Tarbert was a former center of Harris tweed production but is today a close-packed bustling little place and important ferry port; the shortest crossing to mainland Scotland goes from here. Tarbert has an ATM in its large car park, shops, fuel, and other basic facilities.

Accommodations and Food

Cute little **Rockview Bunkhouse** (Main St., tel. 01859/502626, beds £10) is the cheapest place to stay in town. There are 32 beds but this place has the intimate feel of a small hostel. Dorms are mixed, and you get free towels, hot water, and bed linens—none of the niggling hidden charges many hostels impose, and with a waterfront location to beat the vast majority of them. One drawback is how many beds are squeezed into each room.

There are 24 crisp modern rooms at the big, white **Harris Hotel** (tel. 01859/502154, www.harrishotel.com, £55–80 s, £90–140 d) and they are the best 24 places to stay in Tarbert.

They vary in size and view (waterfront or garden) but the vast majority are either en suite or with private bathroom. The residents' lounge backs onto a splendid, lush garden that lends an exotic air to the whole establishment. Lots of malt whiskies wait behind the bar. You can get good food in the restaurant like steak topped with Stornoway black pudding and doused in red wine. It's 500 yards from the ferry pier.

For some good home cooking, head to the ◖ **Firstfruits Tearoom** (tel. 01859/502439, 10 A.M.–4:30 P.M. and 7–9 P.M. Mon.–Sat. Apr.–Sept.), a converted stone cottage near the ferry pier. It now does delicious evening meals in addition to the great daytime menu. Expect oddly shaped tables and a whitewashed interior hung with artwork.

Information
Tarbert has a **TIC** (9 A.M.–5 P.M. Mon.–Sat. Apr.–Oct.; also Tues., Thurs., and Sat. to coincide with arrival time of 7:40 P.M. ferry from Uig on Skye) by the pier.

Getting There and Away
Seven **buses** on weekdays and four on Saturday run between Tarbert and Stornoway.

Tarbert is also a ferry port. **Calmac** (tel. 0870/565 0000, www.calmac.co.uk) offers two ferries a day from Uig on Skye to Tarbert (Mon.–Sat., 1 hr. 45 min., £10 adult, £48 car one-way). Head down to **Leverburgh** in South Harris for ferries to Berneray and North Uist.

NORTH HARRIS
Aside from the main road, the mountainous northern part of Harris only has three roads—a testament to its remoteness rather than its size. It's a stunningly beautiful drive down the Hushinish Road, with seldom-visited beaches and the island of Scarp, site of some bizarre but inventive projects over the years. The high rocky backbone of Harris forms one of Britain's longest and most inhospitable continuous ranges of hills, at their wildest in North Harris.

Sights
Along the **Scarp Road,** the The B887 winds along the sparkling Soay sound to culminate in **Hushinish (Huisinis),** the area's big settlement with about five houses facing a wonderful expanse of golden sand. Just across the water (an extremely dangerous wade at low tide) is the rocky island of **Scarp,** where German inventor Gerhard Zucker developed a scheme to deliver the island's post by rocket mail in 1934. The rocket was fired from Harris to Scarp and exploded, an incident remembered in the film *The Rocket Post,* filmed on Harris.

There is some great isolated walking to be had in the **Rhenigidale (Reinigeadal)** area around the coast of **Loch Seaforth.**

Accommodations
Rhenigidale Hostel (www.gatliff.org.uk, beds £8.50) was the first of the Gatliff Trust hostels opened: it's been going strong over 40 years now. It's a very peaceful spot—a 13-bed white croft cottage on the rocky slopes overlooking the loch. You can walk the six miles to the hostel from Tarbert; allow two to three hours and bring provisions, as there's not a lot out here but the hills.

Getting There and Away
During school time, three or four **buses** run along the Scarp Road from Tarbert. Book a ticket on either of the two buses from Tarbert to Rhenigidale by the day before (North Harris Motors, tel. 01859/502250).

SOUTH HARRIS AND ST. KILDA
There's a far more relaxed feel to South Harris, the undisputed paradise of the northern Outer Hebrides. It manages to follow the knack these islands have for dividing themselves into totally different landscapes—there are grassy slopes laced with shimmering sandy beaches in the west and a barren rock-pockmarked landscape in the east. It's all delightfully remote, and yet South Harris has been able to develop significant industries over the years: fishing and, far more famously, tweed from the island's sheep. South Harris also offers the opportunity to visit the remotest of remote places in Britain: St.

Luskentyre Beach, in South Harris, one of the loveliest beaches in Europe

© LUKE WATERSON

Kilda, a desolate rocky island home to Britain's biggest population of seabirds.

◖ Beaches

The stretch of machair-backed white sand at **Luskentyre (Losgaintir)** has to be one of the most wonderful beaches in Europe. It's sheltered, you can swim safely here, and it's tucked out of the way sufficiently to mean it never gets really crowded. You can park in the cemetery car park and walk down. Farther along the road is **Scarista (Sgarasta),** another wonderful inlet made up of crushed shell sand.

Other South Harris Sights

Seallam! (Northton, tel. 01859/520258, www .seallam.com, 10 A.M.–5 P.M. Mon.–Sat.) has the Western Isles' top-notch genealogy center; you can have your family history traced from £20.

Standing isolated by the roadside in **Rodel (Roghadal)** is the medieval **St. Clement's Church** (year-round, free), built by Alexander MacLeod, clan chief of Harris and Dunvegan on Skye. There are some intriguing tombs on the ground floor of the church, including

MacLeod's and three others depicting knights. You can climb the tower (up a series of steep wooden ladders) for some mesmerizing views of the surrounding lunar landscape. If you visit one church during your time in the Highlands and islands of Scotland, make it this one. Opening hours aren't set in stone but access during reasonable hours is rarely a problem.

The Golden Road is the single-track road that wends its way north from Rodel over the stark east coast of South Harris, so called because of the cost of building it. The predominant color is gray, though. This stretch of land was so rocky that the images of Jupiter in the film *2001: A Space Odyssey* were achieved by panning in on the lunar-like rock formations that rise up above the Road. If you follow the coast road around, you will come to signs for the hamlet of **Plocropool (Plocrapol),** home to **Harris Tweed and Knitwear** (4 Plocropool, tel. 01859/511217, 9 A.M.–6 P.M. daily), where Harris tweed is still made the traditional way. They'll put on weaving demonstrations for tour parties (arrange in advance to avoid disappointment) and have a shop where you can purchase the

© LUKE WATERSON

South Harris looks lunar enough to be used as a setting for *2001: A Space Odyssey.*

finished products. Apart from that, it's rocks, lochs, and the occasional patch of grass.

❰ St. Kilda

The small ferry port of Leverburgh in South Harris is where, weather permitting, cruises with **St. Kilda Cruises** (tel. 01859/502060, www.kildacruises.co.uk, one cruise daily dependent on weather) depart to sheer-sided, deserted St. Kilda. It's a 2.75-hour trip to St. Kilda, a sharp rocky ridge jutting starkly out of the Atlantic 50 miles west of Harris. It's one of Europe's most important sites for seabirds; there are more gannets here than anywhere else in the world. The island once had a human population, too, but they were evacuated at their own request in 1930. Life, as you can imagine, was extremely bleak on the islands: Children would have to be tied down to avoid them falling off the cliffs, and the only way for the men to survive at times was to risk their lives scaling the treacherous cliffs to look for seabird eggs. The trip will give you most of the day ashore to explore the ruined houses and spot seabirds. It's £160 per person round-

trip in a comfortably well-equipped boat. It will be the most memorable £160 you'll spend in Scotland.

If you are planning a visit, a bit of research is a good idea. Have a look at www.kilda.org.uk, where there are also details of other ways you can visit the island (as part of a volunteer group or with your own private boat). When you go, take care to respect the birdlife and take all litter home with you. There is a small, basic **campsite** (tel. 01463/232034 for details) on the island, mainly used by volunteer parties.

Accommodations and Food

Am Bothan (Leverburgh, tel. 01859/520251, www.ambothan.com, beds £12–14) is a brightly painted log chalet in Leverburgh—a clean, friendly place to stay, and pretty convenient for the North Uist ferry as well as for exploring Rodel. There are five rooms with between three and six beds. Try to grab the loft (three beds) for the pick of the rooms. It's possible to pitch a tent in the garden. There are wonderful warm showers and a patio with a barbecue area to soak up the atmosphere. It's also possible to hire bikes—they really have thought of everything here.

Captain Alexander MacLeod, who had the **C Rodel Hotel** (Rodel, tel. 01859/520210, www.rodelhotel.co.uk, £65 s, £100 d) built in the late 18th century, is said to have declared that the real value of Harris was in its sea rather than its land. He constructed a series of fishing stations around this stretch of coast and built this tall white house right next to the pier. It's a tranquil, tucked-away spot. Rooms are big, neat, and white with baths, showers, and fantastic views over the old pier and harbor. The restaurant serves lunch and evening meals like a piece of Minch cod or a steak in red wine from 5:30 P.M. Main courses are £14–16. The hotel can help arrange fishing and sailing trips.

After miles of nothingness it's a bit of a shock to find sophisticated **Skoon Art Café** (4 Geocrab, Gold Road, tel. 01859/530268, www.skoon.com, 10 A.M.–5 P.M. Tues.–Sat. Mar.–Oct., noon–4 P.M. Wed.–Sat. Nov.–Dec.) halfway up the Golden Road. It's a flagstone-floored place displaying local artwork and music and serving a great range of leaf teas, coffees, and cakes (£1–4).

Getting There and Away

Most **buses** from Stornoway to Tarbert continue to Leverburgh to make ferry connections via the South Harris beaches.

Four buses Monday–Friday (three on Saturdays) make the wonderful journey along the Golden Road from Tarbert to Rodel. Some of these continue to Leverburgh to connect with **ferries** to Berneray (three to four daily, 1 hr., £5.75 adult, £26 car one-way).

The Uists and Barra

The isles of North Uist, Benbecula, South Uist, and Eriskay may all be linked by causeways, but these are places of incredible contrasts. Lochs litter the isles to the point where at times, even when on dry land, it feels like you are at sea. There are also wild, seldom-visited mountains and some of Scotland's finest machair-backed, white sand beaches to add to the spectrum of landscapes. The islands are an ornithologist's paradise, with two internationally important bird reserves. A wealth of history is on offer, from prehistoric sites to crofting settlements that time seems not to have touched. The island also has romantic associations with Bonnie Prince Charlie, both his arrival on Scottish soil and his dramatic escape a year later.

NORTH UIST (UIBHIST A TUATH)

Don't come to North Uist if you don't like wilderness. Whether it's the loch-splattered and in-let-riven watery east or the brown-green grassy west with its flanks of sand dunes, absolute isolation is the common theme. It's one of the most important bird-watching sites in Scotland, and lovers of seafood should flock here, too—on the west coast is the best place in Scotland to buy smoked fish. This peaceful place has seen its share of violence in the past, with the last battle fought on British soil without firearms taking place on North Uist in 1601. Lovely Lochmaddy (Loch nam Madah) is the big town of the area, little more than a hamlet divided up by lochs with basic tourist facilities.

Sights

The **Taigh Chearsabhagh Museum and North Uist Sculpture Trail** (tel. 01876/500293, www.taigh-chearsabhagh.org, 10 A.M.–5 P.M. Mon.–Sat.) hosts some amazing exhibitions, which have recently included Andy Goldsworthy works. It displays local art, hosts local music, and has a section devoted to North Uist history. Add to that a very good café, tourist information service, shop, and superb setting on the shores of island-scattered Lochmaddy, and this becomes an unmissable attraction. From right outside the door begins the wonderful **Uist Sculpture**

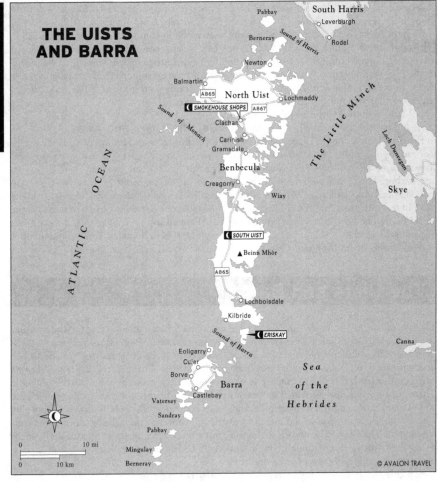

THE UISTS AND BARRA

Pabbay
South Harris
Leverburgh
Berneray
Sound of Harris
Rodel
Newton
Balmartin
A865   North Uist
Lochmaddy
🌑 SMOKEHOUSE SHOPS   A867
Clachan
Carinish
Gramsdale
Benbecula
Creagorry
Wiay
Sound of Monach
The Little Minch
Loch Dunnegan
Skye
ATLANTIC OCEAN
🌑 SOUTH UIST
▲ Beinn Mhòr
A865
Lochboisdale
Kilbride
🌑 ERISKAY
Sound of Barra
Canna
Eoligarry
Cuier
Borve
Barra
Castlebay
Vatersay
Sandray
Pabbay
Mingulay
Berneray
Sea of the Hebrides

0   10 mi
0   10 km

© AVALON TRAVEL

Trail. The highlight is a short walk away at the **Hut of the Shadow** (open year-round).

The west coast is gentler on the eye than the east but still has its fair share of dark hills and ice-blue lochans. The main reason to visit is to check out one of the best places in the British Isles to catch a sight of the shy corncrake, **Balranald RSPB Reserve** (tel. 01463/715000, year-round). The corncrake is one of the country's rarest birds, due to farming methods, but farming on North Uist is strictly corncrake-friendly. There are corncrake displays in the

hut by the car park. If you want to go corncrake-spotting the best time is May to July. You'll find the reserve in the extreme west of the island, signposted from the A865.

🌑 Smokehouse Shops

Continuing clockwise on the west coast loop road, you'll reach the small village of Clachan and the amazing shop of the **Hebridean Smokehouse** (Clachan, tel. 01876/580209, www.hebrideansmokehouse.com, shop open daily), one of the very few places in Britain to peat-smoke their fish. You can buy peat-smoked salmon, trout, and scallops to take away (the shop sells oatcakes and other accompanying foods, too) or you can order online or by phone. The fish has a unique taste, and if you're unsure what to go for there are samples of all the different varieties on the counter. Hot smoked salmon pâté (£6.95) is a real treat.

Sports and Recreation

If you feel like burning some serious energy you should head to the **Uist Outdoor Centre** (tel. 01876/500480, www.uistoutdoorcentre.co.uk) on the outskirts of Lochmaddy. Here you can try your hand at kayaking and scuba diving (there's no shortage of watery spots for these activities) and mountain-climbing, to name but a few of the pursuits on offer. It's signposted down the little lane to the east of Lochmaddy Village.

Accommodations and Food

The island of Berneray is connected to North Uist via a long causeway but the **Berneray Hostel** (www.gatliff.org.uk, Berneray, beds £8.50) is cut off even by the island's standards of isolation. It's a spick-and-span, white, 20-bed thatched croft cottage hostel. Facilities are good but basic. You come here for the location; you will be gazing onto the island-speckled Sound of Harris across a wide stony beach. You can camp in the hostel grounds, too. You can't book in advance; just turn up and it's unlikely you'll be turned away. Check www.isleofberneray.com for details on things to do. To reach the hostel, follow the road through Berneray village until the road turns left at a bus shelter; carry straight on towards the sea.

As its name suggests, the **Old Court House** (Lochmaddy, tel. 01876/500358, oldcourthouse@tiscali.co.uk, room only £20 pp, bed and breakfast £25–30 pp) was once the jail for all the islands down to Barra. Today it's a bed-and-breakfast offering just four relaxed rooms and a fantastic breakfast (anything from kippers to white pudding). You may even hear the owner's husband playing his bagpipes (it's evocative, not intrusive!). Head

up the peaceful road towards Uist Outdoor Centre to get there.

The traditional, whitewashed **Lochmaddy Hotel** (tel. 01876/500331, www.lochmaddy-hotel.co.uk, from £35 pp) overlooks the rocky shoreline at Lochmaddy. It's had a recent refurbishment; rooms are as rustic and traditional as the rest of the place, but they're en suite with TVs in each. Most get waterfront views. Downstairs is a lounge with an open fire and a chilly bar.

Secluded **Langass Lodge Hotel** (Langass, tel. 01876/580285, www.langasslodge.co.uk, £60 s, £90 d) is the best place to stay in North Uist. The six latest rooms to be added are wide, white, high-ceilinged places; all are en suite with flat-screen TVs, but you'll mainly be feasting your eyes on the views over gorgeous sparkling Loch Euphoirt. The rooms in the main part of the lodge are smaller but with just as much character. The restaurant features an array of locally caught seafood. Brown trout, whenever it appears on the menu, has always been caught either by the staff or the guests. Head southwest from Lochmaddy past Bharpa Langais cairn on the A867; you'll see the hotel signposted on your left.

The Lobster Pot (Berneray, tel. 01876/540288, 10 A.M.–4:30 P.M. Mon.–Sat. Apr.–Sept.) is just the place to gather your thoughts before or after embarking on North Uist and the nearest eatery to where the Harris ferry comes in (turn right and right again from the pier). It's a tearoom attached to the village stores, a cozy space of clattering wooden tables with artwork (including lovely stained glass) that gives it a bright cheerful feel. Most of the menu is under £5: huge homebakes, toasted sandwiches, and crisp, simple salads. You can buy maps of the isles in the store here.

Getting There and Away

There are 10 **buses** daily (fewer on Saturdays) between Lochmaddy and Berneray Pier, with some continuing to Berneray village. Three to five buses daily Monday–Saturday head around to the west coast of North Uist from Lochmaddy (for Balranald RSPB Reserve and the Hebridean Smokehouse).

Lochmaddy is also connected by bus to Benbecula and Lochboisdale in the south of South Uist. You'll possibly have to change in Balivanich, and about six Lochmaddy departures arrive daily Monday–Friday in Lochboisdale.

Calmac ferries sail from Lochmaddy to Uig on Skye twice daily (2 hrs. 45 min., £10 adult, £48 car one-way) and from Berneray just north of Lochmaddy to Leverburgh on South Harris three to four times every day of the week (1 hr., £5.75 adult, £26 car one-way).

BENBECULA (BEINN NA FAOGHLA)

Crisscrossed by lochs, Benbecula acts as the largely unspectacular join between North Uist and South Uist. The area is as much sand, pebbles, and water as it is land. Its name translates from the Gaelic as "Mountain of the Fords"; its highest point, Rueval, can hardly be described as a mountain, but you can climb it to get views of the wide, sandy fords that until recently isolated the island from its neighbors to the north and south. Today, you can blink and miss the island; it's scarred by an ugly army base and only worth a mention for a couple of excellent accommodation and food options. Head to the depressing army base village of Balivanich for facilities such as a supermarket, bank, and laundry.

Shopping

Macgillivray's (Balivanich, tel. 01870/602525, www.macgil.co.uk, Mon.–Sat.) is the classic Scottish island shop—a treasure trove of, quite literally, everything, from old books to tweed jackets, music, fishing rods, and pottery.

Accommodations and Food

Shell Bay Campsite (Lionacleit, tel. 01870/602447, tents from £6) occupies a very windy site on some gorgeous grass backing onto the machair. It has very good hot showers and a peaceful atmosphere.

◖ **Nunton Steadings** (Nunton, tel. 01870/603774, www.nuntonsteadings.com, 10 A.M.–4 P.M. Mon.–Sat.) is a traditional 18th-century collection of farm buildings (or steadings) where Flora MacDonald stayed while helping Bonnie Prince Charlie escape in 1746. It's been done up to make Benbecula not only geographically, but also culturally, the center of activity in the Uists. There are two tearooms, regular live performances by Gaelic musicians, and a museum explaining Nunton's somewhat colorful history. There's also a shop, but for the moment the tearoom is the highlight, flanked by shelves of local crafts and serving up heavenly soups, scones, and big homebakes (£2–5).

Getting There and Away

Because of the army base, Balivanich has an **airport** (tel. 01870/602051). You can fly to Stornoway twice daily and Barra daily from here. You may have to change in Balivanich for connecting northbound/southbound bus services. It's the best-connected place on the Uists, with buses running almost hourly north to Lochmaddy and south to Lochboisdale.

◖ SOUTH UIST (UIBHIST A DEAS)

A shrine at the roadside and a huge granite statue of the Madonna and Child mark the beginning of the second-largest island in the Outer Hebrides; the southern part of this archipelago remained strongly Catholic after the reformation, in stark contrast to the staunchly Protestant north. It's an island of two halves: agricultural land fringed by dunes in the west and mountains in the east. The northern part of South Uist is, like Benbecula, daubed in marsh and lochs, making it an important home for Greylag geese. Beach-lovers should head for the sands that line the west coast almost from top to bottom, best appreciable from the magical crofting settlement of Howmore. Wildlife lovers should take to the rugged east, where golden eagles swoop over mountain passes. Whatever you do, it's taking the time to explore the side roads that will make your visit here memorable. The quiet port of Lochboisdale is the main community: It has a hotel, shop, seasonal tourist information point, and garage.

Sights

Standing 33 feet high beneath a yellow-green hill topped by aerial masts, the **Our Lady of the Isles Statue** (north of island off A865, open year-round, free) was raised in 1930. It remains a moving testimony in these wild isles to how, despite many cruel attempts to suppress their faith by successive landlords, people here have remained proudly Catholic. A drivable track leads right up to the statue.

The tiny crofting community of **Howmore (Tobha Mor)** has one of the best collections of thatched cottages anywhere in Scotland. Even so, the houses are outnumbered by the many ruins of churches and chapels in the marshy ground surrounding the settlement, once clearly an important ecclesiastical site. There are four chapels and one church in a somewhat decrepit, lichen-covered state. Head for the walled complex just down from the Gatliff Trust hostel.

One of the few buildings on the long drive south to South Uist's main town Lochboisdale is **Kildonan Museum** (tel. 01878/710343, www.kildonanmuseum.co.uk, 10 A.M.–5 P.M. Mon.–Sat., 2–5 P.M. Sun., free). The highlight is easily the huge **Clanranald Stone,** a carved stone from the ecclesiastical complex at Howmore, possibly over 1,000 years old and said to be cursed. The museum has weaving memorabilia and accounts of island life depicted by photographs. It also offers an important introduction to South Uist archaeology. There is a popular café here, too (the views are better than the food). Farther south 1.5 miles, the tumbled-down blackhouses of Milton are where you will find **Flora MacDonald's Birthplace** (year-round). A cairn marks where McDonald, the Scottish heroine that helped Prince Charlie, was born.

Sports and Recreation

Rothan Cycles (Howmore, tel. 01878/620283, www.rothan.com) rents bikes from £8 per day. They'll do pick-up from various locations in the Uists and at Stornoway for a charge.

Accommodations and Food

Howmore Croft and Campsite (www.gatliff .org.uk, beds £8.50) is a basic croft hostel that overlooks Howmore's series of ruined chapels and churches—one is practically in the back garden. It's a neat little 17-bed hostel with good space for camping and bags of local information. It's one of the prettier and more popular Gatliff Trust hostels. Remember, you can't book this place in advance; just turn up and the warden will collect your money.

Lochside Cottage (northwest of Lochboisdale on A865, tel. 01878/700472, £25 pp) deserves its name with a wonderful lochside setting. Wherever you are in the house, it's flooded by a wonderful natural light. The two rooms are clean, white, and simply furnished. You get a lounge where you can sit by the fire and a conservatory where you can gaze out at the loch. Fishermen have been coming here for years, but anyone who's a fan of great scenery should consider staying. A room-only deal is even cheaper.

Pictures of the **Polochar Inn** (Polochar, tel. 01878/700215, www.polocharinn.com, £55 s, £85 d) invariably feature the standing stone by the garden; it proves almost as much of an incentive to visit as a beer and a bed do in the height of the season. The well-appointed rooms are modern and refurbished, with red leather and furnishings. Each comes with its own bathrooms and TV/DVD set. The inn has a good reputation for food: seafood, meat, and pasta, cooked in an old-fashioned Scottish way, are on offer. The bar has an open fire.

You might think the signs leading you up the dead-end road to the ⚫ **Orasay Inn** (Lochcarnan, tel. 01870/610298, £35 s, £70 d, dinners from £8–30) are a joke. Even when you see this unremarkable building from the outside, you may have your doubts. But this quiet inn is one of the best places to stay on the archipelago and also one of the best to eat. The location makes this one a winner. Big, clean, en suite rooms and the enticing restaurant alike look out on the scattered islands of Loch Carnan and the Minch beyond. Try some of the shellfish and relax by a peat fire with a whisky in the lounge afterwards—paradise. The turn is on the left just after you cross over to South Uist from Benbecula.

cemetery, Eriskay

Getting There and Away

Six **buses** daily head north to Lochmaddy Monday–Friday. Buses go almost hourly as far north as Balivanich from Lochboisdale. The Lochboisdale to Lochmaddy journey is about one hour 40 minutes.

⬤ ERISKAY (EIRIOSGAIGH)

Rejuvenated by the causeway connecting it to South Uist, this island of low grassy hills grazed by sturdy Eriskay ponies and wonderful white sandy beaches has long been the embodiment of the ideal romantic getaway. Its colorful past says it all: Bonnie Prince Charlie first set foot on Scottish soil on a beach on the island's west coast, and Eriskay was more recently catapulted to fame when a ship carrying over 250,000 bottles of whisky was wrecked off its shores during World War II. Islanders are apparently still reaping the benefits to this day. The near-perfect light and beaches to rival the Caribbean in all but temperature make the island a highlight of any trip to the Outer Hebrides.

Eriskay has plenty of gorgeous **beaches,** but none with quite the historic clout of **Coilleag**

a' Phrionnsa, just north of the ferry terminal, the stretch of sand where Bonnie Prince Charlie landed in 1745. White-striped Pink Sea bindweed grows on the shore here, said to have come from seeds dropped from a handkerchief by the Prince.

The best place to **camp** anywhere on the Scottish islands is south of Am Baile village center beyond the cemetery; there's tussocky grass sloping to sandy beaches and the feeling that you are an extra on *Treasure Island.* There is no charge—and no facilities, but it's not far to the pub.

The modern **Am Politician Pub** (Baile, tel. 01878/720246, 11 A.M.–midnight Mon.–Wed., 11 A.M.–1 A.M. Thurs.–Sun.) is the center of island life: a really lively bar, a light restaurant with gorgeous views of the bay, and a bottle of whisky from the cargo of the *Politician* (for looking, not drinking). There's also big-screen sports and rather tasty pub grub.

Getting There and Away

From Eriskay there are almost hourly sailings to Barra (40 min.). There are daily **post buses**

© LUKE WATERSON

WHISKY GALORE

The wreckers that worked the west and north of Scotland used to view it as providence if a ship was wrecked off their patch of coast, standing in merciless silence as the crew and cargo floundered in the sea. It was more open-mouthed shock and uncontrollable excitement with the residents of Eriskay, when the SS *Politician* ran aground off the island's coast in February 1941. The crew members were saved, but lost to the waves were around 264,000 bottles of single malt whisky from Edradour, one of Scotland's finest distilleries. The cargo had been on its way to the United States to pay some of the war debt owed by Britain to America, but for an island in the grip of wartime rationing, this was an opportunity not to be passed over. It's thought over 2,000 cases or 24,000 bottles were "intercepted" by the islanders. A fairy tale come true it may have seemed, but in reality 19 islanders were tried and imprisoned for their part in drinking the goods. Compton Mackenzie wrote a slightly more idealized version of the incident in his book *Whisky Galore*, which was made into a 1949 film of the same name, released by the less romantic title *Tight Little Island* in the United States.

between Eriskay and Lochboisdale on South Uist (40 min.). On Saturday you can get to Ballivanich airport directly from Eriskay.

The Western Isles Bus Service W29 also operates six times daily between Lochboisdale and Eriskay, connecting with ferry departure times.

BARRA (BARRAIGH)

Barra is the most isolated of the main Outer Hebridean islands, yet you'll feel more at home here than on any of them. Perhaps that's because of the number of attractions crammed into such a small area. There's a vivid history to explore, from prehistoric to medieval times, as well as miles of sandy beaches and, for the more adventurous, boat trips to deserted

islands. With a center of grassy uplands and coasts that overflow with golden sand dunes backed by brightly flowering machair, this is a condensed version of the Outer Hebrides in just over 30 square miles. The main village, the port of Castlebay (Bagh a Chaisteil) is a lively little place with shops, a bank with an ATM, and a castle mirrored in its bay.

Sights

Kisimul Castle (tel. 01871/810313, 9:30 A.M.–5:30 P.M. daily Apr.–Sept., 9:30 A.M.–4:30 P.M. Sat.–Wed. Oct.) sticks up from a rocky island some meters off the shore of Castlebay. It's Barra's most distinctive feature and one of Scotland's most splendidly located castles. The fortress is restored to its original 12th-century glory. The magical experience of a visit is heightened by having to get to it by boat. On the island itself, check the ring of rocks to the east of the landing place; this was to catch fish for survival in case the fortress was ever under siege.

Dun Bharpa (Borve, year-round) is one of the best-preserved chambered cairns in the Outer Hebrides, still standing at five meters high. You can get to it from Borve (Borgh) valley, about four miles clockwise from Castlebay.

At the north end of Barra is **Cill Barra** (near Barra Airport, year-round, free), a chapel and graveyard on a steeply sloping hillside. In 1865 a stone with a Celtic cross on one side and a runic inscription on the other was found here: evidence that Vikings who stayed on Barra came to accept Christianity. The Kilbar Stone, as it is known, is on display in Edinburgh. A replica stands by the chapel. Compton Mackenzie, author of *Whisky Galore*, is buried in the graveyard.

Accommodations and Food

It's not just budget travelers who should consider heading to **Dunard Hostel** (tel. 01871/810433, www.dunardhostel.co.uk, beds £12, £30 d). This whitewashed 16-bed cottage just five minutes' walk from the Castlebay ferry terminal also has one of the cheapest double rooms on the island and a welcoming open fire

OUTER HEBRIDES

in the lounge, not to mention a view to rival the very best over sparkling Castle Bay.

Northbay House (tel. 01871/890255, www.barraholidays.co.uk, Apr.–Oct., £30 pp) was once a school; now this 19th-century place just gives lessons in excellent hospitality. There are only two en suite rooms, so service is attentive. Room views are of quiet North Bay itself. There are two residents' lounges, and you get hot drinks and good home baking in the evenings.

The **Castlebay Hotel** (tel. 01871/810223, www.castlebay-hotel.co.uk, £59 s, £89 d) has huge beige-toned rooms with en suite bathrooms, TVs, and vistas of sandy Vatersay island from the windows. In the spacious restaurant you can feast on boar, hare, and Barra lamb.

Information and Services

The **TIC** (tel. 01871/810336, 9 A.M.–5 P.M. Mon.–Sat., 1–4 P.M. Sun., and one hour after ferries arrive Apr.–Oct.) is on Pier Road.

Getting There
◖ FLYING TO BARRA

Loganair (tel. 01871/890823, www.loganair.co.uk, www.britishairways.com) operates daily flights to both Benbecula and Glasgow from Barra. Landing times depend on the tide:

Planes touch down upon a beach on one of the world's only tidal runways. You couldn't hope for a more spectacular introduction to a stay on an island. Many, regardless of whether they are flying, head up to The Big Strand (Traigh Mor), where the famed flight lands and takes off. Watching the plane on the sand is something of a pastime on the island—livestock has to be chased away from the runway beforehand.

GETTING TO BARRA BY SEA

Calmac (www.calmac.co.uk) runs a daily ferry service between Oban on the Scottish mainland in Argyllshire and Castlebay (£21.80 adult, £81 car one-way). Some sailings go via Lochboisdale in South Uist. Direct services from Oban take just under five hours. Service is reduced to 4–5 sailings weekly during winter.

There are 10 sailings per day between Barra and Eriskay (40 min., £6.15 adult, £18.05 car one-way). These arrive in Barra at the north of the island, near Ardmhor.

Getting Around

Buses run from Castlebay fairly regularly up the east side of the island and less often up the west side to meet ferry connections at Ardmhor (Mon.–Sat.). Journey time is 20 minutes.

ORKNEY ISLANDS

Effused at almost any time of year in its own unique, lurid light, this scattered archipelago of some 70 islands lies just off the north coast of the Scottish mainland. Orkney has the highest concentration of prehistoric monuments in Northern Europe, and as soon as you arrive they start appearing everywhere on this flat, green, sparsely vegetated land: standing stones, stone circles, and chambered cairns. There is Skara Brae, Europe's oldest surviving settlement, dating back more than 4,500 years, and other ancient sites without equal in Britain like Maes Howe.

Kirkwall, with its ferry terminal and airport, is, in the eyes of most except Stromness folk, the hub of island activity. It's a charming Norse-founded town with narrow streets full of historic sights and good places to eat. Orkney has a reputation for good food: award-winning seafood, beef, lamb, and cheese. Here you can let your taste buds acclimatize to bliss, your cheeks to the islands' characteristically strong winds, and your ears to the musical Orcadian dialect, which often seems like another language altogether. Stromness on West Mainland is the prettiest town on the Scottish islands, with its cluster of slate-gray houses hugging a harbor full of brightly painted fishing boats.

The isles beyond the mainland are sparsely populated and, like much of Orkney, have stronger ties with Scandinavia than Scotland. A trip to one of these isolated isles is an integral part of any Orkney experience, with birds and ancient stone monuments more in evidence than people. Westray is the best place in Britain to see puffins, and on the most remote

© LUKE WATERSON

HIGHLIGHTS

◖ Highland Park Distillery: Take the tour of the world's most northerly Scotch whisky distillery, one of the few where traditional floor maltings are still carried out (page 537).

◖ Live Music in Kirkwall: Saturday evening at the Reel in Kirkwall is perhaps the best live traditional music experience possible in Scotland, with local musicians getting involved in an atmospheric jamming session (page 540).

◖ The Italian Chapel: On its own rocky island on the way to the South Isles is one of Scotland's most moving buildings: an exquisitely painted chapel made from a Nissen hut by Italian prisoners-of-war (page 546).

◖ Stromness: Let the winding cobbled streets of the prettiest town in the Scottish islands lead you to gourmet restaurants, tucked away craft shops, and a world-class art gallery (page 550).

◖ Maes Howe: This fascinating chambered cairn is considered to be one of prehistoric Europe's finest building feats (page 551).

◖ Skara Brae: At around 5,000 years old, this is northwest Europe's oldest preserved village, with a gorgeous sandy bay alongside (page 553).

◖ Rackwick and the Old Man of Hoy: Hike from isolated Rackwick to one of Britain's most impressive rock stacks, soaring a giddying 450 feet above the sea (page 555).

◖ Shapinsay: This peaceful island has fine restaurants and a special restaurant boat from Kirkwall on summer evenings (page 557).

LOOK FOR ◖ TO FIND RECOMMENDED SIGHTS, ACTIVITIES, DINING, AND LODGING.

◖ Westray: Spy puffins at the Castle o' Burrian and climb brooding Noltland Castle (page 560).

◖ North Ronaldsay: Stay in a bird observatory at one of Europe's most important migratory bird crossroads and see the island's unique seaweed-eating sheep (page 563).

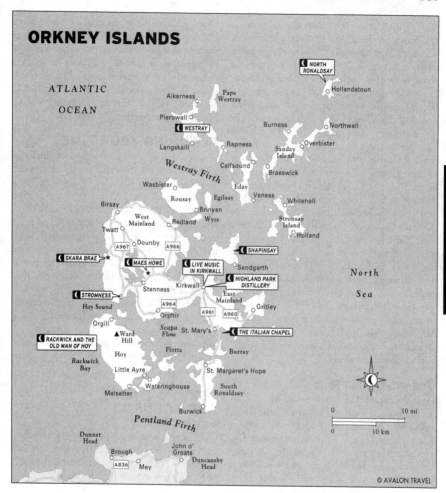

ORKNEY ISLANDS

of all the islands, North Ronaldsay, you can see the world's only seaweed-eating sheep.

It's not only ancient monuments that pack the Orkneys. For such a geographically small spread of land, these islands are peppered with an impossible variety of things to do, from distillery tours to diving to see World War II wrecks. In a way, this region is the antithesis of a typical Scottish island experience: There are better restaurants, bigger tourist attractions, and generally more vitality than on most of mainland Scotland. Away from the main

tourist draws however, it's still a place predominated by sea, sky, and very little else.

HISTORY
Prehistory and Norse Rule

Early hunter-gatherers were most likely the first peoples in Orkney, but the first sign of Orkney's habitation is also the first sign of Northern Europe's: the Knap of Howar, a farm on the island of Papa Westray. Skara Brae, the best example of a prehistoric village community on Orkney, was built by 3000

B.C. Throughout prehistory, Orkney was at the center of the action in Northern Britain. The Iron Age saw many brochs (large stone towers) being built, and perhaps news of wealthy Orkney with its fine stone buildings and good farming land spread to Norway during the middle of the first millennium A.D. By A.D. 800 the Vikings were on the islands; the Viking boom years begun around A.D. 900. The *Orkneyinga Saga,* an important document from this time, describes the golden age as lasting until 1200. Following Norse defeat at the Battle of Largs (which ended their dominion in Scotland), King Hakon spent the winter on the retreat back to Norway in the Bishop's Palace in Kirkwall. His death here after just a few months signified the real demise of Norse rule in Orkney and Shetland, but power did not shift from Norse to Scottish immediately. Norway continued to own the earldom of Orkney and Shetland until well into the 15th century. By 1471 Scotland had struck a somewhat underhand deal with the cash-strapped King Christian I of Norway and Denmark, integrating Orkney and Shetland into the rest of Scotland.

Under Scottish Rule

Several centuries of poverty and often famine followed, dominated by cruel lairds (landlords) who reduced their tenants to a status of virtual slavery. The most notorious figures were the tyrannical Robert Stewart and his even more dislikable son Patrick. Robert Stewart was arrested for various misdeeds, only for his son to rise up and seize control of Kirkwall. It took the King's best army to stop him; father and son were both executed. Patrick Stewart's most lasting impression on Orkney was the construction of Earl's Palace in Kirkwall, described as the finest renaissance building in all Scotland.

As in Shetland, poverty-struck Orcadians went to sea to make ends meet. During the Napoleonic wars, not enough recruits were joining willingly and press gangs were brought in to force people to join. Orcadians, known for their sailing ability, were key press gang targets.

Orkney played a key role in both World Wars: It changed physically with the construction of many new buildings and mentally, with the influence of an outside population of soldiers that vastly outnumbered locals. The oil boom of the 1970s did not affect Orkney as much as Shetland; the discovery of Uranium north of Stromness caused more controversy.

PLANNING YOUR TIME

Orkney's good air and sea connections and proximity to the Scottish mainland means many people "do" Orkney in day trips from Inverness. This gives you time to charge around the Ring of Brodgar and Skara Brae but isn't recommended; the tiny, windy roads of these islands are not geared to rushing around. With two days, you could do the island some justice and see the main Mainland sights; with four you could take in one of the outlying islands like Westray or Hoy (staying overnight is recommended). Not-to-be-missed Mainland sights include Skara Brae and Maes Howe. Listening to some live music in an Orkney pub and staying overnight on one of the outlying islands are fun and will leave visitors with a more rounded impression of the islands.

GETTING THERE AND AROUND
Getting There

Orkney is well connected to the Scottish mainland by a number of sea and air routes, so much so that it's easier to get to the islands than it is to many parts of mainland Scotland.

AIR

The chief operator is **Loganair** (tel. 01856/872494, www.loganair.co.uk or www.britishairways.com). You can fly from Kirkwall airport to Edinburgh (1.5 hrs.), Glasgow (1.5 hrs.), Aberdeen (45 min.), or Inverness (30 min.). You can also fly to Sumburgh Airport on Shetland. Daily flights leave to/from all these destinations, but prices vary depending on how much in advance you book. A sample fare on the shortest flight (to Inverness) is £68 if booked two weeks in advance.

BOAT

Northlink Ferries (tel. 0845/600 0449, www .nortlinkferries.co.uk) has three sailings per day between Scrabster in Caithness on mainland Scotland and Stromness (1.5 hrs., £15.50 adult, £46.40 car one-way) on weekdays and two sailings on weekends. This popular, scenic crossing takes you past the Old Man of Hoy.

Northlink also operates the Aberdeen–Shetland ferry, which calls at Kirkwall (6 hrs., £24.90 adult, £88.40 car one-way). This leaves Aberdeen at 5 and 7 P.M. only on Tuesday, Thursday, Saturday, and Sunday. There's no Tuesday sailing November–March. The crossing can be very rough.

Pentland Ferries (Pier Rd., St. Margaret's Hope, tel. 01856/831226, www.pentland-ferries.co.uk) runs the shortest year-round crossing between Orkney and the Scottish mainland. There are three sailings (1 hr., £10 adult, £25 car one-way) between St. Margaret's Hope on South Ronaldsay and Gills Bay on mainland Scotland in winter and four sailings in summer.

John o' Groats Ferries (tel. 01955/611353, www.jogferry.co.uk) operates the shortest sailing to Orkney, from John o' Groats to the southern tip of South Ronaldsay May–September. It's passengers only; cars are not transported. There are two to four crossings daily (40 min., £16 one-way, £26 round-trip).

BUS

The most efficient way to get to **Scrabster** (the departure point for ferries to Orkney) is by bus from Inverness. **Scottish Citylink** runs one direct bus per day (3.25 hrs., £16.50) to Scrabster to connect with Northlink Ferries; otherwise change in Thurso (five buses per day, about 3.5 hrs., £16.50) some two miles from Scrabster.

Getting Around

Roads on Orkney are good between Kirkwall and Stromness but narrow and slow-going in all other places. Orcadians use any double-track road as a motorway, so be warned. If you're exploring any other island, you will need to use a boat or, occasionally, plane.

BUS

Orkney's main bus stations are the new-look **Kirkwall Travel Centre** (West Castle St., Kirkwall, tel. 01856/872856), where the new tourist information is also now located, and the **Stromness Travel Centre** (Pier Head, Stromness, tel. 01856/850716), alongside the Stromness ferry terminal. The Kirkwall and Stromness Travel Centres are the best places for timetable inquiries. Buses are identified by their number, not their company.

Buses connect the Orkney mainland with the south isles of Burray and South Ronaldsay (via causeways). Bus connections are not bad—there are hourly buses from Kirkwall to Stromness (16 miles to the west, 40 min.) and several daily buses between Kirkwall and St. Margaret's Hope (15 miles to the south, 40 min.), with a round-trip fare from Kirkwall to St. Margaret's Hope or Stromness costing £3.50. But buses are few and far between to the north of the mainland, and many of Orkney's main attractions are outside of these three main towns, well away from bus routes. Sightseeing by public transport on Orkney is therefore not for those on a tight schedule.

There are few public bus services in operation in the Outer Isles, although on Westray a minibus meets the ferry at Rapness to take you to the capital, Pierowall.

CAR

Petrol is pretty pricey on the Orkneys and roads are mostly single-track, country lanes.

A reputable car hire firm is **Orkney Car Hire** (James D. Peace & Co., Junction Rd., Kirkwall, tel. 01856/872866, www.orkney-carhire.co.uk, from £28 per day), with a wide selection of vehicles. Another rental business is **W. R. Tullock** (tel. 01856/875000, www.orkneycarrental.co.uk, from £32 per day), with an office at Kirkwall Airport as well as in town.

BOAT

Orkney Ferries (Shore St., Kirkwall, tel. 01856/ 872044, www.orkneyferries.co.uk) connects mainland Orkney with the outlying islands. Be aware that any printed timetable is subject to change due to weather or other unforeseen circumstances.

AIR
Loganair (tel. 01856/872494, www.loganair .co.uk) flies from Kirkwall Airport to six of the smaller islands. Flights are very cheap (as little as £10 round-trip). Check the website or inquire at the TIC for details. Flight prices to the outer isles are usually cheapest if you spend one night on the island.

Kirkwall and East Mainland

Approaching from the west, the road drops steeply to an expanse of green between two wide bays and reveals a spread of old, gray houses you would not have imagined possible on these far-flung northern islands. Dignified Kirkwall is the thriving capital of Orkney. It's centered on its magnificent red sandstone cathedral with a series of narrow, bumpy lanes lined with packed 17th- and 18th-century buildings housing proudly individual shops and cafés. This 11th-century Norse-planned town's past is fresh and exciting after the Bonnie Prince Charlie–themed history of Highland Scotland. Near the cathedral are the palace ruins of one of Scotland's most tyrannical chieftains, the 2nd Earl of Orkney Patrick Stewart. Grassy, sandy East Mainland spreads out from Kirkwall with some of Orkney's best sandy swimming beaches and a smattering of little-known prehistoric sites.

SIGHTS
Kirkwall is a spread-out place. With the exception of the cathedral, palaces, and museums in the town center, you may want to drive to the other attractions. A nice walk connects Kirkwall with Scapa Beach.

St. Magnus Cathedral
Earl Rognivald founded the cathedral (Broad St., tel. 01856/874894, 9 A.M.–6 P.M. Mon.–Sat., 2–6 P.M. Sun. Apr.–Sept., 9 A.M.–1 P.M. and 2–5 P.M. Mon.–Sat. Oct.–Mar., free) in 1137 in memory of his uncle, Earl Magnus, who had previously inherited the earldom of Orkney. The cathedral is a blend of Norman and early Gothic architecture. Parts dating from the 12th and 13th century remain, including the elaborately carved chapel to St. Rognavald. Other parts, like the roof, impress with their simplicity. The cathedral has some fine stained-glass windows, a monument to the Arctic explorer Dr. John Rae, and plaques to Orkney's great writers, including George Mackay Brown. Tours to the Gothic upper levels of the cathedral on Tuesday and Thursday (11 A.M. and 2 P.M.) cost £5.50; book with the custodian in advance.

Bishop's Palace and Earl's Palace
These two imposing ruins (tel. 01856/871918, 9:30 A.M.–5:30 P.M. Apr.–Sept., 9:30 A.M.–4:30 P.M. Sat.–Wed. Oct., £3.50 adults, £2.50 seniors, £1.75 children) face the Cathedral across Palace Road. The most significant feature of the Bishop's Palace is the round tower, added around 1550. The place saw Norwegian rule in Scotland fizzle out when, following defeat at the Battle of Largs, King Hakon of Norway settled in the palace in 1263 and died there soon after. Earl Patrick Stewart investigated the potential of having the Bishop's Palace as his home before acquiring the land nearby and using slave labor to build the Earl's Palace, in 1607. In its day it is agreed to have been the finest example of a Renaissance building in Scotland. Patrick Stewart's time in the castle was short: He got his comeuppance in 1610 when he was imprisoned. His son Robert Stewart seized the palace briefly in 1614. Today the tree-screened palace is in as ruined a state as the Bishop's Palace but both make for great exploration. Information boards explain the history of the buildings on-site.

Kirkwall, looking toward Shapinsay

© LUKE WATERSON

Tankerness House Museum

This former laird's house is one of the best-preserved 16th-century town houses in Scotland
and gives an appropriately grand setting
for Orkney's main museum (Broad St., tel.
01856/873191, 10:30 A.M.–5 P.M. Mon.–Sat.
Apr., 10:30 A.M.–5 P.M. Mon.–Sat., 2–5 P.M.
Sun. May–Sept., 10:30 A.M.–12:30 P.M. and
1:30–5 P.M. Mon.–Sat. Oct.–Mar., free).
Because of the wealth of historic sites on
Orkney, there are several thousand years to
get through, and the museum is divided into
sections including a recently renewed Bronze
Age/Neolithic section. If you're unfamiliar
with prehistory, pay a visit here before you head
off to any of the sites themselves. A highlight
is the Burrian Stone in the Pictish section, one
of the finest Pictish carved stones to be found
on Orkney. Fees are charged April–September
to display rooms only.

Orkney Wireless Museum

The founder of the Orkney Wireless Museum
(tel. 01856/871400, www.owm.org.uk, Kiln
Corner, 10:30 A.M.–4:30 P.M. Mon.–Sat.
2–4 P.M. Sun. Apr.–Sept., £2), Jim MacDonald,
had a passion for domestic and defense wireless
equipment and amassed an intriguing collection of contraptions, now on view in this intriguing little museum staffed by volunteers.
Visiting really is like stepping into a spy film.
Why should you come? Well, museums stem-
ming from one man's hard collecting simply
don't exist in many places. It's quirky, it's personal, and it just may be the most bizarre thing
you do in Kirkwall.

◖ Highland Park Distillery

Highland Park Distillery (Holm Rd., tel.
01856/874619, www.highlandpark.co.uk,
10 A.M.–5 P.M. Mon.–Sat., noon–5 P.M. Sun.,
tours half-hourly until 4 P.M. May–Aug.,
10 A.M.–5 P.M. Mon.–Fri., tours half-hourly
until 4 P.M. Apr., Sept., and Oct., 1–5 P.M.
Mon.–Fri., tour only at 2 P.M. Nov.–Mar., £5
adults) is one of the best distilleries you can visit
in the whole of Scotland. It's not just that it's the
most northerly Scotch whisky distillery you can

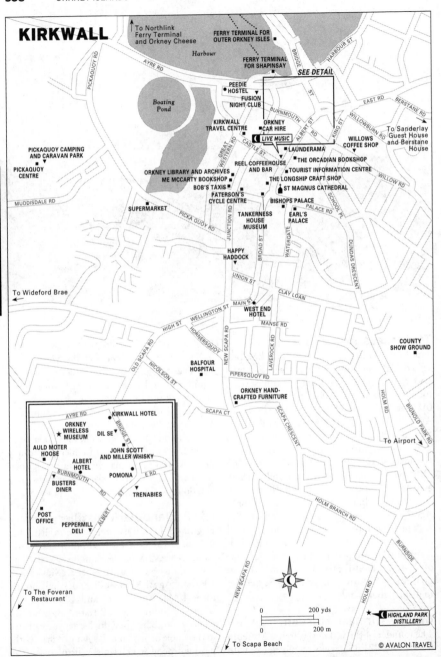

KIRKWALL

To Northlink Ferry Terminal and Orkney Cheese

FERRY TERMINAL FOR OUTER ORKNEY ISLES

Harbour

FERRY TERMINAL FOR SHAPINSAY

SEE DETAIL

PEEDIE HOSTEL

FUSION NIGHT CLUB

Boating Pond

BURNMOUTH

KIRKWALL TRAVEL CENTRE

ORKNEY CAR HIRE

EAST RD

BERSTANE RD

WILLOWS COFFEE SHOP

To Sanderlay Guest House and Berstane House

PICKAQUOY CAMPING AND CARAVAN PARK

PICKAQUOY CENTRE

LIVE MUSIC

LAUNDERAMA

REEL COFFEEHOUSE AND BAR

THE ORCADIAN BOOKSHOP

TOURIST INFORMATION CENTRE

WILLOW RD

ORKNEY LIBRARY AND ARCHIVES

ME MCCARTY BOOKSHOP

BOB'S TAXIS

THE LONGSHIP CRAFT SHOP

ST MAGNUS CATHEDRAL

MUDDISDALE RD

PATERSON'S CYCLE CENTRE

BISHOPS PALACE

PALACE RD

SUPERMARKET

TANKERNESS HOUSE MUSEUM

EARL'S PALACE

WATERGATE

DUNDAS DRESCENT

HAPPY HADDOCK

UNION ST

To Wideford Brae

CLAY LOAN

MAIN ST

WEST END HOTEL

COUNTY SHOW GROUND

HIGH ST

WELLINGTON ST

MANSE RD

HORNERSQUOY

NEW SCAPA RD

LAVEROCK RD

OLD SCAPA RD

NICOLSON ST

BALFOUR HOSPITAL

PIPERSQUOY RD

HOLM RD

BIGNOLD PARK RD

ORKNEY HAND-CRAFTED FURNITURE

To Airport

SCAPA CT

SCAPA CRESCENT

HOLM BRANCH RD

BURNSIDE

AYRE RD

KIRKWALL HOTEL

ORKNEY WIRELESS MUSEUM

DIL SE

BRIDGE ST

AULD MOTER HOOSE

ALBERT HOTEL

JOHN SCOTT AND MILLER WHISKY

BURNMOUTH

POMONA

E RD

BUSTERS DINER

TRENABIES

RD

ALBERT ST

POST OFFICE

PEPPERMILL DELI

To The Foveran Restaurant

| 0 | 200 yds |
| 0 | 200 m |

To Scapa Beach

HIGHLAND PARK DISTILLERY

© AVALON TRAVEL

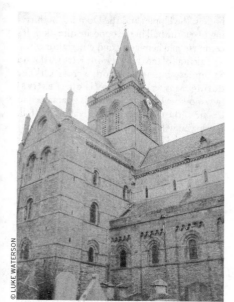

© LUKE WATERSON

St. Magnus Cathedral

Wideford Brae

From this high green hill above Kirkwall (the one with the radio mast), you can do a very pleasant, muddy walk to an impressive chambered cairn (you can slide back the lid and go down inside). Unusually, you can still see the exterior stonework dating from about 3000 B.C. There are good views north toward Finnstown. Admission is free. Access to the hill is from the old Kirkwall-Finnstown road about two miles west of Kirkwall.

Tours

If you plan to be doing the rounds of Skara Brae, Maeshowe, the Brough of Birsay, and the like, buy the **Orkney Explorer Pass,** which will save you money on entrance fees. Visit www.historic-scotland.gov.uk to buy it online for £16 adults, £8 children.

You can almost plan your own itinerary with **Wildabout Tours** (tel. 01856/851011, www.wildaboutorkney.com, day tours £83) due to the choice of the tours on offer. It could be wildlife, it could be archaeology—the choice is yours. The Treasures of Orkney Day Trip is a comprehensive one-day tour of island sights.

It definitely does help to have a company devoted to just archaeology on Orkney. This is where **Orkney Archaeology Tours** (tel. 01856/721450, www.orkneyarchaeology-tours.co.uk, half-day tours for up to four people £145) come in handy. Professional archaeologists run the tours here, and if you make reservations it will be exclusively your party on the tour.

ENTERTAINMENT

It's worth checking out some live music while you're in town; several places can oblige, although the selection of decent places to go out is limited. Buy a copy of the *Orkney Today* newspaper to find out what's on.

Bars and Nightclubs

The **Albert Hotel** (Mounthoolie Ln., tel. 01856/876000, 11 A.M.–midnight Sun.–Wed. 11 A.M.–1 A.M. Thurs.–Sat., open for food noon–2 P.M. and 5–9 P.M. daily) had its much-treasured bar, the Bothy, catch fire a few years

tour in the world or that it's one of the oldest and most photogenic distilleries (built in 1798). It's rather the unique, atmospheric, competently conducted tour that makes Highland Park so special. The distillery is one of the few in the world where hand-turned malting is still done on-site. You get tastings of this fine peaty malt, too, and get to see a film about the history of the distillery. Another special part of the experience is the way Highland Park whisky seems to embody the heart and the spirit of Orkney life. A visit here should get you in the Orcadian swing of things, especially after a dram or three.

Scapa Beach

This sandy, seaweed-covered beach makes for a good bracing walk from Kirkwall. It's a favorite with the locals, who even on days that feel almost arctic to the visitor will buy ice creams and head here for a swim. Out at sea you can see the marker where the HMS *Royal Oak* was torpedoed during World War II. Head out to the beach past the hospital; the road is on the right. A footpath/cycle path runs most of the way.

ago. The good news is that the Bothy, best bar on Orkney by some distance, has finally reopened. It's just as cozy and relaxing as it ever was but still gets pretty lively at weekends. There are lots of Orkney beers to try.

Fusion Nightclub (Ayre Rd., tel. 01856/ 879489, www.fusionclub.co.uk, 10 P.M.– 2:20 A.M. Fri.–Sat.) isn't a bad spot; it's heaven compared to some of the other dire clubs in the north of Scotland. A lot of big names come here for gigs, often to the Firelounge (open Thursdays). You will almost certainly bump into Kirkwall's entire population of just-turned-18-year-olds, though.

Live Music

Checking out some live music in Kirkwall is a magical experience, especially if you head to the **Reel Coffeehouse and Bar** (3 Castle St., 10 A.M.–4 P.M. Mon.–Sat., Sat. evenings until late), owned by a renowned fiddle-playing sister act. There's an air of the sophisticated city wine bar about this place, but also something unique. Sure, it has an eclectic collection of musical instruments displayed on the walls, big battered armchairs, a cozy feel, and a good wine selection. But what makes this stand out from many other places are the impromptu music events that take place on Saturday evenings. It's a pity it is not open every night of the week, but maybe therein lies the charm. This is quite possibly the best, most intense traditional music experience you can have in Scotland as, one after the other, various musicians begin a mesmerizing jamming session. These Orcadians seem to have no end of musical talents—piano playing, fiddle playing, and singing.

During the day Reel is a funky coffeehouse doing lovingly prepared food (huge slabs of cake) as well as alcohol.

EVENTS

Orkney has a lively cultural program: Kirkwall and live music are usually at the heart of it.

The Ba (www.bagame.com) is a bizarre version of street rugby taking place in Kirkwall on Christmas Day and New Year's Day. Two teams of brawny men are mixed in the battle of

bodies: the Uppies and the Doonies, both trying to get the ball in the opposite direction. It's complete mayhem and good entertainment.

Taking place mainly in Kirkwall and Stromness but in locations across Orkney during May, the **Orkney Folk Festival** (www.orkneyfolkfestival.com) is guaranteed to be one of the most magical festivals of live folk music you will witness anywhere in Scotland.

At the end of June, one of the liveliest events of the Orkney Calendar, the **St. Magnus Festival** (www.stmagnusfestival.com), kicks off with everything from poetry to drama to contemporary music performances.

The **County Show** (www.visitorkney.com/ events) is the culmination of a series of agricultural shows held across Orkney during August. East Mainland and West Mainland as well as a couple of the outer islands have shows.

SHOPPING

Orkney produces some of Scotland's finest crafts and food. A well-established and signposted craft trail takes you around a network of different island craft shops and studios; pick up the craft trail leaflet in the TIC. Key inspirations in designs are the sea and the wealth of prehistoric heritage. Orkney jewelry can now be found in stores across England and Scotland.

Bookstores

M. E. McCarty (54 Junction Rd., tel. 01856/ 870860, at least 9:30 A.M.–5 P.M. Mon.–Sat., closes for lunch) is a great old bookstore whose owner believes the ethos of a good bookshop is quality and uniqueness, two attributes that certainly come across here. It's very easy to engage the owner in an illuminating conversation about one obscure title or another. **The Orcadian** (Albert St., tel. 01856/878888, www.orcadian.co.uk, open daily) is Orkney's main new bookshop and stocks a good selection of new books, including plenty of local interest books and maps.

Food

For monster-size slabs and off-cuts of Orkney cheese, head to the factory shop at **Orkney**

Cheese (Crowness Rd., tel. 01856/872824, www.orkneycheese.com, 8:30 A.M.–4 P.M. Mon.–Fri.).

On the drinks front, **John Scott & Miller** (15–19 Bridge St., tel. 01856/873146, www.jsmorkney.co.uk) is one of Scotland's more eclectic whisky shops, with some weird and wonderful special edition bottles.

Jewelry, Crafts, and Photography

Kirkwall's best craft shop is **The Longship** (7–15 Broad St., tel. 01856/888790), home of renowned Ola Gorie jewelry. The young, enthusiastic owner at **Orkney Hand-Crafted Furniture** (New Scapa Rd., tel. 01856/872998, www.orkneyhandcraftedfurniture.co.uk) makes great Orkney chairs, traditional hooded seats to keep out the cold and wet in leaky old croft houses.

If you have photographic problems or requests, head to **Orkney Photographic** (20 Bridge St., tel. 01856/873574, www.orkneyphotographic.co.uk).

SPORTS AND RECREATION
Cycling

Cycling on Orkney is nearly always a battle against the wind, even in the height of summer. The Kirkwall-Stromness road can get very busy, with Stromness being the best bet for bike hire.

Fishing

Many anglers think Orkney is the best place to go fishing in Scotland. The best lochs are the **Loch of Stenness** and the **Loch of Harray;** check www.orkneytroutfishing.co.uk or ask at Kirkwall TIC for comprehensive information.

Fitness Center

A state-of-the-art leisure center, **Pickaquoy Centre** (Pickaquoy Rd., tel. 01856/879900, open daily until at least 10 P.M.) is good for a workout if it proves too wet or windy to be doing outdoor pursuits. There's no swimming pool, though. You'll find a gym, sauna, badminton courts, and other facilities, including a half-decent café.

ACCOMMODATIONS

Staying on Orkney generally is quite cheap. Kirkwall has a good spread of accommodation options; out in the sticks you cannot afford to be so picky.

Under £25

Pickaquoy Camping and Caravan Park (Pickaquoy Centre, tel. 01856/879900, Apr.–Oct., tents £4.40–7.90) is a grassy site, hardly in the most spectacular location, but with decent facilities, including good showers. A new utility block opened in 2008. There's 30 electric hookups and 80 pitches altogether.

The 10-bed **Peedie Hostel** (Ayre Houses, tel. 01856/875477, dorms £10) really is peedie (little). Pine bunks are spread through three rooms. There's none of the sterility you get in some of the larger hostels, and the intimacy of the place means you're bound to get chatting to someone. There's a lounge where you can watch TV. A great thing about this place for budget travelers is that it is open year-round.

£25-50

The **⬛ Pomona** (9 Albert St., tel. 01856/872325, from £40 d) is all about friendly, genuine Orkney hospitality. Right in the center of Kirkwall, down a side street above the café of the same name, it's a four-room bed-and-breakfast with an informal feel. Wallpapered rooms are quite traditionally decked out but have very good en suite facilities, color TVs, and bird's-eye views of the ebb and flow of Kirkwall life. You can also get free use of a washing machine. The café downstairs seems to reserve the hugest portions of food for guests' breakfasts; you may have problems moving after one of these.

You can stay at **Berstane House** (Berstane, St. Ola, tel. 01856/876277, www.berstane.co.uk, from £50 d) in the middle of one of Orkney's only woods above Kirkwall and overlooking fields that slope to the sea. Away from the town center hubbub, this Gothic-looking Victorian house and grounds is the former home of Arctic Explorer John Rae. There are three rooms (blue, pink, and green), two of which are en suite but all are large airy affairs. There are wonderful sea views from the breakfast room. A stay here will make you as laid-back as the owner. There's lots of way-off-the-road parking.

Sanderlay Guest House (2 Viewfield Dr., tel. 01856/875587, from £25 s, £40 d) is a modern guesthouse on the outskirts of Kirkwall with great value rooms. The cheapest rooms are the most basic, with shared bathroom; the en suite doubles are marginally more. Rooms are prettily wallpapered, all with TVs and direct-dial telephones. Wireless Internet access is also available. There is a recently redecorated guest lounge with sumptuous armchairs and a library of books to peruse. Sanderlay is on a dead-end road, so it's a quiet place to stay.

£50-100

The **West End Hotel** (Main St., tel. 01856/872368, from £46 s, £74 d) is a former hospital with a warren of comfortable rooms, high above Kirkwall's main shopping street. It's a pretty place with red-framed windows, and the warming rooms, particularly at the front, have a very continental feel with views onto the narrow street outside. All have color TV, telephones, and en suite bathrooms. It's now all undergone yet another refurbishment, and the management's emphasis is on making this a family-friendly place.

The rooms at the **Albert Hotel** (Mounthoolie Ln., tel. 01856/876000, www.alberthotel.co.uk, from £90 s, £100 d) are some of the most luxurious in town. All have a glossy, manicured feel; you sometimes get the feeling you are in a showroom rather than a hotel. The deluxe double has a sectioned-off lounge area. All 18 double rooms are en suite; then there are the little extras like potted plants and flat-screen TVs. The large, popular stone-built hotel has two of Kirkwall's finest bar/restaurants.

The handsome Victorian **C Kirkwall Hotel** (tel. 01856/872232, www.kirkwall-hotel.co.uk, £40-80 s, £60-140 d) is always going to win the prize for the grandest place to stay in town, and should be where you head

FINE ISLAND CUISINE

Sampling Orkney's distinctive cuisine is an essential part of any trip to the islands. A combination of good marketing, fertile land, and producers committed to quality and healthy living have resulted in several sought-after culinary delights. On the island of North Ronaldsay, the **seaweed-eating sheep** that inhabit the rocky coast have their own distinctively flavored meat. **Orkney beef** is more meat as you've never tasted it before: It's got a fuller, more delicate texture than most beef, and even the fast-food joints serve it! You'll often hear Orcadians rating the quality of their meal out based on how many pieces of **Grimbister deep-fried cheese** they've been given. Two to four pieces is about average, but however little or much you try, it's a mouthwatering experience. **Highland Park whisky** and **Orkney Brewery ales** are about as good as alcohol in Scotland gets. Make sure you try a fruity Red MacGregor ale and one of the potent Skullsplitters. Whatever local delicacy you try, make sure you save room for dessert. **Orkney fudge cheesecake** is a popular, creamy, and irresistible dessert, while **Orkney Ice Cream** is popular across Scotland. The best flavor? Marmalade Cheesecake.

if you want to spoil yourself. It's one of the town's most discernable landmarks. All rooms are good but ask to see several—some are much better than others. The truly gorgeous ones are at the front with incredible harbor views. Standard rooms have to settle for simply good views of the town center. Despite being heavily furnished with rich carpets and comfortable chairs and sofas, a refurbishment has ensured rooms all look clean and sparkling with white coats of paint. You can eat very well here, too; the big challenge during your stay will be whether you can find anywhere better.

FOOD

Cafés and tearooms dominate the eating scene and are an important introduction to the Orcadian way of life (Orcadians like a piece of cake and a gossip). This is balanced by a couple of top-quality restaurants specializing in Scottish cuisine and Kirkwall's very own little pocket of international cuisine.

Cafés, Tearooms, and Snacks

The **Pomona Café** (9 Albert St., tel. 01856/872325, 7 A.M.–5:30 P.M. daily) is where you should go if, at any point during your stay, you feel deprived of a proper, gut-busting Scottish breakfast. You can partake of a cup of tea and a fry-up piled high with goodies at this joint, which will more than compensate for every inadequate breakfast you have had, ever. The customers here are as traditional as the place itself—you can catch up on all the local gossip. Anyone used to big coffee shop chains should be prepared to be stared at. If you don't want a big breakfast, try one of the rather good fancies (cakes). Meals are £2–6.

The high-quality, Fair Trade **(Trenabies** (16 Albert St., tel. 01856/874336, 8 A.M.–6 P.M. Mon.–Thurs. and Sat., 8 A.M.–9 P.M. Fri., noon–5 P.M. Sun.) is a real dose of city sophistication without any of the pretentiousness. Well, OK, with maybe a bit of the pretentiousness, but not much. For people-watching, try to bag one of the tables at the front of this café; otherwise, head for a booth or a comfy sofa at the back. A fair selection of townsfolk pass through here during the day—an indication of the delicious tucker on offer. The coffees, teas, and cakes are first-class; packets of the coffees and teas are for sale if you like what you drink. There's also plenty of vegetarian food, including appetizing salads and Orkney's best paninis. Snacks and meals are £3.50–6.

The **Willows Coffee Shop** (Wellpark Garden Centre, tel. 01856/874203, 10 A.M.–4 P.M. Mon.–Sat. Jan., 10 A.M.–4 P.M. Mon.–Sat., 11 A.M.–4 P.M. Sun. Feb.–Dec.) is in the middle of the town garden center. You can enjoy good coffee, bagels, wraps, and Kirkwall's finest cakes (£1.50–4). It's a slightly bizarre setting surrounded by bird boxes and fertilizer bags but well worth it.

The **Peppermill** (21 Albert St., tel. 01856/878878, 9 A.M.–6 P.M. Mon.–Sat., 11:30 A.M.–4:30 P.M. Sun.) deli works hard to produce quality takeaway goods, including the most gourmet selection of sandwich fillings in town and very good coffee.

Seafood/Scottish

Happy Haddock (69 Junction Rd., tel. 01856/872533, noon–2 P.M. Mon.–Sat. and 4:30–8 P.M. daily) does the best fish supper in Kirkwall. A big piece of fresh battered fish, mammoth chip portions, and a drink will set you back £5. You can also get other delights like battered sausages for £1–5.

The Foveran (St. Ola, tel. 01856/872389, www.foveranhotel.co.uk, 6:30–8:30 P.M. Fri.–Sat. and other evenings during summer) is thought by many to do the best food on Orkney. This hotel-restaurant just outside Kirkwall has great views of Scapa Flow as you feast on such delights as organic salmon and locally caught scallops. There is a lounge to relax in beforehand and after. The restaurant is off the A964 Orphir road three miles southwest of Kirkwall. Opening hours are dependent on the number of guests staying at the hotel out of season (i.e., no guests equals a closed restaurant). Booking beforehand is strongly advised.

(The Kirkwall Hotel (Harbour St., tel. 01856/872232, www.kirkwallhotel.com, food served daily until 9 P.M.) is a popular place to go in the town center—a combination of great views and great cuisine. The restaurant with its plush carpets and crisp tablecloths is very spacious; you could kick-start an evening out with a dram or a glass of wine in the equally spacious Tudor Lounge beforehand. Then choose from a menu including hand-dived Scapa scallops or Orkney lamb as you overlook the harbor. Round off the meal with a piece of Orkney fudge cheesecake. Starters are £4–6, mains £8–18.

sheep, near Kirkwall

Asian

Dil Se (7 Bridge St., tel. 01856/875242, www.dilserestaurant.co.uk, 4–11 P.M. daily) with its bright decor and fabric patterns on the walls is truly one of the finest restaurants in town. A meal here can last hours thanks to the huge portions. Meals are graded according to their spiciness, and just as well: If you've been eating Scottish food for a while it might be a shock to be taste buds! Expect to pay £9–13 for main courses inclusive of sundries.

American

Cheap, cheerful **Busters Diner** (1 Mounthoolie Pl., tel. 01856/876717, noon–2 P.M. and 4:30–9:30 P.M. Mon.–Thurs., noon–2 P.M. and 4:30 P.M.–midnight Fri., noon–midnight Sat., 4:30–9 P.M. Sun.) is as close to the Wild West as Kirkwall gets. You have to enter the restaurant through swinging double doors and get to choose from classic American burgers, big thick milk shakes, gooey pizzas, and even a smattering of Mexican food. Serving such a range of scrumptious carbohydrates means

Busters is popular with young families and teenagers too young to get into the pubs. Meals are £5–10.

INFORMATION AND SERVICES
Tourist Information

Kirkwall Travel Centre (West Castle St., tel. 01856/872856, 8:30 A.M.–8 P.M. daily June–Aug., 9 A.M.–5 P.M. Mon.–Fri., 10 A.M.–4 P.M. Sat. Sept.–May) is a very helpful center for all information on Orkney. There's a good selection of books, maps, and leaflets on different attractions.

Banks

There are many banks with cash machines in Kirkwall. You will find them spread along Broad Street and Albert Street.

Communications

Orkney Library and Archives (Junction Rd., tel. 01856/873166, 9 A.M.–8 P.M. Mon.–Thurs., 9 A.M.–6 P.M. Fri., 9 A.M.–5 P.M. Sat.) is a hugely impressive new building offering free Internet access for up to one hour.

PEAT RIGHTS

All countries have their fair share of obscure laws that have somehow wriggled past the scrutinizing eyes of time to remain on the books, however preposterous they might be. Scotland has a number of such laws, a lot of which are recognized but seldom enforced. One law involves the cutting of peat, decayed vegetable matter that forms a rich, dark, crumbly soil particularly on heathery moor. Peat has been historically at the heart of Scottish goings-on: forming a great deal of its scenery, giving a unique flavor to its whisky, and turning drinking water brown. On Orkney, peat was imperative: There were never many trees, and peat was the fuel that made the fires families' lives revolved around. The right to cut peat probably dates back to medieval times, along with such rights as salmon-netting. The right was part of a very necessary bartering system – fuel in return for services to the landlord, for example. In this modern age of electricity and oil heating, where many houses don't even have open fires, such laws seem a little bizarre. But in peat-rich places like Orkney, not only are these traditional rights recognized, they are also regularly exercised and occasionally enforced. Arguments and family feuds have developed over the years in Orkney through people cutting peat from someone else's supply. Peat-cutting rights are handed down from one crofting generation to the next – they don't come automatically, even to island residents. If you are visiting Orkney and wondering whether you are entitled to cut a bit of peat for your holiday home fire, you are almost certainly not; you might literally be digging up history and a whole lot of trouble.

Kirkwall post office (tel. 0845/722 3344) is at 15 Junction Road.

Medical Services

Balfour Hospital (Old Scapa Rd., tel. 01856/888800) has an outpatient department, although those requiring specialist treatment will have to head over to a hospital on the Scottish mainland (Aberdeen is easiest to access from Orkney).

Laundry

Launderama (47 Albert St., tel. 01856/872982, 8:30 A.M.–5:30 P.M. Mon.–Fri., 9 A.M.–5 P.M. Sat.) is the most central launderette. You can do a wash and dry for £5–7.

GETTING THERE AND AROUND

Kirkwall Airport (tel. 01856/886210) is east of the town on Tankerness. It's a modern little place with an information deck and café. Buses connect Kirkwall Airport with the town center every half hour.

The main bus station is undergoing a transformation into the **Kirkwall Travel Centre** (West Castle St., tel. 01856/872856), where the new tourist information is now located. Island buses also now leave from the Travel Centre. Bus connections are not bad (there are hourly buses to Stromness) but will not run near many of the out-of-the-way attractions.

Bob's Taxis (58 Junction Rd., tel. 01856/876543, www.bobstaxis.com) has normal and seven-seater taxis.

EAST MAINLAND

The mainland east of Kirkwall gets far fewer visitors than most areas of Orkney. The rolling grassy landscape gives way to some great dunes and Mainland's best sandy beaches at places like Newark Bay. It also rears up suddenly to stomach-lurchingly dramatic cliffs at the Gloup and Mull Head. It's a quiet area of Orkney full of the chatter of seabirds and has some of the best walking around.

Mine Howe

Mine Howe (Tankerness, tel. 01856/861234, 11 A.M.–3 P.M. Wed. and Sun. May, 11 A.M.–5 P.M.

daily June–Aug., 11 A.M.–4 P.M. early–mid-Sept., 11 A.M.–2 P.M. Wed. and Sun. late Sept., £2.50) is the lovable little sister to Maes Howe. Its lack of commercialization is half its charm. It's essentially an Iron Age chamber built deep underground into the rock, made all the more an adventure by the fact that you can only enter one or two at a time because of the narrow entrance. Going down into the dark, damp chamber is not for the claustrophobic or faint-hearted, although it's not so often on Orkney that you have an archaeological site almost completely to yourself. There are guided tours of the continuing excavations and an exhibition on the discovery of Mine Howe.

The Gloup and Vicinity

If you like impressive rock formations, you'll love the coast on the eastern edge of the Orkney. Follow the road as far as it goes to a car park. A muddy path leads to the cliff edge, where, out of nowhere a stupendous collapsed sea cave appears. This is **The Gloup.** A path along the springy clifftop grass continues to the **Brough of Deerness,** a steep hill almost cut off by the sea on either side. A path climbs to an Iron Age fortification at the top. Allow two hours to get to the Brough of Deerness and back.

Getting There and Away

Buses run via Tankerness as far as Deerness Village from Kirkwall five times per day.

The South Isles

The islands of Lamb Holm, Glimps Holm, Burray, and South Ronaldsay lie in a long line south of the Orkney mainland, connected to it via the dramatic Churchill Barriers. The barriers were constructed for defensive purposes during World War II but were not completed until just before the war ended. More important than their wartime use has proven to be the vital life link to the mainland they provided the islands. This halted depopulation and made these fertile, low-lying, treeless islands the thriving places they are today. Burray village and St. Margaret's Hope are two of Orkney's liveliest, prettiest villages, and throughout the isles there are some great museums and historic sites. The numerous boats, both German and English, that sunk in Scapa Flow despite the barriers are now dark mysterious wrecks beneath the water that you can dive to explore. It's not all World War II heritage that's on offer: There are unique ancient archaeological sites and peaceful coastal walking, too, not to mention some of Orkney's best pubs and restaurants.

LAMB HOLM AND BURRAY

On tiny Lamb Holm is one of Orkney's major attractions: The Italian Chapel, surely the most beautiful building in Britain to come out of World War II. It's a magical introduction to the friendly island of Burray, its slightly larger neighbor, which has a riveting museum and a good pub. Just off the coast you can dive to some of the shipwrecks you can see sticking up out of the shallow water: many say Britain's most interesting diving is around here (see *Sights and Activities* in *Stromness* section for details).

◖ The Italian Chapel

The hauntingly beautiful chapel (Lamb Holm, 9 A.M.–10 P.M. daily Apr.–Sept. 9 A.M.–4:30 P.M. daily Oct.–Mar., free) stands isolated on tiny Lamb Holm, originally no more than a Nissen hut (tunnel-shaped corrugated steel structure) where Italian prisoners of war were housed while they were working on building the Churchill Barriers. The prisoners designed and built the chapel themselves during their captivity. The exquisitely painted interior is a true mark of genius: Paintwork looks like three-dimensional engraving. The overall effect is one of simple beauty—a testament to what men can do with basic materials while working as a team, even in captivity.

Orkney Fossil and Vintage Centre

This superb collection of fossils (tel. 01856/731255, 10 A.M.–6 P.M. daily Apr.–Sept., £3.50) lies in restored farm buildings on Burray. It includes specimens up to 360 million years old and a dark room where you can see minerals that have an eerie fluorescent glow in darkness. Upstairs there is an archive room and displays on traditional agricultural and domestic life in Orkney. There is a very good shop and a pleasant café with cheap, tasty snacks.

Accommodations and Food

Rooms at the **Sands Hotel** (Burray, tel. 01856/731298, from £55 s, £80 d, food served noon–2 P.M. and 6–9 P.M. daily) by the pier in Burray Village look out over the sea and the Churchill Barriers. The rooms are quite snazzy—a cross between traditional and modern, but all very cozy with en suite bathrooms, TV, and telephones. Six rooms and two suites are available. The hotel has one of the best bar/restaurants in Orkney, light with great waterside views. Mains are £9–17; the Fisherman's Catch for £14.50 changes daily and is very tasty. The bar here has a pool table, not a bad place to knock back Orkney ales as you recuperate after a day's excursions.

Getting There and Away

St. Margaret's Hope **buses** stop on Lamb's Holm and Burray (six per day). Note that there is nothing on Lamb's Holm but the Italian Chapel, and it's a long wait for the next bus. You can, however, walk back across the Churchill Barrier into St. Mary's Holm Village, where the St. Margaret's Hope buses also stop.

SOUTH RONALDSAY

Orkney's most beautiful village, St. Margaret's Hope, is where most of the action goes on in South Ronaldsay—it's squeezed-together 18th-century houses spread around a harbor cluttered with fishing nets and boats moored alongside harborfront cottages. The village has a wealth of eating and drinking places for its size, including Orkney's best seafood restaurant.

Farther south is the unusual attraction of the Tomb of the Eagles, a visitors center with a 5,000-year-old chambered cairn in which some bizarre artifacts have been discovered.

St. Margaret's Hope

Wandering the streets, shoreline, and surrounding countryside of this village is an attraction in itself. In the village center is the **Smiddy Museum** (11:30 A.M.–1:30 P.M. and 2–4 P.M. Mon.–Fri., noon–4 P.M. Sat.–Sun. June–Aug., 1:30–3:30 P.M. Mon.–Fri., 2–4 P.M. Sat.–Sun. May and Sept., 2–4 P.M. Sun. Oct.) with an exhibition on the annual **Boy's Ploughing Match,** one of the more bizarre agricultural events in Scotland on the nearby **Sands o' Wright.** You can walk to a World War II observation tower at **Hoxa Head** from St. Margaret's Hope. Take the lane up past Bellevue Guest House and follow it down to a beach, then up a track to the road by the Sands o' Wright. Bear right here to Hoxa.

Orkney Marine Life Aquarium

You can see a variety of Orkney sealife at this fun center (by South Cara, off A961 east of St. Margaret's Hope, tel. 01856/831700, www.orkneymarinelife.co.uk, 10 A.M.–6 P.M. daily Apr.–Oct., £5.50 adult, £4 child), including phenomenally sized lobsters and other shellfish molded by the waves of the Pentland Firth into their own strange shapes and sizes. Admission includes an optional guided tour.

Tomb of the Eagles

Between 1957 and 1958, a local farmer, Ronnie Simison, discovered his farmland was riddled with Bronze Age sites of international importance. He and his family still own and run the site (tel. 01856/831339, 10 A.M.–noon daily Mar., 9:30 A.M.–5:30 P.M. daily Apr.–Oct., £5.50 adults, £4.50 seniors, £3 children) 50 years on and give guided tours with a passion that makes this rather a special place to visit. There's a visitors center and a walk out to the grassy coastline where the two main archaeological sites are. First up is Orkney's only fully excavated Bronze Age house, where Ronnie himself

© LUKE WATERSON

St. Margaret's Hope

fills you in on his thoughts on Bronze Age life. The second site is a 5,000-year-old chambered cairn on the clifftops. What makes this site fascinating is what was found inside: the remains of over 300 skeletons and 70 white sea-eagle talons. The finds raise a number of interesting questions addressed in the visitors center by the enthusiastic staff. Some people find the initial introduction in the visitors center (a personalized group talk on Neolithic Orkney with a bit of a spiritual slant) a little off-putting.

Accommodations and Food

It is possible to pitch a tent/small caravan on a grassy site at the **Sands o' Wright Camping and Caravan Site** (open year-round, free) at the northern end of the wild Sands o' Wright beach. Shelter is minimal, but the bonus is that the views over Scapa Flow and Hoy from here are second to none. The facilities, however, are accordingly basic: just the washrooms in the car park toilets 50 meters down the road.

St. Margaret's Hope Backpackers and Coach House Cafe (Back Rd., tel. 01856/831225 or 01856/831641, beds £12 pp) is an attractive stone-built cottage in the heart of the village right by the pub. Rooms consist of a dorm, two doubles, and a single: you couldn't ask for cozier, more ideally situated accommodation for the price. There is a well-appointed kitchen and a TV lounge. A shop is also nearby. In summer the courtyard outside is filled with tables from the neighboring café (food available until 8 P.M. May–Sept.), a great place to relax in the sun with a coffee, cake, or famed crabmeat sandwich.

Dating from the 1700s, **Bankburn House** (St. Margaret's Hope, tel. 01856/831310, www.bankburnhouse.co.uk, £30 s, £60 d) is a fabulous guesthouse that overlooks St. Margaret's Hope and the bay. The rooms are done in cool whites and attract a lot of sun; you can gaze down over the grassy stone-walled fields and feel properly in rural bliss. Rooms have TV/DVD players, and Internet access is available. The house is just south of town, off the A961.

The Galley Inn (Harbour, St. Margaret's Hope, tel. 01856/831526, £30 s, £60 d, open for lunch and dinner) is a former village store that is, first and foremost, a bright, cozy pub serving

SCAPA FLOW AND THE WORLD WARS

Scapa Flow ranks among the largest natural harbors in the world. Hoy forms its eastern side, the south coast of Orkney's mainland its northern side, and the southern isles of Burray and South Ronaldsay its eastern side. With very few gaps in between, sole access was from the south, and the harbor was the ideal place to be a haven for British ships during wartime. As Norwegian King Hakon's ships had before them, the British Grand Fleet stationed itself in Scapa Flow. After a German U-Boat breached defenses to gain access to the harbor early in World War I, block ships were sunk and submarine nets set up at all vulnerable points.

After the Armistice, 74 German ships were ordered into Scapa Flow as part of the settlement. For the few months they were there, the ships even proved a popular tourist attraction. To prevent further British gains, the commander of the German fleet in Scapa Flow decided to scuttle the fleet while the majority of British Scapa Flow forces were out of the harbor on exercises. It was a dramatic sight: an entire fleet of German boats, suddenly wrecked and floating in bits and pieces in the water. Nine German sailors were killed by British gunfire as they attempted to scuttle their ship.

However, the Germans would later retake the upper hand at Scapa Flow. Between the two World Wars, the British failed to strengthen Scapa Flow's defenses. When it came to World War II, German U-Boats were able to take advantage of high tide and stole around the block ships to torpedo the battleship HMS *Royal Oak*, costing 833 of the 1400-member crew their lives. Prime Minister Winston Churchill instigated a step-up in harbor security. Further block ships were sunk and batteries built on headlands around the harbor. This did not satisfy Churchill, and in 1942 he gave the order for a series of barriers to be built, connecting the southern isles. Somewhat reluctant Italian prisoners-of-war were recruited for the work, and the barriers were constructed over three years. Ironically, the only defense that guaranteed to keep out invading ships was not finished until the war was almost over.

ORKNEY ISLANDS

hearty meals (£5–9) like Thai curry (£7.95) and Orkney sirloin steak in haggis and whisky sauce. This is the place to try some local ale, such as the delicious Red MacGregor. Buffeted by the waves and recently refurbished after the waves got too high in a storm and flooded the place, it's also a bed-and-breakfast with three clean en suite rooms (two doubles, one single). Rooms yield bird's-eye views over the harbor, and you can open your window and smell the sea salt. Breakfast is served in the restaurant.

The Creel Restaurant with Rooms (Front Rd., St. Margaret's Hope, tel. 01856/831311, www.thecreel.co.uk, rooms £60 s, £90 d, food served 7–8:45 P.M. May–Oct.) has been a dependable name in the Orkney dining scene since the 1980s. It's *the* place on Orkney to feast on seafood while watching the summer sun linger over the harbor. You won't have heard of half the marine offerings on the menu, but just ask—you'll probably get a description of how and where they were caught as well. You can also taste North Ronaldsay lamb. It's worth stretching your wallet that bit further to try mains, which are around £20. Not established as long as the restaurant but almost as promising are the rooms on offer: white-walled, pine-furnished places where you can ogle the harbor and Scapa Flow views a little bit more. Start the next morning off with a spot of homemade muesli followed by haddock, kippers, or smoked salmon.

Getting There and Away

Bus 10 runs six times daily between Kirkwall and St. Margaret's Hope. Connections to Burwick on the A961 run regularly (to meet the ferries) when the Burwick–John o' Groats ferry is running May–September. At other times of the year, it's best to venture beyond St. Margaret's Hope only if you have your own transport.

West Mainland and Hoy

This fertile area makes up the bulk of Orkney's mainland, falling away in the south to the glimmering Hoy Sound. Rearing up out of Hoy Sound is mountainous Hoy itself, with a totally different feel from the rest of the Orkney Islands. A jewel among island ferry ports, photogenic Stromness sits below green hills with a superb location overlooking Hoy. It's the starting point for a number of forays into this archaeologically rich region. All Orkney's key historic sites are here: Whether it's rambling around ruins, fishing, great beaches, dramatic cliff walks, or diving to the wrecks in Orkney's deeps that tickles your fancy, this is where you should head.

◖ STROMNESS

The most idyllic approach to Orkney is by ferry to this timeless gray fishing port, backed by green hills and fronted by its old-world harbor of colorful fishing craft. Stromness is the most charming settlement in the Scottish islands. It has a fiercely independent spirit and has made itself a cultural center not just to rival Kirkwall but to hold its own against any town in Scotland. It's the former home of Orkney poet George Mackay Brown and the current home of a museum and Scotland's finest rural art gallery. Add to that some classy places to stay and to eat and you have your ideal Scottish island base.

Sights and Activities

Even if it was in London or Edinburgh, you would want to make time to check out the recently refurbished, excellently presented **Pier Arts Centre** (Victoria St., tel. 01856/850209, www.pierartscentre.com, 10:30 A.M.–5 P.M. Mon.–Sat., noon–4 P.M. Sun. Apr.–Sept., 10:30 A.M.–5 P.M. Mon.–Sat. Oct.–Mar.); it's that good. Transplant it to anywhere in remote northern Scotland and you have a major tourist attraction; transport it to Stromness and you have a major reason to visit Orkney. The main theme of the museum is Margaret

Gardiner's superb collection of 20th-century art, including works by Barbara Hepworth, Ben Nicholson, and Alfred Wallis.

The stretch of coast around Orkney has a great many tales to tell; that maritime history is explored at the quirky and very thorough **Stromness Museum** (52 Alfred St., tel. 01856/850025, 10 A.M.–5 P.M. Mon.–Sat. 10:30 A.M.–12:30 P.M. and 1:30 P.M. 5 P.M. Sun. May–Sept., 10:30 A.M.–5 P.M. Mon.–Sat. Oct.–Apr., £2.50). The displays on the scuttling of the German Fleet in Scapa Flow are fascinating, and there are exhibits on the port's connections with whaling and Arctic exploration. The former house of **George Mackay Brown** is opposite the museum; Orkney's most famous poet lived here for almost 30 years.

Scapa Scuba (tel. 01856/851218, www.scapascuba.co.uk, £70 for half-day first-time divers' course), based in the lifeboat station at Stromness, is Orkney's best dive company. You can dive to the many World War I and World War II wrecks near the Churchill Barriers or do deeper dives to ships like the *Royal Oak*. All levels of experience can have a go. The company also does a number of specialist PADI courses including a wreck-divers' course.

Hire a bike at **Stromness Cycle Hire** (Victoria St, tel. 01856/850750), where mountain bikes are rented out for £10 per day.

Accommodations and Food

This attractive, quiet, neatly set-out **Point of Ness Caravan Site** (tel. 01856/873535, May–Sept., tents £4.40–7.95) by the shore is right at the end of the long main street in Stromness, yielding fantastic views of Hoy and the town below. Yes, it gets windy, but doesn't everywhere? Washing facilities and laundry are available on-site.

◖ **Browns** (45–47 Victoria St., tel. 01856/850661, £11–12 pp) is an appealing little place fronting the main cobbled Stromness shopping street. It's a gem among Orkney's many hostels. Going strong for 30 years, it provides little touches like free tea and coffee, free Internet access, and hot water bottles to make this a budget accommodation experience to remember. Rooms are spread over three floors; single, double, and family rooms are available. It's a very sociably arranged hostel, too, with everyone eating together at one table in the comfy kitchen.

In the quiet, whitewashed **Millers House and Harbourside Guest House** (13 John St., tel. 01856/851969, from £40 s, £50 d) you can enjoy great views from the equally quiet, white rooms and filling breakfasts in a central spot in town. Breakfast is served in the nearby Millers House, the oldest dated house in Stromness, with options including Orkney salmon.

A large stone-built hotel right on the harborfront, the **Stromness Hotel** (tel. 01856/850298, www.stromnesshotel.com, from £40 s, £80 d) is one of Orkney's most imposing buildings. There are 42 en suite rooms at this mammoth place, done in a mix of pinks and peaches with color TVs and telephones. Many rooms look out on the busy harbor or the tranquil garden at the rear. The hotel has something of a reputation for good cooking: You will not be disappointed come breakfast. You can get discounted winter rates.

Julia's Café/Bistro (opposite ferry car park, tel. 01856/850904, 9 A.M.–5 P.M. Mon.–Sat., 10 A.M.–5 P.M. Sun., evening meals from 7 P.M.) is the brightest, most popular café in Stromness, with a mix of indoor and outdoor seating. Whether it's to eat ice cream on a hot afternoon, dine out with great harbor views in the evening, or huddle with coffee or homemade soup in the bleak weather, Julia's is perfect. There is plenty of space and the mix of people means you won't feel awkward coming in alone. Mains like Moroccan couscous or Wiltshire bake with ham, apples, and caramelized onions are £7–8. The café also does a line in healthy vegetarian food (very tasty lasagna).

A pretty, family-run restaurant with an open fire, the **Hamnavoe Restaurant** (33–35 Dundas St., tel. 01856/850606, 7–10 P.M. Tues.–Thurs. and Sun., noon–2 P.M. and 7–10 P.M. Fri.–Sat. mid-May–Sept., 7–10 P.M. Tues.–Sun. Apr.–mid-May and Oct., 7–10 P.M.

Sat.–Sun. Nov.–Mar.) has one of the most special atmospheres of any restaurant on Orkney. Seafood, caught locally, is the main draw. A summertime lobster lunch or prawn tails in garlic butter (a specialty) are just some of the meals to savor. Remember those fishing boats in the harbor? This food came fresh from them. It is £15–18 for three courses.

Getting There and Away

Buses run between Kirkwall Travel Centre and Stromness Ferry Terminal Travel Centre hourly (40 min.). **Northlink Ferries** (tel. 0845/600 0449, www.northlinkferries.co.uk) has three sailings per day on weekdays from Stromness to Scrabster in Caithness on the Scottish mainland (1.5 hrs., £15.50 adult, £46.40 car one-way); there are two sailings on weekends. Two to four buses daily make their way north en route to **Tingwall Ferry Terminal** from Stromness, stopping at Skaill and Birsay.

STENNESS, ORPHIR, AND SOUTH COAST

Between Stromness and Kirkwall is a tract of open farmland and moor dominated by the two snaking silvery lochs of Stenness and Harray, as fine as any in Scotland for fishing. Commanding views of silvery water and open skies stretch for miles from the crests of the low green-brown hills. Today this part of West Mainland is little changed since the first prehistoric peoples started building in the area, clearly fascinated by the same scenes. And, my, how they built: one of Scotland's most photogenic stone circles and the country's best-preserved chambered cairn are just part of the legacy they left behind. Farther south on the coast near Orphir is a museum explaining the *Orkneyinga Saga,* the most valuable surviving document of Norse rule in these isles.

◀ Maes Howe

This huge grass-topped cairn (by Stenness off A965, tel. 01856/761606, 9:30 A.M.–5 P.M. daily Apr.–Sept., 9:30 A.M.–4 P.M. daily Oct.–Mar., £5.20 adults, £2.60 children) is an eye-turner on the Kirkwall-Stromness road more than 5,000 years after it was initially built. This is the best-preserved chambered cairn in northwest Europe, especially good because you have to crawl along a low passageway to get to the internal chamber. It is a site that has held the interest of many peoples throughout history—note the rather boastful runes etched on the stone inside. To explore Maes Howe you have to go as part of a guided tour. This is a blessing in disguise, as you get to listen to the knowledgeable guides contextualizing the history of the monument. The last tour leaves 45 minutes before the site closes.

Stones of Stenness

These lofty stones (open year-round, free) overlooking Harray Loch are the remains of a stone circle constructed around 3000 B.C. Four significant stones remain standing; the story goes that a local farmer got so fed up with Victorian visitors like Sir Walter Scott traipsing across his land to get a good look that he destroyed one stone and flattened another. Try to get here around sunset, when the views across to Hoy are at their most spectacular. An even taller stone known as the Watch Stone stands at the roadside nearby. Explanatory panels offer background historical information. To get to the stones, take the A965 toward Kirkwall from Stromness and turn left on the B9055. The stones are immediately on the right.

Ring of Brodgar

This is one of the most impressive stone circles (open year-round, free) in Britain. Some 36 stones of varying shapes and sizes form a wide circle, stark against the peaty green ground and silvery gray lochs. The stones were probably erected between 2500 B.C. and 2000 B.C. Ring of Brodgar is on the B9055 between lochs of Stenness and Harray.

Orkneyinga Saga Centre and Orphir Round Church

The Orkneyinga Saga Centre (9 A.M.–5 P.M. daily, free) in Orphir explains the context of the famous Viking document of Norse life during the golden years of their empire. Information panels and a video give you a bit of Viking enlightenment before you walk behind the center to Orphir Round Church (open year-round). The remains of the circular church were modeled on the church of the Holy Sepulchre in Jerusalem, where Earl Hakon went on penance after ordering the murder of his cousin Earl Magnus. This is a dramatic spot. You can look out across the graveyard to the sea pounding against the low cliffs.

Houton

At Houton you can do a memorable trip to see some of the scuttled German shipwrecks in Scapa Flow without even getting wet. It's run by **Roving Eye Enterprises** (tel. 01856/811360, www.rovingeye.co.uk); full marks to them for coming up with such an ingenious concept. The MV *Guide* leaves Houton harbor, beginning by showing a video about the scuttling of the German fleet to get people in the mood, and then uses a remote camera to relay images of the deep, both wrecks and sea creatures alike, to passengers while they sit in the cabin. Trips leave daily at 1:20 P.M. from Houton and cost £28.

Accommodations and Food

The **Mill of Eyrland** (Stenness, tel. 01856/ 850136, www.millofeyrland.co.uk, from £30 s, £50 d) is a scenic converted water mill that has three plump-bedded rooms full of antique furniture and rugs. You can look out on the cranking mill works and the mill burn tumbling right on through. The guest lounge contains grinding stones, and the room where food is served has a host of mill-related artifacts. The mill is unique in Orkney in another sense, too: It has a garden, complete with lots of shrubs and foliage.

Gerri's Ice Cream Parlour (Summerdale Stenness, tel. 01856/850668, 10:30 A.M.–7 P.M. Mon.–Fri., 10:30 A.M.–5 P.M. Sat., 11 A.M.– 6 P.M. Sun.) is probably the best place in the world to come and devour Orkney ice cream, with views out over Stenness Loch. The Orkney fudge is a good flavor. If you can finish a Stenness Monster (we're talking a cone with seven scoops of ice cream in it), like some of the bairns (children) around here can, you really do have a sweet tooth.

Beautifully situated **Scorrabrae Inn** (tel. 01856/811262, 6–10 P.M. Mon.–Fri., noon–2 P.M. and 6–10 P.M. Sat., noon–10 P.M. Sun., extended hours during summer) does the best Sunday roast lunch on Orkney; every ingredient down to the cabbage is done delectably. The pub is split into a spacious bar with pool table and dartboard and a sit-down restaurant full of dark wood. You can watch big screen sports and play board games here, too. Meals are on the pricey side and the tasty side at £9–14.

Getting There and Away

Kirkwall–Stromness **buses** will drop you off at Maes Howe/Stones of Stenness. Up to six buses per day run on weekdays between Kirkwall Travel Centre, Orphir, and Houton Ferry Terminal (for Hoy ferries). For the Ring of Brodgar, you'll need to be part of a tour or have your own wheels (bike or car) to get there.

THE WEST COAST AND INLAND

Grassy cliffs soar and dip between sandy bays and exposed headlands along this scenic stretch of the mainland's coastline; the spectacular shapes they have eroded into at places like Yesnaby would be enough of a reason to linger in this area. But there is also the little matter of Scotland's most important Neolithic site at Skara Brae, the best-preserved prehistoric village in northern Europe. Inland, the damp-looking, gray-green farmland around Dounby provides good access to fishing in the Loch of Harray.

C Skara Brae

Revealed in 1850 when a storm whipped up the sand dunes by Skaill Bay, Skara Brae (Skaill, tel. 01856/841815, 9:30 A.M.–5:30 P.M. daily Apr.–Sept., 9:30 A.M.–4:30 P.M. daily Oct.–Mar., £6.50 adults, £3.25 children, includes Skaill House) is one of the most wonderfully preserved prehistoric villages in Europe. Not only were the 5,000-year-old circular stone houses of this ancient farming community revealed, but uniquely, so were a lot of domestic items, down to the beds inhabitants slept in and the boxes they used for storage. The visitor

experience kicks off in the state-of-the-art visitors center with a short film about Skara Brae and displays of the different artifacts found. Then you walk down on to the windswept site itself. These dwellings were cut into the ground for protection from the weather. Skara Brae has also allowed historians multiple insights into the practicalities of people's lives during this time—how they lit their fires and what their diet would have been—a spellbinding cross-section of life over 3,000 years ago. The visitors center has a shop and restaurant. Try to come either early or late to avoid the crowds. You can get free views of Skara Brae from Skaill Bay.

Skaill House

This 17th-century house (Skaill, tel. 01856/841501, www.skaillhouse.com, 9:30 A.M.–6:30 P.M. daily Apr.–Sept.) has been the traditional residence of Orkney's lairds, including the laird who discovered Skara Brae. It's a charming, creaky old place; if you're in one of the rooms by yourself you will start believing the several ghost stories attached to the house. The house passed to Bishop Graham following the execution of the villainous Earl Patrick Stewart; a bed in an upstairs room bears the inscription Graham me Fieri Fecit—Bishop Graham had me made. You can also see a dinner service belonging to Captain Cook in the dining room. You may catch a glance of the cheery current laird, who is frequently in and around the house. There are cracking views of Skara Brae and the bay of Skaill from the upstairs rooms. The house has a shop full of Orkney souvenirs, which you pass through to leave. Admission is included in the Skara Brae ticket.

Yesnaby Cliffs

You can do a great walk along the cliffs from Skara Brae to Yesnaby. There is a car park at Yesnaby surrounded by information boards and derelict World War II buildings. It's pretty here but only really spectacular farther on at Yesnaby castle sea stack, a huge wedge of rock plastered in seabirds, twisting out of the sea like a corkscrew. It's a six-mile walk along to

© LUKE WATERSON

Skara Brae, by Skaill, the oldest preserved village in northwest Europe

Stromness from here. Road access to Yesnaby is off the B9056 south of Skaill.

Food

You can enjoy magnificent vistas over the Bay of Skaill while you munch the home-cooked food at **Appies Tearoom** (Lower Appiehouse, Sandwick, tel. 01856/841562, 11 A.M.–7 P.M. daily Apr.–Sept.). There is a balcony for fine weather snacking on Orkney oatcakes and cheese (£2.50) and also owner Pam Farmer's pictures to distract the eye.

The large, light, quite sophisticated **Skara Brae Visitor Centre Restaurant** (tel. 01856/ 841815, 9:30 A.M.–5:30 P.M. daily Apr.–Sept., 9:30 A.M.–4:30 P.M. daily Oct.–Mar.) is part of the reason Skara Brae is a five-star tourist attraction. Queue up at the counter to place your order. You can get a good coffee and cake here, and wholesome meals cost £4–8.

BIRSAY AND THE NORTH

The countryside gets progressively hillier, bleaker, and more windswept as you near Birsay at the northern edge of the mainland. It's even considered far enough from Kirkwall for some Orkney urbanites to have holiday homes up here. Shaped around the guttural ruin of former Orkney Earl Robert Stewart's palace, Birsay is the ancient capital of Orkney with 1,000 years worth of history scattered around it. The picturesque village of Evie, farther around the coast to the east, has some good places to stay.

Sights

The tidal island of the **Brough of Birsay** (accessible only at low tide, tel. 01856/721205 or 01856/841815 for tide times, mid-June–Sept. when tides allow, £3 adults, 1.50 children in season, free at other times) was once the ancient capital of Orkney. Earl Thorfinn the Mighty (1014–1065) is said to have had his stronghold here. It would certainly have made an imposing and easily defendable location: Access is at low tide along a boulder-strewn beach to the steep island itself. However, it is as romantic as it is practical to think of the ruins on the Brough in this way—no one really knows what to make of them. It's a bracing, windy walk up to the lighthouse on the clifftop.

Accommodations and Food

Eviedale Campsite (Evie, tel. 01856/751270, tents from £4.50) is one of the best campsites on the Orkney mainland. It's also one of the smallest—there's very little room for caravans. Facilities are basic but it's very clean and well kept. With lots of flowers and trees (by Orkney standards!) and picnic tables this is a lush, grassy place to pitch a tent.

Woodwick House (Evie, tel. 01856/751330, www.woodwickhouse.co.uk, £68–100 d) is a touch of glorious middle England in Evie, the oasis in Orkney's bleak north. Set in bluebell-coated woods with a burn running through en route to its own private bay, this country house is every inch the romantic getaway. Rooms are comfortable and traditional, meals are candle-lit, open fires blaze in the sitting room, and there is even a performance room upstairs hosting various events throughout the year. Don't chance its "open year-round" claim, though: Book this place in advance and give an approximate arrival time. This place is not quite as superb as a single—you'll pay the full double price. Three-course evening meals cost £24.

The **Barony Hotel** (Birsay, tel. 01856/721327, www.baronyhotel.com, Apr.–Sept., from £30 s, £60 d) is an old fishing hotel done up very traditionally. There are nine rooms here, mostly en suite and of varying qualities. Some rooms are large, decorated in cooling whites, and have views over Boardhouse Loch. It's a slightly different environment from most Orkney hotels, very rural and nothing fancy, but it has boats you can take out on the loch and a big, often gloomy bar/restaurant with a number of tables that suggests it is very popular. When you're in the bar of an evening looking out over the loch and getting ready to tuck into some Orkney beef, you will feel this to be an idyllic getaway.

Getting There and Away

Buses 6, 7, or 8 make varying journeys from Kirkwall via Finnstown to the north of the mainland. Around seven buses daily on weekdays (four on Sat.) get as far as Evie; two to three on weekdays go to Birsay, some with a change at Evie. A Kirkwall–Birsay jaunt takes 55 minutes.

HOY

Hoy is, as any Orcadian will tell you, different. For one thing, it's hilly. The rearing brown-green summit of Ward Hill is only 1,570 feet but dominates the Orkney skyline. Driving, cycling, or walking the steep winding hills and roads feels like breaking free after the mainland's neatly fenced farmland. The heather-clad moors culminating in plummeting cliffs offer Orkney's most adventurous and spectacular walking. The main attraction is the spectacular rock stack known as the Old Man of Hoy just off the west coast, but mainly Hoy is designed for hiking and relaxing; it's full of picnicking places and sandy bays to explore.

◖ Rackwick and the Old Man of Hoy

Rackwick is a gorgeous spot: a long drive down a tiny lane cutting between steep grassy ridges.

© LUKE WATERSON

Old Man of Hoy, from the cliffs above Rackwick

It's a tiny crafting community lying just above the wide, sandy Rackwick Bay. Being the only access point to Hoy's wild west coast, there's a real sense of isolation here. Plenty of great picnicking spots lie along the road down to Rackwick from Moaness. About halfway along on the left a boardwalk leads to **The Dwarfie Stane** (year-round, free), Britain's only rock-cut tomb. It's an immense hollowed-out block of red sandstone that Sir Walter Scott maintained was the home of a legendary Norse dwarf. Rackwick car park is the starting-out point for the walk to the **Old Man of Hoy,** a precarious-looking 137-meter red sandstone rock stack. This is Orkney's most beautiful walk, with dramatic clifftop scenery. Note that it can get very windy and the path goes close to the cliff edge. It's three hours there and back to the clifftop viewpoint. You can, if you are an experienced climber, tackle the rock stack itself—20 to 50 people per year manage the tricky, giddying ascent. If you don't have your own wheels, or if you fancy a longer walk, you can do the hilly walk to Rackwick cross-country from Moanness; allow seven to eight hours there and back.

Lyness

If you are interested in the naval history of Scapa Flow, it is well worth stopping by the **Scapa Flow Visitor Centre** (Lyness, tel. 01856/791300, 9 A.M.–4:30 P.M. Mon.–Fri., 10:30 A.M.–4 P.M. Sat.–Sun. mid-May–Sept., 9 A.M.–4:30 P.M. Mon.–Fri. Oct.–mid-May). Many troops were stationed on Hoy during World War II, outnumbering the local population by many times. You can see the remains of buildings everywhere on the island—Martello towers and billets. The center has lots of military artifacts on display, including many from the HMS *Hampshire* which exploded in a mine off Orkney's coast. The moving Lyness Naval Cemetery is also nearby.

Accommodations and Food

Rackwick Youth Hostel (Rack Wick, tel. 01856/873535 or 0870/155 3255, dorms £9.45) is basic, but you won't get a more beautiful

setting for a place to stay on either Hoy or Orkney. This place is mainly used by walkers, and with good reason: There's fantastic hiking in the surrounding hills. There are eight beds in two dormitories; pre-booking is strongly advised and you should bring your own sleeping bag. A modern, newly refurbished building, the **Hoy Centre** (Hoy Village, tel. 01856/876327, beds £12) may lack the spectacular location of Rackwick hostel, but it does have better facilities. You can get en suite rooms here. It's best to pre-book.

The **Stromabank Hotel** (South Walls, tel. 01856/701494, www.stromabank.co.uk, £30–36 s, £60–72 d, food served 6–9 P.M. daily Mon.–Sat., noon–2 P.M. Sun.) surpasses expectations you might have of a provincial hotel. The setting, in grounds amidst open, green farmland with the islands of this shimmering part of Scapa Flow part of the vista to the front, is superb. The four rooms, all en suite, are snug, pastel-colored, soothing places to spend the night. All rooms come with TV and radio. The bar/restaurant is a good place for food (evening meals available throughout the week, lunches available on the weekend); eating in the conservatory-style restaurant will yield great views.

You can stay right next to a Stevenson-built lighthouse at the very tip of South Walls in two former lighthouse-keepers' cottages at **Cantick Head Lighthouse** (tel. 01856/701255, www.cantickhead.com, three-night stay for two people from £195). It's the perfect option if you fancy basing yourself on Hoy for a few days. They are well-appointed, self-catering cottages with pale-colored rooms and wood-burning stoves completing that rustic touch. Views are world-class, and you can sight porpoises and seals off shore.

One thing Hoy is not blessed with are decent places to eat, which is what makes the **Pumphouse Café** (Scapa Flow Visitor Centre, Lyness, tel. 01856/791300, 9:30 A.M.–4:20 P.M. daily Apr.–Oct.) such a good bet for a daytime snack. The fare is simple: soups and rolls and Orkney ice cream for £1–4.

The Inner Isles

The isles of Shapinsay and Rousay offer their fair share of extremes: Shapinsay's mild green agricultural land and Rousay's comparatively mountainous moor scattered with prehistoric sights. Shapinsay's charms are more refined; exploring fortresses and eating in fine restaurants is the order on this island. Rousay is more rough and rugged and is simply littered in ancient ruins from chambered cairns and eerie burial places to grand Iron Age stone towers called brochs.

◖ SHAPINSAY

The lairds of Balfour were notoriously cruel types who had by the 18th century made fertile Shapinsay their permanent home. They were known to give island folk a hard time during their often-tyrannical reign, but the legacy of buildings left behind by the Balfour family makes this island one of the most attractive to visit. The magnificent gray turrets of Balfour Castle, surrounded by woods and formal gardens that beg to be explored, dominate the island. Below, the gorgeous 18th-century Balfour village, designed to house workers on the castle estate, today houses the vibrant restaurants that entice visitors. Shapinsay is all about taking it easy—eating great food, checking out the local craftspeople at work, and watching the wading birds at the RSPB reserve.

Sights and Shopping

On summer Sundays, the best thing to do on the island is the **Balfour Castle Tour** (tel. 01856/711282, May–Sept.). The package, £20 adults/£10 children, includes a ferry from Kirkwall to Shapinsay, a look around the castle and grounds, and afternoon tea in the castle.

At **David Holmes Pottery** (Elwick Mill, east of Balfour, tel. 01856/711211, 10 A.M.–4 P.M. Tues.–Sun.), you can see pottery being made by one of Orkney's top potters and buy the finished products.

Accommodations and Food

Try beating the supremely gothic, many-turreted **Balfour Castle** (Balfour, tel. 01856/711282, www.balfourcastle.com, from £110 pp) for sheer class. For centuries it was the residence of the Balfour family, lairds of Shapinsay. The large, traditional rooms exude dark wood and antique furniture; one has the four-poster bed of the Balfour lairds in it. Guests can also walk the extensive grounds, which contain one of Orkney's largest woods, carpeted with bluebells in the spring. The grandiose gatehouse to Balfour Castle is now an atmospheric but seldom-open pub (tel. 01856/711216).

Relaxed, modern **Hilton Farmhouse** (outside Balfour, tel. 01856/711239, www.hiltonorkneyfarmhouse.co.uk, from £25 s, £50 d) has two large en suite rooms (power showers and baths) with great views across the stone-walled fields to the beach. There's Essence of Orkney toiletries in the bathrooms and color TVs, as well as a sun lounge to properly soak up the peaceful atmosphere. Here's the best bit: a farmhouse tearoom doing warming soups, oatcakes and cheese, cakes, and other snacks. You can get evening meals here, too. The farmhouse offers good-value, two-day, full-board package deals with a tour of the island thrown in for £100 per person.

The specialty at ◖ **The Smithy Restaurant** (Balfour, tel. 01856/711722, 10 A.M.–11 P.M. daily Feb.–Dec.) is seafood from around the Orkney shores. There's nothing like sitting in this light, colorful little restaurant with some scallops and crusty bread washed down by a bottle of white wine, looking out at the seals playing on the shore. Expect to pay £10–15 for mains. For the ultimate magical dining experience, a boat runs from Kirkwall harbor to Shapinsay and back on summer evenings. Inquire at the Smithy or at Kirkwall TIC.

Information

For information on the island, head to the **Smithy Heritage Centre in Balfour** (tel. 01856/711258, May–Sept.).

© LUKE WATERSON

Shapinsay

Getting There

There are six **ferries** per weekday (four or five on weekends) between Shapinsay and Kirkwall (25 min.).

ROUSAY, EGILSAY, AND WYRE

For some reason, people have wanted to cross the treacherous Eynhallow sound that separates Rousay from mainland Orkney and make a living on this hilly yellow-green island for many millennia. The remains of these ancient civilizations are what draw visitors back to this mini archipelago today. There are 166 archaeological sites on Rousay, Egilsay, and Wyre from brochs to cairns to castles to churches. No other area in Europe of this size (all three islands would fit into a 10-km by 10-km square) can boast this wealth and density of ancient monuments. Given this, you would think the crowds would be flocking, but guess what? They're not.

Sights

Cairns, as far as Orkney is concerned, are more than just piles of stones used as waymarks: They are huge prehistoric monuments, ancient burial chambers, and places of sacrifice. Rousay has an awful lot of them. Heading clockwise on the big cairn trail from the ferry terminal, first up is **Taversoe Tuick,** an unusual two-story cairn. **Blackhammer Cairn** is a well-preserved cairn dating from around 3500 B.C. Farther above on the moor overlooking Eynhallow sound is the more interesting **Knowe of Yarso,** a Neolithic cairn where the remains of 29 adults (not all with skulls) and 36 red deer were discovered upon its excavation. Admission to all the cairns is free.

Midhowe Cairn (open year-round, free) is a huge megalithic construction, housed these days by a protective covering. It's Orkney's longest chambered cairn, a dark, eerie place with 25 stalls or sections to bury the dead (or alive). Right behind it is **Midhowe Broch.** Orkney's most impressive broch is all about placement; thick stone walls stand over 4 meters tall, 2,000 years after they were last occupied, perched on a grassy promontory jutting into gray Eynhallow Sound. You get a real sense here of how impressive the original settlement would have been. The ruins cover quite a large area and would originally have housed many families and their livestock. The broch, or stone tower, would have been visible from across on the mainland, but it's as likely the structure was built to impress and deter passersby rather actually withstand attack. You can walk south from here along a path to the substantial ruins of a crofting village.

Trumland House Gardens (tel. 01856/ 821322, 10 A.M.–5 P.M. Mon.–Fri. May–Sept., £1.50) is an enthusiastically restored and peaceful garden, good for a refuge from the biting wind. It's part of the Trumland Estate, built by ex-soldier William Traill-Burroughs. Burroughs managed to die as Orkney's most hated landlord—no mean feat on an island historically inflicted with roguish, ruthless chieftains. The new owners are planning to restore both gardens and house to their previous grandeur and open them to the public.

The island of **Egilsay** occupied an important place in Orkney history; it was here that, having jointly inherited the earldom of the archipelago, Earl Magnus and his cousin Earl Hakon agreed to meet on Egilsay to peacefully settle their quarrels. Hakon's plan was always to have Magnus murdered, but he lacked the courage to do it and got a cook to do the dirty work. Today you can visit **St. Magnus Church** on little Egilsay, a poignant reminder of this turbulent period and one of only two examples of a Norse round-towered church still surviving.

Wyre is a two-mile-long, flat, green island just off to Rousay's southeast with some important sights on its diminutive shores. The ruins of **Cubby Roo's Castle** date from 1145; their builder is said to have links with the renowned Orkney giant Cubby Roo. Orkney poet Edwin Muir also lived on the island. Find out about both events at the **Wyre Heritage Centre** (Community Centre, tel. 01856/821211, Apr.–Sept. or phone to arrange for it to be opened). The center was created by a remarkable community effort and deserves a visit.

Accommodations and Food

The **Taversoe Hotel** (by Knowe of Yarso, south of island, tel. 01856/821325, www.taversoehotel.co.uk, £59.90 d) got a makeover and it's still popular with the locals! The management must be doing something right. The rooms here are wonderful: The two with sea views have wash basins and shared bathrooms, and one en suite overlooks the tangle of garden. All of the pearl-white rooms have color TV. There is a residents' lounge looking on to the Eynhallow Sound, with a collection of books and videos. The bar/lounge in the middle of the complex has big screen sports, a pool table, a dartboard, and a lot of bare stone work. You can get a reasonable meal here, too.

Getting There and Away

Buses (five daily Mon.–Fri., three daily Sat., 25 min.) run between Kirkwall and the Tingwall ferry terminal. On Wednesday and Friday a bus also runs from Stromness to Tingwall.

A **boat** from Tingwall runs frequently to Rousay, Egilsay, and Wyre. Rousay services are hourly, with five to seven boats calling at Egilsay and Wyre daily. It is therefore possible to catch any of these boats to get between the three islands. From Tingwall, it's a 25-minute crossing to Rousay.

Getting Around

A **post bus** makes a once- to twice-daily circuit of Rousay, calling at the island's very own post office (tel. 01856/821352) on the west of the island. It leaves from Rousay Pier in the morning.

The Outer Isles

Each of these sea-bashed isles has a unique character. To get a more vivid sense of what it was traditionally like to be an islander with nothing but the sea, a few shacks, and the wheeling seabirds to see you through life, you should aim to visit at least one during your time on Orkney. Westray is the largest and most tourist-friendly island, with good accommodation options and world-class puffin-watching. Airplane enthusiasts are attracted to taking the world's shortest flight to neighboring laid-back Papa Westray, home to Europe's oldest house. On gangly Stronsay, the ferocity of the sea has formed some of Orkney's best sandy beaches and its most dramatic rock formations. Sanday lives up to its name with excellent swaths of sandy beaches. Most extreme of the isles is North Ronaldsay, a bird-watchers' haven populated by unique seaweed-eating sheep.

◖ WESTRAY

Westray (www.westraypapawestray.co.uk) is a great introduction to what the outer Orkney isles can offer; you can feel isolated here without feeling cut off from civilization. It has a verdant, rolling landscape and its main community, Pierowall, is a pretty, bustling village with a strong community spirit. Birds are still the main reasons to visit. Noup Head in the north boasts more breeding seabirds than anywhere in Britain except St. Kilda, and the Castle o' Burrian in the south has Europe's best puffin-spotting. But there are also a good variety of other distractions: a castle, a heritage center, good coastal walks, and the best accommodations of the outer isles.

Sights

For the best place in Europe to see the clumsy comic cliff-performers otherwise known as puffins, you have to walk along the grassy, part-eroded cliffs to the **Castle o' Burrian.** The "castle" is actually a separate sheer rocky outcrop that should not be climbed under any circumstances, but its here that you can see,

during early summer, the puffins flying backward and forward feeding their young and often just crashing into things. If you don't have your own transport, you can call **Westraak** (tel. 01857/677777, www.westraak.co.uk) to arrange seasonal puffin tours and other excursions.

The best thing about **Noltland Castle** (year-round) is that you have to collect the huge keys to open it yourself. The brooding ruin was erected by Gilbert Balfour, said to hold favor with Mary, Queen of Scots. You can clamber up through several different levels to giddying views from the battlements.

Noup Head Nature Reserve (year-round, free, donations requested) at the northwestern tip of Westray is Britain's second-most-populous seabird colony. More than two miles of the cliffs here are a designated RSPB reserve, full of the squawking chatter of breeding kittiwakes, guillemots, and the like.

Accommodations and Food

The predominantly pine-furnished **Barn Hostel and Campground** (Pierowall, www.thebarnwestray.co.uk, dorm beds £13 adults, £9.50 children, two-person tent £5) has a mix of small rooms that each feel more like your own special island art studio than they do dormitories. It's great for families or groups of three or four who can book a whole room for their own private space. There is a large lounge and self-catering kitchen. The grassy campsite has its own separate kitchen and games room. Showers are hot but metered. Budget accommodation has never had it so good.

The hostel at the working croft of **Bis Geos** (tel. 01857/677420, www.bis-geos.co.uk, beds £10–12) has been converted to three solid pine-furnished rooms. It's a traditional bothy-style place (fish nets and the like for that degree of authenticity) with gorgeous views from the set piece conservatory. There's also underground-heated flagstone and timber floors and Internet access. If you're not happy with the cozy, comfortable hostel, there are self-catering cottages with traditional

Orkney box beds to rent as well. Bis Geos is west of Pierowall on the road to Noup Head.

❰ Number 1 Broughton (near Pierowall, tel. 01857/677726, www.number1brough-ton.co.uk, from £25 pp) is an old house on the coast just outside Pierowall that's had a futuristic makeover. Large en suite rooms are done in whites—it's as if every bit of natural light in Westray was illuminating them. Pictures painted by the owner grace the walls. The wonderfully light conservatory is where the huge breakfasts are served, and it's also good for watching the sun sink across the bay of a summers evening. At the end of a hard day's exploring, the sauna comes in useful.

You get the best of both worlds at white-washed **Cleaton House Hotel** (Cleaton, tel. 01857/677508, www.cleatonhouse.co.uk, £55 s, £85 d): ultimate luxury and ultimate views. Choose between a suite or an en suite double room. The decor is different in each of the five rooms, the common themes being wide comfortable beds and wonderful views. One room has a lovely wood-paneled bath. Many believe this to be the finest place to stay on Orkney; certainly nowhere else this isolated can offer such impeccable accommodations. You can eat at the informal, rustic restaurant in the evening; it is wood-beamed with a bare stone hearth. Seafood is a main feature of the menu, along with North Ronaldsay lamb.

The smell of the fish and chips cooking at the **Pierowall Hotel** (Pierowall, tel. 01857/677472, www.pierowallhotel.com, meals until 8:30 P.M.) will have your belly rumbling long before you taste them. You won't find a better fish supper on Orkney.

Information
There is an abundance of local information available at the **Westray Heritage Centre** (tel. 01857/677414, admission to exhibitions £2) in Pierowall.

Getting There and Away
You can **fly** twice daily between Kirkwall and Westray Monday–Saturday and once on Sunday. There are two daily **ferry** sailings

between Kirkwall and Westray. Prices, as for all the northern isles, are £6.50 adult, £15.05 car one-way. It will take you one hour 25 minutes to sail there.

Getting Around
Westraak (tel. 01857/677777) in Pierowall offers a taxi service and cycle rentals. **Ferries** from Kirkwall come in at Rapness, seven miles south of Pierowall. A Pierowall-bound minibus usually meets the ferry, or you can call in advance to arrange a taxi.

PAPA WESTRAY
This tiny island with its combination of gently rolling agricultural land, sparkling sandy beaches, and sheer rocky cliffs punches above its weight with the attractions it offers. The island is home to the Knap of Howar, northern Europe's oldest dwelling and terminus of the world's shortest flight. It also has the most complete example of a traditional farm on Orkney. It's a very laid-back island with many different seabirds such as skuas and Arctic terns nesting in its angular northern cliffs.

Sights
Farmers were busy living at the grass-topped ruin of the **Knap of Howar** (year-round, free) before the great pyramids of Egypt were built. This is Northern Europe's oldest surviving house, the walls of which were raised over 5,000 years ago. **Holland Farm** (Holland, tel. 01857/644251, year-round, free) is the best surviving example of a traditional Orkney farmstead. There's a collection of agricultural oddities spread around traditional outbuildings, including a doo'cot (dove cote), cotton-drying kiln, and small museum.

Papay Peedie Tours (tel. 01857/644321) does tours of the island's main sights during summer on Tuesday, Thursday, and Saturday. Operators are pretty accommodating.

Accommodations and Food
Beltane Guest House and Youth Hostel (tel. 01857/644321, from £25 s, £50 d, hostel beds £10–12) is a collection of late 19th-century

ORKNEY ISLANDS

converted farm buildings looking out on a wide swath of grass. There are four en suite rooms in the guesthouse, an adjoining 16-bed hostel with self-catering kitchen, and a village shop at Beltane which together make up the real center of things on Papa Westray.

Getting There and Away

If you want to take the **world's shortest scheduled flight** between Westray and Papa Westray, be sure not to nod off—it lasts all of two minutes. All flights to Papa Westray (at least two per day Mon.–Sat., one Sunday) go from Kirkwall, with some stopping off in Westray first. Flights are 15 minutes in total from Kirkwall.

There are three to six sailings daily between Pierowall and Papa Westray in summer. It's a passenger-only service, free if you are making a direct connection from or to Rapness for Kirkwall boats.

STRONSAY

During the herring boom before World War I, it was said that there were so many boats packed into the harbor of Whitehall, Stronsay's main village, that you could walk across it without ever touching water. A century on, this quiet island is not the thriving place it once was. From the air Stronsay looks like it has had three enormous bites taken out of it due to the sandy bays that cut into its flat, grassy ground. It's a peaceful landscape awash with flowers, small lochs, and great, golden dunes. As evidenced by the churning wind farm at one end, however, there's little shelter on these gale-blasted shores. The land does rise, however, to form some of Orkney's most impressive sea cliffs near the Vat of Kirbister.

The most impressive coastal walk on Stronsay and possibly on Orkney is in the southeast of Stronsay to this staggeringly impressive rock arch known as the **Vat of Kirbister.**

Stronsay's once-clamoring fish market has been converted into the laid-back, three-bedroom **Stronsay Fish Mart** (Whitehall, tel. 01857/616386, beds £13 with bedding supplied). It's a small, simple place with great waterside views and not even a whiff of fish. There

is also a café here serving basic meals and a heritage center. The **Stronsay Hotel** (Whitehall Village, tel. 01857/616473) reportedly does good pub food, including seafood.

Two to three **boats** daily sail from Stronsay to Kirkwall, some via Eday. The direct journey will take about 1.5 hours, or over two hours via Eday.

EDAY

Sparsely populated Eday is a bulk of heather-covered uplands, the appropriately remote setting for Britain's last pirate to be captured. The big attraction is Orkney's tallest standing stone, a 15-foot monolith in the north of the island. Eday was a favorite stomping grounds of Orkney writer and poet Eric Linklater; it has a wild, untamed beauty that attracts an important population of skuas, terns, short-eared owls, and very few visitors. That, of course, is just the reason you should visit. Head to the north of the island to see the **Stone of Setter** and for views of the **Calf of Eday,** topped with a chambered cairn. **Carrick House** in northern Eday is where John Gow, Britain's last pirate, was captured; the floor is supposedly still blood-stained from where Gow wounded himself trying to escape. **Eday Hostel** (tel. 01857/622206, Apr.–Sept., £10) is a basic but clean wooden cabin with 13 hard beds and soft chairs in its lounge.

There are weekly **flights** to Eday from Kirkwall on Wednesday, otherwise you are reliant on the two to three daily **ferries** from Kirkwall, usually via Stronsay and Sanday (£6.55 adult, £15.05 car one-way). These will take 1.25–2 hours, depending on the route.

SANDAY

Sanday is just what its name suggests: a collection of wide, white sands that form Orkney's best beaches. The island is essentially a big sand dune held together by tendrils of grassland. So low-lying is Sanday that in days gone by ships often couldn't see it at all. Islanders would watch and wait as ships ran aground and often even entice them to be wrecked on the shores so as to pocket the cargo. The signs of the wrecking trade, as it was known, are still around on the island; look again at that fence-post and see if it isn't really a ship's mast.

Sights

Sanday abounds in beautiful golden **beaches** perfect for a swim. You may have to wade quite a way out before it gets deep enough to swim. There is gorgeous but exposed **Otter's Wick** in the north and the **Bay of Newark** in the southeast.

Standing on Elsness amidst spectacular dunes in southern Sanday, **Quoyness Chambered Tomb** (year-round, free) is a 5,000-year-old cairn. It's very well preserved, and one of Orkney's most visually impressive chambered cairns. The entrance is high and narrow, then you must crawl into the dark central chamber. Remains of 15 adults and children were found upon excavation.

Accommodations and Food

The hostel at **Ayre's Rock** (due north of Kettletoft, north coast of Sanday, tel. 01857/600410, www.ayres-rock-sanday-orkney.co.uk, beds £12, two- to three-man tent £4) is part of a complex of whitewashed converted farm outbuildings. There are three rooms (two twin, one family) and a self-catering kitchen. If you don't want to cook, you can get an evening meal and bed and breakfast for only £22. There is also a grassy campsite with coin-operated showers and washing machine (both £1), a craft shop, and, wait for it, a takeaway chip shop. The latter is open on Saturdays (5–9 P.M. summer, 5–8 P.M. winter).

The **Kettletoft Hotel** (Kettletoft, tel. 01857/600217, http://kettletofthotel.moonfruit.com, from £25 s, £60 d) is at the heart of the island social scene. It's right next to the pier, stacked with lobster pots. The rooms are a mixed bag: singles and doubles both en suite and with shared bathrooms. They're clean, simple, and recently refurbished. The hotel is far and away the best place to eat on Sanday. The light, conservatory-style restaurant has its own unique archaeological attraction: a stone carved with symbols excavated locally. There's a great range of whiskies available in the bar,

which also has a dartboard and wonderful waterside views. Wednesdays and Saturdays are fish and chips takeaway nights.

Getting There and Around

From Monday to Saturday, there are morning and afternoon **flights** from Kirkwall to Sanday. There are two to three **ferries** between Kirkwall and Sanday. Direct sailings (£6.55 adult, £15.05 car one-way) are one hour 25 minutes. Sailings via Eday take a little longer.

Marygarth Manse (by Ayre's Rock Hostel, due north of Kettletoft, tel. 01857/600284) on the island doubles as a taxi service base and cycle hire shop. Bike hire is £8 per day; it's best to book in advance.

◖ NORTH RONALDSAY

As you get off the tiny plane onto Orkney's remotest island, it seems as if the crashing sea is higher than the land itself. This is Orkney's answer to Fair Isle, an ornithologist's paradise with thousands of rare migrant birds visiting from August to November. There are plenty of creatures to capture the imagination here, not least North Ronaldsay's unique seaweed-eating sheep, which are kept off the island by a 13-mile dyke. Kelp is more plentiful than grass on the island and so sheep forge their living on the foreshore. Britain's tallest land-based lighthouse is the island's high point.

Sights

The best way to see the island sights is to walk. Walking right around the edge of the island is possible, and this is where you get the best glimpses of seaweed-eating sheep and seals.

The 13-mile **Sheep Dyke,** built in 1832, is a listed building circling the island. The **seaweed-eating sheep** it keeps out are unique, surviving solely on seaweed, which gives their much-sought-after meat a delectable flavor. At lambing time they are rounded into punds (stone enclosures)—the only time they leave the rocky shore in the year. So plentiful are the sheep that an ailing ship from the Spanish Armada in 1588 badly needed to anchor on North Ronaldsay for supplies but thought better of it, mistaking the sheep for humans with ill intentions.

The poignant ruins of the **Broch of Burrian** (year-round), a once-extensive Iron Age fort, sit on Strom Ness at the island's most southerly point. The tumbled-down walls are good for a roam around. When the site was excavated in the 1880s, a rock was found inscribed with the distinctive Burrian Cross, now one of the most popular motifs in Orkney jewelry.

The **North Ronaldsay Lighthouse** (for tours tel. 01857/633257, £4), in the north of the island, is Britain's tallest land-based lighthouse and one of the last in Britain to be automated. Tours of the red-and-white striped lighthouse are available with the former keeper himself, which makes this one of the best lighthouses to explore in Scotland. Tours run on Sunday sailing days or by prior appointment. There's a small shop at the lighthouse.

Shopping

Whether it's a sweater made of seaweed-eating sheep wool or a nice cold lager to drink

© LUKE WATERSON

North Ronaldsay Lighthouse, the tallest land-based lighthouse in Britain

on the seashore, **North Ronaldsay Wool Shop and Off-Licence** (tel. 01857/633221, Hollandstoun) will sort you out. It even doubles as a tearoom selling tasty homebakes.

Accommodations and Food

In 1986 this croft house in the south of the island was converted into **North Ronaldsay Bird Observatory** (tel. 01857/633200, alison@nrbo.prestel.co.uk, £13 dorm, £30 s, £50 d), a wonderful observation station for North Ronaldsay's diverse birdlife. It's run on wind and solar power and offers dormitory and guesthouse accommodation. There are seven en suite rooms in the guesthouse and four-bed dorms in a separate building with shared bathrooms and a self-catering kitchen. Bed and breakfast is included (except for dorms; breakfast can be ordered at an additional cost of £6 per person), and evening meals can be ordered. Meals are taken at a long table, staff and guests together, and are always good for catching up on the latest bird news. The convivial bar prides itself on having a huge selection of whiskies. It's an open affair with windows looking out on the wild coast. The bird observatory has bags of information on recent bird sightings. Among numerous other species, the observatory is working on a program of encouraging corncrakes to the island. You'll find the observatory near the ferry pier.

Getting There and Away

Boats find it hard to land at the island's exposed pier and won't be able to do so in choppy weather. Boats depart Kirkwall on Friday for North Ronaldsay (2 hrs. 40 min.). Check in the TIC or the *Islands of Orkney* tourist brochure for departure times, which vary according to the week. There are additional Sunday sailings in summer.

While going by sea gives a real sense of the island's isolation, a far more practical way to get there is to fly. Three **flights** daily run between Kirkwall Airport and North Ronaldsay Airstrip on weekdays, with two services on weekends. Flights take 15 minutes and cost as little as £10, provided you stay overnight.

SHETLAND ISLANDS

As far north as Britain gets, Shetland looks and feels like another world, sitting some 40 miles north of the northern tip of the Scottish mainland. Although these islands are often lumped together with Orkney for their common Norse heritage, Shetland has a very different landscape. Scrub-covered uplands culminate in a moonscape of sheer craggy cliffs interrupted by the deep gashes of voes (inlets). In summer, the sun does not set until midnight, and night never really falls. During other times of the year, if you're lucky and get a cloud-free sky, you will see one of the most spectacular sights in the world: the Northern Lights. A far more common sight are Shetland's distinctive, diminutive ponies, roaming wild at the roadside or, more often than not, in front of your car.

The Shetland Islands may be far flung, but if you venture here, you'll uncover an uncommon and fascinating culture with a Norse history that lives on in the villages and festivals. The capital, Lerwick, rises up from the harbor in tiers of old fishing cottages and is rich with overtones of its fishing and smuggling past. It also hosts the annual Up Helly aa festival, where a Viking longship is set alight. Farther south are Shetland's archaeological treasures: Scotland's biggest broch and, at windswept Sumburgh Head, labyrinthine Jarlshof with 3,000 years worth of history in its varied ruins.

Northward, the land gets barer, dotted with shining lochs. North Mainland culminates in dramatic headlands like the Eshaness cliff, a series of strange rock formations with stranger names like Devil's Caves and the Drongs. Yell, Fetlar, and Unst are Shetland's—and

© LUKE WATERSON

HIGHLIGHTS

◖ **Shetland Museum and Archives:** This state-of-the-art museum blends Lerwick's historic docks with a fascinating insight into Shetland heritage from boatbuilding to bird-life (page 569).

◖ **Up Helly Aa:** One of Scotland's most out-landish festivals, in which a Norse longship is set on fire in Lerwick by locals clad in horned helmets (page 571).

◖ **Mousa Broch:** Take a boat trip to Britain's biggest, best-preserved broch (page 575).

◖ **Jarlshof:** At one of Scotland's most impressive prehistoric attractions, you can see the unique archaeological evidence of 3,000 years of continual occupation from Stone Age times through to Norse (page 576).

◖ **Fair Isle:** As remote as inhabited Scotland gets, this island is home to some of Britain's best bird-watching (page 578).

◖ **Eshaness Cliffs:** Northern Shetland rises up into a dizzying series of sheer cliffs, jagged inlets, stacks and arches carved out by the ferocity of the sea (page 584).

◖ **Hermaness:** See thousands of wheeling seabirds and hike to dramatic Muckle Lighthouse at the northern tip of Britain (page 590).

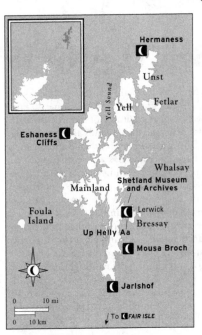

LOOK FOR ◖ TO FIND RECOMMENDED SIGHTS, ACTIVITIES, DINING, AND LODGING.

Britain's—most northerly islands, teeming with varied birdlife. Unst, farthest north, ends in the Hermaness peninsula, a bird reserve bashed on both sides by the sea, and Muckle Flugga, a lighthouse built by Robert Louis Stevenson's father that warns all passing ships not to venture too close to these treacherous outcrops of rock.

HISTORY
Prehistory to 19th Century

The earliest mention of Shetland in the annals of time was during the Roman General Julius Agricola's circumnavigation of the British Isles. "Dispecta est et Thule" (And we even sighted Thule) were his recorded words for rounding the

north of Britain. There is debate as to whether "Thule" was Fair Isle or the Faroes; rocky islands must all have looked similar through the sea mist. Vikings came to Shetland in the 8th to 9th centuries A.D., and Norse rule reached its height in the 12th and 13th centuries when the islands formed the northern half of the great earldom based in Orkney. Norwegian rule ended on Scotland's west coast in 1263 but lasted for another 200 years on Shetland. Scottish rule was slow to assert itself on the islands, and in its absence, various earls vied for power with little regard for the inhabitants.

Keeping Shetland from total collapse was the Hanseatic League of Merchants, which traded Shetland fish at European cities such as

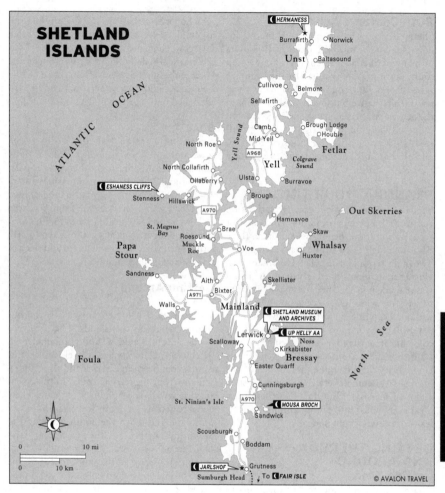

SHETLAND
ISLANDS

ATLANTIC
OCEAN

HERMANESS
Burrafirth   o Norwick
Unst   o Baltasound
Cullivoe o   o Belmont
Sellafirth
Camb o   o Brough Lodge
Mid Yell   o Houbie
North Roe o   A968   **Fetlar**
North Collafirth   **Yell**   Colgrave
Ollaberry o   Ulsta o   Sound
ESHANESS CLIFFS   o Burravoe
Stenness o   o Brough
Hillswick   **Out Skerries**
A970   Hamnavoe o
St. Magnus   o Skaw
Bay   o Brae   **Whalsay**
**Papa   Roesound   Voe   Huxter
Stour**   Muckle   o
Roe
Sandness o   Aith o   o Skellister
Bixter   **North**
Walls o   A971   Sea
Mainland
SHETLAND MUSEUM
AND ARCHIVES
Lerwick o   UP HELLY AA
Scalloway o   Noss
o Kirkabister
Foula   **Bressay**
Easter Quarff o
o Cunningsburgh
St. Ninian's Isle   A970   MOUSA BROCH
Sandwick
Scousburgh o
o Boddam
0   10 mi
0   10 km
JARLSHOF   o Grutness
Sumburgh Head   ¦ To FAIR ISLE
© AVALON TRAVEL

SHETLAND ISLANDS

Bergen in Norway and Hamburg in Germany throughout the 13th to 17th centuries. Trade boomed but was hampered when, following the Union of the Crowns in 1707, the British government kicked out the experienced German and Norwegian merchants in an effort to keep the lucrative fish income within the country. Scots from the mainland now arrived to fill the vacated merchant roles, but they had considerably less skill in the fish trade, and fish was the one resource Shetland had. As a result, Shetland slumped economically. Shetlanders were reduced to near-starvation as tenants on bare land controlled by a minority of often villainous and unpopular landlords (lairds) loyal to the crown. One of the only ways out of these miserable conditions was to go to sea. Many islanders joined the navy in the Napoleonic wars between Britain and France, either willingly or by force at the hands of barbaric navy recruitment groups called press gangs. Even when crofters were freed from landlord tyranny in the 1880s it was impossible to make a living from the land.

20th Century: War and Oil

Shetlanders continued to turn to the sea for employment. World War I claimed the lives of many of Shetland's men; it also put a stop to the herring boom that had finally begun to raise islanders out of poverty. For many, there was no alternative but to go and seek a life in the new world. Mass emigration continued well into the 1950s. Only recently, through agriculture, a rejuvenated fishing industry, tourism, and oil, has Shetland gone from dire poverty to relative wealth.

PLANNING YOUR TIME

Shetland's sights may not exactly be thick on the ground, but are spread out. Allowing for recuperation from the journey out here, three days is enough to fit in the main attractions. Two of the big ones, Jarlshof and Hermaness on Unst (Britain's most northerly point, which, if you've made it to the Shetlands, you will want to see), are as far apart as it's possible to get without a dip in the North Sea. Five to seven days will give you more time to kick back and enjoy life at an island pace, particularly if you want to make a trip to one of the remoter islands. With three days, be sure to include the Shetland Museum in Lerwick, Mousa, Jarlshof, and the Eshaness cliffs. Of the Northern Isles, Unst is the most interesting; aim to spend at least a day and a night here.

GETTING THERE AND AROUND
Getting There

Thanks to the oil industry, connections to Shetland and roads around Shetland are generally of a good standard.

AIR

Sumburgh Airport is in the far south of the island, at Sumburgh Head, and is Shetland's principal airport. It has a car rental office, tourist information, and an insufficient number of bus connections with Lerwick (4–5 per day).

Air connections with other Scottish cities are good. You can fly from Glasgow, Edinburgh, Aberdeen, and Kirkwall to Sumburgh Airport with **Loganair** (tel. 01856/872494, www.loganair.co.uk or www.britishairways.com). From Glasgow, there are at least four flights daily. There are also daily flights between Inverness and Sumburgh. Prices start from around £50 if booked a month in advance, rising up to £150 if booked only a couple of days in advance.

BOAT

Northlink Ferries (tel. 0845/600 0449, www.northlinkferries.co.uk) make a daily run between Aberdeen and Lerwick, usually calling at Kirkwall. It's a sometimes-rough 13- to 14-hour crossing departing Aberdeen at 5 P.M. or 7 P.M. A one-way fare from Aberdeen to Lerwick is £32.70. Cars are £116.60. Don't despair about arriving at a godforsaken time in either port; you can stay on board and sleep or have breakfast until a respectable time.

Getting Around
BUS

Viking Bus Station in Lerwick is the bus transport hub for the islands. The main operator is **John Leask & Son** (Esplanade, tel. 01595/693162, www.leasktravel.co.uk). Bus connections between Lerwick and all points en route to Toft, the ferry terminal to the North Isles (Tingwall, Voe, and Brae), are good. There is also reasonable service to Scalloway in Central Mainland and down the South Mainland to Sumburgh Airport. Although actual driving time across the Shetland mainland from Sumburgh Airport in the south to Toft in the north is only one hour 45 minutes, you'll need to add a good couple of hours on to your journey waiting for the connection in Lerwick. Buses on the Northern Isles and to more remote areas of the mainland are sporadic, with only one or two buses per week in places. For buses to remoter places, it is often necessary to book the night before, or the bus might not show. A bus from Sumburgh Airport to Lerwick (half the length of the mainland) costs £2.70 one-way.

CAR

In spite of the oil industry, petrol is more expensive on Shetland than anywhere else in

Britain. The presence of Summum Voe oil terminal has meant that roads are very good, though. Car rental rates are cheaper in Lerwick than at the airport.

Star Rent-a-Car (airport office tel. 01950/ 460444, www.starrentacar.co.uk) is one of only two companies with an office at Sumburgh Airport.

In Lerwick, **M & R Gair** (Blackhill Industrial Estate, tel. 01595/693246, www .gair.co.uk, from £23 per day) has some of the cheapest rates in town. The company with the biggest fleet of cars on the island is **Bolts Car Hire** (tel. 01595/693636, www.boltscar-hire.co.uk), which also now has an office at Sumburgh Airport.

Lerwick and Vicinity

Sheltered by the islands of Bressay and Noss, the gray town of Lerwick clusters prettily up in tiers from the harbor. Shetland's main ferry port expanded rapidly in the 1970s with the oil boom on the islands, but it's retained its original 17th-century character. The center is full of winding cobbled streets and closely packed houses. These are centered on the town's first building, the ruined Fort Charlotte, built at significant cost to protect the islands from the Dutch who came to the area to fish.

SIGHTS
Fort Charlotte
Built to protect the islands from Dutch fishermen in the 17th century, Fort Charlotte (year-round, free) is nothing but a cavernous ruin with stout worn walls that do give a great view over Lerwick and Bressay beyond. Information boards in the fort explain the history of the town.

◖ Shetland Museum and Archives
This impressive attraction (Hays Dock, tel. 01595/695057, www.shetlandmuseumandarchives.org.uk, 10 A.M.–5 P.M. Mon., Wed., and Fri.–Sat., 10 A.M.–7 P.M. Thurs., noon–4 P.M. Sun., free) is in the refurbished Hays Dock, the only remaining part of the original 19th-century dock in Lerwick. The former fish processing and boat-making buildings lend a highly appropriate theme to the museum, which traces Shetland's varied maritime and knitwear history. There are traditional Shetland boats suspended from the ceilings, an operating lighthouse, and exhibits on the legendary

Shetland fiddlers. The highlight is the boat-building shed, where traditional Shetland boats are now once again being built and restored as they were centuries ago. There's also an extensive section of archives upstairs and a very good restaurant. Check the installation outside: a series of receivers imparting fragmented conversations of Shetland life, which together form a moving patchwork of sound.

Bod of Gremista
This 18th-century bod (Shetland house) (tel. 01595/694386/695057, 10 A.M.–1 P.M. and 2–5 P.M. Wed.–Sun. May–mid-Sept., free) was the former home of Arthur Anderson, joint founder of P&O Ferries. It's typical of the accommodation Shetland fishing families would have had 200 years ago, including living quarters and a working store for the drying of fish. It's done up in traditional, simple Shetland style.

Clickimin Broch
This well-preserved 3,000-year-old broch (year-round during daylight hours, at least 9:30 A.M.–5:30 P.M. Apr.–Sept. 9:30 A.M.–4:30 P.M. Oct.–Mar., free) sits on a promontory into Clickimin Loch. It's a slightly surreal sight—probably one of the few Bronze-age monuments surrounded by a 20th-century housing estate. The thick walls of this family home and farm would originally have been some 15 meters high—little wonder that people chose to occupy it on and off for over 1,000 years.

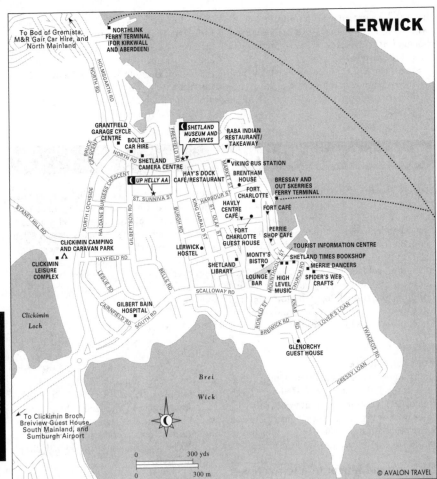

Tours

Shetland Geo Tours (tel. 01595/859218 or 01595/693434, www.shetlandgeotours.com, £145/245 four-day/seven-day tour) offers superb tours that give an insight into Shetland's geology and wildlife. They take in all parts of the island, including many places that are difficult to get to independently. These include "Summer Dim" specials on those balmy evenings when the sun barely sinks below the horizon.

John Leask & Son (Esplanade, tel. 01595/693162), the island's main transport provider, also has minibuses for hire. You can inquire about chartering one for a guided island tour.

ENTERTAINMENT

Lerwick has a poor selection of nightlife offerings for a place of its size; however, remember the best live music events in these parts are often impromptu. Pick up a copy of **The Shetland Times** for the low-down on what is going on where.

The **Lounge Bar** (Mounthooly St., tel. 01595/692231, 11 A.M.–1 A.M. daily) is the pick of

© LUKE WATERSON

Clickimin Broch

Lerwick's dire selection of bars and is your best chance of hearing some live music. There is a comfortable, relaxed upstairs part (downstairs is less captivating).

EVENTS
◖ Up Helly Aa

This festival ensures the Viking influence lives on in Scotland; it's the highlight of Shetland's festival calendar on the last Tuesday in January. It culminates with the torching of a Viking longship in Lerwick Harbour. If you miss this, you can at least have the history of the festival explained to you at the **Up Helly Aa exhibition** (St. Sunniva St., tel. 08701/999440, 2–4 P.M. and 7–9 P.M. Tues., 7–9 P.M. Thurs., 2–4 P.M. Fri. mid-May–Sept., £3 adults, £1 children) with the colorful costumes as props.

Music Festivals

Shetland is renowned for its talented musicians and musical heritage, particularly where fiddling is concerned. There are a couple of key musical festivals on the calendar, including the **Shetland Folk Festival** (www.shetlandfolkfestival.com), the U.K.'s most northerly folk festival, with international acts and a strong focus on fiddle music. There is also the **Shetland Fiddle Frenzy** (www.shetlandfiddlefrenzy.com), held in August. It's a weeklong celebration of the famous Shetland fiddle music, with students getting together with more experienced fiddlers to run workshops and host talks on the art of fiddle playing and, above all, play.

SHOPPING

Shetland is a good place to buy a unique gift.

The **Shetland Times Bookshop** (71–79 Commercial St., tel. 01595/695531, www.shetland-bookshop.co.uk, 9 A.M.–6 P.M. Mon.–Fri., 9 A.M.–5 P.M. Sat.) has a great selection of books and maps on Shetland and good general fiction and nonfiction. It's a simply cavernous place.

Shetland Camera Centre (Toll Clock Shopping Centre or 72 Commercial St., tel. 01595/694345, 9 A.M.–5:30 P.M. Mon.–Sat.) has one of Scotland's biggest stock of binoculars and is where you should head for photographic queries.

UP HELLY AA: VIKING REVELRY OR VICTORIAN WHIM?

While the celebrations that rock Lerwick each January certainly seem on the surface to be Viking-themed (the revelers wearing horned helmets and the carrying of a Viking long-ship to the harbor, for example), there's a lot that's not Norse about the festivities. The setting alight of a ship is, it is true, supposedly what the Vikings once did to give thanks for the coming of the sun for another year. But search before 1800 in the history books and you'll find little more reference to Up Helly Aa than you will to kumquats. The only link is that remote parts of Shetland did celebrate Up Helly night 24 days after Christmas. Festivities in Lerwick only really kicked off after the Napoleonic Wars: Soldiers came back with a thing for firearms and frivolity. By the 1840s there were many reports of brawling and the firing of guns, as well as fiddling and the carrying of blazing tar barrels in the streets of Lerwick.

Wealthy residents complained; the whole process seemed dangerous and unruly.

It was not until the 1870s that the Viking theme was introduced into the festival. This was largely an attempt to intellectualize the revelry and give it a more cultural tone. It was then that the element of disguise or "quizing" was introduced to proceedings. Also very Victorian was the introduction of the first longship to be carried through the streets. However, after World War II Up Helly Aa had almost died out and it was the decision to have the distinctive "quizers" of today's festivals disguised as Vikings that really seems to have brought its popularity back. A Victorian invention Up Helly Aa may be, but try telling a "quizer" that as he hurtles toward you carrying a wooden Viking galley over his head. The festival's popularity is in its wild Viking associations, regardless of their historical accuracy.

Merrie Dancers (59 Commercial St., tel. 01595/693000), a gourmet food and gift shop, is a perfect for stocking up on Shetland products (like the packed hampers) or buying that edible memento.

Spiders Web (51 Commercial St., tel. 01595/695248, 9 A.M.–5 P.M. Mon.–Sat.) has a host of knitwear products made by Shetlanders in their own homes.

High Level Music (1 Gardie Ct., tel. 01595/692618) is a good bet to pick up some local music and, if you really want to get in the Shetland spirit, a fiddle.

SPORTS AND RECREATION

The terrible weather can be a downer when it comes to sport. Tough winds make cycling a challenge.

The weather is often bad so lots of folk head to the superb **Clickimin Leisure Complex** (Lochside, tel. 01595/741000, www.srt.org.uk/clickimin.htl, pool 7 A.M.–9 P.M., other facilities as late as 11 P.M.), which has a gym, swimming pool, health suite, indoor bowls hall (bowls is a game related to petanque and bocce), and plenty of other activities for the health-conscious.

Grantfield Garage Cycle Hire (North Rd., tel. 01595/692709) rents out bikes from £5 per day.

ACCOMMODATIONS

Lerwick's hotels are not the best; places to stay are mostly guesthouses. There is also a good campsite, as well as a youth hostel in town. It's worth noting here that one wonderful accommodation option in Shetland is the island's **camping bods** (£8 per person). These are formerly derelict farm cottages revamped to provide characterful basic accommodation in the wilds. You'll need your own sleeping bag or mat. These places are full of history and have a common room (usually with a fire) and basic kitchen and bathroom facilities. Bods are all reservable through Lerwick TIC (there's not always someone on hand at the bods to pay).

Behind the leisure center, **Clickinin Camping and Caravan Park** (tel. 01595/741000, May–Sept. and possibly other times by arrangement, small tents £7.10) is the only camping ground in town. Sweeping grassy views look down toward Clickimin Broch, and it's a well-appointed if slightly stark site with very little shelter from the rain. There are showering and clothes-drying facilities.

Lerwick Youth Hostel (King Harald St., tel. 01595/692114, Apr.–Sept., dorms £14) is a newly refurbished Victorian house constituting the northerly extent of the youth hostel network. It's a big place with 64 beds in 4- to 12-bed dorms. There is a self-catering kitchen, but with more spirited surroundings is the House Café at the hostel where you can pick up cheap, warming food.

If you're arriving early in Lerwick on the overnight crossing from Aberdeen, **◖ Fort Charlotte** (1 Charlotte St., tel. 01595/692140, www.fortcharlotte.co.uk, £30 s, £55 d) is a wonderful warm welcome to terra firma, both in the temperature sense and in the friendliness sense. You'll get a hearty breakfast if you have to wait for the previous night's guests to check out. The breakfast room overlooks the main shopping street of Lerwick—a good introduction to the bustle of life in this otherworldly place. Then there are the rooms: two floors of them, most with views of the steep back streets of Lerwick and the ruins of the fort, some with harbor views. All are cozy affairs with TVs, en suite bathrooms, and flowers. You could stay here five days and have a different breakfast option each day (porridge, smoked salmon and scrambled eggs, English muffins—the list goes on).

Breiview Guest House (43 Kantersted Rd., tel. 01595/695956, www.breiviewguesthouse.co.uk, £25–35 s, £50–70 d) is a modern house out of the town center near Clickimin Broch. There're eight neat rooms here, done up in bright blues and whites. The owner, a former chef, will cook you an evening meal on request. You can relax in a light lounge full of potted plants and partake of the honesty bar. Stay seven nights and you'll only pay for six. The matter-of-fact owner doesn't try to dress

up **Glenorchy Guest House** (20 Knab Rd., tel. 01595/692031, www.guesthouselerwick.com, £47 s, £74 d) in any way: he just says it's the best Lerwick can offer. Given the disappointing hotels in town, and the size of this place (bigger than many hotels) he may just be right. The rooms are large and immaculate, many with underfloor heating, air-conditioning, and satellite TV. There's a first floor lounge with honesty bar and a downstairs restaurant where breakfast and evening Thai food are served.

Brentham House (7 Harbour St., tel. 01950/460201, www.brenthamhouse.co.uk, £55 s, £75 d) offers some of Lerwick's largest rooms, which, despite their size, still exude coziness. All come with en suite bathrooms, some with stand-alone baths. The decor is kept simple, with the effect that rooms all look clean and modern.

FOOD

Lerwick's eating scene has long been a little disappointing, but with a couple of good new restaurants having opened in recent years, things are looking up. The best places do almost all Scottish cuisine, although you can get Indian and Chinese food.

Fort Café (2 Commercial Rd., tel. 01595/693125, 11 A.M.–10:30 P.M. Mon.–Fri., 11 A.M.–7 P.M. Sat., 5–10:30 P.M. Sun.) is run by the owners of Fort Charlotte Guesthouse and serves the best fish and chips in Lerwick. You can eat in the small restaurant or takeaway. Battered snacks start from £1.

At the **Havly Centre Café** (9 Charlotte St., tel. 01595/692100, 10 A.M.–3 P.M. Mon.–Fri., 10 A.M.–4:45 P.M. Sat.), a small, friendly café/Christian center, you can try homemade bread and Norwegian waffles (£2–5). Families are welcome: Parents can relax on the leather-backed chairs while children play in the kids' corner. This place may be Norwegian-themed, but it also does tasty pizzas.

◖ Peerie Shop Café (Esplanade, tel. 01595/692816, www.peerieshopcafe.com, 9 A.M.–6 P.M. Mon.–Sat.) is about as cool as a Shetland summer, with two floors done up in an industrial-style decor connected by a spiral staircase like a fire escape. Order at the counter: you might come in just fancying a shot of the fine coffee but you would need to be pretty strong-willed to resist a cake like the Malteser slice (a Shetland special) or the carrot cake. There are also good soups and plum smoked salmon; light bites are £2–6.

Hay's Dock Café Restaurant (Hay's Dock, tel. 01595/741569, www.haysdock.co.uk, 11 A.M.–5 P.M. Mon.–Sat., noon–4 P.M. Sun., plus 6:30–11 P.M. Tue.–Sat., telephone in advance) is a breath of fresh air in the Lerwick dining scene: a spacious new restaurant above the Shetland Museum. With large glass windows looking out on the harbor, it's one of the most cosmopolitan places in town and knows it. The menu is as modern as the feel: It's £4–7 for big lunchtime paninis with salad and potato chips or filled potato skins with sour cream. It's a good place to sample local culinary delights, like Unst oysters and Orkney beef sandwiches. Evening mains are £12–14.

With bare stone walls and heavy wooden chairs, **Monty's Bistro** (5 Mounthooly St., tel. 01595/696555, noon–2 P.M. and 6:30–9 P.M. Tues.–Sat.) is the place to eat out in style in Lerwick, and has been for about a decade. You can enjoy the full spectrum of Shetland culinary delights from lamb to seafood. Mains are £10–18. The dining experience is enhanced by being in the steep wynds (narrow paths) that make up Lerwick's back streets—it all adds to the quiet, intimate atmosphere.

INFORMATION AND SERVICES

Shetland's main **TIC** (tel. 01595/693434, 8 A.M.–6 P.M. Mon.–Fri., 8 A.M.–4 P.M. Sat.–Sun. Apr.–Oct., 9 A.M.–5 P.M. Mon.–Fri. Nov.–Mar.) is at Market Cross in the center of town. There is a lot of useful information on Shetland and also maps available. There is an accommodation-booking service and you can change travelers checks here. There's also a small TIC at Sumburgh Airport.

Commercial Street has several banks with ATMs. The **post office** (9 A.M.–5 P.M. Mon.–Fri. 9 A.M.–noon Sat.) is also on Commercial Street.

Shetland Library (Lower Hillhead, tel.

01595/743868, 9:30 A.M.–8 P.M. Mon. and Thurs., 9:30 A.M.–5 P.M. Tues.–Wed. and Fri.–Sat.) has free Internet access and an extensive Shetland information section.

In a health emergency, head to **Gilbert Bain Hospital** (South Rd., tel. 01595/743000), which has outpatients and accident and emergency (A&E) departments.

GETTING THERE AND AROUND

Viking Bus Station, the main transport hub for the islands, is on Commercial Street.

Allied Taxis (tel. 01595/690069) sometimes offer special rates for senior citizens. From Sumburgh Airport to Lerwick costs around £35.

AROUND LERWICK

Just across the sound from Lerwick are two wildlife-rich islands.

Bressay and Noss

Bressay is an island of some 400 people lying across the water from Lerwick. It's a great place to relax, boasting a spa and peaceful coastal walks. Beyond it, Noss is one of the country's most important seabird colonies, with up to 80,000 pairs of birds breeding annually. You can relax for days at the **Northern Lights Holistic Spa** (Sound View, Bressay, tel. 01595/820733, northernlights-holisticspa@fsmail.net, £55 s, £90 d) and choose from a range of soothing treatments from sauna to Turkish steam room to flotation room.

Boats to Noss (tel. 01595/693345 for details, island accessible 10 A.M.–5 P.M. Tues.–Wed. and Fri.–Sun. mid-May–Aug.) give access to the island seabird colonies. A walk around the edge takes three hours. It's a 2.5-mile walk, drive, or cycle across Bressay to Noss Sound, from where the Noss boat (actually a large dinghy) departs. A **Lerwick-Bressay Ferry** (7 min., £3.20 passenger round-trip) makes frequent journeys between Albert Buildings in Lerwick and Bressay.

South Mainland and Fair Isle

The area south of Lerwick is green, fertile land more akin to the landscape of the Orkney Islands. Here is the most fascinating glimpse into Shetland's past with some of Northern Europe's most important archaeological sights at Mousa Broch and Jarlshof. The coast of sand and marram grass rears steeply up to culminate in Sumburgh Head with the sea crashing around it—a dramatic reminder of how cut off Shetland is from the rest of the world.

SANDWICK AND ST. NINIAN'S ISLE

The scattering of houses overlooking Mousa Sound makes a good base for exploring formidable Mousa Broch, with good facilities. It's a very attractive area, especially around Hoswick. A few miles southwest on the other side of the mainland is St. Ninian's Isle with its distinctive sandy tombolo, where one of the world's most important hoards of Celtic silver was found.

◖ Mousa Broch

The island of Mousa is a bird sanctuary on which stands Scotland's grandest broch. This 13-meter-high monster stands like a fat funnel above the island shoreline, one of the most distinctive landmarks in the area. If you visit one archaeological site on Shetland, make it this one. It's the experience of having to get a boat to this tiny deserted island and being able to climb up a spiral staircase inside to its summit that make this place so special. There are several theories as to why this broch has remained so intact when its counterparts across Scotland have fallen into disrepair; most likely is the effort it would have taken to come over here and take the stone. Boat trips (Leebitton, tel. 01950/431367, www.mousaboattrips.co.uk, from Sandwick 12:30 and 2 P.M. June–Aug., 2 P.M. Apr.–May and Sept.) give you a good 2.5 hours ashore. Equally mesmerizing are the late-night trips the same company runs to see storm petrels (small nocturnal seabirds) on Mousa from late May to July. These run currently at 11 P.M. on Wednesday and a Saturday. Day trips are £12 adults, £6 children under 16. Petrel excursions are £14 adults, £7 children.

Hoswick Visitor Centre

This visitors center (Sandwick, tel. 01950/431403, 10 A.M.–5 P.M. Mon.–Sat., 11 A.M.–5 P.M. Sun. May–Sept., free) is housed in a former tweed-weaving building (the industry died out in this part of Shetland in the 1980s). The airy museum focuses on the textile-making and fishing that have shaped the history of the area. There's a café, shop, and Internet point too. In the **Hoswick Woollen Mill** (tel. 01950/431215, Laurence@odie-knitwear.co.uk, 9 A.M.–5 P.M. Mon.–Fri.) across the road is Shetland's largest selection of knitwear, good for souvenir finding.

St. Ninian's Isle

It's hard to say what is more impressive about small, sandy isle: the approach to it or the island itself. West of the village of Bigton, the approach involves crossing Britain's longest active **tombolo,** a sandy spit lapped by waves from both sides. Check the tide before you set off to avoid being cut off. The island has the ruins of a 12th-century **chapel** on its eastern side (to the right of the pathway onto the island). Little now remains, but this is where St. Ninian's Teasure was found beneath the chapel floor in 1958—a hoard of Celtic silver from A.D. 800. The treasure is in the Scottish museum in Edinburgh; Shetland Museum has replicas.

Accommodations

Solbrekke (Sandwick, tel. 01950/431410, £22–24 pp) has a chatty and informative owner who knits Fair Isle sweaters; she may show you her creations. That and the good views over Mousa Broch are the main reasons to stay. It's a homey modern bungalow with a guest lounge for TV watching. The rooms can be as cool temperature-wise as the pastel colors in which they are

© LUKE WATERSON

St. Ninian's Isle

furnished, but there are bucket-loads of local information. Bathrooms are shared.

Up a steep, narrow lane in Hoswick village is **Orca Country Inn** (Hoswick, tel. 01950/431226, www.orcacountryinn.co.uk, £42.50 s, £64.95 d)—you could blink and miss it, and it's certainly remote. The six rooms have pine furnishings and get great light, helped by being white and spacious. The inn is about as informal as you could hope for, with accommodating staff always ready to rustle up a meal for hungry travelers (mains from £7.50). It really does feel like you were being cooked for in your own home. If you're here for the birdlife, chat to the owner, who knows a thing or two about the subject.

Getting There and Away

Bus service 6 heading south will call at Sandwick Central (eight per day Mon.–Fri., six per day Sat., four per day Sun.). It's 25 minutes to Lerwick or 30 minutes to Sumburgh Airport. By the time you've walked up to the main road at **Channerswick** to wait for one of the two buses per day for Bigton and St. Ninian's Isle, you might as well have walked all the way.

SUMBURGH HEAD AND VICINITY

Landing at Sumburgh Airport, your heart will be in your mouth as the small craft seems to be heading straight across sand into the sea on the other side. This is where the south mainland thins out with its dune-backed coast rising up to the lighthouse at Sumburgh Head. Two of Scotland's key archaeological sites sit at the peninsula tip, both unique and begging to be explored. There is more recent history to be explored, too, at the lovely Quendale Watermill in the west.

Jarlshof

It's no small statement, but Jarlshof (Sumburgh, tel. 01950/460112, 9:30 A.M.–5:30 P.M. daily Apr.–Oct., £4.70 adults, £2.35 children) is a top contender for Scotland's most impressive archaeological attraction. It's not that any one of the structures here stands out as spectacular; rather, this is the only place in Scotland where

© LUKE WATERSON

Jarlshof, one of the world's longest continually occupied dwellings

you can see evidence of over 3,000 years of continuous habitation of the same site, right up until the 1600s. There are Stone Age, Bronze Age, Iron Age, Pictish, Norse, and medieval remains here. The **Pictish Wheelhouses** (dwellings in holes dug out of the ground) are the most complete and intriguing of the many monuments; the remains of the **Norse farm** are most extensive. It makes the mind boggle to see such a patchwork of historic remains on one site—without an accompanying explanation, the best history buff in the world would be confused by the complexity. Fortunately, knowledgeable staff are on hand to inform you. A small visitors center on-site also has a very good explanation of which ruins date from which periods of history with a scale model for reference. A final thought: right on the coast, Jarlshof was at various times in its history covered by fluctuating sand dunes after storms. This means it would have been completely rediscovered by subsequent peoples. Perhaps the most interesting thing of all to do here is contemplate that each was probably as fascinated by what they discovered as we are today.

Old Scatness

Old Scatness (near Sumburgh, tel. 01950/461869, 10 a.m.–4:30 p.m. Sun.–Thurs., £4 adults, £3 children) is not only a well-preserved Iron Age broch and village but also the only place currently in the U.K. where you can watch prehistoric conservation work in progress. Guides dressed in period costume enthusiastically show you around the site, which includes reconstructed houses modeled on those being excavated. This makes it good fun for children, too. A visitors center gives insight into Iron Age culture on the Shetlands. The site is on the right-hand side north of Sumburgh on the main Lerwick road.

At **Quendale Mill** (Quendale, tel. 01950/460969, www.quendalemill.shetland.co.uk, 10 a.m.–5 p.m. daily mid-Apr.–mid-Oct., £2 adults, £1 seniors, £0.50 children), a restored water mill dating from 1867, you can see how grain from Shetland's main farming region was handled during the 19th century. Agricultural machinery and tools used in Shetland over the last 200 years are on view. The mill also acts as a local **tourist information point,** and a café.

THE BRAER OIL SPILL

The coast off Garth's Ness near Quendale has a reputation for being the site of one of the greatest man-made environmental disasters. The Braer Oil Tanker was carrying over 85,000 tons of crude oil, twice as much as the Exxon *Valdez*, when it ran aground on rocks to the south of Shetland in January 1993. Despite best efforts, oil from the hold poured into a stretch of sea renowned for its birdlife, seals, otters, and whales. The worst was feared but, fortunately for Shetland, the storm that drove the tanker into difficulties also limited the disaster. The oil was churned up and dispersed by persistently huge waves caused by winds that ravaged the islands throughout the month, reducing the threat to wildlife.

Accommodations

Betty Mouat's Camping Bod (Old Scatness, tel. 01595/693434, £8 per bed) is named after a Shetland heroine who once survived an eight-day drift on a boat in stormy seas by herself. You can stay in her simple stone house, full of displays on her life, with 10 bunk beds and a small kitchen. Rooms are wood paneled and showers are warm. Bring your own bedding. The Iron Age excavations of Old Scatness are right outside.

Sitting above the Loch of Spiggie within a stone's throw of some of Shetland's most unspoiled beaches, the **◖ Spiggie Hotel** (Scousburgh, tel. 01950/460409, www.thespiggiehotel.co.uk, £55 s, £75 d) is a quiet place to get away from it all. It's a small place with only four rooms, all en suite and with great views over the surrounding countryside. The vista of green livestock-grazed fields, a loch, and distant sand dunes are unusual on Shetland—more what you would expect on Orkney to the south. Shuffling Shetland ponies are the only giveaway. Spiggie is recognized by CAMRA (Campaign for Real Ale); try one of the Valhalla ales and you'll know why. You only have to step into the cozy, dark

wood bar for the tone of the whole hotel to be set; it's popular with locals and fishermen (permits to fish in the loch are available here). You can also dine in the light conservatory restaurant.

Getting There and Away

John Leask & Son operates **bus** service 6, which runs just five times a day Monday–Saturday and four times on Sunday between Lerwick and Sumburgh Airport. Sumburgh Airport, in the southern part of the island, has regular flights to Glasgow, Edinburgh, Aberdeen, and Kirkwall on **Loganair** (tel. 01856/872494, www.loganair.co.uk or www.britishairways.com), as well as daily flights between Inverness and Sumburgh.

◖ FAIR ISLE

All alone in the North Sea, tiny Fair Isle is best known for its distinctively patterned jumpers, although most visitors come to catch a sight of the island's diverse birdlife or to soak up the remoteness. Being the only bit of land around for some distance, Fair Isle is on an important migration crossroads for many birds, including two rare species of warbler. There are also a lot of breeding seabirds, including puffins and Arctic terns. Much of the island's human population still makes a living from traditional crafting. The farmland in the south rises to sheer sea cliffs in the north. At five miles long by three miles wide, there's no need to bring a car across to the island. It is best seen on foot or by bike if you want to get close to the birdlife.

Fair Isle Lodge and Bird Observatory (by ferry pier, tel. 01595/760258, www.fairislebirdobs.co.uk, £30 dorm, £44 s, £78 d) is where a lot of the island's activity centers. It offers dormitories with four, five, and six beds, as well as single and double rooms—simple white-painted affairs with hand basins and shared bathrooms. All accommodation offered is full board, with bird observatory staff and guests eating together in an informal eating area at set times. It's a great opportunity to exchange bird-sighting stories and have a good chin wag. There is a bar, too, and a shop selling snacks. The observatory is dedicated to monitoring seabirds and migratory birds and records fluxes in populations. Of

© LUKE WATERSON

traditional Fair Isle sweater

course, it is also a great source of information about birds on the island, what to see, and where to see it. The busy times of year are mid-May to mid-June (the best time to see seabirds) and late September to early October (the best time to see the rarer migratory birds).

Fair Isle Crafts (www.fairisle.org.uk) still produce the only authentic Fair Isle knitting in the world, made by the island cooperative. Visit the website or ask at the observatory for further details. If you want to take home a genuine garment, be prepared to shell out up to £200 for a sweater.

Getting There and Away

There are three weekly **sailings** between mainland Shetland and Fair Isle. The **mailboat** *Good Shepherd IV* runs from Sumburgh on Tuesday and Saturday. On Thursday it makes a run from either Lerwick or Sumburgh to Fair Isle. Journey time is about 2.5 hours and costs an unbelievably cheap £3 for a passenger one-way. While a flight may be quicker, the boat may be your best chance of seeing the varied sealife that populates these waters: dolphins, whales, and up to five species of seal.

You can **fly** from Tingwall on Shetland's mainland to Fair Isle twice a day on Monday, Wednesday, and Friday (£30 one-way, £56 round-trip). **Loganair** (tel. 01856/872494, www.loganair.co.uk or www.britishairways.com) also operates a summer service between Kirkwall on Orkney and Fair Isle via North Ronaldsay.

Central and West Mainland

This grassy swath of the mainland is often passed through by visitors heading for the more exciting northern and southern extremes of the islands, but seldom stopped in. Sights are few and far between, but isolated picnicking spots, walks, and drives are everywhere. It wasn't always so quiet: Scalloway was once capital of the Shetlands, and the island's parliament met at Tingwall. It's also here where you have to head for ferry or air connections to the far-flung provinces of Papa Stour, Foula, and Fair Isle.

SCALLOWAY AND CENTRAL MAINLAND

Once the capital of Shetland and now a busy fishing port, Scalloway with its distinctive castle sticking up above a boat-filled harbor is the nearest thing the islands have to a second town. Scalloway Museum charts the history of the fascinating "Shetland Bus" between Shetland and Norway during wartime. Farther up the thin, loch-strewn isthmus that holds the mainland together is Tingwall, once where parliament met.

Sights and Shopping

The shell of **Scalloway Castle** (tel. 01595/841815 for visitor information, 9:30 A.M.–5 P.M. Mon.–Fri., free) isn't the most aesthetically pleasing ruin you will see, somewhat spoiled by the brash modern fishing port nearby. However, it is an important historical building, built in 1600 by Earl of Shetland **Patrick Stewart** as his main island stronghold in the days when Scalloway was still capital of all the Shetlands. Stewart wasn't a very popular person; he was executed, and the castle's short usage came to an end. Once inside there is still a sense of lingering grandeur with a spiral staircase giving good views of the main hall. Get the key from the **Shetland Woollen Company** Monday–Friday and from the **Scalloway Hotel** weekends.

The main story told at the **Scalloway Museum** (Main St., tel. 01595/880675,

10 A.M.–noon and 2–4:30 P.M. Mon.–Sat. May–Sept., free) through well-presented display panels is that of the "Shetland Bus," a unique service running during World War II between Shetland and Norway. All kinds of fishing craft would make the dangerous journey to Norway to help refugees escape and to bring in arms and other support. The history of Scalloway as a fishing port and capital of Shetland is also touched upon.

Capital of the long thin islands of West and East Burra that lie south of Scalloway, **Hamnavoe Fishing Village** is one of Shetland's most authentic fishing villages, almost totally rows of tiny, one-story fishermen's cottages descending in tiers down the green hillside to the pier. Fishing nets hang over back doors and boats lean by garden fences. Some of the fences are worth checking out in their own right—colorfully decorated iron railings now rarely seen in Britain. It's all good for a wander down maritime memory lane. You can do several walks from here down into the islands, including one around the shore to the lighthouse, passing a good beach. Bridges connect these islands to the Shetland mainland.

Yealtaland Bookshop (Main St., tel. 01595/880335, 10 A.M.–5 P.M. Mon.–Sat.) is a great secondhand bookshop with a wealth of local interest books and a helpful owner.

Accommodations and Food

There's no shortage of ambition when it comes to decor at well-regarded **Herrislea House Hotel** (Veensgarth, tel. 01595/840208, www.herrisleahouse.co.uk, £50–70 s, £80–110 d). Bright red on the outside, the country hotel has 13 brightly decorated rooms done up in sky blues, daffodil yellows, and rosy pinks. Somehow the colors combine to make for heartwarming places to spend the night. It's a good place to eat, too, with a select but stylish menu concentrating on lamb (the hotel rears its own) and seafood, like mussels marinere for starters followed by scallops with fresh tarragon.

The **Da Haaf** (NAFC Marine Centre Port Arthur, tel. 01595/772480, 8 A.M.–8 P.M. Mon.–Fri.) restaurant is part of the North Atlantic Fisheries College on the edge of Scalloway. Consequently the chefs here know a few things about good, fresh, locally caught seafood (£10–15).

Getting There and Away
John Leask & Son operates **bus** service 4, which takes 25 minutes to get from Lerwick to Scalloway. There are at least eight buses per day Monday–Saturday. Two to four buses continue to Hamnavoe and Burra.

WESTSIDE AND PAPA STOUR
Westside refers to the bulky peninsula sticking out west from Shetland's stringy mainland. It's a wildly undulating landscape of hills and lochans (small lochs), particularly in the west near Sandness (where it's positively lunar). Much of it is cultivated, however, so there's not so much of the barrenness you get farther north. Just off to the northeast is Papa Stour, an island with some of the U.K.'s most incredible cave systems.

Walls and Vicinity
Walls is a quiet village overlooking Vaila sound, coming to life for the **Walls Agricultural Show** in July. It's the metropolis of the area with a post office, a café, and a garage. The scattered houses of **Sandness** in the grassy fields overlooking Papa Stour have a pretty formidable approach northwest from Walls—over a creviced boulder-strewn landscape glimmering with lochs. Around Sandness a **coastal walk** has been developed from the car park at the far (west) end of the road; it takes you past some restored **Norse water mills** and continues on to impressive **rock stacks.**

Papa Stour
Low-lying, green-brown Papa Stour can seem a bit bleak at times. Celtic missionaries were the first people to settle here as early as the 6th century A.D.; the sheltered harbor meant it found favor with the Norse. The island was traditionally as much somewhere you were

COME TO PAPA

During the early 20th century, fuel supplies on Papa Stour began to dwindle and the island's already tiny population plummeted rapidly. Then in 1972 one enterprising local put the following advertisement in a national newspaper: "Island needs young people with adventurous spirit. Land and crofts available." Alternative types from around the world flooded in, and it seemed Papa Stour was saved. But at the first sign of winter most of the newcomers found conditions too harsh and left again. A few lingered, however, and the island survived. The island still has a fragile economy, and in recent years a feud between two leading families caused one to leave and the population to once again plunge toward crisis levels. Papa Stour may have to advertise for inhabitants again.

banished to as chose to inhabit: Leprosy sufferers from the Shetland mainland were once exiled here. Today its few visitors come for the birdlife and spectacular coastal scenery, which includes some of Scotland's finest **sea caves.** Ask around if you fancy chartering a boat to explore them—boats outnumber cars here.

Accommodations and Food
Want to get away from it all? You can't get a place that feels farther away from anywhere than **Burrastow House** (Walls, tel. 01595/809307, www.users.zetnet.co.uk/burrastow-house-hotel, £35 s, £70 d). This is the best, if not the only, place to stay in the area in a gorgeously remote location two miles outside Walls. There are now five rooms available at this whitewashed 18th-century house, both in the main house and the extension. Rooms have bathrooms with Victorian style bathtubs. The house overlooks tranquil, sparkling Vaila Sound. Right by the shore, the hotel has a boat for exploring local waters and a seafood-dominated menu (halibut, lobster, squid, mussels). The owners will tell you what is available for that day. On weekends it is open

to nonresidents for dinner. Feast in the conservatory or oak-paneled dining room. To get there, follow the road up the hill in Walls, bear left and keep going until the end.

The lively pine-furnished **Baker's Rest Tearooms** (Springfield, tel. 01595/809308, 10:30 A.M.–4:30 P.M. Mon.–Sat., noon–4:30 P.M. Sun.) is something of an oasis in these parts; it serves up products from the bakery next door like the delicious handmade biscuits (£1–5). You can get a decent cup of coffee, too. It doubles as a local **tourist information point** and shop.

Getting There and Away

Bus number 9 runs five times per day between Lerwick and Walls. A Monday, Friday, and Saturday shopper service operated by **Robinson Transport** (tel. 01595/745745) runs between West Burrafith and Lerwick. Make sure to book this service by the afternoon prior to travel.

A **ferry** runs to Papa Stour from **West Burrafith** (three times a day Mon., Wed., Fri., and Sat., one Sun. service, £2.80). **Flights** go from Tingwall to Papa Stour's airstrip every Tuesday (£26); they're proudly advertised as direct, but one wonders where else they would stop.

FOULA

Jostling with Fair Isle for title of the most isolated inhabited spot in the British Isles, windravaged Foula sits 20 miles off to the west of Walls, often cut off by gales for months at a time in winter. Its Norse name is Fugloy or "bird island"; a multitude of birds, including one of Britain's largest colonies of Great Skuas, make the island's high rocky cliffs their home. If you like remoteness and bird-watching *and* fancy staying, be aware there are no shops or restaurants—you'll have to bring your own provisions. Foula folk are even out on a limb when it comes to their Christmas festivities, celebrating them as Auld Yule on January 6.

You can stay on the island at **Leraback** (tel. 01595/753226, full board £35 pp), a modern bungalow with simple, white rooms (two have sea views). Booking in advance is essential; accommodation besides this is virtually nonexistent.

Getting There and Away

Cycharters Ltd (tel. 01595/693434 or 07787/945480) does a full-day sightseeing trip to Foula every Wednesday through summer. From Walls on Westside, there are ferries on Tuesday and Thursday year-round with **Atlantic Ferries** (tel. 07881/823732, 2-hr. crossing). Additional summer sailings run on Saturday from Walls and alternate Thursdays from Scalloway (3.5-hr. crossing). One-way passenger fares to Foula are £3. **Flights** to Foula are possible from Tingwall on Atlantic Airways (booking tel. 01595/840246, www.flyshetland.com, Mon.–Wed. and Fri., 15 min., £50 adults, £25 children round-trip).

Northmavine and North Mainland

Grassy Northmavine is almost an island, joined only by the evocatively named isthmus of Mavis Grind to the north of Shetland's mainland. Daubed with lochs, it rises in all its finery into superb, dramatic cliffs at Eshaness. This is the prettiest part of Shetland and has the most attractive accommodations on the island. Farther east, the deep Sullum Voe secretes the oil terminal of the same name, Europe's largest exporting oil terminal and Shetland's main economy-booster. Despite the comings and goings of oil tankers transporting millions of barrels worldwide, somehow a few minutes' drive away are the grassy inlets and unspoiled beaches of North Mainland. The area is a good wildlife-spying spot, and one of the best places to see Shetland ponies. You'll need to venture into the region for ferry connections to the North Isles, Whalsay, and Out Skerries.

MUCKLE ROE ISLAND AND BRAE

Muckle Roe is an idyllic red sandstone island connected to the mainland by a bridge. It's mainly just an attractive place to kick back for a while, with good diving (inquire at Lerwick TIC) and tranquil places to stay nearby. Brae is a big place in these parts with a population swelled by Sullum Voe oil workers. It's the unspectacular gateway to Muckle Roe Island and Northmavine.

Sights

From **North Ham** on Muckle Roe there are great views of Muckle Roe's red sandstone **cliffs and stacks.** It's here that you'll find the best **diving spots;** on a dive you can see **sea caves** and hosts of sand eels. The **Brae Hotel** (Brae, tel. 01806/522456) is a good source of local information on diving. North Ham is also the starting point for great walking on the island.

Accommodations and Food

In a quiet location on scenic Muckle Roe, **Westayre** (Muckle Roe, tel. 01806/522368, www.westayre.shetland.co.uk, £35 s, £56 d) has just two en suite rooms (one has a lovely bath). Both are homey, done up in soothing blues and mild pinks. A peat fire is lit in the sitting room/dining room of an evening to accentuate the coziness. Views are jaw-droppingly beautiful wherever you are, be it the dining room or the colorful garden. It's the last house in Muckle Roe after you cross the bridge.

Probably the best place to stay on Shetland, (**Busta House** (Busta, tel. 01806/522506, www.bustahouse.com, £75 s, £100–140 d) is a whitewashed hotel built in stages from the 16th to 18th centuries. Rooms are named after different Shetland Islands; there are light, white-furnished ones and more traditional ones with dark polished wood and four-poster beds. Many rooms have gorgeous views of Busta Voe, like the daffodil-colored Muckle Roe room, which comes with an adjoining lounge. Outside, wooded grounds lead down to the shoreline. Explore away: it's all part of the package. Busta House is also the best place to eat in the area by some way. Muckle Roe mussels and organically farmed cod are among the delights on offer. Mains are £8–11.

Decked out in white and blue, **Da Mish** (tel. 01806/242715, breakfast 9 A.M.–11 P.M., dinner 5–9 P.M.) café/bar does filling no-nonsense Scottish food. In the morning you can feast on piles of pancakes glued with maple syrup (£3.29) or for the evening try fresh haddock and chips (£5.95). It serves a constant flux of hungry oil workers as well as locals. Come evening this little place veritably shakes with discos, karaoke, pool-playing, and the like.

Getting There and Away

John Leask & Son runs six **buses** daily between Brae and Lerwick. The same service will run up to Toft for the Yell ferry from Brae, too.

SHETLAND ISLANDS

© LUKE WATERSON

a welcome to Northmavine

ESHANESS CLIFFS AND VICINITY

The grassy ground rises up slowly from the hamlet of Hillswick; you would never think that lying at the end of the narrow road to Eshaness would be Shetland's finest clifftop scenery. You could spend days wandering this dramatic stretch of coast. Add to that a lively museum and some great accommodation options and you have one of the most enticing areas to linger anywhere on the Shetlands.

◖ Eshaness Cliffs

This is Shetland's most fascinating stretch of coastal scenery: soaring grass-topped cliffs covered in yellow thrifts and ragged robin, towering precariously over a violently crashing sea. By the cliff car park is **Eshaness Lighthouse,** a dumpy square lighthouse built in 1929 by David Stevenson. From the cliffs near the lighthouse are the best views south along the coast to the north. You can peer down to the crashing sea far below in the dark, deep inlets gouged out of the rock. This stretch of coast

also contains **sea arches** and a **blow hole** (where sea water far below is blown up through a hole in the ground above). An information board points out the different phenomena the sea has carved up.

Tangwick Haa Museum

This restored 17th-century laird's house (Tangwick, tel. 01806/503389, 11 a.m.–5 p.m. daily May–Sept., free, donations greatly appreciated) explores the history of Northmavine. The particularly poignant contrasts between the area's wealthy and poor are best illustrated by a mid-19th-century wedding dress belonging to the wife of one of the lairds and details of the hardships of local fishermen. There's an intriguing display of nautical knots.

North Roe

On North Roe, northeast of Eshaness by some 12 miles via the A970, you can climb through a rock-strewn, loch-strewn landscape to **Ronas Hill,** the highest point on Shetland for views of the whole of Shetland and even Fair Isle.

© LUKE WATERSON

Eshaness Cliffs

Accommodations and Food

Braewick Café and Caravan Park (Braewick, tel. 01806/503345, www.eshaness.shetland.co.uk, tent and two people £6.50, café open 10 A.M.–6 P.M. daily Apr.–Sept., 10 A.M.–5 P.M. Wed.–Sun. Oct.–Mar.) is a rather exposed but extremely scenic grassy campsite. Space here is mainly for tents (and up to 10 caravans) overlooking Braewick Bay and the Drongs sea stacks. There is a shower room and coin-op hairdryer and laundry facilities. If the campsite views are good, from inside the café they are even better. Grab a window seat and feast on a range of hot and cold snacks, many made using produce grown on the croft. There's an evening menu available to guests with reservations.

There never used to be a road to Hillswick; visitors to the **(** **St. Magnus Hotel** (tel. 01806/503372, reception@stmagnusbayhotel.co.uk, £110 d) used to arrive by sea. In fact, so did the hotel itself, a unique wooden building made in Norway and reassembled on the cliffs here in the 1890s. New management has only recently taken over and is in the process of giving the place a revamp. The big, traditionally decked out rooms are getting antique furnishings to replace the 1970s greens and browns. All rooms are en suite and have amazing views of the coastline. There's a wood-paneled bar and a more formal restaurant—both get packed, particularly for the very good Sunday roast.

Getting There and Away

Operated by **Johnson Transport** (tel. 01806/522331), one or two **buses** daily connect Eshaness and Hillswick with Lerwick. A bus leaves Lerwick for Eshaness at 5:10 P.M. (service 21). You may have to change in Brae. Buses leave Eshaness at 7:15 A.M. for Hillswick and 9:40 A.M. for Lerwick.

NORTH MAINLAND

Red grouse and mountain hares haunt the inland hills of North Mainland, while seals and otters bask on the flat offshore rocks. Here you'll find one of Shetland's prettiest villages, its most eccentric museum, and the best place to see Shetland ponies.

Sights

With a still-active fishing pier and a colorful, Scandinavian appearance, **Voe** is one of Shetland's prettiest communities, nestled on the grassy slopes of Olna Firth. The owner of **The Cabin** (Wirlie, Vidlin, tel. 01806/577243, 10 A.M.–5 P.M. Tues.–Wed. and Fri.–Sat., 10 A.M.–1 P.M. Thurs., 10 A.M.–noon and 2–5 P.M. Sun., free) has accumulated an extensive collection of war memorabilia. If you have a passion for this sort of thing it's guaranteed the owner will match it. Expect photos, medals, uniforms, and other wartime artifacts, many of which reflect Shetland's part in World War II. Outside of the above hours it's worth phoning to see if the accommodating owner will open up. **Gletness** (open year-round) on Nesting is home to one of the island's main **Shetland pony studs.** This is a good place to get close up to these sturdy little creatures in their natural environment.

Accommodations and Food

In a former knitwear workshop, colorful **Sail Loft Camping Bod** (Voe, Delting, tel. 01595/694434, Apr.–Sept., beds £8) is the largest of Shetland's camping bods and one of the best ones to stay in. There are three public rooms and one bunkroom, all with a polished, open feel and great views down the fjordlike Ronas Voe. It's about as close as you will come in Scotland to feeling like you are in Norway. Book at Lerwick TIC.

Pierhead Bar and Restaurant (Voe, tel. 01806/588332, food served 12:30–2:30 P.M. and 6–9 P.M. daily) serves some of Shetland's best cuisine in an unbelievably picturesque stone restaurant by the pier in Voe. Succulent seafood shapes the menu here, like the seafood medley or fresh mussels in garlic and wine. Main courses are £10–20. The bar is open 11 A.M.–11 P.M. daily.

Getting There and Away

Bus service 23 makes six journeys per day connecting Lerwick with Toft to coincide with Yell ferries. These will all stop off at Voe. Voe is 30 minutes from Lerwick. There is one morning and one evening bus Monday–Saturday between Lerwick and Vidlin (Out Skerries ferry terminal) via Tingwall, Nesting junction, and Laxo (Whalsay ferry terminal).

WHALSAY

Whalsay is one of the most densely populated of the Shetland Islands—around 1,000 people on an island five miles long by two miles wide. The reasons are on display in the harbor—a fleet of glitzy, multimillion-pound fishing vessels. These deep sea trawlers are among Europe's largest fishing boats; they can keep catch fresh at sea for long periods and are thus far more effective at fish-catching than other boats. Whalsay may have wealth, but tourist attractions it does not. There's a photogenic coastline to stroll with plenty of basking seals and lobster pots, but the most interesting thing about the island is its associations with renowned Scottish poet Hugh McDiarmid. You can visit **Greive House** (off main road opposite Loch of Huxter, tel. 01595/693434, beds £6), where McDiarmid lived on the island throughout the 1930s and relive the writer's impoverished life by staying here (it's now a camping bod).

Ferries (tel. 01806/566259) run frequently (about every 45 min.) between Laxo on the mainland and Symbister on Whalsay. It's £7.60 for a car and driver.

OUT SKERRIES

Even when a storm is raging out at sea, the sheltered harbor of Bod Voe where boats arrive on the Out Skerries remains surreally calm. These tiny islands have a history fraught with shipwrecks and smuggling. The rocky coast teems with seabirds like puffins (Taamie Nories in local speak) and oystercatchers. Fishing is still a big thing here; so friendly are the locals that you may even find someone prepared to take you out on their boat looking for mackerel. The best time to visit Out Skerries is in July for the **Eela competition,** when fishermen compete to catch the biggest fish, then party all night. The island has a couple of shops, a post office, a public toilet, and precious little else in the way of amenities.

Accommodations

Rocklea (Out Skerries, tel. 01806/515228, www.rockleaok.co.uk, £23 pp) is a very friendly bed-and-breakfast with three snug, white, centrally heated rooms. Rocklea also offers the handy option of evening meals for an additional £12 in this restaurant-less part of the world.

Getting There and Away

You can reach the Out Skerries by **ferry** (tel. 01806/515226) from Lerwick/Vidlin (Mon., Tues., Thurs., and 3 daily Fri.–Sun., 2.5 hours, £2.80). Lerwick sailings are on Tuesday and Thursday. You can also **fly** from Tingwall on Monday, Wednesday, and Friday. Contact Tingwall Airport (tel. 01595/840246) for flight information.

The Northern Isles

These islands look—and feel—like the furthest extent of Britain. They are dominated by foreboding peaty moorland that alternates from purple-brown to almost black depending on the time of year. They are sparsely populated, wind-swept places even by Shetland standards, littered with the ruins of humans who tried to forge a life here and failed. Where mankind has retreated, nature has thrived. It's to get a glimpse of this nature, or through a fascination with extremes, that visitors come here. Yell is the bleakest island with a wonderful museum and the area's best eating spot; Fetlar is a little-visited haven for birdlife; and Unst is Scotland's most northerly hurrah before plunging into the North Sea. Unst has the internationally important bird reserve of Hermaness and a strong community spirit that has resulted in the creation of several fascinating visitor attractions.

YELL

The main road from Ulsta in the south to Gutcher in the northeast gives you little time to appreciate Yell; impressions are likely to be of a bleak, treeless island with little save the pale yellow-green and purple-brown colors of the moorland to distract the eye. Take time to explore the back roads, though, and you'll see the peaty moor give way to gentler terrain—the pretty hamlet of Burravoe with its museum depicting the history of Yell and a grassy coast, one of the best places in Europe to see otters.

Sights

There are several places on the island to catch a glimpse of **otters:** the east coast between Gossaburgh and Otterswick and south of Gutcher at Burraness (also good for seal-spotting) are some of the best. They are timid creatures, so approach quietly.

The **Old Haa Heritage Centre** (Burravoe, tel. 01957/722339, 10 A.M.–4 P.M. Tues.–Thurs. and Sat., 2–5 P.M. Sun. Apr.–Sept., free, donations appreciated) was originally built in 1672 by a fish merchant; Yell's oldest house is now the home to this museum exploring Yell's history. You might think this wouldn't amount to much, but it will take some time to absorb the detailed displays. One room contains wildlife photographs by renowned Yell naturalist Bobby Tulloch, and there's a lot of time devoted to a display on the *Bohus*, a German ship wrecked off Yell's east coast. The figurehead of the *Bohus*, known now as the **White Wife,** stands on the coast at Otterswick, a poignant memorial to the disaster gazing out to sea. All the hard work that has gone into this museum is incredible.

Just north of Cullivoe are the **Sands of Breckon,** a beach made of crushed shells. Park at the farm and walk down. The fields around are carpeted with wildflowers.

Accommodations and Food

Windhouse Lodge (A968 west of Mid Yell turn-off, Apr.–Sept. and by arrangement, beds £8) is one of the better-equipped of Shetland's atmospheric but basic camping bods. It's the

© LUKE WATERSON

the White Wife, a shipwreck figurehead, Yell

gatehouse to an allegedly haunted lodge on top of the hill. It gets nippy in the evenings but there is a stove to huddle by. Bring your own bedding.

These days **Norwind Guesthouse** (Hillend, tel. 01957/702312, £33 s, £55 d) is about the only guesthouse on the island, a modern house with big, clean, white rooms, en suite bathrooms, and huge breakfasts. Save at least an hour for the latter; the owners are chatty types and will always insist on you having more. It's at the top of Mid Yell village just past the old fire station; the views are of hills thrusting down to the sea at Mid Yell Voe. If you like the idea of the belly-stretching meals and want more of the same, you can also arrange for a dinner, bed, and breakfast package.

In an unassuming, green, wind-buffeted shack, [C] **Wind Dog Café** (tel. 01957/744321, 9 A.M.–5 P.M. Mon.–Fri. 10 A.M.–5 P.M. Sat.–Sun., 6:30–9 P.M. daily mid-May–Aug.) is a busy little place seeing anyone who is anyone passing by en route to Unst, Fetlar, or the mainland. Locals and tourists seem to love it equally. You can get Yell's finest coffee here and a good selection of light snacks and meals (£0.80–5). There are even books to read and speedy Internet access. Inside it's quite spacious, and in summer there is live music.

Services
Aywick Shop (tel. 01957/702077, 8:30 A.M.– 9 P.M. daily) tends to all shopping needs from postcards to compost to camera batteries. It also has a post office and petrol. It's on the east coast near Otterswick.

Getting There and Away
The **ferry** from Toft on the mainland to Ulsta in southwest Yell (tel. 01957/722259) runs almost hourly throughout the week (slightly reduced Sunday service, 20 min., £7.60 car and driver round-trip).

An equally frequent service connects Gutcher in North Yell with Unst. When you buy your ticket on the Toft–Ulsta ferry, this is also valid for travel on to Unst and Fetlar.

An 8 A.M. **overland bus** leaves Lerwick and will connect you through from Ulsta at 9:30 A.M. to the Gutcher ferry terminal for onward Unst and Fetlar services. Up to two or three buses connect Ulsta with Gutcher and Cullivoe Monday–Saturday.

If you miss a connection, call **Yell Hire** (tel. 01957/722280) for a taxi.

FETLAR
Fertile Fetlar is known as the Garden of Shetland and attracts some of Britain's rarest birds around the marshy Loch of Funzie. The island was once home to Britain's only breeding pair of snowy owls; sadly, none have been seen here since 1995. Fetlar's birdlife and its historical connections with the development of antiseptic medicine are explored, along with a host of other intriguing issues, in the Fetlar Interpretive Centre. There are also a smattering of archaeological sites and good beaches on the island.

Sights
Colorfully painted **Fetlar Interpretive Centre** (Beach of Houbie, tel. 01957/733206, www

.fetlar.com, 11 A.M.–3 P.M. Mon.–Fri., 1–4 P.M. Sat.–Sun. May–Sept., £2 adults, £1 seniors) is pretty switched on to the 21st century; interactive presentations on wildlife and Internet access are on offer. Fetlar's natural history is fascinating, but more so are the displays on the history of Sir William Watson Cheyne, Fetlar's very own pioneer of antiseptic surgery. There is a good sandy **beach** at nearby Tresta. The **Loch of Funzie** is an important breeding ground for birds including the red-necked phalarope. The B988 runs past the loch at the east end of the island.

East of the northern end of Finnigert Daek, a possibly Bronze Age wall splitting Fetlar in two, is **Haltadans** (tel. 01957/733246, during bird-breeding season May–Sept., call RSPB Warden to arrange access, free), an ancient ring of stones surrounding an earth bank. Central stones allegedly represent a fiddler and his wife who were playing for a dancing group of trows (trolls) when the sun came up and turned them to stone.

Accommodations

Gord (Houbie, tel. 01957/733227, £25 pp) is about the island's only place to stay inside four solid walls. You'll have no complaints. The whitewashed, orange-roofed house has three comfortable en suite rooms, all enjoying exquisite views. Evening meals are £12 pp.

Getting There and Away

There are up to seven **sailings** from Gutcher on Yell to Hamars Ness on Fetlar. It's a 25- to 30-minute crossing.

UNST

By the time you get to Unst (www.unst.org) you're 160 miles north of mainland Scotland and on the same latitude as Anchorage, Alaska. The catchphrase on the island website says it all: The Island above All Others. As far as Britain goes, that is true. But Unst is not as desolate as Yell or Fetlar, and while it can rival them in walking and wildlife, it can exceed them in tourist facilities. There's generally more to do here and more of a buzz than on any other Shetland island. This includes, besides the array of bird-life, a castle and two fascinating museums.

Even with your own transport, it's stretching things to fit Unst into a day trip; staying on the island is recommended.

South Unst

Lawrence Bruce, the cruel Sheriff of Shetland, built **Muness Castle** (southeast tip of island by Uyeasound, open year-round, free), Britain's most northerly castle because he feared attack from the son of his half-brother, Patrick Stewart, Earl of Orkney. Earl Patrick did come to Unst intent on destroying the castle, as Bruce had predicted, but his forces withdrew at the last minute for reasons that history leaves unexplained. French raiders did Earl Patrick's job for him, ransacking the castle in 1627. You can climb to the first floor of this gray-stoned ruin and see the main hall. The decorative bases of what would once have been turrets are on the outside walls.

North Unst

Unst Bus Shelter (South of Haroldswick, year-round) is Britain's most northerly bus shelter, and easily its most bizarre. It comes with a TV, free snacks, a sofa to sit on, and even whisky to drink. You'll be loath to take the bus when it does arrive, which isn't often.

Housed in a shed in Haroldswick, **Unst Boat Haven** (Haroldswick, tel. 01957/711528, 11 A.M.–5 P.M. daily May–Sept., £2 adults, £1 seniors) is an extensive collection of boats. Among the exhibits are traditional Shetland Sixareens (square-sailed fishing boats manned by six oarsmen and rowed up to 40 miles offshore in the hunt for catch). This is an evocative introduction to how traditional fishing boats in Shetland would have looked and been used. Equally fascinating is how Shetland's history dictated how boats were built. Fishermen had little money and so boats were built simply but also with pride. Up until the 18th century, wood was imported from Norway for building boats, while more recently Scottish larch has been used. Among the other items on display here is a large collection of sea shells.

What makes the **Unst Heritage Centre** (West of Haroldswick, 11 A.M.–5 P.M. daily May–Sept., £2 adults, £1 seniors) stand out from others is that a lot of the history it covers lives on in the Unst community still. Skills like spinning are still practiced by residents; wooden furniture like that in the museum still furnishes their houses. Fishing and Unst's part in the defense of Britain (the island housed until recently the most northerly RAF base) are the main topics. It's housed in a rather ugly building on the edge of Haroldswick. You can get a joint admission ticket for the Boat Haven and the Heritage Centre.

☾ Hermaness

Allegedly Hermaness (northernmost Unst west of Burra Firth, RSPB Warden tel. 01957/711278, Scottish National Heritage Office tel. 01595/693345, year-round, visitors center open daily May–Sept.) took its name from a giant who used this barren ground as a place to hurl rocks at another giant across the voe. Walking through this bird reserve at the northern tip of Unst and thus Great Britain gives you a pretty special feeling. You are as far north as Britain takes you and, for the most part, only accompanied by some of the country's most diverse seabird life, including fulmars and puffins. Then at the northern tip of the reserve, the dramatic Stevenson lighthouse of **Muckle Flugga** comes into view, perched on jagged rocks just off the coast. This really is the last outpost of mankind in a part of the country where nature has triumphed. Keep to the paths (difficult as this can be in the wet) in the reserve to avoid being dive bombed by Great Skuas. There is a white-painted **visitors center** perched on the slopes above the gray Burra Firth. This is a good frame of reference for information on birds in the reserve, and you can get Britain's most northerly coffee at the café. To get there, keep following the signs north from Haroldswick on the B9086.

Muckle Flugga Charters (tel. 01806/522447, www.muckleflugga.co.uk, trips from Baltasound Pier) runs trips to see Britain's most northerly lighthouse, Muckle Flugga. You can spot a whole host of birdlife on the way. Booking is essential. The company also has a boat that can take you diving to see a sunken submarine.

Accommodations and Food

Gardiesfauld Youth Hostel (tel. 01957/755279, www.gardiesfauld.shetland.co.uk, £11) is Britain's most northerly youth hostel. It has carpeted 2- to 11-bed dormitory-style accommodations and a lounge centered on a fire. There's a coin-operated laundry and shower facilities.

No longer is there a reason not to stay overnight on Unst, thanks to **Saxa Vord** (Haroldswick, tel. 01957/711711, www.saxavord.com, bunks £15). This is a simply huge place in a recently converted army base with oodles of rooms. At the time of writing it was offering just self-catering and bunkhouse accommodation (seven warm two-bed rooms, shared bathrooms, a kitchen, and lounge). In its infancy, the layout is still higgledy-piggledy, but you can get warming meals

Unst Bus Shelter, the most northerly bus shelter in Britain

at the bar/restaurant. A study center has now opened in the former officer's mess, and big plans are afoot to add a hotel and spa to this surreal-looking complex.

Buness House (Buness, east of Baltasound, tel. 01957/711315, buness-house@zetnet.co.uk, £65 s, £110 d) is the best guesthouse on the island, reportedly standing since the 15th century. There are four en suite rooms (one decorated with 19th-century decoupage). The **Baltasound Hotel** (Baltasound, tel. 01957/711334, www.baltasound-hotel.shetland.co.uk, £49 s, £78 d) is Britain's northernmost hotel. Accommodation is available in the main building and also in slightly claustrophobic but comfortable log chalets. The bar stocks no fewer than six Valhalla Brewery ales.

Getting There and Away

Regular **ferries** (about hourly) connect Belmont in south Unst with Gutcher on northeast Yell. Journey time is about 10 minutes. Two to three **buses,** operated by **P & T Coaches** (tel. 01957/711666), connect Haroldswick with Baltasound and Belmont. It's best to phone in advance to check the timetable.

SHETLAND ISLANDS

BACKGROUND

The Land

Scotland, along with Wales and England, makes up the country of Great Britain. The landmass of Great Britain is the largest island in Europe, and Scotland occupies the northern third of this island. The country sits at a latitude of mainly between 54° and 61° north and on a longitude between 02°01' west and 07°15' west. It lies on a latitudinal par with the north of Quebec and St. Petersburg in Russia. Scotland's only land border is a 60-mile frontier with England to the south. Scotland's entire north, east, and west borders are with the sea. A cursory glance at a map of Scotland makes it seem geographically modest. The country is just 274 miles long and 154 miles wide at its extremes, and as little as 25 miles wide at its narrowest point. This gives it a total land area of 30,414 miles—Scotland could fit inside the U.S. state of Texas eight times with room to spare. Its highest point, despite its reputation as a mountainous country, is only 4,406 feet. Small-scale on the world stage Scotland may be, but don't underestimate this little country; when you're traveling through it will seem vast. The reason is its tricky topography. The enormous number of inlets and islands gives Scotland one of the longest coastlines in Europe; the region of Argyll and

© LUKE WATERSON

the Inner Hebrides alone has more coastline than all of France. These inlets together with vast freshwater lochs all but cut the country off into pieces, and long mountain ranges finish the job.

GEOLOGY

Scotland's most important geological feature is the Highland boundary fault, which splits Scotland in two from Stonehaven in the northeast to Helensburgh and Arran in the southwest. Everything north of the boundary fault is mountainous upland, while to the south lies fertile lowland. Over the millennia, this has come to define the country's character, down to its agriculture, its urban areas, and the mentality of its people. The fault was formed by a mighty collision of tectonic plates about 400 million years ago. To the north of this line lie waves of hard metamorphic Precambrian or Cambrian rocks, including the Assynt region's gray-green Lewisian Gneiss, some of the world's oldest rock. To the south of the fault lie softer sedimentary rocks like the old red sandstone. Scotland's chaotic seismological thrusts seem to be well behind it; the country's volcanoes are still very evident but all extinct and earthquakes are unheard of in recent times.

GEOGRAPHY

Scotland's geography can be split into two key areas: the area to the north of the Highland Boundary Fault (the Highland) and the area lying immediately south of the Highland Boundary Fault (the lowland). The Highland area comprises raw mountain scenery and, farther north, gives way to expanses of peat bog. The soil in these upland areas is generally thin and acidic; vegetation is therefore dominated by hardy moorland plants like heather and patches of coniferous forest. The lowland area of Scotland, transected by the country's major rivers including the River Tay and the River Forth, is a lush, highly cultivated area with large coverings of trees. Four-fifths of Scotland's population lives in this area of Scotland, which means this region is also significantly more urbanized. The major cities of Edinburgh and Glasgow fall within this region, but Scotland as a whole is still classified as 98 percent rural.

Mountains

Scotland's mountains are not high by the standards of the Himalayas, the Rockies, or even other European mountain ranges. They are, however, often stark, rocky, sheer, and notoriously difficult to climb. They also offer some of Europe's most uninterrupted upland scenery. Many of these mountains are characterized by their sheer-sidedness, the result of chiseling by a number of ice age glaciers. The mountains of Scotland can be classified into three main groups. Most important are the **Grampian Mountain Range,** which follow the path of the Highland Boundary Fault. All Scotland's key peaks, including Ben Nevis, the highest point in Britain, can be found within this range. The Grampians include the **Cairngorm Mountains,** which lie immediately south of the River Spey in the Southern Highlands. These mountains are known as the roof of Britain, as they form the largest unbroken high-altitude plateau in the country. To the northwest of the Cairngorms and to the southeast of the Great Glen lie the **Monadhliath Mountains.** As the Grampian Range continues southwest toward the west coast it divides into the **Mamores and Aonachs Mountains** lying either side of Loch Leven and the **Nevis Range** lying to the north. The Nevis Range ruptures into Scotland's highest peak, Ben Nevis. The Grampians then extend west into the mountains of **Lochalsh** and **Knoydart.** The other important mountain range in Scotland lies on the Isle of Skye in the shape of the **Cuillin Range.** They're the most dramatic peaks of the lot, soaring straight out of the sea in a flurry of pinnacles, corries, and ridges. The Cuillin are the most challenging peaks to scale in the country. The term "Munro" is used to refer to any Scottish mountain over 3,000 feet (914 meters). The term comes from the mountain-compiler Sir Hugh Munro (1856–1919), who made a comprehensive list of these peaks. "Munro-bagging" is a popular activity in Scotland, and there are 284

Munro mountains in Scotland. This figure changes almost yearly, not through any geological phenomenon but through continuous arguments amongst those in the know as to what constitutes a mountain peak.

Besides adventure-seekers, Scotland's mountains also attract much wildlife, including red deer and golden eagles.

Forests

Once, Scotland was nearly all forest. The country-wide arboreal spread was known as the Caledonian pine forest and now only has a few remnants left in Highland Perthshire, Glen Affric, and in the foothills of the Cairngorm Mountains. A hugely significant 14 percent of Scotland is forest, however. Forests in Scotland are enjoyed by recreational users and are also at the heart of a sustainable forestry industry. Scotland's forests are owned and managed by a body known as the **Forestry Commission.** Forest areas are spread fairly equally throughout the country. The wild **Galloway Forest Park** is the largest forest park in Britain, spanning much of the inland areas of Dumfries and Galloway. Perthshire, which dubs itself "Big Tree Country" has several areas of gorgeous forest, including a patch of ancient Caledonian pine forest in the **Tay Forest Park.** One of the most popular areas of forest in the country is in the lovely **Queen Elizabeth Forest Park** in the Trossachs. The area around Inverness is littered with forests important enough to keep timber as one of the city's main sources of income. The **Rothiemurchus Forest** that sits below the Cairngorm Mountains near Aviemore is a great forest park to explore and forms the largest tract of Caledonian pine forest left in Scotland.

Lochs

One of Scotland's key geographical features are its lochs, or lakes, found spattered across the northern half of the country. Lochs are a mix of freshwater and saltwater in Scotland. The largest two freshwater lochs in Scotland are also its most famous. **Loch Lomond** snakes north of Glasgow for 23 miles and has an overall area of 27.5 square miles. **Loch Ness** is 21.8 square miles but due to its depth is the country's largest loch by volume of water. It's deep enough to hide an alleged monster and is far and away the most popular loch to visit in Scotland. Few bodies of freshwater in the world attract so many visitors. **Loch Awe,** while considerably smaller than these two giants, is the third-largest loch (14.9 square miles), still able to fit an area the size of Greater London into its midst. The only significant lowland loch is **Loch Leven.** Lochs usually occur in Scotland between steep mountains in fjordlike valleys.

The predominance of lochs has had several key effects on Scotland. They have, throughout history, been strategic defensive sites, and today lochs contain over 2,000 years of man-made buildings either on their shores or on islands in their midst, from crannogs (basic island fortifications) to castles. Lochs are also extremely important areas for wildlife, none more so than **Loch Maree** in the Northern Highlands, the islands of which form a crucial habitat for birds like black-throated divers. **Loch Druidibeg** in the Outer Hebrides is an important habitat for Greylag Geese. Lochs are also recreational destinations, with Loch Ness and Loch Lomond seeing plenty of cruises, canoeists, and kayakers. **Loch Tay** in Perthshire and **Loch Ken** in Dumfries and Galloway are major water sports destinations. Fishing is another extremely popular loch-based activity in Scotland. There are few better fishing lakes in the world than Loch Awe and on the Orkney Islands at the **Loch of Harray;** both provide stupendous catches.

Rivers

Scotland's main rivers lie for the majority of their course in the central and southern regions of the country. The longest river, the **River Tay,** rises high on the slopes of Ben Lui in Perthshire and flows 120 miles before reaching the sea at Dundee. The River Tay is popular in its upper reaches with water sports enthusiasts, with its rapids east of Loch Tay being the finest white-water rafting destination in Scotland. The **River Spey,** Scotland's second-longest river at 107 miles, has a wide, looping course through the Southern Highlands and Moray. A long-distance footpath runs the length of its course. In Moray it forms the focal point of the prolific whisky-producing Speyside region; the Spey's waters flavor many of Scotland's best single malts. The **River Clyde** has long been at the heart of Scotland's industrial prosperity. At 106 miles long it is Scotland's third-longest river. It powered the cotton mills of South Lanarkshire and brought in the ships so important to Glasgow's 19th-century trade. Scotland's other famous river is the **River Dee,** with a length of 85 miles. It forms the area known as Royal Deeside in Aberdeenshire, the location of the British Royal Family's holiday home, Balmoral. The River Dee generates more in tourism revenue than any other river in Scotland, reaching the sea at Aberdeen.

Fishing, a major recreational activity on Scotland's rivers, is best on the most southerly of Scotland's major rivers, the **River Tweed.** This river is one of Scotland's most richly vegetated rivers. It's not only fish that make their home in Scottish rivers; a huge variety of birdlife also have rivers as the center of their habitat, such as the herons on the **River Don.** Scotland's major rivers form wide valleys called straths. In a predominantly hilly landscape, the wide fertile plains of straths are major farming and population centers.

Coasts and Islands

When all the islands are factored in, Scotland's incredibly indented coast extends to over 10,000 miles. The shoreline is at its most jagged on the west of the country, where steep-sided sea lochs similar to the Norwegian fjords cut deep into the mainland mountains. Scotland's boundary with the sea often takes the form of dramatic cliffs, which are important habitats for maritime flowers and seabirds. In the northwest of the country, and on several Scottish islands, the hard Precambrian rock soars into very high cliffs. In the south and east of the country below the line of the Highland Boundary Fault, the cliffs are made of softer red sandstone, forming a broken series of pinnacles, sea stacks, and cliff overhangs.

Both types of cliffs are favorites with wildlife. Among Scotland's most important cliffs are **Cape Wrath,** the highest series of cliffs on the British mainland, and the cliffs of **St. Kilda** near the Outer Hebrides. Where Scotland's rivers empty into the sea, they form a series of wide estuary mouths called firths, such as the **Firth of Clyde** near Glasgow and the **Firth of Forth** north of Edinburgh. Often these firths are characterized by calm, sheltered water and sandy shallows. Beaches form the other major coastal feature in Scotland. Scotland has some of the most beautiful beaches in Europe in terms of unspoiled, uninterrupted expanses of sand. Scotland's islands, which number around 800, mostly lie off the north and west coasts. The vast majority are north of the Highland Boundary Fault and therefore form similar terrain to the Highlands of Scotland (peat bogs and mountains). The islands fall into four key groups: the **Shetland Islands** and the **Orkney Islands** off the north coast and the **Outer Hebrides** and the **Inner Hebrides,** including Skye, off the west coast. Strong tides like the **Corrywreckan** off Jura and the **Pentland Firth** between the Orkneys and the northern Scottish mainland churn between these islands, due to their exposure to open ocean and the rocky sea beds between them.

CLIMATE

Scottish weather is notoriously disagreeable, changeable, and sometimes just plain awful; Scotland is probably the only country in the world to depend on its poor weather to the extent that it can be a selling point for the tourism industry. Mist and torrential rain are marketed as enhancing the moody beauty of the mountaintops and providing the perfect excuse to sit by a peat fire in a pub with a dram of whisky.

Before complaining about Scottish climate too much, it's worth noting Scotland is on the same latitude as Labrador in Canada, where icebergs and prolonged heavy snow are common winter conditions. Scotland enjoys a far less extreme climate than this location thanks to the Gulf Stream, or North Atlantic Drift. This warm current of water makes for a far milder climate and improves air temperature by several degrees in western Scotland. The climate in Scotland is temperate and temperamental but rarely very hot or very cold. Temperatures in December and January range on average 32–43°F (0–6°C), while in the height of summer between June and August temperatures reach on average 64–68°C (18–20°C). Despite the relatively mild climate, Scotland experiences most of Britain's climatic extremes. The lowest ever temperature in Britain of -17°F (-27.2°C) was recorded at Braemar in Aberdeenshire.

Scotland is a very windy country due to the amount of exposed ground. Rainfall, particularly in western Scotland, is high, with parts of the Highlands getting over 177 inches (4,500 mm) annually. Wet weather in Scotland occurs so frequently because the warm, wet air created by the Gulf Stream is forced to rise over the high Grampian Mountains, where it cools, condenses, and forms precipitation. Scotland may be snowy by British standards, but on a worldwide scale it receives comparatively little snow. Parts of the Highlands see anything from 35 to 105 days of snow per year, most occurring between November and April. The best times of year weather-wise are of course a lottery, but May, September, and October are as likely to produce good weather as the height of summer. Even in summer evenings, the weather can turn very cool.

Keeping Track of the Weather

Whatever the weather is doing, it will be printed in newspapers daily and announced on local and national TV several times daily. If you're going to be out at sea, tune in to National Radio Four for an installment of the *Shipping Forecast*. You can also keep up to date with the weather on nationwide website www.bbc.co.uk.

ENVIRONMENTAL ISSUES

The main areas for environmental concern in Scotland are now the development of renewable energy sources and climate change.

Scottish environmental policy is frequently at odds with U.K. environmental policy, however. The Scottish National Party (SNP) has, since its election in May 2007, implemented a "No New Nuclear Power" strategy in stark contrast to the overall U.K. policy, which has given the green light on nuclear development. Taken as separate from England and Wales, Scotland has one of the best potentials in Europe for sustaining its power by renewable energy sources, having a huge amount of wind, wave, and water energy to tap into. It is anticipated that the U.K. as a whole will rely heavily and, many say, unfairly, on Scotland to meet proposed European Union renewable energy targets. Wind farms, such as the proposed development of the world's largest onshore wind farms on Barvas Moor in the Outer Hebrides, raise two environmental concerns. Firstly, the most unspoiled, scenic parts of the country are being targeted for energy development. Secondly, wind farms have also proven to be hazardous for birds, with the Outer Hebrides being one of the most important seabird sites in the country. It is predicted that birdlife, as other examples of wind farm developments across the country can testify, will suffer fatalities from wind farms as they get caught in the turbine blades.

The other major threat to the Scottish environment from energy resources in the past has been the oil and gas industries. The Braer oil disaster of 1993 off the coast of Shetland would have been more catastrophic (although many seabirds still died) had wind not dispersed the 85,000 tons of oil spilled. Still, the fact that a disaster such as this could occur in the relative nascence of the industry has put Scottish environmentalists on their guard.

While nuclear power is now less of an issue in Scotland than before, high incidences of cancer on the north coast and on the Orkney Islands have been linked with the proximity of these areas to the nuclear power station at Dounreay. Ironically, perhaps the most devastating effect of all on the Scottish environment came through tree-planting. The forestry commission planted large amounts of nonnative forest close to ecologically sensitive peat bog in northeast Scotland, which has still not recovered as an ecosystem.

The effects of global warming have begun to show themselves in the Highlands, with sub-arctic ecosystems that function in the upper reaches of the mountains being forced to retreat farther up onto the ridges to maintain the temperatures they require for survival. Soon simple facts of geology will leave them with nowhere to retreat to.

The story of Scotland's environment is not a completely bleak one. Many environmental bodies are now in place to monitor future environmental changes. Some wield significant power at a national level. The Green Party, a party committed to environmental improvement, currently has two seats in the Scottish Parliament. Groups like the Royal Society for the Protection of Birds (RSPB) have created a series of parks and reserves, which act as safe havens for nature and are committed to the ecological development of Scotland, with land used in a nature-friendly way.

Flora and Fauna

FLORA

The fate of Scotland's flora is, and will continue to be, closely linked to the fate of the animal life, birdlife, and sealife that depend upon it. With a climate ranging from the positively clement to the virtually arctic, the diversity of Scotland's flora is huge. The pine forests of the Cairngorm Mountains seem as if they have been transported from the Alps or the Rocky Mountains, while at the other end of the spectrum are the temperate coastal plant phenomena like lush subtropical gardens and flower-carpeted sand dunes.

Trees

It's a misnomer to think of Scotland as a tree-less place. The vast majority of Scotland has ready access to large tracts of woodland and forest, and forests alone cover 14 percent of the country. Coniferous forests and woodlands are dominated by pine trees, while deciduous forests are dominated by oak. Scotland is the birthplace of commercial forestry, which began in Perthshire in the 18th century. The remains of the ancient **Caledonian pine forest** have been reduced to a paltry 1 percent of their former glory. Once they covered Scotland from head to toe, and now they have been pushed back to areas of the Southern Highlands and Perthshire. These patches of forest are up to 10,000 years old. Rothiemurchus Forest,

clustered below the Cairngorm Mountains, is one of the most ancient patches of forest in Europe. Many individual trees here are over 300 years old and contain a rich variety of bird, plant, and animal life. Around Sunart, by the Ardnamurchan Peninsula, are lush, unique **Atlantic oakwoods,** particularly rich in their array of mosses and ferns and, because of their proximity to the sea, an extraordinary array of wildlife from pine martens and porpoises. Patches of **broadleaf woodland** can be found across Scotland, too.

Flowers

In spring and summer, Scotland becomes a gaudily colorful place where the high moors blaze with yellow gorse and purple heather and the tropical gardens teem with rhododendrons. There are over 500 species of wildflower in Britain, and most of these can be spotted in Scotland. In the woods, look out for bluebells, pungent wild garlic, bright yellow primroses, white ransoms, and some of Europe's most diverse mosses and lichens. On upland slopes and moor, look out for the distinctive bell heather, cloudberry, and bog asphodel, while hogging the sea cliffs are different diminutive flowers like thrift and ragged robin. There are some truly beautiful and spectacular flowers in Scotland, including several different species of white and purple orchids and the rounded red-brown bilberry. There are also several edible (and tasty) wild plants; Scotland is particularly good for wild mushroom-hunting due to its warm, wet climate.

Unique Vegetation Zones
MACHAIR
Machair is the Gaelic word for the low-lying vegetated sand dunes that back many beaches, particularly in the Outer Hebrides. The ecosystem is made unique by the presence of seashell shards in the sandy soil and exposure to sea salt. The machair can include rare flowers like yellow orchids and yellow rattle and are extremely vulnerable to erosion by storms. Rare birds like the corncrake also frequent the machair. The roots of the vegetation bind the sand together.

UPLAND BLANKET BOG
The north of Scotland and the Isle of Lewis in the Outer Hebrides contain two of Europe's prime areas of blanket bog, which grows by a nominal rate each year and is up to 6,000 years old. Virtually all of the 124,000 hectares of blanket bog in Britain is in Scotland. Many notable plants are found in this region, such as bilberries, sundews, dwarf birch, and cowberries. The pools in between the bog are important for otters.

FAUNA
Livestock and Game
Often, Scotland's specially reared animals can produce as much affectionate cooing from visitors as the wildlife. In the case of the much-loved **Highland cattle,** livestock is often placed in fields near the main tourist routes just to enhance the bucolic ambience. Highland Cattle are one of the purest breeds of cattle in existence, identifiable by their shaggy ginger coats and sharp horns. They were traditionally bred to withstand the often-brutal weather and infertile pastures of the Highlands. The other main breed of cow in Scotland is the black **Aberdeen Angus,** sadly more recognizable on a restaurant menu than in reality. The islands of Scotland have their own unique brands of sheep, including the stocky **Shetland sheep** of the Shetland Islands and the brown and white semi-wild **Soay sheep** of St. Kilda. A great time to see a coming together of Scotland's diverse livestock is at a county show. The best county shows are on the islands where community spirit is most concentrated.

Other Mammals
Scotland is not a country for spotting big wild animals. Still, catching sight of one of Scotland's wild creatures is a magical experience and a reaffirmation of the stark beauty of nature in a land where true wildernesses are hard to find. One of the most iconic Scottish animals is the **red deer** which, after a scare, are now on the increase. These are the largest wild animals in Scotland, measuring around four feet (120 cm) in height and up to nine feet (285 cm) in length. Other types of deer include the smaller, brown-colored **roe deer, fallow deer,** and the tiny **muntjac deer,** also found in upland areas. **Moose** have, as of 2008, been reintroduced to Scotland and are roaming free once more in the Highlands. The **pine marten,** once hunted almost to extinction for its valued fur, is now an increasingly common sight in Scotland; they are shy, reddish-brown creatures of the weasel family. European **badgers** are distinctly different from American badgers. Found throughout Scotland, they have more distinctive black and white facial stripes, longer faces, and strong jaws. They are omnivores, living on a diet of grubs but also plants and tree roots. Other wild mammals include foxes, feral goats, and otters. The Cairngorm Mountains also host Britain's only herd of **reindeer,** but they're not wild animals. **Voles** in Scotland have evolved to be so plentiful they even have their own unique subspecies, such as the **Orkney voles** and the **Raasay voles.**

Sealife
Common seals, the larger **grey seals, minke whales, orcas** (killer whales), **common dolphins,** and **bottle-nosed dolphins** can all be sighted off Scotland's coast, as can the world's second-biggest fish, the **basking shark,** at 11 meters long. Scotland's waters are full of

© LUKE WATERSON

Highland cows are some of the world's most placid creatures.

fish, but the comparatively cool water means there isn't the range of sea creatures you get in other areas of the world. **Eels** are common in the Atlantic, where **pike** and **Atlantic salmon** can exceed a meter in length. There are also many types of **shellfish.**

Reptiles and Amphibians

Scotland has one poisonous snake, although the **adder,** on average 20 inches (50 cm) long, is a timid creature likely to bite only in self-defense with a mild venom incapable of imperiling human life. The endangered **natterjack toad** has Scotland as one of its last remaining stomping grounds.

Birds

The single most impressive aspect of Scotland's wildlife is its birdlife, which ranks among the finest in Europe for both volume and species diversity. Scotland's mountains make the perfect habitat for the **golden eagle,** the **white-tailed eagle** (Britain's largest bird of prey) and the **red kite. Ospreys** are bouncing back in Scotland

and now inhabit several different areas, including the coastal areas of Dumfries and Galloway and most notably Loch Garten in the Cairngorm Mountains. You can see five different species of **owl** in Scotland but, contrary to what you may have read, there are currently no known **snowy owls** in Scotland—not even in Shetland, which is wrongly advertised as a snowy owl breeding site on occasion. You may see a snowy owl in the extreme north of Scotland.

Among the several fascinating inland bird species are the colorful **kingfisher,** a common but hard-to-spot bird in riverside areas. More easily spotted are **herons,** found in much the same locations. The **capercaillie** is found in upland forest areas; it's a large woodland grouse with an entertaining mating ritual. The **Scottish crossbill** enjoys the reputation of being the only bird exclusively found in Britain. The crossbill is a member of the finch family and is found in upland pine forests.

Sighting **greylag geese** in the wild is the most memorable water-bird experience you can have in Scotland. These bulky, blundering

THE GLORIOUS TWELFTH

August 12 is the date when the shooting or hunting season for red grouse kicks off in earnest. More game will be shot across Scotland on this day than any other. The occasion is Scotland at its most traditional and, quite often, most unpopular. When you see large groups of men with Eton accents clad in tweed advancing over the moor with rifles on a summer's day, grouse-shooting is what they'll be engaged in. These scenes are both hilarious and tragic to behold. On the one hand, these huntin', shootin', and fishin' chaps look as though they've just stepped out of a 19th-century painting. On the other, vast numbers of grouse are shot on August 12 and in the days thereafter that are not even eaten. The concept of breeding birds for mostly middle-aged men to shoot at point blank is often considered barbaric, and animal rights protestors frequently attend the opening day of the shooting season to make their voice heard.

It's unlikely action is going to be taken to defend the poor old grouse anytime soon, though. Game shooting is big business in Scotland and vital to the rural economy. The hunting season has had a few other setbacks over recent years; poor weather made many moorland areas inaccessible for shooting and the Foot and Mouth crisis of 2001 also meant that the season could not proceed. The Glorious Twelfth is governed by some suitably ancient legislature, too, the laws set out by a Game Act back in 1831. These rules stipulate, amongst other suitably dated small print, that the Glorious Twelfth can never start on a Sunday. In any case, considerably fewer people have a problem with this time-honored August tradition when a tasty piece of pheasant appears on their plates in a restaurant. After red grouse, woodcock and pheasant are up next, with their season starting on October 1.

birds are all too often found tamely begging for scraps in city parks but in remote Scottish RSPB reserves can be found in their wild state. The Solway Firth in Dumfries and Galloway, Islay, and South Uist in the Outer Hebrides are the main places to see them. One of the rarest and most special birds to catch a sight of in Great Britain is the **corncrake,** which had until recently become all but extinct due to farming methods that destroyed its traditional field-side habitat. Corncrakes are now restricted to the very peripheries of Scotland. You can spot them on North Ronaldsay in the Orkney Islands and on North Uist, in the Outer Hebrides. They look a little like moorhens, but you are far more likely just to hear their distinguished, rasping call.

Despite being an all-around ornithological destination, it is seabirds for which Scotland is best known. The seabird colonies across the country are internationally significant and by some ways the most important in Europe. Again, it's the outer islands that have the most abundant seabird life. With over half a million breeding seabirds and more pairs of breeding **gannets** than anywhere else in the world, remote St. Kilda off the coast of the Outer Hebrides is where you should head for the best seabird experience on the planet. You can also see **guillemots, fulmars, shags, kittiwakes, razorbills,** and four species of **gull** on St. Kilda. Outdoing all of these seabirds in the entertainment stakes are the clifftop comedians, the **puffins.** The best place in Britain to see these birds in all their clumsy action is on the island of Westray, in the Orkney Islands. Puffins are identifiable by their large blue, orange, and yellow beaks which can cram in up to 60 fish in one go.

History

No country in the world makes quite so much of its history as Scotland. There's plenty of justification for this: The grand and turbulent signs of past millennia are etched more deeply into the landscape than most countries. Nowhere else in the world can claim to have such an eclectic spread of megalithic monuments or ruined castles. The profusion of the ruins that litter the land can mainly be attributed to a historically divided country. Scotland was, until the 18th century, a place of rival tribes, which displayed their animosity by raiding and destroying each other's property and their profound mistrust of each other by building defensive fortresses.

Evidence suggests that in the far north of the country and on outlying islands like Orkney and the Outer Hebrides, prehistoric tribes possessed incredibly powerful dynasties. These dynasties were exclusively regional, often weakened by feuds and ultimately unable to defend themselves against the continual influx of invaders that would arrive over the next few thousand years. The Romans came from the south, the Gaels came from Ireland to the west, and the Norse came from the northeast. All made various inroads into Scotland's territory. Even when Scotland became united in name, it was still torn apart by disputes with the Norse and, in time, the English. The last seven centuries in Scotland have been predominated by conflicts with the English. This confirmed Scotland's history as one of valiant stands against mightier oppressors, which ultimately resulted in bloody defeat. It's only very recently that the tide of history seems to be turning in favor of the Scots, with devolution from England in 1999.

PREHISTORY

Hunter-gatherers were certainly making a living from fishing and farming in Scotland by 7500 B.C. The first sign of human habitation in the country, on the Isle of Rum, dates from this time. By the beginning of the fourth millennium B.C. Scotland's (and northwest Europe's) oldest surviving building, a farm on the Knap of Howar on the island of Papa Westray, had been erected. By 3000 B.C. there were the first signs of village life at communities like Skara Brae, also on Orkney. Having the community altogether in one place was an important development—it made organizing labor forces far easier. Construction of grand stone monuments was also now possible; these had purposes as varied as burial chambers and lunar observation stations, like Callanish in the Outer Hebrides. The evidence indicates that throughout the Stone Age, Orkney was at the center of the action in Northern Britain; very few other places in Scotland have archaeological sites as old.

The coming of the Bronze Age, which began in Scotland around 2500 B.C., put much of the country at a disadvantage: bronze was an alloy of copper and tin, and the only known tin mines were in Cornwall, in the south of England. Bronze gave a degree of luxury; where stone had been a functional material, bronze was as often a decorative one. Peoples from northern Europe introduced the "Beaker Culture" to Scotland: Now the dead were being honored by individual burial in beaker-like pots rather than mass tombs. Stone Age sites were used and improved by Bronze Age peoples. More complex astronomical alignments like the Clava Cairns near Inverness were further signs of a new and improved culture. By 1000 B.C. to 700 B.C., there is evidence to suggest that many of these individual tribes had become aware of each other's existence and that intertribal feuding had become common. Larger-scale defenses were built around this time. In East Lothian, near Edinburgh, this took the form of a hill fort that would have supported a large community by the beginning of the first millennium B.C. Stone tower houses or brochs were also being constructed by the last half of this millennium; these were built to defend from attack by a local source but it was from farther afield that the major invasion came.

ROMAN OCCUPATION

By A.D. 79, having conquered England, Roman leaders set their sights on pushing their newly acquired empire northward. In the Caledonian tribes of northern Scotland, however, they met their match. As the Romans advanced farther north into Scotland, tribes carried out guerrilla-style raids on various Roman camps. Even after victory at the battle of Mons Grapius, in A.D. 122, Romans could not capitalize on their position. They preferred to keep out these warlike northern tribes rather than conquer them and built Hadrian's Wall, which came to mark the frontier between Scotland and England, and the Antonine Wall, 100 miles to the north. After the joint stand at Mon Grapius, the tribes of Caledonia seem to have become more unified; even if the "Picti" (the nickname the Romans gave them, meaning "painted ones") or Picts did still have divisions amongst themselves, the Pictish kingdom was known as one empire during late Roman occupation in Britain. As the Romans turned to disturbances elsewhere in their vast empire, emboldened parties of Picts performed increasingly daring raids and crossed Hadrian's Wall into Britain during the 4th and 5th centuries. This antagonized not only the Romans but also the Saxons, who resisted Pictish advances. As the Roman threat subsided, the Pictish kingdom was faced with a new threat: the Gaels.

THE DARK AGES

The first Gaelic migrants arrived from Ireland around A.D. 500. They came from the region of Dalriada (or Dal Riata) in Northern Ireland and settled on the southwestern coast of Scotland in modern-day Kintyre. In A.D. 567, another entirely different group of people landed in Scotland from Ireland—a group of Celtic missionaries headed by St. Columba. The saint is credited with introducing Christianity to Scotland. He founded a seat of learning and religious harmony on the Isle of Iona and even succeeded in converting many of the heathen Picts. The coming of the Saint was the high point in an age dominated by tribal skirmishes. In the 9th century A.D., the Pictish kingdom and the kingdom of Dalriada merged. The King of Dalriada, Kenneth I or Kenneth MacAlpin, subdued the Picts and went on to become the first lord of the new unified land, in A.D. 843.

KINGDOM OF ALBA (900-1300)

Alba referred to the kingdom of Scotland as ruled by monarchs of Gaelic descent between A.D. 900 and 1300 (although Macbeth in the mid-11th century is thought to have been the last Gaelic-speaking king). As the new kingdom of Alba was strengthening around A.D. 900, so too was the Norse stranglehold on the northern islands of Orkney and Shetland and on many of Scotland's western islands. The Norse had arrived as a result of overpopulation in the west of Norway. At first, Norse presence in these outlying areas does not seem to have overly troubled the kingdom of Alba. However, in 1263 King Hakon of Norway sailed his mighty fleet of warships into a threatening position on the River Clyde, an event which erupted into the Battle of Largs, where the Norse were heavily defeated and turned tail for home. The Norse influence would last for two more centuries in Orkney and Shetland but essentially, their dominion over Scotland's islands was at an end. After 1263 the Kingdom of Alba was more commonly known as the Kingdom of the Scots. Despite unification, Scotland's ancient tribal divisions were not forgotten. Now these tribes became known as clans, which would continue to play out the same series of intertribal quarrels they always had.

THE WARS OF INDEPENDENCE

The departure of the Norse coincided with a power vacuum in the Kingdom due to King Alexander III's untimely death in 1286. John Balliol, Lord of Galloway, and Robert Bruce, grandfather of future king Robert the Bruce, emerged as the main rivals for the throne, and

Scottish nobles now feared civil war between Balliol and Bruce. They called on Edward I of England to intermediate, who agreed under the proviso that he be named Lord Paramount, supreme ruler of Great Britain. The Scots had little choice but to accept. Edward I continued to press his advantage, which included the rather humiliating request for John Balliol, the appointed king, to do homage to him in London. Edward I had recently defeated the Welsh in battle, and it was clear he wanted to extend his dominion to include Scotland. He soon found the pretext to attack Scotland, beginning the Wars of Independence, in which freedom fighter William Wallace and Robert the Bruce offered Scottish resistance. Robert the Bruce, the one surviving man with a claim to the throne of Scotland, led the Scots to a series of victories against the English, culminating in a famous trouncing of the English at the Battle of Bannockburn in 1314. A treaty was now signed recognizing Scottish independence. Robert the Bruce did not enjoy his reign over an independent Scotland for long; he died in 1329, which reignited conflict with the English.

THE STUART DYNASTY AND THE REFORMATION (1373-1603)

In 1373 the daughter of Robert the Bruce, married Walter, 6th High Steward of Scotland, thereafter known as Robert II. He was the first of the ill-fated Stuart monarchs who would rule Scotland over the following two centuries. The Stuarts had taken over the throne at an unfortunate time. The development of the printing press over the 14th and 15th centuries led to the Renaissance, essentially a rediscovery of the knowledge of ancient Greek and Roman cultures. This would, in the long term, revolutionize Scotland's key institutions: the court and the church. In the short term, it put Scotland on the map as a key center of learning and culture, with universities like St. Andrews flourishing in the 15th century. Scotland during this period became recognized as one of the great powers of Europe. The Stuart monarchs

capitalized on this to marry into the most influential families of Europe in order to stake a claim on the thrones of France and England, a move which would backfire. The Catholic Stuarts were victims of what historians dub "The Modern Age." The 15th century saw an emphasis placed on law rather than family loyalty, and slowly the authority of the monarchy was eroded. In 1517, Martin Luther had begun the Protestant Reformation. This reached Scotland in 1560 courtesy of John Knox. After ransacking several ecclesiastical institutions, Knox and his supporters were asked to help devise a new constitution for the Scottish church, which denied the authority of the Catholic Church and even forbade taking mass.

THE UNION OF THE CROWNS

The fervor of anti-Catholicism did nothing for the popularity of the then monarch Mary, Queen of Scots. Mary was not only despised by Scottish Protestants but feared by English authorities, as she was next in line to the throne after her childless cousin Elizabeth I. Several scandals forced the unfortunate Mary to abdicate in 1567 (she was eventually put to death 20 years later for charges of treason). Her infant son James VI became king in her place. Queen Elizabeth named King James VI as her successor to the English throne, largely to smooth over Anglo-Scottish rifts caused by his mother. In 1603, he became King James VI of Scotland and I of England.

THE COVENANTERS REBELLION (1638-1688)

The new king moved his court to England and returned to Scotland just once in 1617, where he unwisely lectured his countrymen on the superiority of English civilization. It was a bad move, turning many Scots against the monarch. King James also wished to unite the parliaments of England and Scotland, another move in which he was vigorously opposed. His still more unpopular son, Charles I, attempted to Anglicize the Church of Scotland in 1637, which led to Scots signing the National Covenant in 1638, where opposition to Anglicization of the church was put in writing. To be a Covenanter became an offense punishable by death. The Covenanters therefore supported the overthrowing of the monarchy by Oliver Cromwell in 1649. In 1650, the Scots fell out with Cromwell, now with the title of Lord Protector of the Commonwealth, and gave their support to Charles II, son of Charles I. Cromwell's troops now attacked Scotland. With the restoration of King Charles II and the Stuart monarchy in 1660, Scottish Covenanters were again the subject of persecution until 1688, with the abrupt end to the Stuart Monarchy.

THE GLORIOUS REVOLUTION

The son of Charles II, James II, with his staunch Catholicism and belief in the divine right to rule, alienated himself from his parliament. The government openly gave their support to a revolution by Protestant Mary, James II's daughter, and her husband William of Orange, who became joint monarchs. James II was exiled to the continent. Unrest in Scotland rose: James II had been a Catholic, Stuart king with Scottish blood, and a strong Anglo-Scottish rivalry developed. The clans of the Highlands particularly resented the sovereignty of William and Mary, and plots to mount an insurrection to reinstate James II were devised. John Graham of Claverhouse, known as "Bonnie Dundee," led the first Jacobite uprising in 1689, but the rebellion fizzled out after his death. The government focused on permanently subduing the rebellious Highlanders, and in 1692 licensed the Campbell clan to massacre the MacDonald clan of Glencoe to drum home to the Highland clans the price of disobedience. In a further attempt to prevent rebellion, the English parliament decided that merging with the Scottish parliament, with the Act of Union in 1707, would unify Britain.

THE JACOBITE REBELLIONS (1715-1746)

The Highlanders were not so easily subdued. After 1715 when the son of James II, James Stuart, plotted to retake the throne, the government commissioned General Wade to strengthen their Highland defenses by constructing a network of paved roads and improving fortifications. This ultimately helped Jacobite forces more than government troops. In 1745, the grandson of James II, Charles Edward Stuart or "Bonnie Prince Charlie," rallied a sizable force of Highlanders and raised his standard at Glenfinnan. His army enjoyed considerable success but the campaign ended in brutal defeat at Culloden, by Inverness, in 1746. Charles went into hiding and escaped back to France. Jacobite defeat at Culloden also brought the demise of the Scottish clan system. Clans were hunted down and murdered by government forces and replaced by government-friendly estate owners.

ENLIGHTENMENT AND INDUSTRIALIZATION

Scotland would now enjoy a period of calm and, in places, prosperity. Landowners rehoused tenants in smart planned settlements like Inveraray in Argyll with paved roads, schools, and other facilities. The 18th century also saw great Scottish minds like geologist James Hutton and philosopher David Hume profoundly change their respective spheres of expertise. Great architects and engineers like Thomas Telford and Robert Adam were constructing revolutionary canals and elaborate buildings that shouted Scotland's prosperity to the world. In literature, Robert Burns was making a name for himself. In Glasgow, heavy industrialization began to rival agriculture. With rich seams of coal in the area around the city and an abundance of fish in the River Clyde, Glasgow burgeoned as a center of commerce. A tobacco trade with the New World had already begun in earnest by the 1670s, and the dredging of the Clyde in the 18th century, together with the invention of the steam engine, instigated the Industrial Revolution. Along the country's main rivers, water mills manufacturing cotton and other materials sprung up. This was an urban boom period, which masked the continued utter poverty of the rural areas of Scotland.

19TH-CENTURY HIGHLAND CLEARANCES

By the 1820s, an ugly truth was emerging to tarnish the prosperous reputation of Scotland, namely the systematic destruction of the homes of Highland tenant farmers. The potato famine of 1847 to 1856 came as the final blow for Highlanders who lived in infertile areas and could grow nothing else to survive. Estate owners across the Highlands, now faced with tenants who had neither a food source nor a commodity to trade, decided simply to evict people rather than accept any responsibility for them. Eviction allowed landowners to convert the land to more economically viable sheep farming. Highlanders were often smoked out of their homes, with their only remaining option being to emigrate to the New World.

1850-1914

As increasing parts of rural Scotland became economically deprived, several lifelines were thrown their way: the development of the railway and tourism. When Queen Victoria made Balmoral Castle on the River Dee in Aberdeenshire the official Royal holiday home in the 1840s, the public was quick to visit the area, too. Scotland soon had fashionable Victorian spa towns like Crieff in Perthshire. Signs of blight, both rural and urban, were becoming more apparent, however. By the turn of the 20th century, the cities that had boomed only decades before were now grievously overcrowded. In the countryside, mass emigration had given a forlorn feel to many communities.

THE WORLD WARS

For many, the two World Wars came as a relief. War brought an avenue of escape for a generation of men who had perceived themselves as trapped in a provincial Scotland with few prospects. World War II saw Scotland, a largely remote area under less threat from enemy attack, used for training troops. Despite the hive of activity, the two World Wars would have a huge and devastating impact on Scotland. The country was not as badly bombed as other European countries—although Glasgow's shipbuilding industry did make it the target of considerable bombing—but Scotland sustained heavy casualties that hit Scotland's rural communities particularly hard.

THE PATH TO DEVOLUTION (1945 ONWARD)

Mass emigration continued throughout much of Scotland after 1945. This continued unchecked until the discovery of oil and gas in the North Sea, which saw parts of the country like Shetland and Aberdeen reap long-lasting financial benefits. Tourism also took off, and these industries made Scotland more economically independent. The success of these industries again raised the issue of devolution (a central government returning power to a local-level government). In 1997 British Prime Minister Tony Blair's administration held a referendum on the issue of Scottish devolution. A resounding "yes" vote led to a Scottish parliament forming in 1999—for the first time since 1707.

Government and Economy

GOVERNMENT

Scotland is currently run by Alex Salmond's Scottish National Party (SNP), which has just one seat more in the Scottish parliament than the opposition Scottish Labour Party. The SNP is dedicated to complete Scottish independence from England, a contentious issue that has been the cause of debate for over 700 years. The Scottish parliament operates from Holyrood, in Edinburgh.

History and Context

The history of Scotland's government has focused on the age-old question of just what degree of independence from England Scotland should have. When James VI of Scotland and I of England moved his court and parliament to London in 1603, the monarch increasingly believed that having separate English and Scottish parliaments was impractical, and a merged Anglo-Scottish parliament, based of course in London, happened in 1707, in the Act of Union. In all important matters, Scotland answered to the London-based 558-seat House of Commons, in which 45 Scottish Members of Parliament (MP's) represented Scotland with seats in the House of Commons. For the next 292 years, Scotland would not have a parliament of its own.

Devolution in 1999

Devolution, the granting of separate powers from a country's central government to an individual part of that country, was a much-debated subject almost from the moment the Scottish parliament was abolished. In 1997 Tony Blair's Labour Party won a landslide general election, with Scottish-born Gordon Brown appointed to the influential position of Chancellor of the Exchequer. Blair and Brown were in favor of Scottish devolution, and a referendum on the issue passed resoundingly. In 1998 the British Government passed the Scotland Act, which laid down exactly what authority the new Scottish parliament should have. Members of Parliament (MP's) would continue to represent Scotland and sit as before in the House of Commons, which would in turn continue to have authority over the Scottish Parliament on military affairs, international relations, taxes, and certain other matters. In other important respects, such as health, education, and transportation, the Scottish Parliament would have complete authority. This paved the way to the first Scottish parliament in nearly three centuries convening on July 1, 1999, with David Dewar becoming Scotland's First Minister.

Organization and Elections

After almost 300 years of being sidelined, Scottish politics now makes up a significant part of wider British politics. Officially, British politics is decided by one unified sovereign government, in which Scotland has representatives. However, while British politics, decided at the House of Commons in Westminster, London, still presides over Scotland in certain matters, devolution has meant that the Scottish parliament has total power to make most political decisions affecting Scotland. Parliamentary policy is primarily implemented and developed by a First Minister, the Scottish equivalent of a Prime Minister. The Scottish parliament is made up of 129 Members of the Scottish Parliament (MSP's).

For electoral purposes, Scotland is divided into 73 local constituencies and eight larger regions. Each voter has two votes. The first vote is for an MSP to represent his or her respective local constituency. A voter's second vote is for a candidate standing either individually or for a party in one of eight larger regional constituencies. Each region is allocated seven seats in parliament. The 129 seats in the Scottish parliament therefore comprise 73 local constituency MSP's and 56 regional constituency MSP's. A fresh parliament is elected every four years, but there are no limitations on the term of the First Minister, providing their party remains in power. The constitutional system of

Scotland has been criticized—the system of proportional representation increases the likelihood of a coalition and therefore of a weakened government being in power. Scotland was run by a Labour-Liberal coalition until the last elections in 2007.

Current Political Situation

The current breakdown of the Scottish parliament sees the SNP party in control with 47 seats, the key opposition Scottish Labour Party (pro-workers and trade unions) with 46 seats, the Scottish Conservative and Unionist party (center-right) with 17 seats, and the Scottish Liberal Democrat Party (left) represented with 16 seats. The SNP Party, despite having formed in the 1920s, has never before enjoyed as much success as currently. After the last Scottish election in May 2007, First Minister Alex Salmond and his pro-independence SNP party headed the Scottish parliament. Salmond is a colorful character whose outspoken opinions and appearances on TV entertainment shows have earned him plenty of media attention. His decisive, no-nonsense approach and push for complete Scottish political autonomy from England seemed on paper to be exactly what Scotland needed. Salmond has now come under criticism for failing to fully deliver on pre-election promises—and his push for complete Scottish independence is far from universally popular. He plans to hold a referendum on complete Scottish independence before the 2011 elections, with a view to total independence by 2017. Many critics doubt Scotland's ability to function independently, given that its economy has for so long been reliant on England's. Despite such disagreements within the parliament, the political situation in Scotland is a peaceful one.

ECONOMY

Scotland has had something of a seesaw economic ride historically, with periods as one of Europe's key superpowers (the Renaissance, 1400–1700, and the Industrial Revolution, 1750–1900) set against periods of intense poverty (the 19th-century Highland Clearances).

Economic development has often been thoughtlessly followed through and limited to random regions of the country, but since the 1960s, through financial services, the oil and gas industries, and tourism, Scotland's economy has been improving.

Economic Indicators

As Scotland is economically part of the United Kingdom, it is unjust and in many ways inaccurate to compare its economic indicators on anything more than a regional basis. Scotland has a GDP of £86.3 billion, which makes it the second-most affluent region of the U.K. after southeast England. Due to division of wealth disparities, though, this still gives Scotland a per-capita income of £16,944 (2005). The average weekly adult income is £592.70 (2006 figures), based on the percentage of adults of working age in full-time employment (78 percent).

Agriculture

Despite the potato famine of 1849–1857 and the Foot and Mouth crisis of 2001, agriculture has remained imperative to the Scottish economy. It may have been surpassed in its economic contribution by other industries, but it's responsible for all those iconic images of Scotland from shaggy Highland cows to whisky, which helps generate more tourism. Traditionally, agriculture has also delineated the most prosperous areas of Scotland. Areas like Aberdeenshire have remained wealthy because of their fertile farmland. In the 21st century, the use of polytunnels has now extended the growing season in the bleaker regions of Scotland. The country has also cottoned on to the increased industry demands for healthy, organically produced food, which has gone some way to bolstering Scottish agriculture as an income-generator. Scotland is 98 percent rural, yet cultivated land accounts for approximately only 25 percent. This is an indication of the large amounts of barren upland, which makes crop-growing impracticable. The wet, moist climate, while often a bane to visitors, helps to make Scotland an extremely fertile place. The fertile areas are confined generally to the

wind farms, near Thurso

© LUKE WATERSON

lowland and coastal areas in the southern half of the country and in Aberdeenshire. Barley, wheat, potato, and dairy farming are the main agricultural activities here, along with growing fruit. The upland areas mainly rear cows and sheep especially bred for the thin soil and sparse vegetation.

Fishing and Forestry
Scotland's fish-rich waters have meant that ever since prehistoric times, when druids traded fish with the first Romans, fishing has been of key importance to Scotland. Development of harbors in the 18th century allowed the fishing trade to really boom. Peterhead was the leading whitefish port in Europe for much of the 20th century, and a major daily catch is still landed there. Herring, haddock, cod, lobster, and crabs are the main fish caught in Scotland. The European Union's overfishing policy put a limit on the number of fish that could be landed to maintain fish levels in the North Sea, which has brought about a drastic decline in the fishing industry. Today, fishing in Scotland is an income generator in terms of the catch brought in by commercial fishing and also in terms of the visitors wanting to try their hand at reaping the benefits of vast numbers of salmon and trout.

Scotland's forests create more commerce than any other country in Great Britain and account for around 14 percent of the total landmass. A massive 47 percent of British forests are in Scotland. Key activities include timber-felling, the making of wood pulp, and recreational activities.

Industry and Trade
After World War II, with Scotland increasingly unable to compete with Eastern Europe and Asia in heavy industries like coal mining, the country turned to service industries to prop up its economy. Financial services became increasingly important and now account for 6 percent of Scotland's GDP. Edinburgh is the fifth biggest financial center in Europe. By the 1980s, the central belt of Scotland between Glasgow and Edinburgh had been dubbed Silicon Glen

due to the major electronics industries located there. The other huge post-war industrial development was in the fields of oil and gas, now providing employment for 6 percent of Scotland's workforce. The country has some of the best natural resources in Europe, from oil and gas to peat.

As a wild and elemental country, Scotland's churning rivers, high winds, and crashing seas make it perfectly poised to develop alternative energy resources. Hydroelectric power, wind turbines, and wave-powered energy-generating devices have been pioneered in the remoter parts of the country, including a scheme to build one of the world's largest wind farms on Lewis in the Outer Hebrides. It is not surprising that the Scottish government aims to be producing 18 percent of Scotland's energy from renewable energy resources by 2011. Another key Scottish export is, of course, whisky.

Tourism

Tourism has been a major revenue-generator since the late 18th and early 19th centuries and accounts for 3 percent of Scotland's GDP. This statistic does not indicate how crucial tourism is as an income in many rural areas of Scotland. Visitors from the United States supply most of Scotland's overseas tourism, with 24 percent of the tourist income. Most of Scotland's tourism income, however, is derived from domestic tourism (visitors from parts of the U.K.). History and mountains are probably the two biggest tourist draws.

Distribution of Wealth

Highland Clearances in the 19th century had a lasting effect on economic disparity in Scotland. You do not have to look very far to see evidence of this: Landowners' opulent mansions stand next to the ruins of tenants' crofting cottages, illustrating the huge difference in lifestyles between rich and poor that have persisted throughout Scotland's history. As recently as 1976, the rate of owner-occupied dwellings in Scotland was appallingly low, at just over 30 percent. In 1997, just 350 people owned between them half of Scotland's land. Much land was being farmed by tenants who did not own their own land. The Land Reform Acts passed in 1997 gave tenants the chance to buy the land they worked or lived on. Later that year, on the Isle of Eigg, tenants bought out the landlord and took ownership of the island—an act unprecedented in Scottish history. Owner occupancy in Scotland has more than doubled now to around 65 percent, but it's still significantly lower than the U.K. average.

People and Culture

IDENTITY

Never, ever make the mistake of confusing the Scottish and the English. The Scottish are a proud people who consider themselves historically and culturally a very separate country, and you will offend them by classifying them as English. Scottish consider the difference between themselves and the English at least as great as that between Canadians and Americans. One interesting difference between England and Scotland is how people refer to their nationality. English people will often refer to themselves as British, with those who do not often considered ridiculously overpatriotic. Scottish people will almost always refer to themselves as Scottish; there is no such thing as being "too patriotic" in Scotland. Most Scots are incredibly gentle people below a matter-of-fact and down-to-earth exterior. You'll soon come to find that the Scottish have a wonderful, deeply ironic sense of humor, too. This may be based, in part, on a history in which they have largely been on the losing side. A heavy sense of historical injustice is part of the Scottish identity.

DEMOGRAPHICS

Accurate estimates of the Scottish population are hard to judge, as recent years have seen huge influxes of immigrants from areas like Eastern Europe. There are approximately 5,100,000 inhabitants in the country, four-fifths of whom live in the central belt of the country. At last report, the census showed around 98 percent of Scotland's population to be of white British, white Irish, or other white origin. The 2 percent of non-white Scottish citizens (Pakistani, Chinese, or Indian, mostly) are concentrated in the main cities of Glasgow and Edinburgh. The recent influx of Eastern European citizens to Scotland has checked, and to some degree masked, the steadily falling population of the country. Many Scots, especially those starting out in careers, choose to gravitate to other parts of the U.K., particularly London. This has meant that the population of Scotland is not only on a general downward curve but is also getting increasingly older. Life expectancy is a fraction lower than the Western European average of 76.8 years (2005 estimate). Scotland has a 99 percent adult literacy rate.

In a happy turn-around, the Highlands, in stark contrast to the last 200 years, has now seen one of the biggest increases in population anywhere in Scotland, while many inner city areas have seen population decrease. Scotland has a very low population density, due to the sparsely populated Highland region with a density of just 21 people per square mile. In Glasgow, population density reaches over 3,000 people per square mile—still relatively low compared to a metropolis like New York with over 25,000 people per square mile.

RELIGION

Religious divides have been responsible for a lot of Scottish history. Religion is, while by no means overzealous, still a more passionate issue in Scotland than it is south of the border in England. Religious tensions are mainly between the two predominant religions in the country, the Protestant Church of Scotland (47 percent of the population) and the Roman Catholic Church (17.5 percent of the population). Both are branches of Christianity. As significant are the 17.5 percent of Scots who

claim to have no religion at all. The princi minority religion is Islam.

Protestantism Versus Catholicism

Martin Luther made his stand against decadence of the Catholic Church and its necessary "indulgences" or what many saw supercilious riches in 1517. By the middle the 16th century, Protestantism, which dev oped from Lutheranism, had taken a hold Scotland. The Protestant Reformation rag across the country courtesy of John Kn who was preaching against the wrongful re gious beliefs of the Catholic Mary, Queen Scots by the 1560s. The Catholic religion v already well established through the relig of the Stuart Kings of Scotland and, m recently, has been represented by the Ir population of central and western Scotla who arrived during the Industrial Revoluti Since the mid-16th century, a continue stream of incidents has reopened Protesta Catholic rifts, from the development of monarchy to disputes between fans at Rang versus Celtic football matches.

LANGUAGE

The official language of Scotland is Engl and is spoken by nearly 100 percent of population.

Gaelic

Gaelic, which was once spoken as a first l guage from north to south, is now the m tongue only in the Outer Hebrides and ot extremes of Scotland's western islands. Scot Gaelic all but died out as a language when Scottish king James VI also became heir the English throne and took his court south London. The aristocracy, and therefore the ucated classes, spent more time in England adopted English as their preferred langua They were bilingual in English and Gaelic, Gaelic became more and more confined to rural, working community. Thanks to bo like the Comhairle nan Eilean (the West Isles Council) Gaelic is not just rejuvenate

GAELIC PLACE-NAMES

Gaelic may not be the official language of Scotland (that's English), and it's unlikely to be strictly necessary to speak it, but many Scottish place names appear on maps by their Gaelic name only. It's amazing how much more you will be able to understand about the land of Scotland by knowing what the terms below mean.

Gaelic	English	Gaelic	English
Abhainn	River	Eilean	Island
Aird	Promontory	Failte	Welcome
Allt/Ullt	Burn/stream	Fraoch	Heather
Aonach	Steep height	Geodhra	Geo or ravine
Ard	High	Glas	Green
Beag	Little	Kirk	Church
Bealach	Pass	Mor	Large/great
Beinn/Bheinne	Mountain	Na/Nam	The
Caol/Caolas	Kyle or narrow/straight	Rin/Ros	Point, promontory, or isthmus
Carn/Cairn	Heap of stones		
Clachan	Village	Sgurr	Sharp, steep hill
Coille	Wood	Srath	Strath/river valley
Coire	Corrie or rock hollow	Tairbeart	Tarbet or isthmus
Eas	Waterfall	Tigh/Taigh	House

sporadic areas of Scotland but is now taught as a language in schools across the country. Gaelic speakers can all speak English, too.

Scots

Scots is not officially a language but a dialect, although there have been 10-volume dictionaries filled with Scots vocabulary. Some of Scotland's regional accents can certainly sound like other languages, like the dialects of the Orkney and Shetland Islands with a profound influence from old Norse. Anglo-Scottish rivalries meant Scotland often enjoyed closer political ties with the French (a trend called the Auld Alliance), and therefore there are French and Dutch traces to the Scots language. The Irish, Scotland's other significant invading force, have also shaped Scots. All this has meant that the Scottish form of English (Scots) can be difficult to understand to other English speakers. The rich patchwork of Scottish language rarely makes communication difficult; it's more a colorful cultural trait that makes visiting different areas of the country all the more interesting.

The Arts

LITERATURE

Scotland has an extremely rich literary heritage. Tapping into it is an essential step toward understanding Scotland: its language, its deep and vivid history, and its culture. As long ago as the Dark Ages, Scotland was a beacon of literary light, with Celtic missionary monks setting up centers of learning across the country. However it was the 18th century when Scottish wordsmiths really got writing.

Robert Burns (1759–1796) was the most famous of Scotland's writers, honored for his literary achievements far beyond his native country. His birthday is, after Christmas, the most celebrated of any person in the world. The poet became popular for the way he embodied traditional Scottish language into his work and captured the spirit of the common Scot. His best-loved work was the epic poem "Tam o' Shanter" about the dark visions of a man who stays drinking too long at the pub. Burns also wrote other famous poems like "Address to a Haggis," but he was also key in preserving a lot of the traditional songs of his country that had been dying out. *Auld Lang Syne,* the well-known Scottish New Year song, is credited to Burns, but his achievement was not writing the song but reworking its cadence to achieve mass popularity.

Sir Walter Scott (1771–1832) was an incredible multitasker who fitted in sheriff duties and rediscovering Scotland's Crown Jewels around a prolific writing career. He remains Scotland's most important novelist. *Waverley* focuses on the 1745 rebellion that tried to restore a Scottish family to the throne of Britain. However, Scott is best remembered for his overly romantic portrayals of life in Britain as in the adventure novels *Rob Roy* and *Ivanhoe.*

Robert Louis Stevenson (1850–1894) was a masterful story-teller who wrote some of the world's best-loved adventure yarns. *Kidnapped* and *Treasure Island* are inspired by his times following his lighthouse-building family around the far-flung coast of Scotland. He also wrote the gripping, sinister double-identity thriller, *The Strange Case of Dr. Jekyll and Mr. Hyde.*

Sir Arthur Conan Doyle (1859–1930) was another Victorian writer who wrote a world-famous series of books involving the greatest fictional detective of them all, **Sherlock Holmes.** The most famous of these books is *Study in Scarlet.*

John Buchan (1875–1940) is a lesser known but equally riveting adventure writer. His novel *The Thirty-nine Steps* is considered one of the best suspense novels ever written. **J. M. Barrie** (1860–1937) wrote the famous book about the boy who never grows up, *Peter Pan,* based on his brother who died a tragic early death. **Compton Mackenzie** (1883–1972) wrote the hugely entertaining novel *Whisky Galore* about an Outer Hebridean island deprived of whisky during World War II that suddenly has a ship carrying whisky wrecked upon its shores.

Hugh MacDiarmid (1892–1978) and **George Mackay Brown** (1921–1996) were two of Scotland's most important 20th-century poets. MacDiarmid championed a poignant use of the traditional Scottish language in his verse, while Mackay Brown, despite barely leaving his native island of Orkney, wrote vividly about his homeland in a worldly way that tied Scotland not just to its place in the world but to its place in the universe.

More recent exponents of Scottish novel writing have included the hugely important **Alisdair Gray** and **Iain Banks,** who have portrayed their native country in a number of innovative and fascinating ways. Gray's best-known work, *Lanark* details life in a disturbing Glasgow-esque fantasy city and earned him a reputation as one of the best Scottish novelists ever.

VISUAL ARTS

Scotland does not immediately jump out as a land of artists in quite the same way it does as a land of writers. Perhaps the most important of Scotland's portrait painters was **Sir Henry**

Raeburn (1756–1823), who insisted on painting everything directly from real life. He captured some of the most important people of his age in his paintings, including Sir Walter Scott and, most famously, *The Reverend Robert Walker skating on Duddingston Loch.*

In the 1870s, a group of artists known as the **Glasgow Boys** came to prominence, challenging the classically influenced established art scene in Scotland with portrayals of rural life in different parts of Scotland. Making up this rebellious group were **James Guthrie, E. A. Hornel,** and **Joseph Crawhill.** Following more or less in the footsteps of the Glasgow Boys were the **Scottish Colourists** such as **J. D. Fergusson** and **F. C. B. Cadell.** They took the vibrant contemporary French painting of the 1920s and developed it along distinctly Scottish lines with subject matter like Edinburgh buildings and landscape scenes.

The most successful current Scottish artist is **Jack Vettriano,** who started off working in the Scottish coal fields but who has in the last two decades risen to the forefront of Scottish art. His work, often said to be influenced by the Scottish Colourists, is vivid and often comical realist style, epitomized by paintings like *The Singing Butler.* Like much of its home-grown talent, Scotland has almost distanced itself from Vettriano and has none of his work displayed in its galleries.

ARCHITECTURE AND DESIGN

Scotland has produced several outstanding architects who came to prominence in the 18th-century enlightenment era. The father-and-son legacy of **William Adam** (1689–1748) and **Robert Adam** (1728–1792) between them designed many of Scotland's most notable buildings. They reinvented Edinburgh's New Town and designed the grand, classic facades of a large number of Scotland's great country houses. William's work had a strong baroque influence and included **Duff House** in Aberdeenshire and the Duke of Hamilton's glamorous dog kennel at **Chatelherault** near Glasgow. Robert's work included the design of **Charlotte Square** in Edinburgh, **Mellerstain House** in the Scottish Borders, and the **Trades Hall** in Glasgow. The architect and designer **Charles Rennie Mackintosh** (1868–1928) put his home city of Glasgow at the forefront of British art nouveau design. He designed several important buildings in Glasgow and the surrounding area.

MUSIC AND DANCE

It's quite possible that most Scots should be included in the all-time list of their country's musical greats. After all, traditional Scottish music has always been an impromptu, sociable activity with many people participating. There scarcely seems a pub in Scotland you can walk into without about half of the clientele having the capability to pick up and play any number of instruments in perfect harmony of an evening. As if to complement this, the other half seem to be able to get up and dance in time to the music pretty effectively.

Traditional/Folk Music

The bagpipe and the fiddle are at the heart of the Scottish traditional and folk music scene. The grandeur of the sound of the bagpipes has lent itself more to live, ceremonial renditions, while the fiddle translates well to recorded music as well as live music. Fiddle music, therefore, is where most of Scotland's traditional music prodigies have made their name. For a long time, traditional music was very much an underground affair, championed little outside of Scotland until Perthshire fiddler **Neil Gow** (1727–1807) came along. He composed and wrote huge amounts of fiddle music. Scottish traditional music began to receive international recognition from the 19th century onward, with several composers including traditional Scottish music in their compositions. Every rural town you go to in Scotland is likely to have its own celebrated series of musicians. The Orkney and Shetland Islands have a particularly rich and well-preserved traditional music tradition and have bred the finest traditional musicians including **Aly Bain** and, more recently, the **Wrigley Sisters.**

CEILIDHS

You won't have to travel long in Scotland before you see a sign advertising a ceilidh, for many one of the most singly moving aspects of the country's culture. This traditional dance event would have been made obsolete in other countries by the advent of discos and nightclubs, but the Scottish have always made a great deal of their national traditions and the ceilidh remains an important social event enjoyed by young and old alike.

A ceilidh was originally an impromptu social gathering where other activities such as ballad singing, card playing, or even just good old-fashioned *craic* (conversation) took place alongside dance, but these days dancing is the main focus of a ceilidh. Taking place in all types of venues across Scotland, a ceilidh focuses around a band playing traditional Scottish music (ranging from the fiddle to accordion music) for the audience to join in and dance in time to. The steps are easy to learn and all-around participation is encouraged. Ceilidhs are very relaxed affairs (most participants are at least a little tipsy) and offer a great chance for visitors to mingle with locals. The great thing about experiencing a ceilidh is that you are getting involved in an event that has carried on pretty much unchanged for centuries.

Rock and Pop Music

Traditional music typically conjures up images of the Scottish countryside, despite it being played equally in the big towns and cities. Major urban centers like Glasgow, meanwhile, have in the last two or three decades become synonymous with the production of inspirational pop and rock artists/bands. **Annie Lennox,** heralded by some to be the greatest white soul singer alive, rose to prominence in the 1980s both for her career in the rock/synthopop band Eurythmics and her later solo songs. She's widely considered to have one of the most powerful female singing voices ever. Also emerging on the Scottish new music scene around this time were pop band **The Cocteau Twins,** influenced by the Sex Pistols and Joy Division, as well as rock group **Simple Minds.** The 1990s saw hugely important instrumental rock/post-rock band **Mogwai** and indie pop band **Belle and Sebastian,** recently voted in a poll as Scotland's best pop music band ever, rise to the top of British music. Belle and Sebastian became famed for lyrically brilliant early albums like *If You're Feeling Sinister.* Other famous Scottish bands include alternative rock band **Texas** and, more recently, indie band **Franz Ferdinand.** Glasgow is recognized as one of the foremost new music venues in Europe, with a history of being the city where famous bands hit the big time.

Traditional Dance

Scottish country dancing has developed from 18th-century ballrooms and traditional roots and includes the lively quick-step and the more sedate Strathspey step. It's a social dance, the basics of which can be learned without too much difficulty. At Highland festivals, you are likely to see a spot of **Highland dancing,** which is a highly complex form of step dancing and involves considerable foot movement as well and arm and upper body movements. Complemented with lots of tartan, it's done for aesthetics and is unlikely to be something visitors pick up too quickly. Highland Dancers require months of training.

COMEDY

The terrific Scottish sense of humor is looked upon in awe by many outsiders in much the same way as the Irish are looked upon in awe for their "Gift of the Gab" (ability to talk). The foremost exponent of Scottish comedy is Glaswegian **Billy Connolly** otherwise known as the "Big Yin." He is well known for his entertaining stand-up comedy.

HANDICRAFTS

As a general rule in Scotland, the more traditional and therefore more authentic handicrafts are made in remoter areas. In cities, genuine handicrafts are harder to distinguish. For example, **crystal** is made in the Edinburgh area, with the center of the industry at Penicuik, but there are many places in Edinburgh that sell mass-produced crystal as handmade.

Many of Scotland's finest craftspeople work in the Highlands and islands where the light is better and where, in many cases, landscape features are incorporated into designs. A hotbed of the Scottish craft industry is Orkney, where you will find wonderful **pottery** and **jewelry.** There are so many different crafts here that the local council has now produced a Craft Trail encompassing all of them. The Shetland Islands and Fair Isle are known for their striking **wool products** made with the wool of the distinctive local sheep. The Isle of Skye produces some fine **silverware** with fascinating island-themed images worked into it. Portsoy on the Aberdeenshire coast has been renowned for centuries for its fine marble.

Southern Scotland also has some important handicrafts centers. The East Neuk of Fife has several fine places to buy **pottery,** and Kirkcudbright in Dumfries and Galloway has long been known as a center of quality local **art galleries.**

ESSENTIALS

Getting There

Scotland is a very well-connected country, but being small it only has a couple of international airports. This means many international connections are more restricted and also pricier than those to London, England. Excellent road and rail connections from London mean that this city is a feasible means of starting your Scottish holiday, too.

FROM OVERSEAS
Air

Scotland has two major international airports, **Glasgow International Airport** (tel. 0870/040 0008, www.glasgowairport.com) and **Edinburgh International Airport** (tel. 0870/040 0007, www.edinburghairport.com). Of these, Glasgow International handles the most flights. You can fly direct to Glasgow or Edinburgh from most major European cities. **Aberdeen Airport** (tel. 0870/040 0006, www.aberdeenairport.com) also handles flights from some European cities including Amsterdam. **Glasgow Prestwick Airport** (tel. 0871/223 0700, www.gpia.co.uk), in Ayrshire, southwest of Glasgow, is where most of the budget flights arrive in Scotland; it serves a clutch of destinations across Europe.

Scotland has direct flights to several airports

in North America. You can fly to Glasgow direct with **Continental Airlines** (U.S. tel. 800/231-0856, www.continental.com), **Thomas Cook Airways** (tel. 0844/855 0515, www.thomascookairlines.com), and **Flyglobespan** (tel. 0871/271 0415, www.flyglobespan.com) from a number of cities. These cities include New York, Boston, Chicago, Toronto, Vancouver, and Las Vegas. Edinburgh has daily direct flights to and from Atlanta with **Delta Airlines** (U.S. tel. 800/221-1212, www.delta.com) and New York with **Continental Airlines.** Glasgow and Edinburgh both have limited flights to Africa, the Middle East, and parts of Asia, including Dubai and Lahore.

It's not much more hassle to fly in to London and make your way up to Scotland via air or over-ground afterward. This approach would give you a greater flexibility with flight times and flight prices, as London's airports handle more flights. If you are considering getting to Scotland via a London airport, then you should also consider using **British Airways** (tel. 0844/493 0787, www.ba.com).

Flight prices obviously depend on how much in advance you buy the tickets. Booking online with the airline directly is usually cheaper than booking with an agency, although some airlines have websites that are notoriously difficult to use. The cheapest flights from North America to Scotland leave from the east coast of the U.S. (New York and Boston) and from Toronto in Canada. With all these variables, giving an idea of price is difficult. In a worst-case scenario, where you book your flights only a week before your departure and do not have the time or the inclination to hunt around for special offers, round-trip flights from the east coast of the U.S. direct to Glasgow will cost in the region of £800–900 (US$1,550–1,800) per person. However, it is entirely possible to get round-trip flights on the same route for £400 (US$800) or less with some planning. Again, bear in mind that flying to London rather than Glasgow is probably going to be cheaper. Only book a flight to London if the price difference is significant, as it will cost you at least £30 per person to make your way from London to Scotland by bus, at least £100 by train. Direct flight time between Glasgow and New York is 6.5–7.5 hours.

Lots of people prefer to use a travel agency to book flights and save the hassle of searching different flight websites. A good company to use is **STA Travel** (www.statravel.com), which offers the most competitive international flight rates and has offices in the U.S, Canada, and major cities in Scotland.

Sea

You can get ferries to Scotland from both Northern Ireland and Zeebrugge in Belgium. Northern Ireland ferries run from near Stranraer, in Dumfries and Galloway. **Stenna Line** (tel. 0870/707070, www.stennaline.com) operates the Stranraer–Belfast service with up to nine crossings daily. **P&O** (tel. 0870/242 4777, www.poirishsea.com) makes up to eight crossings daily between Cairnryan north of Stranraer to Larne. Journey time is 1–1.75 hours. In either case, prices are extremely variable and depend how much in advance you book.

If you're coming from Europe with a car, one way to beat the hours of driving up through England is with **Superfast Ferries** (www.superfast.com) that run between Rosyth, just north of Edinburgh, and Zeebrugge in Belgium (16 hours, £58 weekday standard to £86 weekend standard).

FROM WITHIN THE UNITED KINGDOM
Air

Once you're in the U.K., you have a few more options for flying to Scotland. You can fly to Inverness, Dundee, and Aberdeen as well as Glasgow Prestwick, Glasgow International, and Edinburgh airports. The major London airports (Heathrow, Gatwick, London City, and Stanstead), as well as other airports like Manchester, have flights to Scottish airports. **British Airways** is the main flight provider but is pricier than the clutch of budget airlines plying the route north. These include **RyanAir, EasyJet,** and **Flybe.** Flight time from London to Edinburgh is one hour 20 minutes; it will take two hours to reach Inverness from London.

Flying to Scotland from within the U.K. can be incredibly cheap and in many cases far cheaper than train travel. Ryan Air regularly posts fares for £1 from London to Glasgow Prestwick. Getting such cheap deals necessitates a degree of forward planning. Even if you book flights within two weeks of your departure date, prices from London to the main Scottish airports won't top £60 as long as you're prepared to be flexible with your arrival times. Bear in mind that if you are flying north to Scotland from within the U.K., taking the train takes around the same amount of time when you factor in time-consuming airport activities like checking in and waiting for your luggage.

Train

The high-speed line from London Kings Cross to Edinburgh now whisks you up to Scotland in under 4.5 hours, leaves hourly, rarely has delays, and costs around £100 one-way (less if the ticket is purchased online in advance). It also gets you directly into the heart of Edinburgh's Old Town. London Euston station also has hourly trains to Glasgow, taking up to six hours for the same price. Some trains from London to Scotland are overnight on what is popularly known as the **Caledonian Sleeper** (www.firstgroup.com), which departs from London Euston station twice nightly. You can go to sleep and wake up in rural Scotland (the train doesn't always stop in Glasgow or Edinburgh but continues to Stirling, Pitlochry, Inverness, and Fort William. One-way reclining seats/berths cost £51/78.

If you do opt to reach Scotland by train, consider buying a National Rail railcard beforehand, which will be more expensive in the short term (an additional £20–30) but will get you up to a 30 percent discount on subsequent rail journeys. You have to be of a certain age to qualify for a railcard (generally under 26 or over 65).

Bus

Bus travel to Scotland is the cheapest and lowest form of reaching the country on offer in the United Kingdom. The main operators are **National Express** (tel. 0870/580 8080, www.nationalexpress.com) and **Megabus** (tel. 0900/160 0900, www.megabus.com) and take 8–10 hours to reach Edinburgh or Glasgow from London. There's usually a choice of day or overnight services. **Silver Choice Travel** (tel. 0141/333 1400, www.silverchoicetravel. co.uk) also runs overnight to Edinburgh and Glasgow from London. There will be a service stop about halfway.

Car

The British road network from major English airports to Scotland is excellent, on three-lane motorways for the entire route. Access from London along the east/central side of England is on the M1, while along the west of England it is the M5/M6. Driving time from London to Edinburgh or Glasgow is 7–8 hours. Edinburgh is 398 miles by road north of London. Coming by car to Scotland offers a different and, in many ways, preferable introduction to Scotland, as you see the scenery of the south of Scotland often bypassed by rail and air connections. If you are driving up to Scotland, bear in mind that it is no fun driving in Scotland's big cities; a car is only necessary for exploring outside of Edinburgh and Glasgow.

Getting Around

Many overseas visitors will wince at the cost of travel in Scotland. While it's cheaper to get around in Scotland than it is in England, by most countries' standards Scotland is on the pricey side, whether you have your own wheels or are using public transportation.

AIR

Scotland is not a big country, and so overland or oversea transport is generally better for getting around. Traveling in this way is also far more fun and more of an adventure on the whole. There are only a few places within Scotland to which it is more practical to fly. Several of the Scottish islands are particularly far-flung and therefore flying saves a lot of time and seasickness. **Tiree** in Argyll and the Inner Hebrides (daily flight Mon.–Sat. from Glasgow, 50 min.), **Stornoway** in the Outer Hebrides (several daily flights from Glasgow, Edinburgh, Aberdeen, and Inverness, 1 hr.), **Kirkwall** in the Orkney Islands (several daily flights from Glasgow, Aberdeen, Inverness, and Sumburgh, 45 min. to 1 hr.) and **Sumburgh** in the Shetland Islands (several daily flights from Glasgow, Edinburgh, Aberdeen, Inverness and Kirkwall 45 min. to 1 hr.) are the only destinations to which you will need to fly.

Within the Outer Hebrides, the Orkney Islands, and the Shetland Islands, there are also a number of interisland flights. These are in tiny, eight-seater planes and are great ways of seeing several different islands. One-way flights in between the Orkney Islands are as little as £12, usually with the proviso of an overnight stay on the island in question. Flying from the mainland to the outer isles can cost anything from £40 to £100 one-way. All flights are operated by **British Airways** (tel. 0844/493 0787, www.britishairways.com).

BOAT

With nigh on 800 islands, boat travel is important in Scotland. In the case of most islands, there is no other transport option but boat.

Boat travel is generally island to island or island to mainland, but in several cases is the only means of getting between two points on the mainland, such as the **Bruce Watt** ferry from Mallaig to Knoydart. Virtually all of the boats to Scotland's islands are run by **Caledonian MacBrayne** or Calmac (tel. 0870/565 0000, www.calmac.co.uk) and are large boats with recliner lounges, bars, and restaurants. Most routes run regularly throughout the year. If you are traveling to the Orkney Islands or the Shetland Islands you will also need to make use of Scotland's other major ferry company, **Northlink Ferries** (tel. 0845/600 0449, www.northlinkferries.co.uk), which runs to the isles from Aberdeen and Scrabster. Some smaller islands are not blessed with ferry connections, but this does not make them impossible to get to. Locals will generally know someone with a boat for charter, or there may be signposts at west coast harbors advertising sailings. Many people underestimate how rough Scotland's seas can get. Many islands lie on the wrong side of some of the most treacherous stretches of water in the world, particularly the ferry crossings to Orkney, Shetland, and the Outer Hebrides. Even if you don't normally suffer from seasickness, take precautions. Eating a huge meal or drinking several pints on a crossing is rarely a good idea even on mild summer crossings; the locals do it, but they're tough.

TRAIN

If train is your preferred method of transportation, Scotland has plenty of gorgeous railways to oblige you. Considering Scotland's remote terrain, the rail network does a decent job of reaching the outlying places. The main cities of Edinburgh, Glasgow, Aberdeen, Dundee, Inverness, and Stirling are connected by regular trains, and there are also memorable scenic journeys, like the West Highland line from Glasgow to Oban. Train journeys on the scenic routes are up to four hours in length but are worth every penny and minute you spend.

POST BUSES

If you get the chance, which you will do if you go to remote parts of Scotland, then make sure you get to ride in the endearingly Scottish form of transportation known as the post bus. Where public transport in isolated regions of Scotland falls down, post buses are there to help travelers get to those far-flung, dream destinations. There is, of course, very little point for a normal bus to run a service along a poorly surfaced, dead-end road that leads to one house and a few mountains, but every place in the country needs mail delivered. This is where the post bus scheme comes in. Riding as a bus passenger in a red Royal Mail van along with the postman and all his parcels is a memorable way for travelers without their own transport to get to outlying places. The post bus system has been sadly cut back of recent years, but especially in the Highlands and islands, many services still run. Post buses will ply their respective routes usually once or twice a day each way Monday–Saturday. Local post offices will have details, or you can check out Royal Mail's website, www.royalmail. com, which has routes and timetables. You can hail a post bus at any point along its route and, traffic permitting, it will stop and pick you up. The driver will tell you the fare as you get on, £2 to £5 depending on how far you are going.

© LUKE WATERSON

Post buses – a cross between post vans and buses – are sometimes the only public transport available in remoter parts of Scotland.

Few places in Europe have railways that traverse such glorious scenery. No train journey in Scotland will cost more than £40 one-way, and usually considerably less. If you have a railcard, you will get further discounts. When purchasing a railcard, you will probably need to give a U.K. address and telephone number (your hotel address will do). Frequency of trains ranges from every 15 minutes between Edinburgh and Glasgow to a few trains per day in remote areas.

BUS

Bus travel in Scotland is good in the sense that even in the rural areas, buses stick to their timetables with relative success. It's bad in the sense that buses are sometimes only slated to run a handful of times per week. The scant supply of roads also means that if one route is blocked, incredibly long detours may be necessary. If a bus is going to be late, it could be very late. Sometimes, bus travel is unavoidable. Buses are the only way of getting via public transport to remote parts of Scotland and, while requiring careful planning at times, can usually get you to the area you want to go. The major operators in Scotland are **Stagecoach** (www. stagecoachbus.com), which covers routes in the central belt and south of Scotland; **Scottish Citylink** (tel. 0870/550 5050, www.citylink. co.uk), which covers routes between main towns across the country; and **Rapsons** (tel. 01463/710555, www.rapsons.co.uk), which covers the Highlands of Scotland.

The good news is that most tourist destinations are reached by very good bus services. Scotland's main bus station, Buchanan Street in Glasgow, is a very efficient and well-served bus station. As you board a bus, it's worth checking the journey time; buses to Skye from Glasgow, for instance, can take up to six hours and make only a very short stop for a toilet break en route. In nearly all cases, you can buy tickets from the driver on board. Glasgow and Edinburgh city buses require exact change for the fares. The long, rural bus journeys, although time-consuming, are usually great adventures.

If you like to have an element of planning to your journey, it's also worth knowing that a number of tour companies run hop-on/hop-off **Backpacker Buses** between major points across the Highlands. These include **Haggis Adventures** (tel. 0131/557 9393, www.haggisadventures.co.uk). There are regular departures to destinations like Skye and Orkney, usually on three- or five-day adventure packages.

Bus Fares

Traveling by bus is the cheapest way of getting around Scotland. Fares on local buses in towns and cities are between £1 and £2. Within a small region, travel is quite reasonable. First Buses and Stagecoach buses will charge £5 or less to ride right across regions like Dumfries and Galloway. In parts of the Southern Highlands and in the islands, costs are greater due to the distances involved. Traveling across the Southern Highlands, for example, from Inverness to Skye will cost £19. Buying tickets online can get you discounts, however, and this fare is at the top end of what you will pay for regional bus travel. Generally, expect to pay around £5–10 for long bus journeys within a particular region. National bus journeys within Scotland can cost anything between £5 and, in the most extreme cases, £40.

CAR

Scottish roads are a mixed bag. If you have driven up from southern England, the first thing you will notice as you cross the border is that the roads almost immediately deteriorate, both in width and surface quality. Dual carriageways or motorways, with two or three lanes in each direction, persist until you reach Glasgow and also connect Edinburgh, Dundee, Aberdeen, and Perth. Beyond these points, even the second-category roads (A-Roads) can be slow going. Single-track roads are a key feature of the Highland transport network. The majority of roads are paved, although many are vulnerable to flash floods, avalanches, and ice or snow. Even main roads in the north of Scotland are often closed for periods in winter. Much of northern Scotland relies on only a slim number of roads to connect it to the south.

PASSING PLACE ETIQUETTE

Once you get away from the main urban areas, Scotland's roads shrink in width not just down to one lane in each direction but to one lane only. Single-track roads are distributed across Scotland and in the Highlands and islands of Scotland constitute the majority of the road network. Even roads marked as second-category roads (A-Roads) can be single-track. Traffic passes by means of passing places, placed at regular intervals along the roads and invariably marked by a white sign on a post. Once you've mastered passing place etiquette, driving on these roads becomes positively enjoyable.

Whether it is you or the oncoming vehicle that moves into the passing place is determined technically by which vehicle passes the last available passing place first. However, a degree of forward planning is necessary here. If you spot that the vehicle approaching is large, or approaching fast, it's wise to pull in to a passing place earlier rather than later. This will save someone having to do a tricky reversing job along often rather precarious roads. Passing place etiquette means that driving becomes a rather more personable experience. At the very least, you'll need to cooperate with vehicles on the road and usually drivers pass each other with a friendly wave or a nod of acknowledgment. Often, where the squeeze to pass is tight or the oncoming vehicle is in no rush, windows might even be rolled down and pleasantries exchanged.

This puts extraordinary pressure on roads like the A82 along Loch Lomond, especially in tourist season. The paucity of road connections also means roads are used by all vehicles; often traffic on major routes crawls along at a snail's pace behind a tractor for hours.

Driving in Glasgow and Edinburgh is to be avoided if at all possible, and it's unnecessary due to good public transportation in each. It's only necessary to hire a car for exploring outside of Glasgow and Edinburgh.

Licenses and Insurance

Holders of overseas driving licenses can drive motor vehicles for up to 12 months in Scotland and the rest of the United Kingdom. If you're bringing your own car across (i.e., shipping it), ensure you have green card insurance (an International Motor Insurance Certificate, which your motor insurance company should be able to provide either free or for a small administrative charge) and the car registration documents of the vehicle you are driving.

Rules of the Road

Driving in Scotland is, particularly in the rural areas, nothing short of exhilarating. You get an enormous degree of freedom that public transport can't offer. Before you get behind the wheel, it is worth bearing several points in mind. In Scotland, as in the rest of the U.K., driving is on the left-hand side. Speed limits on motorways (triple-track roads) and dual carriageways (double-track roads) are 70 miles per hour (mph) or 112 kilometers per hour (kph). If you are towing a caravan or trailer, then you must not exceed 60 mph/96 kph. On other main roads the limit is 60 mph/96 kph for all vehicles. At roundabouts, frequent stumbling blocks for drivers in unfamiliar territory, give priority to vehicles coming from the right and always turn left on entering. Scottish law requires that all passengers in front and back seats wear seatbelts. It is also illegal to use a mobile or cell phone when driving and to drive under the influence of alcohol.

If you are driving, the golden rule to doing so safely is not to rush—and you would hardly want to in most parts of Scotland. Give yourself ample time to reach your destination. Locals in rural areas drive far too fast and will, in their frustration, use even the narrowest double track road as a speedway. This is highly dangerous; roads are narrow and twisting and visibility even on a clear day is usually poor. Always give drivers that hassle you as much room as possible to overtake and slow down on straights to allow them to pass you. A huge cause of road accidents in Scotland is caused by frustration, usually courtesy of a holidaymaker's car slowing down traffic.

Fuel Stations

One of the most shocking elements of driving in Scotland for overseas visitors is the price of fuel. You might think with that with its burgeoning oil industry fuel prices in Scotland would be cheap, but no. Even in the main urban areas where fuel is cheapest, the average price per liter was at last report £1 for unleaded petrol (gas). The more you venture into the remote countryside, the higher the prices go. On islands, most expensive of all, you can pay up to £1.20 a liter for unleaded petrol. Most cars will take unleaded gas, while larger vehicles may use diesel, which is even more expensive. In the urban areas finding a fuel station won't be a problem, with many stations open 24 hours. In rural areas, fuel stations are few and far between, with hours that are not only limited but often nonsensical. Many islands do not even have a petrol station; if you're taking your car or a rental car over to a small island, check before you board the ferry whether there is a fuel station. To be on the safe side, always carry a spare fuel can and hose. Aviemore, by the Cairngorm Mountains, is the only place in the whole of the rural Highlands to have a 24-hour petrol station.

Hitchhiking

Hitching in Scotland is not permitted on motorways or motorway slipways. If the police see you attempting to hitchhike in these locations, they will tell you to move. In urban areas, many drivers are very wary of hitchers and will be less likely to stop. In rural Scotland, the reverse is often true; there, tired hikers and backpackers thumbing a lift is a common sight. Hitching a lift on certain islands is an accepted form of getting around, but on the mainland, despite the magical experiences that may result, hitchhiking is not something to make a habit of. It may be cheap, but you have to ask yourself whether the few pounds you save are worth spending large proportions of your holiday on invariably rain-drenched roadsides having drivers hooting at you. Thumbing a lift is also, of course, potentially dangerous.

Car Rental

The main international rental car companies in Scotland are the usual suspects: **Hertz** (tel. 0870/844 8844, www.hertz.co.uk), **Avis** (tel. 0870/606 0100, www.avis.co.uk), **Budget Rent-A-Car** (tel. 0870/153 9170, www.budget.co.uk), and **Thrifty** (tel. 01494/751600, www.thrifty.co.uk).

All these companies will have offices at Scotland's main airports and also town/city center offices in most major places including Edinburgh, Glasgow, and Aberdeen. Major car hire companies charge a standard £35 to £50 for their smallest car (likely to be manual drive, not automatic, but some companies offer cars with automatic transmissions). Weekly prices are cheaper, around £135 per week for the smallest type of car. Some of these companies have special online deals with specific airlines. The price quoted will not include insurance. This is not essential but will cover you in case of accident on Scotland's often-tricky roads. If you have special requirements (for instance, you need a child seat), it is recommended you let rental car companies know in advance. Rental cars in Scotland generally take unleaded fuel (that's the green pump at the fuel stations!).

Car hire in Scotland can be a lot cheaper with a smaller company, as low as £17 per day or £115 per week. Taking a car on a ferry can be pricey in Scotland. Many Scottish islands are both far away from the mainland and rather large; the best solution to this problem is to hire a car when you get there (relatively easy in the Outer Hebrides, Orkney, and Shetland).

Sports and Recreation

The national sport in Scotland is most certainly football, although rugby is also a popular spectator sport. Tennis is increasingly popular, too, with young Scottish sensation Andy Murray a top 10 player in the men's single rankings. There were nationwide celebrations in 2007 when Glasgow won the bid to host the 2014 Commonwealth Games, although it remains to be seen how much this will inspire Scotland as a nation. Scotland is the birthplace of golf, and it will not take you long to realize this with a vast selection of courses across the country. Walking is another extremely popular recreational activity with many Scots, as is fishing. The country is also getting a growing reputation for its water sports.

WALKING

All factors considered, Scotland is probably the best walking destination in the world. For starters, Scotland has a stunning diversity of terrain contained within a compact area. A day's hike can include mountains, moor, forest, lochside, beach, and low-level cultivated land. Scotland's compactness also means that getting to the really remote spots doesn't take very long. The country's remotest regions can be accessed within a few of hours from its largest city. Trails are well marked, and several long-distance footpaths have been developed. There are websites and substantial free printed information about Scotland's walking routes. Accommodations for walkers are also regularly available. If you don't feel like carrying your own tent, there are a number of well-appointed hostels and guesthouses you can plan your walk around. Mountaineers rate Scotland's high hills on a par with the Himalayas for sheer majesty, and most people in the know rate Scotland's beaches as among Europe's finest. One thing you can guarantee: you will only see the best of Scotland's scenery if you get on those hiking boots and walk out into the middle of it.

Long-Distance Footpaths

Scotland's long-distance footpaths are designed to show off Scotland in all its dramatic diversity. Southern Scotland's 212-mile **Southern Upland Way** (www.southernuplandway.com) is the country's longest and toughest footpath. The **Borders Abbeys Way** is a 65-mile route linking the four Borders abbeys of Melrose, Dryburgh, Jedburgh, and Kelso, heading through rich forests and high hills. A surprisingly little-walked path is the 62-mile **Arran Coastal Way,** which goes right around the coast of the Isle of Arran in Ayrshire. It shows the island at its absolute best: wild rocky beaches and castles peeping from the treetops. The 95-mile **West Highland Way** (www.west-highland-way.co.uk) is Scotland's most popular long-distance path and one of the most satisfying, given that you start on the edge of a city (Milngavie, near Glasgow) and end up in some of the country's remotest scenery. The path is 95 miles long. Farther up in the Highlands is the **Great Glen Way,** while the **Speyside Way** spans the Southern Highlands and Aberdeenshire and passes by some of Scotland's best distilleries.

DESIGNATED NATIONAL AND PROTECTED PARKS

The trend over the last 50 years in Scotland has been to designate specific areas of its outstanding scenery as protected spaces, thereby preserving them for wildlife and visitors alike. Scotland currently has just two national parks, which is perhaps surprising given its wealth of wilderness. The **Cairngorms National Park** (www.cairngorms.co.uk) is 2,360 square miles (3,800 square km) of Scotland's highest and most rugged mountain scenery in the Southern Highlands, containing 25 percent of Britain's threatened birds and plants. There is also **Loch Lomond and the Trossachs National Park.** The parks are popular with walkers, cyclists, water sports enthusiasts, skiers, and mountaineers and have excellent tourist facilities.

Galloway Forest Park (www.forestry.gov. uk) is Britain's largest forest park, located in Dumfries and Galloway, popular with mountain-bikers. Scotland also has many National Nature Reserves, which are given protected area status. The best of these to enjoy exploring include **Beinn Eighe and Loch Maree,** a wild area in the northwest highlands in Wester Ross; gorgeous **Glen Affric** north of Loch Ness, a hiker's mecca; and the outstanding wildlife of the island of **St. Kilda.** National Nature Reserves have notice boards and a number of signed trails to follow as well as information about how to respect these sacred natural habitats. The **Northwest Highlands Geopark,** which stretches from the northwest tip of Scotland down through rocky Assynt is a favorite with geologists and hill walkers alike, drawn by the formidable landscapes formed by Europe's oldest rocks.

CYCLING

Cycling in Scotland, due to the profusion of quiet, winding, single-track roads, is perfect. Roads are generally well serviced and bike hire shops (typical rental is £10–15 per day) and repair shops are common. Even some of the larger cities are safe, cycle-friendly destinations. A wonderful series of canal towpaths and disused railway lines give gorgeous, car-free links between the centers of Edinburgh and Aberdeen and the countryside. Urban and rural routes are linked well with the notable exception of Scotland's largest city, Glasgow, whose ring roads make it the worst place in the country to begin a cycling holiday. With road cycling, you should adhere to the same rules of the road as you would when driving in Scotland. If you want to be really adventurous, then there is ample off-road cycling, like southern Scotland's thrilling **7stanes** (www.7stanes.gov.uk) routes, generally through forest. Check out Visit Scotland's information on cycling and mountain biking in Scotland at http://cycling.visitscotland.com.

GOLF

Scotland's coastal scenery in the east and the southwest forms a gentle landscape of grass-covered, bumpy sand dunes that makes perfect golf-playing terrain. Scotland is the home of golf, and you only have to look at a map to see the number of courses there are to play. There are plenty of inland courses in Scotland but most delightful of all are the links courses by the coast; nothing can quite beat the sensation of playing golf with the sea filling your view. The main golfing regions are **Fife,** the golfing capital of the world, with the Old Course of St. Andrews, the **Angus Coast** north of Fife, and the **Ayrshire and Arran** region.

Even on courses like the Old Course, it's not difficult to book yourself a playing slot. You can book yourself a tee time up to a year in advance; information is available from the **St. Andrews Links Trust** (www.standrews. org.uk). In other parts of the country, it's usually possible to book a time on a course one or two weeks in advance. Most of the golf courses have individual websites with essential information like pricing. Visit www.scotlands -golf-courses.com for information on Scotland's courses. A round will cost anything from £20 on the remoter courses up to £125 for a round on the Old Course in St. Andrews, with deals available for those who want to play multiple rounds. Some lavish hotel resorts contain some of Scotland's finest golf courses, such as **Gleneagles,** but you can still play here even if you are not staying.

DIVING

Scotland is not the likeliest dive destination, but the waters are not as cold and the visibility not as poor as first impressions might suggest. In fact, the country is ranked within the top 10 diving areas in the world. This is largely due to the wide bay of **Scapa Flow** in the Orkney Islands where there are a multitude of sunken World War II ships to explore. When you factor in a whole host of sealife like seals and dolphins, you have a very good reason to visit Scotland for its diving. **Coldingham** in the Borders is another key dive site. Scotland's dive schools have an excellent reputation. The *Stromness* section under *West Mainland and Hoy* of the *Orkney Islands* chapter and *Coldingham and St. Abbs Head* under *East Coast and Lammermuir*

Foothills in the *Borders* chapter have further information on diving.

WATER SPORTS

The combination of fast, churning rivers and long, wide lochs make Scotland a playground for water sports enthusiasts. Pretty much any body of major inland water can offer kayaking, canoeing, sailing, and windsurfing. Excellent inland areas are **Loch Ken** in Dumfries and Galloway and **Loch Tay** in Perthshire. For the finest whitewater rafting in the country, head to the **River Tay** just east of Loch Tay in Perthshire; a number of companies in this area offer white-knuckle rides on the rapids here. Scotland has some of the highest waves in the world and coastal areas like **Coldingham** in the Borders, **Thurso** (cold but hair-raising), and the island of **Tiree** in the Inner Hebrides offer great surfing and windsurfing. There are great surf schools and coaching available at all these destinations.

MOUNTAINEERING

On the face of it, mountain-climbing in Scotland is not too difficult; for a start, there are no peaks over 4,500 feet in the country. Still, with the determination of mountaineers to find the most challenging ways to do everything and the number of sheer craggy faces soaring vertically for upwards of 1,000 feet, mountaineering up here is no easy feat. Unless you are a fully qualified mountaineer you should always go climbing with an experienced, qualified guide: If you don't, you risk death. **Lochaber** in the Southern Highlands is the self-proclaimed outdoor capital of Britain and, along with the nearby **Cuillin Hills** on the Isle of Skye, offers the finest climbing in the country. There is also great climbing on **Ben Nevis** and the **Aoanach Eagach Ridge** in Glencoe.

FISHING

The fish-rich rivers and seas of Scotland have been tempting anglers since prehistory. Among those spots with the best reputation are the **River Tweed** in the Borders, **Loch Awe** in Argyll, and Orkney's **Harray and Stenness Lochs.** Salmon (averaging up to four feet or 120 cm) and brown trout (averaging up to 2.5 feet or 80 cm) are the highlights of Scotland's waters. Far bigger fish have, of course, been caught. Visiting anglers are key to the economy in rural Scotland and are therefore well catered to, including some purpose-built fishing hotels. In Scotland, you do not require a fishing license; just ensure you buy a permit from whoever owns the land you want to fish on.

SPECTATOR FOOTBALL

Scots are passionate about football. On the world stage and even on the European stage, Scotland is far from being at the top of the football hierarchy (although recent world rankings place the national side in the world's top 15). Scotland attracted considerable media coverage by "almost" qualifying for the 2008 European championships yet, as usual, failing to do so. The top division of Scottish domestic football consists of 12 teams that compete over a season that lasts from August to late May. Dominating the domestic scene are the Glasgow-based giants of the **Rangers** and **Celtic** football clubs. They enjoy a smattering of European success and a great deal of rivalry. The best way to feel the passion of Scottish football is to go to a game: matches generally take place on Saturday afternoons, as well as Sunday afternoons and weekday evenings from Monday to Wednesday. Tickets cost from £20 up to £60 or £70 for good seats. All stadiums are now all-seat affairs; standing is not permitted.

Accommodations and Food

ACCOMMODATIONS

There is a huge spectrum of accommodation in Scotland, with rooms to suit every budget and taste. You will seldom be totally stuck for a place to stay but in remote areas, especially at busy times of year, it is advisable to pre-book accommodations. Places to stay can be in old churches, lighthouses, farms, mills, schools, castles, and universities. It is not always necessary to phone up to reserve accommodations; this can often be done online on the establishment's website. Online information is not always regularly updated and is often inaccurate.

Accommodation Types

Scotland has a great network of **camp and caravan sites.** Designated sites, ranging from the basic to large places with shops, playgrounds, and swimming pools, will cost £5–15 for two people and a modest two-person tent per night. If you wish to wild camp (possible in remoter areas of the country), the rules are that you must do so out of the way (and, preferably, sight) of main paths and roads and ensure you leave the site as you found it. Be responsible and preserve the countryside for future visitors to enjoy. Campsites are usually only open in Scotland from Easter to October.

Budget accommodation is plentiful in Scotland. Cheapest of all are **bothies:** simple croft cottages in remote areas, with no bedding provided and designed to provide shelter for walkers. **Hostels** offer cheap accommodation, usually in dormitories with self-catering kitchens; at times they can be a sociable, fun experience and at times synonymous with heavily snoring fellow guests and dirty showers. Scottish Youth Hostel Association (SYHA) hostels can be sterile and sleep guests in single-sex dormitories, while independent hotels often offer a less common sleeping experience, with more elaborate decor, staff that try hard to be cool, mixed dorms, and occasionally private rooms. You will generally pay between £10 and £15 per person per night.

The most widespread accommodation in Scotland is in either a **bed-and-breakfast** or a **guesthouse,** houses owned and lived in by residents of a particular area with parts rented out on a nightly basis to guests. Almost always a breakfast will be included in the price. Rooms will always be private, although cheaper places will have shared bathrooms. Quality varies drastically from small rooms little better than hostels to well-appointed mansions with facilities that outdo most hotels. Most double rooms fall between £50 and £100 per night.

Accommodation in **pubs** and **hotels** is synonymous with quality. Pub rooms are generally cheaper, with prices for a double room from around £60 to well in excess of £100. At top-end hotels you can pay £200 or £300 for one night's stay in a double room. Rooms for these price tags are usually en suite, with good facilities. A **resort** is a glorified hotel usually offering extra facilities to guests like a gym, swimming pool, or golf course. Rooms at Scotland's most lavish golf resort, Gleneagles, can cost over £1,000 per night.

Particularly common in remote areas of Scotland are **self-catering cottages,** which an owner will rent out by the week (which works out as cheap day-to-day as many guesthouses) to paying guests. They have most of the luxuries (TV, self-catering kitchen, good-quality bedding) you would expect in your own home. In urban areas, sometimes self-catering places will let you stay by the night.

FOOD

Scottish food has not traditionally enjoyed good press. Traditionally, the climate was to blame. Wet, windy weather and thin, infertile moorland soil meant that very few things could grow. Flour, potatoes, and meat in the form of beef or lamb were often the only ingredients available for making meals. Scottish cuisine developed along these lines as heavy and often tasteless. The nation's food has come leaps and bounds since those dark times, however, and

© LUKE WATERSON

Many of Scotland's old castles, like Glengorm Castle on Mull, now provide atmospheric accommodations for visitors.

the country is now sought after by food gurus for its variety of fresh, organic local produce and its mix of top-notch restaurants. The great thing about Scotland's restaurants is their tendency to turn up in unexpected places. There are classy dining scenes in remotest Skye and in the Northwest Highlands to equal the dining out in the larger cities. The country can also offer anything from Indian to Mongolian to Australian cuisine, pulled off with varying degrees of authenticity.

Where to Eat

The cheapest bet for food is to cook for yourself, by heading to a local **shop** or **supermarket.** Local shops have higher prices than supermarkets but can, especially in more rural areas, offer more interesting products. Most supermarkets in Scotland are chain stores offering low prices but often-depressing uniformity. They are also often located out of town, geared toward car drivers. You could also head to a **street-side snack stall** where food will be

a basic, quick fix, generally in locations where there are no sources of food like out-of-the-way car parks.

Cafés and tearooms are the best bet for a cheap, filling meal. They vary enormously in quality but open early (between 8 and 10 A.M.) and stay open until 4 or 5 P.M. and occasionally for dinner, too. These places serve simple dishes for around £2–10. Look out for the Italian cafés run by Scotland's significant Italian population—great spots for fine coffee and an Italian snack.

For evening meals, **restaurants** generally open at midday and have last orders around 9 or 9:30 P.M. There are also **pubs,** which offer a more casual eating alternative and serve food during approximately the same hours. Pubs are primarily drinking houses that also serve food on occasion. The food in restaurants is traditionally of a more refined quality and a higher price. The cheapest evening meals in pubs start at around £7, while you'll want to be trying something pretty special to pay over £15 for one course in

Scotland is full of wonderful, traditional old pubs like the Shore Inn in Portsoy.

either a pub or a restaurant. Guesthouses and bed-and-breakfasts sometimes offer evening meals for around £15–25 for three courses.

What to Eat

Scotland has any number of national and regional delicacies but across the board the **full Scottish breakfast,** also known as a fry-up, is a favorite start to the day: a platter of fried eggs, sausages, bacon, fried tomato, baked beans, and sometimes also a potato scone or **black pudding,** which is cooked, congealed cow or pig blood mixed with a suet or meat filling and served in sausage-like slices (incidentally, scrumptious). Another classic Scottish breakfast dish is **porridge,** a steaming bowl of oats, milk, salt, and water, sometimes enhanced by a sprinkle of crusty brown sugar on the top.

Fishy delicacies to check out include **Arbroath Smokies,** a type of lightly smoked herring. Smoked fish is a particularly Scottish concept; look out for peat- or oak-smoked **kippers** and **smoked salmon,** common for breakfast or doused in lemon juice and

served with salad as a starter or snack. In the Shetlands, **gravadlax** is a regional delicacy—raw, seasoned salmon that has been pickled rather than smoked. On the Outer Hebrides, it's not just seafood that is popular to eat but also **seaweed.** A favorite dish across Scotland is **Cullen Skink,** a thick fish and potato soup. Seafood is at the heart of a lot of the food in Scotland; take the opportunity to try gorgeous **langoustines** and **lobster** when it arises. The fish-rich rivers of Scotland also mean that rural delicacies across the country will often feature **salmon** and **brown trout.**

Many simpler snacks also grace Scotland's cuisine, like the **Forfar Bridie,** which is minced flavored meat in a crumbly pastry casing. Cheese is something Scotland does very well, including **Island Cheese** on Arran, which makes beautiful creamy cheddars and blue cheeses. One of the main delicacies on the Orkney Islands is **Grimbister fried cheese** in a bread-crumb case.

By a distance, the most famous Scottish meat dish is **haggis.** This is sheep's heart, liver, and lungs minced with suet, spices, oatmeal, and onion. Scottish meat is highly prized, from juicy **Aberdeen Angus steaks** to **North Ronaldsay lamb.** Sheep on this Orkney Island live on seaweed, which gives the meat a sought-after gourmet flavor. You can have your meat neat or dressed up in a popular dish like a **steak and ale pie** with a pastry topping.

Scotland's traditional desserts are quite plain but there are plenty to choose from. These include the well-known **shortbread,** a thick crumbly biscuit and **flapjack,** a baked dish made with oats and golden syrup. Another popular dessert in the north of Scotland is **tiffin,** a mass of chocolate, fruit, and caramel. Homemade cakes and other sweet things are often referred to as home-bakes, popular as an afternoon tea treat across Scotland. Other sweets to try include **clootie dumpling,** a blend of molasses, fruit, and suet blended and boiled together in a cloth.

Ordering Food and Tipping

Here's the rule in Scotland: in pubs and inns, if you want to eat you generally will be asked to find a table with a table number, then go up to order at the bar, giving the table number when you do so. In busy places, no free table means no food can be ordered. Most pubs have restaurant menus and separate bar food, which is cheaper. With restaurants and many of the better cafés, you'll be escorted to or asked to choose a table where your order will be taken. Service in Britain has never been regarded as particularly high quality, generally because waitstaff assume that they will not generally get tips. There are, however, lots of snazzy restaurants now in Scotland where service is excellent. Scotland is not a country where a tip is expected, except when you are having meals in restaurants, where it's good form to tip (around 10 percent of the total bill is a reasonable amount). Even here, tipping is entirely at your discretion, although better restaurants will include a 10 percent service charge on the bill.

What to Drink

Highland Spring Water is about the best water you will ever taste, often flavored unmistakably with peat. Scotland, like Britain, typically has **tea** as its number one hot drink, but across the land you will also find plenty of great places to have **coffee.** Either way, look out for Scottish company **Brodies** on your travels, a fine Edinburgh-based tea and coffee merchant. The southwest coast of Scotland, thanks to 19th-century Italian immigrants, still serves some of the best coffee in the country. A popular soft drink in Scotland is **Irn Bru,** a fizzy orange bubblegum-flavored drink that you will either love or loathe.

The Scottish tend to favor harder alcoholic drinks. There are many top-notch breweries around the country producing excellent Scottish ales and beers. If you fancy a flavor of heather to your ale then try the tasty **Fraoch.** The Norse-influenced Shetland Islands produce wonderful **vodka** at Blackwood's Distillers, including creamy **JAGO,** the world's only vanilla vodka cream liqueur.

WHISKY AND WHISKY-TASTING

Whisky is the number one drink in Scotland. The country has far too many distilleries to

Whisky is a big part of Scottish culture.

© LUKE WATERSON

go into details about them here, but each of Scotland's distilleries produces its own distinctive single malt. Nowhere else in the world has the right to call any spirits it produces "whisky." Single malt whisky-drinking in Scotland is a whole world of tastes, and if you haven't yet developed a taste for the drink, Scotland is the place to start. To fully appreciate whisky, tasting is done not with the tongue but the nose, which has eight times as many sensory receptors. The color gives away a few clues about the age and how the whisky has been matured; it comes from wood of the cask it's been matured in. A rich red whisky will indicate a sherry cask has been used, while a lighter, sharper color will mean a bourbon cask. Tasting is done by taking a sip and letting the whisky roll over the tongue, which has four sensory areas that bring out the different qualities of whisky. The tip of the tongue determines the sweetness, while the back gauges dryness and bitterness. The sides, crucial when it comes to tasting briny whiskies distilled near the coast, measure the saltiness and sourness.

Tips for Travelers

VISAS AND OFFICIALDOM
Tourist Requirements and Customs

In all immigration and visa matters, Scotland is subject to the policy of the United Kingdom as a whole. If you are a British, Australian, Canadian, U.S.A., Japanese, South African, or other European Union citizen, you do not need a visa to enter the United Kingdom. You will need a passport, valid for at least six months after your arrival date. This will enable you to stay in the U.K. a maximum of six months, provided you do not intend to seek paid work. A stay in the U.K. includes any time spent in England, Scotland, Wales, or Northern Ireland. If you need to extend your stay in the U.K. for any reason, contact **Home Office, Immigration, and Nationality Directorate** (Festival Ct., 200 Brand St., Govan, Glasgow, tel. 0870/606 7766, www.bia.homeoffice.gov.uk). Do this before your existing permit expires, not after!

If you enter Britain at a non-Scottish airport you will not have to go through customs again if you subsequently travel through Britain to reach Scotland. You are not required to show an onward ticket when you arrive in the U.K., but if you possess one, showing it will certainly help cut down on your grilling at customs. British customs officers have a reputation for being firm but fair. Use common sense when dealing with them: dress smartly and be respectful. In the current climate of perceived terrorist threat, security is pretty tight. It is far better to deal with any doubts or queries you have about your eligibility to enter the U.K. in your home country. If you are an American citizen, a great website to help you with officialdom inquiries is www.uk-yankee.com; it may be aimed at Americans who are coming to live in the U.K. long-term but it has lots of information about visas for which you are eligible and problems you may encounter.

It is possible to bring a foreign car into the United Kingdom, usually for a period of up to six months in any one 12 month period. Foreign plates may be displayed, providing all taxes including vehicle excise duty have been paid in the country of origin.

STUDY, EMPLOYMENT, AND VOLUNTEERING

If you want to come to Scotland for more than just a holiday, opportunities exist. As far as study is concerned, American Gap Year students of 18 or 19 years of age may work for up to a year in the United Kingdom, provided they have a written offer of employment from a U.K. educational establishment. They must be able to prove both that they will not be seeking other paid work in the U.K. and that they will be returning to full-time education in the United States upon their return.

DAY-TO-DAY SCOTTISH SURVIVAL TIPS

There are a few day-to-day basics in Scotland worth knowing about that simply can't be categorized elsewhere. Knowing these things might not be essential, but they will certainly help you in social situations. The single most important thing to remember is that living costs in Scotland are higher than most other countries in Europe, although significantly less than in England.

When you wake up in the morning and need a **coffee,** you'll be looking at paying £1-2 depending on the style of the place you frequent. Many hostels and guesthouses provide coffee free of charge, but it's generally instant. Generally, greasy-spoon-type cafés (lower-end) will serve you your coffee with milk already added unless you request otherwise. Most cafés will serve you a decent cup of coffee; this will not be American-style drip coffee but most likely made in a coffee machine.

The first thing you will notice about **shopping** in Scotland is that, in the south at least, High Streets are quite Americanized with lots of samey chain stores. This can actually be a good thing, as you can guarantee finding a shop for a specific need on almost every High Street in central and southern Scotland. In remoter mainland Scotland and on the islands, chain stores are replaced by far more individual stores. Most public amenity and chain store **opening hours** (9 A.M.-5 P.M. Mon.-Sat. and often noon-5 P.M. Sun.) generally apply to smaller independent stores, but not always.

Shops that are useful to know about include **supermarkets,** the cheapest of which are **Tesco** and **Morrisons** and the most high-quality of which are **Waitrose** and **Marks and Spencer.** The **pharmacy** chain **Boots** is found in nearly every town, even in the Highlands, and is a good bet to get contraception and also photographic film. You can get film developed here, too. The main **news agent/newsstand** is **WH Smith,** while **Woolworths** is a good bet for day-to-day items including **square three-pin electrical adapters,** which you will need to use foreign electrical devices. Scottish **department stores** include **Jenners** and **Mackays.** Common **travel agencies** to look out for include **Thomas Cook.** It rarely has the best deals but does have a good spread of stores across the country.

A standard size 1.5-liter **bottle of water** will cost £0.70-1. If you need to fill up with **petrol (gasoline),** you'll pay £1-1.15 per liter. If you're taking a **cross-town or cross-city bus,** typical fares are £1-2. If you are heading out to a **pub** in the evening with Scottish friends, general pub culture dictates that you take it in turns to buy **rounds,** which means buying everyone in the party a drink. A **pint of beer** will cost £2.50-3.50. **Wine** is expensive to buy in a pub or restaurant in Scotland; a decent wine will be in the region of £15-20. This is a 100 percent to 200 percent mark-up on their shop price. If you fancy going to the **cinema,** tickets are cheap by British standards at £4-7. Many **nightclubs** in Scotland will collect a cover charge of £5-15 to get in, depending on what is going on. Finally, it's worth remembering that, as with other parts of the world these days, you can get things cheaper online.

Similar arrangements exist between the U.K. and other countries. Scotland's key universities are in Glasgow, Edinburgh, Aberdeen, and St. Andrews. With the resurgence of Gaelic, study courses are slowly becoming more popular with visitors and are possible at a number of places in Scotland. There is nowhere more atmospheric to learn than on an island where Gaelic is still a big part of everyday life: check out the courses on offer at **Lews Castle College** (www.lews.uhi.ac.uk) on Lewis in the Outer Hebrides. Course fees start around £100 and increase depending on whether you want accommodation thrown in.

European Union citizens can work in Britain free of immigration controls, but citizens of the U.S.A., Canada, Australia, and other countries may only seek employment for limited periods under certain requirements. To see if you are eligible for work in the United Kingdom, check out www.ukvisas. gov.uk or, for citizens of the U.S., www.uk-yankee.com. The work on offer if you do meet U.K. working requirements will most likely be in the catering and tourism industries. In Scotland, a largely rural country, many of these jobs can be very pleasant means of financing a holiday. The tax on your wages will be quite high.

It's likely to be of far more value both to you and Scotland if you come to the U.K. as a volunteer/charity worker. The projects you can become involved with in a small country are limited but meaningful. Volunteer projects can involve working in inner-city areas renovating low-income housing, archaeological work, wildlife surveying, and national park maintenance. The **Volunteer Abroad** program (www.volunteerabroad.com) has details on projects currently on offer in Scotland. If you are a full-time student in another country, coming to volunteer or to work is less hassle. Non-students will require a visa whether they are coming to volunteer or work. Volunteers must be able to prove that they will be paid for no more than essential accommodation and food costs during their stay.

TRAVELERS WITH DISABILITIES

Services for the disabled are improving in Scotland; many bed-and-breakfast inns and most hotels now advertise wheelchair-accessible rooms. There is a policy of providing door ramps on all new buildings, with the majority of public buildings like libraries having good disabled access. The abundance of accommodations and attractions in Scotland in century-old buildings means that disabled access in these cases is restricted. Refreshingly, both Historic Scotland (www.historic-scotland.gov. uk) and the National Trust for Scotland (www. nts.org.uk), which between them own most of the cultural sites in the country, have vastly improved disabled access of late, with ramps and also courtesy buggies. The **Association of Scottish Visitor Attractions** (tel. 01786/ 475172, www.asva.co.uk) is committed to maximizing disabled access at all Scottish attractions, so email them if you have any special requirements prior to visiting.

If you're going to be spending time in a major town or city like Glasgow, Edinburgh, Aberdeen, or Inverness, it's worth knowing about an operation called Shopmobility, dedicated to providing motorized buggies for disabled shoppers and city users. Public transport throughout the country might in practice be disabled friendly (you'll see special Disabled Priority Zone signs) but only a few buses have disabled ramps. Overall, disabled facilities in Scotland are good, and **Mobility Scotland** (www.mobilityscotland.co.uk) has lots of further links to useful resources for disabled travelers.

TRAVELING WITH CHILDREN

Scotland is a hugely child-friendly destination with some areas of the country like Dumfries and Galloway being particularly exciting and welcoming for kids. If you are hiring a car and you have a small child traveling with you, be sure to let the rental car company know, as they can have a special child seat fitted. This isn't just a convenience, but the law. Children have to wear a seatbelt suitable to their size, and if your child is under the age of nine they will not be suited to standard fitted seatbelts.

Children under the age of 16 will generally get in either half price or free to most attractions requiring an entrance fee. You might encounter some obstacles when traveling with children, however; certain accommodations will not accept children under the age of 16 and will usually state if this is the case on their website/brochure.

WOMEN TRAVELERS

Scotland is perfectly safe to travel in for everyone. Women are treated with equal respect to men in Scotland and will seldom encounter any displays of chauvinism. Women traveling alone should merely use the common sense they would in any country, e.g. avoiding walking through red light districts late at night. It is worth noting that in rural areas Scottish women often dress in jeans and sweaters during normal day-to-day activities, due mainly to the weather and the high winds that make dresses impractical. That doesn't mean that female tourists you can't dress revealingly if they want, but bear in mind that it could, as in lots of places, garner a degree of attention from the opposite sex. There are certain pubs, usually in towns and cities, known as "old man pubs," which are still bastions of the Scottish male. You won't be in any danger if you enter these joints but you will get attention.

Bear in mind that the contraceptive pill is only available by prescription in Scotland but you can get the morning-after pill from pharmacies. This is effective against conception for up to 72 hours after unprotected sexual intercourse.

GAY AND LESBIAN TRAVELERS

Scotland is generally gay- and lesbian-friendly. Only its two biggest cities can be said to have anything resembling a gay scene; no other cities are large or cosmopolitan enough. The lovable little pink triangle in Edinburgh (the area around Broughton Street in New Town) and Glasgow's Merchant City (Virginia and Glassford Streets) have established gay areas. Outside of these areas, open displays of affection between same-sex partners are probably not too wise. Scotland has a gay and lesbian magazine, **ScotsGay,** with its own website, www.scotsgay.co.uk, which has links to a wealth of resources for gays and lesbians in Scotland. There are LGBT (Lesbian, Gay, Bisexual, and Transgender) centers in Edinburgh (58a/60 Broughton St.) and Glasgow (the corner of Bell St. and High St., Merchant City).

CONDUCT AND CUSTOMS

The Scots are friendly, polite, unassuming people that exude a quiet self-confidence. Sometimes it can seem that their brusque exterior is hard to get past, but having been historically sidelined, Scots are often just unsure whether visitors are genuinely interested in their culture. If you show an interest in finding out more about them, they will want to find out more about you. Scots have a deeply ironic humor that often goes hand-in-hand, especially in rural areas, with an utterly laid-back approach to life. If you have been used to the hectic pace of England or even other central parts of Scotland, you will find that life in the extremes of the country is relaxed: Conversation is always more important that meeting a schedule. Even if Scots do get panicked, they never show it—portraying emotions to strangers is not a Scottish trait.

Although it's not immediately apparent, religion is hugely important in Scotland, so be sensitive to people's religious beliefs. Most of the population is either protestant or Roman Catholic. On the Outer Hebrides, religion is more widely practiced than in any other part of Scotland. Sunday is a day of religious observation when public services cease. If you do go into a place of worship in the Outer Hebrides, respect local traditions and ensure you are decently attired (smart clothes and no hat for men, a dress and a head covering for women).

On the Orkneys, Shetlands, and other islands of Scotland, you will, sadly, encounter a local policy of littering. This evidences itself in the most bizarre of forms, such as letting the sea reclaim rusting car wrecks when they are no longer roadworthy. What happens, of course, is that the sea doesn't really reclaim them but leaves these bedraggled-looking wrecks right on the shore causing an eyesore.

FESTIVALS, EVENTS, AND NATIONAL PUBLIC HOLIDAYS

Here are a selection of the most important events and festivals in the country, as well public holidays that mean, for the visitor, a shutdown or severe reduction in public services. Many establishments across Scotland will close on festival days (if the particular region celebrates it) and public holidays. You can find more about festivals and events by turning to the destination chapters.

January

Jan. 1: **New Year's Day** (nationwide public holiday)

Jan. 1: **The Ba** (Kirkwall, Orkney)—A bizarre form of street football with what seems like the whole town joining in.

Jan. 11: **Burning of the Clavie** (Burghead, Moray)—A festival with pagan origins where the main event is carrying a blazing barrel filled with tar in a procession through the village.

Jan. 25: **Burns Night** (nationwide)—A traditional remembrance of Scotland's favorite poet, Robert Burns, with Burns suppers and poetry recitals.

Late January: **Celtic Connections** (Glasgow)—Celtic music festival.

Last Tuesday of January: **Up Helly Aa** (Lerwick, Shetland)—A Viking festival with torchlight parades.

February

Feb. 14: **Valentine's Day** (nationwide)

March

March/April: **Easter Weekend** (nationwide

public holidays)—Good Friday and the Monday after Easter Sunday are public holidays.

April

Early April: **Melrose Sevens** (Melrose, Borders)—A highly competitive rugby championship.

April 30: **Beltane fire festival** (Edinburgh)—A commemoration of the ancient Celtic celebration of the coming of spring sees thousands take to Edinburgh's Calton Hill for an evening of fireworks, costumed parades, and the like.

Late April: **Triptych** (Glasgow, Edinburgh, and Aberdeen)—Music and theater festival.

May

Early May: **May Day** (nationwide public holiday)

Early May: **Shetland Folk Festival** (Lerwick and across Shetland)—Shetland is renowned for its fiddling, and there's plenty on offer at this magical festival, with live music in venues across the islands.

Early May: **Isle of Bute Jazz Festival** (Isle of Bute, Inner Hebrides)—Some of the biggest names in U.K. and international jazz converge on this little island for five days of great live music.

Early May: **Spirit of Speyside Whisky Festival** (Dufftown, Moray)—The "world capital" of Scotch whisky, Dufftown, hosts a festival devoted entirely to the nation's favorite drink with events, tastings, and tours going on at the many distilleries in and around town.

Mid-May: **Ullapool Book Festival** (Ullapool, Northern Highlands)—Quirky literary festival in the heart of the Northern Highlands with growing notoriety and a host of Scottish authors doing talks and book signings.

Late May: **Orkney Folk Festival** (Kirkwall,

Stromness, and across Orkney)—The best folk festival in Scotland.

Late May: **Spring Bank Holiday** (nationwide public holiday)

June

During June: **Portsoy Traditional Boat Festival** (Portsoy, Aberdeenshire)—One of Europe's biggest fests of traditional sea vessels, with lots of music and dance and a food fayre (old-fashioned spelling of fair, used to make the occasion sound more traditional).

Mid-June: **Kirkcudbright Jazz Festival** (Kirkcudbright, Dumfries and Galloway)—An atmospheric jazz festival in a picturesque harbor town, with a focus on Dixieland and swing.

Mid-June: **Royal Highland Show** (Edinburgh)—Scotland's premier agricultural event.

Late June: **St. Magnus Festival** (Kirkwall, Orkney)—A music and arts extravaganza.

Late June: **Dundee Blues Bonanza** (Dundee)—One of Scotland's top celebrations of live jazz and blues.

Throughout June: **Common Riding Festivals** (Borders)—Processional checking of the traditional town boundary lines with plenty of pomp in various Borders towns. The festivals at Selkirk, reckoned by many to be Europe's largest equestrian gathering, and Duns are recommended.

July

Early July: **Tarbert Seafood Festival** (Tarbert, Argyll and Bute)—Scotland's best seafood festival with live music, entertainment, and celebrity chefs preparing gourmet seafood dishes, all in one of the country's prettiest coastal villages.

Mid-July: **Hebridean Celtic Festival** (Stornoway, Outer Hebrides)—A cracking Celtic fes-

tival in a Celtic-speaking land—expect music, dance, and revelry at various locations.

Late July: **Edinburgh Jazz and Blues Festival** (Edinburgh)—The prequel to the Edinburgh Festivals and the longest running U.K. jazz festival.

August

Early August: **Summer Bank Holiday** (nationwide public holiday)

During August: **Shetland Fiddle Frenzy** (Lerwick, Shetland)—See the Scottish fiddling maestros in action.

Mid-August: **Blair International Horse Trials** (Blair Atholl, Perthshire)—This is one of Scotland's largest equestrian events. The world's top horse riders go up against each other in a series of show jumping and dressage competitions, with a huge country fair of craft stalls and local produce taking place, too.

All August: **Edinburgh Festival** (Edinburgh)—Music, dance, drama, comedy, books, film: you name it and this city is celebrating it, all month long.

All August and Early September: **Highland Games**—The favorite Highland event of them all, with gatherings throughout the Highlands. You'll see bagpiping and lots of kilt-clad men and women competing against each other in different athletic disciplines. The climax is the Braemar Gathering in early September.

September

During September: **Doors Open Day**—This is a great opportunity to see some fascinating old buildings in Scotland not normally open to the public (see www.cockburnassociation.org for details).

Mid-September: **Loopallu** (Ullapool, Northern Highlands)—One of the coolest rural music festivals in Britain.

Late September: **Wigtown Book Festival** (Wigtown, Dumfries and Galloway)—Scotland's best book festival.

October

Early to Mid-October: **Tour of Mull** (Isle of Mull, Inner Hebrides)—A crazed road race around the island's roads.

Mid-October to Early November: **Enchanted Forest** (Pitlochry, Perthshire)—A magical light show and music festival in the forests of Perthshire.

October and Early November: **Glasgay** (Glasgow)—Scotland's annual celebration of queer culture and the U.K.'s largest multi-arts gay and lesbian festival.

November

Nov. 30: **St. Andrew's Day** (nationwide public holiday)

Late November and December: **Christmas lights switch-ons** (nationwide)

December

Dec. 25 and 26: **Christmas Day and Boxing Day** (nationwide public holidays)

Dec. 28–31: **Hogmanay** (nationwide)—Traditional Scottish New Year celebrations, which run on for days.

Health and Safety

Scotland is one of the safest countries to visit in the world. Health care here is first rate and is available throughout the country, even in the rural areas. For minor ailments, pharmacists offer over-the-counter service and advice. They can also point you in the direction of other medical care should you need it. Most hospitals have outpatient departments, which you should visit unless your medical situation is an emergency.

COMMON COMPLAINTS

Pollen count is high in Scotland, and **hay fever** can affect even those who do not normally suffer. Symptoms include runny nose, runny or bloodshot eyes, fatigue, and itching. Carry antihistamines like Diphenhydramine (Benadryl) with you to relieve symptoms, or gargle with saltwater.

Some visitors to Scotland react badly to the peat content of the **water** in the Highlands. This is water at its most natural and is likely to do you more good than harm, but if you're not used to it, it might make you feel queasy.

The single biggest aggravation you will encounter in Scotland will be the little mosquito-like insect known as the **midge,** prevalent in damp, sheltered areas of the country.

EXPOSURE ILLNESS

If you're exposed to the elements for a long time in Scotland without being adequately prepared for them, it's possible that you could get either heat exposure sickness or hypothermia. This is a possibility particularly if you are planning lots of long-distance hiking. Heat exposure can happen if you're exposed to the sun for long periods of time, particularly if you are in open Highland country with little natural shelter from the elements, and the body does not get adequate supplies of water and salt. Symptoms include tiredness, giddiness, raging thirst, headaches, and painful, dark urine. Preventative measures include covering your head with a hat and carrying plenty of water. This advice might seem straightforward, but it is incredible how many people in Scotland strike out over the moors without taking necessary precautions.

More likely in Scotland than heat exposure is hypothermia, in which the body's core temperature drops too low. This can happen when

THE MIDGE

Stealing all the limelight in the insect world in Scotland is the one pesky little beast you'll have absolutely no interest in seeing: the midge. These tiny, biting flies occur the world over, but the Scottish climate lends itself very well to a particularly vicious strain. These creatures come out at sheltered times of the day like dawn and dusk in damp areas of the country (therefore, just about anywhere). The Scottish Midge, otherwise known as the Highland Midge, generally hangs out in upland areas of north and west Scotland. About the only saving grace of the wind and heavy rain in Scotland is that it keeps away these annoying insects. As soon as the sun breaks out of the cloud and the wind drops, you know you're in for some trouble.

Midges tend to favor arms and ankles for biting spots, and they are very persistent: Even if you are covering up they can crawl down the inside of socks and sleeves to find their perfect piece of flesh. The bite is not a health hazard but is itchy enough to be the bane of your holiday. Wearing sleeves and long trousers when in prime midge country can help minimize risk of getting bitten, as can wearing light-colored clothing (for some reason, midges prefer dark clothes). However, it's extremely advisable to use some form of midge repellent, available for purchase in some in one of the larger cities, where midges are not such a problem. One tried and true repellent is DEET (diethyl toluamide). It doesn't have the most attractive scent but it does the job.

you are exposed to prolonged wind, rain, and icy temperatures without being adequately protected. Signs of hypothermia include acute shivering and loss of orientation, which if not treated can lead to coma. The key preventative action is always having sufficient outdoor gear to deal with high wind, constant rain and sleet, and sub-zero temperatures. If hypothermia sets in, remove the affected individual to a sheltered place and remove wet clothing. Shared body warmth and hot sweet drinks can help the re-warming process.

SAFETY

Scotland is so safe that in most places you could leave your car with the doors open for weeks and it would still be there when you returned. Still, it's always best to err on the side of caution.

Scotland's big cities can be dangerous and intimidating in certain areas late at night; use common sense and keep your money close when traveling in them, particularly Glasgow. Even by the standards of European cities, Edinburgh is extremely safe. Glasgow long had a reputation as being the stabbing capital of the U.K. but is safe by the standards of most European cities.

Stay well clear of Orange marches, which take place from time to time in Glasgow; these pro–Northern Irish independence marches and Protestant-Catholic clashes can often turn to violence. Protestant-Catholic conflicts are also a feature of Glasgow Rangers–versus–Glasgow Celtic football matches. Football fans have been killed for expressing sentiments one way or the other at the wrong time; it's best not to get involved.

One annoyance if you're in Edinburgh or Glasgow at festival times: you are likely to get approached by touts persistently promoting gigs and music events.

Information and Services

MONEY

The currency of Britain is the pound sterling. The pound is doing pretty well at present against nearly every other currency in the world. At last report, one British pound was worth US$1.81. Currency comes in pounds and pennies (pence). There are 100 pennies to one pound. Coin denominations come in 1p, 2p, 5p, 10p, 20p, 50p, £1, and £2. There are £5, £10, £20, and £50 bank notes; in Scotland, there is also the endearing £1 note and the hefty £100 note. Scottish notes look slightly different from English notes. English notes are accepted in Scotland, but south of the border, and in other countries, many shopkeepers will not accept Scottish tender, even though it is technically legal. Scottish notes can still usually be changed at English banks. Coins are the same as in England.

COMMUNICATIONS AND MEDIA

In many respects, Scotland is like the rest of the United Kingdom when it comes to post, telephone, and media, with a few characteristic differences.

Postal Service

Unexpectedly, the postal service in Scotland is better than in many parts of the United Kingdom. There are two kinds of stamps: first-class and second-class. The price depends on the weight of what you are sending but starts at £0.34 for first-class small letters and £0.52 for large letters, and £0.24 for second-class small letters and £0.52 for large letters. First-class is, in theory, next-day delivery while second-class takes three to four working days. Postcards to Europe cost £0.48, to North America £0.54. Air mail is the best way of sending a letter or large package outside of the U.K.: expect it to take three to five days to reach Western Europe and at least five days to reach North America. Mail to Australia and New Zealand takes seven days. If you want your letter to be sent by air

mail rather than on a ship, be sure to place an air mail sticker on the envelope. It's never a good idea to send cash by post.

There have been cutbacks to the number of post offices across Scotland as the national postal service, Royal Mail, struggles to adapt to the financial blow struck by the Internet. Still, most small towns and villages have a post office, with general opening hours being 9 A.M.–5 P.M. Monday–Friday. In larger towns, post offices are open on Saturday mornings, too. Post boxes are red and have collection times written on the side: collections will be at least once daily Monday–Saturday.

If you are going to be in Scotland for a while and want to receive mail, then most post offices in large towns offer a **Post Restante** service (sometimes known as general delivery in the U.S.). This means you can use any participating post office for up to three months to receive mail. Be sure to put the exact address of the post office. When picking up mail abroad, you'll need to have your passport with you for identification. Check www.royalmail.com for further details.

Telephone

To phone Scotland from abroad, dial your country's international access code plus 44 (the U.K.'s country code) and the area code (drop the first 0), followed by the phone number. For example, to call Edinburgh from the U.S., dial 011-44-131 and then the phone number.

To phone abroad from Scotland, dial 00 followed by the country code; then dial the area code (drop the first 0 as necessary) and the rest of the number. Country codes include 001 for the U.S. and Canada, 0061 for Australia, and 0063 for New Zealand.

The iconic red telephone box is alive and well in Scotland, particularly in rural areas. However, these phone boxes are now an endangered species and have in many areas been replaced by dull, gray telephone boxes. Boxes will usually have a list of numbers inside. Some

USEFUL NUMBERS AND CODES

International Operator: 155
Emergency (Fire, Police, Ambulance, Coast Guard): 999/112
Talking Clock: 123
Directory Inquiries: 118118/118500
Toll Free Code: 0800
National Call Rate Code: 0870
Premium Rate Code: 0891

boxes will take coins only, some will take telephone cards only, and some will take both. Coin phones will not give change and are often vandalized. Phone cards give you more for your money and are available in amounts of £5, £10, and £20 from almost every convenience store in Scotland. Call charges from the U.K. to the U.S. are around £0.54 per minute, while from the U.K. to Australia it will cost you a whopping £0.91 per minute.

MOBILE PHONE

Most main areas of Scotland have excellent mobile or cellular phone coverage. In rural areas, coverage is limited to a couple of networks and at the best of times can cut out any moment. You may find yourself wandering up a hill in the rain to find reception or, in remote areas, not getting reception at all. These days, if you are going to be in the country for a long time, it's convenient to purchase a cheap mobile phone on a Pay As You Go or contract basis. All major towns have mobile phone shops and might even be able to help with technical inquiries from those with foreign phones. Mobile phones purchased in Scotland are designed to be compatible with European phone networks only. Cheaper mobile phones are rarely connected to the best networks. The best network for coverage in Scotland is Vodafone.

The U.K. uses the GSM 900/1800 network, which is compatible with Europe, Australia, and New Zealand but not the U.S. or Canada. It's best to check with your service provider beforehand about using a North American mobile phone in the U.K.

Internet Access

Scotland is online in a big way. Because of Scotland's isolated rural nature, the Internet has reinvented the way many people do business in the country. You're as likely to see a Highlander on a laptop these days as on a tractor or a fishing boat. Because most Scots now have Internet in their home, Internet cafés are not as common as they once were. However, the chances are that your hostel or hotel will offer Internet access either free or at a nominal fee. Certain pubs and cafés also now offer wireless Internet access. The Internet can now be used for helping plan your trip to an extent. Many hotels and hostels and an increasing number of bed-and-breakfasts have online booking facilities and, if not, still have information that can help you decide if you want to stay. The big problem with Internet resources is that they are notoriously out of date and it can be nigh on impossible to find the information you want.

Media

For starters, when dealing with electrical items in Scotland, as with all the U.K., you'll need a square three-prong adapter. Like most of Europe, Africa, and Australasia, the country is part of the PAL broadcasting system, which differs from the North American NTSC system—worth bearing in mind when it comes to buying your favorite video and finding it doesn't work back home.

The main TV stations in Scotland are BBC1 and BBC2 (no commercials) and ITV, Channel 4, and Channel 5. The BBC Channels and Channel 4 are where most of the quality programs are. BBC Scotland gives a Scottish flavor to the BBC channels north of the English border.

There are five main radio stations. Radio One is contemporary music; Radio Two is easy listening music (1950s onward); Radio Three plays classical, jazz, and world music along with a selection of drama; Radio Four is the culture station and includes quirky delights like the *Shipping Forecast;* and Radio Five is sports-oriented. In Scotland, you are most likely to pick up BBC Radio Scotland (810 MW, 92–95 FM) for the Scottish take on British events.

It's always interesting to pick up a Scottish newspaper to get a feel for what the nation is all about. *The Scotsman* and the *Glasgow Herald* are the quality daily broadsheets; you could also check out the *Daily Record,* which is a sensationalistic (and quite amusing) tabloid. There are a number of important regional newspapers, too (always worth picking up to find out what's going on) like the *Oban Times,* covering Argyll and the Inner Hebrides; the *Highland News,* covering the Highlands; and *Orkney Today,* covering the Orkney Islands. Local newspapers are far more important than in most countries.

TOURIST INFORMATION AND MAPS
Tourist Information
Scotland is covered by a comprehensive range of tourist information centers (TICs) designed to help visitors with their inquiries in regions across the country. All offices can provide local information; the problem comes when you want them to give an opinion, which they are not technically allowed to do. You will usually get a proficient service, although you might also end up getting fobbed off with a lot of information freebies. Most TICs stock a range of free maps and sell other, more comprehensive maps, too. In the height of the tourist season, TIC offices are open for at least some hours every day of the week. Most TICs are operated by Visit Scotland, the national tourist information organization, and, as such, phone inquiries are often dealt with through a centralized office. This can be annoying, as the person you get put through to can often not give region-specific information. Scotland's TIC system is much more geared toward over-the-counter inquiries.

There is also a lot of tourist information available on Scotland's national tourism website, www.visitscotland.com.

Maps
There is no shortage of high-quality maps of Scotland, and these will be available at all TIC offices and also in bookshops. There are three main types of maps you are going to need in Scotland. Easiest to come by are general touring and driving maps showing all the major roads. It's hard to go wrong with these maps but one of the best fold-out maps of this category are the Automobile Association (AA) road maps which cover Britain in large regional areas, including the **AA Road Map of Scotland.** Then, there are more localized maps and here, Britain's number one mapping company the Ordnance Survey (OS) comes in mighty handy. The OS has a series of pink **Landranger Maps,** which have a 1:50000 scale. Even these, however, might not be enough if you are getting out into the roadless wilds. For off-road adventures, it's highly recommended that you purchase one of the 1:25000 (4 cm to 1 km/2.5 inches to 1 mile) **Ordnance Survey Explorer Maps,** which cover popular walking and outdoor activities areas. Towns and villages close to the outdoor area you want to go to will stock a series of other large-scale maps.

WEIGHTS, MEASURES, AND ELECTRICITY
Britain, and therefore Scotland, has a few endearing and often frustrating traits, of which the weights and measures system is likely to be among the most confusing to overseas visitors. In line with the rest of Europe, the metric system has been adopted in Scotland. The major exceptions are when it comes to road distances (measured in miles and yards) and buying beer in the pub (measured out in pints).

In Scotland, the electrical system runs on 220/240 volts. Scottish electric sockets take square three-pin/three-prong adapters; if you are bringing products with you that need to be plugged in, purchase an adapter either in your own country or in a U.K. store.

RESOURCES

Glossary

When you consider that in standard English, the average educated fluent speaker knows around 20,000 words, it is astonishing that there are an estimated 20,000 additional words used by Scots. Many of these are not nationally used words but rather regional words. Many regional versions of certain words will differ slightly from the "standard" Scots detailed below.

auld old
aw/a' all
aye yes
bairn child
bannock biscuit or scone
ben mountain
besom difficult woman
blackhouse traditional Scottish croft house with a turf roof
blether idle chitchat
body a person
bonnie beautiful
brae slope
broch Iron Age stone tower
burn stream
but and ben cottage
caber a large log, most commonly used in the Highland game of "tossing the caber"
cairn pile of stones used as way-mark, monument, or burial chamber
ceilidh a get-together involving traditional Scottish music and dance
cloot cloth
coo cow
croft/crofter small-scale farm/farmer

dram measure of whisky
dreich dreary, miserable, cold, wet weather
eejit idiot
first foot the first visitor in the New Year
firth a wide estuary mouth, often characterized by calm, sheltered water and sandy shallows
fu full, or drunk (occasionally)
gey rather
glen valley
gloaming dusk
hauf half
heavy a dark beer
hen a woman (endearment)
homebake a homemade cake or sweet snack, usually a tray bake (baked on a tray in an oven)
hoose house
jimmy a man (generic)
ken know
kin family
kirk church
laird land owner or estate owner
lassie girl
loch lake
mac prefix to a family name, normally meaning "son of"
machair grass-covered dunes
manse minister's house
mull headland or promontory
Munro a mountain over 3,000 feet (914 meters)
nae bother it's no trouble
neep turnip
neuk corner
Och! Well!

scunner nuisance
stane stone
tae to
tattie potato
thrawn perverse
toun town
twa two

wabbit pale or weak-looking
wean child
wee small
wife old woman
wynd narrow path
ye you
yin one

Suggested Reading

HISTORICAL AND GENERAL NONFICTION

Atkinson, Tom. *The Lonely Lands.* Edinburgh: Luath Press, 1995. An in-depth, insightful look at the history and culture of Argyll and the Inner Hebrides.

Bathurst, Bella. *The Lighthouse Stevensons.* New York: Harper Perennial, 2000. This is a fascinating and colorful account of the history of Scotland's lighthouses, mostly built by the family of acclaimed writer Robert Louis Stevenson.

Bathurst, Bella. *The Wreckers.* Boston: Houghton Mifflin, 2005. The history of the sea is the history of Scotland: this book focuses on the rather grim "wrecking" trade around Britain's waters and particularly in Scotland, where locals would lure ships onto the rocks in storms in order to procure their cargo.

Jackson, Michael. *Malt Whisky Companion,* 4th edition. London: Dorling Kindersley, 1999. This should be the bible of anyone who has an interest in the history, development, and sampling of the famous Scottish drink.

Laing, Lloyd. *The Picts and the Scots.* Stroud, England: The History Press, 2001. This book focuses on Scotland's origins and the people that shaped the country.

Maclean, Fitzroy. *Highlanders: A History of the Scottish Clans.* London: Everyman's Library, 1995. This wonderfully illustrated book teaches you about the Scottish clan system and its development.

Magnusson, Magnus. *Scotland: The Story of a Nation.* New York: Harper Collins, 2000. Probably the most comprehensive and easy-to-digest of the many histories on Scotland, from prehistoric times until that fateful day in 1746 when hopes of a Scottish king were defeated by the English once and for all.

TRAVEL WRITING AND TRAVELOGUES

Banks, Ian. *Raw Spirit.* London: Arrow Books Ltd, 2004. This book focuses on one man's journey across his native country to discover the secrets of whisky and a whole lot more.

Boswell, James. *A Tour of the Hebrides With Samuel Johnson.* 1785. This is not just the most enlightening and entertaining travel-writing book on Scotland but the definitive and genre-forming travel writing book. It describes 18th-century notables James Boswell and Samuel Johnson's horrific and delightful tour of the Highlands and islands of Scotland in the 1770s.

Griffiths, Neil. *Gurkha Highlander: Walking Mallaig to Stonehaven.* Dunfermline, Scotland: Cualann Press, 2004. An entertaining book about walking across Scotland with four Himalayan Gurkhas: the follow-up to the equally enjoyable *Gurkha Reiver,* which focuses on walking the Southern Upland Way in Southern Scotland.

Martin, Martin. *A Description of the Western Isles of Scotland.* 1703. One of the earliest known travel accounts of Scotland, this contains lots of fascinating information on the lives of islanders at this time. The writing style leaves something to be desired, but the book includes priceless information on life on the now-deserted island of St. Kilda as well as the only written perspective on the Highlands and islands in the early 18th century.

FICTION

It's no surprise that, as a nation of storytellers, writers communicate a lot of Scotland's culture and history through fiction.

Banks, Iain. *The Crow Road.* London: Abacus, 1993. The story of Prentice McHoan, who has over the course of his young life to deal with religion, love, and the eventful history of his family, is told brilliantly against a backdrop of lovingly related Scottish historical and geographical descriptions.

Brown, George Mackay. *Under Brinkie's Brae.* New York: Hyperion, 1989. Brown, one of Scotland's best-loved 20th-century poets, wrote a poetic column for an Orkney newspaper for a time; this is the collection of what he wrote. It's a beautiful snapshot of Orkney and Scotland life mixed with worldly themes from the classical Greek to the biblical.

Buchan, John. *The Thirty-nine Steps.* Edinburgh: William Blackwood and Sons, 1915. John Buchan continued the trend of riveting Scottish adventure stories long after Stevenson was dead. This book, a tale of espionage set against a classic Scottish backdrop, is his most famous.

Burns, Robert. "Tam o' Shanter." 1791. You should read something by Scotland's best-loved poet, and this poem is classic Burns, focusing on common Scots and their lives, for which he is best remembered. The poem tells the tale of one man's prolonged stay at the pub and the terrible events that ensue as he staggers home after one too many.

Gray, Alistair. *Lanark: A Life in Four Books.* Edinburgh: Canongate Press, 1981. This dystopian vision of Gray's home city, Glasgow, put him on the stage of all-time great Scottish authors when it came out in 1981.

Robertson, James. *The Testament of Gideon Mack.* London: Hamish Hamilton, 2006. A hugely entertaining, morbidly fascinating tale of one Scottish Presbyterian church minister, his encounter with the devil, and how it shook the small Scottish town where it happened.

Scott, Sir Walter. *The Heart of Midlothian.* Edinburgh: Archibald Constable and Company, 1818. A harrowing account based on the true story of one woman's journey to London on foot to plead for her sister who has been charged with infanticide, this is considered Scott's best novel.

Shakespeare, William. *Macbeth.* 1603–1606. The classic Scottish play: it might not be historically accurate but it remains a hauntingly evocative portrayal of medieval Scotland.

Spark, Muriel. *The Prime of Miss Jean Brodie.* New York: Macmillan, 1961. Set in an Edinburgh girls' school, this book highlights the snobbishness and social values of those in the city's wealthy suburbs during the 1930s.

Stevenson, Robert Louis. *Kidnapped.* London: Cassell and Company, 1886. A rip-roaring yarn of adventure and intrigue, inspired by a Scottish island and fictionally portraying events in the Scottish Highlands in the aftermath of the Jacobite Revolution.

Stevenson, Robert Louis. *The Body Snatcher.* London: Pall Mall Christmas Extra, 1884. A short story on the grizzly trend of body snatching (grave-robbing) in 19th-century Edinburgh.

Suggested Viewing

The Bill Douglas Trilogy (1972–1978), directed by Bill Douglas. This moving series of three films follow the development of a boy who grows up in desperate poverty and eventually makes cultural discoveries with the help of a middle-class English boy.

Braveheart (1995), directed by Mel Gibson. This film has done more for the Scottish tourist industry than any other: it follows Scottish freedom fighter William Wallace and his campaign to rid Scotland of the English against the odds.

Brigadoon (1954), directed by Vincente Minnelli. This masterful film shows two Americans become lost on a hunting trip and come across a village not marked on any of their maps: Brigadoon, a village with a dark secret that seems trapped in the past.

Local Hero (1983), directed by Bill Forsyth. This film, about a young representative of an American oil company sent to purchase a remote Scottish village for his firm to use as an oil refinery base, is one of the most enjoyable films ever made about Scotland.

Trainspotting (1996), directed by Danny Boyle. A dark, hugely important portrayal of the Edinburgh drug scene, based on the novel by Irvine Welsh.

Whisky Galore! (1949), directed by Alexander Mackendrick. Based on the novel by Compton Mackenzie, this lovable comedy is about islanders deprived of whisky in the war. Things look up when a ship carrying thousands of whisky bottles spills its cargo off the island's coast.

The Wicker Man (1973), directed by Robin Hardy. A staunchly Christian policeman is called to a remote Scottish island to investigate the disappearance of a missing girl and becomes embroiled in Paganism.

Internet Resources

TRAVEL RESOURCES

www.britishairways.com
British Airways operates almost all of the domestic flights within Scotland as well as plenty of international flights into the United Kingdom.

www.continental.com
One of the main airlines with flights to Scotland and the United Kingdom.

www.loganair.co.uk
Logan Air is owned by British Airways but has more specific information on flying to Orkney and Shetland.

www.ryanair.com
Ryan Air is the main cheap-flight airline company.

www.calmac.co.uk
Caledonian MacBrayne operates virtually all Scotland's ferries; you can plan your route to the Scottish isles on its website.

www.qjump.co.uk
This website has information on train connections in Scotland and throughout the United Kingdom.

www.citylink.co.uk
The website of Scotland's main bus company, CityLink.

NATIONAL

www.visitscotland.com

Scotland's official tourist website is well set out, including a clickable map where you can zoom in on regional destinations. It's snazzy enough but the information within is often several years out of date and, in keeping with the Scottish tourist board ethos, it doesn't offer any opinion in writeups. While it may be excellent for a general overview or online exploration of what Scotland has to offer, it is too often inaccurate and questionable in the selection of places it includes to be used for more specific planning.

www.scotland.gov.uk

A national government website with general information on Scottish history, politics, sport, leisure, and other subjects.

www.scotland-inverness.co.uk

This is an insightful travel and resource guide for visitors to Scotland from an individual perspective. It contains lots of travelers tips and, usefully, is not afraid to give an opinion on a destination. It's comprehensive but information is liable to be out of date. It's still one of the most interesting national travel resources available online.

REGIONAL

www.visitscottishheartlands.com

This Internet resource covers all of Central Scotland, with information on Stirling, Loch Lomond, the Trossachs, Argyll, and the Inner Hebrides.

www.visithighlands.com

This website has a good array of information on the whole of the Highlands, although some bits can be out of date.

LOCAL

www.edinburgh-royalmile.com

This is a poorly laid-out but occasionally useful guide to the main attractions and services on offer in Scotland's capital.

www.glasgowguide.co.uk

This is a good source of information on Glasgow, particularly with reference to places to go out.

www.list.co.uk

A handy guide for good places to go and for what's going on in Scotland's major cities.

CULTURAL AND GENERAL

www.historic-scotland.gov.uk

This website has information on a huge array of Scotland's historical sites and attractions.

www.uk-yankee.com

This is aimed at Americans who are coming to live in the U.K. but has bags of information of interest to visitors as well.

Index

Map Index

Acknowledgments

This first edition of *Moon Scotland* would not have been what it is without the collective efforts of various people who went far and beyond the call of duty to help me with my research. First and foremost, from the first typed word to the final edit, thanks to Poppy Clinton for her help, support, and generally keeping me sane when I was phoning her at obscure hours from a callbox somewhere in the Scottish drizzle.

In Scotland, special thanks need to go out to Archie Leith, an incredible mine of Scottish information, and Amanda and Paul Wade-Charters, for their hospitality and insider information on Aberdeenshire and the Orkney Islands respectively.

In almost every town and village I visited, I met a huge array of people from helpful shopkeepers to knowledgeable locals in pubs passionate about making this guidebook a success. Many thanks, guys—you know who you are. I only wish there was room here to give you the praise you deserve for your help!

Among the individuals/organizations that deserve a special mention for their assistance: Alexis Dite for the help with the Glasgow/Edinburgh sections; the guys at the Arch Inn, Ullapool; Dunbeath Heritage Centre; everyone behind the scenes at the Edinburgh Tattoo for your help, even when you had your work cut out as it was; Historic Scotland generally for their informative and exceptional staff (particularly at Jarlshof in Shetland Islands, Urquhart Casle in the Highlands, and Caerlaverock in Dumfries and Galloway); Marcie Hume for her help with the Edinburgh section; Jedburgh Tourist Information; Inverness Tourist Information; all the guys at Loch Ness Backpackers; Mike for the information on Mabie Forest; Neil at Glencloy Farmhouse, Arran; the *Orkney Today* newspaper (especially John!); Simon at Torridon Youth Hostel for his unique perspective on Wester Ross; Sea.Fari Adventures in Argyll; Tobermory Tourist Information; Sandra and Chris Watts in Jedburgh; and almost everybody in Wigtown, Patrick at Bladnoch Distillery and all the staff at Wigtown County Buildings particularly.

Much gratitude is also due to Nigel Waterson, Armorel Clinton (www.armorelclinton.net), and Chris Hassan for their help with photograph images and to my sister Amy for her brilliant marketing campaign on my behalf!

And finally, a token of gratitude to my parents for taking me on countless Scottish holidays as a child and instilling me with an undying love for the country, not to mention ferrying me around the wilds of Lewis and Harris for research for the Outer Hebrides section of this book when a hire car proved impossible to find!

Acknowledgments

www.moon.com

For helpful advice on planning a trip, visit www.moon.com for the **TRAVEL PLANNER** and get access to useful travel strategies and valuable information about great places to visit. When you travel with Moon, expect an experience that is uncommon and truly unique.

MAP SYMBOLS

▦	Expressway	🄲	Highlight	✗	Airfield	⚓	Golf Course
▦	Primary Road	○	City/Town	✗	Airport	🅿	Parking Area
▦	Secondary Road	◉	State Capital	▲	Mountain	⬗	Archaeological Site
▦	Unpaved Road	⊛	National Capital	✚	Unique Natural Feature	⛪	Church
-------	Trail	★	Point of Interest			⛽	Gas Station
··········	Ferry	•	Accommodation	⟍	Waterfall	⬭	Glacier
✖✖✖✖	Railroad	▾	Restaurant/Bar	▲	Park	⬭	Mangrove
▦	Pedestrian Walkway	▪	Other Location	❶	Trailhead	▭	Reef
▦	Stairs	⋀	Campground	⛷	Skiing Area	▭	Swamp

CONVERSION TABLES

$°C = (°F - 32) / 1.8$
$°F = (°C \times 1.8) + 32$
1 inch = 2.54 centimeters (cm)
1 foot = 0.304 meters (m)
1 yard = 0.914 meters
1 mile = 1.6093 kilometers (km)
1 km = 0.6214 miles
1 fathom = 1.8288 m
1 chain = 20.1168 m
1 furlong = 201.168 m
1 acre = 0.4047 hectares
1 sq km = 100 hectares
1 sq mile = 2.59 square km
1 ounce = 28.35 grams
1 pound = 0.4536 kilograms
1 short ton = 0.90718 metric ton
1 short ton = 2,000 pounds
1 long ton = 1.016 metric tons
1 long ton = 2,240 pounds
1 metric ton = 1,000 kilograms
1 quart = 0.94635 liters
1 US gallon = 3.7854 liters
1 Imperial gallon = 4.5459 liters
1 nautical mile = 1.852 km

°FAHRENHEIT °CELSIUS

230 — 110
220
210 — 100 WATER BOILS
200
190 — 90
180
170 — 80
160
150 — 70
140
130 — 60
120
— 50
110
100 — 40
90
80 — 30
70
60 — 20
50
40 — 10
30
20 — 0 WATER FREEZES
10
0 — -10
-10
-20 — -20
-30
-40 — -30
      -40

MOON SCOTLAND

Avalon Travel
a member of the Perseus Books Group
1700 Fourth Street
Berkeley, CA 94710, USA
www.moon.com

Editor and Series Manager: Kathryn Ettinger
Copy Editor: Valerie Sellers Blanton
Graphics Coordinators: Stefano Boni,
    Domini Dragoone
Production Coordinators: Darren Alessi,
    Amber Pirker
Cover Designer: Stefano Boni
Map Editor: Kevin Anglin
Cartographers: Chris Markiewicz, Kat Bennett,
    Tim Lohnes, Bart Wright, Jon Niemczyk
Proofreader: Leah Gordon
Indexer: Greg Jewett

ISBN-10: 1-59880-006-X
ISBN-13: 978-1-59880-006-7
ISSN: 1945-4562

Printing History
1st Edition – January 2009
5 4 3 2 1

Some photos and illustrations are used by permission and are the property of the original copyright owners.

Front cover photo: © Eric Schmidt/Masterfile
Title page photo: Highland cow,
    ©123rf.com/Clara Natoli.
Interior photos: pg. 4 © Purestock.com; pg. 8-12, 14, 18 (top), 22, and 23 © Luke Waterson; pg. 7 (top left) © Purestock.com; pg. 6, 7 (bottom left), 13, 16, 18 (bottom), and 20 (bottom) © 123rf.com/Stephen Finn; pg. 7 (top right) and 24 © 123rf.com/Rafa Irusta Machin; pg. 7 (bottom right) © 123rf.com/Roy Longmuir; pg. 15 (top) © 123rf.com/Mike Markey; pg. 15 (bottom) and 21 © 123rf.com/Jeffrey Banke; pg. 17 © 123rf.com/Juliane Jacobs; p. 19 © 123rf.com/leksele; pg. 20 (top) © 123rf.com/Adrian Fortune.

Printed in the United States by RR Donnelley

KEEPING CURRENT

If you have a favorite gem you'd like to see included in the next edition, or see anything that needs updating, clarification, or correction, please drop us a line. Send your comments via email to feedback@moon.com, or use the address above.